MW01039799

# ENTERTAINMENT, MEDIA, AND THE LAW

## TEXT, CASES, AND PROBLEMS

**Fifth Edition**

■ ■ ■

**Paul C. Weiler**
*Henry J. Friendly Professor of Law, Emeritus*
*Harvard Law School*

**Gary Myers**
*Dean and Earl F. Nelson Professor of Law*
*University of Missouri*

**William W. Berry III**
*Associate Professor of Law and Jessie D. Puckett Lecturer*
*University of Mississippi*

AMERICAN CASEBOOK SERIES®

444 Cedar Street, Suite 700
St. Paul, MN 55101
1-877-888-1330



Printed in the United States of America

**ISBN:** 978-1-63459-883-5

*To the Weiler, Darwin and Guerard families,*
*and my fellow entertainment fans*
*—PW*

*For Professor David Lange, who first introduced me to*
*entertainment law over 30 years ago.*
*—GM*

*For Stephanie, Eleanor, William, and Caroline*
*—WB*

# PREFACE

Since the first edition of *Entertainment, Media, and the Law* appeared almost twenty years ago, the entertainment industry has generated increasingly challenging moral, economic, and legal issues. Various shooting incidents from Columbine to Virginia Tech to Charleston focused popular and political as well as judicial attention on the role that violent entertainment may play in inspiring real events. The fact that we now use personal computers and the Internet for fun, not simply for work, contributed to the decline in record sales, beginning in 2001 because of free access to music, initially on Napster and then to various legal and illegal downloading and streaming sources. And no industry was subject to more dramatic corporate conglomeration, on an international as well as a national basis, than the entertainment business, epitomized by the unfortunate merger of AOL with Time Warner.

An important feature of the entertainment field (like the field of sports law) is that it is an industry, not an intrinsic body of law. Nonetheless, every part of this industry—from novels to movies to music to broadcasting to video games—regularly draws on and is shaped by legal subjects ranging from constitutional law to copyright, contract, corporate, and communications law. To prepare for such a professional career, then, one has to learn about the evolution and current shape of the various branches of the industry, the distinctive features of the law when applied to any of them, and the major legal policy issues that regularly confront courts, legislatures, and even international tribunals dealing with the entertainment world.

*Entertainment, Media, and the Law* is a blend, then, of industry developments and legal responses. It is valuable for students to take this course, as opposed to simply studying the basic subjects that come into play, given the interplay of the legal issues being presented by the same industries. Grappling with the issues posed by the lawsuit filed by the family of a murdered Columbine teacher against the manufacturer of the video game *Doom*, or with the accomplishments of Hollywood union leader Ronald Reagan in generating more equitable distribution of movie revenues among bit players, brings tort and labor law alive. Even more important, though, is the enlightenment that comes from having to place that video game tort suit in the context of the First Amendment rights of the owners of *Doom*, or the effort by Courtney Love to use common law unconscionability doctrine rather than collective labor action to try to make music contracts fairer for her.

The authors of this book wish to thank those who have provided invaluable assistance in producing this and prior editions. Paul Weiler gives thanks to his students, his research assistants (particularly Jol Silversmith, Matt Colman, Ryan Gauthier), and his administrative assistants (particularly Susan Smith and Sheila Vargas).

Gary Myers thanks his research assistants, particularly Taylor Leonard and Micah Uptegrove, as well as Bridget Myers for her comments on the manuscript.

Will Berry thanks his family for all of their support during a summer in Cambridge, England in which much of this edition was updated.

PAUL WEILER, CAMBRIDGE, MA
GARY MYERS, COLUMBIA, MO
WILL BERRY, OXFORD, MS

# SUMMARY OF CONTENTS

# TABLE OF CONTENTS

## PART 2. INTELLECTUAL PROPERTY IN ENTERTAINMENT ASSETS

## PART 4. INDUSTRY ORGANIZATION, ECONOMIC POWER, AND LEGAL REGULATION IN THE ENTERTAINMENT WORLD

# TABLE OF CASES

**The principal cases are in bold type.**

# ENTERTAINMENT, MEDIA, AND THE LAW

## TEXT, CASES, AND PROBLEMS

**Fifth Edition**

# PROLOGUE

## SPEECH FOR FUN AND PROFIT

■ ■ ■

To a casual observer, the phrase "entertainment law" might appear to be something of a contradiction in terms. Entertainment is what we turn to for enjoyment, which certainly is not the experience of those caught up in legal disputes. However, as participants in the entertainment world know and as readers of this book are about to discover, this industry gives rise to an enormous number of legal controversies. Whether the law has helped or hindered the industry's ability to entertain its fans is a judgment the reader should suspend for the next thousand pages.

What we lawyer fans can be pleased about, though, is that often when we go to a movie, watch a television show, listen to a song, read a novel, or play a video game, we are doing research, not just having fun. Illustrating that point, when the first edition of this book was being written in 2001, the movie and book *Harry Potter and the Sorcerer's Stone* was the subject of a major lawsuit about who owned the right to Muggles, a suit that had been scheduled to begin in New York City on September 11, 2001. As the second edition was being edited, the publisher of *The Da Vinci Code* was being sued by two earlier authors claiming that the core idea in their book, the relationship between Jesus and Mary Magdalene, had been "stolen" by Dan Brown. In 2010, "The Social Network" depicted the story behind the founding of Facebook, which resulted in an ownership dispute between its founders. And numerous copyright disputes have arisen regarding online streaming of copyrighted films and television programs. Finally, as this edition goes to press, new forms of media delivery have proliferated that have complicated the picture even further.

The tragic killings in Columbine generated a lawsuit against the video game *Doom* and other entertaining works that are said to have inspired the young students to take that violent action. A very different cause of action was launched by author Faye Kellerman against Disney's Miramax arm the day before its *Shakespeare in Love* won the Oscar for Best Picture of 1998. This was at the same time as the MGM makers of the most popular movie series ever, about James Bond, had used the courts to block Sony Entertainment from making its own Bond films, which eventually inspired Sony to acquire MGM itself. Then the heirs of the creator of *Gone With The Wind* launched their suit to block an

African-American perspective of life in the South around the Civil War, *The Wind Done Gone*. And not long after Stacey Stillman had graduated from law school and taken some time off to play a role in the most watched summer television program, *Survivor*, where she felt denied a fair chance to survive to the finish, she became involved in a major contract and tort suit against CBS.

As illustrated by these and other legal battles we are about to encounter, the title of this book is actually something of a misnomer. Entertainment law is a qualitatively different kind of subject than contract law, for example. Entertainment is a human activity and economic venture. Its internal relationships and products are, of course, shaped by contract, as well as constitutional, copyright, labor, antitrust, and trade law. Yet every one of those branches of the law applies as well to other industries, such as auto manufacturing. Professors do not, however, teach and write books about "automobile law." What is distinctive about entertainment law is the unique way that many crucial features of this industry have shaped and been shaped by the legal system. The aim of this prologue is to provide a brief sketch of those key features and trace how they have dictated the organization of this book.

*Speech.* Americans spend well over $500 billion a year to entertain themselves in their leisure time. However, only a portion of those expenditures fits within the compass of this book. Broadly defined, the entertainment sector includes personal recreation (e.g., rollerblading), amusement parks, spectator sports, and gambling (whose annual net expenditures are well over $100 billion). However, this book focuses just on motion pictures, broadcasting (including cable), music publishing and recording, performing arts, book publishing, and video games.[a]

Each of these forms of entertainment have an essential element in common: they consist of some form of *speech*. Unlike a football game or a roulette wheel, for example, a book, a play, a song, or a movie offers its audience a form of expression. The legal significance of this feature is obvious. The First Amendment to the Constitution ordains that the government "shall make no law . . . abridging the freedom of speech." Yet, the sheer size of this volume is testimony to the fact that the Constitution does not bar every use of the law to shape and control entertaining

[a] By contrast, a leading text on the financial side of the entertainment world, Harold L. Vogel, *Entertainment Industry Economics: A Guide For Financial Analysis* (Cambridge Univ. Press, 9th ed. 2014), has chapters on the sports, toys and games, gambling, and amusement park branches of the entertainment industry, as well as material on movies, music, broadcasting, publishing, and now the Internet. Other recent and important books about different parts of this industry are Michael J. Wolf, *The Entertainment Economy: How Mega Media Forces are Transforming Our Lives* (Random House, 1999); David Putnam, with Neil Watson, *The Undeclared War: The Struggle for Control of the World's Film Industry* (Harper Collins, 1999); Donald S. Passman, *All You Need to Know about the Music Business* (Simon & Schuster, 8th ed., 2012); and Richard E. Caves, *Creative Industries: Contracts Between Art and Commerce* (Harvard U. Press, 2000).

speech. Indeed, it was not until the 1950s that an Italian movie, *The Miracle*, led the Supreme Court to fashion something of a constitutional miracle, and finally rule that movies and other forms of entertainment did fit within the First Amendment. Even in that landmark decision, the Court acknowledged that each method of expression presents its own "peculiar" constitutional problems. A major aim of this book is to help understand why and how the legal treatment of the business of entertaining speech is far more complicated than the simple wording of the First Amendment edict would imply.

One reason, perhaps, is that by contrast with news and public commentary, scholarship, or the "high" arts, entertainment offers people fun and diversion rather than political, scientific, or artistic breakthroughs. Providing such "fun" has become a highly profitable enterprise for the performers and firms whose works people find most entertaining. At the same time, consumer demand for sexy and violent films and songs, or for docudrama portrayals of intriguing events in the lives of real people, has raised a host of social and political concerns. What the law can and cannot do about a movie like *Natural Born Killers* or a brief television exposure of Janet Jackson's bare breast at the 2004 Super Bowl half-time is the focus of Part One of this book.

*Technology.* The modern entertainment industry provides not simply speech, but technologically enhanced speech. Technology is not absolutely essential for entertaining fans. Singers can perform in a live concert, or a theatrical group can present a play, without using anything that resembles what industry insiders are now celebrating as the "celestial jukebox in cyberspace." However, for over 500 years, ever since Johann Gutenberg invented the printing press, which permitted readers to acquire and enjoy books that did not have to be copied by hand, the crucial connection of technology to speech has been axiomatic.

The major components of the entertainment world are outgrowths of technological innovations over the past 130 years. Phonographs were developed in the 1880s, motion pictures in the 1890s, radio transmission at the turn of the century, television and sound movies in the 1920s, audio recorders in the 1950s, video recorders in the 1960s, cable satellite transmission in the 1970s, and digital products in the 1980s. Now, in this millennium, we are experiencing the Internet "superhighway" playing a major role in our entertainment as well as our informational lives.

Technology has two contrasting consequences for the authors of entertainment works. The positive value is the vast increase in the potential audience for their work. Only a limited number of people can enjoy a live performance in a concert hall or theater. Now the same work and performance can be transmitted into hundreds of millions of homes around the world, where people can see and hear it if they wish.

Unfortunately, another consequence of technology is that it makes it nearly as easy for copiers as for creators to deliver versions of the original work to potential consumers. The significance of such entertainment "piracy" was driven home to American movie and music producers not only by Chinese factories producing compact discs and videos of American entertainment for the Asian market, but more recently by worldwide fans using Internet services as Napster and then its Bit-Torrent successors to secure these same works for free.

It is for precisely this reason that Gutenberg's invention of printing technology is credited with inspiring the creation of enforceable property rights in intellectual products. These laws entitle the authors of entertainment works to sue others who copy any significant portion of their original work. The result is that the same companies that ask the courts to stop the government from restricting sex and violence on television are regularly filing suits themselves to block others from saying what they want, on the theory that the defendant's work is derived from speech that the plaintiff "owns." This produced, on the last day of the judicial career of Chief Justice Rehnquist in 2005, the most important Supreme Court entertainment law decision in two decades, *MGM v. Grokster*. What we should see as another complex set of relationships between entertaining speech, technology, intellectual property, and the First Amendment are the subjects of Part Two.

*Collaboration.* Another significant byproduct of technology is a far greater need for collaborative relationships in the entertainment world. Creating and distributing works to broad audiences requires contributions from a host of individuals and firms. Much of the rhetoric of copyright law is still based on the image of a single person laboring away on a novel, a play, or a song. Even these authors need the help of many others for editing, publishing, and distributing their works. Qualitatively different levels of collaboration are required for movies and television programs, and even for major record albums. Making a film in Hollywood today requires not only a sizeable team of actors, screenwriters, cinematographers, producers, and directors, but also investors and insurers to provide the capital to fund the project. Once the movie has been completed, an even broader-based effort is necessary to distribute and promote the work for its showing in thousands of theaters, for the streaming, rental, and sale of copies for home viewing, and for its broadcast on cable and broadcast television, with corollary ventures in marketing soundtrack records, merchandising film characters and images, and perhaps even developing derivative works, such as a movie sequel or a television series.

Defining the precise rights, responsibilities, and relationships of the hundreds of collaborators on a major film or other entertainment project is accomplished through contracts negotiated by or on behalf of the parties. Resolving the inevitable disputes that arise often requires that a judge decide whether there is a binding contract, and, if so, how it should be interpreted and enforced. One case was launched by Courtney Love, seeking the same kind of contractual freedom for recording artists that Olivia De Havilland had secured for movie performers more than a half-century ago. The way in which general contract principles shape entertainment industry collaboration, or what Love alleged to be "involuntary servitude," is the subject of Part Three.

*Economics.* Entertainers (both performers and producers) spend a great deal of money and time on contract negotiation and dispute resolution. This is so not only because their projects are so complex, but also because so much money rides on their success or failure.

For entertainers to reap a significant return on their talent, they need two kinds of representation. The first one, the subject of Chapter 10, is the brand of agent representation in the negotiation of individual contracts that was created more than a century ago by William Morris, working out of his little New York home for vaudeville stars like Will Rogers. The other one, the subject of Chapter 11, is representation by performer labor unions that do the collective bargaining with movie studios, television networks, Broadway theaters, and the like.

We shall also be reading about the career of a person who began his career as a movie actor in the early 1930s, then became the head of the new Screen Actors Guild created soon after. In that role, he criticized the attacks launched against the "Hollywood Ten," who had not only been Oscar-winning screenwriters, but also Communists arguing for economic equality during the Great Depression. He then led the most successful strike in Hollywood history, which enhanced the rewards to the supporting actors even more than to stars like Charlton Heston. Ronald Reagan's success in this entertainment union job proved to be the launching pad for an even more important real-world role in the White House.

On the other side of the bargaining table with agents and unions are the entertainment firms that organize and finance the creative projects and then sell the resulting products. Along with the sheer size of the investment required for such projects, another crucial feature of entertainment economics is the unpredictability of success or failure. Driven by these financial risks, the major entertainment firms have engaged in massive corporate expansion and diversification. New giants like Time Warner, Viacom Paramount CBS, and Disney ABC now operate across the entire entertainment spectrum and generate from tens of billions in revenues and expenditures. From the perspective of entertainment executives, this wave of corporate mergers seems a sensible strategy for diversifying risks and generating a synergistic interplay among the various branches of their firms. So another major issue is the impact of these conglomerates on shareholders, performers, and consumers.

Chapters 12 and 13 examine the key roles that antitrust and telecommunications law have played in shaping entertainment conglomeration and the exercise of market power. For example, in the late 1940s, the Supreme Court required Paramount Pictures and all other movie studios to dispose of company-owned movie theaters, and over the next two decades the Federal Communications Commission established the same principle in the television industry (which, among other things, forced CBS to give up its infant cable arm, Viacom). In the early 1950s, a recent graduate of Harvard Law School, Sumner Redstone, was persuaded by his father to manage their newly purchased theaters in the Boston area, rather than work for a law firm.

*International Dimension.* The expansion and diversification of entertainment firms has not been confined to the United States: it now extends around the globe. The creation, financing, and distribution of entertainment works today are aimed at an international audience whose expenditures far exceed the billions that Americans now spend each year on these products. Several of the top entertainment conglomerates are foreign-based, like the Japanese Sony, which owns both Columbia and MGM, and Rupert Murdoch's Australian News Corp. Yet the actual production of creative works remains dominated by American talent, be they performers, executives, or lawyers. Particularly in the case of movies, but also in the realms of television and music, the United States now enjoys a large comparative advantage in international trade.

This situation has generated very different reactions from countries such as China and France. By contrast with China, where piracy has made it easier and cheaper to enjoy American video and audio products, France has placed limits on how much American film and music can be aired on French television and radio stations. And the Seattle demonstrations at the beginning of this millennium's round of international trade negotiations included many union leaders and members from Hollywood, protesting the way a Canadian policy successfully lured a large amount of movie productions north of the border.

For example, the 1996 Oscar-winning story *Good Will Hunting* about life in Cambridge, Massachusetts was filmed in Toronto with Canadian taxpayer support. In 2002, the Oscar-winning *Chicago* and the profitable *My Big Fat Greek Wedding*, both about life in Chicago, were also made in Toronto. In 2005, the Oscar contending *Brokeback Mountain*, about cowboys in Texas and Wyoming, was made up north in Alberta. While other countries like Australia for the *Matrix* series and Czechoslovakia for Matt Damon's *The Bourne Identity*, followed that Canadian subsidy lead, New Zealand chose not to. Thus, Time Warner had to spend $270 million of its own money filming all three stories of *The Lord of the Rings* without any financial aid there. These kinds of foreign policies pose the question of whether and how the U.S. government should use its own trade law measures to secure the "level" playing field on which American entertainers have been winning the lion's share of the international audience. The Epilogue to this book offers a glimpse of both the controversies and the key tools of trade law that can be used to address these issues.

*Lawyering*. With respect to each of these features of the entertainment world, lawyers play a prominent role greater than in any other industry (except perhaps sports). The bulk of this time and effort (performed by outside lawyers, agents, and corporate executives) is spent negotiating contract deals among protagonists who are trying to extract a fair share of a book deal that may generate $10 million in revenues, a record album that may produce $100 million, or a movie or television show that could yield in excess of a billion dollars. Those negotiations focus on entertainment products whose value (though not their appeal) as speech for fun and profit depends to a considerable extent on their legal base.

The contents of this book are devoted as much to real life entertainment controversies and personalities as to legislative enactments and judicial opinions. The book is not, however, intended to be a how-to guide to drafting precise contract language for the array of issues now facing the industry. Its focus, instead, is on the broader trends in legal doctrine, social and economic policy, and constitutional principle that are vividly displayed in the entertainment world. After all, before one can effectively negotiate a contract on a specific issue, one needs an understanding of the background legal rules that define the options for private agreement and shape the negotiating leverage that the parties bring to the bargaining table. The entertainment industry is one of the best illustrations of the basic truth that all bargaining takes place in the shadow of the law.

Most important of all are the fundamental policy issues now being debated within both the industry and the legal system. The controversies depicted in this book require us to grapple with the analytical concepts we encounter in constitutional, antitrust, copyright, and contract law, as well as the complex relationships among all of them. With that appreciation of the basic themes, new lawyers are better positioned to experience and adapt to the often unexpected ways the entertainment field is going to evolve throughout their professional careers.

# PART 1

# LEGAL RESTRAINTS ON ENTERTAINMENT STORIES

■ ■ ■

# CHAPTER 1

# SEX AND VIOLENCE IN ENTERTAINMENT AND THE LAW

■ ■ ■

Many producers of entertainment content include violent or sexual material in their works. This material presents a number of complex issues regarding whether and how governmental policies should address these issues, as well as fundamental First Amendment questions. Indeed, the regulation of sex and violence in the media has long been an important topic in the field of entertainment law.

In response to public opinion in favor of restricting exposure to sex and violence, government entities regulate the content of television, movies, music, and video games in an effort to minimize any negative impact of public consumption of such media. This requires a balancing of the public appetite for such materials with the desire of some to limit the exposure of the public, particularly minors, to obscene materials.

Any such governmental actions generate not just popular concerns, but also constitutional challenges. The First Amendment states: "Congress shall make no law . . . abridging the freedom of speech." This crucial constitutional edict imposes very steep hurdles to any governmental effort to restrict the content of entertainment products—whether sex, violence, invasions of personal privacy and reputation, or other examples addressed in this part. To be sure, the First Amendment has increasingly become a significant lever in the struggle by entertainment conglomerates to fend off Congressional efforts to shape the underlying structure of the entertainment marketplace, which we will see in Part Four.

The First Amendment poses two fundamental types of questions. The first type, substantive in character, asks *what* kinds of speech regulation, if any, are permissible, and what is "speech" in the first place (e.g., whether speech includes burning a flag or dancing nude). The second theme, this one institutional, is *who* should resolve those controversies about where to draw the line between speech and action, between individual freedom and community values. Should this be a question of courts listening to lawyers, legislators to voters, or businesses to customers?

In studying the cases and materials in this book, it will become apparent that neither Congress nor the courts believe there to be an intrinsic incompatibility between the rule of law and freedom of speech. A major issue for us to consider is why the same companies that appeal to the First Amendment to challenge the laws depicted in Parts I and IV of this book also make affirmative use of copyright (Part II) and contract law (Part III) to preclude others speaking freely with what the companies believe are their intellectual or talent property rights. Thus, a key reason for taking this course and reading this book is to learn not just about the intrinsic features of each legal and industry subject, but also to witness the interplay and hence the complexities of the issues presented by each.

## A. ENTERTAINMENT AND THE FIRST AMENDMENT[a]

To the senior citizens in the entertainment world, this preoccupation with the role of the First Amendment in their business is a comparatively new phenomenon. Indeed, for this nation's first century and a half, the Supreme Court left this provision almost totally unused, even in the explicitly political context. Until the New Deal of the 1930s, the Court considered the most important constitutional freedom to be freedom of contract, along the lines of *Lochner v. New York*, 198 U.S. 45 (1905). The flip side of this judicial preoccupation with the virtues of a private market (shaped to some extent by federal antitrust law) was that the Supreme Court ruled, in *Mutual Film Corp. v. Industrial Commission of Ohio*, 236 U.S. 230 (1915), that as a profit-oriented industry, the entertainment world was not entitled to a constitutional guarantee of "freedom of speech."

The infant motion picture industry first appeared on the American scene at the beginning of the 20th century. One or two-reel films were

[a] Among the countless scholarly books and articles on the First Amendment are two treatments from somewhat different intellectual perspectives: Rodney A. Smolla, *Free Speech In An Open Society* (Alfred Knopf, 1992), and Cass R. Sunstein, *Democracy and the Problem of Free Speech* (The Free Press, 1993). And the subject matter of this chapter has produced a host of books. Among the notable works are Kevin W. Saunders, *Violence as Obscenity: Limiting the Media's First Amendment Protection* (Duke U. Press, 1996); John Leonard, *Smoke and Mirrors: Violence, Television and Other American Cultures* (The New Press, 1997); Sissela Bok, *Mayhem: Violence as Public Entertainment* (Perseus Books, 1998); Jeffrey Goldstein, ed., *Why We Watch: The Attractions of Violent Entertainment* (Oxford U. Press, 1998); James T. Hamilton, *Channeling Violence: The Economic Market for Violent Television Programming* (Princeton U. Press, 1998); and Marjorie Heins, *Not in Front of the Children: "Indecency," Censorship, and the Innocence of Youth* (Hill and Wang, 2001); and among the list of law review articles that engaged in in-depth analysis of the legal treatment of entertaining violent films and songs were Forouzan M. Khalili, *Television Violence: Legislation to Combat the National Epidemic*, 18 Whittier L. Rev. 219 (1996); Sandra Davidson, *Blood Money: When Media Expose Others to Risk of Bodily Harm*, 19 Hast. Comm/Ent L.J. 225 (1997); Jendi Reiter, *Serial Killer Trading Cards and First Amendment Values: A Defense of Content-Based Regulation of Violent Expression*, 62 Albany L. Rev. 183 (1998); Kevin W. Saunders, *Electronic Indecency: Protecting Children in the Wake of the Cable and Internet Cases*, 46 Drake L. Rev. 1 (1998); and R. Polk Wagner, *Filters and the First Amendment*, 83 Minnesota L. Rev. 755 (1999).

shown in "nickelodeon" booths for a five cent admission charge. Civic and religious groups were concerned about the impact of this intense new visual experience on a largely working class audience (whose adults, let alone its children, often could not read). Both local and state authorities quickly responded with laws that sought to ensure the moral quality of this new product.

In *Mutual Film*, a film distribution company challenged the early Ohio legislation that required every film to be shown to the state board of censors, which would only license the film to be shown in the state if it displayed "a moral, educational or amusing and harmless character." At the time, the Court had not yet ruled that the First Amendment guarantees of the federal Constitution were applicable to the states. The Court, however, did have to construe and apply Ohio's state constitution, which precluded passage of any law that "restrains or abridges the liberty of speech, or of the press." The Court felt that it "strained . . . common sense" to try to fit "moving pictures"—or the theater, the circus, and other shows and spectacles—within constitutional guarantees of free opinion, speech, and the public press:

> It cannot be put out of view that the exhibition of moving pictures is a business pure and simple, originated and conducted for profit, like other spectacles, not to be regarded, not intended to be regarded by the Ohio constitution, we think, as part of the press of the country or as organs of public opinion. They are mere representations of events, of ideas and sentiments published and known, vivid, useful and entertaining no doubt, but, as we have said, capable of evil, having power for it, the greater because of their attractiveness and manner of exhibition.

236 U.S. at 244–45.

Four decades later, the Supreme Court reversed the constitutional course of the entertainment industry in a case that provides an intriguing picture of the kinds of movies that people found troubling as late as the 1950s. The subject of this case was a forty minute Italian movie, *The Miracle*, made by one of the great film directors, Roberto Rossellini, and starring Anna Magnani and Federico Fellini. The essence of the movie's story was conveyed through this critic's summary reproduced in Justice Frankfurter's concurring opinion in the decision we are about to read:

> A poor, simple-minded girl is tending a herd of goats on a mountainside one day, when a bearded stranger passes. Suddenly it strikes her fancy that he is St. Joseph, her favorite saint, and that he has come to take her to heaven, where she will be happy and free. While she pleads with him to transport her, the stranger gently plies the girl with wine, and when she is in a

> state of tumult, he apparently ravishes her. (This incident in the story is only briefly and discreetly implied.)
>
> The girl awakens later, finds the stranger gone, and climbs down from the mountain not knowing whether he was real or a dream. She meets an old priest who tells her that it is quite possible that she did see a saint, but a younger priest scoffs at the notion. 'Materialist!' the old priest says.
>
> There follows now a brief sequence—intended to be symbolic, obviously—in which the girl is reverently sitting with other villagers in church. Moved by a whim of appetite, she snitches an apple from the basket of a woman next to her. When she leaves the church, a cackling beggar tries to make her share the apple with him, but she chases him away as by habit and munches the fruit contentedly.
>
> Then, one day, while tending the village youngsters as their mothers work at the vines, the girl faints and the women discover that she is going to have a child. Frightened and bewildered, she suddenly murmurs, 'It is the grace of God!' and she runs to the church in great excitement, looks for the statue of St. Joseph, and then prostrates herself on the floor.
>
> Thereafter she meekly refuses to do any menial work and the housewives humor her gently but the young people are not so kind. In a scene of brutal torment, they first flatter and laughingly mock her, then they cruelly shove and hit her and clamp a basin as a halo on her head. Even abused by the beggars, the poor girl gathers together her pitiful rags and sadly departs from the village to live alone in a cave.
>
> When she feels her time coming upon her, she starts back towards the village. But then she sees the crowds in the streets; dark memories haunt her; so she turns towards a church on a high hill and instinctively struggles towards it, crying desperately to God. A goat is her sole companion. She drinks water dripping from a rock. And when she comes to the church and finds the door locked, the goat attracts her to a small side door. Inside the church, the poor girl braces herself for her labor pains. There is a dissolve, and when we next see her sad face, in close-up, it is full of a tender light. There is the cry of an unseen baby. The girl reaches towards it and murmurs, 'My son! My love! My flesh!'

In Italy, *The Miracle* received mixed reviews, including the review by the movie critic for *L'Osservatore Romano*, the publishing organ of the Vatican. While some critics objected to certain artistic features of the film, as well as its depiction of "illegitimate motherhood" and "carnality," the critic for *Il Popolo*, published by the Christian Democratic Party, called the picture a "beautiful thing." The Vatican's movie reviewing arm, the Catholic Cinematographic Center, called *The Miracle* "an abominable profanation from religious and moral viewpoints." Despite the Center's prerogative under Italian law to block exhibition of movies deemed offensive to Catholics, it did not ask for such censure and *The Miracle* was shown in Italy with mixed box office results. A year later, with the Vatican's approval, Rossellini used Italian members of the Franciscan Order as part of the cast for his filming of the life of St. Francis.

Under New York Education Law at that time, the Motion Picture Division of the New York State Education Department screened pictures and issued licenses for viewing unless the "film or a part thereof is obscene, indecent, immoral, inhumane, sacrilegious, or is of such a character that its exhibition would tend to corrupt morals or incite to crime." For the American market, *The Miracle* was combined with two French films, Jean Renoir's *A Day in the Country* and Marcel Pagnol's *Jofre*, under the joint title, *Ways of Love*, and was licensed for release by film distributor Joseph Burstyn in New York in 1950. Most New York critics praised *Ways of Love*, which was voted best foreign film of the year.

A private Catholic organization, the National Legion of Decency, attacked *The Miracle* as "a sacrilegious and blasphemous mockery of Christian religious truth," and New York's Cardinal Spellman issued a statement for reading at all Masses in the city on Sunday, January 7, 1951, condemning the film and calling for a tightening of state censorship law. Again, a number of notable Catholics, such as Notre Dame professor William Clancy, writing in the Commonweal, and the well-known poet and critic, Allen Tate, firmly disagreed. In response to the religious and political outcry, the Chair of the New York Board of Regents appointed a special three-member committee of the Board to reconsider the Division's original licensing decision. After the committee members had rescreened *The Miracle* and decided that it was sacrilegious, the Board as a whole revoked the picture's license on February 16, 1951. The Board's reasons were that "the mockery or profaning of these beliefs that are sacred to any portion of our citizenship is abhorrent to the laws of this great State." The constitutionality of that Board action eventually reached the Supreme Court.

## JOSEPH BURSTYN, INC. V. WILSON

Supreme Court of the United States, 1952.
343 U.S. 495, 72 S.Ct. 777, 96 L.Ed. 1098.

MR. JUSTICE CLARK delivered the opinion of the court.

[After detailing the above factual background, the opinion for the Court described and quoted from the earlier *Mutual Film* precedent, and then continued.]

* * *

In a series of decisions beginning with *Gitlow v. New York*, 268 U.S. 652 (1925), this Court held that the liberty of speech and of the press which the First Amendment guarantees against abridgment by the federal government is within the liberty safeguarded by the Due Process Clause of the Fourteenth Amendment from invasion by state action. That principle has been followed and reaffirmed to the present day. Since this series of decisions came after the *Mutual* decision, the present case is the first to present squarely to us the question whether motion pictures are within the ambit of protection which the First Amendment, through the Fourteenth, secures to any form of "speech" or "the press."

It cannot be doubted that motion pictures are a significant medium for the communication of ideas. They may affect public attitudes and behavior in a variety of ways, ranging from direct espousal of a political or social doctrine to the subtle shaping of thought which characterizes all artistic expression. The importance of motion pictures as an organ of public opinion is not lessened by the fact that they are designed to entertain as well as to inform. As was said in *Winters v. New York*, 333 U.S. 507, 510 (1948):

> "The line between the informing and the entertaining is too elusive for the protection of that basic right [a free press]. Everyone is familiar with instances of propaganda through fiction. What is one man's amusement, teaches another's doctrine."

It is urged that motion pictures do not fall within the First Amendment's aegis because their production, distribution, and exhibition is a large-scale business conducted for private profit. We cannot agree. That books, newspapers, and magazines are published and sold for profit does not prevent them from being a form of expression whose liberty is safeguarded by the First Amendment. We fail to see why operation for profit should have any different effect in the case of motion pictures.

It is further urged that motion pictures possess a greater capacity for evil, particularly among the youth of a community, than other modes of expression. Even if one were to accept this hypothesis, it does not follow that motion pictures should be disqualified from First Amendment protection. If there be capacity for evil it may be relevant in determining the permissible scope of community control, but it does not authorize substantially unbridled censorship such as we have here.

For the foregoing reasons, we conclude that expression by means of motion pictures is included within the free speech and free press guaranty of the First and Fourteenth Amendments. To the extent that language in the opinion in *Mutual Film Corp. v. Industrial Comm'n*, supra, is out of harmony with the views here set forth, we no longer adhere to it.[12]

To hold that liberty of expression by means of motion pictures is guaranteed by the First and Fourteenth Amendments, however, is not the end of our problem. It does not follow that the Constitution requires absolute freedom to exhibit every motion picture of every kind at all times and all places. That much is evident from the series of decisions of this Court with respect to other media of communication of ideas.[13] Nor does it follow that motion pictures are necessarily subject to the precise rules governing any other particular method of expression. Each method tends to present its own peculiar problems. But the basic principles of freedom of speech and the press, like the First Amendment's command, do not vary. Those principles, as they have frequently been enunciated by this Court, make freedom of expression the rule. There is no justification in this case for making an exception to that rule.

The statute involved here does not seek to punish, as a past offense, speech or writing falling within the permissible scope of subsequent punishment. On the contrary, New York requires that permission to communicate ideas be obtained in advance from state officials who judge the content of the words and pictures sought to be communicated. This Court recognized many years ago that such a previous restraint is a form of infringement upon freedom of expression to be especially condemned. *Near v. Minnesota ex rel. Olson*, 283 U.S. 697 (1931). The Court there recounted the history which indicates that a major purpose of the First Amendment guaranty of a free press was to prevent prior restraints upon publication, although it was carefully pointed out that the liberty of the press is not limited to that protection. It was further stated that "the protection even as to previous restraint is not absolutely unlimited. But the limitation has been recognized only in exceptional cases." In the light of the First Amendment's history and of the *Near* decision, the State has

---

[12] *See United States v. Paramount Pictures, Inc.*, 334 U.S. 131, 166 (1948): "We have no doubt that moving pictures, like newspapers and radio, are included in the press whose freedom is guaranteed by the First Amendment." It is not without significance that talking pictures were first produced in 1926, eleven years after the *Mutual* decision. Hampton, *A History of the Movies* (1931), 382–383.

[13] E.g., *Feiner v. New York*, 340 U.S. 315 (1951); *Kovacs v. Cooper*, 336 U.S. 77 (1949); *Chaplinsky v. New Hampshire*, 315 U.S. 568 (1942); *Cox v. New Hampshire*, 312 U.S. 569 (1941).

a heavy burden to demonstrate that the limitation challenged here presents such an exceptional case.

New York's highest court says there is "nothing mysterious" about the statutory provision applied in this case: "It is simply this: that no religion, as that word is understood by the ordinary, reasonable person, shall be treated with contempt, mockery, scorn and ridicule. . . ." This is far from the kind of narrow exception to freedom of expression which a state may carve out to satisfy the adverse demands of other interests of society. In seeking to apply the broad and all-inclusive definition of "sacrilegious" given by the New York courts, the censor is set adrift upon a boundless sea amid a myriad of conflicting currents of religious views, with no charts but those provided by the most vocal and powerful orthodoxies. New York cannot vest such unlimited restraining control over motion pictures in a censor. Under such a standard the most careful and tolerant censor would find it virtually impossible to avoid favoring one religion over another, and he would be subject to an inevitable tendency to ban the expression of unpopular sentiments sacred to a religious minority. Application of the "sacrilegious" test, in these or other respects, might raise substantial questions under the First Amendment's guaranty of separate church and state with freedom of worship for all. However, from the standpoint of freedom of speech and the press, it is enough to point out that the state has no legitimate interest in protecting any or all religions from views distasteful to them which is sufficient to justify prior restraints upon the expression of those views. It is not the business of government in our nation to suppress real or imagined attacks upon a particular religious doctrine, whether they appear in publications, speeches, or motion pictures.

Since the term "sacrilegious" is the sole standard under attack here, it is not necessary for us to decide, for example, whether a state may censor motion pictures under a clearly drawn statute designed and applied to prevent the showing of obscene films. That is a very different question from the one now before us.[20] We hold only that under the First and Fourteenth Amendments a state may not ban a film on the basis of a censor's conclusion that it is "sacrilegious."

Reversed.

---

[20] In the *Near* case, this Court stated that "the primary requirements of decency may be enforced against obscene publications." 283 U.S. 697, 716. In *Chaplinsky v. New Hampshire*, 315 U.S. 568, 571–572 (1942), Justice Murphy stated for a unanimous Court: "There are certain well-defined and narrowly limited classes of speech, the prevention and punishment of which have never been thought to raise any Constitutional problem. These include the lewd and obscene, the profane, the libelous, and the insulting or 'fighting' words—those which by their very utterance inflict injury or tend to incite an immediate breach of the peace. . . ."

*Burstyn* was a crucial legal event for the entertainment world because it rejected the *Mutual Film* premise that simply because movie distribution was a business for private profit, it did not enjoy the constitutional freedom afforded to "speech." The Court did add that a motion picture, like other methods of expression, might "present its own peculiar problems" that precluded application of "the precise rules" governing other media. We will see later in this chapter (and again in Chapter 13) the significance of that judicial qualification in connection with the Court's treatment of broadcasting. In the meantime, in *Kingsley International Pictures v. Regents of the University of the State of New York*, 360 U.S. 684 (1959), the Supreme Court overturned the New York Motion Picture Division's refusal to license showing of the movie version of D.H. Lawrence's famous novel, *Lady Chatterley's Lover*, because of the Division's judgment that the film portrayed adultery as "desirable, acceptable, or a proper pattern of behavior." In *Kingsley*, the Court made it clear that Americans had as much of a First Amendment right to advocate adultery as they did atheism or socialism.

Ironically, in the same decade in which the Supreme Court was giving the movie industry these favorable verdicts in *Burstyn* and *Kingsley*, the Court was also holding that citizens did not have a First Amendment right to advocate the ideology of the Communist Party (see *Dennis v. United States*, 341 U.S. 494 (1951)), and that while adultery could be portrayed as socially acceptable, its sexual component could not be displayed in a visibly "obscene" fashion (*see Roth v. United States*, 354 U.S. 476 (1957)). Thus, as a prelude to our investigation of the current constitutional status of entertaining "speech for fun and profit," it is important to have at least a capsulized version of the key issues and rulings that have transformed the First Amendment from what it was like at the time of the *Burstyn* ruling.

The one point that nearly everyone now agrees upon is that judges cannot simply apply the text of the First Amendment to every contested case. Indeed, in important respects the literal wording has been expanded by the Court to encompass restraints on speech by state entities (as in *Burstyn*) as well as by Congress, and to protect demonstrative actions (e.g., flag burning in *Texas v. Johnson*, 491 U.S. 397 (1989)) as well as speech in the ordinary meaning of that term. At the same time, not every restraint on expression is considered an "abridgment of the freedom of speech" for constitutional purposes. For example, if director Rossellini had included as part of the opening credits of *The Miracle* an apparent endorsement by the Pope, or the movie's producer had said in its securities offering that the National Legion of Decency had invested in the production, or the American distributor's advertisements pictured Cardinal Spellman telling Catholics to go see the film, the laws of trademark, securities, libel, and unfair trade practices would definitely have been (and still could be) brought to bear on such "speech." And so far the courts have ruled that even stronger restraints can be placed on personal efforts to transmit videos of movies like *The Miracle* to friends and colleagues over the Internet.

That same leeway is afforded the government to deal with speech that constitutes perjury in courts, soliciting or conspiring to commit murder, giving legal or medical advice without a license to practice, requesting sex in return for a promotion, selling confidential information, and the like. The question, then, is what the proper dividing line is between such permissible constraints on speech and what everyone would now agree is an unconstitutional ban on a "sacrilegious" movie like *The Miracle*. Answering that question requires grappling with the fundamental issue of why speech requires qualitatively different protection than other conduct from the legislative policy judgments arrived at via the usual political process.

Shortly after *Mutual Film*, two of the most oft-cited judicial explanations of the First Amendment's role were offered by Justices Oliver Wendell Holmes and Louis Brandeis. Justice Holmes expressed his point of view in *Abrams v. United States*, 250 U.S. 616 (1919), which dealt with federal prosecution of Russian-Jewish immigrants who had criticized the American government for providing military support to those who were trying to fend off the revolution in Russia.

> [W]hen men have realized that time has upset many fighting faiths, they may come to believe even more than they believe the very foundations of their own conduct that the ultimate good desired is better reached by free trade in ideas—that the best test of truth is the power of the thought to get itself accepted in the competition of the market, and that truth is the only grounds upon which their wishes safely can be carried out.

250 U.S. at 630. Justice Brandeis stated his perspective in *Whitney v. California*, 274 U.S. 357 (1927), a case in which a Communist labor leader was prosecuted:

> Those who won our independence . . . believed that freedom to think as you will and to speak as you think are means indispensable to the discovery and spread of political truth; that without free speech and assembly discussion would be futile; that with them discussion affords ordinarily adequate protection against the dissemination of noxious doctrine; that the greatest menace to freedom is an inert people; that public discussion is a public duty; and that this should be a fundamental principle of the American government.

274 U.S. at 375. While there are significant differences between the two Justices' respective "competitive market" and "civic republicanism"

premises for the distinctive value of free speech, a common feature is that the passages were written in cases in which the Court was upholding convictions for the speech of both Abrams and Whitney.

Another constitutional view shared by Justices Holmes and Brandeis, the legitimacy of government regulation of the business market, emerged triumphant in the late 1930s when the Supreme Court did its "switch in time that saved nine" and upheld President Roosevelt's New Deal by repudiating the constitutional version of "liberty of contract" articulated in *Lochner v. New York*, 198 U.S. 45 (1905). The Supreme Court overturned criminal convictions for speech, in *De Jonge v. Oregon*, 299 U.S. 353 (1937), and *Herndon v. Lowry*, 301 U.S. 242 (1937) (involving Communist activists prosecuted for what they had been saying in labor and civil rights disputes respectively). Yet, a conspicuous feature of the political New Deal was the adoption of comprehensive regulation of business practices involving speech: securities offerings, food and drug and other trade advertising, labor representation campaigns, and the allocation and control of broadcasting licenses under the new Communications Act. It is understandable, then, that a posture of judicial restraint in imposing constitutional limits on the actions of popularly elected governments was also exhibited in the context of speech. Besides the *Dennis* and *Roth* cases mentioned above, another noteworthy First Amendment ruling was *Beauharnais v. Illinois*, 343 U.S. 250 (1952), in which the Court upheld a state conviction of the president of a White Circle League for circulating racist leaflets calling on the people of Chicago to block the "Negro invasion of their neighborhoods" in violation of a state law that prohibited libel of racial or religious groups.

In sum, in 1952 when *Burstyn* was being decided, the Court's bringing of the entertainment industry under the umbrella of the First Amendment had somewhat more symbolic than practical significance. After all, the so-called Golden Age of Hollywood in the 1930s and 1940s had taken place when *Mutual Film* was the law on this question. The real impact of *Burstyn* came in the 1960s, when the Supreme Court dramatically enhanced the constitutional protection afforded to any kind of speech. Two of the key rulings were byproducts of the civil rights movements, though from opposing ends of that spectrum.

The first, *New York Times v. Sullivan*, 376 U.S. 254 (1964), was precipitated by a full-page advertisement in the New York Sunday Times, in which a number of civil rights organizations and supporters protested the "wave of terror" that had been instituted by southerners and the police to try to quell the peaceful protest movement of Dr. Martin Luther King and his supporters. Sullivan, one of the elected commissioners in Montgomery, instituted a defamation lawsuit against the Times and several clergymen signatories to the advertisement. Although Sullivan had not been mentioned in the advertisement and only a handful of copies of the Sunday Times were actually sold in Alabama, a jury found that Sullivan had been libeled by several inaccuracies in the ad, and awarded him $500,000 in damages.

This award under state common law was overturned by the Supreme Court in what many scholars believe to be the most important step in the evolution of judicial understanding of "the central meaning of the First Amendment" (376 U.S. at 273).[b] The tort law of defamation had to be constrained by a

> profound national commitment to the principle that debate on public issues should be uninhibited, robust and wide-open, and that it may well include vehement, caustic and sometimes unpleasantly sharp attacks on government and public officials.

376 U.S. at 270. Because it was as much the duty of citizens to criticize government as it was the officials' duty to administer it, citizen performance of that duty required broad constitutional immunity—absent "actual malice" in the sense of knowledge or reckless disregard of the falsity of a harmful statement—from the threat of damage suits by officials concerned about the effect of criticism on their reputations.

The second major precedent, *Brandenburg v. Ohio*, 395 U.S. 444 (1969), afforded constitutional protection to speech by Clarence Brandenburg, leader of an Ohio branch of the Ku Klux Klan. Brandenburg's speech to this gathering of hooded, cross-burning Klan members vilified Blacks and Jews, and ended by saying that:

> If our President, our Congress, our Supreme Court continues to suppress the white Caucasian race, it's possible that there might have to be some revengeance [sic] taken.

Brandenburg, whose speech happened to be filmed and telecast, was prosecuted and convicted under Ohio's Criminal Syndicalism legislation, which prohibited

> advocacy of the duty, necessity or propriety of crime, sabotage, violence, or unlawful methods of terrorism as a means of accomplishing industrial or political reform.

The Supreme Court overturned its earlier precedent, *Whitney v. California*, 274 U.S. 357 (1927), and ruled that it would violate the First Amendment to punish the pure *advocacy* of illegal force. Only "advocacy directed to inciting or producing *imminent* lawless action and [that] is likely to incite or produce such action" could constitutionally be made illegal. Illustrating how far the First Amendment had journeyed from

---

[b] *See* Harry Kalven Jr., *The* New York Times *Case: A Note on the Central Meaning of the First Amendment,* 1964 Sup. Ct. Rev. 191; Anthony Lewis, New York Times v. Sullivan *Reconsidered: Time to Return to "The Central Meaning of the First Amendment,"* 83 Colum. L. Rev. 603 (1983).

*Abrams* (1919), *Dennis* (1951), and other such precedents was the Court's ruling in *Hess v. Indiana*, 414 U.S. 105 (1973), that there was no "clear and present danger" that could justify conviction of the leader of an anti-Vietnam War group who, when the police were breaking up his demonstration, told the sheriff that "we'll take the fucking street later."

A thread running through almost all of the Supreme Court precedents mentioned to this point is that they involved *political* speech by people who were dissenting from actions taken by government over some question of public policy. Later on in this chapter we shall observe the significance of *Brandenburg* and *Hess* for lower court scrutiny of both public and private efforts to control the level of violence portrayed in film and music. The scope and impact of *New York Times* was itself sharply expanded in the late 1960s in a case, *Time, Inc. v. Hill*, 385 U.S. 374 (1967), that involved an early example of what is now a key entertainment industry product—the docudrama.

The Hill family had been the victims of a highly-publicized 1952 hostage-taking by three escaped convicts who were using the Hills' suburban Philadelphia home. Luckily the Hills all emerged unscathed from what had been non-violent, even courteous, treatment by the convicts. Nonetheless, distraught by the experience, the Hills moved to Connecticut and avoided all efforts to remain in the media spotlight.

A year later, a book, *The Desperate Hours*, appeared, a fictional portrayal of a suburban family that had been the victim of similar hostage-taking by escaped convicts, though this one was marked by physical brutality and sexual harassment. When *The Desperate Hours* was turned into a Broadway play for the 1954–55 season, Life Magazine explicitly tied the storyline to the Hills' experience. Indeed, Life had pictures taken in the Philadelphia home of the various actors playing the Hills family and the convicts, reenacting some of the purportedly violent incidents as depictions of the play's "heart-stopping account of how a family rose to heroism in a crisis."

The Hills' reaction to that account was to sue Time-Life for violating New York's "right to privacy" legislation. The New York Court of Appeals had ruled, in *Warren Spahn v. Julian Messner*, 18 N.Y.2d 324, 274 N.Y.S.2d 877, 221 N.E.2d 543 (1966), that while the New York legislation did not preclude "factual reporting of newsworthy persons and events" (even if the persons had been involuntarily rendered newsworthy), it did preclude fictionalized portrayals that were "inaccurate and distorted." The Hills won a $75,000 jury verdict under the legislation. Time-Life then appealed to the Supreme Court, with Richard Nixon serving as the Hills' attorney in his one appearance in the Court as counsel rather than client. A closely-divided Supreme Court overturned the jury verdict on the grounds that "knowing or reckless disregard of falsity"—rather than negligent failure to make a reasonable investigation—was the constitutional predicate to such a privacy suit by a private individual (as well as the defamation claim by the public official in *New York Times Co. v. Sullivan*):

> The guarantees for speech and press are not the preserve of political expression or comment upon public affairs, essential as these are to healthy government. One need only pick up any newspaper or magazine to comprehend the vast range of published matter which exposes persons to public view, both private citizens and public officials. Exposure of the self to others in varying degrees is a concomitant of life in a civilized community. The risk of this exposure is an essential incident of life in a society which places a primary value on freedom of speech and of press . . . We have no doubt that the subject of the *Life* article, the opening of a new play linked to an actual incident, is a matter of public interest . . . We create a grave risk of serious impairment of the indispensable service of a free press in a free society if we saddle the press with the impossible burden of verifying to a certainty the facts associated in news articles with a person's name, picture or portrait, particularly as related to a defamatory matter. Even negligence would be a most elusive standard, especially when the content of the speech itself affords no warning of prospective harm to another through falsity. . . .

385 U.S. at 388–89.

We shall trace in the next chapter the impact of *Time, Inc. v. Hill* on the evolution of individual privacy and publicity rights in a world of docudramas and tabloid television. More immediately relevant to the subject of this chapter was a fifteen-year debate among the Supreme Court's members, following its decision in *Roth v. United States*, 354 U.S. 476 (1957), about whether and to what extent government could restrain depictions of explicit sex—pornography in lay terms, obscenity or indecency in legal terms. Just a year after *Time, Inc. v. Hill*, the Court in *Interstate Circuit, Inc. v. City of Dallas*, 390 U.S. 676 (1968), struck down a Dallas city ordinance that provided for prior viewing of films by a citizen's Motion Picture Classification Board for purposes of classifying certain movies as "not suitable for young persons" (less than 16 years of age). The standards for "lack of suitability for young persons" were:

> (1) Describing or portraying brutality, criminal violence or depravity in such a manner as to be . . . likely to incite or encourage crime or delinquency on the part of young persons; or
>
> (2) Describing or portraying nudity beyond the customary limits of candor in the community, or sexual promiscuity or extra-

> marital or abnormal sexual relations in such a manner as to be . . . likely to incite or encourage delinquency or sexual promiscuity on the part of young persons or to appeal to their prurient interest.
>
> . . . In determining whether a film is "not suitable for young persons," the Board shall consider the film as a whole, rather than isolated scenes, and shall determine whether its harmful effects outweigh artistic or educational values such films may have for young persons.

Films classified by the Board as unsuitable had to be advertised as such by the motion picture exhibitor, and admission was denied to children under 16 unaccompanied by their parents.

Relying on *Burstyn*, the Court concluded that the "vice of vagueness" reflected in these licensing standards was seriously detrimental to the constitutional rights of the motion picture industry and its fans.

> It may be unlikely that what Dallas does in respect to the licensing of motion pictures would have a significant effect upon film makers in Hollywood or Europe. But what Dallas may constitutionally do, so may other cities and States. Indeed, we are told that this ordinance is being used as a model for legislation in other localities. Thus, one who wishes to convey his ideas through that medium, which of course includes one who is interested not so much in expression as in making money, must consider whether what he proposes to film, and how he proposes to film it, is within the terms of classification schemes such as this. If he is unable to determine what the ordinance means, he runs the risk of being foreclosed, in practical effect, from a significant portion of the movie-going public. Rather than run that risk, he might choose nothing but the innocuous, perhaps save for the so-called "adult" picture. Moreover, a local exhibitor who cannot afford to risk losing the youthful audience when a film may be of marginal interest to adults—perhaps a "Viva Maria"—may contract to show only the totally inane. The vast wasteland that some have described in reference to another medium might be a verdant paradise in comparison. The First Amendment interests here are, therefore, broader than merely those of the film maker, distributor, and exhibitor, and certainly broader than those of youths under 16.

390 U.S. at 683–84. And the fact that the technique for Dallas' regulation of film expression was "one of classification rather than direct suppression" could not save this "system of informal censorship" from constitutional challenge by the film in question, *Viva Maria*.

---

An immediate byproduct of *City of Dallas* was that the movie industry, acting through its arm, the Motion Picture Association of America (MPAA), developed its own system of film ratings for sex and violence (which we will examine later in this chapter). Five years later (and sixteen years after *Roth*), the Supreme Court, in *Miller v. California*, 413 U.S. 15 (1973), finally settled on the still-prevailing formula about what kinds of works governments can constitutionally restrict as sexually "obscene." The basic guidelines are

(a) whether the average person, applying contemporary community standards, would find that the work taken as a whole, appeals to the prurient interest,

(b) whether the work depicts or describes, in a patently offensive way, sexual conduct specifically defined by the applicable state law,

(c) and whether the work, taken as a whole, lacks serious literary, artistic, political, or scientific value.

413 U.S. at 24. Having to satisfy all three of these components to the constitutional standard in practice now limits government regulation of movies to those that constitute "hard core pornography"—about which at least some of the Justices believe they "know it when they see it" (*see Jacobellis v. Ohio*, 378 U.S. 184, 197 (1964)).

An intriguing illustration of how far both the movie and legal worlds have moved in the five decades since the *Burstyn* decision was the 1995 movie *Priest*. This was a story about two priests in Liverpool, England, one having an affair with the housekeeper, the other having several homosexual encounters. The movie was distributed in the United States by Miramax, a division of the long-time leader in family pictures, the Walt Disney Company. Though New York's Cardinal O'Connor (and then-Senator Robert Dole) denounced *Priest* as an offensive portrayal of the Catholic clergy, and the Knights of Columbus tried to arrange a boycott of theaters where the movie was being shown, no one would have dreamed of the government banning *Priest* from the screen.

---

The politics of the First Amendment experienced an intriguing twist in the 1980s. Until then, the same people—"liberals"—who had pressed for governmental regulation of contractual relations also vigorously defended freedom of speech from legal constraints, while their opponents—"conservatives"—who were fighting for freedom of contract in business and labor markets also supported governmental controls on speech to preserve public safety and morality. More recently, though, the question of what to do about speech that threatens gender and racial equality has fractured both these left and right coalitions.

In the 1980s, feminist legal scholarship (especially the work of Catherine MacKinnon) sought to reformulate our understanding of the legitimate roles of anti-pornography law in ways that would both narrow and expand the constitutional concept of "obscenity." Rather than focusing as *Miller* did, on works that appeal to *prurient* interests in sexual practices that are *patently offensive* to a community's moral and religious standards of appropriate sexual behavior, MacKinnon argued that the law should target only that sexual content that risks specific kinds of harm to women—their portrayal in violent, degrading, or subordinating sexual encounters with men. The harm this law would aim at might be inflicted on the women actually being portrayed in the product (e.g., a pornographic movie, though not a book), or upon those who were later attacked, sexually harassed, or otherwise mistreated by the male viewers of the product. However prurient and offensive these might seem to the community, explicit portrayals of egalitarian sexual encounters would be legalized. At the same time, violent pornography against women would not enjoy constitutional protection even if it did have "serious literary or artistic value."

In the United States, a number of local governments sought to embody this new intellectual perspective in their legal ordinances—most prominently Indianapolis. A city ordinance of the early 1980s placed pornography within the administratively and judicially-enforceable bars to discrimination against women. For this purpose, the law defined "pornography" as "the graphic sexually explicit subordination of women, whether in pictures or in words" in a variety of ways: women presented as sexual objects who enjoy pain or humiliation; women who experience sexual pleasure in being raped, tied up, cut up, or mutilated; women penetrated by objects or animals; women presented in scenarios of degradation, torture, or hurt, in a context that makes these conditions sexual. More generally, pornography would consist of the presentation of women "as sexual objects for domination, conquest, violation, exploitation, possession or use, or through postures or positions of servility or submission or display." The Indianapolis ordinance was challenged in front of the Seventh Circuit Court of Appeals in *American Booksellers Ass'n v. Hudnut*, 771 F.2d 323 (7th Cir. 1985), authored by Judge Frank Easterbrook.

In the court's view, the fact that the Indianapolis ordinance excluded the most graphic depictions of sex as long as women were portrayed as equals, while deeming pornography to consist in presentation of women as "enjoying pain, humiliation, or rape" or in "positions of servility or display," made the law more, not less, constitutionally offensive:

. . . This is thought control. It establishes an "approved" view of women, of how they may react to sexual encounters, of how the sexes may relate to each other. Those who espouse the approved view may use sexual images; those who do not, may not.

Indianapolis justifies the ordinance on the ground that pornography affects thoughts. Men who see women depicted as subordinate are more likely to treat them so. Pornography is an aspect of dominance. It does not persuade people so much as change them. It works by socializing, by establishing the expected and the permissible. In this view pornography is not an idea; pornography is the injury.

There is much to this perspective. Beliefs are also facts. People often act in accordance with the images and patterns they find around them. People raised in a religion tend to accept the tenets of that religion, often without independent examination. People taught from birth that black people are fit only for slavery rarely rebelled against that creed; beliefs coupled with the self-interest of the masters established a social structure that inflicted great harm while enduring for centuries. Words and images act at the level of the subconscious before they persuade at the level of the conscious. Even the truth has little chance unless a statement fits within the framework of beliefs that may never have been subjected to rational study.

Therefore we accept the premises of this legislation. Depictions of subordination tend to perpetuate subordination. The subordinate status of women in turn leads to affront and lower pay at work, insult and injury at home, battery and rape on the streets. In the language of the legislature, "pornography is central in creating and maintaining sex as a basis of discrimination. Pornography is a systematic practice of exploitation and subordination based on sex which differentially harms women. The bigotry and contempt it produces, with the acts of aggression it fosters, harm women's opportunities for equality and rights [of all kinds]."

Yet this simply demonstrates the power of pornography as speech. All of these unhappy effects depends on mental intermediation. Pornography affects how people see the world, their fellows, and social relations. If pornography is what pornography does, so is other speech. Hitler's orations affected how some Germans saw Jews. Communism is a world view, not simply a Manifesto by Marx and Engels or a set of speeches. Efforts to suppress communist speech in the United States were based on the belief that the public acceptability of such ideas would increase the likelihood of totalitarian government. Religions affect socialization in the most pervasive way. The opinion in *Wisconsin v. Yoder*, 406 U.S. 205 (1972), shows how a religion can dominate an entire approach to life, governing much more than the relation between the sexes. Many people believe that the existence of television, apart from the content of specific programs, leads to intellectual laziness, to a penchant for violence, to many other ills. The Alien and Sedition Acts passed during the administration of John Adams rested on a sincerely held belief that disrespect for the government leads to social collapse and revolution—a belief with support in the history of many nations. Most governments of the world act on this empirical regularity, suppressing critical speech. In the United States, however, the strength of the support for this belief is irrelevant. Seditious libel is protected speech unless the danger is not only grave but also imminent. *See New York Times Co. v. Sullivan*, 376 U.S. 254 (1964).

Racial bigotry, anti-semitism, violence on television, reporters' biases—these and many more influence the culture and shape our socialization. None is directly answerable by more speech, unless that speech too finds its place in the popular culture. Yet all is protected as speech, however insidious. Any other answer leaves the government in control of all of the institutions of culture, the great censor and director of which thoughts are good for us.

Sexual responses often are unthinking responses, and the association of sexual arousal with the subordination of women therefore may have a substantial effect. But almost all cultural stimuli provoke unconscious responses. Religious ceremonies condition their participants. Teachers convey messages by selecting what not to cover; the implicit message about what is off limits or unthinkable may be more powerful than the messages for which they present rational argument. Television scripts contain unarticulated assumptions. People may be conditioned in subtle ways. If the fact that speech plays a role in a process of conditioning were enough to permit governmental regulation, that would be the end of freedom of speech.

771 F.2d at 328–30.

Another argument by the City was that it wanted to protect actresses in violent pornographic films from experiencing the harm of sexual violence depicted in these works. Judge Easterbrook noted that while government can and should directly target this kind of harmful action by producers engaged in making the film, this objective clearly could not justify an ordinance that also banned sexual violence in books. Even with respect to movies, this argument would not suffice:

> The more immediate point, however, is that the image of pain is not necessarily pain. In *Body Double*, a suspense film directed by Brian DePalma, a woman who has disrobed and presented a sexually explicit display is murdered by an intruder with a drill. The drill runs through the woman's body. The film is sexually explicit and a murder occurs—yet no one believes that the actress suffered pain or died. In *Barbarella* a character played by Jane Fonda is at times displayed in sexually explicit ways and at times shown "bleeding, bruised, [and] hurt in a context that makes these conditions sexual"—and again no one believes that Fonda was actually tortured to make the film. In *Carnal Knowledge* a woman grovels to please the sexual whims of a character played by Jack Nicholson; no one believes that there was a real sexual submission, and the Supreme Court held the film protected by the First Amendment. *Jenkins v. Georgia*, 418 U.S. 153 (1974). And this works both ways. The description of women's sexual domination of men in *Lysistrata* was not real dominance. Depictions may affect slavery, war, or sexual roles, but a book about slavery is not itself slavery, or a book about death by poison a murder.

771 F.2d at 330. The Seventh Circuit's ruling striking down the Indianapolis law was upheld by the Supreme Court without argument or opinion: *see* 475 U.S. 1001 (1986).

---

The Supreme Court itself adopted essentially the same position as Judge Easterbrook's in *Hudnut* with respect to the analogous question of the constitutionality of laws that prohibit "hate speech" directed at racial or religious groups. Recall that in the 1950s, the Supreme Court had upheld a law of this kind: *see Beauharnais v. Illinois*, 343 U.S. 250 (1952). In *R.A.V. v. St. Paul*, 505 U.S. 377 (1992), the Court, by a narrow 5–4 margin, struck down a St. Paul ordinance that prohibited the burning of crosses and swastikas with that kind of racial or religious connotation. Though the Minnesota Supreme Court had construed the local ordinance to cover only racist and religious epithets, the kinds of "fighting words" that are assumed to be unprotected by the First Amendment (*see Chaplinsky v. New Hampshire*, 315 U.S. 568 (1942)), the Supreme Court majority found it unconstitutional to target only those hate speech epithets that had a distinctively racist or anti-religious point of view.

---

As sketched in the last several pages, the last five decades have produced a dramatically different First Amendment jurisprudence since the Supreme Court, in *Burstyn*, brought the entertainment industry under that constitutional umbrella. As noted at the outset of this chapter, the issues remain hotly contested in both the popular and political spheres, and there is nothing intrinsic to the wording, historical intent, or philosophical underpinning of the First Amendment that precludes equally radical changes and reversals during this new century. In tracking and appraising the legal treatment of entertaining speech throughout this book, keep the following questions in mind.

1. The current American stance towards freedom of speech is considerably more absolutist than in any other democratic nation. Interestingly, Canada and most members of the European Union, have adopted even more stringent restraints on hate speech than those struck down by the Supreme Court in *R.A.V.* What lessons can be drawn from this contrasting treatment of speech in these various countries and cultures?

2. Interestingly, there is a comparative history of the treatment of speech within the United States itself, derived from the fact that the Supreme Court has long approved the effort by the federal government to hold *broadcast* speech to somewhat more "civilized" standards. Most (though not all) constitutional scholars believe that television and radio stations should now enjoy the same full-bodied freedom of speech as their other media counterparts (more and more of whom are owned by the same corporate entities). It is at least logically possible that the constitutional movement could be in the opposite direction. Reflect on your own experience with television as compared with movies, or radio and music concerts, to assess how these types of media should be treated.

3. From the point of view of philosophical principle rather than legal doctrine, should entertaining speech enjoy the same constitutional stature as the political speech in *Sullivan*, *Brandenburg*, et al.? Recall the passages quoted earlier by Holmes in *Abrams*, with its preference for free trade in ideas, and Brandeis in *Whitney*, with its emphasis on public discussion in a democracy. Why exactly is it crucial to protect speech from unwarranted restraints through the judicial rather than just the political process? Should such First Amendment entitlements apply not just to Robert Rossellini's *The Miracle* or James Joyce's *Ulysses*, but to any

kind of entertainment product whose combination of sex and violence has consumer appeal in the marketplace?

4. As the scope of the First Amendment has expanded over the last fifty years, so also has its use by business entities (e.g., broadcast companies). In the 1990s, for example, the telephone companies have used the First Amendment to challenge the long-standing federal ban on phone companies also offering cable services within their same local areas, on the grounds that this was equivalent to an unconstitutional restraint on political dissent and artistic creativity. *See Chesapeake & Potomac Tel. Co. v. United States*, 830 F. Supp. 909 (E.D. Va. 1993). Should businesses have to make this case for a free market in speech in the political rather than in the judicial arena? (In fact, as we shall see in Chapter 13, the "Baby Bells" did win this struggle in Congress in early 1996 at the very same time that the Supreme Court was grappling with the First Amendment implications of this issue.)

5. The flip side of that latter coin is whether the First Amendment should permit or preclude the use of the law by a business rather than a government entity to restrict speech on or with the business's "private" property. If, as the Supreme Court held in *Metromedia v. San Diego*, 453 U.S. 490 (1981), the First Amendment limits government's power to restrict the use of billboards on public highway space, should it also limit the use of trespass law by a shopping center owner to stop people from passing out anti-Vietnam War leaflets in the part of the mall that was otherwise open to and regularly used by everyone in the neighborhood? *See Lloyd Corp. v. Tanner*, 407 U.S. 551 (1972).

## B. ENTERTAINING SEX

The foregoing is a rather truncated account of several major First Amendment victories won by the entertainment industry over the last half century. It is clearly the case that extending to entertainment products essentially the same constitutional freedom as is enjoyed by public policy debates, scientific inquiry, and artistic creativity has made life much better for entertainment producers. The more fundamental question, though, is whether this has made life better for Americans generally.

While the Supreme Court still has not rendered an explicit verdict about entertaining violence, it continues to produce a host of decisions about entertaining sex. But one of the very few recent occasions in which anti-sex laws, formulated according to the *Miller v. California* guidelines, have been targeted at notable figures in the entertainment world involved a highly controversial recording by the rap music group, 2 Live Crew.[c] The lyrics of the album, *As Nasty as They Wanna Be*, together with its hit single, "Me So Horny," made constant references to the genitalia and to intercourse, cunnilingus, fellatio, and the like. Representative lines included "He'll tear the cunt open 'cause its satisfaction,'" and "Grabbed her by the hair, threw her on the floor, opened up her thighs, and guess what I saw." The unexpurgated *Nasty* version had sold over 2 million copies and soared high on the 1989 Billboard Hits Chart. An alternative version, *As Clean As They Wanna Be*, with the same melodies but different lyrics, sold 250,000 copies.

That winter the South Florida Broward County Sheriff's Department received complaints from local residents about *Nasty*. The Sheriff investigated, secured an *ex parte* probable-cause-of-obscenity determination from a county judge, and used this to warn local record stores not to sell *Nasty* if they wanted to avoid prosecution. All the local stores immediately removed *Nasty* from their shelves. The 2 Live Crew group, led by Luther Campbell, and their record company, Skyywalker Records, filed suit under § 1983 of the United States Code, claiming violation of their federal constitutional rights. After losing in the district court, plaintiffs appealed to the Eleventh Circuit, which in the below opinion applies the *Miller* criteria concerning what constitutes "obscenity."

## SKYYWALKER RECORDS, INC. V. NAVARRO

United States Court of Appeals, Eleventh Circuit, 1992.
960 F.2d 134.

PER CURIAM.

In this appeal, appellants Luke Records, Inc., Luther Campbell, Mark Ross, David Hobbs, and Charles Wongwon seek reversal of the district court's declaratory judgment that the musical recording "As Nasty As They Wanna Be" is obscene under Fla.Stat. § 847.011 and the United States Constitution, contending that the district court misapplied the test for determining obscenity. We reverse.

Appellants Luther Campbell, David Hobbs, Mark Ross, and Charles Wongwon comprise the musical group "2 Live Crew," which recorded "As Nasty As They Wanna Be." In response to actions taken by the Broward

[c] For a review of the constitutional issues posed by this and other such proposals, see Daniel A. Cohen, *Compensating Pornographic Victims: A First Amendment Analysis*, 29 Valparaiso U. L. Rev. 285 (1994). For an insightful debate about the underlying empirical issues, see Daniel Linz, Steven D. Penrod, and Edward Donnerstein, *The Attorney General's Commission on Pornography: The Gap Between "Findings" and Facts*, 1987 Amer. Bar Found. Res. J. 713; Frederick Schauer, *Causation Theory and the Causes of Sexual Violence*, *id.*, 737.

County, Florida Sheriff's Office to discourage record stores from selling "As Nasty As They Wanna Be," appellants filed this action in federal district court to enjoin the Sheriff from interfering further with the sale of the recording. The district court granted the injunction, finding that the actions of the Sheriff's office were an unconstitutional prior restraint on free speech. The Sheriff does not appeal this determination.

In addition to injunctive relief, however, appellants sought a declaratory judgment pursuant to 28 U.S.C.A. § 2201 that the recording was not obscene. The district court found that "As Nasty As They Wanna Be" is obscene under *Miller v. California.*

This case is apparently the first time that a court of appeals has been asked to apply the *Miller* test to a musical composition, which contains both instrumental music and lyrics. Although we tend to agree with appellants' contention that because music possesses inherent artistic value, no work of music alone may be declared obscene, that issue is not presented in this case. The Sheriff's contention that the work is not protected by the First Amendment is based on the lyrics, not the music. The Sheriff's brief denies any intention to put rap music to the test, but states "it is abundantly obvious that it is only the 'lyrical' content which makes "As Nasty As They Wanna Be" obscene." Assuming that music is not simply a sham attempt to protect obscene material, the *Miller* test should be applied to the lyrics and the music of "As Nasty As They Wanna Be" as a whole. The basic guidelines for the trier of fact must be: (a) whether "the average person, applying contemporary community standards" would find that the work, taken as a whole, appeals to the prurient interest; (b) whether the work depicts or describes, in a patently offensive way, sexual conduct specifically defined by the applicable state law; and (c) whether the work, taken as a whole, lacks serious literary, artistic, political, or scientific value. 413 U.S. at 24, 93 S.Ct. at 2615. This test is conjunctive. *Penthouse Intern., Ltd. v. McAuliffe,* 610 F.2d 1353, 1363 (5th Cir.1980). A work cannot be held obscene unless each element of the test has been evaluated independently and all three have been met. *Id.*

Appellants contend that because the central issue in this case is whether "As Nasty As They Wanna Be" meets the definition of obscenity contained in a Florida criminal statute, the thrust of this case is criminal and the Sheriff should be required to prove the work's obscenity beyond a reasonable doubt. In the alternative, appellants assert that at minimum, the importance of the First Amendment requires that the burden of proof in the district court should have been by "clear and convincing evidence," rather than by "a preponderance of the evidence." Assuming, arguendo, that the proper standard is the preponderance of the evidence, we conclude that the Sheriff has failed to carry his burden of proof that the material is obscene by the *Miller* standards under that less stringent standard. Thus, to reverse the declaratory judgment that the work is obscene, we need not decide which of the standards applies.

There are two problems with this case which make it unusually difficult to review. First, the Sheriff put in no evidence but the tape recording itself. The only evidence concerning the three-part *Miller* test was put in evidence by the plaintiffs. Second, the case was tried by a judge without a jury, and he relied on his own expertise as to the prurient interest community standard and artistic value prongs of the *Miller* test.

*First,* the Sheriff put in no evidence other than the cassette tape. He called no expert witnesses concerning contemporary community standards, prurient interest, or serious artistic value. His evidence was the tape recording itself.

The appellants called psychologist Mary Haber, music critics Gregory Baker, John Leland and Rhodes Scholar Carlton Long. Dr. Haber testified that the tape did not appeal to the average person's prurient interest.

Gregory Baker is a staff writer for *New Times Newspaper,* a weekly arts and news publication supported by advertising revenue and distributed free of charge throughout South Florida. Baker testified that he authored "hundreds" of articles about popular music over the previous six or seven years. After reviewing the origins of hip hop and rap music, Baker discussed the process through which rap music is created. He then outlined the ways in which 2 Live Crew had innovated past musical conventions within the genre and concluded that the music in "As Nasty As They Wanna Be" possesses serious musical value.

John Leland is a pop music critic for *Newsday* magazine, which has a daily circulation in New York, New York of approximately six hundred thousand copies, one of the top ten daily newspaper circulations in the country. Leland discussed in detail the evolution of hip hop and rap music, including the development of sampling technique by street disc jockeys over the previous fifteen years and the origins of rap in more established genres of music such as jazz, blues, and reggae. He emphasized that a Grammy Award for rap music was recently introduced, indicating that the recording industry recognizes rap as valid artistic achievement, and ultimately gave his expert opinion that 2 Live Crew's music in "As Nasty As They Wanna Be" does possess serious artistic value.

Of appellants' expert witnesses, Carlton Long testified most about the lyrics. Long is a Rhodes scholar with a Ph.D. in Political Science and was to begin an assistant professorship in that field at Columbia University in New York City shortly after the trial. Long testified that "As Nasty As They Wanna Be" contains three oral traditions, or musical conventions, known as call and response, doing the dozens, and boasting. Long testified that these oral traditions derive their roots from certain segments of Afro-American culture. Long described each of these conventions and cited examples of each one from "As Nasty As They Wanna Be." He concluded that the album reflects many aspects of the cultural heritage of poor, inner city blacks as well as the cultural experiences of 2 Live Crew. Long suggested that certain excerpts from "As Nasty As They Wanna Be" contained statements of political significance or exemplified numerous literary conventions, such as alliteration, allusion, metaphor, rhyme, and personification.

The Sheriff introduced no evidence to the contrary, except the tape.

*Second,* the case was tried by a judge without a jury, and he relied on his own expertise as to the community standard and artistic prongs of the *Miller* test.

The district court found that the relevant community was Broward, Dade, and Palm Beach Counties. He further stated:

> This court finds that the relevant community standard reflects a *more* tolerant view of obscene speech than would other communities within the state. This finding of fact is based upon this court's personal knowledge of the community. The undersigned judge has resided in Broward County since 1958. As a practicing attorney, state prosecutor, state circuit judge, and currently, a federal district judge, the undersigned has traveled and worked in Dade, Broward, and Palm Beach. As a member of the community, he has personal knowledge of this area's demographics, culture, economics, and politics. He has attended public functions and events in all three counties and is aware of the community's concerns as reported in the media and by word of mouth.
>
> In almost fourteen years as a state circuit judge, the undersigned gained personal knowledge of the nature of obscenity in the community while viewing dozens, if not hundreds of allegedly obscene films and other publications seized by law enforcement.
>
> . . . .
>
> The plaintiffs' claim that this court cannot decide this case without expert testimony and the introduction of specific evidence on community standards is also without merit. The law does not require expert testimony in an obscenity case. The defendant introduced the *Nasty* recording into evidence. As noted by the Supreme Court in *Paris Adult Theatre I* [*v. Slaton,* 413 U.S. 49, 93 S.Ct. 2628, 37 L.Ed.2d 446 (1973)], when the material in question is not directed to a 'bizarre, deviant group' not within the experience of the average person, the best evidence is the material, which 'can and does speak for itself.'

> *Paris Adult Theatre I,* 413 U.S. at 56 & n. 6, 93 S.Ct. at 2634 & n. 6.
>
> In deciding this case, the court's decision is not based upon the undersigned judge's personal opinion as to the obscenity of the work, but is an application of the law to the facts based upon the trier of fact's personal knowledge of community standards. In other words, even if the undersigned judge would not find *As Nasty As They Wanna Be* obscene, he would be compelled to do so if the community's standards so required.
>
> It is difficult for an appellate court to review value judgments. Although, generally, these determinations are made in the first instance by a jury, in this case the district judge served as the fact finder, which is permissible in civil cases. Because a judge served as a fact finder, however, and relied only on his own expertise, the difficulty of appellate review is enhanced. A fact finder, whether a judge or jury, is limited in discretion. "Our standard of review must be faithful to both Rule 52(a) and the rule of independent review." "The rule of independent review assigns to appellate judges a constitutional responsibility that cannot be delegated to the trier of fact," even where that fact finder is a judge.

In this case, it can be conceded without deciding that the judge's familiarity with contemporary community standards is sufficient to carry the case as to the first two prongs of the *Miller* test: prurient interest applying community standards and patent offensiveness as defined by Florida law. The record is insufficient, however, for this Court to assume the fact finder's artistic or literary knowledge or skills to satisfy the last prong of the *Miller* analysis, which requires determination of whether a work "lacks serious artistic, scientific, literary or political value."

In *Pope v. Illinois,* the Court clarified that whether a work possesses serious value was not a question to be decided by contemporary community standards. The Court reasoned that the fundamental principles of the First Amendment prevent the value of a work from being judged solely by the amount of acceptance it has won within a given community:

Just as the ideas a work represents need not obtain majority approval to merit protection, neither, insofar as the First Amendment is concerned, does the value of the work vary from community to community based on the degree of local acceptance it has won.

The Sheriff concedes that he has the burden of proof to show that the recording *is* obscene. Yet, he submitted no evidence to contradict the testimony that the work had artistic value. A work cannot be held obscene unless each element of the *Miller* test has been met. We reject the argument that simply by listening to this musical work, the judge could determine that it had no serious artistic value.

Reversed.

### *QUESTIONS FOR DISCUSSION*

1. One ground for the 2 Live Crew appeal was that the Sheriff's case consisted simply of having the trial judge listen to the tape and read the lyrics of "As Nasty As They Wanna Be." Should either (or both) sides in obscenity trials have to present expert testimony on the issues, and if so, with respect to which features of the *Miller* test? Recall the comment by Justice Stewart in *Jacobellis v. Ohio*, 378 U.S. 184, 197 (1964), that while he had trouble defining hardcore pornography, he certainly knew it when he saw it. Do you think the judges in the Georgia state courts might have seen the early 1970s movie, *Carnal Knowledge* (starring Jack Nicholson, Ann Margret, Art Garfunkel, and Candace Bergen), differently than did the members of the Supreme Court? *See Jenkins v. Georgia*, 418 U.S. 153 (1974).

2. Another controversial song, titled "Mind of a Lunatic" and written and performed by the Geto Boys, was filled with lyrics like the following:

> Her body's so beautiful, so I'm thinking rape. Shouldn't have had the curtains open; so that's her fate. Slit her throat and watched her shake.

Does the popularity of songs like these influence your appraisal of the contrasting views of Professor MacKinnon and Judge Easterbrook that we saw detailed in *Hudnut*? Keep this brand of "Gangsta Rap" music in mind while reading the cases and materials in the next section, on **Entertaining Violence**.

3. In *Paris Adult Theatre I v. Slaton*, 413 U.S. 49 (1973), the Supreme Court made it clear that even fully-informed consenting adults had no federal constitutional right to watch movies that passed the *Miller* obscenity test. In *State v. Henry*, 302 Ore. 510, 732 P.2d 9 (1987), however, the Oregon Supreme Court found such a right under that state's constitution. Would you advocate other state courts or legislatures following the Oregon lead and abolishing any legal restrictions on sexual entertainment for adults?

4. Suppose that the South Florida authorities had simply refused to allow 2 Live Crew to perform this music at a concert in a publicly-owned facility that is regularly used for musical events in the area. *See Cinevision v. City of Burbank*, 745 F.2d 560 (9th Cir. 1984). What if the public authority refuses to license use of its facility by "hard rock" bands whose music is judged too loud for the surrounding community? *See Fact Concerts, Inc. v. City of Newport*, 626 F.2d 1060 (1st Cir. 1980), vacated on other grounds, 453 U.S. 247 (1981), and *Ward v. Rock Against Racism*, 491 U.S. 781 (1989). What if the authority requires the band to secure costly liability insurance following prior altercations, drug use, and injuries at rock band concerts? *See Rock Against Racism v. Ward*, 658 F. Supp. 1346 (S.D.N.Y. 1987).

5. The 1995 Thanksgiving weekend witnessed a tragic event in the New York subway system. Early Sunday morning, a Brooklyn token clerk was severely burned when two arsonists squirted inflammable liquid into his booth and ignited it. This was exactly the same scenario that had been depicted in the Wesley Snipes/Woody Harrelson movie, *Money Train*, which had opened that same weekend. As it turned out, the Transit Authority had assisted Columbia Pictures in filming the movie, though the Authority had objected to this scene (which was based on an actual event that had taken place five years earlier). This combination of real and fictional violence gave a real edge to the ongoing debate about whether public authorities should make their facilities available for movies like *Money Train* (or its 1974 predecessor, *The Taking of Pelham One, Two, Three*, about the hijacking of New York subway car for ransom, which was recently remade).

While Senator Robert Dole was calling for a boycott of *Money Train's* "pornography of violence as a way to sell movie tickets," his fellow Republican, New York Mayor Rudy Giuliani, was saying that city officials "should not be reading the script of every movie and acting as a censor." With whom do you agree? Does it affect your judgment on that score to learn that in this case the offenders said they had *not* seen *Money Train*? Even if a city agency (or a state university) might be inclined to withhold permission to film a movie on its premises unless a scene of explicit violence (or sex or drug use) was cut from the script, would such a position be constitutionally permissible? On the broader cultural phenomenon of rap music, see Tricia Rose, *Black Noise* (Wesleyan U. Press, 1994). On the legal issues posed by the 2 Live Crew case, see Margaret A. Blanchard, *The American Urge to Censor: Freedom of Expression Versus the Desire to Sanitize Society—From Anthony Comstock to 2 Live Crew*, 33 William & Mary L. Rev. 741 (1992); Blake D. Morant, *Restraint of Controversial Musical Expression After* Skyywalker Records v. Navarro *and* Barnes v. Glen Theater: *Can the Band Play On?,* 70 Denver U. L. Rev. 5 (1992).[d]

6. In some ways, the growth of the Internet has diffused some of the conflicts concerning the regulation of sex on network television and radio airwaves. Television shows that contain sexual or violent scenes simply choose alternative networks or venues, including cable channels like HBO or online providers like Netflix to offer their materials. Similarly, the ability to listen to music through online providers like iTunes or Spotify allows artists more freedom to provide uncensored works of music. Still, many artists offer "clean" versions of their songs in hope for widespread distribution. Do you think that Internet-based providers provide acceptable alternatives to complying with government regulations? Why or why not?

---

[d] For an in-depth analysis of the economic as well as the First Amendment features of this problem, see Jon Garon, Star Wars: *Film Permitting, Prior Restraint, & Government's Role in the Entertainment Industry,* 17 Loyola of L.A. Enter. L. Rev. 1 (1996).

In the spring of 2000, the Supreme Court rendered its verdict about another form of sexual entertainment, one that was not based on the *Miller* obscenity standards. In 1994, the City of Erie, Pennsylvania proclaimed that it "has, at various times over more than a century, expressed its findings that certain lewd, immoral activities carried on in public places for profit are highly detrimental to the public health, safety and welfare, and lead to the debasement of both women and men, promote violence, public intoxication, prostitution and the serious criminal activity . . ." The Council then passed a general ban on anyone appearing in public space in "a state of nudity."

A company called Pap's A.M. had been operating an entertainment establishment called Kandyland, which featured totally nude and erotic dancing performed by women. When told that the only way to avoid prosecution under the new Ordinance was to clothe the women in at least some "pasties" and a "G-string," the company sued the City, alleging an infringement of its First Amendment right to free speech.

There had been a prior Supreme Court decision, *Barnes v. Glen Theatre*, 501 U.S. 560 (1991), which had upheld an analogous state-wide law in Indiana. However, the five different opinions written by Justices in *Barnes* satisfied the Supreme Court of Pennsylvania that *Barnes* was too much of a "hodgepodge" to be a binding First Amendment verdict. *See Pap's A.M. v. City of Erie*, 553 Pa. 348, 719 A.2d 273 (1998). After characterizing nude dancing as a form of "speech," the Pennsylvania Court dismissed as "highly circuitous" the notion that the city could "prevent rape, prostitution, and other sex crimes by requiring a dancer in a legal establishment to wear pasties and a G-string before appearing on stage." But when the City of Erie took this case up to the U.S. Supreme Court, the majority of a still-divided court (at 529 U.S. 277 (2000)) found that banning nude dancing was constitutional.

The majority opinion written by Justice O'Connor found nude dancing to be a form of "expressive conduct," though "it falls only within the outer ambit of the First Amendment protection." *Id.* at 289. However, this city ordinance was "a content neutral restriction that regulates conduct, not First Amendment expression." *Id.* at 298. Erie did have a legitimate objective of trying "to deter crime and the other deleterious effects caused by the presence of such a [nude dancing] establishment in the neighborhood." *Id.* at 297. Finally, "the requirement that dancers wear pasties and G-strings is a minimal restriction in favor of the asserted government interests, and the restriction leaves ample capacity to convey the dancer's erotic message." *Id.* at 301.

Justice Souter's dissent accepted the basic jurisprudential principles in the O'Connor opinion, but wanted the case sent back to require Erie to provide some evidence that its ordinance was "reasonably designed to mitigate real harms." *Id.* at 317. The concurring opinion of Justices Scalia and Thomas was "highly skeptical . . . that the addition of pasties and G-strings will at all reduce the tendency of establishments such as Kandyland to attract crime and prostitution, and hence to foster sexually transmitted disease." They believed, however, that there was no constitutionally-protected "expression" here at all, and that instead the traditional power of government to foster good morals and the acceptability of the "traditional judgment that nude public dancing *itself* is immoral, have not been repealed by the First Amendment." *Id.* at 310. By contrast, the other dissent (by Justices Stevens and Ginsburg) found unconstitutional Erie's total ban (rather than zoning locational regulation) on nude dancing, which was "a species with expressive conduct that is protected by the First Amendment" because it "fits well within a broad cultural tradition." *Id.* at 326.

In reflecting on these rather diverse First Amendment perspectives on nude dancing, consider as well how they fit with the constitutional treatment we have and will be seeing courts giving in this (and the next) chapter to a host of other forms of entertainment.

In the spring of 2002, the Supreme Court issued a major—and divided—ruling on the application of that kind of First Amendment exception to technological rather than real depiction of child sex. Two decades before, in *New York v. Ferber*, 458 U.S. 747 (1982), the Court had ruled that the *Miller* obscenity standard did not bind the government's power to prohibit pornography using children having sex. However, the development of the new computer technology facilitated the creation of these virtual images without any real children actually engaged in the sex.

Thus, the Congress, led here by Missouri Senator John Ashcroft, placed in the 1996 budget legislation a Child Pornography Prevention Act that was signed by President Clinton. This broadened the definition of child pornography to include "any visual depiction, including any photograph, film, video, picture, or computer-generated image or picture [that] is, or appears to be, of a minor engaging in sexually explicit conduct." Among the congressional aims in this new "virtual child pornography" was to preclude pornographers who had actually used children from defending by claiming they had just used their computer; to prevent "pedophiles" from using just digital images to recruit real children who had witnessed films apparently showing their counterparts "having fun" with sex; and also to insulate from these images adults who might "harbor illicit desires for children and commit criminal acts to gratify these impulses" (with reports that annually, more than 90,000 children were the victims of such child sexual abuse).

Over the next five years, four different circuit courts had upheld the constitutionality of this legislation in cases involving criminal prosecution of the offenders. However, a body called the Free Speech Coalition, an organization of California adult movie producers and video stores, brought a class action suit claiming a violation of their First Amendment rights, which the full Ninth Circuit accepted in *Free Speech Coalition v. Reno*, 220 F.3d 1113 (2000). This appeal followed:

## ASHCROFT V. FREE SPEECH COALITION

Supreme Court of the United States, 2002.
535 U.S. 234, 122 S.Ct. 1389, 152 L.Ed.2d 403.

MR. JUSTICE KENNEDY delivered the opinion of the Court.

II

* * *

The Child Pornography Prevention Act (CPPA) prohibits speech despite its serious literary, artistic, political, or scientific value. The statute proscribes the visual depiction of an idea—that of teenagers engaging in sexual activity—that is a fact of modern society and has been a theme in art and literature throughout the ages. Under the CPPA, images are prohibited so long as the persons appear to be under 18 years of age. This is higher than the legal age for marriage in many States, as well as the age at which persons may consent to sexual relations. *See* U.S. National Survey of State Laws 384–388 (R. Leiter ed., 3d ed. 1999) (48 States permit 16-year-olds to marry with parental consent); W. Eskridge & N. Hunter, *Sexuality, Gender, and the Law* 1021–1022 (1997) (in 39 States and the District of Columbia, the age of consent is 16 or younger). It is, of course, undeniable that some youths engage in sexual activity before the legal age, either on their own inclination or because they are victims of sexual abuse.

Both themes—teenage sexual activity and the sexual abuse of children—have inspired countless literary works. William Shakespeare created the most famous pair of teenage lovers, one of whom is just 13 years of age. *See Romeo and Juliet*, act I, sc. 2, l. 9 ("She hath not seen the change of fourteen years"). In the drama, Shakespeare portrays the relationship as something splendid and innocent, but not juvenile. The work has inspired no less than 40 motion pictures, some of which suggest that the teenagers consummated their relationship. E.g., *Romeo and Juliet* (B. Luhrmann director, 1996). Shakespeare may not have written sexually explicit scenes for the Elizabethean audience, but were modern directors to adopt a less conventional approach, that fact alone would not compel the conclusion that the work was obscene.

Contemporary movies pursue similar themes. Last year's Academy Awards featured the movie, *Traffic*, which was nominated for Best Picture. The film portrays a teenager, identified as a 16-year-old, who becomes addicted to drugs. The viewer sees the degradation of her addiction, which in the end leads her to a filthy room to trade sex for drugs. The year before, *American Beauty* won the Academy Award for Best Picture. In the course of the movie, a teenage girl engages in sexual relations with her teenage boyfriend, and another yields herself to the gratification of a middle-aged man. The film also contains a scene where, although the movie audience understands the act is not taking place, one character believes he is watching a teenage boy performing a sexual act on an older man.

Our society, like other cultures, has empathy and enduring fascination with the lives and destinies of the young. Art and literature express the vital interest we all have in the formative years we ourselves once knew, when wounds can be so grievous, disappointment so profound, and mistaken choices so tragic, but when moral acts and self-fulfillment are still in reach. Whether or not the films we mention violate the CPPA, they explore themes within the wide sweep of the statute's prohibitions. If these films, or hundreds of others of lesser note that explore those subjects, contain a single graphic depiction of sexual activity within the statutory definition, the possessor of the film would be subject to severe punishment without inquiry into the work's redeeming value. This is inconsistent with an essential First Amendment rule: The artistic merit of a work does not depend on the presence of a single explicit scene. *See Book Named "John Cleland's Memoirs of a Woman of Pleasure" v. Attorney General of Mass.*, 383 U.S. 413, 419, 16 L. Ed. 2d 1, 86 S. Ct. 975 (1966) (plurality opinion) ("The social value of the book can neither be weighed against nor canceled by its prurient appeal or patent offensiveness"). Under *Miller*, the First Amendment requires that redeeming value be judged by considering the work as a whole. Where the scene is part of the narrative, the work itself does not for this reason become obscene, even though the scene in isolation might be offensive. For this reason, and the others we have noted, the CPPA cannot be read to prohibit obscenity, because it lacks the required link between its prohibitions and the affront to community standards prohibited by the definition of obscenity.

The Government seeks to address this deficiency by arguing that speech prohibited by the CPPA is virtually indistinguishable from child pornography, which may be banned without regard to whether it depicts works of value. *See New York v. Ferber*, 458 U.S. at 761. Where the images are themselves the product of child sexual abuse, *Ferber* recognized that the State had an interest in stamping it out without regard to any judgment about its content. The production of the work, not its content, was the target of the statute. The fact that a work contained serious literary, artistic, or other value did not excuse the harm it caused to its child participants. It was simply "unrealistic to equate a community's toleration for sexually oriented materials with the permissible scope of legislation aimed at protecting children from sexual exploitation." *Id.* at 761, n. 12.

*Ferber* upheld a prohibition on the distribution and sale of child pornography, as well as its production, because these acts were "intrinsically related" to the sexual abuse of children in two ways. *Id.* at 759. First, as a permanent record of a child's abuse, the continued circulation itself would harm the child who had participated. Like a defamatory statement, each new publication of the speech would cause new injury to the child's reputation and emotional well-being. *See id.* at 759, and n. 10. Second, because the traffic in child pornography was an economic motive for its production, the State had an interest in closing the distribution network. "The most expeditious if not the only practical method of law enforcement may be to dry up the market for this material by imposing severe criminal penalties on persons selling, advertising, or otherwise promoting the product." *Id.* at 760. Under either rationale, the speech had what the Court in effect held was a proximate link to the crime from which it came.

* * *

In contrast to the speech in *Ferber*, speech that itself is the record of sexual abuse, the CPPA prohibits speech that records no crime and creates no victims by its production. Virtual child pornography is not "intrinsically related" to the sexual abuse of children, as were the materials in *Ferber*. While the Government asserts that the images can lead to actual instances of child abuse, the causal link is contingent and indirect. The harm does not necessarily follow from the speech, but depends upon some unquantified potential for subsequent criminal acts.

The Government says these indirect harms are sufficient because, as *Ferber* acknowledged, child pornography rarely can be valuable speech. This argument, however, suffers from two flaws. First, *Ferber's* judgment about child pornography was based upon how it was made, not on what it communicated. The case reaffirmed that where the speech is neither obscene nor the product of sexual abuse, it does not fall outside the protection of the First Amendment.

The second flaw in the Government's position is that *Ferber* did not hold that child pornography is by definition without value. On the contrary, the Court recognized some works in this category might have significant value, but relied on virtual images—the very images prohibited by the CPPA—as an alternative and permissible means of expression. . . . *Ferber*, then, not only referred to the distinction between actual and virtual child pornography, it relied on it as a reason supporting its holding. *Ferber* provides no support for a statute that eliminates the distinction and makes the alternative mode criminal as well.

III

The CPPA, for reasons we have explored, is inconsistent with *Miller* and finds no support in *Ferber*. The Government seeks to justify its prohibitions in other ways. It argues that the CPPA is necessary because pedophiles may use virtual child pornography to seduce children. . . .

Here, the Government wants to keep speech from children not to protect them from its content but to protect them from those who would commit other crimes. The principle, however, remains the same: The Government cannot ban speech fit for adults simply because it may fall into the hands of children. The evil in question depends upon the actor's unlawful conduct, conduct defined as criminal quite apart from any link to the speech in question. This establishes that the speech ban is not narrowly drawn. The objective is to prohibit illegal conduct, but this restriction goes well beyond that interest by restricting the speech available to law-abiding adults.

The Government submits further that virtual child pornography whets the appetites of pedophiles and encourages them to engage in illegal conduct. This rationale cannot sustain the provision in question. The mere tendency of speech to encourage unlawful acts is not a sufficient reason for banning it. The government "cannot constitutionally premise legislation on the desirability of controlling a person's private thoughts." *Stanley v. Georgia*, 394 U.S. 557, 566, 22 L. Ed. 2d 542, 89 S. Ct. 1243 (1969). First Amendment freedoms are most in danger when the government seeks to control thought or to justify its laws for that impermissible end. The right to think is the beginning of freedom, and speech must be protected from the government because speech is the beginning of thought.

To preserve these freedoms, and to protect speech for its own sake, the Court's First Amendment cases draw vital distinctions between words and deeds, between ideas and conduct. . . . There is here no attempt, incitement, solicitation, or conspiracy. The Government has shown no more than a remote connection between speech that might encourage thoughts or impulses and any resulting child abuse. Without a significantly stronger, more direct connection, the Government may not prohibit speech on the ground that it may encourage pedophiles to engage in illegal conduct.

The Government next argues that its objective of eliminating the market for pornography produced using real children necessitates a prohibition on virtual images as well. Virtual images, the Government contends, are indistinguishable from real ones; they are part of the same market and are often exchanged. In this way, it is said, virtual images promote the trafficking in works produced through the exploitation of real children. The hypothesis is somewhat implausible. If virtual images were identical to illegal child pornography, the illegal images would be driven from the market by the indistinguishable substitutes. Few pornographers would risk prosecution by abusing real children if fictional, computerized images would suffice.

In the case of the material covered by *Ferber*, the creation of the speech is itself the crime of child abuse; the prohibition deters the crime by removing the profit motive. Even where there is an underlying crime, however, the Court has not allowed the suppression of speech in all cases. We need not consider where to strike the balance in this case, because here, there is no underlying crime at all. Even if the Government's market deterrence theory were persuasive in some contexts, it would not justify this statute.

Finally, the Government says that the possibility of producing images by using computer imaging makes it very difficult for it to prosecute those who produce pornography by using real children. Experts, we are told, may have difficulty in saying whether the pictures were made by using real children or by using computer imaging. The necessary solution, the argument runs, is to prohibit both kinds of images. The argument, in essence, is that protected speech may be banned as a means to ban unprotected speech. This analysis turns the First Amendment upside down.

The Government may not suppress lawful speech as the means to suppress unlawful speech. Protected speech does not become unprotected merely because it resembles the latter. The Constitution requires the reverse. The overbreadth doctrine prohibits the Government from banning unprotected speech if a substantial amount of protected speech is prohibited or chilled in the process.

To avoid the force of this objection, the Government would have us read the CPPA not as a measure suppressing speech but as a law shifting the burden to the accused to prove the speech is lawful. In this connection, the Government relies on an affirmative defense under the statute, which allows a defendant to avoid conviction for nonpossession offenses by showing that the materials were produced using only adults and were not otherwise distributed in a manner conveying the impression that they depicted real children.

The Government raises serious constitutional difficulties by seeking to impose on the defendant the burden of proving his speech is not unlawful. An affirmative defense applies only after prosecution has begun, and the speaker must himself prove, on pain of a felony conviction, that his conduct falls within the affirmative defense. In cases under the CPPA, the evidentiary burden is not trivial. Where the defendant is not the producer of the work, he may have no way of establishing the identity, or even the existence, of the actors. If the evidentiary issue is a serious problem for the Government, as it asserts, it will be at least as difficult for the innocent possessor. The statute, moreover, applies to work created before 1996, and the producers themselves may not have preserved the records necessary to meet the burden of proof. Failure to establish the defense can lead to a felony conviction.

We need not decide, however, whether the Government could impose this burden on a speaker. Even if an affirmative defense can save a statute from First Amendment challenge, here the defense is incomplete and insufficient, even on its own terms. It allows persons to be convicted in some instances where they can prove children were not exploited in the production. A defendant charged with possessing, as opposed to distributing, proscribed works may not defend on the ground that the film depicts only adult actors. So while the affirmative defense may protect a movie producer from prosecution for the act of distribution, that same producer, and all other persons in the subsequent distribution chain, could be liable for possessing the prohibited work. Furthermore, the affirmative defense provides no protection to persons who produce speech by using computer imaging, or through other means that do not involve the use of adult actors who appear to be minors. In these cases, the defendant can demonstrate no children were harmed in producing the images, yet the affirmative defense would not bar the prosecution. For this reason, the affirmative defense cannot save the statute, for it leaves unprotected a substantial amount of speech not tied to the Government's interest in distinguishing images produced using real children from virtual ones.

In sum, § 2256(8)(B) covers materials beyond the categories recognized in *Ferber* and *Miller*, and the reasons the Government offers in support of limiting the freedom of speech have no justification in our precedents or in the law of the First Amendment. The provision abridges the freedom to engage in a substantial amount of lawful speech. For this reason, it is overbroad and unconstitutional.

* * *

The judgment of the Court of Appeals is affirmed.

JUSTICE THOMAS, concurring in the judgment.

In my view, the Government's most persuasive asserted interest in support of the Child Pornography Prevention Act of 1996 (CPPA), 18 U.S.C. § 2251 et seq., is the prosecution rationale—that persons who possess and disseminate pornographic images of real children may escape conviction by claiming that the images are computer-generated, thereby raising a reasonable doubt as to their guilt. At this time, however, the Government asserts only that defendants raise such defenses, not that they have done so successfully. In fact, the Government points to no case in which a defendant has been acquitted based on a "computer-generated images" defense. While this speculative interest cannot support the broad reach of the CPPA, technology may evolve to the point where it becomes impossible to enforce actual child pornography laws because the Government cannot prove that certain pornographic images are of real children. In the event this occurs, the Government should not be foreclosed from enacting a regulation of virtual child pornography that contains an appropriate affirmative defense or some other narrowly drawn restriction.

The Court suggests that the Government's interest in enforcing prohibitions against real child pornography cannot justify prohibitions on virtual child pornography, because "this analysis turns the First Amendment upside down. The Government may not suppress lawful speech as the means to suppress unlawful speech." But if technological advances thwart prosecution of "unlawful speech," the Government may well have a compelling interest in barring or otherwise regulating some narrow category of "lawful speech" in order to enforce effectively laws against pornography made through the abuse of real children. The Court does leave open the possibility that a more complete affirmative defense could save a statute's constitutionality, implicitly accepting that some regulation of virtual child pornography might be constitutional. I would not prejudge, however, whether a more complete affirmative defense is the only way to narrowly tailor a criminal statute that prohibits the possession and dissemination of virtual child pornography. Thus, I concur in the judgment of the Court.

CHIEF JUSTICE REHNQUIST, with whom JUSTICE SCALIA joins in part, dissenting.

* * *

We normally do not strike down a statute on First Amendment grounds "when a limiting instruction has been or could be placed on the challenged statute." *Broadrick v. Oklahoma*, 413 U.S. 601, 613 (1973). This case should be treated no differently.

Other than computer generated images that are virtually indistinguishable from real children engaged in sexually explicitly conduct, the CPPA can be limited so as not to reach any material that was not already unprotected before the CPPA. The CPPA's definition of "sexually explicit conduct" is quite explicit in this regard. It makes clear that the statute only reaches "visual depictions" of:

"Actual or simulated . . . sexual intercourse, including genital-genital, oral-genital, anal-genital, or oral-anal, whether between persons of the same or opposite sex; . . . bestiality; . . . masturbation; . . . sadistic or masochistic abuse; . . . or lascivious exhibition of the genitals or pubic area of any person." 18 U.S.C. § 2256(2).

The Court and Justice O'Connor suggest that this very graphic definition reaches the depiction of youthful looking adult actors engaged in suggestive sexual activity, presumably because the definition extends to "simulated" intercourse. Read as a whole, however, I think the definition reaches only the sort of "hard core of child pornography" that we found without protection in *Ferber*, 458 U.S. at 773–774. So construed, the CPPA bans visual depictions of youthful looking adult actors engaged in actual sexual activity; mere suggestions of sexual activity, such as youthful looking adult actors squirming under a blanket, are more akin to written descriptions than visual depictions, and thus fall outside the purview of the statute.

* * *

Indeed, we should be loath to construe a statute as banning film portrayals of Shakespearian tragedies, without some indication—from text or legislative history—that such a result was intended. In fact, Congress explicitly instructed that such a reading of the CPPA would be wholly unwarranted. As the Court of Appeals for the First Circuit has observed:

> "The legislative record, which makes plain that the [CPPA] was intended to target only a narrow class of images—visual depictions 'which are virtually indistinguishable to unsuspecting viewers from unretouched photographs of actual children engaging in identical sexual conduct.'" *United States v. Hilton*, 167 F.3d 61, 72 (1999) (quoting S. Rep. No. 104–358, pt. I, p. 7 (1996)).

* * *

This narrow reading of "sexually explicit conduct" not only accords with the text of the CPPA and the intentions of Congress; it is exactly how the phrase was understood prior to the broadening gloss the Court gives it today. Indeed, had "sexually explicit conduct" been thought to reach the sort of material the Court says it does, then films such as *Traffic* and *American Beauty* would not have been made the way they were. *Traffic* won its Academy Award in 2001. *American Beauty* won its Academy Award in 2000. But the CPPA has been on the books, and has been enforced, since 1996. The chill felt by the Court ("Few legitimate movie producers . . . would risk distributing images in or near the uncertain reach of this law"), has apparently never been felt by those who actually make movies.

To the extent the CPPA prohibits possession or distribution of materials that "convey the impression" of a child engaged in sexually explicit conduct, that prohibition can and should be limited to reach "the sordid business of pandering" which lies outside the bounds of First Amendment protection. This is how the Government asks us to construe the statute, and it is the most plausible reading of the text, which prohibits only materials "advertised, promoted, presented, described, or distributed in such a manner that conveys the impression that the material is or contains a visual depiction of a minor engaging in sexually explicit conduct." 18 U.S.C. § 2256(8)(D) (emphasis added).

The First Amendment may protect the video shop owner or film distributor who promotes material as "entertaining" or "acclaimed" regardless of whether the material contains depictions of youthful looking adult actors engaged in nonobscene but sexually suggestive conduct. The First Amendment does not, however, protect the panderer. Thus, materials promoted as conveying the impression that they depict actual minors engaged in sexually explicit conduct do not escape regulation merely because they might warrant First Amendment protection if promoted in a different manner. I would construe "conveys the impression" as limited to the panderer, which makes the statute entirely consistent with Ginzburg and other cases.

* * *

In sum, while potentially impermissible applications of the CPPA may exist, I doubt that they would be "substantial . . . in relation to the statute's plainly legitimate sweep." Broadrick, 413 U.S. at 615. The aim of ensuring the enforceability of our Nation's child pornography laws is a compelling one. The CPPA is targeted to this aim by extending the definition of child pornography to reach computer-generated images that are virtually indistinguishable from real children engaged in sexually explicit conduct. The statute need not be read to do any more than precisely this, which is not offensive to the First Amendment.

For these reasons, I would construe the CPPA in a manner consistent with the First Amendment, reverse the Court of Appeals' judgment, and uphold the statute in its entirety.

JUSTICE O'CONNOR, concurring in the judgment in part and dissenting in part.

[Justice O'Connor agreed with the majority striking down the CPPA ban on material that "conveys the impression that it contains actual-child pornography," but with the dissent upholding "the ban on pornographic depictions that appear to be of minors so long as it is not applied to youthful-adult pornography."]

* * *

II

I disagree with the Court, however, that the CPPA's prohibition of virtual-child pornography is overbroad. Before I reach that issue, there are two preliminary questions: whether the ban on virtual-child pornography fails strict scrutiny and whether that ban is unconstitutionally vague. I would answer both in the negative.

The Court has long recognized that the Government has a compelling interest in protecting our Nation's children. This interest is promoted by efforts directed against sexual offenders and actual-child pornography. These efforts, in turn, are supported by the CPPA's ban on virtual-child pornography. Such images whet the appetites of child molesters, who may use the images to seduce young children. Of even more serious concern is the prospect that defendants indicted for the production, distribution, or possession of actual-child pornography may evade liability by claiming that the images attributed to them are in fact computer-generated. Respondents may be correct that no defendant has successfully employed this tactic. But, given the rapid pace of advances in computer-graphics technology, the Government's concern is reasonable. Computer-generated images lodged with the Court by Amici Curiae National Law Center for Children and Families et al. bear a remarkable likeness to actual human beings. Anyone who has seen, for example, the film *Final Fantasy: The Spirits Within* (H. Sakaguchi and M. Sakakibara directors, 2001) can understand the Government's concern. Moreover, this Court's cases do not require Congress to wait for harm to occur before it can legislate against it.

Respondents argue that, even if the Government has a compelling interest to justify banning virtual-child pornography, the "appears to be . . . of a minor" language is not narrowly tailored to serve that interest. They assert that the CPPA would capture even cartoon-sketches or statues of children that were sexually suggestive. Such images surely could not be used, for instance, to seduce children. I agree. A better interpretation of "appears to be . . . of" is "virtually indistinguishable from"—an interpretation that would not cover the examples respondents provide. Not only does the text of the statute comfortably bear this narrowing interpretation, the interpretation comports with the language that Congress repeatedly used in its findings of fact . . .

Reading the statute only to bar images that are virtually indistinguishable from actual children would not only assure that the ban on virtual-child pornography is narrowly tailored, but would also assuage any fears that the "appears to be . . . of a minor" language is vague. The narrow reading greatly limits any risks from "discriminatory enforcement." Respondents maintain that the "virtually indistinguishable from" language is also vague because it begs the question: from whose perspective? This problem is exaggerated. This Court has never required "mathematical certainty" or "meticulous specificity" from the language of a statute.

The Court concludes that the CPPA's ban on virtual-child pornography is overbroad. The basis for this holding is unclear. Although a content-based regulation may serve a compelling state interest, and be as narrowly tailored as possible while substantially serving that interest, the regulation may unintentionally ensnare speech that has serious literary, artistic, political, or scientific value or that does not threaten the harms sought to be combated by the Government. If so, litigants may challenge the regulation on its face as overbroad, but in doing so they bear the heavy burden of demonstrating that the regulation forbids a substantial amount of valuable or harmless speech. Respondents have not made such a demonstration. Respondents provide no examples of films or other materials that are wholly computer-generated and contain images that "appear to be . . . of minors" engaging in indecent conduct, but that have serious value or do not facilitate child abuse. Their overbreadth challenge therefore fails.

[Justice O'Connor then explained why she judged the ban on "youthful-adult pornography to violate the First Amendment," as the majority had held, but why that did *not* require holding unconstitutional the SPPA "ban on virtual-child pornography." Even though this was in the same "appears to be" of children text, drawing that key distinction would "preserve the CPPA's prohibition of the material that Congress found most dangerous to children."]

---

While the Court majority was not prepared to accept his narrower reading of the CPPA to save its constitutionality, while he was still Attorney-General, Ashcroft did ask Congress to have that explicitly written in for the future, though they have not done so yet. Among the key questions posed by such action is whether it still does make sense as a matter of public policy in this new millennium; is it politically viable on Capitol Hill and in the White House; and if such a new CPPA law is enacted, should the Justices consider that it does pass their First Amendment standards.

---

The National Endowment for the Arts (NEA) was created in 1965. By the late 1960s it was awarding grants of around $10 million annually, and over $300 million in the late 1980s. The NEA could take credit for such major accomplishments as supplying the initial seed money for what eventually became the Academy Award-winning movie *Driving Miss Daisy*. By the early 1990s, though, the NEA was engulfed in controversy for having given money for exhibition of the work of photographer Robert Mapplethorpe, including his portfolio of homoerotic and child nudity scenes. This and a few other sexually explicit NEA projects did not strengthen the NEA's hand in the broader political debate over whether any such government spending program should be preserved.

Whatever the politics, though, there was a basic question of constitutional principle about whether it was legitimate for a body like the NEA to apply a standard established by a 1980 federal statutory amendment directing NEA personnel to "take into consideration general standards of decency and respect for the values of the American public," as well as the "artistic excellence and artistic merit" of the applicants and proposals in deciding which were to get NEA funding for their projects. In *NEA v. Finley*, 524 U.S. 569 (1998), the Supreme Court addressed this issue for the first time with a dissent by Justice Souter, and a skeptical concurrence by Justices Scalia and Thomas. Justice O'Connor reversed the lower court decisions and upheld this provision against a challenge to its facial constitutionality.

The first key distinction drawn by the Court majority was from its ruling in *R.A.V. v. St. Paul*, 505 U.S. 377 (1992), which had struck down as facially invalid a municipal ordinance prohibiting anyone placing a symbol on property (e.g., a swastika) that would "arouse anger, alarm, or resentment in others on the basis of race, color, creed, religion, or gender." Here, by contrast, the NEA was awarding a grant rather than punishing a crime, and this "decency" factor was just one of many for the NEA to consider.

In striking down this NEA directive, the D.C. Circuit had relied on the Supreme Court's recent decision in *Rosenberger v. Rector and Visitors of University of Virginia*, 515 U.S. 819 (1995), which had found it unconstitutional for a public university to refuse to grant funding to a particular student newspaper because it was *religious* in content. The distinction drawn by Justice O'Connor between *Rosenberger* and *NEA* was that the latter body was conducting a competition among a large number of notable artists for a scarce amount of public funding, and the "decency" of this work was only one factor to be taken into consideration in what was inherently a "content-based" NEA verdict. And in response to the claim that simply making "decency" a factor on the face of the statute had a chilling effect on First Amendment speech, the Court noted that the Act also told the NEA that in displaying respect for the diverse beliefs and values of the American public in its grant-making decisions, it should treat as a *positive* feature of a proposal the fact that it "reflects the culture of a minority. . . ."

Justice O'Connor did say that "if the NEA were to leverage its power to award subsidies on the basis of subjective criteria into a penalty on disfavored viewpoints, then we would confront a different case." However, this would require proof that Karen Finley, for example, had topped her competitors on all other artistic scores, and thus the reason she had not won an NEA grant was because of the sexual indecency of her work. In view of the fact that two of Finley's co-plaintiffs in this case had actually secured NEA grants since their suit was filed, the Court was not prepared to assume that the NEA was actually exercising its discretionary power "in a manner that raises concern about the suppression of disfavored viewpoints."

Given that qualifications added by Justice O'Connor to her *NEA* opinion, Justice Scalia characterized Congress' apparent victory here as the equivalent of "the operation was a success, but the patient died." Justice Scalia believed that this statute was clearly "mandating" consideration of decency, such that if the other artistic factors were equal, an indecent work was supposed to lose the competition. However, this unquestionable "viewpoint discrimination" in the spending of public money on Finley should not be said to *abridge* her First Amendment freedom of speech because there were a host of other sources of money for her artistic works.

Just a year later, a major artistic battle took place in New York, one that had Mayor Rudy Giuliani agreeing with Justice Scalia. The Brooklyn Museum of Art had been located on the Eastern Parkway for over a century and receiving financial support from the City for that time as well. The fall of 1999 had a special exhibition coming there, *Sensation*, consisting of 90 paintings from the private Saatchi collection from Britain. One of these paintings, by Chris Ofili (a Roman Catholic of Nigerian descent), was called *The Holy Virgin Mary*, but depicted the Madonna with a breast made from elephant dung and surrounded by female genitalia from pornographic magazine cutouts. Giuliani called this "sick stuff" that was "Catholic-bashing"; his administration not only cut off all financial aid for the museum, but set out to terminate its lease.

The museum responded by going to court, and found federal district Judge Nina Gershon agreeing with its position in *Brooklyn Institute of Arts and Sciences v. City of New York and Rudolph W. Giuliani*, 64 F. Supp. 2d 184 (E.D.N.Y. 1999). Judge Gershon characterized what had happened here as an "effort by governmental officials to censor works of expression and to threaten the vitality of a major cultural institution, as punishment for failing to abide by governmental demands for orthodoxy." She rejected the Giuliani administration's argument that "hard-working taxpayers shouldn't have to foot the bill for offensive displays and the desecration of religion." In her view, the relevant Supreme Court precedent was not *Finley*, but *Burstyn* (discussed above), from which she quoted the following passage:

> It is not the business of government in our nation to suppress real or imagined attacks upon a particular religious doctrine, whether they appear in publications, speeches, or motion pictures.

The Judge then enjoined the City from cutting either the museum's funding or ending its lease. Mayor Giuliani immediately said he would be appealing what he characterized as "the usual knee-jerk reaction" of judges under the First Amendment. However, just before the Senate race got underway in the spring of 2000, Giuliani dropped his appeal and the City gave the Museum an additional $800,000. But what do you think is the appropriate reaction by either the courts or the government to *The Holy Virgin Mary*? Suppose that, rather than cutting off all financial support of the Brooklyn Museum and terminating its lease, Mayor Giuliani had just deducted funds for the space and time when *Sensation* was being exhibited: should that make a difference in the legal verdict? From the perspective of artists generally, what is the most productive reading of the First Amendment here?

---

One part of the entertainment world we have not yet seen in any of the cases is the medium that is now most prominent in our daily lives—television and radio broadcasting. As we shall explore in Chapter 13, so far this branch of the entertainment industry has received significantly different regulatory and First Amendment treatment than its counterparts in movies, music, and print. Indeed, in the same period when the Supreme Court was sharply expanding the constitutional rights of newspapers, magazines, and motion picture distributors, the Court was upholding government regulation of the broadcast industry.

In *Red Lion Broadcasting v. Federal Communications Commission*, 395 U.S. 367 (1969), the Court approved use of the FCC's "fairness doctrine," which gave subjects of personal, over-the-air attacks a right to free air time in order to reply. Though just a few years later the Court rejected application of such a right-of-reply doctrine to newspapers, *see Miami Herald Publishing v. Tornillo*, 418 U.S. 241 (1974), it has continued to endorse this and other special treatment of broadcasting because of the latter's use of part of the scarce, governmentally-allocated spectrum for communicating messages directly into the privacy of people's homes.

Besides "fairness," another problem that attracted the attention of the FCC in the 1970s was the phenomenon of "topless radio." These were mid-day call-in shows in which the radio hosts graphically talked about a variety of intimate sexual topics—e.g., favored techniques for oral sex—with callers. After a formal proceeding, the FCC found this kind of talk to violate § 1464 of the *Communications Act,* which forbids "obscene, indecent, or profane language" on broadcasts. That ruling was upheld by an appeals court against constitutional challenge in *Illinois Citizens Committee for Broadcasting v. FCC*, 515 F.2d 397 (D.C.Cir. 1974). Then came the Supreme Court's crucial ruling in the following case.

## FEDERAL COMMUNICATIONS COMMISSION V. PACIFICA FOUNDATION

Supreme Court of the United States, 1978.
438 U.S. 726, 98 S.Ct. 3026, 57 L.Ed.2d 1073.

JUSTICE STEVENS delivered the principal opinion of the Court.

[In this case, a performer named George Carlin recorded a 12-minute monologue—aptly entitled, "Filthy Words"—that he had delivered on a live stage in a California theater. Some time later, Pacifica broadcast the recording on a Tuesday afternoon over its New York station. A man who had heard the broadcast while driving his car with his young son, wrote to the Federal Communications Commission (FCC), saying that while he could understand the record being sold for private use, he could not accept it being broadcast over the air. Pacifica responded to this complaint by stating that Carlin was "a significant social satirist" who "like Twain and Sahl before him, examined the language of ordinary people . . . not mouthing obscenities . . . [but] merely using words to satirize as harmless and essentially silly our attitudes toward these words."

A five-member majority of the Court upheld the FCC's finding that Carlin's language violated the terms of the Communication Act which barred "indecent", though not necessarily "obscene," broadcasts. Dissenting from that statutory interpretation were Justices Brennan, Stewart, White, and Marshall, who would limit the Act's prohibition to "obscene" broadcasts. Given the majority's statutory construction, the question was posed of whether such federal legislation was constitutional. As to this issue Justice Stevens wrote simply for Chief Justice Burger and Justice Rehnquist.]

* * *

### IV

Pacifica makes two constitutional attacks on the Commission's order. First, it argues that the Commission's construction of the statutory language broadly encompasses so much constitutionally protected speech that reversal is required even if Pacifica's broadcast of the "Filthy Words" monologue is not itself protected by the First Amendment. Second, Pacifica argues that inasmuch as the recording is not obscene, the Constitution forbids any abridgment of the right to broadcast it on the radio.

*A*

[The Court rejected Pacifica's first argument on the grounds that judicial review was "limited to the question whether the Commission has the authority to proscribe this particular broadcast." In the Court's view, "invalidating any rule on the basis of its hypothetical application to situations not before the Court is 'strong medicine' to be applied 'sparingly and only as a last resort.' "]

*B*

When the issue is narrowed to the facts of this case, the question is whether the First Amendment denies government any power to restrict the public broadcast of indecent language in any circumstances.[19] For if the government has any such power, this was an appropriate occasion for its exercise. . . .

The words of the Carlin monologue are unquestionably "speech" within the meaning of the First Amendment. It is equally clear that the Commission's objections to the broadcast were based in part on its content. The order must therefore fall if, as Pacifica argues, the First Amendment prohibits all governmental regulation that depends on the content of speech. Our past cases demonstrate, however, that no such absolute rule is mandated by the Constitution.

The classic exposition of the proposition that both the content and the context of speech are critical elements of First Amendment analysis is Mr. Justice Holmes' statement for the Court in *Schenck v. United States*, 249 U.S. 47:

> "We admit that in many places and in ordinary times the defendants in saying all that was said in the circular would have been within their constitutional rights. But the character of every act depends upon the circumstances in which it is done. . . . The most stringent protection of free speech would not protect a man in falsely shouting fire in a theater and causing a panic. It

---

[19] Pacifica's position would, of course, deprive the Commission of any power to regulate erotic telecasts unless they were obscene under *Miller v. California* 413 U.S. 15. Anything that could be sold at a newsstand for private examination could be publicly displayed on television.

We are assured by Pacifica that the free play of market forces will discourage indecent programming. "Smut may," as Judge Leventhal put it, "drive itself from the market and confound Gresham;" the prosperity of those who traffic in pornographic literature and films would appear to justify skepticism.

does not even protect a man from an injunction against uttering words that may have all the effect of force. . . . The question in every case is whether the words used are used in such circumstances and are of such a nature as to create a clear and present danger that they will bring about the substantive evils that Congress has a right to prevent."

249 U.S. at 52. Other distinctions based on content have been approved in the years since *Schenck*. The government may forbid speech calculated to provoke a fight. *See Chaplinsky v. New Hampshire*, 315 U.S. 568 (1942). It may pay heed to the "commonsense differences between commercial speech and other varieties." *Bates v. State Bar of Arizona*, 433 U.S. 350, 381 (1977). It may treat libels against private citizens more severely than libels against public officials. *See Gertz v. Robert Welch, Inc.*, 418 U.S. 323 (1974). Obscenity may be wholly prohibited. *Miller v. California*, 413 U.S. 15. And only two Terms ago we refused to hold that a "statutory classification is unconstitutional because it is based on the content of communication protected by the First Amendment." *Young v. American Mini Theatres, Inc.*, 427 U.S. 50, 52 (1976).

The question in this case is whether a broadcast of patently offensive words dealing with sex and excretion may be regulated because of its content. Obscene materials have been denied the protection of the First Amendment because their content is so offensive to contemporary moral standards. *Roth v. United States*, 354 U.S. 476 (1957). But the fact that society may find speech offensive is not a sufficient reason for suppressing it. Indeed, if it is the speaker's opinion that gives offense, that consequence is a reason for according it constitutional protection. For it is a central tenet of the First Amendment that the government must remain neutral in the marketplace of ideas. If there were any reason to believe that the Commission's characterization of the Carlin monologue as offensive could be traced to its political content—or even to the fact that it satirized contemporary attitudes about four-letter words[22]—First Amendment protection might be required. But that is simply not this case. These words offend for the same reasons that obscenity offends.[23] Their place in the hierarchy of First Amendment values was aptly sketched by Mr. Justice Murphy when he said: "[Such] utterances are no

22 The monologue does present a point of view; it attempts to show that the words it uses are "harmless" and that our attitudes toward them are "essentially silly." The Commission objects, not to this point of view, but to the way in which it is expressed. The belief that these words are harmless does not necessarily confer a First Amendment privilege to use them while proselytizing, just as the conviction that obscenity is harmless does not license one to communicate that conviction by the indiscriminate distribution of an obscene leaflet.

23 The Commission stated: "Obnoxious, gutter language describing these matters has the effect of debasing and brutalizing human beings by reducing them to their mere bodily functions. . . ." Our society has a tradition of performing certain bodily functions in private, and of severely limiting the public exposure or discussion of such matters. Verbal or physical acts exposing those intimacies are offensive irrespective of any message that may accompany the exposure.

essential part of any exposition of ideas, and are of such slight social value as a step to truth that any benefit that may be derived from them is clearly outweighed by the social interest in order and morality." *Chaplinsky v. New Hampshire*, 315 U.S., at 572.

Although these words ordinarily lack literary, political, or scientific value, they are not entirely outside the protection of the First Amendment. Some uses of even the most offensive words are unquestionably protected. Indeed, we may assume, *arguendo*, that this monologue would be protected in other contexts. Nonetheless, the constitutional protection accorded to a communication containing such patently offensive sexual and excretory language need not be the same in every context. It is a characteristic of speech such as this that both its capacity to offend and its "social value," to use Mr. Justice Murphy's term, vary with the circumstances. Words that are commonplace in one setting are shocking in another. To paraphrase Mr. Justice Harlan, one occasion's lyric is another's vulgarity. Cf. *Cohen v. California*, 403 U.S. 15, 25.

In this case it is undisputed that the content of Pacifica's broadcast was "vulgar," "offensive," and "shocking." Because content of that character is not entitled to absolute constitutional protection under all circumstances, we must consider its context in order to determine whether the Commission's action was constitutionally permissible.

### *C*

We have long recognized that each medium of expression presents special First Amendment problems. *Joseph Burstyn, Inc. v. Wilson*, 343 U.S. 495, 502–503. And of all forms of communication, it is broadcasting that has received the most limited First Amendment protection. Thus, although other speakers cannot be licensed except under laws that carefully define and narrow official discretion, a broadcaster may be deprived of his license and his forum if the Commission decides that such an action would serve "the public interest, convenience, and necessity." Similarly, although the First Amendment protects newspaper publishers from being required to print the replies of those whom they criticize, *Miami Herald Publishing Co. v. Tornillo*, 418 U.S. 241, it affords no such protection to broadcasters; on the contrary, they must give free time to the victims of their criticism. *Red Lion Broadcasting Co. v. FCC*, 395 U.S. 367.

The reasons for these distinctions are complex, but two have relevance to the present case. First, the broadcast media have established a uniquely pervasive presence in the lives of all Americans. Patently offensive, indecent material presented over the airwaves confronts the citizen, not only in public, but also in the privacy of the home, where the individual's right to be left alone plainly outweighs the First Amendment rights of an intruder. *Rowan v. Post Office Dept.*, 397 U.S. 728 (1970).

Because the broadcast audience is constantly tuning in and out, prior warnings cannot completely protect the listener or viewer from unexpected program content. To say that one may avoid further offense by turning off the radio when he hears indecent language is like saying that the remedy for an assault is to run away after the first blow. One may hang up on an indecent phone call, but that option does not give the caller a constitutional immunity or avoid a harm that has already taken place.[27]

Second, broadcasting is uniquely accessible to children, even those too young to read. Although *Cohen's* written message might have been incomprehensible to a first grader, Pacifica's broadcast could have enlarged a child's vocabulary in an instant. Other forms of offensive expression may be withheld from the young without restricting the expression at its source. Bookstores and motion picture theaters, for example, may be prohibited from making indecent material available to children. We held in *Ginsberg v. New York*, 390 U.S. 629 (1968), that the government's interest in the "well-being of its youth" and in supporting "parents' claim to authority in their own household" justified the regulation of otherwise protected expression.[28] The ease with which children may obtain access to broadcast material, coupled with the concerns recognized in *Ginsberg*, amply justify special treatment of indecent broadcasting.

It is appropriate, in conclusion, to emphasize the narrowness of our holding. This case does not involve a two-way radio conversation between a cab driver and a dispatcher, or a telecast of an Elizabethan comedy. We have not decided that an occasional expletive in either setting would justify any sanction or, indeed, that this broadcast would justify a criminal prosecution. The Commission's decision rested entirely on a

---

[27] Outside the home, the balance between the offensive speaker and the unwilling audience may sometimes tip in favor of the speaker, requiring the offended listener to turn away. *See Erznoznik v. Jacksonville*, 422 U.S. 205. As we noted in *Cohen v. California*:

> "While this Court has recognized that government may properly act in many situations to prohibit intrusion into the privacy of the home of unwelcome views and ideas which cannot be totally banned from the public dialogue . . . , we have at the same time consistently stressed that 'we are often "captives" outside the sanctuary of the home and subject to objectionable speech.' "

403 U.S. at 21. The problem of harassing phone calls is hardly hypothetical. Congress has recently found it necessary to prohibit debt collectors from "[placing] telephone calls without meaningful disclosure of the caller's identity"; from "engaging any person in telephone conversation repeatedly or continuously with intent to annoy, abuse, or harass any person at the called number"; and from "[using] obscene or profane language or language the natural consequence of which is to abuse the hearer or reader." *Consumer Credit Protection Act Amendments*, 91 Stat. 877, 15 U.S.C. § 1692d (1976 ed., Supp. II).

[28] The Commission's action does not by any means reduce adults to hearing only what is fit for children. Cf. *Butler v. Michigan*, 352 U.S. 380, 383 (1957). Adults who feel the need may purchase tapes and records or go to theaters and nightclubs to hear these words. In fact, the Commission has not unequivocally closed even broadcasting to speech of this sort; whether broadcast audiences in the late evening contain so few children that playing this monologue would be permissible is an issue neither the Commission nor this Court has decided.

nuisance rationale under which context is all-important. The concept requires consideration of a host of variables. The time of day was emphasized by the Commission. The content of the program in which the language is used will also affect the composition of the audience,[29] and differences between radio, television, and perhaps closed-circuit transmissions, may also be relevant. As Mr. Justice Sutherland wrote, a "nuisance may be merely a right thing in the wrong place,—like a pig in the parlor instead of the barnyard." *Euclid v. Ambler Realty Co.*, 272 U.S. 365, 388. We simply hold that when the Commission finds that a pig has entered the parlor, the exercise of its regulatory power does not depend on proof that the pig is obscene.

The judgment of the Court of Appeals is reversed.

APPENDIX TO OPINION OF THE COURT

The following is a verbatim transcript of "Filthy Words" prepared by the Federal Communications Commission.

Aruba-du, ruba-tu, ruba-tu. I was thinking about the curse words and the swear words, the cuss words and the words that you can't say, that you're not supposed to say all the time, ['cause] words or people into words want to hear your words. Some guys like to record your words and sell them back to you if they can, (laughter) listen in on the telephone, write down what words you say. A guy who used to be in Washington knew that his phone was tapped, used to answer, Fuck Hoover, yes, go ahead (laughter). Okay, I was thinking one night about the words you couldn't say on the public, ah, airwaves, um, the ones you definitely wouldn't say, ever, [']cause I heard a lady say bitch one night on television, and it was cool like she was talking about, you know, ah, well, the bitch is the first one to notice that in the litter Johnie right (murmur) Right. And, uh, bastard you can say, and hell and damn so I have to figure out which ones you couldn't and ever and it came down to seven but the list is open to amendment, and in fact, has been changed, uh, by now, ha, a lot of people pointed things out to me, and I noticed some myself. The original seven words were, shit, piss, fuck, cunt, cocksucker, motherfucker, and tits. Those are the ones that will curve your spine, grow hair on your hands and (laughter) maybe, even bring us, God help us, peace without honor (laughter) um, and a bourbon (laughter). And now the first thing that we noticed was that word fuck was really repeated in there because the word motherfucker is a compound word and it's another form of the word fuck. (laughter) You want to be a purist it doesn't really—it can't be on the list of basic words. Also, cocksucker is a compound word and neither half of that is really dirty. The word—the

[29] Even a prime-time recitation of Geoffrey Chaucer's *Miller's Tale* would not be likely to command the attention of many children who are both old enough to understand and young enough to be adversely affected by passages such as: "And prively he caughte hire by the queynte." *The Canterbury Tales*, Chaucer's Complete Works (Cambridge ed. 1933), p. 58, l. 3276.

half sucker that's merely suggestive (laughter) and the word cock is a half-way dirty word, 50% dirty—dirty half the time, depending on what you mean by it. (laughter) Uh, remember when you first heard it, like in 6th grade, you used to giggle. And the cock crowed three times, heh (laughter) the cock—three times. It's in the Bible, cock in the Bible. (laughter) And the first time you heard about a cock-fight, remember—What? Huh? naw. It ain't that, are you stupid? man. (laughter, clapping) It's chickens, you know, (laughter) Then you have the four letter words from the old Anglo-Saxon fame. Uh, shit and fuck. The word shit, uh, is an interesting kind of word in that the middle class has never really accepted it and approved it. They use it like, crazy but it's not really okay. It's still a rude, dirty, old kind of gushy word (laughter). They don't like that, but they say it, like, they say it like, a lady now in a middle-class home, you'll hear most of the time she says it as an expletive, you know, it's out of her mouth before she knows. She says, Oh shit oh shit, (laughter) oh shit. If she drops something, Oh, the shit hurt the broccoli. Shit. Thank you (footsteps fading away) (papers ruffling).

* * *

[The transcript continued for two more pages in the same vein.]

---

Justice Powell wrote a concurring opinion with which Justice Blackmun agreed. The two accepted the major premise of Justice Stevens' opinion (in Part IV–C) that broadcasting requires different treatment under the First Amendment because of the practical problems faced in protecting children from programs being carried directly into the home:

> . . . Sellers of printed and recorded matter and exhibitors of motion pictures and live performances may be required to shut their doors to children, but such a requirement has no effect on adults' access. The difficulty is that such a physical separation of the audience cannot be accomplished in the broadcast media. During most of the broadcast hours, both adults and unsupervised children are likely to be in the broadcast audience, and the broadcaster cannot reach willing adults without also reaching children. This, as the Court emphasizes, is one of the distinctions between the broadcast and other media to which we often have adverted as justifying a different treatment of the broadcast media for First Amendment purposes. In my view, the Commission was entitled to give substantial weight to this difference in reaching its decision in this case.
>
> A second difference, not without relevance, is that broadcasting—unlike most other forms of communication—comes directly into the home, the one place where people

> ordinarily have the right not to be assaulted by uninvited and offensive sights and sounds.... The Commission also was entitled to give this factor appropriate weight in the circumstances of the instant case. This is not to say, however, that the Commission has an unrestricted license to decide what speech, protected in other media, may be banned from the airwaves in order to protect unwilling adults from momentary exposure to it in their homes. Making the sensitive judgments required in these cases is not easy. But this responsibility has been reposed initially in the Commission, and its judgment is entitled to respect.
>
> * * *
>
> The Commission's holding does not prevent willing adults from purchasing Carlin's record, from attending his performances, or, indeed, from reading the transcript reprinted as an appendix to the Court's opinion. On its face, it does not prevent respondent Pacifica Foundation from broadcasting the monologue during late evening hours when fewer children are likely to be in the audience, nor from broadcasting discussions of the contemporary use of language at any time during the day. The Commission's holding, and certainly the Court's holding today, does not speak to cases involving the isolated use of a potentially offensive word in the course of a radio broadcast, as distinguished from the verbal shock treatment administered by respondent here. In short, I agree that on the facts of this case, the Commission's order did not violate respondent's First Amendment rights.

438 U.S. at 758–61. By contrast, Justices Powell and Blackmun refused to endorse the theme developed in Part IV–B of the Court's principal opinion, to the effect that there are variations in the "value" of particular brands of speech, and thence their levels of constitutional protection. Justice Powell did have to acknowledge, however, that he and the rest of the Court had just made that kind of differential value judgment for *commercial* speech.

Justice Brennan, with whom Justice Marshall joined, filed a dissent on the First Amendment issues. Comparing Carlin's "Filthy Words" broadcast with the "Fuck the Draft" jacket worn in a Los Angeles courtroom in *Cohen v. California*, 403 U.S. 15 (1971), Justice Brennan said it was much easier for Carlin's listeners to protect their privacy by turning off their radios than for Cohen's viewers to leave the courtroom:

> ... Whatever the minimal discomfort suffered by a listener who inadvertently tunes into a program he finds offensive during the brief interval before he can simply extend his arm and switch

> stations or flick the "off" button, it is surely worth the candle to preserve the broadcaster's right to send, and the right of those interested to receive, a message entitled to full First Amendment protection. To reach a contrary balance, as does the Court, is clearly to follow Mr. Justice Stevens' reliance on animal metaphors, ante, at 750–751, "to burn the house to roast the pig." *Butler v. Michigan*, 352 U.S. 380, 383 (1957).
>
> The Court's balance, of necessity, fails to accord proper weight to the interests of listeners who wish to hear broadcasts the FCC deems offensive. It permits majoritarian tastes completely to preclude a protected message from entering the homes of a receptive, unoffended minority. No decision of this Court supports such a result. Where the individuals constituting the offended majority may freely choose to reject the material being offered, we have never found their privacy interests of such moment to warrant the suppression of speech on privacy grounds. . . .

438 U.S. at 765–66. Justice Brennan rejected the notion that parents wanting to protect their children from Carlin were the only ones with a claim here. Not only did this FCC rule bar access by all adults to Carlin's material in order to protect children, but it actually misapplied the crucial parental right at issue:

> [T]he time-honored right of a parent to raise his child as he sees fit—[is] a right this Court has consistently been vigilant to protect. *See Wisconsin v. Yoder*, 406 U.S. 205 (1972); *Pierce v. Society of Sisters*, 268 U.S. 510 (1925). Yet this principle supports a result directly contrary to that reached by the Court. *Yoder* and *Pierce* hold that parents, not the government, have the right to make certain decisions regarding the upbringing of their children. As surprising as it may be to individual Members of this Court, some parents may actually find Mr. Carlin's unabashed attitude towards the seven "dirty words" healthy, and deem it desirable to expose their children to the manner in which Mr. Carlin defuses the taboo surrounding the words. Such parents may constitute a minority of the American public, but the absence of great numbers willing to exercise the right to raise their children in this fashion does not alter the right's nature or its existence. Only the Court's regrettable decision does that.

438 U.S. at 769–70. The Justice was also concerned about the absence of any principled limit to the FCC's "privacy and children-in-the-audience" rationales for excluding "offensive" broadcasts from the air waves:

> . . . Taken to their logical extreme, these rationales would support the cleansing of public radio of any "four-letter words" whatsoever, regardless of their context. The rationales could justify the banning from radio of a myriad of literary works, novels, poems, and plays by the likes of Shakespeare, Joyce, Hemingway, Ben Jonson, Henry Fielding, Robert Burns, and Chaucer; they could support the suppression of a good deal of political speech, such as the Nixon tapes; and they could even provide the basis for imposing sanctions for the broadcast of certain portions of the Bible.[5]

438 U.S. at 770–71. Finally, Justice Brennan observed that both the FCC and the Court majority were affected by an "acute ethnocentric myopia" that left them depressingly unable "to appreciate that in our land of cultural pluralism there are many . . . who do not share their fragile sensibilities." *Id.* at 776–77.

## *QUESTIONS FOR DISCUSSION*

1. Having read key segments of the opinions authored by these three different groups on the Court, with whose positions do you disagree? Is radio (or television) special? Should the airwaves be protected from the "Filthy Words" (which, incidentally, Carlin and Pacifica developed as protest action against this FCC rule)? Is it relevant that the FCC has refused to take action against Pacifica's annual "Bloomsday" readings from the most erotic passages in James Joyce's *Ulysses*? From a more general perspective, does the "spectrum scarcity" rationale for the Supreme Court's endorsement of the FCC "fairness" policy in *Red Lion* also support the "indecency" policy under the First Amendment? Are radio and television stations really scarce anymore? (For the later history of the scarcity-fairness issue, see *Syracuse Peace Council v. FCC*, 867 F.2d 654 (D.C.Cir. 1989), and Chapter 13 generally.) If not, in what other ways are broadcasts different from books, movies, records, or live performances by groups such as 2 Live Crew?

2. What does the Court's rationale in *Pacifica* imply for the problem that confronted the Supreme Court in *Erznoznik v. City of Jacksonville*, 422 U.S. 205 (1975)—a local ordinance that barred showing at open-air, drive-in theaters of movies with nude scenes? (Suppose the ordinance barred only nude *sex* scenes at open-air drive-ins?) Or the problem that faced the Court in *City of Renton v. Playtime Theatres, Inc.*, 475 U.S. 41 (1986)—an ordinance

---

[5] *See*, e.g., I Samuel 25:22: "So and more also do God unto the enemies of David, if I leave of all that pertain to him by the morning light any that pisseth against the wall"; II Kings 18:27 and Isaiah 36:12: "[Hath] he not sent me to the men which sit on the wall, that they may eat their own dung, and drink their own piss with you?"; Ezekiel 23:3: "And they committed whoredoms in Egypt; they committed whoredoms in their youth; there were their breasts pressed, and there they bruised the teats of their virginity."; Ezekiel 23:21: "Thus thou calledst to remembrance the lewdnes of thy youth, in bruising thy teats by the Egyptians for the paps of thy youth." The Holy Bible (King James Version) (Oxford 1897).

that barred location of "adult" motion picture theaters within 1,000 feet of a church, school, park, or residential neighborhood?

---

For the decade following the Supreme Court's *Pacifica* verdict, the FCC limited this policy to shows which used one or more of the "filthy words" before ten o'clock in the evening. Then came two controversial decisions in 1987. One involved a new Pacifica broadcast—a late night play, "Jerker," which included the extremely erotic sexual fantasies of two gay men dying of AIDS. This led the FCC to postpone the "safe harbor" period to midnight. The other involved Howard Stern's new brand of early-morning "shock radio" via Infinity Broadcasting. The following excerpts targeted by the FCC convey some of the Stern show's flavor of constant references to sexual bodily parts and actions.

**FCC Excerpts from Howard Stern Broadcasts**

* * *

*Excerpt 1*

Howard Stern: "God, my testicles are like down to the floor. Boy, Susan, you could really have a party with these. I'm telling you honey."

*Excerpt 2*

Howard Stern: "Let me tell you something honey. These homos you are with are all limp."

Ray: "Yeah. You've never even had a real man."

Howard Stern: "You've probably never been with a man with a full erection."

*Excerpt 3*

Susan: "No, I was in a park in New Rochelle, N.Y."

Howard Stern: "In a park in New Rochelle? On your knees?"

Susan: "No, no."

Ray: "And squeezing someone's testicles, probably."

*Excerpt 4*

Howard Stern: "I mean to go around porking other girls with vibrating rubber products and they [lesbians] want the whole world to come to a standstill."

*Excerpt 5*

| | |
|---|---|
| Howard Stern: | "The closest I came to making love to a black woman was, I masturbated to a picture of Aunt Jemima." |

*Excerpt 6*

| | |
|---|---|
| Howard Stern: | "First I want to just strip and rape [rival Los Angeles disc jockeys] Mark and Brian. I want my two bitches laying there in the cold, naked . . . I want them bleeding from the buttocks." |

*Excerpt 7*

| | |
|---|---|
| Howard Stern: | [About Michelle Pfeiffer]: "I would not even need a vibrator. . . . Boy, her rump would be more black and blue than a Harlem cub scout." |

* * *

The *Stern* case produced a new generic standard for "indecent" broadcasting:

> "Language or material that depicts or describes, in terms patently offensive as measured by contemporary community standards for the broadcast medium, sexual or excretory activities or organs."

Stating that it was now concerned about the impact of broadcast indecency on teenagers (from 12–17 years old), not just children younger than 12, the FCC reaffirmed this new policy in Matter of *Infinity Broadcasting Corp. of Pennsylvania*, 64 R.R.2d 211 (F.C.C. 1987). The FCC also found, in *Gannett Publishing*, 5 F.C.C.R. 7688 (1990), a violation of its indecency standard by the broadcast of a song by the feminist folk group, Uncle Bursai, whose "Penis Envy" began and ended with the following verses:

> If I had a penis I'd wear it outside, In cafes and car lots With pomp and with pride.
>
> * * *
>
> If I had a penis I'd still be a girl, But I'd make much more money, And conquer the world.

Thence came a fascinating interaction among the FCC, the D.C. Circuit Court, the Congress, and the industry (particularly Howard Stern). The new FCC policy was quickly appealed to the D.C. Circuit which, in an opinion authored by then-Judge Ruth Bader Ginsburg, upheld the new "indecency" standard against vagueness and overbreadth challenges, but struck down the shortened safe harbor time as inadequately justified by the FCC in terms of its concern for teenagers. *See Action For Children's Television v. FCC*, 852 F.2d 1332 (D.C.Cir. 1988) (*ACT I*).

Shortly after the Circuit Court ruling in *ACT I*, the Congress passed a rider to an appropriations bill that required the FCC to consider and promulgate new indecency regulations with a 24-hour ban. The FCC conducted an extended rulemaking proceeding in 1989 and 1990, and concluded that the 24-hour ban on broadcast indecency was appropriate. *See Enforcement of Prohibition Against Broadcast Indecency*, 67 Rad. Reg. 2d 1714 (F.C.C. 1990). The D.C. Circuit again reversed, with Judge Abner Mikva concluding that the Supreme Court's recent ruling in *Sable Communications of California, Inc. v. FCC*, 492 U.S. 115 (1989), which had struck down a federal statutory ban on dial-a-porn 900-number telephone services, meant that adults were also entitled to some access to sexual indecency on radio as well as over the phone. *See Action for Children's Television v. FCC*, 932 F.2d 1504 (D.C.Cir. 1991) (*ACT II*).

Congress intervened once more, in the *Public Communications Act of 1992* § 16(a), which required the FCC to consider a new regulation that allowed a safe harbor for indecency just from midnight to 6 a.m., with the exception of public stations that could broadcast indecent programs after 10 p.m. if the station was going off the air at or before midnight. The Commission again accepted this congressional directive, in *Re Broadcast Indecency*, 71 Rad. Reg. 2d 1116 (F.C.C. 1993), which spelled out three objectives to be served by the policy.

1. Ensuring that parents had the opportunity to supervise their children listening to or viewing over-the-air broadcasts;
2. Ensuring the well-being of minors regardless of parental supervision;
3. Protecting the right of all members of the listening public to be insulated from indecent material in the privacy of their homes.

Again, the case went back to the D.C. Circuit, and again the FCC policy was struck down as constitutionally overbroad. *See Action for Children's Television v. FCC*, 11 F.3d 170 (D.C.Cir. 1993) (*ACT III*). This time, though, the case took an unexpected legal twist. The panel decision was reargued *en banc* in late 1994.

While the D.C. Circuit decision was pending, the issue was assuming major economic as well as moral interest. Howard Stern himself had become a major media figure. Besides his nationally-syndicated shock radio show, Stern's book, *Private Parts*, was a 1993 best-seller, and his New Year's Eve television special that year (with John Wayne Bobbitt as one of the bit players) set the new record as the most lucrative non-boxing, pay-for-view show. (At $40 a home, *The Miss Howard Stern New Year's Eve Pageant* grossed over $15 million. The biggest prior pay-TV show was a 1990 New Kids on the Block concert that had grossed $5.4 million at $20 a home.) The only down-side for Stern was that the content of the New Year's Eve show led the Fox Broadcasting Network to break off negotiations for a regular Stern television series.

Meanwhile, Stern's host network, Infinity Broadcasting, had expanded into the largest radio network in the country, with 22 stations and three more purchases pending. The latter three included the highly-rated Westwood station in Los Angeles whose existing syndicated programs included Larry King and Pat Buchanan, which Infinity wanted to combine with its existing stable (including Stern, Don Imus, and Gordon Liddy). The problem was that purchase of these new stations needed FCC approval for transfer of the broadcast licenses, and the FCC had by then assessed a total of nearly $2 million in fines against Infinity for "indecent" Stern broadcasts that the network was refusing to pay on constitutional grounds. Eventually, following receipt of the D.C. Circuit ruling in *ACT III* and before its *en banc* revocation, the FCC gave the go-ahead to these three station transfers. Several more acquisitions were still pending, though, as Infinity sought to expand its radio syndication network.

Finally, in the summer of 1995 the full D.C. Circuit issued its ruling, *Action for Children's TV. v. FCC*, 58 F.3d 654 (D.C.Cir. 1995) (*ACT IV*), upholding the constitutionality of restrictions on "indecent" broadcast programming between 6 a.m. and midnight. The majority opinion authored by Judge Buckley found that this legal policy was based on two "compelling government interests"—support for parental supervision of children and the social concern for the emotional and ethical well-being of the nation's children. Relying on recent survey evidence that two-thirds of children live in homes with several television sets and half have sets in their own bedrooms, the court decided that restraints upon what could be broadcast on television (or radio) is a measure that is narrowly tailored to serve one or both of these independent governmental interests:

> The government's dual interest in assisting parents and protecting minors necessarily extends beyond merely channeling broadcast indecency to those hours when parents can be at home to supervise what their children see and hear. It is fanciful to believe that the vast majority of parents who wish to shield their children from indecent material can effectively do so without meaningful restriction on the airing of broadcast indecency.

58 F.2d at 663. Shortly thereafter, and without admitting to any wrongdoing by Howard Stern, Infinity agreed to make a "voluntary

contribution to the United States Treasury" in the amount of the still-unpaid FCC fines and interest. In early 1996, the Supreme Court rejected ACT's petition for review of the D.C. Circuit's decision.

### *QUESTIONS FOR DISCUSSION*

1. The *ACT IV* en banc dissent argued that there was a potential tension between parental and governmental concerns about what kinds of programming children would see or hear, and that parents must have the final say on this score. Even if parents want their children to watch or listen to materials that the FCC considers indecent, do parents have alternatives to over-the-air shows for that purpose? And even if there are no adequate alternatives, should parental views on that score always override social concerns about the ethical development of its citizenry?

2. In yet another ruling in the "indecency" saga, *Action for Children's Television v. FCC*, 59 F.3d 1249 (D.C.Cir. 1995) (*ACT V*), a divided D.C. Circuit panel upheld the FCC's procedures for enforcing its rules through the imposition of fines ("forfeitures"), even though as a practical matter the validity of the ruling did not get to court for years, and in the interim the FCC felt entitled to levy higher fines for subsequent instances of indecency on that broadcast outlet. The majority rejected the analogy of the Supreme Court's ruling in *Bantam Books v. Sullivan*, 372 U.S. 58 (1963), which had struck down Rhode Island's Commission to Encourage Morality in Youth, a body that investigated publications felt to be objectionable for children, and asked book stores selling the item to remove it from their shelves or have the matter referred to the local police for possible prosecution under state obscenity law. Do you think that the FCC procedures warrant the same judgment as the Supreme Court gave to this Rhode Island Commission—*de facto* government censorship without effective recourse to the courts?

3. Is the FCC policy narrowly tailored to the emotional and moral protection of children and their parents? In particular, should the FCC have focused only on children 12 and under, rather than on teenagers between 13 and 17? Would that somewhat more relaxed stance afford greater freedom to broadcasters seeking to reach adults earlier than midnight (how much earlier)? Or is the real social concern about the impact of indecent programming precisely at that early teenage stage?

4. Does indecent programming actually pose a significant social problem—as a general matter and as applied to Howard Stern? Is there any countervailing value in Howard Stern and George Carlin's right to talk over the air in the manner you have seen?

5. The scope of regulatory authority over broadcast speech was at issue in *Capital Broadcasting Co. v. Mitchell*, 333 F. Supp. 582 (D.D.C. 1971), *aff'd without opinion*, 405 U.S. 1000 (1972), which upheld a 1969 statutory ban on cigarette advertising on radio or television. Then *Yale Broadcasting v. FCC*, 478 F.2d 594 (D.C.Cir. 1973), upheld an FCC requirement that broadcasters take active steps to learn of "drug-oriented" music lyrics on their

stations so as to be able to exercise "licensee responsibility" for what they were transmitting over the air. Should either of these legal policies be maintained? Can they be distinguished from each other? From the issues of sexual content we have been exploring?

6. One of the numerous provisions included by Congress in the 1996 Telecommunications Act required cable operators with channels "primarily dedicated to sexually-oriented programming" to ensure that those signals were "fully scrambled" to block "signal bleed" of these programs into the homes of general cable subscribers who had not subscribed to that particular show. This scrambling process had originally been designed to ensure that only paying subscribers could have access to such special programming. The Act, though, directed cable operators that did not have complete scrambling (which most did not) to place such sexually oriented programs in the "safe harbor" period of 10 p.m. to 6 a.m. when children were more likely to be asleep rather than watching television.

Unhappy about the impact of that new law on its various sexual programs, Playboy launched a suit asserting that its First Amendment rights had been violated. A closely-divided Supreme Court rendered its verdict four years later in *United States v. Playboy Entertainment Group*, 529 U.S. 803 (2000). How do you think this case came out? What are your own views about the appropriate constitutional and policy treatment of such programming?

---

In 1996, a Republican-led Congress passed and Democratic President Clinton signed into law a major *Telecommunications Reform Act*. The principal thrust of this legislation involved a host of marketplace/regulation issues in the broadcasting industry which will be addressed in Chapter 13. Among the politically appealing features of the bill, though, were two that are directly relevant to this chapter. One related to the issue of violence on television, which will be taken up in detail shortly. The other provision, titled the Communications Decency Act, made it a federal crime to transmit or allow to be transmitted on a public computer network any "indecent" material—defined as "any comment, request, suggestion, proposal, image or other communication that, in context, depicts or describes, in terms patently offensive as measured by contemporary community standards, sexual or excretory activities or organs." An affirmative defense was provided to those who, in "good faith," take "effective . . . action" to restrict access to the messages by minors: e.g., by requiring designated forms of age proof (such as a credit card). As soon as the bill became law, the American Civil Liberties Union and other groups went to court to block enforcement of this particular provision, labeling it the "cyberspace equivalent of book burning." They were victorious in *Reno v. American Civil Liberties Union*, 521 U.S. 844 (1997), where the Supreme Court defined the First Amendment status of the Internet. In an extended opinion authored by

Justice Stevens the Court majority rejected the federal government's reliance on the familiar precedent: *Ginsberg v. New York*, 390 U.S. 629 (1968) (an expansive definition of obscenity for children); *City of Renton v. Playtime Theatres*, 475 U.S. 41 (1986) (barring "adult" movie theaters from residential neighborhoods); and *FCC v. Pacifica Foundation*, 438 U.S. 726 (1978) (barring "indecent" language from over-the-air broadcasting). The Court found none of these situations were analogous to the contemporary technological and cultural development of cyberspace.

With respect to *Pacifica*, the Court found a qualitative difference between broadcasting over the air and sending messages via the Internet. In particular, broadcasting was said to have an extensive history of regulation, a scarcity of available frequencies (at least at the time of *Pacifica*), and an invasive nature of the programs coming into American homes. It was these factors that had led the Court to grant that medium a lower level of First Amendment protection than movies or newspapers. According to the *Reno* Court, the clearest analogy to sex on the Internet was sex on pre-recorded telephone messages (i.e., commercial "dial-a-porn"), which was found to be constitutionally free of FCC bans of "indecent" speech in *Sable Communications v. FCC*, 492 U.S. 115 (1989). The *Reno* Court felt that applying the *Pacifica* standard to the Internet would likely generate a *de facto* ban on such sexual speech reaching adults who wanted to experience it via this medium, something the Court found to be unconstitutional here.

The partial dissent of Justice O'Connor found it to be a legitimate constitutional objective to carve out "adults-only zones" on the Internet. Thus, the *Communications Decency Act* should be found constitutional where the party submitting the indecent message knows that all of the recipients were children. However, given the fact that on the Internet (by contrast to theaters), minors can still readily enter into a "sex chat room" on cyberspace, it should now be unconstitutional for the law to force indecent sex messages to be shut down at the expense of the adults who want to receive them.

The 2004 Super Bowl produced not only a last minute 32–29 victory for the New England Patriots against the Carolina Panthers and a record-setting TV audience of 147 million people around the world, but also a major controversy about what had happened at half-time. The risqué duet team of Justin Timberlake and Janet Jackson planned to have him pulling off part of her black leather bustier as he was singing, as part of their "Rock Your Body" piece, "I'll have you naked by the end of this song." Unfortunately, though, Jackson's red lace bra also came off, displaying for a second or two her breast—and the medallion ring she had on the naked nipple—to everyone in that Houston Stadium and those watching the game on television, which included around one in five Americans aged 2 to 11.

FCC Chairman Michael Powell (son of Secretary of State Colin Powell) was shocked by that "classless, crass and deplorable stunt" as part of an entire performance he chose to label as "onstage copulation." After more than 200,000 (and eventually more than 555,000) complaints flooded in about this "wardrobe malfunction," he quickly had the FCC staff processing an "indecency" complaint. In the fall of 2004 the FCC issued its decision, finding Viacom's CBS arm and TV stations liable for this "indecency" and fining them a total of $550,000. Rather than appeal this ruling, Viacom shortly afterwards made a "voluntary contribution" of $3.5 million to the U.S. Treasury.

This moment of Super Bowl nudity also produced an FCC reversal of its treatment of the U2 singer Bono. In 2002, when he was singled out on NBC's live broadcast as the person winning the Golden Globe award for the best original song that year, he excitedly said, "this is really, really fucking brilliant." After a rash of complaints were received, the FCC ruled in 2003 that this did not meet their "indecency" standards. "The word 'fucking' may be crude and offensive, but, in the context presented here, did not describe sexual or excretory organs or activities. Rather the performer used this word as an adjective or expletive to emphasize an exclamation."

For its 2004 Golden Globe program, NBC developed a new ten-second delay system to be able to edit out these kinds of words, and ABC followed that lead for the 2004 Oscars. Then, following the Janet Jackson event, the FCC also decided to reverse its earlier ruling, about Bono.

> We believe that, given the core meaning of the F-word, any use of this word or a variation in any context, inherently has a sexual connotation. [It is] "potentially offensive" because the F-word is one of the most vulgar, graphic and explicit descriptions of sexual activity in the English language. The fact that the use of this word may have been unintentional is irrelevant; it still has the same affect of exposing children to indecent language."

The Bono case was also the first one in which the FCC found a word to be "profane" as well as "indecent," because that former term had previously been used to decide only whether a word or phrase was blasphemous. While this substantive ruling was unanimous, a 3–2 FCC majority decided not to fine NBC the standard $27,500 because the rule had just been changed. However, President Bush introduced and the House quickly enacted a bill to raise the fine for television or radio "indecency" from $27,500 to $500,000 for each such incident. The proposal being debated in the Senate would raise the maximum fine to $275,000 for the first offence, $375,000 for the second and $500,000 for the third and later ones. A more important source of debates and political controversy is the addition to the Senate Commerce Commission definition of "indecency" of any unduly "violent," as well as "sexual images" and words.

The 2006 Utah Child Protection Registry Act enabled parents to register their children's email addresses with the state Consumer Protection Division, and made it a crime to send sexual content or enticements to the children's emails. The Free Speech Coalition immediately filed a lawsuit claiming the Act was preempted by the 2003 federal CANSPAM Act, violated the dormant Commerce Clause of the Constitution, and violated the First Amendment. In the opening decision on this Internet case, *Free Speech Coalition v. Shurtleff*, 2007 WL 922247 (D. Utah), U.S. district judge Dale Kimball thoroughly rejected all those claims.

The spring of 2008 brought a major ruling about the 2004 Super Bowl "wardrobe malfunction" of the pop star Janet Jackson, who experienced her breasts being bared for an international audience. The Federal Communications Commission (FCC) fined the network CBS $550,000 for what it said was "consciously and deliberately broadcasting the halftime show and . . . fail[ing] to take reasonable precaution to ensure that no actionably indecent material was broadcast." The Third Circuit, in *CBS Corp. v. Federal Communications Commission*, 535 F.3d 167 (3rd Cir. 2008), overturned that administrative decision as deviating from a 30-year policy of not sanctioning such isolated and fleeting moments on television. While President Tim Winter of the Parents Television Council condemned this decision as "making a mockery of federal broadcast decency laws," the ACLU's senior attorney Chris Hansen praised it, saying "Whatever one's view on what constitutes indecency, the government can't change the rules halfway through the game."

The fall of 2008 brought to the US Supreme Court a major case and legal policy issue for this section of this chapter, produced by the U2 rock band's lead singer Bono uttering a profanity, "This is really, really f—ing brilliant," while accepting an award on the 2003 broadcast of the Golden Globe Awards, and the 2004 broadcast of the Super Bowl where at half-time pop singer Janet Jackson bared one of her breasts. Inspired in particular by the "fleeting profanities" used by entertainers Cher and Nicole Richie during Fox network's broadcasts of the Billboard Music Awards in 2002 and 2003, the FCC substantially expanded its broadcasting "indecency" to include any "fleeting expletives" being aired on television. In addition, Congress dramatically increased the potential maximum penalty for each indecency infraction from $32,500 to $325,000. In *Complaints Regarding Various Television Broadcasts,* 21 FCC 2664 (2006), the FCC found the telecast of Bono's award statement to be a violation of its new rule. The Commission stressed that "any use of that word f—ing inherently has a sexual connotation" and that this word "is one of the most vulgar, graphic and explicit description of sexual activity in the English language."

The four major television networks, Fox, ABC, CBS, and NBC, immediately filed a legal challenge to this new FCC rule, even though in this particular case the FCC refrained from imposing any fine, stating that "existing precedent would have permitted the broadcast," and thus the networks "necessarily did not have the requisite notice to justify a penalty." In June 2007, by a two-to-one vote a panel of the Second Circuit Court of Appeals, in *Fox Television Stations v. FCC* (2d Cir. 2007), agreed with that network position, striking down this new rule basically on statutory grounds but also as dubious under the federal constitution. As Judge Rosemary Pooler put it, "We are skeptical that the commission can provide a reasoned explanation for its 'fleeting expletive' regime that would pass constitutional muster." Dissenting Judge Pierre Leval observed that "a court's disagreement with the commission on this question is of no consequence. The commission's position is not irrational; it is not arbitrary and capricious."

## FEDERAL COMMUNICATIONS COMMISSION V. FOX TELEVISION STATIONS

Supreme Court of the United States, 2009.
129 S.Ct. 1800, 173 L.Ed.2d 738.

SCALIA, JUSTICE.

* * *

This case concerns utterances in two live broadcasts aired by Fox Television Stations, Inc., and its affiliates prior to the Commission's *Golden Globes Order*. The first occurred during the 2002 Billboard Music Awards, when the singer Cher exclaimed, "I've also had critics for the last 40 years saying that I was on my way out every year. Right. So f* * * 'em." Brief for Petitioners 9. The second involved a segment of the 2003 Billboard Music Awards, during the presentation of an award by Nicole Richie and Paris Hilton, principals in a Fox television series called "The Simple Life." Ms. Hilton began their interchange by reminding Ms. Richie to "watch the bad language," but Ms. Richie proceeded to ask the audience, "Why do they even call it 'The Simple Life?' Have you ever tried to get cow s* * * out of a Prada purse? It's not so f* * *ing simple." *Id.*, at 9–10. Following each of these broadcasts, the Commission received numerous complaints from parents whose children were exposed to the language.

On March 15, 2006, the Commission released Notices of Apparent Liability for a number of broadcasts that the Commission deemed actionably indecent, including the two described above. *In re Complaints Regarding Various Television Broadcasts Between February 2, 2002 and March 8, 2005,* 21 FCC Rcd. 2664 (2006). Multiple parties petitioned the Court of Appeals for the Second Circuit for judicial review of the order, asserting a variety of constitutional and statutory challenges. Since the order had declined to impose sanctions, the Commission had not previously given the broadcasters an opportunity to respond to the indecency charges. It therefore requested and obtained from the Court of Appeals a voluntary remand so that the parties could air their objections. 489 F.3d 444, 453 (2007). The Commission's order on remand upheld the indecency findings for the broadcasts described above. *See In re Complaints Regarding Various Television Broadcasts Between February 2, 2002, and March 8, 2005,* 21 FCC Rcd. 13299 (2006) *(Remand Order).*

The order first explained that both broadcasts fell comfortably within the subject-matter scope of the Commission's indecency test because the 2003 broadcast involved a literal description of excrement and both broadcasts invoked the "F-Word," which inherently has a sexual connotation. *Id.,* at 13304, 13323. The order next determined that the broadcasts were patently offensive under community standards for the medium. Both broadcasts, it noted, involved entirely gratuitous uses of "one of the most vulgar, graphic, and explicit words for sexual activity in the English language." *Id.,* at 13305, 13324. It found Ms. Richie's use of the "F-Word" and her "explicit description of the handling of excrement" to be "vulgar and shocking," as well as to constitute "pandering," after Ms. Hilton had playfully warned her to " 'watch the bad language.' " *Id.,* at 13305. And it found Cher's statement patently offensive in part because she metaphorically suggested a sexual act as a means of expressing hostility to her critics. *Id.,* at 13324. The order relied upon the "critically important" context of the utterances, *id.,* at 13304, noting that they were aired during prime-time awards shows "designed to draw a large nationwide audience that could be expected to include many children interested in seeing their favorite music stars." *Id.,* at 13305, 13324. Indeed, approximately 2.5 million minors witnessed each of the broadcasts. *Id.,* at 13306, 13326.

The order asserted that both broadcasts under review would have been actionably indecent under the staff rulings and Commission dicta in effect prior to the *Golden Globes Order*—the 2003 broadcast because it involved a literal description of excrement, rather than a mere expletive, because it used more than one offensive word, and because it was planned, 21 FCC Rcd., at 13307; and the 2002 broadcast because Cher used the F-Word not as a mere intensifier, but as a description of the sexual act to express hostility to her critics, *id.,* at 13324. The order stated, however, that the pre-*Golden Globes* regime of immunity for isolated indecent expletives rested only upon staff rulings and Commission dicta, and that the Commission itself had never held "that the isolated use of an expletive . . . was not indecent or could not be indecent," 21 FCC Rcd., at 13307. In any event, the order made clear, the *Golden Globes Order* eliminated any doubt that fleeting expletives could be actionably indecent, 21 FCC Rcd., at 13308, 13325, and the Commission disavowed the bureau-level decisions and its own dicta that had said otherwise, *id.,* at 13306–1330. Under the new policy, a lack of repetition "weigh[s] against a finding of indecency," but is not a safe harbor. *Id.,* at 13325.

The order explained that the Commission's prior "strict dichotomy between 'expletives' and 'descriptions or depictions of sexual or excretory functions' is artificial and does not make sense in light of the fact that an 'expletive's' power to offend derives from its sexual or excretory meaning." *Id.,* at 13308. In the Commission's view, "granting an automatic exemption for 'isolated or fleeting' expletives unfairly forces viewers (including children)" to take " 'the first blow' " and would allow broadcasters "to air expletives at all hours of a day so long as they did so one at a time." *Id.,* at 13309. Although the Commission determined that Fox encouraged the offensive language by using suggestive scripting in the 2003 broadcast, and unreasonably failed to take adequate precautions in both broadcasts, *id.,* at 13311–13314, the order again declined to impose any forfeiture or other sanction for either of the broadcasts, *id.,* at 13321, 13326.

* * *

[Fox appealed the Commission's order to the Second Circuit, which reversed the order, finding that the Commission's reasoning was inadequate under the Administrative Procedure Act. The Second Circuit was unsure whether the order could pass constitutional muster, but declined to consider the constitutional question.]

* * *

[T]he Commission's new enforcement policy and its order finding the broadcasts actionably indecent were neither arbitrary nor capricious. First, the Commission forthrightly acknowledged that its recent actions have broken new ground, taking account of inconsistent "prior Commission and staff action" and explicitly disavowing them as "no longer good law." *Golden Globes Order,* 19 FCC Rcd., at 4980. To be sure, the (superfluous) explanation in its *Remand Order* of why the Cher broadcast would even have violated its earlier policy may not be entirely convincing. But that unnecessary detour is irrelevant. There is no doubt that the Commission knew it was making a change. That is why it declined to assess penalties; and it relied on the *Golden Globes Order* as removing any lingering doubt. *Remand Order,* 21 FCC Rcd., at 13308, 13325.

Moreover, the agency's reasons for expanding the scope of its enforcement activity were entirely rational. It was certainly reasonable to determine that it made no sense to distinguish between literal and nonliteral uses of offensive words, requiring repetitive use to render only the latter indecent. As the Commission said with regard to expletive use of the F-Word, "the word's power to insult and offend derives from its sexual meaning." *Id.,* at 13323. And the Commission's decision to look at the patent offensiveness of even isolated uses of sexual and excretory words fits with the context-based approach we sanctioned in *Pacifica,* 438 U.S., at 750. Even isolated utterances can be made in "pander[ing,] . . . vulgar and shocking" manners, *Remand Order,* 21 FCC Rcd., at 13305, and can constitute harmful " 'first blow[s]' " to children, *id.,* at 13309. It is surely rational (if not inescapable) to believe that a safe harbor for single words would "likely lead to more widespread use of the offensive language," *Golden Globes Order, supra,* at 4979.

When confronting other requests for *per se* rules governing its enforcement of the indecency prohibition, the Commission has declined to create safe harbors for particular types of broadcasts. *See In re Pacifica Foundation, Inc.,* 2 FCC Rcd., at 2699 (repudiating the view that the Commission's enforcement power was limited to "deliberate, repetitive use of the seven words actually contained in the George Carlin monologue"); *In re Infinity Broadcasting Corp. of Pa.,* 3 FCC Rcd., at 932 ("reject[ing] an approach that would hold that if a work has merit, it is *per se* not indecent"). The Commission could rationally decide it needed to step away from its old regime where nonrepetitive use of an expletive was *per se* nonactionable because that was "at odds with the Commission's overall enforcement policy." *Remand Order, supra,* at 13308.

The fact that technological advances have made it easier for broadcasters to bleep out offending words further supports the Commission's stepped-up enforcement policy. *Golden Globes Order, supra,* at 4980. And the agency's decision not to impose any forfeiture or other sanction precludes any argument that it is arbitrarily punishing parties without notice of the potential consequences of their action.

* * *

The Court of Appeals found the Commission's action arbitrary and capricious on three grounds. First, the court criticized the Commission for failing to explain why it had not previously banned fleeting expletives as "harmful 'first blow[s].' " 489 F.3d, at 458. In the majority's view, without "evidence that suggests a fleeting expletive is harmful [and] . . . serious enough to warrant government regulation," the agency could not regulate more broadly. *Id.*, at 461. As explained above, the fact that an agency had a prior stance does not alone prevent it from changing its view or create a higher hurdle for doing so. And it is not the Commission, but Congress that has proscribed "any . . . indecent . . . language." 18 U.S.C. § 1464.

There are some propositions for which scant empirical evidence can be marshaled, and the harmful effect of broadcast profanity on children is one of them. One cannot demand a multiyear controlled study, in which some children are intentionally exposed to indecent broadcasts (and insulated from all other indecency), and others are shielded from all indecency. It is one thing to set aside agency action under the Administrative Procedure Act because of failure to adduce empirical data that can readily be obtained. *See, e.g., State Farm,* 463 U.S., at 46–56 (addressing the costs and benefits of mandatory passive restraints for automobiles). It is something else to insist upon obtaining the unobtainable. Here it suffices to know that children mimic the behavior they observe—or at least the behavior that is presented to them as normal and appropriate. Programming replete with one-word indecent expletives will tend to produce children who use (at least) one-word indecent expletives. Congress has made the determination that indecent material is harmful to children, and has left enforcement of the ban to the Commission. If enforcement had to be supported by empirical data, the ban would effectively be a nullity.

The Commission had adduced no quantifiable measure of the harm caused by the language in *Pacifica,* and we nonetheless held that the "government's interest in the 'well-being of its youth' . . . justified the regulation of otherwise protected expression." 438 U.S., at 749 (quoting *Ginsberg v. New York,* 390 U.S. 629, 640, 639, 88 S.Ct. 1274, 20 L.Ed.2d 195 (1968)). If the Constitution itself demands of agencies no more scientifically certain criteria to comply with the First Amendment, neither does the Administrative Procedure Act to comply with the requirement of reasoned decision making.

The court's second objection is that fidelity to the agency's "first blow" theory of harm would require a categorical ban on *all* broadcasts of expletives; the Commission's failure to go to this extreme thus undermined the coherence of its rationale. 489 F.3d, at 458–459. This objection, however, is not responsive to the Commission's actual policy under review—the decision to include patently offensive fleeting expletives within the definition of indecency. The Commission's prior enforcement practice, unchallenged here, already drew distinctions between the offensiveness of particular words based upon the context in which they appeared. Any complaint about the Commission's failure to ban only some fleeting expletives is better directed at the agency's context-based system generally rather than its inclusion of isolated expletives.

More fundamentally, however, the agency's decision to consider the patent offensiveness of isolated expletives on a case-by-case basis is not arbitrary or capricious. "Even a prime-time recitation of Geoffrey Chaucer's Miller's Tale," we have explained, "would not be likely to command the attention of many children who are both old enough to understand and young enough to be adversely affected." *Pacifica, supra,* at 750, n. 29. The same rationale could support the Commission's finding that a broadcast of the film Saving Private Ryan was not indecent—a finding to which the broadcasters point as supposed evidence of the Commission's inconsistency. The frightening suspense and the graphic violence in the movie could well dissuade the most vulnerable from watching and would put parents on notice of potentially objectionable material. *See In re Complaints Against Various Television Licensees Regarding Their Broadcast on Nov. 11, 2004 of the ABC Television Network's Presentation of the Film "Saving Private Ryan,"* 20 FCC Rcd. 4507, 4513 (2005) (noting that the broadcast was not "intended as family entertainment"). The agency's decision to retain some discretion does not render arbitrary or capricious its regulation of the deliberate and shocking uses of offensive language at the award shows under review—shows that were expected to (and did) draw the attention of millions of children.

Finally, the Court of Appeals found unconvincing the agency's prediction (without any evidence) that a *per se* exemption for fleeting expletives would lead to increased use of expletives one at a time. 489 F.3d, at 460. But even in the absence of evidence, the agency's predictive judgment (which merits deference) makes entire sense. To predict that complete immunity for fleeting expletives, ardently desired by broadcasters, will lead to a substantial increase in fleeting expletives seems to us an exercise in logic rather than clairvoyance. The Court of Appeals was perhaps correct that the Commission's prior policy had not yet caused broadcasters to "barrag[e] the airwaves with expletives," *ibid.* That may have been because its prior permissive policy had been confirmed (save in dicta) only at the staff level. In any event, as the *Golden Globes* order demonstrated, it did produce more expletives than the Commission (which has the first call in this matter) deemed in conformity with the statute.

* * *

[The Court recognized that the Commission's orders might be considered unconstitutional in some cases, but refused to consider the constitutionality of the Commission's orders until a lower court had considered the issues and ruled.]

---

On remand, the D.C. Circuit has addressed the constitutionality of the FCC rule on fleeting expletives, deeming it unconstitutionally vague, with the potential to chill speech. *Fox Television Stations, Inc. v. FCC*, 613 F.3d 317 (2010).

Two years later, the Supreme Court affirmed the holding of the D.C. Circuit, finding that the FCC had not given the broadcasters adequate notice of its rules. *Fox Television Stations, Inc. v. FCC*, 132 S.Ct. 2307 (2012).

In evaluating the FCC rule from a policy perspective, consider that the indecency rule did not apply to either cable TV or satellite programming, even though these now come into around 85 percent of American homes.

In 2008 the Supreme Court rendered another decision about entertaining sex, *United States v. Williams*, 553 U.S. 285 (2008). This time the 7-to-2 majority upheld Congress's effort to respond to the Court's 2002 decision, *Ashcroft v. Free Speech Coalition*, 535 U.S. 234 (2002), discussed above. This time the dissenter in the earlier case, Justice Antonin Scalia, wrote for the majority upholding the 2003 Prosecutorial Remedies and Other Tools to End the Exploitation of Children Today Act—or PROTECT Act—making it a federal crime to either offer or solicit sexually explicit images of children. The defendant was found to have been offering 22 images of real children on his Internet service. By limiting its newly defined crime to "pandering," Congress had produced "a carefully crafted attempt to eliminate the First Amendment problems we identified" in the *Ashcroft* ruling. In their concurring opinion, Justices Stevens and Breyer said that Scalia's narrow reading of this statute had allayed "any constitutional concerns that might arise"—though Justices Souter and Ginsburg disagreed.

On regulation of fleeting expletives, see Edward L. Carter & R. Trevor Hall, *Broadcast Profanity and the "Right to Be Let Alone": Can the FCC Regulate Non-indecent Fleeting Expletives under a Privacy Model?* 31 Hast.Comm/Ent L.J. 1 (2008); Lindsay Weiss, *S!*T, P*@S, C*?T, F*#K, C*@!S* & !ER, M*!#$*@!*#?R, T*!S—The FCC'S Crackdown On Indecency, 28 J. Nat'l Ass'n L. Jud. 577 (2008).* A recent commentator suggests that the solution to the question of indecent material on television is to have distinct brand identity for stations/networks that carry explicit material. *See* Kristin L. Rakowski, *Branding as an Antidote to Indecency Regulation*, 16 UCLA Ent. L. Rev. 1 (2009). Would this type of market-based approach address the problem without raising constitutional problems? For recent commentary on explicit song lyrics, see Tracy Reilly, *The "Spiritual Temperature" of Contemporary Popular Music: an Alternative to the Legal Regulation of Death-metal and Gangsta-rap Lyrics*, 11 Vand. J. Ent. & Tech. L. 335 (2009).

## C. ENTERTAINING VIOLENCE

Federal and state legislatures and administrative bodies like the FCC have devoted a great deal of regulatory attention to the sexual content of broadcasts and other forms of entertainment. Until recently, almost no action had been taken with respect to violence, whether over the air, on the screens, or in the songs. This began to change for various reasons, most importantly the killings at Columbine High School. Now there is much more popular and political attention and concern about the potential impact of entertaining violence on real safety in schools, homes, and other parts of the community.

Historically, the principal instrument of legal action has been tort litigation rather than legislation or administrative regulation.[e] The principal tort precedent for such litigation was a decision by the Supreme Court of California in *Weirum v. RKO General*, 15 Cal. 3d 40, 123 Cal. Rptr. 468, 539 P.2d 36 (1975). KHJ, a Los Angeles radio station with a large teenage audience broadcast a summer program that featured its disk jockey, Don Steele, driving around the area in an identifiable vehicle. Steele regularly broadcast his location, with prizes for the first listeners to locate and identify Steele from what he was wearing. Two teenage drivers saw Steele's vehicle on a freeway and started chasing him to identify his clothes and win the prize. Tragically, the young listeners accidentally killed another driver on the way. The California court found the radio station liable for the fatal injury, because it actively created a foreseeable and unreasonable risk that a listener would endanger a third party. In this innovative tort ruling, the California court stated, without citing the Supreme Court's *Brandenburg* precedent that we read about in Section A, that it was irrelevant to legal accountability for personal injury that the harm was done by word rather than by deed.

The Supreme Court did not take on the *Weirum* case for review and has not yet explicitly addressed the question of what is the appropriate

[e] This litigation has produced a large body of law review literature. See, for example, Andrew B. Sims, *Tort Liability for Physical Injuries Resulting From Media Speech: A Comprehensive First Amendment Approach*, 34 Arizona L. Rev. 231 (1992); Jeffrey B. Kahan, *Bach, Beethoven and the Homeboys: Censoring Violent Rap Music in America*, 66 Southern Calif. L. Rev. 2583 (1993); Laura W. Brill, *The First Amendment and the Power of Suggestion: Protecting "Negligent" Speakers in Cases of Imitative Harm*, 94 Columbia L. Rev. 984 (1994); David Crump, *Camouflaged Incitement: Freedom of Speech, Communicative Torts, and the Borderland of the Brandenburg Test*, 29 Georgia L. Rev. 1 (1994); Forouzan M. Khalili, *Television* Violence: *Legislation to Combat the National Epidemic*, 18 Whittier L. Rev. 219 (1996); Sandra Davidson, *Blood Money: When Media Expose Others to Risk of Bodily Harm*, 19 Hast. Comm/Ent L.J. 225 (1997); Jendi Reiter, *Serial Killer Trading Cards and First Amendment Values: A Defense of Content-Based Regulation of Violent Expression*, 62 Albany L. Rev. 183 (1998); Kevin W. Saunders, *Electronic Indecency: Protecting Children in the Wake of the Cable and Internet Cases*, 46 Drake L. Rev. 1 (1998); R. Polk Wagner, *Filters and the First Amendment*, 83 Minnesota L. Rev. 755 (1999); Robert Firester and Kendall T. Jones, *Catchin' the Heat of the Beat: First Amendment Analysis of Music Claimed to Incite Violent Behavior*, 20 Loyola of L.A. Ent. L. Rev. 1 (2000); and Richard C. Ausness, *The Application of Product Liability Principles to Publishers of Violent or Sexually Explicit Material*, 52 Florida L. Rev. 603 (2000).

constitutional status of violent themes in entertaining speech, rather than the political diatribes of the Ku Klux Klan in *Brandenburg*. But the lower courts have recently had to tackle precisely this issue in considering lawsuits by people who felt they were the victims of violence portrayed in movies like *Natural Born Killers* and *The Basketball Diaries*, rap albums like Tupac Shakur's album *2Pacalypse Now,* or video games like *Mortal Kombat* and *Doom*.

The first such suit was directed at Time Warner, then the owner of Shakur's record studio, Interscope Records. Back in 1992, a young black teenager driving a stolen Chevy Blazer, was pulled over by a Texas state trooper, Bill Davidson. When Davidson reached the Blazer, Howard pulled out a gun and shot and killed the police officer. It turned out that for the previous 45 minutes Howard had been playing and replaying *2Pacalypse Now* on the blazer's tape deck, with songs like "Soulja's Story" and "Crooked Ass Nigga." With Shakur following the lead of his gangsta rap colleague Ice-T and his "Cop Killer,"[f] his songs had lyrics such as these:

> Cops on my tail So I bail till I dodge them, They finally pull me over And I laugh . . . Remember Rodney King, And I blast his punk ass

The murderer himself testified that he had been partly motivated to kill the police officer by these lyrics, though this did not persuade the criminal jury to refrain from imposing the death penalty for this capital offense. Notwithstanding the factual bases for the tort suit filed by Davidson's widow Linda against Shakur, Interscope Records, and the record company's owner Time Warner, in *Davidson v. Time Warner*, 25 Media L. Rep. 170 (S.D. Tex. 1997), the District Judge Rainey granted the defendants summary dismissal of the lawsuit, principally for the following reasons.

> To create a duty requiring Defendants to police their recordings would be enormously expensive and would result in the sale of only the most bland, least controversial music.
>
> * * *
>
> In support of the first prong, the Davidsons argue that Shakur describes his music as "revolutionary" that has a purpose of angering the listener. This argument may place too much

[f] The following lyrics conveyed Ice-T's message in this song from his 1992 album, *The Body Count*.

> I got my 12-gauge sawed off I got my headlights turned off I'm 'bout to bust some shots off I'm 'bout to dust some cops off
>
> Chorus
>
> Cop killer, it's better you than us Cop killer, fuck police brutality Cop killer, I know your family's grievin' Cop killer, but tonight we get even

importance on Shakur's rhetoric. Calling one's music revolutionary does not, by itself, mean that Shakur intended his music to produce imminent lawless conduct. At worst, Shakur's intent was to cause violence some time after the listener considered Shakur's message.[24]

While *2Pacalypse Now* is both insulting and outrageous, it does not appear that Shakur intended to incite imminent illegal conduct when he recorded *2Pacalypse Now*.

* * *

The Davidsons are the first to claim that *2Pacalypse Now* caused illegal conduct, three years after the recording *2Pacalypse Now* and after more than 400,000 sales of the album. The Davidsons argue that, because Howard shot Officer Davidson while listening to *2Pacalypse Now*, that Davidson was killed because Howard was listening to *2Pacalypse Now*. The Court will not engage in the fallacy of *post hoc, ergo propter hoc*. Courts addressing similar issues have repeatedly refused to find a musical recording or broadcast incited certain conduct merely because certain acts occurred after the speech. In this case, it is far more likely that Howard, a gang member driving a stolen automobile, feared his arrest and shot officer Davidson to avoid capture. Under the circumstances, the Court cannot conclude that *2Pacalypse Now* was likely to cause imminent illegal conduct. . . .

* * *

Moreover, Shakur's music, however, was not overtly directed at Howard. The Davidsons argue that *2Pacalypse Now* is directed to the violent black "gangsta" subculture in general. However, this group is necessarily too large to remove First Amendment protection from the album: to hold otherwise would remove constitutional protection from speech directed to marginalized groups . . .

* * *

*2Pacalypse Now* is both disgusting and offensive. That the album has sold hundreds of thousands of copies is an indication of society's aesthetic and moral decay. However, the First

[24] In one of his interviews discussing a later recording, Shakur states "I think of me as fighting for the black man. . . . I'd rather die than go to jail." In another interview, Shakur is more forthcoming: "I think that my music is revolutionary because it's for soldiers. It makes you want to fight back. It makes you want to think. It makes you want to ask questions. It makes you want to struggle, and if struggling means when he swings you swing back, then hell yeah, it makes you swing back."

Amendment became part of the Constitution because the Crown sought to suppress the Framers' own rebellious, sometimes violent views. Thus, although the Court cannot recommend *2Pacalypse Now* to anyone, it will not strip Shakur's free speech rights based on the evidence presented by the Davidsons.

---

A similar lawsuit was filed against the heavy metal band Slayer and its record label Sony Music. A young 15-year-old girl, Elyse Pahler, was stabbed to death by three young neighbors who had formed their own band (named Hatred) to emulate the band Slayer. Based on the killers' own statements on the way to guilty pleas and long-term sentences for murder, the Pahler family sued Slayer and Sony for the inspiration these youngsters allegedly drew from such songs as "Dead Skin Mask" and "Post-Mortem."

While Slayer and Sony were relying on the *Davidson* ruling to have this wrongful death tort suit dismissed, the Pahler family based their case on an apparently contrary judicial verdict that was rendered in a lawsuit involving director Oliver Stone's controversial film, *Natural Born Killers* (based on a story originally authored by Quentin Tarantino, the creator of *Pulp Fiction*). Woody Harrelson and Juliette Lewis played murderous lovers who spend the first half of the film embarking on a journey west during which they gunned down 52 people to show they really loved each other. In the movie's second half, the pair go to prison and escape, becoming media celebrities—not just on the covers of *Newsweek* and *People* magazines, but even more on a fictional television hit show, *American Maniacs*.

Unfortunately for Stone, not only did he not win his third Oscar for *Natural*, but this film turned out to have exactly the kind of media results he was supposedly parodying. Indeed, Stone himself acknowledged that "the most pacifist people in the world said they came out of this movie wanting to kill somebody." So far a total of 14 murderers have told the authorities they were inspired by what they saw on the *Natural Born Killers* screen (including two women viewers in France). Among those who went out on such a killing spree were Benjamin Darrus and his girlfriend Sara Edmondson (the daughter of an Oklahoma state judge). After watching the movie on home video several times, the teenaged couple then began driving down to New Orleans and committing several killings on the way. One of the victims was Bill Savage, a close friend of John Grisham in Mississippi, and another, just across the border in Louisiana, was Patsy Byers, who was working in a convenience store.

John Grisham is a practicing lawyer who turned himself into a best-selling author, telling fictional law stories that have been regularly turned into movies (e.g., *The Firm* and *A Time To Kill)*. When Grisham heard that Edmondson and Darrus had been inspired by *Natural Born Killers* to shoot his friend Savage as well as Byers, he wrote an article in the literary journal, *The Oxford American*, advocating product liability suits against filmmakers causing such "copycat" crimes. An early such lawsuit filed in Georgia was summarily dismissed. *See Miller v. Warner Brothers*, 228 Ga.App. 469, 492 S.E.2d 353 (1997).

The opposite result was initially reached in the suit filed (against Warner Brothers as well as Edmondson) by Byers when she was paralyzed from the shooting, and continued by her family after she died. In *Byers v. Edmondson*, 712 So.2d 681 (La. App. 1998), a Louisiana Court of Appeals overturned the district judge's grant of peremptory dismissal to Warner Brothers (and Stone). The key reason for that appellate ruling was that the lawyers for the Byers family had formulated their claim as alleging that Warner Bros. had made and released "a film containing violent imagery which was intended to cause its viewers to imitate the violent imagery." Based on *Weirum v. RKO General*, 15 Cal.3d 40, 123 Cal. Rptr. 468, 539 P.2d 36 (1975), that assertion stated a viable claim under tort law. And at this stage, at least, the tort claim also passed the First Amendment test in *Brandenburg v. Ohio*, 395 U.S. 444 (1969), which excludes from First Amendment protection any "advocacy" of violence that is "directed to inciting or producing imminent lawless action." The Court of Appeals did make it clear that if and when the *Byers* case came to trial, the plaintiff would face the major obstacle that "foreseeability or knowledge that the publication might be misused for criminal purposes is not sufficient for liability," and that "proof of intent necessary for liability in cases such as the instant one will be remote and even rare. . . ."

So the parties then engaged in extensive discovery proceedings, where this was one additional piece of evidence in the affidavit sworn to by Edmondson herself.

> During the two weeks prior to the robbery and shooting of Mr. Savage on March 7, 1995 and the robbery and shooting of Mrs. Byers on March 8, 1995, Benjamin Darrus [and] I watched Natural Born Killers several times in Oklahoma. We also ingested a quantity of LSD, a hallucinogen, during this time. Had we not seen the movie repeatedly we would not have taken a gun. It wouldn't have occurred to me. As well, had we not been under the influence of LSD; we never would have left Oklahoma. The movie did have a numbing influence concerning the effects of violence and a desire to experience it. The shooting did not take place as much from a need for money as from a desire to experience the power of violence. Benjamin had told me before leaving while watching the film that I was "his Mallory," and during the trip I quoted, "I'm a new woman." The effect the

movie had on us is a factor. It is one of several elements all-contributing to a dangerous chemistry with roots in very bad choices.

Notwithstanding this uncontradicted evidence of the role this movie had played in the killings of both Byers and Savage, the Louisiana First Circuit Court of Appeals eventually felt compelled by the Supreme Court's first amendment jurisprudence to dismiss this tort suit in *Byers v. Edmondson*, 826 So.2d 551 (La. App. 2002). Chief Justice Carter wrote

> This court is aware that, because of the abundance of imagery used in the film, there is certainly room for a wide variety of interpretations. It is not the prerogative of this court to provide an allegorical interpretation of this movie or to provide an artistic critique. Based on our viewing of the film, we conclude that nothing in it constitutes incitement. *Natural Born Killers* is not just about the killing spree of its main characters, Mickey and Mallory Knox, but also portrays how their exploits are glorified by the media to the point where they become cultural icons. The basic plot of the movie follows Mickey and Mallory as they meet, murder her abusive parents, and then engage in a killing spree. It also chronicles their capture, imprisonment, and Mickey's interview with a tabloid journalist that causes a prison riot facilitating their escape.
>
> Throughout the film, images frequently switch from color to black and white, and even live-action video. Some of the scenes employ facial distortions, sitcom laugh tracks, newspaper and cartoon clips, slow motion and oblique camera angles. Such techniques place this film in the realm of fantasy. *Natural Born Killers* is permeated with violent imagery, which goes to the core of the issue. The violence in the film is presented in the format of imagery and fictionalized violence. Although we acknowledge that such a portrayal of violence can be viewed as a glorification and glamorization of such actions, such a portrayal does not rise to the level of incitement, such that it removes the film from First Amendment protection.
>
> When considering the guidelines that courts have used in determining whether speech is classified as inciteful, we cannot say that *Natural Born Killers* exhorts, urges, entreats, solicits, or overtly advocates or encourages unlawful or violent activity on the part of viewers. *Natural Born Killers* does not purport to order or command anyone to perform any concrete action immediately or at any specific time. At no point during this film is the viewer directed or urged to commit any type of imminent lawless activity.

> We are mindful of the United States Supreme Court's guideline that speech does not lose its First Amendment protection merely because it has "a tendency to lead to violence." *Hess v. Indiana*, 414 U.S. 105 at 109 (1973). Edmondson and Darrus may very well have been inspired to imitate the actions of Mickey and Mallory Knox, but the film does not direct or encourage them to take such actions. Accordingly, as a matter of law, we find Natural Born Killers cannot be considered inciteful speech that would remove it from First Amendment protection.
>
> It is an unfortunate aspect of our society that certain individuals seek to emulate fictional representations. However, the constitutional protection accorded to the freedom of speech and of the press is not based on the naive belief that speech can do no harm, but on the confidence that the benefits society reaps from the free flow and exchange of ideas outweigh the costs society endures by receiving reprehensible or dangerous ideas.

Another major lawsuit and decision was produced by the 1995 New Line Cinema movie *The Basketball Diaries*, starring Leonardo DiCaprio in one of his early lead roles. The principal focus of *Basketball* was the personal life and problems of DiCaprio's character as a high school student and basketball player. At one point in the movie, while lying in his bathtub and doing that day's diary entry, DiCaprio's character falls asleep and has a daydream. During this 80-second imaginary dream scene, DiCaprio is pictured going into the classroom, pulling out his gun from his long leather coat and shooting the teacher and several students, while being cheered by his other classmates who were not being shot.

Two years later, in May 1997, a young Kentucky high school freshman, Michael Carneal, did much the same thing in real life. After a morning prayer meeting at his private high school, he pulled out a gun and shot and killed three students and wounded five others. That same day, Carneal admitted to the police that he had seen *Basketball* and remembered what DiCaprio's character was portrayed as doing. Thus, after reading in April 1999 of the Supreme Court's non-reversal of *Byers*, lawyers for the Kentucky families expanded their lawsuits against Carneal's parents and school administrators to include New Line Cinema and its movie. Indeed, the lawyers also added the media manufacturers of such violent interactive computer games as *Mortal Kombat*, *Oracle*, and *Doom* (the latter, recall, being a favorite of the Littleton high school killers). After learning what had taken place in Kentucky and Colorado, DiCaprio said he would never again make such a violent film.

After Carneal had been found guilty of second degree murder and sentenced to 25 years in prison without any possible parole, Time Warner and other media conglomerates received favorable news from a federal district judge in Kentucky. In *James v. Meow Media*, 90 F. Supp.2d 798 (W.D.Ky.2000) the judge refused to follow the *Byers* precedent and summarily dismissed the claim, but simply on tort, not constitutional, law grounds. The judge's basic rationale was that even if one accepted the fact that Carneal "was an avid consumer of violent video games, nihilistic movies, and obscene Internet materials, and was influenced by all of these events," it was not legally viable to impute either foreseeability or causation to media defendants: "that as a result of disseminating their products and failing to warn of the materials contained therein, a fourteen-year old boy who played their video games, watched their violent movies, and viewed their provocative website materials, would go to a friend's house, steal guns, take the guns to school the next day, and gun down his classmates during a prayer session." The families then took their case to the Sixth Circuit, with the following result.

## JAMES V. MEOW MEDIA

United States Court of Appeals, Sixth Circuit, 2002.
300 F.3d 683.

BOGGS, CIRCUIT JUDGE.

* * *

III

The court began by pointing out that under tort law, the first issue was whether such an entertainment body owed any duty of a care to these Kentucky High School students.

A. The Existence of a Duty of Care

The "existence of a duty of care" as an element of a tort cause of action is of relatively recent vintage. At early English common law, the existence of a duty of care was not considered as an element of an actionable tort. Then, tort law attached strict liability for any damages that resulted from "wrongful acts." Prosser on Torts § 53. The requirement that the plaintiff establish that he was owed a specific duty of care by the defendant came with the advent of negligence in place of strict liability. As a separate basis of liability, negligence was simply too broad, according to later English courts. Accordingly, the concept of limited duty disciplined the concept of negligence, requiring the plaintiff to establish a definite legal obligation.

* * *

Thus, Kentucky courts have held that the determination of whether a duty of care exists is whether the harm to the plaintiff resulting from the defendant's negligence was "foreseeable." Foreseeability is an often invoked, but not terribly well defined, concept in the common law of tort. . . . Kentucky's particular use of foreseeability in the duty inquiry finds its roots in perhaps the most famous application of the foreseeability principle. In *Palsgraf v. Long Island Railroad Co.*, 162 N.E. 99 (N.Y. 1928), then-Judge Cardozo determined that the defendant's duty is to avoid "risks reasonably to be perceived." *Id.* at 100. As every former law student remembers, the plaintiff in Palsgraf had bought a train ticket to travel to the Rockaways for the afternoon and was waiting on the station platform. Two men were rushing to catch a departing train, one easily hopped on board and the other struggled to pull himself onto the rear car. A conductor on the train pulled him on board, but in the process, the struggling passenger dropped onto the rails the brown-paper package he was carrying. The package was full of fireworks and exploded. The explosion overturned a large set of scales on the platform, which struck Palsgraf, and Palsgraf sued the railroad for her injuries.

Cardozo determined that the railroad simply did not owe a duty to Palsgraf to protect against the injury that she suffered. For Cardozo, the harm that Palsgraf suffered was not sufficiently probable that the railroad employees could have been expected to anticipate it occurring from their actions. Cardozo's reasoning, although implying that Palsgraf was the unforeseeable plaintiff, rested on the improbability of the harm that she suffered arising from the defendant's particular actions. *Id.* at 101. For Cardozo too, the existence of a duty of care was a creature of circumstance.

Cardozo's opinion in *Palsgraf*, while cited as the cornerstone of the American doctrine of a limited duty of care, has been criticized for its conclusory reasoning regarding whether Palsgraf's harm really was sufficiently unforeseeable. *See* William L. Prosser, *Palsgraf Revisited*, 52 Mich. L. Rev. 1, 7–9 (1953). Such conclusory reasoning has been endemic in the jurisprudence of determining duty by assessing foreseeability. Courts often end up merely listing factual reasons why a particular harm, although having materialized, would have appeared particularly unlikely in advance and then simply asserting that the harm was too unlikely to be foreseeable and to create a duty to exercise due care in protecting against it. What has not emerged is any clear standard regarding what makes a projected harm too improbable to be foreseeable.

* * *

Thus, we are called, as best we can, to implement Kentucky's duty of care analysis in this case. Our inquiry is whether the deaths of James, Steger, and Hadley were the reasonably foreseeable result of the defendants' creation and distribution of their games, movie, and internet sites. Whether an event was reasonably foreseeable is not for us to determine with the assistance of hindsight. The mere fact that the risk may have materialized does little to resolve the foreseeability question.

[Judge Boggs then described some Kentucky precedents, especially those saying a bar could be held liable for serving too much alcohol to a person who then went out and drove very negligently into a fatal car accident but not when he used his gun to intentionally shoot and kill someone else in the same bar.]

Intentional violence is less likely to result from intoxication than negligent operation of a motor vehicle. Yet, the Kentucky Supreme Court never makes clear how unlikely is too unlikely for a particular type of harm to be unforeseeable. The cases do not create a principle, portable to the context of this case, for evaluating the probability of harm.

This court has encountered this foreseeability inquiry under Kentucky law before in a situation similar to this case. In *Watters v. TSR, Inc.*, 904 F.2d 378 (6th Cir. 1990), the mother of a suicide victim sued TSR for manufacturing the game "Dungeons and Dragons." The suicide victim regularly played the game. The mother contended that the game's violent content "desensitized" the victim to violence and caused him to undertake the violent act of shooting himself in the head. We held that the boy's suicide was simply not a reasonably foreseeable result of producing the game, notwithstanding its violent content. To have held otherwise would have been "to stretch the concepts of foreseeability and ordinary care to lengths that would deprive them of all normal meaning." *Id.* at 381.

Foreseeability, however, is a slippery concept. Indeed, it could be argued that we ourselves confused it with some concept of negligence. We noted in *Watters*: "The defendant cannot be faulted, obviously, for putting its game on the market without attempting to ascertain the mental condition of each and every prospective player." *Ibid.* We almost appeared to say that the costs of acquiring such knowledge would so outweigh the social benefits that it would not be negligent to abstain from such an investigation. We can put the *foreseeability* point a little more precisely, however. It appears simply impossible to predict that these games, movie, and internet sites (alone, or in what combinations) would incite a young person to violence. Carneal's reaction to the games and movies at issue here, assuming that his violent actions were such a reaction, was simply too idiosyncratic to expect the defendants to have anticipated it. We find that it is simply too far a leap from shooting characters on a video screen (an activity undertaken by millions) to shooting people in a classroom (an activity undertaken by a handful, at most) for Carneal's actions to have been reasonably foreseeable to the manufacturers of the media that Carneal played and viewed.

At first glance, our conclusion also appears to be little more than an assertion. Mental health experts could quite plausibly opine about the manner in which violent movies and video games affect viewer behavior.

We need not stretch to imagine some mixture of impressionability and emotional instability that might unnaturally react with the violent content of the "Basketball Diaries" or "Doom." Of course, Carneal's reaction was not a normal reaction. Indeed, Carneal is not a normal person, but it is not utter craziness to predict that someone like Carneal is out there.

We return, however, to the Kentucky court's observation that the existence of a duty of care reflects a judicial policy judgment at bottom. From the Kentucky cases on foreseeability, we can discern two relevant policies that counsel against finding that Carneal's violent actions were the reasonably foreseeable result of defendants' distribution of games, movies, and internet material.

1. The Duty to Protect Against Intentional Criminal Actions

First, courts have held that, except under extraordinary circumstances, individuals are generally entitled to assume that third parties will not commit intentional criminal acts. The reasons behind this general rule are simple enough. The first reason is a probabilistic judgment that foreseeability analysis requires. Individuals generally are significantly deterred from undertaking intentional criminal conduct given the sanctions that can follow. The threatened sanctions make the third-party intentional criminal conduct sufficiently less likely that, under normal circumstances, we do not require the putative tort defendant to anticipate it. Indeed, this statistical observation explains the distinction drawn by Kentucky courts in the dram shop liability cases.

The second reason is structural. The system of criminal liability has concentrated responsibility for an intentional criminal act in the primary actor, his accomplices, and his co-conspirators. By imposing liability on those who did not endeavor to accomplish the intentional criminal undertaking, tort liability would diminish the responsibility placed on the criminal defendant. The normative message of tort law in these situations would be that the defendant is not entirely responsible for his intentional criminal act.

Does this case involve the extraordinary circumstances under which we would require the defendants to anticipate a third party's intentional criminal act? Kentucky courts have found such circumstances when the tort defendant had previously developed "a special relationship" with the victim of a third-party intentional criminal act. This duty to protect can be triggered by placing the putative plaintiff in custody or by taking other affirmative steps that disable the plaintiff from protecting himself against third-party intentional criminal acts. Of course, a special relationship can be created by a contract between the plaintiff and the defendant.

We can find nothing close to a "special relationship" in this case. The defendants did not even know James, Steger, and Hadley prior to

Carneal's actions, much less take any affirmative steps that disabled them from protecting themselves.

Courts have held, under extremely limited circumstances, that individuals, notwithstanding their relationship with the victims of third-party violence, can be liable when their affirmative actions "create a high degree of risk of [the third party's] intentional misconduct." Restatement of Torts (Second) § 302B, cmt. e.H. Generally, such circumstances are limited to cases in which the defendant has given a young child access to ultra-hazardous materials such as blasting caps, *Vills v. City of Cloquet*, 138 N.W. 33 (Minn. 1912), or firearms. *Spivey v. Sheeler*, 514 S.W.2d 667 (Ky. 1974). Even in those cases, courts have relied on the third party's severely diminished capacity to handle the ultra-hazardous materials. With older third parties, courts have found liability only where defendants have vested a particular person, under circumstances that made his nefarious plans clear, with the tools that he then quickly used to commit the criminal act. *See Meers v. McDowell*, 62 S.W. 1013 (Ky. 1901). Arguably, the defendants' games, movie, and internet sites gave Carneal the ideas and emotions, the "psychological tools," to commit three murders. However, this case lacks such crucial features of our jurisprudence in this area. First, the defendants in this case had no idea Carneal even existed, much less the particular idiosyncrasies of Carneal that made their products particularly dangerous in his hands. In every case that this court has discovered in which defendants have been held liable for negligently creating an unreasonably high risk of third-party criminal conduct, the defendants have been specifically aware of the peculiar tendency of a particular person to commit a criminal act with the defendants' materials.

Second, no court has ever held that ideas and images can constitute the tools for a criminal act under this narrow exception. Beyond their intangibility, such ideas and images are at least one step removed from the implements that can be used in the criminal act itself. In the cases supporting this exception, the item that the defendant has given to the third-party criminal actor has been the direct instrument of harm.

2. First Amendment Problems

Moreover, we are loath to hold that ideas and images can constitute the tools for a criminal act under this exception, or even to attach tort liability to the dissemination of ideas. We agree with the district court that attaching tort liability to the effect that such ideas have on a criminal actor would raise significant constitutional problems under the First Amendment that ought to be avoided. *See NLRB v. Catholic Bishop of Chicago*, 440 U.S. 490, 500 (1979) (suggesting that non-constitutional questions of law ought to be construed, where possible, to avoid significant constitutional problems). Although the plaintiffs' contentions in this case do not concern the absolute proscription of the defendants' conduct, courts have made clear that attaching tort liability to protected speech can violate the First Amendment. *See New York Times v. Sullivan*, 376 U.S. 254, 265 (1964).

The first inquiry is whether the defendants' activity constitutes protected speech under the First Amendment. One thing is perfectly clear to this court: the plaintiffs' argument does not seek to attach liability to the cassettes and cartridges distributed by the defendants, but the ideas and images communicated to Carneal by those products. Although the defendants' products may be a mixture of expressive and inert content, the plaintiffs' theory of liability isolates the expressive content of the defendants' products.

Expression, to be constitutionally protected, need not constitute the reasoned discussion of the public affairs, but may also be for purposes of entertainment. *See Time, Inc. v. Hill*, 385 U.S. 374, 388 (1967). Clearly, the various media distributed in this case fall along a spectrum of expressive content. It is long settled that movies can constitute protected speech. *Joseph Burstyn, Inc. v. Wilson*, 343 U.S. 495, 501 (1952). Of more recent, but no less definitive, resolution is that internet sites are similarly entitled to protection. *See Reno v. American Civil Liberties Union*, 521 U.S. 844 (1997) (striking down the Communications Decency Act regulating indecent material on the internet). The constitutional status of video games has been less litigated in federal courts. Yet most federal courts to consider the issue have found video games to be constitutionally protected. *American Amusement Mach. Ass'n v. Kendrick*, 244 F.3d 572 (7th Cir. 2001) (Posner, J.); *Wilson v. Midway Games, Inc.*, 198 F. Supp. 2d 167 (D. Conn. 2002); *Sanders v. Acclaim Entm't, Inc.*, 188 F. Supp.2d 1264 (D. Colo. 2002). *But see Interactive Digital Software Ass'n v. St. Louis County, Mo.*, 200 F. Supp. 2d 1126 (E.D. Mo. 2002) (holding that video games were not protected expression under the First Amendment).

Extending First Amendment protection to video games certainly presents some thorny issues. After all, there are features of video games which are not terribly communicative, such as the manner in which the player controls the game. The plaintiffs in this case, however, complain about none of those non-expressive features. Instead, they argue that the video game, somehow, communicated to Carneal a disregard for human life and an endorsement of violence that persuaded him to commit three murders. Because the plaintiffs seek to attach tort liability to the communicative aspect of the video games produced by the defendants, we have little difficulty in holding that the First Amendment protects video games in the sense uniquely relevant to this lawsuit. Our decision here today should not be interpreted as a broad holding on the protected status of video games, but as a recognition of the particular manner in which James seeks to regulate them through tort liability.

To say that the features of the defendants' products of which the plaintiffs complain are protected by the First Amendment is not necessarily to say that attaching tort liability to those features raises significant constitutional problems. The plaintiffs' argument is more nuanced: they do not seek to hold the defendants responsible merely for distributing their materials to anyone, but to young, impressionable children or, even more specifically, to Carneal. The protections of the First Amendment have always adapted to the audience intended for the speech. Specifically, we have recognized certain speech, while fully protected when directed to adults, may be restricted when directed towards minors. *See, e.g., Sable Communications v. FCC*, 492 U.S. 115, 126 (1989); *Connection Distrib. Co. v. Reno*, 154 F.3d 281, 291–92 (6th Cir. 1998). We have also required, however, that such regulations be narrowly tailored to protecting minors from speech that may improperly influence them and not effect an "unnecessarily broad suppression of speech" appropriate for adults. *Reno v. American Civil Liberties Union*, 521 U.S. 844, 874–75 (1997); *United States v. Playboy Entm't Group, Inc.*, 529 U.S. 803, 812–13 (2000); *Connection Distrib.*, 154 F.3d at 292.

Of course, the measure here intended to protect minors from the improper influence of otherwise protected speech is quite different from the regulations that we have countenanced in the past. Those regulations were the product of the reasoned deliberation of democratically elected legislative bodies, or at least regulatory agencies exercising authority delegated by such bodies. It was legislative bodies that had demarcated what otherwise protected speech was inappropriate for children and that had outlined in advance the measures that speakers were required to take in order to protect children from the speech.

In contrast, the question before us is whether to permit tort liability for protected speech that was not sufficiently prevented from reaching minors. At trial, the plaintiff would undoubtedly argue about the efficient measures that the defendants should have taken to protect the children. But at the end of this process, it would be impossible for reviewing courts to evaluate whether the proposed protective measures would be narrowly tailored regulations. Who would know what omission the jury relied upon to find the defendants negligent? Moreover, under the concept of negligence, there is no room for evaluating the value of the speech itself. The question before a jury evaluating James's claim of negligence would ask whether the defendants took efficient precautions, in keeping their material from Carneal, that would be less expensive than the amount of the loss, the three deaths.

We cannot adequately exercise our responsibilities to evaluate regulations of protected speech, even those designed for the protection of children, that are imposed pursuant to a trial for tort liability. Crucial to the safeguard of strict scrutiny is that we have a clear limitation, articulated in the legislative statute or an administrative regulation, to evaluate. "Whither our children," as Appellant's brief states at 3, is an important question, but their guidance through the regulation of protected speech should be directed in the first instance to the legislative and executive branches of state and federal governments, not the courts.

Our concerns about adequately evaluating the narrow tailoring of regulations wane if the underlying expression is completely unprotected. Whether certain speech is not protected at all is a question that courts are regularly called upon to answer. James argues that to the extent that the content distributed by the defendants is at all expressive, it constitutes obscene material that is unprotected by the First Amendment. *See Paris Adult Theatre I v. Slaton*, 413 U.S. 49, 69 (1973). It would be novel to argue that the video games and *The Basketball Diaries* are obscene. As we understand James's complaint, he complains that the video games and the movie are excessively violent—yet we have generally applied our obscenity jurisprudence only to material of a sexual nature, appealing only to prurient interest and lacking any other socially redeeming value. *See Miller v. California*, 413 U.S. 15, 23–24 (1973) ("We now confine the scope of [obscene material] to works which depict or describe sexual conduct."); *United States v. Thoma*, 726 F.2d 1191, 1200 (7th Cir. 1984) (holding that because depictions of violence are not sexual, obscenity jurisprudence does not apply).

With the sexually-oriented internet defendants, James has an arguable basis to allege that the material is unprotected speech under our conventional obscenity jurisprudence. Nevertheless, where the First Amendment concerns wane the most with the possibility of obscenity, the foreseeability problems loom the largest. In his complaint, James contends that the sexual content displayed by the internet sites made "virtual sex pleasurable and attractive" for Carneal and caused him to undertake his violent actions. To us, however, James's allegations regarding his exposure to violence seem much closer to the mark. After all, James does not seek to hold the internet defendants responsible for a sexual crime: Carneal never endeavored sexually to abuse his victims, just to kill them.

With the movie and video game defendants, James contends that their material is excessively violent and constitutes obscene, non-protected speech. We decline to extend our obscenity jurisprudence to violent, instead of sexually explicit, material. Even if we were to consider such an expansion, James's arguments are not conceptually linked to our obscenity jurisprudence. The concept of obscenity was designed to permit the regulation of "offensive" material, that is, material that people find "disgusting" or "degrading." *See American Amusement Mach. Ass'n v. Kendrick*, 244 F.3d 572, 574 (7th Cir. 2001). James's argument, on the other hand, is that the violent content of these video games and the movie shapes behavior and causes its consumers to commit violent acts. This is a different claim than the obscenity doctrine, which is a limit on the extent to which the community's sensibilities can be shocked by speech, not a protection against the behavior that the speech creates. *Id.* at 574–75 (holding that the law of obscenity does not apply to the argument that violence in video games causes players to commit violent acts).

This is not to say that protecting people from the violence that speech might incite is a completely impermissible purpose for regulating speech. However, we have generally handled that endeavor under a different category of our First Amendment jurisprudence, excluding from constitutional protection those communicated ideas and images that incite others to violence. Speech that falls within this category of incitement is not entitled to First Amendment protection. *See R.A.V. v. City of St. Paul*, 505 U.S. 377, 384–85 (1992). The Court firmly set out the test for whether speech constitutes unprotected incitement to violence in *Brandenburg v. Ohio*, 395 U.S. 444 (1969). In protecting against the propensity of expression to cause violence, states may only regulate that speech which is "*directed to* inciting or producing *imminent* lawless action and *is likely to incite* or produce such action." *Id.* at 447 (emphasis added).

The violent material in the video games and *The Basketball Diaries* falls well short of this threshold. First, while the defendants in this case may not have exercised exquisite care regarding the persuasive power of the violent material that they disseminated, they certainly did not "intend" to produce violent actions by the consumers, as is required by the *Brandenburg* test. *Hess v. Indiana*, 414 U.S. 105, 108 (requiring evidence that the speaker "intended" his words to produce violent conduct under the *Brandenburg* test). Second, the threat of a person like Carneal reacting to the violent content of the defendants' media was not "imminent." Even the theory of causation in this case is that persistent exposure to the defendants' media gradually undermined Carneal's moral discomfort with violence to the point that he solved his social disputes with a gun. This glacial process of personality development is far from the temporal imminence that we have required to satisfy the *Brandenburg* test. Third, it is a long leap from the proposition that Carneal's actions were foreseeable to the *Brandenburg* requirement that the violent content was "likely" to cause Carneal to behave this way.

James contends that the *Brandenburg* test for speech inciting violence does not apply to depictions of violence, but instead only to political discourse advocating imminent violence. James suggests that the suppression of expression that is not advocacy, but does tend to inspire violence in its viewers or consumers, is governed by a less stringent standard. Federal courts, however, have generally demanded that all expression, advocacy or not, meet the *Brandenberg* test before its regulation for its tendency to incite violence is permitted. *See Dworkin v.*

*Hustler Magazine, Inc.*, 867 F.2d 1188, 1199–1200 (9th Cir. 1989) (applying the Brandenburg test to arguments that pornography causes viewers to engage in conduct that is violent and degrading to women); *Herceg v. Hustler Magazine, Inc.*, 814 F.2d 1017, 1024 (5th Cir. 1987) (rejecting suggestion "that a less stringent standard than the *Brandenburg* test be applied in cases involving non-political speech that has actually produced harm.").

Like the district court, we withhold resolution of these constitutional questions given the adequacy of the state law grounds for upholding the dismissal. Attaching such tort liability to the ideas and images conveyed by the video games, the movie, and the internet sites, however, raises grave constitutional concerns that provide yet an additional policy reason not to impose a duty of care between the defendants and the victims in this case.

* * *

IV

James also contends that the district court erred in dismissing his products liability claims. In his complaint, James alleged that the defendants' video games, movie, and internet transmissions constitute "products," and their violent content "product defects." Under Kentucky law, manufacturers, distributors, and retailers of "products" are strictly liable for damages caused by "defects" in those products. *Clark v. Hauck Mfg. Co.*, 910 S.W.2d 247, 250 (Ky. 1995); Restatement (Second) of Torts § 402A. If this theory of liability were to apply, James's failure to establish a duty to exercise ordinary care to prevent the victims' injuries would be irrelevant. Under strict liability, James would only be required to establish causation.

James's theory of product liability in this case is deeply flawed. First, and something none of the parties have mentioned, the "consumers or ultimate users" of the alleged products are not the ones claiming physical harm in this case. Restatement (Second) of Torts § 402A. Carneal was the person who "consumed" or "used" the video games, movie, and internet sites. Allegedly because of Carneal's consumption of the products, he killed the victims in this case. In early products liability law, courts had required privity between the final retailer of the product and the injured plaintiff for strict liability to attach. Eventually, courts broadened the class of plaintiffs who could avail themselves of strict liability to include those who consumed or ultimately used the product. Kentucky courts, but certainly not all courts, have extended the protection of products liability to "bystanders" who are injured by the product, but are not "using" or "consuming" the product. *Embs v. Pepsi-Cola Bottling Co. of Lexington*, 528 S.W.2d 703 (Ky. Ct. App. 1975) (holding that bystander could recover on strict liability basis for injuries caused by exploding soda bottle);

Restatement (Second) of Torts § 402A, n.1 (noting the split in authority regarding whether bystanders may recover on a strict liability basis). Imposing strict liability for the injuries suffered in this case would be an extension of Kentucky's bystander jurisprudence, as the decedents were not directly injured by the products themselves, but by Carneal's reaction to the products.

We place this open question of Kentucky law aside as the parties apparently have. James has failed to demonstrate a prior requirement, that the video games, movies, and internet sites are "products" for purposes of strict liability. This was the basis on which the district court dismissed James's products liability claims, holding that the video games, movie, and internet transmissions were not "products," at least in the sense that James sought to attach liability to them.

This court has already substantially resolved the question of Kentucky law presented. In *Watters v. TSR*, 904 F.2d 378 (6th Cir. 1990), this court held that "words and pictures" contained in a board game could not constitute "products" for purposes of maintaining a strict liability action. We cannot find any intervening Kentucky authority that persuades us that *Watters* no longer correctly states Kentucky law. James's theory of liability, that the ideas conveyed by the video games, movie cassettes and internet transmissions, caused Carneal to kill his victims, attempts to attach product liability in a nearly identical way.

James argues that, at least in this case, we are not just dealing with "words and pictures." Carneal, of course, had video game cartridges and movie cassettes. James argues that the test for determining whether an item is a product for purposes of Kentucky law is whether it is "tangible," and that the cartridges and cassettes are "tangible." As for the internet sites, James points us to a court that has held that "electricity" is a "product" for purposes of strict liability under Kentucky law. *See C.G. Bryant v. Tri-County Elec. Membership Corp.*, 844 F. Supp. 347, 352 (W.D. Ky. 1994). Internet sites are nothing more than communicative electrical pulses, James contends. James argues that there is no relevant difference between the internet transmissions and the electricity.

And of course James is partially correct. Certainly if a video cassette exploded and injured its user, we would hold it a "product" and its producer strictly liable for the user's physical damages. In this case, however, James is arguing that the words and images purveyed on the tangible cassettes, cartridges, and perhaps even the electrical pulses through the internet, caused Carneal to snap and to effect the deaths of the victims. When dealing with ideas and images, courts have been willing to separate the sense in which the tangible containers of those ideas are products from their communicative element for purposes of strict liability. *See*, e.g., *Winter v. G.P. Putnam's Sons*, 938 F.2d 1033,

1036 (9th Cir. 1991); *Jones v. J.B. Lippincott Co.*, 694 F. Supp. 1216, 1217–18 (D. Md. 1988). We find these decisions well reasoned. The video game cartridges, movie cassette, and internet transmissions are not sufficiently "tangible" to constitute products in the sense of their communicative content.

V

For all the foregoing reasons, we AFFIRM the district court's dismissal of all James's claims.

* * *

---

Another big legal event in this era of entertaining violence took place in May 1999, involving the lawsuits that had been filed against the producers of *The Jenny Jones Show.* In March 1995, Jenny Jones had invited Jonathan Schmitz, a 24-year old waiter in Detroit, to fly to Chicago for a televised meeting with his "secret admirer." But when he showed up for this event, Schmitz was stunned to learn that the person describing the erotic fantasies was Schmitz's gay neighbor, Scott Amedure. After filming and viewing Schmitz's emotional reactions to that disclosure, Jones and her colleagues decided not to air this episode. However, three days after Schmitz and Amedure had flown back to Detroit together, Schmitz bought a shotgun and murdered Amedure.

Four years later, Schmitz was convicted for the second time of second degree murder, and sentenced to spend between 25 and 50 years in prison. Just prior to that, though, the Amedure family won its big tort suit against Time Warner, the studio-producer of *The Jenny Jones* syndicated daytime hit show. The family's lawyer, Geoffrey Fieger, who had made his name by defending Doctor Jack Kevorkian against mercy killing charges, was able to persuade the civil jury that the defendants were partially responsible for the killing of Schmitz, and that the family that had lost their son were entitled to slightly more than $25 *million* in damages.

Supporters of this verdict against the "public humiliation" industry (epitomized by the Jerry Springer Show) applauded the Detroit jury for saying that "when you draw ratings from suffering, they'll make you pay for it." Needless to say, Time Warner said it would be appealing a decision that would have a "chilling effect on anyone involved in the business of interviewing ordinary people," at least unless they first did a "psychological pre-screening" of everyone. But the family of one of the Littleton high school victims immediately hired Fieger as their attorney to bring a lawsuit against everyone potentially responsible for this tragic event—not just the parents, school administrators, and local authorities, but also the producers and suppliers of media (and firearm) products to these teenage killers.

---

## DIANE HERCEG AND ANDY V. v. HUSTLER MAGAZINE, INC.

United States Court of Appeals, Fifth Circuit, 1987.
814 F.2d 1017.

ALVIN B. RUBIN, CIRCUIT JUDGE.

* * *

In its August 1981 issue, as part of a series about the pleasures—and dangers—of unusual and taboo sexual practices, Hustler Magazine printed "Orgasm of Death," an article discussing the practice of autoerotic asphyxia. This practice entails masturbation while "hanging" oneself in order to temporarily cut off the blood supply to the brain at the moment of orgasm. The article included details about how the act is performed and the kind of physical pleasure those who engage in it seek to achieve. The heading identified "Orgasm of Death" as part of a series on "Sexplay," discussions of "sexual pleasures [that] have remained hidden for too long behind the doors of fear, ignorance, inexperience and hypocrisy" and are presented "to increase [readers'] sexual knowledge, to lessen [their] inhibitions and—ultimately—to make [them] much better lovers."

An editor's note, positioned on the page so that it is likely to be the first text the reader will read, states: "Hustler emphasizes the often-fatal dangers of the practice of 'autoerotic asphyxia,' and recommends that readers seeking unique forms of sexual release DO NOT ATTEMPT this method. The facts are presented here solely for an educational purpose."

The article begins by presenting a vivid description of the tragic results the practice may create. It describes the death of one victim and discusses research indicating that such deaths are alarmingly common: as many as 1,000 United States teenagers die in this manner each year. Although it describes the sexual "high" and "thrill" those who engage in the practice seek to achieve, the article repeatedly warns that the procedure is "neither healthy nor harmless," "it is a serious—and often-fatal—mistake to believe that asphyxia can be controlled," and "beyond a doubt—. . . auto-asphyxiation is one form of sex play you try only if you're anxious to wind up in cold storage, with a coroner's tag on your big toe." The two-page article warns readers at least ten different times that the practice is dangerous, self-destructive and deadly. It states that persons who successfully perform the technique can achieve intense physical pleasure, but the attendant risk is that the person may lose consciousness and die of strangulation.

Tragically, a copy of this issue of Hustler came into the possession of Troy D., a fourteen-year-old adolescent, who read the article and attempted the practice. The next morning, Troy's nude body was found, hanging by its neck in his closet, by one of Troy's closest friends, Andy V. A copy of Hustler Magazine, opened to the article about the "Orgasm of Death," was found near his feet.

* * *

[On the basis of those facts, the deceased's family filed a tort suit based on negligence and other grounds. Following a judicial ruling, the claim was amended to include an incitement allegation and allowed to go to the jury on that ground alone. The jury returned a verdict of $69,000 in compensatory damages (for psychological harm) and $100,000 in exemplary damages. On appeal the majority found that the verdict could not be supported under the *Brandenburg* "incitement" doctrine. The third member of this Fifth Circuit panel agreed that the jury verdict had to be overturned, but only on procedural grounds. For the following reasons, Judge Jones believed that a cause of action was defensible as a matter of substantive constitutional and tort law.]

* * *

EDITH JONES, CIRCUIT JUDGE, Concurring and Dissenting.

* * *

What disturbs me to the point of despair is the majority's broad reasoning which appears to foreclose the possibility that any state might choose to temper the excesses of the pornography business by imposing civil liability for harms it directly causes. Consonant with the First Amendment, the state can protect its citizens against the moral evil of obscenity, the threat of civil disorder or injury posed by lawless mobs and fighting words, and the damage to reputation from libel or defamation, to say nothing of the myriad dangers lurking in "commercial speech." Why cannot the state then fashion a remedy to protect its children's lives when they are endangered by suicidal pornography? To deny this possibility, I believe, is to degrade the free market of ideas to a level with the black market for heroin. Despite the grand flourishes of rhetoric in many First Amendment decisions concerning the sanctity of "dangerous" ideas, no federal court has held that death is a legitimate price to pay for freedom of speech.

In less emotional terms, I believe the majority has critically erred in its analysis of this case under existing First Amendment law. The majority decide at the outset that Hustler's "Orgasm of Death" does not embody child pornography, fighting words, incitement to lawless conduct, libel, defamation or fraud, or obscenity, all of which categories of speech are entirely unprotected by the First Amendment. Nor do they find in the article "an effort to achieve a commercial result," which would afford it modified First Amendment protection. Comforted by the inapplicability of these labels, they then accord this article full First Amendment protection, holding that in the balance struck between society's interest in Troy's life and the chilling effect on the "right of the public to receive . . . ideas," Troy loses. Any effort to find a happier medium, they conclude, would not only be hopelessly complicated but would raise substantial concerns that the worthiness of speech might be judged by "majoritarian notions of political and social propriety and morality." I agree that "Orgasm of Death" does not conveniently match the current categories of speech defined for First Amendment purposes. Limiting its constitutional protection does not, however, disserve any of these categories and is more appropriate to furthering the "majoritarian" notion of protecting the sanctity of human life. Finally, the "slippery slope" argument that if Hustler is held liable here, Ladies Home Journal or the publisher of an article on hang-gliding will next be a casualty of philistine justice simply proves too much: This case is not a difficult one in which to vindicate Troy's loss of life.

I.

Proper analysis must begin with an examination of Hustler generally and this article in particular. Hustler is not a bona fide competitor in the "marketplace of ideas." It is largely pornographic, whether or not technically obscene. One need not be male to recognize that the principal function of this magazine is to create sexual arousal. Consumers of this material so partake for its known physical effects much as they would use tobacco, alcohol or drugs for their effects. By definition, pornography's appeal is therefore non-cognitive and unrelated to, in fact exactly the opposite of, the transmission of ideas.

Not only is Hustler's appeal noncognitive, but the magazine derives its profit from that fact. If Hustler stopped being pornographic, its readership would vanish.

According to the trial court record, pornography appeals to pubescent males. Moreover, although sold in the "adults only" section of newsstands, a significant portion of its readers are adolescent. Hustler knows this. Such readers are particularly vulnerable to thrill seeking, recklessness, and mimicry. Hustler should know this. Hustler should understand that to such a mentality the warnings "no" or "caution" may be treated as invitations rather than taboos.

"Orgasm of Death" provides a detailed description how to accomplish autoerotic asphyxiation. The article appears in the "Sexplay" section of the magazine which, among other things, purports to advise its readers on "how to make you a much better lover." The warnings and cautionary comments in the article could be seen by a jury to conflict with both the explicit and subliminal message of Hustler, which is to tear down custom, explode myths and banish taboos about sexual matters. The article trades on the symbiotic connection between sex and violence. In sum, as Hustler knew, the article is dangerously explicit, lethal, and likely to be distributed to those members of society who are most vulnerable to its message. "Orgasm of Death," in the circumstances of its publication and dissemination, is not unlike a dangerous nuisance or a stick of dynamite in the hands of a child. Hustler's publication of this particular article bears the seeds of tort liability although, as I shall explain, the theory on which the case was tried is incorrect.

II.

First Amendment analysis is an exercise in line-drawing between the legitimate interests of society to regulate itself and the paramount necessity of encouraging the robust and uninhibited flow of debate which is the life-blood of government by the people. That some of the lines are blurred or irregular does not, however, prove the majority's proposition that it would be hopelessly complicated to delineate between protected and unprotected speech in this case. Such a formulation in fact begs the critical question in two ways. First, a hierarchy of First Amendment speech classifications has in fact developed largely in the last few years, and there is no reason to assume the hierarchy is ineluctable. Second, the essence of the judicial function is to judge. If it is impossible to judge, there is no reason for judges to pretend to perform their role, and it is a non sequitur for them to conclude that society's or a state's judgment is "wrong." Hence, in novel cases like this one, the reasons for protecting speech under the First Amendment must be closely examined to properly evaluate Hustler's claim to unlimited constitutional protection.

* * *

The interest in protecting life is recognized specifically for First Amendment purposes and, analytically, can be no less important than the interest in reputation. The state's interest in this case is to protect the lives of adolescents who might be encouraged by pornographic publications and specifically instructed how to attempt life-threatening activities. In *NAACP v. Claiborne Hardware Company*, 458 U.S. 886 (1982), the Supreme Court assumed that if violence had broken out as a result of Charles Evers' incendiary speech, both the mob and the speaker could have been subjected to damage claims by the victims. For similar reasons, "fighting words" have long been outside the sphere of First Amendment protection. *See Chaplinsky v. New Hampshire*, 315 U.S. 568 (1942). The Supreme Court has also dealt favorably with state regulations designed to protect minors from performing sexual acts by prohibiting distribution of films containing such acts. *New York v. Ferber*,

458 U.S. 747 (1982). . . . The Court has even gone so far as to uphold an FCC regulation banning "indecent" speech from the airwaves at the times when children would be in the audience. *F.C.C. v. Pacifica Foundation*, 438 U.S. 726 (1978). States already regulate the distribution of pornography to minors, and a remedy for the collateral consequences of unauthorized distribution, by way of a civil action for damages, would only serve to reinforce that regulation.

Permitting recovery of damages in defamation cases offers an analogous framework. Balanced against the state interest, the Court held in *Dun & Bradstreet v. Greenmoss Builders*, 472 U.S. 749 (1985), that the First Amendment interest at stake was less important than the one weighed in *Gertz v. Robert Welch*, 418 U.S. 323 (1974). While *Gertz* involved a libelous publication on a matter of public concern, the false information in *Dun & Bradstreet* was contained in a credit report distributed to merchants. . . . Speech on matters of "private concern," the Court found, while not wholly unprotected, is not as substantial relative to important state interests. Thus, the credit report was prepared solely for the individual interest of the speaker and a specific business, it was false and clearly damaging, and, like advertising, it represents a form of speech unlikely to be deterred by incidental state regulation: The credit report involved a matter of "private concern."

Measured by this standard, both Hustler in general and "Orgasm of Death" in particular deserve limited only First Amendment protection. Hustler is a profitable commercial enterprise trading on its prurient appeal to a small portion of the population. It deliberately borders on technical obscenity, which would be wholly unprotected, to achieve its purposes, and its appeal is not based on cognitive or intellectual appreciation. Because of the solely commercial and pandering nature of the magazine, neither Hustler nor any other pornographic publication is likely to be deterred by incidental state regulation . . .

To place Hustler effectively on a par with *Dun & Bradstreet's* "private speech" or with commercial speech, for purposes of permitting tort lawsuits against it hardly portends the end of participatory democracy, as some might contend. First, any given issue of Hustler may be found legally obscene and therefore entitled to no First Amendment protection. Second, tort liability would result after-the-fact, not as a prior restraint, and would be based on harm directly caused by the publication in issue. Third, to the extent any chilling effect existed from the exposure to tort liability, this would, in my view, protect society from loss of life and limb, a legitimate, indeed compelling, state interest. Fourth, obscenity has been widely regulated by prior restraints for over a century. Before *Roth v. United States*, 354 U.S. 476 (1957), there was no Hustler magazine and it would probably have been banned. Despite such regulation, it does not appear that the pre-*Roth* era was a political dark age. Conversely, increasing leniency on pornography in the past three decades has allowed pornography to flourish, but it does not seem to have corresponded with an increased quality of debate on "public" issues. These observations imply that pornography bears little connection to the core values of the First Amendment and that political democracy has endured previously in the face of "majoritarian notions of social propriety."

Rendering accountable the more vicious excesses of pornography by allowing damage recovery for tort victims imposes on its purveyors a responsibility which is insurable, much like a manufacturer's responsibility to warn against careless use of its products. A tort remedy which compensates death or abuse of youthful victims clearly caused by a specific pornographic publication would be unlikely to "chill" the pornography industry any more than unfavorable zoning ordinances or the threat of obscenity prosecution has done. The reasonableness of allowing a tort remedy in cases like this is reinforced by the fact that only one lawsuit was filed in regard to "Orgasm of Death." The analogy with regulations on commercial speech is not inappropriate: pornography should assume a lower value on the scale of constitutional protection; and the state regulation by means of tort recovery for injury directly caused by pornography is appropriate when tailored to specific harm and not broader than necessary to accomplish its purpose.

* * *

Eliminating the *Brandenburg* incitement theory as a basis for recovery would have been sufficient to reverse the jury award here. The majority go much further, however, and afford Hustler virtually complete protection from tort liability under the First Amendment. I vigorously oppose their unnecessary elaboration on First Amendment law, which, I believe, will undercut the ability of the states to protect their youth against a reckless and sometimes dangerous business which masquerades as a beneficiary of the First Amendment.

## *QUESTIONS FOR DISCUSSION*

1. *Herceg* involved a suicide allegedly triggered by the contents of a magazine story. An even more difficult legal policy problem was presented by *Olivia N. v. National Broadcasting Company*, 126 Cal.App.3d 488, 178 Cal. Rptr. 888 (1981). Following is the judicial synopsis of the facts of that case.

> At 8 p.m. on September 10, 1974, NBC telecast nationwide, and Chronicle Broadcasting Company broadcast locally, a film entitled *Born Innocent*. "The subject matter of the television film was the harmful effect of a state-run home upon an adolescent girl who had become a ward of the state. In one scene of the film, the young girl enters the community bathroom of the facility to take a shower. She

is then shown taking off her clothes and stepping into the shower, where she bathes for a few moments. Suddenly, the water stops and a look of fear comes across her face. Four adolescent girls are standing across from her in the shower room. One of the girls is carrying a 'plumber's helper,' waving it suggestively by her side. The four girls violently attack the younger girl, wrestling her to the floor. The young girl is shown naked from the waist up, struggling as the older girls force her legs apart. Then, the television film shows the girl with the plumber's helper making intense thrusting motions with the handle of the plunger until one of the four says, 'That's enough.' The young girl is left sobbing and naked on the floor." It is alleged that on September 14, 1974, appellant, aged 9, was attacked and forcibly "artificially raped" with a bottle by minors at a San Francisco beach. The assailants had viewed and discussed the "artificial rape" scene in *Born Innocent*, and the film allegedly caused the assailants to decide to commit a similar act on appellant. Appellant offered to show that NBC had knowledge of studies on child violence and should have known that susceptible persons might imitate the crime enacted in the film. Appellant alleged that *Born Innocent* was particularly likely to cause imitation and that NBC televised the film without proper warning in an effort to obtain the largest possible viewing audience. Appellant alleged that as a proximate result of respondents' telecast, she suffered physical and psychological damage.

(a) Should there be greater legal receptivity to a tort claim that a third party has been raped (even killed) as a result of the immediate consumer watching, reading, or listening to an entertainment product?

(b) Given *Pacifica*, can television (or radio) broadcasts be subjected to more expansive tort liability than books, recordings, or films shown in theaters?

2. In reflecting on the fundamental question of how the law should treat personal injuries or deaths that may have been precipitated by someone (perpetrator or victim) having read, watched, or listened to entertaining speech, keep the following array of cases in mind.

(a) A book, *The Encyclopedia of Mushrooms*, identifies and describes which mushrooms are safe to eat. Two readers pick and eat a supposedly safe type of mushroom which turns out to be so poisonous that the two eventually need liver transplants. Should they be able to sue the book publisher under the law of strict liability for defective products? Or the law of negligent misrepresentation? *See Winter v. G.P. Putnam's Sons*, 938 F.2d 1033 (9th Cir. 1991).

(b) After the killing of two people outside California movie theaters following a showing of the film *The Warriors*, the producer advises theaters to hire extra security for the film. Notwithstanding that warning, the plaintiff's son is killed outside a Boston theater in a fight that began with the perpetrator imitating a scene he had just witnessed in the movie. *See Yakubowicz v. Paramount Pictures*, 404 Mass. 624, 536 N.E.2d 1067 (1989), and compare the facts and verdict in *Bill v. Superior Court*, 137 Cal.App.3d 1002, 187 Cal. Rptr. 625 (1982).

(c) After listening (while drinking and smoking dope) for hours to a Judas Priest album, *Stained Glass,* that allegedly has subliminal lyrics with suicidal overtones, two young men, aged 18 and 20, go to a nearby playground where they shoot themselves to death. *See Vance v. Judas Priest*, 104 Nev. 424, 760 P.2d 137 (1990). Compare a variation on the same theme with Ozzy Osbourne's song, "Suicide Solution" from the album, *Blizzard of Oz. Waller v. Osbourne*, 763 F. Supp. 1144 (M.D. Ga. 1991), *aff'd,* 958 F.2d 1084 (11th Cir. 1992). (Professor Myers, one of the book coauthors, worked on this case while in private practice.)

---

In the early 1990s, Paladin Press tested the limits of First Amendment protection by publishing a text entitled *Hit Man*. This work instructed its readers how hired killers could secure profitable assignments, do the killings unheard and unseen, and then escape without any witnesses being left behind.

One of the 13,000 copies sold in the next few years was bought by a man named Perry who then got the job from the divorced Horn to kill both the latter's ex-wife and eight-year old son so that he could secure a large trust fund in the son's name. When these facts came out, Paladin was sued in tort by the other relatives of the victims. Eventually, in *Rice v. Paladin Enterprises*, 128 F.3d 233 (4th Cir. 1997), the Fourth Circuit rejected the publisher's motion for summary dismissal based on the First Amendment.

The defense lawyers relied, in part, on the fact that the book explicitly said it was written "for informational purposes only." Indeed, apparently among its purchasers had been police officers, criminologists, and fictional crime story authors. The Fourth Circuit, however, found *Hit Man* to be "so effectively written that its protagonist seems to be present at the planning, commission, and cover-up of the murders the book inspires. [T]he book is arrestingly effective in the accomplishment of its objectives of counseling others to murder and assisting them in its commission and cover-up." This was judged to be fundamentally different from the *Brandenburg*-like "vague, rhetorical threats of politically and socially motivated violence that have historically been considered part and parcel of the impassioned criticisms of laws, policies and government indispensable to a free society." Paladin then decided to settle the case, paying substantial sums to the plaintiff and ceasing publication and sales of *Hit Man*.

In the spring of 2001, the family of the teacher killed in Columbine, Dave Sanders, sued a variety of media companies; not just those that made movies like *The Basketball Diaries*, but also those that made video games like *Doom* and *Quake* (which these high school killers regularly played). However, at the same time as the Sanders family was suing in the Eighth Circuit, a Seventh Circuit panel was ruling in *American Amusement Machine v. Kendrick*, 244 F.3d 572 (7th Cir. 2001), that such "martial arts" games were fully protected by the First Amendment.

This decision involved an Indianapolis ordinance that restricted children's access to certain video games in arcades or similar public sites unless accompanied by the parent or another adult. The games deemed "harmful to minors" were those that "predominantly appeal" to children's "morbid interest in graphic violence" or "prurient interest in sex." Distinguishing the constitutional status of restraints on sexual games, Judge Posner found it unconstitutional to deny full access by children 17 and younger to game machines with a "visual depiction . . . of realistic serious injury to a human," including "decapitation, dismemberment, bloodshed, mutilation, maiming," and the like.

Recognizing that minors can constitutionally be insulated from "sexually graphic expression," this court reasoned that "violence has always been and remains a central interest of humankind and a recurrent, even obsessive theme of culture both high and low . . . To shield children right up to the age of 18 from exposure to violent descriptions and images would not only be quixotic but deforming; it would leave them unequipped to cope with the world as we know it." 244 F.3d at 577. Judge Posner did recognize that video games are "interactive," but attempting to distinguish this product from literature as a whole (including visual movies and television) was fallacious. Indeed, Judge Posner believed that the better the literature, the more it was interactive. "[It] draws the reader into the story, makes him identify with the characters, invites him to judge them and quarrel with them, to experience their joys and sufferings from the reader's own." *Id.*

What about the City's reliance on some recent empirical studies displaying the impact of violent video games on children's psychology and behavior? These studies

> do not suggest it is the *interactive* character of the games, as opposed to the violence of the images in them, that is the cause of the aggressive feelings. The studies thus are not evidence that

> violent video games are any more harmful to the consumers or to the public safety than violent movies or other violent, but passive, entertainments. It is highly unlikely that they are more harmful, because "passive" entertainment aspires to be interactive too and often succeeds. When Dirty Harry or some other avenging hero kills off a string of villains, the audience is expected to identify with him, to revel in his success, to feel their own finger on the trigger. It is conceivable that pushing a button or manipulating a toggle stick engenders an even deeper urge of aggressive joy, but of that there is no evidence at all.

---

Essentially, the same results have been reached in the other major cases here. For example, in the most notorious of all, the Columbine killings, we saw at the start of this chapter Chief Judge Lewis Babcock of the U.S. District Court of Colorado was summarily dismissing all the tort suits launched against the entertainment industry for the role it may have played in inspiring the killings in Columbine. In his decision, *Sanders et al. v. Acclaim Entertainment, et al.*, Judge Babcock accepted the position formulated by Judge Posner in *Kendrick* that a video game like *Mortal Kombat* (produced by Acclaim) or *Doom* (produced by I.D. Software) enjoyed the same First Amendment status as a film like *The Basketball Diaries* (produced and distributed by what is now AOL Time Warner).

With respect to the video game, the Sanders family had claimed that "these violent games . . . made violence pleasurable and attractive and . . . disconnected the violence from the natural consequences thereof, thereby causing Harris and Klebold to act out the violence . . . [and] trained [them] how to point and shoot a gun effectively without teaching either of them any of the constraints, responsibilities, or consequences necessary to inhibit such an extremely dangerous killing capacity." This claim was based on "massive volumes of scientific research [which] show that children who witness acts of violence and/or who are interactively involved with creating violence or violent images often act more violently themselves and sometimes recreate the violence to which they have been exposed."

Just on the basis of the parties' briefs, Judge Babcock ruled that the producers of a *Mortal Kombat* or *Doom* "have no reason to believe that a shooting spree was a likely or probable consequence of exposure to their video games. . . . At most, these Defendants might have speculated that their video game had the potential to stimulate an idiosyncratic reaction in the minds of some disturbed individuals. A speculative possibility, however, is not enough to create a legal duty." Having reviewed the judicial opinions in other states largely dismissing these tort actions against various entertainment products, the judge then concluded that "under similar Colorado tort law, there is no basis for determining that violence would be considered the likely consequence of exposure to video games or movies," which meant the court should not be imposing on the producers a legal duty to try to prevent that.

It was possible that on appeal, the court might rule that product liability can be justified if there is evidence that violent behavior was a significant possibility, even if not the "likely consequence," of exposure to entertaining violence (especially here, given that the two Columbine killers had left a home video stating that their forthcoming massacre was based on what they had learned from their favorites like *Doom*). Thus, Judge Babcock began his analysis of the First Amendment protection by stating that "creating and distributing works of imagination, whether in the form of video games, movies, television, books, visual art, or song, is an integral component of a society dedicated to the principle of free expression." After citing the *Burstyn* decision as establishing that movies like *The Basketball Diaries* "are a significant medium for the communication of ideas," the judge relied on Judge Posner's ruling in *Kendrick* to find that video games were entitled to the same status as "expressive and imaginative forms of entertainment even if they contain violence." That meant that "makers of works of imagination including video games and movies may not be held liable in tort based merely on the content or ideas expressed in their creative works. Placing a duty of care on Defendants . . . would chill their rights of free expression."

While the Columbine victim families eventually decided not to appeal to the Eighth Circuit, entertainment products, especially the Matrix series, have played a role in insanity defenses to murder charges against those who viewed them and then were allegedly inspired to go out and do the same thing.

Young Lee Malvo (one of the D.C. snipers) trained by playing the video game *Ghost Recon* and watching a *Matrix* home video more than 100 times. Although Malvo was not acquitted, he was able to avoid the death penalty. Among those who have succeeded in this *Matrix* insanity defense were the 27-year old Vadim Mieseges who had killed his San Francisco landlord in 2000 and the 37-year old Tanda Lynn Ansley who in May 2003 killed a Miami University professor in Ohio. That same year Josh Cooke, a 19-year old obsessed *Matrix* fan dressed himself in the same brand and color of trench coat worn by actor Keanu Reeve playing the lead character Neo, armed himself with a Neo-like 12-gauge shotgun, and went down to the family basement to shoot and kill both his mother and father (the latter being the President of the University of the District of Columbia). After calling the police to come and arrest him, Cooke had a lawyer, Rachel Fierro, appointed to defend him. Fierro then filed a motion claiming that his client had a "bona fide belief that he was living in the virtual reality of *The Matrix*," and thus had the Fairfax Circuit Court appoint a psychiatrist to examine whether Cooke had become insane under criminal law.

Although the trial judge in the Columbine case accepted the Paines principle about the First Amendment status of video games, another trial judge disagreed, in *Interactive Digital Software Ass'n v. St. Louis County, Missouri*, 200 F. Supp.2d 1126 (E.D. Mo. 2002). Unlike *Sanders*, but like *American Amusement*, this case involved municipal regulation rather than private litigation.

St. Louis County had adopted an ordinance requiring that those running video stores or arcades restrict games judged "harmful to minors" in a separate "Restricted-17" room, preventing purchases by minors without the consent of a parent or guardian. The industry did not challenge that "harmful to minors" ordinance as it was applied to games with sexual content, but just those that "predominantly appeal to minors' morbid interest in violence." To be subject to that restraint, the game had to be both lacking a "serious, literary, artistic, political or scientific value as a whole for minors," but contain "graphic violence," which consisted of the visual depiction or representation of realistic serious injury to a human or human-like being . . . "And the Ordinance included a 'rebuttable' presumption that video games rate 'M' or 'AO' by the [industry's] Entertainment Software Review Board (ESRB) are harmful to minors."

The major video game bodies quickly went off to court to challenge this ordinance as an improper restraint on their free speech rights under the First Amendment. After viewing the video games that had been presented to him, *The Resident of Evil Creek*, *Mortal Kombat*, *Doom*, and *Fear Effect*, and then reviewing the evolution and current nature of both video games and constitutional jurisprudence, District Judge Stephen Limbaugh found these games to have

> no conveyance of ideas, expression, or anything else that could possibly amount to speech. The Court finds that video games have more in common with board games and sports than they do with motion pictures. A few courts have looked at whether "Bingo" is speech and protected under the First Amendment. In this instance, the Seventh Circuit held that "Bingo" does not convey ideas, nor does it contain "expression", and therefore, it is not protected by the First Amendment. *There to Care, Inc. v. Commissioner of the Ind. Dep't of Revenue*, 19 F.3d 1165, 1167 (7th Cir. 1994). The Seventh Circuit also implied that a game of blackjack is not expressive. Another court has held that a Bingo game is wholly devoid of the requisite communicative and informative elements necessary for First Amendment protection.

*Allendale Leasing, Inc. v. Stone*, 614 F. Supp. 1440, 1454 (D.R.I. 1985). The court went on to hold that Bingo may involve interaction and communication between runners and participants, but any such communication is "singularly in furtherance of the game; it is totally divorced from a purpose of expressing ideas, impressions, feelings, or information unrelated to the game itself." *Id.*

It might seem odd that the Court is comparing video games to games of Bingo, however, most of these simple games can and have been created in video form. The Court has trouble seeing how an ordinary game with no First Amendment protection, can suddenly become expressive when technology is used to present it in "video" form. For instance, the game of baseball is not a form of expression entitled to free speech protection. It is often times surrounded by speech and expressive ideas—music between innings, fans carrying signs with expressive messages—however, these expressive elements do not transform the game of baseball into "speech." Rather it remains, just what it is—a game. Nor does the Court think there is some magical transformation when this game of baseball appears in video form. The objectives are still the same—to score runs—and the only difference is a player pushes a button or swings a "computer bat," rather than swinging a wooden bat. Just like Bingo, the Court fails to see how video games express ideas, impressions, feelings, or information unrelated to the game itself.

The Court also finds that "violent" video games do not have any more expressive elements than other video games just because they are deemed to be violent. In other words, "violence" does not automatically create expression. Just as a baseball game is not a form of expression, neither is a hockey game. If within that hockey game, two players get in a fight, or someone gets sliced with a hockey stick and blood flies, the game does not suddenly become a form of expression. Another applicable analogy is boxing, where the main objective is to punch and knock out the opponent. However, boxing is still just a sport, not speech. In the same light, video games do not become a form of expression just because they contain violence.

Plaintiffs provided the Court with "scripts" from various video games. The Court admits that these "scripts" were creative and very detailed. However, almost every new creation and/or invention, starts as a "creative concept in the minds of the [ ] developers, who brainstorm, collaborate, and sketch scripts." Every product put on the market came from a creative concept. Most of the developers had to write down their ideas, and had to

> sketch pictures in order to convey their ideas to others working on the project. However, this "background" expression does not make every automobile, gadget, or machine created, a form of expression. The Supreme Court has held that it is "possible to find some kernel of expression in almost every activity . . . but such a kernel is not sufficient to bring the activity within the protection of the First Amendment." *City of Dallas v. Stanglin*, 490 U.S. 19, 25, 109 S.Ct. 1591, 1595, 104 L.Ed.2d 18 (1989).
>
> Plaintiffs claim that the final product contains "extensive plot and character development." However, plaintiffs did not show the Court the final product, the video game, and the issue in this cause of action is whether plaintiffs' video games are a form of expression, not whether plaintiffs' "scripts" are a form of expression. The Court must look at the video games in their context, in the environment in which they are presented. *See Spence v. State of Washington*, 418 U.S. 405, 410, 94 S.Ct. 2727, 2730, 41 L.Ed.2d 842 (1974) (the context in which a symbol is used for purposes of expression is important, for the context may give meaning to the symbol). The only video games given to the Court were those presented by defendants, and the Court simply did not find the "extensive plot and character development" referred to by the plaintiffs in the games it viewed. For all of these reasons, the Court finds that plaintiffs failed to meet their burden of showing that video games are a protected form of speech under the First Amendment.

200 F. Supp.2d at 1135–36.

The judge then went on to consider if the First Amendment did indeed cover video games, whether this St. Louis ordinance still did pass the "strict scrutiny" test required of any restraint on free speech. The judge here reviewed not only a few recent scientific studies relied on by St. Louis as showing that violent video games are "physically and emotionally harmful to children," and the host of studies demonstrating "that there is a causal connection between viewing violent movies and TV programs and violent acts," but also the industry's own rating process which, for example, rated some videos 'M,' as "suitable for persons aged 17 and older," because they "may include more intense violence or language." Thus, he concluded that this kind of ordinance readily passed the "strict scrutiny" test.

> The Court also finds that the statute is narrowly drawn to regulate only that expression which is necessary to address the government's compelling interests. In coming to this conclusion, the Court has looked at the right of the video game "creators" to speak, the right of minors to receive that speech, the right of

> parents to decide what is suitable for their children, and the right of the County to protect the welfare of its children. The Ordinance does not prohibit video game "creators" from making any video games, however, the Ordinance does limit the number of people video game makers can reach with their video games. Non-violent video games can be purchased and played by everyone. According to plaintiffs, that is the majority of the games. Violent video games can be purchased and played by all those over seventeen, which according to plaintiffs are the majority of the purchasers. Violent video games can also be purchased and played by those under the age of seventeen if the parents have given their consent. So in practice, the video game industry is only restricted in conveying their violent "message" to those under seventeen years of age whose parents do not want their children viewing and/or playing that particular type of game.

200 F. Supp.2d at 1138.

Needless to say, Interactive Digital Software and its colleagues in this industry, which has now reached the $10 billion annual revenue level, immediately filed an appeal with the Eighth Circuit. Especially if this court reaches a contrary First Amendment appraisal of violent video games than the Seventh Circuit did in *American Amusement*, this issue will likely then be going up to the Supreme Court. The Justices will then have to be rendering their appraisal of how this popular form of child entertainment in this new millennium fits into that First Amendment created back in 1790.

An important array of legal policy issues are posed in these major tragedies that took place in the 1990's. One set of questions relates to the appropriate operation of tort law. For example, should a recording, a movie, or a video game be viewed as just another potentially dangerous product, governed by the same products liability standards that apply to motor vehicles or medical devices? Indeed, a key feature of present-day products litigation is that often the suits are based not on some physical defect in the product itself, but rather on misleading instructions or inadequate warnings about use of the product in question. What distinction can one draw between this kind of speech associated with a prescription drug and the speech contained in a rap music record or a *Born Innocent* television movie? Should the *Brandenburg* incitement test continue to govern suits against record or television producers? Or, as argued by Judge Jones in her *Herceg* opinion, should the claims triggered by a dangerous record or film receive the same First Amendment leeway as that given to the victims of personal defamation (under the *Gertz* test) or commercial falsehood (under the *Dun & Bradstreet* test)?

Consider the breakdown of the *Jenny Jones* damage verdict: $5 million for pain and suffering by Amedure before he died; $10 million for the distress suffered by the family for loss of their loved one; $10 million for their loss of money that Amedure would have earned and saved in his working life; and $6,500 for his funeral expenses. What is the appropriate role of tort damages in any personal injury case, not just those injuries to which a television show may have contributed? And, of course, in all of these cases there is the further issue of whether the producers of movies and television shows—or interactive games such as *Doom* and *Mortal Kombat*—were at "fault" in producing a "defective" product because of its occasional motivating impact (as compared, for example, to the producers of the weapons used to do these killings).

Should the producers of movies and all other brands of "speech" have a legally protected right to create such a risk, at least unless their works were specifically intended to immediately induce such actions by the viewer or player? Given the possible disparity between the *Paladin Press* and *American Amusement Machine* circuit court rulings, it may be that events like the Columbine killings and resulting tort suits against games like *Doom* will eventually move the Supreme Court to address the key issue posed at the start of this Chapter 1, of whether the First Amendment formulation in *Brandenburg v. Ohio*, 395 U.S. 444 (1969), governs not just criminal prosecution of those engaged in political speech (there, on behalf of the Ku Klux Klan), but also tort suits against the producers of entertainment products.

With respect to *ex ante* legislative regulation rather than *ex post* private litigation, the Columbine killings generated essentially the same political logjams as in the past. For example, the House rejected Congressman Hyde's proposal to expand the federal offense barring sales of "obscene" materials to minors under 17, by encompassing not just sexual material but also "the kind of violence that appeals to the prurient, morbid, or shameful interest of children without redeeming social value." The MPAA and its then head Jack Valenti said that any such congressional action "by piling on Hollywood, [would be] distracting from the real issues—like guns." The NRA, in turn, appealed to the Second Amendment to block any expansion of current legal restraints on teenager access to guns, including the Colorado gun shows where the guns were secured for the Littleton killers. *Cf. Morial v. Smith & Wesson*, 785 So.2d 1 (La. 2001) (dismissing New Orleans suit against gun manufacturers).

---

Returning to the broader issue of entertaining violence, there is a significant *causal* as well as *constitutional* question posed by a lawsuit which claims that the viewing of a movie or the listening to a record in fact precipitated the violent act in question.[g] It may well be the case that certain kinds of movies and records increase the statistical incidence of violence in the community, even though it is not possible to identify any one individual injury or death that is directly tied to the perpetrator having watched a particular show or listened to a particular song. If that is so, the preferred governmental mechanism for addressing the social problem of entertaining violence would be administrative regulation before the violence occurs in real life, not litigation in court after the fact.

The last two decades have witnessed a huge amount of attention—scientific, popular, and political—being paid to the violence issue. Television programming is likely the most significant because of its dominant role in daily family lives.[h] A study by the Center for Media and Public Affairs found that the 50 top-grossing films in 1998 averaged 46 violent scenes apiece, music videos (typically 3 minutes long) averaged four such scenes, and television or cable shows averaged six "serious" violent scenes (i.e., murder, rape, kidnapping, or assault with a weapon). It should be noted, though, that television violence levels have actually dropped slightly since Senator Estes Kefauver raised the issue in the early 1950s.

One of the original systematic surveys, Mediascope's *National Television Violence Study* (1996) (commissioned by the cable channels but conducted by scholars from four universities), found that 57 percent of television shows in the 1994–95 season had at least one violent episode. The proportions ranged from 18 percent on public television to 44 percent on network programming, to 55 percent on independent stations, to 59 percent on basic cable, to 85 percent on pay cable. A more contextual analysis of these violent episodes, commissioned by the four networks and conducted by the UCLA Center For Communication Policy, *Television Violence Monitoring Report* (1995), concluded that gratuitous violence was less a problem with prime-time television series than is usually supposed. From this perspective, *NYPD Blue* and *Law & Order* were judged not to

---

[g] Besides the pieces cited in note e above, see Frederick Schauer, *Mrs. Palsgraf and the First Amendment*, 47 Wash. & Lee L. Rev. 161 (1990); and Jonathan Seiden, *Screaming for a Solution: Regulating Hollywood Violence: An Analysis of Legal and Legislative Remedies*, 31 U. Penn. J. Const. L. 1010 (2001).

[h] *See* Symposium, *Television & Violence*, 22 Hofstra L. Rev. 773 (1994); Brandon S. Centerwall, *Television & Violence: The Scale of the Problem & Where to Go From Here*, 267 JAMA 3059 (1992); Timothy B. Dyk & Barbara McDowell, *The Congressional Assault on Television Violence*, 11 Communic. Law. 3 (Fall 1993); George Vradenburg III, *Understanding Violence on Television*, 11 Communic. Law. 9 (Fall 1993); Julia W. Schlegel, *The Television Violence Act of 1990: A New Program for Government Censorship*, 46 Fed. Comm. L.J. 187 (1993); "Stephen J. Kim, *Viewer Discretion Is Advised": A Structural Approach to the Issue of Television Violence*, 142 U. Pa. L. Rev. 1383 (1994); Harry T. Edwards & Mitchell N. Berman, *Regulating Violence on Television*, 89 Nw. U. L. Rev. 1487 (1995). For empirical studies, see Susan Villani, *Impact of Media on Children & Adolescents: A 10-year Review of the Research*, 40 J. Amer. Acad. Child & Adolescent Psych. 39 (2001); Thomas N. Robinson, et al., *Effects of Reducing Children's Television & Video Game Use on Aggressive Behavior*, 155 Arch. Pediatric Adolescent Med. 17 (2001).

be a problem, though *Walker, Texas Ranger* and *The X-Files* were. Much more serious was the level of gratuitous violence in the broadcasting of theatrical films: this was true of 50 out of 118 shown during the 1994–95 season, as compared to 23 out of 161 made-for-television movies and miniseries. A second UCLA Study found a slight overall drop in television violence, but the same distribution among network programs, made-for-television movies, and theatrical movies. The biggest concern was about "sinister combat violence" in children's programming, e.g., *The Mighty Morphin Power Rangers* and *X-Men*, whose characters were fighting at the slightest provocation. Young children on average watch 22 hours of television a week (the availability of home videos has reduced this from 27 hours in the mid-1980s), and one quarter watch nearly 40 hours a week. It is estimated, then, that by the time a child leaves elementary school, he or she will have witnessed 8,000 made-for-television murders and 100,000 fictional acts of violence at this most impressionable age.

Psychological studies have found that more (and more violent) television viewing produces more aggressive childhood behavior. The limited number of long-term comparative studies indicate that these early psychological experiences contribute to higher crime rates. For example, one study consisted of 875 Midwesterners who were first investigated as children in 1960: it was found that childhood television viewing rates were the best index of adolescent aggressive behavior by 1970, and of adult criminal behavior by 1980.

An even more striking study compared the national experience in the United States, Canada, and South Africa—the first two countries gaining television in the late 1940s, but South Africa not until 1975 (because the Afrikaaner government was worried about the impact of television on apartheid). In the United States and Canada, white homicide rates nearly doubled from 1945 to 1975: in the United States, from 3.0 to 5.8 homicides per 100,000 people, in Canada from 1.3 to 2.5/100,000. South Africa's white homicide rate dropped slightly in that period (from 2.7 to 2.5/100,000). Then, when television came to South Africa in 1975 as a result of a new government policy, that country's homicide rates more than doubled in the next dozen years (from 2.5 to 5.8/100,000), while North American rates were stable.

Respected psychologists have criticized both the design of and conclusions drawn from this research. Nor is there any scientific assertion that television (or other entertainment) portrayal of violence does any more than aggravate a propensity to engage in violent behavior that is also heavily influenced by family relationships, economic conditions, easy availability of guns, and the like. For example, another international comparison found that the level of violence on prime-time network television in Japan was more than double that in the United States, though real-life homicides and other violent crimes in Japan are at only a fraction of the level in this country. Still, a 1995 poll showed that over 90 percent of Americans believe that television programming is making some contribution to real-life violence, and over 80 percent (including groups like the American Medical Association) believe that the government should do something about it.

Throughout the last two decades, two basic models for action were being debated in Congress. One would direct the FCC to treat "violent" programming as it now does "indecent" programming, and specify a "safe harbor" period when such programs could only be shown because children would not likely be viewing at that time (e.g., perhaps after 10 p.m.). The other would require installation in all new television sets of a built-in circuitry (originally called the V-for-violence-chip) that would receive signals of the rating of violence for a particular show and automatically block any channel which was carrying shows above the rating levels programmed by families into their sets.

The "safe harbor" concept had been pushed by a number of members of Congress, particularly Democratic Senator Hollings, but did not receive majority support there, nor within the FCC itself. The "V-chip" concept was pressed by a large number of Democrats, including then President Clinton. It was opposed not only by the television industry, but by the Republican leaders in Congress who were pressing for less rather than more regulation of the telecommunications marketplace. Thus, during 1995 both Senate Majority Leader Dole and House Speaker Gingrich voted against this specific feature of the reform legislation. However, what could now be labeled a C-for-choice chip (because it would be activated by sexually indecent ratings as well), was part of the vast Telecommunications Act which was passed by Congress and signed by the President in February, 1996. We shall see in Section D the host of controversies that Americans have experienced about what they see on the screen and what some of them see in the courts.[i]

### *QUESTIONS FOR DISCUSSION*

1. In analyzing statistics about the levels of violent programming on prime-time dramas or Saturday morning cartoons, what does (and should) be meant by "violence?" Recall the definition quoted earlier that is used by researchers for monitoring broadcasts. Is this too broad, too insensitive to the context, tone, and outcome of a violent scene? Should one simply count the number of homicides that take place in *Schindler's List*, for example, and compare the numbers to those in *Natural Born Killers*? How would you compare the psychological and behavioral impact of the extremely graphic depiction of a police officer executing the serial killer he has been chasing throughout the movie and a more discreet and artistic portrayal of an

---

[i] The first scholarly analysis of the issues was J.M. Balkin, *Media Filters, The V-Chip and the Foundations of Broadcast Regulation*, 45 Duke L.J. 1131 (1996).

attractive outlaw hero slaying his criminal rivals with no untoward consequences for him? With respect to the impact on young children, are the "sugarcoated" incidents in a cartoon likely to have as much (or perhaps more) impact than the unvarnished homicides in an adult film?

2. What do you believe are the actual consequences of violent broadcasting? Do statistical relationships between violence on television and violence in real life evidence only correlation or actual causation? Might one argue that watching violence could prove an antidote to performing it? Has entertainment violence made the public unduly insensitive and/or unduly insecure about violent incidents? Can broadcasters fairly claim that viewers are not influenced by what they see on the television screen?

3. Why is violent programming so prevalent on American television? For example, one study found that from 1988 to 1993, Nielsen ratings for more violent shows averaged 11, while ratings for non-violent shows averaged 14. Does the production pattern actually have more to do with the foreign market, in which American actors like Sylvester Stallone and Arnold Schwarzenegger were then considered among the most valuable commodities in the motion picture industry (and why would that be so)?

4. How effective has the V-chip been in altering industry programming and family viewing? How would you compare the positive and negative impact of the V-chip policy with an FCC expansion of its "safe harbor" policy to encompass "violent" programming as well as the "indecent" programming seen in *Pacifica* and its successors? Why are the networks more concerned about the eventual impact of V-chip rating than cable channels? A 2000 survey by the Kaiser Family Foundation found that 39 percent of parents had never heard of the V-Chip, only 9 percent had bought one, and of these just one-third (or 3 percent of all parents) had used it to block the viewing of programs they considered unsuitable for their children.

5. How legitimate are any or all of these policy instruments in light of broader social values? Is it consistent with First Amendment principles for a government agency simply to put a "violent" label on different shows? Compare *Bantam Books v. Sullivan*, 372 U.S. 58 (1963) (holding unconstitutional the labeling under a state law of certain books as "objectionable" because of their "obscene, indecent, or impure" content), with *Meese v. Keene*, 481 U.S. 465 (1987) (holding constitutional the labeling under the Foreign Agents Registration Act of three films on nuclear war and acid rain as "political propaganda," though one had won the 1983 Academy Award as best documentary). Suppose the law combines those labels with built-in lock-boxes on the television set in the home. Should non-fictional violence be treated the same as fictional violence, e.g., should the V-chip be triggered by a newscast film clip of the Rodney King beating or by an instant replay of a hockey player slashing an opponent's head with his stick?

6. In 1990, Congress enacted the Children's Television Act which directed the FCC to ensure that licensed broadcasters were providing appropriate levels of "educational and informational" programming at times

that children would be able to watch it if they (or their parents) so choose. For the next six years the FCC was locked in a fierce debate about whether to adopt regulations that would make this statutory goal precise and enforceable. Some Democrats argued for a rule that specified a minimum of three hours a week (between 7:00 a.m. and 9:00 p.m.) of programming that met an objective educational standard. Republican members considered this rule to be an intrusion upon the First Amendment rights of stations and networks. In Chapter 13, Section B, we shall see more of the context and details of this debate, as well as its apparent resolution in the summer of 1996. Would such FCC programming *requirements* be more or less compatible with constitutional freedom of speech and consumer sovereignty than FCC *bars* on indecent (or violent) programming?

7. While broadcasting is within Congress's bailiwick, movies and music (as well as books) have often been regulated by the states. When state legislatures began to turn their attention to the violent rather than the sexual content of entertainment products, they ran into constitutional hurdles.[j] For example, in *Video Software Dealers Ass'n v. Webster*, 968 F.2d 684 (8th Cir. 1992), the Eighth Circuit struck down as unconstitutionally "vague" a Missouri statute that barred the rental and sale of excessively violent videos to minors. Unduly violent videos were defined by Missouri as those that:

> taken as a whole and applying contemporary community standards . . . [have] a tendency to cater or appeal to morbid interests in violence for persons under the age of seventeen [minors] . . . and depict violence in a way which is patently offensive to the average person applying contemporary adult community standards with respect to what is suitable for viewing by [minors] . . . and, taken as a whole, lacks serious literary, artistic, political or scientific value for [minors].

Similarly, *Davis-Kidd Booksellers v. McWherter*, 866 S.W.2d 520 (Tenn.1993), struck down on that same constitutional "vagueness" ground a Tennessee law that barred rental or sale to minors of any material that contained "excess violence," defined as follows:

> Depiction of acts of violence in such a graphic and/or bloody manner as to exceed common limits of custom and candor, or in such a manner that the predominant appeal of the material is portrayal of violence for violence's sake.

Do you agree with either or both of these rulings? Is this judicial treatment of anti-violence legislation consistent with the Supreme Court's endorsement of anti-obscenity or indecency laws in *Miller* and *Pacifica*? How would you redraft the statutory language to satisfy the appropriate standards of constitutional clarity?

---

[j] *See* Jessalyn Hershinger, *State Restrictions on Violent Expression: The Impropriety of Extending Obscenity Analysis*, 46 Vand. L. Rev. 473 (1993).

8. Industry representatives and others have regularly testified that focusing on television (or movie or music) violence is no more than a symbolic response to the crime problem—ignoring the real issues such as guns, drugs, and broken families. At the same time, making this symbolic gesture threatens creative artistic expression much more than it does garden-variety programming. What are your views about these concerns?

Another vivid illustration of how entertainment products can shape our lives occurred in the spring of 2007, when a Virginia Tech college student, the 23-year-old Seung-Hui Cho, a South Korean who was an avid fan in particular of the video game *Counter-Strike*, killed a total of 32 people, and then himself. This quite popular game (that perhaps taught Cho how to produce the largest mass murder by an individual in American history) has its players portraying either a terrorist or a counter-terrorist.

Despite calls for strict legal regulation of such games as this one, *Doom* and *Grand Theft Auto III*, Dr. Karen Sternheimer, a sociology professor at the University of Southern California and the author of the book, *Kids These Days: Facts and Fiction about Today's Youth*, said "not only have youth violence rates decreased but violence rates in the U.S. have declined precipitously." So while the national debate so far is about gun control—both banning students having guns and arming the university police—we also have to be reflecting and debating even more this major entertainment legal policy issue.

That same April 2007 month produced a debate within and a report by the Federal Communications Commission, titled *Violent Television Programming and Its Impact on Children*. This report not only referred to that Virginia Tech tragedy—where NBC's *Dateline NBC* show also had reportedly inspired Cho by telling the story of the psychotic murderer Robert Hyde—but began by pointing out, among other things, that not only does the average child by the time they reach the age of 18 have watched 10,000 to 15,000 hours of television, but also "by the time most children begin the first grade, they will have spent the equivalent of three school years in front of the television set." And by age 18 an American child will have seen on TV about 15,000 simulated murders and 200,000 acts of violence, with a Time Magazine poll finding 66 percent of Americans believing there was too much violence on television. Thus, the U.S. Congress asked the FCC to undertake yet another inquiry into television violence, its impact on personal behavior, and whether it was both in the public interest and constitutional for the government to define and regulate "excessively violent programming that is harmful to children."

Among the major recent studies relied on by the FCC, *Youth Violence: A Report of the Surgeon General*, found that:

> for both boys and girls, habitual early exposure to TV violence is predictive of more aggression by them later in life independent of their own initial childhood aggression, their own intellectual capabilities, their social status as measured by parents' education or

> their father's occupation, their parents' TV viewing habits, and their parents' rejection, nurturance, and punishment of them in childhood.

The study concluded that Congress should impose time channeling restrictions on excessively violent TV programs. The rating systems were judged not only inaccurate but also likely to attract children to inappropriate programming. On the other hand, the Media Institute pointed out the difficulties in judging whether there was excessive violence not only in the *Star Wars* science fiction and the Holocaust drama *Schindler's List*, but also the Super Bowl.

The Commission concluded that "there is strong evidence that exposure to violence in the media can increase aggressive behavior in children," and that action, perhaps by Congress, "should be taken to address violent programming." To avoid legislation, not only should the industry adopt a family hour with no violent programming at the beginning of prime time, but also the multi-channel video programming providers (MVPDs) should adopt an a la carte regime allowing parents to opt out of paying for channels showing excessive violence.

Among others, California tried to regulate the use of violence in video games. The state's law, though, was challenged by video game manufacturers under the First Amendment. In 2011, the Supreme Court considered the constitutionality of the California statute.

## BROWN V. ENTERTAINMENT MERCHANTS ASS'N

Supreme Court of the United States, 2011.
131 S.Ct. 2729, 180 L.Ed.2d 708.

JUSTICE SCALIA delivered the opinion of the court.

We consider whether a California law imposing restrictions on violent video games comports with the First Amendment.

### I

California Assembly Bill 1179 (2005), Cal. Civ. Code Ann. §§ 1746–1746.5 (West 2009) (Act), prohibits the sale or rental of "violent video games" to minors, and requires their packaging to be labeled "18." The Act covers games "in which the range of options available to a player includes killing, maiming, dismembering, or sexually assaulting an image of a human being, if those acts are depicted" in a manner that "[a] reasonable person, considering the game as a whole, would find appeals to a deviant or morbid interest of minors," that is "patently offensive to prevailing standards in the community as to what is suitable for minors," and that "causes the game, as a whole, to lack serious literary, artistic, political, or scientific value for minors." § 1746(d)(1)(A). Violation of the Act is punishable by a civil fine of up to $1,000. § 1746.3.

Respondents, representing the video-game and software industries, brought a preenforcement challenge to the Act in the United States District Court for the Northern District of California. That court concluded that the Act violated the First Amendment and permanently enjoined its enforcement. *Video Software Dealers Assn. v. Schwarzenegger*, No. C–05–04188 RMW (2007), App. to Pet. for Cert. 39a. The Court of Appeals affirmed, *Video Software Dealers Assn. v. Schwarzenegger*, 556 F. 3d 950 (CA9 2009), and we granted certiorari, 559 U.S. ___ (2010).

II

California correctly acknowledges that video games qualify for First Amendment protection. The Free Speech Clause exists principally to protect discourse on public matters, but we have long recognized that it is difficult to distinguish politics from entertainment, and dangerous to try. "Everyone is familiar with instances of propaganda through fiction. What is one man's amusement, teaches another's doctrine." *Winters v. New York*, 333 U.S. 507, 510 (1948). Like the protected books, plays, and movies that preceded them, video games communicate ideas—and even social messages—through many familiar literary devices (such as characters, dialogue, plot, and music) and through features distinctive to the medium (such as the player's interaction with the virtual world). That suffices to confer First Amendment protection. Under our Constitution, "esthetic and moral judgments about art and literature . . . are for the individual to make, not for the Government to decree, even with the mandate or approval of a majority." *United States v. Playboy Entertainment Group, Inc.*, 529 U.S. 803, 818 (2000). And whatever the challenges of applying the Constitution to ever-advancing technology, "the basic principles of freedom of speech and the press, like the First Amendment's command, do not vary" when a new and different medium for communication appears. *Joseph Burstyn, Inc. v. Wilson*, 343 U.S. 495, 503 (1952).

The most basic of those principles is this: "[A]s a general matter, . . . government has no power to restrict expression because of its message, its ideas, its subject matter, or its content." *Ashcroft v. American Civil Liberties Union*, 535 U.S. 564, 573 (2002) (internal quotation marks omitted). There are of course exceptions. " 'From 1791 to the present,' . . . the First Amendment has 'permitted restrictions upon the content of speech in a few limited areas,' and has never 'include[d] a freedom to disregard these traditional limitations.' " *United States v. Stevens*, 559 U.S. ___, ___ (2010) (slip op., at 5) (quoting *R.A.V. v. St. Paul*, 505 U.S. 377, 382–383 (1992)). These limited areas—such as obscenity, *Roth v. United States*, 354 U.S. 476, 483 (1957), incitement, *Brandenburg v. Ohio*, 395 U.S. 444, 447–449 (1969) *(per curiam)*, and fighting words, *Chaplinsky v. New Hampshire*, 315 U.S. 568, 572 (1942)—represent "well-defined and narrowly limited classes of speech, the prevention and punishment of which have never been thought to raise any Constitutional problem," *id.*, at 571–572.

Last Term, in *Stevens*, we held that new categories of unprotected speech may not be added to the list by a legislature that concludes certain speech is too harmful to be tolerated. *Stevens* concerned a federal statute purporting to criminalize the creation, sale, or possession of certain depictions of animal cruelty. *See* 18 U.S.C. § 48 (amended 2010). The statute covered depictions "in which a living animal is intentionally maimed, mutilated, tortured, wounded, or killed" if that harm to the animal was illegal where the "the creation, sale, or possession t[ook] place," §48(c)(1). A saving clause largely borrowed from our obscenity jurisprudence, *see Miller v. California*, 413 U.S. 15, 24 (1973), exempted depictions with "serious religious, political, scientific, educational, journalistic, historical, or artistic value," § 48(b). We held that statute to be an impermissible content-based restriction on speech. There was no American tradition of forbidding the *depiction of* animal cruelty—though States have long had laws against *committing* it.

The Government argued in *Stevens* that lack of a historical warrant did not matter; that it could create new categories of unprotected speech by applying a "simple balancing test" that weighs the value of a particular category of speech against its social costs and then punishes that category of speech if it fails the test. *Stevens*, 559 U.S., at ___ (slip op., at 7). We emphatically rejected that "startling and dangerous" proposition. *Ibid.* "Maybe there are some categories of speech that have been historically unprotected, but have not yet been specifically identified or discussed as such in our case law." *Id.*, at ___ (slip op., at 9). But without persuasive evidence that a novel restriction on content is part of a long (if heretofore unrecognized) tradition of proscription, a legislature may not revise the "judgment [of] the American people," embodied in the First Amendment, "that the benefits of its restrictions on the Government outweigh the costs." *Id.*, at ___ (slip op., at 7).

That holding controls this case. As in *Stevens*, California has tried to make violent-speech regulation look like obscenity regulation by appending a saving clause required for the latter. That does not suffice. Our cases have been clear that the obscenity exception to the First Amendment does not cover whatever a legislature finds shocking, but only depictions of "sexual conduct," *Miller, supra,* at 24. *See also Cohen v. California*, 403 U.S. 15, 20 (1971); *Roth, supra,* at 487, and n. 20.

*Stevens* was not the first time we have encountered and rejected a State's attempt to shoehorn speech about violence into obscenity. In *Winters*, we considered a New York criminal statute "forbid[ding] the massing of stories of bloodshed and lust in such a way as to incite to crime against the person," 333 U.S., at 514. The New York Court of Appeals upheld the provision as a law against obscenity. "[T]here can be no more precise test of written indecency or obscenity," it said, "than the continuing and changeable experience of the community as to what types of books are likely to bring about the corruption of public morals or other analogous injury to the public order." *Id.*, at 514 (internal quotation marks omitted). That is of course the same expansive view of governmental power to abridge the freedom of speech based on interest-balancing that we rejected in *Stevens*. Our opinion in *Winters*, which concluded that the New York statute failed a heightened vagueness standard applicable to restrictions upon speech entitled to First Amendment protection, 333 U.S., at 517–519, made clear that violence is not part of the obscenity that the Constitution permits to be regulated. The speech reached by the statute contained "no indecency or obscenity in any sense heretofore known to the law." *Id.*, at 519.

Because speech about violence is not obscene, it is of no consequence that California's statute mimics the New York statute regulating obscenity-for-minors that we upheld in *Ginsberg v. New York*, 390 U.S. 629 (1968). That case approved a prohibition on the sale to minors of *sexual* material that would be obscene from the perspective of a child. 2 We held that the legislature could "adjus[t] the definition of obscenity 'to social realities by permitting the appeal of this type of material to be assessed in terms of the sexual interests . . .' of . . . minors. " *Id.*, at 638 (quoting *Mishkin v. New York*, 383 U.S. 502, 509 (1966)). And because "obscenity is not protected expression," the New York statute could be sustained so long as the legislature's judgment that the proscribed materials were harmful to children "was not irrational." 390 U.S., at 641.

The California Act is something else entirely. It does not adjust the boundaries of an existing category of unprotected speech to ensure that a definition designed for adults is not uncritically applied to children. California does not argue that it is empowered to prohibit selling offensively violent works *to adults*—and it is wise not to, since that is but a hair's breadth from the argument rejected in *Stevens*. Instead, it wishes to create a wholly new category of content-based regulation that is permissible only for speech directed at children.

That is unprecedented and mistaken. "[M]inors are entitled to a significant measure of First Amendment protection, and only in relatively narrow and well-defined circumstances may government bar public dissemination of protected materials to them." *Erznoznik v. Jacksonville*, 422 U.S. 205, 212–213 (1975) (citation omitted). No doubt a State possesses legitimate power to protect children from harm, *Ginsberg*, *supra*, at 640–641; *Prince v. Massachusetts*, 321 U.S. 158, 165 (1944), but that does not include a free-floating power to restrict the ideas to which children may be exposed. "Speech that is neither obscene as to youths nor subject to some other legitimate proscription cannot be suppressed solely to protect the young from ideas or images that a legislative body thinks unsuitable for them." *Erznoznik, supra,* at 213–214.

California's argument would fare better if there were a longstanding tradition in this country of specially restricting children's access to depictions of violence, but there is none. Certainly the *books* we give children to read—or read to them when they are younger—contain no shortage of gore. Grimm's Fairy Tales, for example, are grim indeed. As her just deserts for trying to poison Snow White, the wicked queen is made to dance in red hot slippers "till she fell dead on the floor, a sad example of envy and jealousy." The Complete Brothers Grimm Fairy Tales 198 (2006 ed.). Cinderella's evil stepsisters have their eyes pecked out by doves. *Id.*, at 95. And Hansel and Gretel (children!) kill their captor by baking her in an oven. *Id.*, at 54.

High-school reading lists are full of similar fare. Homer's Odysseus blinds Polyphemus the Cyclops by grinding out his eye with a heated stake. The Odyssey of Homer, Book IX, p. 125 (S. Butcher & A. Lang transls. 1909) ("Even so did we seize the fiery-pointed brand and whirled it round in his eye, and the blood flowed about the heated bar. And the breath of the flame singed his eyelids and brows all about, as the ball of the eye burnt away, and the roots thereof crackled in the flame"). In the Inferno, Dante and Virgil watch corrupt politicians struggle to stay submerged beneath a lake of boiling pitch, lest they be skewered by devils above the surface. Canto XXI, pp. 187–189 (A. Mandelbaum transl. Bantam Classic ed. 1982). And Golding's Lord of the Flies recounts how a schoolboy called Piggy is savagely murdered *by other children* while marooned on an island. W. Golding, Lord of the Flies 208–209 (1997 ed.).

This is not to say that minors' consumption of violent entertainment has never encountered resistance. In the 1800's, dime novels depicting crime and "penny dreadfuls" (named for their price and content) were blamed in some quarters for juvenile delinquency. *See* Brief for Cato Institute as *Amicus Curiae* 6–7. When motion pictures came along, they became the villains instead. "The days when the police looked upon dime novels as the most dangerous of textbooks in the school for crime are drawing to a close. . . . They say that the moving picture machine . . . tends even more than did the dime novel to turn the thoughts of the easily influenced to paths which sometimes lead to prison." Moving Pictures as Helps to Crime, N. Y. Times, Feb. 21, 1909, quoted in Brief for Cato Institute, at 8. For a time, our Court did permit broad censorship of movies because of their capacity to be "used for evil," *see Mutual Film Corp. v. Industrial Comm'n of Ohio*, 236 U.S. 230, 242 (1915), but we eventually reversed course, *Joseph Burstyn, Inc.*, 343 U.S., at 502; *see also Erznoznik, supra,* at 212–214 (invalidating a drive-in movies restriction designed to protect children). Radio dramas were next, and then came comic books. Brief for Cato Institute, at 10–11. Many in the late 1940's and early 1950's blamed comic books for fostering a "preoccupation with violence and horror" among the young, leading to a rising juvenile crime rate. *See* Note, Regulation of Comic Books, 68 Harv.L.Rev. 489, 490 (1955). But efforts to convince Congress to restrict comic books failed. Brief for Comic Book Legal Defense Fund as *Amicus Curiae* 11–15. And, of course, after comic books came television and music lyrics.

California claims that video games present special problems because they are "interactive," in that the player participates in the violent action on screen and determines its outcome. The latter feature is nothing new: Since at least the publication of The Adventures of You: Sugarcane Island in 1969, young readers of choose-your-own-adventure stories have been able to make decisions that determine the plot by following instructions about which page to turn to. Cf. *Interactive Digital Software Assn. v. St. Louis County,* 329 F. 3d 954, 957–958 (CA8 2003). As for the argument that video games enable participation in the violent action, that seems to us more a matter of degree than of kind. As Judge Posner has observed, all literature is interactive. "[T]he better it is, the more interactive. Literature when it is successful draws the reader into the story, makes him identify with the characters, invites him to judge them and quarrel with them, to experience their joys and sufferings as the reader's own." *American Amusement Machine Assn. v. Kendrick,* 244 F. 3d 572, 577 (CA7 2001) (striking down a similar restriction on violent video games).

Justice Alito has done considerable independent re-search to identify, *see post,* at 14–15, nn. 13–18, video games in which "the violence is astounding," *post,* at 14. "Victims are dismembered, decapitated, disemboweled, set on fire, and chopped into little pieces. . . . Blood gushes, splatters, and pools." *Ibid.* Justice Alito recounts all these disgusting video games in order to disgust us—but disgust is not a valid basis for restricting expression. And the same is true of Justice Alito's description, *post,* at 14–15, of those video games he has discovered that have a racial or ethnic motive for their violence—" 'ethnic cleansing' [of] . . . African Americans, Latinos, or Jews." To what end does he relate this? Does it somehow increase the "aggressiveness" that California wishes to suppress? Who knows? But it does arouse the reader's ire, and the reader's desire to put an end to this horrible message. Thus, ironically, Justice Alito's argument highlights the precise danger posed by the California Act: that the *ideas* expressed by speech—whether it be violence, or gore, or racism—and not its objective effects, may be the real reason for governmental proscription.

III

Because the Act imposes a restriction on the content of protected speech, it is invalid unless California can demonstrate that it passes strict scrutiny—that is, unless it is justified by a compelling government interest and is narrowly drawn to serve that interest. *R. A. V.*, 505 U.S., at 395. The State must specifically identify an "actual problem" in need of solving, *Playboy*, 529 U.S., at 822–823, and the curtailment of free speech must be actually necessary to the solution, *see R. A. V., supra,* at 395. That is a demanding standard. "It is rare that a regulation restricting speech because of its content will ever be permissible." *Playboy, supra,* at 818.

California cannot meet that standard. At the outset, it acknowledges that it cannot show a direct causal link between violent video games and harm to minors. Rather, relying upon our decision in *Turner Broadcasting System, Inc. v. FCC*, 512 U.S. 622 (1994), the State claims that it need not produce such proof because the legislature can make a predictive judgment that such a link exists, based on competing psychological studies. But reliance on *Turner Broadcasting* is misplaced. That decision applied *intermediate scrutiny* to a content-neutral regulation. *Id.*, at 661–662. California's burden is much higher, and because it bears the risk of uncertainty, *see Playboy, supra,* at 816–817, ambiguous proof will not suffice.

The State's evidence is not compelling. California relies primarily on the research of Dr. Craig Anderson and a few other research psychologists whose studies purport to show a connection between exposure to violent video games and harmful effects on children. These studies have been rejected by every court to consider them, and with good reason: They do not prove that violent video games *cause* minors to *act* aggressively (which would at least be a beginning). Instead, "[n]early all of the research is based on correlation, not evidence of causation, and most of the studies suffer from significant, admitted flaws in methodology." *Video Software Dealers Assn.* 556 F. 3d, at 964. They show at best some correlation between exposure to violent entertainment and minuscule real-world effects, such as children's feeling more aggressive or making louder noises in the few minutes after playing a violent game than after playing a nonviolent game.

Even taking for granted Dr. Anderson's conclusions that violent video games produce some effect on children's feelings of aggression, those effects are both small and indistinguishable from effects produced by other media. In his testimony in a similar lawsuit, Dr. Anderson admitted that the "effect sizes" of children's exposure to violent video games are "about the same" as that produced by their exposure to violence on television. App. 1263. And he admits that the *same* effects have been found when children watch cartoons starring Bugs Bunny or the Road Runner, *id.*, at 1304, or when they play video games like Sonic the Hedgehog that are rated "E" (appropriate for all ages), *id.*, at 1270, or even when they "vie[w] a picture of a gun," *id.*, at 1315–1316.

Of course, California has (wisely) declined to restrict Saturday morning cartoons, the sale of games rated for young children, or the distribution of pictures of guns. The consequence is that its regulation is wildly underinclusive when judged against its asserted justification, which in our view is alone enough to defeat it. Underinclusiveness raises serious doubts about whether the government is in fact pursuing the interest it invokes, rather than disfavoring a particular speaker or viewpoint. *See City of Ladue v. Gilleo*, 512 U.S. 43, 51 (1994); *Florida Star v. B.J.F.*, 491 U.S. 524, 540 (1989). Here, California has singled out the purveyors of video games for disfavored treatment—at least when compared to booksellers, cartoonists, and movie producers—and has given no persuasive reason why.

The Act is also seriously underinclusive in another respect—and a respect that renders irrelevant the contentions of the concurrence and the dissents that video games are qualitatively different from other portrayals of violence. The California Legislature is perfectly willing to leave this dangerous, mind-altering material in the hands of children so long as one parent (or even an aunt or uncle) says it's OK. And there are not even any requirements as to how this parental or avuncular relationship is to be verified; apparently the child's or putative parent's, aunt's, or uncle's say-so suffices. That is not how one addresses a serious social problem.

California claims that the Act is justified in aid of parental authority: By requiring that the purchase of violent video games can be made only by adults, the Act ensures that parents can decide what games are appropriate. At the outset, we note our doubts that punishing third parties for conveying protected speech to children *just in case* their parents disapprove of that speech is a proper governmental means of aiding parental authority. Accepting that position would largely vitiate the rule that "only in relatively narrow and well-defined circumstances may government bar public dissemination of protected materials to [minors]." *Erznoznik*, 422 U.S., at 212–213.

But leaving that aside, California cannot show that the Act's restrictions meet a substantial need of parents who wish to restrict their children's access to violent video games but cannot do so. The video-game industry has in place a voluntary rating system designed to inform consumers about the content of games. The system, implemented by the Entertainment Software Rating Board (ESRB), assigns age-specific ratings to each video game submitted: EC (Early Childhood); E

(Everyone); E10+ (Everyone 10 and older); T (Teens); M (17 and older); and AO (Adults Only—18 and older). App. 86. The Video Software Dealers Association encourages retailers to prominently display information about the ESRB system in their stores; to refrain from renting or selling adults-only games to minors; and to rent or sell "M" rated games to minors only with parental consent. *Id.*, at 47. In 2009, the Federal Trade Commission (FTC) found that, as a result of this system, "the video game industry outpaces the movie and music industries" in "(1) restricting target-marketing of mature-rated products to children; (2) clearly and prominently disclosing rating information; and (3) restricting children's access to mature-rated products at retail." FTC, Report to Congress, Marketing Violent Entertainment to Children 30 (Dec. 2009), online at http://www.ftc.gov/os/2009/12/P994511violent entertainment.pdf (as visited June 24, 2011, and available in Clerk of Court's case file) (FTC Report). This system does much to ensure that minors cannot purchase seriously violent games on their own, and that parents who care about the matter can readily evaluate the games their children bring home. Filling the remaining modest gap in concerned-parents' control can hardly be a compelling state interest.

And finally, the Act's purported aid to parental authority is vastly overinclusive. Not all of the children who are forbidden to purchase violent video games on their own have parents who *care* whether they purchase violent video games. While some of the legislation's effect may indeed be in support of what some parents of the restricted children actually want, its entire effect is only in support of what the State thinks parents *ought* to want. This is not the narrow tailoring to "assisting parents" that restriction of First Amendment rights requires.

* * *

California's effort to regulate violent video games is the latest episode in a long series of failed attempts to censor violent entertainment for minors. While we have pointed out above that some of the evidence brought forward to support the harmfulness of video games is unpersuasive, we do not mean to demean or disparage the concerns that underlie the attempt to regulate them—concerns that may and doubtless do prompt a good deal of parental oversight. We have no business passing judgment on the view of the California Legislature that violent video games (or, for that matter, any other forms of speech) corrupt the young or harm their moral development. Our task is only to say whether or not such works constitute a "well-defined and narrowly limited clas[s] of speech, the prevention and punishment of which have never been thought to raise any Constitutional problem," *Chaplinsky*, 315 U.S., at 571–572 (the answer plainly is no); and if not, whether the regulation of such works is justified by that high degree of necessity we have described as a compelling state interest (it is not). Even where the protection of children is the object, the constitutional limits on governmental action apply.

California's legislation straddles the fence between (1) addressing a serious social problem and (2) helping concerned parents control their children. Both ends are legitimate, but when they affect First Amendment rights they must be pursued by means that are neither seriously underinclusive nor seriously overinclusive. *See Church of Lukumi Babalu Aye, Inc. v. Hialeah*, 508 U.S. 520, 546 (1993). As a means of protecting children from portrayals of violence, the legislation is seriously underinclusive, not only because it excludes portrayals other than video games, but also because it permits a parental or avuncular veto. And as a means of assisting concerned parents it is seriously overinclusive because it abridges the First Amendment rights of young people whose parents (and aunts and uncles) think violent video games are a harmless pastime. And the overbreadth in achieving one goal is not cured by the underbreadth in achieving the other. Legislation such as this, which is neither fish nor fowl, cannot survive strict scrutiny.

We affirm the judgment below.

*It is so ordered.*

---

Finally, in the summer of 2015, 21-year old Dylann Roof interrupted a church service in Emanuel African Methodist Episcopal Church, pulling out a gun and firing at others in the church in a racially motivated act. He killed nine people, including the senior pastor and a state senator. Roof had published a manifesto on his website detailing his beliefs on race and containing photographs of him posing with emblems of white supremacy. Roof's photos with the Confederate battle flag sparked a national outcry against the use of the symbol, with several states discussing removing it from all public places. Golfer Bubba Watson tweeted that he would paint over the top of the "General Lee," a car used in the television show "The Dukes of Hazzard," which had a Confederate flag painted on the roof.

Suppose a film maker wanted to make a new spin-off television show based on the Dukes of Hazzard and wanted to use the Confederate flag in the show. Assuming a network wanted to televise the show, could the government prevent the use of that symbol? Why or why not?

## D. SELF REGULATION BY THE ENTERTAINMENT INDUSTRY

The entertainment industry claims there is no need for governmental regulation of the content of their products because there is fully-developed self-regulation for each type—from movies to video games. This ratings process provides parents with everything they need to know about what television shows their children should not be watching or what music they should not be listening to. Those killings in Columbine did produce a major government study of the operation of such entertainment self-regulation, whose key findings we will be reading about soon. First, though, we should learn about the history and current state of these industry programs.

The latest form of entertainment ratings was created in the television industry in the late 1990's, as a by-product of the V-chip provision of the 1996 Telecommunications Act. Its immediate predecessor had been fashioned by the record industry. At the beginning of the 1990's the Recording Industry Association of America (RIAA) had been conscious of the fact that roughly one third of domestic record sales were made to adolescents 12 to 19 years old. There was growing popular concern about the tone of contemporary music, precipitated by a group called the Parent's Music Resource Center (PMRC) and comprising a number of prominent Washington wives—e.g., Tipper Gore, Susan Baker, Beryl Ann Bentsen, and Nancy Thurmond. The PMRC wanted the RIAA to print song lyrics on album covers, and to attach labels such as V (violent), X (sexually explicit), D/A (drugs/alcohol) to those albums that warranted it. Eventually in 1990, the RIAA agreed to have a single warning label—Parental Advisory Explicit Lyrics—attached by individual record distributors to those albums which they (and the artists in question) believed justified the label.[k]

These television and music industries advisories are quite limited by comparison with the long-standing regime in the motion picture industry.[l] In the early 1930s, under pressure from the Catholic Legion of Decency, the MPAA created the Production Code Administration. Under this system of self-regulation, the studios agreed that while there could be sex and violence themes in their movies, to get the Production Code Seal of Approval the scenes themselves had to be discreet, and by the end of the story evil had to be punished and good rewarded. That system appeared to work very well throughout the 1930s and 1940s as the movie industry flourished both artistically and financially. In the 1950s, though, the Production Code began to unravel. Facing a huge competitive threat from free television at home, film-makers looked for ways to induce people to go out and pay to watch a movie in a theater. The financial virtues of more explicit sex were illustrated by such controversial hits as

[k] *See* Ann Galligan and Timothy Brown, *Warning Labels on Records and Tapes: The Mapping of Two Conflicting Policy Positions*, 21 J. of Arts, Management, and Law 355 (1992).

[l] Frank Miller, *Censored Hollywood: Sex, Sin, and Violence on Screen* (Turner Publishing, 1994), and Jon Lewis, *Hollywood v. Hard Core: How the Struggle Over Censorship Saved the Modern Film Industry* (NYU Press, 2000), are readable and insightful historical accounts and appraisals of Hollywood's efforts at self-regulation.

Otto Preminger's *The Moon is Blue* (1953) and Roger Vadim's *And God Created Woman* (1956), starring Brigitte Bardot in the nude. Indeed, many producers were no longer very concerned about whether their movies had secured the Seal of Approval. The appearance of Stanley Kubrick's *Lolita* in 1962 sparked reactions by both local and state authorities, and moved the MPAA to create a very different Voluntary Movie Rating System in 1968.

The immediate occasion was a pair of Supreme Court decisions that year. One decision we saw earlier in this chapter—*Interstate Circuit v. City of Dallas*, 391 U.S. 53 (1968), which struck down the Dallas film classification system as unduly vague, but held out the prospect that more tightly-formulated standards could pass constitutional muster. (Earlier in the decade, in *Times Film Corp. v. Chicago*, 365 U.S. 43 (1961), the Court had upheld local requirements for pre-screening movie clearance, at least as long as the ordinance offered immediate *de novo* judicial review of an unfavorable designation. *See Freedman v. Maryland*, 380 U.S. 51 (1965).) In the companion case to *Interstate*, *Ginsberg v. New York*, 390 U.S. 629 (1968), the Court made it clear that governments had even greater leeway to block dissemination of certain kinds of material to children. At the time, there were more than forty local censorship boards operating around the country. The Motion Picture Association of America (MPAA)—comprising the then largest motion picture studios, Universal, Twentieth Century-Fox, MGM/UA, Warner Brothers, Paramount Pictures, Disney, and Columbia Pictures—established a new, self-administered rating system. The objective was two-fold: to provide American parents with useful information about the suitability of films for their children, and to stave off the threat of censorship presented by federal, state or local attempts to regulate films.

The MPAA's rating system is jointly administered with the National Association of Theater Owners (NATO). Presently, there are five different ratings which may be applied to a film:

G—"General Audience. All ages admitted."

PG—"Parental Guidance Suggested. Some material may not be suitable for children."

PG-13—"Parents Strongly Cautioned. Some material may be inappropriate for children under 13."

R—"Restricted. Under 17 requires accompanying parent or adult guardian." (Age varies in some jurisdictions).

NC-17—"No children Under 17 Admitted." (Age varies in some jurisdictions).

Ratings are chosen by the Rating Board within the MPAA's Classification and Rating Administration (CARA). The Rating Board consists of a group of seven to eleven American parents who serve terms of varying lengths, and is headed by a Rating Board Chairman chosen by the MPAA President. The identity and number of Board members, who are appointed by the Board Chairman and MPAA President, are kept secret. This is how the MPAA describes its qualifications for Board membership:

> There are no special qualifications for Board membership, except the members must have a shared parenthood experience, must be possessed of an intelligent maturity, and most of all, have the capacity to put themselves in the role of most American parents so they can view a film and apply a rating that most parents would find suitable and helpful in aiding their decisions about their children's movie going.

After films are screened by the Rating Board, the only question asked of Board members is: "Do you think most American parents will want this film restricted or not? If yes: R or NC-17? If not: G, PG or PG-13? Write your reasons." Criteria used include "theme, violence, language, nudity, sensuality, drug abuse, and other elements." The only automatic rules relate to drug use and sexual language: if there is any reference to drug use, a film is automatically rated at least PG-13, subject to reversal by three-fourths of the Board; if there is any use of a sexually derived word, the film gets at least a PG rating, unless the word is used more than once or is used in a sexual sense, in which case an R rating is imposed, subject to reversal by two-thirds of the Board. The final rating is chosen by the majority of Board members, and then communicated to the film producer.

If a film's producers are unhappy with the film's rating, they have two options. They can ask the Board for reasons why the film was given a particular rating, and then edit the film in an attempt to address any concerns the Board may have. Films often have to be re-edited several times before the Board will change the rating. Another option is to appeal the rating decision to the MPAA Appeal Board, which consists of fourteen to eighteen members from the MPAA and NATO. The Appeal Board screens the film, and then hears arguments from the producer and the Rating Board Chairman as to why a particular rating should or should not be changed. An initial rating will not be overturned unless two-thirds of the Appeal Board members present decide to do so. That decision is based upon a screening of the film, the arguments of the film's producers, and the counter-arguments of the MPAA Rating Board Chairman. The Appeal Board does not issue reasoned opinions to explain its decisions, and there is no further appeal from an Appeal Board decision.

There is a third option for those producers who are not members of the MPAA—they may release a film unrated. Members of the MPAA are bound by contract to submit their films to the MPAA Rating Board. This is, however, an unattractive option because there are very few general distributors, exhibitors, video stores, and newspapers who will accept unrated films for distribution, exhibition, sale, or advertising.

Over the last quarter century, the MPAA has regularly attracted criticism from both filmmakers and outside observers. One recurring concern has been the lack of meaningful rating standards. A second concern is the lack of film-making, child psychology, or other membership qualifications besides parenting. A third criticism is the preoccupation with sex as compared to violence. (As illustration, the Bruce Willis film, *Die Hard II*, got an R rating despite a total of 264 killings.) The last is that the system tends to be tilted towards the films made by major studios that make up the MPAA, at the expense of their independent film-making competitors.

---

Before we return to the effort by the television industry to adjust the MPAA model to the special characteristics of the broadcasting world, it is useful to read the following effort by what was then an independent movie producer to have these concerns about MPAA ratings aired in court.

## MIRAMAX FILMS CORP. V. MOTION PICTURE ASSOCIATION OF AMERICA, INC.

Supreme Court of New York, New York County, 1990.
148 Misc.2d 1, 560 N.Y.S.2d 730.

RAMOS, JUDGE.

[In this case the MPAA movie rating board had given an "X" rating to *Tie Me Up! Tie Me Down!*, a film made by the Spanish director, Pedro Almodovar, starring Antonio Banderas, and distributed in the United States by Miramax. The distributor brought this action asking the court to find the film's "X" rating to be arbitrary and capricious, and to substitute an "R" rating in its place. While the MPAA, a not-for-profit New York corporation, did not dispute the court's jurisdiction over the case, it did argue that the court had no legal authority to reverse its movie ratings.]

* * *

Traditionally, any controversy regarding the content of a motion picture focused on the issues of censorship and free speech, not on the fairness of action taken with regard to a particular film by an industry rating board.

Censorship is an anathema to our Constitution and to this court. The respondent which created and administers the present rating system also proclaims that it is against censorship. However, notwithstanding the denials of censorship by the respondent, the present system of rating motion pictures "G", "PG", "PG-13", "R" and "X" is an effective form of censorship. It is censorship from within the industry rather than imposed from without, but censorship nevertheless.

The repeatedly expressed concern by the MPAA that its rating system is the industry's only defense to government censorship is unwarranted in light of First Amendment guarantees. The courts of this State and of the United States have sought to articulate a standard which would reconcile the interests that conflict—the preservation of individual liberties and creative freedoms on the one hand, and the protection of legitimate public concerns such as the emotional well-being of our children, on the other. The effort has produced a balancing point, the point at which speech stops and obscenity begins. Justice Brennan stated the present view in *Roth v. United States*, 354 U.S. 476 (1957):

> "All ideas having even the slightest redeeming social importance—unorthodox ideas, controversial ideas, even ideas hateful to the prevailing climate of opinion—have the full protection of the guaranties, unless excludable because they encroach upon the limited areas of more important interests. But implicit in the history of the First Amendment is the rejection of obscenity as utterly without redeeming social importance."

354 U.S. at 484.

There is nothing inherent in the rating system that would modify or extend the *Roth* standard. The standard in *Roth* was intended to apply in cases of governmental action to suppress or to prosecute and cannot be imposed upon the MPAA as its standard.

For its part, the MPAA contends that because First Amendment issues are not at stake, its rating determination must stand unless there is overt administrative misconduct. Once there is a finding of no administrative misconduct, the argument goes, its expertise ought to be deferred to as a legitimately authorized and duly constituted administrative body. Omitted from this analysis is the question of the reasonableness of the standard which the MPAA applies. If the MPAA is to avoid the relief sought herein then that standard must be rational, not arbitrary.

* * *

With regard to *Tie Me Up! Tie Me Down!* a seven-member [MPAA Rating] Board viewed the film and unanimously determined that the film should be classified with an "X" rating. The board members individually filled out, in their usual course of operations, rating forms which detailed the basis for the "X" rating. Each of the raters found that two sexually explicit scenes warranted giving the film an "X" rating. The board also found the visual depiction of the sex acts and language accompanying one scene to justify an "X" rating.

Petitioners were afforded an opportunity to delete or edit the objectionable scenes and declined. An appeal of the ruling was heard by the rating appeals board which split down the middle on whether the film warranted an "X" rating. As a two-thirds vote of the appeals board is required to reverse the underlying determination, the "X" rating was upheld.

Petitioners point to no deviance from standard procedures of the MPAA in the rating of the film.

The court notes that at any time a producer may withdraw a film from consideration by respondent and distribute the film unrated. The negative economic impact of not obtaining a satisfactory rating is clear and severe. Petitioners chose to distribute the film unrated.

The MPAA's standard for rating films was described in a memo to the rating board members from the chair of CARA, Mr. Richard D. Heffner. In that memo Mr. Heffner states that the MPAA rates films "as we honestly believe most American parents will want us to". It is evident that the MPAA standard is to rate films "G" through "X" based upon the tastes of the average American parent (AAP). The stated purpose of the rating system is "to provide advance information to enable parents to make judgments on movies they wanted their children to see or not to see." As such the MPAA rating system is clearly not designed to rate the merits of a film or even to advise adults as to which films they may wish to see.

The MPAA's list of cinematic no-nos is predictable: language, violence, nudity, drug use and sex. Notably absent is any sensitivity to the offenses suffered by women, minorities, the disabled and those who may not share the values of the AAP.

This court cannot avoid the notion that the standard is reasonable only if one agrees with it. This standard, by definition, restricts material not because it is harmful, but because it is not average fare . . . The manner in which the MPAA rates all films, not just *Tie Me Up! Tie Me Down!* causes this court to question the integrity of the present rating system.

The court notes that the initial rating board and the Ratings Appeals Board members have no special qualifications [and here the judge quoted the MPAA statement about this feature that was reproduced in the text before this decision.]

* * *

Petitioners allege in conclusory fashion that the board members and Ratings Appeals Board are selected and subject to the control of the major motion picture producers and distributor establishment. This court is unable to address this issue because no attempt at offering a factual underpinning for such allegations has been made.

An even more substantial concern is the question, not addressed by the parties, of whether respondent is adequately meeting the needs of America's children in film rating. Having voluntarily taken on this responsibility there may well be the obligation to competently address the task. An often leveled criticism of the MPAA is that violence in films is condoned to a far greater extent than displays of sexual activity. Without professional guidance or input it may well be that the interests of children are not adequately protected or are even endangered by providing color of acceptability to extremely violent and psychologically damaging films.

Although each of the categories which the rating system uses is cloaked in terms which suggest that they are fashioned to protect America's children, the inference of concern for the welfare of children is not borne out by any scrutiny of the standard and the guidance given to the rating board members. The standard is not scientific. There are no physicians, child psychiatrists or child care professionals on the board, nor is any professional guidance sought to advise the board members regarding any relative harm to minor children. No effort is made to professionally advise the board members on the impact of a depiction of violent rape on the one hand and an act of love on the other, nor is any distinction made between levels of violence. In this regard, the court notes the following from Mr. Heffner's December 1988 memo to rating board members: "Be concerned about violence, for American parents increasingly are. . . . but remember always how much violence seems to be accepted, perhaps even expected, in television and films."

Excerpts of Valenti's description of what the ratings indicate are probative of the relative tolerance with which violence in films is permitted related to material of a sexual nature:

> R: Restricted, under 17, requires accompanying or adult guardian (Age varies in some jurisdictions) * * *.
>
>> The language may be rough, the violence may be hard, drug use content may be included, and while explicit sex is not to be found in R-rated films, nudity and lovemaking may be involved * * *.
>
> X: No one under 17 admitted * * *.

> The reason for not admitting children to X-rated films can relate to the accumulation of sexually connected language or of explicit sex, or of excessive and sadistic violence.

Thus, the MPAA rates films on a purely subjective basis of what they believe is the AAP criteria for their children. A film may be viewed by children that may contain "hard violence" and "drug use" but not "explicit sex". Only "excessive and sadistic violence" will result in an "X" rating. It may well be that the MPAA ratings are skewed towards permitting film makers huge profits pandering to the appetite for films containing "hard violence" and "drug use" while neglecting the welfare of children intended to be protected by the rating system. This court concludes that reliance upon a nonprofessional rating board is misplaced and that the effort by the MPAA to encourage a more lenient policy toward violence is indefensible.

The failure of the rating system to provide a professional basis leaves only the viewing taste of the AAP, the consumers, as the standard. This standard may serve as a basis for a successful marketing strategy but may not coincide with the advice child care professionals might offer.

It may make good business sense not to ask a question if you might not like the answer, but it does render as hypocritical Mr. Heffner's claim that the sole rationale for the "X" rating is to avoid psychological abuse of children. The industry that profits from scenes of mass murder, dismemberment, and the portrayal of war as noble and glamorous apparently has no interest in the opinions of professionals, only the opinions of its consumers.

The record also reveals that films are produced and negotiated to fit the ratings. After an initial "X" rating of a film whole scenes or parts thereof are cut in order to fit within the "R" category. Contrary to our jurisprudence which protects all forms of expression, the rating system censors serious films by the force of economic pressure. The MPAA requires that American films deal with adult subjects in nonadult terms, or face an "X" rating. Films shown under the present system tend to be restricted to those fit for children under 17, as defined by the AAP.

The heart of petitioners' grievance is that an "X" rating stigmatized their film and lumped it into a category with pornographic films which none of the parties or serious critics contend should be done. Petitioners wish the court to award an "R" rating or alternatively seek to have the court determine that the rating system itself is patently arbitrary and capricious or without rational basis.

At its inception, the rating system denoted the various levels by the use of symbols and registered those symbols as trademarks, with the notable exception of the "X" rating. The effect of that exception (not explained in the papers submitted or during oral argument) has been to permit those who characterize themselves as pornographers to appropriate the "X" rating for their own purposes. "X rated" is now synonymous with pornography. For a film not intended for the pornography market, the rating of "X" is a stigma that relegates the film to limited advertising, distribution and income.

While it may be true that the MPAA has permitted the "X" rating to be appropriated by the pornography industry with a concomitant tainting of any film awarded an "X" rating, petitioners do not allege any bad faith or foresight in respondent's failing to register the "X" rating. While arguing in conclusory fashion that the current system works to the detriment of certain types of films and film makers, petitioners do not set forth an adequate factual basis on the papers before this court, or oral argument, to warrant such findings.

The court notes that it is clearly precluded in judicial review from substituting its judgment for that of the body reviewed or from considering the facts de novo. This principle will also apply to a review of a determination of a private nongovernmental organization. This court is also precluded from imposing a different (professional) standard because the MPAA may not be required to do so under the First Amendment. Therefore, the burden is on petitioners to set forth facts indicating that respondent acted arbitrarily, capriciously and without rational basis in applying the standard of the AAP. This petitioners have clearly failed to do. Within the context of this rating system for parental guidance there has been no showing that the "X" rating afforded *Tie Me Up! Tie Me Down!* was without a rational basis or arbitrary and capricious. Petitioners themselves acknowledge that the film contains material that is not suitable for those under the age of 18 and there is no dispute that the film contains language and sexually explicit scenes that parents might not wish their children to view.

As a part of this proceeding, the court has been requested to view selected scenes from *Tie Me Up! Tie Me Down!* and scenes from other films rated "R" in order to determine if the "X" rating was arbitrary. That determination this court declines to make.

This court will not dignify the present system by rendering an opinion on so frivolous a standard as the wishes of the AAP. What is offensive is the unprofessional standard itself, not the manner in which the rating board applies it. The standard of the AAP is a marketing standard, a tool to aid in promoting films. There is no basis in the record for the court to conclude that the MPAA does not know how to label its products for market, there is only a question as to the significance of the labeling.

At best the offering of clips of "R" rated films into evidence amounts to an argument of discriminatory enforcement of the rating standards.

That over the course of more than two decades a handful of films may have been as sexually explicit as *Tie Me Up! Tie Me Down!* or arguably, in the eyes of the beholder, more explicit and unsuitable for youthful viewers and have obtained an "R" rating is not inherently arbitrary and capricious or without rational basis. To find respondent's actions of affording the "R" rating to certain films and not to *Tie Me Up! Tie Me Down!* to be wrongful, the court believes petitioners need offer evidence of clear and intentional discrimination. Petitioners have failed to do so. Merely alluding in conclusory fashion to possible vague discrimination is not sufficient. Additionally, the overriding concern is whether respondent acted in good faith in furtherance of its own legitimate purpose. Petitioners do not, other than by cursory conjecture, substantiate any basis to indicate respondent acted in bad faith or outside of its stated function in its rating of *Tie Me Up! Tie Me Down!*

* * *

This court is mindful of constitutional limitations on the imposition of a governmental system of censorship (*see Interstate Circuit v. Dallas*, 390 U.S. 676 (1968)). The courts would thus be reluctant to tamper with a voluntary independent system of film rating. However, in view of the dominant and preemptive role played by the MPAA in the film industry there is an obligation to administer the system fairly and with a foundation that is rationally based. This proceeding has raised certain issues which need be addressed by respondent although no relief may be afforded herein. The initial problem is the need to avoid stigmatizing films of an adult nature, which ought not be seen by children, but which are clearly not pornographic. The MPAA, having acquiesced in the use of the "X" rating by the pornography industry, may well have some affirmative responsibility to avoid stigmatizing films with an "X" rating.

This court also concludes that the rating system's categories have been fashioned by the motion picture industry to create an illusion of concern for children, imposing censorship, yet all the while facilitating the marketing of exploitive and violent films with an industry seal of approval.

While the petition before this court does not adequately present a case for addressing these serious issues, it appears that the MPAA should strongly consider some changes in its methods of operations to properly perform its stated mission. Unless such concerns are meaningfully dealt with, the MPAA may find its rating system subject to viable legal challenge by those groups adversely affected herein, including organizations charged with the responsibility of protecting children.

If the MPAA chooses to rate films for the benefit of children it is its duty to do so with standards that have a rational and professional basis or to leave the task to others whose interests are not subject to the powerful economic forces at work within the industry. The respondent is strongly advised either to consider proposals for a revised rating system that permits a professional basis for rating films or to cease the practice altogether. The petition before this court is, however, not the appropriate vehicle to afford such relief.

Dismissed.

---

Though Miramax lost this particular case, a significant change was soon made in the movie rating system. The MPAA added a new NC-17 rating, which still bars children under 17 from being admitted to the theater to watch the movie, but which would not impose on serious movies like *Tie Me Up* the stigma of an X-rating that had been co-opted by pornographic movies like *Deep Throat*. The reaction of the mainstream film industry, though, was to be nearly as leery about distributing an NC-17 as an X-rated film. And following such artistic and financial successes as *The Crying Game* and *The Piano*, Miramax itself joined that mainstream. In 1993, the Walt Disney Company bought Miramax for $80 million and brought its principals, the Weinstein brothers, in to run this branch of its movie financing and distribution system. A year later, in 1994, Miramax brought two box office hits (*Pulp Fiction* and *The Crow*) and 22 Academy Award nominations back to Disney.

Miramax and the Weinsteins, however, have had to confront the tension between the artistic inclinations of some film producers and Disney's corporate policy against releasing any NC-17 or X-rated films. (That was not an issue with *Priest*, notwithstanding its controversial content and boycott efforts by certain religious groups.) With the help of Alan Dershowitz, Miramax was able to persuade the MPAA to revise its initial rating of *Clerks*, and give it an R. In the summer of 1995, that same effort was unsuccessful for the movie *Kids*, which received an NC-17 rating for its "explicit sex, language, drug use and violence involving children." Though Miramax paid $3.5 million for the distribution rights to *Kids*, the Weinsteins had to spin off a separate distribution arm, Excalibur Films, which released the film without any rating at all.

Another MPAA member, MGM/United Artists, decided to confront the rating challenge head on. MGM/UA paid huge amounts for the services of the director (Paul Verhoeven) and screenwriter (Joe Eszterhas) of *Basic Instinct* to produce a movie, *Showgirls*, which turned out to be far racier than even that earlier notorious hit. As expected, *Showgirls* got an NC-17 from the MPAA. That rating posed a large financial gamble for MGM/United Artists, an old major studio that was trying to revive itself after more than a decade in the movie business doldrums. The reason is that a number of theater chains will not exhibit NC-17 movies, partly because of restrictions placed by many shopping malls where theaters are located. Major video distributors such as Red Box, Wal-Mart, and Kmart will not sell or rent NC-17 (as well as X-rated) movies. Moreover, a number of newspapers will not accept advertisements for NC-17 films in what they consider to be "family papers." There are a few NC-17 films like *Henry and June*, *Bad Lieutenant*, and *You So Crazy* that have made a profit by grossing $10 million or so at the domestic box office. Given the average $75 million production and distribution costs of the major studios' movie releases, those kinds of financial prospects are unacceptable to the studios. There is, however, a large international market for movies that concentrate on sex and violence rather than on dialogue. Thus *Showgirls'* release in the fall of 1995 was to be the test case of whether the MPAA's NC-17 rating is a *de facto* economic control on explicit sex (if not violence) in big-time movies.

As it turned out, though, while *Showgirls* was able to book a large number of theater screens and get a lot of pre-release media attention, the movie also received very negative reviews and low-box office results after the first weekend. With the film having grossed less than $25 million at the domestic box office after costing $40 million to produce, Verhoeven, the director, agreed to edit out 60 seconds of explicit sex for a video version that now-defunct Blockbuster was willing to carry once it got an R-rating. (The original NC-17 version was distributed on video in most other video stores.) The verdict about the impact of an NC-17 rating on a better-made movie is still unclear. The *Showgirls* experience has now made it essentially impossible for big budget movies to have an NC-17 rating.

### *QUESTIONS FOR DISCUSSION*

1. As a matter of general legal principle, should ratings by an industry body such as the MPAA be subject to the same searching judicial scrutiny as the Constitution requires for municipal agencies (as we saw in the earlier quotation from *Interstate Circuit v. City of Dallas*, 391 U.S. 53 (1968))? How much weight should be given to the public-private distinction in the context of movie "censorship" through advisory ratings? Put yourself in the position of a director like *Pulp Fiction's* Quentin Tarantino or a rap artist like Snoop Doggy Dogg: if there is going to be labeling or regulation of the sexual and violent content of your work, would you rather have this done by an industry or government-appointed body? What are the risks in each and how do they compare?

2. What was the legal theory on which Miramax based its ratings claim? What if any circumstances might have led the judge to uphold a claim on this theory? Are there other legal predicates with which to attack an MPAA rating in the courts? For example, what about the "covenant of good faith and fair dealing" implied in the relationship between MPAA and

producer? *See Maljack Productions, Inc. v. MPAA*, 52 F.3d 373 (D.C. Cir. 1995) (involving *Henry: Portrait of a Serial Killer*).

3. Alternatively, what about an antitrust claim based on the relationship between MPAA and NATO—as well as the *de facto* exclusionary impact of NC-17 ratings on newspaper advertisements and video distributors such as Red Box and Wal-Mart? For an early such effort, see *Tropic Film Corp. v. Paramount Pictures Corp. and MPAA*, 319 F. Supp. 1247 (S.D.N.Y. 1970) (*Tropic of Cancer*). We shall return to this issue in Chapter 12 which deals in depth with the antitrust status of the motion picture industry. For the moment, though, did the television networks have a sufficient concern about antitrust liability to warrant Illinois Senator Paul Simon introducing and getting adopted the 1990 *Television Program Improvement Act*, which made antitrust laws inapplicable for three years to joint television industry development and adoption of "voluntary guidelines designed to alleviate the negative impact of violence in telecast material?" *See United States v. National Association of Broadcasters*, 553 F. Supp. 621 (D.D.C.1982).

---

Turning now to the policy merits rather than its legal status, there are many calls for improvements in the MPAA and other industry ratings systems. One question is who should be doing the ratings. For example, of the several dozen countries that now have film rating regimes (for motion pictures, television, or both), the MPAA program in the United States is the only one that makes "parenting" the sole explicit qualification for inclusion on the ratings boards. Should the MPAA include members with backgrounds in filmmaking, child psychology, criminal justice administration, and/or any other experiences that might be considered relevant to this task?

The next issue is whether the content of the current movie ratings can be enhanced. One possibility is to go to a single Parental Advisory warning, as in music? Another is to follow the new model for video game ratings adopted in 1994 (under congressional pressure) by the industry's Interactive Digital Software Association (IDSA)? The IDSA's Entertainment Software Rating Board, headed by a specialist in child psychology, has five ratings: EC (early childhood, from 3 years up); KA (kids to adult, ages 6 and older and permitting some violence); T (teens, aged 13 and older, and permitting violence and strong language); M (mature, aged 17 and older, and permitting violence and sex scenes); and AO (adults only, permitting graphic sex and violence). Every video game carries with it both a description of the rating system and a toll-free number that offers explanations for the ratings of individual games. Following creation of this IDSA program, Wal-Mart announced that it would not stock any AO video games and would require proof of age to purchase an M-rated game.

In 1997, the television industry in the United States introduced its age-based rating system, following the MPAA model for movie ratings. Children's programming is rated as either TV-Y (All children) or TV-Y7 (Older children); all other programming is divided into TV-G (General Audience), TV-PG (Parental Guidance), TV-14 (Parents Strongly Cautioned), and TV-M (Mature Audience Only). Under pressure from family and educational groups as well as the Clinton administration, the networks (except for NBC) decided to follow the Canadian model, which differentiates between the violence (V), sex (S) and language (L) content of a program. Two different kinds of questions were posed by this debate. First, does an age-based or a content-based rating system best serve the policy objectives of the Telecommunications Act? Second, if the FCC were eventually to mandate a specific content model for rating television programs, would this infringe upon the First Amendment rights of television producers and programmers?

In 2000, the FTC found that the record companies marketed to children under 17 years old 100 percent of the 55 albums labeled with "explicit" content, the movie studios did this with 80 percent (35 of 44) of movies rated R, and the video game firms with 70 percent (83 of 118) games rated M (mature). This FTC Report accentuated a mid-1990's survey done by Variety that while just 16 percent of moviegoers over 50 liked R-rated movies, these were the preference for 59 percent of those between 18 and 24 and 41 percent of those between 12 and 17 years old.

A later FTC Report, *Marketing Entertainment Violence to Children,* found that the movie and video game industries had reduced somewhat the amount of advertising of R-rated movies and M-rated games at least on those television shows with 35 percent or more of their audiences less than 18 years old, and that they were now more likely to be including the ratings and their reasons in newspapers, magazines, and Internet ads. The music industry had taken neither of those steps.

More important, perhaps, were the FTC's findings from Undercover Mystery Shop Surveys conducted to find out how often children were able to obtain unsuitable material. With respect to movie theaters, 46 percent of 13–16 year-olds bought tickets for R-rated movies unaccompanied by adults; this went up slightly to 48 percent in 2001, including 33 percent of 13-year-olds (of course, many other teenagers were buying a ticket for a PG-13 film and then going inside to see the R film on another screen in the standard megaplex theaters). With respect to video games, while the sale of M-rated games to 13–16 year-olds dropped from 85 percent to 78 percent, 66 percent of 13-year-olds were able to buy them. And in the music industry, the numbers went up from 85 percent to 90 percent of young teenagers purchasing explicit-content recordings, including 87 percent of 13 year-old children who wanted to listen to them.

Around the same time, the California Court of Appeals addressed yet another tort suit about a movie, this one filed against the theater that had shown the movie by the parents of a child who had been killed as a result. The film in question, *Dead Presidents*, was an urban crime drama set in the Bronx, with an R rating because of its "extremely graphic depiction of violence and bodily injury." A theater in Los Angeles allowed a number of 13 year-old children to come in and watch it. One of them, Raymond Aiolentunu, became very "agitated" by what he was seeing on the screen and said to his friends, "I am going to leave and shoot somebody." In fact, immediately after *Dead Presidents* was over, Aiolentunu walked a couple of blocks, pulled out his gun, and killed Marcos Delgado, Jr.

The parents' tort suit against the theater owner for letting in these children was summarily dismissed in *Delgado v. American Multi-Cinema*, 72 Cal.App.4th 1403, 85 Cal. Rptr.2d 838, 840 (1999). The appeals court said that "the movie industry's film rating system is designed to allow parents to exercise control over what their children see," and "basic to the [ratings] program was and is responsibility of the parents to make the decision." Thus, as the *Delgado* court put it,

> . . . [M]easured by its goal of protecting children from objectionable films, the movie-rating system's duty flows to parents; it was not designed or intended to protect society at large . . . Therefore [American Multi Cinema] breached no duty to [the Delgado's] . . . who are not [the viewing child's] parents . . . by letting [Aiolentunu] view a movie he should not have seen without an adult.

85 Cal. Rptr. at 841. Do you agree with that position as a matter of state tort law (e.g., as applied to other product warning systems)? And do you believe that it would be desirable and/or constitutional for a state to enact a law that made it illegal and punishable for a movie theater to sell tickets for R-rated movies to those under 17 (without their parents), or to sell AO (adults only) video games to anyone under 21? *See Soundgarden v. Eikenberry*, 123 Wash.2d 750, 871 P.2d 1050 (1994).

Events such as these have generated even more intense political debates about the entertainment industry in the last decade. Some action has also been taken by the industry. For example, as part of the MPAA effort to require its studio members to "set a goal of not *inappropriately* specifically targeting children for R-rated movies" (which can include a *Schindler's List*), newspaper and billboard ads (but not Internet or television ads) must include not just letter ratings but also the explanation provided by the Ratings. In addition, the National Association of Theater Owners (NATO) is seeking to enforce the MPAA rating system by requiring all teenagers to show photo IDs with their age on it before being sold tickets for R-rated movies like *Natural Born Killers.* NATO did add, though, that if there were to be guards controlling entrance into the room showing R-rated films in a megaplex, the cost of this must be paid for by the MPAA studios members.

---

All of the cases and episodes we have read in this chapter display the institutional dimensions (and dilemmas) of entertainment and the law. What is the appropriate vehicle for delivering the final verdict on this hotly-contested issues? As was advocated by 2 Live Crew, for example, should the judgment about whether to listen to *As Nasty As They Wanna Be*, rather than to the *Clean* version, be left to individual choice in the marketplace of ideas? Or should the judgment about whether certain messages about sex and violence are to come into the neighborhood (not just the home) ultimately be made by community choice through the democratic process? Is there something about the entertainment market that seems to require collective action in favor of a more attractive social and cultural environment? Or is there something about the political market that renders it unsympathetic to contemporary renditions of the iconoclastic message of *The Miracle*, the movie with which this chapter began? These are questions needing extensive discussion not only in the courts and the Congress, but also in the classroom.

# CHAPTER 2

# ENTERTAINING THE PUBLIC WITH INDIVIDUAL LIVES

■ ■ ■

In Chapter 1, we saw that judicial construction of the First Amendment has left the media largely immune from legal intervention aimed at the public interest in reducing antisocial behavior. In this and the next chapter, we shall see that the private interest in being treated fairly by the media—even better, in being left alone—has found a slightly more responsive judicial ear.

Elizabeth Taylor provided one illustration. In 1982, ABC announced that it was planning a miniseries about Taylor's life. Taylor responded with a lawsuit in New York, saying that any such film would have to be "completely fictionalized unless there was somebody under the carpet or under the bed during my [then] 50 years." ABC soon dropped the project for "creative reasons." In 1994, NBC announced that it was planning a Taylor program, based on a controversial biography by David Heymann, *Liz: An Intimate Biography*. Taylor again went to court, this time in California, to try to block the showing. The judge refused to issue an injunction, saying that this would amount to unconstitutional "prior restraint" of speech; however, Taylor was left free to pursue her suit for damages if NBC went ahead with this venture. While NBC did show its four-hour production of *Liz*, a detailed comparison of the book and the film by the New York Times concluded that the television portrayal had considerably watered down the book's assertions about Taylor's personal and professional life.

The reason for that muted portrayal is that the prospect of litigation requires the producer of a docudrama about Elizabeth Taylor or anyone else to undertake a painstaking analysis of the film project from initial treatment, to script, to rough cut, to final product. Every scene must be annotated with detailed references to all the substantiating material found in publications, trial transcripts, or interviews. Those story lines that are both provocative and shakily-documented may well be cut from the script.

These "program standards" are necessary in order to secure the "errors and omissions" insurance that television networks require before showing a movie. Both the documentation costs and liability premiums can, of course, be sharply reduced if the producer is able to secure waivers and releases from the key subjects of the story. Such authorization and cooperation by the subjects may contribute to the original production and marketing of the docudrama. For example, James and Jennifer Stolpa received $650,000 for recounting the details of their story of how they survived being trapped for eight days in a Nevada mountain snowfall with their six-month-old baby. The shadow the law casts over docudramas is another important reason why the costs of these legal rights and releases has been soaring even for very public events. Hence, the figure-skating rivals Tonya Harding and Nancy Kerrigan each received a half million dollars for their consent to made-for-television movies about their lives.

In this chapter and the next, we shall explore the kinds of legal claims that either an Elizabeth Taylor or a Jessica McClure might bring challenging their portrayal in a film, as well as the crucial limitations that have been placed on an individual's right to be left alone in order to serve the public's right to know what happened. Although the First Amendment serves as a constraint, the affirmative source of individual protection is state law, largely judge-made. At present, the bulk of such legal claims rest on the rights of privacy and publicity. The law of defamation, however, was the original source of common law regulation of what the media can say about the individual, and thus of constitutional restrictions on the types of such suits that individuals can pursue against the media for things that have been said. We shall begin, then, with an overview of defamation law in the entertainment world.

## A. DEFAMATION

The tort of defamation was developed in Britain centuries ago as a regime for settling disputes where comments by one person had insulted another's honor and integrity. Rather than leaving them to resort to duels on the streets, the courtroom gave the injured parties a peaceful forum for clearing the subject's name and securing redress for the damage inflicted on the person's reputation.

The key components of a defamation claim were that (i) a statement had been made of and concerning the plaintiff; (ii) the statement had been published to at least one other party; (iii) the statement was false (presumed at common law); and (iv) the statement harmed the subject's reputation by lowering his or her standing in at least some part of the community. If these conditions were established, then liability would generally follow, irrespective of whether the author actually knew, or should reasonably have known, that the statement about the subject was untrue. And with respect at least to assertions published to the broader community, general tort damages could be awarded on such a strict liability footing even though the subject had suffered no tangible physical or economic harm.

That brand of defamation law posed considerable risk to the media. Given a popular subject and an unpopular publisher, a jury might well award very sizable damages for provocative observations. Recognizing the possibly chilling effects of such liability on freedom of expression in the community, state courts had fashioned a number of special privileges or fair comment defenses to suits about mistaken statements that were made in good faith. In quite a number of situations, though, the safest path for the media was to publish only innocuous assertions about people who looked like they were willing and able to sue in court. Finally, as we saw in Chapter 1, in 1964 the Supreme Court moved to constitutionalize key features of the tort of defamation, in a ruling that has had major implications for all of First Amendment jurisprudence.

## 1. THE CONSTITUTIONALIZATION OF DEFAMATION LAW[a]

In 1960, the New York Times published a fund-raising advertisement by civil rights groups. The advertisement described non-violent demonstrations by civil rights advocates in Montgomery, Alabama, and the "wave of terror" undertaken by local officials to thwart those efforts. L.B. Sullivan was one of three elected commissioners of the City of Montgomery, and the one in charge of the police department. Though he had not been named in the advertisement, Sullivan filed suit against the Times, alleging that it had wrongfully implied that he was guilty of misconduct. Four similar suits were filed by other government officials. The evidence demonstrated that some of the statements in the advertisement regarding the incidents in question were incorrect. The trial jury awarded Sullivan $500,000 damages, the full amount demanded, and the Alabama Supreme Court affirmed that verdict.

In a unanimous opinion, *New York Times v. Sullivan*, 376 U.S. 254 (1964), the Court reversed and curtailed the reach of state defamation law by announcing two sweeping changes in constitutional doctrine. First, the Court held that in defamation actions brought by public officials, the plaintiff must prove that the statement was made with " 'actual malice'—that is, with knowledge that it was false or reckless disregard of whether it was false or not." *Id.* at 279–80. The Court reasoned that any other rule would deter "would-be-critics" of official conduct from voicing their criticisms, even those believed to be true, because of their inability to prove the factual basis or because of the expense involved in doing so. Second, the Court held that in defamation cases, appellate courts must

[a] For a fascinating account of *Sullivan* and its aftermath, see Anthony Lewis, *Make No Law: The Sullivan Case and its Aftermath* (Random House 1991).

examine the entire record to insure that a trial judgment does not impinge upon First Amendment freedoms.

In *Curtis Publishing Co. v. Butts*, 388 U.S. 130 (1967), the Court applied the *New York Times* standard to public figures. The *Saturday Evening Post* had published an article alleging that Wally Butts, athletic director for the University of Georgia, had conspired to "fix" a college football game. The accusation was based on a revelation by a Georgia insurance salesman that he accidentally overheard a conversation in which Butts revealed his key strategies to a coach on an opposing team. Butts sued the *Post* for libel and won a trial verdict (for $460,000) before *New York Times* was decided. A narrow majority of the Supreme Court reversed, holding that the actual malice standard for public *officials* should also apply to public *figures* like Butts (Justice Harlan and three of his colleagues preferred the gross negligence standard). Even so, Chief Justice Warren concurred in Justice Harlan's judgment that on the facts of this case, the Post's new editorial policy of "sophisticated muckraking" and its shoddy research into this story about Butts (admittedly a public figure) satisfied the actual malice standard.

Determining what constitutes "actual malice" is thus critical to defamation analysis. The pivotal inquiry is whether at the time the defamatory comment is made, the defendant either knows that the statement is false or acts with reckless disregard as to the statement's truth. *See Bose Corp. v. Consumers Union of U.S., Inc.*, 466 U.S. 485, 498–513 (1984). With respect to assertions made by the media itself, where deliberate falsehoods are rarely published, the legal focus is on whether the author entertained significant doubt about the truth of the assertion but went ahead with it anyway, without undertaking a real investigation of the facts (as happened in *Butts*).

The Court has not, however, pursued the same approach with respect to private figures. In fact, in *Gertz v. Robert Welch, Inc.*, 418 U.S. 323 (1974), a divided Court ruled that where the plaintiff is neither a public official nor a public figure, the Constitution does not require application of the "actual malice" standard. In 1968, Chicago policeman Richard Nuccio shot and killed a young boy. Nuccio was convicted of murder, and the boy's family retained Elmer Gertz, a lawyer, to bring a civil suit against Nuccio. *American Opinion*, a publication of the John Birch Society, published an article alleging that Nuccio was framed as part of a Communist conspiracy against the police. Although Gertz played no role in the criminal proceeding against Nuccio, the article alleged that Gertz was the "architect" of the Nuccio "frame-up." Gertz sued *American Opinion* for libel. The jury awarded Gertz $50,000. Even though Gertz was not a public figure, the judge entered judgment notwithstanding the verdict for *American Opinion*, on the grounds that the *New York Times* standard applies to discussion of any public issue without regard to the status of the person defamed therein. The Seventh Circuit affirmed.

On appeal, the Supreme Court reversed. The Court noted that private individuals are much less able than public figures to rebut libelous assertions about them. What is more, unlike most public figures, private figures do not voluntarily expose themselves to the risk of damaged reputation. The Court did, however, see the need to strike a balance between the state's legitimate interest in compensating private individuals for reputational injury and shielding the media from unavoidable defamation liability. The Court thus held that states should be free to establish a negligence standard of liability for defamation of private figures, but that their courts could not award presumed or punitive damages in these cases absent proof of actual malice.

One further Supreme Court decision on this topic involved a reporter quoting the subject of an interview as having said something that had not been said in those words. In *Masson v. The New Yorker Magazine*, 501 U.S. 496 (1991), Janet Malcolm, a regular contract writer for The New Yorker, conducted extensive interviews with Dr. Jeffrey Masson, a psychoanalyst and recently-fired Project Director for the Sigmund Freud Archives outside London. In her two-part article and subsequent book on Freud and the Archives, Malcolm quoted Masson extensively.

In initial complaints to the magazine's fact-checking department, Masson claimed that he had not in fact said many of the things attributed to him. For example, Masson was quoted as saying to his Archives superiors, "I was like an intellectual gigolo—you take your pleasure from him, but you don't take him out in public." From a tape recording of the interview, it is clear that Masson actually said ". . . I was, in a sense, much too junior within the hierarchy of analysis for these important training analysts to be caught dead with." The crux of Masson's defamation action was that the discrepancies between what he did say and what he was quoted as saying amounted to defamation.

In their summary judgment motions, Malcolm and *The New Yorker* defended on the grounds that Malcolm had done extensive interviews with Masson over and above what had been tape-recorded, and the quotations attributed to Masson were a fair and substantially accurate interpretation of the gist of what he had been saying. The Supreme Court rejected that position. A writer might claim lack of "actual malice" even in an article that inaccurately reconstructed the essence of what the interviewee may have said. By contrast, knowingly placing quotation marks around a supposed interviewee statement that materially altered the meaning of what in fact had been said would be defamatory if that alteration damaged the person's reputation. In other words, Malcolm could legally say that Masson was an "intellectual gigolo," but she could not say that that Masson used that term to describe himself.

## 2. DEFAMATION IN ENTERTAINMENT

The vast bulk of defamation cases, including those we have seen the Supreme Court grappling with, involve the *news* media rather than the *entertainment* world. Quite a number of entertainers have been involved in defamation suits about things said *off* their shows—for example, as plaintiff, *Newton (Wayne) v. NBC*, 930 F.2d 662 (9th Cir. 1990), and as defendant, *Edwards v. Arsenio Hall*, 234 Cal.App.3d 886, 285 Cal. Rptr. 810 (2d Dist.1991). Newton initially won a jury verdict of around $20 million that was the largest in history at that time (though later overturned on appeal of the "actual malice" point). And in 2001, Tom Cruise launched a $100 million suit against Kyle Bradford for being quoted in the French magazine *Actustar* as saying the reason why Cruise was being divorced by Nicole Kidman was that he had been having a real (not a fictional) affair with the "erotic wrestler" Bradford.

Indeed, *Newton* is a case study of what more systematic surveys disclose about defamation litigation generally. Defendants win approximately three quarters of defamation suits by way of summary dismissal (usually on the "actual malice" issue); of cases that go to trial, plaintiffs win more than three quarters of the jury verdicts with median awards over a million dollars; but nearly three quarters of the time, the defendant on appeal gets the verdict at least partially reversed. The combination of low plaintiff odds of winning high damage verdicts, at substantial legal expense to both sides, has left numerous scholars dubious about whether *New York Times* was the best constitutional accommodation of the values of free speech and personal reputation.[b] Does the "actual malice" test do justice to the victim of an untruthful and damaging comment that has been widely circulated by the media? Does the likelihood of eventually winning a suit at some stage in the proceedings, based on this constitutional standard, eliminate the chilling effect of such litigation on fearless reporting? Should the Supreme Court rethink its opinion in *Miami Herald Publishing Co. v. Tornillo*, 418 U.S. 241 (1974), and find it compatible with the First Amendment for states to require the media to offer a reasonable right of reply to the subjects of

[b] For just a sampling of the range of scholarly views, see Paul C. Weiler, *Defamation, Enterprise Liability, & Freedom of Speech*, 17 U. Tor. L.J. 278 (1967); Harry Kalven, *The Reasonable Man & the First Amendment*; Hill, Butts, *and* Walker, 1967 Sup. Ct. Rev. 267; Rodney A. Smolla, *Let the Author Beware: The Rejuvenation of the American Law of Libel*, 132 U. Penn. L. Rev. 1 (1983); Richard Epstein, *Was* New York Times v. Sullivan *Wrong?*, 53 U. Chi. L. Rev. 782 (1986); Stanley Ingber, *Rethinking Intangible Injuries: A Focus On Remedy*, 73 Cal. L. Rev. 772 (1985); Robert C. Post, *The Social Foundations of Defamation Law: Reputation & the Constitution*, 74 Cal. L. Rev. 691 (1986); Russell L. Weaver & Geoffrey Bennett, *Is the New York Times "Actual Malice" Standard Really Necessary? A Comparative Perspective*, 53 La. L. Rev. 1153 (1993).

critical personal stories, perhaps as part of legislation that puts a cap on the size of damage awards in defamation actions?

---

Returning to the world of entertainment more narrowly-defined—speech for fun and profit—one recurring source of defamation suits is actually the converse of the *Masson* case. Rather than attribute direct quotations to a real and identifiable person, the author or producer of a book or movie explicitly labeled as fiction arguably creates the impression (at least among some of its readers) that the book is "of and concerning" a real person. Here, the "actual malice" test is of little help, because the author has deliberately fictionalized the person in question. The question is whether the person has been defamed. *See* Richard C. Giller, *Defamation in Fiction: The Need for a Clear "Of and Concerning" Standard*, 3 Ent. & Sports L.J. 253 (1986).

A significant early treatment of this issue came in *Wheeler v. Dell Publishing*, 300 F.2d 372 (7th Cir. 1962), about the best-selling book and hit movie *Anatomy of a Murder*. The book and movie story was based on a real-life, small-town murder trial of a man charged with killing another man for raping his wife. In the fictional story, as in real life, the defendant's attorney (played by James Stewart) got his client acquitted by reason of insanity. To add human drama to the actual events, though, the author had embellished a number of the characters and their personal lives. The plaintiff, Hazel Wheeler, the widow of the dead man, was presented as an unsavory "harridan," with dyed red hair, a livid facial scar, and extremely foul language. Though her friends and neighbors knew that Wheeler was the widow, they also knew that she did not actually look and sound like the widow portrayed in the book and on the screen. Even so, the court held that Wheeler could not sue for defamation.

Is such a ruling sound? What is the rationale for holding that embellishing a real person with a host of unpleasant fictional features means that there is (or is not) actionable harm to their reputation? In thinking about these legal policy issues, we have what has become a rather significant variation on the docudrama theme.

Ray Davis had been the Commander of the United States Military Group and Chief of the United States Mission to Chile in the early 1970s. He was in that position in 1973 when the Chilean military led by General Pinochet staged a coup to remove Allende from power. Charles Horman, a young American residing in Chile, then disappeared, and his parents went to Chile to look for him. Eventually they discovered that Charles had been executed by Chilean soldiers.

Thomas Hauser wrote a book, *The Execution of Charles Horman*, which developed the thesis of Ed Horman, Charles' father, suggesting that the U.S. military in Chile had known and approved of the killing of his son by Pinochet's troops. Four years later, Costa-Gavras made a well-received movie, *Missing*, starring Jack Lemmon in the role of Ed Horman and Sally Field as his wife. *Missing* was a fictionalized version of the book, *Execution*, with the U.S. military head named Ray Tower. Davis, who had not sued the book's author or publisher, sued the movie director and studio for defamation. The legal issue posed by the case was whether there was any evidence of "actual malice" that would satisfy the *New York Times* standard.

## DAVIS V. COSTA-GAVRAS

United States District Court, Southern District of New York, 1987.
654 F. Supp. 653.

POLLACK, SENIOR DISTRICT JUDGE.

* * *

Designated Evidence Offered by Plaintiff

Plaintiff alleges that there are four general categories of purported evidence in the paper defense to the motion from which to find actual malice on behalf of defendants: (1) that defendants' "entire purpose in making *Missing* was to show plaintiff as responsible for Charles Horman's death"; (2) that defendants' reliance on Thomas Hauser's book, *The Execution of Charles Horman* (*Execution*), was unreasonable; (3) that defendants never consulted with plaintiff on the facts presented in the film; and (4) that *Missing* contains scenes portraying certain episodes which defendants knew were embroidered.

An analysis of the record shows that to accept the plaintiff's opposition to summary judgment would require a distortion of the proofs, deviation from applicable law, and wrenching of the film out of its plain context.

A. *The Thesis of the Film*

Plaintiff has produced no evidence in his papers to substantiate his assertion that the purpose of *Missing* was to make a non-fictional film establishing that Ray Davis, the plaintiff, was responsible for Charles Horman's death. To the contrary, the papers unalterably establish that the film is not a non-fictional documentary or aimed at Ray Davis as an individual, and that it cannot be understood as other than a dramatization of a true story. The film includes fictional characters and a composite portrayal of the American military presence in Chile at the time of the uprising and Allende coup.

The theme of the film is the search for a missing man by his father and his wife. The man who disappeared is finally found to have been executed by the Chilean military. The film is based upon a true story. It is only in that setting that the composite conduct of the American governmental representatives in Chile at the time and the degree of their assistance in that search comes under scrutiny and criticism. There is no person named Ray Davis referred to in the film at any time. Ray Tower, with whom the plaintiff associates himself, is a symbolic fictional composite of the entire American political and military entourage in Chile.

The film derives from and is solidly documented and supported by the stories relied on by the filmmakers, taken from the acts and statements of the concerned father and the anguished wife set forth in detail in Thomas Hauser's book, *Execution*. Those sources are shown to have been heavily investigated and confirmed by the filmmakers, who entertained no serious doubts of their truth or knowledge to the contrary of what they portrayed.

* * *

### *B. Defendants' Reliance on Hauser's Book*

*Missing* is a dramatic portrayal of events and interpretations detailed in Thomas Hauser's book, *Execution*. The substance of the movie's scenes is extracted directly from *Execution*. To meet those facts, plaintiff purports to suggest that defendants' reliance on Hauser's book was unreasonable and that Hauser's credentials would have disclosed him to be "suspect" had a good faith search by defendants been made.

* * *

There is nothing in the record tending to show that the filmmakers questioned Hauser's credentials or his book in any respect at the time *Missing* was made. The record is to the contrary. The filmmakers met with Hauser, went over his investigation and sources, supplied him with drafts of the script under preparation and were satisfied that there was no reason to doubt his work. No evidence whatever challenges those facts. Certainly the filmmakers obtained no knowledge contradicting the veracity or accuracy of Hauser's book and the stories of the Hormans as told to them and reflected in the book. There is no suggestion to the contrary from any provable sources. Indeed, nothing in plaintiff's papers demonstrates that either Hauser's credentials or his book, which was nominated for a Pulitzer Prize, are in fact "suspect" in any way.

The filmmakers knew that Hauser was a lawyer who had served as a judicial clerk in the Chambers of a Federal Judge and then worked for a prestigious Wall Street law firm. They knew that Hauser interviewed Captain Ray Davis, as well as other United States officials in Chile and numerous other persons when preparing *Execution*. The filmmakers also knew that no legal action whatsoever was taken against the book in the approximately four years since its publication. In an August 1980 meeting where Costa-Gavras, the film's director, and Stewart, the co-scriptwriter, met with Hauser to verify the accuracy of his book, Hauser described his meticulous research methods and broad inquiries. There is no evidence to the contrary.

The filmmakers then met with Charles Horman's parents, his wife, and one Terry Simon, a close friend who was in Chile with Charles around the time of his disappearance. Each of these individuals made clear to Costa-Gavras and Stewart that Hauser's book accurately and reliably depicted events as they knew and believed them. There is no evidence that any of defendants' further research and review of documents regarding Horman and events in Chile during the coup caused them to doubt the veracity of Hauser's book.

* * *

*C. Failure to Consult Plaintiff Prior to Making Film*

Plaintiff argues that defendant's failure to consult plaintiff personally prior to presentation of the film is evidence of actual malice.

However, plaintiff cannot prove actual malice merely by asserting that a publisher failed to contact the subject of his work. The actual malice standard cannot be satisfied by evidence of a failure to check with third parties prior to publication without proof that a publisher knew his publication was false, entertained serious doubts as to its truth, or had obvious reasons to doubt the veracity or accuracy of the source of published information.

While "verification of facts" of a story with its subjects and with others is a desirable and responsible practice and "an important reporting standard, a reporter, without a 'high degree of awareness of their probable falsity,' may rely on statements made by a single source even though they reflect only one side of the story without fear of libel prosecution. . . ." *New York Times v. Connor*, 365 F.2d 567, 576 (5th Cir. 1966). Plaintiff has not designated specific facts suggesting an awareness or even suspicion by defendants of probable falsity of their source material.

*D. Scenes in Missing as Evidence of Actual Malice*

Plaintiff enumerates nine scenes in *Missing* which the filmmakers allegedly created, or in which they distorted the context, or made baseless suggestions. None of these scenes provides or contributes to the requisite evidence of actual malice.

It should be made clear that *Missing* is not a documentary, but a dramatization of the Horman disappearance and search. The film does not purport to depict a chronology of the events precisely as they actually occurred; it opens with the prologue: "This film is based on a true story. The incidents and facts are documented. Some of the names have been changed to protect the innocent and also to protect the film." No one challenged the accuracy and veracity of Hauser's book to the knowledge of defendants. Defendants concede that although the substance of the film's scenes is extracted almost directly from Thomas Hauser's book, not everything in their film is literally faithful to the actual historical record as if in a documentary. That is not to say that which was not historical was set out in bad faith, portrayed with actual malice, or established or increased the defamatory impact.

The film is not a documentary. A documentary is a non-fictional story or series of historical events portrayed in their actual location; a film of real people and real events as they occur. A documentary maintains strict fidelity to fact.

*Missing*, on the other hand, is an art form sometimes described as "Docu-Drama." The line separating a documentary from a docudrama is not always sharply defined, but is nonetheless discernible. Both forms are necessarily selective, given the time constraints of movies and the attention span of the viewing audience. The docudrama is a dramatization of an historical event or lives of real people, using actors or actresses. Docudramas utilize simulated dialogue, composite characters, and a telescoping of events occurring over a period into a composite scene or scenes. This treatment is singularly appropriate and unexceptionable if the context is not distorted when dealing with public and political figures.

Self-evidently a docudrama partakes of author's license—it is a creative interpretation of reality—and if alterations of fact in scenes portrayed are not made with serious doubts of truth of the essence of the telescoped composite, such scenes do not ground a charge of actual malice.

Each scene questioned by the plaintiff is a telescoped composite of events, personalities, and of the American representatives in Chile who are involved therein. Each uses permissible literary license to fit historical detail into a suitable dramatic context. Such dramatic embellishments as are made do not distort the fundamental story being told—the frantic search by his family for a missing man who has suddenly disappeared, their emotions, anxieties, impatience, frustration, and doubts of assistance from American officialdom. The scenes are thus a hybrid of fact and fiction which however do not materially distort the analysis. Always to be remembered is that they fairly represent the source materials for the film believed to be true by the filmmakers. Leeway is properly afforded to an author who thus attempts to recount a true event.

As a matter of law, the dramatic overlay supplied by the film does not serve to increase the impact of what plaintiff charges as defamatory since it fairly and reasonably portrays the unassailable beliefs of the Hormans, the record thereof in the Hauser book, and the corroborative results of the authors' inquiries. In docudrama, minor fictionalization cannot be considered evidence or support for the requirement of actual malice.

The nine scenes selected by plaintiff as support for the requirement of actual malice do no such thing. Each is related solely and unquestionably to the theme of this film. The movie's Ray Tower character is a fictional composite of the American presence operating in Chile at the time. He is a symbolic figure. The artistic input in the scenes questioned is found in permissible syntheses and composite treatment in the film. Although in actuality particular individuals were not physically present when certain dialogue occurred, in the movie scene the composite character portrayed was.

The content of the film reflects what happened according to the book, the persons who complained, and the sources relied on by defendants. While the actual persons involved in the events portrayed do not appear in on-scene interviews to describe their experiences, actions, and motivations, the real names of some individuals are employed. But the name Ray Davis is never mentioned. Real life personalities are accordingly represented by telescoped composites in many instances.

The cases on point demonstrate that the First Amendment protects such dramatizations and does not demand literal truth in every episode depicted; publishing a dramatization is not of itself evidence of actual malice.

* * *

Conclusion

The issue on the motion is not the truth of whether Davis (qua Ray Tower) ordered or approved a Chilean order to kill Charles Horman because he "knew too much" about alleged American involvement in the Chilean coup; the issue is whether the filmmakers intentionally portrayed such a defamatory suggestion, knowing that it was false or with serious doubts of its truth. There is no doubt that Ed Horman, the father of the missing man, asserted such a theory and that assertion is documented in Hauser's book. Plaintiff has not presented evidence that defendants knew the theory of the father was false, or entertained serious doubts as to its truth. There is no evidence that defendants acted with actual malice or disbelieved what the Hormans thought and said or what Hauser wrote.

* * *

Complaint dismissed.

### *QUESTIONS FOR DISCUSSION*

1. What were the key features of the movie that led to this ruling? Was it the court's judgment that the movie, *Missing*, could not actually have "defamed" plaintiff Davis' reputation, or that the movie director, Costa-Gavras, could not actually have been "malicious" in his characterization of Davis? What was—what should be—the significance of a film maker's reliance on a book's portrayal of events rather than on direct conversations with the protagonists, especially of those depicted in an unfavorable light?

2. Palmyra is an uninhabited island in the Pacific Ocean. During the summer of 1974, Stephanie Stearns and Rick Walker sailed to Palmyra. When they arrived on the island, the two discovered that their boat was no longer seaworthy. Shortly thereafter another couple, the Grahams, arrived on Palmyra. By the end of October, Stearns and Walker had managed to get to Hawaii in the Grahams' boat, but the Grahams had disappeared. Seven years later, the bones of the Grahams were found washed up on Palmyra Island. The authorities in Hawaii indicted both Stearns and Walker for murder. Walker was tried first, defended by Earle Partington, and convicted. Stearns was tried next, defended by Vincent Bugliosi, and acquitted.

Bugliosi had become a famous legal personality both for prosecuting Charles Manson, and then for writing a best-seller, *Helter Skelter*, about the crime and conviction. Not surprisingly, Bugliosi wrote a book about the Palmyra case, titled *And The Sea Will Tell*, which Random House published and CBS then turned into a television miniseries. Partington was greatly offended by the way he was portrayed in the book and the television program—as a lawyer who, unlike Bugliosi, had not understood the best trial strategy for getting his client off. Thence came another legal byproduct of the Palmyra case, *Partington v. Bugliosi*, 56 F.3d 1147 (9th Cir. 1995), in which the Ninth Circuit addressed an important question in the law of both defamation and false light invasion of privacy.

At this stage of the case, the court assumed that Partington was not a "public figure" for even a limited purpose. The legal issue was whether Bugliosi's judgment calls about Partington's trial performance could be made actionable. In another important First Amendment case, *Milkovich v. Lorain Journal*, 497 U.S. 1 (1990), the Supreme Court had rejected the view that any statement labeled an "opinion" was automatically protected by the First Amendment; in a particular context such an opinion statement could readily convey an implied and false factual assertion to the reader or listener. Here, however, Bugliosi had described in detail what had happened in the two trials. Thus, when he made his unfavorable assertions about Partington's trial strategy, Bugliosi was simply giving his "personal viewpoint" about this issue, not purporting to assert "objective facts."

> When, as here, an author writing about a controversial occurrence fairly describes the general events involved and offers his personal perspective about some of the ambiguities and disputed facts, his statements should generally be protected by the First

> Amendment. Otherwise, there would be no room for expressions of opinion by commentators, experts in a field, figures closely involved in a public controversy, or others whose perspectives might be of interest to the public.

56 F.3d at 1154. While the inherent differences between Bugliosi's book and CBS' television show made the latter a more difficult case, the court was satisfied that the same conclusion was appropriate:

> Although the made-for-television movie represents a distinct type of forum [from a book], we conclude that the general tenor of the docudrama also tends to negate the impression that the statements involved represented a false assertion of objective fact . . . Docudramas, as their names suggest, often rely heavily upon dramatic interpretations of events and dialogue filled with rhetorical flourishes in order to capture and maintain the interest of their audience. We believe that viewers in this case would be sufficiently familiar with this genre to avoid assuming that all statements within them represent assertions of verifiable facts. To the contrary, most of them are aware by now that parts of such programs are more fiction than fact.

56 F.3d at 1154–55. Indeed, just as the D.C. Circuit had decided in *Moldea v. New York Times*, 22 F.3d 310 (D.C.Cir. 1994) (involving a defamation suit by an author against his book reviewer), the court here felt that "assessments of trial lawyers' performance" are "inherently subjective and therefore not susceptible to being proved true or false." Do you agree with these judicial sentiments—including the last one (and what would Bugliosi say about that, as either a lawyer or an author)?

3. Lisa Springer attended Columbia University from 1974 to 1978. During that same period, a man named Tine began working on a novel, *State of Grace*, about Vatican finances and politics, with some editorial assistance from Springer. Tine himself testified that he had "loosely patterned" the hero-heroine relationship in the book on his relationship with Springer. Following a rancorous breakup of the two, the book was completed and published. One chapter, ten pages long, explicitly describes the sexual relations of one of the villains, an Italian industrialist, and his mistress, Lisa Blake, formerly a psychology student living on Springer's Manhattan Street, now a well-kept "whore" living on Fifth Avenue. Springer, by then a college tutor, sued for defamation, relying on letters from former Columbia lecturers and students who saw a connection between her and Blake, whose physical description resembled Springer. Should these facts justify a defamation verdict? Whose perspective on the comparison should govern—Springer's, Tine's, acquaintances of the two, or the general reader's? *See Springer v. Viking Press*, 60 N.Y.2d 916, 470 N.Y.S.2d 579, 458 N.E.2d 1256 (1983).

4. Andrew Fetler's first novel was called *The Travelers*. The chief character in the novel, Maxim, apparently has a closer relationship with a Nazi organization than he does with his father. Fetler's brother, Daniel, a

teacher, alleges that Maxim is actually based on him. The following similarities between the novel and Fetler's life were asserted:

> The novel depicts events in the life of the Solovyov family, composed of a father, mother, and thirteen children of whom ten are boys and the third, fourth and eighth are girls. This is the exact composition of the Fetler family. In the novel, Maxim is the eldest child and is twenty-three years old in 1938; in life, the same is true of Daniel. In the novel, Maxim is a Latvian by birth; in fact, Daniel, although born in Leningrad, was a Latvian citizen at the time the events in the novel occurred. In the novel, the father is an itinerant Russian Protestant minister whose wife and children perform as a band and choir where the father preaches. Maxim is generally responsible for their temporal needs and to that end dominates them. The family travels about Europe in an old bus. In fact, Daniel's father was a Russian Protestant (Baptist) minister; the rest of his family gave concerts as a family band and choir. Daniel looked after them, and they journeyed through Europe during the 1930s in an old bus. Both families bought homes in Stockholm.

Does this state a viable defamation claim? *See Fetler v. Houghton Mifflin*, 364 F.2d 650, 651 (2d Cir. 1966).

5. Dr. Paul Bindrim is a licensed psychologist who uses a group therapy technique called "Touching," which seeks to remove patients' inhibitions by having them remove all their clothes. Gwen Mitchell, author of an earlier best-selling novel, was allowed to attend a session only after giving oral and written assurances that her presence was solely for therapeutic reasons, and that she would not write about the session. Two months later, Mitchell signed a contract with Doubleday, with a $150,000 advance, to write a novel called *Touching*. The novel was about a psychiatrist, Dr. Simon Herford, who seemed very different from Bindrim. Herford, however, also had nude encounter sessions with his patients, one of which resembled the session that Mitchell had attended with Bindrim. Herford was portrayed as using sexually explicit and profane language about a clergyman-patient and his wife—something Bindrim did not do. An issue that can be raised later in this chapter is whether Mitchell's conduct was an invasion of Bindrim's *privacy* rights. Here the question is whether Bindrim was *defamed* by the novel *Touching*. *See Bindrim v. Mitchell*, 92 Cal.App.3d 61, 155 Cal. Rptr. 29 (1979).

6. One of the top movies of 1997 was Sony Entertainment's *Donnie Brasco*, which was about an FBI undercover agent investigating the notorious Bonnano crime family. Brasco's efforts succeeded in producing the 1982 prosecutions and convictions of the Bonnanos, a 1987 best-selling book, and then the 1997 movie that starred Al Pacino and had Johnny Depp playing Brasco himself. The initial pre-release screening of *Donnie Brasco* portrayed John "Boobie" Cerasani as a murderer working for the Bonnanos, even though he was acquitted of that charge at the 1982 trial. After Cerasani

heard of that screening and threatened to sue, Sony executives renamed the Cerasani character as "Paulie," and removed his explicit depiction as a murderer, even though he was still shown playing a role in a killing. When Cerasani filed suit, his claim was dismissed in *Cerasani v. Sony*, 991 F. Supp. 343 (S.D.N.Y. 1998), because the plaintiff was deemed a "libel-proof" character. Because his reputation had been "badly tarnished" as a convicted racketeer, bank robber, drug dealer, and Mafia associate, and he had already received ample publicity as the actual killer at the trial and in the 1987 book, Cerasani could not file a suit now just because this implied claim was portrayed in a Hollywood movie.

7. In light of the above cases, consider a lawsuit involving *The Hurricane*, a 1999 movie made by an Oscar-winning Canadian director, Norman Jewison. The subject was the life of the notable black boxer, Hurricane Carter, played by Denzel Washington, who was convicted by an all-white jury of a murder he did not commit. This conviction put Carter in prison, ended his boxing career, and became a major civil rights cause in the 1970s. Despite a *New York Times* investigation and Bob Dylan's song "Hurricane," this effort failed. Carter was eventually freed in the 1980s. A white middleweight champion of the early 1960s, Joey Giardello, was depicted losing a fight in the opening 3-minute scene, but then winning the bout by a verdict rendered by white boxing judges. When Giardello went to see the movie, he was shocked at this presentation of the opening of Carter's civil rights cause. Giardello sued producer Universal Pictures, claiming the movie had defamed his reputation as a Hall of Fame boxer. Though the parties reached a confidential settlement, what was the likely impact of the current state of defamation law on the relative terms of the settlement?

8. Jonathan Harr's book, *A Civil Action*, generated litigation over statements in the book indicating that a tannery operator had lied, committed perjury, and run a business that produced toxins that killed numerous residents in the area. The First Circuit Court affirmed a grant of summary judgment dismissing the tannery operator's defamation action in *Riley v. Harr*, 292 F.3d 282 (1st Cir. 2002). The decision was based on the court's understanding of the limits placed by the First Amendment on defamation law, even when the allegedly defamed plaintiff is not a public figure, if the speech addresses a matter of public concern. The court stressed that when the author makes clear that the allegedly defamatory statements are only his interpretation of underlying facts from which readers can draw their own conclusions, the statements are normally protected by the First Amendment. The First Amendment also protects "rhetorical hyperbole" and "imaginative expression" to enliven prose. *Accord Horsley v. Rivera*, 292 F.3d 695 (11th Cir. 2002).

9. Defamation lawsuits continue to arise where films offer unflattering portrayals of individuals, even when not mentioning them by name. For instance, Wall Street stockbroker Andrew Greene recently sued the producers of Martin Scorcese's hit movie, *The Wolf of Wall Street*. Greene claims that he was the inspiration for the character of Nicky "Rugrat"

Koskoff, who is the butt of many jokes riffing off of his unfortunate hairpiece. Greene seeks $25 million in his lawsuit. In light of the prior material, what will he have to show to prevail?

10. Another example of a casual mention in a film leading to a defamation lawsuit was an offhand comment made by Jennifer Lawrence's character in the 2013 film *American Hustle*. Lawrence's character commented that "microwaves take the nutrition out of food." When her husband challenged her, she said, "I read it in an article. Look, by Paul Brodeur." Brodeur, who gave interviews during the late 1970's promoting the safety of food cooked by microwaves, has filed a $1 million defamation lawsuit against the producers of *American Hustle*. Interestingly, the producers have argued, among other things, that the comment was made by a "ditzy" person, and that audiences would recognize that the comment was not meant to be taken seriously. The trial judge denied the producers' motion to dismiss, saying that the "ditzy defense" was a jury question. What should the outcome in this case be?

---

Yet another Oscar-winning movie to produce a defamation suit was Michael Moore's documentary, *Bowling for Columbine*. Timothy McVeigh was executed for masterminding the Oklahoma City bombing, and Terry Nichols is now serving *two* life sentences for helping McVeigh carry out the bombing that killed 168 people. Nichols' brother James sued Moore, asking for $20 million in damages, because the movie portrayed him helping carrying out the bombing. Moore had recorded a lengthy interview with James Nichols and then included around ten minutes of it in the film. One apparent theme of the movie was that James had helped his brother and McVeigh by giving them use of his Michigan farm to practice effective bombing. Moore went on the Oprah Winfrey television show and made essentially the same point about James Nichols' role. And his website stated:

> I can guarantee to you, without equivocation, that every fact in my movie is true. Three teams of fact-checkers and two groups of lawyers went through it with a fine tooth comb to make sure that every statement of fact is indisputable fact. Trust me, no film company would ever release a film like this without putting it through the most vigorous vetting process possible.

After two years of litigation, the court, in *Nichols v. Moore*, 396 F. Supp.2d 783 (E.D.Mich.2005), granted summary dismissal of suit. There were two key legal reasons offered. The first was that Moore's allegation was a "substantially true statement" because he was essentially saying that the police believed James to be part of a conspiracy with his brother Terry and McVeigh. In any event, even if this was untrue, James was deemed to be "a public figure and he failed to meet that significant constitutional hurdle of actual malice." Not only was James Terry's brother and host on his farm, but the police had arrested him and he had then given dozens of interviews to the media. Thus, Nichols had made himself "a limited public figure because he had voluntarily injected himself into the public controversy surrounding the bombing." The Sixth Circuit affirmed. 477 F.3d 396 (6th Cir. 2007).

## B. INFLICTION OF EMOTIONAL DISTRESS[c]

A closely related legal remedy is the tort of "intentional infliction of emotional distress." The elements of the tort generally require that the defendant's conduct not only be intentional or reckless, but also extreme and outrageous, and the resulting emotional distress must be severe. Medical science has recognized that words can inflict anxiety, nervousness, and grief on others—a form of mental battery. The law has followed suit by providing a means by which victims of psychological injury can collect compensation.

Public figures have attempted to bring claims of intentional infliction of emotional distress as substitutes for defamation claims. The Supreme Court, however, largely foreclosed this avenue in *Hustler Magazine v. Falwell*, 485 U.S. 46 (1988). In its November 1983 issue, Larry Flynt's notorious Hustler Magazine featured a parody of minister and activist Jerry Falwell. The parody was modeled on a series of Campari Liqueur advertisements that featured celebrities discussing their "first times" drinking the liqueur. In the parody, Falwell's "first time" occurs during a sexual rendezvous with his mother in an outhouse. The parody included a Hustler disclaimer noting that it was fictitious.

Falwell filed suit. Although the jury refused to find the parody defamatory because it could not reasonably be understood as describing actual facts about Falwell, the jury did find in favor of Falwell's emotional distress claim. The Supreme Court reversed the verdict:

* * *

> The sort of robust political debate encouraged by the First Amendment is bound to produce speech that is critical of those who hold public office or those public figures who are "intimately involved in the resolution of important public questions or, by reason of their fame, shape events in areas of concern to society at large." Justice Frankfurter put it succinctly in *Baumgartner v.*

[c] *See* Daniel Givelber, *The Right to Minimum Social Decency & the Limits of Evenhandedness: Intentional Infliction of Emotional Distress by Outrageous Conduct*, 82 Columbia L. Rev. 42 (1982), Rodney A. Smolla, *Emotional Distress and the First Amendment*, 20 Arizona State L.J. 423 (1988); Paul A. LeBel, *Emotional Distress, The First Amendment, & "This Kind of Speech": A Heretical Perspective on* Hustler Magazine v. Falwell, 60 Colorado L. Rev. 315 (1989); Robert C. Post, *The Constitutional Concept of Public Discourse: Outrageous Opinion, Democratic Deliberation, and* Hustler Magazine v. Falwell, 103 Harvard L. Rev. 601 (1990).

*United States*, 322 U.S. 665, 673–674 (1944), when he said that "one of the prerogatives of American citizenship is the right to criticize public men and measure." Such criticism, inevitably, will not always be reasoned or moderate; public figures as well as public officials will be subject to "vehement, caustic, and sometimes unpleasantly sharp attacks. . . ."

Of course, this does not mean that any speech about a public figure is immune from sanction in the form of damages. Since *New York Times Co. v. Sullivan*, we have consistently ruled that a public figure may hold a speaker liable for the damage to reputation caused by publication of a defamatory falsehood, but only if the statement was made "with knowledge that it was false or with reckless disregard of whether it was false or not. . . ."

Respondent argues, however, that a different standard should apply in this case because here the State seeks to prevent not reputational damage, but the severe emotional distress suffered by the person who is the subject of an offensive publication . . . In respondent's view, and in the view of the Court of Appeals, so long as the utterance was intended to inflict emotional distress, was outrageous, and did in fact inflict serious emotional distress, it is of no constitutional import whether the statement was a fact or an opinion, or whether it was true or false. It is the intent to cause injury that is the gravamen of the tort, and the State's interest in preventing emotional harm simply outweighs whatever interest a speaker may have in speech of this type.

[I]n the world of debate about public affairs, many things done with motives that are less than admirable are protected by the First Amendment. In *Garrison v. Louisiana*, 379 U.S. 64 (1964), we held that even when a speaker or writer is motivated by hatred or ill-will his expression was protected by the First Amendment:

Debate on public issues will not be uninhibited if the speaker must run the risk that it will be proved in court that he spoke out of hatred; even if he did speak out of hatred, utterances honestly believed contribute to the free interchange of ideas and the ascertainment of truth.

*Id.* at 73. Thus while such a bad motive may be deemed controlling for purposes of tort liability in other areas of the law, we think the First Amendment prohibits such a result in the area of public debate about public figures.

> Were we to hold otherwise, there can be little doubt that political cartoonists and satirists would be subjected to damages awards without any showing that their work falsely defamed its subject. . . . The appeal of the political cartoon or caricature is often based on exploration of unfortunate physical traits or politically embarrassing events—an exploration often calculated to injure the feelings of the subject of the portrayal. The art of the cartoonist is often not reasoned or evenhanded, but slashing and one-sided.
>
> Despite their sometimes caustic nature, from the early cartoon portraying George Washington as an ass down to the present day, graphic depictions and satirical cartoons have played a prominent role in public and political debate. . . . From the viewpoint of history it is clear that our political discourse would have been considerably poorer without them.
>
> * * *
>
> We conclude that public figures and public officials may not recover for the tort of intentional infliction of emotional distress by reason of publications such as the one here at issue without showing in addition that the publication contains a false statement of fact which was made with "actual malice," i.e., with knowledge that the statement was false or with reckless disregard as to whether or not it was true. . . .

485 U.S. at 51–56.

This triumph by Hustler publisher Larry Flynt over Jerry Falwell later made another contribution to the entertainment world. One of the most notable movies of 1996 was *The People vs. Larry Flynt,* starring Woody Harrelson as Flynt, Courtney Love as his wife Althea, and Edward Norton as his lawyer. Movie critics praised the film's artistic qualities, and First Amendment fans once again lauded the Rehnquist Court for having protected Flynt's parody of Falwell. However, feminists such as Gloria Steinem were harshly critical of the way that the movie glossed over Hustler's typical depiction of women, for essentially the same reasons we read about in Chapter 1.

### *QUESTIONS FOR DISCUSSION*

1. The claim of intentional infliction of emotional distress does increase a *private* figure's ability to secure redress. As we have seen, jokes, parodies, and fictional accounts are not actionable defamation even if the plaintiff is a private figure, unless a reasonable person could read or view the expression as describing actual facts about the plaintiff. No similar requirement exists for emotional distress claims, and the Supreme Court's ruling in *Hustler* imposes the "actual malice" standard only on public figures.

With respect to public figures, is the implication of the Supreme Court's First Amendment formulation in *Falwell* that they can never sue for emotional distress if they cannot also recover for harm to their reputation? Keep these questions in mind when you read the materials later in this chapter on the scope of this constitutional concept of a "public figure."

2. Angie Geary, a model, has appeared in a television commercial for the Swedish-made Wasa Crispbread, which also featured the tag line "You Can Have It In America!" Al Goldstein, executive producer of a sexually explicit late-night cable program, *Midnight Blue*, used the ad's voice-over and several images of Geary blended together with pornographic sexual scenes. Can Geary sue for infliction of emotional distress? For defamation? For false light invasion of privacy (which we will see later in this chapter)? *See Geary v. Al Goldstein*, 831 F. Supp. 269 (S.D.N.Y. 1993).

3. Howard Stern's "shock radio" show, which was deemed indecent (see Chapter 1), has also made a contribution to the development of individual rights of privacy over the air. Deborah Roach (using the name Debbie Tay) had been a topless dancer and regular guest on Stern's show as the Space Lesbian. Sadly, though, Roach suddenly died from a drug overdose. Following her funeral, Roach's family gave her cremated remains to Roach's close friend Chaunce Hayden, saying those remains were to be "preserved and honored in an appropriate and private manner." Instead, though, Hayden took Roach's remains to Stern where (on both his radio and cable shows) the two fondled Roach's remains while discussing her past life and death. When the family launched a tort action against both Stern and Infinity Broadcasting, a divided appeals court decided they had a legally viable claim for a jury to decide whether Stern's conduct was "extreme and outrageous"—rather than just "vulgar and disrespectful"—behavior inflicting intense emotional distress on the Roach family. *See Roach v. Stern*, 252 A.D.2d 488, 675 N.Y.S.2d 133 (1998).

4. A more recent case shows that the First Amendment does not always protect the media from intentional infliction of emotional distress claims. In 2005, Natalee Holloway disappeared on a senior class trip to Aruba. Despite extensive searches, criminal investigations, and intense media coverage, 18 year old Natalee was never found. The *National Enquirer* published three articles that purported to describe details of the death and/or burial of Natalee, in June and December 2010, and April 2011. Specifically, the articles described a map that purported to show where Natalee's body was located, a "secret graveyard" where Natalee had been "buried alive," and other details about the treatment of her "corpse," including that it had been secreted temporarily in a coffin with another corpse before being moved to a final location. Natalee's mother sued American Media, *National Enquirer*'s parent company, and alleged, among other things, intentional infliction of emotional distress for publication of facts that the newspaper knew were false. Finding that the First Amendment did not protect American Media's publication of this material, the Alabama district court held that Mrs. Holloway's tort claim for intentional infliction of emotional distress could

proceed. *See Holloway v. American Media*, 947 F. Supp.2d 1252 (N.D. Ala. 2013).

---

Illustrative of the complex interplay between the First Amendment and tort law (even after *Falwell*) was a controversy involving CBS' *60 Minutes*. This television show had planned a 1995 segment in which Mike Wallace uncovered an alleged cover-up by Brown & Williamson (B & W) of the dangers of its tobacco products. The confidential source for this item was B & W's ex-research director, Jeffrey Weigand. Weigand had been put on retainer by CBS as a consultant to *60 Minutes* and guaranteed indemnity against any libel suit brought by B & W against him. When the CBS lawyers learned that Weigand had signed a nondisclosure agreement while he was an employee of the tobacco company, they advised *60 Minutes* producer Don Hewitt to kill this item on the show.

The source of the lawyers' concern was a Supreme Court ruling, *Cohen v. Cowles Media*, 501 U.S. 663 (1991). This decision had upheld the constitutionality of a suit against the Minneapolis Star Tribune for having published the name of a political campaign official who, in return for an explicit promise that his identity would be kept confidential, had leaked information about the rival candidate to the paper. The Supreme Court in *Cohen* held that "generally applicable laws do not offend against the First Amendment simply because their enforcement against the press has incidental effects on its ability to gather and report news." *Id.* at 669. In response to the dissent's argument that this case was not distinguishable from *Falwell*, which involved a general tort of infliction of emotional distress, the majority stated that while Falwell was suing for "injury to his reputation and state of mind," Cohen was suing for "breach of a promise that caused him to lose his job and lowered his earning capacity." *Id.* at 671. CBS counsel was reportedly concerned that B & W could sue the program for the tort of inducing Weigand to breach his confidentiality promise. Not until the *Wall Street Journal* published a 1996 story describing a sworn deposition by Weigand in a Mississippi lawsuit (containing all the significant points made in the *60 Minutes* segment), did the CBS show get the legal go-ahead to be aired.

This part of the ongoing tobacco legal battle eventually generated a 1999 movie, *The Insider*, which displayed to the general public the potential impact of private contracts on public interest news stories. Should the *Cohen* and B & W situations have been judged distinguishable either as a matter of liability or First Amendment policy? As they do in most states, courts in New York use the Restatement standard for inducing breach of contract suits, one that requires not just *intentional* but also *improper* interference with existing contract relations. The latter factor requires a balancing of the private and public interests at stake. Did the tobacco company have a stronger or weaker claim to protect its interest against CBS than Jerry Falwell had against *Hustler*?

## C. PRIVACY: INTRUSION ON SOLITUDE[d]

This brings us to the most commonly used tort claim in this entertainment setting—invasion of privacy. This legal concept was born in a Harvard Law Review article written a century ago, which developed the case for giving citizens the means of protecting their personal lives from intrusions by "yellow journalism." *See* Samuel D. Warren and Louis Brandeis, *The Right To Privacy*, 4 Harvard L. Rev. 193 (1890). The authors argued that people badly needed a legal "right to be left alone."

> The press is overstepping in every direction the obvious bounds of propriety and of decency. Gossip is no longer the resource of the idle and of the vicious, but has become a trade . . . To occupy the indolent, column upon column is filled with idle gossip which can only be procured by intrusion upon the domestic circle. The intensity and complexity of life . . . have rendered necessary some retreat from the world . . . but modern enterprise and invention have, through invasions upon his privacy, subjected [people] to mental pain and duress far greater than could be inflicted by mere bodily injury.

*Id.* at 196. After suffering an initial defeat at the hands of New York courts, in *Roberson v. Rochester Folding Box*, 171 N.Y. 538, 64 N.E. 442 (1902), privacy rights finally received common law endorsement from the Georgia Supreme Court in *Pavesich v. New England Life Insurance*, 122 Ga. 190, 50 S.E. 68 (1905).

Beginning with *Pavesich*, the initial concern of Warren and Brandeis about privacy invasions through public gossip has blossomed into four distinct causes of action: unreasonable intrusion on personal solitude; public disclosure of true but embarrassing private facts; presentation of people in a false light in the public eye; and appropriation of one's name and likeness. The last component, protection of a proprietary interest in a commercially valuable name and likeness, is the subject of the next chapter on Celebrity Publicity Rights. Here, we shall develop the first three components of privacy law, which relate to essentially the same personal and psychological concerns that underlie the torts of defamation and emotional distress.

---

[d] *See* William Prosser, *Privacy*, 48 California L. Rev. 383 (1960); Robert C. Post, *The Social Foundations of Privacy: Community & Self in the Common Law Tort*, 77 California L. Rev. 957 (1989); Rodney A. Smolla, *Free Speech In An Open Society* (Random House 1992) (Chapter 5—"Personal Reputation & Privacy").

As noted above, the privacy tort was originally proposed not as a response to fictionalized docudrama (such as *Anatomy of a Murder*) or offensive parodies (such as *Hustler's* mock Jerry Falwell), but as a protection against media intrusion into people's personal lives and the publication of embarrassing facts about them. In the world of contemporary tabloid television, this brand of journalism has attained new technological heights. Television networks, cable systems, and independent syndication producers seek to fill the continually expanding amounts of channel time with pictures and sounds of real people in emotionally gripping situations. Often, though, the subjects of these video and audio tapes feel violated and aggrieved when their friends and acquaintances view a program depicting them in tragic or humiliating situations.

The law provides at least some protection of the subject's privacy.[e] For example, a CBS News camera crew from the program *Street Stories* accompanied federal secret service agents in the search of the Ayeni home in Brooklyn. The husband was a suspect in a credit-card fraud case, but was not at home at the time. The crew, however, filmed the frightened wife and crying child in their home. District Judge Jack Weinstein refused to dismiss a lawsuit that he said posed "grave issues of the right of privacy in the home from the intruding eye and ear of a private broadcaster's television camera," aimed at "broadcasting to the world at large, pictures of intimate secrets of the household." CBS then settled the suit for an undisclosed amount. *See also Ayeni v. Mottola*, 35 F.3d 680 (2d Cir. 1994), in which the Court endorsed the validity, in principle, of the Ayeni suit against the Secret Service for violation of their Fourth Amendment rights.

In 1999, the Supreme Court unanimously decided that the police violated "the right of residential privacy at the core of the Fourth Amendment" when they invited these television or newspaper people to accompany them in what would be a defensible intrusion by law enforcement personnel themselves. One of the cases, *Wilson v. Layne*, 526 U.S. 603 (1999), involved *Washington Post* reporter/photographers accompanying a joint federal/local police task force, which in the middle of the night went into the wrong residence—the home of the parents, not the fugitive himself. The other ride-along case, *Hanlon v. Berger,* 526 U.S. 808 (1999), had a CNN camera crew joining federal agents searching a Montana ranch for evidence of violations of wildlife laws. Chief Justice Rehnquist's opinion stated that "surely the possibility of good public

---

[e] *See* Lyrissa C. Barnett, *Intrusion & the Investigative Reporter*, 71 Texas L. Rev. 433 (1992); Andrew Jay McClurg, *Bringing Privacy Law Out of the Closet. A Tort Theory of Liability for Intrusions In Public Places*, 73 North Carolina L. Rev. 989 (1995); David A. Logan, *Masked Media: Judges, Juries, & the Law of Surreptitious Newsgathering*, 83 Iowa L. Rev. 161 (1997); Jeffrey Malkan, *Stolen Photographs: Personality, Publicity, & Privacy*, 75 Texas L. Rev. 779 (1997).

relations for the police is simply not enough, standing alone, to justify the ride-along intrusion into a private home." 526 U.S. at 613.

Though the Court did not address tort law, it is likely that the media entities would be liable for intruding on the solitude of private residents. The principal basis for such a legal claim is the privacy tort that bars "unreasonable intrusion on personal solitude." An important case in the evolution of this doctrine was *Dietemann v. Time, Inc.*, 449 F.2d 245 (9th Cir. 1971). Life Magazine, as part of a story on medical "quackery," featured pictures of the plaintiff practicing medicine without a license and being arrested for doing so. Life obtained the pictures by cooperating with the Los Angeles District Attorney's Office to gain entrance to the plaintiff's home by passing Life reporters off as persons seeking treatment. Once in the home, the reporters used electronic devices to transmit their conversations with the plaintiff. Quoting *Briscoe v. Reader's Digest Ass'n*, 4 Cal. 3d 529, 93 Cal. Rptr. 866, 869, 483 P.2d 34, 37 (1971), the court noted "the increasing capabilit[ies] of . . . electronic devices with their capacity to destroy an individual's anonymity, intrude upon his most intimate activities, and expose his most personal characteristics to public gaze." According to the court, such electronic intrusions can be even more harmful than physical intrusion. The court thus held that under the invasion of privacy tort, "surreptitious electronic recording of a plaintiff's conversation causing him emotional distress" is actionable.

Public as well as private figures are protected from such intrusion, as illustrated by *Galella v. Onassis*, 487 F.2d 986 (2d Cir. 1973). Ronald Galella, a free-lance photographer, was a "paparazzo" specializing in taking and selling photographs of famous people. Galella's favorite target was Jacqueline Kennedy Onassis, the widow of President Kennedy and wife of shipping tycoon Aristotle Onassis, as well as her children. In the quest for pictures, Galella interrupted tennis games and invaded the children's private school. He pursued Onassis in a power boat while she was swimming, and he even romanced a family employee in order to keep him informed regarding Onassis' whereabouts. In an effort to snap a photo of Onassis' son John, Jr., Galella leaped into the boy's bicycle path. Fearing for John, Secret Service agents (who are assigned to the children of former presidents until they reach sixteen) arrested Galella. He was eventually acquitted in state court.

Following his acquittal, Galella filed suit against Onassis and the Secret Service, alleging that they had maliciously prosecuted him and, under the guise of protecting Onassis, had unlawfully interfered with Galella's trade as part of the media world. Onassis counterclaimed, charging that Galella had invaded her privacy and engaged in a campaign of harassment. The district court dismissed the claim against the agents on the grounds that they acted within their scope of authority. After trial, the court dismissed Galella's claim against Onassis and granted her relief by enjoining Galella from placing Onassis and her family under surveillance, approaching within 100 yards of Onassis' home or her children, using the name or portrait of Onassis or her children for advertising, and attempting to communicate with Onassis or her children. On appeal the Second Circuit acknowledged that legitimate social needs warrant some intrusions on a person's privacy. However, in light of the facts as determined by the lower court, the appellate court held:

> . . . Galella's action went far beyond the reasonable bounds of news gathering. When weighed against the de minimis public importance of the daily activities of [Onassis], Galella's constant surveillance, his obtrusive and intruding presence, was unwarranted and unreasonable. If there were any doubt in our minds, Galella's inexcusable conduct toward [Onassis'] minor children would resolve it.

*Id.* at 995. The majority did rule, though, that the lower court's injunction was broader than required to protect Onassis, and it decreased the distance restrictions under the injunction. Finally, the court lifted the prohibition on Galella taking pictures of Onassis, finding this to be "improper and unwarranted by the evidence." *Id.* at 998.

---

None of these cases dealt with media personnel accompanying police or other authorities in *public* rather than in private space to discover and film the plight of private individuals. In 1998, the Supreme Court of California addressed the scope of personal privacy (rather than Fourth Amendment) rights. Ruth Shulman and her family were in a car being driven by her daughter when it fell off a Los Angeles freeway and plunged 100 feet. Shulman was trapped under the car, and had to be cut free from the vehicle by a device known as "the jaws of life." This was done by a private paramedic team that Mercy Air dispatched to the scene, who then flew Shulman to a hospital. This Mercy Air team also had a ride-along cameraman, Joel Cooke, whose videotape of the bloodied and severely-injured mother was eventually shown on the syndicated program, *On Scene: Emergency Response*, though just referring to her as "Ruth." The flight nurse working on Shulman, Laura Carnahan, was wearing a tiny microphone which taped the patient saying "I just want to die. I don't want to go through this." Shulman did survive, though as a paraplegic, and three months later saw herself on this nine-minute segment of *On Scene*. Her response was to sue for invasion of privacy.

## SHULMAN V. GROUP W. PRODUCTIONS

Supreme Court of California, 1998.
18 Cal.4th 200, 74 Cal. Rptr.2d 843, 955 P.2d 469.

WERDEGAR, JUSTICE.

More than 100 years ago, Louis Brandeis and Samuel Warren complained that the press, armed with the then recent invention of "instantaneous photographs" and under the influence of new "business methods," was "overstepping in every direction the obvious bounds of propriety and of decency." (Warren & Brandeis, *The Right to Privacy* (1890) 4 Harv. L. Rev. 193, 195–196 (hereafter Brandeis).) Even more ominously, they noted the "numerous mechanical devices" that "threaten to make good the prediction that 'what is whispered in the closet shall be proclaimed from the house tops.' " Today, of course, the newspapers of 1890 have been joined by the electronic media; today, a vast number of books, journals, television and radio stations, cable channels and Internet content sources all compete to satisfy our thirst for knowledge and our need for news of political, economic and cultural events—as well as our love of gossip, our curiosity about the private lives of others, and "that weak side of human nature is never wholly cast down by the misfortunes and frailties of our neighbors." Moreover, the "devices" available for recording and transmitting what would otherwise be private have multiplied and improved in ways the 19th century could hardly imagine.

Over the same period, the United States has also seen a series of revolutions in mores and conventions that has moved, blurred and, at times, seemingly threatened to erase the line between public and private life. While even in their day Brandeis and Warren complained that "the details of sexual relations are spread broadcast in the columns of the daily papers," today's public discourse is particularly notable for its detailed and graphic discussion of intimate personal and family matters—sometimes as topics of legitimate public concern, sometimes as simple titillation. More generally, the dominance of the visual image in contemporary culture and the technology that makes it possible to capture and, in an instant, universally disseminate a picture or sound allows us, and leads us to expect, to see and hear what our great-grandparents could have known only through written description.

The sense of an ever-increasing pressure on personal privacy notwithstanding, it has long been apparent that the desire for privacy must at many points give way before our right to know, and the news media's right to investigate and relate, facts about the events and individuals of our time. Brandeis and Warren were themselves aware that recognition of the right to privacy requires a line to be drawn between properly private events, words and actions and those of "public and general interest" with which the community has a "legitimate concern." As early as 1931, in the first California case recognizing invasion of privacy as a tort, the court observed that the right of privacy "does not exist in the dissemination of news and news events." (*Melvin v. Reid* (1931) 112 Cal.App. 285, 290, 297 P. 91.)

Also clear is that the freedom of the press, protected by the supreme law of the First and Fourteenth Amendments to the United States Constitution, extends far beyond simple accounts of public proceedings and abstract commentary on well-known events. "The guarantees for speech and press are not the preserve of political expression or comment on public affairs, essential as those are to healthy government. One need only pick up any newspaper or magazine to comprehend the vast range of published matter which exposes persons to public view, both private citizens and public officials. Exposure of the self to others in varying degrees is a concomitant of life in a civilized community. The risk of this exposure is an essential incident of life in a society which places a primary value on freedom of speech and of press" (*Time, Inc. v. Hill* (1967) 385 U.S. 374, 388). Thus, "[t]he right to keep information private was bound to clash with the right to disseminate information to the public." (*Briscoe v. Reader's Digest Association, Inc.* (1971), 93 Cal. Rptr. 866, 483 P.2d 34.)

Despite, then, the intervening social and technological changes since 1890, the fundamental legal problems in defining a right of privacy vis-a-vis the news media have not changed—have, if anything, intensified. At what point does the publishing or broadcasting of otherwise private words, expressions and emotions cease to be protected by the press's constitutional and common law privilege—its right to report on matters of legitimate public interest—and become an unjustified, actionable invasion of the subject's private life? How can the courts fashion and administer meaningful rules for protecting privacy without unconstitutionally setting themselves up as censors or editors? Publication or broadcast aside, do reporters, in their effort to gather the news, have any special privilege to intrude, physically or with sophisticated photographic and recording equipment, into places and conversations that would otherwise be private? Questions of this nature have concerned courts and commentators at least since Brandeis and Warren wrote their seminal article, and continue to do so to this day.

* * *

## I. Publication of Private Facts

* * *

The element critical to this case is the presence or absence of legitimate public interest, i.e., newsworthiness, in the facts disclosed. After reviewing the decisional law regarding newsworthiness, we conclude, inter alia, that lack of newsworthiness is an element of the "private facts" tort, making newsworthiness a complete bar to common law liability. We further conclude that the analysis of newsworthiness inevitably involves accommodating conflicting interests in personal privacy and in press freedom as guaranteed by the First Amendment to the United States Constitution, and that in the circumstances of this case—where the facts disclosed about a private person involuntarily caught up in events of public interest bear a logical relationship to the newsworthy subject of the broadcast and are not intrusive in great disproportion to their relevance—the broadcast was of legitimate public concern, barring liability under the private facts tort.

* * *

Our prior decisions have not explicitly addressed the type of privacy invasion alleged in this case: the broadcast of embarrassing pictures and speech of a person who, while generally not a public figure, has become involuntarily involved in an event or activity of legitimate public concern. We nonetheless draw guidance from those decisions, in that they articulate the competing interests to be balanced. First, the analysis of newsworthiness does involve courts to some degree in a normative assessment of the "social value" of a publication. All material that might attract readers or viewers is not, simply by virtue of its attractiveness, of legitimate public interest. Second, the evaluation of newsworthiness depends on the degree of intrusion and the extent to which the plaintiff played an important role in public events, and thus on a comparison between the information revealed and the nature of the activity or event that brought the plaintiff to public attention.

* * *

An analysis measuring newsworthiness of facts about an otherwise private person involuntarily involved in an event of public interest by their relevance to a newsworthy subject matter incorporates considerable deference to reporters and editors, avoiding the likelihood of unconstitutional interference with the freedom of the press to report truthfully on matters of legitimate public interest. In general, it is not for a court or jury to say how a particular story is best covered. The constitutional privilege to publish truthful material "ceases to operate only when an editor abuses his broad discretion to publish matters that are of legitimate public interest." By confining our interference to extreme cases, the courts "avoid . . . unduly limiting . . . the exercise of effective editorial judgment." Nor is newsworthiness governed by the tastes or limited interests of an individual judge or juror; a publication is newsworthy if some reasonable members of the community could entertain a legitimate interest in it. Our analysis thus does not purport to distinguish among the various legitimate purposes that may be served by truthful publications and broadcasts . . .

* * *

On the other hand, no mode of analyzing newsworthiness can be applied mechanically or without consideration of its proper boundaries. To observe that the newsworthiness of private facts about a person involuntarily thrust into the public eye depends, in the ordinary case, on the existence of a logical nexus between the newsworthy event or activity and the facts revealed is not to deny that the balance of free press and privacy interests may require a different conclusion when the intrusiveness of the revelation is greatly disproportionate to its relevance. Intensely personal or intimate revelations might not, in a given case, be considered newsworthy, especially where they bear only slight relevance to a topic of legitimate public concern . . .

* * *

Turning now to the case at bar, we consider whether the possibly private facts complained of here—broadly speaking, Ruth's appearance and words during the rescue and evacuation—were of legitimate public interest . . . We agree at the outset with defendants that the subject matter of the broadcast as a whole was of legitimate public concern. Automobile accidents are by their nature of interest to that great portion of the public that travels frequently by automobile. The rescue and medical treatment of accident victims is also of legitimate concern to much of the public, involving as it does a critical service that any member of the public may someday need. The story of Ruth's difficult extrication from the crushed car, the medical attention given her at the scene, and her evacuation by helicopter was of particular interest because it highlighted some of the challenges facing emergency workers dealing with serious accidents.

The more difficult question is whether Ruth's appearance and words as she was extricated from the overturned car, placed in the helicopter and transported to the hospital were of legitimate public concern. Pursuant to the analysis outlined earlier, we conclude the disputed material was newsworthy as a matter of law. One of the dramatic and interesting aspects of the story as a whole is its focus on flight nurse Carnahan, who appears to be in charge of communications with other emergency workers, the hospital base and Ruth, and who leads the medical assistance to Ruth at the scene. Her work is portrayed as demanding and important and as involving a measure of personal risk (e.g., in crawling under the car to aid Ruth despite warnings that gasoline may be dripping from the car). The broadcast segment makes apparent that this type of emergency care requires not only medical knowledge, concentration and courage, but an ability to talk and listen to severely traumatized patients. One of the challenges Carnahan faces in assisting Ruth is the confusion, pain and fear that Ruth understandably feels in the aftermath of the accident. For that reason the broadcast video depicting Ruth's injured physical state (which was not luridly shown) and audio showing her disorientation and despair were substantially relevant to the segment's newsworthy subject matter.

* * *

One might argue that, while the contents of the broadcast were of legitimate interest in that they reflected on the nature and quality of emergency rescue services, the images and sounds that potentially allowed identification of Ruth as the accident victim were irrelevant and of no legitimate public interest in a broadcast that aired some months after the accident and had little or no value as "hot" news. We do not take that view. It is difficult to see how the subject broadcast could have been edited to avoid completely any possible identification without severely undercutting its legitimate descriptive and narrative impact. As broadcast, the segment included neither Ruth's full name nor direct display of her face. She was nonetheless arguably identifiable by her first name (used in recorded dialogue), her voice, her general appearance and the recounted circumstances of the accident (which, as noted, had previously been published, with Ruth's full name and city of residence, in a newspaper). In a video documentary of this type, however, the use of that degree of truthful detail would seem not only relevant, but essential to the narrative.

## II. Intrusion

Of the four privacy torts identified by Prosser, the tort of intrusion into private places, conversations or matter is perhaps the one that best captures the common understanding of an "invasion of privacy." It encompasses unconsented-to physical intrusion into the home, hospital room or other place the privacy of which is legally recognized, as well as unwarranted sensory intrusions such as eavesdropping, wiretapping, and visual or photographic spying. It is in the intrusion cases that invasion of privacy is most clearly seen as an affront to individual dignity.

* * *

We ask first whether defendants "intentionally intrude[d], physically or otherwise, upon the solitude or seclusion of another," that is, into a place or conversation private to Wayne or Ruth . . . To prove actionable intrusion, the plaintiff must show the defendant penetrated some zone of physical or sensory privacy surrounding, or obtained unwanted access to data about, the plaintiff. The tort is proven only if the plaintiff had an objectively reasonable expectation of seclusion or solitude in the place, conversation or data source. . . .

Cameraman Cooke's mere presence at the accident scene and filming of the events occurring there cannot be deemed either a physical or sensory intrusion on plaintiffs' seclusion. Plaintiffs had no right of ownership or possession of the property where the rescue took place, nor any actual control of the premises. Nor could they have had a reasonable expectation that members of the media would be excluded or prevented from photographing the scene; for journalists to attend and record the scenes of accidents and rescues is in no way unusual or unexpected.

Two aspects of defendants' conduct, however, raise triable issues of intrusion on seclusion. First, a triable issue exists as to whether both plaintiffs had an objectively reasonable expectation of privacy in the interior of the rescue helicopter, which served as an ambulance. Although the attendance of reporters and photographers at the scene of an accident is to be expected, we are aware of no law or custom permitting the press to ride in ambulances or enter hospital rooms during treatment without the patient's consent. . . .

Second, Ruth was entitled to a degree of privacy in her conversations with Carnahan and other medical rescuers at the accident scene, and in Carnahan's conversations conveying medical information regarding Ruth to the hospital base. Cooke, perhaps, did not intrude into that zone of privacy merely by being present at a place where he could hear such conversations with unaided ears. But by placing a microphone on Carnahan's person, amplifying and recording what she said and heard, defendants may have listened in on conversations the parties could reasonably have expected to be private.

* * *

We turn to the second element of the intrusion tort, offensiveness of the intrusion . . . In deciding . . . whether a reporter's alleged intrusion into private matters (i.e., physical space, conversation or data) is "offensive" and hence actionable as an invasion of privacy, courts must consider the extent to which the intrusion was, under the circumstances, justified by the legitimate motive of gathering the news. Information collecting techniques that may be highly offensive when done for socially unprotected reasons—for purposes of harassment, blackmail or prurient curiosity, for example—may not be offensive to a reasonable person when employed by journalists in pursuit of a socially or politically important story . . . [However,] on this summary judgment record, we believe a jury could find defendants' recording of Ruth's communications to Carnahan and other rescuers, and filming in the air ambulance, to be " 'highly offensive to a reasonable person.' " With regard to the depth of the intrusion, a reasonable jury could find highly offensive the placement of a microphone on a medical rescuer in order to intercept what would otherwise be private conversations with an injured patient. In that setting, as defendants could and should have foreseen, the patient would not know her words were being recorded and would not have occasion to ask about, and object or consent to, recording. Defendants, it could reasonably be said, took calculated advantage of the patient's "vulnerability and confusion." Arguably, the last thing an injured accident victim should have to worry about while being pried from her wrecked car is that a television producer may be recording everything she says to medical personnel for the possible edification and entertainment of casual television viewers.

For much the same reason, a jury could reasonably regard entering and riding in an ambulance—whether on the ground or in the air—with two seriously injured patients to be an egregious intrusion on a place of expected seclusion. Again, the patients, at least in this case, were hardly in a position to keep careful watch on who was riding with them, or to inquire as to everyone's business and consent or object to their presence. A jury could reasonably believe that fundamental respect for human dignity requires the patients' anxious journey be taken only with those whose care is solely for them and out of sight of the prying eyes (or cameras) of others.

Nor can we say as a matter of law that defendants' motive—to gather usable material for a potentially newsworthy story—necessarily privileged their intrusive conduct as a matter of common law tort liability. A reasonable jury could conclude the producers' desire to get footage that would convey the "feel" of the event—the real sights and sounds of a difficult rescue—did not justify either placing a microphone on Nurse Carnahan or filming inside the rescue helicopter. Although defendants' purposes could scarcely be regarded as evil or malicious (in the colloquial sense), their behavior could, even in light of their motives, be thought to show a highly offensive lack of sensitivity and respect for plaintiffs' privacy. A reasonable jury could find that defendants, in placing a microphone on an emergency treatment nurse and recording her conversation with a distressed, disoriented and severely injured patient, without the patient's knowledge or consent, acted with highly offensive disrespect for the patient's personal privacy comparable to, if not quite as extreme as, the disrespect and insensitivity demonstrated in *Miller*.

Turning to the question of constitutional protection for newsgathering, one finds the decisional law reflects a general rule of nonprotection: the press in its newsgathering activities enjoys no immunity or exemption from generally applicable laws . . . "It is clear that the First Amendment does not invalidate every incidental burdening of the press that may result from the enforcement of civil and criminal laws of general applicability. Under prior cases, otherwise valid laws serving substantial public interests may be enforced against the press as against others, despite the possible burden that may be imposed." (*Branzburg v. Hayes*, (1972), 408 U.S. 665, at 682–683). California's intrusion tort and section 632 are both laws of general applicability. They apply to all private investigative activity, whatever its purpose and whoever the investigator, and impose no greater restrictions on the media than on anyone else. (If anything, the media enjoy some degree of favorable treatment under the California intrusion tort, as a reporter's motive to discover socially important information may reduce the offensiveness of the intrusion.) These laws serve the undisputedly substantial public interest in allowing each person to maintain an area of physical and sensory privacy in which to live. Thus, defendants enjoyed no constitutional privilege, merely by virtue of their status as members of the news media, to eavesdrop in violation of section 632 or otherwise to intrude tortiously on private places, conversations or information.

* * *

As should be apparent from the above discussion, the constitutional protection accorded newsgathering, if any, is far narrower than the protection surrounding the publication of truthful material; consequently, the fact that a reporter may be seeking "newsworthy" material does not in itself privilege the investigatory activity. The reason for the difference is simple: the intrusion tort, unlike that for publication of private facts, does not subject the press to liability for the contents of its publications. Newsworthiness, as we stated earlier, is a complete bar to liability for publication of private facts and is evaluated with a high degree of deference to editorial judgment. The same deference is not due, however, when the issue is not the media's right to publish or broadcast what they choose, but their right to intrude into secluded areas or conversations in pursuit of publishable material. . . .

* * *

Conclusion

The claim of these accident victims that their privacy was invaded by the production and broadcast of a documentary segment on their rescue raises questions about how the news media obtain their material (the intrusion claim), as well as about what they choose to publish or broadcast (the publication of private facts claim). Largely for constitutional reasons, the paths we have taken in analyzing these two privacy claims have diverged and led to different results.

The broadcast details of Ruth's rescue of which she complains were, as a matter of law, of legitimate public concern because they were substantially relevant to the newsworthy subject of the piece and their intrusiveness was not greatly disproportionate to their relevance. That analytical path is dictated by the danger of the contrary approach; to allow liability because this court, or a jury, believes certain details of the story as broadcast were not important or necessary to the purpose of the documentary, or were in poor taste or overly sensational in impact, would be to assert impermissible supervisory power over the press.

The intrusion claim calls for a much less deferential analysis. In contrast to the broad privilege the press enjoys for publishing truthful, newsworthy information in its possession, the press has no recognized constitutional privilege to violate generally applicable laws in pursuit of material. Nor, even absent an independent crime or tort, can a highly offensive intrusion into a private place, conversation, or source of information generally be justified by the plea that the intruder hoped thereby to get good material for a news story. Such a justification may be available when enforcement of the tort or other law would place an impermissibly severe burden on the press, but that condition is not met in this case.

In short, the state may not intrude into the proper sphere of the news media to dictate what they should publish and broadcast, but neither may the media play tyrant to the people by unlawfully spying on them in the name of newsgathering. Summary judgment for the defense was proper as to plaintiffs' cause of action for publication of private facts (the second cause of action), but improper as to the cause of action for invasion of privacy by intrusion (the first cause of action).

Affirmed in part, reversed in part.

---

Several other concurring or dissenting opinions were written about one or more of these privacy rights issues. For our purposes here, the most significant one was by Judge Brown, objecting to the majority's new standard for legalizing the publication of private facts—wherever they bear a "logical relationship to a matter of legitimate public concern." Judge Brown preferred an earlier doctrine that required consideration of a variety of factors in determining the "newsworthiness" of private facts: "the social value of the facts published, the depth of the article's intrusion into ostensibly private affairs, and the extent to which the party voluntarily acceded to a position of public notoriety." And Judge Brown felt that, at a minimum, the *Shulman* case itself presented triable issues of material fact on the question of newsworthiness.

> The private facts broadcast had little, if any, social value. The public has no legitimate interest in witnessing Ruth's disorientation and despair. Nor does it have any legitimate interest in knowing Ruth's personal and innermost thoughts immediately after sustaining injuries that rendered her a

> paraplegic and left her hospitalized for months. "I just want to die. I don't want to go through this."

955 P.2d at 503. Keep this part of the *Shulman* decision in mind when you get to the next section, about **Public Disclosure of Embarrassing Personal Facts**.

### *QUESTIONS FOR DISCUSSION*

1. Yolanda Baugh called Alameda County's 911 number during a physical attack by her husband. The County's Mobile Crisis Intervention Team went to the Baugh home, accompanied by a CBS *Street Stories* news team which was producing an episode, "Stand By Me," about Elaine Lopes, a Crisis Team member who provided emotional support and guidance to crime or abuse victims. When Baugh saw the camera crew come in with the Crisis Team and begin filming her with Lopes, the police told her that the tapes were being made for the District Attorney's office. A few days later, when Baugh learned that scenes of her weeping in her living room were to be broadcast on *Street Stories*, she asked that these be cut from the program. CBS refused. Assuming the truth of these allegations, does Baugh have a legal claim against CBS? *See Baugh v. CBS*, 828 F. Supp. 745 (N.D. Cal. 1993).

2. Recall the facts from *Bindrim v. Mitchell*, 92 Cal.App.3d 61, 155 Cal. Rptr. 29 (1979), synopsized in the earlier section on **Defamation**. Would Bindrim, the psychologist, have an intrusion claim against the novelist, Mitchell, who violated her commitment not to write about the "Nude Marathon" session that Mitchell was allegedly attending just for therapeutic reasons?

3. Micki Free, lead guitarist for the music group Shalamar, was the target of an arrest warrant for failure to meet child support payments. When the police went to execute the warrant at 5:30 a.m., a television crew from NBC's *Hard Copy* accompanied them. The crew videotaped Free, just awakened and in his underwear, asking the police to call his ex-wife to verify that he was not behind in the support payments. The video clips of Free were part of a *Hard Copy* item on "Deadbeat Dads." Actionable or not? Should it make a difference as a matter of *privacy* law whether Free was filmed by the crew inside his house, or from the street while he was standing on the front steps? *See* 16 National L. J., 12/27/1993, at 1, for a description of the claim in *Free v. Paramount*. *See also Taylor v. KTVB*, 96 Idaho 202, 525 P.2d 984 (1974) (local television station videotaped from the street and later aired clip showing a naked Otis Taylor being arrested and taken from his home by the police).

4. Dr. Stuart M. Berger was a New York doctor whose diet program and medical techniques had generated national interest and concern. He had personally appeared on many radio and television shows and been the subject of critical articles by media organizations such as the Wall Street Journal

and ABC News. Berger was also under investigation by the state's Health Department. King World Productions' syndicated show *Inside Edition* sent in a television reporter with a hidden camera, posing as a patient, and taped Berger's alleged unethical behavior and medical malpractice. Can Berger sue for damages from the program (and what would the damages be for)? If he learns about the pending program beforehand, can he get an injunction to block the broadcast? *See In re King World Productions*, 898 F.2d 56 (6th Cir. 1990).

5. ABC's *PrimeTime Live* planned a segment about cataract surgery, based on material gathered from the Desnick Eye Center. John Entine, the *PrimeTime* producer, asked the Eye Center director, Dr. James Desnick, if he could interview Desnick and his staff and film cataract surgery being performed on their patients. Desnick agreed to let ABC do this, based on Entine's assurances that the program was intended to take a serious look at ophthalmological services for senior citizens, and would not involve "ambush" journalism involving "undercover" techniques. In fact, though, ABC sent a number of fake patients into the Eye Center, supposedly accompanied by a friend or relative who used hidden equipment to film and record the patient's consultation with the doctor. The *PrimeTime* segment used these various pieces to show the Eye Center as tampering with its patients' test results to indicate a need for cataract surgery that independent tests demonstrated were unnecessary. Assess Dr. Desnick's legal claims of trespass, invasion of privacy, defamation, fraud, breach of contract, and wiretapping. *See Desnick v. ABC, Inc.*, 44 F.3d 1345 (7th Cir. 1995).

6. Tabloid print and broadcast media have regularly shown nude photos or videotapes of women such as Paris Hilton, Paula Jones, and Tonya Harding, which their ex-boyfriends or husbands had taken years earlier in private, and then sold to the media when the women became embroiled in highly-publicized legal controversies. Should the media have the right to use such material handed to them by someone who himself has violated the privacy rights of the subject?

7. Internet pornography websites increasingly host images and videos of "revenge porn," posted by individuals to get "revenge" against ex-girlfriends. States are increasingly passing statutes in an attempt to regulate, and in some cases, criminalize such behavior. To date, only California, Florida, North Dakota, and Wisconsin have adopted dedicated laws authorizing civil lawsuits.

8. In September, 2014, a massive hack of Apple's iCloud purportedly stole thousands of private nude photographs and videos of famous celebrities, including Jennifer Lawrence, Kate Upton, and Kirsten Dunst. A number of celebrities have filed lawsuits against Apple, which hosted the photos, and Google, for failing to take down the photos and videos. To what extent should Apple be responsible for protecting the privacy of these individuals? To what extent should Google have a right to allow the photographs and videos to

remain in the public domain? Is it realistic to require Google to monitor the possible use of the purloined photos and videos?

---

One of the major dilemmas in this branch of privacy law is whether there can be a legal invasion of someone's right to solitude by observing and recording what the person is doing in public. On its face it would seem strange to label as an invasion of privacy something that takes place in public space. On reflection, though, there is a considerable difference between being seen by a few bystanders and a recording on film for display in a tabloid newspaper or television show. So far, the broad concept of a legal right to "privacy in public" has not generated much judicial support. In *Gill v. Hearst Publishing Co.*, 239 P.2d 636 (Cal.1952), *rehearing after remand*, 40 Cal.2d 224, 253 P.2d 441 (1953), the California Supreme Court first announced and then retreated from the position that a newspaper could be liable for publication (under the caption "Love") of a picture of a young couple sitting outside with their arms around each other. The court's judgment was that even if this romantic portrait was "taken in a pose voluntarily assumed in a public place . . . has no particular news value . . . , the constitutional guarantees of freedom of expression apply with equal force to the publication . . . as an entertainment feature." 253 P.2d at 444. This led Dean Prosser, Chief Reporter of the *Restatement (Second) of Torts,* to draft in the early 1960s an exclusion from the privacy tort of pictures taken as well as direct observation of what people were doing out in public. (§ 652 B, Comment C). A qualification had to be added, though, to accommodate a decision by the Alabama Supreme Court in *Daily Times Democrat v. Graham*, 276 Ala. 380, 162 So.2d 474 (1964), which found a newspaper liable for publishing a snapshot taken of a woman inside a state carnival's "Fun House" with her skirt blown over her head by a concealed air jet.

Around the same time that the *Shulman* decision was being considered by the Supreme Court of California, that state's legislature was debating a statutory reform being sought by bodies like the Screen Actors Guild to protect their celebrity union members like Sylvester Stallone and Will Smith from being stalked by the paparazzi. Needless to say, the person whose 1997 death rendered "stalkerazzi" efforts especially offensive was Princess Diana, divorced wife of Prince Charles. Princess Diana had turned the paparazzi role into a large, but very controversial business venture. Federico Fellini could never have imagined this when he was making his *La Dolce Vita* movie, with Anita Ekberg who aimed a bow and arrow at the paparazzi photographer planted outside her villa. For example, in 1997, one paparazzo secured a $720,000 payment from London's *Sunday Mirror* for his photo of Diana embracing her male friend Emod Mohamad Al-Fayed (Dodi) on the St. Tropez beach.

Shortly afterwards, Di and Dodi went to Paris for their fateful last weekend. Thirty years earlier, Jacqueline Kennedy Onassis had imported this business from Italy to America, with 3 to 4 paparazzi pursuing her for photographs, in a market that had put Jackie on a total of 14 covers of *People*. By the late 1990s, Diana regularly had 30 to 40 paparazzi chasing a woman who made *People*'s cover 43 times *before* her death. On their last evening, Diana and Dodi took off for the family villa, driven by Henri Paul. This time, there were even more paparazzi on motorcycles chasing the vehicle on the road up the Seine, where the car suddenly crashed into the wall of a tunnel, killing Diana, Dodi, and Henri. It turned out that Henri had been intoxicated that night, and his drunk driving precipitated this tragic auto accident. It also seems clear, though, that the paparazzi chase had something significant to do with the speed of the car and the resulting accident. In Paris, the authorities said they would start enforcing their already quite restrictive French privacy law that bars newspapers from "intruding on the private life of any person," e.g., by publishing "unauthorized photographs of the life," or "publicizing the real and imaginary liaisons of anybody."

Meanwhile, in the United States, California's legislature added to Section 1708.8 of its *Civil Code* this new subsection:

> (b) A person is liable for constructive invasion of privacy when the defendant attempts to capture, in a manner that is offensive to a reasonable person, any type of visual image, sound recording, or other physical impression of the plaintiff engaging in a personal or familial activity under circumstances in which the plaintiff had a reasonable expectation of privacy, through the use of a visual or auditory enhancing device, regardless of whether there is a physical trespass, if this image, sound recording, or other physical impression could not have been achieved without a trespass unless the visual or auditory enhancing device was used.

In 2005, Governor Arnold Schwarzenegger, who had himself been stalked by paparazzi in his previous role as a movie star, signed into law an amendment to this California statute that tripled the potential damages and forfeited any profits from photos taken during an altercation or as a result of an assault by the photographer. This bill had been sparked by incidents involving stars such as Reese Witherspoon. And while the new Screen Actors Guild leader Alan Rosenberg was celebrating this bill, the California Newspaper Publisher Association was attacking it as detracting from their First Amendment rights.

Meanwhile, the Supreme Court of Canada was taking an even more dramatic step in the expansion of privacy rights—by endorsing the constitutional validity of a Quebec provincial court decision that was the opposite of the California ruling in *Hearst Publishing* (supra). In *Les Editions Vice Versa and Duclos v. Aubry*, 157 DLR (4th) 577 (1998), the Canadian Court found that the 17-year old girl Aubry had a valid privacy claim against photographer Duclos and his art magazine when they published a photo of Aubry sitting on the steps in front of a public building in Montreal, apparently looking somewhat pensive. The Court did say that the constitutional protection of "freedom of expression" across Canada required certain exceptions to any provincially-created privacy rights. One exception was "when a person appears in an incidental manner in a photograph of a public place," such as the "photograph of a sporting event or a demonstration." When people chose to go into such crowds, they gave "express or tacit consent to the publication of his or her image." A second exception related to public figures—not just those "engaged in a public activity," but also those who have "acquired a certain notoriety," including entertainment performers "whose professional success depends on public opinion." Even a "previously unknown" person could be transformed into such a public figure when "called on to play a high-profile role in a matter within the public domain." But in Quebec now, a picture or film taken of an ordinary person sitting on a public stairwell herself, or on a beach with her arm around a friend, can no longer be placed on a media page or screen without her consent.

As we saw with *Gill*, supra, the approach of American courts has long been different on this score. For example, in *Jackson v. Playboy Enterprises*, 574 F. Supp. 10 (S.D.Ohio 1983), a photo was taken of three young boys on a sidewalk with a policewoman who was helping them fix their bicycle. Sometime later that picture appeared in *Playboy*, in a feature about the officer that also showed her in several nude photos (without the youngsters present). But the Ohio judge rejected the lawsuit filed on behalf of the children and their family, saying there was no privacy right barring publication even in *Playboy* of photos taken "on a city sidewalk in plain view of the public eye."

There have been more recent legal challenges to that American tradition. In 2000, a Florida State business school student, Becky Gritzke, had gone to New Orleans for its annual Mardi Gras celebration. Like many other young women, while marching through the French Quarter, Gritzke accepted the requests of the audience and bared her breasts in return for beads and trinkets. A month later, though, Gritzke was shocked to learn from her friends that they had seen her breasts on TV ads for M.R.A. Holdings' latest version of its *Girls Gone Wild* video series, about *Mardi Gras College Coeds*. On investigating, Gritzke learned that not only was she prominently depicted inside the video, but also on the cover box, a web site promotion, and even on billboards a family friend had seen in Italy. As a result, Gritzke filed a lawsuit in Florida, claiming both intentional infliction of emotional distress and invasion of her privacy rights, including the "false light" portrayal of her as someone who was "willing to be associated with and participate in the risqué and sometimes pornographic displays in the videotape." The defense of M.R.A. Holdings is that "once Gritzke bared it all for the people on Bourbon Street in New Orleans, this sacrificed her right to privacy" because "Mardi Gras is a newsworthy event . . . What happens in public is not private. It's there for all to see." What should be the result here? *See Gritzke v. M.R.A. Holding, LLC*, 2002 WL 32107540 (N.D. Fla. 2002).

How should the courts or legislatures decide whether there is a difference between being viewed on a city sidewalk and in a national magazine, television network, or video (and its advertisements around the world)? Should this be considered a more or less important public policy concern than "technological trespassing" (from the streets) on the private homes, yards, or vehicles of celebrities like Julia Roberts or Tiger Woods? And by the way, is there now a technological device that would allow a *Playboy*, *Vice Versa*, or *On Screen* television show, as well as a *Girls Gone Wild* video, to get material without intruding on the privacy of a Jackson, Aubry, Shulman, or Gritzke? How, for instance, would this apply to videos taken by drones?

What is the appropriate treatment of this legal policy issue in the 21st century? Is the right to personal solitude forfeited when people leave their homes? What about the workplace? Or should the right be available where one's visible actions are made the focus of pictures taken and published or broadcast? What is the appropriate line between legitimate and illegitimate use of such pictures? Does any attempt to draw such a line in litigation pose an unacceptable threat to freedom of the press?

---

Consider the implications of this variation on the *Shulman* case: ABC's *Prime Time Live* sent undercover reporters with false resumes to get jobs at stores in the *Food Lion* supermarket chain. Using hidden cameras, the reporters taped Food Lion staff doctoring up and selling rotten meat and spoiled produce. When Diane Sawyer presented this story over the air, it shocked viewers and severely harmed Food Lion's business. Food Lion did not file a defamation suit challenging the accuracy of the ABC story. Instead, it sued the network for trespass and fraud in the manner in which it gathered its material. The judge initially rejected ABC's First Amendment and common law defense of its actions on the grounds that the story was true and the public needed to learn about it. *See Food Lion v. Capital Cities/ABC Inc.,* 887 F. Supp. 811 (M.D.N.C. 1995). The jury then found that Food Lion was owed $1,402 in compensatory damages for wages paid to the reporters, plus $5.5 million in punitive damages for ABC's violation of Food Lion's legal rights.

With ABC's lawyers saying any such award would operate as a major deterrent to effective journalistic investigation of wrongdoing, the trial judge reduced the verdict to $316,402, consisting of the $1 awards for trespass and breach of employee loyalty, with $315,000 for "business deception" under North Carolina's *Unfair and Deceptive Trade Practices Act*, and $1,400 in punitive damages. The Fourth Circuit then went much further to leave the company with just $2. *See Food Lion v. Capital Cities/ABC, Inc.*, 194 F.3d 505 (4th Cir. 1999). Over a vigorous dissent, the majority refused to allow an "end run" on the First Amendment right to publish these facts via a punitive damages claim attacking the method through which the facts had been discovered and filmed. What would (and should) happen if a future jury, instructed by the judge on this point, were to award $5.5 million (or just $316,402) specifically for trespass and employee disloyalty?

A 2001 decision, *Bartnicki v. Vopper*, 532 U.S. 514 (2001), involved a lawsuit filed by two teacher union leaders in Pennsylvania, Gloria Bartnicki and Anthony Kane, against Fred Vopper, a local radio talk show host. The suit was precipitated by a conversation between Bartnicki, the union negotiator, and Kane, the local union president, about the difficulties they were having in securing a pay increase for their members. After commenting on the rather intransigent school board and the likelihood of a long strike, Kane said "If they're not gonna move for three points, we're gonna have to go to their homes . . . To blow off their front porches, we'll have to do some work on those guys."

What made this case special was not the fact that Vopper quoted Kane on his show, but the way he was able to do so. The two union leaders were talking on their cell phones, which an unknown person tracking the two had intercepted, taped, dropped off in the mail box of a supporter of the school board, who then delivered it to Vopper. After the union secured a salary increase, Vopper played the taped conversation on the air. The lawsuit against Vopper was based on the federal Electronic Communications Privacy Act, which prohibits not only the "interception," but also the "disclosure" of any "electronic communication," e.g., cell phones. Though Vopper had violated this provision, he claimed a First Amendment right to disclose information that he had not illegally intercepted himself. When this issue reached the Supreme Court, the Justices were divided into three different positions on how to resolve this latest conflict between personal privacy and media expression.

Chief Justice Rehnquist (joined by Justices Scalia and Thomas) felt that this was a large social problem that had to be accommodated under the First Amendment. Over 20 million cell phone "scanners" were being used a decade after they had been made illegal. In order to "dry up this market" that had proven "difficult to police" by itself, the statutory policy was to prevent "the wrongdoer from enjoying the fruits of the crime. Were there no prohibition on disclosure, an individual eavesdropper who wanted to disclose the conversation could anonymously launder the interception through a third party and thereby avoid detection. Indeed, demand for illegally obtained private information would only increase if it would be disclosed without repercussion." 532 U.S. at 551.

Justice Stevens (joined by Justices Kennedy, Souter, and Ginsburg) gave more weight to the First Amendment. He recognized that what was special about the privacy interests in this context was that it involved "privacy of communication," and thus "the fear of public disclosure of private conversation might well have a chilling effect on private speech." *Id.* at 533. Although the latter interests might be "strong enough to justify [this federal ban on] disclosure of trade secrets or domestic gossip or other information of purely private concern . . . in this case, privacy concerns give way when balanced against the interest in publishing matters of public importance," especially when uttered by union leaders involved in a public labor dispute. "One of the costs associated with participation in public affairs is an attendant loss of privacy." *Id.* at 534.

Justices Breyer's extended concurring opinion (joined by Justice O'Connor) placed a modest First Amendment limit to this federal privacy protection. The purpose of this legislation is to "ensure the privacy of telephone conversations much as a trespass statute ensures privacy within the home. That assurance of privacy helps to overcome our natural reluctance to discuss private matters when we fear that our private conversation may become public. And the statutory restriction consequently encourages conversation that otherwise might not take place." *Id.* at 537. Why, though, should the law prohibit disclosure, not just interception? "Media dissemination of an intimate conversation to an entire community will often cause the speakers serious harm over and above the harm caused by an initial disclosure to the person who intercepted the phone call. And the threat of that widespread dissemination can create a far more powerful disincentive to speak privately than the comparatively minor threat of disclosure to an interceptor and perhaps to a handful of others." *Id.* Justice Breyer was ready to carve out an exception to that legal policy in *Bartnicki* because "the information publicized involved a matter of unusual public concern, namely a threat of potential physical harm to others." Thus, "the law recognizes a privilege allowing the reporting of threats to public safety." *Id.* at 536–37.

This case shows diversity of viewpoints on the conflict between personal privacy and free speech. Chief Justice Rehnquist would permit a ban on disclosure of the content of any intercepted electronic communications, Justice Breyer would relax this for "public safety," and Justice Stevens would do so for anything of "public importance" or "public concern" (while acknowledging that the latter would likely not include more "domestic gossip"). No Justice was prepared to grant a full-blown right of media disclosure of all communication that happened to have been intercepted by a third party. Which of these positions do you find to be the most sensible legal treatment of such electronic communications? And should the Congress as well as the Court be applying its favored policy to intercepted exchanges on the Internet as well as on cell phones? Compare the Obama Administration's 2010 effort to increase monitoring of Internet communications in the interest of national security.

## D. PUBLIC DISCLOSURE OF EMBARRASSING PRIVATE FACTS[f]

The last several pages involve situations in which the source of individual unhappiness is not so much the location where the information was obtained as it is the sensitive quality of the images being portrayed for the public at large. A second privacy doctrine restricts public disclosure of embarrassing private facts. In the entertainment industry, what often happens is that rather than portraying the private individual on the screen or in print, the story is turned into an apparently fictionalized movie or television show based on the key facts of the incident. A professional actor is now playing the real world character on the screen, often with the name changed. Still, the person involved in the actual event knows who is being portrayed in the film, as do family, friends, and neighbors.

For example, in 1997, Disney announced that it would be making the movie *A Civil Action*, based on the best-selling novel by Jonathan Harr. The book had recounted the story of how families in Woburn, Massachusetts, near Boston, had lost their children from leukemia caused by drinking water that apparently was polluted by the operations of W.R. Grace and Beatrice Foods. The families and their lawyer, Jan Schlichtmann, then went to court. To make the movie, Disney agreed to pay Harr for the right to use his book and Schlichtmann for the right to use his name and life in the movie. It offered nothing to the families whose real names were *not* to be used. Disney's inaction produced another lawsuit by the Woburn families (with different lawyers), as well as a bill passed by the Massachusetts legislature that would specifically require film producers to obtain consent of people whose life stories were to be depicted, even in fictional films, television shows, or plays. After protests by MPAA President Jack Valenti that such a law would "shackle one of the dearest freedoms we possess as a nation, our right to free expression"

---

[f] *See* Peter Gielniak, *Tipping the Scales: Courts Struggle to Strike a Balance Between the Public Disclosure of Private Facts Tort & the First Amendment*, 39 Santa Clara L. Rev. 1217 (1999); Paul Marcus & Tara L. McMahon, *Limiting Disclosure of Rape Victims' Identities*, 64 Southern California L. Rev. 1019 (1991).

(and a warning that not many movies would be made in a state that passed such a law), Governor Paul Cellucci vetoed the bill.

The families continued their second "civil action" under existing Massachusetts common law of privacy, a suit that was eventually settled, with Disney paying the families an undisclosed sum. *A Civil Action* appeared on the screen, starring John Travolta and Robert Duvall, and won good reviews and several Oscar nominations. The question remains whether the law should give families a right to control fictionalized portrayals of their lives. And should there be any difference in the treatment of the families, the lawyer Schlichtmann, Judge Skinner, or the companies W.R. Grace and Beatrice Foods?

The standard formulation of the relevant common law doctrine bars revelation of information that would be "highly offensive and objectionable to a reasonable person of ordinary sensibilities." W. Page Keeton, et al., *Prosser and Keeton on the Law of Torts*, § 117, 857 (5th ed. 1984). Courts and scholars continue to debate the crucial ingredients of such a standard. Is it the specific factual revelation that has to be "shocking" or the general category of private material being disclosed? Should courts balance the individual's sensibilities against public fascination with the topic, or deem that the individual's privacy rights must always give way to any "legitimate" public interest in the material?

Needless to say, these situations raise issues not only about the appropriate scope of state privacy law, but also about the federal constitutional rights of the media to communicate with their readers and viewers. That is an especially sensitive debate when the news story in question relates to sexual matters or forcible rapes. State legislatures have rightly sought to protect the privacy of rape victims from public disclosure of what has happened to them. The problem, though, is that under both tort and constitutional law, courts are inclined to rule that once individuals have become involved in a public event, however involuntarily, they lose their right to have their identity and fate kept confidential.

It is clear that once a fact is included in a public record to which the public has a legal right of access (however sparingly that right would be exercised), the media may truthfully broadcast that fact without fear of reprisal. In *Cox Broadcasting v. Cohn*, 420 U.S. 469 (1975), the Supreme Court held that states cannot bar publication of truthful information contained in public records that are open to public inspection. A reporter for WSB-TV, a Cox Broadcasting television station, obtained the name of a deceased rape victim by reviewing criminal indictments of accused rapists that were available for public inspection. Despite a Georgia law prohibiting the broadcast or publication of a rape victim's identity, the reporter broadcast the victim's name in a news report concerning the rape. The victim's father filed suit alleging violation of the Georgia law and invasion of privacy. The Supreme Court held that state law could not both leave the information accessible to the general public, and bar publication by the print or broadcast media.

The Court noted that unlike other privacy claims, the tort of public disclosure protects individuals from publication of even truthful factual accounts of their especially private affairs. Thus, "[b]ecause the gravamen of the claim is the publication of information . . . it is here that claims of privacy most directly confront the constitutional freedoms of speech. . . ." *Id.* at 489. The court underscored that the general public relies on the media to report on public records. Further, the Court noted that the tort of privacy itself usually denies liability where publicity is given to information that is already public knowledge. Therefore, the Court held that when the state places information in the public domain in official court records, there is a presumption that the information is in the public interest and may be freely reported. According to the Court, "[p]ublic records by their very nature are of interest to those concerned with the administration of government. . . ." *Id.* at 495. The Court refused, however, to decide whether a state may ever define and protect an area of privacy free from unwanted publicity.

In *Gates v. Discovery Communications, Inc.*, 34 Cal. 4th 679, 21 Cal. Rptr. 3d 663, 101 P.3d 552 (2004), the California Supreme Court recently interpreted *Cox Broadcasting* to protect the publication by a television show, *The Prosecutor*, of a man's thirteen year old guilty plea to an accessory to murder charge. The man had since lived a lawful life and become a respected member of his community. The court stated that it made no difference that the information was no longer "newsworthy" because it could be found in publicly available official records. However, because of that distinctive feature of *Cox Broadcasting*—the information in question was already in court documents—the *Cox* holding has left lower courts to struggle to figure out which facts should be deemed private and which considered to be in the public domain. How much information is in the public record, whether the public can gain access to this record, how much time has passed since the plaintiff was a topic of public interest, and what steps the plaintiff has taken to secure a private life, are all factors that figure in the legal analysis.

In *Diaz v. Oakland Tribune, Inc.*, 139 Cal.App.3d 118, 188 Cal. Rptr. 762 (1983), the court grappled with a number of these issues. Toni Ann Diaz was the student body president of the College of Alameda and a student representative on the College Board of Trustees. In that capacity, Diaz became involved in a campus controversy and as a result received some media attention. Shortly thereafter a couple of students told Sidney Jones, a reporter at the Oakland Tribune, that Diaz was transsexual. Jones checked police files, and found a reference to Diaz that confirmed that she had once been a man. Jones subsequently revealed the information with the following item in his Tribune column:

> More Education Stuff: The students at the College of Alameda will be surprised to learn that their student body president, Toni Diaz, is no lady, but is in fact a man whose real name is Antonio.
>
> Now I realize, that in these times, such a matter is no big deal, but I suspect his female classmates in P.E. 97 may wish to make other showering arrangements.

*Id.* at 766.

Distraught by this revelation, Diaz sued for invasion of privacy. It turned out that Diaz had been born in 1942 as a male named Antonio Diaz. In 1975, the sex (and name) change took place, which Diaz disclosed only to family and long-time friends, not to new acquaintances. The revealing fact discovered by the reporter in the police files was that in 1971, before the sex change, Antonio Diaz had been arrested for soliciting an undercover woman police officer. Putting this fact together with other clues gave Jones the confirmation he needed to write his column. Should Diaz have a privacy action in this situation? Recall the debate within the California Supreme Court in the *Shulman* case about whether and when there should be any such rights under state common law. In addition, how would such a claim by Diaz square with the Supreme Court's First Amendment ruling in *Cox Broadcasting*? With the analysis of the privacy-speech issues in the following case?

## ROSS V. MIDWEST COMMUNICATIONS, INC.

United States Court of Appeals, Fifth Circuit, 1989.
870 F.2d 271.

HIGGINBOTHAM, CIRCUIT JUDGE.

[The person who raped Marla Ross in 1983 was never caught by the police. At one point in the police investigation, Ross viewed a suspects' lineup that included Steven Fossum, but Ross said that her rapist was not in the lineup. Fossum was, however, convicted of two other rapes during that period.

In 1986, WCCO-TV, owned by Midwest Communications, presented a documentary designed to show that Fossum was actually innocent. A key feature of the production was that significant details in the other two rapes were very similar to those of the Ross case (including the pretext used by the rapist to get into the private residence, his sexual demands on the victims, and the rapist's fixation with baths and showers). Since Ross had explicitly rejected Fossum as her attacker, the argument was that someone else had committed the two other crimes for which Fossum had been convicted. Not only did WCCO win the Dupont Columbia Award for this broadcast, but Fossum got a pardon from the Governor of Texas for his second conviction and a pending motion for retrial of the first.

During the television show, WCCO specifically identified Ross by her first name and showed the house in which she was living at the time of her rape. The station neither sought nor received Ross' consent for her portrayal. Ross and her husband sued for invasion of their privacy. The issue in this motion for summary dismissal of the claim was whether the newsworthiness of Ross' identity as a rape victim precluded as a matter of law a privacy suit against WCCO.]

* * *

II

* * *

Ross, "in order to recover for public disclosure of private facts about [herself], must show (1) that publicity was given to matters concerning [her] private life, (2) the publication of which would be highly offensive to a reasonable person of ordinary sensibilities, and (3) that the matter publicized is not of legitimate public concern." *Industrial Foundation of the South v. Texas Industrial Accident Board*, 540 S.W.2d 668, at 682, citing W. Prosser, *Law of Torts* § 117, p. 809 (4th ed. 1971).

To apply this test, we must first ascertain what "private facts" Ross is alleging WCCO to have disclosed. There are at least three possibilities: (A) the details of the rape itself; (B) the allegedly false details included in the report; and (C) Ross's first name and the appearance of her former residence.

Ross has contended vigorously that the details of the rape were themselves "private facts." Yet these facts were clearly of "legitimate public concern." The Ross brief itself effectively concedes as much. With respect to WCCO's suggestion that Fossum is innocent of the Lewis rape because innocent of the Ross rape, the brief says, "WCCO's theory was intriguing and, if verifiable, undoubtedly worthy of public disclosure in one form or another." The brief adds the proviso that "the facts of Mrs. Ross's rape did not fit the theory," but this proviso amounts at most to an argument that WCCO's theory was wrong. That argument does not generate a material issue of fact as to whether the theory addressed a matter of legitimate public concern. The details of the Ross rape are relevant to Fossum's innocence, a legitimate matter of public concern, so long as the Ross and Lewis rapes are sufficiently similar to generate a reasonable argument that the rapes were committed by the same individual. The argument need not be convincing to all, or even most, of its auditors. It need only be, as Ross's brief nicely puts it, reasonably "intriguing" to a concerned public.

There is no doubt that WCCO's report on the Ross and Lewis rapes meets this standard. The excuses used by each rapist to enter the victims' homes were strikingly similar: both attackers claimed to be employed by Genex homes, and to have lost a dog. Even absent the details contested by Ross, the demands made by the two rapists were, again, strikingly similar. So were the descriptions provided by the victims. We have no difficulty finding that, under Texas law, WCCO's report of these details does not give rise to a cause of action for invasion of privacy, for the details are evidently of "legitimate public concern."

The second possibility, that the "private facts" are the allegedly false details of the Ross rape, is inconsistent with Ross's apparent theory of liability. She did not file a libel claim. Indeed, the problem with such a cause of action, from Ross's perspective, would be that the damages she seeks stem from the disclosure of the uncontested, rather than the disputed, details of her rape. Nor would the inclusion of some inaccuracies in WCCO's documentary detract from the newsworthiness of the facts correctly reported. We do not understand Ross to rely on these allegedly false details as a ground for her suit. Rather, we understand her to suggest that WCCO's inclusion of some false claims is evidence that the true material was not newsworthy.

The third possibility, that the "private fact" is Ross's identity as the rape victim, is the basis for Ross's strongest argument. She contends that even if the details of her rape were newsworthy, the documentary could have been produced without mentioning her name, and thus without disclosing the indignities of her rape to the world. This argument, however, is difficult to accommodate within the literal terms of the privacy tort definition, quoted above. Ross's name, residence, or "identity" are not easily characterized as "private, embarrassing facts." The more common form of privacy tort involves the disclosure of facts which are interesting precisely because the facts are about a known, specified individual. *See, e.g., Gill v. Snow*, 644 S.W.2d 222; *Campbell v. Seabury Press*, 614 F.2d 395 (5th Cir. 1980). The public concern over these facts is inseparable from the public concern over the connection between the facts and the individual involved.

To bring this case within the ambit of the *Industrial South* test, we must characterize the essential question as whether Ross's connection to the rape details—themselves a subject of public concern—was itself also a matter of public concern. This issue is apparently one of first impression in Texas. We have not found any Texas cases contesting the newsworthiness of an individual's personal connection to the details of an event which are concededly newsworthy in themselves.

The Tenth Circuit did, however, consider this question in *Gilbert v. Medical Economics Co.*, 665 F.2d 305 (10th Cir. 1981). *Gilbert* involved a periodical article describing an alleged breakdown in the evaluation of a doctor's fitness, and a consequent malpractice problem. The plaintiff, Gilbert, was the subject of the story. Her name was used, and details of her personal life were revealed. The trial court granted summary judgment for the defendant on constitutional grounds. The Tenth Circuit affirmed. The court cited with approval our decision in *Campbell*, and construed the scope of the First Amendment protection against liability for publication by reference to the elements of the privacy tort: the constitution barred liability for the dissemination of true, private information if no liability would exist under the common law tort. The Court of Appeals concluded that Gilbert's connection to the malpractice incident was a matter of legitimate public concern. The court stated that "plaintiff's photograph and name" were "substantially relevant to a newsworthy topic because they strengthen the impact and credibility of the article. They obviate any impression that the problems raised in the article are remote or hypothetical, thus providing an aura of immediacy and even urgency that might not exist had plaintiff's name and photograph been suppressed."

WCCO and its reporters make a similar argument for its use of Ross's first name, and for its photograph of her former residence. The journalists argue that the use of Ross's name, and the picture of her residence, provides a "personalized frame of reference that fosters perception and understanding," and avoids the loss of credibility that comes with anonymity.

This argument has force. The infamous Janet Cooke controversy (about the fabricated, Pulitzer-Prize winning Washington Post series on the child-addict, Jimmy) suggests the legitimate ground for doubts that may arise about the accuracy of a documentary that uses only pseudonyms. On the other hand, WCCO did use some pseudonyms in its documentary, and WCCO could have demonstrated the accuracy of its report by using the police department's offense number for each incident. Numbers, however, are easily forgotten, and would most likely have less impact.

The argument establishing a logical nexus between the rape victim's name and a matter of legitimate public concern is peculiarly strong in this case because the point of the publication was to persuade the public, and in turn authorities, to a particular view of particular incidents. Communicating that this particular victim was a real person with roots in the community, and showing WCCO's knowledge of the details of the attack upon her, were of unique importance to the credibility and persuasive force of the story. We thus may, and now do, decide that Ross's connection to the details of the rape in this case was a matter of legitimate public interest, without also deciding that the name of a rape victim is always a matter of public concern if her rape is a matter of public concern.

We reach this conclusion aware that judges, acting with the benefit of hindsight, must resist the temptation to edit journalists aggressively. Reporters must have some freedom to respond to journalistic exigencies without fear that even a slight, and understandable, mistake will subject them to liability. Exuberant judicial blue-pencilling after-the-fact would blunt the quills of even the most honorable journalists. Yet we need not now decide the extent of judicial deference to editorial discretion. Here, it is at least arguable, even with the benefit of hindsight, that WCCO was correct in its judgment about the newsworthiness of the victim's identity. That conclusion, although it no way diminishes the victim's legitimate distress, justifies the district court's grant of summary judgment to defendants.

III

Our holding today is narrow. Our decision turns upon the peculiar facts present in this case. We point out that the doctrine we announce today, although it justifies the district court's award of summary judgment against Ross, does not leave rape victims without any protection against public disclosure of their names. First, the discussion above leaves open the possibility that the rape victim's name may be irrelevant when the details of the rape victim's experience are not so uniquely crucial to the story as they are in this case, or when the publisher's "public concern" goes to a general, sociological issue. Second, the discussion leaves open the state's power to protect rape victims' privacy by preserving the confidentiality of the state's records, and punishing any who steal the information. Liability for the wrongful taking of information could encompass damages resulting from the foreseeable publication of the information. Consider *Landmark Communications, Inc. v. Virginia*, 435 U.S. 829, 836–37 (1978) (suggesting that Virginia might preserve the confidentiality of judicial disciplinary proceedings by punishing those who disclose the information, rather than third parties who publish the information).

* * *

Affirmed.

## *QUESTIONS FOR DISCUSSION*

1. A key reason advanced by the court in ruling against Ross was that use of her first name and the picture of her home "personalized" the story and thus "avoided the loss of credibility that comes with anonymity." Does this mean—should it mean—that the media must have an overriding First

Amendment right to enhance the emotional impact, rather than just the intellectual content, of its stories?

2. Nancy Tatum shot and killed a male intruder when the man entered her bedroom late at night, and approached her with a knife in his hand and his penis exposed. The police judged the case to be a justifiable homicide. When they gave reporters details of the case, the police said they informed the reporters that this was a sexual assault. Under the Georgia Rape Shield Act, publication of the name of a sexual assault victim is prohibited. The *Macon Telegraph*, though, published both Tatum's name and address in its story about the case, titled "Macon Woman Kills Attacker in Bedroom." Can Tatum's privacy claim be upheld, given the ruling in *Cox Broadcasting*, described earlier? *See Macon Telegraph Publishing v. Tatum*, 263 Ga. 678, 436 S.E.2d 655 (1993). *See generally The Florida Star v. B.J.F.*, 491 U.S. 524 (1989) (rejecting privacy claim where police accidentally place details of rape incident in press room, though leaving open the possibility of suit in some circumstances).

3. A Georgia man with AIDS agreed to go on a live television show about this topic, on condition that his face would not be recognizable to the audience. Because of an initial mistake in the level of electronic digitization used by the station to distort the telecast image of the man's face, he was recognizable for the first seven seconds of the program. The result was that the man's condition became known in the community and he felt compelled to leave his job. Should a $500,000 jury verdict for breach of privacy be upheld? *See Multimedia WMAZ v. Kubach*, 212 Ga. App. 707, 443 S.E.2d 491 (1994).

---

Another decision, *Howell v. New York Post*, 81 N.Y.2d 115, 596 N.Y.S.2d 350, 612 N.E.2d 699 (1993), posed even more starkly the policy question of what relationship there must be between the individual whose private facts are being disclosed and the story in which there is a public interest. The case arose, though, in New York, whose privacy law remains severely truncated by comparison with other states. New York was the first state to consider and reject a common law privacy right (in *Roberson v. Rochester Folding Box*, 171 N.Y. 538, 64 N.E. 442 (1902)), then the first to enact such a right by statute, Sections 50 and 51 of its Civil Rights Act, and then (by contrast to California) the first to exclude any supplemental common law privacy rights that were being developed by courts around the country (*Stephano v. News Group Publ., Inc.*, 64 N.Y.2d 174, 485 N.Y.S.2d 220, 474 N.E.2d 580 (1984)).

The plaintiff in the *Howell* case, Pamela Howell, was a patient in a private psychiatric hospital, Four Winds, located in Westchester County. To aid in her recovery, Howell's hospitalization was kept secret from all but her immediate family. A fellow patient was Hedda Nussbaum, who a year before was involved in a notorious homicide case, in which Nussbaum's live-in lover, Joel Steinberg, had abused and then killed his six-year-old child Lisa. Though Hedda had become Lisa's "adoptive" mother, she had done little or nothing to protect the child, partly because Steinberg was regularly abusing her as well.

In 1988, the New York Post sneaked a photographer onto Four Winds' secluded grounds to take a picture of Nussbaum, who then happened to be walking with Howell. The hospital director called and asked the Post editor not to run the picture. Nonetheless, the photo appeared on the front page of the Post the next day, side-by-side with a picture of Nussbaum taken a year earlier, just after her arrest. The caption read:

> The battered face above belongs to the Hedda Nussbaum people remember—the former live-in lover of accused child-killer, Joel Steinberg. The serene woman in jeans at left is the same Hedda, strolling with a companion in the grounds of the upstate psychiatric center where her face and mind are healing from the terrible wounds Steinberg inflicted.

Howell sued the Post for both invasion of privacy and intentional infliction of emotional distress. The Court of Appeals stated that the statutory privacy provision simply barred the use of a person's name or picture for "advertising or trade" purposes, and did not embody a distinct tort for public disclosure of true but embarrassing private facts. The reading of that statute in *Stephano* and other decisions precluded any liability for "publication concerning newsworthy events or matters of public interest," which could also include pictures unless the latter bore "no real relationship to the article." Clearly the story about and picture of Nussbaum were newsworthy. With respect to Howell's claim that her inclusion in the photo was unnecessary, the court said:

> . . . The photograph of a visibly healed Nussbaum, interacting with her smiling, fashionably clad "companion," offers a stark contrast to the adjacent photograph of Nussbaum's disfigured face. The visual impact would not have been the same had the Post cropped plaintiff out of the photograph, as she suggests was required.

612 N.E.2d at 704. The court went on to hold that because the Post had a "right" under the state's privacy law to publish Howell's picture, she could not attack that "privileged conduct" under the general tort of intentional infliction of emotional distress.

### *QUESTIONS FOR DISCUSSION*

1. Suppose this case were to arise under broader common law privacy doctrine—for example, under Texas law as seen in *Ross*? What is the appropriate legal—and editorial—treatment of a photograph of Howell taken together with Nussbaum?

2. Miriam Booher appeared as a guest on the *Phil Donahue Show* to tell the story of how her second husband, William Booher (a police officer), had had sex with Miriam's 11-year old daughter by her first marriage (whom Booher had adopted following their marriage). The result of that incest and statutory rape was that the daughter, Nancy, became pregnant and gave birth to a boy, William Booher, Jr. Miriam, who did not then know who was the boy's father, agreed that they should adopt and raise him as Nancy's apparent brother. Five years later, Miriam learned that her husband was actually William Jr.'s father; the couple did, however, continue to live together. After another ten years had passed, William Jr. finally learned the truth about his birth. He decided to stay with his father, and Miriam left and divorced her husband. Miriam then sent this story of her life to several national television talk shows, and Donahue responded with an invitation to appear on his program. Miriam's daughter Nancy (now married and named Anonsen) asked her mother not to go on the show and disclose to the public these facts that only a few close friends and relatives now knew about. Miriam decided to go on *Donahue* anyway. The resulting publicity from her appearance forced the son, William Jr., to transfer to another high school to avoid harassment from his classmates. Should the daughter, Nancy, and the son, William Jr., be able to sue both Miriam and Donahue for invasion of their privacy? *See Anonsen v. Donahue*, 857 S.W.2d 700 (Tex. App. 1993).

3. In 1975, Oliver Sipple stopped Sara Jane Moore from shooting President Gerald Ford on the streets of San Francisco. Two days later, in the midst of the national attention to this near-assassination, San Francisco Chronicle columnist Herb Caen wrote in his column that Sipple, "the man who saved the President's life," was the hero of San Francisco's gay community, of which Sipple was a locally-known member. Unfortunately for Sipple, the national media picked up this item, which brought news of Sipple's homosexuality back to his parents and siblings in the Midwest and led to his being abandoned by his family and suffering severe embarrassment and anguish. (Indeed, a number of years later, Sipple took his own life.) Sipple sued the Chronicle for invasion of his privacy rights. What is the appropriate result? *See Sipple v. Chronicle Publishing*, 154 Cal. App. 3d 1040, 201 Cal. Rptr. 665 (1984).

4. Nicholas Lemann's book *The Promised Land*, published by Alfred A. Knopf, was one of the leading non-fiction works of 1991. The book presented its account of *The Great Black Migration* (from the rural south to the industrial north) and through the stories of a number of African-American families. One of the individuals depicted in the book was Ruby Daniels. Ruby had been married to and had several children by Luther Daniels, until Luther left her and married (now) Dorothy Daniels who had lived in the same Chicago building. The book detailed Luther's sex life with Dorothy while married to Ruby, his drinking, joblessness, and criminal record, and the impact this had on Ruby and their children. Luther and Dorothy, who are now "upstanding, church-going members of their community," sued for invasion of privacy (as well as defamation). Should this book's treatment of

Luther and Dorothy's lives be actionable? Are these facts "truly private," given that many of them—particularly the sexual relations—are described in divorce documents, though they were embellished in Lemann's interviews with Ruby? Suppose there had been a "no-fault" divorce proceeding with none of these facts depicted in court records. Should the fact that Luther often drank in bars and regularly lost his jobs be deemed "private" or "public?" Should the law require that the author secure the consent of everyone portrayed in such fashion, or fictionalize the names and identities? *See Haynes v. Alfred A. Knopf, Inc.*, 8 F.3d 1222 (7th Cir. 1993).

5. Another New York Privacy Act case involved two construction workers, one male and one female, who were observed by a CBS television crew walking down Madison Avenue, hand in hand, on a beautiful spring day. The crew filmed the two and ran a brief segment on an evening broadcast, *Couples in Love in New York*, depicting the intriguing "hard hats in love" angle. The item ran against the vehement objections of the couple, the man being married and the woman engaged to be married. Can they sue? *See De Gregorio v. CBS*, 123 Misc.2d 491, 473 N.Y.S.2d 922 (1984).

6. A newspaper runs a story about a young teenager who has concealed her entire pregnancy from her parents, given birth to the child while alone in her bedroom at home, and then had her brother deliver the infant to a nearby hospital. Should the girl be able to sue the newspaper for identifying her by name? *See Pasadena Star-News v. Superior Court*, 203 Cal.App.3d 131, 249 Cal. Rptr. 729 (1988).

## E. FALSE LIGHT PORTRAYALS[g]

This brings us to a third category of privacy doctrine—"false light." Plaintiffs in these cases assert that untrue facts have been published which place them in a false light in the public eye. Though the historical antecedents and legal technicalities are different, there is a common core to false light privacy and defamation. In entertainment docudrama cases, for example, it is quite common for the plaintiff to assert both causes of action. The justification offered for preserving the two torts is that defamation is focused on the damage to the plaintiff's reputation in the community, while false light privacy concentrates on the psychological harm caused by objectionable misrepresentations.

Given the similar impact of the two torts on media defendants, it is not surprising that just three years after its momentous *New York Times*

[g] *See* Melville B. Nimmer, *The Right To Speak From* Times *To* Time: *First Amendment Theory Applied To Libel & Misapplied To Privacy*, 56 California L. Rev. 935 (1968); Diana L. Zimmerman, *Requiem For a Heavyweight: A Farewell To Warren & Brandeis' Privacy Tort*, 68 Cornell L. Rev. 291 (1983); Gary Schwartz, *Explaining & Justifying A Limited Tort Of False Light Invasion Of Privacy*, 41 Case Western Reserve L. Rev. 885 (1991); Randall P. Bezanson, *The Right To Privacy Revisited: Privacy, News, & Social Change, 1810–1990*, 80 California L. Rev. 1133 (1992); and Ruth Gavison, *Too Early For A Requiem: Warren & Brandeis Were Right On Privacy vs. Free Speech*, 43 South Carolina L. Rev. 437 (1992).

holding about the First Amendment and defamation, the Court returned to the same issue in the privacy context. As we saw in Chapter 1, *Time v. Hill*, 385 U.S. 374 (1967), was concerned with the Hill family which had been held hostage in their suburban Pennsylvania home by escaped convicts.[h] Happily the Hills had been treated decently by their captors and were released unharmed from the ordeal. The incident drew enormous media attention, and partly to escape the public spotlight and restore their private lives, the Hills moved to Connecticut.

Unfortunately for the Hills, Joseph Hayes used their story as the basis for a book and then a play, *The Desperate Hours*. This fictionalized treatment depicted a family that had been both brutalized by their captors and heroic in their resistance. On the occasion of the Broadway opening of *The Desperate Hours*, Life Magazine wrote an article that described the play as a "reenactment" of the Hills' ordeal. Complementing the article were pictures of the Broadway actors playing the Hills and the convicts in the Pennsylvania home. The Hills filed suit against Life (not Hayes) under the New York Privacy Act, alleging that the article portrayed them in a "false light" by implying that they had had the same hostage experience as the family in the play. The Life reporter's testimony was that while he knew the play was "fictionalized" to some extent, he believed its facts were sparked by the Hill story. No effort had been made to check Life's own file of press clippings on the Hill's actual experience to see exactly how the play had altered the original facts.

This time a closely-divided Supreme Court ruled that the *New York Times*' "actual malice" standard—in the sense of "knowing or reckless disregard" of the falsity—must also apply to "false light" privacy claims. Tort liability could not be imposed for "an innocent or negligent" misstatement, because to do so "would present a grave hazard of discouraging the press from exercising its constitutional guarantees." The jury verdict in favor of the Hills was overturned. This is not to imply that plaintiffs can never prevail under the "knowing or reckless disregard" standard. Indeed, the Hills and their attorney, Richard Nixon, eventually settled the case for nearly the same amount as had been awarded by the jury. Tragically, Mrs. Hill committed suicide five years later.

In *Cantrell v. Forest City Publishing*, 419 U.S. 245 (1974), Margaret Cantrell's husband had been killed along with 43 others when an Ohio River bridge collapsed. Five months later, as a follow-up to the original stories, the Cleveland Plain Dealer published a feature article that used the Cantrell family's condition to illustrate the impact of this disaster on local family lives. The article had a number of inaccuracies in its depiction of the "abject poverty" of the Cantrell's, including a comment attributed to Margaret Cantrell though she had not been there when the

[h] For an engaging account of the Hills' story by one of their counsel, see Leonard Garment, *Annals of Law: The Hill Case*, The New Yorker 90 (April 17, 1989).

reporter spoke to her children and took pictures of them and the home. On these facts, the Supreme Court upheld a "false light" privacy verdict against the newspaper.

With respect to fictionalized entertainment products—i.e., the docudrama—the "actual malice" test may be even easier to meet. A particularly striking case is *Spahn v. Julian Messner*, 21 N.Y.2d 124, 286 N.Y.S.2d 832, 233 N.E.2d 840 (1967). This case involved a largely imaginary biography of Warren Spahn, a Hall-of-Fame pitcher for the National League Braves. The biography was aimed at a children's audience. The author had never met Spahn, let alone interviewed him. Instead, the writer began with news stories about the basic facts of Spahn's life and career, and then made up a host of imaginary but dramatic episodes in Spahn's life: a heroic World War II career that produced a Bronze Star; the serious psychological impact on his father of the war injury to Spahn's pitching arm; several romantic (non-sexual) incidents in Spahn's relationship with his wife; Spahn's mid-season preoccupation with his wife's first pregnancy; and fictional conversations between Spahn and Casey Stengel, Jackie Robinson, and other baseball notables. (These and other examples are detailed in the trial decision at 43 Misc.2d 219, 250 N.Y.S.2d 529 (1964).) The New York Court of Appeals concluded (at 18 N.Y.2d 324, 274 N.Y.S.2d 877, 221 N.E.2d 543 (1966)) that fictionalizing the "personality" of a public figure for purposes of commercial publishing constituted a violation of New York's Privacy Act, and the court issued an injunction against distribution of the book.

*Spahn* was litigated at a crucial time in the evolution of this branch of First Amendment law. The path-breaking *New York Times Co. v. Sullivan* decision was rendered by the Supreme Court in the early rounds of the *Spahn* litigation. *Spahn* was then appealed to the Supreme Court along with *Time Inc. v. Hill*; after the Court used *Hill* to expand the scope of the "actual malice" requirement, it remanded *Spahn* back to the New York courts for another look. The verdict of the state Court of Appeals was the same. However attractive it might be for readers of a book to have the story livened up with a host of dramatic incidents, the author was not entitled to use "imaginary incidents, manufactured dialogue and a manipulated chronology" that was based on no serious research effort to document the truth of these parts of the story.

> To hold that this [largely nonexistent] research effort entitles the defendants to publish the kind of knowing fictionalization presented here would amount to granting a literary license which is not only unnecessary to the protection of free speech but destructive of an individual's right—albeit a limited one in the case of a public figure—to be free of the commercial exploitation of his name and personality.

286 N.Y.S.2d at 836, 233 N.E.2d at 843. The injunction was maintained.

---

Perhaps because of how the law has developed since *Spahn*, but more likely because of the way the movie portrayed him, the Nobel prize-winning scientist John Nash did not sue Universal for the way its Oscar-winning *A Beautiful Mind* had Russell Crowe displaying his life and character as much more beautiful than it really was. However, a far more dramatic set of events in the early 1990's produced both a hit movie and a lawsuit. A young woman named Teena Brandon living in Lincoln, Nebraska decided that she would start to live as a man. She changed her name to Brandon Teena, altered her appearance as well as her clothing, and moved to nearby Falls City. There she met and fell in love with a woman named Lana Tisdel. Brandon ended up being killed by a pair of male ex-convicts who knew the Tisdel family and were appalled to learn that Brandon was really a woman. The resulting murder produced not only a criminal prosecution, but a book *All She Wanted*, a television documentary *The Teena Brandon Story*, and then the Fox Searchlight movie *Boys Don't Cry*. In that movie Hillary Swank played Brandon and Chloe Sevigny played Tisdel, using the girls' real names. Tisdel's attorney filed suit against Fox after the studio refused to remove her name from the film.

Tisdel claimed a violation of her right to control the use of her personal name and likeness, false light invasion of privacy, and defamation. In particular, she objected to the movie depicting her as someone who overindulges in alcohol and drugs, who maintains her sexual relations with Brandon even after learning she is a woman, and at the end falls asleep in the room next to where Brandon is being raped and killed. Tisdel's suit alleged that this portrayal of her as "lazy . . . white trash . . . [and] skanky snake" not only cost her a job in Fall City, but left her "scorned and abandoned by her friends and family, some of whom will now believe she is a lesbian who did nothing to stop a murder." Fox initially dismissed this lawsuit as groundless because the film had portrayed her relationship with Brandon in an "emotionally true" fashion. But just before the 2000 Oscar night (where Swank won Best Actress) Fox opted for an "amicable" settlement of the suit.

### *QUESTIONS FOR DISCUSSION*

1. *Boys Don't Cry* poses broader legal questions. First, assuming that the basic facts are accurate, should Tisdel have a right of privacy to block use of her real name in such a fictional movie (as opposed to nonfiction news reports, books, or documentaries)? Second, assuming some of the movie facts are inaccurate but that the Fox script-writers believed them to be true, what

is the appropriate standard for determining the liability for such a false portrayal with Tisdel's actual name (or even without it)?

2. A.J. Quinnel has authored a work of fiction entitled *In the Name of the Father*, which was published by NAL publishing. The novel's plot involves a scheme by three Vatican officials to kill the then-Soviet Premier Yuri Andropov in an effort to prevent future assassination attempts on the Pope's life. Quinnel gives a character in the novel the real name and office of Archbishop Marcinkus, a well-known Roman Catholic prelate, in order, he said, to give the story a sense of historical accuracy. Marcinkus' role in the novel is a prominent one, for it is he who conceives of the plan and proposes it to his co-conspirators.

In the preface to the novel, Quinnel inserted the following statement:

> This book is a work of fiction. Names, characters, places, and incidents are used fictitiously, and any resemblance to actual persons, living or dead, except as noted below . . . is entirely coincidental. Some real people such as . . . Paul Marcinkus . . . appear as characters in the book to give a sense of historical accuracy. However, their actions and motivations are entirely fictitious and should not be considered real or factual.

Marcinkus has filed suit against NAL Publishing alleging that his name, office and background have been used in violation of New York Privacy Act. What are the competing arguments? *See Marcinkus v. NAL Publishing Inc.*, 138 Misc.2d 256, 522 N.Y.S.2d 1009 (1987).

3. Nellie Mitchell is a ninety-seven-year-old woman who has operated a local newsstand in Arkansas since 1963. Her newsstand made her something of a local legend in her small town community. In 1980, a picture of Mitchell was featured in a story in the Examiner, one of Globe International Publishing's supermarket tabloids, portraying Mitchell as a "paperboy" at age 85. In 1990, the Sun, another Globe supermarket tabloid, published a story featuring a picture of Nellie Mitchell under a heading, "Pregnancy forces Granny to quit work at age 101." The text of the story inside refers to an Australian "paper gal" named Audrey Wiles, with another picture of Mitchell. Some residents in Mitchell's small town saw only the picture and the Sun headline while waiting in a grocery store check-out line. That edition of the Sun was, however, a quick sellout in Mitchell's local area.

Mitchell filed suit against the Globe and won a jury award of $650,000 in compensatory and $850,000 in punitive damages. The Globe appealed, arguing that Mitchell has no claim as a matter of law. What kind of legal claims do you think were filed by Mitchell against the Globe? What defenses would you advance on the Globe's behalf? What should be the outcome? *See Peoples Bank & Trust Company of Mountain Home v. Globe International Publishing, Inc.*, 978 F.2d 1065 (8th Cir. 1992).

4. Reporters from a Cleveland television station accompanied federal Drug Enforcement Agency (DEA) officials on a drug raid of an apartment.

Kim Rogers happened to be in the apartment picking up her children from a babysitter. The babysitter/tenant, though, was also allowing crack dealers to make and sell crack in her apartment. After verifying that Rogers was not involved in drug dealing or use, the reporter on this story excluded her from footage on his show. However, another station reporter working on a special, *The Silent Victims*, portraying the child-victims of drug use, happened to include the shot of Rogers in the station's film footage. The particular segment on which Rogers' face appeared referred to her children as "silent victims . . . caught in a parental crack trap." Should Rogers be able to sue for false light privacy, as well as for defamation? *See Rogers v. Buckel*, 83 Ohio App.3d 653, 615 N.E.2d 669 (1992).

5. Joseph Wambaugh has written a book, *Lines and Shadows*, about San Diego police officers assigned to the Border Alien Robbery Force (BARF), a unit whose role is to combat crime in the Mexican border area. A current member of the BARF squad, Kenneth Kelly, agreed, for $5,000, to assign Wambaugh "the right to depict and/or portray [him] . . . to such extent and in such manner, either factually or fictionally, as [Wambaugh] in [his] discretion and pursuant to any contract with [Kelly] may determine . . ." The book does depict Kelly by name, but portrays him (allegedly inaccurately) as a heavy-drinking, promiscuous man who fights with his wife and pimps for his fellow officers. Does that contract language suffice to block a defamation and false light privacy action by Kelly? *See Kelly v. William Morrow*, 186 Cal.App.3d 1625, 231 Cal. Rptr. 497 (1986).

6. Eminem's 1989 breakthrough album, The Slim Shady LP, contained a song entitled "Brain Damage." A sanitation worker, Deangelo Bailey, who had gone to elementary school with Eminem (when he was Marshall Mathers III), was shocked to hear this song beginning with "Way before my baby daughter Hailey, I was harassed daily by this fat kid named D'Angelo Bailey," and then went on with many more lines about Bailey beating Eminem up, like "He banged my head against the urinal til he broke my nose, soaked my clothes in blood, grabbed me and choked my throat." Bailey admitted that as an eighth grader he had "bullied" the fourth grader Eminem by occasionally giving him a "little shove," he firmly denied anything like the behavior described in "Brain Damage." What was the appropriate Michigan ruling on whether this case should be allowed to go to trial, after the lower court judge's finding that "The lyrics are stories no one would take as fact, they're an exaggeration of a childish act?" *See Bailey v. Mathers III, a/k/a Eminem Slim Shady*, 33 Media L. Rep. 205 (Mich. App. 2005).

---

A number of important issues are still unsettled regarding the content, and even the value, of the false light privacy tort.[i] It is clear after

[i] Before this appellate verdict had come down, Professor Don T. Carter had authored a revised and updated version of his book, *Scottsboro: A Tragedy of the American South* (Louisiana State U. Press, 1979). A key addition to the book was Carter's personal account of the final Scottsboro trial that had taken place in 1977, pitting Victoria Price against both Carter's

*Hill* and *Spahn* that "actual malice" is a requirement of false light as well as defamation claims brought by public figures. Does that mean, though, that the *Gertz* negligence standard for defamation of private figures also applies to false light claims by the latter? Is there any reason why the *Gertz* federal constitutional rule should not be applied to false light liability?

The more fundamental question is why have a false light tort in addition to defamation (as illustrated by the two-part claim in the *Rogers* case noted above). Under conventional formulations, defamation protects people from untrue statements that are disparaging of their reputations, while false light protects against untrue statements that are highly offensive to one's sensibilities. The Supreme Court of North Carolina, in *Renwick v. News & Observer Publishing Co.*, 310 N.C. 312, 312 S.E.2d 405 (1984), found that the latter protection was simply duplicative and refused to adopt an independent false light tort for that state. The contrary view was elaborated by Judge Richard Posner, in *Douglass v. Hustler Magazine, Inc.*, 769 F.2d 1128 (7th Cir. 1985), as a predicate for the Seventh Circuit's judgment that Illinois would adopt false light liability.

In reflecting on this issue, consider a number of examples from actual cases. In *Mitchell*, a 101-year-old woman was said to be pregnant. In *Spahn*, a great pitcher was said to have won a Bronze Star and to have agonized in mid-season about his wife's first pregnancy. In *Chuy v. Philadelphia Eagles*, 595 F.2d 1265 (3d Cir. 1979), an NFL team doctor said that one of his team's players was suffering from a rare and potentially fatal disease. (Several years ago, Elizabeth Taylor was said to be dying of lupus.) In *Hill*, a family was said to have been brutally abused by escaped convicts. In *Youssoupoff v. CBS Inc.*, 48 Misc.2d 700, 265 N.Y.S.2d 754 (1965), a Russian exile was portrayed as having been raped by Rasputin. Assume that these assertions are false. Are they defamatory in the sense of disparaging the subject's reputation? Are the non-defamatory statements still highly offensive to one's sensibilities? Is there a significant area of personal protection that false light adds to traditional defamation law?

If you agree with Judge Posner about the independent value of false light protection, this poses a second question about the interplay of the "false light" and the "true but embarrassing" categories of privacy law. Recall the *Diaz* case from the previous section, which indicated that the Oakland Tribune's *truthful* assertion that a student president had undergone a sex change was actionable. Suppose that the Tribune's assertion about Diaz had been *false*, but the reporter honestly and reasonably believed it to be true. Does the *Hill* and *Gertz* requirement of

---

Bancroft Prize-winning book and the NBC's docudrama, both of which had assumed that Price (as well as any possible defamation or privacy claim) had already passed away.

constitutional "fault" mean that Diaz could not sue for a false statement about her *persona*, but could sue for a true one? What exactly is the significance of "falsity" in designing legal protection against invasions of individual privacy?

There is another potential difference between defamation and privacy that may explain the practical difference in family reactions to two movies. The first movie, *Hoodlum,* released by MGM/USA in late 1997, depicted the 1930s battle between an African American Ellsworth "Bumpy" Johnson (played by Laurence Fishburne) and a Jewish mobster Dutch Schultz (played by Tim Roth) for control of the numbers racket in Harlem. Thomas Dewey (played by William Atherton) was named and portrayed as a corrupt New York prosecutor who was then on the take from the Mafia gangster leader Lucky Luciano (played by Andy Garcia) to help Schultz try to defeat Bumpy Johnson's effort.

The truth of the matter, though, was that Dewey had actually been a "crime-busting" prosecutor in New York City whom Schultz had plotted to kill, and Dewey had racked up 72 convictions of organized crime members (including Luciano) before he went on to become Governor of New York State and almost President of the United States. When the family of Dewey (who had been dead for many years) learned of *Hoodlum*, they immediately wrote the studio, strongly protesting this portrayal of their relative. MGM head Frank Mancuso replied that "the film was a work of fiction, and it was presented as such to the public. MGM has not violated any legally-cognizable right of either your father or your family." With respect to defamation law, the right to sue clearly passes away with the person whose reputation was defamed. Yet, that doctrine does not necessarily apply to the newer privacy right to protection from false light portrayals.

That distinction was subsequently tested by the 2000 movie, *The Perfect Storm*. This movie tells a story of what might have happened on a commercial fishing ship, Andrea Gail, which left Massachusetts for a late-season expedition in 1991, and became caught up in a gigantic storm that eventually sunk the ship and killed the six people on it. The family of the ship captain Bill Tyne, who was played by George Clooney, sued Time Warner for having tarnished the image of their deceased relative. They claimed the movie portrayed Tyne "in a false and unflattering light," as someone who had "piloted Andrea Gail in an unprofessional, unseaworthy and incompetent manner and as having suffered a self-imposed death, abandoning his crew and any hope of survival," because he was depicted as "emotionally aloof, reckless, excessive risk-taking, self-absorbed, emasculated, despondent, obsessed and maniacal." No such lawsuit had been filed regarding the best-selling book, *The Perfect Storm*, on which the movie was explicitly based under a licensing contract.

In 2002, Judge Conway dismissed *The Perfect Storm* lawsuit just before it was to go to trial. The judge relied on a Florida decision, *Loft v. Fuller*, 408 So.2d 619 (Fla.App. 1981), involving a book and movie, *The Ghost of Flight 401*, about an Eastern Airlines plane crash and the role of the dead pilot, to dismiss this case because the Andrea Gail ship captain was dead. As the Florida appeals court had said in *Loft*:

> A cause of action for invasion of the common law right of privacy is strictly personal and may be asserted only by the person who is the subject of the challenged publication. Relatives of a deceased person have no right of action for invasion of privacy of the deceased person regardless of how close such personal relationship was with the deceased.

And while Tyne's daughters were briefly depicted in *The Perfect Storm* (e.g., attending their father's memorial service), these scenes were factually accurate, and "the picture's portrayal of the Tyne daughters is not sufficiently egregious in nature to establish a claim of invasion of privacy."

*Tyne v. Time Warner Entertainment*, 204 F. Supp. 2d 1338, 1347 (M.D.Fla. 2002). This part of Judge Conway's decision was affirmed in *Tyne v. Time Warner Entertainment,* 336 F.3d 1286 (11th Cir. 2003).

The broader question of legal policy remains for state legislatures as well as courts across the country. Should the heirs of Thomas Dewey, for example, have a right to block an entirely false portrayal of their antecedents in a docudrama like *Hoodlum*?

## F. PUBLIC FIGURES UNDER DEFAMATION AND PRIVACY LAW

It is difficult (but not impossible) for public figure plaintiffs to satisfy a court that the producers of an entertainment work failed the "actual malice" test for purposes of either a defamation or false light privacy action. Illustrative of the force of that legal obstacle is the case earlier in this chapter by the U.S. military leader Ray Davis, against the producers of the film *Missing*, who did not even talk to Davis about what had taken place in the Chilean military coup a decade earlier. *See Davis v. Costa-Gavras*, 654 F. Supp. 653 (S.D.N.Y. 1987). Assuming a false statement has been made "of and concerning" the plaintiff, a critical factor in the litigation is whether the plaintiff is a "public figure" for purposes of the subject of the book, film, or broadcast.

In *Gertz v. Robert Welch, Inc.*, 418 U.S. 323 (1974), the Supreme Court outlined two ways in which someone can be judged a "public figure." Some people attain such "pervasive fame and notoriety" that they are public figures "for all purposes and in all contexts." More common, however, are those people who become public figures with regard to a particular set of facts or circumstances. These people either "voluntarily inject" themselves or are "drawn into" a public controversy that renders them public figures "for a limited range of issues." *Id.* at 351.

Although *Gertz* provided a basis for public figure analysis, it did not formulate a specific test for determining at what point someone becomes a public figure. Lower courts have determined that many "high profile" or prominent public citizens meet the "pervasiveness" standard. A newspaper publisher, *see Loeb v. Globe Newspaper Co.*, 489 F. Supp. 481 (D.Mass. 1980), the wife of a television celebrity, *see Carson v. Allied News Co.*, 529 F.2d 206 (7th Cir. 1976), and candidates for public office, *see Ocala Star-Banner Co. v. Damron*, 401 U.S. 295 (1971), have all been deemed public figures under this standard. Nonetheless, absent "clear evidence of general fame or notoriety in the community, and pervasive involvement in the affairs of society, an individual should not be deemed a public personality for all aspects of his life." *Gertz*, 418 U.S. at 352.

Courts have differed, however, over the proper test for determining when someone has become a public figure for a limited purpose. Some courts have outlined a three-part test for such determinations. Applying an objective standard, one must 1) isolate and define a public controversy, 2) analyze the plaintiff's role in the controversy, and 3) find the false statement to be "germane" to the plaintiff's participation in the controversy. *See Waldbaum v. Fairchild Publications*, 627 F.2d 1287 (D.C.Cir. 1980). Other courts have outlined additional factors for consideration, such as the degree to which the plaintiff "voluntarily injected" himself into a controversy or the degree to which the plaintiff maintained "regular and continuing access to the media." *See Lerman v. Flynt Distributing Co.*, 745 F.2d 123, 136–37 (2d Cir. 1984).

Doctors involved in public controversies, *see Park v. Capital Cities Communications,* 181 A.D.2d 192, 585 N.Y.S.2d 902 (1992), Nobel Prize winners, *see Pauling v. National Review*, 49 Misc.2d 975, 269 N.Y.S.2d 11 (1966), union officials, *see Lins v. Evening News Ass'n*, 129 Mich.App. 419, 342 N.W.2d 573 (1983), and prominent attorneys with high profile clients, *see Schwartz v. Worrall Publications, Inc.*, 258 N.J.Super. 493, 610 A.2d 425 (1992), have all been deemed public figures for a limited purpose. Yet courts are often hesitant to conclude that someone has voluntarily injected himself into a public controversy. What is more, many courts are hostile to the notion that someone can become a public figure involuntarily. One of the major "limited purpose" cases resulted in the Supreme Court declining to classify the person as a public figure.

In *Time, Inc. v. Firestone*, 424 U.S. 448 (1976), the ex-wife of the heir to the Firestone Tire fortune filed a libel suit against *Time* magazine for featuring a brief paragraph summarizing the Firestone divorce action.

The divorce had received considerable media attention, and Firestone herself gave press conferences about it. The *Time* story summarized the judge's finding that the divorce should be granted on grounds of extreme cruelty and several extramarital affairs. Nonetheless, the Supreme Court held that Firestone was not a public figure, and therefore was not required to meet the *New York Times* "actual malice" standard. Specifically, the Court held that Firestone had not thrust herself into the forefront on a matter of controversy. The dissolution of a marriage, even though the subject of a judicial proceeding, was not the kind of public issue that required proof of actual malice.

Cases involving private persons suddenly thrust into the limelight generally require difficult determinations as to whether the person is a public figure for a limited purpose. Under "limited purpose analysis," an individual may be entitled to public figure status as to some facts, and private figure status as to others. In the following case, the court attempted to address some of these issues.

## DRESBACH V. DOUBLEDAY & COMPANY

United States District Court, District of Columbia, 1981.
518 F. Supp. 1285.

GREEN, DISTRICT JUDGE.

[In 1980, Michael Mewshaw authored and Doubleday published a book, *Life For Death*, about the murder of the parents of Lee Dresbach by Lee's brother, Wayne. At that time Lee was fourteen years old and Wayne was fifteen. Mewshaw and his family had been summertime neighbors of the Dresbachs. Following the killings, the Mewshaws took Lee into their home, where he lived for three years (and dated Michael's sister). The Mewshaws also became intensely involved with Wayne, regularly visiting him in prison (often with Michael) and assisting in the appeal from his conviction. Mewshaw's book, written nearly twenty years later, described not only the original events but also what happened afterwards, and thus was "significantly autobiographical." Lee objected to the book's portrayal of him after the killings—in particular, his alienation from Wayne, his rare prison visits, his unwillingness to share or use his inheritance from the murdered parents to give Wayne financial support, and his concealment of his whereabouts from Wayne after the latter was released from prison.

Lee contended that some of these assertions in the book were untrue, and he thus challenged them under false light privacy doctrine. Others he accepted as true, but challenged their publication as "private facts in which the public has no legitimate concern, and whose publication would cause suffering, shame, or humiliation to a person of ordinary sensibilities." In particular, Lee objected to the publication of such private facts about him in 1980, even conceding a legitimate public interest in those events at the time of the murders two decades earlier.]

* * *

In support of the argument that the passage of time has rendered private subject matter which was admittedly at one time a legitimate subject of public interest, plaintiff cites cases holding that a cause of action may be stated where a publication identifies a rehabilitated criminal with his crime of many years past. *Melvin v. Reid*, 112 Cal.App. 285, 297 P. 91 (1931); *Bernstein v. National Broadcasting Co.*, 129 F. Supp. 817 (D.D.C.1955); *Briscoe v. Reader's Digest Association*, 4 Cal.3d 529, 93 Cal. Rptr. 866, 483 P.2d 34 (1971). *Melvin v. Reid* involved a movie about a woman who eight years previous had been a prostitute and was tried for murder and acquitted. She had since reformed and become a respectable member of society. Many of her present acquaintances did not know of her past. The Court found that although the republication of events in the public record was not actionable, a cause of action for invasion of privacy was stated based upon the use of plaintiff's correct maiden name in connection with unsavory incidents of her past life. A major reason for allowing such an action, in the eyes of the Court, was society's interest in the "rehabilitation of the fallen and the reformation of the criminal." In *Bernstein*, while finding no privacy cause of action on the facts of that case, the Court stated that there could be a cause of action for unreasonable public identification of a person in his present setting referring to earlier actions which took place at a time when the plaintiff was a legitimate object of public interest. *Briscoe* held that the plaintiff has a cause of action for a publication concerning his involvement in a truck hijacking incident eleven years earlier. Plaintiff alleged that he had been completely rehabilitated since, and that he had many friends, as well as a daughter, who were not previously aware of his involvement in that offense. The Court stated that truthful reports about recent crimes are privileged, as are the facts about past crimes. However, identification of the actors in long past crimes, where the actors had done nothing to reattract public attention, could be found by a jury to be without legitimate public interest and grossly offensive to the average person. The Court believed that a jury could find that the article in question concerning truck hijacking would have lost none of its value by deleting the plaintiff's name. An important factor in the decision was the State's interest in the rehabilitative process.

The State interest in the rehabilitative process was characterized as "most important" in the *Briscoe* case in a recent California Supreme Court case, *Forsher v. Bugliosi*, 26 Cal.3d 792, 163 Cal. Rptr. 628, 608 P.2d 716 (1980), stating that *Briscoe* was "an exception to the more general rule that 'once a man has become a public figure, or news, he remains a matter of legitimate recall to the public mind to the end of his days.' "

In our case we must decide whether true matters in the Book were matters of public interest at the time they were published, and whether the inclusion of plaintiff in connection with those matters was legitimate, or whether the countervailing interest in plaintiff's privacy concerning those matters many years after the events renders the publication actionable.

Given the generally broad public interest exception to the right of privacy action, and the fact that the few cases plaintiff has been able to cite in his favor rest strongly upon the plaintiffs' status as rehabilitated criminals, there is no doubt that for the purpose of a privacy action, the subject matter of this Book was of legitimate public interest at the time it was published. (We need not decide whether Wayne Dresbach, as a rehabilitated criminal, could have brought a privacy action concerning this Book, as he has given his consent to its publication.) The public has a legitimate interest in the facts about past crimes and their investigation and prosecution, as well as the possible motivating forces in the background of the criminal. Plaintiff cannot prevail on a theory that the subject matter of the Book had become private with the passage of time. He also cannot object to republication of matters which are in the public record of the trial and related proceedings, no matter how private or offensive, as information in the public record is absolutely privileged. Nor could the Book have been written, with its implication that the circumstances of Wayne's home life drove him to murder, without including private facts about plaintiff's home life, which obviously was intimately bound up with his brother's. This is even more true here than in the usual case of brothers growing up in the same home, since much of the friction between Wayne and his parents concerned their unfavorable comparison of him with Lee.

Plaintiff's relationship with his brother after the murders and plaintiff's own subsequent history are less obviously integral to the subject matter of the Book. However, we tread on dangerous ground deciding exactly what matters are sufficiently relevant to a subject of legitimate public interest to be privileged. First Amendment values could obviously be threatened by the uncertainty such decisions could create for writers and publishers. "Only in cases of flagrant breach of privacy which has not been waived or obvious exploitation of public curiosity where no legitimate public interest exists should a court substitute its judgment for that of the publisher." This is not such a case. The subject matter of Wayne's rehabilitation after his murder conviction, focusing both on prison conditions and the support or lack thereof he received from friends and family, cannot be said to be without legitimate public interest, and facts about Wayne's relationship with his brother are clearly related to that subject. In *Campbell v. Seabury Press*, 614 F.2d 395 (5th Cir. 1980), the plaintiff was found not to have a cause of action for invasion of privacy for the disclosure of private facts regarding her marriage and home life. The book in question was the autobiography of a man whose brother, plaintiff's former husband, was a religious and civil rights leader. The challenged disclosures were included in the context of plaintiff's relationship with the brother and the impact of that relationship upon the author. The Court held that there is a constitutional privilege to publish news or other matters of public interest, and that the privilege "extends to information concerning interesting phases of human activity and embraces all issues about which information is needed or appropriate so that individuals may cope with the exigencies of their period. . . . (The privilege applies even to) information relating to individuals who have not sought or have attempted to avoid publicity. . . . The privacy of such individuals is protected, however, by requiring that a logical nexus exist between the complaining individual and the matter of legitimate public interest." The Court found that the accounts of the brother's marriage as they impacted upon the author had the requisite logical nexus to fall within the ambit of constitutional protection. Although this Court might not go as far as the *Campbell* court in extinguishing the right to privacy, clearly here, where the important public issues of crime, the criminal justice system, and rehabilitation are concerned, the defendants have shown an adequate nexus between matters of legitimate public interest and the disclosures about the plaintiff to merit constitutional protection.

We are not without compassion for Lee Dresbach's plight. The exercise of defendants' First Amendment rights has imposed a heavy burden upon plaintiff. It is easy to sympathize with his objection to the Book having been written at all, and certainly to his inclusion in it. In his own words in response to the question, "What else do you find objectionable?", he replied, "Me being in the book at all. I asked not to be in the book. I have a right to my own privacy. I can go probably weeks without thinking about seeing two people murdered. Every day since then all I do is think about it." Additionally, a great deal of very sensitive information about plaintiff's past which he has chosen to keep secret is now available to friends, employers, customers, his wife, and in-laws. Yet, there is no doubt that a cause of action based upon truthful material in the Book cannot be permitted consistent with the First Amendment. Clearly, this society has put a higher value on open criminal proceedings and on public discussion of all issues than on the individual's right to privacy. To guard against the possible evils of abuse of power if the criminal justice system were to operate away from the public eye, and of suppression of freedom of thought if writers could not freely explore the causes and handling of past crimes of public interest, the plaintiff's right to bury the past must be sacrificed. Freedom of speech would be crippled if discussions of matters of public interest were narrowly circumscribed in the manner suggested by plaintiff to protect privacy. Summary judgment must be granted in favor of both defendants on plaintiff's privacy claim as to accurate material in the Book.

* * *

[For purposes of this motion for summary dismissal, the court accepted that there was some basis for Dresbach's claim that certain of the assertions about him in the Book were untrue: e.g., that Lee had been abused by his parents before their death; that Lee had refused to give Wayne any money to fix his teeth; and that on leaving for Vietnam, Lee's will left Wayne just five dollars. The court also concluded that because *Gertz v. Robert Welch*, 418 U.S. 323 (1974) had adopted the negligence standard for defamation of private figures, the same standard must apply to false light privacy claims, notwithstanding the Supreme Court's use of "actual malice" language in *Time Inc. v. Hill*, 385 U.S. 374 (1967), seven years prior to *Gertz*. This posed the question, then, of whether Lee was a private or public figure under the law.]

* * *

The Supreme Court has defined "public figure" for the purpose of libel claims in *Gertz v. Robert Welch, Inc.*, supra.

> Hypothetically, it may be possible for someone to become a public figure through no purposeful action of his own, but the instances of truly involuntary public figures must be exceedingly rare. For the most part those who attain this status have assumed roles of especial prominence in the affairs of society. Some occupy positions of such pervasive power and influence that they are deemed public figures for all purposes. More commonly, those classed as public figures have thrust themselves to the forefront of particular public controversies in order to influence the resolution of the issues involved. In either event, they invite attention and comment.

418 U.S. at 345. Private individuals are entitled to a greater degree of protection from defamation than public figures, first because they usually have less access to the channels of effective communication to counteract false statements, and more importantly, because public officials and public figures have generally voluntarily exposed themselves to increased risk of injury from defamatory falsehoods by the positions they have assumed.

The application of these principles in this Circuit has required the Court, in order to find that a plaintiff is a public figure for limited purposes (it is not claimed that plaintiff here is a public figure for all purposes), to first isolate a public controversy which is a real dispute whose outcome affects the general public or some segment of it in an appreciable way, and which is actually being publicly discussed; and then determine whether the plaintiff has thrust himself into the forefront of that controversy so as to become a factor in its ultimate resolution. Defendants claim that the crime, prosecution and rehabilitation of Wayne Dresbach formed a part of the public controversy over child abuse, violent youth, rehabilitation, and the problems of the criminal justice system in general; and that plaintiff, as the only surviving witness of the killings, an important witness at Wayne's trial, and the innocent victim of a home life that drove his brother to murder their parents, is an involuntary public figure. If in fact this situation meets the first test set forth in *Waldbaum* [*v. Fairchild Publications*, 627 F.2d 1287 (D.C.Cir. 1980)], a public controversy, it still cannot be said that plaintiff thrust himself into the forefront of that controversy so as to become a factor in its ultimate resolution. A fourteen year old child at the time, he merely described what he witnessed when required to do so by police and the Court. He never took a position on any issue, and was not the object of controversy himself. At most, he was casually mentioned as Wayne's brother in some of the newspaper articles about the murders. His trial testimony was not determinative or controversial, since Wayne repeatedly confessed the murders himself. Referring to the rationales for the public/private distinction put forth in *Gertz*, plaintiff did not, by his involvement in the events described in the Book, gain any special access to the channels of communication to enable him to rebut falsehoods about him. And he certainly did not voluntarily expose himself to the risk of defamatory falsehoods. "A private individual is not automatically transformed into a public figure just by becoming involved in or associated with a matter that attracts public attention. . . . A libel defendant must show more than mere newsworthiness to justify application of the demanding burden of *New York Times*."

* * *

[With respect to the false light cause of action, the court permitted Dresbach to pursue his claim that the author, Mewshaw, had been negligent in asserting certain facts that may have placed Dresbach in a false light in the public eye.]

Partial summary dismissal.

## *QUESTIONS FOR DISCUSSION*

1. Do you agree with the judge's approach to the specific issue of Lee Dresbach's "public figure" status? What impact does the overall treatment of the facts of this case have on your views about the appropriate balance between speech and privacy?

2. The National Enquirer published a story about Tamara Hood and her infant son Christian, a child fathered out of wedlock by the movie star

Eddie Murphy. The Enquirer story described not only the Hoods' relationship with Murphy and the large sums of money he was contributing to their support, but also Tamara's prior romances with other men. Attached to the story was a picture of both Tamara and Christian that had been taken at a private dinner party and later sold by the photographer to the Enquirer. The Hoods sued the National Enquirer and the photographer for both "intrusion upon solitude" and "public disclosure of private facts." Relevant especially to the latter question is whether either of the plaintiffs is a public figure for purposes of privacy law. What is your view? *See Hood v. The National Enquirer*, 17 Enter. L. Rep. 3 (Feb. 1996).

---

The next case, involving a fateful event in American constitutional history, poses in even more dramatic fashion the tension between the public's right to know and the individual's right to be left alone. One of the most infamous events in the history of American criminal law took place in the 1930s. In 1931, nine young blacks were accused of raping two white women while all were riding a freight train from Chattanooga, Tennessee to Huntsville, Alabama. The black youths were quickly tried in Scottsboro, Alabama without legal counsel, convicted by all-white juries, and sentenced to death by white male judges. While the Supreme Court of Alabama affirmed the convictions, the U.S. Supreme Court reversed them all because of the denial of a right to counsel under the Sixth Amendment. *See Powell v. Alabama,* 287 U.S. 45 (1932). A host of further trials took place, again with white-jury guilty findings and eventual Supreme Court reversals because blacks had been systematically excluded from the juries. *See Norris v. Alabama,* 294 U.S. 587 (1935), and *Patterson v. Alabama,* 294 U.S. 600 (1935). In the final round of trials, five of the nine defendants were convicted by their respective juries.

One of the key early trials involved defendant Patterson, whose initial jury conviction was the only one set aside by an Alabama trial judge, Judge Horton, who was soon voted out of office. Eventually, though, a later judge upheld the final jury conviction and sentenced Patterson to 75 years in prison for allegedly raping a white woman. Four decades later, NBC broadcast a 1970s made-for-television movie, *Judge Horton and the Scottsboro Boys,* based on one chapter in historian Dr. Daniel Carter's 1969 book, *Scottsboro: A Tragedy of the American South.* The principal focus of this TV drama (which won numerous awards) was on Judge Horton, who was portrayed as a courageous figure struggling to bring justice to a southern community then "gripped by racial prejudice and intent on vengeance" against any blacks accused of raping white women.

Another theme of the movie was a very critical portrayal of the one woman who continued to be an accuser throughout the trials, Victoria

Price Street. Street was "pictured as a prostitute who had traveled from Alabama to Chattanooga to 'hustle' for business, had engaged in voluntary sex on the train, and had then falsely told the police that she had been raped by young black men who had been engaged in an altercation with whites that halted the train." At the time of the trial, Price (her name then) had given numerous press interviews as well as trial testimony; she then married and dropped out of public view for the next three decades. Indeed, the reason that neither Dr. Carter nor NBC's producers interviewed Street for the book or film was their belief (stated in both works) that Street was now dead.

When Street saw this TV drama, along with her husband and friends, she immediately filed a suit against NBC, claiming both defamation of her reputation and false light invasion of her privacy. The basis of this tort suit was that NBC had "portrayed her as a perjurer, a woman of bad character (a prostitute), a woman who falsely accused the Scottsboro boys of rape knowing that the result would likely be the electric chair." This suit produced a major debate on whether Street was still a "public figure" who must persuade a jury not only of the falsity of her portrayal and negligence on the part of the movie makers, but also full-blown "actual malice."

## STREET V. NATIONAL BROADCASTING CO.

United States Court of Appeals, Sixth Circuit, 1981.
645 F.2d 1227.

MERRITT, CIRCUIT JUDGE.

* * *

### III. The First Amendment Defenses

#### A. *Plaintiff was a Public Figure During the Scottsboro Trials*

* * *

[Under *Gertz v. Welch*, 418 U.S. 323 (1974), the first issue was whether Street had had the required "participation" in a public controversy. With respect to the latter factor, the court found the answer to be an easy one.] The Scottsboro trials were the focus of major public debate over the ability of our courts to render even-handed justice. It generated widespread press and attracted public attention for several years. It was also a contributing factor in changing public attitudes about the right of black citizens to equal treatment under law and in changing constitutional principles governing the right to counsel and the exclusion of blacks from the jury.

The first factor in determining the nature and extent of plaintiff's participation is the prominence of her role in the public controversy. She was the only alleged victim, and she was the major witness for the State in the prosecution of the nine black youths. Ruby Bates, the other young woman who earlier had testified against the defendants, later recanted her incriminating testimony. Plaintiff was left as the sole prosecutrix. Therefore, she played a prominent role in the public controversy.

The second part of the test of public figure status is also met. Plaintiff had "access to the channels of effective communication and hence a realistic opportunity to counteract false statements." The evidence indicates that plaintiff recognized her importance to the criminal trials and the interest of the public in her as a personality. The press clamored to interview her. She clearly had access to the media and was able to broadcast her view of the events.

The most troublesome issue is whether plaintiff "voluntarily" "thrust" herself to the forefront of this public controversy. It cannot be said that a rape victim "voluntarily" injects herself into a criminal prosecution for rape. *See Time, Inc. v. Firestone*, 424 U.S. 448, 457 (1976). In such an instance, voluntariness in the legal sense is closely bound to the issue of truth. If she was raped, her participation in the initial legal proceedings was involuntary for the purpose of determining her public figure status; if she falsely accused the defendants, her participation in this controversy was "voluntary." But legal standards in libel cases should not be drawn so that either the courts or the press must first determine the issue of truth before they can determine whether an individual should be treated as a public or a private figure. The principle of libel law should not be drawn in such a way that it forces the press, in an uncertain public controversy, to guess correctly about a woman's chastity.

When the issue of truth and the issue of voluntariness are the same, it is necessary to determine the public figure status of the individual without regard to whether she "voluntarily" thrust herself in the forefront of the public controversy. If there were no evidence of voluntariness other than that turning on the issue of truth, we would not consider the fact of voluntariness. In such a case, the other factors—prominence and access to media alone—would determine public figure status. But in this case, there is evidence of voluntariness not bound up with the issue of truth. Plaintiff gave press interviews and aggressively promoted her version of the case outside of her actual courtroom testimony. In the context of a widely-reported, intense public controversy concerning the fairness of our criminal justice system, plaintiff was a public figure under *Gertz* because she played a major role, had effective access to the media, and encouraged public interest in herself.

*B. Plaintiff Remains a Public Figure for Purposes of Later Discussion of the Scottsboro Case*

The Supreme Court has explicitly reserved the question of "whether or when an individual who was once a public figure may lose that status by the passage of time." *Wolston v. Reader's Digest Ass'n, Inc.*, 443 U.S. 157, 166 n. 7 (1979). In *Wolston* the District of Columbia Circuit found that plaintiff was a public figure and retained that status for the purpose of later discussion of the espionage case in which he was called as a witness. The Supreme Court found that the plaintiff's role in the original public controversy was so minor that he was not a public figure. It therefore reserved the question of whether a person retains his public figure status.

Plaintiff argues that even if she was a public figure at the time of the 1930s trial, she lost her public figure status over the intervening forty years. We reject this argument and hold that once a person becomes a public figure in connection with a particular controversy, that person remains a public figure thereafter for purposes of later commentary or treatment of that controversy. This rule finds support in both case law and analysis of the constitutional malice standard.

On this issue the Fifth Circuit has reached the same conclusion as the District of Columbia Circuit in *Wolston*. In *Brewer v. Memphis Publishing Co., Inc.*, 626 F.2d 1238 (5th Cir. 1980), plaintiff sued when a newspaper implied that she was reviving a long-dormant romantic relationship with Elvis Presley. The Fifth Circuit concluded that although the passage of time might narrow the range of topics protected by a malice standard, plaintiff remained a public figure when the defendant commented on her romantic relationship. The court noted that plaintiff's name continued to be connected with Presley even after her retirement from show business.

* * *

Our analytical view of the matter is based on the fact that the Supreme Court developed the public figure doctrine in order that the press might have sufficient breathing room to compose the first rough draft of history. It is no less important to allow the historian the same leeway when he writes the second or the third draft.

Our nation depends on "robust debate" to determine the best answer to public controversies of this sort. The public figure doctrine makes it possible for publishers to provide information on such issues to the debating public, undeterred by the threat of liability except in cases of actual malice. Developed in the context of contemporaneous reporting, the doctrine promotes a forceful exchange of views.

Considerations that underlie the public figure doctrine in the context of contemporaneous reporting also apply to later historical or dramatic treatment of the same events. Past public figures who now live in obscurity do not lose their access to channels of communication if they choose to comment on their role in the past public controversy. And although the publisher of history does not operate under journalistic deadlines it generally makes little difference in terms of accuracy and verifiability that the events on which a publisher is reporting occurred decades ago. Although information may come to light over the course of time, the distance of years does not necessarily make more data available to a reporter: memories fade; witnesses forget; sources disappear.

There is no reason for the debate to be any less vigorous when events that are the subject of current discussion occurred several years earlier. The mere passage of time does not automatically diminish the significance of events or the public's need for information. A nation that prizes its heritage need have no illusions about its past. It is no more fitting for the Court to constrain the analysis of past events than to stem the tide of current news. From Alfred Dreyfus to Alger Hiss, famous cases have been debated and reinterpreted by commentators and historians. A contrary rule would tend to restrain efforts to shed new light on historical events and reconsideration of past errors.

The plaintiff was the pivotal character in the most famous rape case of the twentieth century. It became a political controversy as well as a legal dispute. As the white prosecutrix of nine black youths during an era of racial prejudice in the South, she aroused the attention of the nation. The prosecutions were among the first to focus the conscience of the nation on the question of the ability of our system of justice to provide fair trials to blacks in the South. The question persists today. As long as the question remains, the Scottsboro boys case will not be relegated to the dusty pages of the scholarly treatise. It will remain a living controversy.

### C. *Evidence Insufficient to Support Malice*

A plaintiff may not recover under the malice standard unless there is "clear and convincing proof" that the defamation was published "with knowledge of its falsity or with reckless disregard for the truth." There is no evidence that NBC had knowledge that its portrayal of Victoria Price was false or that NBC recklessly disregarded the truth. The derogatory portrayal of Price in the movie is based in all material respects on the detailed findings of Judge Horton at the trial and Dr. Carter in his book. When the truth is uncertain and seems undiscoverable through further investigation, reliance on these two sources is not unreasonable.

We gain perspective on this question when we put to ourselves another case. Dr. Carter, in his book, persuasively argues, based on the evidence, that the Communist Party financed and controlled the defense of the Scottsboro boys. A different playwright might choose to portray Judge Horton as some Southern newspapers portrayed him at the time, as an evil judge who associated himself with a Communist cause and gave his approval to interracial rape in order to curry favor with the eastern press. The problem would be similar had Judge Horton, for many years before his death an obscure private citizen, sued the publisher for libel.

* * *

The malice standard is flexible and encourages diverse political opinions and robust debate about social issues. It tolerates silly arguments and strange ways of yoking facts together in unusual patterns. But it is not infinitely expandable. It does not abolish all the common law of libel even in the political context. It still protects us against the "big political lie," the conscious or reckless falsehood. We do not have that in this case.

Affirmed.

JOHN W. PECK, SENIOR CIRCUIT JUDGE, dissenting.

The majority offers no convincing reasons in law or policy for extending to NBC the protection of the *New York Times* privilege of freedom from liability for defamatory statements made without "malice." Forty years after the events that made Mrs. Street famous (or infamous), the purposes behind the legal distinction (not the everyday distinction) between public figures and private individuals are served only by ranking Mrs. Street among the latter.

The majority exalts "robust debate on social issues." So do we all. If that were the only interest of weight in defamation and privacy cases, there would be no need to distinguish between public figures and private persons in our law. It would be much better to apply the *New York Times* "malice" test in all cases; yet it is no mystery why this is not our rule of law.

The Constitution does not protect damaging misstatements of fact because of their intrinsic worth. "(T)here is no constitutional value in false statements of fact." *Gertz v. Robert Welch, Inc.*, 418 U.S. 323, 340 (1974). False reports are protected because they are "inevitable in free debate." The inevitability of demonstrable error lessens with the passage of time. Accordingly, when the pressures of contemporaneous reporting subside, the need for the protection of the "malice" standard disappears. A negligence standard is enough. I would follow the reasoning of Justices Blackmun and Marshall, and hold that the passage of time can extinguish public figure status. *See Wolston v. Reader's Digest Ass'n, Inc.*, 443 U.S. 157, 169–72 (1979) (concurring opinion).

The majority adopts the rule, not that public figure status is eternal, but that it persists as long as the public controversy that gave rise to it.

For my brethren, Scottsboro persists as a public controversy because the trials have taken on "an overlay of political meaning." In short, Mrs. Street is a public figure today because the majority thinks the Scottsboro affair merits public attention. This reasoning resurrects the "newsworthiness" test for applying the "malice" standard in defamation cases, a test proposed by a plurality of the Supreme Court in *Rosenbloom v. Metromedia, Inc.*, 403 U.S. 29 (1971), and rejected by a majority of the Court in *Gertz*. It is not the business of judges to decide "what information is relevant to self-government."

* * *

By making a plaintiff's status hinge on its determination of the significance of a defendant's speech, the majority pushes the Court into a quagmire where the law of defamation is standardless, easily manipulated, and no more speech-protective than the judges who happen to be applying it. The better approach is to take the distinction between public and private figures back to its roots, and examine the present status of the plaintiff in light of the reasons behind the distinction, as did Justices Blackmun and Marshall in *Wolston*.

The First Amendment affords less protection to the reputations of public figures not because news of them is deemed significant, but because they can more easily rebut falsehoods in public media, and because they have as a rule assumed the risk of public commentary. In short, the law encourages and expects those labeled public figures to be uninhibited, robust debaters.

Over forty years ago, the prominence Mrs. Street gained through the Scottsboro trials allowed her to speak through public media. She was unquestionably a public figure in the current legal sense. Today her voice cannot rebut network "docudramas," which literally reach the entire nation in "gripping" displays. Few people assume the risk that the most personal aspects of their lives will be presented to the nation as dramatic entertainments. The majority hold that Mrs. Street assumed that risk by her involvement in an unspecified number of interviews over forty years ago.

When NBC broadcast *Judge Horton*, Mrs. Street was not only not a public figure, she was a nonentity. Dr. Carter, historian and author of the book on which *Judge Horton* was loosely based, had been unable to trace Mrs. Street, and had described her death in some detail. The majority offers no convincing reason why those who would write of her today should not be liable for damages caused by their failure to make reasonable efforts to get their facts straight.

*Gertz* and its progeny compel the conclusion that public figure status is determined by looking at a plaintiff's media power or public involvement at the time of the alleged defamation. I know of no case holding a person as presently obscure as Mrs. Street a public figure. [After reviewing the facts, the dissenting judge concluded that there was no basis for a negligence claim in the first broadcast of Judge Horton, when everyone assumed Street was dead and thus could not be interviewed. However, the second broadcast of Judge Horton took place after Street had seen and sued it, and the lack of any effort by NBC to do any more investigation and possible adjustments could potentially justify a jury finding of negligence in this showing.]

* * *

My fundamental disagreement with the majority concerns the constitutionality of permitting states to impose liability for negligence in defamation cases where the pressures of contemporaneous reporting are totally absent. The majority argues that different pressures work on historians, since "the distance of years does not necessarily make more data available to a reporter: memories fade; witnesses forget; sources disappear." Obviously, a negligence standard does not expect a writer to discover what is forever lost. When truth is unknowable, falsity, and hence defamation, cannot be proven.

III

The majority's unstated assumption is that application of the *New York Times* "malice" standard necessarily creates "breathing space" for uninhibited speech.

> Yet a publisher's decision to print or broadcast a libelous story is only partly influenced by the probability of winning or losing a lawsuit. While the publication decision involves a complex calculus, the salient cost factors are likely to be the probability that the publisher will be sued, and the cost of defending if suit is brought. Rules affecting the publisher's ultimate liability are thus likely to be marginal considerations in the decision to publish.

L. Tribe, *American Constitutional Law*, § 12–13 at 643 (1978). Since no evidentiary privilege protects the editorial process, *Herbert v. Lando*, 441 U.S. 153, 159–67 (1979), litigation costs are not likely to vary with the application of *New York Times* "malice" or *Gertz* "fault" rules. In the present case, the district court did not decide the question of Mrs. Street's status until the close of all proof. Had this action been brought after *Lando*, and had the trial judge (contrary to his actual ruling) early in the trial held Mrs. Street a public figure, the evidence (and outcome) in the trial might have been different, but it is incredible that either the hypothetical or the actual outcomes would significantly influence future publishing decisions. Invocation of *New York Times v. Sullivan* does not exorcise what to the majority is the demon of self-censorship. Only abolition of the torts of defamation and invasion of privacy can do that, and that abolition is a price measured in individual dignity that our Constitution does not exact.

A living person is not a means to an end. Events may be symbolic, but individuals are not mere symbols. The dramatic effect of *Judge Horton*, and the merit of its historical interpretation, however important they may be to the majority, are not matters before us, nor were they before any jury. The substantial truth of factual assertions in the work, and the liability of the network for any material errors in them, were questions for the jury to decide.[j]

### *QUESTIONS FOR DISCUSSION*

1. Do you agree with the majority or the dissenting opinion? What are the reasons for imputing and maintaining "public figure" status to the subject of a book or film? What are the consequences for the producers if they cannot assert this particular response to a defamation or false light claim? Should the First Amendment judgment on this score vary depending on whether the story is published close to the time of the controversy, or is produced decades later?

2. Mary Miles Minter, a young movie actress, met the noted film director, William Taylor, in 1919, when she was seventeen. Taylor directed Minter in several movies that made her a major star. The two became engaged, and good friends of another young actress, Mabel Normand. However, in early 1922, Taylor was murdered before the planned wedding, and Minter left the motion picture industry. This famous murder mystery was never solved.

In 1970, while watching television, Minter happened to see a CBS show, *Rod Serling's Wonderful World of Crime*. Following is part of the transcript for the show:

> We are inclined to feel nostalgic about anything old, including crime, and especially murder. Murder is the unlawful taking of human life with malice aforethought. It is forbidden by the sixth of the Ten Commandments, and though some crimes are held equal to it, none is more blameworthy. Yet the act of murder is at the core of our most enduring literature. From the story of Genesis to the story of Hamlet, in literature as in history, we not only tolerate murder, we relish it. The locality of a murder, as soon as the mists of time have closed in on it, becomes a special place. The deed itself becomes an historical event. And the [murderer] an historical figure. There is no such historic figure in the murder of William

[j] Besides the articles cited in note g above, see Ruth Waldren and Emile Netzhammer, *False Light Invasion of Privacy: Untangling the Web of Uncertainty*, 9 Hast. Comm/Ent L.J. 347 (1987).

> Desmond Taylor. No murderer was ever caught, nor does the murder scene exist. It did exist on South Alvarado Street, in Los Angeles, but has since been murdered by a shopping center. The victim was a movie director of the kind likely to arouse warm feelings in some women, and jealousy. His name was linked romantically with Mabel [Normand], ingenue of the Mack Sennett Comedies, but he had other strings to his bow; it was no secret that Mary Miles Minter considered herself engaged to William Desmond Taylor. Miss Minter was the first star ever to sign a million-dollar contract, and since her mother, Charlotte Shelby, was still the guardian of the girl's wealth, she did not view her daughter's impending marriage with any great favor. Nor could Miss [Normand], who was still on the warmest terms with Taylor and whose picture set next to his bed inscribed 'Oh, My Dearest!' At any rate, la dolce vita came to an end for Taylor one February night in 1922. He was left on the floor of his Alvarado Street apartment the worse for a 38 slug. A shrouded figure was observed by a neighbor running from the scene. It could have been a man. It could have been a woman. Today, forty-eight years after death and funeral, no one knows which it was. Given the choice, both police and posterity like to think it was a woman. In the annals of crime, the murderer is tolerated. The murderess is preferred . . .

The show then went on to describe two notorious murderers, Louise Peete and Winnie Roth Judd. At one point the screen pictured Peete and Judd together with Normand, Minter, and Minter's mother, Charlotte Shelby. Minter sued CBS for invasion of her privacy. What are the key issues? What should be the outcome? *See O'Hilderbrandt v. CBS*, 40 Cal.App.3d 323, 114 Cal. Rptr. 826 (1974).

3. In 2007, Dixie Chicks lead singer Natalie Maines Pasdar participated in several rallies to "free the West Memphis Three," three men who were believed to have been falsely accused of murdering three 8 year old boys in 1993 (the West Memphis three were released from prison in 2012). As part of the campaign, Pasdar posted a letter on the Dixie Chicks' MySpace page that implicated Terry Hobbs, one of the victims' stepfathers, in the murders. Hobbs sued Pasdar and the Dixie Chicks, alleging defamation and false light invasion of privacy. In granting summary judgment for the defendants, the federal district court held that Hobbs was a limited purpose public figure, and that Hobbs could not demonstrate actual malice by clear and convincing evidence. *See Hobbs v. Pasdar*, 682 F. Supp.2d 909 (E.D. Ark. 2009).

---

We have now seen situations in two dozen or so portrayals of real people in entertainment works on the television or movie screen or in books and magazines. We have read a half dozen explorations by different courts about where the line should be drawn between the right to speak freely and the right to be left alone. It is worth underscoring that the key interests that producers and subjects fight about in court are shared within the broader community. Most Americans love to watch television shows with a real-life human twist. Most Americans also love the privacy, tranquility, and solitude that comes from not being portrayed as the villain or the freak in such a show. We are now in a position to make a more informed judgment about how well the courts have accommodated those competing interests in a variety of contexts.

One last example should help focus that question in our minds. One of the best-received movies of 1992 was *A Few Good Men*, whose estimated world-wide earnings were several hundred million dollars. The subject of the movie was a 1986 hazing incident at the U.S. Marine base at Guantanamo Bay, Cuba. The target of the hazing was a young Marine, William Santiago, who had broken the Marines' "code of silence" by writing Washington officials about his fellow Marines firing rifles into Cuban territory. As it turned out, the trigger for the hazing was a "Code Red" signal given by the Marine base commander, played by Jack Nicholson. Tragically, Santiago died as a result of the hazing and his two assailants were charged with murder in court martial proceedings. One legal defender, played by Demi Moore, persuaded another, a recent Harvard Law grad played by Tom Cruise, to take on the case. Cruise was eventually able to implicate Nicholson and use the defense of "official orders" to get the charges reduced against his young clients, though they were dishonorably discharged from the Marines and forced to start their life anew. The movie closed with the standard disclaimer that the events and characters were purely fictional and any resemblance between the film and reality was unintended and coincidental.

The disclaimer was not accurate. An almost identical event took place in 1986 at Guantanamo Bay, with the victim, named William Alvarado (not Santiago), having also broken the "code of silence," and the commanding officer having given the "Code Red" signal. The key differences were that the role of the commander was discovered early and punished, Alvarado was injured, not killed, and the Marines who contested the charges (represented by Don Marcari) were found guilty only of assault and were not discharged from the Marines. The more exciting fictional variations on these events were the work of writer Aaron Sorkin, whose product first appeared as a play on Broadway and then on the screen. And the reason why Sorkin first became acquainted with this case was that his sister, Lt. Debra Sorkin, was on the defense team and gave Aaron the trial transcripts (which apparently are not publicly available in the case of Marine Corps court-martials).

In 1994, the Marines decided to sue. If you were their lawyer, how would you have formulated the causes of action? If you had been the judge, what else would you have wanted to know, and how would you have been inclined to rule (in a case the parties eventually settled on confidential terms)? Suppose that the actual events at Guantanamo Bay had involved just a "roughing up" of the victim who suffered no injuries, and only the commander, not the Marines, had received discipline for the Code Red. Would these further variations in the facts have significantly altered the legal prospects of a suit involving *A Few Good Men*?

---

One final concern often raised in defamation and privacy litigation is that the people who feel most damaged by what was said about them are the least likely to sue (and vice versa). Airing the matter in court may well draw more public attention to the private event than what often was a brief and fleeting mention on television. After having read the cases and problems in this chapter, do you think that factual observation is true? Even if you think there is some truth to the point, how relevant is it to the broader policy question of whether tort litigation protects people's lives and reputations from unwarranted exposure by the media?

# CHAPTER 3

# CELEBRITY PUBLICITY RIGHTS[a]

■ ■ ■

Some intrusions on personal privacy neither reveal nor falsify facts about the individual. They may do no more than feature the person's name or picture—for example, the picture of a famous chef on the cover of a cookbook or the name of a sports star on a sweatshirt. When unauthorized, this use may leave the individual feeling personally invaded by having his or her identity exploited. More important, perhaps, the celebrity feels deprived of the revenue that he or she would otherwise have received for endorsing the product.

Every year commercial endorsements generate billions of dollars in the entertainment industry. By appearing in advertisements or lending their names to products, celebrities like Elizabeth Taylor, Michael Jordan, Peyton Manning, and Tiger Woods have earned more money from endorsements than from the trades that made them famous. That is only possible, though, if the law gives celebrities the necessary legal resources for protecting their identities from unauthorized uses.

The right of publicity provides that protection. Often referred to as the fourth branch of the privacy tort, the right of publicity embodies a right to control the use of one's identity for commercial purposes. Unlike its privacy brethren, the focus of this right is on the ability of a person to enhance a product's value. Absent commercial exploitation by one side or the other, a publicity action is unavailable.

## A. EVOLUTION AND NATURE OF PUBLICITY RIGHTS

The right of publicity deserves special attention because, unlike other aspects of privacy, most states now conceive of publicity rights as a form

---

[a] *See* Michael Madow, *Private Ownership of Public Image: Popular Culture & Publicity Rights*, 81 Cal. L. Rev. 127 (1993); Mark F. Grady, *A Positive Economic Theory of the Right of Publicity*, 1 UCLA Enter. L. Rev. 97 (1994); Roberta R. Kwall, *The Right of Publicity vs. The First Amendment: A Property & Liability Rule Analysis*, 70 Ind. L.J. 47 (1994); Oliver R. Goodenough, *Go Fish: Evaluating the Restatement's Formulation of the Law of Publicity*, 47 S.C. L. Rev. 709 (1996); Arlen W. Langvardt, *The Troubling Implications of a Right of Publicity "Wheel" Spun Out of Control*, 45 U. Kan. L. Rev. 329 (1997); Roberta R. Kwall, *Fame*, 73 Ind. L.J. 1 (1997); Jonathan Kahn, *Bringing Dignity Back to Light: Publicity Rights & the Eclipse of the Tort of Appropriation of Identity*, 17 Cardozo Arts & Enter. L. Rev. 213 (1999); David Westfall & David Landau, Publicity Rights as Property Rights, 23 Cardozo Arts & Enter. L. Rev. 71 (2005).

of *property* (thence both transferable and descendible). To understand how publicity rights can have both tort and property components, it is helpful to canvass briefly their historical evolution.

New York was the first state to offer any protection to a person's name and likeness. In 1903, after the New York Court of Appeals rejected a claim that a person's name and likeness should be protected at common law (in *Roberson v. Rochester Folding Box Co.*, 171 N.Y. 538, 64 N.E. 442 (N.Y. 1902)), the New York legislature enacted what are now Sections 50 and 51 of the New York Civil Rights Law, making it both a misdemeanor and a tort to use the "name, portrait or picture of any living person . . . for advertising purposes, or for the purposes of trade . . . without having first obtained the written consent of such person."

Two years later, in *Pavesich v. New England Life Insurance Co.*, 122 Ga. 190, 50 S.E. 68 (1905), the Georgia Supreme Court recognized that unauthorized use of a person's photograph in an advertisement was a violation of a new common law right to privacy. The Georgia court adopted the Warren and Brandeis view that appropriation of someone's name and likeness is a tort—a violation of the personal and non-assignable right not to have one's feelings hurt.

For the next half century, the appropriation of a person's name and likeness was treated as a brand of tort similar to the privacy rights discussed in Chapter 2. Plaintiffs were awarded modest compensation for the psychological injury they experienced from having their names and likenesses used publicly without their consent. (*See, e.g.*, *Fisher v. Murray M. Rosenberg, Inc.*, 175 Misc. 370, 23 N.Y.S.2d 677 (Sup.Ct.1940), awarding $300 to a famous dancer whose unauthorized photo was used in a shoe advertisement.) Depending upon the context in which the name or likeness was used, the appropriation might also give rise to a defamation claim.

Indicative of the underdeveloped state of this component of privacy law was a decision rendered by the Fifth Circuit—*O'Brien v. Pabst Sales Co.*, 124 F.2d 167 (5th Cir. 1941). Davey O'Brien had been the heavily-publicized All-American quarterback for the Texas Christian University football team in 1938, before being drafted to play for the NFL's Philadelphia Eagles. In 1939, Pabst Brewing put out its annual football calendar containing college and professional schedules. At the top of the calendar was a picture of O'Brien in his TCU uniform and throwing stance, side by side with a glass of Pabst Blue Ribbon Beer. Pabst had obtained O'Brien's picture from the TCU Publicity Department for this explicit purpose. In dismissing O'Brien's suit, the Fifth Circuit (applying Texas law) said that O'Brien, who had authorized countless mailings of his picture to the media and football fans, could not now complain of an intrusion on his privacy; that the calendar did not contain an explicit endorsement of Pabst beer by O'Brien; and that he had no independent right to sell the commercial value of his name and likeness. The result was that sports celebrities like Babe Ruth and entertainment celebrities like Mae West never enjoyed a right of publicity during their careers.

A decade later, that legal situation was dramatically altered in another sports-related case, *Haelan Laboratories, Inc. v. Topps Chewing Gum, Inc.*, 202 F.2d 866 (2d Cir. 1953). The dispute here was actually between two firms that had signed agreements with baseball players authorizing use of their names and pictures on cards sold with chewing gum. Haelan, the firm with the first and supposedly "exclusive" license to that effect, sued Topps for inducing breach of its contract. Topps' defense was that both sets of contracts amounted to no more than the players giving a release from liability for invasion of the privacy right not to have their feelings hurt by unconsented-to publication; under the governing New York law there was no separate right in the commercial value of one's name and likeness. A divided Second Circuit rejected that position. Besides the statutory right of privacy, there existed an independent and assignable common law right (which might or might not be labeled "property") in the publicity value of one's name and picture:

> This right might be called a "right of publicity." For it is common knowledge that many prominent persons (especially actors and ball-players), far from having their feelings bruised through public exposure of their likenesses, would feel sorely deprived if they no longer received money for authorizing advertisements, popularizing their countenances, displayed in newspapers, magazines, busses, trains and subways. This right of publicity would usually yield them no money unless it could be made the subject of an exclusive grant which barred any other advertiser from using their pictures.

202 F.2d at 868.

The ruling in *Haelan*, combined with a crucial law review exposition of its potential (Melville B. Nimmer, *The Right of Publicity*, 19 Law and Contemp. Prob. 203 (1954)), gave an entirely different property twist to the traditional tort slant to privacy doctrine. Inextricably intertwined with this property/personality debate was the question of what interests the right of publicity protects. Is this right supposed to protect a personal interest in keeping one's identity private, or a moral claim to reap the benefits of one's labor and accomplishments, or an accurate and economic allocation of celebrity likenesses across the spectrum of commercial products? And whatever are the positive values generated by this legal concept, does enforcement of this individual right unduly restrain freedom of speech—even for fun and profit?

Adding to these complexities, the right of publicity overlaps with other areas of the law, specifically trademark and unfair competition. In cases where celebrities themselves use their own names to promote their own businesses, courts may liken a claim against another party to trade name infringement. Other judges have applied unfair competition analysis, designed to prohibit someone from "reaping where he has not sown" by appropriating the goodwill that a public person has worked hard to develop. A recurring theme in the judicial and scholarly debate is what additional value is served by publicity rights, and at what costs to the economy and the culture.

---

Since the Second Circuit in *Haelan* first devised the right of publicity for baseball players and baseball cards, this right has been asserted by a host of major figures in American life: Jacqueline Onassis, Muhammad Ali, Johnny Carson, Arnold Palmer, Woody Allen, Dustin Hoffman and Tiger Woods. The greatest of them all was Dr. Martin Luther King, Jr., who was the subject of a suit filed more than a decade after his assassination. That suit was brought in Dr. King's native Georgia—the state that first developed the right of *privacy* at the beginning of this century. Now Georgia had to decide whether adding a distinctive right of *publicity* was sensible legal policy as well.

## MARTIN LUTHER KING, JR. CENTER FOR SOCIAL CHANGE v. AMERICAN HERITAGE PRODUCTS, INC.

Supreme Court of Georgia, 1982.
250 Ga. 135, 296 S.E.2d 697.

HILL, JUSTICE.

[James E. Bolen, doing business through his American Heritage Products company, produced and sold plastic busts of Dr. Martin Luther King, Jr., accompanied by a booklet on Dr. King's life and death. Advertisements in Ebony Magazine and brochures depicted the bust as an "exclusive memorial" to Dr. King, and as an opportunity to support the Martin Luther King, Jr. Center for Social Change. Though the Center had refused to endorse or participate in this bust project, Bolen set aside ninety cents of the $29.95 purchase price for future donations to the Center. Rather than accept this money, the Center filed suit, along with Coretta Scott King, Dr. King's widow and estate administratrix, and Motown Records, assignee of the copyright in Dr. King's speeches.]

* * *

The right of publicity may be defined as a celebrity's right to the exclusive use of his or her name and likeness. *Price v. Hal Roach Studios*, 400 F. Supp. 836, 843 (S.D.N.Y. 1975); *Estate of Presley v. Russen*, 513 F.

Supp. 1339, 1353 (D.N.J. 1981), and cases cited. The right is most often asserted by or on behalf of professional athletes, comedians, actors and actresses, and other entertainers. This case involves none of those occupations. As is known to all, from 1955 until he was assassinated on April 4, 1968, Dr. King, a Baptist minister by profession, was the foremost leader of the civil rights movement in the United States. He was awarded the Nobel Prize for Peace in 1964. Although not a public official, Dr. King was a public figure, and we deal in this opinion with public figures who are neither public officials nor entertainers. Within this framework, we turn to the questions posed.

1. Is the "right of publicity" recognized in Georgia as a right distinct from the right of privacy?

Georgia has long recognized the right of privacy. Following denial of the existence of the right of privacy in a controversial decision by the New York Court of Appeals in *Roberson v. Rochester Folding Box Co.*, 171 N.Y. 538 (64 N.E. 442) (1902), the Georgia Supreme Court became the first such court to recognize the right of privacy in *Pavesich v. New England Life Ins. Co.*, 122 Ga. 190 (50 S.E. 68) (1905).

In *Pavesich v. New England Life Ins. Co.*, supra, the picture of an artist was used without his consent in a newspaper advertisement of the insurance company. Analyzing the right of privacy, this court held: "The publication of a picture of a person, without his consent, as a part of an advertisement, for the purpose of exploiting the publisher's business, is a violation of the right of privacy of the person whose picture is reproduced, and entitles him to recover without proof of special damage." If the right to privacy had not been recognized, advertisers could use photographs of private citizens to promote sales and the professional modeling business would not be what it is today.

In the course of its opinion the *Pavesich* court said several things pertinent here. It noted that the commentators on ancient law recognized the right of personal liberty, including the right to exhibit oneself before the public at proper times and places and in a proper manner. As a corollary, the court recognized that the right of personal liberty included the right of a person not to be exhibited before the public, saying: "The right to withdraw from the public gaze at such times as a person may see fit, when his presence in public is not demanded by any rule of law is also embraced within the right of personal liberty. Publicity in one instance and privacy in the other is each guaranteed. If personal liberty embraces the right of publicity, it no less embraces the correlative right of privacy; and this is no new idea in Georgia law."

Recognizing the possibility of a conflict between the right of privacy and the freedoms of speech and press, this court said: "There is in the publication of one's picture for advertising purposes not the slightest semblance of an expression of an idea, a thought, or an opinion, within the meaning of the constitutional provision which guarantees to a person the right to publish his sentiments on any subject." The defendants in the case now before us make no claim under these freedoms and we find no violation thereof.

Observing in dicta that the right of privacy in general does not survive the death of the person whose privacy is invaded, the *Pavesich* court said: "While the right of privacy is personal, and may die with the person, we do not desire to be understood as assenting to the proposition that the relatives of the deceased can not, in a proper case, protect the memory of their kinsman, not only from defamation, but also from an invasion into the affairs of his private life after his death. This question is not now involved, but we do not wish anything said to be understood as committing us in any way to the doctrine that against the consent of relatives the private affairs of a deceased person may be published and his picture or statute exhibited."

Finding that *Pavesich*, although an artist, was not recognized as a public figure, the court said: "It is not necessary in this case to hold, nor are we prepared to do so, that the mere fact that a man has become what is called a public character, either by aspiring to public office, or by holding public office, or by exercising a profession which places him before the public, or by engaging in a business which has necessarily a public nature, gives to everyone the right to print and circulate his picture." Thus, although recognizing the right of privacy, the *Pavesich* court left open the question facing us involving the likeness of a public figure.

* * *

In *Palmer v. Schonhorn Enterprises*, 232 A.2d 458 (N.J.Super.Ch.1967), Arnold Palmer, Gary Player, Doug Sanders and Jack Nicklaus obtained summary judgment against the manufacturer of a golf game which used the golfers' names and short biographies without their consent. Although written as a right of privacy case, much of what was said is applicable to the right of publicity. In its opinion the court said:

> It would therefore seem, from a review of the authorities, that although the publication of biographical data of a well-known figure does not per se constitute an invasion of privacy, the use of that same data for the purpose of capitalizing upon the name by using it in connection with a commercial project other than the dissemination of news or articles or biographies does.
>
> The names of plaintiffs have become internationally famous, undoubtedly by reason of talent as well as hard work in perfecting it. This is probably true in the cases of most so-called

> celebrities, who have attained national or international recognition in a particular field of art, science, business or other extraordinary ability ... It is unfair that one should be permitted to commercialize or exploit or capitalize upon another's name, reputation or accomplishments merely because the owner's accomplishments have been highly publicized.

232 A.2d at 462. . . . At this point it should be emphasized that we deal here with the unauthorized use of a person's name and likeness for the commercial benefit of the user, not with a city's use of a celebrity's name to denominate a street or school.

* * *

The right of publicity was first recognized in Georgia by the Court of Appeals in *Cabaniss v. Hipsley*, 151 S.E.2d 496 (1966). There the court held that the plaintiff, an exotic dancer, could recover from the owner of the Atlanta Playboy Club for the unauthorized use of the dancer's misnamed photograph in an entertainment magazine advertising the Playboy Club. Although plaintiff had had her picture taken to promote her performances, she was not performing at the Playboy Club. The court used Dean William L. Prosser's four-pronged analysis of the right of privacy, saying:

* * *

> Unlike intrusion, disclosure, or false light, appropriation does not require the invasion of something secret, secluded or private pertaining to plaintiff, nor does it involve falsity. It consists of the appropriation, for the defendant's benefit, use or advantage, of the plaintiff's name or likeness. . . . The interest protected (in the "appropriation" cases) is not so much a mental as a proprietary one, in the exclusive use of the plaintiff's name and likeness as an aspect of his identity.

Although Ms. Hipsley was an entertainer (i.e., a public figure), the court found she was entitled to recover from the Playboy Club (but not from the magazine which published the Club's ad) for the unauthorized use of her photograph. However the court noted a difference in the damages recoverable in traditional right of privacy cases as opposed to right of publicity cases saying:

> Recognizing, as we do, the fundamental distinction between causes of action involving injury to feelings, sensibilities or reputation and those involving an appropriation of rights in the nature of property rights for commercial exploitation, it must necessarily follow that there is a fundamental distinction between the two classes of cases in the measure of damages to be applied. In the former class (which we take to include the

intrusion, disclosure, and false light aspects of the privacy tort), general damages are recoverable without proof of special damages. In the latter class, the measure of damages is the value of the use of the appropriated publicity.

In *McQueen v. Wilson*, 117 Ga. App. 488 (161 S.E.2d 63), reversed on other grounds, 224 Ga. 420 (1968), the Court of Appeals upheld the right of an actress, Butterfly McQueen, who appeared as "Prissie" in the movie *Gone With the Wind*, to recover for the unauthorized use of her photograph, saying: "Both before and since *Pavesich* it has been recognized that the appropriation of another's identity, picture, papers, name or signature without consent and for financial gain might be a tort for which an action would lie. . . ."

Thus, the courts in Georgia have recognized the rights of private citizens, as well as entertainers, not to have their names and photographs used for the financial gain of the user without their consent, where such use is not authorized as an exercise of freedom of the press. We know of no reason why a public figure prominent in religion and civil rights should be entitled to less protection than an exotic dancer or a movie actress. Therefore, we hold that the appropriation of another's name and likeness, whether such likeness be a photograph or sculpture, without consent and for the financial gain of the appropriator is a tort in Georgia, whether the person whose name and likeness is used is a private citizen, entertainer, or as here a public figure who is not a public official.

[The court then went on to consider whether publicity rights might be descendible to Dr. King's estate. Those portions of the decision will be reproduced in the last section of this chapter.]

* * *

WELTNER, JUSTICE, concurring specially.

* * *

In this opinion, we have taken the "right of privacy" as enumerated in *Pavesich*, supra, and added thereto a new thing, now called a "right of publicity." That seems to me to be more an exercise in verbal juxtaposition than a careful examination of legal issues and practical results.

At heart, the whole body of tort law is but an expression of what the community perceives to be the civil, as opposed to moral or ethical, responsibility of its members to each other. That concept changes with the cumulative experiences and assessments of succeeding generations, through constitutional, legislative, and judicial pronouncement. And well it should, for, in Thomas Jefferson's words, "Laws and institutions must go hand in hand with the progress of the human mind."

[The judge agreed that in *King,* as in *Pavesich*, the court had properly granted a civil remedy for defendants' behavior that was "contrary to the good conscience of the community." However, by] . . . proclaiming this new "right of publicity," wc have created an open-ended and ill-defined force which jeopardizes a right of unquestioned authenticity—free speech.

* * *

But the majority says that the fabrication and commercial distribution of a likeness of Dr. King is not "speech," thereby removing the inquiry from the ambit of First Amendment or Free Speech inquiries.

To this conclusion I most vigorously dissent. When our Constitution declares that anyone may "speak, write and publish his sentiments, on all subjects" it does not confine that freedom exclusively to verbal expression. Human intercourse is such that oft-times the most powerful of expressions involve no words at all, e.g., Jesus before Pilate; Thoreau in the Concord jail; King on the bridge at Selma.

Do not the statues of the Confederate soldiers which inhabit so many of our courthouse squares express the sentiments of those who raised them?

Are not the busts of former chief justices, stationed within the rotunda of this very courthouse, expressions of sentiments of gratitude and approval?

Is not the portrait of Dr. King which hangs in our Capitol an expression of sentiment? Manifestly so.

If, then, a two-dimensional likeness in oil and canvas is an expression of sentiment, how can it be said that a three-dimensional likeness in plastic is not?

But, says the majority, our new right to publicity is violated only in cases involving financial gain.

Did the sculptors of our Confederate soldiers, and of our chief justices, labor without gain? Was Dr. King's portraitist unpaid for his work?

If "financial gain" is to be the watershed of violation vel non of this new-found right, it cannot withstand scrutiny. It is rare, indeed, that any expression of sentiment beyond casual conversation is not somehow connected, directly or indirectly, to "financial gain." For example, a school child wins a $25 prize for the best essay on Dr. King's life. Is this "financial gain?" Must the child then account for the winnings?

The essay, because of its worth, is reprinted in a commercial publication. Must the publisher account?

The publication is sold on the newsstand. Must the vendor account?

The majority will say "free speech." Very well. The same child wins a $25 prize in the school art fair. His creation—a bust of Dr. King.

Must he account?

The local newspaper prints a photograph of the child and of his creation. Must it account?

The school commissions replicas of the bust to raise money for its library. Must it account?

UNICEF reproduces the bust on its Christmas cards. Must it account?

Finally, a purely commercial venture undertakes to market replicas of the bust under circumstances similar to those of this case. Must it account?

Obviously, the answers to the above questions will vary, and properly so, because the circumstances posited are vastly different. The dividing line, however, cannot be fixed upon the presence or absence of "financial gain." Rather, it must be grounded in the community's judgment of what, ex aequo et bono, is unconscionable.

Were it otherwise, this "right of publicity," fully extended, would eliminate scholarly research, historical analysis, and public comment, because food and shelter, and the financial gain it takes to provide them, are still essentials of human existence.

Were it otherwise, no newspaper might identify any person or any incident of his life without accounting to him for violation of his "right to publicity."

Were it otherwise, no author might refer to any event in history wherein his reference is identifiable to any individual (or his heirs!) without accounting for his royalties.

---

Two decades later, a major ally of Martin Luther King produced another significant publicity case, *Parks v. LaFace Records,* 329 F.3d 437 (6th Cir. 2003). Indeed, it was Rosa Parks who had taken the crucial first step that soon made King the leader of the civil rights movement. In 1955, Parks refused to give up her seat to a white passenger and move to the back of the bus to which the city of Montgomery, Alabama confined blacks. When Parks was arrested for violating that state law, King accepted her request to institute the boycotts and other peaceful protests against these forms of racial segregation. This eventually produced both the *Civil Rights Act* and a much more integrated America.

But while King had been murdered back in 1968, Parks was still alive to receive the honors granted to historic Americans at the end of the millennium. Thus, unlike King's estate, it was Parks herself who was filing a lawsuit that posed some important issues about the publicity rights of civil rights celebrities. The targets of this suit were a rap (or "hip hop") music group called OutKast that had included a song called "Rosa Parks" in its 1998 album *Aquarium* that was produced by LaFace Records and distributed by its Bertelsmann BMG Entertainment affiliate Arista Records. The song did not mention Parks by name in its lyrics which were not specifically about the civil rights movement. But the chorus repeated ten different times the phrase, "Ah, ha, hush that fuss. Everybody move to the back of the bus!" Not only did the song bring OutKast a Grammy nomination, but it made *Aquarium* one of the best-selling albums (2.5 million) that year.

Rosa Parks had never been told of this song, let alone asked for her consent to the use of her name. When she heard it played, she was offended by the overall lyrics that she found had "profanity, racial slurs, and derogatory language directed at women." Thus Parks filed suit for violation of her publicity rights (as well as defamation, false light privacy, and trademark law). The Sixth Circuit, in rejecting the record label's motion for summary dismissal, stated: "we believe that Parks' right of publicity claim presents a genuine issue of material fact . . .". They also said "whether we personally regard [the song] as repulsive trash or a work of genius is immaterial to a determination of the legal issues presented to us." Instead, they quoted Shakespeare from his play *Othello* to explain why Rosa Parks was entitled to a full trial here.

> Who steals my purse steals trash; 'tis something, nothing;
>
> 'Twas mine, 'tis his, and has been slave to thousands;
>
> But he that filches from me my good name
>
> Robs me of that which not enriches him
>
> And makes me poor indeed.

Thus, in 2005, the parties settled this lawsuit before trial. The record label agreed to pay the 92-year-old Rosa Parks an undisclosed amount to be used for her health and financial care, and OutKast gained an explicit right to keep playing and selling that song—which the following September was ranked one of the top ten best songs of the South by the *Atlanta Journal Constitution*. But if these two sides had not finally been able to reach such an amicable settlement, what are your views about the likely and appropriate treatment at trial of a song like "Rosa Parks"?

One of the major present-day African American figures is Tiger Woods, who has now succeeded Michael Jordan as the most financially valuable celebrity figure (earning over $70 million a year in endorsement contracts with Nike and other businesses). As such a celebrity, Woods sued a "sports artist," Rich Rush, when he saw the latter's work *The*

*Masters of Augusta.* This work had an art print and accompanying narrative insert that placed Tiger Woods in the center "displaying that awesome swing" that had won him the 1997 Masters as the youngest golfer ever to do so (with the faces of Jack Nicklaus and Arnold Palmer looking down on him). The 700 serigraph editions of *Masters* sold for $700 each, and the small lithographs for $15 apiece. Woods, through his personal endorsement agency ETW Group, responded with a lawsuit claiming violation of his publicity rights in his name and image (and also of trademark rights we will be learning about in Chapter 6).

In *ETW Corp. v. Jireh Publishing*, 332 F.3d 915 (6th Cir. 2003), a divided Sixth Circuit panel rejected this claim. After reviewing the history and application of publicity rights, Judge Graham for the majority wrote

> The evidence in the record reveals that Rush's work consists of much more than a mere literal likeness of Woods. It is a panorama of Woods's victory at the 1997 Masters Tournament, with all of the trappings of that tournament in full view, including the Augusta clubhouse, the leader board, images of Woods's caddy, and his final round partner's caddy. These elements in themselves are sufficient to bring Rush's work within the protection of the *First Amendment.* The Masters Tournament is probably the world's most famous golf tournament and Woods's victory in the 1997 tournament was a historic event in the world of sports. A piece of art that portrays a historic sporting event communicates and celebrates the value our culture attaches to such events. It would be ironic indeed if the presence of the image of the victorious athlete would deny the work *First Amendment* protection. Furthermore, Rush's work includes not only images of Woods and the two caddies, but also carefully crafted likenesses of six past winners of the Masters Tournament: Arnold Palmer, Sam Snead, Ben Hogan, Walter Hagen, Bobby Jones, and Jack Nicklaus, a veritable pantheon of golf's greats. Rush's work conveys the message that Woods himself will someday join that revered group.
>
> * * *
>
> In balancing these interests against Woods's right of publicity, we note that Woods, like most sports and entertainment celebrities with commercially valuable identities, engages in an activity, professional golf that in itself generates a significant amount of income which is unrelated to his right of publicity. Even in the absence of his right of publicity, he would still be able to reap substantial financial rewards from authorized appearances and endorsements. It is not at all clear

> that the appearance of Woods's likeness in artwork prints which display one of his major achievements will reduce the commercial value of his likeness.
>
> While the right of publicity allows celebrities like Woods to enjoy the fruits of their labors, here Rush has added a significant creative component of his own to Woods's identity. Permitting Woods's right of publicity to trump Rush's right of freedom of expression would extinguish Rush's right to profit from his creative enterprise.
>
> After balancing the societal and personal interests embodied in the *First Amendment* against Woods's property rights, we conclude that the effect of limiting Woods's right of publicity in this case is negligible and significantly outweighed by society's interest in freedom of artistic expression.

*Id.* at 936, 938. Dissenting Judge Clay, however, disagreed on both issues. After reviewing the history of publicity rights under the First Amendment, he emphasized that

> the rendition done by Rush is nearly identical to that in the poster distributed by Nike. Although the faces and partial body images of other famous golfers appear in blue sketch blending in the background of Rush's print, the clear focus of the work is Woods in full body image wearing his red shirt and holding his famous swing in the pose which is nearly identical to that depicted in the Nike poster. Rush's print does not depict Woods in the same vein as the other golfers, such that the focus of the print is not the Masters Tournament or the other golfers who have won the prestigious green jacket award, but that of Woods holding his famous golf swing while at that tournament. Thus, although it is apparent that Rush is an adequately skilled artist, after viewing the prints in question it is also apparent that Rush's ability in this regard is "subordinated to the overall goal of creating literal, conventional depictions of [Tiger Woods] so as to exploit his . . . fame [such that Rush's] right of free expression is outweighed by [Woods'] right of publicity."
>
> * * *
>
> Accordingly, contrary to the majority's conclusion otherwise, it is clear that the prints gain their commercial value by exploiting the fame and celebrity status that Woods has worked to achieve. Under such facts, the right of publicity is not outweighed by the right of free expression.

*Id.* at 959. What are your views on these two key legal cases and how would you compare the claims of Woods and Parks?

## *QUESTIONS FOR DISCUSSION*

1. In appraising these cases, consider the assertion in the concurring opinion in *King,* that by characterizing the creation and distribution of a likeness as something other than "speech," the majority had diluted the value of the First Amendment. The concurrence suggests, instead, that these cases be decided by relying on "community standards" to determine which appropriations are "unconscionable." Which approach do you find more appealing? What would amount to an "unconscionable" appropriation under "community" standards? By the way, in 1993, the King estate filed suit against USA Today for printing the text of Dr. King's "I Have A Dream" address on the occasion of Martin Luther King Day, a suit that USA Today settled by agreeing to pay a fee for that privilege. Backed by the various legal tools we will encounter in this and the next two chapters, the King estate announced in early 1997 that it had signed a multimillion dollar deal with Time Warner, which will be selling to the American public Martin Luther King's speeches, sermons, thoughts, and images via books, audio cassettes, CD–ROMs, along with a website.

2. One can put a real-life face on some of the hypothetical examples mentioned in the concurring opinion, regarding the potential scope of judge-made publicity rights. Beginning in the late 1950s, Andy Warhol helped create a new brand of Pop Art. Along with tins of Campbell Soup, Warhol's favorite image was Marilyn Monroe, who by the end of that century had been ranked the top actress of the twentieth century and the sex symbol of America. In a number of works, he used a publicity still photo of Monroe's face taken for her 1953 movie *Niagara*, (the year she also started dating her future husband, Joe DiMaggio) enlarged it photomechanically, silkscreened the picture onto canvass, and then surrounded it with other images and colors to present his artistic theme. Warhol received the consent of neither Monroe (before her death), nor her estate afterwards, for this use of her likeness on these now famous works of art (which made Warhol into a celebrity as well). Can an artistic creation such as *Gold Marilyn Monroe*, prominently displayed at the New York Museum of Modern Art, be judged a violation of its subject's common law publicity rights? Is it permissible under the First Amendment for a court to treat differently Warhol's depiction of Monroe and Bolen's treatment of King in the above case?

3. A recent case involved wrestler "Pretty Boy" Doug Somerson illustrates the limits to the right of publicity claim under the First Amendment (as discussed in Chapter 1). Somerson alleged, among other things, that World Wrestling Entertainment ("WWE") and Vince McMahon violated his right of publicity by using his name and likeness in certain merchandise without paying him royalties, and without his consent or authorization. The Court, however, dismissed Somerson's right of publicity claim because the information used was factual in nature and described his public actions as a wrestler. The Court compared it to the cataloging of historical information in baseball statistics. Why is this case different than *King*? *See Somerson v. WWE*, 956 F. Supp. 1360 (N.D. Ga. 2013).

4. By contrast, where the violation of the right of publicity is clear, courts are not reluctant to enforce it. From the late 1940's until his death in 2000, Jack Gibson was known as radio personality "Jack the Rapper." Gibson's heirs continue to use and promote the alias. In 2012, Billy Foster and others hosted a series of events called "The New Jack the Rapper Convention." Heirs of Gibson objected, and won a temporary restraining order, before reaching a settlement for payment of one-time use of the moniker. Foster failed to pay as required by the settlement, and then continued to use the name in a new series of events the following year. The Court granted summary judgment for the plaintiffs recognizing the tortious use of Gibson's right of publicity. *See Bell v. Foster*, 109 U.S.P.Q. 1249 (N.D. Ga. 2013). In light of this case, why do you think the right of publicity is so important?

5. On spring break, fourteen-year old Lindsey Bullard exposed her breasts to two unknown men in a Panama City parking lot. She consented to their videotaping her, and did not discuss what they might do with the videotape. The men subsequently sold the footage to MRA Holding, which included in their *College Girls Gone Wild* video series. MRA did not obtain Bullard's permission to use the video. In addition, a photo of Bullard was included on the cover of the video box, with the phrase "Get Educated!" superimposed over Bullard's breasts. Bullard sued MRA, alleging misappropriation of her likeness. Result? *See Bullard v. MRA Holding*, 292 Ga. 748 (2013).

---

In 1999, the movie, *Bowfinger* had Steve Martin playing "down-and-out" producer-director Bobby Bowfinger, who was told by a major studio executive (played by Robert Downey, Jr.) that in order to get a deal for financing and distributing his current movie project, *Chubby Rain*, he needed to have Hollywood's action star Kit Ramsey (played by Eddie Murphy) in it. Bowfinger was clearly unable to afford signing Ramsey up to the star's usual $20 million salary fee. Instead, he came up with the idea of having his film crew track Ramsey around the streets of Los Angeles and surreptitiously film real world encounters with other unknown actors crossing his path. Suppose that *Bowfinger* was a true story: would and should his lawyers eventually have had to sign up Ramsey (or Murphy) as accepting this new role before releasing *Chubby Rain* to the movie audience?

*Bowfinger* may have been inspired by ongoing discussions in Hollywood about one aspect of Paramount's famous movie, *Forrest Gump*, which became the third largest-grossing movie in history while sweeping the 1994 Academy Awards. But rather than having his film crews tracking celebrities around the streets, the producers of this movie used the brand-new digital imaging technology to portray extremely realistic likenesses of Presidents John Kennedy, Lyndon Johnson, and Richard

Nixon conversing with Gump as played by Tom Hanks. Much the same thing had been done in the 1993 hit *In the Line of Fire*, starring Clint Eastwood as an aging Secret Service agent trying to protect a current president from assassination. The film inserted clips of Eastwood in his early *Dirty Harry* movie days (though with his hair digitally shortened from the 1970s stylistic look) into actual footage of President Kennedy's 1963 motorcade from the airport into Dallas, in order to depict Eastwood as a young Secret Service agent who had not been able to prevent the assassination of JFK. Digital imaging also saved the 1994 movie *The Crow*, when its star, Brandon Lee, died before filming had been completed. Indeed, some movie financiers and insurers are reportedly now considering a contractual requirement that all the lead actors be digitally scanned before a project gets underway.

The digital imaging process will be detailed in Chapter 5 where we consider some of the intellectual property issues posed by using film of these famous personages. Assume, though, that there was no copyright problem, perhaps because the motion picture studio was using its own film sources. If Martin Luther King had been depicted in conversation with Gump, would that be actionable if done without the consent of his estate? Are the relevant policy issues the same as they would be if Paramount used material from *Gump* to create an image of Tom Hanks for another movie portraying an entirely different character? Suppose the latter movie brought back Humphrey Bogart and Marilyn Monroe to portray new characters in their unique personal styles? The movie industry has now developed the kind of digital technology which permits computerized close-ups of facial expressions, lip movements, and the like for depicting real-life rather than animated characters. Suppose, though, that the studios would like to economize its production costs by not paying for the use of the previously-filmed images of either deceased or living actors. Such entertainment industry action would pose the kinds of legal and policy questions you must keep in mind as you delve into the array of cases and materials that surround the *King* decision that you have just read.[b]

## B. PUBLICITY RIGHTS AND ENTERTAINMENT SHOWS[c]

Publicity rights come into play in two quite different contexts. The first is the entertainment show itself, whether it be a live event or a

[b] *See* Joseph J. Beard, *Casting Call at Forest Lawn: The Digital Resurrection of Deceased Entertainers, a 21st Century Challenge to Intellectual Property Law*, 8 High Tech. L.J. 101 (1993); Roberta R. Kwall, *Preserving Personality & Reputational Interests of Constructed Personas Through Moral Rights: A Blueprint for the Twenty-First Century*, 2001 U. Ill. L. Rev. 151.

[c] *See* Peter L. Felcher & Edward L. Rubin, *Privacy, Publicity & the Portrayal of Real People by the Media*, 88 Yale L.J. 1577 (1979); *see also* Josh Blackman, *Omniveillance, Google, Privacy in Public, & the Right to Your Digital Identity*, 49 Santa Clara L. Rev. 313 (2009).

filmed or recorded product. The second context is commercial marketing or advertising, which is often inserted in commercial breaks on entertainment broadcasts. With respect to the creation of entertainment products, just as we saw with privacy rights, the assertion of common law publicity claims raises countervailing constitutional rights to freedom of speech. In the following case, the Supreme Court addressed these issues while exploring the distinctive features of entertainer publicity rights.

## ZACCHINI V. SCRIPPS-HOWARD BROADCASTING CO.

Supreme Court of the United States, 1977.
433 U.S. 562, 97 S.Ct. 2849, 53 L.Ed.2d 965.

MR. JUSTICE WHITE delivered the opinion of the court.

[Hugo Zacchini's fifteen-second entertainment act had him being shot from a cannon into a net 200 feet away. In 1972, Zacchini was performing at an Ohio county fair in an enclosed grandstand site to which anyone who paid the general admission fee had access. Against Zacchini's wishes, a reporter from the defendant's local radio station used a small movie camera to tape the entire performance. The station aired the tape on that night's eleven o'clock newscast with favorable commentary about this thrilling "human cannonball act" that one had to see in person to really appreciate. When Zacchini sued the station for unlawful appropriation of his professional property rights, the Ohio Supreme Court recognized that while performers did have such a state law publicity right, the television station also had a First Amendment privilege to report such a "matter of legitimate public interest." Zacchini appealed to the Supreme Court.]

* * *

. . . It is clear enough from the opinion of the Ohio Supreme Court that in adjudicating the crucial question of whether respondent had a privilege to film and televise petitioner's performance, the court placed principal reliance on *Time, Inc. v. Hill*, 385 U.S. 374 (1967), a case involving First Amendment limitations on state tort actions. It construed the principle of that case, along with that of *New York Times Co. v. Sullivan*, 376 U.S. 254 (1964), to be that "the press has a privilege to report matters of legitimate public interest even though such reports might intrude on matters otherwise private," and concluded, therefore, that the press is also "privileged when an individual seeks to publicly exploit his talents while keeping the benefits private." The privilege thus exists in cases "where appropriation of a right of publicity is claimed."

* * *

The Ohio Supreme Court held that respondent is constitutionally privileged to include in its newscasts matters of public interest that would otherwise be protected by the right of publicity, absent an intent to injure or to appropriate for some nonprivileged purpose. If under this standard respondent had merely reported that petitioner was performing at the fair and described or commented on his act, with or without showing his picture on television, we would have a very different case. But petitioner is not contending that his appearance at the fair and his performance could not be reported by the press as newsworthy items. His complaint is that respondent filmed his entire act and displayed that film on television for the public to see and enjoy. This, he claimed, was an appropriation of his professional property. . . .

* * *

[The Supreme Court next asserted that *Time, Inc. v. Hill*, 385 U.S. 374 (1967), which the Ohio Supreme Court had relied heavily on here, did not] mandate a media privilege to televise a performer's entire act without his consent . . . *Time, Inc. v. Hill*, which was hotly contested and decided by a divided Court, involved an entirely different tort from the "right of publicity" recognized by the Ohio Supreme Court . . . The Court [in *Time, Inc.*] was aware that it was adjudicating a "false light" privacy case involving a matter of public interest, not a case involving "intrusion," "appropriation" of a name or likeness for the purposes of trade, or "private details" about a non-newsworthy person or event. It is also abundantly clear that *Time, Inc. v. Hill* did not involve a performer, a person with a name having commercial value, or any claim to a "right of publicity." This discrete kind of "appropriation" case was plainly identified in the literature cited by the Court and had been adjudicated in the reported cases.

The differences between these two torts are important. First, the State's interests in providing a cause of action in each instance are different. "The interest protected" in permitting recovery for placing the plaintiff in a false light "is clearly that of reputation, with the same overtones of mental distress as in defamation." Prosser, supra, 48 Calif. L. Rev., at 400. By contrast, the State's interest in permitting a "right of publicity" is in protecting the proprietary interest of the individual in his act in part to encourage such entertainment. As we later note, the State's interest is closely analogous to the goals of patent and copyright law, focusing on the right of the individual to reap the reward of his endeavors and having little to do with protecting feelings or reputation. Second, the two torts differ in the degree to which they intrude on dissemination of information to the public. In "false light" cases the only way to protect the interests involved is to attempt to minimize publication of the damaging matter, while in "right of publicity" cases the only question is who gets to do the publishing. An entertainer such as petitioner usually has no objection to the widespread publication of his act as long as he gets the commercial benefit of such publication. . . .

Nor does it appear that our later cases, such as *Rosenbloom v. Metromedia, Inc.*, 403 U.S. 29 (1971); *Gertz v. Robert Welch, Inc.*, 418 U.S. 323 (1974); and *Time, Inc. v. Firestone*, 424 U.S. 448 (1976), require or furnish substantial support for the Ohio court's privilege ruling. These cases, like *New York Times*, emphasize the protection extended to the press by the First Amendment in defamation cases, particularly when suit is brought by a public official or a public figure. None of them involve an alleged appropriation by the press of a right of publicity existing under state law.

Moreover, *Time, Inc. v. Hill, New York Times, Metromedia, Gertz*, and *Firestone* all involved the reporting of events; in none of them was there an attempt to broadcast or publish an entire act for which the performer ordinarily gets paid. It is evident, and there is no claim here to the contrary, that petitioner's state-law right of publicity would not serve to prevent respondent from reporting the newsworthy facts about petitioner's act. . . . The Constitution no more prevents a State from requiring respondent to compensate petitioner for broadcasting his act on television than it would privilege respondent to film and broadcast a copyrighted dramatic work without liability to the copyright owner, Copyrights Act, 17 U.S.C. App. § 101 et seq. (1976 ed.); cf. *Kalem Co. v. Harper Bros.*, 222 U.S. 55 (1911); *Manners v. Morosco*, 252 U.S. 317 (1920), or to film and broadcast a prize fight, *Ettore v. Philco Television Broadcasting Corp.*, 229 F.2d 481 (CA3), cert. denied, 351 U.S. 926 (1956); or a baseball game, *Pittsburgh Athletic Co. v. KQV Broadcasting Co.*, 24 F. Supp. 490 (W.D.Pa.1938), where the promoters or the participants had other plans for publicizing the event. There are ample reasons for reaching this conclusion.

The broadcast of a film of petitioner's entire act poses a substantial threat to the economic value of that performance. As the Ohio court recognized, this act is the product of petitioner's own talents and energy, the end result of much time, effort, and expense. Much of its economic value lies in the "right of exclusive control over the publicity given to his performance"; if the public can see the act free on television, it will be less willing to pay to see it at the fair. The effect of a public broadcast of the performance is similar to preventing petitioner from charging an admission fee. . . . Moreover, the broadcast of petitioner's entire performance, unlike the unauthorized use of another's name for purpose of trade or the incidental use of a name or picture by the press, goes to the heart of petitioner's ability to earn a living as an entertainer. Thus, in this case, Ohio has recognized what may be the strongest case for a "right of publicity"—involving, not the appropriation of an entertainer's reputation to enhance the attractiveness of a commercial product, but the appropriation of the very activity by which the entertainer acquired his reputation in the first place.

Of course, Ohio's decision to protect petitioner's right of publicity here rests on more than a desire to compensate the performer for the time and effort invested in his act; the protection provides an economic incentive for him to make the investment required to produce a performance of interest to the public. This same consideration underlies the patent and copyright laws long enforced by this Court. As the Court stated in *Mazer v. Stein*, 347 U.S. 201 (1954):

> The economic philosophy behind the clause empowering Congress to grant patents and copyrights is the conviction that encouragement of individual effort by personal gain is the best way to advance public welfare through the talents of authors and inventors in 'Science and useful Arts.' Sacrificial days devoted to such creative activities deserve rewards commensurate with the services rendered.

347 U.S. at 219. These laws perhaps regard the "reward to the owner [as] a secondary consideration," *United States v. Paramount Pictures*, 334 U.S. 131, 158 (1948), but they were "intended definitely to grant valuable, enforceable rights" in order to afford greater encouragement to the production of works of benefit to the public. *Washingtonian Publishing Co. v. Pearson*, 306 U.S. 30, 36 (1939). The Constitution does not prevent Ohio from making a similar choice here in deciding to protect the entertainer's incentive in order to encourage the production of this type of work.

There is no doubt that entertainment, as well as news, enjoys First Amendment protection. It is also true that entertainment itself can be important news. But it is important to note that neither the public nor respondent will be deprived of the benefit of petitioner's performance as long as his commercial stake in his act is appropriately recognized. Petitioner does not seek to enjoin the broadcast of his performance; he simply wants to be paid for it. Nor do we think that a state-law damages remedy against respondent would represent a species of liability without fault contrary to the letter or spirit of *Gertz v. Robert Welch, Inc.*, 418 U.S. 323 (1974). Respondent knew that petitioner objected to televising his act but nevertheless displayed the entire film.

We conclude that although the State of Ohio may as a matter of its own law privilege the press in the circumstances of this case, the First and Fourteenth Amendments do not require it to do so.

Reversed.

### *QUESTION FOR DISCUSSION*

Justice Powell's dissent objected to the majority's characterization of this case as "comparable to unauthorized commercial broadcasts of sporting events, theatrical performances, and the like where the broadcaster keeps the profits." Instead, the dissenters believed that this was simply a routine fifteen-second feature of a television newscast, and that imposing liability could produce "media self-censorship" by substituting verbal commentary with still pictures for live film footage. With whose views do you agree? Note also the several references in the judicial opinions to "commercial exploitation." What should be the meaning and implications of that phrase in this entertainment law context?

---

Just a few years after *Zacchini* was decided, a judge had to explore its implications for a far more celebrated figure, in *Estate of Presley v. Russen*, 513 F. Supp. 1339 (D.N.J. 1981). Elvis Presley, "The King of Rock and Roll," had enchanted music fans around the world with his characteristic style—wearing a jump suit, wildly gyrating his hips and legs on the stage, and singing into a hand-held microphone. Presley's musical tours were billed as *Elvis in Concert*, his back-up band was called the TCB Band, and his insignia was a lightning bolt design. Following his death, Presley's popularity soared even higher. His estate received large royalties from record sales, videotapes of his several movies (such as *Viva Las Vegas*), marketing licenses to such firms as Boxcar Enterprises and Factors, and visits to Elvis' Memphis home, Graceland Mansion. (By the late 1980s, the Presley estate was reportedly earning $15 million a year.) However, beginning in 1975, Rob Russen developed "The Big El Show," starring Larry Seth, who sang songs made popular by Presley, performed in the same voice, style and dress, and used a back-up musical group called the TCB Band. Advertisements for concert tours and recordings described the performance as "Reflections on a Legend . . . A Tribute to Elvis Presley. . . . Looks and Sounds LIKE THE KING." While Elvis had not sued Russen, his estate did.

The district court acknowledged that the First Amendment did protect the right to depict celebrities in both factual and fictional works, quoting the following passage from a California Supreme Court ruling in *Guglielmi v. Spelling-Goldberg Productions*, 25 Cal. 3d 860, 160 Cal. Rptr. 352, 603 P.2d 454 (1979):

> Contemporary events, symbols and people are regularly used in fictional works. Fiction writers may be able to more persuasively, more accurately express themselves by weaving into the tale persons or events familiar to their readers. The choice is theirs. No author should be forced into creating mythological worlds or characters wholly divorced from reality. The right of publicity derived from public prominence does not confer a shield to ward off caricature, parody and satire. Rather, prominence invites creative comment.

160 Cal. Rptr. at 358, 603 P.2d at 460 (Bird C.J. concurring). However, the judge concluded that "The Big El Show" was simply an imitation of Presley, not a creative parody, burlesque, satire, or criticism.

> [T]he show serves primarily to commercially exploit the likeness of Elvis Presley without contributing anything of substantial value to society . . . [E]ntertainment that is merely a copy or imitation, even if skillfully and accurately carried out, does not really have its own creative component and does not have a significant value as pure entertainment.

513 F. Supp. at 1359. After *Zacchini*, an entertainer's right to block such appropriation of his celebrity value was found to override anyone else's First Amendment claim to do this kind of show.

## *QUESTIONS FOR DISCUSSION*

1. As we saw from the materials in Chapter 1, New Jersey could not legally ban a live performance by Elvis Presley or his musical successors on the grounds that it was "indecent" or "violent." Why should the state's law be able to ban a performance because it is "imitative" (and how does pure imitation differ from parody)? What are the precise distinctions in both the affirmative social policies and the free speech constraints? Should these distinctions make a legal difference?

2. *Janis* is a play with two acts. Act One consists of imaginary dialogue between Janis Joplin and other deceased personages of her time (such as Jack Kerouac and Bessie Smith) on a fictional day that is to end in a Joplin concert. Act Two is the concert, with a performer singing a number of Joplin's hit songs in her characteristic style. The producers of the play have a license from the music publishing society to use the music, but have no license from Joplin's estate to use her likeness. Should this play constitute a violation of the common law rights of publicity of a musician (whether dead or alive)? Assume the case is to be resolved under California law, which makes publicity rights descendible, but exempts treatments in plays (as well as films and books) from claims of infringement of inherited publicity rights. *See Joplin Enterprises v. Allen*, 795 F. Supp. 349 (W.D. Wash. 1992). Compare *Groucho Marx Productions v. Day & Night Co.*, 523 F. Supp. 485 (S.D.N.Y. 1981), reversed on other grounds, 689 F.2d 317 (2d Cir. 1982) (involving a musical comedy that used a parody of the Marx brothers as one of the devices in its satire on Hollywood movies).

3. Ginger Rogers and her musical partner, Fred Astaire, starred in a number of highly successful Hollywood musicals in the 1930s and 1940s. Rogers herself won the 1940 Oscar Award for Best Actress. Together the two, generally known as "Fred and Ginger," were considered the movie world's "paragons of style, elegance, and grace." Even in the 1980s, Rogers was still licensing her name for use on products and was writing an autobiography which she hoped would be adapted into a movie. In 1986, Frederico Fellini,

the equally illustrious Italian film director, made a movie entitled *Ginger and Fred*, about the careers and relationship of two fictional Italian cabaret performers billed as "Ginger and Fred" because their standard performance was an imitation of Rogers and Astaire. The Fellini movie was shown briefly in the United States, attracting not only mixed reviews but a lawsuit by Rogers. What is the appropriate result? *See Rogers v. Grimaldi*, 875 F.2d 994 (2d Cir. 1989).

---

Next comes a case about two people who became celebrities for the wrong reasons. One capitalized on her newfound celebrity status by writing a book account that became a docudrama movie, while the other sought to use publicity law to secure a share of the proceeds.

## MATTHEWS V. WOZENCRAFT

United States Court of Appeals, Fifth Circuit, 1994.
15 F.3d 432.

SMITH, CIRCUIT JUDGE.

[In the late 1970s, Creig Matthews and Kim Wozencraft were narcotic officers in the Tyler, Texas police force, engaged in an undercover operation against a suspected drug dealer. During that operation the two became romantically involved, were later attacked and wounded by an assailant with a shotgun, produced over 100 arrests, and were taken to a safe-house by Ross Perot, then head of a Texas crime commission. It turned out, though, that Matthews and Wozencraft had themselves become drug-addicted, and that the two had planted a "phony stash" on their principal target to try to incriminate him. When these facts (and their perjured testimony) became known, Matthews and Wozencraft (now married) went to prison.

While in prison, the two agreed to collaborate on a book about their story. However, when Wozencraft was released, she went to New York to do graduate work at Columbia. Her thesis became the basis for a successful book, *Rush,* published by Random House, and then the sale to MGM (for $1 million) of the right to make a fictionalized movie of the same name, featuring Jason Patric as the Matthews character and Jennifer Jason Leigh as Wozencraft.

Meanwhile, Matthews, whom it was conceded was recognizably featured in *Rush*, had received no compensation from this project. Instead, he had cooperated in the authorship of a much less visible, non-fiction account of the same events, *Smith County Justice*. Thus Matthews sued Wozencraft, Random House, and MGM for their appropriation of the rights to his story. In this appeal from summary dismissal of Matthews's suit, the Fifth Circuit had to decide whether there was any viable appropriation claim here, since Matthews conceded that he had become a public figure in an incident that was a matter of public concern.]

* * *

II

C.

There are three elements to a misappropriation claim under Texas law: (i) that the defendant appropriated the plaintiff's name or likeness for the value associated with it, and not in an incidental manner or for a newsworthy purpose; (ii) that the plaintiff can be identified from the publication; and (iii) that there was some advantage or benefit to the defendant. Under this test, Matthews is unable to create any issue of material fact as to liability.

There is no question that Matthews can be identified from the publication, at least to the point of creating a genuine issue of fact as to the identity of the Jim Raynor character. He claims that his life story was appropriated for Wozencraft's commercial benefit. The protection of "name or likeness" under Texas law, however, does not include a person's life story. If Texas law did protect such a right, it was not "appropriated." And, even if Matthews could state a claim, Wozencraft would be protected by an exception in the state tort law.

Tortious liability for appropriation of a name or likeness is intended to protect the value of an individual's notoriety or skill. Thus, the Restatement notes, "In order that there may be liability under the rule stated in this Section, the defendant must have appropriated to his own use or benefit the reputation, prestige, social or commercial standing, public interest or other values of the plaintiff's name or likeness." Restatement § 652C, comment c. The misappropriation tort does not protect one's name per se; rather, it protects the value associated with that name.

Appropriation of a name or likeness generally becomes actionable when used "to advertise the defendant's business or product, or for some similar commercial purpose." Restatement § 652C, comment b. The value of one's likeness is not "appropriated when it is published for purposes other than taking advantage of his reputation, prestige, or other value associated with him, for purposes of publicity. . . . It is only when the publicity is given for the purpose of appropriating to the defendant's benefit the commercial or other values associated with the name or the likeness that the right of privacy is invaded." Restatement § 652C, comment.

There is nothing unique about Matthew's name or likeness that creates value for Wozencraft to appropriate. She is not "cashing-in" on goodwill associated with his name but is simply converting factual events that happen to include Matthews into fiction. The use of his name does not provide value to the book, nor is she using his name to "endorse" the book to the public, because his name has no independent value. In short, Matthew's life story, while interesting to readers and film-goers, is not a "name or likeness" for purposes of applying the misappropriation doctrine.

Protecting one's name or likeness from misappropriation is socially beneficial because it encourages people to develop special skills, which then can be used for commercial advantage. Associating one's goodwill with a product transmits valuable information to consumers. Without the artificial scarcity created by the protection of one's likeness, that likeness would be exploited commercially until the marginal value of its use is zero.[2]

For instance, if a well-known public figure's picture could be used freely to endorse commercial products, the value of his likeness would disappear. Creating artificial scarcity preserves the value to him, to advertisers who contract for the use of his likeness, and in the end, to consumers, who receive information from the knowledge that he is being paid to endorse the product.[3] *See Kimbrough v. Coca-Cola/USA*, 521 S.W.2d 719, 722 (Tex.Civ.App.1975) (in which former Texas A & M football star stated valid claim for misappropriation where his picture was used, over his objection, as part of an advertisement for Coca-Cola in a football game program).

As Judge Posner writes,

> It might seem that creating a property right in such uses would not lead to any socially worthwhile investment but would simply enrich already wealthy celebrities. However, whatever information value a celebrity's endorsement has to consumers will be lost if every advertiser can use the celebrity's name and picture. . . . The value of associating the celebrity's name with a

---

[2] If the appropriation of an individual's goodwill were left untrammelled, it soon would be overused, as each user will not consider the externality effect his use will have on others. Each use of the celebrity's name or face will reduce the value that other users can derive from it. The use of a name or face, therefore, is analogous to the overuse of a public highway: in deciding whether to use the road, each user does not consider the increased congestion that his use will inflict on others. *See* Frank H. Knight, *Some Fallacies in the Interpretation of Social Cost*, 38 Q.J. Econ. 582 (1924).

We can ration the use of highways by imposing tolls. *See id.* We grant celebrities a property right to ration the use of their names in order to maximize their value over time.

[3] The information transmitted is both direct and indirect in nature. It is direct because of any goodwill (or ill-will) associated with the person's link to the product. Indirect information is transmitted because the payment by the advertiser to him is an investment in nonsalvageable capital signaling a commitment to quality by the advertiser. *See* Benjamin Klein & Keith B. Leffler, *The Role of Market Forces in Assuring Contractual Performance*, 89 J. Pol. Econ. 615, 630–31 (1981).

particular product will be diminished if others are permitted to use the name in association with their products.

Richard A. Posner, *Economic Analysis of Law* § 3.3, at 43 (4th ed. 1992). The tort of misappropriation of name or likeness, therefore, creates property rights only where the failure to do so would result in the excessive exploitation of its value.[4]

Thus, the term "likeness" includes such things as pictures, *National Bank of Commerce v. Shaklee Corp.*, 503 F. Supp. 533 (W.D.Tex.1980); drawings, *Benavidez v. Anheuser Busch, Inc.*, 873 F.2d 102 (5th Cir. 1989); and the use of a singer's distinctive voice, *Waits v. Frito-Lay, Inc.*, 978 F.2d 1093 (9th Cir. 1992) (reasoning that "a voice is as distinctive as a face" and thus cannot be imitated in order to sell a product), that one could exploit for commercial advantage. If exploitation of this beneficial information were not limited, its value soon would be dissipated.

The term "likeness" does not include general incidents from a person's life, especially when fictionalized. The narrative of an individual's life, standing alone, lacks the value of a name or likeness that the misappropriation tort protects. Unlike the goodwill associated with one's name or likeness, the facts of an individual's life possess no intrinsic value that will deteriorate with repeated use. As Posner observes, "If Brand X beer makes money using Celebrity A's picture in its advertising, competing brands might use the same picture until the picture ceased to have any advertising value at all. In contrast, the multiple use of a celebrity's photograph by competing newspapers is unlikely to reduce the value of the photograph to the newspaper-reading public." Richard A. Posner, *The Economics of Justice* 258 (2d ed. 1983).

Far from reducing the value of Matthews's story, *Rush* increased the value, as reflected in the publication of articles about Matthews and Wozencraft in New York Magazine, The Washington Post, and The Guardian, among others. Similarly, *Smith County Justice*, although published first, did not reduce the sales of *Rush*. As there is no fear that any valuable information provided by the facts of one's life will be reduced by repeated use, the law does not forbid the "appropriation" of this information.

Further, because most of the material facts are a matter of public record because of the highly-publicized trial, it is especially difficult for Matthews to claim that his likeness was unfairly appropriated, as a name cannot be appropriated by reference to it in connection with the legitimate mention of public activities. "No one has the right to object

[4] The social goals misappropriation furthers are identical to those animating the prohibition of fraud. *See, e.g., Moore v. Big Picture Co.*, 828 F.2d 270, 277 (5th Cir. 1987) (misappropriation occurs when plaintiff's name used by defendant without permission in order to secure a contract); *see also* Posner, supra, § 4.6, at 109–10 (fraud reduces societal wealth by encouraging investment in wealth-redistributing, rather than wealth-creating, activity).

merely because his name or his appearance is brought before the public, since neither is in any way a private matter and both are open to public observation." Restatement § 652C, comment d.

III.

[The Court then sketched the reasons why, even if Texas had "recognized a cause of action for misappropriation of events in one's life," for freedom of speech reasons it would also have incorporated an exception for biographies of public figures based on information "in the public domain."] As one court has commented,

> [A] public figure has no exclusive rights to his or her own life story. . . . Such life story of the public figure may legitimately extend, to some reasonable degree, to . . . information concerning the individual, and to facts about him, which are not public. . . . Thus the life history of one accused of [crime], together with such heretofore private facts may throw some light upon what kind of person he is, his possible guilt or innocence, or his reasons for committing a crime, are a matter of legitimate public interest.

*Corabi v. Curtis Publishing Co.*, 273 A.2d 899, 919 (Pa.1971).

In the time since his participation in the Tyler drug investigation and his subsequent conviction and prison time for his illegal activity, Matthews voluntarily submitted to numerous interviews with the national media. He also cooperated in the publication of *Smith County Justice* and testified about his activities in Hardy's criminal trial. All the material facts underlying *Rush* were a matter of public knowledge and were in the public domain.

Thus, Matthews became a public figure through his activities. The subject matter of his statements—narcotics officers using drugs, perjuring themselves, and making fraudulent charges—was a matter of public interest. Because all of the events were a part of the public domain, defendants were entitled to their fair use, including their narration in fictionalized form.

[The court also upheld summary dismissal of Matthews's contract claim against Wozencraft.]

* * *

Affirmed.

---

We shall soon encounter a number of controversial cases that test the validity of the *Matthews* court's affirmative justification for an exclusive publicity right for advertising and merchandising purposes—the belief that such a right is socially beneficial because it preserves the value of a celebrity's name and identity. Before tackling that problem, we will see one more treatment (under New York privacy law as then understood) of the fictionalized depiction of a period in the real life of a celebrity. Intriguingly, the celebrity in this case was herself an author of mystery fiction.

## HICKS V. CASABLANCA RECORDS

United States District Court, Southern District of New York, 1978.
464 F. Supp. 426.

PIERCE, DISTRICT JUDGE.

[Agatha Christie was perhaps the best-known mystery writer of all time. Over the five decades of her career, she wrote scores of books, most starring Hercule Poirot, and most of which were made into movies and television series with the consent of Christie and her estate. However, shortly after Christie died in 1976, the defendant began filming a movie, *Agatha*, that its subject had not consented-to. The film was based on a real-life incident in Christie's life. Back in 1926, she suddenly dropped from sight, leaving her husband and family in distress at home, and the people in England and elsewhere stunned. Eleven days later, Christie reappeared, but never disclosed her whereabouts or what she had been doing. The script for *Agatha* provided a totally fictionalized explanation of this real-life mystery. "Christie is portrayed as an emotionally unstable woman, who, during her eleven-day disappearance, engages in a sinister plot to murder her husband's mistress, in an attempt to regain the alienated affections of her husband." When Christie's daughter and heir, Rosalind Christie Hughes, learned of this film project, she filed suit, alleging violation of her mother's right of publicity. (Defamation and privacy claims die with the person so portrayed.) Following is the court's verdict.]

* * *

Here, the Court is faced with the novel and rather complex question of "whether the right of publicity attaches where the name or likeness is used in connection with a book or movie?" The question is novel in view of the fact that more so than posters, bubble gum cards, or some other such "merchandise", books and movies are vehicles through which ideas and opinions are disseminated and, as such, have enjoyed certain constitutional protections, not generally accorded "merchandise." It is complex because this Court is unaware of any other cases presenting a similar fact pattern or similar constitutional question with respect to this issue of the right of publicity. [The Court then noted that New York's statutory right of privacy, § 51 of the Civil Rights Act, had been read in *Spahn v. Julian Messner*, 23 A.D.2d 216, 260 N.Y.S. 2d 451, 453 (1965), as including a privilege to use "matters of news, history, biography, and other factual subjects of public interest despite the necessary references to the names, portraits, identities, or histories of living persons."] . . . This Court finds that the same privileges and exemptions "engrafted" upon the privacy statute are engrafted upon the right of publicity.

In addressing defendants' argument that the book *Agatha* is a biography protected under *Spahn*, this Court, while noting that the affidavit of the author of the book details her investigation with respect to the "facts" surrounding the disappearance, finds the book to be fiction, not biography. Indeed, defendant Ballantine Books' use of the word "novel" on the cover of the book, as well as the notable absence of any cited source or reference material therein, belie its contention that the book is a biography. Moreover, the only "facts" contained in the book appear to be the names of Mrs. Christie, her husband, her daughter, and Ms. Neeley; and that Mrs. Christie disappeared for eleven days. The remainder is mainly conjecture, surmise, and fiction. Accordingly, the Court finds that the defendants in both cases cannot avail themselves of the biography privilege in connection with the book or movie. Further since the book and the movie treat these few scant facts about the disappearance of Mrs. Christie as mere appendages to the main body of their fictional accounts, neither can be considered privileged as "fair comment."

Thus, finding none of the *Spahn* privileges available to the defendants herein, the Court must next inquire as to whether the movie or the novel, as fictionalizations, are entitled to any constitutional protection. In so doing, it is noted that other courts, in addressing the scope of First Amendment protections of speech, have engaged in a balancing test between society's interest in the speech for which protection is sought and the societal, commercial or governmental interests seeking to restrain such speech. And unless there appears to be some countervailing legal or policy reason, courts have found the exercise of the right of speech to be protected . . . Here, this Court is of the opinion that the interests in the speech sought to be protected, i.e., the movie and the novel, should be protected and that there are no countervailing legal or policy grounds against such protection.

In support of this position, resort is again made to cases in the privacy field, of which two are found to be particularly relevant: *Spahn*, cited supra, and *University of Notre Dame Du Lac v. Twentieth Century-Fox Film Corp.*, 22 A.D.2d 452, 256 N.Y.S.2d 301 (1965), Aff'd upon the opinion of the Appellate Division, 15 N.Y.2d 940, 259 N.Y.S.2d 832, 207 N.E.2d 508 (1965) (hereinafter cited as *Notre Dame*). The *Spahn* case, like the book case here, involved the distribution of a book which was presented by the defendant as being a biography of the well-known baseball player Warren Spahn. However, presented in the book were deliberate falsifications of events represented to be true, manufactured dialogue, and erroneous statistical data. Defendant argued that this material was presented in an effort to make the book more attractive to youngsters. Plaintiff sued on the ground that the book constituted a violation of his right of privacy under § 51. The New York Court of Appeals agreed, stating:

> We hold in conformity with our policy of construing sections 50 and 51 so as to fully protect free speech, that, before recovery by a public figure may be had for an unauthorized presentation of his life it must be shown, in addition to the other requirements of the statute, that the presentation is infected with material and substantial falsification . . . Or with a reckless disregard for the truth.
>
> To hold that this research effort (on the part of the author) entitled the defendants to publish the kind of knowing fictionalization presented here would amount to granting a literary license which is not only unnecessary to the protection of free speech but destructive of an individual's right, albeit a limited one in the case of a public figure, to be free of the commercial exploitation of his name. . . .

The *Notre Dame* case involved the distribution of a movie, entitled, *John Golfarb, Please Come Home* which satirized modern-day events, people, and institutions, including a football team, identified as that of Notre Dame. Notre Dame University and its president, Father Hesburg, brought suit against the defendant pursuant to the New York Civil Rights Act and the common law on unfair competition. The Appellate Division, in denying the relief requested, stated:

> Motion pictures, as well as books, are "a significant medium for the communication of ideas"; their importance "as an organ of public opinion is not lessened by the fact that they are designed to entertain as well as to inform"; and like books, they are a constitutionally protected form of expression notwithstanding that "their production, distribution and exhibition is a large-scale business conducted for private profit".

And by way of dicta, the Court stated:

> Defendants argue that injunctive relief would violate the First Amendment, but that is an issue we do not reach. It is permissible to express praise or derision of a college's athletic activities in a journal of news or opinion. If such a journal, a novel and a photoplay are on a parity in law as media of expression, extension of the doctrine of unfair competition to interdict praise or derision by means of the novel or photoplay would seem without justification. Social cost may properly be considered in these matters . . . and the granting of an injunction

in this case would outlaw large areas heretofore deemed permissible subject matter for literature and the arts. . . .[8]

In applying the holdings of these two cases to those at bar, it would appear that the later decided *Spahn* case which curiously did not cite *Notre Dame* would dictate the result herein. However, upon closer scrutiny of *Spahn*, this Court is of the opinion that the *Spahn* holding should be and was intended to be limited to its facts, and that the result here should follow the holding in the *Notre Dame* case. The Court reaches this conclusion based on the very language of the New York Court of Appeals' decision in *Spahn*. In essence, the Court in *Spahn* stressed the fact that the lower court had found that the defendant had engaged in deliberate falsifications of the circumstances surrounding the life of plaintiff and that such falsifications, which the reader might accept as true, were capable of presenting plaintiff in a false light. Thus, the Court of Appeals in *Spahn* balanced the plaintiff's privacy rights against the First Amendment protection of fictionalization qua falsification and, after finding there to be no such protection, held for the plaintiff. Conversely, in the *Notre Dame* case, the Appellate Division, as affirmed by the New York Court of Appeals, found that the defendant had not represented the events in the movie to be true and that a viewer of the film would certainly know that the circumstances involved therein were fictitious; thus, the finding for the defendants.

It is clear from the review of these two cases that the absence or presence of deliberate falsifications or an attempt by a defendant to present the disputed events as true, determines whether the scales in this balancing process, shall tip in favor of or against protection of the speech at issue. Since the cases at bar are more factually similar to the *Notre Dame* case, i.e., there were no deliberate falsifications alleged by plaintiffs, and the reader of the novel in the book case by the presence of the word "novel" would know that the work was fictitious, this Court finds that the First Amendment protection usually accorded novels and movies outweighs whatever publicity rights plaintiffs may possess and for this reason their complaints must be dismissed.

Accordingly, the Court finds that the right of publicity does not attach here, where a fictionalized account of an event in the life of a public figure is depicted in a novel or a movie, and in such novel or movie it is evident to the public that the events so depicted are fictitious.

* * *

Summary dismissal granted.

---

[8] Defendants' point to the developing literary genre involving fictionalization of the lives of deceased figures, e.g., *Burr* by Gore Vidal, to buttress their argument that if plaintiffs prevail publishers may be unable to publish such books.

### *QUESTIONS FOR DISCUSSION*

1. If Agatha Christie had been alive at the time the movie was made, should the result have been the same? Suppose, for example, a television network were to run a movie about an alleged episode in the life of a Madonna or Woody Allen, one which presents them as plotting to murder a rival for their lover's affections. Would it be legally sufficient for the broadcast to begin with a rider stating that the story was just fiction?

2. Compare the *Christie* case (especially with Agatha Christie still alive) with the *Ginger Rogers* case noted above, and also with *Marcinkus v. NAL Publishing Inc.*, 138 Misc.2d 256, 522 N.Y.S.2d 1009 (1987), in which a book had a real Vatican official, Archbishop Marcinkus, involved in a fictional plot to murder the then-Soviet Premier, Yuri Andropov. How would you rate the competing interests in those cases?

---

A more recent decision illustrating the limits to any such legal claims against movies is *Polydoros v. Twentieth Century Fox*, 67 Cal. App. 4th 318, 79 Cal. Rptr. 2d 207 (2 Dist. 1997). This case involved a 1993 fictional movie titled *The Sandlot*, one of whose characters was named Michael Palledorous and nicknamed "Squints." That film then produced a lawsuit by a Michael Polydoros, who had grown up in the setting for the film as a schoolmate of writer-director David Mickey Evans, who had known Polydoros as "Squints" back then. The court, however, dismissed the lawsuit, saying there was no violation of a person's privacy or publicity rights from an author working into a totally different story someone who had essentially the same name and nickname, and considerable resemblance in character. The court here relied heavily on *Maggio v. Charles Scribner's Sons*, 205 Misc. 818, 130 N.Y.S.2d 514 (1954), which had dismissed a suit by Maggio whose name and certain personal traits were used for a character authored by Maggio's World War II army colleague, James Jones, in *From Here to Eternity* (the predecessor to *The Thin Red Line*). As the *Maggio* court explained:

> It is generally understood that novels are written out of the background and experiences of the novelist. The characters portrayed are fictional, but very often they grow out of real persons the author has met or observed. This is so also with respect to places which are the setting of the novel. The end result may be so fictional as to seem wholly imaginary, but the acorn of fact is usually progenitor of the oak, which when fully grown no longer has any resemblance to the acorn. In order to disguise the acorn and to preserve the fiction, the novelist disguises the names of the actual persons who inspired the characters of the book. Since a novel is not a biography, the details of the character's life and deeds usually have, beyond

> possible faint outlines, no resemblance to the life and deeds of the actual person known to the author. Thus, the public has come to accept novels as pure fiction and does not attribute their characters to real life.

The California appellate division in *Polydoros* believed the same was true of movies:

> There is no question that *The Sandlot* is a fanciful work of fiction and imagination. In the movie, the dog next door to the sandlot assumes the proportions of a grizzly bear (having been magnified by the boys' fear); baseball hero Babe Ruth appears and offers advice (notwithstanding Ruth's death some 20 years before the movie takes place); the dog's owner just happens to be a former teammate of Babe Ruth; the "Squints" character fakes his own drowning death in order to sneak a kiss from the pretty female lifeguard, and so on. Appellant does not attempt to suggest that any of this is true or actually happened to him. Because the film is obvious fantasy, appellant could not reasonably suffer injury to his feelings or his peace of mind. This film is not a portrait of appellant's life and reveals no private facts about appellant: his name and former physical appearance are not private facts.

67 Cal. Rptr. at 211.

By contrast with Polydoros, Bobby Seale was both a notable public figure and one who was made the explicit subject of a movie. Along with Eldridge Cleaver and Huey Newton, Bobby Seale had been one of the founders and first Chairman of the Black Panther Party movement of the late 1960s, reacting against Martin Luther King's *non*-violent style of civil rights activism. In the mid-1990s, Gramercy Pictures made a docudrama movie titled *Panthers*, with a soundtrack album released by Polygram. Seale filed suit because this movie had been made without his consent. The false light privacy claim lost on the facts, while the celebrity publicity claim was rejected as a matter of principle. In *Seale v. Gramercy Pictures*, 949 F. Supp. 331 (E.D.Pa. 1996), the district judge applied to this effect Section 46 of ALI's *Restatement (Third) of Unfair Competition* (1995), that bars "appropriat[ion] of the commercial value of a person's identity by using without consent the person's name, likeness, . . . for the purpose of trade." This standard was said *not* to encompass the making of news stories, books, or films, or the advertising of them, unless "the person's name and/or likeness is used solely to attract attention to a work that is not related to the [life and situation of the] identified person."

Tony Twist had been a hockey player for various NHL teams like the Quebec Nordiques and the St. Louis Blues, where he was regarded as a notable violent "enforcer" out on the ice. After retiring, he not only did some amateur coaching but created *The Tony Twist Show* for a local TV station.

During that same period, Todd McFarlane, a comic writer, was forming in 1992 his Image Comics company and bringing out his very popular violent comic book, *Spawn*. This starred Al Simmons as a CIA agent who had been murdered by some corrupt colleagues, gone down to Hell and made a deal with the Devil to return to earth as Spawn, a creature with superhuman power, though controlled by the Devil. In 1993, he added to *Spawn* a new Mafia character named "Tony Twist," who as Spawn's antagonist committed child abductions and murders. This has produced not only a series of comic book spin-offs, but an animated series, a feature-length movie, a line of toys based on the *Spawn* characters, clothes bearing the *Spawn* logo, and finally a lawsuit.

While the only evident resemblance between the comic and the real Tony Twist was their name, McFarlane had told the media several times that this hockey player was the actual source of his fictional character's name. As he once wrote in the April 1996 edition of Wizard:

> The Mafia don that has made life exceedingly difficult for Al Simmons and his loved ones, in addition to putting out an ill-advised contract on the Violator, is named for former Quebec Nordique's hockey player Tony Twist, now a renowned enforcer (i.e., "Goon") for the St. Louis Blues of the National Hockey League.

When he learned of this, Twist filed a suit against McFarlane and the other bodies displaying his works, claiming violation of his publicity rights through a defamatory misappropriation of his name. When the case went to trial, a Missouri jury not only found a violation of his rights but awarded him $24.5 million in compensatory damages. Then, both the trial judge and the Missouri Court of Appeals in *John Doe a.k.a. Tony Twist v. TCI Cablevision, Todd McFarlane, et al.*, 30 Media L. Rep. 240 (Mo.App. 2002) reversed this verdict as violating McFarlane's First Amendment rights, but the Supreme Court of Missouri, in 110 S.W.3d 363 (2003), disagreed.

The Court of Appeals had first noted that "Twist cites no case that allows a public figure, celebrity or sports figure to recover on a 'misappropriation of name' or 'right of publicity' theory simply because a fiction writer names a character after them. Every court to address this issue has concluded that name-sameness alone does not give rise to a claim under either of these tests." By contrast with "a purely commercial purpose" in the form of advertising, "here, the alleged use of Twist's identity appears in a comic book with significant re-publication of the stories in the television and video mediums."

This court wanted the readers of its opinion to be aware that "our ruling today should not be read as an approval of the ethics of McFarlane's practice of naming characters, but leaves that to the readers and viewers of the *Spawn* story." The reason these judges felt that the First Amendment had to leave it up to *Spawn* readers rather than litigators to preserve Twist's real identity was exhibited in the following passage they quoted from the Supreme Court of California's decision in *Comedy III Productions v. Gary Saderup*, 25 Cal. 4th 387, 106 Cal. Rptr.2d 126, 21 P.3d 797, 803 (2001).

> Entertainment and sports celebrities are the leading players in our Public Drama. We tell tales, both tall and cautionary, about them. We monitor their comings and goings, their missteps and heartbreaks. We copy their mannerisms, their styles and their modes of conversation and consumption. Whether or not celebrities are 'the chief agents of moral change in the United States' they certainly are widely used—far more than are institutionally anchored elites—to symbolize individual aspirations, group identities, and cultural values. Their images are thus important expressive and communicative resources: the peculiar, yet familiar idiom in which we conduct a fair portion of our cultural business and everyday conversation.

The Missouri Supreme Court explicitly disagreed with this California "transformative" effort to guarantee full First Amendment protection "wherever the use of a name is in any way expressive, regardless of the commercial exploitation." Instead, they adopted the balancing test, "a sort of predominant use test" that had just been advocated by Mark Lee in his 2003 Loyola Entertainment Law Review article.

> If a product is being sold that predominantly exploits the commercial value of an individual's identity, that product should be held to violate the right of publicity and not be protected by the First Amendment, even if there is some "expressive" content in it that might qualify as "speech" in other circumstances. If, on the other hand, the predominant purpose of the product is to make an expressive comment on or about a celebrity, the expressive values could be given greater weight.

Then, after examining the *Spawn* comic, the court judged that "on the record here, the use and identity of Twist's name has become predominantly a ploy to sell comic books and related products rather than an artistic or literary expression, and under these circumstances, free speech must give way to the right of publicity."

The Missouri Supreme Court did find that the trial judge had made a "right of publicity" tort error in his instructions to the jury, and thus sent the case back for a new trial. After the U.S. Supreme Court had refused to take on McFarlane's First Amendment appeal, another trial was held in the summer of 2004, and this time a St. Louis jury awarded Twist $15 million in damages.

With McFarlane going to the bankruptcy court under Chapter 11, what are your views about both the right of a McFarlane to use a celebrity name for his evil rather than holy character and also a jury awarding Twist a "mere" $15 million rather than the original $24.5 million in tort damages for the emotional as well as financial harm caused by his name sake in *Spawn*?

Needless to say, President Clinton was a much more notable (and more notorious) public figure in the 1990s than Tony Twist then or Bobby Seale back in the 1960s. While still in the White House, the President was the clear subject of the 1998 movie *Primary Colors* (with John Travolta playing Clinton in a somewhat fictionalized version of his 1992 Presidential campaign), and an implicit character in Dustin Hoffman's *Wag the Dog* (which became a big home video hit in the spring of 1998 when the Clinton-Lewinsky affair hit the news screen). The previous summer of 1997, Warner Studios had released the movie *Contact*, starring Jodie Foster and Matthew McConaughey, and directed by Robert Zemeckis who had earlier made *Forrest Gump*. And just as he had done with ex-Presidents Kennedy, Johnson, and Nixon in *Forrest Gump*, Zemeckis had President Clinton playing himself in *Contact*. This was done by taking real statements that Clinton had made on the news for CNN (also owned by Time Warner) and then incorporating these pictures and words into *Contact*'s fictional story about extraterrestrials coming to America.

Much of *Contact*'s plot took place in Washington, in particular the theme of political maneuvering "Inside the Beltway," with the National Security Advisor played by James Wood trumping the scientific objectives of Jodie Foster's character out in the Rockies. In one scene, with Wood "morphed" into the background of a Clinton press conference inserted into the movie, Zemeckis used Clinton's statement about possible traces of life on Mars: "If this discovery is confirmed, it will surely be remarkable." This was made in the movie into a comment about extraterrestrials contacting Foster. Another use was of Clinton's statement after he had just heard of the Oklahoma City bombing: "I would warn everybody not to be influenced by suggestions beyond the known facts. We are monitoring what has actually happened." In the movie this was used as the President's comment about the possible disaster of Foster's planned trip up into the stars.

While Warner Studios did send Clinton a print of the movie to watch in the White House before it appeared in theaters, his White House Counsel Charles Ruff issued a statement saying it was "fundamentally unfair" for the studio to incorporate into the movie these statements, taken totally out of context and put into a very different plot for commercial purposes. However, counsel said, Clinton would *not* be suing Time Warner. Still, in appraising the viability of any such suit, what is the significance of the fact that the original 1985 novel *Contact* by Carl Sagan has a *woman* President, in deciding whether this was "for a legitimate story purpose or merely to enhance the marketability of the movie" (by comparison to the films *Primary Colors* or *Wag the Dog*)? In addition, would the President be judged to be "in the public domain" not only for the movie, but also for movie previews or advertisements? And suppose that in the *Polydoros* case, *supra*, that the parents of Director David Evans had long ago taken and saved motion pictures of Polydoros and Evans playing together on a Little League ballfield, and that Evans now used the same digital technology employed to put Clinton into *Contact* to work these shots of Polydoros into *Sandlot*.

Perhaps Hollywood will feel the need to follow the path of *Men in Black*, the big hit of the summer of 1997. This had a brief scene showing a Big Board grid of TV screens monitoring the extraterrestrials that had come to America, and whom Tommy Lee Jones and Will Smith were chasing down as INS officers. Among the "extraterrestrials" displayed on the screen were such entertainment celebrities as Sylvester Stallone, Danny DeVito, and Dionne Warwick who had consented, but not Michael Jackson who had refused. But *Men in Black* had not even asked for, let alone secured the consent of then-House Speaker Newt Gingrich for this brief portrayal of him. Is there a legal policy justification for this disparate treatment of Jackson and Gingrich (or Clinton in *Contact*)?

---

An interesting variation on these episodes involved a different brand of "fiction"—the tabloid print and broadcast media whose pioneer, and still its leader, is the *National Enquirer*, with its weekly circulation of around four million. In 1982, the *Enquirer* published a cover story about an alleged "Love Triangle" of Clint Eastwood with his then live-in girlfriend, the actress Sandra Locke, and a supposed competitor for his affections, singer Tanya Tucker. Alleging that the *Enquirer* article was knowingly false, Eastwood sued for violation of both his privacy and publicity rights. The *National Enquirer* conceded that the story might constitute a violation of the "false light" aspect of privacy law, but contended that there was no cause of action here for commercial misappropriation of Eastwood's "publicity" rights under California law. In *Eastwood v. The Superior Court of Los Angeles County*, 149 Cal.App.3d 409, 198 Cal. Rptr. 342 (1983), a California appellate court disagreed with the *Enquirer*.

The court held that Eastwood's publicity rights in his name and likeness had been commercially appropriated by the *Enquirer* when these were deliberately used to sell its newspaper product, irrespective of whether there was any implication that Eastwood was endorsing this effort:

> The first step toward selling a product or service is to attract the consumers' attention. Because of a celebrity's audience appeal, people respond almost automatically to a celebrity's name or picture. Here, the Enquirer used Eastwood's personality and fame on the cover of the subject publication and in related telecast advertisements. To the extent their use attracted the readers' attention, the Enquirer gained a commercial advantage. Furthermore, the Enquirer used Eastwood's personality in the context of an alleged news account, entitled "Clint Eastwood in Love Triangle with Tanya Tucker" to generate maximum curiosity and the necessary motivation to purchase the newspaper.

198 Cal. Rptr. at 349. The court recognized that for both constitutional and statutory reasons, media vehicles such as the *Enquirer* had the right to describe Eastwood's actions and character for enlightenment of the public—including any participation in a "love triangle." Drawing upon *New York Times v. Sullivan*, 376 U.S. 254 (1964), the court held that the appropriate dividing line between these competing rights of Eastwood and the *Enquirer* was whether the story was being published with knowledge or reckless disregard of its false content.

> As noted earlier, all fiction is literally false, but enjoys constitutional protection. However, the deliberate fictionalization of Eastwood's personality constitutes commercial exploitation, and becomes actionable when it is presented to the reader as if true with the requisite *scienter* [knowing or reckless falsity].

198 Cal. Rptr. at 352.

## *QUESTIONS FOR DISCUSSION*

1. Within days after release of the 1995 movie, *To Wong Foo, Thanks For Everything! Julie Newmar*, a comedy about three New York "drag queens" stranded in a small Nebraska town, a then notable golfing personality, Chi Chi Rodriguez, filed suit against the producers for having assigned his name to one of the characters who (according to the complaint) "engages in numerous disreputable acts and is portrayed as sexually promiscuous." What were the legal prospects for *Rodriguez v. Universal Pictures* (now settled)?

2. Dyna Taylor, a student at the California Institute of Arts (founded by Walt Disney Studios in 1961), was paid $200 to model for the animators of Disney's *Pocahontas* movie production. Apparently Taylor's facial features were reflected in Pocahontas's face (while the body features of another student-model, Jamie Pillow, served as the base for Pocahontas's physique). Shortly after *Pocahontas* appeared on the screen in June, 1995, Taylor lamented that she had not received any screen credit or additional compensation (she would have liked a Disney scholarship at the Arts Institute). Taylor did not suggest she would sue, and it was unclear from the news stories whether the model release form she signed with Disney gave the latter the right to use her features in an animation film. Suppose there was no such contractual license. Is there an independent basis in the right of publicity to bar the use of one's distinctive facial (or other physical) features in a movie? Should it make a difference if the features used are not those of a (then) unknown like Dyna Taylor, but rather belong to a celebrity like Elizabeth Taylor? For an analogous case involving a Playgirl Magazine drawing of a nude black boxer sitting in the ring, captioned as the "Mystery Man," but whose appearance was very reminiscent of Muhammad Ali, see *Ali v. Playgirl*, 447 F. Supp. 723 (S.D.N.Y. 1978).

3. In 2013, Gita May Hall, a fashion model in the 1950's and 60's, sued Lionsgate Entertainment. She alleges that a Richard Avedon photograph used in the opening sequence of the hit television show "Mad Men," is being used without her consent. Ironically, Hall did not become aware of the use of the photo until 2012, even though the photo had been used since 2007, because she did not subscribe to cable television. Assuming that they are using the photo without permission, what defenses might Lionsgate have, if any?

4. In 2015, rock stars Daryl Hall and John Oates filed a lawsuit against an artisan granola company from Brooklyn. They allege that the hipster-friendly product "Haulin' Oats" is a use of their name and likeness, and . . . they won't go for that. Putting aside the trademark claim for now, do they have a valid right of publicity claim?

## C. CRIMINAL CELEBRITIES[d]

There is one group of celebrities who often do not object to their stories being told on television—criminals. Indeed, the protagonists in highly-publicized criminal ventures are now finding that television producers, book publishers, and magazine editors are bidding higher and higher sums to get an "exclusive" angle on their stories. (Recall that in the *Matthews* case, Kim Wozencraft, the drug-using undercover narcotics officer, received $1 million for the movie rights to her story, *Rush*.) While

[d] *See* Garrett Epps, *Wising Up: "Son of Sam" Laws & the Speech & Press Clauses*, 70 N.C. L. Rev. 493 (1992) (written just before the Supreme Court's ruling in *Simon & Schuster* that is the subject of this Section); Lori F. Zavack, *Can States Enact Constitutional "Son of Sam" Laws After Simon & Schuster?* 37 St. Louis L.J. 701 (1993).

there had been earlier examples of this genre—e.g., Truman Capote's *In Cold Blood* and Norman Mailer's *The Executioner's Song*—the real surge in the "true crime" book world was triggered by the early 1980s best-seller, Joe McGinness's *Fatal Vision*, the story of Green Beret Jeffrey MacDonald and his conviction for the killing of his family. It is estimated that approximately 10 percent of nonfiction best-sellers are true stories of celebrity crimes and criminals. Then, after the television portrayals of *Fatal Vision* and *The Burning Bed* garnered the biggest audiences of the 1984–85 television season, true crime docudramas began to account for as much as 40 percent of made-for-television movies. On occasion, multiple networks might create their own versions of particularly unusual stories, like that Amy Fisher and Joey Buttafuoco. (Fisher collected $100,000, while Buttafuoco and his wife got $750,000.) Another major source of revenue is tabloid television—such as *Inside Edition*, *A Current Affair*, and *Hard Copy*—and tabloid publications like *The National Enquirer*. These "infotainment" vehicles pay huge sums of money for immediate appearances and stories by the John and Lorena Bobbitts, the Tonya Hardings and Jeff Gilloolys of the world, and others who have been at the center of violent episodes that have caught the gruesome fancy of the nation. Even non-violent crimes with a titillating twist can prove to be a monetary jackpot for a previously unknown offender. For example, the Los Angeles prostitute Divine Brown's sexual encounter with movie star Hugh Grant brought Brown a $1,350 fine for her offense and over $300,000 for interviews, public appearances, even for commercials.

Probably the biggest media celebrity of all—criminal or non-criminal—was O.J. Simpson. While he languished in jail, his colleagues were marketing O.J. autographs, coins, and busts for many millions of dollars. Just before trial, Simpson's own book appeared, *I Want to Tell You*—O.J.'s response to the hundreds of thousands of letters he had received from people around the world. Lawrence Schiller, who had collaborated with Norman Mailer on the Pulitzer Prize-winning *The Executioner's Song*, wrote the book for O.J., which was published by the respected firm Little, Brown (a division of Time-Warner Inc.). Little, Brown had paid O.J. an advance of more than a million dollars—a worthwhile investment in a book that within days had soared to the top of the best-seller charts. However, because of the huge controversy over his acquittal, O.J. was not able to go forward with his plan for an exclusive pay-television interview that his advisors had believed would net him over $10 million.

This trend in celebrity criminal stories has generated popular concern and political reaction—not about the crime stories being told, but about the criminals being paid for the stories. The issue first surfaced in the late 1970s in the case of a serial killer, David Berkowitz. Berkowitz, who billed himself as "Son of Sam," had terrorized New York neighborhoods and filled New York newspapers with stories about his dozen murders and maimings in 1976 and 1977. After finally being apprehended by the police, Berkowitz sold his story rights for nearly $100,000. The State of New York responded immediately with a "Son of Sam law" whose basic concept was soon adopted in approximately forty other states. The New York law applied to contracts by convicted (and later accused) persons for

> . . . reenactment of such crimes by way of a movie, book, magazine article, tape recording, phonograph record, radio or television presentation, live entertainment of any kind, or from the expression of such accused or convicted person's thoughts, feelings, opinions, or emotions regarding such crimes.

The law required the publisher or producer in such a contract to pay over to the New York State Crime Victims Board the monies owed to the convicted or accused person. These funds would be held in escrow by the Board for five years for purposes of reimbursing the victims of the crime in question if, during that period, the victim secured a civil damage award for the injuries. The Board also could pay up to twenty percent of the money to the representative of the convicted or accused person who had arranged for production and sale of the story. Those accused persons who were acquitted of their criminal charges were immediately paid the monies owed them. Those convicted got the balance of the funds left in the escrow account after the five years were up. "Conviction" for purposes of this law included not just formal conviction in criminal court, but also "voluntary and intelligent" admission in the book of having committed the crime.

During the next fifteen years, the fund accumulated just $165,000, which did not include Berkowitz's money, because he was found mentally incompetent to stand trial: the original version of the law was triggered just by "conviction," not "accusation." (Apparently Berkowitz voluntarily paid his book revenues to the estates of his victims.) The first major use of and challenge to the law involved a book by Jean Harris, the lover and convicted murderer of Herman Tarnower, the "Scarsdale Diet Doctor." Harris's book, *Stranger In Two Worlds*, dealt principally with her life in prison, but also recounted the crime and what led up to it. Harris had agreed to donate her roughly $100,000 in royalties to the Children of Bedford, a charitable organization that looked after the children of prisoners. When the Crime Victims Board found that the Harris book came within the terms of New York's "Son of Sam" law, it denied the charity any of the book's proceeds. Thus the charity sought, unsuccessfully, to challenge the constitutionality of New York's law in the state courts: *see Children of Bedford v. Petromelis*, 77 N.Y.2d 713, 570 N.Y.S.2d 453, 573 N.E.2d 541 (1991).

Then came another criminal turned celebrity, Henry Hill, who had been a low-level member of a Mafia crime family. When faced with charges of drug dealing, Hill agreed to testify against his former "family" members in return for immunity from prosecution and placement in the federal Witness Protection Program. Hill's lawyer also negotiated a deal with Simon & Schuster for a book about his life, *Wiseguy: Life in a Mafia Family*, authored by Nicholas Pileggi, which movie director Martin Scorsese turned into an award-winning movie, *Goodfellas*. Hill's publisher, Simon & Schuster, brought the constitutionality of Son of Sam laws before the Supreme Court to determine whether the company could pay Hill his royalties.

## SIMON & SCHUSTER, INC. V. NEW YORK STATE CRIME VICTIMS BOARD

Supreme Court of the United States, 1991.
502 U.S. 105, 112 S.Ct. 501, 116 L.Ed.2d 476.

JUSTICE O'CONNOR delivered the opinion of the court.

* * *

I

A

In the summer of 1977, New York was terrorized by a serial killer popularly known as the Son of Sam. The hunt for the Son of Sam received considerable publicity, and by the time David Berkowitz was identified as the killer and apprehended, the rights to his story were worth a substantial amount. Berkowitz's chance to profit from his notoriety while his victims and their families remained uncompensated did not escape the notice of New York's Legislature. The State quickly enacted the statute at issue.

The statute was intended to "ensure that monies received by the criminal under such circumstances shall first be made available to recompense the victims of that crime for their loss and suffering." As the author of the statute explained, "it is abhorrent to one's sense of justice and decency that an individual . . . can expect to receive large sums of money for his story once he is captured—while five people are dead, [and] other people were injured as a result of his conduct."

* * *

B

[The Court then turned from the Son of Sam to the Wiseguy.] Looking back from the safety of the Federal Witness Protection Program, Henry Hill recalled: "At the age of twelve my ambition was to be a gangster. To be a wiseguy. To me being a wiseguy was better than being president of the United States." N. Pileggi, *Wiseguy: Life in a Mafia Family* 19 (1985). Whatever one might think of Hill, at the very least it can be said that he realized his dreams. After a career spanning 25 years, Hill admitted engineering some of the most daring crimes of his day, including the 1978–1979 Boston College basketball point-shaving scandal, and the theft of $6 million from Lufthansa Airlines in 1978, the largest successful cash robbery in American history. Most of Hill's crimes were more banausic: he committed extortion, he imported and distributed narcotics, and he organized numerous robberies.

Hill was arrested in 1980. In exchange for immunity from prosecution, he testified against many of his former colleagues. Since his arrest, he has lived under an assumed name in an unknown part of the country.

In August 1981, Hill entered into a contract with author Nicholas Pileggi for the production of a book about Hill's life. The following month, Hill and Pileggi signed a publishing agreement with Simon & Schuster. Under the agreement, Simon & Schuster agreed to make payments to both Hill and Pileggi. Over the next few years, according to Pileggi, he and Hill "talked at length virtually every single day, with not more than an occasional Sunday or holiday skipped. We spent more than three hundred hours together; my notes of conversations with Henry occupy more than six linear file feet." Because producing the book required such a substantial investment of time and effort, Hill sought compensation.

The result of Hill and Pileggi's collaboration was *Wiseguy*, which was published in January 1986. The book depicts, in colorful detail, the day-to-day existence of organized crime, primarily in Hill's first-person narrative. Throughout *Wiseguy*, Hill frankly admits to having participated in an astonishing variety of crimes. He discusses, among other things, his conviction of extortion and the prison sentence he served. In one portion of the book, Hill recounts how members of the Mafia received preferential treatment in prison:

> The dorm was a separate three-story building outside the wall, which looked more like a Holiday Inn than a prison. There were four guys to a room, and we had comfortable beds and private baths. There were two dozen rooms on each floor, and each of them had mob guys living in them. It was like a wiseguy convention—the whole Gotti crew, Jimmy Doyle and his guys, Ernie Boy' Abbamonte and Joe Crow' Delvecchio, Vinnie Aloi, Frank Cotroni.
>
> It was wild. There was wine and booze, and it was kept in bath-oil or after-shave jars. The hacks in the honor dorm were almost all on the take, and even though it was against the rules, we used to cook in our rooms. Looking back, I don't think Paulie

> went to the general mess five times in the two and a half years he was there. We had a stove and pots and pans and silverware stacked in the bathroom. We had glasses and an ice-water cooler where we kept the fresh meats and cheeses. When there was an inspection, we stored the stuff in the false ceiling, and once in a while, if it was confiscated, we'd just go to the kitchen and get new stuff.
>
> We had the best food smuggled into our dorm from the kitchen. Steaks, veal cutlets, shrimp, red snapper. Whatever the hacks could buy, we ate. It cost me two, three hundred a week. Guys like Paulie spent five hundred to a thousand bucks a week. Scotch cost thirty dollars a pint. The hacks used to bring it inside the walls in their lunch pails. We never ran out of booze, because we had six hacks bringing it in six days a week. Depending on what you wanted and how much you were willing to spend, life could be almost bearable.

*Wiseguy* was reviewed favorably: The Washington Post called it an "amply detailed and entirely fascinating book that amounts to a piece of revisionist history," while New York Daily News columnist Jimmy Breslin named it "the best book on crime in America ever written." The book was also a commercial success: within 19 months of its publication, more than a million copies were in print. A few years later, the book was converted into a film called *Goodfellas*, which won a host of awards as the best film of 1990.

From Henry Hill's perspective, however, the publicity generated by the book's success proved less desirable. The Crime Victims Board learned of *Wiseguy* in January 1986, soon after it was published. [By that time Simon & Schuster had already paid Hill's literary agent approximately $96,000 in advance royalties and another $28,000 was to be paid out soon. After reviewing the contents of *Wiseguy*, the Board directed Hill to pay over the $96,000, and Simon & Schuster the $28,000 together with any future royalties. Instead, the publisher went to court to have the Son of Sam law declared a violation of the First Amendment. After the Second Circuit upheld the statute, at 916 F.2d 777 (2d Cir. 1990), the case was appealed to the Supreme Court.]

* * *

II

A

A statute is presumptively inconsistent with the First Amendment if it imposes a financial burden on speakers because of the content of their speech. As we emphasized in invalidating a content-based magazine tax, "official scrutiny of the content of publications as the basis for imposing a tax is entirely incompatible with the First Amendment's guarantee of freedom of the press." *Arkansas Writers' Project, Inc. v. Ragland*, 481 U.S. 221, 230 (1987).

This is a notion so engrained in our First Amendment jurisprudence that last Term we found it so "obvious" as to not require explanation. *Leathers v. Medlock*, 499 U.S. 439 (1991). It is but one manifestation of a far broader principle: "Regulations which permit the Government to discriminate on the basis of the content of the message cannot be tolerated under the First Amendment." *Regan v. Time, Inc.*, 468 U.S. 641, 648–649 (1984). *See also Police Dept. of Chicago v. Mosley*, 408 U.S. 92, 95 (1972). In the context of financial regulation, it bears repeating, as we did in *Leathers*, that the Government's ability to impose content-based burdens on speech raises the specter that the Government may effectively drive certain ideas or viewpoints from the marketplace. The First Amendment presumptively places this sort of discrimination beyond the power of the Government. As we reiterated in *Leathers*, " 'The constitutional right of free expression is . . . intended to remove governmental restraints from the arena of public discussion, putting the decision as to what views shall be voiced largely into the hands of each of us . . . in the belief that no other approach would comport with the premise of individual dignity and choice upon which our political system rests.' "

The Son of Sam law is such a content-based statute. It singles out income derived from expressive activity for a burden the State places on no other income, and it is directed only at works with a specified content. Whether the First Amendment "speaker" is considered to be Henry Hill, whose income the statute places in escrow because of the story he has told, or Simon & Schuster, which can publish books about crime with the assistance of only those criminals willing to forgo remuneration for at least five years, the statute plainly imposes a financial disincentive only on speech of a particular content.

The Board tries unsuccessfully to distinguish the Son of Sam law from the discriminatory tax at issue in *Arkansas Writers' Project*. While the Son of Sam law escrows all of the speaker's speech-derived income for at least five years, rather than taxing a percentage of it outright, this difference can hardly serve as the basis for disparate treatment under the First Amendment. Both forms of financial burden operate as disincentives to speak; indeed, in many cases it will be impossible to discern in advance which type of regulation will be more costly to the speaker.

* * *

The Son of Sam law establishes a financial disincentive to create or publish works with a particular content. In order to justify such differential treatment, "the State must show that its regulation is necessary to serve a compelling state interest and is narrowly drawn to achieve that end."

### B

The Board disclaims, as it must, any state interest in suppressing descriptions of crime out of solicitude for the sensibilities of readers. As we have often had occasion to repeat, " 'The fact that society may find speech offensive is not a sufficient reason for suppressing it. Indeed, if it is the speaker's opinion that gives offense, that consequence is a reason for according it constitutional protection.' " *Hustler Magazine, Inc. v. Falwell*, 485 U.S. 46, 55 (1988) (quoting *FCC v. Pacifica Foundation*, 438 U.S. 726, 745 (1978)). The Board thus does not assert any interest in limiting whatever anguish Henry Hill's victims may suffer from reliving their victimization.

There can be little doubt, on the other hand, that the State has a compelling interest in ensuring that victims of crime are compensated by those who harm them. Every State has a body of tort law serving exactly this interest. The State's interest in preventing wrongdoers from dissipating their assets before victims can recover explains the existence of the State's statutory provisions for prejudgment remedies and orders of restitution.

The State likewise has an undisputed compelling interest in ensuring that criminals do not profit from their crimes. Like most if not all States, New York has long recognized the "fundamental equitable principle," that "no one shall be permitted to profit by his own fraud, or to take advantage of his own wrong, or to found any claim upon his own iniquity, or to acquire property by his own crime." *Riggs v. Palmer*, 115 N. Y. 506, 511–512, 22 N. E. 188, 190 (1889). The force of this interest is evidenced by the State's statutory provisions for the forfeiture of the proceeds and instrumentalities of crime.

The parties debate whether book royalties can properly be termed the profits of crime, but that is a question we need not address here. For the purposes of this case, we can assume without deciding that the income escrowed by the Son of Sam law represents the fruits of crime. We need only conclude that the State has a compelling interest in depriving criminals of the profits of their crimes, and in using these funds to compensate victims.

The Board attempts to define the State's interest more narrowly, as "ensuring that criminals do not profit from storytelling about their crimes before their victims have a meaningful opportunity to be compensated for their injuries." Here the Board is on far shakier ground. The Board cannot explain why the State should have any greater interest in compensating victims from the proceeds of such "storytelling" than from any of the criminal's other assets. Nor can the Board offer any justification for a distinction between this expressive activity and any other activity in connection with its interest in transferring the fruits of crime from criminals to their victims. Thus even if the State can be said to have an interest in classifying a criminal's assets in this manner, that interest is hardly compelling.

* * *

In short, the State has a compelling interest in compensating victims from the fruits of the crime, but little if any interest in limiting such compensation to the proceeds of the wrongdoer's speech about the crime. We must therefore determine whether the Son of Sam law is narrowly tailored to advance the former, not the latter, objective.

C

As a means of ensuring that victims are compensated from the proceeds of crime, the Son of Sam law is significantly overinclusive. As counsel for the Board conceded at oral argument, the statute applies to works on any subject, provided that they express the author's thoughts or recollections about his crime, however tangentially or incidentally. In addition, the statute's broad definition of "person convicted of a crime" enables the Board to escrow the income of any author who admits in his work to having committed a crime, whether or not the author was ever actually accused or convicted.

These two provisions combine to encompass a potentially very large number of works. Had the Son of Sam law been in effect at the time and place of publication, it would have escrowed payment for such works as *The Autobiography of Malcolm X*, which describes crimes committed by the civil rights leader before he became a public figure; *Civil Disobedience*, in which Thoreau acknowledges his refusal to pay taxes and recalls his experience in jail; and even the *Confessions of Saint Augustine*, in which the author laments "my past foulness and the carnal corruptions of my soul," one instance of which involved the theft of pears from a neighboring vineyard. *The Confessions of Saint Augustine*, 31, 36–37 (Franklin Library ed. 1980). Amicus Association of American Publishers, Inc., has submitted a sobering bibliography listing hundreds of works by American prisoners and ex-prisoners, many of which contain descriptions of the crimes for which the authors were incarcerated, including works by such authors as Emma Goldman and Martin Luther King, Jr. A list of prominent figures whose autobiographies would be subject to the statute if written is not difficult to construct: the list could include Sir Walter Raleigh, who was convicted of treason after a dubiously conducted 1603 trial; Jesse Jackson, who was arrested in 1963 for trespass and resisting arrest after attempting to be served at a lunch counter in North Carolina; and Bertrand Russell, who was jailed for seven days at the age of 89 for participating in a sit-down protest against nuclear weapons. The argument that a statute like the Son of Sam law would prevent publication of all of these works is hyperbole—some would have been written without compensation—but the Son of Sam law clearly reaches a wide range of literature that does not enable a criminal to profit from his crime while a victim remains uncompensated.

Should a prominent figure write his autobiography at the end of his career, and include in an early chapter a brief recollection of having stolen (in New York) a nearly worthless item as a youthful prank, the Board would control his entire income from the book for five years, and would make that income available to all of the author's creditors, despite the fact that the statute of limitations for this minor incident had long since run. That the Son of Sam law can produce such an outcome indicates that the statute is, to say the least, not narrowly tailored to achieve the State's objective of compensating crime victims from the profits of crime.

III

The Federal Government and many of the States have enacted statutes designed to serve purposes similar to that served by the Son of Sam law. Some of these statutes may be quite different from New York's, and we have no occasion to determine the constitutionality of these other laws. We conclude simply that in the Son of Sam law, New York has singled out speech on a particular subject for a financial burden that it places on no other speech and no other income. The State's interest in compensating victims from the fruits of crime is a compelling one, but the Son of Sam law is not narrowly tailored to advance that objective. As a result, the statute is inconsistent with the First Amendment.

The judgment of the Court of Appeals is accordingly

Reversed.

---

The summer of 1999 saw the release of a new Spike Lee film, *Summer of Sam*, graphically depicting the story of the "Son of Sam" (i.e., David Berkowitz) killing or wounding numerous New Yorkers in the summer of 1977. While this movie received favorable movie reviews and did reasonably well at the box office, it received some strong objections from the families of those victims. One parent of a murdered daughter said that "Spike Lee is making the families relive this all over again . . . He is making money off my sorrow and my family's hurt." When Berkowitz was interviewed in prison where he still had approximately 300 years left to serve on his sentence, this born-again Christian said that "I deserve to be in prison for the rest of my life," but that Lee should not be inflicting this "needless pain" on his victims' families. Lee's response was that "I feel deeply for the parents of the victims of Son of Sam. At the same time, I'm an artist and this is a story I wanted to tell" (including a depiction of life in New York when Berkowitz was doing his killing, and Lee was in college there preparing for his film career). Needless to say, neither Lee nor his studio, Walt Disney's Touchstone Pictures, had offered any money to Berkowitz to get an "inside scoop" of what had moved him to these murders (which he had said at the time were ordered by the Black Labrador dog owned by his neighbor Sam).

## *QUESTIONS FOR DISCUSSION*

1. In *Simon & Schuster*, Justice O'Connor characterized most of Henry Hill's crimes (e.g., extortion, robbery, and drug-dealing) as "banausic." What exactly is a *banausic* crime? Would you know one if you saw it?

2. What are your views about the constitutional issues? Is this the kind of law that imposes a direct restraint on speech, and thus requires strict scrutiny to determine whether the government has a "compelling interest" in it? Or is this a law that imposes only an incidental burden on speech, thus sustainable if it serves an "important substantial interest?" The Court had applied the latter test in *City of Renton v. Playtime Theatres, Inc.*, 475 U.S. 41 (1986), to uphold a city bylaw that prohibited location of "adult" motion picture theaters close to churches, schools, parks, and residential neighborhoods. How would you analyze the comparative constitutionality of these different public policies?

3. Another decision not mentioned by the Supreme Court was *Snepp v. United States*, 444 U.S. 507 (1980). Snepp, a former Central Intelligence Agency (CIA) agent, had written a book, *Decent Interval*, after leaving the Agency. Snepp had complied with one of the Agency rules, that ex-agents not reveal any classified information, but not with another rule, that all books be submitted to the Agency for prepublication review. The Supreme Court (by a 6–3 margin) upheld against a First Amendment challenge a constructive trust imposed on all proceeds from the book for the benefit of the Agency. How would you compare the First Amendment claims of Hill and of Snepp to the financial returns from books about their respective careers?

4. One more possible analogy is *Richardson v. Ramirez*, 418 U.S. 24 (1974), in which the Supreme Court upheld a California law that denied convicted felons the right to vote even after their prison terms had been served. How would you compare the constitutional values and criminal justice policies in *Simon & Schuster* with those in *Richardson*?

5. Katherine Ann Power had been an anti-Vietnam student radical and accomplice in a 1970 Boston bank holdup that left a police officer, Walter Schroeder, dead. In 1993, Power finally turned herself in to the Boston authorities after living for twenty years in rural Oregon with a new name, identity, and family. This story aroused huge popular interest, not simply because it was revisiting the nation's trauma over Vietnam—the series of

bank robberies was designed to secure funds to arm the Black Panthers to fight against the war after the invasion of Cambodia and the National Guard killing of student protesters at Kent State—but also because of Power's subsequent remorse and felt need for atonement. Within days after Power's surrender to the police, her attorney had received dozens of proposals for book, television, and movie portrayals of Power's life. The trial judge accepted the 8–12 year prison sentence that Power's attorney had negotiated with the state prosecutors as a prelude to her surrender. However, the judge surprised both sides by adding a subsequent 20-year probation period that was explicitly conditioned on Power not selling the rights to her story. The judge said that "I will not permit profit on the lifeblood of a Boston police officer by someone responsible for the killing." Power, who stated she would give any money she received for such story rights to the Schroeder family as compensation, appealed that probation condition. How would you compare the *Power* situation with that in *Simon & Schuster*? Should the fact that this is a judicially-imposed condition on probation, rather than a general legislative requirement, make a difference? *See Commonwealth v. Power*, 420 Mass. 410, 650 N.E.2d 87 (1995).

6. While the Supreme Court was careful to state that it was addressing only New York's law, the implications of *Simon & Schuster* were inevitably broader. As illustration, following the attack on her figure skating rival, Nancy Kerrigan, Tonya Harding received $600,000 from *Inside Edition* and $500,000 from a movie producer. Harding's ex-husband, Jeff Gillooly, who arranged the attack, got $275,000 from *A Current Affair*. The attackers, Shane Stant and David Smith, got $200,000 from *Hard Copy*. Though all were convicted of some criminal offense, Oregon's Son of Sam law has not been applied to any of these media proceeds. Does that create any significant social problems?

7. A year after the *Simon & Schuster* ruling, then-Governor Mario Cuomo signed a new "Son of Sam" law for New York. This law targeted all "profits of crime," which were defined as "any payments obtained through or generated from commission of a crime . . . including any assets obtained through the use of unique knowledge about the commission of the crime." The law requires any party contracting to pay any such *profits of crime* to a person *convicted* of crime to give notice to the Crime Victims Board. The victims are then given three years from the date that such a profit-making venture is disclosed to sue to collect damages for their injuries from those profits. As a matter of statutory interpretation, can royalties from a book or payments from a television docudrama be considered the criminal's "profits of crime?" Would such an interpretation pass constitutional muster after *Simon & Schuster*?

The expected answers to some of these questions may be indicated by the settlement of the first claim under this New York law, filed in early 1995. This claim was lodged against Time Warner by the Kellogg children, whose parents had been depicted in a 1994 television movie, *Lies of the Heart: The Story of Laurie Kellogg*, telling the story of how their mother, Laurie Kellogg, had her teenage lover shoot and kill her husband and their father, Malcolm Kellogg. The children were seeking the $5,000 that Time Warner Entertainment paid to Laurie, and the $45,000 paid to her lawyer. The studio ended up paying them just $5,000 to match the sum paid to Laurie, but not the much larger sum paid to her lawyer, a potential loophole to this New York legislative effort.

8. During its 15-year life, the original New York law attracted a number of cases which posed the question of how to treat proceeds from "crimes without victims"—at least immediate victims. *In re Halmi*, 128 A.D.2d 411, 512 N.Y.S.2d 650 (1987), upheld a lower court verdict about the proceeds from the book *Mayflower Madam*, about Sydney Biddle Barrows, the socialite-turned expensive Call Girl operator. *St. Martin's Press v. Zweibel*, 203 N.Y. L.J. 25 (1990), involved a book about the exploits of R. Foster Wynans, the Wall St. Journal reporter-turned insider trader. Even Henry Hill, the protagonist in *Wiseguy*, *Goodfellas*, and *Simon & Schuster*, had previously sold to Sports Illustrated (for $10,000) the inside story on how he had gotten Boston College players to "shave points" in their 1978–79 college basketball games. What is the appropriate treatment of these earnings from stories about crimes that do not have identifiable victims seeking compensation?

---

We now have a second major "Son of Sam" judicial ruling, involving a rather important celebrity name and image, Frank Sinatra. This involved the Supreme Court of California addressing the question of whether the distinctive features of that state's legislation did or did not interfere with the constitutional freedom of speech that the U.S. Supreme Court had provided to New York criminals in Simon & Schuster.

The overall thrust of this California law was the same as New York's, to prevent criminals making a financial gain from their crimes while leaving the victims uncompensated. Thus, its Section 2225(b)(1) required the placing in a fund for the benefit of the victim all money earned by a criminal from a book, movie, magazine article, television show, or other means of "depiction, portrayal, or reenactment of a felony."

There were, however, several important differences between these two statutes. The California law applied only to people who were actually convicted of a felony (or acquitted by reason of insanity), though when judged guilty by a court, the trust was then applied to any money "earned, accrued or paid before or after the conviction." The law also excluded from the trust any publications that made only a passing mention of the crime "as in a footnote or bibliography," and it also allowed up to 40 percent of the proceeds of such a covered publication to be used to pay the criminal's attorney fees. Following the rather notorious O.J. Simpson episode (where the law would not be applied because he was found to have killed his wife just in a tort, not a criminal, court), the California statute was amended in 1999, to make it applicable to the proceeds of any of the offender's goods (including publicity rights) whose sale value had gone up because of criminal notoriety. And any balance left in the trust account after the criminal's victims had been compensated was placed in the state's Restitution Fund for criminal victims generally.

The case that finally brought this very popular California legislation before its Supreme Court involved the Sinatra family. Back in 1963, the entertainment celebrity's son, Frank Sinatra, Jr., had been kidnapped from his Nevada hotel room and held for ransom by Barry Keenan and his partner until the father paid them off in Los Angeles. Sometime later, the Keenan team was captured, convicted, and sentenced to lengthy time in prison.

However, after they had been released from jail, the kidnappers reached a deal with the tabloid *New Times of Los Angeles* and one of its authors, Peter Gilstrop, to tell the story of *Snatching Sinatra*, first in the *New Times*, and then on a made-for-television movie. Indeed, shortly after this *New Times* article appeared in the January 1998 issue, its people negotiated an agreement with Sony's Columbia Pictures to sell the movie rights for up to $1.5 million. And the earlier contract that *New Times* and Gilstrop had signed with Keenan and his accomplices had the parties splitting up all the revenues generated by this popular kidnapping story.

Frank Sinatra, Jr., had suffered not only physical pain, economic loss, and emotional distress from the kidnapping, but also some serious reputational harm when the kidnaper told the media and the court what turned out to be clearly false—that he had been part of a conspiracy to extort this money from his father. Thus, when *Snatching Sinatra* appeared, Sinatra Jr. went to court to require Columbia Pictures to pay the kidnappers' share of its advance into the state's "involuntary trust fund" for the benefit of victims like him. This is the verdict of the Supreme Court of California on that score.

## KEENAN V. SUPERIOR COURT OF LOS ANGELES COUNTY

Supreme Court of California, 2002.
40 P.3d 718.

BAXTER, JUSTICE.

[After reviewing the above facts and legislative history, as well as analyzing the Simon & Schuster opinion in detail, the Court then began its own First Amendment analysis. It first held that the fact that another provision of this same statute targeted other parts of the criminal's property, whose value had been enhanced by the felony, did not mean that this particular subsection was anything but a "suspect content-based regulation of speech" that would clearly be "unconstitutional unless, at a minimum, it is narrowly tailored to serve compelling state interests." The court then turned to the question of whether this test had been satisfied by a law whose clear purpose "is to assure that the 'fruits' of one's crimes—in this case, proceeds from exploiting the story of those crimes—will be used to compensate crime victims." It did assume "that the fruits of crime include a criminal's proceeds from exploiting the story of the crime." The key question, though, was whether section 2225(b)(1) is "narrowly tailored to ensure that the fruits of crime are used to compensate the victims of crime."]

* * *

We are persuaded that section 2225(b)(1), like the New York law at issue in Simon & Schuster, is overinclusive and therefore invalid. As did the New York statute, section 2225(b)(1) penalizes the content of speech to an extent far beyond that necessary to transfer the fruits of crime from criminals to their uncompensated victims. Even if the fruits of crime may include royalties from exploiting the story of one's crimes, section 2225(b)(1) does not confine itself to such income. Instead, it confiscates all a convicted felon's proceeds from speech or expression on any theme or subject which includes the story of the felony, except by mere passing mention. By this financial disincentive, section 2225(b)(1), like its New York counterpart, discourages the creation and dissemination of a wide range of ideas and expressive works which have little or no relationship to the exploitation of one's criminal misdeeds.

In at least one respect, the involuntary trust provision of section 2225(b)(1) operates more harshly against expressive materials that depict the creator's past crimes than did the escrow account provided for by the New York law at issue in Simon & Schuster. Under the New York statute, proceeds from a crime story contract were to be turned over to the New York Board for placement in escrow, but if, at the end of five years, no valid claims of the criminal's victims or creditors were pending, remaining funds in the account were returned to the criminal. Under section 2225(b)(1), by contrast, any entrusted amounts not subject to legitimate individual claims at the end of the five-year trust period are turned over to the Controller for allocation to the Restitution Fund.

[The court then turned to the Sinatra argument that the California statute had cured the overinclusive problem identified in Simon & Schuster by applying the law "only to persons actually found guilty of felonies" and "only to expressive materials that include the 'story' of a felony—and exempt mere 'passing mention'." However, this court said] . . . we do not read Simon & Schuster as suggesting that a statute which exhibited marginal narrowing in these particular regards would necessarily pass constitutional muster.

Instead, the [Supreme Court's] concern was with the essential values of the First Amendment. As the court's lengthy discussion discloses, the vice of the New York law was that in order to serve a relatively narrow interest—compensating crime victims from the fruits of crime—the statute targeted, segregated, and confiscated all income from, and thus unduly discouraged, a wide range of expressive works containing protected speech on themes and subjects of legitimate interest, simply because material of a certain content—reference to one's past crimes—was included.

Thus, the California statute's limitation to felony convictions does not suffice to avoid an overbroad infringement of speech. As Simon & Schuster made clear, one motivated in part by compensation might discuss his or her past crimes, including those that led to felony convictions, in many contexts not directly connected to exploitation of the crime. One might mention past felonies as relevant to personal redemption warn from experience of the consequences of crime; critically evaluate one's encounter with the criminal justice system; document scandal and corruption in government and business; describe the conditions of prison life; or provide an inside look at the criminal underworld.

Mention of one's past felonies in these contexts may have little or nothing to do with exploiting one's crime for profit, and thus with the state's interest in compensating crime victims from the fruits of crime. Yet section 2225(b)(1) entrusts and permanently confiscates all income, whenever received, from all expressive materials, whatever their subject, theme, or commercial appeal, that include a substantial description of such offenses, whatever their nature and however long in the past they were committed. Thus, even as so limited to felony convictions, section 2225(b)(1) is not narrowly tailored to achieve the compelling interests it purports to serve.

[The court then turned to the Sinatra argument that, contrary to New York's, this California law excluded "mere passing mention of the felony," and instead its requirement of a "story," in the sense of a "depiction, portrayal, or reenactment of the criminal episode" meant that this law "applies only when an expressive work provides narrative detail about a felony for which the work's author or creator was convicted."]

* * *

These arguments do not convince us that section 2225(b)(1) focuses with sufficient precision on the fruits of crime, while leaving other speech-related income undisturbed. Simon & Schuster illustrated the overbreadth of the New York statute by observing that it reached even incidental and tangential mention of past crimes, but nothing in Simon & Schuster suggests the New York law could have cured its overinclusive effect simply by providing an exemption for tangential or incidental references. Moreover, Simon & Schuster neither stated nor implied that the federal Constitution might allow confiscation, on behalf of crime victims, of all proceeds from any expressive work that includes a descriptive account, or even a vivid account, of a past crime committed by the author.

Such arbitrary demarcation lines do not comport with the basic rationale of Simon & Schuster. A statute that confiscates all profits from works which make more than a passing, nondescriptive reference to the creator's past crimes still sweeps within its ambit a wide range of protected speech, discourages the discussion of crime in nonexploitative contexts, and does so by means not narrowly focused on recouping profits from the fruits of crime.

* * *

Had section 2225(b)(1) been in effect at the time and place of publication, the statute would have applied to numerous works by authors whose discussions of larger subjects make substantial, and often vividly descriptive, contextual reference to prior felonies of which they were convicted.[20]

Appeal granted.

---

In his Concurring Opinion, Justice Brown did agree that this California statute had "the same essential constitutional flaws condemned in Simon & Schuster." However, "lest it seem the moral of the story is crime does pay," he wrote a separate opinion

> . . . to dispel the understandable misconception that every "Son of Sam" law is unconstitutional. A properly drafted statute can separate criminals from profits derived from their crimes while complying with the First Amendment.
>
> The Simon & Schuster court recognized the fundamental difference between works like The Confessions of Saint Augustine or Letter from Birmingham Jail and a ghost-written work entitled Snatching Sinatra. In the former examples, it is

[20] These include, for example, Alex Haley and Malcolm X's *The Autobiography of Malcolm X* (Ballantine Books ed. 1992), in which the murdered civil rights leader describes early burglaries for which he was convicted (*id.*, pp. 161–172); Eldridge Cleaver's *Soul on Ice* (1968), which discusses his rapes of White women, for which he was incarcerated, as since-repented acts of racial rage (*id.*, pp. 14–15); memoirs by Charles Colson (*Born Again* (1976)), G. Gordon Liddy (*Will!* (1980)), and John Dean (*Blind Ambition: The White House Years* (1976)) detailing their criminal roles in the Watergate coverup; and the memoirs of Patricia Hearst, the scion of a publishing dynasty, who was kidnapped by the Symbionese Liberation Army and later participated with her captors in an armed bank robbery for which she was imprisoned (Hearst & Moscow, *Every Secret Thing* (1981)).

> the public prominence, fame, wit, passion and eloquence of the authors that make these stories valuable. The "crimes" caused negligible harm to any actual victim and added nothing to the marketability of the stories. In contrast, Mr. Keenan's crime involved both a serious harm and is the source of his work's profitability; judging by the title of his literary effort, it is the celebrity status of his victim that makes the story noteworthy.
>
> Notwithstanding today's decision, the state may constitutionally seize any asset of a criminal to redress the harm inflicted upon his victim. Additionally, the state may seize the fruits of the crime to render it unprofitable. For some works, like The Autobiography of Malcolm X, it may be difficult to determine the extent to which royalties result from the author's criminal involvement or his literary skill. But the existence of hard cases that might win an as-applied challenge does not mean all such laws are facially unconstitutional. The First Amendment protects schlock journalism as well as great literature. Thus, Mr. Keenan has every right to tell his story. That does not mean the First Amendment guarantees he can keep the money. And therein lies the tale.

Justice Brown noted that Simon & Schuster had endorsed "two compelling state interests" here, ensuring "that crimes should neither impoverish the victim nor enrich the criminal. The fulfillment of these interests restores both victim and criminal to the status quo ante and nullifies the tangible effects of the crime." However, to avoid being overinclusive, any such legislation must be "seizing only assets that would compensate the victim or render crime unprofitable."

* * *

> The hypothetically prominent figure who mentions a minor theft in his autobiography bears a strong resemblance to Saint Augustine, and very little to defendant. Defendant's kidnapping created more than trivial harm, and it appears the notoriety of his criminal conduct is substantially responsible for the salability of his literary efforts. Thus, seizure of defendant's royalties serves one or both of the compelling state interests. If so, the state may constitutionally distinguish between Snatching Sinatra and The Confessions of Saint Augustine.

40 P.3d at 736.

* * *

Justice Brown then observed that the key flaws found by Simon & Schuster in the New York Son of Sam law was its underinclusivity from both a compensation and prevention perspective. For example, "a law that shields assets such as Ms. Harris' home or stock portfolio from a compensation order hardly serves that interest." Similarly, from the point of view of "pursuing the compelling interest of depriving criminals of their profits" the key defect of New York's law is that

> . . . if Jean Harris exploited her criminal notoriety by writing a book, the state could confiscate those royalties. If instead of telling her story she chose to exploit her notoriety by charging $25 for underwear depicting the "Scarsdale Diet" logo with a red slash through it, these royalties would be protected from seizure. The law's message was not that crime doesn't pay but that speaking about crime doesn't pay. Deterring crime is a compelling state interest, deterring speech is not.

* * *

Whether the law pursues the compensation or anti-profit interest, a limitation in the law's scope to storytelling is the Achilles' heel of a Son of Sam provision. Virginia law, therefore, bars a defendant from exploiting her criminal notoriety through any means. It seizes "any proceeds or profits received or to be received directly or indirectly by a defendant or a transferee of that defendant from any source, as a direct or indirect result of his crime or sentence, or the notoriety which such crime or sentence has conferred upon him." (Va. Code Ann. § 19.2–368.20.) Regardless of whether a Virginia criminal profited by selling her account of the crime, her autograph, or her furniture for an exorbitant price, she could not enjoy such revenues under this law.

Section 2225(b)(2) similarly avoids content discrimination in its seizure of profits. In conjunction with section 2225, subdivision (a)(10), it authorizes seizure of "all income from anything sold or transferred by the felon . . . including any right, the value of which thing or right is enhanced by the notoriety gained from the commission of a felony. . . ." The statute is indifferent to the thing's expressive or nonexpressive character, and if expressive, its content. The majority correctly observes section 2225, subdivision (b)(2) is "clearly severable" from subdivision (b)(1), and today's decision does not affect the continuing validity of the former provision.

The content neutrality of section 2225(b)(2) is arguable, insofar as the law distinguishes between income-generating activity that exploits criminal notoriety and that which does not. For example, if Mr. Keenan published a book of poetry anonymously, the royalties would probably not qualify as profits as defined by the subdivision. But if he marketed the poems as "Sizzling Sonnets from the Sinatra Snatcher," the royalties would be enhanced by his criminal notoriety, and thus subject to seizure.

On the other hand, *Simon & Schuster* observed statutes may be content neutral, and thus avoid strict scrutiny, where they are intended to serve purposes unrelated to the content of the regulated speech, notwithstanding their incidental effects on some speakers or messages but not others. Although New York's law was too overinclusive to qualify, a more narrowly drawn statute might face only intermediate scrutiny under *Ward* and *City of Renton*. Moreover, even if held to be content based, a statute that pursues a compelling interest (depriving criminals of all their profits) and is narrowly drawn (seizing only profits) could survive strict scrutiny.

A law that neutrally seizes all profits of crime comports with *Simon & Schuster*, 502 U.S. 105, and thus the First Amendment. Even when his victim has been fully compensated, a criminal is not entitled to profit from his crimes.

As the foregoing analysis shows, a state may constitutionally seize assets by pursuing the compelling interest of compensating victims, in which case the state may seize assets from any source (including assets that are not the fruits of the crime) up to the amount of the victim's damages. Likewise, a state may constitutionally seize assets by pursuing the compelling interest of depriving criminals of assets that are the fruits of crime. And there is no apparent reason why a state must select only one compelling interest to pursue. A state may pursue both interests separately; seizing all assets up to the amount of damage under the compensation rationale, and then all fruits of crime under the antiprofit theory. Because each phase would neutrally seize assets in furtherance of a compelling state interest, the law would avoid the constitutional pitfalls noted in *Simon & Schuster*, 40 P.3d at 738–39.

---

Is the implication of Justice Brown's concurring opinion that the California authorities are still entitled to seize the Keenan group's revenues from *Snatching Sinatra*, but under Section 2225(b)(2), rather than § 2225(a)(1)? And what are your views about whether any such law makes sense from the point of view of criminal justice policy, and can and should such a policy be legitimately implemented from the point of view of constitutional free speech principle?

In 2004, a California court of appeals (in an unpublished opinion) did reject Keenan's claim to collect from Sinatra his $197,000 in attorney fees from winning that lawsuit. He had claimed that this amount was significantly more than the $165,000 that Columbia Pictures had paid him to secure the right to that *Snatching Sinatra* movie. Not only might he make lots more money as his share of the eventual profits from this venture, but they firmly rejected Keenan's claim under the California Code of Civil Procedure awarding such fees when inter alia, "the litigation has resulted in the enforcement of an important right affecting the public interest." The appeals court panel said "we are satisfied that the primary and overriding benefit from this litigation inures to Keenan and other felons who have committed crimes of notoriety, not to the general public or a large class of persons, and that his motion for fees was for this reason properly denied."

Even if there is not such a specific statute, there is another legal instrument that may be available to victims. For a period in the late 1990s, Louise Woodward seemed to have replaced O.J. Simpson as the media's favorite homicide story—what Court TV named *The Nanny Murder Trial*. Woodward had been brought from England to Massachusetts in 1996 as an 18-year old *au pair* supplied by EF Au Pair to Doctors Sunil and Deborah Eappen to look after their new baby Matthew while the two practiced medicine. Several months later, in February 1997, Matthew was dead from head trauma, which the parents and their medical experts attributed to Woodward-inflicted "shaken-baby syndrome." Thus Woodward was arrested and charged with murder (and jailed rather than bailed as a foreigner). This heavily-publicized trial produced a great deal of sympathy for Woodward, especially in England where people contributed a total of several hundred thousand dollars for her defense. Eventually the jury found Woodward guilty of unintended second degree murder, for which the trial judge immediately substituted manslaughter and sentenced her to the 279 days she had already spent in jail.

A year later (with Woodward out on bail), the Supreme Judicial Court of Massachusetts dismissed appeals from both sides, and Woodward immediately took off for England where there was a lot of talk about a lucrative book deal. (Woodward's parents, for example, had been paid $60,000 just for an in-depth interview with the tabloid *Daily Mail*.) Because Massachusetts had repealed its Son of Sam law following the Supreme Court's ruling in *Simon & Schuster*, and the Massachusetts courts had not imposed a *Power* probation condition on Woodward, the Eappen family decided to sue her themselves. Given the criminal conviction (requiring proof beyond reasonable doubt), there was no doubt about Woodward's "wrongful death" tort liability to the Eappens, with the only issue being the amount of damages: thus, the family also secured an interim order barring Woodward from spending any money earned from selling her story. This Massachusetts order (and suit) posed some real enforceability challenges in Britain (as opposed to other states within America). Nonetheless, by early 1999 Woodward was a law student at South Bank University in London, and she and her lawyers decided to settle this case with the Eappens. Woodward is totally free to tell her own version of the story to try to exonerate herself, but she contractually agreed with the Eappens to donate any money paid for those stories (estimated as possibly ranging from $10,000 to $500,000) to the charity of *her* choice—UNICEF, the United Nation's children's arm. While Massachusetts politicians highlighted the *Woodward* case as the reason to restore a more carefully-crafted Son of Sam law to the state, one question is whether this case really serves as evidence that tort law can effectively do the same thing.

---

In thinking about the ideal scope of a law that seeks to remove from the criminal the proceeds of a crime, consider the following range of examples. Assume that an imaginative but illegal Enron-like securities scheme has generated initial profits for the scheme's mastermind in the capital market, then sizeable proceeds for the "exclusive" story rights in the entertainment market, and then (after jail time) a well-paying job in the labor market—e.g., as an expert advisor on how the securities industry can protect itself from future such "scams." Does the story-rights category strike you as being closer to the initial crime profits or to the earnings from the eventual job? Having reflected on these analogies and issues, what is your view about how the Supreme Court should resolve the fundamental question about whether a better-drafted Son of Sam law can satisfy the Court's First Amendment concerns?

---

The experiences of crime witnesses, crime investigators, and crime jurors often generate as much popular interest and potential financial rewards as the stories of the criminals themselves. For example, in the William Kennedy Smith rape case in Palm Beach, Florida, Anne Mercer, the woman who went out to the Kennedy estate to pick up the alleged rape victim, sold her story (for $40,000) to *A Current Affair* before she testified. Several years ago, two jurors in the trial of Bernard Goetz, the man who used his gun in a New York subway car, sold their exclusive stories to the *New York Daily News* and *New York Post*. More recently, two Atlanta police officers in the midst of an investigation of whether Frederic Tokar, a lawyer drug dealer, had hired a killer to execute his wife Sara in front of their young children, sold their story rights; the price was $100,000 apiece if there was both a murder charge and a two-hour television docudrama, and double that amount if there was a four-hour miniseries. And while the jurors in the Simpson case did not get the huge financial advances paid by publishers to the lawyers for both the prosecution and the defense, they have certainly earned considerable money from book royalties, television appearances, and the like.

California enacted legislation in 1994 to bar witnesses from selling their story rights before testifying, and jurors from selling their story rights until ninety days after the trial is complete. So far the only restraints placed on police and prosecutors have come via civil service administration. Do these legal restrictions have any material impact on the value and likelihood of such stories being told? How do they square with *Simon & Schuster's* treatment of the stories of the criminal accused? *See California First Amendment Coalition v. Lungren*, 1995 WL 482066 (N.D.Cal.1995), for the first judicial ruling on the constitutionality of the state's ban on people selling and telling their stories until after their role in the trial is completed.

## D. CELEBRITY PUBLICITY AS A MARKETING VEHICLE[e]

The principal use of celebrity names and likenesses comes not in entertainment events or stories, but in media advertisements and on posters, clothes, or other consumer products. It is in precisely this setting that the role of commercial publicity rights has diverged the farthest from the original legal policy favoring personal privacy. Businesses now find that it makes good sense to pay large sums of money to entertainment stars who are willing to license use of their identities to enhance the attractiveness of a commercial product. The lucrative feature of these transactions is precisely why some businesses would prefer not to have to pay the prices for their creative marketing ventures, and why the celebrity is prepared to pay legal counsel to create new doctrinal roadblocks to such utilization of their personas. The entertainment world plays an important role on both sides of this legal and economic struggle—as the place where entertainers earn the reputation that generates endorsement revenues, and also where the costs of media advertising are increased by the amounts that must be paid for the privilege of associating celebrity names and identities with their products. We shall see this happening with major celebrities who helped to create publicity rights for product merchandising and then for commercial advertising.

---

[e] Again along with the articles cited earlier, see Todd F. Simon, *Right of Publicity Reified: Fame As a Business Asset*, 30 N.Y. School L. Rev. 699 (1985); Theodore H. Haas, *Storehouse of Starlight: The First Amendment Privilege To Use Names and Likenesses in Commercial Advertising*, 19 U.C. Davis L. Rev. 539 (1986); Barbara A. Barnett, *The Property Right of Publicity & the First Amendment: Popular Culture and the Commercial Persona*, 3 Hofstra Prop. L.J. 171 (1992).

## JOHNNY CARSON V. HERE'S JOHNNY PORTABLE TOILETS, INC.

United States Court of Appeals, Sixth Circuit, 1983.
698 F.2d 831.

BROWN, CIRCUIT JUDGE.

[Johnny Carson was the long-time star of NBC's *The Tonight Show*. Right from the beginning in 1962, he had always been introduced by his sidekick, Ed McMahon, as "He-e-e-re's Johnny!" in a distinctively drawn-out tone. As part of Carson's large number of commercial ventures, he licensed the use of this phrase to the "Here's Johnny Restaurant" chain and to a "Here's Johnny" clothing label (produced by his own Johnny Carson Apparel Company).

In 1976, the defendant company owned and operated by Earl Braxton began renting and selling portable toilets under the name "Here's Johnny," coupled with another turn of phrase, "The World's Foremost Commodian." Carson filed suit under both federal trademark and state publicity law. With respect to the trademark claim, the court applied the "likelihood of confusion" test (derived from *Frisch's Restaurants, Inc. v. Elby's Big Boy of Steubenville, Inc.*, 670 F.2d 642 (6th Cir. 1982)), and found neither an intent nor a risk of inducing the public to think that Carson was personally connected with these toilets. That left the court with the question of whether Carson's publicity rights had been infringed.]

* * *

The right of publicity has developed to protect the commercial interest of celebrities in their identities. The theory of the right is that a celebrity's identity can be valuable in the promotion of products, and the celebrity has an interest that may be protected from the unauthorized commercial exploitation of that identity. In *Memphis Development Foundation v. Factors Etc., Inc.*, 616 F.2d 956 (6th Cir. 1980), we stated: "The famous have an exclusive legal right during life to control and profit from the commercial use of their name and personality."

The district court dismissed appellants' claim based on the right of publicity because appellee does not use Carson's name or likeness. It held that it "would not be prudent to allow recovery for a right of publicity claim which does not more specifically identify Johnny Carson." We believe that, on the contrary, the district court's conception of the right of publicity is too narrow. The right of publicity, as we have stated, is that a celebrity has a protected pecuniary interest in the commercial exploitation of his identity. If the celebrity's identity is commercially exploited, there has been an invasion of his right whether or not his "name or likeness" is used. Carson's identity may be exploited even if his name, John W. Carson, or his picture is not used.

In *Motschenbacher v. R.J. Reynolds Tobacco Co.*, 498 F.2d 821 (9th Cir. 1974), the court held that the unauthorized use of a picture of a distinctive race car of a well known professional race car driver, whose name or likeness were not used, violated his right of publicity. In this connection, the court said:

> We turn now to the question of "identifiability." Clearly, if the district court correctly determined as a matter of law that plaintiff is not identifiable in the commercial, then in no sense has plaintiff's identity been misappropriated nor his interest violated.
>
> Having viewed a film of the commercial, we agree with the district court that the "likeness" of plaintiff is itself unrecognizable; however, the court's further conclusion of law to the effect that the driver is not identifiable as plaintiff is erroneous in that it wholly fails to attribute proper significance to the distinctive decorations appearing on the car. As pointed out earlier, these markings were not only peculiar to the plaintiff's cars but they caused some persons to think the car in question was plaintiff's and to infer that the person driving the car was the plaintiff.

*Id.* at 826–827.

> In *Ali v. Playgirl, Inc.*, 447 F. Supp. 723 (S.D.N.Y. 1978), Muhammad Ali, former heavyweight champion, sued Playgirl magazine under the New York "right of privacy" statute and also alleged a violation of his common law right of publicity. The magazine published a drawing of a nude, black male sitting on a stool in a corner of a boxing ring with hands taped and arms outstretched on the ropes. The district court concluded that Ali's right of publicity was invaded because the drawing sufficiently identified him in spite of the fact that the drawing was captioned "Mystery Man." The district court found that the identification of Ali was made certain because of an accompanying verse that identified the figure as "The Greatest." The district court took judicial notice of the fact that "Ali has regularly claimed that appellation for himself."

In *Hirsch v. S.C. Johnson & Son, Inc.*, 90 Wis. 2d 379, 280 N.W.2d 129 (1979), the court held that use by defendant of the name "Crazylegs" on a shaving gel for women violated plaintiff's right of publicity. Plaintiff, Elroy Hirsch, a famous football player, had been known by this nickname. The court said:

The fact that the name, "Crazylegs," used by Johnson was a nickname rather than Hirsch's actual name does not preclude a cause of action. All that is required is that the name clearly identify the wronged person. In the instant case, it is not disputed at this juncture of the case that the nickname identified the plaintiff Hirsch. It is argued that there were others who were known by the same name. This, however, does not vitiate the existence of a cause of action . . . [I]t would be absurd to say that Samuel L. Clemens would have a cause of action if that name had been used in advertising, but he would not have one for the use of "Mark Twain." If a fictitious name is used in a context which tends to indicate that the name is that of the plaintiff, the factual case for identity is strengthened.

280 N.W. 2d at 137.

* * *

That the "Here's Johnny" name was selected by [defendant] Braxton because of its identification with Carson was the clear inference from Braxton's testimony. . . . The proof showed without question that appellee had appropriated Carson's identity in connection with its corporate name and its product.

Although this opinion holds only that Carson's right of publicity was invaded because appellee intentionally appropriated his identity for commercial exploitation, the dissent, relying on its interpretation of the authorities and relying on policy and constitutional arguments, would hold that there was no invasion here. We do not believe that the dissent can withstand fair analysis.

* * *

With respect to the dissent's general policy arguments, it seems to us that the policies there set out would more likely be vindicated by the majority view than by the dissent's view. Certainly appellant Carson's achievement has made him a celebrity which means that his identity has a pecuniary value which the right of publicity should vindicate. Vindication of the right will tend to encourage achievement in Carson's chosen field. Vindication of the right will also tend to prevent unjust enrichment by persons such as appellee who seek commercially to exploit the identity of celebrities without their consent.

The dissent also suggests that recognition of the right of publicity here would somehow run afoul of federal monopoly policies and First Amendment proscriptions. If, as the dissent seems to concede, such policies and proscriptions are not violated by the vindication of the right of publicity where the celebrity's "name, likeness, achievements, identifying characteristics or actual performances" have been appropriated for commercial purposes, we cannot see why the policies and proscriptions would be violated where, as here, the celebrity's identity has admittedly been appropriated for commercial exploitation by the use of the phrase "Here's Johnny Portable Toilets."

Reversed and remanded.

KENNEDY, CIRCUIT JUDGE, dissenting.

I respectfully dissent from that part of the majority's opinion which holds that appellee's use of the phrase "Here's Johnny" violates appellant Johnny Carson's common law right of publicity. While I agree that an individual's identity may be impermissibly exploited, I do not believe that the common law right of publicity may be extended beyond an individual's name, likeness, achievements, identifying characteristics or actual performances, to include phrases or other things which are merely associated with the individual, as in the phrase "Here's Johnny." The majority's extension of the right of publicity to include phrases or other things which are merely associated with the individual permits a popular entertainer or public figure, by associating himself or herself with a common phrase, to remove those words from the public domain.

* * *

I. Policies Behind Right of Publicity

The three primary policy considerations behind the right of publicity are succinctly stated in Hoffman, *Limitations on the Right of Publicity*, 28 Bull. Copr. Soc'y, 111, 116–22 (1980). First, "the right of publicity vindicates the economic interests of celebrities, enabling those whose achievements have imbued their identities with pecuniary value to profit from their fame." Second, the right of publicity fosters "the production of intellectual and creative works by providing the financial incentive for individuals to expend the time and resources necessary to produce them." Third, "[t]he right of publicity serves both individual and societal interests by preventing what our legal tradition regards as wrongful conduct: unjust enrichment and deceptive trade practices."

None of the above-mentioned policy arguments supports the extension of the right of publicity to phrases or other things which are merely associated with an individual. First, the majority is awarding Johnny Carson a windfall, rather than vindicating his economic interests, by protecting the phrase "Here's Johnny" which is merely associated with him. In *Zacchini v. Scripps-Howard Broadcasting*, 433 U.S. 562 (1977), the Supreme Court stated that a mechanism to vindicate an individual's economic rights is indicated where the appropriated thing is "the product of . . . [the individual's] own talents and energy, and the end result of much time, effort and expense." There is nothing in the record to suggest that "Here's Johnny" has any nexus to Johnny Carson other than being the introduction to his personal appearances. The phrase is not part of an identity that he created. In its content "Here's Johnny" is a very simple and common introduction. The content of the phrase neither originated with Johnny Carson nor is it confined to the world of entertainment. The phrase is not said by Johnny Carson, but said of him. Its association with him is derived, in large part, by the context in which it is said—generally by Ed McMahon in a drawn out and distinctive voice[5] after the theme music to "The Tonight Show" is played, and immediately prior to Johnny Carson's own entrance. Appellee's use of the content "Here's Johnny," in light of its value as a double entendre, written on its product and corporate name, and therefore outside of the context in which it is associated with Johnny Carson, does little to rob Johnny Carson of something which is unique to him or a product of his own efforts.

The second policy goal of fostering the production of creative and intellectual works is not met by the majority's rule because in awarding publicity rights in a phrase neither created by him nor performed by him, economic reward and protection is divorced from personal incentive to produce on the part of the protected and benefited individual. Johnny Carson is simply reaping the rewards of the time, effort and work product of others.

Third, the majority's extension of the right of publicity to include the phrase "Here's Johnny" which is merely associated with Johnny Carson is not needed to provide alternatives to existing legal avenues for redressing wrongful conduct. The existence of a cause of action under section 42(a) of the Lanham Act, 15 U.S.C.A. § 1125(a) (1976) and Michigan common law does much to undercut the need for policing against unfair competition through an additional legal remedy such as the right of publicity. The majority has concluded, and I concur, that the District Court was warranted in finding that there was not a reasonable likelihood that members of the public would be confused by appellee's use of the "Here's Johnny" trademark on a product as dissimilar to those licensed by Johnny Carson as portable toilets. In this case, this eliminates the argument of wrongdoing. Moreover, the majority's extension of the right of publicity to phrases and other things merely associated with an individual is not conditioned upon wrongdoing and would apply with equal force in the case of an unknowing user. With respect to unjust enrichment, because a celebrity such as Johnny Carson is himself enriched by phrases and other things associated with him in which he has made no personal investment of time, money or effort, another user of such a phrase or thing may be enriched somewhat by such use, but this enrichment is not at Johnny Carson's expense. The policies behind the right of publicity are not furthered by the majority's holding in this case.

---

[5] Ed McMahon arguably has a competing publicity interest in this same phrase because it is said by him in a distinctive and drawn out manner as his introduction to entertainers who appear on "The Tonight Show," including Johnny Carson.

## II. Countervailing Interests and Considerations

The right of publicity, whether tied to name, likeness, achievements, identifying characteristics or actual performances, etc. conflicts with the economic and expressive interests of others. Society's interests in free enterprise and free expression must be balanced against the interests of an individual seeking protection in the right of publicity where the right is being expanded beyond established limits. In addition, the right to publicity may be subject to federal preemption where it conflicts with the provisions of the Copyright Act of 1976.

### A. *Federal Policy: Monopolies*

Protection under the right of publicity creates a common law monopoly that removes items, words and acts from the public domain. That federal policy favors free enterprise was recently reaffirmed by the Supreme Court in *National Society of Professional Engineers v. United States*, 435 U.S. 679, in which the Supreme Court indicated that outside of the "rule of reason," only those anticompetitive restraints expressly authorized by Congress would be permitted to stand. Concern for the impact of adopting an overbroad approach to the right of publicity was also indicated in this Court's decision in *Memphis Development Foundation v. Factors Etc., Inc.*, 616 F.2d 956 (6th Cir.) (1980). In *Memphis Development*, this Court held that the right of publicity does not survive a celebrity's death under Tennessee law. In so holding, this Court recognized that commercial and competitive interests are potentially compromised by an expansive approach to the right of publicity. This Court was concerned that an extension of the right of publicity to the exclusive control of the celebrity's heirs might compromise the efficiency, productivity and fairness of our economic system without enlarging the stock or quality of the goods services, artistic creativity, information, invention or entertainment available and detract from the equal distribution of economic opportunity available in a free market system. *Memphis Development* recognized that the grant of a right of publicity is tantamount to the grant of a monopoly, in that case, for the life of the celebrity. The majority's grant to Johnny Carson of a publicity right in the phrase "Here's Johnny" takes this phrase away from the public domain, giving him a common law monopoly for it, without extracting from Johnny Carson a personal contribution for the public's benefit. Protection under the right of publicity confers a monopoly on the protected individual that is potentially broader, offers fewer protections and potentially competes with federal statutory monopolies. As an essential part of three federal monopoly rights, copyright, trademark and patents, notice to the public is required in the form of filing with the appropriate governmental office and use of an appropriate mark. This apprises members of the public of the nature and extent of what is being removed from the public domain and subject to claims of infringement.

The right of publicity provides limited notice to the public of the extent of the monopoly right to be asserted, if one is to be asserted at all. As the right of privacy is expanded beyond protections of name, likeness and actual performances, which provide relatively objective notice to the public of the extent of an individual's rights, to more subjective attributes such as achievements and identifying characteristics, the public's ability to be on notice of a common law monopoly right, if one is even asserted by a given famous individual, is severely diminished. Protecting phrases and other things merely associated with an individual provides virtually no notice to the public at all of what is claimed to be protected. By ensuring the invocation of the adjudicative process whenever the commercial use of a phrase or other associated thing is considered to have been wrongfully appropriated, the public is left to act at their peril. The result is a chilling effect on commercial innovation and opportunity.

Also unlike the federal statutory monopolies, this common law monopoly right offers no protections against the monopoly existing for an indefinite time or even in perpetuity.

* * *

[The dissent went on to argue that federal policy favoring "free expression" as well as "free enterprise" precluded expansion of the state law right of publicity beyond its established components]—name, likeness, achievements, identifying characteristics, actual performances, and fictitious characters created by a performer. Research reveals no case which has extended thc right to publicity to phrases and other things which are merely associated with an individual. [The dissent then sought to distinguish the cases relied on the majority—*Hirsch*, *Ali*, and *Motschenbacher*—as well as another decision, *Lombardo v. Doyle, Dane & Bernbach*, 58 A.D.2d 620, 396 N.Y.S.2d 661 (1977), which had found a violation in a television commercial involving a band playing "Auld Lang Syne" on New Year's Eve, with the same music beat and bandleader gestures as traditionally performed by Guy Lombardo.]

## *QUESTIONS FOR DISCUSSION*

1. A scholarly skeptic about the right of publicity, Michael Madow (see his *Private Ownership of Public Image: Popular Culture and Publicity Rights*, 81 Calif. L. Rev. 127, 233 (1993)), questions whether the *Carson* ruling means that Clint Eastwood, for example, could block marketing of "Make My Day" vitamins, or former President George Bush could block "Read My Lips" lipstick. Do you think *Carson's* "Here's Johnny" is distinguishable from these hypotheticals? If not, is that an argument for or against the *Carson* holding? What are your views about the merits of the publicity rights claims in *Hirsch*, *Motschenbacher*, and the other cases described in *Carson*?

2. Under the court's ruling, Carson can control the use of a phrase associated with him. Does the phrase "Here's Johnny" fall within the traditional scope of publicity protection of name, likeness, achievements, identifying characteristics or actual performances? The defendant might have called his company the "John William Carson Portable Toilet Company." Is it possible that one can appropriate another's name without appropriating his identity? Would the public understand any such reference to Carson? Does the photograph in *Motschenbacher* identify Motschenbacher in a different way than the phrase "Here's Johnny" identifies Carson?

3. The New Kids on the Block became one of the hottest musical groups of the early 1990s, with over 500 marketing ventures, one of which was a 900 number that fans could call to hear the New Kids talk or to leave messages for them. *USA Today* and *Star Magazine* each announced in their papers a popular poll (via a 900 number) that asked fans to name their "fave" Kid (USA Today) or the "sexiest" Kid (Star). Should the Kids be able to sue for violation of their publicity rights (the trademark issues we will see later in Chapter 6)? *See The New Kids on the Block v. News America Publishing*, 971 F.2d 302 (9th Cir. 1992).

4. After quarterback Joe Montana led the San Francisco 49ers to their fourth Super Bowl victory in the 1980s, the *San Jose Mercury* published a special Souvenir Section of the paper devoted exclusively to the 49ers. The front page of the Section had an artistic rendition of Montana. Two or three weeks later, the *Mercury* had this Section's pages reprinted in poster form, with each page-poster selling for $5 (though many were given away at charity functions). Montana then sued the *Mercury*, not with respect to the original newspaper picture and story, but just for the poster-page featuring his likeness. Was the latter a violation of Montana's publicity rights under state law? Would upholding such a state law claim violate the First Amendment rights of the newspaper? *See Montana v. San Jose Mercury News*, 34 Cal.App.4th 790, 40 Cal. Rptr.2d 639 (1995). Compare the earlier case in which a photo of the wrestler Hulk Hogan is inserted at the center of a magazine, folded to accommodate the fact that it is four times the size of the regular page, and the paper is the kind that can be used for a poster on the wall. Is Hogan's claim weaker or stronger than Montana's? *See Titan Sports v. Comics World*, 870 F.2d 85 (2d Cir. 1989). Suppose an artist like Leroy Neiman wants to paint Shaquille O'Neal doing a "slam dunk," or an impression of Martin Luther King stating "I Have a Dream." Does Neiman need the celebrity's consent for the original painting and its sale? For selling a limited number of artistic reproductions?

5. What about satirical posters, greeting cards, or T-shirts? During the late-1980s debate about legislative expansion of New York law via a Celebrity Rights Act, proponents of the law showed two greeting cards that had been circulated by gay rights groups. One card pictured John Wayne wearing a cowboy hat and bright red lipstick, saying "It's such a bitch being butch!" Another had Clark Gable standing before the main staircase at Tara with a scantily clad young man in his arms, saying "Frankly my dear, I *do* give a

damn!" Does giving live or dead celebrities the right to block such products make this country better or worse off? For an example of publicity litigation about a satirical T-shirt depicting Howard Hughes, see *Rosemont Enterprises v. Choppy Productions*, 74 Misc.2d 1003, 347 N.Y.S.2d 83 (Sup.Ct. 1972).

6. A set of baseball cards, described as "Cardtoons," includes caricatures of a significant number of players who are renamed Fowl Boggs, Tony Twynn, Cal Ripkenwinkle, Treasury Bonds, Ozzie Myth, Don Battingly, and so on, and who are said to be playing for teams such as the St. Louis Credit Cards and the Los Angeles Codgers. Should the manufacturers be able to assert a "parody" defense to the players' *Haelan*-based publicity claim, relying on the Supreme Court's endorsement (in *Campbell v. Acuff-Rose Music*, 510 U.S. 569 (1994)) of such "fair use" in a copyright suit about 2 Live Crew's rap music version of the Roy Orbison classic, *Oh Pretty Woman*? *See Cardtoons v. MLB Players Association*, 95 F.3d 959 (10th Cir. 1996).

7. Suppose a state enacts a law that denies any publicity rights to *convicted* criminals, such as the 1990s serial killer, Jeffrey Dahmer. Suppose the law is applied to *accused* criminals, such as O.J. Simpson. Can the convicted or accused criminal sue to block sale of merchandise that capitalizes on his name and criminal *modus operandi*? Can such a law be distinguished from the one struck down in *Simon & Schuster*, and if so, how?

---

As the *Carson* case demonstrates, the scope of publicity rights has expanded in many states. Ironically, New York is the exception. Although the Second Circuit was the first to recognize a common law right of publicity in a case based on New York law, *Haelan Laboratories, Inc. v. Topps Chewing Gum*, 202 F.2d 866 (2d Cir. 1953), the New York Court of Appeals later ruled in *Stephano v. News Group Publications, Inc.*, 64 N.Y.2d 174, 485 N.Y.S.2d 220, 474 N.E.2d 580 (1984), that the *Haelan* court had misinterpreted New York law. The Court of Appeals concluded that New York's Civil Rights Law, Sections 50 and 51, provides the exclusive remedy for appropriation of one's name and likeness for any commercial purposes. The impact of *Stephano* on New York privacy law is unclear, though the court did suggest that the impact on publicity doctrine would be minimal: "By its terms the statute applies to any use of a person's [name], picture or portrait for advertising or trade purposes whenever the defendant has not obtained the person's written consent to do so." *Id.* at 224.

Later cases, however, have interpreted *Stephano* to deny publicity claims for any form of identity appropriation beyond name, picture or portrait. Thus, *Tin Pan Apple, Inc. v. Miller Brewing Co., Inc.*, 737 F. Supp. 826 (S.D.N.Y. 1990), dismissed a suit by Tin Pan Apple, owner of the registered service mark for the rap group FAT BOYS, alleging that Miller Brewing Company's use of sound-alikes of the FAT BOYS' voices violated Sections 50 and 51. The court held that because the New York Civil Rights Law did not mention voice, Tin Pan Apple failed to state a claim under New York privacy law. As we will see in Chapter 4, the way that Miller secured the Fat Boys' sound-alikes may well have violated federal copyright law. In any event, New York amended its Civil Rights Law in 1995 to add "voice" to the statutory list of personal assets protected against commercial use by others.

In other states, the right of publicity has been interpreted to protect all aspects of a celebrity's identity, extending not just to voice but to style of performance and professional characteristics as well. For example, in the late 1980s, the California courts protected singing superstar Bette Midler from Ford Motor Company's attempt to impersonate her voice in an advertisement. (This was something of a reversal from earlier California decisions, such as *Davis v. TWA*, 297 F. Supp. 1145 (C.D.Cal. 1969), which dismissed the Fifth Dimension's suit against TWA for the latter's use in its commercials of the theme from the group's hit song, "Up, Up and Away," and *Sinatra v. Goodyear Tire & Rubber*, 435 F.2d 711 (9th Cir. 1970), which did the same thing to Nancy Sinatra's suit against Goodyear Tire's use of the theme from "These Boots Are Made for Walkin'." In both cases, the firms had purchased the right to use the copyrighted songs, but there was no felt need then to secure an additional license from the singers identified with the songs.) After Midler refused an offer by Ford's advertising agency, Young and Rubicam, to take part in Ford's Lincoln-Mercury advertising campaign, the agency hired a former Midler backup singer to impersonate her. Young and Rubicam instructed the impersonator to "sound as much as possible like Bette Midler. . . ." California Civil Code Section 3344 prevents appropriation of a celebrity's "name, voice, signature, photograph or likeness." Although Young and Rubicam never used Midler's voice, name or picture, Midler filed suit alleging that Ford appropriated Midler's voice without her authorization.

The district court held that no legal principle prevents imitation of a voice, and granted Ford summary dismissal of the suit. The Ninth Circuit reversed, interpreting California common law to hold that "when a distinctive voice of a professional singer is widely known and is deliberately imitated . . . to sell a product, the sellers have appropriated what is not theirs and have committed a tort in California." The court reasoned that because California protects against appropriation of the attributes of one's identity, and a "voice is as distinctive and personal as a face," the impersonation of a distinctive voice constitutes appropriation of the person's identity. *See Midler v. Ford Motor Co.*, 849 F.2d 460 (9th Cir. 1988).

Building on the *Midler* rationale, singer Tom Waits prevailed in a claim against Frito-Lay, the makers of Dorito's corn chips. Waits is a well-known singer whose voice sounds like he "drank a quart of bourbon, smoked a pack of cigarettes, and swallowed a pack of razor blades. . . ." Waits is also a purist—opposed to making commercials because they detract from his "artistic integrity." Frito-Lay, wanting to use a Waits' song in a Doritos advertisement, hired Stephen Carter, who "had consciously perfected" an impersonation of Waits' voice. Frito-Lay claimed that Carter captured Waits' style and feeling without duplicating Waits' voice. Nonetheless, Waits sued and the jury found in Waits' favor. On appeal, the court reaffirmed *Midler* and upheld Waits' judgment on that basis, holding that whether Waits' voice is "distinctive" was a jury question. *See Waits v. Frito-Lay*, 978 F.2d 1093 (9th Cir. 1992).[f]

Another legal issue posed by this dramatic difference between the shape of publicity rights in New York and California is the appropriate application, if any, of the latter state's law to actions also taken in the former state. For example, should the injunction as well as damages remedies given by a federal judge in California to block Frito-Lay using Waits' image prohibit any such advertising in New York City as well as Los Angeles? One judicial exploration of this issue took place at a later stage in the Johnny Carson case: *see Carson v. Here's Johnny Portable Toilets*, 810 F.2d 104 (6th Cir. 1987).

Voice impersonations were only the beginning of this development of an expansive conception of publicity rights under California law. The next case displayed how far the courts were prepared to go on this legal venture.

## VANNA WHITE V. SAMSUNG ELECTRONICS AMERICA, INC.

United States Court of Appeals, Ninth Circuit, 1992.
971 F.2d 1395.

GOODWIN, CIRCUIT JUDGE.

[Vanna White is the hostess of *Wheel of Fortune*, a television game show watched by 40 million viewers every day. David Deutsch Associates developed a national advertising campaign for Samsung Electronics, which sought to produce a humorous combination of a Samsung product and a 21st-century twist on a current feature of popular culture. One example was a depiction of the irreverent "news" host Morton Downey, Jr. in front of an American flag with the caption: "Presidential Candidate 2008 A.D."

The "Vanna White ad" had a robot dressed in a wig, gown and jewelry designed to resemble White's hair and dress. The robot was posed in White's recognizable stance next to a Wheel-of-Fortune type game

---

[f] In both *Midler* and *Waits* the Ninth Circuit rejected the argument that voice appropriation claims under state law were preempted by Section 114 of the federal Copyright Act. Keep that issue in mind when reading the copyright cases and materials in Part Two of this book.

board, with a caption reading "Longest running game show. 2012 A.D." Unlike other celebrities used in the campaign, White neither consented to nor was paid for this ad. A district court granted summary judgment against White's suit, and the issues on appeal were whether any state law publicity rights of White had been infringed and whether Samsung had a First Amendment right to do so.]

* * *

II. Right of Publicity

* * *

[Under common law, the question was whether the right of publicity was confined to appropriation of the "name or likeness" of celebrities such as White.] It is not important how the defendant has appropriated the plaintiff's identity, but whether the defendant has done so. *Motschenbacher*, *Midler*, and *Carson* teach the impossibility of treating the right of publicity as guarding only against a laundry list of specific means of appropriating identity. A rule which says that the right of publicity can be infringed only through the use of nine different methods of appropriating identity merely challenges the clever advertising strategist to come up with the tenth.

Indeed, if we treated the means of appropriation as dispositive in our analysis of the right of publicity, we would not only weaken the right but effectively eviscerate it. The right would fail to protect those plaintiffs most in need of its protection. Advertisers use celebrities to promote their products. The more popular the celebrity, the greater the number of people who recognize her, and the greater the visibility for the product. The identities of the most popular celebrities are not only the most attractive for advertisers, but also the easiest to evoke without resorting to obvious means such as name, likeness, or voice.

Consider a hypothetical advertisement which depicts a mechanical robot with male features, an African-American complexion, and a bald head. The robot is wearing black hightop Air Jordan basketball sneakers, and a red basketball uniform with black trim, baggy shorts, and the number 23 (though not revealing "Bulls" or "Jordan" lettering). The ad depicts the robot dunking a basketball one-handed, stiff-armed, legs extended like open scissors, and tongue hanging out. Now envision that this ad is run on television during professional basketball games. Considered individually, the robot's physical attributes, its dress, and its stance tell us little. Taken together, they lead to the only conclusion that any sports viewer who has registered a discernible pulse in the past five years would reach: the ad is about Michael Jordan.

Viewed separately, the individual aspects of the advertisement in the present case say little. Viewed together, they leave little doubt about the celebrity the ad is meant to depict. The female-shaped robot is wearing a long gown, blond wig, and large jewelry. Vanna White dresses exactly like this at times, but so do many other women. The robot is in the process of turning a block letter on a game-board. Vanna White dresses like this while turning letters on a game-board but perhaps similarly attired Scrabble-playing women do this as well. The robot is standing on what looks to be the Wheel of Fortune game show set. Vanna White dresses like this, turns letters, and does this on the Wheel of Fortune game show set. She is the only one. Indeed, defendants themselves referred to their ad as the "Vanna White" ad. We are not surprised.

Television and other media create marketable celebrity identity value. Considerable energy and ingenuity are expended by those who have achieved celebrity value to exploit it for profit. The law protects the celebrity's sole right to exploit this value whether the celebrity has achieved her fame out of rare ability, dumb luck, or a combination thereof. We decline Samsung and Deutsch's invitation to permit the evisceration of the common law right of publicity through means as facile as those in this case. Because White has alleged facts showing that Samsung and Deutsch had appropriated her identity, the district court erred by rejecting, on summary judgment, White's common law right of publicity claim.

* * *

## IV. The Parody Defense

In defense, defendants cite a number of cases for the proposition that their robot ad constituted protected speech. The only cases they cite which are even remotely relevant to this case are *Hustler Magazine v. Falwell*, 485 U.S. 46 (1988) and *L.L. Bean, Inc. v. Drake Publishers, Inc.*, 811 F.2d 26 (1st Cir. 1987). Those cases involved parodies of advertisements run for the purpose of poking fun at Jerry Falwell and L.L. Bean, respectively. This case involves a true advertisement run for the purpose of selling Samsung VCRs. The ad's spoof of Vanna White and Wheel of Fortune is subservient and only tangentially related to the ad's primary message: "buy Samsung VCRs." Defendants' parody arguments are better addressed to non-commercial parodies.[3] The difference between a "parody" and a "knock-off" is the difference between fun and profit.

---

[3] In warning of a First Amendment chill to expressive conduct, the dissent reads this decision too broadly. This case concerns only the market which exists in our society for the exploitation of celebrity to sell products, and an attempt to take a free ride on a celebrity's celebrity value. Commercial advertising which relies on celebrity fame is different from other forms of expressive activity in two crucial ways.

First, for celebrity exploitation advertising to be effective, the advertisement must evoke the celebrity's identity. The more effective the evocation, the better the advertisement. If, as Samsung claims, its ad was based on a "generic" game-show hostess and not on Vanna White, the ad would not have violated anyone's right of publicity, but it would also not have been as humorous or as effective.

V. Conclusion

In remanding this case, we hold only that White has pleaded claims which can go to the jury for its decision.

Affirmed in part, reversed in part, and remanded.

---

While there was a brief dissent by one of the members of the original panel in *White*, the countervailing intellectual property and First Amendment points were elaborated in much greater detail by Judge Kozinski in his dissent from the Ninth Circuit's refusal to rehear this case *en banc* in *White v. Samsung Electronics*, 989 F.2d 1512 (9th Cir. 1993).

> Something very dangerous is going on here. Private property, including intellectual property, is essential to our way of life. It provides an incentive for investment and innovation; it stimulates the flourishing of our culture; it protects the moral entitlements of people to the fruits of their labors. But reducing too much to private property can be bad medicine. Private land, for instance, is far more useful if separated from other private land by public streets, roads and highways. Public parks, utility rights-of-way and sewers reduce the amount of land in private hands, but vastly enhance the value of the property that remains.
>
> So too it is with intellectual property. Overprotecting intellectual property is as harmful as underprotecting it. Creativity is impossible without a rich public domain. Nothing today, likely nothing since we tamed fire, is genuinely new: culture, like science and technology, grows by accretion, each new creator building on the works of those who came before. Overprotection stifles the very creative forces it's supposed to nurture.
>
> The panel's opinion is a classic case of overprotection. Concerned about what it sees as a wrong done to Vanna White, the panel majority erects a property right of remarkable and dangerous breadth: under the majority's opinion, it's now a tort for advertisers to remind the public of a celebrity. Not to use a

---

Second, even if some forms of expressive activity, such as parody, do rely on identity evocation, the First Amendment hurdle will bar most right of actions against those activities. Cf. *Falwell*, 485 U.S. at 46 (1988). In the case of commercial advertising, however, the First Amendment hurdle is not so high. *Central Hudson Gas & Electric Corp. v. Public Service Comm'n of New York*, 447 U.S. 557, 566 (1980). Realizing this, Samsung attempts to elevate its ad above the status of garden-variety commercial speech by pointing to the ad's parody of Vanna White. Samsung's argument is unavailing. Unless the First Amendment bars all right of publicity actions—and it does not, *see Zacchini v. Scripps-Howard Broadcasting Co.*, 433 U.S. 562 (1977)—then it does not bar this case.

> celebrity's name, voice, signature or likeness; not to imply the celebrity endorses a product; but simply to evoke the celebrity's image in the public's mind. This Orwellian notion withdraws far more from the public domain than prudence and common sense allow. It conflicts with the Copyright Act and the Copyright Clause. It raises serious First Amendment problems. It's bad law, and it deserves a long, hard second look.

989 F.2d at 1513. But while Judge Kozinski did win two other subscribers to his point of view, this was just a small minority on the Ninth Circuit. With the basic viability of Vanna White's legal position having been upheld, at the later trial, she won a jury verdict for $400,000 in damages, roughly the same amount as had been won by Bette Midler a few years earlier. Tom Waits won a jury verdict of more than $2 million in compensatory and punitive damages. Celebrity publicity rights have certainly come a long way since Davey O'Brien, the 1938 All-American quarterback from TCU, lost his suit against Pabst Brewing.

### *QUESTIONS FOR DISCUSSION*

1. Christian Dior developed an advertising campaign featuring a trio of imaginary Diors, one female and two males, whose personalities were based on the characters from Noel Coward's 1933 play, *Design For Living.* The series of sixteen ads featured the trio in a host of settings wearing Dior clothes. One such ad had the female marrying one of the men with the other as best man, in a scene billed as the "legendary private affair." What made it legendary was the presence in the picture of the television personality Gene Shalit, the movie actress Ruth Gordon, the model Shari Belafonte, and especially the secretary Barbara Reynolds, who bore a striking resemblance to Jacqueline Kennedy Onassis. As the wife and widow of both President John Kennedy and super-rich Aristotle Onassis and one of the world's most notable figures in her own right, Onassis had never allowed her name to be used for commercial promotions. The Dior ad ran in *Esquire, Harper's Bazaar, The New Yorker*, the *New York Times Magazine*, and other upscale magazines, and generated widespread news comment and a surge in Dior sales. It also produced an Onassis lawsuit. What are the various interests involved in a case such as this? What should be the legal result? *See Onassis v. Christian Dior-New York, Inc.*, 122 Misc.2d 603, 472 N.Y.S.2d 254 (1984).

2. A model named Stephano agreed to pose for an article about 1981 men's fall fashions, which appears as scheduled in the September 7, 1981 issue of *New York* magazine under the title "Fall Fashions." The article contained two photographs of Stephano. A week before, though, *New York* had published another picture taken of Stephano in a Giorgio Armani jacket, as part of its regular column "Best Bets" which describes new and unusual products and services appearing in the metropolitan area. Can Stephano sue the magazine for this unauthorized use of his picture? *See Stephano v. News Group Publications*, 64 N.Y.2d 174, 485 N.Y.S.2d 220, 474 N.E.2d 580 (1984).

3. A photograph of the New York Jets' Joe Namath was originally published by Sports Illustrated in its story about the 1969 Super Bowl, and then reused by S.I. in its advertisements in *Cosmopolitan* (under the heading, "The Man You Love Loves Joe Namath") and *Life Magazine* ("How To Get Close to Joe Namath"). Can Namath sue about the advertisement? *See Namath (Joe) v. Sports Illustrated*, 39 N.Y.2d 897, 386 N.Y.S.2d 397, 352 N.E.2d 584 (1976); compare *Cher v. Forum International*, 692 F.2d 634 (9th Cir. 1982), and *Booth (Shirley) v. Curtis Publishing Co.*, 15 A.D.2d 343, 223 N.Y.S.2d 737 (1962).

4. Suppose a car commercial includes a picture of Johnny Carson or Vanna White driving their Cadillac, or Mercedes, or whatever car they own: is that actionable? What about sneaker or golf club advertisements which truthfully state that Michael Jordan and Tiger Woods used this equipment while developing their respective games as youngsters? For contrasting judicial views, see *Nature's Way Prods. v. Nature-Pharma*, 736 F. Supp. 245 (D.Utah 1990), and *Vinci v. American Can Co.*, 69 Ohio App.3d 727, 591 N.E.2d 793 (1990).

5. If the perceived vice in the advertising case is the implication that the subject is actually endorsing use of the product, would it be sufficient to allow the celebrity to assert a Lanham Act claim of consumer confusion? Woody Allen has filed such claims in look-alike cases: *Allen v. National Video*, 610 F. Supp. 612 (S.D.N.Y. 1985), and *Allen v. Men's World Outlet*, 679 F. Supp. 360 (S.D.N.Y. 1988).

6. Should the flip side of such a truth-in-advertising policy be that celebrities are potentially liable for negligently failing to check the veracity of the claims they agreed to have put in their mouths? *See Kramer v. John Unitas*, 831 F.2d 994 (11th Cir. 1987); *Ramson v. Layne*, 668 F. Supp. 1162 (N.D.Ill. 1987) (involving Lloyd Bridges); and *In re Diamond Mortgage Corp.*, 118 B.R. 588 (Bkrtcy. N.D.Ill. 1989) (involving George Hamilton).

7. The Oldsmobile division of General Motors did a television commercial during the 1993 NCAA basketball championship which celebrated the fact that Oldsmobile had just won Consumers Digest's "Best Buy" award for the third year in a row. The lead-in was a trivia quiz about "Who holds the record for being voted the MVP in this tournament three times in a row," and the answer was UCLA's Lew Alcindor from 1967 through 1969. Shortly afterwards Alcindor changed his name to Kareem Abdul-Jabbar, under which he became the NBA's all-time scoring leader and a member of basketball's Hall of Fame. Should Abdul-Jabbar be able to sue for a violation of his publicity rights consisting of the use of his former name, or is "abandonment" a defense in a case such as this? Even if the Oldsmobile ad used his current name in the quiz answer, should that type of commercial be actionable? *See Abdul-Jabbar v. General Motors Corp.*, 75 F.3d 1391 (9th Cir. 1996).

---

In the summer of 2001, the Supreme Court of California finally addressed the compatibility of the publicity rights created by their state legislators with the federal constitutional First Amendment. This case involved The Three Stooges, which had been created after World War I by a team of Larry Fein, Moe Howard, and Jerome (Curly) Howard. This team of Larry, Moe and Curly began performing as live vaudeville and eventually turned into movie shorts. The Three Stooges became the most celebrated brand of slapstick comedy from the 1920s into the 1940s, decades before Johnny Carson and Vanna White had appeared on the scene.

Eventually, these partners had fashioned a Comedy III arm, not only to become the registered owner of federal copyright in their stories and characters, but also of their own personal publicity rights. But sometime after all three had passed away, they became the subject of work by an experienced artist, Gary Saderup, who had long done charcoaled drawings of celebrities that he then turned into lithographs and silkscreens that could easily be reproduced and sold in products like T-shirts. Since Saderup had done this to The Three Stooges without any permission from Comedy III (and had made $75,000 in net profit from their sales), he became the target of a lawsuit against whom the trial judge awarded not only that amount in damages, but double that figure in attorney fees. As a result, Saderup appealed the case to the Supreme Court of California, claiming that this violated his First Amendment right to freedom of artistic expression.

## COMEDY III PRODUCTIONS V. GARY SADERUP, INC.

Supreme Court of California, 2001.
25 Cal.4th 387, 106 Cal. Rptr.2d 126, 21 P.3d 797.

MOSK, JUSTICE.

[After addressing the statutory issues about the scope and limits of the California definition of publicity rights, which the court found was violated here, it set out to "formulate . . . a balancing test between the First Amendment and the right of publicity." It started by judging that Saderup's works did not involve purely commercial speech that created "a false and misleading impression that the celebrity is endorsing a product." And although his "work was done for financial gain, 'the First Amendment is not limited to those who publish without charge,'" but instead also covers those "undertaken for profit" (quoting from *Guglielmi v. Spelling-Goldberg Productions*, 25 Cal.3d 860, 868, 160 Cal. Rptr. 352, 603 P.2d 454 (1979)).]

* * *

The tension between the right of publicity and the First Amendment is highlighted by recalling the two distinct, commonly acknowledged purposes of the latter. First, " 'to preserve an uninhibited marketplace of ideas' and to repel efforts to limit the 'uninhibited, robust and wide-open' debate on public issues." (*Guglielmi, supra*, 25 Cal.3d at p. 866.) Second, to foster a "fundamental respect for individual development and self-realization. The right to self-expression is inherent in any political system which respects individual dignity. Each speaker must be free of government restraint regardless of the nature or manner of the views expressed unless there is a compelling reason to the contrary."

The right of publicity has a potential for frustrating the fulfillment of both these purposes. Because celebrities take on public meaning, the appropriation of their likenesses may have important uses in uninhibited debate on public issues, particularly debates about culture and values. And because celebrities take on personal meanings to many individuals in the society, the creative appropriation of celebrity images can be an important avenue of individual expression. As one commentator has stated: "Entertainment and sports celebrities are the leading players in our Public Drama. We tell tales, both tall and cautionary, about them. We monitor their comings and goings, their missteps and heartbreaks. We copy their mannerisms, their styles, their modes of conversation and of consumption. Whether or not celebrities are 'the chief agents of moral change in the United States,' they certainly are widely used—far more than are institutionally anchored elites—to symbolize individual aspirations, group identities, and cultural values. Their images are thus important expressive and communicative resources: the peculiar, yet familiar idiom in which we conduct a fair portion of our cultural business and everyday conversation." (Madow, *Private Ownership of Public Image: Popular Culture and Publicity Rights* (1993) 81 Cal.L.Rev. 125, 128 (Madow).)

As Madow further points out, the very importance of celebrities in society means that the right of publicity has the potential of censoring significant expression by suppressing alternative versions of celebrity images that are iconoclastic, irreverent, or otherwise attempt to redefine the celebrity's meaning. A majority of this court recognized as much in *Guglielmi*: "The right of publicity derived from public prominence does not confer a shield to ward off caricature, parody and satire. Rather, prominence invites creative comment."

For similar reasons, speech about public figures is accorded heightened First Amendment protection in defamation law. As the United States Supreme Court held in *Gertz v. Robert Welch, Inc.* (1974) 418 U.S. 323, public figures may prevail in a libel action only if they prove that the defendant's defamatory statements were made with actual malice, i.e., actual knowledge of falsehood or reckless disregard for the truth, whereas private figures need prove only negligence. The rationale for such differential treatment is, first, that the public figure has greater access to the media and therefore greater opportunity to rebut defamatory statements, and second, that those who have become public figures have done so voluntarily and therefore "invite attention and comment." Giving broad scope to the right of publicity has the potential of allowing a celebrity to accomplish through the vigorous exercise of that right the censorship of unflattering commentary that cannot be constitutionally accomplished through defamation actions.

Nor do Saderup's creations lose their constitutional protections because they are for purposes of entertaining rather than informing. As Chief Justice Bird stated in *Guglielmi*, invoking the dual purpose of the First Amendment: "Our courts have often observed that entertainment is entitled to the same constitutional protection as the exposition of ideas. That conclusion rests on two propositions. First, '[t]he line between informing and entertaining is too elusive for the protection of the basic right. Everyone is familiar with instances of propaganda through fiction. What is one man's amusement, teaches another doctrine.' " "Second, entertainment, as a mode of self-expression, is entitled to constitutional protection irrespective of its contribution to the marketplace of ideas. 'For expression is an integral part of the development of ideas, of mental exploration and of the affirmation of self. The power to realize his potentiality as a human being begins at this point and must extend at least this far if the whole nature of man is not to be thwarted.' "

Nor does the fact that expression takes a form of nonverbal, visual representation remove it from the ambit of First Amendment protection. In *Bery v. City of New York* (2d Cir. 1996) 97 F.3d 689, the court overturned an ordinance requiring visual artists—painters, printers, photographers, sculptors, etc.—to obtain licenses to sell their work in public places, but exempted the vendors of books, newspapers or other written matter. As the court stated: "Both the [district] court and the City demonstrate an unduly restricted view of the First Amendment and of visual art itself. Such myopic vision not only overlooks case law central to First Amendment jurisprudence but fundamentally misperceives the essence of visual communication and artistic expression. Visual art is as wide ranging in its depiction of ideas, concepts and emotions as any book, treatise, pamphlet or other writing, and is similarly entitled to full First Amendment protection. . . . One cannot look at Winslow Homer's paintings on the Civil War without seeing, in his depictions of the boredom and hardship of the individual soldier, expressions of anti-war sentiments, the idea that war is not heroic."

Moreover, the United States Supreme Court has made it clear that a work of art is protected by the First Amendment even if it conveys no discernable message: "[A] narrow, succinctly articulable message is not a condition of constitutional protection, which if confined to expressions conveying a 'particularized message,' would never reach the unquestionably shielded painting of Jackson Pollock, music of Arnold Schoenberg, or Jabberwocky verse of Lewis Carroll." (*Hurley v. Irish-American Gay, Lesbian and Bisexual Group of Boston, Inc.* (1995) 515 U.S. 557, 569.)

Nor does the fact that Saderup's art appears in large part on a less conventional avenue of communications, T-shirts, result in reduced First Amendment protection. As Judge Posner stated in the case of a defendant who sold T-shirts advocating the legalization of marijuana, "its T-shirts . . . are to [the seller] what the New York Times is to the Sulzbergers and the Ochses—the vehicle of her ideas and opinions." (*Ayres v. City of Chicago* (7th Cir. 1997) 125 F.3d 1010, 1017; *see also Cohen v. California* (1971) 403 U.S. 15.) First Amendment doctrine does not disfavor nontraditional media of expression.

But having recognized the high degree of First Amendment protection for noncommercial speech about celebrities, we need not conclude that all expression that trenches on the right of publicity receives such protection. The right of publicity, like copyright, protects a form of intellectual property that society deems to have some social utility. "Often considerable money, time and energy are needed to develop one's prominence in a particular field. Years of labor may be required before one's skill, reputation, notoriety or virtues are sufficiently developed to permit an economic return through some medium of commercial promotion. For some, the investment may eventually create considerable commercial value in one's identity." (*Lugosi, supra,* 25 Cal.3d at pp. 834–835 (dis. opn. of Bird, C. J.).)

* * *

In sum, society may recognize, as the Legislature has done here, that a celebrity's heirs and assigns have a legitimate protectible interest in exploiting the value to be obtained from merchandising the celebrity's image, whether that interest be conceived as a kind of natural property right or as an incentive for encouraging creative work. Although critics have questioned whether the right of publicity truly serves any social purpose, there is no question that the Legislature has a rational basis for permitting celebrities and their heirs to control the commercial exploitation of the celebrity's likeness.

Although surprisingly few courts have considered in any depth the means of reconciling the right of publicity and the First Amendment, we follow those that have in concluding that depictions of celebrities amounting to little more than the appropriation of the celebrity's economic value are not protected expression under the First Amendment.

* * *

[The Court then began reviewing the few decisions that had addressed this issue, beginning with the U.S. Supreme Court's verdict in *Zacchini* that we read earlier in this chapter. After doing so, it provided this formulation of the governing principles.]

. . . (1) State law may validly safeguard forms of intellectual property not covered under federal copyright and patent law as a means of protecting the fruits of a performing artist's labor; and (2) the state's interest in preventing the outright misappropriation of such intellectual property by others is not automatically trumped by the interest in free expression or dissemination of information; rather, as in the case of defamation, the state law interest and the interest in free expression must be balanced, according to the relative importance of the interests at stake.

* * *

It is admittedly not a simple matter to develop a test that will unerringly distinguish between forms of artistic expression protected by the First Amendment and those that must give way to the right of publicity. Certainly, any such test must incorporate the principle that the right of publicity cannot, consistent with the First Amendment, be a right to control the celebrity's image by censoring disagreeable portrayals. Once the celebrity thrusts himself or herself forward into the limelight, the First Amendment dictates that the right to comment on, parody, lampoon, and make other expressive uses of the celebrity image must be given broad scope. The necessary implication of this observation is that the right of publicity is essentially an economic right. What the right of publicity holder possesses is not a right of censorship, but a right to prevent others from misappropriating the economic value generated by the celebrity's fame through the merchandising of the "name, voice, signature, photograph or likeness" of the celebrity.

* * *

[The opinion then addressed the question of whether the "fair use" defense to copyright claims (which we shall be learning about in Chapter 4) should be incorporated into state publicity rights law. This court was not prepared to endorse a wholesale importation of federal fair use, but it did find that] the first fair use factor—"the purpose and character of the use" (17 U.S.C. § 107(1))—does seem particularly pertinent to the task of reconciling the rights of free expression and publicity. As the Supreme Court has stated, the central purpose of the inquiry into this fair use factor "is to see, in Justice Story's words, whether the new work merely 'supersede[s] the objects' of the original creation [citations], or instead adds something new, with a further purpose or different character, altering the first with new expression, meaning, or message; it asks, in other words, whether and to what extent the new work is 'transformative.' [Citation.] Although such transformative use is not absolutely necessary for a finding of fair use, [citation] the goal of copyright, to promote science and the arts, is generally furthered by the creation of transformative works." (*Campbell v. Acuff-Rose Music, Inc.* (1994) 510 U.S. 569, 579.)

This inquiry into whether a work is "transformative" appears to us to be necessarily at the heart of any judicial attempt to square the right of publicity with the First Amendment. As the above quotation suggests, both the First Amendment and copyright law have a common goal of encouragement of free expression and creativity, the former by protecting such expression from government interference, the latter by protecting the creative fruits of intellectual and artistic labor. The right of publicity, at least theoretically, shares this goal with copyright law. When artistic expression takes the form of a literal depiction or imitation of a celebrity for commercial gain, directly trespassing on the right of publicity without adding significant expression beyond that trespass, the state law interest in protecting the fruits of artistic labor outweighs the expressive interests of the imitative artist.

On the other hand, when a work contains significant transformative elements, it is not only especially worthy of First Amendment protection, but it is also less likely to interfere with the economic interest protected by the right of publicity. As has been observed, works of parody or other distortions of the celebrity figure are not, from the celebrity fan's viewpoint, good substitutes for conventional depictions of the celebrity and therefore do not generally threaten markets for celebrity memorabilia that the right of publicity is designed to protect. (*See Cardtoons, L.C. v. Major League Baseball Players Association* (10th Cir. 1996) 95 F.3d 959, 974 (*Cardtoons*).) Accordingly, First Amendment protection of such works outweighs whatever interest the state may have in enforcing the right of publicity. The right-of-publicity holder continues to enforce the right to monopolize the production of conventional, more or less fungible, images of the celebrity.

*Cardtoons, supra*, 95 F.3d 959, cited by Saderup, is consistent with this "transformative" test. There, the court held that the First Amendment protected a company that produced trading cards caricaturing and parodying well-known major league baseball players against a claim brought under the Oklahoma right of publicity statute. The court concluded that "[t]he cards provide social commentary on public figures, major league baseball players, who are involved in a significant commercial enterprise, major league baseball," and that "[t]he cards are no less protected because they provide humorous rather than serious commentary." The *Cardtoons* court weighed these First Amendment rights against what it concluded was the less-than-compelling interests advanced by the right of publicity outside the advertising context—especially in light of the reality that parody would not likely substantially impact the economic interests of celebrities—and found the cards to be a form of protected expression. While *Cardtoons* contained dicta calling into question the social value of the right of publicity, its conclusion that works parodying and caricaturing celebrities are protected by the First Amendment appears unassailable in light of the test articulated above.

We emphasize that the transformative elements or creative contributions that require First Amendment protection are not confined to parody and can take many forms, from factual reporting to fictionalized portrayal (*Guglielmi, supra,* 25 Cal.3d at pp. 871–872; *see also Parks v. LaFace Records* (E.D.Mich.1999) 76 F. Supp.2d 775, 779–782 [use of civil rights figure Rosa Parks in song title is protected expression]), from heavy-handed lampooning (*see Hustler Magazine v. Falwell* (1988) 485 U.S. 46) to subtle social criticism (*see* Coplans et al., Andy Warhol (1970) pp. 50–52 [explaining Warhol's celebrity portraits as a critique of the celebrity phenomenon]).

Another way of stating the inquiry is whether the celebrity likeness is one of the "raw materials" from which an original work is synthesized, or whether the depiction or imitation of the celebrity is the very sum and substance of the work in question. We ask, in other words, whether a product containing a celebrity's likeness is so transformed that it has become primarily the defendant's own expression rather than the celebrity's likeness. And when we use the word "expression," we mean expression of something other than the likeness of the celebrity.

We further emphasize that in determining whether the work is transformative, courts are not to be concerned with the quality of the artistic contribution—vulgar forms of expression fully qualify for First Amendment protection. On the other hand, a literal depiction of a celebrity, even if accomplished with great skill, may still be subject to a right of publicity challenge. The inquiry is in a sense more quantitative than qualitative, asking whether the literal and imitative or the creative elements predominate in the work.[11]

[11] Saderup also cites *ETW Corp. v. Jireh Publishing, Inc.* (N.D.Ohio 2000) 99 F. Supp.2d 829, 835–836, in which the court held that a painting consisting of a montage of likenesses of the well-known professional golfer Eldridge "Tiger" Woods, reproduced in 5000 prints, was a work of art and therefore protected under the First Amendment. We disagree with the *ETW Corp.* court if its holding is taken to mean that any work of art, however much it trespasses on the right of publicity and however much it lacks additional creative elements, is categorically shielded from liability by the First Amendment. Whether the work in question in that case would be judged to be exempt from California's right of publicity, either under the First Amendment test articulated in this opinion or under the statutory exception for material of newsworthy value, is, of course, beyond the scope of this opinion.

Furthermore, in determining whether a work is sufficiently transformative, courts may find useful a subsidiary inquiry, particularly in close cases: does the marketability and economic value of the challenged work derive primarily from the fame of the celebrity depicted? If this question is answered in the negative, then there would generally be no actionable right of publicity. When the value of the work comes principally from some source other than the fame of the celebrity—from the creativity, skill, and reputation of the artist—it may be presumed that sufficient transformative elements are present to warrant First Amendment protection. If the question is answered in the affirmative, however, it does not necessarily follow that the work is without First Amendment protection—it may still be a transformative work.

In sum, when an artist is faced with a right of publicity challenge to his or her work, he or she may raise as affirmative defense that the work is protected by the First Amendment inasmuch as it contains significant transformative elements or that the value of the work does not derive primarily from the celebrity's fame.

Turning to the present case, we note that the trial court, in ruling against Saderup, stated that "the commercial enterprise conducted by [Saderup] involves the sale of lithographs and T-shirts which are not original single works of art, and which are not protected by the First Amendment; the enterprise conducted by the [Saderup] was a commercial enterprise designed to generate profits solely from the use of the likeness of The Three Stooges which is the right of publicity . . . protected by section 990." Although not entirely clear, the trial court seemed to be holding that *reproductions* of celebrity images are categorically outside First Amendment protection. The Court of Appeal was more explicit in adopting this rationale: "Simply put, although the First Amendment protects speech that is sold [citation], reproductions of an image, made to be sold for profit do not per se constitute speech." But this position has no basis in logic or authority. No one would claim that a published book, because it is one of many copies, receives less First Amendment protection than the original manuscript. It is true that the statute at issue here makes a distinction between a single and original work of fine art and a reproduction. Because the statute evidently aims at preventing the illicit merchandising of celebrity images, and because single original works of fine art are not forms of merchandising, the state has little if any interest in preventing the exhibition and sale of such works, and the First Amendment rights of the artist should therefore prevail. But the inverse—that a reproduction receives no First Amendment protection—is patently false: a reproduction of a celebrity image that, as explained above, contains significant creative elements is entitled to as much First Amendment protection as an original work of art. The trial court and the Court of Appeal therefore erred in this respect.

Rather, the inquiry is into whether Saderup's work is sufficiently transformative. Correctly anticipating this inquiry, he argues that all portraiture involves creative decisions, that therefore no portrait portrays a mere literal likeness, and that accordingly all portraiture, including reproductions, is protected by the First Amendment. We reject any such categorical position. Without denying that all portraiture involves the making of artistic choices, we find it equally undeniable, under the test formulated above, that when an artist's skill and talent is manifestly subordinated to the overall goal of creating a conventional portrait of a celebrity so as to commercially exploit his or her fame, then the artist's right of free expression is outweighed by the right of publicity. As is the case with fair use in the area of copyright law, an artist depicting a celebrity must contribute something more than a " 'merely trivial' " variation, [but must create] something recognizably " 'his own' " (*L. Batlin & Son, Inc. v. Snyder* (2d Cir. 1976) 536 F.2d 486, 490), in order to qualify for legal protection.

On the other hand, we do not hold that all reproductions of celebrity portraits are unprotected by the First Amendment. The silkscreens of Andy Warhol, for example, have as their subjects the images of such celebrities as Marilyn Monroe, Elizabeth Taylor, and Elvis Presley. Through distortion and the careful manipulation of context, Warhol was able to convey a message that went beyond the commercial exploitation of celebrity images and became a form of ironic social comment on the dehumanization of celebrity itself.[12] Such expression may well be entitled to First Amendment protection. Although the distinction between protected and unprotected expression will sometimes be subtle, it is no more so than other distinctions triers of fact are called on to make in First Amendment jurisprudence.

Turning to Saderup's work, we can discern no significant transformative or creative contribution. His undeniable skill is manifestly subordinated to the overall goal of creating literal, conventional depictions of The Three Stooges so as to exploit their fame. Indeed, were we to decide that Saderup's depictions were protected by the First Amendment, we cannot perceive how the right of publicity would remain a viable right other than in cases of falsified celebrity endorsements.

Moreover, the marketability and economic value of Saderup's work derives primarily from the fame of the celebrities depicted. While that fact alone does not necessarily mean the work receives no First

[12] The novelist Don DeLillo gives this fictional account of an encounter with Warhol's reproductions of images of Mao Zedong: "He moved along and stood finally in a room filled with images of Chairman Mao. Photocopy Mao, silk-screen Mao, wallpaper Mao, synthetic-polymer Mao. A series of silkscreens was installed over a broader surface of wallpaper serigraphs, the Chairman's face a pansy purple here, floating nearly free of its photographic source. Work that was unwitting of history appealed to [him]. He found it liberating. Had he ever realized the deeper meaning of Mao before he saw these pictures?" (DeLillo, Mao II (1991) p. 21.)

Amendment protection, we can perceive no transformative elements in Saderup's works that would require such protection.

Saderup argues that it would be incongruous and unjust to protect parodies and other distortions of celebrity figures but not wholesome, reverential portraits of such celebrities. The test we articulate today, however, does not express a value judgment or preference for one type of depiction over another. Rather, it reflects a recognition that the Legislature has granted to the heirs and assigns of celebrities the property right to exploit the celebrities' images, and that certain forms of expressive activity protected by the First Amendment fall outside the boundaries of that right. Stated another way, we are concerned not with whether conventional celebrity images should be produced but with who produces them and, more pertinently, who appropriates the value from their production. Thus, under section 990, if Saderup wishes to continue to depict The Three Stooges as he has done, he may do so only with the consent of the right-of-publicity holder.

Affirmed.

---

Just two months after the Supreme Court of California had released this decision upholding the publicity rights of the heirs of The Three Stooges against the First Amendment claim of an artist, the Ninth Circuit was rendering the verdict about the claim of a major contemporary celebrity, Dustin Hoffman. Hoffman was one of the most successful actors over the past four decades, with seven Oscar nominations and two victories. Back in the 1960s, he made some commercials (for Volkswagen), but after starring in *The Graduate*, Hoffman ceased doing that. Thus, he was the first of only two stars to sue Disney when its subsidiary *Los Angeles Magazine* had a story appear in 1997.

This 15-page story, titled "Grand Illusion," used the new technology to alter some famous scenes from such classic movies as *Gone With the Wind*, *Rear Window*, and *Saturday Night Fever*, and digitally create a new still-life picture of the big stars wearing and praising brand-new styles of clothing. For example, besides Elizabeth Taylor, Marilyn Monroe, Jane Russell, John Travolta, Marlene Dietrich, Elvis Presley, and a few others, the story had Cary Grant with his new image characterized as "still ducking that pesky place in *North by Northwest*, but now he is doing it as a runway model, wearing a suit from Maschino's spring collection. We know purists will be upset, but who could resist the opportunity to produce a 1997 fashion show with mannequins who have classic links." In Hoffman's case, his 1982 Oscar-nominated *Tootsie* movie had a scene where Hoffman was wearing a long red dress, standing in front of an American flag, and saying "What do you get when you cross a hopelessly straight starving actor with a dynamite red sequined dress? You get America's hottest new actress." *L.A. Magazine* used computer imaging to put Dustin and his pose on the page, but in a yellow silk gown with spaghetti straps and high-heeled shoes, and the phrase "Dustin Hoffman isn't a drag in a butter-colored silk gown by Richard Taylor and Ralph Lauren heels." While the magazine said the aim of the article was to display these historic movie scenes dressed in brand-new clothing as a window into the style of the late 1990s, the story did refer readers to a page 147 "Shoppers Guide" regarding the prices and stores for these and all other clothes depicted in the article.

After a full trial, the federal district judge upheld the claim that this Disney magazine had violated Hoffman's publicity rights through "the exploitative commercial use of [his] name and likeness," and awarded him $1.5 million in compensatory, and another $1.5 million in punitive damages. However, in *Hoffman v. Capital Cities*, 255 F.3d 1180 (9th Cir. 2001), a Ninth Circuit panel rejected the basic assumption that this was commercial (rather than entertaining) speech.

> These facts are not enough to make the "Tootsie" photograph pure commercial speech. If the altered photograph had appeared in a Ralph Lauren advertisement, then we would be facing a case much like those cited above. But LAM did not use Hoffman's image in a traditional advertisement printed merely for the purpose of selling a particular product. Insofar as the record shows, LAM did not receive any consideration from the designers for featuring this clothing in the fashion article containing the altered movie stills. Nor did the article simply advance a commercial message. "Grand Illusions" appears as a feature article on the cover of the magazine and in the table of contents. It is a complement to and a part of the issue's focus on Hollywood past and present. Viewed in context, the article as a whole is a combination of fashion photography, humor, and visual and verbal editorial comment on classic films and famous actors. Any commercial aspects are "inextricably entwined" with expressive elements, and so they cannot be separated out "from the fully protected whole." . . . "[T]here are commonsense differences between speech that does no more than propose a commercial transaction and other varieties," *Va. State Bd. of Pharmacy v. Va. Citizens Consumer Council, Inc.*, 425 U.S. 748, 771 n. 24, and common sense tells us this is not a simple advertisement.

255 F.3d at 1185–86. And in a footnote to the *Hoffman* opinion, this panel distinguished the recent *Comedy III* ruling on the ground that "there is no question that LAM's publication of the 'Tootsie' photography contained

'significant transformative elements.' Hoffman's body was eliminated and a new differently clothed body was substituted in its place."

Hoffman's attorney immediately filed an appeal to the full Ninth Circuit and said that, if necessary, they would be taking this case to the U.S. Supreme Court. However, just before the hearing was scheduled before the Ninth Circuit, the parties settled the case for the typical "undisclosed amount."

Since all such legal negotiations take place in the shadow of the governing law, how would you have compared Hoffman's claim to that of his celebrity predecessors, Johnny Carson, Vanna White, and the Three Stooges? What are your views not only about these various rulings, but also about the broader legal policy justifications that have been offered for the major expansions of publicity rights that have taken place over the previous quarter century—that these are necessary to provide effective incentives and just rewards to the Carsons, the Whites, and the Three Stooges and to prevent unjust enrichment of the makers of toilets, VCRs, and T-shirts by excessive use of celebrity personas. Clearly such celebrities benefit from conferral of such an exclusive property in their name and identity. But are Americans generally made better or worse off when their suppliers have to pay a significant premium in the price of their consumer products to have them identified with notable personalities? Or, as Judge Smith asserted in *Matthews*, *supra*, are we all better off because exclusive celebrity control of the use and abuse of their identities preserves their popular appeal? And if that is so, should a Hoffman also have a legal right to keep his image out of Taylor's clothes and Lauren's shoes, like the Three Stooges did with Saderup T-shirts?

## E. WHO OWNS PUBLICITY AND ITS VALUE

We have now seen the host of settings in which publicity rights can be asserted in the entertainment world. Legal creation of such property rights confers substantial economic value on the people whose consent is needed before their names and likenesses can be used. The bigger the name, the higher the price for such consent.[g]

Once a valuable property right has been created, another question that naturally arises is who "owns" this right and the flow of revenue it can generate. For example, one of the points made by the dissent to the original panel decision in *White* is that the key features of Vanna White's identity supposedly being appropriated by the Samsung ad were really the byproduct of *Wheel of Fortune* and thus the property right of the

[g] For a critique of White and its broader implications, see Stephen R. Barnett, *First Amendment Limits on the Right of Publicity*, 30 Tort & Ins. L.J. 635 (1995). But for an authoritative endorsement of the expansion of publicity rights we have traced in this chapter, see American Law Institute, Restatement of the Law Third, *Unfair Competition*, at 527–572 (1995).

show's producer, not its performer. (Interestingly, Sony's Columbia Pictures, the producer and copyright owner of Hoffman's *Tootsie* movie and character, did not file a suit against their fellow entertainment conglomerate, Disney/ABC, for the latter's use of its film still of *Tootsie* in the *Los Angeles Magazine.*) The *Cheers* case, though, has already produced two circuit court rulings, in *Wendt and Ratzenberger v. Host International, Inc.*, 50 F.3d 18 (9th Cir. 1995), and *Paramount Pictures Corp.*, 125 F.3d 806 (9th Cir. 1997).

In the decade-long television hit, *Cheers*, George Wendt and John Ratzenberger had played the characters "Norm" and "Cliff" and who sat at the bar, drinking beer and chatting about life. Paramount, the producer and copyright owner of *Cheers*, licensed Host International to operate Cheers-like bars, one feature of which were life-size talking characters, Hank and Blue, who closely resembled Cliff and Norm in their usual location at the corner of the *Cheers* bar. Since there was a much closer resemblance here than in the *Vanna White* case, and Host had not secured licenses from Wendt and Ratzenberger, the latter sued both Host and Paramount for violation of their publicity rights. (Because *Cheers* had by then been put to rest, except for syndication purposes, the two actors had no compunction about suing their producer.) The defense raised by both Host and Paramount was that in circumstances such as these, the assertion of state publicity rights was preempted by the federal trademark rights of producers in the identities of their fictional characters (which we shall explore in Chapter 6).

In its second ruling, the Ninth Circuit panel said this case needed a full-blown trial with the jury having to decide whether Host's robots "resemble, caricature, or bear an impressionistic resemblance" to Wendt, Ratzenberger, and their characters. But is there a fundamental conflict between those publicity and trademark rights that is sufficient to trigger the constitutional preemption doctrine? How would one compare the *Wendt/Cheers* case with the *White/Wheel of Fortune* case in this regard?

When the Supreme Court refused to take the *Wendt/Cheers* case, the parties chose to settle it on undisclosed terms. Given that all such negotiated deals are arrived at within the shadow of the relevant laws, what is your view about whether there is a fundamental conflict between state publicity rights and federal trademark rights, one that would trigger the federalism preemption (rather than First Amendment) doctrine?

An analogous issue has been generated in the sports rather than the entertainment world, but it has important implications for the latter industry as well. The case of *Allison v. Vintage Sports Plaques,* 136 F.3d 1443 (11th Cir. 1998), involved suits by both a notable baseball pitcher, Orel Hershiser, and the widow of the star race car driver Richard Allison.

Both of these athletes had licensed the use of their names and images on trading cards in return for a share of the receipts (with Hershiser doing so as part of the MLBPA group sales). Vintage Sports Plaques bought a large group of such cards from their producer-distributors, and then framed them between a transparent acrylic sheet and a wood back (sometimes with a small sports motif clock attached) that were then resold as a "Limited Edition of Authentic Collectibles" at a much higher price for these plaques.

The Eleventh Circuit dismissed the athletes's claims that this Vintage action had violated their publicity rights under state common law, by deciding to apply the "first sale" doctrine that federal statutes had long applied to copyright, trademark, and patent claims.

> Appellants argue that the right of publicity differs from other forms of intellectual property because the former protects "identity," whereas the latter protect "a particular photograph or product." The first-sale doctrine should not apply, they reason, because a celebrity's identity continues to travel with the tangible property in which it is embodied after the first sale. We find two significant problems with appellants' argument. First, the distinction that appellants draw between what is protected by the right of publicity and what is protected by other forms of intellectual property rights, such as copyright, is not sound. Copyright law, for example, does not exist merely to protect the tangible items, such as books and paintings, in which the underlying expressive material is embodied; rather, it protects as well the author's or artist's particular expression that is included in the tangible item. The copyright law thus would be violated not only by directly photocopying a protected work, but also by publishing language or images that are substantially similar to that contained in the copyrighted work.
>
> Second, and more important in our view, accepting appellants' argument would have profoundly negative effects on numerous industries and would grant a monopoly to celebrities over their identities that would upset the delicate "balance between the interests of the celebrity and those of the public." *White v. Samsung Electronics Amer., Inc.*, 989 F.2d 1512, 1515 (9th Cir. 1993) (Kozinski, J., dissenting from the order rejecting the suggestion for rehearing en banc.). Indeed, a decision by this court not to apply the first-sale doctrine to right of publicity actions would render tortious the resale of sports trading cards and memorabilia and thus would have a profound effect on the market for trading cards, which now supports a multi-billion dollar industry . . . Such a holding presumably also would prevent, for example, framing a magazine advertisement that

bears the image of a celebrity and reselling it as a collector's item, reselling an empty cereal box that bears a celebrity's endorsement, or even reselling a used poster promoting a professional sports team. Refusing to apply the first-sale doctrine to the right of publicity also presumably would prevent a child from selling to his friend a baseball card that he had purchased, a consequence that undoubtedly would be contrary to the policies supporting that right.

A holding that the first-sale doctrine does limit the right of publicity, on the other hand, would eliminate completely a celebrity's control over the use of her name or image; the right of publicity protects against unauthorized use of an image, and a celebrity would continue to enjoy the right to license the use of her image in the first instance—and thus enjoy the power to determine when, or if, her image will be distributed. Appellants in this case, for example, have received sizable royalties from the use of their images on the trading cards at issue, images that could not have been used in the first place without permission.

136 F.3d at pp. 1448–49. The court then went on to rule that Vintage was just reselling the cards themselves in a different and more elegant-looking frame, rather than attaching the cards, for example, to a baseball glove or a toy car and selling these as the "official" Hershiser glove or Allison race car. Those transformations of the initially-licensed and sold works would violate publicity rights as much as copyright law.

For the past several decades the most contentious ownership issue has involved the descendibility of publicity rights.[h] Ironically, for many celebrities their publicity value actually increases rather than decreases at death. No better example can be given than that of Elvis Presley. While Presley was the King of Rock and Roll from the mid-1950s to the mid-1960s, both his music and movie career had fallen considerably by the 1970s. However, American fans were shocked to learn of Presley's sudden death at Graceland in 1977, and his appeal suddenly soared. By the late 1980s, the Presley estate was earning $15 million a year, with more coming in from sale of Presley's identity than of his music. The estate and the firms to which it had licensed use of Presley's identity quickly became embroiled in litigation addressing the complex legal question of whether and to what extent publicity rights could outlive the celebrities themselves. For a more recent judicial exploration of this issue (including the Presley cases), we shall now read the remaining portion of the *Martin Luther King* decision with which this chapter began.

---

[h] For scholarly commentary, see Peter L. Felcher & Edward L. Rubin, *The Descendibility of the Right of Publicity: Is There Commercial Life After Death?*, 89 Yale L.J. 1125 (1980); Timothy P. Terrell & Jane S. Smith, *Publicity, Liberty, & Intellectual Property: A Conceptual and Economic Analysis of the Inheritability Issue*, 34 Emory L.J. 1 (1985).

## MARTIN LUTHER KING, JR. CENTER FOR SOCIAL CHANGE, INC. v. AMERICAN HERITAGE PRODUCTS, INC.

Supreme Court of Georgia, 1982.
250 Ga. 135, 296 S.E.2d 697.

HILL, JUSTICE.

* * *

2. Does the "right of publicity" survive the death of its owner (i.e., is the right inheritable and devisable)?

Although the *Pavesich* court expressly did not decide this question, the tenor of that opinion is that the right to privacy at least should be protectable after death.

The right of publicity is assignable during the life of the celebrity, for without this characteristic, full commercial exploitation of one's name and likeness is practically impossible. That is, without assignability the right of publicity could hardly be called a "right." Recognizing its assignability, most commentators have urged that the right of publicity must also be inheritable.

The courts that have considered the problem are not as unanimous. In *Price v. Hal Roach Studios*, 400 F. Supp. 836 (S.D.N.Y. 1975), the court reasoned that since the right of publicity was assignable, it survived the deaths of Stanley Laurel and Oliver Hardy. Other decisions from the Southern District of New York recognize the descendibility of the right of publicity, which has also been recognized by the Second Circuit Court of Appeals.

In *Factors Etc., Inc. v. Pro Arts, Inc.*, 579 F.2d 215 (2d Cir. 1978), Elvis Presley had assigned his right of publicity to Boxcar Enterprises, which assigned that right to Factors after Presley's death. Defendant Pro Arts published a poster of Presley entitled "In Memory." In affirming the grant of injunction against Pro Arts, the Second Circuit Court of Appeals said:

> The identification of this exclusive right belonging to Boxcar as a transferable property right compels the conclusion that the right survives Presley's death. The death of Presley, who was merely the beneficiary of an income interest in Boxcar's exclusive right, should not in itself extinguish Boxcar's property right. Instead, the income interest, continually produced from Boxcar's exclusive right of commercial exploitation, should inure to Presley's estate at death like any other intangible property right. To hold that the right did not survive Presley's death, would be to grant competitors of Factors, such as Pro Arts, a windfall in the form of profits from the use of Presley's name and likeness. At the same time, the exclusive right purchased by

> Factors and the financial benefits accruing to the celebrity's heirs would be rendered virtually worthless.

579 F.2d at 221.

In *Lugosi v. Universal Pictures*, 160 Cal. Rptr. 323 (603 P.2d 425) (1979), the Supreme Court of California, in a 4 to 3 decision, declared that the right of publicity expires upon the death of the celebrity and is not descendible. *See Guglielmi v. Spelling-Goldberg Productions*, 160 Cal. Rptr. 352, 603 P.2d 454 (1979), decided two days after *Lugosi*. Bela Lugosi appeared as Dracula in Universal Picture's movie by that name. Universal had acquired the movie rights to the novel by Bram Stoker. Lugosi's contract with Universal gave it the right to exploit Lugosi's name and likeness in connection with the movie. The majority of the court held that Lugosi's heirs could not prevent Universal's continued exploitation of Lugosi's portrayal of Count Dracula after his death. The court did not decide whether Universal could prevent unauthorized third parties from exploitation of Lugosi's appearance as Dracula after Lugosi's death.

In *Memphis Development Foundation v. Factors Etc., Inc.*, 616 F.2d 956 (6th Cir. 1980), Factors, which had won its case against Pro Arts in New York (see above), lost against the Memphis Development Foundation under the Court of Appeals for the Sixth Circuit's interpretation of Tennessee law. There, the Foundation, a non-profit corporation, planned to erect a statue of Elvis Presley in Memphis and solicited contributions to do so. Donors of $25 or more received a small replica of the proposed statue. The Sixth Circuit reversed the grant of an injunction favoring Factors, holding that a celebrity's right of publicity was not inheritable even where that right had been exploited during the celebrity's life. The court reasoned that although recognition of the right of publicity during life serves to encourage effort and inspire creative endeavors, making the right inheritable would not. The court also was concerned with unanswered legal questions which recognizing inheritability would create. We note, however, that the court was dealing with a non-profit foundation attempting to promote Presley's adopted home place, the City of Memphis. The court was not dealing, as we do here, with a profit-making endeavor.

In *Estate of Presley v. Russen*, 513 F. Supp. 1339, the court found in favor of descendibility, quoting from Chief Justice Bird's dissent in *Lugosi v. Universal Pictures*, 603 P.2d at 434, and saying:

> If the right is descendible, the individual is able to transfer the benefits of his labor to his immediate successors and is assured that control over the exercise of the right can be vested in a suitable beneficiary. 'There is no reason why, upon a celebrity's death, advertisers should receive a windfall in the form of freedom to use with impunity the name or likeness of the

> deceased celebrity who may have worked his or her entire life to attain celebrity status. The financial benefits of that labor should go to the celebrity's heirs. . . .'

513 F. Supp. at 1315.

For the reasons which follow, we hold that the right of publicity survives the death of its owner and is inheritable and devisable. Recognition of the right of publicity rewards and thereby encourages effort and creativity. If the right of publicity dies with the celebrity, the economic value of the right of publicity during life would be diminished because the celebrity's untimely death would seriously impair, if not destroy, the value of the right of continued commercial use. Conversely, those who would profit from the fame of a celebrity after his or her death for their own benefit and without authorization have failed to establish their claim that they should be the beneficiaries of the celebrity's death. Finally, the trend since the early common law has been to recognize survivability, notwithstanding the legal problems which may thereby arise. We therefore answer question 2 in the affirmative.

3. Must the owner of the right of publicity have commercially exploited that right before it can survive?

Exploitation is understood to mean commercial use by the celebrity other than the activity which made him or her famous, e.g., an inter vivos transfer of the right to the use of one's name and likeness.

[The court noted several cases which had suggested that the right of publicity must "be exploited by the celebrity during his or her lifetime in order to render the right inheritable," and then continued.] The cases which have considered this issue involved entertainers. The net result of following them would be to say that celebrities and public figures have the right of publicity during their lifetimes (as others have the right of privacy), but only those who contract for bubble gum cards, posters and tee shirts have a descendible right of publicity upon their deaths. That we should single out for protection after death those entertainers and athletes who exploit their personae during life, and deny protection after death to those who enjoy public acclamation but did not exploit themselves during life, puts a premium on exploitation. Having found that there are valid reasons for recognizing the right of publicity during life, we find no reason to protect after death only those who took commercial advantage of their fame.

Perhaps this case more than others brings the point into focus. A well known minister may avoid exploiting his prominence during life because to do otherwise would impair his ministry. Should his election not to take commercial advantage of his position during life ipso facto result in permitting others to exploit his name and likeness after his death? In our view, a person who avoids exploitation during life is entitled to have his image protected against exploitation after death just as much if not more than a person who exploited his image during life.

Without doubt, Dr. King could have exploited his name and likeness during his lifetime. That this opportunity was not appealing to him does not mean that others have the right to use his name and likeness in ways he himself chose not to do. Nor does it strip his family and estate of the right to control, preserve and extend his status and memory and to prevent unauthorized exploitation thereof by others. Here, they seek to prevent the exploitation of his likeness in a manner they consider unflattering and unfitting. We cannot deny them this right merely because Dr. King chose not to exploit or commercialize himself during his lifetime.

* * *

---

As is evident from the *King* decision above, a variety of answers have been given in different jurisdictions about whether celebrity property rights should be descendible. In New York, for example, the Court of Appeals has ruled (in *Stephano v. News Group Publications*, 64 N.Y.2d 174, 485 N.Y.S.2d 220, 474 N.E.2d 580 (1984)) that there is no independent common law of publicity, and the Privacy Act statutory right of action is by its terms confined to "a living person." For this reason, the Second Circuit, in *Pirone v. MacMillan*, 894 F.2d 579 (2d Cir. 1990), had to tell the heirs of that rather well-known figure, Babe Ruth, that the commercial use of his name was not actionable under New York law. Notwithstanding that Second Circuit verdict, news reports in 1995 on the 100th anniversary of "Babe's" birth disclosed that the estate was now earning over a million dollars a year in licensing rights. Indeed, not only has the digital imaging technology described earlier in this chapter brought Humphrey Bogart back to the television show *Tales From the Crypt*, but it has enabled Marilyn Monroe to do television commercials for Chanel.

In California, a divided Supreme Court reached the same verdict as New York's Supreme Court about this issue, in *Lugosi v. Universal Pictures*, 25 Cal. 3d 813, 160 Cal. Rptr. 323, 603 P.2d 425 (1979) and *Guglielmi v. Spelling-Goldberg*, 25 Cal. 3d 860, 160 Cal. Rptr. 352, 603 P.2d 454 (1979). A number of years later, the state legislature enacted amendments to the California Civil Code that created a descendible publication right in the "name, voice, signature, photograph, and likeness" of deceased persons. Two significant restrictions were placed on that new right. First, it endured for just fifty years following the death of the person: Babe Ruth's California publicity rights would have expired in 1998. Second, the *deceased* figure's publicity rights are confined to commercial advertising and marketing, and explicitly exclude both news and entertainment products (other than the commercials). Similar variations can be found in other states' legislative and judicial treatment of these issues; for example, publicity rights survive for twenty years after death in Virginia but for one hundred years in Indiana and Oklahoma.

Then, in October 1999, California enacted a new *Astaire Celebrity Image Protection Act.* This legislative action had been precipitated by the judicial ruling in *Astaire v. Best Film & Video Corp.*, 116 F.3d 1297 (9th Cir. 1997), rehg. 136 F.3d 1208 (9th Cir. 1998). There, Fred Astaire's widow Robyn had lost her suit to block the incorporation of Astaire movie dancing scenes (with the consent of the film producer) as the introduction of an instructional dance video captioned as "Fred Astaire teaches you how to dirty dance." The Ninth Circuit concluded that the use of a "deceased image" for this purpose was permissible under the current California statute as an entertainment rather than a commercial product.

Robyn Astaire then went to the state legislature seeking elimination of that entire "entertainment" exemption. Faced with opposition from the ACLU as well as the MPAA, Astaire and her supporters only succeeded in obtaining a more modest expansion of publicity rights. First, the deceased celebrity's rights have now been expanded from 50 to 70 years, post-mortem. Second, the permissible uses of their images are now reduced somewhat to "fictional or nonfiction entertainment, dramatic, literary, musical work," and even then, only if the deceased personalities are not shown as endorsing specific products being placed in the works. Thus, in California at least, future instructional videos using clips of an Astaire dancing will likely violate his estate's publicity rights, but a film using the same clips would not.

Two sets of problems are posed by this legislation. First, as a substantive legal matter, what is the preferable legal policy? Should New York, for example, enact legislation that both expands publicity rights for living celebrities (to encompass the *Midler* and *White* situations, for example), and then makes this right descendible? Should publicity rights be the same for people who are alive and those who are dead, or vary as they do in California (and perhaps in other fashions)?

The second problem relates to the choice of law. Assuming the stark variations that exist among Georgia, California, and New York law, for example, which state's law should govern? Should it be the law of the state where the public figure is (or was) resident or domiciled? Should it be the state where the firm that is using the name and likeness is based and does business? Should it be the state where the allegedly offending product is being distributed and sold to consumers? These choice of law questions apply equally to other state law doctrines such as defamation, privacy, and obscenity that have been canvassed in earlier chapters. (In *New York Times v. Sullivan*, for example, the plaintiff, the Montgomery Commissioner, used the law of his home state of Alabama to sue the *New York Times* for $500,000 for selling in that state a total of 300 copies of the Sunday Times.) What is the appropriate choice-of-law analogy here: is it property, tort, or some other area of law? Which state law should be used to resolve such disputes in a national (indeed, an international) entertainment marketing industry? For early explorations by the Second Circuit, see *Factors Etc. v. Pro Arts*, 652 F.2d 278 (2d Cir. 1981) (about Elvis), and *Groucho Marx Productions v. Day & Night*, 689 F.2d 317 (2d Cir. 1982) (about Groucho). And look back at § 5 of Judge Kozinski's dissent in the *White* case for a brief comment about why interstate enforcement of the state law selected under conflict of laws doctrine makes the latter issue so crucial in shaping the economic value of publicity rights.

---

As noted earlier in this section, "descendibility" is just one of the variety of "ownership" issues that have to be addressed once the basic substantive right has been created in the first place. The following cases and problems pose several of the other key legal questions.

### *QUESTIONS FOR DISCUSSION*

1. In 1985, Continental Telephone (Contel) ran an advertisement featuring a photograph of a Contel employee named Cindy Staruski. The text accompanying the photo said "Hi, I'm Cindy Staruski," and attributed the following fictitious quotation to Staruski, "[I]t has been exciting . . . to know that Continental continues to expand its equipment and services to meet its obligation to serve you." Contel never sought Staruski's permission for use of her name and likeness. Staruski, upset by the advertisement, filed suit for invasion of privacy. Should she succeed? *See Staruski v. Continental Telephone Co. of Vermont*, 154 Vt. 568, 581 A.2d 266 (1990): compare *Jackson v. Playboy Enterprises*, 574 F. Supp. 10 (S.D.Ohio 1983).

2. In 1975, at the age of ten, Brooke Shields posed nude for a publication entitled "Portfolio 8," financed by Playboy Press, with the written consent of her mother. The photos were also used, again with the consent of Shields's mother, in other publications and public displays. Five years later, after learning that the photos were to appear in "Photo" magazine, Shields filed suit in tort and contract seeking damages and an injunction against future use of the pictures.

Assuming that at common law a minor could disaffirm her consent or a consent executed for her by another, should Section 51 of New York's Civil Rights Law (the privacy statute) prohibit liability where written consent has been obtained? What significance should be attached to New York's General

Obligations Law, Section 3–105, which requires prior court approval of minor's contracts in the "performing arts"? *See Shields v. Gross*, 58 N.Y.2d 338, 461 N.Y.S.2d 254, 448 N.E.2d 108 (1983).

3. Frederica von Stade Elkus was a celebrated recording artist and performer with the Metropolitan Opera. During her marriage, Elkus enjoyed tremendous professional success. Her income rose from $2,000 in 1973 to $622,000 in 1989. Elkus's husband travelled with her, serving as performance instructor, voice coach, photographer, and caretaker of the couple's children. In 1991, Elkus sued her husband for divorce. The question arose whether her celebrity status constituted marital property that must be divided with her husband. What should be the verdict? *See Elkus v. Elkus*, 169 A.D.2d 134, 572 N.Y.S.2d 901 (1991) (and also *Piscopo v. Piscopo*, 232 N.J.Super. 559, 557 A.2d 1040 (1989)). Any difference if the husband (or wife) simply stayed in and looked after the home?[i]

---

Thirty years after *New York Times v. Sullivan* created the major federal constitutional law dimension to state law efforts to protect the reputational, privacy, and publicity rights of their citizens, a 1994 decision, *Estate of Andrews v. United States*, 850 F. Supp. 1279 (E.D.Va. 1994), introduced the federal tax law dimension, with equally unpredictable results. The *Andrews* case both provides a revealing window on the book publishing world and poses some serious questions about the nature and future prospects for publicity rights.[j]

Virginia Andrews' first book, *Flowers in the Attic*, published in 1979 under the acronym V.C. Andrews, quickly made her a major figure in the world of Gothic romance novels about children in peril, aimed principally at an audience of teenage girls and young women. The $35,000 advance for that first best-selling book had, seven years and seven books later, blossomed into a November 1986 contract for two books for $3 million. Suddenly, though, Andrews died in December, having written just 100 pages for her next book, *Garden of Shadows*, a prequel to *Flowers in the Attic*.

Andrews' family, her publisher, Simon & Schuster, and her agent, Anita Diamant, decided to try to have another Andrews book written by another author, Andrew Niederman—also a client of Diamant who had written other less successful horror stories. Niederman used his computer to immerse himself in Andrews' characters, plots, dialogue, and overall style. *Garden of Shadows* came out a year later, billed as written by V.C.

---

[i] *See* Robin P. Rosen, *A Critical Analysis of Celebrity Careers as Property Upon Dissolution of Marriage*, 61 George Washington L. Rev. 522 (1993).

[j] For a first look at these issues, see the Note (by Dean Newton), *Federal Estate Tax and the Right of Publicity: Taxing Estates for Celebrity Value*, 108 Harv. L. Rev. 683 (1995), and more recently, Ray D. Madoff, *Taxing Personhood: Estate Taxes and the Compelled Commodification of Identity*, 17 Va. Tax Rev. 759 (1998).

Andrews, and it sold equally well as its predecessors. By 1993, Niederman had written nine books for and by Andrews (as compared to seven by Andrews herself), and the books were continuing to command advances of $1.5 million apiece, of which the Andrews estate was giving Niederman one third. His highest-ever advance in his own name had been $70,000. Unlike other ghostwriters for deceased authors—such as John Gardner writing books about Ian Fleming's James Bond, or Robert Goldsborough writing books about Rex Stout's Nero Wolfe—Niederman was entirely invisible on the jacket and title pages of Andrews' Gothic romance novels. Indeed, reviewers of the first book assumed that the manuscript had actually been written by Andrews before her death.

In the early 1990s, though, Joann Levinstein, an Andrews' fan who was also an IRS auditor, happened to be browsing through a bookstore when she saw some Andrews' books with titles and dates that puzzled her. The eventual result of her literary investigation was an IRS assessment of an additional $1.25 million value to the Andrews estate (which had already paid $2 million for the initial $8 million valuation), which translated into a $950,000 bill for back taxes plus interest. The estate paid the bill under protest and took the dispute to court. The estate conceded that in the distinctive circumstances of this case, the deceased's name and associated publicity rights were a taxable form of descendible property. The contested question was exactly how much to value that right as of 1986. The district court's verdict was for $700,000.

## *QUESTIONS FOR DISCUSSION*

1. How generalizable is the *Andrews* taxability ruling? Recall some of the cases we have seen in this chapter. Should Elvis Presley's name and likeness have been taxable as part of his estate? Tom Waits'? Dr. Martin Luther King's? Jacqueline Kennedy Onassis'? What are the relevant factors in making such judgments?

2. What methods should be used to calculate the value of the right? Based on how the right had been exploited by the celebrity prior to his death? On all the ways in which the right could possibly be exploited by the estate in the future? Or by some other method?

3. Does the blend of state law inheritability and federal taxability raise some questions about the original creation and social value of publicity rights? Consider the implications of this recent incident. Janis Joplin, whose post-death publicity rights had been the subject of *Joplin Enterprises v. Allen*, 795 F. Supp. 349 (W.D. Wash.1992) (noted earlier), had once recorded a song, "Mercedes Benz," that was a sardonic critique of contemporary materialism. The Joplin estate, though, sold to Mercedes Benz the right to use her image (as well as some of the lyrics) in a 1995 television commercial for its cars. Could a musical successor to Joplin (e.g., Tom Waits) write into his will a bar on the use of his name or likeness in any (or just some) commercial

advertising or merchandising? Could that restriction serve to reduce the level of taxation of the estate? How might such restraints be enforced in practice?

4. By the way, suppose that Andrew Niederman, dissatisfied with his share of the proceeds for his writing, decides to author further Gothic romances in the same style, published under his name but describing him on the book jacket as the long-time "Ghost" for V.C. Andrews. Could the Andrews estate assert a right of publicity against such a self-identity? (The next Part will address the question of whether a copyright claim could be asserted against the contents of the book itself.)

---

Finally, some individuals face restrictions on their right to publicity based on their status as amateurs. Intercollegiate athletes, per National Collegiate Athletic Association (NCAA) rules, are forbidden to profit from the use of their name or likeness while a student-athlete attending a university. Breaking these rules results in loss of eligibility.

Former UCLA basketball star Ed O'Bannon challenged the NCAA's sale of student-athlete likenesses to EA Sports for its video games. The lawsuit evolved from its filing into an even broader challenge to the denial of the right of publicity of student-athletes, including sharing in the profits of television, tickets, and merchandise sold with the athletes' likenesses.

Specifically, the student-athletes argued that the NCAA's prohibitions violated antitrust law, as all of the universities colluded to deny the athletes the ability to profit off of their likenesses while a student.

To what promises to be a much-litigated question over the next decade—the question of student-athlete rights to compensation—the district court of California offered an initial answer: maybe. If they want to remain amateurs, student-athletes have a right to share in the profits of the university, to a degree, but not the right to profit from third parties directly for use of their likenesses.

## O'BANNON V. NATIONAL COLLEGIATE ATHLETIC ASS'N

U.S. Court of Appeals, Ninth Circuit.
2015 WL 5712106.

BYBEE, CIRCUIT JUDGE:

Section 1 of the Sherman Antitrust Act of 1890, 15 U.S.C. § 1, prohibits "[e]very contract, combination . . . , or conspiracy, in restraint of trade or commerce." For more than a century, the National Collegiate Athletic Association (NCAA) has prescribed rules governing the eligibility of athletes at its more than 1,000 member colleges and universities.

Those rules prohibit student-athletes from being paid for the use of their names, images, and likenesses (NILs). The question presented in this momentous case is whether the NCAA's rules are subject to the antitrust laws and, if so, whether they are an unlawful restraint of trade.

After a bench trial and in a thorough opinion, the district court concluded that the NCAA's compensation rules were an unlawful restraint of trade. It then enjoined the NCAA from prohibiting its member schools from giving student-athletes scholarships up to the full cost of attendance at their respective schools and up to $5,000 per year in deferred compensation, to be held in trust for student-athletes until after they leave college. As far as we are aware, the district court's decision is the first by any federal court to hold that any aspect of the NCAA's amateurism rules violate the antitrust laws, let alone to mandate by injunction that the NCAA change its practices.

We conclude that the district court's decision was largely correct. Although we agree with the Supreme Court and our sister circuits that many of the NCAA's amateurism rules are likely to be procompetitive, we hold that those rules are not exempt from antitrust scrutiny; rather, they must be analyzed under the Rule of Reason. Applying the Rule of Reason, we conclude that the district court correctly identified one proper alternative to the current NCAA compensation rules—*i.e.,* allowing NCAA members to give scholarships up to the full cost of attendance—but that the district court's other remedy, allowing students to be paid cash compensation of up to $5,000 per year, was erroneous. We therefore affirm in part and reverse in part.

## I

### A. *The NCAA*

American colleges and universities have been competing in sports for nearly 150 years: the era of intercollegiate athletics began, by most accounts, on November 6, 1869, when Rutgers and Princeton met in the first college football game in American history—a game more akin to soccer than to modern American football, played with "25 men to a side." Joseph N. Crowley, In the Arena: The NCAA's First Century 2 (2006), *available at* https://www.ncaapublications.com/p–4039–in–the–arena–the–ncaas–first–century.aspx. College football quickly grew in popularity over the next few decades.

*Fin de siècle* college football was a rough game. Serious injuries were common, and it was not unheard of for players to be killed during games. Schools were also free to hire nonstudent ringers to compete on their teams or to purchase players away from other schools. By 1905, these and other problems had brought college football to a moment of crisis, and President Theodore Roosevelt convened a conference at the White House to address the issue of injuries in college football. Later that year, the presidents of 62 colleges and universities founded the Intercollegiate Athletic Association to create uniform rules for college football. In 1910, the IAA changed its name to the National Collegiate Athletic Association (NCAA), and it has kept that name to this day.

The NCAA has grown to include some 1,100 member schools, organized into three divisions: Division I, Division II, and Division III. Division I schools are those with the largest athletic programs—schools must sponsor at least fourteen varsity sports teams to qualify for Division I—and they provide the most financial aid to student-athletes. Division I has about 350 members.

For football competition only, Division I's membership is divided into two subdivisions: the Football Bowl Subdivision (FBS) and the Football Championship Subdivision (FCS). FBS schools are permitted to offer more full scholarships to their football players and, as a result, the level of competition is generally higher in FBS than in FCS. FBS consists of about 120 of the nation's premier college football schools.

**B. *The Amateurism Rules***

One of the NCAA's earliest reforms of intercollegiate sports was a requirement that the participants be amateurs. President C.A. Richmond of Union College commented in 1921 that the competition among colleges to acquire the best players had come to resemble "the contest in dreadnoughts" that had led to World War I, and the NCAA sought to curb this problem by restricting eligibility for college sports to athletes who received no compensation whatsoever. But the NCAA, still a voluntary organization, lacked the ability to enforce this requirement effectively, and schools continued to pay their athletes under the table in a variety of creative ways; a 1929 study found that 81 out of 112 schools surveyed provided some sort of improper inducement to their athletes.

The NCAA began to strengthen its enforcement capabilities in 1948, when it adopted what became known as the "Sanity Code"—a set of rules that prohibited schools from giving athletes financial aid that was based on athletic ability and not available to ordinary students. *See* Daniel E. Lazaroff, *The NCAA in Its Second Century: Defender of Amateurism or Antitrust Recidivist?,* 86 Or. L.Rev. 329, 333 (2007). The Sanity Code also created a new "compliance mechanism" to enforce the NCAA's rules—"a Compliance Committee that could terminate an institution's NCAA membership." *Id.*

In 1956, the NCAA departed from the Sanity Code's approach to financial aid by changing its rules to permit its members, for the first time, to give student-athletes scholarships based on athletic ability. These scholarships were capped at the amount of a full "grant in aid," defined as the total cost of "tuition and fees, room and board, and required course-related books." Student-athletes were prohibited from receiving any "financial aid based on athletics ability" in excess of the value of a grant-in-aid, on pain of losing their eligibility for collegiate athletics. Student-athletes could seek additional financial aid not related to their athletic skills; if they chose to do this, the total amount of athletic and nonathletic financial aid they received could not exceed the "cost of attendance" at their respective schools.

In August 2014, the NCAA announced it would allow athletic conferences to authorize their member schools to increase scholarships up to the full cost of attendance. The 80 member schools of the five largest athletic conferences in the country voted in January 2015 to take that step, and the scholarship cap at those schools is now at the full cost of attendance. Marc Tracy, *Top Conferences to Allow Aid for Athletes' Full Bills,* N.Y. Times, Jan. 18, 2015, at SP8.

In addition to its financial aid rules, the NCAA has adopted numerous other amateurism rules that limit student-athletes' compensation and their interactions with professional sports leagues. An athlete can lose his amateur status, for example, if he signs a contract with a professional team, enters a professional league's player draft, or hires an agent. And, most importantly, an athlete is prohibited—with few exceptions—from receiving *any* "pay" based on his athletic ability, whether from boosters, companies seeking endorsements, or would-be licensors of the athlete's name, image, and likeness (NIL).

### C. *The* O'Bannon *and* Keller *Litigation*

In 2008, Ed O'Bannon, a former All-American basketball player at UCLA, visited a friend's house, where his friend's son told O'Bannon that he was depicted in a college basketball video game produced by Electronic Arts (EA), a software company that produced video games based on college football and men's basketball from the late 1990s until around 2013. The friend's son turned on the video game, and O'Bannon saw an avatar of himself—a virtual player who visually resembled O'Bannon, played for UCLA, and wore O'Bannon's jersey number, 31. O'Bannon had never consented to the use of his likeness in the video game, and he had not been compensated for it.

In 2009, O'Bannon sued the NCAA and the Collegiate Licensing Company (CLC), the entity which licenses the trademarks of the NCAA and a number of its member schools for commercial use, in federal court. The gravamen of O'Bannon's complaint was that the NCAA's amateurism rules, insofar as they prevented student-athletes from being compensated for the use of their NILs, were an illegal restraint of trade under Section 1 of the Sherman Act, 15 U.S.C. § 1.

Around the same time, Sam Keller, the former starting quarterback for the Arizona State University and University of Nebraska football teams, separately brought suit against the NCAA, CLC, and EA. Keller alleged that EA had impermissibly used student-athletes' NILs in its video games and that the NCAA and CLC had wrongfully turned a blind eye to EA's misappropriation of these NILs. The complaint stated a claim under Indiana's and California's right of publicity statutes, as well as a number of common-law claims.

The two cases were consolidated during pretrial proceedings. The defendants moved to dismiss Keller's right-of-publicity claims on First Amendment grounds. The district court denied the motion to dismiss, and we affirmed that decision, holding that "[u]nder California's transformative use defense, EA's use of the likenesses of college athletes like Samuel Keller in its video games is not, as a matter of law, protected by the First Amendment." *In re NCAA Student-Athlete Name & Likeness Licensing Litig. ("Keller"),* 724 F.3d 1268, 1284 (9th Cir.2013).

In November 2013, the district court granted the plaintiffs' motion for class certification. The court held that certification of a damages class under Rule 23(b)(3) was inappropriate, but it certified the following class under Rule 23(b)(2) for injunctive and declaratory relief:

All current and former student-athletes residing in the United States who compete on, or competed on, an NCAA Division I (formerly known as "University Division" before 1973) college or university men's basketball team or on an NCAA Football Bowl Subdivision (formerly known as Division I–A until 2006) men's football team and whose images, likenesses and/or names may be, or have been, included or could have been included (by virtue of their appearance in a team roster) in game footage or in videogames licensed or sold by Defendants, their co-conspirators, or their licensees.

After class certification was granted, the plaintiffs voluntarily dismissed their damages claims with prejudice. The plaintiffs also settled their claims against EA and CLC, and the district court preliminarily approved the settlement. *O'Bannon* and *Keller* were deconsolidated, and in June 2014, the antitrust claims against the NCAA at issue in *O'Bannon* went to a bench trial before the district court.

* * *

### III

On appeal, the NCAA contends that the plaintiffs' Sherman Act claim fails on the merits, but it also argues that we are precluded altogether from reaching the merits, for three independent reasons: (1) The Supreme Court held in *NCAA v. Board of Regents of the University of Oklahoma,* 468 U.S. 85, 104 S.Ct. 2948, 82 L.Ed.2d 70 (1984), that the NCAA's amateurism rules are "valid as a matter of law"; (2) the compensation rules at issue here are not covered by the Sherman Act at all because they do not regulate commercial activity; and (3) the plaintiffs have no standing to sue under the Sherman Act because they have not suffered "antitrust injury." We find none of these three arguments persuasive.

### A. Board of Regents *Did Not Declare the NCAA's Amateurism Rules "Valid as a Matter of Law"*

We consider, first, the NCAA's claim that, under *Board of Regents,* all NCAA amateurism rules are "valid as a matter of law."

*Board of Regents* concerned the NCAA's then-prevailing rules for televising college football games. The rules allowed television networks to negotiate directly with schools and conferences for the right to televise games, but they imposed caps on the total number of games that could be broadcast on television each year and the number of games that any particular school could televise. *Id.* at 91–94. The University of Oklahoma and the University of Georgia challenged this regime as an illegal restraint of trade under Section 1.

The Court observed that the television rules resembled two kinds of agreements that are ordinarily considered per se unlawful when made among horizontal competitors in the same market: a price-fixing agreement (in that the rules set a minimum aggregate price that the television networks were required to pay the NCAA's members) and an output-restriction agreement (in that the rules artificially capped the number of televised game licenses for sale). *Id.* at 99–100. But it concluded that applying a per se rule of invalidity to the NCAA's television rules would be "inappropriate" because college football is "an industry in which horizontal restraints on competition are essential if the product is to be available at all." *Id.* at 100–01. The Court elaborated:

> What the NCAA and its member institutions market in this case is competition itself—contests between competing institutions. Of course, this would be completely ineffective if there were no rules on which the competitors agreed to create and define the competition to be marketed. A myriad of rules affecting such matters as the size of the field, the number of players on a team, and the extent to which physical violence is to be encouraged or proscribed, all must be agreed upon, and all restrain the manner in which institutions compete. Moreover, the NCAA seeks to market a particular brand of football—college football. . . . *In order to preserve the character and quality of th[is] "product," athletes must not be paid, must be required to attend class, and the like.* And the integrity of the "product" cannot be preserved except by mutual agreement; if an institution adopted such restrictions unilaterally, its effectiveness as a competitor on the playing field might soon be destroyed. Thus, the NCAA plays a vital role in enabling college football to preserve its character,

> and as a result enables a product to be marketed which might otherwise be unavailable. In performing this role, its actions widen consumer choice—not only the choices available to sports fans but also those available to athletes—and hence can be viewed as procompetitive.

*Id.* at 101–02 (emphasis added). The Court held that the NCAA's rules should therefore be analyzed under the Rule of Reason.

Applying the Rule of Reason, the Court struck down the television rules on the ground that they did not serve any legitimate procompetitive purpose. *Id.* at 113–20. It then concluded its opinion by stating:

> The NCAA plays a critical role in the maintenance of a revered tradition of amateurism in college sports. There can be no question but that it needs ample latitude to play that role, *or that the preservation of the student-athlete in higher education adds richness and diversity to intercollegiate athletics and is entirely consistent with the goals of the Sherman Act.* But consistent with the Sherman Act, the role of the NCAA must be to preserve a tradition that might otherwise die; rules that restrict output are hardly consistent with this role. Today we hold only that the record supports the District Court's conclusion that by curtailing output and blunting the ability of member institutions to respond to consumer preference, the NCAA has restricted rather than enhanced the place of intercollegiate athletics in the Nation's life.

*Id.* at 120 (emphasis added).

Quoting heavily from the language in *Board of Regents* that we have emphasized, the NCAA contends that any Section 1 challenge to its amateurism rules must fail as a matter of law because the *Board of Regents* Court held that those rules are presumptively valid. We disagree.

The *Board of Regents* Court certainly discussed the NCAA's amateurism rules at great length, but it did not do so in order to pass upon the rules' merits, given that they were not before the Court. Rather, the Court discussed the amateurism rules for a different and particular purpose: to explain why NCAA rules should be analyzed under the Rule of Reason, rather than held to be illegal per se. The point was a significant one. Naked horizontal agreements among competitors to fix the price of a good or service, or to restrict their output, are usually condemned as per se unlawful. *See, e.g., United States v. Trenton Potteries Co.*, 273 U.S. 392, 398, 47 S.Ct. 377, 71 L.Ed. 700 (1927); *see also, e.g., Broad. Music, Inc. v. CBS, Inc.*, 441 U.S. 1, 19–20, 99 S.Ct. 1551, 60 L.Ed.2d 1 (1979) (arrangements that "almost always tend to restrict competition and decrease output" are usually per se illegal). The *Board of Regents* Court decided, however, that because college sports could not exist without certain horizontal agreements, NCAA rules should not be held per se unlawful even when—like the television rules in *Board of Regents*—they appear to be pure "restraints on the ability of member institutions to compete in terms of price and output." *Bd. of Regents,* 468 U.S. at 103.

*Board of Regents,* in other words, did not approve the NCAA's amateurism rules as categorically consistent with the Sherman Act. Rather, it held that, because many NCAA rules (among them, the amateurism rules) are part of the "character and quality of the [NCAA's] 'product,"' *id.* at 102, no NCAA rule should be invalidated without a Rule of Reason analysis. The Court's long encomium to amateurism, though impressive-sounding, was therefore dicta. To be sure, "[w]e do not treat considered dicta from the Supreme Court lightly"; such dicta should be accorded "appropriate deference." *United States v. Augustine,* 712 F.3d 1290, 1295 (9th Cir.2013). Where applicable, we will give the quoted passages from *Board of Regents* that deference. But we are not bound by *Board of Regents* to conclude that every NCAA rule that somehow relates to amateurism is automatically valid.

What is more, even if the language in *Board of Regents* addressing amateurism were *not* dicta, it would not support the tremendous weight that the NCAA seeks to place upon it. The Court's opinion supports the proposition that the preservation of amateurism is a legitimate procompetitive purpose for the NCAA to pursue, but the NCAA is not asking us to find merely that its amateurism rules are procompetitive; rather, it asks us to hold that those rules are essentially exempt from antitrust scrutiny. Nothing in *Board of Regents* supports such an exemption. To say that the NCAA's amateurism rules are procompetitive, as *Board of Regents* did, is not to say that they are automatically lawful; a restraint that serves a procompetitive purpose can still be invalid under the Rule of Reason if a substantially less restrictive rule would further the same objectives equally well. *See Bd. of Regents,* 468 U.S. at 101 n. 23 ("While as the guardian of an important American tradition, the NCAA's motives must be accorded a respectful presumption of validity, it is nevertheless well settled that good motives will not validate an otherwise anticompetitive practice.").

The NCAA cites decisions of three of our sister circuits, claiming that each adopted its view of *Board of Regents.* Two of these three cases, however, ultimately subjected the NCAA's rules to Rule of Reason scrutiny—the very approach we adopt today. *See Smith v. NCAA,* 139 F.3d 180, 186 (3d Cir.1998), *vacated on other grounds by NCAA v. Smith,* 525 U.S. 459, 119 S.Ct. 924, 142 L.Ed.2d 929 (1999); *McCormack v. NCAA,* 845 F.2d 1338, 1344–45 (5th Cir.1988). Only one—the Seventh Circuit's decision in *Agnew v. NCAA,* 683 F.3d 328 (7th Cir.2012)—comes close to agreeing with the NCAA's interpretation of *Board of Regents,* and we find it unpersuasive.

In *Agnew,* two former college football players who lost their scholarships challenged certain NCAA rules that prohibited schools from offering multi-year scholarships and capped the number of football scholarships each school could offer. *Id.* at 332–33. The *Agnew* court read *Board of Regents* broadly and concluded that, "when an NCAA bylaw is clearly meant to help maintain the 'revered tradition of amateurism in college sports' or the 'preservation of the student-athlete in higher education,' the bylaw [should] be presumed procompetitive." *Id.* at 342–43 (quoting *Bd. of Regents,* 468 U.S. at 120). The court concluded, however, that the scholarship limitations that were before it did not "implicate the preservation of amateurism," since awarding more or longer scholarships to college athletes would not change their status as amateurs. *Id.* at 344. Thus, no "procompetitive presumption" applied to the scholarship rules. *Id.* at 345. Instead of dismissing the plaintiffs' antitrust claims on the merits, the court dismissed them on the unrelated ground that the plaintiffs had failed to plead the existence of a cognizable market. *Id.*

Like the amateurism language in *Board of Regents, Agnew's* "procompetitive presumption" was dicta that was ultimately unnecessary to the court's resolution of that case. But we would not adopt the *Agnew* presumption even if it were not dicta. *Agnew's* analysis rested on the dubious proposition that in *Board of Regents,* the Supreme Court "blessed" NCAA rules that were not before it, and did so to a sufficient degree to virtually exempt those rules from antitrust scrutiny. *Id.* at 341. We doubt that was the Court's intent, and we will not give such an aggressive construction to its words.

In sum, we accept *Board of Regents*' guidance as informative with respect to the procompetitive purposes served by the NCAA's amateurism rules, but we will go no further than that. The amateurism rules' validity must be proved, not presumed.

### B. *The Compensation Rules Regulate "Commercial Activity"*

The NCAA next argues that we cannot reach the merits of the plaintiffs' Sherman Act claim because the compensation rules are not subject to the Sherman Act at all. The NCAA points out that Section 1 of the Sherman Act applies only to "restraint[s] of trade or commerce," 15 U.S.C. § 1, and claims that its compensation rules are mere "eligibility rules" that do not regulate any "commercial activity."

This argument is not credible. Although restraints that have no effect on commerce are indeed exempt from Section 1, the modern legal understanding of "commerce" is broad, "including almost every activity from which the actor anticipates economic gain." Phillip Areeda & Herbert Hovenkamp, *Antitrust Law: An Analysis of Antitrust Principles and Their Application,* ¶ 260b (4th ed.2013). That definition surely encompasses the transaction in which an athletic recruit exchanges his labor and NIL rights for a scholarship at a Division I school because it is undeniable that both parties to that exchange anticipate economic gain from it. *See, e.g., Agnew,* 683 F.3d at 340 ("No knowledgeable observer could earnestly assert that big-time college football programs competing for highly sought-after high school football players do not anticipate economic gain from a successful recruiting program."). Moreover, *Board of Regents*' discussion of the procompetitive justifications for NCAA amateurism rules shows that the Court "presume[d] the applicability of the Sherman Act to NCAA bylaws, since no procompetitive justifications would be necessary for noncommercial activity to which the Sherman Act does not apply." *Id.* at 339.

It is no answer to these observations to say, as the NCAA does in its briefs, that the compensation rules are "eligibility rules" rather than direct restraints on the terms of agreements between schools and recruits. True enough, the compensation rules are written in the form of eligibility rules; they provide that an athlete who receives compensation other than the scholarships specifically permitted by the NCAA loses his eligibility for collegiate sports. The mere fact that a rule can be characterized as an "eligibility rule," however, does not mean the rule is not a restraint of trade; were the law otherwise, the NCAA could insulate its member schools' relationships with student-athletes from antitrust scrutiny by renaming every rule governing student-athletes an "eligibility rule." The antitrust laws are not to be avoided by such "clever manipulation of words." *Simpson v. Union Oil Co. of Cal.,* 377 U.S. 13, 21–22, 84 S.Ct. 1051, 12 L.Ed.2d 98 (1964).

In other words, the substance of the compensation rules matters far more than how they are styled. And in substance, the rules clearly regulate the terms of commercial transactions between athletic recruits and their chosen schools: a school may not give a recruit compensation beyond a grant-in-aid, and the recruit may not accept compensation beyond that limit, lest the recruit be disqualified and the transaction vitiated. The NCAA's argument that its compensation rules are "eligibility" restrictions, rather than substantive restrictions on the price terms of recruiting agreements, is but a sleight of hand. There is real money at issue here.

As the NCAA points out, two circuits have held that certain NCAA rules are noncommercial in nature. In *Smith v. NCAA,* the Third Circuit dismissed a student-athlete's challenge to the NCAA's "Postbaccalaureate Bylaw," which prohibited athletes from participating in athletics at postgraduate schools other than their undergraduate schools, on the grounds that the Sherman Act did not apply to that Bylaw. The *Smith* court held that eligibility rules such as the Postbaccalaureate Bylaw "are not related to the NCAA's commercial or business activities. Rather than intending to provide the NCAA with a commercial advantage, the eligibility rules primarily seek to ensure fair competition in intercollegiate athletics." *Smith,* 139 F.3d at 185.

The Sixth Circuit, meanwhile, held in *Bassett v. NCAA,* 528 F.3d 426, 430, 433 (6th Cir.2008), that the NCAA's rules against giving recruits "improper inducements" were "explicitly noncommercial."

The court explained:

> In fact, th[e]se rules are *anti-commercial* and designed to promote and ensure competitiveness amongst NCAA member schools. Violation of the applicable NCAA rules gives the violator a decided competitive advantage in recruiting and retaining highly prized student athletes. It also violates the spirit of amateur athletics by providing remuneration to athletes in exchange for their commitments to play for the violator's football program. Finally, violators of these rules harm the student-athlete academically when coaches and assistants complete coursework on behalf of the student-athlete.

*Id.* at 433.

Neither *Smith* nor *Bassett* convinces us that the NCAA's Postbaccalaureate Bylaw challenged in *Smith* was a true "eligibility" rule, akin to the rules limiting the number of years that student-athletes may play collegiate sports or requiring student-athletes to complete a certain number of credit hours each semester. As the *Smith* court expressly noted, the Postbaccalaureate Bylaw was "not related to the NCAA's commercial or business activities." *Smith,* 139 F.3d at 185. By contrast, the rules here—which regulate what compensation NCAA schools may give student-athletes, and how much—*do* relate to the NCAA's business activities: the labor of student-athletes is an integral and essential component of the NCAA's "product," and a rule setting the price of that labor goes to the heart of the NCAA's business. Thus, the rules at issue here are more like rules affecting the NCAA's dealings with its coaches or with corporate business partners—which courts have held to be commercial—than they are like the Bylaw challenged in *Smith. See Bd. of Regents,* 468 U.S. at 104–13 (applying Sherman Act to rules governing NCAA members' contracts with television networks); *Law v. NCAA,* 134 F.3d 1010, 1024 (10th Cir.1998) (applying Sherman Act to NCAA rules limiting compensation of basketball coaches).

*Bassett* cannot be distinguished here in the way that *Smith* can since it involved an NCAA rule relating to payments to athletic recruits, but we believe *Bassett* was simply wrong on this point. Bassett's reasoning, in fine, is that rules that seek to combat*commercialism* in college sports by preventing schools from competing to pay student-athletes cannot be considered restraints on "commerce." We simply cannot understand this logic. Rules that are "*anti-commercial* and designed to promote and ensure competitiveness," *Bassett,* 528 F.3d at 433, surely *affect* commerce just as much as rules promoting commercialism. The intent behind the NCAA's compensation rules does not change the fact that the exchange they regulate—labor for in-kind compensation—is a quintessentially commercial transaction.

We therefore conclude that the NCAA's compensation rules are within the ambit of the Sherman Act.

### C. *The Plaintiffs Demonstrated that the Compensation Rules Cause Them Injury in Fact*

The NCAA's last argument antecedent to the merits is that the plaintiffs' Section 1 claim fails at the threshold because the plaintiffs have failed to show that they have suffered "antitrust injury." Antitrust injury is a heightened standing requirement that applies to private parties suing to enforce the antitrust laws. To satisfy the antitrust-injury requirement, a plaintiff must show "injury of the type the antitrust laws were intended to prevent and that flows from that which makes defendants' acts unlawful." *Glen Holly Entm't, Inc. v. Tektronix Inc.,* 343 F.3d 1000, 1007–08 (9th Cir.2003) (quoting *Brunswick Corp. v. Pueblo Bowl-O-Mat, Inc.,* 429 U.S. 477, 489, 97 S.Ct. 690, 50 L.Ed.2d 701 (1977)) (internal quotation marks omitted).

Although the NCAA purports to be making an antitrust-injury argument, it is mistaken. The NCAA has not contended that the plaintiffs' injuries are not "of the type the antitrust laws were intended to prevent." Rather, the NCAA has made a garden-variety standing argument: it alleges that the plaintiffs have not been *injured in fact* by the compensation rules because those rules do not deprive them of any NIL compensation they would otherwise receive. Addressing each of the potential markets for NIL rights that the district court identified, the NCAA argues that (1) there are no legally-recognized NIL rights for participants in live game broadcasts; (2) the NCAA's compensation rules do not deprive the plaintiffs of compensation for use of their NILs in video games because the NCAA no longer permits college sports video games to be made and has a separate policy forbidding the use of student-athletes' NILs in video games; and (3) the NCAA's licensing agreement for archival footage with T3Media does not deprive athletes of NIL compensation for archival footage because it prevents T3Media from licensing student-athletes' NILs while they are in school and requires the company to obtain consent once student-athletes have left school.

We conclude that the plaintiffs have shown that they are injured in fact as a result of the NCAA's rules having foreclosed the market for their NILs in video games. We therefore do not reach the thornier questions of whether participants in live TV broadcasts of college sporting events have enforceable rights of publicity or whether the plaintiffs are injured by the NCAA's current licensing arrangement for archival footage.

**1. Absent the NCAA's compensation rules, video game makers would negotiate with student-athletes for the right to use their NILs**

As we have explained, the district court found that, if permitted to do so, video game makers such as EA would negotiate with college athletes for the right to use their NILs in video games because these companies want to make games that are as realistic as possible. *O'Bannon,* 7 F.Supp.3d at 970. The district court noted that EA currently negotiates with the NFL and NBA players' unions for the right to use their members' NILs in pro sports video games. *Id.* The plaintiffs also put into evidence a copy of a 2005 presentation by EA representatives to the NCAA, which stated that EA's inability to use college athletes' NILs was the "number one factor holding back NCAA video game growth."

The NCAA argues, however, that we cannot find that the plaintiffs have suffered an injury in fact based on lost compensation from video game companies because the NCAA has terminated its relationship with EA and is not currently working with any other video game maker. We disagree. The district court found that it is entirely possible that the NCAA will resume its support for college sports video games at some point in the future, given that the NCAA found such games to be profitable in the past, *id.,* and that finding of fact was not clearly erroneous. Given the NCAA's previous, lengthy relationship with EA and the other evidence presented, it was reasonable for the district court to conclude that the NCAA may well begin working with EA or another video game company in the future.

Our conclusion is unaffected by the NCAA's claim that other rules and policies, not directly at issue here, would forbid video game makers from using student-athletes' NILs in their games if such games were to be made again. The NCAA did, after all, permit EA to continue making NCAA video games for some time after EA began incorporating recognizable player avatars into the games. Moreover, Joel Linzner, an EA executive, testified at trial that EA "made a long-sustained effort to work with the NCAA" to change the policy against using student-athletes' NILs, and that NCAA executives were "supportive" of the idea. It was not clearly erroneous for the district court to conclude on the basis of this evidence that the NCAA might well either change its policy barring the use of athletes' NILs in video games or decline to enforce it.

**2. Whether the Copyright Act preempts right-of-publicity claims based on sports video games is tangential to this case and irrelevant to the plaintiffs' standing**

In addition to arguing that its current policies against college sports video games defeat the plaintiffs' claims to standing, the NCAA also contends that there are legal barriers that would prevent the plaintiffs from being compensated by a video game maker. Specifically, the NCAA argues that the Copyright Act would preempt any right-of-publicity claim arising out of the use of those NILs in sports video games. Thus, the NCAA maintains, if it were to resume its support for college sports video games and permit video game companies to use student-athletes' NILs, the video game makers would not *pay* student-athletes for their NILs; rather, they could use the NILs for free.

We decline to consider this argument, for two reasons. First, it is convoluted and far afield from the main issues in this case. The NCAA asks us to decide whether, assuming that EA or some other video game company were to make a college sports video game that incorporated student-athletes' NILs and then refuse to pay student-athletes for those NILs, the game maker would have a viable Copyright Act defense to a right-of-publicity lawsuit brought by the athletes. That question is a complex one, implicating both Section 301 of the Copyright Act, 17 U.S.C. § 301, which expressly preempts certain common-law claims, and a murky body of case law holding that, in some circumstances, the Act impliedly preempts claims that fall outside of Section 301's scope. *See, e.g., Facenda v. NFL Films, Inc.*, 542 F.3d 1007, 1028–32 (3d Cir.2008) (suggesting, on the basis of a conflict preemption analysis, that federal copyright law can "impliedly preempt[ ]" right-of-publicity claims). It is scarcely fit for resolution within the confines of a standing inquiry in an antitrust suit between the NCAA and its student-athletes that involves neither EA nor any other video game company as a party. Should a college sports video game be made in the future and the right-of-publicity suit envisioned by the NCAA come to pass, the court hearing that suit will be in a far better position to resolve the question of Copyright Act preemption than we are.

Second and more importantly, the NCAA's argument about the Copyright Act, even if correct, is irrelevant to whether the plaintiffs lack standing. On the NCAA's interpretation of the Copyright Act, *professional* football and basketball players have no enforceable right-of-publicity claims against video game makers either—yet EA currently pays NFL and NBA players for the right to use their NILs in its video games. *O'Bannon,* 7 F.Supp.3d at 970. Thus, there is every reason to believe that, if permitted to do so, EA or another video game company would pay NCAA athletes for their NIL rights rather than test the enforceability of those rights in court. That the NCAA's rules deny the plaintiffs all opportunity to receive this compensation is sufficient to endow them with standing to bring this lawsuit. *See* 13A Charles Alan Wright & Arthur R. Miller, Federal Practice and Procedure § 3531.4 (3d ed. 1998) ("[L]oss of an opportunity may constitute injury, even though it is not certain that any benefit would have been realized if the opportunity had been accorded." (collecting cases)); *cf., e.g., United States v. Students Challenging Regulatory Agency Procedures (SCRAP),* 412 U.S. 669, 689 n. 14, 93 S.Ct. 2405, 37 L.Ed.2d 254 (1973) (rejecting the government's argument that standing should be limited "to those who have been 'significantly' affected by agency action"); *Preminger v. Peake,* 552 F.3d 757, 763 (9th Cir.2008) ("The injury may be minimal.").

Because the plaintiffs have shown that, absent the NCAA's compensation rules, video game makers would likely pay them for the right to use their NILs in college sports video games, the plaintiffs have satisfied the requirement of injury in fact and, by extension, the requirement of antitrust injury.

## IV

Having rejected all of the NCAA's preliminary legal arguments, we proceed to review the plaintiffs' Section 1 claim on the merits. Although in another context the NCAA's decision to value student-athletes' NIL at zero might be per se illegal price fixing, we are persuaded—as was the Supreme Court in *Board of Regents* and the district court here—that the appropriate rule is the Rule of Reason. As the Supreme Court observed, the NCAA "market[s] a particular brand . . . [that] makes it more popular than professional sports to which it might otherwise be comparable." *Board of Regents,* 468 U.S. at 101–02. Because the "integrity of the 'product' cannot be preserved except by mutual agreement," "restraints on competition are essential if the product is to be available at all." *Id.*at 101, 102; *see also id.* at 117 ("Our decision not to apply a per se rule to this case rests in large part on our recognition that a certain degree of cooperation is necessary if the type of competition that [the NCAA] and its member institutions seek to market is to be preserved." (footnote omitted)).

Like the district court, we follow the three-step framework of the Rule of Reason: "[1] The plaintiff bears the initial burden of showing that the restraint produces significant anticompetitive effects within a relevant market. [2] If the plaintiff meets this burden, the defendant must come forward with evidence of the restraint's procompetitive effects. [3] The plaintiff must then show that any legitimate objectives can be achieved in a substantially less restrictive manner." *Tanaka v. Univ. of S. Cal.,* 252 F.3d 1059, 1063 (9th Cir.2001) (citations and internal quotation marks omitted).

A. ***Significant Anticompetitive Effects Within a Relevant Market***

As we have recounted, the district court made the following factual findings: (1) that a cognizable "college education market" exists, wherein colleges compete for the services of athletic recruits by offering them scholarships and various amenities, such as coaching and facilities; (2) that if the NCAA's compensation rules did not exist, member schools would compete to offer recruits compensation for their NILs; and (3) that the compensation rules therefore have a significant anticompetitive effect on the college education market, in that they fix an aspect of the "price" that recruits pay to attend college (or, alternatively, an aspect of the price that schools pay to secure recruits' services). These findings have substantial support in the record.

By and large, the NCAA does not challenge the district court's findings. It does not take issue with the way that the district court defined the college education market. Nor does it appear to dispute the district court's conclusion that the compensation rules restrain the NCAA's member schools from competing with each other within that market, at least to a certain degree. Instead, the NCAA makes three modest arguments about why the compensation rules do not have a significant anticompetitive effect. First, it argues that because the plaintiffs never showed that the rules reduce output in the college education market, the plaintiffs did not meet their burden of showing a significant anticompetitive effect. Second, it argues that the rules have no anticompetitive effect because schools would not pay student-athletes anything for their NIL rights in any event, given that those rights are worth nothing. And finally, the NCAA argues that even if the district court was right that schools would pay student-athletes for their NIL rights, any such payments would be small, which means that the compensation rules' anticompetitive effects cannot be considered significant.

We can dispose of the first two arguments quickly. First, the NCAA's contention that the plaintiffs' claim fails because they did not show a decrease in output in the college education market is simply incorrect. Here, the NCAA argues that output in the college education market "consists of opportunities for student-athletes to participate in FBS football or Division I men's basketball," and it quotes the district court's finding that these opportunities have "increased steadily over time." *See O'Bannon,* 7 F.Supp.3d at 981. But this argument misses the mark. Although output reductions are one common kind of anticompetitive effect in antitrust cases, a "reduction in output is not the *only* measure of anticompetitive effect." Areeda & Hovenkamp ¶ 1503b(1) (emphasis added).

The "combination[s] condemned by the [Sherman] Act" also include "price-fixing . . . by purchasers" even though "the persons specially injured . . . are sellers, not customers or consumers." *Mandeville Island Farms, Inc. v. Am. Crystal Sugar Co.,* 334 U.S. 219, 235, 68 S.Ct. 996, 92 L.Ed. 1328 (1948). At trial, the plaintiffs demonstrated that the NCAA's compensation rules have just this kind of anticompetitive effect: they fix the price of one component of the exchange between school and recruit, thereby precluding competition among schools with respect to that component. The district court found that although consumers of NCAA football and basketball may not be harmed directly by this price-fixing, the "student-athletes themselves are harmed by the price-fixing agreement among FBS football and Division I basketball schools." *O'Bannon,* 7 F.Supp.3d at 972–73. The athletes accept grants-in-aid, and no more, in exchange for their athletic performance, because the NCAA schools have agreed to value the athletes' NILs at zero, "an anticompetitive effect." *Id.* at 973. This anticompetitive effect satisfied the plaintiffs' initial burden under the Rule of Reason. *Cf. Cal. Dental Ass'n v. FTC,* 526 U.S. 756, 777, 119 S.Ct. 1604, 143 L.Ed.2d 935 (1999) ("[R]aising price, reducing output, and dividing markets have the same anticompetitive effects." (quoting *Gen. Leaseways, Inc. v. Nat'l Truck Leasing Ass'n,* 744 F.2d 588, 594–95 (7th Cir.1984))).

Second, the NCAA's argument that student-athletes' NILs are, in fact, worth nothing is simply a repackaged version of its arguments about injury in fact, which we have rejected.

Finally, we reject the NCAA's contention that any NIL compensation that student-athletes might receive in the absence of its compensation rules would be de minimis and that the rules therefore do not significantly affect competition in the college education market. This "too small to matter" argument is incompatible with the Supreme Court's holding in *Catalano, Inc. v. Target Sales, Inc.,* 446 U.S. 643, 100 S.Ct. 1925, 64 L.Ed.2d 580 (1980) (per curiam). In *Catalano,* a group of beer retailers sued a group of beer wholesalers, alleging that the wholesalers had secretly agreed to end their customary practice of extending the retailers interest-free credit for roughly a month after the delivery of beer. *Id.* at 644. The Court unanimously held that this agreement was unlawful per se. It reasoned that the agreement was clearly a means of "extinguishing one form of [price] competition among the sellers," given that credit terms were part of the price of the beer, and that the agreement was therefore tantamount to price-fixing. *Id.* at 649. The Court was not concerned with whether the agreement affected the market adversely: "It is no excuse that the prices fixed are themselves reasonable." *Id.* at 647.

The NCAA's compensation rules function in much the same way as the agreement at issue in *Catalano:* they "extinguish[ ] one form of competition" among schools seeking to land recruits. We acknowledge that *Catalano* was a per se case in which the Court did not analyze the anticompetitive effect of the wholesalers' agreement in detail, but the decision nonetheless indicates that an antitrust court should not dismiss an anticompetitive price-fixing agreement as benign simply because the agreement relates only to one component of an overall price. That proposition finds further support in *Board of Regents:* in *Board of Regents,* a Rule of Reason case, the Court held that the NCAA's television plan had "a significant potential for anticompetitive effects" without delving into the details of exactly how much the plan restricted output of televised games or how much it fixed the price of TV contracts. 468 U.S. at 104–05. While the precise value of NIL compensation is uncertain, at this point in the analysis and in light of *Catalano* and *Board of Regents,* we conclude that the plaintiffs have met their burden at the first step of the Rule of Reason by showing that the NCAA's compensation rules fix the price of one component (NIL rights) of the bundle that schools provide to recruits.

Because we agree with the district court that the compensation rules have a significant anticompetitive effect on the college education market, we proceed to consider the procompetitive justifications the NCAA proffers for those rules.

### B. *Procompetitive Effects*

As discussed above, the NCAA offered the district court four procompetitive justifications for the compensation rules: (1) promoting amateurism, (2) promoting competitive balance among NCAA schools, (3) integrating student-athletes with their schools' academic community, and (4) increasing output in the college education market. The district court accepted the first and third and rejected the other two.

Although the NCAA's briefs state in passing that the district court erred in failing to "credit all four justifications fully," the NCAA focuses its arguments to this court entirely on the first proffered justification—the promotion of amateurism. We therefore accept the district court's factual findings that the compensation rules do not promote competitive balance, that they do not increase output in the college education market, and that they play a limited role in integrating student-athletes with their schools' academic communities, since we have been offered no meaningful argument that those findings were clearly erroneous. *See, e.g., Md. Cas. Co. v. Knight,* 96 F.3d 1284, 1291 (9th Cir.1996).

The district court acknowledged that the NCAA's current rules promote amateurism, which in turn plays a role in increasing consumer demand for college sports. *O'Bannon,* 7 F.Supp.3d at 978. The NCAA does not challenge that specific determination, but it argues to us that the district court gave the amateurism justification short shrift, in two respects. First, it claims that the district court erred by focusing solely on the question of whether amateurism increases consumers' (*i.e.,* fans') demand for college sports and ignoring the fact that amateurism also increases choice for student-athletes by giving them "the only opportunity [they will] have to obtain a college education while playing competitive sports *as students.*" Second, it faults the district court for being inappropriately skeptical of the NCAA's historical commitment to amateurism. Although we might have credited the depth of the NCAA's devotion to amateurism differently, these arguments do not persuade us that the district court clearly erred.

The NCAA is correct that a restraint that broadens choices can be procompetitive. The Court in *Board of Regents* observed that the difference between college and professional sports "widen[s]" the choices "available to athletes." *Bd. of Regents,* 468 U.S. at 102. But we fail to see how the restraint at issue in this particular case—*i.e.,* the NCAA's limits on student-athlete compensation—makes college sports more attractive to recruits, or widens recruits' spectrum of choices in the sense that *Board of Regents* suggested. As the district court found, it is primarily "the opportunity to earn a higher education" that attracts athletes to college sports rather than professional sports, *O'Bannon,* 7 F.Supp.3d at 986, and that opportunity would still be available to student-athletes if they were paid some compensation in addition to their athletic scholarships. Nothing in the plaintiffs' prayer for compensation would make student-athletes something other than students and thereby impair their ability to become student-athletes.

Indeed, if anything, loosening or abandoning the compensation rules might be the best way to "widen" recruits' range of choices; athletes might well be more likely to attend college, and stay there longer, if they knew that they were earning some amount of NIL income while they were in school. *See* Jeffrey L. Harrison & Casey C. Harrison, *The Law and Economics of the NCAA's Claim to Monopsony Rights,* 54 Antitrust Bull. 923, 948 (2009). We therefore reject the NCAA's claim that, by denying student-athletes compensation apart from scholarships, the NCAA increases the "choices" available to them.

The NCAA's second point has more force—the district court probably underestimated the NCAA's commitment to amateurism. *See Bd. of Regents,* 468 U.S. at 120 (referring to the NCAA's "revered tradition of amateurism in college sports"). But the point is ultimately irrelevant. Even if the NCAA's concept of amateurism had been perfectly coherent and consistent, the NCAA would still need to show that amateurism brings about some procompetitive *effect* in order to justify it under the antitrust laws. *See id.* at 101–02 & n. 23. The NCAA cannot fully answer the district court's finding that the compensation rules have significant anticompetitive effects simply by pointing out that it has adhered to those rules for a long time. Nevertheless, the district court found, and the record supports that there is a concrete procompetitive effect in the NCAA's commitment to amateurism: namely, that the amateur nature of collegiate sports increases their appeal to consumers. We therefore conclude that the NCAA's compensation rules serve the two procompetitive purposes identified by the district court: integrating academics with athletics, and "preserving the popularity of the NCAA's product by promoting its current understanding of amateurism." *O'Bannon,* 7 F.Supp.3d at 1005.

We note that the district court's findings are largely consistent with the Supreme Court's own description of the college football market as "a particular brand of football" that draws from "an academic tradition [that] differentiates [it] from and makes it more popular than professional sports to which it might otherwise be comparable, such as, for example, minor league baseball." *Bd. of Regents,* 468 U.S. at 101–02. "Thus, the NCAA plays a vital role in enabling college football to preserve its character, and as a result enables a product to be marketed which might otherwise be unavailable." *Id.* at 102. But, as *Board of Regents* demonstrates, not every rule adopted by the NCAA that restricts the market is necessary to preserving the "character" of college sports. We thus turn to the final inquiry—whether there are reasonable alternatives to the NCAA's current compensation restrictions.

### C. *Substantially Less Restrictive Alternatives*

The third step in the Rule of Reason analysis is whether there are substantially less restrictive alternatives to the NCAA's current rules. We bear in mind that—to be viable under the Rule of Reason—an alternative must be "virtually as effective" in serving the procompetitive purposes of the NCAA's current rules, and "without significantly increased cost." *Cnty. of Tuolumne v. Sonora Cmty. Hosp.,* 236 F.3d 1148, 1159 (9th Cir.2001) (internal quotation marks omitted). We think that plaintiffs must make a strong evidentiary showing that its alternatives are viable here. Not only do plaintiffs bear the burden at this step, but the Supreme Court has admonished that we must generally afford the NCAA "ample latitude" to superintend college athletics. *Bd. of Regents,* 468 U.S. at 120; *see also Law v. Nat'l Collegiate Athletic Ass'n,* 134 F.3d 1010, 1022 (10th Cir.1998) ("[C]ourts should afford the NCAA plenty of room under the antitrust laws to preserve the amateur character of intercollegiate athletics."); *Race Tires Am., Inc. v. Hoosier Racing Tire Corp.,* 614 F.3d 57, 83 (3d Cir.2010) (noting that, generally, "sports-related organizations should have the right to determine for themselves the set of rules that they believe best advance their respective sport").

The district court identified two substantially less restrictive alternatives: (1) allowing NCAA member schools to give student-athletes grants-in-aid that cover the full cost of attendance; and (2) allowing member schools to pay student-athletes small amounts of deferred cash compensation for use of their NILs. *O'Bannon,* 7 F.Supp.3d at 1005–07. We hold that the district court did not clearly err in finding that raising the grant-in-aid cap would be a substantially less restrictive alternative, but that it clearly erred when it found that allowing students to be paid compensation for their NILs is virtually as effective as the NCAA's current amateur-status rule.

**1. Capping the permissible amount of scholarships at the cost of attendance**

The district court did not clearly err in finding that allowing NCAA member schools to award grants-in-aid up to their full cost of attendance would be a substantially less restrictive alternative to the current compensation rules. All of the evidence before the district court indicated that raising the grant-in-aid cap to the cost of attendance would have virtually no impact on amateurism: Dr. Mark Emmert, the president of the NCAA, testified at trial that giving student-athletes scholarships up to their full costs of attendance would not violate the NCAA's principles of amateurism because all the money given to students would be going to cover their "legitimate costs" to attend school. Other NCAA witnesses agreed with that assessment. *Id.* at 983. Nothing in the record, moreover, suggested that consumers of college sports would become less interested in those sports if athletes' scholarships covered their full cost of attendance, or that an increase in the grant-in-aid cap would impede the integration of student-athletes into their academic communities. *Id.*

The NCAA, along with fifteen scholars of antitrust law appearing as *amici curiae,* warns us that if we affirm even this more modest of the two less restrictive alternative restraints identified by the district court, we will open the floodgates to new lawsuits demanding all manner of incremental changes in the NCAA's and other organizations' rules. The NCAA and these *amici* admonish us that as long as a restraint (such as a price cap) is "reasonably necessary to a valid business purpose," it should be upheld; it is not an antitrust court's function to tweak every market restraint that the court believes could be improved.

We agree with the NCAA and the *amici* that, as a general matter, courts should not use antitrust law to make marginal adjustments to broadly reasonable market restraints. *See, e.g., Bruce Drug, Inc. v. Hollister, Inc.,* 688 F.2d 853, 860 (1st Cir.1982) (noting that defendants are "not required to adopt the least restrictive" alternative); *Am. Motor Inns, Inc. v. Holiday Inns, Inc.,* 521 F.2d 1230, 1249 (3d Cir.1975) (denying that "the availability of an alternative means of achieving the asserted business purpose renders the existing arrangement unlawful if that alternative would be less restrictive of competition no matter to how small a degree"). The particular restraint at issue here, however—the grant-in-aid cap that the NCAA set below the cost of attendance—is not such a restraint. To the contrary, the evidence at trial showed that the grant-in-aid cap has no relation whatsoever to the procompetitive purposes of the NCAA: by the NCAA's own standards, student-athletes remain amateurs as long as any money paid to them goes to cover legitimate educational expenses.

Thus, in holding that setting the grant-in-aid cap at student-athletes' full cost of attendance is a substantially less restrictive alternative under the Rule of Reason, we are not declaring that courts are free to micromanage organizational rules or to strike down largely beneficial market restraints with impunity. Rather, our affirmance of this aspect of the district court's decision should be taken to establish only that where, as here, a restraint is *patently and inexplicably* stricter than is necessary to accomplish all of its procompetitive objectives, an antitrust court can and should invalidate it and order it replaced with a less restrictive alternative.

A compensation cap set at student-athletes' full cost of attendance is a substantially less restrictive alternative means of accomplishing the NCAA's legitimate procompetitive purposes. And there is no evidence that this cap will significantly increase costs; indeed, the NCAA already permits schools to fund student-athletes' full cost of attendance. The district court's determination that the existing compensation rules violate Section 1 of the Sherman Act was correct and its injunction requiring the NCAA to permit schools to provide compensation up to the full cost of attendance was proper.

**2. Allowing students to receive cash compensation for their NILs**

In our judgment, however, the district court clearly erred in finding it a viable alterative to allow students to receive NIL cash payments untethered to their education expenses. Again, the district court identified two procompetitive purposes served by the NCAA's current rules: "preserving the popularity of the NCAA's product by promoting its current understanding of amateurism" and "integrating academics and athletics." *O'Bannon,* 7 F.Supp.3d at 1005; *see also Board of Regents,* 468 U.S. 117 ("It is reasonable to assume that most of the regulatory controls of the NCAA are justifiable means of fostering competition among amateur athletic teams and therefore procompetitive because they enhance public interest in intercollegiate athletics."). The question is whether the alternative of allowing students to be paid NIL compensation unrelated to their education expenses, is "virtually as effective" in preserving amateurism as *not* allowing compensation. *Cnty. of Tuolumne,* 236 F.3d at 1159 (internal quotation marks omitted).

We cannot agree that a rule permitting schools to pay students pure cash compensation and a rule forbidding them from paying NIL compensation are both *equally* effective in promoting amateurism and preserving consumer demand. Both we and the district court agree that the NCAA's amateurism rule has procompetitive benefits. But in finding that paying students cash compensation would promote amateurism as effectively as not paying them, the district court ignored that not paying student-athletes is *precisely what makes them amateurs.*

Having found that amateurism is integral to the NCAA's market, the district court cannot plausibly conclude that being a poorly-paid professional collegiate athlete is "virtually as effective" for that market as being as amateur. Or, to borrow the Supreme Court's analogy, the market for college football is distinct from other sports markets and must be "differentiate[d]" from professional sports lest it become "minor league [football]." *Bd. of Regents,* 468 U.S. at 102.

Aside from the self-evident fact that paying students for their NIL rights will vitiate their amateur status as collegiate athletes, the court relied on threadbare evidence in finding that small payments of cash compensation will preserve amateurism as well the NCAA's rule forbidding such payments. Most of the evidence elicited merely indicates that paying students large compensation payments would harm consumer demand more than smaller payments would—not that small cash payments will preserve amateurism. Thus, the evidence was addressed to the wrong question. Instead of asking whether making small payments to student-athletes served the same procompetitive purposes as making no payments, the evidence before the district court went to a different question: Would the collegiate sports market be better off if the NCAA made small payments or big payments? For example, the district court noted that a witness called by the NCAA, Bernard Muir, the athletic director at Stanford University, testified that paying student-athletes modest sums raises less concern than paying them large sums. The district court also relied on Dr. Dennis's opinion survey, which the court read to indicate that in the absence of the NCAA's compensation rules, "the popularity of college sports would likely depend on the size of payments awarded to student-athletes." *O'Bannon,* 7 F.Supp.3d at 983. Dr. Dennis had found that payments of $200,000 per year to each athlete would alienate the public more than would payments of $20,000 per year. *Id.* at 975–76, 983. At best, these pieces of evidence indicate that small payments to players will impact consumer demand less than larger payments. But there is a stark difference between finding that small payments are less harmful to the market than large payments—and finding that paying students small sums is virtually as effective in promoting amateurism as not paying them.

The other evidence cited by the district court is even less probative of whether paying these student-athletes will preserve amateurism and consumer demand. The district court adverted to testimony from a sports management expert, Daniel Rascher, who explained that although opinion surveys had shown the public was opposed to rising baseball salaries during the 1970s, and to the decision of the International Olympic Committee to allow professional athletes to compete in the Olympics, the public had continued to watch baseball and the Olympics at the same rate after those changes. *Id.* at 976–77. But professional baseball and the Olympics are not fit analogues to college sports. The Olympics have not been nearly as transformed by the introduction of professionalism as college sports would be.

Finally, the district court, and the dissent, place particular weight on a brief interchange during plaintiffs' cross-examination of one of the NCAA's witnesses, Neal Pilson, a television sports consultant formerly employed at CBS. Pilson testified that "if you're paid for your performance, you're not an amateur," and explained at length why paying students would harm the student-athlete market. Plaintiffs then asked Pilson whether his opinions about amateurism "depend on the level of the money" paid to players, and he acknowledged that his opinion was "impacted by the level." When asked whether there was a line that "should not be crossed" in paying players, Pilson responded "that's a difficult question. I haven't thought about the line. And I haven't been asked to render an opinion on that." When pressed to come up with a figure, Pilson repeated that he was "not sure." He eventually commented that "I tell you that a million dollars would trouble me and $5,000 wouldn't, but that's a pretty good range." When asked whether deferred compensation to students would concern him, Pilson said that while he would not be as concerned by deferred payments, he would still be "troubled by it."

So far as we can determine, Pilson's offhand comment under cross-examination is the sole support for the district court's $5,000 figure. But even taking Pilson's comments at face value, as the dissent urges, his testimony cannot support the finding that paying student-athletes small sums will be virtually as effective in preserving amateurism as not paying them. Pilson made clear that he was not prepared to opine on whether pure cash compensation, of any amount, would affect amateurism. Indeed, he was never asked about the impact of giving student-athletes small cash payments; instead, like other witnesses, he was asked only whether big payments would be worse than small payments. Pilson's casual comment—"[I] haven't been asked to render an opinion on that. It's not in my report"—that he would not be troubled by $5,000 payments is simply not enough to support the district court's far-reaching conclusion that paying students $5,000 per year will be as effective in preserving amateurism as the NCAA's current policy.

The difference between offering student-athletes education-related compensation and offering them cash sums untethered to educational expenses is not minor; it is a quantum leap. Once that line is crossed, we see no basis for returning to a rule of amateurism and no defined stopping point; we have little doubt that plaintiffs will continue to challenge the arbitrary limit imposed by the district court until they have captured the full value of their NIL. At that point the NCAA will have surrendered its amateurism principles entirely and transitioned from its "particular brand of football" to minor league status. *Bd. of Regents,* 468 U.S. at 101–02. In light of that, the meager evidence in the record, and the Supreme Court's admonition that we must afford the NCAA "ample latitude" to superintend college athletics, *Bd. of Regents,* 468 U.S. at 120, we think it is clear the district court erred in concluding that small payments in deferred compensation are a substantially less restrictive alternative restraint. We thus vacate that portion of the district court's decision and the portion of its injunction requiring the NCAA to allow its member schools to pay this deferred compensation.

## V

By way of summation, we wish to emphasize the limited scope of the decision we have reached and the remedy we have approved. Today, we reaffirm that NCAA regulations are subject to antitrust scrutiny and must be tested in the crucible of the Rule of Reason. When those regulations truly serve procompetitive purposes, courts should not hesitate to uphold them. But the NCAA is not above the antitrust laws, and courts cannot and must not shy away from requiring the NCAA to play by the Sherman Act's rules. In this case, the NCAA's rules have been more restrictive than necessary to maintain its tradition of amateurism in support of the college sports market. The Rule of Reason requires that the NCAA permit its schools to provide up to the cost of attendance to their student athletes. It does not require more.

We vacate the district court's judgment and permanent injunction insofar as they require the NCAA to allow its member schools to pay student-athletes up to $5,000 per year in deferred compensation. We otherwise affirm. The parties shall bear their own costs on appeal.

**AFFIRMED IN PART** and **VACATED IN PART**.

THOMAS, CHIEF JUDGE, concurring in part and dissenting in part:

I largely agree with all but one of the majority's conclusions. I respectfully disagree with the majority's conclusion that the district court clearly erred in ordering the NCAA to permit up to $5,000 in deferred compensation above student-athletes' full cost of attendance.

* * *

There was sufficient evidence in the record to support the award. The district court's conclusion that the proposed alternative restraint satisfied the Rule of Reason was based on testimony from at least four experts-including three experts presented by the NCAA-that providing student-athletes with small amounts of compensation above their cost of attendance most likely would not have a significant impact on consumer interest in college sports. *O'Bannon,* 7 F.Supp.3d at 976–77, 983–84, 1000–01. It was also based on the fact that FBS football players are currently permitted to accept Pell grants in excess of their cost of attendance, and the fact that Division I tennis recruits are permitted to earn up to $10,000 per year in prize money from athletic events before they enroll in college. *Id.* at 974, 1000. The majority characterizes the weight of this evidence as "threadbare." Op. at 58. I respectfully disagree.

The NCAA's own expert witness, Neal Pilson, testified that the level of deferred compensation would have an effect on consumer demand for college athletics, but that paying student-athletes $5,000 per year in trust most likely would not have a significant impact on such demand. He also testified that any negative impact that paying student-athletes might have on consumer demand could be partially mitigated by placing the compensation in a trust fund to be paid out after graduation.

The majority dismisses this testimony because it was made in a very "offhand" manner, and because Pilson proffered the $5,000 amount on cross-examination "[w]hen pressed." Op. at 60. However, the NCAA presented this witness as an expert on the issue of whether paying college athletes will negatively impact consumer demand for college sports. Pilson testified at length on the topic, and his qualifications were not challenged. It is not appropriate for us on appeal to assess demeanor we did not see. As a result, I would take the testimony at face value, and the district court did not clearly err in crediting it.

The majority also dismisses the testimony given by expert witness Dr. Daniel Rascher demonstrating that consumer interest in major league baseball and the Olympics increased after baseball players' salaries rose and professional athletes were allowed to compete in the Olympics. The majority reasons that major league baseball and the Olympics are "not fit analogues to college sports," speculating that college sports would be more significantly transformed by professionalism than have the Olympics. Op. at 59. However, the majority does not offer any evidentiary support for the distinction, nor explain how or why the district court clearly erred in crediting this testimony.

Moreover, Rascher also testified that consumer demand in sports such as tennis and rugby increased after the sports' governing boards permitted athletes to receive payment. *O'Bannon,* 7 F.Supp.3d at 977. In my view, the majority errs in dismissing this testimony. The import of Rascher's testimony was that consumer demand typically does not decrease when athletes are permitted to receive payment, and that this general principle holds true across a wide variety of sports and competitive formats. The district court did not clearly err in crediting it.

The district court accepted the testimony of multiple experts that small amounts of compensation would not affect consumer demand, and then used the lowest amount suggested by one of the NCAA's experts. The district court was within its right to do so.

### II

The disagreement between my view and the majority view largely boils down to a difference in opinion as to the procompetitive interests at stake. The majority characterizes our task at step three of the Rule of Reason as determining "whether the alternative of allowing students to be paid NIL compensation unrelated to their education expenses is 'virtually as effective' in preserving *amateurism* as not allowing compensation." Op. at 56 (emphasis added). This conclusion misstates our inquiry. Rather, we must determine whether allowing student-athletes to be compensated for their NILs is 'virtually as effective' in preserving *popular demand for college sports* as not allowing compensation. In terms of antitrust analysis, the concept of amateurism is relevant only insofar as it relates to consumer interest.

The district court found that there are two, limited procompetitive benefits to the current rule. It found that limits on large amounts of student-athlete compensation preserve the popularity of the NCAA's product, and that limits on large amounts of student-athlete compensation promote the integration of academics and athletics. *O'Bannon,* 7 F.Supp.3d at 1004–05. In reaching these conclusions, the district court explained:

> [S]ome restrictions on compensation may still serve a limited procompetitive purpose if they are necessary to maintain the popularity of FBS football and Division I basketball. If the challenged restraints actually play a substantial role in maximizing consumer demand for the NCAA's product—specifically, FBS football and Division I basketball telecasts, re-broadcasts, ticket sales, and merchandise—then the restrictions would be procompetitive. *Id.* at 1000 (emphasis added).

The district court recounted the testimony of NCAA expert witness Dr. J. Michael Dennis, who conducted a survey of consumer attitudes concerning college sports in 2013. The court found that "[w]hat Dr. Dennis's survey does suggest is that the public's attitudes toward student-athlete compensation depend heavily on the level of compensation that student-athletes would receive." *Id.*at 1000–01. It noted that this conclusion "is consistent with the testimony of the NCAA's own witnesses, including [Stanford athletic director Bernard] Muir and Mr. Pilson, who both indicated that smaller payments to student-athletes would bother them less than larger payments." *Id.* at 1001.

The district court determined that "the evidence presented at trial suggests that consumer demand for FBS football and Division I basketball-related products is not driven by the restrictions on student-athlete compensation but instead by other factors, such as school loyalty and geography." *Id.* The court therefore concluded that:

> the NCAA's restrictions on student-athlete compensation play a limited role in driving consumer demand for FBS football and Division I basketball-related products. Although they might justify a restriction on large payments to student-athletes while in school, they do not justify the rigid prohibition on compensating student-athletes, in the present or in the future, with any share of licensing revenue generated from the use of their names, images, and likenesses.
>
> *Id.*

The district court's findings of fact provide that one procompetitive benefit of the current rule is that restricting large payments to student-athletes plays a limited role in preserving the popularity of the NCAA's products. In the context of this antitrust suit, the concept of "amateurism" is useful only to the extent that it furthers this goal. In terms of antitrust analysis, amateurism is relevant only insofar as popular demand for college sports is increased by *consumer* perceptions of and desire for amateurism. Viewed through the antitrust lens, it is consumer desire that we must credit; not the NCAA's preferred articulation of the term.

Plaintiffs are not required, as the majority suggests, to show that the proposed alternatives are "virtually as effective" at preserving the concept of amateurism as the NCAA chooses to define it. Indeed, this would be a difficult task, given that "amateurism" has proven a nebulous concept prone to ever-changing definition. *See O'Bannon,* 7 F.Supp.3d at 973–75 (describing the ways that the NCAA's definition of amateurism has changed over time). Even today, the NCAA's conception of amateurism does not fall easily into a bright line rule between paying student-athletes and not paying them. Tennis players are permitted to receive payment of up to $10,000 per year for playing their sport. A tennis player who begins competing at a young age could presumably earn upwards of $50,000 for playing his sport and still be considered an amateur athlete by the NCAA.

The NCAA insists that consumers will flee if student-athletes are paid even a small sum of money for colleges' use of their NILs. This assertion is contradicted by the district court record and by the NCAA's own rules regarding amateurism. The district court was well within its right to reject it. Division I schools have spent $5 billion on athletic facilities over the past 15 years. The NCAA sold the television rights to broadcast the NCAA men's basketball championship tournament for 12 years to CBS for $10.8 billion dollars. The NCAA insists that this multi-billion dollar industry would be lost if the teenagers and young adults who play for these college teams earn one dollar above their cost of school attendance. That is a difficult argument to swallow. Given the trial evidence, the district court was well within its rights to reject it.

### III

The national debate about amateurism in college sports is important. But our task as appellate judges is not to resolve it. Nor could we. Our task is simply to review the district court judgment through the appropriate lens of antitrust law and under the appropriate standard of review. In the end, my disagreement with the majority is founded on the appropriate standard of review. After an extensive bench trial, the district court made a factual finding that payment of $5,000 in deferred compensation would not significantly reduce consumer demand for college sports. This finding was supported by extensive testimony from at least four expert witnesses. There was no evidence to the contrary. Therefore, on this record, I cannot agree with the majority that the district court clearly erred when it determined that paying student-athletes up to $5,000 per year would be "virtually as effective" at preserving the pro-competitive benefits of the current rule. Therefore, I would affirm the district court in all respects.

For these reasons, I concur in part and dissent in part.

### *QUESTIONS FOR DISCUSSION*

1. Do you agree with how the Court split the difference here? Is the outcome fair? Why or why not?

2. Do you agree that amateurism can serve, at least partially, as a pro-competitive justification?

3. Finally, which do you think is more lucrative—receiving a salary for playing or being able to profit from endorsements? Does this apply to all athletes equally? Who are the real winners and losers, then, in this case?

---

Take one last moment to look back at the variety of cases and problems depicted in this Part of the book. Running through all of the disputes is the theme of the legitimacy of legal constraints on entertaining speech. In this chapter, we saw Vanna White collect $400,000 from Samsung for the latter having mimicked White's *Wheel of Fortune* routine in a television commercial. In Chapter 2, we saw Victoria Sweet denied the chance to sue NBC for a prime-time docudrama that allegedly falsified her role as the rape victim-accuser of the Scottsboro Boys four decades earlier. And in Chapter 1, so far we have seen the apparent real-life victims of *Natural Born Killers* being barred from any recovery for their physical injuries or deaths.

Clearly there are differences in both the brands of entertainment expression and the kinds of personal harms involved in these and other cases in this Part. How would you appraise the legal balance struck by the courts among these competing human, social, and economic values? Reflection on these examples and problems is important not only in its own right, but also as a prelude to essentially the same fundamental challenges portrayed in the next Part, on **Intellectual Property in Entertainment Assets.**[k]

[k] An illuminating analysis and critique of what the courts have been doing with these cases and issues under both the "publicity" and the "intellectual property" legal rubrics is David Lange, *Recognizing the Public Domain*, 44 L. & Contemp. Prob. 147 (1981).

# PART 2

# INTELLECTUAL PROPERTY IN ENTERTAINMENT ASSETS

■ ■ ■

# CHAPTER 4

# ELEMENTS OF COPYRIGHT PROTECTION[a]

■ ■ ■

The constitutional and statutory creation of intellectual property law plays an indispensable role in the world of entertainment performers, producers, and fans. Copyright law, in particular, serves as the bridge that connects artistic creation, technological distribution, and economic returns between producers and consumers of entertainment works. Though a detailed treatment of copyright law is beyond the scope of this book, the next two chapters examine the basic concepts of copyright law and their intersection with the development and operation of the entertainment industry.

The flip side of intellectual property is intellectual "piracy"—one person copies (for personal use or sale) a book, song, or movie whose copyright is owned by someone else. A tension in relations between the United States and China involves Chinese music and video factories that turn out large numbers of bootleg copies of American-made records and movies for sale in the huge Asian market. Such covert action has long been a feature of the *domestic* music, movie, and publishing industries as well. Indeed, it was not until the 1970s that copying of music recordings was made a violation of federal law, and just a quarter century later we witnessed the dramatic challenge that Napster and its Internet successors posed in the definition and enforcement of that law.

Copyright can cut two ways in the entertainment field. For example, Random House, publisher of a popular novel, Dan Brown's *The Da Vinci Code* (which had also just been made into a movie starring Tom Hanks) was itself sued for copyright infringement. The plaintiffs were two British historians whose 1983 book, *Holy Blood, Holy Grail*, Random House also published and which Brown had definitely read. They claimed Brown borrowed their theory that Jesus Christ had married Mary Magdalene and fathered several children by her—which Brown's fictional Harvard professor protagonist investigated after a murder in front of the *Mona Lisa* in the Louvre. The essence of the lawsuit was that Brown had "appropriated the architecture" of their book, while the defense was that the copying was merely "incidental." The British court ruled that the

[a] An engaging introduction to this subject is Paul Goldstein, Copyright's Highway: The Law & Lore of Copyright from Gutenberg to the Celestial Jukebox (Hill & Wang 1994), by the author of a major scholarly treatise in this area.

alleged relationship between Jesus and Mary Magdalene was not copyrightable. Ironically, during the trial, world-wide sales of *Holy Blood, Holy Grail* soared by over 800 percent.

When one reflects on the alleged entertainment piracy, though, it reveals the distinctive features of intellectual products themselves. The "theft" that the original authors complain about is not theft of the physical goods in question. The new books, videos and albums being sold are turned out with the second manufacturer's own labor and materials. What is being taken from the copyright owner is the *content* of the movie or music contained in the original video or album, an item that the copier bought from the owner. Viewed by itself, such use of one's own video or album copy would not seem to infringe on anyone else's enjoyment of the work in question. Entertainment and other intellectual works are a form of public good. In contrast to the drinking of a bottle of wine, one person's listening to a song does not intrude upon anyone else's ability to hear that same song. It is only copyright law that turns the content of the song (or film or book) into a private good whose authors can grant or withhold consent to others to use and distribute it. As we shall see in the next chapter, in the early 1980s, the movie industry came close to getting the Supreme Court to rule that taping a television program on their home sets for later viewing was a form of entertainment piracy. Now, in the early 21st Century, the music industry has been legally, though not yet technologically or practically, successful in its effort to block people from downloading music from the Internet.

In recent years, the rise of fan fiction has made these rules even more challenging to apply. Fan fiction is the creation of independent, new material using characters from other works. Perhaps the most famous works of "fan fiction" are E.L. James "Fifty Shades of Grey" series, which sold 125 million copies worldwide. Based on the "Twilight" series, E.L. James changed the names of the characters to avoid litigation, partially as a result of the sexually provocative nature of its content.

Absent special exceptions for "fair use," copyright law not only places significant constraints on private action, but even more so on public speech. The preceding chapters of this book illustrate the far-reaching First Amendment rights media outlets enjoy against government constraints on the content of their programs (though not of their commercials). In *Harper & Row Publishers v. Nation Enterprises*, 471 U.S. 539 (1985), however, the Supreme Court held that the news magazine, *The Nation*, violated copyright law when it published its account of why Gerald Ford had pardoned Richard Nixon, simply because the *Nation*'s "scoop" story quoted, without authorization, 300 words from ex-President Ford's unpublished memoirs. Whereas the Court held, in *New York Times v. Sullivan*, 376 U.S. 254 (1964), that the First Amendment overrode libel law's ability to provide relief to the victim of an inaccurate and defamatory newspaper item, in *Harper & Row* the Court ruled that an author and publisher's private property rights in their expression trumped the First Amendment rights of a reporter to quote that expression accurately.

Why do the legal systems in the United States and every other major country (now including China) confer such private property rights in intellectual works? The reason is that this legal instrument is viewed as doing far more to encourage than to discourage entertainment and other forms of creative expression. Only with the benefit of such property rights can the original authors and producers recoup their investment in works (like President Ford's memoirs) that readers, viewers, and listeners will pay to enjoy.

The stakes in development and enforcement of copyright are far greater than they are for publicity rights. It is true that the ability of a Vanna White or a Johnny Carson to control use of their personal identities in commercials or merchandise does give these celebrities a valuable asset. Nonetheless, the ability of the producers of *Wheel of Fortune* or *The Tonight Show* to control and sell these programs at a price reflecting what advertisers will pay to reach their viewing audience is crucial to the original investment needed to develop the entertainment shows that have made Vanna White and Johnny Carson famous in the first place. Only if movie fans must purchase the right to view the movie from the producers (or their licensees) of its *content*, rather than just the producers of the *print*, will the investment to create the movie be made in the first place.

Copyright law became an indispensable intermediary between the producer and consumer of intellectual works when technology appeared on the scene. Before Johann Gutenberg invented his printing press in the fifteenth century, it was almost as difficult and expensive to copy a book by hand as it was to author the work in the first place. The printing process suddenly made written works accessible to a far larger audience, but the ability of anyone with a press to produce and sell copies of the original manuscript threatened to erase the economic gains expected by the author and publisher of the original work.

The initial response of European governments was to confer a public monopoly on the printing process itself, a step that gave the government real power to block distribution of works it disapproved. However, in 1710, the British Parliament enacted the Statute of Anne, which instead conferred a private monopoly on the author of each individual work; once published, the new work would compete with other works for their respective audiences. When the American colonies won their independence, one power that the framers of the U.S. Constitution conferred upon the federal government (in Article 1, Section 8, Clause 8) was

> the power . . . To promote the progress of Science and useful Arts by securing for limited Times to Authors and Inventors the exclusive Right to their respective Writings and Discoveries.

Using that constitutional prerogative, Congress quickly enacted the Copyright Act of 1790, which gave the authors of "books, maps, or charts" copyright protection for 14 years (with a limited option to renew for another 14 years).

Over the next two centuries, the legal force of copyright has dramatically expanded in several directions. One such direction has involved the *scope* of intellectual products (basically tracking the evolving technology): prints were added in 1802; musical compositions in 1831; dramatic compositions in 1856; photographs in 1865; paintings, drawings, and sculptures in 1870; motion pictures in 1912; musical recordings in 1971; television and cable broadcasts in 1976; and architectural works in 1990. A second trend has lengthened the *duration* of copyright protection: in 1831, the term was extended to 28 years, while retaining the initial author/family renewal right of 14 years; in 1909, the renewal term was enlarged to 28 years, making the total life of copyright 56 years (and eventually to 75 years). In 1976, the term was changed to encompass the remaining life of the author plus 50 years (and where the copyright owner is a business entity rather than a real person, the term was 75 years from publication or 95 from creation, whichever came first). Finally, in 1998 Congress passed and President Clinton signed the *Sonny Bono Act*, which extended all copyright terms once more, to life plus 70 and 95/120 years respectively.

Since the 1970s, Congress has also relaxed the various formalities for securing copyright protection. Authors no longer need to publish their works, notify the public of their authorship, and register the work with the government in order to receive the exclusive property right in the use and performance of their work. As a practical matter, publication, notification and registration are still significant steps on the way to securing effective enforcement of copyright in one's works,[b] but the failure to take one or more of these steps no longer risks forfeiture of the underlying right itself. And as we shall see throughout this Part, the "bundle of rights" secured through copyright law—in particular, under Section 106 of the Copyright Act—includes production of both the initial work and derivative works (e.g., making movies out of books); distribution of the product by sale or rental (e.g., of DVDs, CDs, or downloads); public

[b] For example, after the 1988 *Berne Convention Implementation Act*, copyright owners need not attach notice of copyright to their works to enjoy legal rights in them. However, addition of such a notice eliminates the "innocent infringement" defense that the copier might otherwise assert to mitigate damages.

performance (e.g., playing songs on radio stations or in clubs); and public display (e.g., of artworks or photographs).

Authors, songwriters, and film producers labor long and hard to create a product that their fans will pay to read, listen to, or watch. Crucial to the economic value of this entertainment work is its author's exclusive prerogative to decide whether, and on what financial terms, the work can be produced, distributed, and performed. The running theme in copyright lore is that such *economic* rights are what make possible the investment of time, talent, and money that ultimately produces a work for consumers to enjoy. Serious questions remain, though, about whether current doctrine provides the correct blend of private property and public use to generate optimal incentives for consumer welfare in this vital sector of the nation's economy and life.

After two hundred years of statutory and doctrinal evolution, copyright law has become the base for a vast entertainment industry (and what sometimes seems nearly as vast a scholarly literature on the range of topics).[c] This chapter will present some of the key components of copyright protection. Section A addresses the scope of copyrightable works, particularly the elements of originality and fixation; Section B deals with infringement actions, especially the need to prove both access and substantial similarity; Section C covers unprotectable story parts, such as stock scenes and characters; and Section D examines the elusive and controversial doctrine of fair use. The next chapter delves more deeply into the issues of technological change and copyright doctrine and enforcement. Chapter 6 addresses other forms of intellectual property law—e.g., trademark, contract, and the "moral" rights of authors, which are still much less developed in America than in Europe.

---

[c] *See* Stephen Breyer, *The Uneasy Case For Copyright: A Study Of Copyright In Books, Photocopies & Computer Programs*, 84 Harv. L. Rev. 281 (1970); William W. Fisher III, *Reconstructing the Fair Use Doctrine*, 101 Harv. L. Rev. 1661 (1988); Wendy J. Gordon, *An Inquiry Into the Merits of Copyright: The Challenges of Consistency, Consent & Encouragement Theory*, 41 Stan. L. Rev. 1343 (1989); William Landes & Richard A. Posner, *An Economic Analysis of Copyright Law*, 18 J. of Legal Stud. 325 (1989); Neil Weinstock Netanel, *Copyright & a Democratic Civil Society*, 106 Yale L.J. 283 (1996); William F. Patry, *The Failure of the American Copyright System: Protecting the Idle Rich*, 72 Notre Dame L. Rev. 907 (1997); Lloyd L. Weinreb, *Copyright for Functional Expression*, 111 Harv. L. Rev. 1149 (1998); William M. Landes, *Copyright, Borrowed Images, & Appropriation Art: An Economic Approach*, 9 Geo. Mason L. Rev. 1 (2000); Arthur R. Miller, *Common Law Protection for Products of the Mind: An Idea Whose Time Has Come*, 119 Harv. L. Rev. 703 (2006). On the interplay of intellectual property and free speech, see Paul Goldstein, *Copyright & the First Amendment*, 70 Colum. L. Rev. 983 (1970); Eugene Volokh & Brett McDonnell, *Freedom of Speech & Independent Judgment Review in Copyright Cases*; Robert C. Denicola, *Copyright & Free Speech: Constitutional Limitations on the Protection Of Expression*, 67 Cal. L. Rev. 283 (1979); Rebecca Tushnet, *Copyright as a Model for Free Speech Law: What Copyright Has in Common with Anti-Pornography Laws, Campaign Finance Reform, & Telecommunications Regulation*, 42 B.C. L. Rev. 1 (2001); Jed Rubenfeld, *The Freedom of Imagination: Copyright's Constitutionality*, 112 Yale L. J. 1 (2002); David McGowan, *Some Realism About the Free-Speech Critique of Copyright*, 74 Fordham L. Rev. 101 (2005).

## A. COPYRIGHTABLE WORKS

In thinking about these issues, we should begin with a key feature of copyright doctrine that the Supreme Court announced in *Bleistein v. Donaldson Lithographing Co.*, 188 U.S. 239 (1903). In *Bleistein*, the products in question were chromolithograph sketches designed for use in advertising for a circus. The appeals court dismissed a suit to prevent copying and sale of these sketches, stating that because the sketches had "no other use than as a pure advertisement," and had no "connection with the fine arts to give [them] intrinsic value," it would not further the constitutional objective of promoting the "useful arts" through copyright to give the authors of these advertisements the exclusive use of this product.

When the case reached the Supreme Court, it drew as author Justice Oliver Wendell Holmes, who had an expansive view of the role and scope of copyright. (Holmes's mindset may have been influenced by the fact that before reaching the Court as a Justice, he had lost a copyright case as a litigant—*Holmes v. Hurst*, 174 U.S. 82 (1899), involving his father's book, *The Autocrat of the Breakfast Table*.) In his *Bleistein* opinion, Holmes first observed that it was by no means an easy artistic task to design and create the particular combination of figures, lines, and colors exhibited in these advertisements. The Justice continued:

* * *

> Certainly works are not the less connected with the fine arts because their pictorial quality attracts the crowd and therefore gives them a real use—if use means to increase trade and to help to make money. A picture is none the less a picture and none the less a subject of copyright that it is used for an advertisement. And if pictures may be used to advertise soap, or the theater, or monthly magazines, as they are, they may be used to advertise a circus. Of course, the ballet is as legitimate a subject for illustration as any other. A rule cannot be laid down that would excommunicate the paintings of Degas.

* * *

> It would be a dangerous undertaking for persons trained only to the law to constitute themselves final judges of the worth of pictorial illustrations, outside of the narrowest and most obvious limits. At the one extreme some works of genius would be sure to miss appreciation. Their very novelty would make them repulsive until the public had learned the new language in which their author spoke. It may be more than doubted, for instance, whether the etchings of Goya or the paintings of Manet would have been sure of protection when seen for the first time. At the

> other end, copyright would be denied to pictures which appealed to a public less educated than the judge. Yet if they command the interest of any public, they have a commercial value—it would be bold to say that they have not an aesthetic and educational value—and the taste of any public is not to be treated with contempt. It is an ultimate fact for the moment, whatever may be our hopes for a change. That these pictures had their worth and their success is sufficiently shown by the desire to reproduce them without regard to the plaintiffs' rights.

188 U.S. at 251–52.

The Court's reading of the Constitution and the statute thus imposes no requirement of aesthetic quality in an intellectual product to merit copyright protection, but a key substantive standard must still be satisfied. By reason of Section 102(c) of the Copyright Act, copyright protection extends only to "original works of authorship fixed in any tangible medium of expression." The requirements of "originality" and "fixation" run through numerous copyright disputes in the entertainment world.

## 1. ORIGINALITY[d]

One manifestation of this issue is the dividing line between fact and fiction. As the Supreme Court put it in another of its major copyright rulings, *Feist Publications v. Rural Telephone Service*, 499 U.S. 340 (1991), "originality" requires independent creation of new intellectual products, something that is intrinsically different from research and discovery of already-existing facts. The reason is that "copyright assures authors the right to their original expression, but encourages others to build upon the ideas and information conveyed by a work."

*Feist* and similar cases have involved the question of where to draw the line between painstakingly-gathered but unprotected facts contained in telephone and other directories, and the protected manner in which such facts are compiled and portrayed. An analogous problem is raised in the entertainment industry by the increasingly popular docudrama film. In Chapters 2 and 3, we considered whether such productions might violate the personal rights of the characters being portrayed on the screen. The next case involves a dispute about whether docudramas might infringe the property rights of an earlier treatment (typically in a book) of the same topic.

---

[d] *See* Howard B. Abrams, *Originality & Creativity in Copyright Law*, 55 Law & Contemp. Prob. 3 (Spring 1992).

## MILLER V. UNIVERSAL CITY STUDIOS, INC.

United States Court of Appeals, Fifth Circuit, 1981.
650 F.2d 1365.

RONEY, CIRCUIT JUDGE.

A sensational kidnapping, committed over a decade ago, furnishes the factual backdrop for this copyright infringement suit. The issue is whether a made-for-television movie dramatizing the crime infringes upon a copyrighted book depicting the unsuccessful ransom attempt.

* * *

In December 1968 the college-aged daughter of a wealthy Florida land developer was abducted from an Atlanta motel room and buried alive in a plywood and fiberglass capsule. A crude life-support system kept her alive for the five days she was underground before her rescue. Gene Miller, a reporter for the Miami Herald, covered the story and subsequently collaborated with the victim to write a book about the crime. Published in 1971 under the title *83 Hours 'Til Dawn*, the book was copyrighted along with a condensed version in Reader's Digest and a serialization in the Ladies Home Journal. The co-author has assigned her interest in this litigation to Miller.

In January 1972 a Universal City Studios (Universal) producer read the condensed version of the book and thought the story would make a good television movie. He gave a copy of the book to a scriptwriter, who immediately began work on a screenplay. Although negotiations for purchase of the movie rights to *83 Hours 'Til Dawn* were undertaken by Universal, no agreement with Miller was ever reached. The scriptwriter was eventually advised that use of the book in completing the script was "verboten." The movie was completed, however, and aired as an ABC Movie of the Week, *The Longest Night*.

The evidence at trial was conflicting on whether the scriptwriter relied almost entirely on the book in writing the screenplay or whether he arrived at his version of the kidnapping story independently. Both plaintiff and his expert witness testified to numerous similarities between the works. The jury, which had copies of the book and viewed the movie twice during the trial, found the movie infringed Miller's copyright and awarded him over $200,000 in damages and profits.

The most substantial question presented on appeal is whether the district court erred in instructing the jury that "research is copyrightable . . ."

Is Research Copyrightable?

* * *

It is well settled that copyright protection extends only to an author's expression of facts and not to the facts themselves. *See, e.g., Rosemont Enterprises, Inc. v. Random House, Inc.*, 366 F.2d 303, 309 (2d Cir. 1966) . . . This dichotomy between facts and their expression derives from the concept of originality which is the premise of copyright law. Under the Constitution, copyright protection may secure for a limited time to "Authors . . . the exclusive Right to their respective Writings." U.S.Const. Art. I, § 8, cl. 8. An "author" is one "to whom anything owes its origin; originator; maker; one who completes a work of science or literature." *Burrow-Giles Lithographic Co. v. Sarony*, 111 U.S. 53, 58 (1884). Obviously, a fact does not originate with the author of a book describing the fact. Neither does it originate with one who "discovers" the fact. "The discoverer merely finds and records. He may not claim that the facts are 'original' with him although there may be originality and hence authorship in the manner of reporting, i. e., the 'expression,' of the facts." 1 M. Nimmer, *Nimmer on Copyright* § 2.03(E), at 2–34 (1980). Thus, since facts do not owe their origin to any individual, they may not be copyrighted and are part of the public domain available to every person.

The district court's charge to the jury correctly stated that facts cannot be copyrighted. Nevertheless, in its order denying defendants' motion for a new trial the court said it viewed "the labor and expense of the research involved in the obtaining of those uncopyrightable facts to be intellectually distinct from those facts and more similar to the expression of the facts than to the facts themselves." *Miller v. Universal City Studios, Inc.*, 460 F. Supp. at 987. The court interpreted the copyright law to reward not only the effort and ingenuity involved in giving expression to facts, but also the efforts involved in discovering and exposing facts. In its view, an author could not be expected to expend his time and money in gathering facts if he knew those facts, and the profits to be derived therefrom, could be pirated by one who could then avoid the expense of obtaining the facts himself. Applying this reasoning to the case at bar, the court concluded "(i)n the age of television 'docudrama,' to hold other than research is copyrightable is to violate the spirit of the copyright law and to provide to those persons and corporations lacking in requisite diligence and ingenuity a license to steal."

Thus the trial court's explanation of its understanding of its charge undercuts the argument to this Court that the word "research" was intended to mean the original expression by the author of the results of the research, rather than the labor of research.

* * *

. . . [T]he labor involved in news gathering and distribution is not protected by copyright although it may be protected under a misappropriation theory of unfair competition. *International News Service v. The Associated Press*, 248 U.S. 215 (1918). In the *International News* case, the Supreme Court commented in dicta that while a newspaper story, as a literary production, can be copyrighted,

> the news element, the information respecting current events contained in the literary production, is not the creation of the writer, but is a report of matters that ordinarily are *publici juris*; it is the history of the day. It is not to be supposed that the framers of the Constitution . . . intended to confer upon one who might happen to be the first to report a historic event the exclusive right for any period to spread the knowledge of it.

*Id.* at 234.

Apart from the [distinguishable] directory cases, the only decision cited to this Court which lends support for the challenged instruction is *Toksvig v. Bruce Publishing Co.*, 181 F.2d 664 (7th Cir. 1950). In *Toksvig*, plaintiff had written a biography of Hans Christian Anderson after extensive research of primary Danish sources. Defendant, who could not read Danish, copied twenty-four specific passages from plaintiff's book in writing her own biography. The Seventh Circuit held the copying of these passages, original translations from Danish separately copyrightable under 17 U.S.C. § 6 (1970), constituted copyright infringement. The court went on to reject defendant's fair use defense, primarily because defendant's use of the translations from Danish had allowed her to write her biography in one-third the time it took plaintiff. The court said the question was not whether defendant could have obtained the same information by going to the sources plaintiff had used, but whether she in fact had done her own independent research.

Although most circuits apparently have not addressed the question, the idea that historical research is copyrightable was expressly rejected by the Second Circuit in the more soundly reasoned case of *Rosemont Enterprises, Inc. v. Random House, Inc.*, 366 F.2d 303 (2d Cir. 1966). In *Rosemont*, it was alleged that defendant's biography of Howard Hughes infringed the copyright on a series of Look articles about Hughes. The district court had asserted in sweeping language that an author is not entitled to utilize the fruits of another's labor in lieu of independent research, relying on *Toksvig*. The Second Circuit reversed. While not challenging the holding of *Toksvig* that substantial copying of specific passages amounted to copyright infringement, it rejected the language regarding independent research:

> We . . . cannot subscribe to the view that an author is absolutely precluded from saving time and effort by referring to

> and relying upon prior published material. . . . It is just such wasted effort that the proscription against the copyright of ideas and facts, and to a lesser extent the privilege of fair use, are designed to prevent.

366 F.2d at 310.

The Second Circuit has adhered to its position in the most recent appellate case to address the question, *Hoehling v. Universal City Studios, Inc.*, 618 F.2d 972 (2d Cir.). *Hoehling* involved various literary accounts of the last voyage and mysterious destruction of the German dirigible Hindenberg. Plaintiff A. A. Hoehling published a book in 1962 entitled, *Who Destroyed the Hindenberg?* Written as a factual account in an objective, reportorial style, the premise of his extensively researched book was that the Hindenberg had been deliberately sabotaged by a member of its crew to embarrass the Nazi regime. Ten years later, defendant Michael McDonald Mooney published his book, *The Hindenberg*. While a more literary than historical account, it also hypothesized sabotage. Universal City Studios purchased the movie rights to Mooney's book and produced a movie under the same title, although the movie differed somewhat from the book. During the litigation, Mooney acknowledged he had consulted Hoehling's book and relied on it for some details in writing his own, but he maintained he first discovered the sabotage theory in Dale Titler's, *Wings of Mystery*, also released in 1962.

Hoehling sued Mooney and Universal for copyright infringement. The district court granted defendants' motion for summary judgment and the Second Circuit affirmed, holding that, assuming both copying and substantial similarity, all the similarities pertained to categories of noncopyrightable material. The court noted the sabotage hypothesis espoused in Hoehling's book was based entirely on interpretation of historical fact and was not copyrightable. The same reasoning applied to Hoehling's claim that a number of specific facts, ascertained through his personal research, were copied by defendants. Relying on the *Rosemont* case, the court stated that factual information is in the public domain and "each (defendant) had the right to 'avail himself of the facts contained' in Hoehling's book and to 'use such information, whether correct or incorrect, in his own literary work.' " 618 F.2d at 979 (quoting *Greenbie v. Noble*, 151 F. Supp. 45, 67 (S.D.N.Y. 1957)).

We find the approach taken by the Second Circuit in *Hoehling* and *Rosemont* to be more consistent with the purpose and intended scope of protection under the copyright law than that implied by *Toksvig*. The line drawn between uncopyrightable facts and copyrightable expression of facts serves an important purpose in copyright law. It provides a means of balancing the public's interest in stimulating creative activity, as embodied in the Copyright Clause, against the public's need for unrestrained access to information. It allows a subsequent author to build upon and add to prior accomplishments without unnecessary duplication of effort. As expressed by the Second Circuit in *Hoehling*:

> The copyright provides a financial incentive to those who would add to the corpus of existing knowledge by creating original works. Nevertheless, the protection afforded the copyright holder has never extended to history, be it documented fact or explanatory hypothesis. The rationale for this doctrine is that the cause of knowledge is best served when history is the common property of all, and each generation remains free to draw upon the discoveries and insights of the past. Accordingly, the scope of copyright in historical accounts is narrow indeed, embracing no more than the author's original expression of particular facts and theories already in the public domain.

618 F.2d at 974.

The valuable distinction in copyright law between facts and the expression of facts cannot be maintained if research is held to be copyrightable. There is no rational basis for distinguishing between facts and the research involved in obtaining facts. To hold that research is copyrightable is no more or no less than to hold that the facts discovered as a result of research are entitled to copyright protection. Plaintiff argues that extending copyright protection to research would not upset the balance because it would not give the researcher/author a monopoly over the facts but would only ensure that later writers obtain the facts independently or follow the guidelines of fair use if the facts are no longer discoverable. But this is precisely the scope of protection given any copyrighted matter, and the law is clear that facts are not entitled to such protection. We conclude that the district court erred in instructing the jury that research is copyrightable.

* * *

Reversed and Remanded.

---

Consider the *Amistad* movie and lawsuit in light of this decision. One of the historic, though long-forgotten, civil rights events in America took place back in 1839–41. A group of black Africans were captured on their home continent to be auctioned off for slavery in the Spanish colonies in the Caribbean. While being transported on the ship L'Amistad, the slaves revolted under the leadership of Joseph Cinque, seized the ship, and sought to return to Africa. Sadly, though, they ended up grounded on Long Island, where they were imprisoned while "salvage property" claims were lodged against them by their purported "owners." The resulting lawsuit, with Roger Baldwin as trial lawyer for the Africans, had former President John Quincy Adams returning to Washington in 1841 to argue and win a precedent-setting Supreme Court decision, *U.S. v. The Amistad*, 40 U.S. 518 (1841). The Court ruled that the illegality of slavery in the northern states overrode individual property claims or trade treaties with other countries.

More than 150 years later, this case produced the movie *Amistad*, directed by Stephen Spielberg, and starring Djimon Hounsou as Cinque, Anthony Hopkins as Adams, Matthew McConaughey as Baldwin, and Morgan Freeman as Theodore Joadson, a fictional stand-in for the historical James Covey. *Amistad* produced a lawsuit pitting two of Hollywood's top litigators against each other—Bert Fields for Spielberg and Pierce O'Donnell for author Barbara Chase-Riboud.

A number of historic accounts have been written about the *Amistad* episode, beginning with *Black Mutiny* in 1953. In the late 1980s, Chase-Riboud, a notable black author, wrote the first-ever fictional treatment of this event—*Echo of Lions*. Indeed, a year before publication of *Echo of Lions*, Chase-Riboud's editor had sent the manuscript to Spielberg's then-production company, Amblin Entertainment. Chase-Riboud had a meeting with Amblin executives, who praised the novel but believed it "was not readily adaptable to a feature film," and instead was better-suited for a television mini-series like *Roots*. Chase-Riboud book sold 500,000 copies and was "pitched" by Hollywood writer David Franzoni to studios like Warner Brothers.

Several years later, though, after Spielberg had combined with Jeffrey Katzenberg and David Geffen to create Dreamworks, he accepted a proposal from the producer Deborah Allen to make an *Amistad* movie, supposedly based on the *Black Mutiny* history. After Spielberg announced his project, Chase-Riboud asked to have her book credited as a source of the movie, and offered to consult in its production. When Spielberg refused (but did give Franzoni credit as the screenwriter), Chase-Riboud filed suit as the movie was about to appear in 1997.

The essence of Chase-Riboud's claim was that a number of key features of the movie plot had been created in her novel, rather than actually having taken place back in 1839–41. These features related, in particular, to the nature of the Cinque character and his conversations with and influences upon Adams, the creation of the Joadson character (called Henry Braithwaite in the novel), the depiction of Baldwin's trial strategy to make this a case about *civil*, rather than *property*, rights, and the destruction of the slave colony in Africa at the same time the Court was rendering its verdict in *The Amistad*. The response of Spielberg was that (i) there was some historical basis for at least some of these facts; (ii) if not, these were non-copyrightable features of characters and/or scenes a faire; and (iii) in any event, there were significant differences in the manner in which *Amistad* depicted these features by comparison with *Echo of Lions*.

This lawsuit produced one ruling in which the court refused Chase-Riboud's request to block release of the movie. *Chase-Riboud v. Dreamworks*, 987 F. Supp. 1222 (C.D. Cal. 1997). After a detailed analysis of the alleged fictional similarities between *Echo of Lions* and *Amistad*, Judge Collins concluded that at least at this stage, Chase-Riboud had "failed to demonstrate a probability of success on the merits." Moreover, though the author "has raised serious questions going to the merits of her copyright infringement claims," she was not entitled to a preliminary injunction for practical reasons. Dreamworks had already spent $75 million in producing and promoting the film, and Chase-Riboud would be able to collect full damages for copyright infringement if she proved at trial that this had taken place. The parties then decided to settle the case for a reportedly "significant" amount; Spielberg likely paid a lot more money than if he had accepted Chase-Riboud's original proposal. And as noted earlier, there was no doubt about the full "access" of Spielberg's team to Chase-Riboud's work because the original manuscript had been sent to them by Chase-Riboud's editor—who just happened to be Jacqueline Kennedy Onassis.

From a legal as well as historical perspective, we should also be aware of a predecessor to the *Amistad* lawsuit, one that also involved the author Chase-Riboud: *Burgess v. Chase-Riboud*, 765 F. Supp. 233 (E.D. Pa. 1991). The subject matter was a political scandal in the early 1800s, which became a Merchant-Ivory movie in 1995, *Jefferson in Paris*, and in the meantime produced several books, a play, and a lawsuit.

In 1802, during Thomas Jefferson's first term as President, an item appeared in a Richmond newspaper asserting that Jefferson had made one of his slaves, Sally Hemings, his concubine, and that she had given birth to a son named Tom, said to bear a striking resemblance to the President. Although Jefferson said that his accuser was a "lying renegade," there were few objective facts with which either to document or refute the charge. Hemings was a slave in Jefferson's household; after Jefferson's wife died, he went to Paris as the U.S. Ambassador, where he was joined shortly thereafter by his two daughters, as well as the 15-year-old Hemings; in 1789, Jefferson returned to the United States to be President Washington's Secretary of State; and while living and working at Jefferson's Monticello estate for the next four decades, Hemings gave birth to several light-skinned children. There is no historical record of any comment by Hemings about whether Jefferson had fathered any of these children.

In 1974, Fawn Brodie published a best-selling book, *Thomas Jefferson: An Intimate History*. This work involved a brand of psychological biography in which Brodie conducted a Freudian-type analysis of Jefferson's actions and writings to develop a picture of what he had done and felt in his life. Though Jefferson had never once mentioned Hemings in his writings, Brodie surmised from her psychoanalytical diagnosis that the story of the Jefferson-Hemings affair was true, and she sketched a series of incidents in their relationship, which she set in Paris and then Monticello.

A quarter century later, scientists produced a possibly physiological basis for Brodie's psychological assertions on behalf of Hemings' heirs. In the meantime, though, her book served as the cornerstone for a 1979 novel by Barbara Chase-Riboud, *Sally Hemings*, and then a 1982 play by Granville Burgess, *Dusty Sally*. The bulk of the documented facts in Jefferson's and Heming's lives, together with those added by Brodie's psychological implications, were incorporated in both of these fictional works. To flesh out their stories, though, both Chase-Riboud and Burgess had to create numerous additional incidents and accompanying dialogue. A number of these incidents imagined by Chase-Riboud in her novel also appeared in Burgess's later play. Chase-Riboud claimed in court that Burgess had illegally copied her work.

The key question in that suit, and one we shall see throughout this chapter, was whether the Burgess play was "substantially similar" in its "creative expression" to the Chase-Riboud novel, or had simply used scenes-à-faire that were natural in a story such as this (e.g., the reaction of Sally Hemings to the storming of the Bastille during the French Revolution). To what extent should that judgment be influenced by the fact that both books used Brodie's analysis? Indeed, could Brodie (by then, her estate) have sued both Chase-Riboud and Burgess for borrowing her psychological speculations about what had taken place between Jefferson and Hemings? For two earlier and important analyses by Judge Learned Hand of the issues posed by the *Burgess* case, see *Sheldon v. Metro-Goldwyn Pictures Corp.*, 81 F.2d 49 (2d Cir. 1936) (in which the movie Letty Lynton was claimed to have copied the play *Dishonored Lady*, both of which were about a nineteenth-century Scottish girl who had been charged with poisoning her previous lover in order to be able to marry a new and more attractive candidate), and *Nichols v. Universal Pictures Corp.*, 45 F.2d 119 (2d Cir. 1930) (discussed in Section C infra).

### *QUESTIONS FOR DISCUSSION*

1. A notable 1930s police story was the FBI's killing of John Dillinger, the nation's Public Enemy Number One, as Dillinger emerged from Chicago's Biograph Theater with his friend, Anna Sage. Sage was the "lady in red" who, for $10,000, had betrayed Dillinger to the police. The Biograph Theater is

now a national historic site with a plaque commemorating this 1934 event. Historian Jay Robert Nash believed that Dillinger was not in fact killed that night; he thought that Dillinger had learned of the trap from Sage and sent a look-alike hoodlum to be killed in his place. Nash published two books and numerous articles detailing his theory and the supporting evidence, including his tracking down of an elderly man whom he said was Dillinger living on the West Coast. CBS saw an interesting story line in his heavily disputed theory. In 1984, CBS ran an episode, *The Dillinger Print*, on its *Simon & Simon* series, in which the Simon brothers, San Diego private detectives, are portrayed tracking down the still-living Dillinger. Do you agree with Nash that CBS should be required to get his consent to use his theory (and supporting evidence) about what had actually taken place? *See Nash v. CBS*, 899 F.2d 1537 (7th Cir. 1990). By analogy, did Oliver Stone, producer of the 1993 movie hit *JFK*, have to get the consent of New Orleans district attorney Jim Garrison to use the latter's published theory about the supposed political conspiracy that produced the assassination of President Kennedy? As we shall see in Chapter 8, while Stone did contract with Garrison to use his story idea and the movie was a box office hit (starring Kevin Costner as Garrison), Garrison's estate sued the movie studio over its "net profits" formula, which had not generated any payments to the estate.

2. Does a book about the *Twin Peaks* television series violate the copyright in the series because one chapter contains detailed descriptions (plus commentary) of the plot twists and character development of eight episodes in the series? Is it crucial whether or not the chapter has extensive quotations of the dialogue from these episodes? *See Twin Peaks Productions v. Publications International, et al.*, 996 F.2d 1366 (2d Cir. 1993).

3. When a film has elements that reflect aspects of an artist's work, is demonstration of such elements enough to demonstrate substantial similarity? Artist William Roger Dean sued James Cameron and Twentieth Century Fox, alleging that the blockbuster film *Avatar* infringed on copyrights of his artwork. But isolated instances of similar representations typically do not give rise to a successful claim for substantial similarity, which focuses on the work as a whole. Should Dean prevail here? *See Dean v. Cameron, et al.*, 53 F. Supp. 3d 641 (S.D.N.Y. 2014).

---

## 2. FIXATION

While an "original" work does not have to be published to enjoy copyright protection, it does have to be "fixed in a tangible medium of expression." Section 101(3) of the Copyright Act states that "a work is 'fixed' . . . when its embodiment in a copy or phonorecord . . . is sufficiently permanent or stable to permit it to be perceived, reproduced, or otherwise communicated for a period of more than transitory duration." This standard is easy to understand and apply in the case of books (such as this one). It is more complex in the case of other forms of artistic expression, such as choreography. Prior to 1976, choreography could be copyrighted only as part of a larger musical or dramatic production. In its major 1976 revision of copyright law, Congress extended copyright protection to pure choreography compositions, but did not address the issue of how such abstract expressions could come to be "fixed in a tangible medium."

The major ruling on that score is *Horgan v. Macmillan*, 789 F.2d 157 (2d Cir. 1986).[e] This case involved a suit brought by Barbara Horgan, who was executrix of the estate of the renowned choreographer George Balanchine (once described as "an artist of the same magnitude as Picasso"). Balanchine's most notable work was his creation in 1954 of the choreography for the ballet *The Nutcracker*, set to music by Tchaikovsky. For the next 30 years until Balanchine died, this was performed by the New York City Ballet every Christmas season, as reportedly the nation's most successful ballet. Balanchine had copyrighted his choreography and received royalties every time the ballet was performed.

In 1985, Horgan learned that MacMillan was planning to publish a book entitled *The Nutcracker: A Story & A Ballet*, portraying the New York presentation of the ballet in text and photographs. The book's title page displays three black and white photographs of George Balanchine directing a rehearsal of the ballet. The book begins with a 15-page text by defendant Switzer regarding the origins of *The Nutcracker* as a story and as a ballet. The main section of the book consists of 60 color photographs of scenes from the New York City Ballet Company production of *The Nutcracker*, following the sequence of the ballet's story and dances. The photographs are interspersed with Switzer's narration of the story, including those portions not portrayed visually. The final section of the book contains interviews with ten of the dancers, with black and white photographs of them out of costume. The defendants obtained this material through their access to company rehearsals and performances. Carras and Costas were considered "official photographers" of the New York City Ballet, who were authorized to take photographs of the Company, some of which might be purchased by the Company for publicity and related purposes.

Attorneys for the estate questioned the publisher's right to "create such a derivative work" and suggested that "in light of the Estate's ownership of the work in question," it suspend any further production until "appropriate licenses" were in place. Horgan eventually filed suit, but the district judge denied a preliminary injunction because he believed the book did not infringe the copyright in Balachine's choreography because

[e] *See* Adaline J. Hilgard, *Can Choreography & Copyright Waltz Together in the Wake of* Horgan v. MacMillan, Inc., 27 U.C. Davis. L. Rev. 757 (1994).

> choreography has to do with the flow of the steps in a ballet. The still photographs in the *Nutcracker* book, numerous though they are, catch dancers in various attitudes at specific instants of time; they do not, nor do they intend to, take or use the underlying choreography. The staged performance could not be recreated from them—just as a Beethoven symphony could not be recreated from a document containing only every twenty-fifth chord of the symphony.

Horgan appealed to the Second Circuit, which had a different view. It recognized that prior to the 1976 Copyright Act revisions, choreographic works were not copyrightable at all.

> Dance was protectable only if it told a story, developed or characterized an emotion, or otherwise conveyed a dramatic concept or idea. The rights of a choreographer in his work were not clearly defined, in part because the means for reducing choreography to tangible form had become readily available only comparatively recently, and in part because of resistance to the acceptance of abstract, non-literary dance as a worthy form of artistic expression.

789 F.2d at 160. But now with choreographic works given legal protection without being specifically defined, the issue was whether "still photographs of a ballet" infringed the latter's new rights.

Horgan's position, then, was that the book was a "reproduction" of Balanchine's copyrighted work because it portrayed the essence of the *Nutcracker*, or, in the alternative, that the book was an infringing "derivative work," with the key "test for infringement, being not whether the original work may be reproduced from the copy—as the district judge held—but whether the alleged copy is substantially similar to the original." MacMillan's response was that

> the photographs in the Switzer book do not capture the flow of movement, which is the essence of dance, and thus cannot possibly be substantially similar to the choreographic component of the production of the ballet . . . Since each photograph in the book captures only a fraction of an instant, even the combined effect of 60 color photographs does not reproduce the choreography itself, nor provide sufficient details of movement to enable a choreographic work to be reproduced from the photographs.

789 F.2d at 161–162.

The Second Circuit disagreed with the relevance of that factor where there were different media at play. "It surely would not be a defense to an infringement claim against the movie version of *Gone With The Wind* that a viewer of the movie could not create the book." More important, taking small but qualitatively significant amounts of the original work (e.g., the ten minute burning of Atlanta in the three-hour *Gone With the Wind*), violates copyright law even if viewers of the latter cannot use these excerpts to recreate the full original. This court held that the district judge had taken

> . . . a far too limited view of the extent to which choreographic material may be conveyed in the medium of still photography. A snapshot of a single moment in a dance sequence may communicate a great deal. It may, for example, capture a gesture, the composition of dancers' bodies or the placement of dancers on the stage. Such freezing of a choreographic moment is shown in a number of the photographs in the Switzer book. A photograph may also convey to the viewer's imagination the moments before and after the split second recorded. On pages 76–77 of the Switzer book, for example, there is a two-page photograph of the "Sugar Canes," one of the troupes that perform in *The Nutcracker*. In this photograph, the Sugar Canes are a foot or more off the ground, holding large hoops above their heads. One member of the ensemble is jumping through a hoop, which is held extended in front of the dancer. The dancer's legs are thrust forward, parallel to the stage and several feet off the ground. The viewer understands instinctively, based simply on the laws of gravity, that the Sugar Canes jumped up from the floor only a moment earlier, and came down shortly after the photographed moment. An ordinary observer, who had only recently seen a performance of *The Nutcracker*, could probably perceive even more from this photograph. The single instant thus communicates far more than a single chord of a Beethoven symphony—the analogy suggested by the district judge.

789 F.2d at 163. Having concluded that the district judge had erred in assuming that "still photographs cannot infringe choreography," the panel sent the case back for a full trial on whether there was sufficient "quantity and sequency" of the ballet's choreography to constitute infringement.

### *QUESTIONS FOR DISCUSSION*

1. The parties then settled the *Horgan* suit, so we do not know the ultimate verdict on these facts. What issues should have been decisive? For example, how could Balanchine get his choreographic version of *The Nutcracker Ballet* "fixed in a tangible medium of expression"? What techniques might be used for this purpose (e.g., written notation, video tapes, or computer graphics), and what are their relative merits? Can a book of

photographs constitute a "reproduction" of, or derivative work based on, a choreography.

2. Can figure skating routines be copyrighted—perhaps to block competitors using any significant parts of the routine in Olympic competitions? Or consider the following controversy: in 1996, Broadway director Joe Mantello attended a local performance by a Florida theatrical group of *Love! Valour! Compassion!*, a Terrence McNally play that Mantello had directed on Broadway in 1994–95. Mantello was shocked to observe that the staging of the Florida production was virtually identical to his Broadway version. While the Florida company had secured the right to perform the play from McNally, the playwright, Mantello's lawyers said that the company should also have secured (and paid for) Mantello's consent to use his staging arrangements (which had been attached to the back of the script by McNally's licensing company) and his music selection (which had not been mentioned in the script at all). After a Florida judge refused to summarily dismiss the director's claim, the two parties settled. What would you have predicted (or advised) as the relative terms of such a settlement being negotiated in the shadow of copyright law?

3. Turning now to even less tangible but probably more valuable entertainment routines, should a personality trait be protectible? For example, the cable network Comedy Central sued to try to stop comedian Jackie Mason from using the name *Politically Incorrect* for the title of his one-man show, alleging that it was "ripping off" the network's own series of the same name. Mason replied that "I can't imagine somebody would have the nerve to pretend not to know that I've been identified as the politically incorrect man for years now." Is Mason correct? Would he have a valid counterclaim against Comedy Central (and what about the ABC show with that same name)?

4. Are "Top Ten" lists copyrightable? When David Letterman left NBC to join CBS, NBC threatened to sue him if he used either his Top Ten List or his Stupid Pet Tricks segments on his new show. Should such routines be protected under copyright law? Or should this depend on whether there are substantial differences between the earlier *Late Night With David Letterman* on NBC and the recently concluded *Late Show With David Letterman* on CBS?[f]

5. Recall the facts of Vanna White's "publicity rights" suit from Chapter 3. Should her *Wheel of Fortune* routine be copyrightable? What if White had plotted out and written exactly what she would do, where she would stand, and so on? If White's routine were held copyrightable, that would raise another legal question about who owned this property—the performer or the producer. Keep this issue in mind when you read the materials in Chapter 5 about copyright ownership and licensing.

---

[f] *See* Leslie Kurtz, *A Knight Without Armour In A Savage Land: Victor DeCosta & Intellectual Property Law in the United States*, 4 Ent. L. Rev. 103 (1993).

6. An analogous scenario actually played itself out in three First Circuit rulings over the last four decades—*Columbia Broadcasting System v. DeCosta*, 377 F.2d 315 (1st Cir. 1967); *DeCosta v. CBS*, 520 F.2d 499 (1st Cir. 1975); and *DeCosta v. Viacom International*, 981 F.2d 602 (1st Cir. 1992). The following passage capsulizes the nature of this dispute:

* * *

The story of this case—more bizarre than most television serial installments—is one of "coincidence" run riot. The plaintiff, of Portuguese parents, is a Rhode Island mechanic whose formal education ceased after the fourth grade. During the Depression, having tired of factory work, he hopped a freight for the West, lived in hobo jungles, and eventually became a range hand on a Texas ranch. After two years of riding and roping he returned to Rhode Island to work as a mechanic and later received training as a motor machinist in the Coast Guard. But he retained his passion for all things western. In 1947 he began to participate in rodeos, horse shows, horse auctions, and parades.

From the beginning plaintiff indulged a penchant for costume. He was already equipped with a moustache. He soon settled on a black shirt, black pants, and a flat-crowned black hat. He had acquired a St. Mary's medal at a parade and affixed this to his hat. He adopted the name Paladin after an onlooker of Italian descent had hurled an epithet at him containing the word "Paladino." On looking up the word Paladin in a dictionary, he found it meant "champion of Knights" and was content that people began so to call him. One day when he had donned his costume in preparation for a horse show, and was about to mount his horse, one of a group waiting for him shouted "Have Gun Will Travel," a cry immediately picked up by the children present.

The finishing touches were a chess knight, bought for fifteen cents at an auction, which plaintiff thought was a good symbol, and which he used on a business card along with the words "Have," "Gun," "Will," "Travel," and "Wire Paladin, N. Court St., Cranston, R.I.," hand-printed with separate rubber stamps; a silver copy of the chess piece on his holster; and an antique derringer strapped under his arm. So accoutered, he would appear in parades, and openings and finales of rodeos, auctions, horse shows, and a pony ring he once operated. From time to time at rodeos he would stage a western gunfight, featuring his quick draw and the timely use of his hidden derringer. He would pass out photographs of himself and cards—printed versions soon replacing the rubber-stamped ones. Hospitals, drug stores, barber shops, sports shops, diners—all were the repositories of his cards, some 25,000 of them. Children clamored for the cards, and clustered about him to the extent that he was likened to the Pied Piper and Gene Autry. This was perhaps one of the

> purest promotions ever staged, for plaintiff did not seek anything but the entertainment of others. He sold no product, services, or institution, charged no fees, and exploited only himself.
>
> Ten years after [DeCosta] had begun to live his avocational role of Paladin, he and his friends saw the first CBS television production of *Have Gun Will Travel*, starring mustachioed Richard Boone, who played the part of an elegant knight errant of the Old West, always on the side of Good—for a fee. The television Paladin also wore a black costume, a flat-crowned black hat bearing an oval silver decoration, and a silver chess knight on his holster, and announced himself with a card featuring a chess piece virtually—if not absolutely—identical with the plaintiff's and the words "HAVE GUN WILL TRAVEL, WIRE PALADIN, SAN FRANCISCO." The series was notably successful; it appeared in 225 first-run episodes in the United States, was licensed in foreign countries, and by the time of trial had grossed in excess of fourteen million dollars.
>
> * * *

377 F.2d at 316–17. Assume (as was found by the court) that CBS did in fact "copy" these particular features of *Have Gun Will Travel* from DeCosta's persona and routine, and also (though this did not happen in that case) that DeCosta had once had his routine recorded on film. Under current copyright doctrine, should his routine be protected?

---

The case of *Mitchell Brothers Film Group v. Cinema Adult Theater*, 604 F.2d 852 (5th Cir. 1979), raised a question that the Copyright Act does not explicitly address. Plaintiff's movie, *Behind the Green Door*, was shown in defendant's movie theater, without license from or payment to the plaintiffs. In response to the suit for infringement of the plaintiff's public performance right in its movie, the defendants raised the issue that *Behind the Green Door* (like many of Mitchell Brothers' lucrative movies) had been found to be obscene by a trial judge, applying the Supreme Court's First Amendment standard in *Miller v. California*, 413 U.S. 15 (1973). Should violation of locally-enacted (and constitutionally-permitted) obscenity laws be a reason for denying copyright to a pornographic movie (or to choreography involving live sex acts)? Is it relevant that federal law now makes interstate shipments of obscene materials a crime? Or that the Lanham Act, governing trademark rights, bars registration of a trademark that "consists of or comprises immoral, deceptive, or scandalous matter?" (On the meaning and application of the latter statutory condition, see *In re Mavety Media Group*, 33 F.3d 1367 (Fed. Cir. 1994).) What is the appropriate accommodation of copyright protection for expression and the objectives of constitutionally-permissible restraints on such expression? Consider also the analogous problem of copyright in writings with fraudulent content: *see Belcher v. Tarbox*, 486 F.2d 1087 (9th Cir. 1973).

## B. INFRINGEMENT

### 1. ACCESS: THE MUSIC SCENE

Unlike patent law, a copyright is violated only if the prior work has been copied, not simply *duplicated*. Copyright law does not preclude the independent creation and sale of an identical work by a subsequent author. In a characteristically elegant passage, Judge Learned Hand illustrated this point as follows:

> [I]t is plain beyond peradventure that anticipation as such cannot invalidate a copyright. Borrowed the work must indeed not be, for a plagiarist is not himself pro tanto an "author," but if by some magic a man who had never known it were to compose anew Keats's *Ode on a Grecian Urn*, he would be an "author," and if he copyright it, others might not copy that poem, though they might of course copy Keats's. . . .

*Sheldon v. Metro-Goldwyn Pictures Corp.*, 81 F.2d 49, 54 (2d Cir. 1936), aff'd, 309 U.S. 390 (1940).[g]

To demonstrate impermissible copying rather than independent creation, the copyright owner must establish that the later author had *access* to the protected work and that the later work displayed undue *similarity* to the original creation. While these issues are logically distinguishable, in practice evidence about one may also indicate the presence of the other. For example, if two works are "strikingly similar," the trier of fact may be able to infer that the author of the later work had enjoyed access to the earlier one.

The next case, based on a finding of subconscious access and recall, poses the question of how far courts can go in relaxing the standards for access while preserving the *copying* feature of copyright law.

### BRIGHT TUNES MUSIC CORP. V. HARRISONGS MUSIC

United States District Court, Southern District of New York, 1976.
420 F. Supp. 177.

OWEN, DISTRICT JUDGE.

This is an action in which it is claimed that a successful song, "My Sweet Lord," listing George Harrison as the composer, is plagiarized from

[g] *See* Arthur R. Miller, *Copyright Protection for Computer Programs, Databases, & Computer-Generated Works: Is Anything New Since CONTU?*, 106 Harv. L. Rev. 977, 1042 (1993) (discussing "the proverbial roomful of monkeys striking the keys of typewriters . . . with one of the monkeys eventually 'producing' Shakespeare's Hamlet").

an earlier successful song, "He's So Fine," composed by Ronald Mask, recorded by a singing group called the "Chiffons," the copyright of which is owned by plaintiff, Bright Tunes Music Corp.

"He's So Fine," recorded in 1962, is a catchy tune consisting essentially of four repetitions of a very short basic musical phrase, "sol-mi-re," (hereinafter motif A), altered as necessary to fit the words, followed by four repetitions of another short basic musical phrase, "sol-la-do-la-do," (hereinafter motif B). While neither motif is novel, the four repetitions of A, followed by four repetitions of B, is a highly unique pattern. In addition, in the second use of the motif B series, there is a grace note inserted making the phrase go "sol-la-do-la-re-do."

"My Sweet Lord," recorded first in 1970, also uses the same motif A (modified to suit the words) four times, followed by motif B, repeated three times, not four. In place of He's So Fine's fourth repetition of motif B, "My Sweet Lord" has a transitional passage of musical attractiveness of the same approximate length, with the identical grace note in the identical second repetition. The harmonies of both songs are identical.[6]

George Harrison, a former member of The Beatles, was aware of "He's So Fine." In the United States, it was No. 1 on the billboard charts for five weeks; in England, Harrison's home country, it was No. 12 on the charts on June 1, 1963, a date upon which one of the Beatle songs was, in fact, in first position. For seven weeks in 1963, "He's So Fine" was one of the top hits in England.

According to Harrison, the circumstances of the composition of My Sweet Lord were as follows. Harrison and his group, which include an American black gospel singer named Billy Preston, were in Copenhagen, Denmark, on a singing engagement. There was a press conference involving the group going on backstage. Harrison slipped away . . . and went to a room upstairs and began "vamping" some guitar chords, fitting on to the chords he was playing the words, "Hallelujah" and "Hare Krishna" in various ways. During the course of this vamping, he was alternating between what musicians call a Minor II chord and a Major V chord.

At some point, . . . he went down to meet with others of the group, asking them to listen, . . . and everyone began to join in, taking first "Hallelujah" and then "Hare Krishna" and putting them into four part harmony. Harrison obviously started using the "Hallelujah," etc., as repeated sounds, and from there developed the lyrics, to wit, "My Sweet Lord," "Dear, Dear Lord," etc. In any event, from this very free-flowing

[6] Expert witnesses for the defendants asserted crucial differences in the two songs. These claimed differences essentially stem, however, from the fact that different words and number of syllables were involved. This necessitated modest alterations in the repetitions or the places of beginning of a phrase, which, however, has nothing to do whatsoever with the essential musical kernel that is involved.

exchange of ideas, with Harrison playing his two chords and everybody singing "Hallelujah" and "Hare Krishna," there began to emerge the My Sweet Lord text idea, which Harrison sought to develop a little bit further during the following week as he was playing it on his guitar. Thus developed motif A and its words interspersed with "Hallelujah" and "Hare Krishna."[8]

Approximately one week after the idea first began to germinate, the entire group flew back to London because they had earlier booked time to go to a recording studio with Billy Preston to make an album. In the studio, Preston was the principal musician. Harrison did not play in the session. He had given Preston his basic motif A with the idea that it be turned into a song, and was back and forth from the studio to the engineer's recording booth, supervising the recording "takes." Under circumstances that Harrison was utterly unable to recall, while everybody was working toward a finished song, in the recording studio, somehow or other the essential three notes of motif A reached polished form. [The judge then stated that] it appears that motif B emerged in some fashion at the recording session as did motif A. This is also true of the unique grace note in the second repetition of motif B.

* * *

The Billy Preston recording, listing George Harrison as the composer, was thereafter issued by Apple Records. The music was then reduced to paper by someone who prepared a "lead sheet" containing the melody, the words and the harmony for the United States copyright application.

Seeking the wellsprings of musical composition—why a composer chooses the succession of notes and the harmonies he does—whether it be George Harrison or Richard Wagner—is a fascinating inquiry. It is apparent from the extensive colloquy between the Court and Harrison . . . that neither Harrison nor Preston were conscious of the fact that they were utilizing the "He's So Fine" theme. However, they in fact were, for it is perfectly obvious to the listener that in musical terms, the two songs are virtually identical except for one phrase. . . . [The judge then noted that "even Harrison's own expert witness acknowledged that although the two motifs were in the public domain, their use here was so unusual that he, in all his experience, had never come across this unique sequential use of these materials."]

What happened? I conclude that the composer, in seeking musical materials to clothe his thoughts, was working with various possibilities. As he tried this possibility and that, there came to the surface of his mind

---

[8] These words ended up being a "responsive" interjection between the eventually copyrighted words of "My Sweet Lord." In "He's so fine" the Chiffons used the sound "dulang" in the same places to fill in and give rhythmic impetus to what would otherwise be somewhat dead spots in the music.

a particular combination that pleased him as being one he felt would be appealing to a prospective listener; in other words, that this combination of sounds would work. Why? Because his subconscious knew it already had worked in a song his conscious mind did not remember. Having arrived at this pleasing combination of sounds, the recording was made, the lead sheet prepared for copyright and the song became an enormous success. Did Harrison deliberately use the music of "He's So Fine?" I do not believe he did so deliberately. Nevertheless, it is clear that My Sweet Lord is the very same song as "He's So Fine" with different words,[13] and Harrison had access to "He's So Fine." This is, under the law, infringement of copyright, and is no less so even though subconsciously accomplished. *Sheldon v. Metro-Goldwyn Pictures Corp.*, 81 F.2d 49, 54 (2d Cir. 1936); *Northern Music Corp. v. Pacemaker Music Co., Inc.*, 147 U.S.P.Q. 358, 359 (S.D.N.Y. 1965).

* * *

Claim upheld.

---

On appeal, the Second Circuit affirmed the district court's decision in *Bright Tunes. See ABKCO Music, Inc. v. Harrisongs Music*, 722 F.2d 988 (2d Cir. 1983). In response to the argument that "it is unsound policy to permit a finding of copyright infringement on the basis of subconscious copying," because this would "bring the law of copyright improperly close to patent law, which imposes a requirement of novelty," the court made the following observations:

> It is not new law . . . that when a defendant's work is copied from the plaintiff's, but the defendant in good faith has forgotten that the plaintiff's work was the source of his own, such "innocent copying" can nevertheless constitute an infringement. . . . We do not find this stance in conflict with the rule permitting independent creation of copyrighted material. It is settled that "[i]ntention to infringe is not essential under the [Copyright] Act," *Buck v. Jewell-LaSalle Realty Co.*, 283 U.S. 191 (1931). . . . Moreover, as a practical matter, the problems of proof inherent in a rule that would permit innocent intent as a defense to copyright infringement could substantially undermine the protections Congress intended to afford to copyright holders. We therefore see no reason to retreat from this circuit's prior position that copyright infringement can be subconscious.

[13] Harrison himself acknowledged on the stand that the two songs were substantially similar. This same conclusion was obviously reached by a recording group called the "Belmonts" who recorded My Sweet Lord at a later time. With "tongue in cheek" they used the words from both He's So Fine and My Sweet Lord interchangeably at certain points.

722 F.2d at 998–99.[h] Are you convinced?

In a more recent case, *Three Boys Music v. Bolton, et al.*, 212 F.3d 477 (9th Cir. 2000), the Ninth Circuit endorsed the "subconscious access" principle of the Second Circuit. *Three Boys* was much more challenging than ABKCO, though, with its six year gap between the release of the first song and the creation of the second. Here, there were 25 years between the time the future Rock and Roll Hall of Fame Isley Brothers released their single song "Love Is a Wonderful Thing" in 1964 and the time that Michael Bolton and Andrew Goldmark began working on their 1989 album with a hit song of the same title. (Apparently, that title has been given to 129 copyright-registered songs, 85 of them released before the Isley Brothers version.) The appeals court upheld the reasonability of the jury's funding of "access" on the grounds that "teenagers are generally avid music listeners. It is entirely plausible that two Connecticut teenagers obsessed with rhythm and blues music could remember an Isley Brothers' song that was played on the radio and television for a few weeks and subconsciously copy it twenty years later." 212 F.3d at 484. This subconscious memory of Bolton and Goldmark not only cost them $1.2 million in damages, but meant that Sony Music, which had released their album had to pay the Isley Brothers an additional $4.2 million from the jury verdict.

A more recent example of subconscious memory resulting in a successful copyright infringement claim occurred in 2015 when a jury awarded the family of Marvin Gaye $7.4 million. Gaye's family sued Pharrell Williams and Robin Thicke, and claimed that Williams' and Thicke's 2013 hit song "Blurred Lines" copied the melody from Marvin Gaye's song "Got to Give It Up." Williams, who wrote the song in 2012, claims that it was his original composition, but admits that it may have been inspired subconsciously by listening to Gaye's song. Williams denounced the jury's verdict as killing the creativity of artists. Should copyright lawsuits be limited to replication, instead of including inspiration? Why or why not?

---

The next case in this section reinforces the independent value of the "access" requirement as a corollary to the "independent creation" right. Should a copyright-holder have to adduce tangible evidence of access even in cases where there is a particularly "striking" level of similarity

[h] *See also Fred Fisher, Inc. v. Dillingham*, 298 F. 145, 148 (S.D.N.Y. 1924) (L. Hand, J.) ("Once it appears that another has in fact used the copyright as the source of his production, he has invaded the author's rights. It is no excuse that in so doing his memory has played him a trick."); *Sheldon v. Metro-Goldwyn Pictures Corp.*, 81 F.2d 49, 54 (2d Cir. 1936) (L. Hand, J.) ("[N]obody knows the origin of his inventions; memory and fancy merge even in adults. Yet unconscious plagiarism is actionable quite as much as deliberate."), *cert. denied*, 298 U.S. 669 (1936).

between the two works? Does judicial insistence on such evidence have a disparate impact on entertainment novices as compared to star performers? We shall now see an important illustration in a lawsuit filed by a relatively unknown musician Ronald Selle against the Bee Gees.

## SELLE V. GIBB

United States Court of Appeals, Seventh Circuit, 1984.
741 F.2d 896.

CUDAHY, CIRCUIT JUDGE.

I

[Selle had composed his song "Let It End" in 1975, secured copyright for it shortly afterward, and played the song a few times with his small band in Chicago. He sent a tape and lead sheet of the song to a number of record companies to have it recorded, but none were willing to do that. In 1978, Selle saw the movie *Saturday Night Fever,* which featured a new Bee Gees' song, "How Deep Is Your Love," whose music (though not its lyrics) he thought were identical to his own. He filed suit against the Gibb brothers, their record company now known as Polygram, and Paramount Pictures which had made and distributed *Saturday Night Fever*.

The Bee Gees were then one of the top music composers and performers in the world. They had composed over 160 songs and some of their albums had totaled more than 30 million sales. Their evidence at the trial was that "How Deep Is Your Love" had been composed (along with the other songs in its album) when the Gibbs brothers and their staff went to a studio outside of Paris to do this work—without, they said, ever having heard "Let It End."]

* * *

The only expert witness to testify at trial was Arrand Parsons, a professor of music at Northwestern University who has had extensive professional experience primarily in classical music. . . . Prior to this case, however, he had never made a comparative analysis of two popular songs. Dr. Parsons testified on the basis of several charts comparing the musical notes of each song and a comparative recording prepared under his direction.

According to Dr. Parsons' testimony, the first eight bars of each song (Theme A) have twenty-four of thirty-four notes in plaintiff's composition and twenty-four of forty notes in defendants' composition which are identical in pitch and symmetrical position. Of thirty-five rhythmic impulses in plaintiff's composition and forty in defendants, thirty are identical. In the last four bars of both songs (Theme B), fourteen notes in each are identical in pitch, and eleven of the fourteen rhythmic impulses are identical. Both Theme A and Theme B appear in the same position in each song but with different intervening material.

Dr. Parsons testified that, in his opinion, "the two songs had such striking similarities that they could not have been written independent of one another." He also testified that he did not know of two songs by different composers "that contain as many striking similarities" as do the two songs at issue here. However, on several occasions, he declined to say that the similarities could only have resulted from copying.

Following presentation of the case, the jury returned a verdict for the plaintiff. . . . Judge Leighton, however, granted the defendants' motion for judgment notwithstanding the verdict and, in the alternative, for a new trial. He relied primarily on the plaintiff's inability to demonstrate that the defendants had access to the plaintiff's song, without which a claim of copyright infringement could not prevail regardless how similar the two compositions are. Further, the plaintiff failed to contradict or refute the testimony of the defendants and their witnesses describing the independent creation process of "How Deep Is Your Love." Finally, Judge Leighton concluded that "the inferences on which plaintiff relies is not a logical, permissible deduction from proof of 'striking similarity' or substantial similarity; it is 'at war with the undisputed facts,' and it is inconsistent with the proof of non-access to plaintiff's song by the Bee Gees at the time in question." [Selle appealed this ruling.]

* * *

III

Proof of copying is crucial to any claim of copyright infringement because no matter how similar the two works may be (even to the point of identity), if the defendant did not copy the accused work, there is no infringement. However, because direct evidence of copying is rarely available, the plaintiff can rely upon circumstantial evidence to prove this essential element, and the most important component of this sort of circumstantial evidence is proof of access. The plaintiff may be able to introduce direct evidence of access when, for example, the work was sent directly to the defendant (whether a musician or a publishing company) or a close associate of the defendant. On the other hand, the plaintiff may be able to establish a reasonable possibility of access when, for example, the complaining work has been widely disseminated to the public. *See, e.g., ABKCO Music, Inc. v. Harrisongs Music, Ltd.*, 722 F.2d 988 (2d Cir. 1983) (finding of access based on wide dissemination).

If, however, the plaintiff does not have direct evidence of access, then an inference of access may still be established circumstantially by proof of similarity which is so striking that the possibilities of independent creation, coincidence and prior common source are, as a practical matter, precluded. If the plaintiff presents evidence of striking similarity sufficient to raise an inference of access, then copying is presumably proved simultaneously, although the fourth element (substantial similarity) still requires proof that the defendant copied a substantial amount of the complaining work. The theory which Selle attempts to apply to this case is based on proof of copying by circumstantial proof of access established by striking similarity between the two works.

One difficulty with plaintiff's theory is that no matter how great the similarity between the two works, it is not their similarity per se which establishes access; rather, their similarity tends to prove access in light of the nature of the works, the particular musical genre involved and other circumstantial evidence of access. In other words, striking similarity is just one piece of circumstantial evidence tending to show access and must not be considered in isolation; it must be considered together with other types of circumstantial evidence relating to access.

As a threshold matter, therefore, it would appear that there must be at least some other evidence which would establish a reasonable possibility that the complaining work was available to the alleged infringer. As noted, two works may be identical in every detail, but, if the alleged infringer created the accused work independently or both works were copied from a common source in the public domain, then there is no infringement. Therefore, if the plaintiff admits to having kept his or her creation under lock and key, it would seem logically impossible to infer access through striking similarity. Thus, although it has frequently been written that striking similarity alone can establish access, the decided cases suggest that this circumstance would be most unusual. The plaintiff must always present sufficient evidence to support a reasonable possibility of access because the jury cannot draw an inference of access based upon speculation and conjecture alone.

* * *

Judge Leighton . . . based his decision on what he characterized as the plaintiff's inability to raise more than speculation that the Bee Gees had access to his song. The extensive testimony of the defendants and their witnesses describing the creation process went essentially uncontradicted, and there was no attempt even to impeach their credibility. Judge Leighton further relied on the principle that the testimony of credible witnesses concerning a matter within their knowledge cannot be rejected without some impeachment, contradiction or inconsistency with other evidence on the particular point at issue. Judge Leighton's conclusions . . . seem correct. . . .

IV

[The court noted that its decision "is also supported by a more traditional analysis of proof of access based only on the proof of 'striking similarity' between the two compositions."]

* * *

"Striking similarity" is not merely a function of the number of identical notes that appear in both compositions. . . . An important factor in analyzing the degree of similarity of two compositions is the uniqueness of the sections which are asserted to be similar.

If the complaining work contains an unexpected departure from the normal metric structure or if the complaining work includes what appears to be an error and the accused work repeats the unexpected element or the error, then it is more likely that there is some connection between the pieces. *See, e.g., Nordstrom v. Radio Corporation of America,* 251 F. Supp. 41, 42 (D.Colo.1965). If the similar sections are particularly intricate, then again it would seem more likely that the compositions are related. Finally, some dissimilarities may be particularly suspicious. *See, e.g., Meier Co. v. Albany Novelty Manufacturing Co.*, 236 F.2d 144, 146 (2d Cir. 1956) (inversion and substitution of certain words in a catalogue in a "crude effort to give the appearance of dissimilarity" are themselves evidence of copying); *Blume v. Spear*, 30 F. 629, 631 (S.D.N.Y. 1887) (variations in infringing song were placed so as to indicate deliberate copying). . . . While some of these concepts are borrowed from literary copyright analysis, they would seem equally applicable to an analysis of music.

The judicially formulated definition of "striking similarity" states that "plaintiffs must demonstrate that 'such similarities are of a kind that can only be explained by copying, rather than by coincidence, independent creation, or prior common source.'" *Testa v. Janssen*, 492 F. Supp. 198, 203 (W.D.Pa.1980) (quoting *Stratchborneo v. Arc Music Corp.*, 357 F. Supp. 1393, 1403 (S.D.N.Y. 1973)). . . .

* * *

[T]he plaintiff relies almost entirely on the testimony of his expert witness, Dr. Arrand Parsons. The defendants did not introduce any expert testimony, apparently because they did not think Parsons' testimony needed to be refuted. Defendants are perhaps to some degree correct in asserting that Parsons, although eminently qualified in the field of classical music theory, was not equally qualified to analyze popular music tunes. More significantly, however, although Parsons used the magic formula, "striking similarity," he only ruled out the possibility of independent creation; he did not state that the similarities could only be the result of copying. In order for proof of "striking similarity" to establish a reasonable inference of access, especially in a case such as this one in which the direct proof of access is so minimal, the plaintiff must show that the similarity is of a type which will preclude any explanation other than that of copying.

In addition, to bolster the expert's conclusion that independent creation was not possible, there should be some testimony or other evidence of the relative complexity or uniqueness of the two compositions. Dr. Parsons' testimony did not refer to this aspect of the compositions and, in a field such as that of popular music in which all songs are relatively short and tend to build on or repeat a basic theme, such testimony would seem to be particularly necessary. . . .

To illustrate this deficiency more concretely, we refer to [a cassette tape and chart]. These exhibits were prepared by the defendants but introduced into evidence by the plaintiff. The tape has recorded on it segments of both themes from both the Selle and the Gibb songs interspersed with segments of other compositions as diverse as "Footsteps," "From Me To You" (a Lennon-McCartney piece), Beethoven's 5th Symphony, "Funny Talk," "Play Down," and "I'd Like To Leave If I May" (the last two being earlier compositions by Barry Gibb). There are at least superficial similarities among these segments, when played on the same musical instrument, and the plaintiff failed to elicit any testimony from his expert witness about this exhibit which compared the Selle and the Gibb songs to other pieces of contemporary, popular music. These circumstances indicate that the plaintiff failed to sustain his burden of proof on the issue of "striking similarity" in its legal sense. . . .

The plaintiff's expert witness does not seem to have addressed any issues relating to the possibility of prior common source in both widely disseminated popular songs and the defendants' own compositions. At oral argument, plaintiff's attorney stated that the burden of proving common source should be on the defendant; however, the burden of proving "striking similarity," which, by definition, includes taking steps to minimize the possibility of common source, is on the plaintiff. In essence, the plaintiff failed to prove to the requisite degree that the similarities identified by the expert witness—although perhaps "striking" in a non-legal sense—were of a type which would eliminate any explanation of coincidence, independent creation or common source, including, in this case, the possibility of common source in earlier compositions created by the Bee Gees themselves or by others. In sum, the evidence of striking similarity is not sufficiently compelling to make the case when the proof of access must otherwise depend largely upon speculation and conjecture.

* * *

Affirmed.

---

Another ruling, *Associated Artists Entertainment v. Walt Disney Pictures*, 172 F.3d 875 (9th Cir. 1999), displays the importance of judicial definitions of the scope and limits of author rights. Dorothy Gilman had written a novel entitled *A Nun in the Closet*, whose movie rights were optioned in 1985 by Associated Artists Entertainment. AAE was a partnership of Curt Wilson and Donna Douglas (who had played Elly Mae Clampett on the television hit *The Beverly Hillbillies)*. AAA developed *A Nun in the Closet* into a screenplay, which they submitted to Walt Disney Pictures, Bette Midler's All Girls Production, and Whoopi Goldberg's production company Whoopi Inc. None of these recipients accepted the AAA proposal.

In 1992, though, a hit comedy appeared, *Sister Act*. Although it was initially supposed to have Midler in the lead role, Whoopi Goldberg ended up playing the nun character, Delores, in what proved to be a big box office hit. Credits as producer went to Scott Rudin (who later made *The Truman Show*), and as screenwriter to Paul Rudnick (later making *First Wives Club*), with Disney being the movie's studio financier and distributor. After the AAA people saw the movie, they filed suit. The Ninth Circuit summarily dismissed the case even though the plaintiffs identified more than 200 similarities between their original *A Nun in the Closet* script and the *Sister Act* movie. The circuit panel concluded there was no independent proof of access, relying on an earlier dictum in *Kouf v. Walt Disney Pictures*, 16 F.3d 1042 (9th Cir. 1994) (involving *Honey, I Shrunk the Kids*). Although AAA had clearly delivered the script to Disney, Midler, and Goldberg, they had no proof that any of these had passed that script along to Rudnick and Rudin (who created *Sister Act)*. By contrast, the Second Circuit has stated in *Gaste v. Kaiserman*, 863 F.2d 1061 (2d Cir. 1988), that the "access" requirement can be satisfied by demonstrating a "striking similarity between the two works."

---

### *QUESTIONS FOR DISCUSSION*

1. Derrick Moore, a young Minneapolis songwriter and musician, through his agent, James Selmer, gave to Cheryl Dickerson, the Los Angeles Director of Artists and Repertoire for a division of MCA, a cassette tape with an instrumental version of Moore's song, "She Can't Stand It." Around the same time, Dickerson's supervisor, Louil Silas, had suggested to Los Angeles songwriters Antoine Reid and Kenny Edmonds that they compose a song for the MCA's Bobby Brown to record for the soundtrack of Columbia Pictures's forthcoming *Ghostbusters II*. Should these facts be sufficient under a "corporate receipt" doctrine to establish the access component of Moore's copyright infringement claim regarding the eventual Reid-Edmunds-Brown

song, "On Our Own," for *Ghostbusters II*? *See Moore v. Columbia Pictures*, 972 F.2d 939 (8th Cir. 1992). What about the fact that at the time that a National Lampoon group was doing an initial screenplay for Universal City Studios of what eventually became *Animal House*, an allegedly similar treatment, *Frat Rats*, was submitted to the director, John Badham, who was doing post-production work at Universal's Hollywood studio on another film for Universal? *See Meta-Film Associates v. MCA*, 586 F. Supp. 1346 (C.D. Cal. 1984).

2. *Jason v. Fonda*, 526 F. Supp. 774 (C.D. Cal. 1981), illustrates that more direct proof of access may be required in the literary world than in the music context. In that case, Sonya Jason sued the producers and broadcasters of the movie *Coming Home* for copyright violations. Jason claimed that Jane Fonda and her partners had copied her book, *Concomitant Soldier-Woman and War*, in making the movie. Undisputed testimony established that the idea for the movie originated in the late 1960s and early 1970s. Defendant Nancy Dowd began to write the screenplay in late 1972, and completed a draft in late 1973. Filming began in January 1977, the film was released in theaters in February 1978, and it was shown on NBC in 1979. Jason's book was apparently written over a 20-year period and ultimately was published in April 1974. The first printing was approximately 1100 copies. Jason submitted her book to United Artists in December 1977, but it was returned; Jason also alleged that she had submitted her book to NBC and that Nancy Dowd might have been given a copy of the book at some point.

In granting summary dismissal of Jason's suit, the court noted that "[w]hether 'access' be defined as the actual reading or knowledge of plaintiff's work by the defendants, . . . or as a 'reasonable opportunity to view' the plaintiff's work, . . . plaintiff has not controverted the explicit denial by each defendant that they had never heard of her book prior to the lawsuit." He went on to make the following assessment of Jason's access claim:

> In sum, there is not one shred of evidence that any of the defendants who were involved in producing *Coming Home* had access to Jason's book during production except for plaintiff's undisputed claim that between 200 and 700 copies were available through various Southern California bookstores. That level of availability creates no more than a "bare possibility" that defendants may have had access to plaintiff's book. In and of itself, such a bare possibility is insufficient to create a genuine issue of whether defendants copied plaintiff's book.

Is this result consistent with *Bright Tunes v. Harrisongs Music*?

3. Contrast the judicial view of the creative process in *Selle v. Gibb* with the view in *Bright Tunes* above. Would the judges in *Selle v. Gibb* be likely to find subconscious infringement in *Bright Tunes*? Is there a difference between the factual background of those cases?

4. An interesting variation on the same theme can be seen in *Fantasy, Inc. v. Fogerty*, 664 F. Supp. 1345 (N.D. Cal. 1987). John Fogerty was the lead singer and songwriter for Creedence Clearwater Revival, one of the major bands of the late 1960s and early 1970s. In 1970, Fogerty wrote the song "Run Through the Jungle," which was part of a hit Creedence album that year. Under the terms of his contract with Fantasy Records, the band's music recording firm, Fogerty transferred the copyright in the song to Fantasy but retained a contractual right to half the royalties it earned. In the mid-1970s, Creedence split up and litigation ensued with Fantasy about what had happened to their money. Fantasy's principal owner, Saul Zaentz, moved from the music to the movie industry, where he produced hits such as *One Flew Over the Cuckoo's Nest, Amadeus,* and *The English Patient.*

In the mid-1980s, Fogerty began a comeback with Warner Records. One of the songs on his hit album, *Centerfield,* was "Old Man Down the Road." Fantasy and Zaentz claimed that this song illegally copied "Jungle." Though the lyrics were totally different, both songs were examples of Fogerty's "swamp rock" genre, a variation on traditional blues music. There were both significant similarities and differences in the sounds of the two songs. Fogerty testified that while he had written "Jungle," he had not listened to it for more than a decade because of his feelings about the breakup of Creedence and the rift with Fantasy.

What is the appropriate legal treatment of a case such as this? Should the fact that an author clearly has "access" to his own work mean that the current owners have correspondingly less need to establish *substantial* similarity (on an "inverse ratio" theory)? Is application of an "unconscious" creation theory here (as well as in *Bright Tunes*) compatible with the "independent creativity" rights of Fogerty (or George Harrison)? Similar legal issues have arisen in the world of fine art. *See, e.g., Franklin Mint Corp. v. National Wildlife Art Exchange,* 575 F.2d 62 (3d Cir. 1978). Suppose, by analogy, that the great French Impressionist painter Monet had sold the copyright as well as the canvas of his first painting of the Cathedral in Rouen. Should that have barred Monet from doing his many later artistic treatments of the same scene, with their subtle changes in time of day and lighting?

5. How would a plaintiff go about proving that "the similarity [between the plaintiff's work and the allegedly infringing work] is of a type which will preclude any explanation other than that of copying," as the court in *Selle v. Gibb* requires? In the view of the *Selle v. Gibb* court, can there ever be "striking similarity" such that access will be presumed, or is some sort of proof always required? If two works are truly strikingly similar, would it make more sense for the defendant to have to prove that it did *not* have access?

6. Access issues also arise with respect to film productions. Bryant Moore sued James Cameron, Twentieth Century Fox, and Lightstorm Entertainment, alleging that the film *Avatar* was substantially similar to two

of his screenplays, *Aquatica* and *Descendants: The Pollination*. Moore claimed that he had previously sent the screenplays to both Cameron and Lightstorm. The Court, however, found that the director and studio did not have "access" to his work. Particularly persuasive was evidence that Cameron had drafted a detailed overview of the film prior to receiving Moore's work. *See Moore v. Lightstorm Entertainment, et al.*, 992 F. Supp.2d 543 (D. Md. 2014).

## 2. SUBSTANTIAL SIMILARITY: BOOKS, PLAYS, MOVIES

Substantial similarity between the copyrighted work and the alleged infringing work is the second requirement for a finding of infringement. The prevailing test for "substantial similarity" originated more than six decades ago, in *Nichols v. Universal Pictures Corporation*, 45 F.2d 119 (2d Cir. 1930). In *Nichols*, Judge Learned Hand undertook a detailed comparison of a play, *Abie's Irish Rose*, and a movie, *The Cohens and The Kellys*, which allegedly copied the play. Judge Hand first noted that copyright in literary works "cannot be limited literally to the text, else a plagiarist would escape by immaterial variations." He then explained the appropriate way to analyze whether works are substantially similar, articulating what is now known as the "abstractions" test for copyright infringement:

> Upon any work, and especially upon a play, a great number of patterns of increasing generality will fit equally well, as more and more of the incident is left out. The last may perhaps be no more than the most general statement of what the play is about, and at times might consist only of its title; but there is a point in this series of abstractions where they are no longer protected, since otherwise the playwright could prevent the use of his "ideas," to which, apart from their expression, his property is never extended. . . . Nobody has ever been able to fix that boundary, and nobody ever can. In some cases the question has been treated as though it were analogous to lifting a portion out of the copyrighted work; but the analogy is not a good one, because, though the skeleton is a part of the body, it pervades and supports the whole. In such cases we are rather concerned with the line between expression and what is expressed.

45 F.2d at 121. The court concluded that the movie did not infringe the play, noting that "[a] comedy based upon conflicts between Irish and Jews, into which the marriage of their children enters, is no more susceptible of copyright than the outline of *Romeo and Juliet*."

Years later, courts have not been able to improve on Judge Hand's test, which, as Judge Hand himself admitted, is "inevitably ad hoc."[i] What is crucial in all these cases is close scrutiny of the facts—the different versions of two scripts or the melodies in two songs—in light of the principles and policies of copyright law. The judge must make the initial judgment about whether an objective comparison of the two works, as dissected by the parties' experts and lawyers, permits a finding of substantial similarity. If the copying claim passes that test, the jury makes its judgment on the ultimate issue.

In some of these cases, the court found the copying to be obvious. For example, in 1975, Universal Studios released the hit movie *Jaws*. Five years later, Film Venture International released a movie called *Great White*. The two films shared the same general story idea about a great white shark attacking and terrorizing inhabitants of a town on the Atlantic coast. What established the illegal copying were striking resemblances in story details and characters. In both movies, a local politician was trying to play down news of the shark to help preserve local tourism. Both had a salty, English-accented skipper whose boat was used to hunt down the shark, but who was killed at the end. They also starred a police chief (played by Roy Scheider in *Jaws*) and shark expert (played by James Franciscus in *Great White*), each of whom had a blond wife and a child injured by the shark, who tried to warn their towns of the dangers, and eventually were able to kill the giant shark in essentially the same risky fashion. From start to finish, there were a host of similar incidents in the two movies. Indeed in several foreign countries, *Great White* was distributed under the title, *The Last Jaws*. The district judge quickly granted an injunction against the showing of *Great White* in the United States. *See Universal City Studios v. Film Ventures International*, 543 F. Supp. 1134 (C.D. Cal. 1982).

The movie *Shakespeare in Love* shows the complexities of those issues. In the same week in 1999 that its producers won the Oscar for Best Picture, they also received a copyright complaint filed by the popular novelist Faye Kellerman. A decade earlier, Kellerman had written a (not-so-best-selling) book *The Quality of Mercy*. As the movie later did, *Quality* portrayed William Shakespeare as a young, impoverished actor-playwright trying to develop his theatrical career in London while his wife and children lived in Stratford-on-Avon. Shakespeare develops a relationship with a young woman, Rebecca, whom he first met while she was dressed like a man. Rebecca's well-to-do Lopez family was then betrothing her to another man. Shakespeare and Rebecca begin an affair that inspired him to write *Romeo and Juliet*. While Rebecca applauds the

---

[i] *See generally*, Amy B. Cohen, *Copyright Law & the Myth of Objectivity: The Idea-Expression Dichotomy & the Inevitability of Artistic Value Judgments*, 66 Ind. L.J. 175 (1990).

unveiling of the play, she does marry her betrothed and leaves for another country. Shakespeare then writes his next play in her honor.

The above features of the book are certainly similar to what viewers later saw in the movie: both works had *Romeo and Juliet* being written in 1593, a period of theatrical unrest in London, though the play was actually written in 1595. But there were also some significant differences in the stories. In the movie, the woman Viola (played by Gwyneth Paltrow) was told to marry an impoverished aristocrat, Lord Wessex. Kellerman's novel had Rebecca's Jewish family (with her father, Queen Elizabeth's physician) betrothing her to her cousin Miguel, who was a gay man leading the effort to save Jews from the Spanish Inquisition. And rather than masquerading as a man to play Romeo in Shakespeare's new play (as Viola does in the movie), Rebecca plays a significant role in the Jewish rescue effort, while Shakespeare is investigating the murder of his playwright friend in London. Near the end of *Quality*, the Lopez family has to flee Britain for Egypt because the anti-Semitic Lord Essex has framed the father with attempting to poison the queen. Thus Shakespeare writes in her memory *The Merchant of Venice*, about the persecution of Jews. At the end of *Shakespeare in Love*, Viola and Lord Wessex depart for an American colony, and Shakespeare starts writing *Twelfth Night* about a woman beginning life on an Atlantic shore as the only survivor of a shipwreck.

Kellerman's lawyer, Barry Novak, applauded *Shakespeare's* winning of Oscars including Best Screenplay, but felt that award should have been for best "adapted," not "original," screenplay. One of the screenwriters, Tom Stoppard, responded that in Hollywood being sued is "one of the accolades of success." Several months later, the defense lawyers were unsuccessful in securing summary dismissal of the claim, with the judge in the unreported *Kellerman v. Miramax Films*, (C.D. Cal. 1999), saying that a full-blown investigation was needed about whether there was "substantial similarity" between those two works. As typically happens in these lawsuits, the parties negotiated a confidential settlement whose actual terms are shaped by the legal background. That gives us the benefit of being able to discuss how a case such as this would have been resolved if it had gone to trial. Suppose that Kellerman had actually begun her career by authoring *The Quality of Mercy* just after *Shakespeare in Love* had won the Oscar; would there be a different treatment of the lawsuit that Miramax would certainly have filed against Kellerman?

The next case illustrates an application of Judge Hand's *Nichols* standard to a new set of facts.

## DENKER V. UHRY

United States District Court, Southern District of New York, 1992.
820 F. Supp. 722.

MICHAEL B. MUKASEY, DISTRICT JUDGE.

In these copyright infringement actions, plaintiff Henry Denker, author of the novel *Horowitz and Mrs. Washington* and the play of the same title, sues defendant Alfred Uhry, author of the play *Driving Miss Daisy* and the screenplay of the same title, and others involved in the production and distribution of the play and film versions of *Driving Miss Daisy*. Defendants have moved jointly for summary judgment on the issue of improper appropriation. . . .

I.

Plaintiff is a respected and prolific author. He has written 24 novels, more than 1,000 scripts for radio and television, screenplays for three feature films and teleplays for 12 network specials. Seven of his plays have been produced on Broadway and two at the Kennedy Center for Performing Arts in Washington D.C. Plaintiff's *Horowitz and Mrs. Washington*, the subject of these lawsuits, originally was published as a novel in 1979 by G.P. Putnam's Sons and then as a condensed book by Reader's Digest in 1980. Later rewritten for the stage, *Horowitz and Mrs. Washington* had a run of seven performances at the Joshua Golden Theater on Broadway in April 1980.

Alfred Uhry, a defendant in both actions, has been writing lyrics, plays and screenplays since 1958. *Driving Miss Daisy*, his Pulitzer Prize winning play, first was produced in New York by defendant Playwrights Horizons in 1987. . . . Adapted for the screen by Uhry in 1988, *Driving Miss Daisy* won four Academy Awards including Best Picture and Best Screenplay. . . .

*A. Horowitz and Mrs. Washington*

Plaintiff's works depict the relationship between Samuel Horowitz, a crusty, bigoted, 72-year-old Jewish man and Harriet Washington, his black physical therapist. The play is set in New York City during July 1977. The action in the novel takes place over a few months sometime in the late 1970's.

Early in the novel, and at the beginning of the play, Horowitz, recovering from a stroke, is brought home from the hospital to his Upper West side apartment by his son Marvin Hammond. Immediately apparent is Horowitz's hostility to the non-white, non-Jewish world. We learn at the outset that he believes, notwithstanding his doctor's insistence to the contrary, that his stroke was precipitated by an earlier mugging at the hands of a gang of "black bastards," and that his doorman, Juan, who refuses to accept a tip because of Horowitz's illness, is really a "shrewd little Puerto Rican . . . setting him up for bigger tips."

Upon arriving at his apartment, Horowitz is horrified to learn that Marvin and his sister Mona Fields have hired Harriet Washington, a "schvartzer," to assist in his rehabilitation. "You can't trust them!" he warns his son. "They mug me, slash me, give me a stroke. . . ." Marvin, however, is adamant, and Horowitz relents when he learns the alternative is a nursing home.

The next few sequences in both novel and play depict Mrs. Washington's patient but firm attempts to overcome Horowitz's hostility and proceed with his physical therapy. Mrs. Washington, to whom Horowitz refers as the "Black Hitler," insists that Horowitz perform a variety of tasks designed to rehabilitate his hand and leg, including cutting his food, crumpling newspapers, shuffling cards, walking, and buttoning his clothes. The nature of Denker's work and its characters is illustrated by the following exchange from the play [which culminates with Horowitz saying] . . . "There is nothing worse than an educated Negro."

Despite Horowitz's offensive manner, Mrs. Washington refuses to quit because the job allows her to help her widowed daughter who is raising two children.

As the novel and play progress, Horowitz increasingly is impressed by Mrs. Washington's integrity and determination, and his attitude towards her gradually softens. During a visit to Central Park the two talk of the loss of their respective spouses. Later Horowitz, who is saddened by eating alone in the dining room where he used to eat with his wife, asks Mrs. Washington if she would join him for dinner. When Mrs. Washington agrees to have coffee while Horowitz eats, it is the first time she sees him smile. Eventually, as the friendship develops Horowitz's racial remarks become more humorous than hostile and he uses them, albeit awkwardly and insensitively, in an attempt to express his growing admiration for Mrs. Washington. Later . . . New York City erupts in rioting and looting during a citywide electrical blackout. The following morning, Mrs. Washington returns to Horowitz's apartment visibly upset. Mrs. Washington's grandson Conrad, after listening to his grandmother's recent complaints of being unable to sleep because of the heat, tried to steal an air conditioner and was arrested. Moved by the story, Horowitz calls his son Marvin, a lawyer, and demands he help Conrad. When Mrs. Washington expresses her appreciation, Horowitz replies, it is "little enough to do for a friend."

A lawyer from Marvin's firm secures Conrad's release with "just a warning." In the novel, Horowitz, Mrs. Washington and her grandchildren celebrate by having dinner at a French restaurant and attending a Shakespeare play in Central Park. In both the novel and play, Horowitz gives Conrad a gold coin that he received from his father on his bar mitzvah. He tells Conrad that when he is angered by his inability to be helpful to his mother and grandmother the coin will serve as a reminder that the answer is hard work.

[A week later Conrad is stabbed. Horowitz assumes the injury took place in the course of a drug deal and says that Conrad should be "locked up with the other animals." Mrs. Washington tells Horowitz that in fact Conrad was stabbed by two men trying to steal the gold coin, and she then storms out in anger. Later that evening, alone, tired, and embarrassed, Horowitz ignores his low cholesterol diet and orders rich food and drink from his delicatessen. He then suffers a mild heart attack. However, driven by the fear of being moved by his daughter to a San Diego home for the aged, and helped by Mrs. Washington, Horowitz experiences remarkable recovery.]

* * *

At the end of the novel and play, Mrs. Washington informs Horowitz that she must leave to care for other patients. Horowitz gives Mrs. Washington "her pinochle winnings"—a sizable gift for her grandchildren's education—and the two vow to remain friends. The novel's final scene occurs almost one year after Horowitz's stroke. Unbeknownst to Horowitz, Mrs. Washington watches as he walks to and from the synagogue to honor the anniversary of his wife's death.

### *B. Driving Miss Daisy*

Uhry's *Driving Miss Daisy* tells the story of Daisy Werthan, an elderly, Jewish woman, and her 25-year relationship with Hoke Coleburn, her black chauffeur. Set in Atlanta between 1948 and 1973, *Driving Miss Daisy* is a distinctively southern story. Daisy is a refined southern woman, who, like Horowitz, is strong-willed and struggles to maintain her independence in the face of advancing age. Hoke, a product of the segregated south, is uneducated but possessed of a strong sense of dignity and, together with Daisy, adjusts to advancing age and changing times. Uhry's works begin with Daisy, 72 years old, inadvertently putting her car in reverse and crashing into her neighbor's yard. In the next scene in the film, and the first in the play, Daisy and Boolie, her 40-year-old son, argue about whether Daisy should continue to drive. Despite his mother's protests, Boolie hires Hoke Coleburn as her chauffeur.

Initially, Daisy ignores Hoke. She walks and takes public transportation rather than being driven. When Hoke attempts to perform household chores to relieve his boredom, Daisy demands that he stop. In both the movie and the play, Hoke eventually convinces Daisy to allow him to drive her to the supermarket. Daisy begins barking out orders from the moment she gets into the car. She accuses Hoke of speeding although he is driving 19 miles an hour in a 35-mile-an-hour zone; she becomes panic stricken when Hoke decides to take a more direct route to the supermarket than the one Daisy is used to; she demands he park the car in the shade; and she takes the keys when entering the supermarket. While Daisy is shopping Hoke calls Boolie to tell him he drove Daisy to the market: "Yassuh, only took six days. Same time it take the Lawd to make the worl'."

In a subsequent scene, Daisy telephones Boolie early in the morning and insists that he come to the house immediately. When Boolie arrives, Daisy triumphantly displays evidence of a missing can of salmon as proof that Hoke is stealing from her. Shortly thereafter, Hoke arrives for work, and before either Daisy or Boolie can mention the missing salmon, Hoke hands Daisy a new can to replace the salmon he had eaten the previous day. An embarrassed Daisy quickly bids Boolie good-bye.

We next see Daisy tending to her husband's grave on what is referred to in the screenplay as a "full, fuzzy-green, warm morning." She asks Hoke, who is standing nearby, to put a pot of azaleas on Leo Bauer's grave. Hoke cannot locate the Bauer grave and, deeply embarrassed, is forced to admit to Daisy that he is unable to read. Daisy, formerly an elementary school teacher, teaches Hoke to sound out the name Bauer. Throughout the works Daisy helps Hoke learn to read and write.

* * *

A few years later, we see Hoke and Boolie discussing the new car Boolie bought for Daisy. Hoke tells Boolie he bought Daisy's old car from a dealer. Although he could have saved money by buying it directly from Daisy, Hoke tells Boolie "yo' mama in my business enough as it is. I ain' studyin' makin' no monthly car payments to her. Dis mine the regular way."

In the film we next see Daisy and Hoke on the way to Mobile, Alabama to visit Daisy's relatives. While they are picnicking on the side of the road two Alabama state troopers pull over. The troopers inspect Hoke's drivers license and the car registration. Walking away, one comments: "An old nigger and an old Jew woman takin off down the road together. Now that is one sorry sight." The other replies: "I'll tell you one sorrier. They're sitting in a Cadillac and I'm sittin' next to you."

Later in the journey, Hoke tells Daisy that he has to stop the car to "make water." When Daisy tells him to wait until they arrive. Hoke drives on a minute and then abruptly stops the car. He tells Daisy quietly but firmly: "I ain' no dog and I ain' no chile and I ain' jes' a back of the neck you look at while you goin' wherever you want to go. I am a man nearly seventy-two years old and I know when my bladder full and I gettin' out dis car and goin' off down the de road like I got to do. And I'm takin' de car key dis time. And that's de end of it."

We next see Hoke in Boolie's office at the Werthan Company telling Boolie that Boolie's cousin Jeannette Lewis has offered him a job. Hoke indicates that it "got him thinking." When Boolie offers a raise to sixty-five dollars a week, Hoke counters with seventy-five and Boolie agrees. As Hoke leaves Boolie's office he tells him it "feel good" to have "people fightin' over you."

After an unstated passage of time, we join a frightened Daisy alone in her home during a winter ice storm. To Daisy's surprise, Hoke shows up for work. Because they are unable to drive, Daisy asks Hoke to keep her company for the day. He agrees and lights a fire. While Daisy "sits contented in her chair" the focus shifts to Boolie who is calling to check up on Daisy. He offers to visit her once the storm subsides, but Daisy declines because Hoke is with her. When Daisy describes Hoke as "very handy," Boolie is startled and remarks that he has never heard his mother "say loving things about Hoke before."

Some years later, Hoke and Daisy are caught in a traffic jam on the way to synagogue. Hoke, who has asked a police officer, informs Daisy that the synagogue was bombed. Distressed, Daisy vehemently insists that it must have been the conservative or orthodox synagogue, rather than the reform synagogue she attends, that was the intended target. Hoke replies: "It doan' matter to them people. A Jew is a Jew to them folks. Jes like light or dark we all the same nigger." Daisy begins to cry.

In the next sequence, Boolie tells Daisy that he cannot accompany her to a United Jewish Appeal dinner at which Martin Luther King will be speaking. Boolie explains that his business would be threatened if associates believed he supported Martin Luther King, and suggests that Daisy invite Hoke. On the way to the dinner Daisy mentions the ticket to Hoke. Hoke, offended by the last-minute invitation, refuses: "Next time you ask me someplace, ask me regular. . . . Things changin', but they ain't change all that much."

Several years pass. Hoke arrives at the house to find Daisy, who is 90, overwrought. She is searching frantically for her students' homework and insists that she is late for school. After calling Boolie, Hoke calms Daisy down. Daisy eventually regains her composure and tells Hoke that he is her best friend. The scene fades with Daisy and Hoke silently holding hands.

The final scenes take place on Thanksgiving two years later. In the film, we first see the outside of Daisy's home with a real estate agent's "For Sale" sign an the lawn and a "sold" sticker pasted over the sign. Boolie, 65 years old, is walking through the house when Hoke, 85, enters. The two briefly walk through the house and then leave to visit Daisy who has been living at a nursing home. When they arrive the patients are finishing their dinner. Daisy is sitting at a table vacantly staring into space when Hoke and Boolie join her. When Daisy does not respond, Boolie starts to make some forced small talk with Hoke. Daisy, who either has been listening or has just become lucid, tells Boolie that Hoke has come to see her not him and sends Boolie to "charm the nurses."

Daisy, regaining for a moment her feisty manner, ensures that Boolie is still paying Hoke. Hoke notices that Daisy has not eaten her pumpkin pie. The play and movie close with Hoke carefully cutting the pie and feeding it to her.

## II.

* * *

### *A. Theme*

The summary judgment standard is easier stated than applied. There is no bright line rule to distinguish between idea and expression, and in comparing works of fiction the distinction "is especially elusive." The inquiry, however, is not without its guiding principles. [The court synopsized Judge Learned Hand's approach in *Nichols v. Universal Pictures*, and noted that *Nichols* "also involv[ed] ethnic conflict depicted on the stage and screen."]

* * *

In the case at hand, as in *Nichols*, there are indeed similarities between the works. Each is about an elderly, white Jewish person, who, in the face of advancing age and resulting loss of independence, requires the assistance of a black helper, and after initial resistance, develops a friendship with the helper. Beyond this level of abstraction, however, the works are markedly dissimilar.

*Horowitz and Mrs. Washington*, which spans one month in the play and several months in the novel, tells the story of the crass, opinionated Horowitz, who with Mrs. Washington's help quickly overcomes his prejudice and the physical handicaps and threatened loss of independence caused by age. Evident throughout the work are racial tensions as they occur in the cultural and ethnic mix of New York City. In addition to Horowitz's overt racism, such tensions manifest themselves in the urban problems that form the background of the work such as the street crime that is the cause of much of Horowitz's fear and which has taken the life of Mrs. Washington's son-in-law.

By contrast, *Driving Miss Daisy* spans 25 years in the deep south and although plaintiff relies heavily on the fact that it too depicts the development of a friendship between an elderly Jewish character and a black helper, *Driving Miss Daisy* is defined by its setting. The political and social climate in the post-war South is evident in all aspects of the work from the character's personalities—Daisy's refinement, Hoke's lack of education and initial subservience—to the events that cause that relationship to develop—the bombing of the synagogue, the racism of the state troopers, Martin Luther King's speech. Similarly, because of the 25-year span of the work, the theme of aging is expressed differently. Whereas Horowitz is handicapped by the sudden onset of illness and eventually regains his independence, in *Driving Miss Daisy* the audience sees Hoke and Daisy age slowly over time with the inevitable result that at the works' close Daisy, unlike Horowitz, is unable to overcome the physical effects of her advanced age.

Plaintiff is correct in his assertion that racism is a major theme in both [works]. However, the expression of this theme differs. Horowitz is knowingly and overtly racist, believing that the men who assaulted him and the residents of Harlem who took advantage of the blackout to loot and riot are typical of all blacks. Eventually, through his interaction with Mrs. Washington, he learns "that you can no more make a general rule about blacks than you can about Jews." Daisy, by contrast, resists all suggestions that she harbors racist attitudes. When Boolie compares her resistance to Hoke to the racism of other southern whites, she responds: "Why, Boolie! What a thing to say! I'm not prejudiced! Aren't you ashamed?" Yet, evident in instances such as Daisy's inability to invite Hoke to the Martin Luther King dinner, is that Daisy has to some extent been affected by her environment. The overt racism in *Driving Miss Daisy* comes from outside the relationship in the attitude of the state troopers and the bombing of synagogue and forms the background of the work. *Driving Miss Daisy* is concerned primarily with Daisy's growing awareness of her own attitudes and eventual ability to recognize Hoke as a friend, set against this background. In essence, unlike plaintiff's works, Uhry's works address the racism in a society in addition to the racism in a particular person.

### *B. Total Concept and Feel*

The works also differ in total concept and feel; such a difference provides a proper basis for determining that a defendant's work does not infringe a plaintiff's. Despite its serious themes, *Horowitz and Mrs. Washington* is principally a comedy. Horowitz, although a bigot, is a comedic character. His racial and ethnic slurs, interaction with Mona, temper tantrums and social commentary on topics ranging from detente to The New York Times are used by Denker for comedic purposes as well as to establish Horowitz's ignorance and insensitivity. By the end of the works . . . even the normally proper Mrs. Washington joins in some of Horowitz's antics. By contrast, *Driving Miss Daisy* is more of a poignant and sentimental work. Conspicuously absent in defendants' works is the television situation comedy tone so prevalent in *Horowitz and Mrs. Washington*.

* * *

### *C. Plot*

Plaintiff attempts to overcome these differences in theme, setting and tone by pointing to certain discrete similarities between the works. The purported similarities, however, either involve unprotected scenes-à-faire—"scenes that necessarily result from the choice of a setting or situation"—or are not similarities at all.

Plaintiff points out that each of the works opens with an "accident" befalling the main character. Notwithstanding plaintiff's recommendation that the Court "take judicial notice of the common use of the term 'cerebral accident' to refer to a stroke" to claim that the events are similar in that both are "accidents" is less an argument than a pun; the events are distinct not only as expression but also in the ideas they express. Horowitz is mugged and subsequently suffers a stroke while Daisy inadvertently drives her car into her neighbor's yard. These are not similar events. Further, the underlying ideas are dissimilar. Although in both *Horowitz and Mrs. Washington* and *Driving Miss Daisy* these events give rise to the need for a helper, Horowitz overcomes the physical effects of the stroke whereas Daisy's accident is the first manifestation of the aging process that ultimately destroys her independence. Thus, at most plaintiff has alleged that Uhry used a somewhat similar plot device to that employed in *Horowitz and Mrs. Washington*, which does not constitute infringement.

Similarly, plaintiff maintains that the plot device used by Uhry to depict Hoke's devotion to Daisy is identical to that used by plaintiff to depict Mrs. Washington's loyalty to Horowitz. In plaintiff's work, Mrs. Washington travels to Horowitz's apartment despite a citywide power outage and climbs 11 flights of stairs to do so. In what plaintiff characterizes as a remarkably similar scene, Hoke reports for work despite an ice storm and hazardous driving conditions. Although plaintiff is correct in the sense that in both works the helper demonstrates loyalty by traveling to work at some personal risk, such generalized plot devices, like the so-called "accidents" discussed above, are not entitled to copyright protection. In *Smith v. Weinstein*, 578 F. Supp. 1297 (S.D.N.Y.), aff'd without op., 738 F.2d 419 (2d Cir. 1984), both plaintiff's screenplay and defendant's allegedly infringing movie included scenes wherein convicts escaped during a rodeo. In granting summary judgment for defendant, Judge Sofaer reasoned that "the development of the rodeo as an escape vehicle is protectible, but only at a level that particularizes the general into characters, details, and events." Here defendant Uhry's use of a plot device that differs as to "characters, details, and events" does not amount to infringement. Plaintiff is not entitled to copyright protection for all instances of misfortune that befall the elderly or all demonstrations of dedication by a servant or helper.

I fail also to see a similarity in expression between Mrs. Washington surreptitiously watching Horowitz walk to synagogue at the end of *Horowitz and Mrs. Washington* and Hoke visiting Daisy at the nursing home at the end of *Driving Miss Daisy*. Although both are methods of expressing the helper's devotion, it is clear that this idea is expressed in dissimilar fashion. In fact, the differences underscore the authors' divergent treatment of the age theme. Mrs. Washington can watch from afar because she has helped Horowitz regain his independence and her assistance is no longer needed. Uhry, however, depicts age as depriving Daisy of her independence. Hoke, himself unable to drive because of failing eyesight, must feed his friend who, because of physical infirmities caused by age, is unable to care for herself.

Plaintiff relies on several other similarities between the works that amount, if anything, to similarities in general themes or ideas. For instance, citing Daisy teaching Hoke to read and write and Horowitz giving Mrs. Washington a check to further the education of her grandchildren, plaintiff argues that "striking is the fact that they (Daisy and Horowitz) assist both Hoke and Mrs. Washington in ways that are educational." Plaintiff also points to the fact that both Hoke and Mrs. Washington previously had worked for Jewish families. In *Driving Miss Daisy* Uhry's only use of this fact is when Hoke tells Boolie that he worked for Judge Stone for seven years and finds that despite what people say, Jews are quite generous. By contrast, it is evident in plaintiff's works that Mrs. Washington has a genuine appreciation for Jewish culture. While in the employ of the Rosengartens, or in the play the Schenks, Mrs. Washington took the time not only to learn to cook traditional dishes which she serves to Horowitz but also to learn about Jewish culture. Plaintiff uses this as a foil for Horowitz's racism. For instance, early in the play, Mrs. Washington tells Horowitz a story about a tzaddik, a righteous scholar, which she learned while working for the Schencks. Horowitz, angry at what he perceives as Mrs. Washington's flippant reference to the tzaddik, explains that a tzaddik is "[a] scholar, a philosopher, with enormous love of all God's creatures, even the smallest." Mrs. Washington retorts: "And the blackest?" Again, although plaintiff may have established that the works used like themes or ideas, here the helper's previous exposure to Jews and Judaism, the expression differs.

The remainder of the similarities alleged by plaintiff involve scenes-B-faire. . . . It is well-accepted that copyright protection, does not extend "to 'stock' themes commonly linked to a particular genre."

* * *

Because, based on the differences discussed above, no reasonable juror could find the works substantially similar and because the few similarities between *Horowitz and Mrs. Washington* and *Driving Miss Daisy* involve non-copyrightable elements of plaintiff's work, summary judgment on the issue of improper appropriation of the work as a whole is warranted.

*D. Characters*

[The court held that the plaintiff did not establish substantial similarity between the main or supporting characters in the two works.]

* * *

Complaint dismissed.

---

Courts regularly distinguish unprotected ideas from protected expression, but it is important to appreciate the analytical point that, absent a literal reproduction of the original, the second work is usually a taking of the ideas out of the first. Thus, the judge found that *Great White* had taken enough of the pattern of ideas from Jaws to make the former a concrete copy of the latter. In *Denker*, by contrast, the judge concluded that the story pattern reflected in both *Driving Miss Daisy* and *Horowitz and Mrs. Washington* was sufficiently limited and abstract to preclude an infringement verdict. What courts have to do, then, is to trace a rather delicate line between protecting enough of the original story line to ensure the returns from and incentives for its creative authorship, but not protecting too much of the story's concepts so as to block the creation of new stories that build on key features of their predecessors.

Another example is *Sandoval v. New Line Cinema*, 147 F.3d 215 (2d Cir. 1998), involving the hit movie *Seven*, starring Morgan Freeman and Brad Pitt investigating a fictional photographer murderer. Without having secured his permission the New Line people had placed ten copies of photographer Sandoval's self-portraits on the wall of the suspect where, from a distance, they were shown briefly while affixed to a light box. The Second Circuit dismissed the copyright claim because, since "Sandoval's photographs appear fleetingly and are obscured, severely out of focus and virtually unidentifiable, we find the use of those photographs to be de minimis." 147 F.3d at 219.

In the literature on this subject, an example often used is the comparison between Shakespeare's immortal *Romeo and Juliet* and Stephen Sondheim's and Leonard Bernstein's Academy-Award winning *West Side Story*. Obviously Shakespeare's heirs did not bring a copyright suit, because *Romeo and Juliet* had been authored long before copyright law was even invented. Suppose, though, that *Romeo and Juliet* had been written recently enough to enjoy copyright protection. Notwithstanding the obvious differences between a drama set in Italy in the sixteenth century and a musical set in New York in the mid-twentieth century, there are definite resemblances between the story lines in the two works. As detailed in the leading treatise, *Nimmer on Copyright* (1995), § 13.03 [A], 36–37, in both works a boy and a girl who are members of rival groups meet at a dance and fall in love; while the girl is committed to someone else, nonetheless they exchange marriage vows with each other; in an encounter between their groups, a relative of the girl kills the boy's best friend after the boy has stayed his friend's hand to try to prevent violence; angry at what he has seen, the boy kills the girl's relative and goes into hiding; the girl tries to send a message to the boy about how they can get together, but the message never reaches him; instead, after receiving the erroneous word that the girl is dead, the boy kills himself (or allows himself to be killed). Even granting the huge number of differences in the events, setting, and tone of *Romeo and Juliet* and *West Side Story*, does that common story pattern amount to just an unprotected "idea" or a protected "expression?"

In 2005, a judgment had to be made on that score about Dan Brown's *The Da Vinci Code*. The author (Lewis Perdue) of two previous relatively low-selling books, *The Da Vinci Legacy* (1983) and *Daughter of God* (2000), accused Brown in the media of stealing more than 50 of his story lines, including making the same historical error of what Leonardo himself had done with his *The Codex Leicestor*. Making regular threats to sue Brown and publisher Random House and expecting an apology and substantial compensation, instead Perdue found himself to be the defendant in a suit filed by Brown seeking a declaratory judgment that he had not engaged in illegal copying. Purdue responded with a countersuit and a claim of $150 million in damages. In *Brown v. Perdue*, 76 U.S.P.Q.2d 1012 (S.D.N.Y. 2005), the court provided an extensive examination of the story lines and characters, noting that the test for "substantial similarity" was "whether an average lay person would recognize the alleged copy as having been appropriated from the copyrighted work." Carefully examining these novels and finding that the ordinary reader would not feel that way, the court found that the novels "involve the unprotectable idea of a mystery thriller set against a religious backdrop." Perdue's were more action stories "with several gun fights and violent deaths," while *The Da Vinci Code* was essentially "an intellectual complex treasure hunt rather than a basically physical adventure." As we saw at the start of this chapter, that did not preclude them from being sued by the authors of *Holy Blood, Holy Grail*.

## BEAL V. PARAMOUNT PICTURES

United States District Court, Northern District of Georgia, 1992.
806 F. Supp. 963.

CARNES, DISTRICT JUDGE.

* * *

Alveda King Beal describes her *The Arab Heart*, on its cover, as a "historical tale of romance and adventure." The book's protagonist is Sharaf Ammar Hakim Riad, an Arabian prince in the country of Whada.

The book opens with Sharaf riding on a horse across the desert, contemplating his grandfather's, the king's, "command" that he travel to the United States to "attend an American college with a great reputation for technical training." Whada is a poor country, and the king wants the prince to receive a technical education that will enable him to improve the country's oil production. Initially reluctant, Sharaf agrees to go and decides to attend the Georgia Institute of Technology (Georgia Tech) in Atlanta, where he lives in a comfortable boarding house near campus with a roommate and the bodyguards that the king has sent with him. Meanwhile, Sharaf's grandfather has had a long war with his half-brother, Mansur, who repeatedly launches terrorist attacks against the king.

At Christmas break, the king orders Sharaf home, under the guise of a trip with his roommate, to prepare him to lead the country should the king be killed. In the spring, Sharaf returns to Whada to help fight Mansur in a battle in which Sharaf and the king kill one of Mansur's sons. Sharaf then finishes the year at Georgia Tech.

While Sharaf is in Atlanta, he first dates a woman named Claire Eastman, a cold, opportunistic, white woman from a wealthy family in Boston. Sharaf and Claire share a passionate, extremely physical relationship and Sharaf considers proposing marriage to her, but is concerned whether Claire, whom he suspects of harboring racial prejudices, would be tolerant of and adapt to the very different cultural traditions of Whada.

At the same time that he is involved with Claire, Sharaf becomes interested in another woman, Flora Johnston, a quiet, reserved woman from an affluent family in Savannah. Flora is the offspring of a marriage between a white man and a black woman. Smitten with Sharaf, Flora attempts to gain his attention by performing a sensual belly dance at a Halloween party at which Sharaf and a jealous Claire attend. Although her provocative dance does succeed in capturing the attention of Sharaf, he believes that his feelings for Flora are "brotherly" and he continues his relationship with Claire, still pondering whether he should ask her to marry him.

Sharaf's dilemma is resolved later when he overhears Claire telling a friend that she would never accept Whadan customs. At that point, he ceases his involvement with Claire and begins a passionate relationship with Flora.

Notwithstanding his grandfather's previously expressed wish that Sharaf agree to an arranged marriage in Whada, four weeks later Sharaf and Flora marry during a small, ceremony in Savannah, after which they return to Whada. In Whada, Flora has difficulty adjusting to the Whadan customs, particularly the treatment of women. Indeed, Sharaf's grandfather, the king, will not accept her into the family until she bears a son. Flora is also concerned about the social conditions in the country, particularly the poverty.

Flora and Sharaf's relationship becomes extremely strained when Flora, who is pregnant at the time, discovers Sharaf in bed with a servant girl. Flora bears a son, and while she and Sharaf are still estranged, Mansur attacks once again, trying, with the assistance of Sharaf's servant girl paramour, to kidnap his and Flora's infant son. In the ensuing altercation, Mansur and the king are killed, and Sharaf stabs the servant girl.

At the end of the book, Sharaf has become the king of Whada. Flora and Sharaf also seem to reconcile, although, because Sharaf's father has advised him that he may continue to pursue extramarital affairs, as long as he is more discreet, the reader is left with the impression that Sharaf has not totally renounced his philandering ways.

*Coming to America* begins by panning miles of lush African jungle. The movie opens on the day of the twenty-first birthday of Prince Akeem of Zamunda, a seemingly opulent and exotic kingdom. On that day, Akeem is to marry the woman that his parents, the king and queen, have chosen for him.

Postponing the wedding, Prince Akeem convinces his father that he should have 40 days to "sow his royal oats." He intends to go to America to find a woman who thinks for herself and who will love him for himself, not for his title or his wealth. His father agrees, sending along Akeem's best friend, Semmi. In deciding which city would be the best place to find his wife, the future Queen, Akeem decides that the appropriate locale for such a search is logically Queens, New York.

Arriving in Queens, Akeem rents a rat-infested apartment. Before he even has time to carry his luggage to his apartment, the residents of the neighborhood steal all his belongings, a fact which does not seem to perturb Akeem. Indeed, Akeem tries to hide his identity as a wealthy prince throughout his stay in New York.

In searching for a wife, Akeem and Semmi first go to bars in Queens to meet women, but instead meet only comically inappropriate women there. Another character tells Akeem to go to a Black Awareness Rally to meet a "nice girl." He sees Lisa McDowell there, likes her, and decides to acquire a job in her father's fast-food restaurant in order to meet her. While Akeem and Semmi work in the restaurant, humorous events occur, including Akeem's foiling of an armed robbery with a mop. Shortly thereafter, Lisa breaks up with her boyfriend because of his presumption in having her father announce their engagement at a social occasion, before he had even asked Lisa to marry him. Akeem and Lisa then begin to date. Several times, in comical scenes, Akeem tries to hide his true identity from Lisa.

Semmi, however, who has tired greatly of the poor lifestyle that he and Akeem are leading, wires Prince Akeem's parents for money. Akeem's parents, the king and queen, became disturbed at the news of the impoverished life that Akeem is leading and come to Queens to check on him.

When Akeem's parents arrive, Lisa discovers his identity and, as a result, angrily turns down his marriage proposal. Akeem then heads home to Zamunda to enter into the marriage previously arranged by his parents. Akeem's parents have apparently intervened and persuaded Lisa to marry Akeem, however, for, in the last scene of the movie, at the moment that Akeem lifts the veil, expecting to see the face of the "arranged" bride, he instead is pleased to see that Lisa is his bride. Akeem and Lisa drive away to the cheers of jubilant Zamundan citizens and the smiles of their parents.

* * *

806 F. Supp. at 964–65.

---

The next judicial excerpts from an earlier case spell out both the plaintiff's script for a proposed television series, *The Coward*, and the pilot script for a 1965–66 series, *Branded*, which was alleged to have copied *The Coward*.

## FINK V. GOODSON-TODMAN ENTERPRISES, LTD.

Court of Appeal of California, Second Appellate District, 1970.
9 Cal.App.3d 996, 88 Cal. Rptr. 679.

REPPY, JUDGE.

* * *

Plaintiff's proposed program is called *The Coward*. Its basic theme is the concept that a person who has undergone an experience which casts his courage in doubt, both to himself and others, may have a continuing compulsion to place himself in positions of peril and, by his conduct in meeting the dangerous circumstances, to prove to himself and others that he was and is not a coward, that he does have the attribute of courage. The hero is Dundee. His initial motivating experience occurs in World War II when, as a young lieutenant, he takes command of a company at the time his superior officer is killed. The commander had received orders from General Patton not to surrender, but before dying he directs Dundee to use his best judgment in the deployment of his troops. Although, after Dundee took over, Patton's order is repeated over a loud-speaker, under circumstances wherein resistance would have meant annihilation, Dundee surrenders his company, asking the enemy commander to honor the Geneva convention with respect to his men. The enemy commander acknowledges that Dundee acted in good faith, but he ignores the convention except as to Dundee as an officer, and has all of Dundee's men machine-gunned to death. Dundee is court-martialled. His attorney gets him acquitted on the technicality that his superior's direction had relieved him of the obligation of following Patton's explicit command, it being found inconsequential whether or not he had heard the Patton order or had made the surrender in an effort to save the men from annihilation. Afterwards, Dundee tells his attorney that he really did not know if he [was] guilty or innocent, but the attorney, dropping a nickel in front of Dundee, says, "[Your] courage . . . is worth this much. . . ." The question of the validity of this aspersion rankles in Dundee's mind.

After the war Dundee becomes a police officer in Greenwich Village. The time setting for the depicted events is around 1960. Each episode finds Dundee involved in an encounter with crime, mostly murder. He conducts himself with daring and bravery. To remind himself of his psychological mission, he carries nickels and has the habit of tossing one away at the end of each exploit. Although he is admired by young recruits for his courage, there are those who know of his military experience and his reaction to it.

The motivating back story is briefly brought out in what is proposed as the signature for each episode, and it is fully depicted in a dream flashback included in the pilot script. In the presentation plaintiff indicates that through similar techniques the audience will be kept mindful of the back story and motivation for Dundee's conduct and attitude in the various episodes.

A segment of the presentation . . . advises that music unique to "The Village" will be a strong factor in depicting the atmosphere of Dundee's area of operations; and it makes the comparative observation, incidentally, that "[the] western has its 'ballad'."

The alleged offending series, which was telecast about five years after plaintiff submitted his proposed program to defendants, is called *Branded* (a title which plaintiff suggests means, when all is known, "branded as a coward"). The basic theme of the *Branded* series is the same as that of plaintiff's program. Its hero is McCord. His initial experience which ends up with him in perplexity about his courage occurs at a time when United States troops are battling American Indians in the early West. The company to which McCord is attached as a young officer comes under attack by a vastly superior force of Indians. McCord's commanding officer, who had had a distinguished career in the service, unfortunately has become senile. He does not appreciate the impossible odds; rather, in a dreamy trance of past exploits, he sees another glorious victory. When the situation is extremely desperate McCord, who out of devotion to his superior had been delaying the move, finally relieves him of command. Immediately thereafter the commander is killed. McCord starts a last-minute retreat, but it is too late. He is hit and put in a coma. The others are killed or are seriously wounded and ultimately die. McCord is the only survivor. He is court-martialled, apparently on the basis of a report by one of the dying men that he had run off from the affray. Out of respect for his beloved commander, he refuses to put up his only defense. He is found guilty. In the course of what is akin to an allocution he is stripped of military insignia and has his sword broken in front of him. The incident is publicized and McCord gets the reputation of being a coward. Although McCord is to be considered innocent in a sense, it is made known that he, himself, is not so sure. He feels that he did not have the inner courage to put the lives of the men above his concern for the reputation of his commanding officer. So, he is at least ambivalent about his courage and feels that he needs to prove to himself, as well as to others, that he has that attribute.

Each episode of *Branded* commences with a "signature" (or prologue), the scene of McCord being stripped of the emblem of his uniform and having his sword broken. The singing of a ballad is a prominent feature of the prologue. It tells that it was false that McCord had run off from the battle, but that, although such abstention will mark him as a coward, he will never reveal the truth. McCord carries the hilt part of the broken sword with him, obviously as a reminder of his life's mission. It is featured in such a way as to remind the audience of McCord's motivation.

McCord becomes an itinerant cowhand in the western frontier. The various episodes involve him in circumstances of danger and combat, wherein, in one way or another, he displays virility and courage, at times by way of restraint, at times in ultimate counter-aggression.

In addition to the signature sequence of McCord being drummed out of the service, there are flashbacks in some of the episodes to the Indian encounter by way of dream or recollection sequences.

* * *

88 Cal. Rptr. at 683–84.

---

The question of substantial similarity can be quite difficult to assess in the context of music. This is particularly true with respect to "intrinsic similarity." The below lawsuit involving Usher and Justin Bieber illustrates these difficulties.

## COPELAND V. BIEBER

United States Court of Appeals, Fourth Circuit, 2015.
789 F.3d 484.

HARRIS, CIRCUIT JUDGE.

Musician Devin Copeland ("Copeland"), together with his songwriting partner, appeals the dismissal of his copyright infringement claim against recording artists Justin Bieber and Usher Raymond IV. Copeland alleges that three recorded songs by the defendants, each titled "Somebody to Love," infringe upon his copyright over his own, earlier song of the same name. The district court granted the defendants' motions to dismiss on the ground that no reasonable jury could find Copeland's song and the defendants' songs sufficiently similar to give rise to liability for infringement. We disagree, and therefore vacate the district court's order and remand the case for further proceedings.

### I.

### A.

Because Copeland appeals from an order granting a motion to dismiss under Rule 12(b)(6) of the Federal Rules of Civil Procedure, we recount the facts as alleged by Copeland, accepting them as true for purposes of this appeal.

Copeland is a Virginia-based R & B singer and songwriter who performs under the name "De Rico." In 2008, together with his songwriting partner Mareio Overton, Copeland began writing and recording songs to perform on his upcoming album, *My Story II*. Among them was "Somebody to Love," the song that is the subject matter of this case (the "Copeland song"). Copeland registered a copyright for the *My Story II* songs, including "Somebody to Love," later that year.

In late 2009, Copeland entered into discussions with Sangreel Media ("Sangreel"), a company that recruits artists for record labels including Island Records, Sony Music, and RCA Records. Sangreel was interested in promoting Copeland's music, and Copeland turned over copies of *My Story II* so that Sangreel could provide promotional copies to its clients. Among the figures to whom Sangreel presented Copeland's music was Usher Raymond IV, a world-famous recording artist who performs under the name "Usher."

According to Copeland's complaint, Usher liked what he heard. Usher's mother and manager, Jonetta Patton ("Patton"), scheduled a conference call with Copeland, during which she informed Copeland that both she and Usher had listened to *My Story II,* and that they were interested in having Copeland re-record the album and join Usher on tour. Yet the plans never materialized, and that was the last Copeland heard from anyone in Usher's camp.

Within a few months of Copeland's phone conversation with Patton, however, Usher had recorded and posted on his YouTube channel a demo song also titled "Somebody to Love" (the "Usher demo song"). Usher did not commercially release this song, but instead allegedly brought it to his protégé and fellow recording artist, Justin Bieber ("Bieber"). Bieber recorded his own "Somebody to Love" (the "Bieber album song") and released it on his debut album, *My World 2.0,* in the spring of 2010. Bieber's "Somebody to Love" was a hit, peaking at number 15 on the U.S. Billboard Hot 100 chart. Finally, Bieber released a fourth and final "Somebody to Love," a remix with lead vocals by both himself and Usher (the "Bieber-Usher remix song") in June 2010. Bieber has continued to perform live versions of those songs while on tour.

* * *

A.

As noted above, intrinsic similarity is assessed from the perspective of a work's intended audience. *See Universal Furniture,* 618 F.3d at 435. That means that the first step in undertaking an analysis of intrinsic similarity is identifying the right audience. The district court concluded that the general public was the intended audience for the Copeland song, and we agree.

In *Dawson,* we clarified our intrinsic similarity analysis by introducing the "intended audience" formulation. Because a primary purpose of copyright law is to "protect[ ] a creator's market," we reasoned, the intrinsic similarity inquiry should be keyed to the impressions of the intended audience for a creator's work—the impressions that count for purposes of marketability. 905 F.2d at 734. So where the market for a given work consists of a discrete and specialized class, the reactions of a generic ordinary observer will not be particularly relevant. *See id.* But in most cases, we cautioned, the general public is in fact the intended audience, and "a court should be hesitant" to find otherwise. *Id* . at 737; *see Lyons,* 243 F.3d at 801.

Copeland argues that this case is the exception to the ordinary rule. According to Copeland, the intended audience for his song was not the general public but instead the "industry professionals" to whom he distributed his song by way of Sangreel. The "market" Copeland was trying to reach, in other words, was the Ushers of the world, and Copeland would be harmed if industry professionals believed his song was substantially similar to those of the defendants even if the general public saw no resemblance.

Like the district court, we are unpersuaded. It may be that Copeland intended to promote his music directly to industry professionals. But "[i]f . . . industry professionals reject [Copeland's] song because it is too similar to the [d]efendants' songs, it would be because those companies fear that the *public* will find the songs to be overly similar." J.A. 252 (emphasis in original). There is a reason that the *Dawson* formulation uses the word "audience," rather than "buyer" or "recipient": Ultimate marketability is not always determined by the impressions of a first-hand purchaser or recipient, but may sometimes rest on the impressions of third parties—the work's actual "audience"—whose preferences the buyer or recipient has in mind when acquiring the work.

Our decision in *Lyons* illustrates the point. There, we considered whether the intended audience for a purple dinosaur costume resembling the character "Barney" from the television series *Barney & Friends* was the adult performers who would buy the costumes or the young children they sought to entertain. 243 F.3d at 802. We concluded that it was the children's reactions that mattered to the intrinsic similarity inquiry, because even though they were not themselves the intended purchasers of the costumes, it was their impressions (or misimpressions) that could lead adults to buy the infringing costumes. *Id.* at 802–03. Adults might discern differences between the two costumes, but if children could not, then there would be no reason for adults to insist on the original—with the result that the "knock-off" costumes would cut into Barney's market and the profits of Barney's owner. *Id.* at 803. The same reasoning applies here. Though industry professionals may have been the intended direct recipients of Copeland's music, the impressions that matter are those of the general public that constitutes the market for popular music—because, as Copeland admits, J.A. 252, those are the impressions that industry professionals would have in mind in choosing whether to do business with Copeland.

Again, this should come as no surprise. When we left open in *Dawson* the possibility that the intended audience for a choral arrangement of a spiritual song was more specialized than the general public and might be limited to choral directors, we also made clear that we were crafting a narrow rule for exceptional circumstances. We specifically distinguished the subject matter there from popular music, for which we noted approvingly that courts "routinely" apply the lay observer test. *Dawson,* 905 F.2d at 737. That is because the intended audience for popular music is usually an ordinary listener or, put differently, the general public. And indeed, the entire premise of Copeland's case is that his song is substantially similar to one that appears on a multi-platinum album by one of the world's most recognizable popular music stars. This is not a case about niche audience appeal, and there is no reason to think of the "intended audience" as anything other than the general public.

B.

Finally, we come to the question at the heart of this case: Whether the songs at issue, assessed from the perspective of the intended audience—here, the general public—and taking into account their "total concept and feel," *Lyons,* 243 F.3d at 801, are sufficiently intrinsically similar to give rise to a valid infringement claim. The district court answered in the negative, holding that no reasonable jury could find the requisite intrinsic similarity. But under the applicable de novo standard of review, *see Peters,* 692 F.3d at 632, we must listen for ourselves and come to our own conclusion. And because the general public typically encounters popular music songs by hearing them from start to finish, we undertake that analysis by listening to the songs in their entirety and side by side, to determine whether a reasonable jury could find that they are subjectively similar.

1.

As a preliminary matter, we should clarify that the "songs" to which we refer include all three of the defendants' versions of "Somebody to Love": the Usher demo version, the Bieber album version, and the Bieber-Usher remix version. At oral argument, Copeland suggested that each of those songs must be considered individually, and separately compared to the Copeland song. We disagree. In our view, the defendants' three songs are sufficiently similar to each other that they may be grouped together, and the same intrinsic analysis applied to all. If any one of them fails to meet the threshold for intrinsic similarity, then all of them do.

The Bieber album song and the Bieber-Usher remix are to our ears identical; the only difference we can hear is that Bieber is the only singer featured on the album song, whereas Usher provides lead vocals in the second verse and backing vocals elsewhere on the remix. On the Usher demo song, Usher is the only singer featured, and that song is in a

different key than the others, presumably to accommodate his different vocal range. But the Usher demo song is otherwise in lock-step with the others down to minor details—everything from the lead singer's exclamation of "oh" in the introductory section to the distinctive synthesizer chords in the verses and the bass line in the pre-chorus. By the unscientific intrinsic standard, the three Bieber and Usher songs are not just substantially similar to one another; they are the same.

2.

We turn now to a comparison of the Copeland song with, collectively, the three Bieber and Usher songs. The district court acknowledged that the Usher and Bieber songs "have some elements in common" with the Copeland song. J.A. 253. But for the district court, what was dispositive was a significant difference in the overall "aesthetic appeal" of the respective songs. J.A. 254. We cannot agree. In our view, that analysis attaches too much weight to what the district court termed a difference in "mood" and "tone," and too little to similarities between the "element" of the songs—their choruses—that is most important.

First, if by "mood" and "tone" the district court meant genre, then we agree with this much: The Copeland song belongs to a different genre than the three Bieber and Usher songs. Though all fall under the same broad umbrella of popular music, the Copeland song is squarely within the R & B subgenre, while the Bieber and Usher songs would be labeled dance pop, perhaps with hints of electronica. Indeed, that difference is striking upon first listen, and at least as a linguistic matter, the very fact of these different genres might be thought to make the songs different in "concept and feel," *Lyons,* 243 F.3d at 801, or, in the words of the district court, in "aesthetic appeal," J.A. 254.

But as Bieber's counsel conceded at oral argument, while genre may be relevant to intrinsic analysis of musical works, it cannot be dispositive under copyright law. For if a difference in genre were enough by itself to preclude intrinsic similarity, then nothing would prevent someone from translating, say, the Beatles' songbook into a different genre, and then profiting from an unlicensed reggae or heavy metal version of "Hey Jude" on the ground that it is different in "concept and feel" than the original. From Copeland's perspective, it may be true that the "aesthetic appeal" of an R & B song is different, in some sense, than that of a dance pop song—but if there is going to be a dance pop version of his R & B "Somebody to Love," then it is his to record or to license, so that he can reap the full return on his creative efforts. *Cf. Castle Rock Entm't, Inc. v. Carol Pub. Grp., Inc.,* 150 F.3d 132, 140 (2d Cir.1998) ("total concept and feel" analysis must take account of fact that works from different genres "must necessarily have a different concept and feel"). And by the same token, of course, were we to put too much stock in *identity* of genre at the intrinsic stage, we would risk deeming each successive work in a genre—whether it be R & B, ragtime, or bossa nova—an appropriation of the same-genre works that came before it.

Second, we do not doubt that the songs at issue here are in many respects dissimilar. And if substantial similarity were a purely quantitative inquiry, asking only whether the majority of the works in question overlapped, we would agree with the district court that no reasonable jury could find the requisite intrinsic similarity. For instance, while the Copeland song concludes with a repeated instrumental figure, the Bieber and Usher songs end more abruptly, after ad-libbed vocal lines. The Bieber and Usher songs include a post-chorus interval, with the lyric "I-I need somebody" sung in a syncopated manner, that has no equivalent in the Copeland song. And perhaps most significantly, the songs' verses feature different vocal melodies and beats as well as different lyrical content, with the Copeland verses lamenting the end of a relationship gone sour and the Bieber and Usher verses conveying the hope and optimism of the start of a relationship with an unidentified love interest. The district court may have had some or all of these in mind when it referred to differences in "mood, tone, and subject matter," J.A. 253, and we agree that taken numerically, the points of dissimilarity may well exceed the points of similarity.

But what that analysis fails to account for, we think, is the relative importance of these differences as compared to what the songs reasonably could be heard to have in common: their choruses. Even when quantitative majorities of two works bear little resemblance, courts routinely permit a finding of substantial similarity where the works share some especially significant sequence of notes or lyrics. *See Swirsky v. Carey,* 376 F.3d 841, 851 (9th Cir.2004) (overlap in first measure of chorus—seven total notes—enough to make pop songs substantially similar); *Fisher v. Dees,* 794 F.2d 432, 434 & n. 2 (9th Cir.1986) (similarity in first six measures of songs, amounting to twenty-nine seconds on a forty-minute album, enough to constitute appropriation of album); *Elsmere Music, Inc. v. Nat'l Broad. Co.,* 482 F.Supp. 741, 744 (S.D.N.Y.), *aff'd,* 623 F.2d 252 (2d Cir.1980) (four-note phrase accompanying lyrics "I love New York" protectable because it is "the heart of the composition"); *Santrayll v. Burrell,* No. 91 Civ. 3166, 1996 WL 134803, at *1–2 (S.D.N.Y. Mar.25, 1996) (repetition of the phrase "uh-oh" four times in a distinctive rhythm for one measure is protectable). And we think it is clear that when it comes to popular music, a song's chorus may be the kind of key sequence that can give rise to intrinsic similarity, even when works differ in other respects.

It is the chorus—often termed the "hook," in recognition of its power to keep a listener coming back for more—that many listeners will recognize immediately or hear in their minds when a song title is mentioned. As the part of a song that is most often repeated and remembered, a chorus hook is important not only aesthetically but also commercially, where it may be central to a song's economic success. *See, e.g.*, Gary Burns, A *Typology of 'Hooks' in Popular Records,* 6 Popular Music 1 (1987) (cataloging characteristics and definitions of term "hook," and noting that "the hook is 'what you're selling' " and that hooks are "the foundation of commercial songwriting, particularly hit-single writing"). From "Respect" by Aretha Franklin to "Seven Nation Army" by the White Stripes, the choruses or hooks of popular music songs are often disproportionately significant, relative to the amount of time or number of measures they occupy. *See id.* at 1 ("[V]irtually no hit record is without a bit of music or words so compelling that it worms its way into one's memory and won't go away .").

After listening to the Copeland song and the Bieber and Usher songs as wholes, we conclude that their choruses are similar enough and also significant enough that a reasonable jury could find the songs intrinsically similar. The most obvious similarity, of course, is the shared chorus lyric, mirrored in the songs' titles: "I [ ] need somebody to love." As Bieber and Usher point out, this phrase is common in popular music, appearing most famously in songs also titled "Somebody to Love" by psychedelic-rock band Jefferson Airplane and arena-rock band Queen, and common lyrical phrases generally are not copyrightable, *see Peters,* 692 F.3d at 635–36 (discussing rap songs' use of the maxim "what does not kill me, makes me stronger"). That might preclude consideration of this similarity under the extrinsic prong, where analysis is preceded by analytic dissection to determine which portions of a work are protectable. But as Bieber and Usher concede, under the intrinsic prong, we do not engage in analytic dissection. Instead, we examine the chorus's lyrics together with the accompanying music, taking the works in their entirety, as an ordinary musical listener would.

And when we listen to the choruses that way, and in the context of the entire songs, we hear the kind of meaningful overlap on which a reasonable jury could rest a finding of substantial similarity. It is not simply that both choruses contain the lyric "somebody to love"; it is that the lyric is delivered in what seems to be an almost identical rhythm and a strikingly similar melody. To us, it sounds as though there are a couple of points in the respective chorus melodies where the Bieber and Usher songs go up a note and the Copeland song goes down a note, or vice versa. In our view, however, a reasonable jury could find that these small variations would not prevent a member of the general public from hearing substantial similarity.

We also conclude that the choruses of the Copeland song and the Bieber and Usher songs are sufficiently important to the songs' overall effect that they may be the basis for a finding of intrinsic similarity. In both the Copeland song and the Bieber and Usher songs, the singing of the titular lyric is an anthemic, sing-along moment, delivered at a high volume and pitch. Quite simply, it is "the heart of the composition[s]," *Elsmere Music,* 482 F.Supp. at 744, the most prominent and memorable part of the songs, and just the sort of significant sequence that courts have found sufficient to render musical works substantially similar. Whether a member of the general public could experience these songs primarily through their choruses and thus find them substantially similar, notwithstanding the differences catalogued above, is in our view a close enough question that it cannot be disposed of as a matter of law and should instead be decided by a jury.

IV.

In summary, we hold that a reasonable jury could find that the Copeland song and the Bieber and Usher songs are intrinsically similar. Because our holding is sufficient to dispose of this appeal, we decline to reach Copeland's other arguments. For the reasons set forth above, we vacate the judgment of the district court and remand the case for further proceedings.

VACATED AND REMANDED.

### *QUESTIONS FOR DISCUSSION*

1. In the *Fink* case, the court said that the best way to judge whether there is substantial similarity between two works is to penetrate beneath the concrete details of their scenes and characters and focus on the "structural spine" of the two story lines and the themes they are seeking to portray. What kind of verdicts would you have rendered in these two cases? How similar and how relevant are the overall messages in each pair of works? In Chapter 6 we will encounter another *Coming to America* suit, this one filed by Art Buchwald against Paramount Pictures.

2. In 1983, a 22-year-old named Samuel Segal sent Paramount Pictures an unsolicited screenplay entitled *Star Trek IV: Inside the Klingon Empire*, which he had previously registered with the Copyright Office. Paramount returned the screenplay to Segal, stating that it was in the process of developing its own sequels to *Star Trek I and II.* Four more sequels followed, the last being *Star Trek VI: The Undiscovered Country*, in 1991. In 1992, Segal filed suit against Paramount, actor-producer Leonard Nimoy, director Nicholas Meyer, writer Denny Martin Flinn, and producer Ralph Winter, alleging that *The Undiscovered Country* infringed his screenplay.

In holding that summary judgment was appropriate in favor of the defendants, the district judge made the following observations:

> *The Undiscovered Country* . . . is a science fiction tale of the efforts of the long-warring United Federation of Planets, the Klingon Empire, and various other nations of the universe to

> change the course of their destructive history of violent confrontation and bring about intergalactic peace. The motion picture was developed and produced in 1990 and 1991, and although the movie is set in the 23rd century, its plot is a metaphor for the end of the Cold War.
>
> Based upon any reading, . . . Segal's screenplay *Inside the Klingon Empire* stands in stark contrast to *The Undiscovered Country*. Whereas *The Undiscovered Country* expressed a tale of the efforts of enemy empires to beat swords into plowshares and to forge a fundamentally new relationship founded on peace, *Inside the Klingon Empire* expresses a story of territorial aggrandizement which fuels violent confrontation among the nations. Apropos for the thorough dissimilarity between the two works, *The Undiscovered Country* concludes with the foil of conspirators who had been bent on disrupting the peace process, while *Inside the Klingon Empire* ends on the brink of an all-out war among the empires, precipitated by the escalation of hostilities throughout the story.
>
> In short, the two works constitute opposites of expression. Segal's *Inside the Klingon Empire* expresses beliefs and prejudices regarding an enemy empire and the concomitant need to relate to those "others" through war. *The Undiscovered Country*, on the other hand, expresses a vision of peaceful relations among nations.[2] In its expression of glasnost and peace, it may be said that *The Undiscovered Country* boldly went where Segal's screenplay had not gone before.

*Segal v. Paramount Pictures*, 841 F. Supp. 146, at 149 (E.D. Pa. 1993). The court acknowledged that "the two works at issue do share many of the same characters, as well as a similar setting and certain common action sequences," but noted that these features were "common to the *Star Trek* television and movie series developed over many years since 1966." Are you persuaded? How much similarity would you require between Star Trek episodes or movie scripts to go to trial on the issue of substantial similarity? For further variations on these themes, see *Twentieth Century-Fox Film v. MCA, Inc.*, 715 F.2d 1327 (9th Cir. 1983), assessing whether the first *Star Wars* hit had been copied by a later film, *Battlestar Galactica*, and *Williams v. Crichton*, 860 F. Supp. 158 (S.D.N.Y. 1994), deciding whether Michael Crichton's novel and Steven Spielberg's movie *Jurassic Park* had infringed Geoffrey Williams' four children's *Dinosaurs Wars* books.

3. In his partial concurrence in *Moore v. Columbia Pictures* (see Subsection 1, Access, above), Senior Circuit Judge Lay concluded that the

---

[2] Indeed, when Segal penned his screenplay in 1983, the manifestations of this vision of post-Cold War peaceful relations upon which *The Undiscovered Country* was based remained years away. For example, the actions of one of the key characters in *The Undiscovered Country* appear to be based upon the role that former Soviet President Gorbachev played in the peace process.

majority should not have resolved the case based on the "substantial similarity" test, when the district court had not passed on that issue. Judge Lay made the following observations:

> I have played the tape which contains the two musical compositions and although I do not know the difference between be-bop, hip-hop, and rock and roll, the tunes all sound the same to me. This may be because I have no ear for music other than reflecting my generation's preference for the more soothing rhythms of Glen Miller and Wayne King or the sophisticated beat of Woody Herman playing the Wood Chopper's Ball. Obviously judges have no expertise to resolve this kind of question—which is why jurors should tell us whether a composite vote of reasonable minds can or cannot find similarity of expression.

972 F.2d at 948. Do you agree that juries are better equipped than judges to make these types of findings? What should be the role of expert testimony in these cases?

4. In *Bieber*, the Court emphasized that the substantial similarity determination rested on a view of whether the general public would find the songs substantially similar. Should this be the standard? Or should the court rely on expert testimony to determine similarity? The Court also seemed wary of judicial determinations of musical similarity, which factored into its decision to vacate the motion to dismiss to allow a jury to determine the similarity question. Are judges or jurors better situated to make such a determination?

## 3. SIMULTANEOUS BROADCASTS AND EXCLUSIVITY

Recently, the United States Supreme Court considered whether an Internet service transmitting a television program at the same time of its initial on-air broadcast infringes on its copyright. Here is the Court's decision.

### AMERICAN BROADCASTING COS. V. AEREO

United States Supreme Court, 2015.
134 S.Ct. 2498.

JUSTICE BREYER.

The Copyright Act of 1976 gives a copyright owner the "exclusive righ[t]" to "perform the copyrighted work publicly." 17 U.S.C. § 106(4). The Act's Transmit Clause defines that exclusive right as including the right to

"transmit or otherwise communicate a performance . . . of the [copyrighted] work . . . to the public, by means of any device or process, whether the members of the public capable of receiving the performance

. . . receive it in the same place or in separate places and at the same time or at different times." § 101.

We must decide whether respondent Aereo, Inc., infringes this exclusive right by selling its subscribers a technologically complex service that allows them to watch television programs over the Internet at about the same time as the programs are broadcast over the air. We conclude that it does.

I

A

For a monthly fee, Aereo offers subscribers broadcast television programming over the Internet, virtually as the programming is being broadcast. Much of this programming is made up of copyrighted works. Aereo neither owns the copyright in those works nor holds a license from the copyright owners to perform those works publicly.

Aereo's system is made up of servers, transcoders, and thousands of dime-sized antennas housed in a central warehouse. It works roughly as follows: First, when a subscriber wants to watch a show that is currently being broadcast, he visits Aereo's website and selects, from a list of the local programming, the show he wishes to see.

Second, one of Aereo's servers selects an antenna, which it dedicates to the use of that subscriber (and that subscriber alone) for the duration of the selected show. A server then tunes the antenna to the over-the-air broadcast carrying the show. The antenna begins to receive the broadcast, and an Aereo transcoder translates the signals received into data that can be transmitted over the Internet.

Third, rather than directly send the data to the subscriber, a server saves the data in a subscriber-specific folder on Aereo's hard drive. In other words, Aereo's system creates a subscriber-specific copy—that is, a "personal" copy—of the subscriber's program of choice.

Fourth, once several seconds of programming have been saved, Aereo's server begins to stream the saved copy of the show to the subscriber over the Internet. (The subscriber may instead direct Aereo to stream the program at a later time, but that aspect of Aereo's service is not before us.) The subscriber can watch the streamed program on the screen of his personal computer, tablet, smart phone, Internet-connected television, or other Internet-connected device. The streaming continues, a mere few seconds behind the over-the-air broadcast, until the subscriber has received the entire show. *See* A Dictionary of Computing 494 (6th ed. 2008) (defining "streaming" as "[t]he process of providing a steady flow of audio or video data so that an Internet user is able to access it as it is transmitted").

Aereo emphasizes that the data that its system streams to each subscriber are the data from his own personal copy, made from the broadcast signals received by the particular antenna allotted to him. Its system does not transmit data saved in one subscriber's folder to any other subscriber. When two subscribers wish to watch the same program, Aereo's system activates two separate antennas and saves two separate copies of the program in two separate folders. It then streams the show to the subscribers through two separate transmissions—each from the subscriber's personal copy.

B

Petitioners are television producers, marketers, distributors, and broadcasters who own the copyrights in many of the programs that Aereo's system streams to its subscribers. They brought suit against Aereo for copyright infringement in Federal District Court. They sought a preliminary injunction, arguing that Aereo was infringing their right to "perform" their works "publicly," as the Transmit Clause defines those terms.

The District Court denied the preliminary injunction. 874 F.Supp.2d 373 (S.D.N.Y.2012). Relying on prior Circuit precedent, a divided panel of the Second Circuit affirmed. *WNET, Thirteen v. Aereo, Inc.*, 712 F.3d 676 (2013) (citing *Cartoon Network LP, LLLP v. CSC Holdings, Inc.*, 536 F.3d 121 (2008)). In the Second Circuit's view, Aereo does not perform publicly within the meaning of the Transmit Clause because it does not transmit "to the public." Rather, each time Aereo streams a program to a subscriber, it sends a *private* transmission that is available only to that subscriber. The Second Circuit denied rehearing en banc, over the dissent of two judges. *WNET, Thirteen v. Aereo, Inc.*, 722 F.3d 500 (2013). We granted certiorari.

II

This case requires us to answer two questions: First, in operating in the manner described above, does Aereo "perform" at all? And second, if so, does Aereo do so "publicly"? We address these distinct questions in turn.

Does Aereo "perform"? *See* § 106(4) ("[T]he owner of [a] copyright . . . has the exclusive righ[t] . . . to *perform* the copyrighted work publicly" (emphasis added)); § 101 ("To *perform* . . . a work 'publicly' means [among other things] to transmit . . . a performance . . . of the work . . . to the public . . ." (emphasis added)). Phrased another way, does Aereo "transmit . . . a performance" when a subscriber watches a show using Aereo's system, or is it only the subscriber who transmits? In Aereo's view, it does not perform. It does no more than supply equipment that "emulate[s] the operation of a home antenna and [digital video recorder (DVR)]." Brief for Respondent 41. Like a home antenna and DVR, Aereo's equipment simply responds to its subscribers' directives. So it is only the subscribers who "perform" when they use Aereo's equipment to stream television programs to themselves.

Considered alone, the language of the Act does not clearly indicate when an entity "perform[s]" (or "transmit[s]") and when it merely supplies equipment that allows others to do so. But when read in light of its purpose, the Act is unmistakable: An entity that engages in activities like Aereo's performs.

A

History makes plain that one of Congress' primary purposes in amending the Copyright Act in 1976 was to overturn this Court's determination that community antenna television (CATV) systems (the precursors of modern cable systems) fell outside the Act's scope. In *Fortnightly Corp. v. United Artists Television, Inc.,* 392 U.S. 390, 88 S.Ct. 2084, 20 L.Ed.2d 1176 (1968), the Court considered a CATV system that carried local television broadcasting, much of which was copyrighted, to its subscribers in two cities. The CATV provider placed antennas on hills above the cities and used coaxial cables to carry the signals received by the antennas to the home television sets of its subscribers. The system amplified and modulated the signals in order to improve their strength and efficiently transmit them to subscribers. A subscriber "could choose any of the . . . programs he wished to view by simply turning the knob on his own television set." *Id.,* at 392, 88 S.Ct. 2084. The CATV provider "neither edited the programs received nor originated any programs of its own." *Ibid.*

Asked to decide whether the CATV provider infringed copyright holders' exclusive right to perform their works publicly, the Court held that the provider did not "perform" at all. *See* 17 U.S.C. § 1(c) (1964 ed.) (granting copyright holder the exclusive right to "perform . . . in public for profit" a nondramatic literary work), § 1(d) (granting copyright holder the exclusive right to "perform . . . publicly" a dramatic work). The Court drew a line: "Broadcasters perform. Viewers do not perform." 392 U.S., at 398, 88 S.Ct. 2084 (footnote omitted). And a CATV provider "falls on the viewer's side of the line." *Id.,* at 399, 88 S.Ct. 2084.

The Court reasoned that CATV providers were unlike broadcasters:

> "Broadcasters select the programs to be viewed; CATV systems simply carry, without editing, whatever programs they receive. Broadcasters procure programs and propagate them to the public; CATV systems receive programs that have been released to the public and carry them by private channels to additional viewers." *Id.,* at 400, 88 S.Ct. 2084.

Instead, CATV providers were more like viewers, for "the basic function [their] equipment serves is little different from that served by the equipment generally furnished by" viewers. *Id.,* at 399, 88 S.Ct. 2084. "Essentially," the Court said, "a CATV system no more than enhances the viewer's capacity to receive the broadcaster's signals [by] provid[ing] a well-located antenna with an efficient connection to the viewer's television set." *Ibid.* Viewers do not become performers by using "amplifying equipment," and a CATV provider should not be treated differently for providing viewers the same equipment. *Id.,* at 398–400, 88 S.Ct. 2084.

In *Teleprompter Corp. v. Columbia Broadcasting System, Inc.,* 415 U.S. 394, 94 S.Ct. 1129, 39 L.Ed.2d 415 (1974), the Court considered the copyright liability of a CATV provider that carried broadcast television programming into subscribers' homes from hundreds of miles away. Although the Court recognized that a viewer might not be able to afford amplifying equipment that would provide access to those distant signals, it nonetheless found that the CATV provider was more like a viewer than a broadcaster. *Id.,* at 408–409, 94 S.Ct. 1129. It explained: "The reception and rechanneling of [broadcast television signals] for simultaneous viewing is essentially a viewer function, irrespective of the distance between the broadcasting station and the ultimate viewer." *Id.,* at 408, 94 S.Ct. 1129.

The Court also recognized that the CATV system exercised some measure of choice over what to transmit. But that fact did not transform the CATV system into a broadcaster. A broadcaster exercises significant creativity in choosing what to air, the Court reasoned. *Id.,* at 410, 94 S.Ct. 1129. In contrast, the CATV provider makes an initial choice about which broadcast stations to retransmit, but then " 'simply carr[ies], without editing, whatever programs [it] receive[s].' " *Ibid.* (quoting *Fortnightly, supra,* at 400, 88 S.Ct. 2084 (alterations in original)).

B

In 1976 Congress amended the Copyright Act in large part to reject the Court's holdings in *Fortnightly* and *Teleprompter*. *See* H.R.Rep. No. 94–1476, pp. 86–87 (1976) (hereinafter H.R. Rep.) (The 1976 amendments "completely overturned" this Court's narrow construction of the Act in *Fortnightly* and *Teleprompter*). Congress enacted new language that erased the Court's line between broadcaster and viewer, in respect to "perform [ing]" a work. The amended statute clarifies that to "perform" an audiovisual work means "to show its images in any sequence or to make the sounds accompanying it audible." § 101; *see ibid.* (defining "[a]udiovisual works" as "works that consist of a series of related images which are intrinsically intended to be shown by the use of machines . . . , together with accompanying sounds"). Under this new language, *both* the broadcaster *and* the viewer of a television program "perform," because they both show the program's images and make audible the program's sounds. *See* H.R. Rep., at 63 ("[A] broadcasting network is performing when it transmits [a singer's performance of a song] . . . and any individual is performing whenever he or she . . . communicates the performance by turning on a receiving set").

Congress also enacted the Transmit Clause, which specifies that an entity performs publicly when it "transmit[s] . . . a performance . . . to the public." § 101; *see ibid.* (defining "[t]o 'transmit' a performance" as "to communicate it by any device or process whereby images or sounds are received beyond the place from which they are sent"). Cable system activities, like those of the CATV systems in *Fortnightly* and *Teleprompter,* lie at the heart of the activities that Congress intended this language to cover. *See* H.R. Rep., at 63 ("[A] cable television system is performing when it retransmits [a network] broadcast to its subscribers"); *see* also *ibid.* ("[T]he concep[t] of public performance . . . cover[s] not only the initial rendition or showing, but also any further act by which that rendition or showing is transmitted or communicated to the public"). The Clause thus makes clear that an entity that acts like a CATV system itself performs, even if when doing so, it simply enhances viewers' ability to receive broadcast television signals.

Congress further created a new section of the Act to regulate cable companies' public performances of copyrighted works. *See* § 111. Section 111 creates a complex, highly detailed compulsory licensing scheme that sets out the conditions, including the payment of compulsory fees, under which cable systems may retransmit broadcasts. H.R. Rep., at 88 (Section 111 is primarily "directed at the operation of cable television systems and the terms and conditions of their liability for the retransmission of copyrighted works").

Congress made these three changes to achieve a similar end: to bring the activities of cable systems within the scope of the Copyright Act.

C

This history makes clear that Aereo is not simply an equipment provider. Rather, Aereo, and not just its subscribers, "perform[s]" (or "transmit[s]"). Aereo's activities are substantially similar to those of the CATV companies that Congress amended the Act to reach. *See id.,* at 89 ("[C]able systems are commercial enterprises whose basic retransmission operations are based on the carriage of copyrighted program material"). Aereo sells a service that allows subscribers to watch television programs, many of which are copyrighted, almost as they are being broadcast. In providing this service, Aereo uses its own equipment, housed in a centralized warehouse, outside of its users' homes. By means of its technology (antennas, transcoders, and servers), Aereo's system "receive[s] programs that have been released to the public and carr[ies] them by private channels to additional viewers." *Fortnightly,* 392 U.S., at 400, 88 S.Ct. 2084. It "carr[ies] . . . whatever programs [it] receive[s]," and it offers "all the programming" of each over-the-air station it carries. *Id.,* at 392, 400, 88 S.Ct. 2084.

Aereo's equipment may serve a "viewer function"; it may enhance the viewer's ability to receive a broadcaster's programs. It may even emulate equipment a viewer could use at home. But the same was true of the equipment that was before the Court, and ultimately before Congress, in *Fortnightly* and *Teleprompter.*

We recognize, and Aereo and the dissent emphasize, one particular difference between Aereo's system and the cable systems at issue in *Fortnightly* and *Teleprompter*. The systems in those cases transmitted constantly; they sent continuous programming to each subscriber's television set. In contrast, Aereo's system remains inert until a subscriber indicates that she wants to watch a program. Only at that moment, in automatic response to the subscriber's request, does Aereo's system activate an antenna and begin to transmit the requested program.

This is a critical difference, says the dissent. It means that Aereo's subscribers, not Aereo, "selec[t] the copyrighted content" that is "perform [ed]," *post,* at 2513 (opinion of SCALIA, J.), and for that reason they, not Aereo, "transmit" the performance. Aereo is thus like "a copy shop that provides its patrons with a library card." *Post,* at 2514. A copy shop is not directly liable whenever a patron uses the shop's machines to "reproduce" copyrighted materials found in that library. *See* § 106(1) ("exclusive righ [t] . . . to reproduce the copyrighted work"). And by the same token, Aereo should not be directly liable whenever its patrons use its equipment to "transmit" copyrighted television programs to their screens.

In our view, however, the dissent's copy shop argument, in whatever form, makes too much out of too little. Given Aereo's overwhelming likeness to the cable companies targeted by the 1976 amendments, this sole technological difference between Aereo and traditional cable companies does not make a critical difference here. The subscribers of the *Fortnightly* and *Teleprompter* cable systems also selected what programs to display on their receiving sets. Indeed, as we explained in *Fortnightly,* such a subscriber "could choose any of the . . . programs he wished to view by simply turning the knob on his own television set." 392 U.S., at 392, 88 S.Ct. 2084. The same is true of an Aereo subscriber. Of course, in *Fortnightly* the television signals, in a sense, lurked behind the screen, ready to emerge when the subscriber turned the knob. Here the signals pursue their ordinary course of travel through the universe until today's "turn of the knob"—a click on a website—activates machinery that intercepts and reroutes them to Aereo's subscribers over the Internet. But this difference means nothing to the subscriber. It means nothing to the broadcaster. We do not see how this single difference, invisible to subscriber and broadcaster alike, could transform a system that is for all practical purposes a traditional cable system into "a copy shop that provides its patrons with a library card."

In other cases involving different kinds of service or technology providers, a user's involvement in the operation of the provider's equipment and selection of the content transmitted may well bear on whether the provider performs within the meaning of the Act. But the many similarities between Aereo and cable companies, considered in light of Congress' basic purposes in amending the Copyright Act, convince us that this difference is not critical here. We conclude that Aereo is not just an equipment supplier and that Aereo "perform[s]."

III

Next, we must consider whether Aereo performs petitioners' works "publicly," within the meaning of the Transmit Clause. Under the Clause, an entity performs a work publicly when it "transmit[s] . . . a performance . . . of the work . . . to the public." § 101. Aereo denies that it satisfies this definition. It reasons as follows: First, the "performance" it "transmit[s]" is the performance created by its act of transmitting. And second, because each of these performances is capable of being received by one and only one subscriber, Aereo transmits privately, not publicly. Even assuming Aereo's first argument is correct, its second does not follow.

We begin with Aereo's first argument. What performance does Aereo transmit? Under the Act, "[t]o 'transmit' a performance . . . is to communicate it by any device or process whereby images or sounds are received beyond the place from which they are sent." *Ibid.* And "[t]o 'perform' " an audiovisual work means "to show its images in any sequence or to make the sounds accompanying it audible." *Ibid.*

Petitioners say Aereo transmits a *prior* performance of their works. Thus when Aereo retransmits a network's prior broadcast, the underlying broadcast (itself a performance) is the performance that Aereo transmits. Aereo, as discussed above, says the performance it transmits is the *new* performance created by its act of transmitting. That performance comes into existence when Aereo streams the sounds and images of a broadcast program to a subscriber's screen.

We assume *arguendo* that Aereo's first argument is correct. Thus, for present purposes, to transmit a performance of (at least) an audiovisual work means to communicate contemporaneously visible images and contemporaneously audible sounds of the work. Cf. *United States v. American Soc. of Composers, Authors and Publishers,* 627 F.3d 64, 73 (C.A.2 2010) (holding that a download of a work is not a performance because the data transmitted are not "contemporaneously perceptible").

When an Aereo subscriber selects a program to watch, Aereo streams the program over the Internet to that subscriber. Aereo thereby "communicate[s]" to the subscriber, by means of a "device or process," the work's images and sounds. § 101. And those images and sounds are contemporaneously visible and audible on the subscriber's computer (or other Internet-connected device). So under our assumed definition, Aereo transmits a performance whenever its subscribers watch a program.

But what about the Clause's further requirement that Aereo transmit a performance "to the public"? As we have said, an Aereo subscriber receives broadcast television signals with an antenna dedicated to him alone. Aereo's system makes from those signals a personal copy of the selected program. It streams the content of the copy to the same subscriber and to no one else. One and only one subscriber has the ability to see and hear each Aereo transmission. The fact that each transmission is to only one subscriber, in Aereo's view, means that it does not transmit a performance "to the public."

In terms of the Act's purposes, these differences do not distinguish Aereo's system from cable systems, which do perform "publicly." Viewed in terms of Congress' regulatory objectives, why should any of these technological differences matter? They concern the behind-the-scenes way in which Aereo delivers television programming to its viewers' screens. They do not render Aereo's commercial objective any different from that of cable companies. Nor do they significantly alter the viewing experience of Aereo's subscribers. Why would a subscriber who wishes to watch a television show care much whether images and sounds are delivered to his screen via a large multisubscriber antenna or one small dedicated antenna, whether they arrive instantaneously or after a few seconds' delay, or whether they are transmitted directly or after a personal copy is made? And why, if Aereo is right, could not modern CATV systems simply continue the same commercial and consumer-oriented activities, free of copyright restrictions, provided they substitute such new technologies for old? Congress would as much have intended to protect a copyright holder from the unlicensed activities of Aereo as from those of cable companies.

The text of the Clause effectuates Congress' intent. Aereo's argument to the contrary relies on the premise that "to transmit . . . a performance" means to make a single transmission. But the Clause suggests that an entity may transmit a performance through multiple, discrete transmissions. That is because one can "transmit" or "communicate" something through a *set* of actions. Thus one can transmit a message to one's friends, irrespective of whether one sends separate identical e-mails to each friend or a single e-mail to all at once. So can an elected official communicate an idea, slogan, or speech to her constituents, regardless of whether she communicates that idea, slogan, or speech during individual phone calls to each constituent or in a public square.

The fact that a singular noun ("a performance") follows the words "to transmit" does not suggest the contrary. One can sing a song to his family, whether he sings the same song one-on-one or in front of all together. Similarly, one's colleagues may watch a performance of a particular play—say, this season's modern-dress version of "Measure for Measure"—whether they do so at separate or at the same showings. By the same principle, an entity may transmit a performance through one or several transmissions, where the performance is of the same work.

The Transmit Clause must permit this interpretation, for it provides that one may transmit a performance to the public "whether the members of the public capable of receiving the performance . . . receive it . . . at the same time or at different times." § 101. Were the words "to transmit . . . a performance" limited to a single act of communication, members of the public could not receive the performance communicated "at different times." Therefore, in light of the purpose and text of the Clause, we conclude that when an entity communicates the same contemporaneously perceptible images and sounds to multiple people, it transmits a performance to them regardless of the number of discrete communications it makes.

We do not see how the fact that Aereo transmits via personal copies of programs could make a difference. The Act applies to transmissions "by means of any device or process." *Ibid.* And retransmitting a television program using user-specific copies is a "process" of transmitting a performance. A "cop[y]" of a work is simply a "material objec[t] . . . in which a work is fixed . . . and from which the work can be perceived, reproduced, or otherwise communicated." *Ibid.* So whether Aereo transmits from the same or separate copies, it performs the same work; it shows the same images and makes audible the same sounds. Therefore, when Aereo streams the same television program to multiple subscribers, it "transmit[s] . . . a performance" to all of them.

Moreover, the subscribers to whom Aereo transmits television programs constitute "the public." Aereo communicates the same contemporaneously perceptible images and sounds to a large number of people who are unrelated and unknown to each other. This matters because, although the Act does not define "the public," it specifies that an entity performs publicly when it performs at "any place where a substantial number of persons outside of a normal circle of a family and its social acquaintances is gathered." *Ibid.* The Act thereby suggests that "the public" consists of a large group of people outside of a family and friends.

Neither the record nor Aereo suggests that Aereo's subscribers receive performances in their capacities as owners or possessors of the underlying works. This is relevant because when an entity performs to a set of people, whether they constitute "the public" often depends upon their relationship to the underlying work. When, for example, a valet parking attendant returns cars to their drivers, we would not say that the parking service provides cars "to the public." We would say that it provides the cars to their owners. We would say that a car dealership, on the other hand, does provide cars to the public, for it sells cars to individuals who lack a pre-existing relationship to the cars. Similarly, an entity that transmits a performance to individuals in their capacities as owners or possessors does not perform to "the public," whereas an entity like Aereo that transmits to large numbers of paying subscribers who lack any prior relationship to the works does so perform.

Finally, we note that Aereo's subscribers may receive the same programs at different times and locations. This fact does not help Aereo, however, for the Transmit Clause expressly provides that an entity may perform publicly "whether the members of the public capable of receiving the performance . . . receive it in the same place or in separate places and at the same time or at different times." *Ibid.* In other words, "the public" need not be situated together, spatially or temporally. For these reasons, we conclude that Aereo transmits a performance of petitioners' copyrighted works to the public, within the meaning of the Transmit Clause.

## IV

Aereo and many of its supporting *amici* argue that to apply the Transmit Clause to Aereo's conduct will impose copyright liability on other technologies, including new technologies, that Congress could not possibly have wanted to reach. We agree that Congress, while intending the Transmit Clause to apply broadly to cable companies and their equivalents, did not intend to discourage or to control the emergence or use of different kinds of technologies. But we do not believe that our limited holding today will have that effect.

For one thing, the history of cable broadcast transmissions that led to the enactment of the Transmit Clause informs our conclusion that Aereo "perform [s]," but it does not determine whether different kinds of providers in different contexts also "perform." For another, an entity only transmits a performance when it communicates contemporaneously perceptible images and sounds of a work. *See* Brief for Respondent 31 ("[I]f a distributor . . . sells [multiple copies of a digital video disc] by mail to consumers, . . . [its] distribution of the DVDs merely makes it possible for the recipients to perform the work themselves—it is not a 'device or process' by which the *distributor* publicly performs the work" (emphasis in original)).

Further, we have interpreted the term "the public" to apply to a group of individuals acting as ordinary members of the public who pay primarily to watch broadcast television programs, many of which are copyrighted. We have said that it does not extend to those who act as owners or possessors of the relevant product. And we have not considered whether the public performance right is infringed when the user of a service pays primarily for something other than the transmission of copyrighted works, such as the remote storage of content. *See* Brief for United States as *Amicus Curiae* 31 (distinguishing cloud-based storage services because they "offer consumers more numerous and convenient means of playing back copies that the consumers have *already* lawfully acquired" (emphasis in original)). In addition, an entity does not transmit to the public if it does not transmit to a substantial number of people outside of a family and its social circle.

We also note that courts often apply a statute's highly general language in light of the statute's basic purposes. Finally, the doctrine of "fair use" can help to prevent inappropriate or inequitable applications of the Clause. *See Sony Corp. of America v. Universal City Studios, Inc.,* 464 U.S. 417, 104 S.Ct. 774, 78 L.Ed.2d 574 (1984).

We cannot now answer more precisely how the Transmit Clause or other provisions of the Copyright Act will apply to technologies not before us. We agree with the Solicitor General that "[q]uestions involving cloud computing, [remote storage] DVRs, and other novel issues not before the Court, as to which 'Congress has not plainly marked [the] course,' should await a case in which they are squarely presented." Brief for United States as *Amicus Curiae* 34 (quoting *Sony, supra,* at 431, 104 S.Ct. 774 (alteration in original)). And we note that, to the extent commercial actors or other interested entities may be concerned with the relationship between the development and use of such technologies and the Copyright Act, they are of course free to seek action from Congress. Cf. Digital Millennium Copyright Act, 17 U.S.C. § 512.

* * *

In sum, having considered the details of Aereo's practices, we find them highly similar to those of the CATV systems in *Fortnightly* and *Teleprompter.* And those are activities that the 1976 amendments sought to bring within the scope of the Copyright Act. Insofar as there are differences, those differences concern not the nature of the service that Aereo provides so much as the technological manner in which it provides the service. We conclude that those differences are not adequate to place Aereo's activities outside the scope of the Act.

For these reasons, we conclude that Aereo "perform[s]" petitioners' copyrighted works "publicly," as those terms are defined by the Transmit Clause. We therefore reverse the contrary judgment of the Court of Appeals, and we remand the case for further proceedings consistent with this opinion.

*It is so ordered.*

## C. UNPROTECTABLE STORY PARTS

Under the Copyright Act, *ideas* as such do not receive protection; it is only the *expression* of an idea that is protected. The line between idea and expression, however, is rarely an easy one to draw. At stake is whether the copyright will extend too far and stifle creativity by preventing later artists and musicians from making use of ideas that came before them. Of particular concern is whether copyright precludes use of memorable scenes and characters in later stories whose overall themes and feel are quite different.

### 1. SCENES-À-FAIRE[j]

One tool intended to prevent this intellectual stagnation is the scenes-à-faire doctrine. In the context of literature, scenes-à-faire are "incidents, characters, or settings which are as a practical matter indispensable, or at least standard, in the treatment of a given topic." *Alexander v. Haley*, 460 F. Supp. 40, 45 (S.D.N.Y. 1978) (dealing with the claim that Alex Haley's book and television show, *Roots*, had unlawfully drawn upon material in plaintiff's earlier book, *Jubilee*, involving fleeing slaves pursued by dogs through the woods, sex between male slave owners and female slaves, and the auction sales of slave children away from their families). Copyright protection is not extended to such story parts and thus they are available to later authors for use in later works.

*Walker v. Time Life Films, Inc.*, 784 F.2d 44 (2d Cir. 1986), dealt with the claim that the movie *Fort Apache: The Bronx* had copied the book, *Fort Apache*. The book was a non-fictional account of the plaintiff's fifteen months as a police officer in the South Bronx, labeled "Fort Apache" by the New York police because of its high crime rate. The book described Walker's experiences, the countless crimes that occurred, the social and family environment in which they took place, and the safety and morale problems confronted by the department. The movie focused on two fictional "Fort Apache" police officers, and dramatized events in their personal and professional lives. The Second Circuit found no significant resemblance—i.e., "comprehensive literal similarity"—in the two works as a whole, and rejected Walker's claim that the movie had illegally copied—i.e., via "fragmented literal similarity"—his accounts of specific incidents.

> [Walker] notes that both the book and the film begin with the murder of a black and a white policeman with a handgun at close range; both depict cockfights, drugs, stripped cars,

[j] *See* Leslie A. Kurtz, *Copyright: The Scenes-À-Faire Doctrine*, 41 Fla. L. Rev. 79 (1989). The term, scenes-à-faire, first coined by a nineteenth century French drama critic, was imported into U.S. copyright law in a judicial opinion about alleged film copying, *Cain v. Universal Pictures*, 47 F. Supp. 1013 (S.D. Cal. 1942).

> prostitutes and rats; both feature as central characters third-or fourth-generation Irish policemen who live in Queens and frequently drink; both show disgruntled, demoralized police officers and unsuccessful foot chases of fleeing criminals.
>
> These similarities, however, relate to uncopyrightable material. The killing of the two police officers actually occurred and was reported in the news media, which placed the historical fact of the murders in the public domain and beyond the scope of copyright protection. Elements such as drunks, prostitutes, vermin and derelict cars would appear in any realistic work about the work of policemen in the South Bronx. These similarities therefore are unprotectible as "scenes-à-faire," that is, scenes that necessarily result from the choice of a setting or situation. Neither does copyright protection extend to "stock" themes commonly linked to a particular genre. Foot chases and morale problems of policemen, not to mention the familiar figure of the Irish cop, are venerable and often-recurring themes of police fiction. As such, they are not copyrightable except to the extent they are given unique—and therefore protectable—expression in an original creation.

784 F.2d at 50.

### *QUESTIONS FOR DISCUSSION*

1. The following facts, drawn from *Reyher v. Children's Television Workshop*, 533 F.2d 87 (2d Cir. 1976), capsulize the legal claim that an episode in the *Sesame Street* magazine, titled "The Most Beautiful Woman in the World," had unlawfully copied the plaintiff's earlier illustrated children's book, *My Mother Is the Most Beautiful Woman In the World.*

* * *

> Reyher's thirty-five page book focuses on a Russian family living in the Ukraine . . . The main protagonists are the mother, father and six year old daughter. The first few pages describe the duties of each family member in harvesting the wheat crop. There is also narrative about the customary feast days during harvesting as Reyher describes, through the literary device of the little girl helping her mother, the preparation of distinctive Russian foods. The feast day itself is depicted with vivid details of costume and entertainment. We have now progressed through fifteen pages of appellant's book. On the last day of field work prior to the feast, the little girl is separated from her parents. Meeting a group of villagers unfamiliar to her, she describes her mother as the most beautiful woman in the world. The village leader sends boys to bring back all the likely candidates; none, of course, is the mother. Finally, a

homely woman, in fact the girl's mother, approaches the crowd and is joyfully reunited with her child. The village leader presents the moral of the story: "We do not love people because they are beautiful, but they seem beautiful to us because we love them." At the feast day, the little girl tells her mother that, although other children have teased her about her feelings, she thinks her mother is the most beautiful woman in the world. The mother expresses her happiness that her child sees with her heart as well as with her eyes.

The Sesame Street Magazine version of the story, two pages long, presumably is set in Africa. There is no textual detail about African life; any information comes from the five illustrations, which show African dress on the characters, a woman carrying a basket on her head, and thatched huts. The story opens with a little boy crying in the fields because he has become separated from his mother. He describes her as the most beautiful woman in the world. The village leader gathers all the beautiful women from surrounding villages to no avail. An old unattractive woman, the missing mother, is reunited with her son. The village leader states that although he doesn't find her beautiful, the important thing is what the little boy thinks. The lesson to be learned is "[what's] not so beautiful to some can be very, very beautiful to others."

* * *

533 F.2d at 92. What is your conclusion?

2. In *Desny v. Wilder*, 46 Cal.2d 715, 299 P.2d 257, 271 (Cal. 1956), discussed in Chapter 6 below, in the section on **Contract Rights in Story Ideas**, the Supreme Court of California observed that "[i]t has been said . . . that 'There are only thirty-six fundamental dramatic situations, various facets of which form the basis of all human drama.' " The court concluded that "[i]t is manifest that authors must work with and from ideas or themes which basically are in the public domain." *See also Gaste v. Kaiserman*, 863 F.2d 1061, 1068 (2d Cir. 1988) ("In assessing [the] evidence, we are mindful of the limited number of notes and chords available to composers and the resulting fact that common themes frequently reappear in various compositions, especially in popular music" and thus "striking similarity between pieces of popular music" required more than common sources and themes that appear in many compositions). How much room does this sentiment leave for copyright protection of valuable entertainment products?

3. Courts require more than similar archetypes in finding substantial similarity. A lawsuit against Stephen King provides an example. Yolanda Acker claimed that a character in her short story, "The Haunting of Addie Lockwood," was used in King's novel "Doctor Sleep." In denying Acker's claim for copyright infringement against King, the court explained that "using psychic abilities to save people, seeing and doing supernatural things, and

defeating villains are scenes a faire that flow necessarily from the idea of a character using her psychic abilities to triumph over evil." *See Acker v. King*, 46 F. Supp.3d 168 (D.Conn. 2014).

## 2. CHARACTERS[k]

Section 102 of the 1976 Copyright Act lists various works of authorship that are subject to copyright protection. These include literary works, dramatic works, pictorial, graphic, and sculptural works, and motion pictures. Characters are often part of these protected works. The Copyright Act does not directly address the protection to be given to the characters themselves. In *Nichols v. Universal Pictures Corp.*, 45 F.2d 119 (2d Cir. 1930), Judge Learned Hand commented on the potential copyright protection for characters:

> If Twelfth Night were copyrighted, it is quite possible that a second comer might so closely imitate Sir Toby Belch or Malvolio as to infringe, but it would not be enough that for one of his characters he cast a riotous knight who kept wassail to the discomfort of the household, or a vain and foppish steward who became amorous of his mistress. These would be no more than Shakespeare's 'ideas' in the play, as little capable of monopoly as Einstein's Doctrine of Relativity, or Darwin's theory of the Origin of Species. It follows that the less developed the characters, the less they can be copyrighted; that is the penalty an author must bear for marking them too indistinctly.

45 F.2d at 121. In Judge Hand's formulation, the protectibility of characters was a specific instance of the broader distinction between idea and expression. A quarter century later, in *Warner Bros. Pictures v. Columbia Broadcasting System*, 216 F.2d 945 (9th Cir. 1954), the Ninth Circuit expressed the view that characters enjoyed qualitatively less copyright protection than other features of a story.

*Warner Bros.* actually turned on the terms of an agreement whereby the author Dashiell Hammett had sold Warner the right to make a film of Hammett's book *The Maltese Falcon*, whose principal character was the detective, Sam Spade. The question was whether Hammett had thereby surrendered the right to author future detective stories starring Spade (which might thereafter also be turned into movies). After construing the contract and intent, the Court went on to state its views about whether it

---

[k] *See* Leslie A. Kurtz, *The Independent Legal Lives of Fictional Characters*, 1986 Wis. L. Rev. 429; Kenneth E. Spahn, *The Legal Protection of Fictional Characters*, 9 U. Miami Ent. & Sports L. Rev. 331 (1992); Michael T. Helfand, *When Mickey Mouse Is as Strong as Superman: The Convergence of Intellectual Property Laws to Protect Fictional Literary & Pictorial Characters*, 44 Stan. L. Rev. 623 (1992); Michael A. Kaplan, *Rosencrantz & Guilderstern Are Dead, But Are They Copyrightable? Protection of Literary Characters With Respect to Secondary Works*, 30 Rut. L. Rev. 817 (1999).

was ever intended that the copyright statute would protect story characters as such:

> The practice of writers to compose sequels to stories is old, and the copyright statute, though amended several times, has never specifically mentioned the point. It does not appear that it has ever been adjudicated, although it is mentioned in *Nichols v. Universal Pictures Corp.*, 2 Cir., 1930, 45 F.2d 119. If Congress had intended that the sale of the right to publish a copyrighted story would foreclose the author's use of its characters in subsequent works for the life of the copyright, it would seem Congress would have made specific provision therefor. Authors work for the love of their art no more than other professional people work in other lines of work for the love of it. There is the financial motive as well. The characters of an author's imagination and the art of his descriptive talent, like a painter's or like a person with his penmanship, are always limited and always fall into limited patterns. The restriction argued for is unreasonable, and would effect the very opposite of the statute's purpose which is to encourage the production of the arts.
>
> It is our conception of the area covered by the copyright statute that when a study of the two writings is made and it is plain from the study that one of them is not in fact the creation of the putative author, but instead has been copied in substantial part exactly or in transparent re-phrasing to produce essentially the story of the other writing, it infringes.
>
> It is conceivable that the character really constitutes the story being told, but if the character is only the chessman in the game of telling the story he is not within the area of the protection afforded by the copyright. . . .

216 F.2d at 950.

---

A quarter century later, in *Walt Disney Productions v. Air Pirates*, 581 F.2d 751 (9th Cir. 1978), the Ninth Circuit ruled that cartoon characters were copyrightable, and that Disney's copyrighted mice had been violated by their bawdy depiction in defendant's adult comic books as "active members of a free-thinking, promiscuous, drug-ingesting counterculture." The court found that cartoon characters like Donald Duck or Mickey Mouse, unlike a literary character like Sam Spade, had a visual image rather than just a conceptual quality that easily made them a form of protected expression.

Shortly thereafter, the Second Circuit returned to this question in the following case pitting Warner's "Superman" against ABC's *The Greatest American Hero*, "Ralph Hinckley."

## WARNER BROTHERS, INC. V. AMERICAN BROADCASTING COMPANIES, INC.

United States Court of Appeals, Second Circuit, 1981.
654 F.2d 204.

MESKILL, CIRCUIT JUDGE.

### Background

Plaintiffs are the owners of the copyrights and other rights in the character Superman and the works embodying him, including comic books depicting the cartoon character Superman; television series depicting Superman in animated and unanimated features; and the motion picture *Superman, The Movie*. The plaintiffs have enjoyed remarkable commercial success for over forty years; they have derived substantial revenue from both domestic and international commercial exploitation of Superman.

The character "evolved" over the years in comic strips, cartoons, television shows, and motion pictures under the ostensible protection of copyright. A glance at the record, for example, reveals that originally Superman was only capable of leaping in the position of a hurdler over tall buildings, while in a recent film version, *Superman, The Movie*, the character is shown demonstrating an apparently later-acquired power of self-propelled flight; Superman assumes a more sophisticated and streamlined style, flying in the prone position, with arms extended in front of him and red cape billowing in the wind.

The entire fictional biographical account of Superman is retold in *Superman, The Movie*. The character is depicted as a superhuman being from a fictional planet, Krypton, who was sent to earth to escape the fatal consequences of the imminent destruction of his planet. Superman is found by the Kents, a midwestern couple, who name the boy Clark and raise him as their son in a bucolic setting. The Kents instill in Clark a strong sense of moral conviction and faith in the "American way," and counsel the boy not to reveal his superhuman powers to anyone. Clark matures into a tall, well-built, dark-haired, and strikingly handsome young man. Ultimately, Clark leaves his pastoral home, finding himself drawn by a mysterious force to a place where he encounters the image of his deceased father, Jor-El. There, Jor-El informs him of his true identity and instructs him to use his superpowers to protect the world from evil. Clark emerges from his fantastic encounter with Jor-El wearing for the first time his Superman costume, a skin-tight blue leotard with red briefs, boots and cape, and a large "S" emblazoned in red and gold upon the chest and cape.

Clark subsequently obtains a position as a reporter for the Daily Planet, but reveals his true identity to no one, assuming instead the appearance of a shy, bumbling, but well-intentioned young man. There he soon meets and becomes infatuated with a beautiful colleague, Lois Lane. Later he appears clad in his Superman regalia to perform amazing feats of strength and courage which immediately attract wide attention, acclaim, and the amorous interest of Lois Lane.

Superman is continually confronted by villains in all of his adventures, but eventually overcomes all evil opponents by exploiting his superpowers of self-propelled flight, imperviousness to bullets, blinding speed, X-ray vision, fantastic hearing, and seemingly immeasurable strength. He fights for "TRUTH, JUSTICE AND THE AMERICAN WAY" and is often described as "FASTER THAN A SPEEDING BULLET," "MORE POWERFUL THAN A LOCOMOTIVE," and "ABLE TO LEAP TALL BUILDINGS IN A SINGLE BOUND." For decades, startled pedestrians in comic strips have shouted, "LOOK, UP IN THE SKY . . . IT'S A BIRD . . . IT'S A PLANE . . . IT'S 'SUPERMAN'!"

The protagonist in *Hero*, Ralph Hinkley, is portrayed as a young high school teacher who is trying to cope with a recent divorce, a resultant dispute over the custody of his son, and the strain that his domestic problems place upon his work and his relationship with an attractive girlfriend. Hinkley's physical attributes are far from extraordinary; he is of medium height, and has a scrawny build and curly blond hair. According to the testimony of his creator, Hinkley is intended to typify the "ordinary guy."

In the premiere episode of *Hero*, Hinkley's van breaks down en route to a high school field trip in the desert. While walking along a road in search of help, Hinkley is nearly run over by an out-of-control automobile driven by Bill Maxwell, an American undercover agent. Maxwell has been searching the desert for his missing FBI partner who, unbeknownst to Maxwell, has been murdered by a band of extremists. Maxwell and Hinkley are suddenly approached by a brightly glowing spaceship from which descends the image of Maxwell's deceased partner. Hinkley is handed a magical caped costume a red leotard with a tunic top, no boots, and a black cape which, when worn, endows him with fantastic powers. Unfortunately, however, Hinkley loses the instruction book that accompanied the intergalactic gift and is left only with the verbal instruction that he should use his powers to save the world from self-destruction. Hinkley grudgingly accepts the mission after being importuned to do so by Maxwell.

While in the privacy of his bedroom the next day, Hinkley holds the suit in front of himself before a mirror and says, "IT'S A BIRD! IT'S A PLANE! IT'S RALPH HINKLEY!" Shortly thereafter he states cynically, "What the world needs is another flying superhero." Hinkley later reveals his newly acquired powers to his girlfriend and begs her understanding. Eventually, he uses his powers to overcome a villain's plan to destroy a portion of southern California.

Although Hinkley ultimately wins the battle with his evil opponent, he does not achieve this goal with the majestic grace, strength, skill, and panache characteristic of Superman. For example, when flying he hollers in fright, and invariably crash-lands, rather than landing with the aplomb of Superman. On one occasion while flying, Hinkley crashes into a building, is nearly knocked unconscious, and then is unceremoniously arrested for vagrancy. And though his magical costume renders him impervious to bullets, when being shot at by villains Hinkley cringes and cowers. Finally, after winning the day in his first adventure, Hinkley shakes the hand of his partner, Maxwell, but unfortunately fractures it, neglecting to restrain his super strength.

On March 16, 1981, two days before the scheduled broadcast of the premiere of *Hero*, plaintiffs filed their complaint seeking the injunctive relief previously described . . . Judge Motley concluded that the parties' works were not substantially similar, and that even if they were, *Hero* was a parody of *Superman* and therefore protected under the fair use doctrine . . . Thus, the defendant was permitted to televise the premiere of *Hero* on March 18, 1981 as scheduled.

Discussion

* * *

This is not the first occasion we have been called upon to decide this issue [of "distill(ing) the nonprotected idea from protected expression"] in an action involving the copyrights in the famous character Superman. *See Detective Comics, Inc. v. Bruns Publications, Inc.*, 111 F.2d 432 (2d Cir. 1940); *see also National Comics Publications, Inc. v. Fawcett Publications, Inc.*, 191 F.2d 594 (2d Cir. 1951). In *Bruns*, we held that while "the pictorial representations and verbal descriptions of 'Superman'" presented more than "a benevolent Hercules" and thus constituted "proper subjects of copyright," we cautioned that the owners of the Superman copyrights were not "entitled to a monopoly of the mere character of a 'Superman' who is a blessing to mankind." This admonition was, of course, consistent with our earlier decisions in *Nichols v. Universal Pictures Corp.*, 45 F.2d 119 (2d Cir. 1930), and *Sheldon v. Metro-Goldwyn Pictures Corp.*, 81 F.2d 49 (2d Cir. 1936), in which this Court ruled that generalized themes and ideas lie in the public domain and are not copyrightable. In deciding in *Bruns* that the defendant's

"Wonderman" comic character infringed the plaintiff's copyrighted Superman works, the Court reviewed the parties' works, identified the similarities between them and concluded that the "only real difference between them is that Superman wears a blue uniform and Wonderman a red one." The Court concluded that the defendants "used more than general types and ideas and . . . appropriated the pictorial and literary details embodied in the complainant's copyrights." While our subsequent decision in *Fawcett Publications* did not turn on the issue of substantial similarity, Judge Hand made the following remark which sheds additional light on the subject:

> (A) copyright never extends to the "idea" of the "work," but only to its "expression," and . . . no one infringes, unless he descends so far into what is concrete as to invade that "expression."

191 F.2d at 600.

* * *

Plaintiffs offer an extensive list of similarities between their works and those of the defendants to establish substantial similarity; for example, both superheroes are shown performing feats of miraculous strength; both wear tight acrobatic costumes; both do battle with villains; both fly with their arms extended in front of them and cape billowing behind; both are impervious to bullets; both have X-ray type vision; both have fantastic hearing and sight; both fly gracefully in the night sky past a city's lit skyscrapers; both lift a car with one hand; both lead a double life; both heroes' power emanates from another planet; and both are drawn to a mysterious spot to meet an extraterrestrial being. We find it unnecessary to recount several other purported similarities between the works suggested by the plaintiffs, since a close examination of the items already listed reveals the fallacy of their argument.

Though it is true that both heroes perform feats of miraculous strength, that is too common and general a characteristic or theme to even approach the degree of concreteness and particularity deserving of copyright protection. In any event, the expression of the general idea of a hero with miraculous strength in *Hero* and *Superman* substantially differs. In *Hero*, Ralph Hinkley derives his power exclusively from his magic suit, whereas in *Superman*, the hero's strength is a natural attribute of his extraterrestrial physical makeup. Additionally, Superman's exploitation of his strength is controlled, whereas Ralph Hinkley struggles at times to conjure it up and at other times to contain it. As to the common use of tight-fitting acrobatic costumes, the defendants convincingly established below that such garb is common in the superhero genre rather than unique to Superman. Moreover, while Superman wears a blue leotard with red briefs, boots and cape, Ralph

Hinkley's costume is a red leotard with a tunic top, no boots, and a black cape. The plaintiffs suggest similarity between the works in that both heroes fight wealthy megalomaniacal villains; however, this suggested similarity concerns something hardly more specific or particular than the classic theme of good versus evil. With respect to the two heroes' common power of self-propelled flight, the defendants demonstrated satisfactorily that several comic strip superheroes possess the power of self-propelled flight and fly with their arms extended in front of them and capes billowing behind. But more important in this regard, the style of flying employed by Superman and Ralph Hinkley hardly could be more different. Superman has mastered the art of self-propelled flight and accomplishes the feat with grace and verve. Ralph Hinkley, on the other hand, seems to be terrified when flying and each time, without fail, crash-lands. Concededly both heroes at some point are shown lifting a car with one hand, but this display would seem to constitute a stereotypical means of demonstrating great strength, within the scenes-à-faire doctrine. The latter notwithstanding, the scenes in each work in which a car is lifted differ substantially; in *Superman*, an infant lifts a pickup truck revealing fantastic strength to the Kents, his future step-parents, whereas in *Hero*, Ralph Hinkley lifts up an automobile to reveal and prove his supernatural strength to his girlfriend. As to the heroes' imperviousness to bullets, while the trait is shared, the expression of the concept differs dramatically. Ralph Hinkley cringes and cowers in the face of gunfire, whereas Superman boldly holds his ground when being fired upon. With respect to the plaintiffs' claim that both heroes share X-ray vision, Ralph Hinkley experiences holographic visions, whereas Superman sees through objects. Nor does the fact that both heroes lead double lives persuade us that the works are substantially similar. The defendants demonstrated below that other personages in the superhero genre lead double lives, their heroic side being kept in deep secrecy. And even more important, the expression of this classic literary idea differs between the two works in this case. In Superman, Clark Kent never reveals his true identity, whereas in *Hero*, Ralph Hinkley voluntarily discloses his part-time superhero status to his girlfriend. With respect to the scenes in which both heroes are shown flying at night with a lit city skyline in the background, the impact of the scene in *Superman* is majestic whereas the impact of the scene in *Hero* is humorous. Superman is shown flying gracefully; Ralph Hinkley flies holding a skylight in one hand for balance. Finally, the scenes in which the hero of each work is drawn mysteriously to a spot to meet an extraterrestrial being are hardly similar in expression. Superman encounters his deceased father's image at some polar icecap location; Ralph Hinkley encounters an unidentified flying object while sitting in an automobile with his future sidekick, Bill Maxwell, and is greeted by Maxwell's deceased partner.

We do not interpret Judge Motley's opinion to suggest that sufficient differences between two works will preclude a finding of substantial similarity notwithstanding the presence of similarities that would otherwise be sufficient to support such a finding. Judge Motley's opinion indicates that she properly focused upon "the similarities, not the differences," and simply adhered to the logic inherent in our statement in *Durham Industries, Inc. v. Tomy Corp.*, 630 F.2d 905, 913 (2d Cir. 1980), that "numerous differences tend to undercut substantial similarity." While "no plagiarist can excuse the wrong by showing how much of his work he did not pirate," "a defendant may legitimately avoid infringement by intentionally making sufficient changes in a work which would otherwise be regarded as substantially similar to that of the plaintiff's." Thus, far from being irrelevant, in cases such as this where the alleged plagiarist "does not take out a block in situ," *Nichols v. Universal Pictures Corp.*, supra, 45 F.2d at 121, an examination of the differences between two works may reveal the absence of substantial similarity.

Finally, plaintiffs cannot seriously contend that the pattern of scenes, sequence of incidents, principal characters, or the general theme between *Hero* and *Superman, The Movie*, for example, are substantially similar. Quite to the contrary, the "total concept and feel" of the two works greatly differ. The *Superman* works portray a benevolent superhuman who seeks to achieve noble goals through the exercise of innate superpowers while at the same time trying to maintain the secrecy of his true identity in order to occupy a position in society as an ordinary person. *Hero* on the other hand, is a "mirror image" of the *Superman* character. *Hero* depicts a typical, young American man with common everyday problems who attempts to cope with the impact upon his life caused by the superhuman powers that are foisted upon him by unidentified alien beings. We conclude that plaintiffs have attempted to demonstrate substantial similarity between the parties' works "by an analysis which alters the actual sequence or construction of plaintiff(s') work in order to achieve a juxtaposition that makes for greater similarity with defendant(s') work."

* * *

Affirmed.

## QUESTIONS FOR DISCUSSION

1. How different from Superman would a superhero have to be to avoid infringement? In *Detective Comics, Inc. v. Bruns Publications, Inc.*, 111 F.2d 432 (2d Cir. 1940), the court found that the defendants' Wonderman infringed the copyright in the *Superman* comic books. Wonderman's powers were quite similar to Superman's, leading the court to note that the only real difference between the two was the color of their costumes. The court also rejected the defendants' argument that Wonderman's and Superman's powers were both

generic and unoriginal. Which features of a character are simply *ideas* and which actually constitute protectible *expression*?

2. Should characters like Superman or Donald Duck receive more protection than literary characters like James Bond? Does the status of the latter character change when Albert Broccoli starts producing movies that make Bond's features more apparent for the viewer, as Sylvester Stallone did with his Rocky and Rambo characters. *See Anderson v. Stallone*, 1989 WL 206431 (C.D. Cal. 1989)?

3. Is the implication of *Warner Bros.* that Dashiell Hammett could not object to *another* author writing a detective story featuring Sam Spade? In light of the underlying goals of copyright law, do literary creations need and merit less protection than cartoon or other visual creations?

4. If someone created a sculpture of a literary character, would this constitute infringement? For example, would a bust of *Tom Sawyer* infringe the copyright on the novel Tom Sawyer (assuming the copyright were still in existence)? What if the bust was done as an abstract sculpture, but was entitled "Artist's Impression of Tom Sawyer"? The Copyright Act does not give a great deal of guidance. Section 106 does list the right to create derivative works as one of the exclusive rights of a copyright holder. But is the above example a derivative work? Section 113 also provides that for pictorial, graphic, and sculptural works, the exclusive right of Section 106 to reproduce the work "includes the right to reproduce the work in or on any kind of article, whether useful or otherwise." Note, however, that this section does not apply to literary works.

5. In *Mattel, Inc. v. Goldberger Doll Manufacturing Co.*, 365 F.3d 133, 136 (2d Cir. 2004), Mattel had created a doll that eventually came to be known as the world-famous "Super-Star Barbie," with worldwide sales exceeding $1 billion. Radio City in New York, to celebrate the new millennium, had Goldberger Doll Mfg. create a doll they named "Rockette 2000." In the ensuing lawsuit, it was clear that there were resemblances between Barbie's and Rockette's eyes, nose and mouth, but the parties disagreed about whether such facial features warranted copyright protection. What are your views about the likely and the appropriate judgment on that doll copyright score?

6. How detailed must a character be to receive copyright protection? *Olson v. NBC*, 855 F.2d 1446 (9th Cir. 1988), involved an allegation of copying by NBC's television series *The A-Team*, of elements in Olson's earlier treatment and screenplay for a television pilot called *Cargo*. The focus of the claim and the judicial opinion was on the characters in the two works:

* * *

> *Cargo* features a unit of three Vietnam veterans—Van Druten, Tronski and Brown—who developed a group practice of conducting scams in Vietnam and continue to conduct such scams as civilians. While in Vietnam, they alienated Col. Kilgore and Lt. Brite by

humiliating them in order to prevent them from uncovering a scam. Today, Tronski and Brown work together for an air cargo business in Miami. Tronski is romantically involved with Marsha Bainwright, the daughter of the owner of the air freight company.

Olson provides three-to four-line descriptions of each of his characters. He compares Van Druten to John Ritter, describing him as an old-money New York intellectual who has studied medicine; he was the group's navigator in Vietnam, and he is reluctant to become involved in the group's scams but agrees to participate. Tronski, who is compared to Nick Nolte, is an impulsive, quick-thinking "good old boy" from the South; he was a pilot in Vietnam and serves as the trio's leader and strategist. Brown, described as a "Rosie Greer [sic] type," is depicted as a physically large athletic, sensitive, emotionally deep man from the deep South. Kilgore is a "militaristic, extremist, schizoid" Southerner. Marsha Bainwright, who resembles Kate Jackson, is said to be wealthy and elegant.

*Cargo* is set in the present. Kilgore and Brite, who are now corrupt Drug Enforcement agents, threaten Tronski and Brown with unjustified smuggling charges, which are to be dropped if they cooperate in breaking up a large Colombian cocaine smuggling ring. Because Van Druten closely resembles the ringleader's son, the DEA agents force Tronski and Brown to enlist his help. After a series of plot episodes that lead the trio to New York City, Florida, Colombia, and much of the adjacent airspace, the unit escapes in a cargo plane carrying a load of drugs, unaware that Kilgore and Brite have sabotaged the plane. After the trio crash lands the plane in the ocean, Kilgore and Brite take them captive, then send divers to salvage the drugs from the plane. The Coast Guard arrives and arrests Kilgore and Brite. The trio flies clothes and gifts to a children's mission in South America.

*The A-Team* includes three members—Peck, Baracus, and Smith—who were wrongly faced with a court martial because, acting under orders from a colonel who died without verifying their story, they robbed the Bank of Hanoi of 100 million yen shortly after the end of the Vietnam war. A fourth man, Murdock, was the trio's pilot in Vietnam. Colonel Lynch, who ran the prison from which the group escaped more than 10 years before, still seeks to find them.

Peck is a suave con artist who is reluctant to participate in the A-Team's adventures. Baracas is a huge, mohawked, pugnacious, mechanical genius. Smith, the leader of the unit in Vietnam, continues to lead the group here. Murdock serves as the group's eccentric, possibly insane pilot. Lynch is a career military man. Amy Allen is an impetuous, dedicated newspaper reporter.

*The A-Team* is set in the present. In the pilot episode, Allen hires the A-Team to help her find a reporter who is missing in

Mexico. The A-Team goes to Mexico and with the reporter's assistance, accomplishes its mission. In the process, it rescues a terrorized town from a band of Mexican revolutionaries.

* * *

855 F.2d at 1449. What is your verdict on *The A-Team*?

7. Titles of stories or names of characters are not copyrightable as such, though use of the same titles and names can be evidence of substantial similarity between two works as a whole. Should merchandise bearing the phrases, "I Love You E.T." and "E.T.-Phone Home," constitute violation of the copyright in the *E.T.* movie? (We shall look at the trademark issues later in Chapter 6.) *See Universal City Studios, Inc. v. Kamar Indus., Inc.*, 1982 Copr.L.Dec. CCH ¶ 25,452, 217 U.S.P.Q. 1162 (S.D. Tex. 1982).

8. Are cars used in comic books "copyrightable?" In 2013, D.C. Comics sued Mark Towle, who was selling replica "Batmobiles" from his "Gotham Garage." Putting aside the obvious trademark violations, can D.C. Comics sustain a copyright claim against Towle? Is the Batmobile copyrightable? *See D.C. Comics v. Towle*, 989 F.Supp.2d 948 (C.D. Cal. 2013).

## D. FAIR AND UNFAIR USES OF ENTERTAINMENT WORKS[1]

The fact that an author has acquired copyright in an intellectual product and then somebody else has copied that work does not inevitably mean that copyright infringement has taken place. The same law that confers property rights on the original author also grants everyone else a privilege of "fair use" of such work. Defining and applying the boundary line between fair and unfair uses requires the courts regularly to return to the fundamental questions of why we create intellectual property in the first place and when enforcement of such a right may detract from the very values the law was designed to promote.

For nearly two centuries, fair use was an entirely judge-made doctrine. Not until the 1976 Copyright Act did Congress enact Section 107 and thence erect an explicit statutory platform for fair use. This Section incorporated the key concepts from the common law, but it was not intended to freeze the evolution of this doctrine.

1 *See* L. Ray Patterson, *Free Speech, Copyright, & Fair Use*, 40 Vand. L. Rev. 1 (1987); William W. Fisher III, *Reconstructing the Fair Use Doctrine*, 101 Harv. L. Rev. 1661 (1988); Pierre N. Leval, *Toward A Fair Use Standard*, 103 Harv. L. Rev. 1105 (1990); Lloyd L. Weinreb, *Fair Use*, 4 Fordham L. Rev. 1291 (1999); Matthew Sag, *God in the Machine: A New Structural Analysis of Copyright's Fair Use Doctrine*, 11 Mich. Tech. L. Rev. 1 (2005); Steven Horowitz, *A Free Speech Theory of Copyright*, 2009 Stan. Tech. L. Rev. 2 (2009). An interesting comparative piece is Tyler G. Newby, *What's Fair Here is Not Fair Everywhere: Does the American Fair Use Doctrine Violate International Copyright Law*, 51 Stan. L. Rev. 1633 (1999).

Section 107 begins by stating that "the fair use of a copyrighted work . . . for purposes such as criticism, comment, news reporting, teaching . . . , scholarship, or research," is not an infringement of copyright. The Section goes on to say that when courts are deciding whether

> the use made of a work in any particular case is a fair use, the factors to be considered shall include:
>
> (1) the purpose and character of the use, including whether such use is of a commercial nature or is for nonprofit educational purposes;
>
> (2) the nature of the copyrighted work;
>
> (3) the amount and substantiality of the portion used in relation to the copyrighted work as a whole; and
>
> (4) the effect of the use upon the potential market for or value of the copyrighted work.

Though there had been considerable debate about fair use, not until the mid-1980s did the Supreme Court finally begin to commit itself on this issue. The next decade, though, witnessed several major court rulings on this topic. One of those cases, *Sony Corp. v. Universal City Studios*, 464 U.S. 417 (1984), is in the next chapter as a major illustration of the response of copyright law to new technologies. The following case required the Court to decide how to reconcile traditional copyright doctrine with the Court's more recent commitment to uninhibited freedom of speech, viewed as the underpinning of self-government in the public arena.

---

Like many former presidents, Gerald Ford negotiated a lucrative book contract for his memoirs. As a byproduct of that deal, publisher Harper & Row agreed to give *Time* magazine the exclusive right to publish excerpts from *A Time To Heal: The Autobiography of Gerald R. Ford* in the week before the book was to appear in stores. A couple of weeks before the book's publication, an unidentified person secretly provided a copy of the manuscript to Victor Navasky, editor of the *Nation* magazine. For his next issue, Navasky quickly authored an article—"Behind the Nixon Pardon"—about that one key item in the memoirs. Interspersed throughout the brief, 2250-word article were approximately 300 words directly quoted from Ford's 300,000-word manuscript. With the appearance of the *Nation* piece and wide reporting of its contents in the national media, *Time* cancelled its article and refused to pay the $12,500 balance due to Harper & Row. The publisher then sued the *Nation* in a case, *Harper & Row Publishers v. Nation Enterprises*, 471 U.S. 539

(1985), that raised major questions about fair use and the line between copyright law and free speech.

Justice O'Connor's majority opinion reversed the Second Circuit and upheld the publisher's claim against the magazine. The Court began by emphasizing the fact that the *Nation* had copied passages from Ford's unpublished memoirs, thereby "seriously infringing the author's right to decide when and whether [the work] will be made public." Nor was it relevant that, unlike a confidential letter, Ford intended to publish this material shortly.

> The obvious benefit to author and public alike of assuring authors the leisure to develop their ideas free from fear of expropriation outweighs any short-term "news value" to be gained from premature publication of the author's expression.

471 U.S. at 555. In response to the *Nation*'s First Amendment claim to print its "scoop" about Ford's reasons for pardoning Nixon, Justice O'Connor wrote:

> Copyright assures those who write and publish factual narratives such as *A Time To Heal* that they may at least enjoy the right to market the original expression contained therein as just compensation for their investment.

471 U.S. at 556–57.

The Court then turned to the four statutory factors governing fair use.

1. *Purpose of the Use*. The Court characterized the *Nation*'s actions not as news reporting for the public benefit, but as a bad faith, commercial effort "to profit from exploitation of the copyrighted material without paying the customary price" (i.e., by outbidding *Time* for the right to this preview of the book), while making use of a stolen manuscript.

2. *Nature of the Copyrighted Work*. Although there is greater latitude to disseminate historical or biographical facts than works of fiction, the Court concluded that this was outweighed by President Ford's interest in confidentiality and creative control over the timing and context of *A Time To Heal*'s publication.

3. *Amount and Substantiality of the Portion Used*. Although quantitatively the words quoted were only a tiny portion of *A Time To Heal*, in qualitative terms they were among the most "powerful passages" in the book—precisely the reason why they constituted such a substantial portion (13 percent) of the *Nation*'s article. The heart of the work was taken.

4. *Effect on the Market.* The Court's opinion underlined that this factor "is undoubtedly the single most important element of fair use." *Time*'s cancellation of its serialization and payment damaged this portion of the market:

> Placed in a broader perspective, a fair use doctrine that permits extensive prepublication quotations from an unreleased manuscript without the copyright owner's consent poses substantial potential for damage to the marketability of first serialization rights in general.

471 U.S. at 569. Having concluded from this analysis of the factors that the *Nation* had no fair use defense, the Court declined to create "a compulsory license permitting unfettered access to the unpublished copyrighted expression of public figures."

In an extended dissent, Justice Brennan objected to the majority's characterization of the *Nation* story as "thievery" or "piracy" of President Ford's property. The dissent depicted the majority as defending private economic prerogatives at the expense of broad dissemination of ideas and robust debate about public issues. More specifically, Justice Brennan emphasized that the true source of the financial damage done by the *Nation* article was its "scoop" about President Ford's actual reasons for pardoning President Nixon, not the quoting of Ford's expression of those reasons; and this fact is not protectable by copyright law irrespective of the disincentives thereby created for research and writing about current or historical events.

## *QUESTIONS FOR DISCUSSION*

1. Justice O'Connor noted at the outset of her opinion that *A Time To Heal* had taken two years to produce, requiring President Ford to "draft essays and word portraits of public figures and participate in hundreds of taped interviews that were later distilled to chronicle his personal viewpoint." Is that position consistent with Justice O'Connor's subsequent opinion in *Feist*, in which she rejected a pure "sweat of the brow" basis for copyright protection—there the gathering of all the names and addresses needed for a telephone directory? Do you think any significant harm would have been done to the writing of political memoirs had the Supreme Court gone the other way in *Harper & Row*? On the other hand, do you sense any constraints on current media coverage from the legal risks posed by the Court's ruling? Should the financial impact on spin-off works such as the *Time* excerpts be given the same weight as the impact on the principal work (e.g., book sales)?

2. Martin Luther King's 1963 "I Have a Dream" speech is likely the most important creative work in the history of American civil rights. Understandably, CBS devoted an episode of its 1994 documentary series on

*The 20th Century* to "Martin Luther King, Jr. & The March on Washington," including about 60 percent of "I Have A Dream" which the CBS news crew had filmed back in 1963. Just as in the contemporary newscasts, CBS had not sought or paid for a license from King or his heirs to broadcast any of the speech. Was it fair use? *See Estate of Martin Luther King v. CBS*, 194 F.3d 1211 (11th Cir. 1999)

3. In 1995, General Colin Powell's long-awaited memoirs, *An American Journey*, were to be published. *Time* magazine had outbid *Newsweek* and *U.S. News* by paying $300,000 to print excerpts to coincide with Random House's publication of the book. Somehow *Newsweek* got a copy of the manuscript and ran a cover story the week before, containing extensive details from and impressions of Powell and his autobiography. The *Newsweek* story was immediately picked up by newspapers across the country. One thing that *Newsweek* did *not* do, though, was to quote any passages from Powell's book. Random House and Time were highly critical of *Newsweek* for breaking "just about every journalistic ethic you can think of" by "having failed in the auction and simply stolen a copy." Time, however, decided to run its own cover story and excerpts the next week, saying that "the only people who will be satisfied by *Newsweek*'s synopsis are people who read Cliff Notes instead of actual literature." A week later, *An American Journey* became a best seller. Still, Random House's lawyers looked into the question of whether *Newsweek* had violated the law with its "scoop." Do you think *Newsweek* violated copyright (or perhaps even contract) law? Do you think it violated journalistic ethics?

4. In 1991, a Los Angeles plumber and amateur photographer, George Holliday, happened to videotape ten minutes of the police arrest and beating of a black motorist, Rodney King. Before he appreciated the political significance and potential value of the tape, Holliday gave it to the KTLA television station to show on this and other stations and networks (in return for the standard $500 licensing fee paid by stations for amateur videos). Holliday later argued that there were implied limits on the scope and terms of that license, requiring future users to secure (and pay for) fresh licenses from him. The case was settled while under appeal from an unreported rejection of the claim. Suppose that Holliday had given KTLA a strictly-limited right to play the tape on the air—would KTLA or other stations have a fair use or First Amendment right to replay it? Recall earlier examples, such as the My Lai photo in the Vietnam War or the Zapruder filming of the shooting of President Kennedy. *See Time, Inc. v. Bernard Geis Associates*, 293 F. Supp. 130 (S.D.N.Y. 1968). Should uses in movies be treated differently than television or newspaper accounts? Spike Lee paid Holliday $65,000 to use his Rodney King film in Lee's *Malcolm X* and Oliver Stone paid Zapruder $40,000 to use his film in *JFK*.

5. Eight years after *Harper & Row*, Congress amended Section 107 to make it clear that the fact a work was unpublished should not by itself bar a finding of fair use based on consideration of all other relevant factors. That legislative debate was influenced by subsequent cases that had tested the

contours of property rights in private writings.[m] *See Salinger v. Random House*, 811 F.2d 90 (2d Cir. 1987) (quotes from unpublished J.D. Salinger letters); *Wright v. Warner Books, Inc.*, 953 F.2d 731 (2d Cir. 1991) (Richard Wright letters). While the fact that the original work was unpublished can no longer be the decisive, should this be at least a relevant factor?

---

George Lucas and his Lucasfilm Ltd. filed suit against Little Brown, the publishing arm of Time Warner, regarding Ted Edwards' book, *The Unauthorized Star Wars Compendium: The Complete Guide to the Movies, Comics, Books, Novels, & More*. Besides its overview of how *Star Wars* evolved from an initial film idea in the 1970s to three movie hits, Edwards recounted numerous anecdotes about what happened backstage (with photos of cast and crews). To tell this story, *Compendium* also contained synopses of prior *Star Wars* movies and books. The Lucasfilm claim was that Little Brown had "copied substantial protectable material from the *Star Wars* trilogy," including its published catalogue and annotated screenplays. While the *Compendium* book had a disclaimer on both its front and back cover saying "[t]his book had not been prepared, approved, licensed, or endorsed by any entity that created or produced the '*Star Wars* properties,'" Lucas' counsel Bert Fields argued that "Little Brown's book trades in the fame of *Star Wars* films, stories and books. They've misappropriated portions of the entire range of copyrighted Lucasfilm publications."

Of course, such unauthorized books have had a number of predecessors to *Star Wars*. For example, Carol Publishing Group published a book, *The Seinfeld Aptitude Test* (SAT), written by Beth Golub. This book contained 643 "trivia" questions about events and characters in the *Seinfeld* show, the answers to which author Golub had learned while watching *Seinfeld* over the years. While NBC actually distributed some copies of this "fun little book" to promote this crucial Thursday night program, *Seinfeld's* producer Castle Rock Entertainment sued for violation of its copyright in the show. Should such a work be deemed a violation of the right to produce or license such a derivative work? Or should the book be judged just a reprint of the "facts" of the series, or a "transformative" use of the original expression for a very different offering to *Seinfeld* fans? What about a similar book about baseball trivia? *See Castle Rock Entertainment v. Carol Publishing Group*, 955 F. Supp. 260 (S.D.N.Y. 1997).

---

[m] *See* Karen Burke LeFevre, *The Tell-Tale "Heart": Determining "Fair" Use of Unpublished Texts*, 55 Law & Contemp. Probs. 153 (Spring 1992).

The Supreme Court returned to the fair use fray a decade after *Harper & Row*—this time in the context of "parody."[n] Parody has long posed a challenge to copyright doctrine, dating back to vaudeville performers impersonating popular stars by singing songs associated with the latter. Parody as an art form predates copyright, as evidenced by the work of Shakespeare and Cervantes. The hoped-for benefits of parody are not only entertainment, but also artistic innovation and social criticism. The legal problem, though, is that in order to parody a work, one also has to copy it sufficiently to create a recognizable "derivative" work, something that ordinarily requires consent of the copyright holder which often is not forthcoming. Lower courts had grappled for decades with this legal and intellectual dilemma. The Supreme Court finally faced this problem in a 1994 case involving a recording by 2 Live Crew on their *As Clean As They Wanna Be* album, parodying "Pretty Woman," Roy Orbison's 1960s country rock hit, "Oh Pretty Woman" (a song whose popularity had soared again as the theme song in Julia Roberts's movie *Pretty Woman*).

## CAMPBELL A.K.A. LUKE SKYYWALKER V. ACUFF-ROSE MUSIC, INC.

Supreme Court of the United States 1994.
510 U.S. 569, 114 S.Ct. 1164, 127 L.Ed.2d 500.

JUSTICE SOUTER delivered the opinion of the Court.

* * *

### I

In 1964, Roy Orbison and William Dees wrote a rock ballad called "Oh, Pretty Woman" and assigned their rights in it to Acuff-Rose Music, Inc. Acuff-Rose registered the song for copyright protection.

Petitioners Luther R. Campbell, Christopher Wongwon, Mark Ross, and David Hobbs, are collectively known as 2 Live Crew, a popular rap music group. In 1989, Campbell wrote a song entitled "Pretty Woman," which he later described in an affidavit as intended, "through comical lyrics, to satirize the original work. . . ." On July 5, 1989, 2 Live Crew's manager informed Acuff-Rose that 2 Live Crew had written a parody of "Oh, Pretty Woman," that they would afford all credit for ownership and authorship of the original song to Acuff-Rose, Dees, and Orbison, and that they were willing to pay a fee for the use they wished to make of it. Enclosed with the letter were a copy of the lyrics and a recording of 2 Live Crew's song. Acuff-Rose's agent refused permission, stating that "I am

---

[n] *See* Alfred C. Yen, *When Authors Won't Sell: Parody, Fair Use, & Efficiency in Copyright Law*, 62 U. Colo. L. Rev. 79 (1991); Richard A. Posner, *When Is Parody Fair Use?*, 21 J. Legal Stud. 67 (1992).

aware of the success enjoyed by 'The 2 Live Crews,' but I must inform you that we cannot permit the use of a parody of 'Oh, Pretty Woman.'" Nonetheless, in June or July 1989, 2 Live Crew released records, cassette tapes, and compact discs of "Pretty Woman" in a collection of songs entitled "As Clean As They Wanna Be." The albums and compact discs identify the authors of "Pretty Woman" as Orbison and Dees and its publisher as Acuff-Rose.

Almost a year later, after nearly a quarter of a million copies of the recording had been sold, Acuff-Rose sued 2 Live Crew and its record company, Luke Skywalker Records, for copyright infringement. The District Court granted summary judgment for 2 Live Crew, reasoning that the commercial purpose of 2 Live Crew's song was no bar to fair use; that 2 Live Crew's version was a parody, which "quickly degenerates into a play on words, substituting predictable lyrics with shocking ones" to show "how bland and banal the Orbison song" is; that 2 Live Crew had taken no more than was necessary to "conjure up" the original in order to parody it; and that it was "extremely unlikely that 2 Live Crew's song could adversely affect the market for the original." The District Court weighed these factors and held that 2 Live Crew's song made fair use of Orbison's original.

The Court of Appeals for the Sixth Circuit reversed and remanded. 972 F.2d 1429, 1439 (1992). Although it assumed for the purpose of its opinion that 2 Live Crew's song was a parody of the Orbison original, the Court of Appeals thought the District Court had put too little emphasis on the fact that "every commercial use . . . is presumptively . . . unfair," *Sony Corp. of America v. Universal City Studios, Inc.*, 464 U.S. 417, 451 (1984), and it held that "the admittedly commercial nature" of the parody "requires the conclusion" that the first of four factors relevant under the statute weighs against a finding of fair use. Next, the Court of Appeals determined that, by "taking the heart of the original and making it the heart of a new work," 2 Live Crew had, qualitatively, taken too much. Finally, after noting that the effect on the potential market for the original (and the market for derivative works) is "undoubtedly the single most important element of fair use," *Harper & Row, Publishers, Inc. v. Nation Enterprises*, 471 U.S. 539, 566 (1985), the Court of Appeals faulted the District Court for "refusing to indulge the presumption" that "harm for purposes of the fair use analysis has been established by the presumption attaching to commercial uses." In sum, the court concluded that its "blatantly commercial purpose . . . prevents this parody from being a fair use."

* * *

II

It is uncontested here that 2 Live Crew's song would be an infringement of Acuff-Rose's rights in "Oh, Pretty Woman," under the Copyright Act of 1976, but for a finding of fair use through parody. From the infancy of copyright protection, some opportunity for fair use of copyrighted materials has been thought necessary to fulfill copyright's very purpose, "to promote the Progress of Science and useful Arts. . . ." U.S. Const., Art. I, § 8, cl. 8. For as Justice Story explained, "in truth, in literature, in science and in art, there are, and can be, few, if any, things, which in an abstract sense, are strictly new and original throughout. Every book in literature, science and art, borrows, and must necessarily borrow, and use much which was well known and used before." *Emerson v. Davies*, 8 F. Cas. 615, 619 (No. 4,436) (C.C.D.Mass.1845) . . .

In *Folsom v. Marsh*, Justice Story distilled the essence of law and methodology from the earlier cases: "look to the nature and objects of the selections made, the quantity and value of the materials used, and the degree in which the use may prejudice the sale, or diminish the profits, or supersede the objects, of the original work." 9 F. Cas. 342, 348 (No. 4,901) (C.C.D. Mass. 1841). Thus expressed, fair use remained exclusively judge-made doctrine until the passage of the 1976 Copyright Act, in which Story's summary is discernible . . .

* * *

. . . Congress meant § 107 "to restate the present judicial doctrine of fair use, not to change, narrow, or enlarge it in any way" and intended that courts continue the common law tradition of fair use adjudication. The fair use doctrine thus "permits [and requires] courts to avoid rigid application of the copyright statute when, on occasion, it would stifle the very creativity which that law is designed to foster." *Stewart v. Abend*, 495 U.S. 207, 236 (1990).

The task is not to be simplified with bright-line rules, for the statute, like the doctrine it recognizes, calls for case-by-case analysis. The text employs the terms "including" and "such as" in the preamble paragraph to indicate the "illustrative and not limitative" function of the examples given in § 101, which thus provide only general guidance about the sorts of copying that courts and Congress most commonly had found to be fair uses. Nor may the four statutory factors be treated in isolation, one from another. All are to be explored, and the results weighed together, in light of the purposes of copyright.

*A*

The first factor in a fair use enquiry is "the purpose and character of the use, including whether such use is of a commercial nature or is for nonprofit educational purposes." This factor draws on Justice Story's formulation, "the nature and objects of the selections made." *Folsom v. Marsh*, 9 F. Cas., at 348. The enquiry here may be guided by the examples given in the preamble to § 107, looking to whether the use is for criticism, or comment, or news reporting, and the like. The central purpose of this investigation is to see, in Justice Story's words, whether the new work merely "supersedes the objects" of the original creation, *Folsom v. Marsh*, supra, at 348; accord, *Harper & Row*, supra, at 562 ("supplanting" the original), or instead adds something new, with a further purpose or different character, altering the first with new expression, meaning, or message; it asks, in other words, whether and to what extent the new work is "transformative." Leval 1111. Although such transformative use is not absolutely necessary for a finding of fair use, the goal of copyright, to promote science and the arts, is generally furthered by the creation of transformative works. Such works thus lie at the heart of the fair use doctrine's guarantee of breathing space within the confines of copyright, and the more transformative the new work, the less will be the significance of other factors, like commercialism, that may weigh against a finding of fair use.

This Court has only once before even considered whether parody may be fair use, and that time issued no opinion because of the Court's equal division. *Benny v. Loew's Inc.*, 239 F.2d 532 (C.A.9 1956), aff'd sub nom. *Columbia Broadcasting System, Inc. v. Loew's Inc.*, 356 U.S. 43 (1958). Suffice it to say now that parody has an obvious claim to transformative value, as Acuff-Rose itself does not deny. Like less ostensibly humorous forms of criticism, it can provide social benefit, by shedding light on an earlier work, and, in the process, creating a new one. We thus line up with the courts that have held that parody, like other comment or criticism, may claim fair use under § 107.

The germ of parody lies in the definition of the Greek parodeia, quoted in Judge Nelson's Court of Appeals dissent, as "a song sung alongside another." 972 F.2d, at 1440, quoting 7 *Encyclopedia Britannica* 768 (15th ed. 1975). Modern dictionaries accordingly describe a parody as a "literary or artistic work that imitates the characteristic style of an author or a work for comic effect or ridicule," or as a "composition in prose or verse in which the characteristic turns of thought and phrase in an author or class of authors are imitated in such a way as to make them appear ridiculous." For the purposes of copyright law, the nub of the definitions, and the heart of any parodist's claim to quote from existing material, is the use of some elements of a prior author's composition to create a new one that, at least in part, comments on that author's works. If, on the contrary, the commentary has no critical bearing on the substance or style of the original composition, which the alleged infringer merely uses to get attention or to avoid the drudgery in working up something fresh, the claim to fairness in borrowing from another's work diminishes accordingly (if it does not vanish), and other factors, like the extent of its commerciality, loom larger.[14] Parody needs to mimic an original to make its point, and so has some claim to use the creation of its victim's (or collective victims') imagination, whereas satire can stand on its own two feet and so requires justification for the very act of borrowing. The fact that parody can claim legitimacy for some appropriation does not, of course, tell either parodist or judge much about where to draw the line. Like a book review quoting the copyrighted material criticized, parody may or may not be fair use, and petitioner's suggestion that any parodic use is presumptively fair has no more justification in law or fact than the equally hopeful claim that any use for news reporting should be presumed fair, *see Harper & Row*, 471 U.S., at 561 . . . Accordingly, parody, like any other use, has to work its way through the relevant factors, and be judged case by case, in light of the ends of the copyright law.

* * *

We have less difficulty in finding the element [of criticism of the original] in 2 Live Crew's song than the Court of Appeals did, although having found it we will not take the further step of evaluating its quality. The threshold question when fair use is raised in defense of parody is whether a parodic character may reasonably be perceived. Whether, going beyond that, parody is in good taste or bad does not and should not matter to fair use. As Justice Holmes explained, "it would be a dangerous undertaking for persons trained only to the law to constitute themselves final judges of the worth of [a work], outside of the narrowest and most obvious limits. At the one extreme some works of genius would be sure to miss appreciation. Their very novelty would make them repulsive until the public had learned the new language in which their author spoke."

While we might not assign a high rank to the parodic element here, we think it fair to say that 2 Live Crew's song reasonably could be perceived as commenting on the original or criticizing it, to some degree. 2 Live Crew juxtaposes the romantic musings of a man whose fantasy comes true, with degrading taunts, a bawdy demand for sex, and a sigh of relief from paternal responsibility. The later words can be taken as a comment on the naivete of the original of an earlier day, as a rejection of

---

[14] A parody that more loosely targets an original than the parody presented here may still be sufficiently aimed at an original work to come within our analysis of parody. If a parody whose wide dissemination in the market runs the risk of serving as a substitute for the original or licensed derivatives (*see* infra, discussing factor four), it is more incumbent on one claiming fair use to establish the extent of transformation and the parody's critical relationship to the original. By contrast, when there is little or no risk of market substitution, whether because of the large extent of transformation of the earlier work, the new work's minimal distribution in the market, the small extent to which it borrows from an original, or other factors, taking parodic aim at an original is a less critical factor in the analysis, and looser forms of parody may be found to be fair use, as may satire with lesser justification for the borrowing than would otherwise be required.

its sentiment that ignores the ugliness of street life and the debasement that it signifies. It is this joinder of reference and ridicule that marks off the author's choice of parody from the other types of comment and criticism that traditionally have had a claim to fair use protection as transformative works.

The Court of Appeals, however, immediately cut short the enquiry into 2 Live Crew's fair use claim by confining its treatment of the first factor essentially to one relevant fact, the commercial nature of the use. The court then inflated the significance of this fact by applying a presumption ostensibly culled from Sony, that "every commercial use of copyrighted material is presumptively . . . unfair. . . ." In giving virtually dispositive weight to the commercial nature of the parody, the Court of Appeals erred.

The language of the statute makes clear that the commercial or nonprofit educational purpose of a work is only one element of the first factor enquiry into its purpose and character. Section 107(1) uses the term "including" to begin the dependent clause referring to commercial use, and the main clause speaks of a broader investigation into "purpose and character." As we explained in *Harper & Row*, Congress resisted attempts to narrow the ambit of this traditional enquiry by adopting categories of presumptively fair use, and it urged courts to preserve the breadth of their traditionally ample view of the universe of relevant evidence. Accordingly, the mere fact that a use is educational and not for profit does not insulate it from a finding of infringement, any more than the commercial character of a use bars a finding of fairness. If, indeed, commerciality carried presumptive force against a finding of fairness, the presumption would swallow nearly all of the illustrative uses listed in the preamble paragraph of § 107, including news reporting, comment, criticism, teaching, scholarship, and research, since these activities "are generally conducted for profit in this country." Congress could not have intended such a rule, which certainly is not inferable from the common-law cases, arising as they did from the world of letters in which Samuel Johnson could pronounce that "no man but a blockhead ever wrote, except for money." 3 *Boswell's Life of Johnson* 19 (G. Hill ed. 1934).

*Sony* itself called for no hard evidentiary presumption. There, we emphasized the need for a "sensitive balancing of interests," noted that Congress had "eschewed a rigid, bright-line approach to fair use," and stated that the commercial or nonprofit educational character of a work is "not conclusive," but rather a fact to be "weighed along with others in fair use decisions." The Court of Appeals's elevation of one sentence from *Sony* to a per se rule thus runs as much counter to *Sony* itself as to the long common-law tradition of fair use adjudication. Rather, as we explained in *Harper & Row, Sony* stands for the proposition that the "fact that a publication was commercial as opposed to nonprofit is a separate factor that tends to weigh against a finding of fair use." But that is all, and the fact that even the force of that tendency will vary with the context is a further reason against elevating commerciality to hard presumptive significance. The use, for example, of a copyrighted work to advertise a product, even in a parody, will be entitled to less indulgence under the first factor of the fair use enquiry, than the sale of a parody for its own sake, let alone one performed a single time by students in school.[18]

B

The second statutory factor, "the nature of the copyrighted work," draws on Justice Story's expression, the "value of the materials used." *Folsom v. Marsh*, 9 F. Cas., at 348. This factor calls for recognition that some works are closer to the core of intended copyright protection than others, with the consequence that fair use is more difficult to establish when the former works are copied. We agree with both the District Court and the Court of Appeals that the Orbison original's creative expression for public dissemination falls within the core of the copyright's protective purposes. This fact, however, is not much help in this case, or ever likely to help much in separating the fair use sheep from the infringing goats in a parody case, since parodies almost invariably copy publicly known, expressive works.

C

The third factor asks whether "the amount and substantiality of the portion used in relation to the copyrighted work as a whole," § 107(3) (or, in Justice Story's words, "the quantity and value of the materials used," *Folsom v. Marsh*, supra, at 348) are reasonable in relation to the purpose of the copying. Here, attention turns to the persuasiveness of a parodist's justification for the particular copying done, and the enquiry will harken back to the first of the statutory factors, for, as in prior cases, we recognize that the extent of permissible copying varies with the purpose and character of the use. The facts bearing on this factor will also tend to address the fourth, by revealing the degree to which the parody may serve as a market substitute for the original or potentially licensed derivatives.

The District Court considered the song's parodic purpose in finding that 2 Live Crew had not helped themselves overmuch. The Court of Appeals disagreed, stating that "while it may not be inappropriate to find that no more was taken than necessary, the copying was qualitatively

[18] Finally, regardless of the weight one might place on the alleged infringer's state of mind, we reject Acuff-Rose's argument that 2 Live Crew's request for permission to use the original should be weighed against a finding of fair use. Even if good faith were central to fair use, 2 Live Crew's actions do not necessarily suggest that they believed their version was not fair use; the offer may simply have been made in a good faith effort to avoid this litigation. If the use is otherwise fair, then no permission need be sought or granted. Thus, being denied permission to use a work does not weigh against a finding of fair use.

substantial. . . . We conclude that taking the heart of the original and making it the heart of a new work was to purloin a substantial portion of the essence of the original."

The Court of Appeals is of course correct that this factor calls for thought not only about the quantity of the materials used, but about their quality and importance, too. In *Harper & Row*, for example, the Nation had taken only some 300 words out of President Ford's memoirs, but we signaled the significance of the quotations in finding them to amount to "the heart of the book," the part most likely to be newsworthy and important in licensing serialization. We also agree with the Court of Appeals that whether "a substantial portion of the infringing work was copied verbatim" from the copyrighted work is a relevant question, for it may reveal a dearth of transformative character or purpose under the first factor, or a greater likelihood of market harm under the fourth; a work composed primarily of an original, particularly its heart, with little added or changed, is more likely to be a merely superseding use, fulfilling demand for the original.

Where we part company with the court below is in applying these guides to parody, and in particular to parody in the song before us. Parody presents a difficult case. Parody's humor, or in any event its comment, necessarily springs from recognizable allusion to its object through distorted imitation. Its art lies in the tension between a known original and its parodic twin. When parody takes aim at a particular original work, the parody must be able to "conjure up" at least enough of that original to make the object of its critical wit recognizable. What makes for this recognition is quotation of the original's most distinctive or memorable features, which the parodist can be sure the audience will know. Once enough has been taken to assure identification, how much more is reasonable will depend, say, on the extent to which the song's overriding purpose and character is to parody the original or, in contrast, the likelihood that the parody may serve as a market substitute for the original. But using some characteristic features cannot be avoided.

We think the Court of Appeals was insufficiently appreciative of parody's need for the recognizable sight or sound when it ruled 2 Live Crew's use unreasonable as a matter of law. It is true, of course, that 2 Live Crew copied the characteristic opening bass riff (or musical phrase) of the original, and true that the words of the first line copy the Orbison lyrics. But if quotation of the opening riff and the first line may be said to go to the "heart" of the original, the heart is also what most readily conjures up the song for parody, and it is the heart at which parody takes aim. Copying does not become excessive in relation to parodic purpose merely because the portion taken was the original's heart. If 2 Live Crew had copied a significantly less memorable part of the original, it is difficult to see how its parodic character would have come through.

This is not, of course, to say that anyone who calls himself a parodist can skim the cream and get away scot free. In parody, as in news reporting, *see Harper & Row, supra*, context is everything, and the question of fairness asks what else the parodist did besides go to the heart of the original. It is significant that 2 Live Crew not only copied the first line of the original, but thereafter departed markedly from the Orbison lyrics for its own ends. 2 Live Crew not only copied the bass riff and repeated it, but also produced otherwise distinctive sounds, interposing "scraper" noise, overlaying the music with solos in different keys, and altering the drum beat. This is not a case, then, where "a substantial portion" of the parody itself is composed of a "verbatim" copying of the original. It is not, that is, a case where the parody is so insubstantial, as compared to the copying, that the third factor must be resolved as a matter of law against the parodists.

Suffice it to say here that, as to the lyrics, we think the Court of Appeals correctly suggested that "no more was taken than necessary," but just for that reason, we fail to see how the copying can be excessive in relation to its parodic purpose, even if the portion taken is the original's "heart." As to the music, we express no opinion whether repetition of the bass riff is excessive copying, and we remand to permit evaluation of the amount taken, in light of the song's parodic purpose and character, its transformative elements, and considerations of the potential for market substitution sketched more fully below.

### *D*

The fourth fair use factor is "the effect of the use upon the potential market for or value of the copyrighted work." It requires courts to consider not only the extent of market harm caused by the particular actions of the alleged infringer, but also "whether unrestricted and widespread conduct of the sort engaged in by the defendant . . . would result in a substantially adverse impact on the potential market" for the original. The enquiry "must take account not only of harm to the original but also of harm to the market for derivative works."

Since fair use is an affirmative defense, its proponent would have difficulty carrying the burden of demonstrating fair use without favorable evidence about relevant markets. In moving for summary judgment, 2 Live Crew left themselves at just such a disadvantage when they failed to address the effect on the market for rap derivatives, and confined themselves to uncontroverted submissions that there was no likely effect on the market for the original. They did not, however, thereby subject themselves to the evidentiary presumption applied by the Court of Appeals. In assessing the likelihood of significant market harm, the Court of Appeals quoted from language in *Sony* that " 'if the intended use is for commercial gain, that likelihood may be presumed. But if it is for a noncommercial purpose, the likelihood must be demonstrated.'" The court reasoned that because "the use of the copyrighted work is wholly commercial, . . . we presume a likelihood of future harm to Acuff-Rose exists." In so doing, the court resolved the fourth factor against 2 Live Crew, just as it had the first, by applying a presumption about the effect of commercial use, a presumption which as applied here we hold to be error.

No "presumption" or inference of market harm that might find support in Sony is applicable to a case involving something beyond mere duplication for commercial purposes. *Sony's* discussion of a presumption contrasts a context of verbatim copying of the original in its entirety for commercial purposes, with the non-commercial context of *Sony* itself (home copying of television programming). In the former circumstances, what *Sony* said simply makes common sense: when a commercial use amounts to mere duplication of the entirety of an original, it clearly "supersedes the objects," of the original and serves as a market replacement for it, making it likely that cognizable market harm to the original will occur. But when, on the contrary, the second use is transformative, market substitution is at least less certain, and market harm may not be so readily inferred. Indeed, as to parody pure and simple, it is more likely that the new work will not affect the market for the original in a way cognizable under this factor, that is, by acting as a substitute for it ("superseding [its] objects"). This is so because the parody and the original usually serve different market functions.

We do not, of course, suggest that a parody may not harm the market at all, but when a lethal parody, like a scathing theater review, kills demand for the original, it does not produce a harm cognizable under the Copyright Act. Because "parody may quite legitimately aim at garroting the original, destroying it commercially as well as artistically," B. Kaplan, *An Unhurried View of Copyright* 69 (1967), the role of the courts is to distinguish between "biting criticism [that merely] suppresses demand [and] copyright infringement[, which] usurps it."

This distinction between potentially remediable displacement and unremediable disparagement is reflected in the rule that there is no protectable derivative market for criticism. The market for potential derivative uses includes only those that creators of original works would in general develop or license others to develop. Yet the unlikelihood that creators of imaginative works will license critical reviews or lampoons of their own productions removes such uses from the very notion of a potential licensing market. "People ask . . . for criticism, but they only want praise." S. Maugham, *Of Human Bondage* 241 (Penguin ed. 1992). Thus, to the extent that the opinion below may be read to have considered harm to the market for parodies of "Oh, Pretty Woman," the court erred.

In explaining why the law recognizes no derivative market for critical works, including parody, we have, of course, been speaking of the later work as if it had nothing but a critical aspect. But the later work may have a more complex character, with effects not only in the arena of criticism but also in protectable markets for derivative works, too. In that sort of case, the law looks beyond the criticism to the other elements of the work, as it does here. 2 Live Crew's song comprises not only parody but also rap music, and the derivative market for rap music is a proper focus of enquiry. Evidence of substantial harm to it would weigh against a finding of fair use, because the licensing of derivatives is an important economic incentive to the creation of originals. Of course, the only harm to derivatives that need concern us, as discussed above, is the harm of market substitution. The fact that a parody may impair the market for derivative uses by the very effectiveness of its critical commentary is no more relevant under copyright than the like threat to the original market.[24]

Although 2 Live Crew submitted uncontroverted affidavits on the question of market harm to the original, neither they, nor Acuff-Rose, introduced evidence or affidavits addressing the likely effect of 2 Live Crew's parodic rap song on the market for a non-parody, rap version of "Oh, Pretty Woman." And while Acuff-Rose would have us find evidence of a rap market in the very facts that 2 Live Crew recorded a rap parody of "Oh, Pretty Woman" and another rap group sought a license to record a rap derivative, there was no evidence that a potential rap market was harmed in any way by 2 Live Crew's parody, rap version. The fact that 2 Live Crew's parody sold as part of a collection of rap songs says very little about the parody's effect on a market for a rap version of the original, either of the music alone or of the music with its lyrics. The District Court essentially passed on this issue, observing that Acuff-Rose is free to record "whatever version of the original it desires;" the Court of Appeals went the other way by erroneous presumption. Contrary to each treatment, it is impossible to deal with the fourth factor except by recognizing that a silent record on an important factor bearing on fair use disentitled the proponent of the defense, 2 Live Crew, to summary judgment. The evidentiary hole will doubtless be plugged on remand.

III

It was error for the Court of Appeals to conclude that the commercial nature of 2 Live Crew's parody of "Oh, Pretty Woman" rendered it presumptively unfair. No such evidentiary presumption is available to

---

[24] In some cases it may be difficult to determine whence the harm flows. In such cases, the other fair use factors may provide some indicia of the likely source of the harm. A work whose overriding purpose and character is parodic and whose borrowing is slight in relation to its parody will be far less likely to cause cognizable harm than a work with little parodic content and much copying.

address either the first factor, the character and purpose of the use, or the fourth, market harm, in determining whether a transformative use, such as parody, is a fair one. The court also erred in holding that 2 Live Crew had necessarily copied excessively from the Orbison original, considering the parodic purpose of the use.

Reversed and remanded.

Appendix A

"Oh, Pretty Woman" by Roy Orbison and William Dees

Pretty Woman, walking down the street, Pretty Woman, the kind I like to meet, Pretty Woman, I don't believe you, you're not the truth, No one could look as good as you Mercy.

Pretty Woman, won't you pardon me, Pretty Woman, I couldn't help but see, Pretty Woman, that you look lovely as can be, Are you lonely just like me?

Pretty Woman, stop a while, Pretty Woman, talk a while, Pretty Woman give your smile to me Pretty Woman, yeah, yeah, yeah, Pretty Woman, look my way, Pretty Woman, say you'll stay with me, 'Cause I need you, I'll treat you right, Come to me baby, Be mine tonight.

Pretty Woman, don't walk on by, Pretty Woman, don't make me cry, Pretty Woman, don't walk away, Hey, O.K. If that's the way it must be, O.K. I guess I'll go on home, it's late. There'll be tomorrow night, but wait!

What do I see, Is she walking back to me? Yeah, she's walking back to me! Oh, Pretty Woman.

Appendix B

"Pretty Woman" as Recorded by 2 Live Crew

Pretty woman walkin' down the street, Pretty woman girl you look so sweet, Pretty woman you bring me down to that knee, Pretty woman you make me wanna beg please, Oh, pretty woman.

Big hairy woman you need to shave that stuff Big hairy woman you know I bet it's tough, Big hairy woman all that hair it ain't legit, Cause you look like 'Cousin It,' Big hairy woman.

Bald headed woman girl your hair won't grow, Bald headed woman you got a teeny weeny afro, Bald headed woman you know your hair could look nice, Bald headed woman first you got to roll it with rice, Bald headed woman here, let me get this hunk of biz for ya, Ya know what I'm saying you look better than rice a roni, Oh bald headed woman.

> Big hairy woman come on in, And don't forget your bald headed friend, Hey pretty woman let the boys, Jump in.
>
> Two timin' woman girl you know you ain't right, Two timin' woman you's out with my boy last night, Two timin' woman that takes a load off my mind, Two timin' woman now I know the baby ain't mine, Oh, two timin' woman, Oh pretty woman.

---

The complexities of fair use in parodies is further illustrated by a case involving the book, *Gone With the Wind.* Margaret Mitchell's book was published in 1936, won the Pulitzer Prize, sold over 25 million copies, and was turned into a classic movie. Six decades later, Houghton Mifflin (whose early authors included such notables as Emerson, Hawthorne, Longfellow, and Thoreau) was preparing to release a new novel, *The Wind Done Gone*, written by Alicia Randall. Her book retold and extended the *Gone With the Wind* story from an African-American perspective. Presumably on the advice of counsel, she gave new names to the 15 original characters she was using, with the exception of Mammy. Her 200-page book is written as a memoir of a brand-new character Cynara, who is the half-sister of Scarlett (now Other). The reason is that Scarlett's father Gerald (now Planter) had had an affair with his slave Mammy who gave birth to Cynara. Randall's novel does reminisce about many of the key events in its predecessor, but all presented from the point of view of Cynara, Mammy, and the other blacks who are portrayed as quite unhappy with their lives as Tara (now Tata) slaves (from which Cynara was sold off at the age of eleven), and then enchanted after being freed by the Civil War.

The essence of the new story line is captured in this first paragraph of *The Wind Done Gone*, set in 1873.

> My father, Planter, was the master of the place; my mother was the Mammy. My half-sister, Other, was the belle of five counties. She was not beautiful, but men seldom recognized this, caught up in the cloud of commotion and scent in which she moved. R [Rhett] certainly didn't; he married her. But then again, he just left her. Maybe that means something to me.

What it did mean for Cynara was that after Wilkes (now "Dreary Gentleman") returns to Scarlett-Other, Rhett-RB, who had earlier bought and freed Cynara, and even sent her on a Grand Tour of Europe, becomes her lover and then marries her after Scarlett-Other dies. The two return to Washington where she becomes part of the new group of black intellectuals and politicians and then leaves Rhett-RB for one of the first blacks elected to the Congress. The book closes with Cynara saying "for all those we love for whom tomorrow will not be another day, we send the sweet prayer of resting in peace."

Randall had never spoken to the Mitchell estate about her sequel, and when they heard about it, they set out to block its release. While Margaret Mitchell had thought about writing a sequel herself, she had never done so. After she and her husband died, her brother Stephen inherited the copyright and was against sequels to his sister's masterpiece (even filing a lawsuit that blocked MGM's efforts to renew itself as a major studio by doing a movie sequel to *Gone With the Wind*). Eventually, his sons became the copyright owners, authorizing a 1991 sequel, called *Scarlett*. Written by Alexander Ripley and turned into a TV miniseries, it earned the Mitchell family $9 million in royalties. A decade later, they were planning another sequel, one which would have the same conditions of no explicit sex, homosexuality, miscegenation, nor deaths of Scarlett or Rhett (to protect further sequels).

The Mitchell's trustee, Suntrust Bank, filed suit against Houghton Mifflin and secured an injunction from an Atlanta district judge barring its release. *See Suntrust Bank v. Houghton Mifflin*, 136 F. Supp. 2d 1357 (N.D. Ga. 2001) Judge Charles Pannell, Jr. found that there was a substantial similarity in the copyrighted characters and plot of *Gone With the Wind*, rejecting the defendant's argument that changing almost all the names and compressing a 1000-page story into a 100-page preview of a sequel from a different perspective was not copying. "The fact that the two works present polar viewpoints of the same fictional work fails to mitigate the fact that it is the same fictional world, described in the same way and inhabited by the same people, who are doing the same things." *Id.* at 1369.

Judge Pannell then addressed the defendant's fair use claim, that "*The Wind Done Gone* provides a fresh and unwritten perspective from the same characters in the same scenes, but does so to criticize the earlier work's one-sided view, as well as to provide a more complete picture of the antebellum South . . . as 'an exuberant art of literary revenge' from which black Americans will derive emotional satisfaction, vindication and fun." Since Randall believed that *Gone With the Wind* "depicts a south that never ever exists," she believes it was fair use to retell the original story in a way that was "giving voice to her modern political viewpoint" on such issues as "the flying of the Confederate flag and the debate over affirmative action."

Judge Pannell responded that "the question before the court is not who gets to write history, but rather whether Ms. Randall can permeate most of her new critical work with the copyrighted characters, plot, and scenes from *Gone With the Wind* in order to correct the 'pain, humiliation and outrage' of the 'ahistorical representation' of the previous work [as

Nobel-prize winner Toni Morrison had declared], while simultaneously criticizing the antebellum and more recent South. Parody has its place in copyright law, but the extent of the use of the copyrighted work and the purpose of the author's prose may limit the parodical effect and nullify the fair use defense." *Id.* at 1378.

Having characterized *Gone With the Wind* as "certainly a work of fiction that is creative, imaginative, and written to gain a financial return for the author's efforts, [and therefore] deserving more protection than a scholarly, historical or newsworthy work" [which, the judge said, accounts for the "lesser" protection given to Ford's autobiography in *Harper & Row*], he went on to rule that "Ms. Randall's use cannot receive the benefit of the fair use defense because she uses far more of the original than necessary . . . thus removing the new work from the safe harbor of parody and, as written, becomes piracy." *Id.* at 1381. Finally, the judge rejected Randall's defense that *The Wind Done Gone* was "criticism" of *Gone With the Wind* and thus not doing any "market harm" to the Mitchell estate's "derivative use market," because they would "never license a 'stinging critique' " of their book. The judge concluded that this "new work is distinguishable from pure parody, because it does not simply engage in 'literary criticism' that may or may not suppress demand for the original but, instead, usurps the original's right to create its own sequel . . . thus constituting 'market substitution.' "

Just three weeks later, an Eleventh Circuit panel lifted the preliminary injunction, allowing Randall's work to appear in bookstores. The panel later released its opinion, *Suntrust v. Houghton Mifflin*, 268 F.3d 1257 (11th Cir. 2001), essentially agreeing that there was substantial similarity because, particularly in the first half, *The Wind Done Gone* was "largely 'an encapsulation of *Gone With the Wind* [that] exploits its copyrighted characters, story lines, and settings as the palette for the new story.' " However, the panel found that, at least in the context of injunctive relief purposes, there was a very plausible fair use defense. Judge Stanley Birch noted that "parody, which is directed towards a particular literary or artistic work, is distinguishable from satire, which more broadly addresses the institutions and mores of a slice of society." 268 F.3d at 1268. He considered as just a dictum the Supreme Court's reliance on the dictionary in *Campbell* to "suggest that the aim of parody is 'comic effect or ridicule,' " and stated instead that a work like *The Wind Done Gone* should be judged to be "a parody if its aim is to comment upon or criticize a prior work by appropriating elements of the original in creating a new artistic, as opposed to scholarly or journalistic, work." From that perspective, *The Wind Done Gone* was judged to be "more than an abstract, pure functional work. It is principally and purposefully a critical statement that seeks to rebut and destroy the perspective, judgments, and mythology of *Gone With the Wind*. Randall's literary goal is to explode the romantic, idealized portrait of the antebellum South during and after the Civil War." *Id.* at 1268–70.

With this as the legal backdrop, the court concluded that it was too early to decide whether (as the district judge had said) Randall had used "far more of the original than necessary" to convey her political (rather than comic) parody message. And at such a trial, SunTrust was going to have to prove that *The Wind Done Gone*'s use of such copyrighted material from *Gone With the Wind* had generated the cognizable harm by reducing sales of the latter work and its sequels through "market substitution" rather than "critical commentary." The two sides settled their lawsuit before trial, just as *The Wind Done Gone* was coming out in paperback. Their agreement specifically stated that it did not cover any "adaptation" of the Randall novel.[o]

## *QUESTIONS FOR DISCUSSION*

1. Which do you think is a more defensible use of the earlier works—"Pretty Woman" by 2 Live Crew or *The Wind Done Gone* by Alice Randall? What is your view of an analogy advanced by the Mitchell estate: if an anti-Semitic group were to make its own version of *Schindler's List*?

2. The Supreme Court's *Campbell* ruling adds another doctrine to established "fair use" jurisprudence—the proposition that use for commercial profit is not *ipso facto* unfair. What if the parody takes place in a commercial advertisement analogous to those we saw in the *Johnny Carson* and *Vanna White* cases in Chapter 3? Should Congress change that ruling (as it did with Court's emphasis on the "unpublished material" factor in *Harper & Row*)?

3. A host of other issues lurk in the Court's opinion. For example, what is a "transformative" as contrasted with a "substitutional" parody? Would you agree with Justice Kennedy's observation in his concurring opinion that the court has drawn an implicit distinction between *parody* and *satire* versus other forms of *humor*? What might that entertainment distinction be, and what if any legal difference should it make? Should "parody" be limited to the bawdy humor of "Pretty Woman," or be expanded to include the kind of social and cultural critique we saw in *The Wind Done Gone*?

4. In 1991, the photographer Annie Liebovitz produced one of the most celebrated of all cover pictures in *Vanity Fair*. It was a photograph of Demi Moore, posing nude with her right hand covering her breasts when she was eight months pregnant. Several years later this picture produced a lawsuit filed by Leibovitz (who had retained copyright) against Paramount Pictures for having used a revised version to promote its 1994 movie *Naked Gun 33 1/3: The Final Insult*. The plot involved marriage and child-bearing, and Paramount hired a photographer and a pregnant model to pose in the same setting and posture as Leibovitz's. The studio then used digital technology to

[o] *See* Neil W. Netanel, *Locating Copyright Within the First Amendment*, 54 Stan. L. Rev. 1 (2001).

match Moore's body configuration and skin tone, while superimposing the smirking face of *Naked Gun* (male) star Leslie Nielsen clutching *his* pregnant body. The aim was to mount an irreverent advertising campaign for this forthcoming release, including ads placed in *Vanity Fair* itself.

The case eventually got to the Second Circuit in *Leibovitz v. Paramount Pictures*, 137 F.3d 109 (2d Cir. 1998). Since there was no doubt about copying, the key legal issue was whether Paramount had a fair use defense. Is the Nielsen image a truly "transformative" parody, given the very careful digital replication of the light and skin tone in Leibovitz's photo? Even if "transformative," is such a work fair use when employed to advertise a movie, rather than placed on the screen itself? What is the relevance of the fact that Leibovitz had apparently modeled Moore after famous Renaissance artist Botticelli's *Birth of Venus* (part of the classical art genre known as *Venus Pudica*)? Suppose Demi Moore had filed a right of publicity claim—how would this compare with the *Vanna White* case?

5. After having read *Campbell*, if you were the lawyer for another contemporary performer, Weird Al Yankovic, would you advise him still to secure and pay for licenses to use the tunes and arrangements from songs like Michael Jackson's "Bad," or "Beat It," along with his new comic lyrics for "Fat" and "Eat It"? *See New Line Cinema v. Bertlesman Music Group*, 693 F. Supp. 1517 (S.D.N.Y. 1988) (rap music video featuring the lead, Freddie Krueger, in the plaintiff's movie, *Nightmare on Elm Street*); *MGM, Inc. v. Showcase Atlanta Co-op. Prods., Inc.*, 479 F. Supp. 351 (N.D. Ga. 1979) (humorous theatrical version of *Gone With the Wind*, titled *Scarlett Fever*).

6. Another issue involves the "raunchy" parody. For example, in *Elsmere Music v. NBC*, 482 F. Supp. 741 (S.D.N.Y. 1980), *aff'd*, 623 F.2d 252 (2d Cir. 1980), the television show *Saturday Night Live* did a skit about the Chamber of Commerce in the Biblical town of Sodom. One feature of this skit was a chorus singing the lines, "I Love Sodom" to the tune of "I Love New York"—the highly successful commercial song developed by New York City in 1977 to restore its image and appeal following near bankruptcy. *See also MCA, Inc. v. Wilson*, 677 F.2d 180 (2d Cir. 1981) ("erotic nude show" in a Greenwich Village cafe with the song "Cunnilingus Champion of Company C," set to the music from "Boogie Woogie Bugle Boy").

7. What about a parody of a character? After *Campbell*, what is your view of the situation in *Walt Disney Productions v. Air Pirates*, 581 F.2d 751 (9th Cir. 1978)? There the defendants published a series of adult, counter-culture, comic books that portrayed Disney's Donald Duck, Mickey Mouse, and other figures as drug-sniffing, free-loving characters. Fair use?

8. Does a biographical film of an actor's life infringe on the copyrights of their original films where the biographical film recreates scenes from the original films? The 2013 film *Lovelace* depicts the life of pornographic film star Linda Lovelace. In particular, the film shows the background behind Lovelace's decision to enter into the adult film industry, and her first big hit film, *Deep Throat*. Arrow Productions, who owns the copyright to a number of

Ms. Lovelace's films, including *Deep Throat*, sued the Weinstein Company, alleging that certain scenes in *Lovelace* infringed on their copyrights. Result? *See Arrow Productions, Ltd. v. Weinstein Co., LLC*, 44 F. Supp.3d 359 (S.D.N.Y. 2014).

---

It is worth concluding this chapter with some instances in which fine art and architecture played a role in movies. One movie, *The Thomas Crown Affair*, used an intriguing creative step to avoid any such lawsuit. The 1999 version was basically a remake of the 1968 original which featured Steve McQueen and Faye Dunaway, and in 1999 had Pierce Brosnan and Rene Russo in these same roles (and Dunaway in another one). The one key change in the story was that McQueen staged a bank heist in Boston, while Brosnan did an art heist in New York. The original creators of the story had to and did authorize this substantially similar version.

Most viewers assumed the unnamed museum from which the fictional Monet was stolen was New York's Metropolitan Museum of Art. The film regularly displayed the exterior of the Metropolitan, but the inside of *Thomas Crown* (especially the entranceway) was actually New York's Public Library, which the city officials were happy to see used.

Contrast the movie, *Batman Forever*, the third in the *Batman* series, opened in 1995 to a then-record weekend box office take of over $52 million. Less than a week later, *Batman Forever* was facing a copyright infringement suit. Apparently a key feature of the movie's mythical Gotham City is an actual piece of art by Andrew Leicester, a sculptor. Leicester had designed a sculptured courtyard, *Zanja Madre* (Mother Ditch), for a new building, 801 Figueroa Tower, in downtown Los Angeles. The courtyard consists of nine 60-feet tall steel and ceramic columns with sculptural works mounted on top of these pilasters. A scale model of *Zanja Madre* was allegedly used for the gates to Gotham City in *Batman Forever*, as well as displayed in some *Batman* merchandise. Permission to film the courtyard site and building was given to Warner Bros. by R & T Development, its owner. But no contact was made with Leicester, although a marble plaque beside the sculpture credited the work to him. Leicester contended that he would never have consented to having his artistic work play a role in a film like *Batman Forever*:

> *Zanja Madre*, which was carefully crafted to create an oasis and allegorical garden of calm and tranquility, is portrayed in *Batman Forever* as an integral part of an openly lurid, frenetic and violent Gotham City.

Leicester lost his lawsuit in *Leicester v. Warner Brothers*, 47 U.S.P.Q.2d 1501 (C.D. Cal. 1998). The key reason was section 120(a) of the Copyright Act, which states that "copyright in any architectural work . . . does not include the right to prevent the making, distributing, or public display of . . . pictorial representations of the work, if the building in which the work is embodied is located in or ordinarily visible from a public place." The judge concluded that a motion picture was a "pictorial representation" of an "architectural work," such that a movie like *King Kong* was free to show the giant gorilla scaling the Empire State Building. He also decided that the "sculptural courtyard" was an "artistic embellishment" of the architectural work itself that was "ordinarily, visible from a public space." The circuit court agreed, especially because Leicester's sculptural courtyard was not "conceptually separate" from the architectural tower. Thus, by contrast with the inside parts of the Metropolitan Museum of Art in *The Thomas Crown Affair*, Warner did not need the consent of Leicester to show his artistic work in *Batman Forever*.

Warner also faced suit involving *The Devil's Advocate*, which starred Al Pacino as the Devil who had assumed the guise of a high-powered Manhattan lawyer. The Devil's apartment had a bas-relief sculpture on its wall, which was displayed for about twenty minutes of the movie, most prominently at the end, when several of the sculptural figures came to life and saw their angelic faces turn to hideous demons. As it turned out, the Devil's sculpture bore an uncanny resemblance to a sculpture that sits above the main entrance to the National Cathedral in Washington. That work, created in 1982 by Frederick Hart, was entitled *Ex Nihilo: Creation of Mankind Out of Nothing, as Narrated in the Book of Genesis*. Shortly after release of the movie, Hart started receiving letters from friends asking why he had allowed this religious work to be "perverted" on screen.

Warner Brothers' response to Hart's lawsuit was that there really was no copying of his work, because the movie sculpture was actually inspired by European classics such as Rodin's *Gates of Hell* in Paris. Even if a court were to find some resemblance between the two, the studio had a "fair use" and First Amendment right to depict such a national monument (at least in the movie, if not in advertising from which the art was removed). Warner could not rely on the ruling from *Batman Forever* because while *Ex Nihil* was clearly "visible from a public space," it was not given its "pictorial representation" as part of the National Cathedral's "architectural work." Thus, just as *The Devil's Advocate* was to be released on video, the trial judge indicated he would likely issue an injunction unless the parties could settle the case. Warner then agreed to make a substantial payment to Hart and to digitally "exorcise" this sculptural resemblance from its video and foreign prints.

There are two significant policy issues posed by these three movies. First, should there be either full copyright or no copyright at all in the publicly-visible architectural expression of the Metropolitan Museum or the sculptural expression on the National Cathedral? Second, should the Metropolitan be able to claim instead a violation of the *trademark* in the outside image of its building? Registration and enforcement of architectural trademarks for landmarks such as the Chrysler, Rockefeller, and Empire State Buildings has now been sought (e.g., to block a future *King Kong* from being portrayed on top of Empire State without owner's consent). The trademark law issues will be addressed in Chapter 6.

# CHAPTER 5

# ENTERTAINMENT INNOVATIONS AND INTELLECTUAL PROPERTY

■ ■ ■

In earlier editions, this chapter focused on technological changes in the world of entertainment over the previous century. The challenges posed by these innovations involved the basic copyright doctrines and their relationships to derivative rights and fair use. The rise of new entertainment media has led to new legal challenges, many of which remain unresolved. An early illustration of how new media platforms have changed the entertainment law world is the Supreme Court's decision in the Grokster case, involving the successor company to Napster, the creation of 19-year old college freshman Shawn Fanning using his own nickname.

Illustrating how far copyright law has expanded, the courts told Harriet Beecher Stowe, author of that era's best-seller *Uncle Tom's Cabin*, that the original Copyright Act did not preclude others from translating her book into a new language, let alone into a dramatized version. *See Stowe v. Thomas*, 23 Fed. Cas. 201 (E.D.Pa. 1853). At that time, illegal copying encompassed only use of the exact words from the original version.

Even so, Congress has regularly brought new forms of entertainment media within the scope of the Copyright Act. Perhaps more important was the adoption at the beginning of the 20th century of the general principle that the creator of the original work had the exclusive right to produce (or authorize) a derivative version in a new medium. The importance of this new principle was made clear by the Supreme Court when it ruled, in *Kalem Co. v. Harper Bros.*, 222 U.S. 55 (1911), that the movie *Ben Hur* violated the copyright of the author of the original book with that classic story.

The past century has witnessed a transformation of both entertainment technology and organization. People no longer just read books or watch plays or listen to live music. They play records, view movies, listen to radio, watch television, cable, and home video, use digital sound and imaging, and now read, listen to, and watch entertainment transmitted over the Internet onto their computers. A single creative work regularly goes from a book to a film shown on movie screens, home videos, pay cable and television series, and now over the Internet (as happened with *Star Wars* and *The Blair Witch Project* just a week after these big hits appeared on movie screens in the summer of 1999). Associated with this transformation of entertainment has been an industrial revolution from the days of lone authors and small printers to a complex network of businesses performing the above functions and more. Some of the businesses are divisions of large conglomerates like Time Warner, Paramount/Viacom/CBS, and Disney/ABC. Congress and the courts have struggled to keep the conception of copyright, the allocation of original authorship, and the interpretation of licenses given the changes in entertainment technology, with the latest challenge posed by file-sharing.

## A. FAIR USE AND HOME VIDEO[a]

Before the Internet, the complex interplay of technology, economics, and law in the entertainment world could be seen in the industry's experience with home video recording systems in the 1970s and 1980s. Home video constituted the third major transformation of the audiovisual world after World War II. Television, whose technology was actually developed in the late 1920s and early 1930s, did not appear in the consumer market until the late 1940s. Similarly, cable television, which was initially devised in the late 1950s as a technique to facilitate clear reception of broadcast signals, first became an independent source of entertainment programming with the creation of Home Box Office (HBO) in the early 1970s. Sony invented and introduced home video into the marketplace in the mid-1970s, and within five years had found a huge demand in American homes. This generated a fierce financial, political, and legal struggle between the American motion picture industry and the Japanese consumer electronics industry. One major byproduct, *Sony Corporation of America v. Universal City Studios*, 464 U.S. 417 (1984), was the Supreme Court's first attempt to interpret the fair use provision of the 1976 Copyright Act.

While television had (and has) an even more powerful economic impact than home video on the entertainment industry, it did not generate anywhere near as compelling an intellectual property dispute. As we will see in Chapter 12, the availability of free audiovisual entertainment in the home drastically reduced the number of people who were prepared to go out and pay to watch a movie in the theater. By the late 1950s the studios had begun to license to the networks the right to show television movies that had previously appeared in theaters. These

[a] *See* James Lardner, *Fast Forward: Hollywood, the Japanese & the Onslaught of the VCR* (W.W. Norton 1987); Paul Goldstein, *Copyright's Highway: The Law & Lore of Copyright from Gutenberg to the Celestial Jukebox* (Hill & Wang 1994); Wendy J. Gordon, *Fair Use as Market Failure: A Structural & Economic Analysis of the Betamax Case & its Predecessors*, 82 Colum. L. Rev. 1600 (1982).

secondary markets for theatrical movies produced a number of intellectual property disputes between the studios and their creative talent, which we will encounter in this and later chapters. (For example, does an author or composer's consent to the use of her book or song in a movie also apply to its showing on television, and if so, what should be the author's share in the revenues from these residual sources? Or, can the studio authorize the network to cut or colorize the original work without regard to the "moral" rights of the director-author?) By the 1960s, the movie and network companies had developed a close and symbiotic relationship after MCA/Universal and other studios began producing the television series and made-for-television movies that came to dominate prime-time.

Cable posed a more central question to copyright law, one that the Supreme Court had to answer in the late 1960s. Cable television—or as it was then called, community antenna television (CATV)—originated in the 1950s as a vehicle for receiving and retransmitting into rural communities the stations that otherwise would not have been accessible to viewers in those areas. In the 1960s, when cable was extended into larger cities whose subscribers wanted a better signal than those being deflected by large buildings in the sky, the revenue stream became much more lucrative. Naturally enough, the producers of the television programs being viewed on cable wanted a share of this financial pie.

The basis for their copyright claim was that the owners of shows had simply licensed the performance of their works by networks and stations broadcasting over the air. When the cable systems captured these signals and retransmitted the programs to their subscribers, this involved a distinct use and public performance of the programs that required the consent and payment to the producer-owners. The Supreme Court first confronted this argument in *Fortnightly Corp. v. United Artists Television*, 392 U.S. 390 (1968), and forthrightly rejected it:

> . . . . Television viewing results from combined activity by broadcasters and viewers. Both play active and indispensable roles in the process; neither is wholly passive. The broadcaster selects and procures the program to be viewed. He may produce it himself, whether "live" or with film or tape, or he may obtain it from a network or some other source. He then converts the visible images and audible sounds of the program into electronic signals, and broadcasts the signals at radio frequency for public reception. Members of the public, by means of television sets and antennas that they themselves provide, receive the broadcaster's signals and reconvert them into the visible images and audible sound of the program. The effective range of the broadcast is determined by the combined contribution of the equipment employed by the broadcaster and that supplied by the viewer.

The television broadcaster in one sense does less than the exhibitor of a motion picture or stage play; he supplies his audience not with visible images but only with electronic signals. The viewer conversely does more than a member of a theater audience; he provides the equipment to convert electronic signals into audible sound and visible images. Despite these deviations from the conventional situation contemplated by the framers of the Copyright Act, broadcasters have been judicially treated as exhibitors, and viewers as members of a theater audience. Broadcasters perform. Viewers do not perform. Thus, while both broadcaster and viewer play crucial roles in the total television process, a line is drawn between them. One is treated as active performer; the other, as passive beneficiary.

When CATV is considered in this framework, we conclude that it falls on the viewer's side of the line. Essentially, a CATV system no more than enhances the viewer's capacity to receive the broadcaster's signals; it provides a well-located antenna with an efficient connection to the viewer's television set. It is true that a CATV system plays an "active" role in making reception possible in a given area, but so do ordinary television sets and antennas. CATV equipment is powerful and sophisticated, but the basic function the equipment serves is little different from that served by the equipment generally furnished by a television viewer. If an individual erected an antenna on a hill, strung a cable to his house, and installed the necessary amplifying equipment, he would not be "performing" the programs he received on his television set. The result would be no different if several people combined to erect a cooperative antenna for the same purpose. The only difference in the case of CATV is that the antenna system is erected and owned not by its users but by an entrepreneur.

The function of CATV systems has little in common with the function of broadcasters. CATV systems do not in fact broadcast or rebroadcast. Broadcasters select the programs to be viewed; CATV systems simply carry, without editing, whatever programs they receive. Broadcasters procure programs and propagate them to the public; CATV systems receive programs that have been released to the public and carry them by private channels to additional viewers. We hold that CATV operators, like viewers and unlike broadcasters, do not perform the programs that they receive and carry.

392 U.S. at 397–401. Six years later, in *Teleprompter Corp. v. Columbia Broadcasting System*, 415 U.S. 394 (1974), the Court reiterated this ruling even though cable systems had become more sophisticated in

transmitting signals from across the country and adding commercials to their subscription revenues.

As part of its massive 1976 overhaul of the Copyright Act, Congress qualified that legal position. The statutory definition of "public performance" was expanded to cover cable transmission. However, a new section 111(a)(3) gave a special exemption for simple retransmission of broadcast signals by

> [A]ny carrier who has no direct or indirect control of the primary transmission or over the particular recipients of the secondary transmission, and whose activities with respect to the secondary transmission consist solely of providing wires, cable, or other communications channels for the use of others.

The flip side of that statutory ("mechanical") license afforded to cable operators was a requirement that they pay a royalty to the program owners, in an amount to be determined by a new Copyright Royalty Tribunal. Around that same time, Ted Turner was pioneering the development of his new superstation, the Atlanta-based WTBS, which was designed to be transmitted to and carried by cable systems around the country. Notwithstanding the fact that the satellite technology facilitated the insertion (and sale) of separate commercials aimed at this national audience, WTBS (along with WGN and WOR) were still found to fit within the Copyright Act's new compulsory license/royalty system. *See Hubbard Broadcasting, Inc. v. Southern Satellite Systems, Inc.*, 777 F.2d 393 (8th Cir. 1985).

By the early 1990s, the Copyright Royalty system was distributing approximately $200 million a year to the film industry from cable system transmission of its television programming (and comparable sums to sports franchises, game or talk show owners, and the like). As we shall see in Chapter 13, this statutory license system quickly paled in comparison to the huge expansion in program production and viewing afforded by dozens of additional channels available exclusively on cable systems, a field occupied by basic cable channels like USA Network, sports channels like ESPN, and movie pay channels like HBO and Showtime. As Congress was rewriting the rules for this rapidly-changing cable universe, a new consumer product was appearing on the scene, the Sony Betamax, which posed a new challenge to the film industry.

Video tape recording had actually appeared two decades earlier, in the form of a magnetic recording system developed by Ampex, an American firm. This device was large, expensive, and designed for industrial rather than consumer use. Indeed, its major impact was to allow television production to move readily from live broadcasts to taped programming that was much more attractive to networks broadcasting across three or more time zones. The fact that much of the talent for producing those programs was located in Hollywood was crucial in saving a film industry that had seen television quickly cutting movie admissions from over four billion a year in the late 1940s to around one billion in the 1950s.

For the next two decades, a number of electronic firms, led by the major Japanese rivals, Sony and Matsushita, sought to develop a video tape recorder that was comparable in size and usability to the audio tape recorders that had appeared in the consumer market in the 1950s. In the late 1960s, Sony and Matsushita had cooperated in the development of a portable video recorder, the U-matic, which helped make electronic newsgathering and editing viable for television networks and stations. It was not until 1975, though, that Sony independently launched the Betamax videocassette recorder, designed to allow people to tape and view television shows in their homes.

The Betamax was reasonably simple to use, and it sold at a price ($1300 for the recorder alone) that was viable in a consumer market. The use that Betamax advertising advocated was "time-shifting"—taping a program for viewing at a later and more convenient time. The flip side of the equipment's small size (the cassette was the same size as a paperback book), the Betamax recording capacity was limited to one hour. If someone wanted to record a longer program, they had to use more than one blank tape. And unlike what happened with the U-matic, Sony was not able to agree with Matsushita and other Japanese firms on a common technological format for this potentially huge market.

Shortly after Betamax appeared in the stores, the people at Universal City Studios received one of Sony's advertising brochures telling American television viewers that they could finally watch both *Kojak* and *Colombo*, even though these two Universal shows appeared on television on Sunday night at 9:00 o'clock. Whatever the reaction of viewers, the Universal leadership was very concerned about this new "time-shifting" device. Universal was worried about the reaction of television advertisers to the prospect of viewers watching taped shows at different times than those planned by producer and network. The bigger concern, though, was the prospect of viewers taping a movie when it was first shown on television and then not having to watch the replay two or three years later. Universal was worried about the impact of such "librarying" on the broadcast value of its recent hits, *Jaws* and *The Sting*; even more so, Walt Disney Studios worried about its classics, such as *Sleeping Beauty* and *Snow White*, which were regularly reshown to successive generations of children.

Universal and Disney sued Sony, alleging violations of the copyright in their films. First, the studios claimed that the taping of television programs by viewers constituted illegal copying of works that had been licensed for broadcast viewing only at specified times. Second, the studios charged that Sony was a participant in such illegal copying because it was producing and selling the equipment that made it possible. The studios wanted Sony to pay for the right to have its Betamax used to tape copyrighted shows; otherwise, the court should bar the sale of this copying device.

Trial of this lawsuit did not begin until 1979, and in the interim both home video technology and its market were transformed. In 1976, Matsushita introduced (through its affiliate, JVC) its new Video Home System (VHS), whose key difference from Betamax was a longer taping capacity (two, then four, then six hours). Though Betamax provided a somewhat higher quality home recording, the combination of longer playing time and the marketing capacity of VHS distributors in the United States (RCA, GE, and others) soon gave VHS the bulk of the VCR market. More important for Universal, its surveys indicated that the average VCR owner (whether Betamax or VHS) had thirty or so tapes in the home, clear evidence that librarying was as important a use as time-shifting.

Then, in 1977, a Detroit businessman, Andre Blay, conceived a plan for selling prerecorded film cassettes for home viewing. Blay was able to persuade Twentieth Century Fox to license fifty films from its library for this purpose. All the films were at least five years old and had been shown on network television, but they included such hits as *The Sound of Music*, *M*A*S*H*, and *Butch Cassidy and the Sundance Kid*. This venture proved so successful that within one year Fox bought it back from Blay for $7 million, and several other studios entered this new market as well.

Next, in 1978, another entrepreneur, George Atkinson, hit upon the idea of buying film cassettes himself and then renting them out at five dollars a day. For the vast majority of viewers, it made far more sense to spend a small sum to watch a movie once, rather than a much larger amount to store the film on their home library shelves. Within two years, there were over 10,000 such video rental outlets across the country, the vast majority being small, family-run businesses. Like the video sales market, video rental was a viable venture only because a Betamax or a VHS was in the viewing home.

The availability of prerecorded movies made the initial Matsushita lead over Sony irreversible, even after Sony enlarged the Betamax taping and viewing length to match that of the VHS. Once both stores and viewers had become more likely to stock up on VHS tapes to match the equipment's general market share, future VCR purchasers were more likely to buy that equipment, which in turn reinforced the tape inventory policies of the stores. By the mid-1980s, Matsushita's market advantage forced Sony to replace the Betamax with a VHS format in its machines.

An analogous problem confronted the studios: the tension between the video sale and rental markets. Studios were inclined to license their films for sale because their $50 royalty share of an $80 retail price promised a lucrative return from potential sales to the millions of homes that had VCRs. But if only 10,000 dealers had to buy one (or even two or three) cassettes for rental to their customers, this offered only a small return to the studios, at the same time as home video rentals were reducing the audience for showing the movie on television. While a studio could insist in its licensing contract with an Andre Blay that the latter just sell, not rent, the prerecorded movie, a rental dealer such as George Atkinson was not bound by that contract. Once Atkinson and his counterparts had purchased the cassette, the "first sale" doctrine incorporated in section 109 of the Copyright Act gave them the right "to sell or otherwise dispose of the possession of that copy or phonorecord." The result was that in 1980 the studios as a group earned only $20 million or so from the home video market.

Sony, of course, could not be held responsible for deficiencies in the market for prerecorded film cassettes that the studios had licensed for this purpose. Its liability, if any, extended only to the unauthorized taping of television programs or films. The core allegation was that such copying of an entire work was an infringement on Universal and Disney's exclusive property rights in their creative works. Sony's first response was that such taping by viewers in the privacy of their homes, for personal convenience rather than for commercial sale or rental, was fair use. By analogy, a listener's taping of music from radio on audio recorders had never been asserted to be a violation of the Copyright Act. The counter from Universal was that home videotaping had none of the creative and social values mentioned in section 107, and that the spread of this practice posed a severe economic threat to the studios' ability to sell their audiovisual products.

Sony's second line of defense was that even if unauthorized copying by a private viewer was unlawful, Sony was not liable for any such copyright violation. Sony was selling a machine that was also capable of a host of authorized and legitimate uses. By analogy, even though the 1976 Copyright Act made "systematic photocopying" illegal, this would not leave Xerox and other manufacturers liable for such use of their machines, given the host of legal uses to which photocopiers were put. Thus, Sony introduced testimony from the commissioners of various sports leagues, religious broadcasters, and Fred Rogers of *Mister Roger's Neighborhood*, to the effect that these program owners approved of the use of a machine that permitted people to tape and watch their shows even if the viewers were not home at the time of the broadcast.

The *Sony-Universal* litigation took five years to make its way through the lower courts. The trial verdict in favor of Sony came down in

1979, with the home video industry in the midst of the transformation depicted above. Two years later, a panel of the Ninth Circuit ruled that Sony was contributorily liable for what was deemed to be illegal copying by home viewers, and remanded the case to the trial judge to fashion an appropriate remedy. By that time, with three million households owning VCRs and Johnny Carson doing *Late Show* bits about "Video Police" invading the home to check whether and what people were taping, no one believed that *banning* VCRs was a viable option. (Indeed, one notable episode of Universal's own *Colombo* series had Peter Falk, as Lt. Colombo, solving a murder mystery with the help of a suspect's VCR.) Instead, what the movie industry sought from Congress, if not the courts, was a specified royalty for the sale of each machine ($40 to $50) and blank cassette ($1 to $2), which would be distributed among the studios in the same way that the Copyright Royalty Tribunal allocated payments for cable transmission of television programs.

There was considerable intellectual and political support for this proposal. Analysts as politically diverse as President Reagan's Justice Department and Harvard Law Professor Larry Tribe contended that at stake were both the free speech and private property rights of the studios. MPAA head Jack Valenti put it somewhat more pungently when he said that millions of "video tapeworms" were eating away at the foundations of Hollywood. Adding to the proposal's political allure was depiction of the issue as a struggle between the American movie industry and the Japanese manufacturing industry, at a time when the U.S. trade deficit with Japan was beginning to soar. Though there was considerable bipartisan support for legislative action, Congress was happy to postpone taking a stand when the Supreme Court agreed to hear Sony's appeal.

## SONY CORPORATION OF AMERICA V. UNIVERSAL CITY STUDIOS, INC.

Supreme Court of the United States, 1984.
464 U.S. 417, 104 S.Ct. 774, 78 L.Ed.2d 574.

JUSTICE STEVENS delivered the opinion of the Court.

IV

* * *

### *A. Authorized Time-Shifting.*

[The Court noted the District Court's finding that a considerable number of copyright owners of television programs—sports leagues, religious broadcasters, and educational communication agencies—wished to have home video tape recorders (VTRs, as they were then called) available for viewers to use to tape their programs for viewing at a later time.] . . . Although the District Court made these statements in the context of considering the propriety of injunctive relief, the statements constitute a finding that the evidence concerning "sports, religious, educational and other programming" was sufficient to establish a significant quantity of broadcasting whose copying is now authorized, and a significant potential for future authorized copying. That finding is amply supported by the record.

* * *

If there are millions of owners of VTRs who make copies of televised sports events, religious broadcasts, and educational programs such as *Mister Rogers' Neighborhood*, and if the proprietors of those programs welcome the practice, the business of supplying the equipment that makes such copying feasible should not be stifled simply because the equipment is used by some individuals to make unauthorized reproductions of respondents' works. The respondents do not represent a class composed of all copyright holders. Yet a finding of contributory infringement would inevitably frustrate the interests of broadcasters in reaching the portion of their audience that is available only through time-shifting.

Of course, the fact that other copyright holders may welcome the practice of time-shifting does not mean that respondents should be deemed to have granted a license to copy their programs. Third-party conduct would be wholly irrelevant in an action for direct infringement of respondents' copyrights. But in an action for contributory infringement against the seller of copying equipment, the copyright holder may not prevail unless the relief that he seeks affects only his programs, or unless he speaks for virtually all copyright holders with an interest in the outcome. In this case, the record makes it perfectly clear that there are many important producers of national and local television programs who find nothing objectionable about the enlargement in the size of the television audience that results from the practice of time-shifting for private home use. The seller of the equipment that expands those producers' audiences cannot be a contributory infringer if, as is true in this case, it has had no direct involvement with any infringing activity.

### B. *Unauthorized Time-Shifting.*

Even unauthorized uses of a copyrighted work are not necessarily infringing. An unlicensed use of the copyright is not an infringement unless it conflicts with one of the specific exclusive rights conferred by the copyright statute. *Twentieth Century Music Corp. v. Aiken*, 422 U.S. 151, at 154–155 (1975). Moreover, the definition of exclusive rights in § 106 of the present Act is prefaced by the words "subject to sections 107 through 118." Those sections describe a variety of uses of copyrighted material that "are not infringements of copyright" "notwithstanding the provisions of section 106." The most pertinent in this case is § 107, the legislative endorsement of the doctrine of "fair use."

That section identifies various factors that enable a court to apply an "equitable rule of reason" analysis to particular claims of infringement. Although not conclusive, the first factor requires that "the commercial or nonprofit character of an activity" be weighed in any fair use decision. If the Betamax were used to make copies for a commercial or profit-making purpose, such use would presumptively be unfair. The contrary presumption is appropriate here, however, because the District Court's findings plainly establish that time-shifting for private home use must be characterized as a noncommercial, nonprofit activity. Moreover, when one considers the nature of a televised copyrighted audiovisual work, and that time-shifting merely enables a viewer to see such a work which he had been invited to witness in its entirety free of charge, the fact that the entire work is reproduced, *see* § 107(3), does not have its ordinary effect of militating against a finding of fair use.

This is not, however, the end of the inquiry because Congress has also directed us to consider "the effect of the use upon the potential market for or value of the copyrighted work." § 107(4). The purpose of copyright is to create incentives for creative effort. Even copying for noncommercial purposes may impair the copyright holder's ability to obtain the rewards that Congress intended him to have. But a use that has no demonstrable effect upon the potential market for, or the value of, the copyrighted work need not be prohibited in order to protect the author's incentive to create. The prohibition of such noncommercial uses would merely inhibit access to ideas without any countervailing benefit.

Thus, although every commercial use of copyrighted material is presumptively an unfair exploitation of the monopoly privilege that belongs to the owner of the copyright, noncommercial uses are a different matter. A challenge to a noncommercial use of a copyrighted work requires proof either that the particular use is harmful, or that if it should become widespread, it would adversely affect the potential market for the copyrighted work. Actual present harm need not be shown; such a requirement would leave the copyright holder with no defense against predictable damage. Nor is it necessary to show with certainty that future harm will result. What is necessary is a showing by a preponderance of the evidence that some meaningful likelihood of future harm exists. If the intended use is for commercial gain, that likelihood may be presumed. But if it is for a noncommercial purpose, the likelihood must be demonstrated.

In this case, respondents failed to carry their burden with regard to home time-shifting. The District Court described respondents' evidence as follows:

"Plaintiffs' experts admitted at several points in the trial that the time-shifting without librarying would result in 'not a great deal of harm.' Plaintiffs' greatest concern about time-shifting is with 'a point of important philosophy that transcends even commercial judgment.' They fear that with any Betamax usage, 'invisible boundaries' are passed: 'the copyright owner has lost control over his program.' "

* * *

There was no need for the District Court to say much about past harm. "Plaintiffs have admitted that no actual harm to their copyrights has occurred to date."

On the question of potential future harm from time-shifting, the District Court offered a more detailed analysis of the evidence. It rejected respondents' "fear that persons 'watching' the original telecast of a program will not be measured in the live audience and the ratings and revenues will decrease," by observing that current measurement technology allows the Betamax audience to be reflected. It rejected respondents' prediction "that live television or movie audiences will decrease as more people watch Betamax tapes as an alternative," with the observation that "[there] is no factual basis for [the underlying] assumption." It rejected respondents' "fear that time-shifting will reduce audiences for telecast reruns," and concluded instead that "given current market practices, this should aid plaintiffs rather than harm them." And it declared that respondents' suggestion that "theater or film rental exhibition of a program will suffer because of time-shift recording of that program" "lacks merit."

* * *

The District Court's conclusions are buttressed by the fact that to the extent time-shifting expands public access to freely broadcast television programs, it yields societal benefits. In *Community Television of Southern California v. Gottfried*, 459 U.S. 498, 508 (1983), we acknowledged the public interest in making television broadcasting more available. Concededly, that interest is not unlimited. But it supports an interpretation of the concept of "fair use" that requires the copyright holder to demonstrate some likelihood of harm before he may condemn a private act of time-shifting as a violation of federal law.

When these factors are all weighed in the "equitable rule of reason" balance, we must conclude that this record amply supports the District Court's conclusion that home time-shifting is fair use. In light of the findings of the District Court regarding the state of the empirical data, it is clear that the Court of Appeals erred in holding that the statute as presently written bars such conduct.

In summary, the record and findings of the District Court lead us to two conclusions. First, Sony demonstrated a significant likelihood that substantial numbers of copyright holders who license their works for broadcast on free television would not object to having their broadcasts time-shifted by private viewers. And second, respondents failed to demonstrate that time-shifting would cause any likelihood of nominal harm to the potential market for, or the value of, their copyrighted works. The Betamax is, therefore, capable of substantial noninfringing uses. Sony's sale of such equipment to the general public does not constitute contributory infringement of respondents' copyrights.

V

"The direction of Art. I is that Congress shall have the power to promote the progress of science and the useful arts. When, as here, the Constitution is permissive, the sign of how far Congress has chosen to go can come only from Congress." *Deepsouth Packing Co. v. Laitram Corp.*, 406 U.S. 518, 530 (1972).

One may search the Copyright Act in vain for any sign that the elected representatives of the millions of people who watch television every day have made it unlawful to copy a program for later viewing at home, or have enacted a flat prohibition against the sale of machines that make such copying possible.

It may well be that Congress will take a fresh look at this new technology, just as it so often has examined other innovations in the past. But it is not our job to apply laws that have not yet been written. Applying the copyright statute, as it now reads, to the facts as they have been developed in this case, the judgment of the Court of Appeals must be reversed.

It is so ordered.

---

Justice Blackmun's dissent disagreed with the majority on almost every analytical point. For example, rather than focusing on the personal and noncommercial character of home videotaping, the dissent emphasized its lack of creative value:

> The intent of § 107(1) is to encourage users to engage in activities the primary benefit of which accrues to others. Time-shifting involves no such humanitarian impulse. It is likewise something of a mischaracterization of time-shifting to describe it as noncommercial in the sense that that term is used in the statute. As one commentator has observed, time-shifting is noncommercial in the same sense that stealing jewelry and wearing it—instead of reselling it—is noncommercial. Purely

> consumptive uses are certainly not what the fair use doctrine was designed to protect, and the awkwardness of applying the statutory language to time-shifting only makes clearer that fair use was designed to protect only uses that are productive.

464 U.S. at 496. Because home copying amounted to personal consumption rather than social production, greater weight had to be given to the risk of harm to the studio copyright owners.

> The Studios have identified a number of ways in which VTR recording could damage their copyrights. VTR recording could reduce their ability to market their works in movie theaters and through the rental or sale of prerecorded videotapes or videodiscs; it also could reduce their rerun audience, and consequently the license fees available to them for repeated showings. Moreover, advertisers may be willing to pay for only "live" viewing audiences, if they believe VTR viewers will delete commercials or if rating services are unable to measure VTR use; if this is the case, VTR recording could reduce the license fees the Studios are able to charge even for first-run showings. Library-building may raise the potential for each of the types of harm identified by the Studios, and time-shifting may raise the potential for substantial harm as well.[35]
>
> The Studios introduced expert testimony that both time-shifting and librarying would tend to decrease their revenue from copyrighted works. The District Court's findings also show substantial library-building and avoidance of commercials. Both sides submitted surveys showing that the average Betamax user owns between 25 and 32 tapes. The Studios' survey showed that at least 40% of users had more than 10 tapes in a "library"; Sony's survey showed that more than 40% of users planned to view their tapes more than once; and both sides' surveys showed that commercials were avoided at least 25% of the time.

464 U.S. at 483. Nor was the fact that the studio copyright owners had licensed a "free" over-the-air television broadcast a reason for denying them protection against copying and replaying that broadcast.

> Although a television broadcast may be free to the viewer, this fact is equally irrelevant; a book borrowed from the public library may not be copied any more freely than a book that is purchased.

[35] A VTR owner who has taped a favorite movie for repeated viewing will be less likely to rent or buy a tape containing a movie, watch a televised rerun, or pay to see the movie at a theater. Both library-builders and time-shifters may avoid commercials; the library-builder may use the pause control to record without them, and all users may fast-forward through commercials on playback.

464 U.S. at 480.

> The development of the VTR has created a new market for the works produced by the Studios. That market consists of those persons who desire to view television programs at times other than when they are broadcast, and who therefore purchase VTR recorders to enable them to time-shift. Because time-shifting of the Studios' copyrighted works involves the copying of them, however, the Studios are entitled to share in the benefits of that new market. Those benefits currently go to Sony through Betamax sales. Respondents therefore can show harm from VTR use simply by showing that the value of their copyrights would increase if they were compensated for the copies that are used in the new market. The existence of this effect is self-evident.

464 U.S. at 497–98. Nor was the dissent persuaded by the majority's argument that classifying videotaping as illegal copying rather than as fair use would actually harm some program owners who wanted home viewers to be able to tape their shows and view them at times when they could.

> Such reasoning . . . simply confuses the question of liability with the difficulty of fashioning an appropriate remedy. It may be that an injunction prohibiting the sale of VTRs would harm the interests of copyright holders who have no objection to others making copies of their programs. But such concerns should and would be taken into account in fashioning an appropriate remedy once liability has been found. Remedies may well be available that would not interfere with authorized time-shifting at all. The Court of Appeals mentioned the possibility of a royalty payment that would allow VTR sales and time-shifting to continue unabated, and the parties may be able to devise other narrowly tailored remedies. Sony may be able, for example, to build a VTR that enables broadcasters to scramble the signal of individual programs and "jam" the unauthorized recording of them. Even were an appropriate remedy not available at this time, the Court should not misconstrue copyright holders' rights in a manner that prevents enforcement of them when, through development of better techniques, an appropriate remedy becomes available.

464 U.S. at 494. Justice Blackmun, however, was not able to persuade a fifth Justice to subscribe to this alternative analysis of the fair use issue.

### *QUESTIONS FOR DISCUSSION*

1. While *Sony* was being litigated, a new commercial use of videotaping was being developed—the taping for sale of newscasts on local television stations. The stations themselves routinely erased their videos of

each program within a week or so after its broadcast. Entrepreneurs contacted individuals who had appeared or figured in the newscast and offered to sell them a copy of the program for their personal viewing. When the stations heard that this was being done, they sued for violation of their copyright in the show. Should this be deemed illegal copying or fair use under the *Sony* analysis? How would you compare the consumer value and economic impact of the two uses of videotaping technology? *See Pacific & Southern Company v. Duncan*, 744 F.2d 1490 (11th Cir. 1984); *Cable News Network v. Video Monitoring Services*, 940 F.2d 1471 (11th Cir. 1991).

2. With respect to television shows, does the availability of time-shifting benefit the producer by expanding the audience for and hence the value of the copyrighted show? Or are there other features of video recording that may cause problems even for those program owners (e.g., of NFL games or *Survivor* episodes) who are not worried about library-building? Why would the NBA, for example, have come out against the *Sony* decision shortly after the Court rendered it?

3. Do you agree with Sony's analogy to a manufacturer of photocopying machines that are on occasion misused (or the manufacturer of guns, some of which are used for crimes, others for sport)? Alternatively, if Sony did not want to have to pay a royalty for the unauthorized tapings that its machines made possible, should it have had to redesign its machines so that they were not able to tape any programs that (unlike *Mister Rogers' Neighborhood*) did not carry a signal authorizing such taping? Can and should courts be able to fashion V-chip-like remedies for what they find to be Copyright Act violations, or should judges be confined to ordering that illegal conduct simply be discontinued?

4. Contrary to the fears of the MPAA, the home video "tapeworms" did not erode the financial foundations of the American film industry. In 1980, the studios were receiving $20 million, or one percent of their overall revenues, from home video. In 1983, when the case was being argued in the Supreme Court, video earnings were more than $600 million, or nearly 15 percent of the studio total (and the bulk of video revenues came from sales to rental dealers). By 2005, home video and DVD was generating over $8 billion for studios, approximately half of their total earnings. Americans now spend $25 billion to watch movies at home (around two thirds for purchase rather than rental of prerecorded films), nearly three times what they spend for tickets to watch movies in theaters. In other countries, this disparity is even greater.

5. The structure of the industry has also been transformed in several ways. Wayne Huizenga opened Blockbuster Video in 1985, and by 1995 it had 2,000 outlets and $2 billion in revenues. The next largest, West Coast Video, had 500 stores and $200 million in revenues. Retail chains like Wal-Mart and Kmart were also major sources of video rentals and sales. The need for investments in a large library of videotapes had made this business better suited to large diversified enterprises. Many of the key players in the home

video drama have also played major roles in the more recent wave of entertainment mergers. Sony and Matsushita became members of the MPAA that they had earlier been battling in both Congress and the courts. In an effort to unite the worlds of entertainment hardware (Japanese) and software (American), Sony acquired Columbia Pictures and Columbia Music for a total of $5.5 billion, and Matsushita acquired MCA/Universal for nearly $6 billion. Then, in 1993, Blockbuster Video's huge cash flow became a critical factor in Sumner Redstone's successful effort to weld together (for over $10 billion) his Viacom cable and theater arms, Blockbuster's video dealerships, and Paramount Communication's much larger film and publishing businesses. Whether or not the synergies of these entertainment conglomerates justify the prices being paid to create them is an issue addressed later in this book. More recently, the market for movie rentals was transformed again, as Internet-based Netflix and low-cost provider Red Box have made the Blockbuster brick-and-mortar model obsolete.

6. At this stage, the key issues to reflect upon relate to the intellectual property framework for the entertainment industry. What is the appropriate balance in benefits and burdens felt by viewers, those who ultimately pay the price for entertainment? Even after losing the *Sony* case, the film studios have made a great deal of money from home viewing of their movies. But would they (and should they) have been able to make more money from the viewing of these movies in theaters and on television? In this connection, consider the impact of the distribution cycle that has evolved over the last decade: exhibition of the movie in theaters for anywhere from a week to several months; then, four to six months after release, sale and rental of home videos; six months later, playing of the movie on pay cable channels like HBO and Showtime; and after another year or more, broadcast of the movie on television (though rarely in network prime-time).

---

As digital video recorders have largely replaced VCRs (and their successors DVD and Blu-Ray devices) as the primary tool by which individuals record television broadcasts (including movies), the question arose as to whether use of such devices violated copyright laws. The next case explains why such devices are acceptable, and ironically does not even utilize principles of fair use.

## CARTOON NETWORK, LP v. CSC HOLDINGS, INC.

United States Court of Appeals, Second Circuit, 2008.
536 F.3d 121.

WALKER, CIRCUIT JUDGE.

Defendant-Appellant Cablevision Systems Corporation ("Cablevision") wants to market a new "Remote Storage" Digital Video Recorder system ("RS-DVR"), using a technology akin to both traditional, set-top digital video recorders, like TiVo ("DVRs"), and the video-on-demand ("VOD") services provided by many cable companies. Plaintiffs-Appellees produce copyrighted movies and television programs that they provide to Cablevision pursuant to numerous licensing agreements. They contend that Cablevision, through the operation of its RS-DVR system as proposed, would directly infringe their copyrights both by making unauthorized reproductions, and by engaging in public performances, of their copyrighted works. The material facts are not in dispute. Because we conclude that Cablevision would not directly infringe plaintiffs' rights under the Copyright Act by offering its RS-DVR system to consumers, we reverse the district court's award of summary judgment to plaintiffs, and we vacate its injunction against Cablevision.

## BACKGROUND

Today's television viewers increasingly use digital video recorders ("DVRs") instead of video cassette recorders ("VCRs") to record television programs and play them back later at their convenience. DVRs generally store recorded programming on an internal hard drive rather than a cassette. But, as this case demonstrates, the generic term "DVR" actually refers to a growing number of different devices and systems. Companies like TiVo sell a stand-alone DVR device that is typically connected to a user's cable box and television much like a VCR. Many cable companies also lease to their subscribers "set-top storage DVRs," which combine many of the functions of a standard cable box and a stand-alone DVR in a single device.

In March 2006, Cablevision, an operator of cable television systems, announced the advent of its new "Remote Storage DVR System." As designed, the RS-DVR allows Cablevision customers who do not have a stand-alone DVR to record cable programming on central hard drives housed and maintained by Cablevision at a "remote" location. RS-DVR customers may then receive playback of those programs through their home television sets, using only a remote control and a standard cable box equipped with the RS-DVR software. Cablevision notified its content providers, including plaintiffs, of its plans to offer RS-DVR, but it did not seek any license from them to operate or sell the RS-DVR.

Plaintiffs, which hold the copyrights to numerous movies and television programs, sued Cablevision for declaratory and injunctive relief. They alleged that Cablevision's proposed operation of the RS-DVR would directly infringe their exclusive rights to both reproduce and publicly perform their copyrighted works. Critically for our analysis here, plaintiffs alleged theories only of direct infringement, not contributory infringement, and defendants waived any defense based on fair use.

* * *

"Section 106 of the Copyright Act grants copyright holders a bundle of exclusive rights. . . ." *Id.* at 607–08. This case implicates two of those rights: the right "to reproduce the copyrighted work in copies," and the right "to perform the copyrighted work publicly." 17 U.S.C. § 106(1), (4). As discussed above, the district court found that Cablevision infringed the first right by 1) buffering the data from its programming stream and 2) copying content onto the Arroyo Server hard disks to enable playback of a program requested by an RS-DVR customer. In addition, the district court found that Cablevision would infringe the public performance right by transmitting a program to an RS-DVR customer in response to that customer's playback request. We address each of these three allegedly infringing acts in turn.

I. The Buffer Data

It is undisputed that Cablevision, not any customer or other entity, takes the content from one stream of programming, after the split, and stores it, one small piece at a time, in the BMR buffer and the primary ingest buffer. As a result, the information is buffered before any customer requests a recording, and would be buffered even if no such request were made. The question is whether, by buffering the data that make up a given work, Cablevision "reproduce[s]" that work "in copies," 17 U.S.C. § 106(1), and thereby infringes the copyright holder's reproduction right.

"Copies," as defined in the Copyright Act, "are material objects . . . in which a work is fixed by any method . . . and from which the work can be . . . reproduced." *Id.* § 101. The Act also provides that a work is " 'fixed' in a tangible medium of expression when its embodiment . . . is sufficiently permanent or stable to permit it to be . . . reproduced . . . *for a period of more than transitory duration.*" *Id.* (emphasis added). We believe that this language plainly imposes two distinct but related requirements: the work must be embodied in a medium, i.e., placed in a medium such that it can be perceived, reproduced, etc., from that medium (the "embodiment requirement"), and it must remain thus embodied "for a period of more than transitory duration" (the "duration requirement"). *See* 2 Melville B. Nimmer & David Nimmer, *Nimmer on Copyright* § 8.02[B][3], at 8–32 (2007). Unless both requirements are met, the work is not "fixed" in the buffer, and, as a result, the buffer data is not a "copy" of the original work whose data is buffered.

The district court mistakenly limited its analysis primarily to the embodiment requirement. As a result of this error, once it determined that the buffer data was "[c]learly . . . capable of being reproduced," i.e., that the work was embodied in the buffer, the district court concluded that the work was therefore "fixed" in the buffer, and that a copy had thus been made. *Cablevision I,* 478 F.Supp.2d at 621–22. In doing so, it relied on a line of cases beginning with *MAI Systems Corp. v. Peak*

*Computer Inc.,* 991 F.2d 511 (9th Cir.1993). It also relied on the United States Copyright Office's 2001 report on the Digital Millennium Copyright Act, which states, in essence, that an embodiment is fixed "[u]nless a reproduction manifests itself so fleetingly that *it cannot be copied.*" U.S. Copyright Office, *DMCA Section 104 Report* 111 (Aug.2001) ("*DMCA Report*") (emphasis added), *available at* http://www.copyright.gov/reports/studies/dmca/sec–104–report–vol–1.pdf.

* * *

Cablevision does not seriously dispute that copyrighted works are "embodied" in the buffer. Data in the BMR buffer can be reformatted and transmitted to the other components of the RS-DVR system. Data in the primary ingest buffer can be copied onto the Arroyo hard disks if a user has requested a recording of that data. Thus, a work's "embodiment" in either buffer "is sufficiently permanent or stable to permit it to be perceived, reproduced," (as in the case of the ingest buffer) "or otherwise communicated" (as in the BMR buffer). 17 U.S.C. § 101. The result might be different if only a single second of a much longer work was placed in the buffer in isolation. In such a situation, it might be reasonable to conclude that only a minuscule portion of a work, rather than "a work" was embodied in the buffer. Here, however, where every second of an entire work is placed, one second at a time, in the buffer, we conclude that the work is embodied in the buffer.

Does any such embodiment last "for a period of more than transitory duration"? *Id.* No bit of data remains in any buffer for more than a fleeting 1.2 seconds. And unlike the data in cases like *MAI *130 Systems,* which remained embodied in the computer's RAM memory until the user turned the computer off, each bit of data here is rapidly and automatically overwritten as soon as it is processed. While our inquiry is necessarily fact-specific, and other factors not present here may alter the duration analysis significantly, these facts strongly suggest that the works in this case are embodied in the buffer for only a "transitory" period, thus failing the duration requirement.

Against this evidence, plaintiffs argue only that the duration is not transitory because the data persist "long enough for Cablevision to make reproductions from them." Br. of Pls.-Appellees the Cartoon Network et al. at 51. As we have explained above, however, this reasoning impermissibly reads the duration language out of the statute, and we reject it. Given that the data reside in no buffer for more than 1.2 seconds before being automatically overwritten, and in the absence of compelling arguments to the contrary, we believe that the copyrighted works here are not "embodied" in the buffers for a period of more than transitory duration, and are therefore not "fixed" in the buffers. Accordingly, the acts of buffering in the operation of the RS-DVR do not create copies, as the Copyright Act defines that term. Our resolution of this issue renders it unnecessary for us to determine whether any copies produced by buffering data would be de minimis, and we express no opinion on that question.

II. Direct Liability for Creating the Playback Copies

In most copyright disputes, the allegedly infringing act and the identity of the infringer are never in doubt. These cases turn on whether the conduct in question does, in fact, infringe the plaintiff's copyright. In this case, however, the core of the dispute is over the authorship of the infringing conduct. After an RS-DVR subscriber selects a program to record, and that program airs, a copy of the program—a copyrighted work—resides on the hard disks of Cablevision's Arroyo Server, its creation unauthorized by the copyright holder. The question is *who* made this copy. If it is Cablevision, plaintiffs' theory of direct infringement succeeds; if it is the customer, plaintiffs' theory fails because Cablevision would then face, at most, secondary liability, a theory of liability expressly disavowed by plaintiffs.

Few cases examine the line between direct and contributory liability. Both parties cite a line of cases beginning with *Religious Technology Center v. Netcom On-Line Communication Services,* 907 F.Supp. 1361 (N.D.Cal.1995). In *Netcom,* a third-party customer of the defendant Internet service provider ("ISP") posted a copyrighted work that was automatically reproduced by the defendant's computer. The district court refused to impose direct liability on the ISP, reasoning that "[a]lthough copyright is a strict liability statute, there should still be some element of volition or causation which is lacking where a defendant's system is merely used to create a copy by a third party." *Id.* at 1370. Recently, the Fourth Circuit endorsed the *Netcom* decision, noting that

> to establish *direct* liability under . . . the Act, something more must be shown than mere ownership of a machine used by others to make illegal copies. There must be actual infringing conduct with a nexus sufficiently close and causal to the illegal copying that one could conclude that the machine owner himself trespassed on the exclusive domain of the copyright owner."

*CoStar Group, Inc. v. LoopNet, Inc.*, 373 F.3d 544, 550 (4th Cir.2004).

Here, the district court pigeon-holed the conclusions reached in *Netcom* and its progeny as "premised on the unique attributes of the Internet." *Cablevision I,* 478 F.Supp.2d at 620. While the *Netcom* court was plainly concerned with a theory of direct liability that would effectively "hold the entire Internet liable" for the conduct of a single user, 907 F.Supp. at 1372, its reasoning and conclusions, consistent with precedents of this court and the Supreme Court, and with the text of the Copyright Act, transcend the Internet. Like the Fourth Circuit, we reject the contention that "the *Netcom* decision was driven by expedience and that its holding is inconsistent with the established law of copyright," *CoStar,* 373 F.3d at 549, and we find it "a particularly rational interpretation of § 106," *id.* at 551, rather than a special-purpose rule applicable only to ISPs.

When there is a dispute as to the author of an allegedly infringing instance of reproduction, *Netcom* and its progeny direct our attention to the volitional conduct that causes the copy to be made. There are only two instances of volitional conduct in this case: Cablevision's conduct in designing, housing, and maintaining a system that exists only to produce a copy, and a customer's conduct in ordering that system to produce a copy of a specific program. In the case of a VCR, it seems clear—and we know of no case holding otherwise—that the operator of the VCR, the person who actually presses the button to make the recording, supplies the necessary element of volition, not the person who manufactures, maintains, or, if distinct from the operator, owns the machine. We do not believe that an RS-DVR customer is sufficiently distinguishable from a VCR user to impose liability as a direct infringer on a different party for copies that are made automatically upon that customer's command.

The district court emphasized the fact that copying is "instrumental" rather than "incidental" to the function of the RS-DVR system. *Cablevision I,* 478 F.Supp.2d at 620. While that may distinguish the RS-DVR from the ISPs in *Netcom* and *CoStar,* it does not distinguish the RS-DVR from a VCR, a photocopier, or even a typical copy shop. And the parties do not seem to contest that a company that merely makes photocopiers available to the public on its premises, without more, is not subject to liability for direct infringement for reproductions made by customers using those copiers. They only dispute whether Cablevision is similarly situated to such a proprietor.

The district court found Cablevision analogous to a copy shop that makes course packs for college professors. In the leading case involving such a shop, for example, "[t]he professor [gave] the copyshop the materials of which the coursepack [was] to be made up, and the copyshop [did] the rest." *Princeton Univ. Press v. Mich. Document Servs.,* 99 F.3d 1381, 1384 (6th Cir.1996) (en banc). There did not appear to be any serious dispute in that case that the shop itself was directly liable for reproducing copyrighted works. The district court here found that Cablevision, like this copy shop, would be "doing" the copying, albeit "at the customer's behest." *Cablevision I,* 478 F.Supp.2d at 620.

But because volitional conduct is an important element of direct liability, the district court's analogy is flawed. In determining who actually "makes" a copy, a significant difference exists between making a request to a human employee, who then volitionally operates the copying system to make the copy, and issuing a command directly to a system, which automatically obeys commands and engages in no volitional conduct. In cases like *Princeton University Press,* the defendants operated a copying device and sold the product they made using that device. *See* 99 F.3d at 1383 ("The corporate defendant . . . is a commercial copyshop that reproduced substantial segments of copyrighted works of scholarship, bound the copies into 'coursepacks,' and sold the coursepacks to students. . . ."). Here, by selling access to a system that automatically produces copies on command, Cablevision more closely resembles a store proprietor who charges customers to use a photocopier on his premises, and it seems incorrect to say, without more, that such a proprietor "makes" any copies when his machines are actually operated by his customers. *See Netcom,* 907 F.Supp. at 1369. Some courts have held to the contrary, but they do not explicitly explain why, and we find them unpersuasive. *See, e.g., Elektra Records Co. v. Gem Elec. Distribs., Inc.,* 360 F.Supp. 821, 823 (E.D.N.Y.1973) (concluding that, "regardless" of whether customers or defendants' employees operated the tape-copying machines at defendants' stores, defendant had actively infringed copyrights).

The district court also emphasized Cablevision's "unfettered discretion in selecting the programming that it would make available for recording." *Cablevision I,* 478 F.Supp.2d at 620. This conduct is indeed more proximate to the creation of illegal copying than, say, operating an ISP or opening a copy shop, where all copied content was supplied by the customers themselves or other third parties. Nonetheless, we do not think it sufficiently proximate to the copying to displace the customer as the person who "makes" the copies when determining liability under the Copyright Act. Cablevision, we note, also has subscribers who use home VCRs or DVRs (like TiVo), and has significant control over the content recorded by these customers. But this control is limited to the channels of programming available to a customer and not to the programs themselves. Cablevision has no control over what programs are made available on individual channels or when those programs will air, if at all. In this respect, Cablevision possesses far less control over recordable content than it does in the VOD context, where it actively selects and makes available beforehand the individual programs available for viewing. For these reasons, we are not inclined to say that Cablevision, rather than the user, "does" the copying produced by the RS-DVR system. As a result, we find that the district court erred in concluding that Cablevision, rather than its RS-DVR customers, makes the copies carried out by the RS-DVR system.

Our refusal to find Cablevision directly liable on these facts is buttressed by the existence and contours of the Supreme Court's doctrine of contributory liability in the copyright context. After all, the purpose of any causation-based liability doctrine is to identify the actor (or actors) whose "conduct has been so significant and important a cause that [he or she] should be legally responsible." W. Page Keeton et al., *Prosser and Keeton on Torts* § 42, at 273 (5th ed.1984). But here, to the extent that we may construe the boundaries of direct liability more narrowly, the doctrine of contributory liability stands ready to provide adequate protection to copyrighted works.

Most of the facts found dispositive by the district court—e.g., Cablevision's "continuing relationship" with its RS-DVR customers, its control over recordable content, and the "instrumental[ity]" of copying to the RS-DVR system, *Cablevision I*, 478 F.Supp.2d at 618–20—seem to us more relevant to the question of contributory liability. In *Sony Corp. of America v. Universal City Studios, Inc.*, the lack of an "ongoing relationship" between Sony and its VCR customers supported the Court's conclusion that it should not impose *contributory* liability on Sony for any infringing copying done by Sony VCR owners. 464 U.S. 417, 437–38, 104 S.Ct. 774, 78 L.Ed.2d 574 (1984). The *Sony* Court did deem it "just" to impose liability on a party in a "position to control" the infringing uses of another, but as a contributory, not direct, infringer. *Id.* at 437, 104 S.Ct. 774. And asking whether copying copyrighted material is only "incidental" to a given technology is akin to asking whether that technology has "commercially significant noninfringing uses," another inquiry the *Sony* Court found relevant to whether imposing *contributory* liability was just. *Id.* at 442, 104 S.Ct. 774.

The Supreme Court's desire to maintain a meaningful distinction between direct and contributory copyright infringement is consistent with congressional intent. The Patent Act, unlike the Copyright Act, expressly provides that someone who "actively induces infringement of a patent" is "liable as an infringer," 35 U.S.C. § 271(b), just like someone who commits the underlying infringing act by "us[ing]" a patented invention without authorization, *id.* § 271(a). In contrast, someone who merely "sells . . . a material or apparatus for use in practicing a patented process" faces only liability as a "contributory infringer." *Id.* § 271(c). If Congress had meant to assign direct liability to both the person who actually commits a copyright-infringing act and any person who actively induces that infringement, the Patent Act tells us that it knew how to draft a statute that would have this effect. Because Congress did not do so, the *Sony* Court concluded that "[t]he Copyright Act does not expressly render anyone liable for infringement committed by another." 464 U.S. at 434, 104 S.Ct. 774. Furthermore, in cases like *Sony*, the Supreme Court has strongly signaled its intent to use the doctrine of contributory infringement, not direct infringement, to "identify[ ] the circumstances in which it is just to hold one individual accountable for the actions of another." *Id.* at 435, 104 S.Ct. 774. Thus, although *Sony* warns us that "the lines between direct infringement, contributory infringement, and vicarious liability are not clearly drawn," *id.* at 435 n. 17, 104 S.Ct. 774 (internal quotation marks and citation omitted), that decision does not absolve us of our duty to discern where that line falls in cases, like this one, that require us to decide the question.

The district court apparently concluded that Cablevision's operation of the RS-DVR system would contribute in such a major way to the copying done by another that it made sense to say that Cablevision was a direct infringer, and thus, in effect, was "doing" the relevant copying. There are certainly other cases, not binding on us, that follow this approach. *See, e.g., Playboy Enters. v. Russ Hardenburgh, Inc.,* 982 F.Supp. 503, 513 (N.D.Ohio 1997) (noting that defendant ISP's encouragement of its users to copy protected files was "crucial" to finding that it was a direct infringer). We need not decide today whether one's contribution to the creation of an infringing copy may be so great that it warrants holding that party directly liable for the infringement, even though another party has actually made the copy. We conclude only that on the facts of this case, copies produced by the RS-DVR system are "made" by the RS-DVR customer, and Cablevision's contribution to this reproduction by providing the system does not warrant the imposition of direct liability. Therefore, Cablevision is entitled to summary judgment on this point, and the district court erred in awarding summary judgment to plaintiffs.

III. Transmission of RS-DVR Playback

Plaintiffs' final theory is that Cablevision will violate the Copyright Act by engaging in unauthorized public performances of their works through the playback of the RS-DVR copies. The Act grants a copyright owner the exclusive right, "in the case of . . . motion pictures and other audiovisual works, to perform the copyrighted work publicly." 17 U.S.C. § 106(4). Section 101, the definitional section of the Act, explains that

> [t]o perform or display a work "publicly" means (1) to perform or display it at a place open to the public or at any place where a substantial number of persons outside of a normal circle of a family and its social acquaintances is gathered; or (2) to transmit or otherwise communicate a performance or display of the work to a place specified by clause (1) or to the public, by means of any device or process, whether the members of the public capable of receiving the performance or display receive it in the same place or in separate places and at the same time or at different times.

*Id.* § 101.

The parties agree that this case does not implicate clause (1). Accordingly, we ask whether these facts satisfy the second, "transmit clause" of the public performance definition: Does Cablevision "transmit

. . . a performance . . . of the work . . . to the public"? *Id.* No one disputes that the RS-DVR playback results in the transmission of a performance of a work—the transmission from the Arroyo Server to the customer's television set. Cablevision contends that (1) the RS-DVR customer, rather than Cablevision, does the transmitting and thus the performing and (2) the transmission is not "to the public" under the transmit clause.

As to Cablevision's first argument, we note that our conclusion in Part II that the customer, not Cablevision, "does" the copying does not dictate a parallel conclusion that the customer, and not Cablevision, "performs" the copyrighted work. The definitions that delineate the contours of the reproduction and public performance rights vary in significant ways. For example, the statute defines the verb "perform" and the noun "copies," but not the verbs "reproduce" or "copy." *Id.* We need not address Cablevision's first argument further because, even if we assume that Cablevision makes the transmission when an RS-DVR playback occurs, we find that the RS-DVR playback, as described here, does not involve the transmission of a performance "to the public."

The statute itself does not expressly define the term "performance" or the phrase "to the public." It does explain that a transmission may be "to the public . . . whether the members of the public capable of receiving the performance . . . receive it in the same place or in separate places and at the same time or at different times." *Id.* This plain language instructs us that, in determining whether a transmission is "to the public," it is of no moment that the potential recipients of the transmission are in different places, or that they may receive the transmission at different times. The implication from this same language, however, is that it is relevant, in determining whether a transmission is made to the public, to discern who is "capable of receiving" the performance being transmitted. The fact that the statute says "capable of receiving the performance," instead of "capable of receiving the transmission," underscores the fact that a transmission of a performance is itself a performance. *Cf. Buck v. Jewell-La Salle Realty Co.,* 283 U.S. 191, 197–98, 51 S.Ct. 410, 75 L.Ed. 971 (1931).

The legislative history of the transmit clause supports this interpretation. The House Report on the 1976 Copyright Act states that

> [u]nder the bill, as under the present law, a performance made available *by transmission to the public at large* is "public" even though the recipients are not gathered in a single place, and even if there is no proof that any of the *potential recipients* was operating his receiving apparatus at the time of the transmission. The same principles apply whenever the *potential recipients of the transmission* represent a limited segment of the

public, such as the occupants of hotel rooms or the subscribers of a cable television service.

H.R.Rep. No. 94–1476, at 64–65 (1976), *reprinted in* 1976 U.S.C.C.A.N. 5659, 5678 (emphases added).

Plaintiffs also reference a 1967 House Report, issued nearly a decade before the Act we are interpreting, stating that the same principles apply where the transmission is "*capable of reaching* different recipients at different times, as in the case of sounds or images stored in an information system and *capable of being performed or displayed* at the initiative of individual members of the public." H.R.Rep. No. 90–83, at 29 (1967) (emphases added). We question how much deference this report deserves. But we need not belabor the point here, as the 1967 report is consistent with both legislative history contemporaneous with the Act's passage and our own interpretation of the statute's plain meaning.

From the foregoing, it is evident that the transmit clause directs us to examine who precisely is "capable of receiving" a particular transmission of a performance. Cablevision argues that, because each RS-DVR transmission is made using a single unique copy of a work, made by an individual subscriber, one that can be decoded exclusively by that subscriber's cable box, only one subscriber is capable of receiving any given RS-DVR transmission. This argument accords with the language of the transmit clause, which, as described above, directs us to consider the potential audience of a given transmission. We are unpersuaded by the district court's reasoning and the plaintiffs' arguments that we should consider a larger potential audience in determining whether a transmission is "to the public."

The district court, in deciding whether the RS-DVR playback of a program to a particular customer is "to the public," apparently considered all of Cablevision's customers who subscribe to the channel airing that program and all of Cablevision's RS-DVR subscribers who request a copy of that program. Thus, it concluded that the RS-DVR playbacks constituted public performances because "Cablevision would transmit the *same program* to members of the public, who may receive the performance at different times, depending on whether they view the program in real time or at a later time as an RS-DVR playback." *Cablevision I,* 478 F.Supp.2d at 623 (emphasis added). In essence, the district court suggested that, in considering whether a transmission is "to the public," we consider not the potential audience of a particular transmission, but the potential audience of the underlying work (i.e., "the program") whose content is being transmitted.

We cannot reconcile the district court's approach with the language of the transmit clause. That clause speaks of people capable of receiving a particular "transmission" or "performance," and not of the potential audience of a particular "work." Indeed, such an approach would render the "to the public" language surplusage. Doubtless the *potential* audience for every copyrighted audiovisual work is the general public. As a result, any transmission of the content of a copyrighted work would constitute a public performance under the district court's interpretation. But the transmit clause obviously contemplates the existence of non-public transmissions; if it did not, Congress would have stopped drafting that clause after "performance."

On appeal, plaintiffs offer a slight variation of this interpretation. They argue that both in its real-time cablecast and via the RS-DVR playback, Cablevision is in fact transmitting the "same performance" of a given work: the performance of the work that occurs when the programming service supplying Cablevision's content transmits that content to Cablevision and the service's other licensees. *See* Br. of Pls.-Appellees Twentieth Century Fox Film Corp. et al. at 27 ("Fox Br.") ("The critical factor . . . is that the same *performance* is transmitted to different subscribers at different times . . . . more specifically, the *performance* of that program *by HBO or another programming service*." (third emphasis added)).

Thus, according to plaintiffs, when Congress says that to perform a work publicly means to transmit . . . a performance . . . to the public, they really meant "transmit . . . the 'original performance' . . . to the public." The implication of this theory is that to determine whether a given transmission of a performance is "to the public," we would consider not only the potential audience of that transmission, but also the potential audience of any transmission of the same underlying "original" performance.

Like the district court's interpretation, this view obviates any possibility of a purely private transmission. Furthermore, it makes Cablevision's liability depend, in part, on the actions of legal strangers. Assume that HBO transmits a copyrighted work to both Cablevision and Comcast. Cablevision merely retransmits the work from one Cablevision facility to another, while Comcast retransmits the program to its subscribers. Under plaintiffs' interpretation, Cablevision would still be transmitting the performance to the public, solely because Comcast has transmitted the same underlying performance to the public. Similarly, a hapless customer who records a program in his den and later transmits the recording to a television in his bedroom would be liable for publicly performing the work simply because some other party had once transmitted the same underlying performance to the public.

We do not believe Congress intended such odd results. Although the transmit clause is not a model of clarity, we believe that when Congress speaks of transmitting a performance to the public, it refers to the performance created by the act of transmission. Thus, HBO transmits its own performance of a work when it transmits to Cablevision, and Cablevision transmits its own performance of the same work when it retransmits the feed from HBO.

Furthermore, we believe it would be inconsistent with our own transmit clause jurisprudence to consider the potential audience of an upstream transmission by a third party when determining whether a defendant's own subsequent transmission of a performance is "to the public." In *National Football League v. PrimeTime 24 Joint Venture* (NFL), 211 F.3d 10 (2000), we examined the transmit clause in the context of satellite television provider PrimeTime, which captured protected content in the United States from the NFL, transmitted it from the United States to a satellite ("the uplink"), and then transmitted it from the satellite to subscribers in both the United States and Canada ("the downlink"). PrimeTime had a license to transmit to its U.S. customers, but not its Canadian customers. It argued that although the downlink transmission to its Canadian subscribers was a public performance, it could not be held liable for that act because it occurred entirely outside of the United States and therefore was not subject to the strictures of the Copyright Act. It also argued that the uplink transmission was not a public performance because it was a transmission to a single satellite. *See id.* at 12.

The *NFL* court did not question the first assumption, but it flatly rejected the second on a specific and germane ground:

> We believe the most logical interpretation of the Copyright Act is to hold that a public performance or display includes each step in the process by which a protected work wends its way to its audience. Under that analysis, it is clear that PrimeTime's uplink transmission of signals captured in the United States is a step in the process by which NFL's protected work wends its way *to a public audience.*

*Id.* at 13 (emphasis added) (internal quotation and citation omitted). Thus, while the uplink transmission that took place in the United States was not, in itself, "to the public," the *NFL* court deemed it so because it ultimately resulted in an undisputed public performance. Notably, the *NFL* court did not base its decision on the fact that an upstream transmission by another party (the NFL) might have been to the public. Nor did the court base its decision on the fact that Primetime simultaneously transmitted a performance of the work to the public in the United States. Because *NFL* directs us to look downstream, rather than upstream or laterally, to determine whether any link in a chain of transmissions made by a party constitutes a public performance, we reject plaintiffs' contention that we examine the potential recipients of the content provider's initial transmission to determine who is capable of receiving the RS-DVR playback transmission.

Plaintiffs also rely on *NFL* for the proposition that Cablevision publicly performs a work when it splits its programming stream and transmits the second stream to the RS-DVR system. Because *NFL* only supports that conclusion if we determine that the final transmission in the chain (i.e., the RS-DVR playback transmission) is "to the public," plaintiffs' reliance on *NFL* is misplaced. *NFL* dealt with a chain of transmissions whose final link was undisputedly a public performance. It therefore does not guide our current inquiry.

In sum, none of the arguments advanced by plaintiffs or the district court alters our conclusion that, under the transmit clause, we must examine the potential audience of a given transmission by an alleged infringer to determine whether that transmission is "to the public." And because the RS-DVR system, as designed, only makes transmissions to one subscriber using a copy made by that subscriber, we believe that the universe of people capable of receiving an RS-DVR transmission is the single subscriber whose self-made copy is used to create that transmission.

Plaintiffs contend that it is "wholly irrelevant, in determining the existence of a public performance, whether 'unique' *copies* of the same work are used to make the transmissions." Fox Br. at 27. But plaintiffs cite no authority for this contention. And our analysis of the transmit clause suggests that, in general, any factor that limits the *potential* audience of a transmission is relevant.

Furthermore, no transmission of an audiovisual work can be made, we assume, without using a copy of that work: to transmit a performance of a movie, for example, the transmitter generally must obtain a copy of that movie. As a result, in the context of movies, television programs, and other audiovisual works, the right of reproduction can reinforce and protect the right of public performance. If the owner of a copyright believes he is injured by a particular transmission of a performance of his work, he may be able to seek redress not only for the infringing transmission, but also for the underlying copying that facilitated the transmission. Given this interplay between the various rights in this context, it seems quite consistent with the Act to treat a transmission made using Copy A as distinct from one made using Copy B, just as we would treat a transmission made by Cablevision as distinct from an otherwise identical transmission made by Comcast. Both factors—the identity of the transmitter and the source material of the transmission—limit the potential audience of a transmission in this case and are therefore germane in determining whether that transmission is made "to the public."

Indeed, we believe that *Columbia Pictures Industries, Inc. v. Redd Horne, Inc.,* 749 F.2d 154 (3d Cir.1984), relied on by both plaintiffs and the district court, supports our decision to accord significance to the existence and use of distinct copies in our transmit clause analysis. In that case, defendant operated a video rental store, Maxwell's, which also housed a number of small private booths containing seats and a television. Patrons would select a film, enter the booth, and close the door. An employee would then load a copy of the requested movie into a bank of VCRs at the front of the store and push play, thereby transmitting the content of the tape to the television in the viewing booth. *See id.* at 156–57.

The Third Circuit found that defendants' conduct constituted a public performance under both clauses of the statutory definition. In concluding that Maxwell's violated the transmit clause, that court explicitly relied on the fact that defendants showed the same copy of a work seriatim to its clientele, and it quoted a treatise emphasizing the same fact:

> Professor Nimmer's examination of this definition is particularly pertinent: "*if the same copy* . . . of a given work is repeatedly played (*i.e.*, 'performed') by different members of the public, albeit at different times, this constitutes a 'public' performance." 2 M. Nimmer, § 8.14[C][3], at 8–142 (emphasis in original). . . . Although Maxwell's has only one copy of each film, it shows each copy repeatedly to different members of the public. This constitutes a public performance.

*Id.* at 159 (first omission in original).

Unfortunately, neither the *Redd Horne* court nor Prof. Nimmer explicitly explains *why* the use of a distinct copy affects the transmit clause inquiry. But our independent analysis confirms the soundness of their intuition: the use of a unique copy may limit the potential audience of a transmission and is therefore relevant to whether that transmission is made "to the public." Plaintiffs' unsupported arguments to the contrary are unavailing.

Given that each RS-DVR transmission is made to a given subscriber using a copy made by that subscriber, we conclude that such a transmission is not "to the public," without analyzing the contours of that phrase in great detail. No authority cited by the parties or the district court persuades us to the contrary.

In addition to *Redd Horne,* the district court also cited and analyzed *On Command Video Corp. v. Columbia Pictures Industries,* 777 F.Supp. 787 (N.D.Cal.1991), in its transmit clause analysis. In that case, defendant On Command developed and sold "a system for the electronic delivery of movie video tapes," which it sold to hotels. *Id.* at 788. The hub of the system was a bank of video cassette players, each containing a copy of a particular movie. From his room, a hotel guest could select a movie via remote control from a list on his television. The corresponding cassette player would start, and its output would be transmitted to that guest's room. During this playback, the movie selected was unavailable to other guests. *See id.* The court concluded that the transmissions made by this system were made to the public "because the relationship between the transmitter of the performance, On Command, and the audience, hotel guests, is a commercial, 'public' one regardless of where the viewing takes place." *Id.* at 790.

Thus, according to the *On Command* court, any commercial transmission is a transmission "to the public." We find this interpretation untenable, as it completely rewrites the language of the statutory definition. If Congress had wished to make all commercial transmissions public performances, the transmit clause would read: "to perform a work publicly means . . . to transmit a performance for commercial purposes." In addition, this interpretation overlooks, as Congress did not, the possibility that even non-commercial transmissions to the public may diminish the value of a copyright. Finally, like *Redd Horne, On Command* is factually distinguishable, as successive transmissions to different viewers in that case could be made using a single copy of a given work. Thus, at the moment of transmission, any of the hotel's guests was capable of receiving a transmission made using a single copy of a given movie. As a result, the district court in this case erred in relying on *On Command.*

Plaintiffs also rely on *Ford Motor Co. v. Summit Motor Products, Inc.,* 930 F.2d 277 (3d Cir.1991), in which the Third Circuit interpreted § 106(3) of the Copyright Act, which gives the copyright holder the exclusive right "to distribute copies . . . of the copyrighted work *to the public,*" 17 U.S.C. § 106(3) (emphasis added). The court concluded that "even one person can be the public *for the purposes of section 106(3).*" *Ford,* 930 F.2d at 299 (emphasis added). Commentators have criticized the *Ford* court for divesting the phrase "to the public" of "all meaning whatsoever," 2 Nimmer & Nimmer, *supra,* § 8.11[A], at 8–149, and the decision does appear to have that result. Whether this result was justified in the context of the distribution right is not for us to decide in this case. We merely note that we find no compelling reason, in the context of the transmit clause and the public performance right, to interpret the phrase "to the public" out of existence.

In sum, we find that the transmit clause directs us to identify the potential audience of a given transmission, i.e., the persons "capable of receiving" it, to determine whether that transmission is made "to the public." Because each RS-DVR playback transmission is made to a single subscriber using a single unique copy produced by that subscriber, we conclude that such transmissions are not performances "to the public," and therefore do not infringe any exclusive right of public performance. We base this decision on the application of undisputed facts; thus, Cablevision is entitled to summary judgment on this point.

This holding, we must emphasize, does not generally permit content delivery networks to avoid all copyright liability by making copies of each item of content and associating one unique copy with each subscriber to the network, or by giving their subscribers the capacity to make their own individual copies. We do not address whether such a network operator would be able to escape any other form of copyright liability, such as liability for unauthorized reproductions or liability for contributory infringement.

In sum, because we find, on undisputed facts, that Cablevision's proposed RS-DVR system would not directly infringe plaintiffs' exclusive rights to reproduce and publicly perform their copyrighted works, we grant summary judgment in favor of Cablevision with respect to both rights.

CONCLUSION

For the foregoing reasons, the district court's award of summary judgment to the plaintiffs is REVERSED and the district court's injunction against Cablevision is VACATED. The case is REMANDED for further proceedings consistent with this opinion.

---

## B. FAIR USE ON THE INTERNET

In light of the ongoing technological transformation of our entertainment world, this section examines the copyright challenges posed by the Internet. Music first began to circulate on the Motion Picture Experts Group Audio Layer 3 (MP3) Internet format, and then movies followed suit. The pioneering Napster service made it easy for listeners to download music, and the Rio device enabled them to make that music portable. After a decade of litigation over music-file sharing, Apple's iPod and iPhone (along with competing alternatives) have become ubiquitous, along with a robust market for paid music downloads which has partially ameliorated the steep decline in CD sales. New revenue streams have developed, including "apps" and ringtones. Webcasting and podcasting have emerged, each presenting its own set of unique copyright questions.

The emergence of these technologies offered important benefits to performers as well as consumers of music. Music, movie and television fans now have ready online access to old as well as new music, films, and TV shows, and they have the ability to create, for example, their own personally-favored playlists of songs. New artists, who are often unable to get a CD placed in their own neighborhood stores, now have a way to deliver their music to potential fans around the entire world.

From the point of view of the record companies, late 1990s surveys had predicted that music downloading systems could actually add a bit to sales, by bringing into the market people who were unlikely to buy a traditional CD album. Thus, Title IV of the 1998 *Digital Millennium Copyright Act* made it clear that the transmission of recordings online must be licensed not just by the songwriters (as with over-the-air broadcasts), but also by the record companies when the music is being played by webcasters that function, in effect, as digital jukeboxes and Internet radio stations. Indeed, in 1999, the American Society of Composers, Authors, and Publishers (ASCAP), the songwriter association whose origins and functions we will read about in Chapter 11, had reached an agreement with MP3.com about the fees to be paid to songwriters.

The understandable concern felt by the music industry, though, was that people could purchase the CD (or video), download its contents to their computer, and then transmit it to others who had not bought the album or video (perhaps in return for copies of other works). It is harder for the copyright owners to discover this kind of online infringement of their works than it would be to find unlicensed concerts and plays, let alone broadcasts. Thus, the last decade has witnessed numerous lawsuits and rulings about fair use and third-party liability on the Internet.

An early suit involved the Rio, a pioneering Diamond Multimedia Systems device that emerged in 1998. This portable instrument (about the size of a deck of cards) that could extract music from a computer hard drive, resulting in personalized music collection of CD sound quality. With 200,000 units sold (at $200 apiece) in its first six months, its portability posed a different threat to CD sales than music downloaded on computers. Rather than seek a legislative expansion of copyright law, the Recording Industry Association of America (RIAA) instead went to court under the existing 1992 *Audio Home Recording Act* (AHRA). The RIAA claimed that the Rio violated the AHRA as a "digital audio recording device" that did not have built into it the Serial Copy Management System (SCMS), i.e., copy protection. In *RIAA v. Diamond Multimedia Systems*, 180 F.3d 1072 (9th Cir. 1999), the court ruled that Rio did not meet the AHRA test.

Under section 1001(3) of the AHRA, a "digital audio recording device" is "any machine or device of a type commonly distributed . . . for use by individuals . . . the digital recording function of which is designed or marketed for the primary purpose of . . . making a digital audio copied recording for private use. . . ." In turn, "digital audio copied recording" is defined by section 1001(1) as the "reproduction in a digital recording format of a digital musical recording"; the latter is defined by section 1001(5)(A) as a "material object . . . in which are fixed, in a digital recording format, only sounds, and material statements, or instructions incidental to those fixed sounds, if any. . . ." Since the Rio extracted music directly from a computer hard drive, the key statutory question was whether the computer itself was a "digital musical recording."

The Court's ruled it was not. Computers certainly were "material objects," but they "contain numerous programs (e.g., for word processing, scheduling, etc.) and databases that are not incidental to any sound files that may be stored on the hard drive," 180 F.3d at 1076, means that computers do not fall within Congress' focus on "recorded compact discs, digital audio tapes, audio cassettes, long-playing albums, digital compact cassettes, and mini-discs." *Id.* at 1077. Although some songs may have reached the computer system from broadcast stations and the like, the fact that Rio itself took the songs from the computer hard drive meant that it was not reproducing the song even "indirectly from a transmission."

The circuit panel felt quite comfortable with the policy implications of this literal reading of the AHRA's wording, because "the Rio's operation is entirely consistent with the Act's main purpose—the facilitation of personal use. . . . The Rio merely makes copies in order to render portable, or 'space-shift', those files that already reside on a user's hard-drive. [Just as the Supreme Court had ruled in its major *Sony* decision], that 'time-shifting' of copyrighted television shows with VCRs constitutes fair use . . . [so too Rio] copying is paradigmatic noncommercial personal use entirely consistent with the purposes of the Act." *Id.* at 1079. Needless to say, the RIAA did not agree on that score, stating afterwards that "unfortunately, the Internet culture and unlicensed use means that theft of intellectual property is rampant, and the music business and its artists are the biggest victims."

The RIAA's immediate response was to agree with the software and hardware manufacturers' *Secure Digital Music Initiative* ("SDMI") that attempted to address this issue through private industry action. Under the SDMI, the manufacturers (including Microsoft and Sony) can offer consumers equipment that initially permits extraction from computers and playback of music that has not been licensed for this purpose. But the manufacturers have all agreed that their equipment—both the digital download players and the portable hardware—will have integrated into it screening technology that blocks the downloading and playing of new music that has not been licensed for that purpose. The record companies (including Sony Music) sought to develop a new electronic "fingerprint" system, combining a *robust* watermark that identifies a CD's protection and a *fragile* watermark that prevents music from being compressed by software not conforming to the SDMI standard. When this happens the owners of this new equipment would have to take it in to be upgraded for access to any of the music being released from then on.

The combination of the *Diamond* ruling and the SDMI industry pact posed a host of challenging questions. The first is whether, from a technological perspective, these efforts will effectively bar listeners from copying music off the Internet without paying the established fees. The second question concerns whether the presence of unsatisfied consumer demand will induce new manufacturers to produce and sell Rio-like equipment that does not screen for and reject watermarked music and films. Alternatively, assuming that the SDMI pact effectively blocks any such equipment from emerging to satisfy this market demand, does such private industry action amount to a reasonable or unreasonable combination of restraint of trade under the *Sherman Antitrust Act* (the subject of Chapter 12)? Finally, supposing that technological, financial, or antitrust obstacles preclude effective enforcement of the SDMI, should the *Diamond* interpretation of the Copyright Act be overridden by the Supreme Court or Congress? In other words, was the *Diamond* court correct in its assumption that production and use of Rio-like equipment is fair in the new Internet music and movie market?

Soon after *Diamond* came a battle over MP3.com's new service called My.MP3.com. MP3.com purchased nearly 100,000 albums, copied them onto its own servers, and permitted My.MP3.com subscribers to draw upon these over the Internet. To gain access to a record, however, the subscriber had to prove he or she already owned the CD or was purchasing it from an online retailer. Four months later, this free My.MP3.com service had over 500,000 subscriber-users. In *UMG Recordings v. MP3.Com*, 92 F. Supp. 2d 349 (S.D.N.Y. 2000), the basic issue was whether that action was "fair use." MP3.com's lawyers argued that the new service was providing "a transformative 'space shift' by which subscribers can enjoy the sound recordings contained on their CD's without lugging around the physical discs themselves." Relying on *Castle Rock Entertainment v. Carol Publishing Group*, 150 F.3d 132 (2d Cir. 1998), which said that transformation requires adding "new aesthetics, new insights, and understandings" to the original, the district court found My.MP3.com to be providing just an "innovative" service, "repackaging these recordings to facilitate their transmission through another medium."

The major defense of MP3.com was that rather than detracting from the plaintiff's market prospects, this service was actually enhancing them. Consumers who were attracted to playing music on their computers could only do so by proving that they had or were now purchasing the music themselves, rather than simply relying on "pirates." The court responded:

> Copyright, however is not designed to afford consumer protection or convenience but, rather, to protect the copyrightholders' property interests. Moreover, as a practical matter, plaintiffs have indicated no objection in principle to licensing their recordings to companies like MP3.com; they simply want to make sure they get the remuneration the law reserves for them as holders of copyrights on creative works. Stripped to its essence, defendant's "consumer protection" argument amounts to nothing more than a bold claim that defendant should be able to misappropriate plaintiffs' property simply because there is a consumer demand for it. This hardly appeals to the conscience of equity.

92 F. Supp. 2d at 352.

After settlements with four of the five major labels (Sony Music, BMG Entertainment, Time Warner Music Group, and EMI Recorded Music) for $20 million apiece, the case proceeded because Seagram's Universal Music Group was not prepared to accept that "modest" settlement amount. Universal obtained a ruling from the trial judge that the appropriate damages were $25,000 for each CD included in My.MP3.com's accessible database, producing a $53 million payment by MP3.com in November 2000. This period of entertainment innovation saw MP3.com's stock price drop from $61 a share in 1999 to $4 a year later.

As part of its settlement, MP3.com restarted its My.MP3.com service, but only by charging all members an annual $50-a-year subscription fee. These revenues, along with advertising income, are then used to pay copyright holders a royalty whenever their music is downloaded. Newspaper readers as well as music fans were far more conscious of the contemporary legal battle over Napster than over My.MP3.com. Unlike My.Mp3.com, Napster did not itself store any CDs into its own computer files; and unlike Sony, the original creator of home video recording, Napster did not produce the technology for users to do that. Instead Napster offered a pioneering new system for "peer-to-peer file-sharing" over the Internet.

The essence of this system had Napster compiling and constantly updating a giant list of all record owners around the world who were prepared to enter their names and the records they had on their computer files which they would exchange with others. Any individual member, after having downloaded the Napster.com software, would simply enter the name of the song and artist. Napster would then immediately display the names of all the other members with that song, and the user could then have the song transmitted to and stored to a computer hard drive.

By 2000 there were nearly 60 million users downloading an average of 200,000 songs every *minute*. Napster faced a lawsuit by the record industry, which feared this to be an economic "time bomb" about to go off. To defend itself, Napster brought in litigator David Boies, who had won the antitrust trial against Microsoft and lost the Bush-Gore election battle in the Supreme Court. Unlike MP3.com, Napster itself could not be charged with direct copying, storing, and transmission of copyrighted music. However, just as the film industry had claimed in *Sony*, the music industry accused Napster of "contributory infringement" by facilitating copying by tens of millions of service users around the planet. Ironically, Sony Music was among those claiming that the fair use defense was not available here.

In the initial district court ruling in this case, *A & M Records v. Napster*, 114 F. Supp. 2d 896 (N.D. Cal. 2000), Judge Marilyn Hall Patel granted them an injunction against Napster's service being used for any copyrighted or unlicensed recordings. With respect to whether the members' use of Napster was commercial or noncommercial, Judge Patel stated:

> Although downloading and uploading MP3 music files is not paradigmatic commercial activity, it is also not personal use in the traditional sense. Plaintiffs have not shown that the majority of Napster users download music to sell—that is, for profit. However, given the vast scale of Napster use among anonymous individuals, the court finds that downloading and uploading MP3 music files with the assistance of Napster are not private uses. At the very least, a host user sending a file cannot be said to engage in a personal use when distributing that file to an anonymous requester. Moreover, the fact that Napster users get for free something they would ordinarily have to buy suggests that they reap economic advantages from Napster use.

*Id.* at 912. The judge accepted the plaintiffs' argument that widespread use of Napster could adversely affect the record industry's financial prospects via "a decrease in retail sales, especially among college students; an obstacle to the record companies' future entry into the digital downloading of music stemming from its free distribution." *Id.* at 914.

Judge Patel also rejected Napster's assertion of "several potential fair uses of the Napster service—including sampling, space-shifting, and the authorized distribution of new artists' work." With respect to the first,

> Sampling on Napster is not a personal use in the traditional sense that courts have recognized—copying which occurs within the household and does not confer any financial benefit on the user. Instead, sampling on Napster amounts to obtaining permanent copies of songs that users would otherwise have to purchase; it also carries the potential for viral distribution to millions of people. Defendant ignores critical differences between

> sampling songs on Napster and VCR usage in *Sony*. First, while "time-shifting [TV broadcasts] merely enables a viewer to see . . . a work which he has been invited to witness in its entirety free of charge," plaintiffs in this action almost always charge for their music—even if it is downloaded song-by-song. They only make promotional downloads available on a "highly restricted basis." Copyright owners also earn royalties from streamed song samples on retail websites like Amazon.com. Second, the majority of VCR purchasers in *Sony* did not distribute taped television broadcasts, but merely enjoyed them at home. In contrast, a Napster user who downloads a copy of a song to her hard drive may make that song available to millions of other individuals, even if she eventually chooses to purchase the CD. So-called sampling on Napster may quickly facilitate unauthorized distribution at an exponential rate.

*Id.* at 913. With respect to "space-shifting" of music users already had on a remote location, the judge found that the defendant had failed to show that this "constitutes a commercially significant use of Napster. Indeed, the most credible explanation for the exponential growth of traffic to the website is the vast array of free MP3 files offered by other users—not the ability of each individual to space-shift music she already owns. Thus, even if space-shifting is a fair use, it is not substantial enough to preclude liability under the staple article of commerce doctrine." *Id.* at 916. And essentially the same conclusion was reached about Napster's argument that another substantial use of its service was "the authorized promotion of independent artists," almost all of whom did not enjoy contracts with and promotion by the established record companies. This appeal followed.

## A & M RECORDS, ET AL. V. NAPSTER

United States Court of Appeals, Ninth Circuit, 2001.
239 F.3d 1004.

BEEZER, CIRCUIT JUDGE.

[After walking through the basic doctrinal issues of whether Napster users were engaging in copyright infringement or fair use, the Circuit then turned to Napster's principal defense of the legality of its registered users' actions.]

### 5. Identified Uses

Napster maintains that its identified uses of sampling and space-shifting were wrongly excluded as fair uses by the district court.

#### *a. Sampling*

Napster contends that its users download MP3 files to "sample" the music in order to decide whether to purchase the recording. Napster argues that the district court: (1) erred in concluding that sampling is a commercial use because it conflated a noncommercial use with a personal use; (2) erred in determining that sampling adversely affects the market for plaintiffs copyrighted music, a requirement if the use is noncommercial; and (3) erroneously concluded that sampling is not a fair use because it determined that samplers may also engage in other infringing activity.

The district court determined that sampling remains a commercial use even if some users eventually purchase the music. We find no error in the district court's determination. Plaintiffs have established that they are likely to succeed in proving that even authorized temporary downloading of individual songs for sampling purposes is commercial in nature. The record supports a finding that free promotional downloads are highly regulated by the record company plaintiffs and that the companies collect royalties for song samples available on retail Internet sites. Evidence relied on by the district court demonstrates that the free downloads provided by the record companies consist of thirty-to-sixty second samples or are full songs programmed to "time out," that is, exist only for a short time on the downloader's computer. In comparison, Napster users download a full, free and permanent copy of the recording. The determination by the district court as to the commercial purpose and character of sampling is not clearly erroneous.

The district court further found that both the market for audio CDs and market for online distribution are adversely affected by Napster's service. As stated in our discussion of the district court's general fair use analysis: the court did not abuse its discretion when it found that, overall, Napster has an adverse impact on the audio CD and digital download markets. Contrary to Napster's assertion that the district court failed to specifically address the market impact of sampling, the district court determined that "even if the type of sampling supposedly done on Napster were a non-commercial use, plaintiffs have demonstrated a substantial likelihood that it would adversely affect the potential market for their copyrighted works if it became widespread." *Napster,* 114 F. Supp. 2d at 914. The record supports the district court's preliminary determinations that: (1) the more music that sampling users download, the less likely they are to eventually purchase the recordings on audio CD; and (2) even if the audio CD market is not harmed, Napster has adverse effects on the developing digital download market.

Napster further argues that the district court erred in rejecting its evidence that the users' downloading of "samples" increases or tends to increase audio CD sales. The district court, however, correctly noted that "any potential enhancement of plaintiffs' sales . . . would not tip the fair use analysis conclusively in favor of defendant." *Id.* at 914. We agree that increased sales of copyrighted material attributable to unauthorized use should not deprive the copyright holder of the right to license the material. *See Campbell*, 510 U.S. at 591 n.21 ("Even favorable evidence, without more, is no guarantee of fairness. Judge Leval gives the example of the film producer's appropriation of a composer's previously unknown song that turns the song into a commercial success; the boon to the song does not make the film's simple copying fair."). Nor does positive impact in one market, here the audio CD market, deprive the copyright holder of the right to develop identified alternative markets, here the digital download market.

We find no error in the district court's factual findings or abuse of discretion in the court's conclusion that plaintiffs will likely prevail in establishing that sampling does not constitute a fair use.

*b. Space-Shifting*

Napster also maintains that space-shifting is a fair use. Space-shifting occurs when a Napster user downloads MP3 music files in order to listen to music he already owns on audio CD. Napster asserts that we have already held that space-shifting of musical compositions and sound recordings is a fair use. *See Recording Indus. Ass'n of Am. v. Diamond Multimedia Sys., Inc.*, 180 F.3d 1072, 1079 (9th Cir. 1999) ("Rio [a portable MP3 player] merely makes copies in order to render portable, or 'space-shift,' those files that already reside on a user's hard drive. Such copying is a paradigmatic noncommercial personal use."). *See also generally Sony*, 464 U.S. at 423 (holding that "time-shifting," where a video tape recorder owner records a television show for later viewing, is a fair use).

We conclude that the district court did not err when it refused to apply the "shifting" analyses of *Sony* and *Diamond*. Both *Diamond* and *Sony* are inapposite because the methods of shifting in these cases did not also simultaneously involve distribution of the copyrighted material to the general public; the time or space-shifting of copyrighted material exposed the material only to the original user. In *Diamond*, for example, the copyrighted music was transferred from the user's computer hard drive to the user's portable MP3 player. So too *Sony*, where "the majority of VCR purchasers did not distribute taped television broadcasts, but merely enjoyed them at home." *Napster*, 114 F. Supp.2d at 913. Conversely, it is obvious that once a user lists a copy of music he already owns on the Napster system in order to access the music from another location, the song becomes "available to millions of other individuals," not just the original CD owner. *See UMG Recordings*, 92 F. Supp.2d at 351–52 (finding space-shifting of MP3 files not a fair use even when previous ownership is demonstrated before a download is allowed).

* * *

(The Circuit then turned to the question of whether Napster was itself liable for contributing to the infringement by its users.)

IV

A. *Knowledge*

Contributory liability requires that the secondary infringer "know or have reason to know" of direct infringement. The district court found that Napster had both actual and constructive knowledge that its users exchanged copyrighted music. The district court also concluded that the law does not require knowledge of "specific acts of infringement" and rejected Napster's contention that because the company cannot distinguish infringing from noninfringing files, it does not "know" of the direct infringement.

It is apparent from the record that Napster has knowledge, both actual and constructive, of direct infringement. Napster claims that it is nevertheless protected from contributory liability by the teaching of *Sony Corp. v. Universal City Studios, Inc.*, 464 U.S. 417 (1984). We disagree. We observe that Napster's actual, specific knowledge of direct infringement renders *Sony's* holding of limited assistance to Napster. We are compelled to make a clear distinction between the architecture of the Napster system and Napster's conduct in relation to the operational capacity of the system.

We are bound to follow *Sony*, and will not impute the requisite level of knowledge to Napster merely because peer-to-peer file sharing technology may be used to infringe plaintiffs' copyrights. *See* 464 U.S. at 436 (rejecting argument that merely supplying the " 'means' to accomplish an infringing activity" leads to imposition of liability). We depart from the reasoning of the district court that Napster failed to demonstrate that its system is capable of commercially significant noninfringing uses. The district court improperly confined the use analysis to current uses, ignoring the system's capabilities. *See generally Sony*, 464 U.S. at 442–43 (framing inquiry as whether the video tape recorder is "capable of commercially significant noninfringing uses"). Consequently, the district court placed undue weight on the proportion of current infringing use as compared to current and future noninfringing use. Nonetheless, whether we might arrive at a different result is not the issue here. The instant appeal occurs at an early point in the proceedings and "the fully developed factual record may be materially different from that initially before the district court. . . ." Regardless of the number of Napster's infringing versus noninfringing uses, the evidentiary record here supported the district court's finding that plaintiffs would likely prevail in establishing that Napster knew or had reason to know of its users' infringement of plaintiffs' copyrights.

* * *

We agree that if a computer system operator learns of specific infringing material available on his system and fails to purge such material from the system, the operator knows of and contributes to direct infringement. Conversely, absent any specific information which identifies infringing activity, a computer system operator cannot be liable for contributory infringement merely because the structure of the system allows for the exchange of copyrighted material. *See Sony*, 464 U.S. at 436, 442–43. To enjoin simply because a computer network allows for infringing use would, in our opinion, violate *Sony* and potentially restrict activity unrelated to infringing use.

We nevertheless conclude that sufficient knowledge exists to impose contributory liability when linked to demonstrated infringing use of the Napster system. The record supports the district court's finding that Napster has actual knowledge that specific infringing material is available using its system, that it could block access to the system by suppliers of the infringing material, and that it failed to remove the material.

*B. Material Contribution*

Under the facts as found by the district court, Napster materially contributes to the infringing activity. Relying on *Fonovisa v. Cherry Auction*, 76 F.3d 259 (9th Cir. 1996), the district court concluded that "without the support services defendant provides, Napster users could not find and download the music they want with the ease of which defendant boasts." *Napster*, 114 F. Supp.2d at 919–20 ("Napster is an integrated service designed to enable users to locate and download MP3 music files."). We agree that Napster provides "the site and facilities" for direct infringement. The district court correctly applied the reasoning in *Fonovisa*, and properly found that Napster materially contributes to direct infringement.

V

We turn to the question whether Napster engages in vicarious copyright infringement. Vicarious copyright liability is an "outgrowth" of respondeat superior. *Fonovisa*, 76 F.3d at 262. In the context of copyright law, vicarious liability extends beyond an employer/employee relationship to cases in which a defendant "has the right and ability to supervise the infringing activity and also has a direct financial interest in such activities."

Before moving into this discussion, we note that *Sony's* "staple article of commerce" analysis has no application to Napster's potential liability for vicarious copyright infringement. The issues of *Sony's* liability under the "doctrines of 'direct infringement' and 'vicarious liability' " were not before the Supreme Court, although the Court recognized that the "lines between direct infringement, contributory infringement, and vicarious liability are not clearly drawn." Consequently, when the *Sony* Court used the term "vicarious liability," it did so broadly and outside of a technical analysis of the doctrine of vicarious copyright infringement. *Id.* at 435 ("Vicarious liability is imposed in virtually all areas of the law, and the concept of contributory infringement is merely a species of the broader problem of identifying the circumstances in which it is just to hold one individual accountable for the actions of another.").

*A. Financial Benefit*

The district court determined that plaintiffs had demonstrated they would likely succeed in establishing that Napster has a direct financial interest in the infringing activity. We agree. Financial benefit exists where the availability of infringing material "acts as a 'draw' for customers." Ample evidence supports the district court's finding that Napster's future revenue is directly dependent upon "increases in userbase." More users register with the Napster system as the "quality and quantity of available music increases." We conclude that the district court did not err in determining that Napster financially benefits from the availability of protected works on its system.

*B. Supervision*

The district court determined that Napster has the right and ability to supervise its users' conduct. We agree in part. The ability to block infringers' access to a particular environment for any reason whatsoever is evidence of the right and ability to supervise. Here, plaintiffs have demonstrated that Napster retains the right to control access to its system. Napster has an express reservation of rights policy, stating on its website that it expressly reserves the "right to refuse service and terminate accounts in [its] discretion, including, but not limited to, if Napster believes that user conduct violates applicable law . . . or for any reason in Napster's sole discretion, with or without cause."

To escape imposition of vicarious liability, the reserved right to police must be exercised to its fullest extent. Turning a blind eye to detectable acts of infringement for the sake of profit gives rise to liability . . . The district court correctly determined that Napster had the right and ability to police its system and failed to exercise that right to prevent the exchange of copyrighted material. The district court, however, failed to recognize that the boundaries of the premises that Napster "controls and patrols" are limited. Put differently, Napster's reserved "right and ability" to police is cabined by the system's current architecture. As shown by the record, the Napster system does not "read" the content of indexed files, other than to check that they are in the proper MP3 format.

Napster, however, has the ability to locate infringing material listed on its search indices, and the right to terminate users' access to the system. The file name indices, therefore, are within the "premises" that

Napster has the ability to police. We recognize that the files are user-named and may not match copyrighted material exactly (for example, the artist or song could be spelled wrong). For Napster to function effectively, however, file names must reasonably or roughly correspond to the material contained in the files, otherwise no user could ever locate any desired music. As a practical matter, Napster, its users and the record company plaintiffs have equal access to infringing material by employing Napster's "search function."

Our review of the record requires us to accept the district court's conclusion that plaintiffs have demonstrated a likelihood of success on the merits of the vicarious copyright infringement claim. Napster's failure to police the system's "premises," combined with a showing that Napster financially benefits from the continuing availability of infringing files on its system, leads to the imposition of vicarious liability.

VIII

[The one change of consequence in the Circuit Court ruling related to the nature of the interim injunctive relief to be granted the music industry against this Napster service.]

The district court correctly recognized that a preliminary injunction against Napster's participation in copyright infringement is not only warranted but required. We believe, however, that the scope of the injunction needs modification in light of our opinion. Specifically, we reiterate that contributory liability may potentially be imposed only to the extent that Napster: (1) receives reasonable knowledge of specific infringing files with copyrighted musical compositions and sound recordings; (2) knows or should know that such files are available on the Napster system; and (3) fails to act to prevent viral distribution of the works. The mere existence of the Napster system, absent actual notice and Napster's demonstrated failure to remove the offending material, is insufficient to impose contributory liability. *See Sony,* 464 U.S. at 442–43.

Conversely, Napster may be vicariously liable when it fails to affirmatively use its ability to patrol its system and preclude access to potentially infringing files listed in its search index. Napster has both the ability to use its search function to identify infringing musical recordings and the right to bar participation of users who engage in the transmission of infringing files.

The preliminary injunction which we stayed is overbroad because it places on Napster the entire burden of ensuring that no "copying, downloading, uploading, transmitting, or distributing" of plaintiffs' works occur on the system. As stated, we place the burden on plaintiffs to provide notice to Napster of copyrighted works and files containing such works available on the Napster system before Napster has the duty to disable access to the offending content. Napster, however, also bears the burden of policing the system within the limits of the system. Here, we recognize that this is not an exact science in that the files are user named. In crafting the injunction on remand, the district court should recognize that Napster's system does not currently appear to allow Napster access to users' MP3 files.

Based on our decision to remand, Napster's additional arguments on appeal going to the scope of the injunction need not be addressed. We, however, briefly address Napster's First Amendment argument so that it is not reasserted on remand. Napster contends that the present injunction violates the First Amendment because it is broader than necessary. The company asserts two distinct free speech rights: (1) its right to publish a "directory" (here, the search index) and (2) its users' right to exchange information. We note that First Amendment concerns in copyright are allayed by the presence of the fair use doctrine. There was a preliminary determination here that Napster users are not fair users. Uses of copyrighted material that are not fair uses are rightfully enjoined. *See Dr. Seuss Enters. v. Penguin Books USA, Inc.*, 109 F.3d 1394, 1403 (9th Cir. 1997) (rejecting defendants' claim that injunction would constitute a prior restraint in violation of the First Amendment).

Affirmed in Part, Reversed in Part, and Remanded.

---

Eventually Napster was sold to one of the copyright plaintiffs, which then offered a new Internet service we will be reading about soon. RIAA members were also developing their own Internet music services. Three of the major labels, Warner Music, EMI, and BMG, combined with RealNetwork and AOL to create a new MusicNet, while the other two majors, Sony and Universal Music, did the same with their own new Pressplay (with EMI offering its songs on this service as well). After having developed what they considered to be safe technology and securing acceptable contracts from the music publishers who also had copyrights in the songs, these systems both started operating in 2001. For a fee of $10 a month, a subscriber had access to around 100,000 songs, but was entitled to stream or download just 100 songs, all of which would be extinguished after that month unless the service and fee was renewed.

By the summer of 2001, Internet services emerged employing new software created by FastTrack: Kazaa, run by a FastTrack partner out of Amsterdam, MusicCity Morpheus (a branch of Streamcast Networks) based in Franklin, Tennessee, and Grokster, operated from Nevis Island in the Caribbean West Indies. These new services were more decentralized than Napster, which had required its users to log on to its own server containing a central directory of everyone who had available songs. By September 2001, more music files were being exchanged on the new FastTrack software than back in February 2001 on Napster.

MusicCity provided this service for free (as had Napster), but displayed advertisements on its webpages.

Another potentially important difference between MusicCity and Napster was that the former provided access not only to music, but to movies, photo images, and documents. Thus, not only albums from Bob Dylan and 'N Sync, but movies like *Planet of the Apes* and *Legally Blonde* were appearing on computers round the world a day or two after they had been released in American movie theaters. Movie "fans" would bring video cameras into the theater to tape the movie while they were watching it, and then compressing the film into their computers for distribution via MusicCity, Kazaa, and Grokster over the FastTrack software. By the fall of 2001, surveys found millions of exchanges of thousands of movies over the Internet, and these numbers were growing as higher-speed connections became available to exchange three-hour movies like *The Lord of the Rings*, or even an entire series of *The Sopranos*, rather than just a three-minute song.

Thus, in October 2001, the MPAA and RIAA members filed suit against these file-sharing services. *MGM v. Grokster, Ltd.*, 243 F. Supp. 2d 1073 (C.D. Cal. 2003). According to the complaint, these "defendants have created a 21st Century piratical bazaar where the unlawful exchange of protected material takes place across the vast expanse of the Internet." The defendants responded that their new service made it possible for people to learn about such public events as the "World Trade Center terrorist tragedy," as well as for young musicians to share their new work; and that they had neither knowledge of any specific items people were seeking to exchange, nor any ability to control the illegal ones.

## METRO-GOLDWYN-MAYER STUDIOS INC. V. GROKSTER, LTD.

Supreme Court of the United States, 2005.
545 U.S. 913, 125 S.Ct. 2764, 162 L.Ed.2d 781.

JUSTICE SOUTER delivered the opinion of the Court.

The question is under what circumstances the distributor of a product capable of both lawful and unlawful use is liable for acts of copyright infringement by third parties using the product. We hold that one who distributes a device with the object of promoting its use to infringe copyright, as shown by clear expression or other affirmative steps taken to foster infringement, is liable for the resulting acts of infringement by third parties.

# I

## A

Respondents, Grokster, Ltd., and StreamCast Networks, Inc., defendants in the trial court, distribute free software products that allow computer users to share electronic files through peer-to-peer networks, so called because users' computers communicate directly with each other, not through central servers. The advantage of peer-to-peer networks over information networks of other types shows up in their substantial and growing popularity. Because they need no central computer server to mediate the exchange of information or files among users, the high-bandwidth communications capacity for a server may be dispensed with, and the need for costly server storage space is eliminated. Since copies of a file (particularly a popular one) are available on many users' computers, file requests and retrievals may be faster than on other types of networks, and since file exchanges do not travel through a server, communications can take place between any computers that remain connected to the network without risk that a glitch in the server will disable the network in its entirety. Given these benefits in security, cost, and efficiency, peer-to-peer networks are employed to store and distribute electronic files by universities, government agencies, corporations, and libraries, among others.

Other users of peer-to-peer networks include individual recipients of Grokster's and StreamCast's software, and although the networks that they enjoy through using the software can be used to share any type of digital file, they have prominently employed those networks in sharing copyrighted music and video files without authorization. A group of copyright holders (MGM for short, but including motion picture studios, recording companies, song-writers, and music publishers) sued Grokster and StreamCast for their users' copyright infringements, alleging that they knowingly and intentionally distributed their software to enable users to reproduce and distribute the copyrighted works in violation of the Copyright Act. MGM sought damages and an injunction.

Discovery during the litigation revealed the way the software worked, the business aims of each defendant company, and the predilections of the users. Grokster's eponymous software employs what is known as FastTrack technology, a protocol developed by others and licensed to Grokster. StreamCast distributes a very similar product except that its software, called Morpheus, relies on what is known as Gnutella technology. A user who downloads and installs either software possesses the protocol to send requests for files directly to the computers of others using software compatible with FastTrack or Gnutella. On the FastTrack network opened by the Grokster software, the user's request goes to a computer given an indexing capacity by the software and designated a supernode, or to some other computer with comparable power and capacity to collect temporary indexes of the files available on the computers of users connected to it. The supernode (or indexing computer) searches its own index and may communicate the search request to other supernodes. If the file is found, the supernode discloses its location to the computer requesting it, and the requesting user can download the file directly from the computer located. The copied file is placed in a designated sharing folder on the requesting user's computer, where it is available for other users to download in turn, along with any other file in that folder.

In the Gnutella network made available by Morpheus, the process is mostly the same, except that in some versions of the Gnutella protocol there are no supernodes. In these versions, peer computers using the protocol communicate directly with each other. When a user enters a search request into the Morpheus software, it sends the request to computers connected with it, which in turn pass the request along to other connected peers. The search results are communicated to the requesting computer, and the user can download desired files directly from peers' computers. As this description indicates, Grokster and StreamCast use no servers to intercept the content of the search requests or to mediate the file transfers conducted by users of the software, there being no central point through which the substance of the communications passes in either direction.

Although Grokster and StreamCast do not therefore know when particular files are copied, a few searches using their software would show what is available on the networks the software reaches. MGM commissioned a statistician to conduct a systematic search, and his study showed that nearly 90% of the files available for download on the FastTrack system were copyrighted works.[5] Grokster and StreamCast dispute this figure, raising methodological problems and arguing that free copying even of copyrighted works may be authorized by the rightholders. They also argue that potential noninfringing uses of their software are significant in kind, even if infrequent in practice. Some musical performers, for example, have gained new audiences by distributing their copyrighted works for free across peer-to-peer networks, and some distributors of unprotected content have used peer-to-peer networks to disseminate files, Shakespeare being an example. Indeed, StreamCast

---

[5] By comparison, evidence introduced by the plaintiffs in A & M *Records, Inc. v. Napster, Inc.*, 239 F. 3d 1004 (CA9 2001), showed that 87% of files available on the Napster filesharing network were copyrighted, *id.*, at 1013. Among the key early scholarly treatments of these issues are Lawrence Lessig, *The Future of Ideas: The Fate of the Commons in a Connected World* (Random House, 2001); Jane C. Ginsburg, *Copyright Use and Excuse on the Internet*, 24 Colum. VLA J. L. & the Arts 1 (2000); R. Anthony Reese, *Copyright & Internet Music Transmissions: Existing Law, Major Controversies, Possible Solutions*, 55 U. Miami L. Rev. 237 (2001). The major one now is the book by William Fisher, *Promises to Keep: Technology Law and the Future of Entertainment* (Stanford Univ. Press 2004).

has given Morpheus users the opportunity to download the briefs in this very case, though their popularity has not been quantified.

As for quantification, the parties' anecdotal and statistical evidence entered thus far to show the content available on the FastTrack and Gnutella networks does not say much about which files are actually downloaded by users, and no one can say how often the software is used to obtain copies of unprotected material. But MGM's evidence gives reason to think that the vast majority of users' downloads are acts of infringement, and because well over 100 million copies of the software in question are known to have been downloaded, and billions of files are shared across the FastTrack and Gnutella networks each month, the probable scope of copyright infringement is staggering. Grokster and StreamCast concede the infringement in most downloads, and it is uncontested that they are aware that users employ their software primarily to download copyrighted files, even if the decentralized FastTrack and Gnutella networks fail to reveal which files are being copied, and when. From time to time, moreover, the companies have learned about their users' infringement directly, as from users who have sent e-mail to each company with questions about playing copyrighted movies they had downloaded, to whom the companies have responded with guidance. And MGM notified the companies of 8 million copyrighted files that could be obtained using their software. Grokster and StreamCast are not, however, merely passive recipients of information about infringing use. The record is replete with evidence that from the moment Grokster and StreamCast began to distribute their free software, each one clearly voiced the objective that recipients use it to download copyrighted works, and each took active steps to encourage infringement.

After the notorious file-sharing service, Napster, was sued by copyright holders for facilitation of copyright infringement. StreamCast gave away a software program of a kind known as OpenNap, designed as compatible with the Napster program and open to Napster users for downloading files from other Napster and OpenNap users' computers. Evidence indicates that "[i]t was always [StreamCast's] intent to use [its OpenNap network] to be able to capture email addresses of [its] initial target market so that [it] could promote [its] StreamCast Morpheus interface to them," indeed, the OpenNap program was engineered " 'to leverage Napster's 50 million user base.' "

StreamCast monitored both the number of users downloading its OpenNap program and the number of music files they downloaded. It also used the resulting OpenNap network to distribute copies of the Morpheus software and to encourage users to adopt it. Internal company documents indicate that StreamCast hoped to attract large numbers of former Napster users if that company was shut down by court order or otherwise, and that StreamCast planned to be the next Napster. A kit developed by

StreamCast to be delivered to advertisers, for example, contained press articles about StreamCast's potential to capture former Napster users, and it introduced itself to some potential advertisers as a company "which is similar to what Napster was." It broadcast banner advertisements to users of other Napster-compatible software, urging them to adopt its OpenNap. An internal e-mail from a company executive stated: " 'We have put this network in place so that when Napster pulls the plug on their free service . . . or if the Court orders them shut down prior to that . . . we will be positioned to capture the flood of their 32 million users that will be actively looking for an alternative.' "

Thus, StreamCast developed promotional materials to market its service as the best Napster alternative. One proposed advertisement read: "Napster Inc. has announced that it will soon begin charging you a fee. That's if the courts don't order it shut down first. What will you do to get around it?"

Another proposed ad touted StreamCast's software as the "#1 alternative to Napster" and asked "[w]hen the lights went off at Napster . . . where did the users go?" StreamCast even planned to flaunt the illegal uses of its software; when it launched the OpenNap network, the chief technology officer of the company averred that "[t]he goal is to get in trouble with the law and get sued. It's the best way to get in the new[s]." The evidence that Grokster sought to capture the market of former Napster users is sparser but revealing, for Grokster launched its own OpenNap system called Swaptor and inserted digital codes into its Web site so that computer users using Web search engines to look for "Napster" or "[f]ree filesharing" would be directed to the Grokster Web site, where they could download the Grokster software. And Grokster's name is an apparent derivative of Napster.

StreamCast's executives monitored the number of songs by certain commercial artists available on their networks, and an internal communication indicates they aimed to have a larger number of copyrighted songs available on their networks than other file-sharing networks. The point, of course, would be to attract users of a mind to infringe, just as it would be with their promotional materials developed showing copyrighted songs as examples of the kinds of files available through Morpheus. Morpheus in fact allowed users to search specifically for "Top 40" songs, which were inevitably copyrighted. Similarly, Grokster sent users a newsletter promoting its ability to provide particular, popular copyrighted materials.

In addition to this evidence of express promotion, marketing, and intent to promote further, the business models employed by Grokster and StreamCast confirm that their principal object was use of their software to download copyrighted works. Grokster and StreamCast receive no revenue from users, who obtain the software itself for nothing. Instead, both companies generate income by selling advertising space, and they stream the advertising to Grokster and Morpheus users while they are employing the programs. As the number of users of each program increases, advertising opportunities become worth more. While there is doubtless some demand for free Shakespeare, the evidence shows that substantive volume is a function of free access to copyrighted work. Users seeking Top 40 songs, for example, or the latest release by Modest Mouse, are certain to be far more numerous than those seeking a free Decameron, and Grokster and StreamCast translated that demand into dollars. Finally, there is no evidence that either company made an effort to filter copyrighted material from users' downloads or otherwise impede the sharing of copyrighted files. Although Grokster appears to have sent e-mails warning users about infringing content when it received threatening notice from the copyright holders, it never blocked anyone from continuing to use its software to share copyrighted files. StreamCast not only rejected another company's offer of help to monitor infringement, but blocked the Internet Protocol addresses of entities it believed were trying to engage in such monitoring on its networks.

B

[Justice Souter noted the lower courts' reading of *Sony*] as holding that distribution of a commercial product capable of substantial noninfringing uses could not give rise to contributory liability for infringement unless the distributor had actual knowledge of specific instances of infringement and failed to act on that knowledge. The fact that the software was capable of substantial noninfringing uses in the Ninth Circuit's view meant that Grokster and StreamCast were not liable, because they had no such actual knowledge, owing to the decentralized architecture of their software. The court also held that Grokster and StreamCast did not materially contribute to their users' infringement because it was the users themselves who searched for, retrieved, and stored the infringing files, with no involvement by the defendants beyond providing the software in the first place.

* * *

II

A

MGM and many of the *amici* fault the Court of Appeals's holding for upsetting a sound balance between the respective values of supporting creative pursuits through copyright protection and promoting innovation in new communication technologies by limiting the incidence of liability for copyright infringement. The more artistic protection is favored, the more technological innovation may be discouraged; the administration of copyright law is an exercise in managing the trade-off.

The tension between the two values is the subject of this case, with its claim that digital distribution of copyrighted material threatens copyright holders as never before, because every copy is identical to the original, copying is easy, and many people (especially the young) use file-sharing software to download copyrighted works. This very breadth of the software's use may well draw the public directly into the debate over copyright policy, and the indications are that the ease of copying songs or movies using software like Grokster's and Napster's is fostering disdain for copyright protection. As the case has been presented to us, these fears are said to be offset by the different concern that imposing liability, not only on infringers but on distributors of software based on its potential for unlawful use, could limit further development of beneficial technologies.[8]

The argument for imposing indirect liability in this case is, however, a powerful one, given the number of infringing downloads that occur every day using StreamCast's and Grokster's software. When a widely shared service or product is used to commit infringement, it may be impossible to enforce rights in the protected work effectively against all direct infringers, the only practical alternative being to go against the distributor of the copying device for secondary liability on a theory of contributory or vicarious infringement. *See In re Aimster Copyright Litigation*, 334 F. 3d 643, 645–646 (CA7 2003).

One infringes contributorily by intentionally inducing or encouraging direct infringement, and infringes vicariously by profiting from direct infringement while declining to exercise a right to stop or limit it.[9] Although "[t]he Copyright Act does not expressly render anyone liable for infringement committed by another," *Sony Corp. v. Universal City*

---

[8] The mutual exclusivity of these values should not be overstated, however. On the one hand technological innovators, including those writing filesharing computer programs, may wish for effective copyright protections for their work. *See, e.g.*, Wu, When Code Isn't Law, 89 Va. L. Rev. 679, 750 (2003). (StreamCast itself was urged by an associate to "get [its] technology written down and [its intellectual property] protected.") On the other hand the widespread distribution of creative works through improved technologies may enable the synthesis of new works or generate audiences for emerging artists. *See Eldred v. Ashcroft,* 537 U.S. 186, 223–226 (2003) (STEVENS, J., dissenting); Van Houweling, *Distributive Values in Copyright*, 83 Texas L. Rev. 1535, 1539–40, 1562–64 (2005).

[9] We stated in *Sony Corp. of America v. Universal City Studios, Inc.*, 464 U.S. 417 (1984), that " 'the lines between direct infringement, contributory infringement and vicarious liability are not clearly drawn' [R]easoned analysis of [the *Sony* plaintiffs' contributory infringement claim] necessarily entails consideration of arguments and case law which may also be forwarded under the other labels, and indeed the parties . . . rely upon such arguments and authority in support of their respective positions on the issue of contributory infringement,". In the present case MGM has argued a vicarious liability theory, which allows imposition of liability when the defendant profits directly from the infringement and has a right and ability to supervise the direct infringer, even if the defendant initially lacks knowledge of the infringement. Because we resolve the case based on an inducement theory, there is no need to analyze separately MGM's vicarious liability theory.

*Studios*, 464 U.S., at 434, these doctrines of secondary liability emerged from common law principles and are well established in the law.

B

* * *

In sum, where an article is "good for nothing else" but infringement, there is no legitimate public interest in its unlicensed availability, and there is no injustice in presuming or imputing an intent to infringe. Conversely, the doctrine absolves the equivocal conduct of selling an item with substantial lawful as well as unlawful uses, and limits liability to instances of more acute fault than the mere understanding that some of one's products will be misused. It leaves breathing room for innovation and a vigorous commerce.

The parties and many of the *amici* in this case think the key to resolving it is the *Sony* rule and, in particular, what it means for a product to be "capable of commercially significant noninfringing uses." MGM advances the argument that granting summary judgment to Grokster and StreamCast as to their current activities gave too much weight to the value of innovative technology, and too little to the copyrights infringed by users of their software, given that 90% of works available on one of the networks was shown to be copyrighted. Assuming the remaining 10% to be its noninfringing use, MGM says this should not qualify as "substantial," and the Court should quantify *Sony* to the extent of holding that a product used "principally" for infringement does not qualify. As mentioned before, Grokster and StreamCast reply by citing evidence that their software can be used to reproduce public domain works, and they point to copyright holders who actually encourage copying. Even if infringement is the principal practice with their software today, they argue, the noninfringing uses are significant and will grow.

We agree with MGM that the Court of Appeals misapplied *Sony*, which it read as limiting secondary liability quite beyond the circumstances to which the case applied. *Sony* barred secondary liability based on presuming or imputing intent to cause infringement solely from the design or distribution of a product capable of substantial lawful use, which the distributor knows is in fact used for infringement. The Ninth Circuit has read *Sony's* limitation to mean that whenever a product is capable of substantial lawful use, the producer can never be held contributorily liable for third parties' infringing use of it; it read the rule as being this broad, even when an actual purpose to cause infringing use is shown by evidence independent of design and distribution of the product, unless the distributors had "specific knowledge of infringement at a time at which they contributed to the infringement, and failed to act upon that information." Because the Circuit found the StreamCast and Grokster software capable of substantial lawful use, it concluded on the basis of its reading of *Sony* that neither company could be held liable, since there was no showing that their software, being without any central server, afforded them knowledge of specific unlawful uses.

This view of *Sony*, however, was error, converting the case from one about liability resting on imputed intent to one about liability on any theory. Because *Sony* did not displace other theories of secondary liability, and because we find below that it was error to grant summary judgment to the companies on MGM's inducement claim, we do not revisit *Sony* further, as MGM requests, to add a more quantified description of the point of balance between protection and commerce when liability rests solely on distribution with knowledge that unlawful use will occur. It is enough to note that the Ninth Circuit's judgment rested on an erroneous understanding of *Sony* and to leave further consideration of the *Sony* rule for a day when that may be required.

C

*Sony's* rule limits imputing culpable intent as a matter of law from the characteristics or uses of a distributed product. But nothing in *Sony* requires courts to ignore evidence of intent if there is such evidence, and the case was never meant to foreclose rules of fault-based liability derived from the common law. Thus, where evidence goes beyond a product's characteristics or the knowledge that it may be put to infringing uses, and shows statements or actions directed to promoting infringement, *Sony's* staple-article rule will not preclude liability. The classic case of direct evidence of unlawful purpose occurs when one induces commission of infringement by another, or "entic[es] or persuad[es] another" to infringe, Black's Law Dictionary 790 (8th ed. 2004), as by advertising. Thus at common law a copyright or patent defendant who "not only expected but invoked [infringing use] by advertisement" was liable for infringement "on principles recognized in every part of the law."

The rule on inducement of infringement as developed in the early cases is no different today.[11] Evidence of "active steps . . . taken to encourage direct infringement," *Oak Industries, Inc. v. Zenith Electronics Corp.*, 697 F. Supp. 988, 992 (N.D.Ill.1988), such as advertising an infringing use or instructing how to engage in an infringing use, show an affirmative intent that the product be used to infringe, and a showing that infringement was encouraged overcomes the law's reluctance to find liability when a defendant merely sells a commercial product suitable for some lawful use. Cf. W. Keeton, D. Dobbs, R. Keeton, & D. Owen, Prosser and Keeton on Law of Torts 37 (5th ed. 1984) ("There is a definite tendency to impose greater responsibility upon a defendant whose conduct was intended to do harm, or was morally wrong").

---

[11] Inducement has been codified in patent law. *See* 35 U.S.C. § 271(b).

For the same reasons that *Sony* took the staple-article doctrine of patent law as a model for its copyright safe-harbor rule, the inducement rule, too, is a sensible one for copyright. We adopt it here, holding that one who distributes a device with the object of promoting its use to infringe copyright, as shown by clear expression or other affirmative steps taken to foster infringement, is liable for the resulting acts of infringement by third parties. We are, of course, mindful of the need to keep from trenching on regular commerce or discouraging the development of technologies with lawful and unlawful potential. Accordingly, just as *Sony* did not find intentional inducement despite the knowledge of the VCR manufacturer that its device could be used to infringe, mere knowledge of infringing potential or of actual infringing uses would not be enough here to subject a distributor to liability. Nor would ordinary acts incident to product distribution, such as offering customers technical support or product updates, support liability in themselves. The inducement rule, instead, premises liability on purposeful, culpable expression and conduct, and thus does nothing to compromise legitimate commerce or discourage innovation having a lawful promise.

III

A

The only apparent question about treating MGM's evidence as sufficient to withstand summary judgment under the theory of inducement goes to the need on MGM's part to adduce evidence that StreamCast and Grokster communicated an inducing message to their software users. The classic instance of inducement is by advertisement or solicitation that broadcasts a message designed to stimulate others to commit violations. MGM claims that such a message is shown here. It is undisputed that StreamCast beamed onto the computer screens of users of Napster-compatible programs ads urging the adoption of its OpenNap program, which was designed, as its name implied, to invite the custom of patrons of Napster, then under attack in the courts for facilitating massive infringement. Those who accepted StreamCast's OpenNap program were offered software to perform the same services, which a fact finder could conclude would readily have been understood in the Napster market as the ability to download copyrighted music files. Grokster distributed an electronic newsletter containing links to articles promoting its software's ability to access popular copyrighted music. And anyone whose Napster or free file-sharing searches turned up a link to Grokster would have understood Grokster to be offering the same file-sharing ability as Napster, and to the same people who probably used Napster for infringing downloads; that would also have been the understanding of anyone offered Grokster's suggestively named Swaptor software, its version of OpenNap. And both companies communicated a clear message by responding affirmatively to requests for help in locating and playing copyrighted materials.

In StreamCast's case, of course, the evidence just described was supplemented by other unequivocal indications of unlawful purpose in the internal communications and advertising designs aimed at Napster users ("When the lights went off at Napster . . . where did the users go?" App. 836 (ellipsis in original)). Whether the messages were communicated is not to the point on this record. The function of the message in the theory of inducement is to prove by a defendant's own statements that his unlawful purpose disqualifies him from claiming protection (and incidentally to point to actual violators likely to be found among those who hear or read the message). Proving that a message was sent out, then, is the preeminent but not exclusive way of showing that active steps were taken with the purpose of bringing about infringing acts, and of showing that infringing acts took place by using the device distributed. Here, the summary judgment record is replete with other evidence that Grokster and StreamCast, unlike the manufacturer and distributor in *Sony*, acted with a purpose to cause copyright violations by use of software suitable for illegal use.

Three features of this evidence of intent are particularly notable. First, each company showed itself to be aiming to satisfy a known source of demand for copyright infringement, the market comprising former Napster users. StreamCast's internal documents made constant reference to Napster, it initially distributed its Morpheus software through an OpenNap program compatible with Napster, it advertised its OpenNap program to Napster users, and its Morpheus software functions as Napster did except that it could be used to distribute more kinds of files, including copyrighted movies and software programs. Grokster's name is apparently derived from Napster, it too initially offered an OpenNap program, its software's function is likewise comparable to Napster's, and it attempted to divert queries for Napster onto its own Web site. Grokster and StreamCast's efforts to supply services to former Napster users, deprived of a mechanism to copy and distribute what were overwhelmingly infringing files, indicate a principal, if not exclusive, intent on the part of each to bring about infringement.

Second, this evidence of unlawful objective is given added significance by MGM's showing that neither company attempted to develop filtering tools or other mechanisms to diminish the infringing activity using their software. While the Ninth Circuit treated the defendants' failure to develop such tools as irrelevant because they lacked an independent duty to monitor their users' activity, we think this evidence underscores Grokster's and StreamCast's intentional facilitation of their users' infringement.[12]

Third, there is a further complement to the direct evidence of unlawful objective. It is useful to recall that StreamCast and Grokster make money by selling advertising space, by directing ads to the screens of computers employing their software. As the record shows, the more the software is used, the more ads are sent out and the greater the advertising revenue becomes. Since the extent of the software's use determines the gain to the distributors, the commercial sense of their enterprise turns on high-volume use, which the record shows is infringing.[13]

This evidence alone would not justify an inference of unlawful intent, but viewed in the context of the entire record its import is clear.

The unlawful objective is unmistakable.

B

In addition to intent to bring about infringement and distribution of a device suitable for infringing use, the inducement theory of course requires evidence of actual infringement by recipients of the device, the software in this case. As the account of the facts indicates, there is evidence of infringement on a gigantic scale, and there is no serious issue of the adequacy of MGM's showing on this point in order to survive the companies' summary judgment requests. Although an exact calculation of infringing use, as a basis for a claim of damages, is subject to dispute, there is no question that the summary judgment evidence is at least adequate to entitle MGM to go forward with claims for damages and equitable relief.

* * *

In sum, this case is significantly different from *Sony* and reliance on that case to rule in favor of StreamCast and Grokster was error. *Sony*

---

[12] Of course, in the absence of other evidence of intent, a court would be unable to find contributory infringement liability merely based on a failure to take affirmative steps to prevent infringement, if the device otherwise was capable of substantial noninfringing uses. Such a holding would tread too close to the Sony safe harbor.

[13] Grokster and StreamCast contend that any theory of liability based on their conduct is not properly before this Court because the rulings in the trial and appellate courts dealt only with the present versions of their software, not "past acts . . . that allegedly encouraged infringement or assisted . . . known acts of infringement." This contention misapprehends the basis for their potential liability. It is not only that encouraging a particular consumer to infringe a copyright can give rise to secondary liability for the infringement that results. Inducement liability goes beyond that, and the distribution of a product can itself give rise to liability where evidence shows that the distributor intended and encouraged the product to be used to infringe. In such a case, the culpable act is not merely the encouragement of infringement but also the distribution of the tool intended for infringing use. *See Kalem Co. v. Harper Brothers*, 222 U.S. 55, 62–63 (1911); *Cable/Home Communication Corp. v. Network Productions, Inc.*, 902 F. 2d 829, 846 (CA11 1990); *A & M Records, Inc. v. Abdallah*, 948 F. Supp. 1449, 1456 (CD Cal. 1996).

dealt with a claim of liability based solely on distributing a product with alternative lawful and unlawful uses, with knowledge that some users would follow the unlawful course. The case struck a balance between the interests of protection and innovation by holding that the product's capability of substantial lawful employment should bar the imputation of fault and consequent secondary liability for the unlawful acts of others. MGM's evidence in this case most obviously addresses a different basis of liability for distributing a product open to alternative uses. Here, evidence of the distributors' words and deeds going beyond distribution as such shows a purpose to cause and profit from third-party acts of copyright infringement. If liability for inducing infringement is ultimately found, it will not be on the basis of presuming or imputing fault, but from inferring a patently illegal objective from statements and actions showing what that objective was.

There is substantial evidence in MGM's favor on all elements of inducement, and summary judgment in favor of Grokster and StreamCast was error. On remand, reconsideration of MGM's motion for summary judgment will be in order.

The judgment of the Court of Appeals is vacated, and the case is remanded for further proceedings consistent with this opinion.

It is so ordered.

JUSTICE GINSBURG, with whom THE CHIEF JUSTICE and JUSTICE KENNEDY join, concurring.

* * *

[Justice Ginsburg began this opinion by stating that while she fully concurred with Justice Souter vacating the lower court's summary dismissal of the plaintiffs' claim that Grokster and Streamcast could be liable "for actively inducing copyright infringement," she also judged that the claim of "contributory copyright infringement" should be reinstated as at least potentially viable.]

At bottom, however labeled, the question in this case is whether Grokster and StreamCast are liable for the direct infringing acts of others. Liability under our jurisprudence may be predicated on actively encouraging (or inducing) infringement through specific acts (as the Court's opinion develops) or on distributing a product distributees use to infringe copyrights, if the product is not capable of "substantial" or "commercially significant" noninfringing uses. While the two categories overlap, they capture different culpable behavior. Long coexisting, both are now codified in patent law. Compare 35 U.S.C. § 271(b) (active inducement liability), with § 271(c) (contributory liability for distribution of a product not "suitable for substantial noninfringing use").

* * *

"The staple article of commerce doctrine" applied to copyright, the *Sony* Court stated, "must strike a balance between a copyright holder's legitimate demand for effective—not merely symbolic—protection of the statutory monopoly, and the rights of others freely to engage in substantially unrelated areas of commerce." "Accordingly," the Court held, "the sale of copying equipment, like the sale of other articles of commerce, does not constitute contributory infringement if the product is widely used for legitimate, unobjectionable purposes. Indeed, it need merely be capable of substantial noninfringing uses." Thus, to resolve the *Sony* case, the Court explained, it had to determine "whether the Betamax is capable of commercially significant noninfringing uses."

To answer that question, the Court considered whether "a significant number of [potential uses of the Betamax were] noninfringing." The Court homed in on one potential use—private, noncommercial time-shifting of television programs in the home (i.e., recording a broad-cast TV program for later personal viewing). Time-shifting was noninfringing, the Court concluded, because in some cases trial testimony showed it was authorized by the copyright holder, and in others it qualified as legitimate fair use. Most purchasers used the Betamax principally to engage in time-shifting, a use that "plainly satisfie[d]" the Court's standard. Thus, there was no need in *Sony* to "give precise content to the question of how much [actual or potential] use is commercially significant."[1] Further development was left for later days and cases.

The Ninth Circuit went astray, I will endeavor to explain, when that court granted summary judgment to Grokster and StreamCast on the charge of contributory liability based on distribution of their software products. Relying on its earlier opinion in *A & M Records, Inc. v. Napster,*

[1] Justice Breyer finds in *Sony Corp. of America v. Universal City Studios, Inc.*, 464 U.S. 417 (1984), a "clear" rule permitting contributory liability for copyright infringement based on distribution of a product only when the product "will be used almost exclusively to infringe copyrights." But cf. *Sony*, 464 U.S., at 442 (recognizing "copyright holder's legitimate demand for effective—not merely symbolic—protection"). Sony, as I read it, contains no clear, near-exclusivity test. Nor have Courts of Appeals unanimously recognized Justice Breyer's clear rule. Compare *A & M Records, Inc. v. Napster, Inc.*, 239 F. 3d 1004, 1021 (CA9 2001) ("[E]vidence of actual knowledge of specific acts of infringement is required to hold a computer system operator liable for contributory copyright infringement."), with In *re Aimster Copyright Litigation*, 334 F. 3d 643, 649–650 (CA7 2003) ("[W]hen a supplier is offering a product or service that has noninfringing as well as infringing uses, some estimate of the respective magnitudes of these uses is necessary for a finding of contributory infringement . . . But the balancing of costs and benefits is necessary only in a case in which substantial noninfringing uses, present or prospective, are demonstrated."). *See also Matthew Bender & Co., Inc. v. West Pub. Co.*, 158 F. 3d 693, 707 (CA2 1998) ("The Supreme Court applied [the *Sony*] test to prevent copyright holders from leveraging the copyrights in their original work to control distribution of . . . products that might be used incidentally for infringement, but that had substantial noninfringing uses . . . The same rationale applies here [to products] that have substantial, predominant and noninfringing uses as tools for research and citation."). All Members of the Court agree, moreover, that "the Court of Appeals misapplied *Sony*," at least to the extent it read that decision to limit "secondary liability" to a hardly-ever category, "quite beyond the circumstances to which the case applied."

*Inc.*, 239 F. 3d 1004 (CA9 2001), the Court of Appeals held that "if substantial noninfringing use was shown, the copyright owner would be required to show that the defendant had reasonable knowledge of specific infringing files." "A careful examination of the record," the court concluded, "indicates that there is no genuine issue of material fact as to noninfringing use." The appeals court pointed to the band Wilco, which made one of its albums available for free downloading, to other recording artists who may have authorized free distribution of their music through the Internet, and to public domain literary works and films available through Grokster's and StreamCast's software. Although it acknowledged MGM's assertion that "the vast majority of the software use is for copyright infringement," the court concluded that Grokster's and StreamCast's proffered evidence met *Sony*'s requirement that "a product need only be capable of substantial noninfringing uses."

This case differs markedly from *Sony*. Here, there has been no finding of any fair use and little beyond anecdotal evidence of noninfringing uses. In finding the Grokster and StreamCast software products capable of substantial noninfringing uses, the District Court and the Court of Appeals appear to have relied largely on declarations submitted by the defendants. These declarations include assertions (some of them hearsay) that a number of copyright owners authorize distribution of their works on the Internet and that some public domain material is available through peer-to-peer networks including those accessed through Grokster's and StreamCast's software.

The District Court declared it "undisputed that there are substantial noninfringing uses for Defendants' software," thus obviating the need for further proceedings. This conclusion appears to rest almost entirely on the collection of declarations submitted by Grokster and StreamCast. Review of these declarations reveals mostly anecdotal evidence, sometimes obtained second-hand, of authorized copyrighted works or public domain works available online and shared through peer-to-peer networks, and general statements about the benefits of peer-to-peer technology. [Here, Justice Ginsburg mentioned various examples cited, including not only the Bible and the Declaration of Independence but also the "search on Morpheus for President Bush's speeches."] These declarations do not support summary judgment in the face of evidence, proffered by MGM, of overwhelming use of Grokster's and StreamCast's software for infringement.[3]

[3] Justice Breyer finds support for summary judgment in this motley collection of declarations and in a survey conducted by an expert retained by MGM. That survey identified 75% of the files available through Grokster as copyrighted works owned or controlled by the plaintiffs, and 15% of the files as works likely copyrighted.

As to the remaining 10% of the files, "there was not enough information to form reasonable conclusions either as to what those files even consisted of, and/or whether they were infringing or non-infringing." Even assuming, as Justice Breyer does, that the Sony Court would have

Even if the absolute number of noninfringing files copied using the Grokster and StreamCast software is large, it does not follow that the products are therefore put to substantial noninfringing uses and are thus immune from liability. The number of noninfringing copies may be reflective of, and dwarfed by, the huge total volume of files shared. Further, the District Court and the Court of Appeals did not sharply distinguish between uses of Grokster's and StreamCast's software products (which this case is about) and uses of peer-to-peer technology generally (which this case is not about).

In sum, when the record in this case was developed, there was evidence that Grokster's and StreamCast's products were, and had been for some time, overwhelmingly used to infringe, and that this infringement was the overwhelming source of revenue from the products. Fairly appraised, the evidence was insufficient to demonstrate, beyond genuine debate, a reasonable prospect that substantial or commercially significant noninfringing uses were likely to develop over time. On this record, the District Court should not have ruled dispositively on the contributory infringement charge by granting summary judgment to Grokster and StreamCast.

If, on remand, the case is not resolved on summary judgment in favor of MGM based on Grokster and StreamCast actively inducing infringement, the Court of Appeals, I would emphasize, should reconsider, on a fuller record, its interpretation of *Sony*'s product distribution holding.

JUSTICE BREYER, with whom JUSTICE STEVENS and JUSTICE O'CONNOR join, concurring.

I

A

[Justice Breyer began by stating that while he fully agreed with Souter's basis for judging that the defendants could potentially be held liable as "the distributor of a dual-use technology" for "actively" encouraging its use for infringement, he disagreed with Ginsburg's reading of *Sony* for purposes of contributory liability. After describing the *Sony* evaluation of the VCR and whether it had produced "substantial"

---

absolved Sony of contributory liability solely on the basis of the use of the Betamax for authorized time-shifting, summary judgment is not inevitably appropriate here. Sony stressed that the plaintiffs there owned "well below 10%" of copyrighted television programming, and found, based on trial testimony from representatives of the four major sports leagues and other individuals authorized to consent to home-recording of their copyrighted broadcasts, that a similar percentage of program copying was authorized. Here, the plaintiffs allegedly control copyrights for 70% or 75% of the material exchanged through the Grokster and StreamCast software, and the District Court does not appear to have relied on comparable testimony about authorized copying from copyright holders.

non-infringing—i.e., "authorized"—taping, he then turned to the same issue on the Internet.]

B

When measured against *Sony's* underlying evidence and analysis, the evidence now before us shows that Grokster passes *Sony*'s test—that is, whether the company's product is capable of substantial or commercially significant noninfringing uses. For one thing, petitioners' (hereinafter MGM) own expert declared that 75% of current files available on Grokster are infringing and 15% are "likely infringing." That leaves some number of files near 10% that apparently are noninfringing, a figure very similar to the 9% or so of authorized time-shifting uses of the VCR that the Court faced in *Sony*.

As in *Sony*, witnesses here explained the nature of the noninfringing files on Grokster's network without detailed quantification. Those files include:

— Authorized copies of music by artists such as Wilco, Janis Ian, Pearl Jam, Dave Matthews, John Mayer, and others.

— Free electronic books and other works from various online publishers, including Project Gutenberg.

— Public domain and authorized software, such as WinZip 8.1.

— Licensed music videos and television and movie segments distributed via digital video packaging with the permission of the copyright holder.

The nature of these and other lawfully swapped files is such that it is reasonable to infer quantities of current lawful use roughly approximate to those at issue in *Sony*. At least, MGM has offered no evidence sufficient to survive summary judgment that could plausibly demonstrate a significant quantitative difference. To be sure, in quantitative terms these uses account for only a small percentage of the total number of uses of Grokster's product. But the same was true in *Sony*, which characterized the relatively limited authorized copying market as "substantial." Importantly, *Sony* also used the word "capable," asking whether the product is "*capable of*" substantial noninfringing uses. Its language and analysis suggest that a figure like 10%, if fixed for all time, might well prove insufficient, but that such a figure serves as an adequate foundation where there is a reasonable prospect of expanded legitimate uses over time. And its language also indicates the appropriateness of looking to potential future uses of the product to determine its "capability."

Here the record reveals a significant future market for noninfringing uses of Grokster-type peer-to-peer software. Such software permits the exchange of *any* sort of digital file—whether that file does, or does not, contain copyrighted material. As more and more uncopyrighted information is stored in swappable form, it seems a likely inference that lawful peer-to-peer sharing will become increasingly prevalent.

And that is just what is happening. Such legitimate noninfringing uses are coming to include the swapping of: *research information* (the initial purpose of many peer-to-peer networks); *public domain films* (e.g., those owned by the Prelinger Archive); *historical recordings and digital educational materials* (e.g., those stored on the Internet Archive); *digital photos* (OurPictures, for example, is starting a P2P photo-swapping service); *"shareware"* and *"freeware"* (e.g., Linux and certain Windows software); *secure licensed music and movie files* (Intent MediaWorks, for example, protects licensed content sent across P2P networks); *news broadcasts past and present* (the BBC Creative Archive lets users "rip, mix and share the BBC"); *user-created audio and video files* (including "podcasts" that may be distributed through P2P software); *and all manner of free "open content" works collected by Creative Commons* (one can search for Creative Commons material on StreamCast). I can find nothing in the record that suggests that this course of events will not continue to flow naturally as a consequence of the character of the software taken together with the foreseeable development of the Internet and of information technology.

There may be other now-unforeseen noninfringing uses that develop for peer-to-peer software, just as the home-video rental industry (unmentioned in *Sony*) developed for the VCR. But the foreseeable development of such uses, when taken together with an estimated 10% noninfringing material, is sufficient to meet *Sony*'s standard. And while *Sony* considered the record following a trial, there are no facts asserted by MGM in its summary judgment filings that lead me to believe the outcome after a trial here could be any different. The lower courts reached the same conclusion.

Of course, Grokster itself may not want to develop these other noninfringing uses. But *Sony*'s standard seeks to protect not the Groksters of this world (which in any event may well be liable under today's holding), but the development of technology more generally. And Grokster's desires in this respect are beside the point.

II

The real question here, I believe, is not whether the record evidence satisfies *Sony*. As I have interpreted the standard set forth in that case, it does. And of the Courts of Appeals that have considered the matter, only one has proposed interpreting *Sony* more strictly than I would do—in a case where the product might have failed under any standard. *In re Aimster Copyright Litigation,* 334 F. 3d 643, 653 (CA7 2003) (defendant "failed to show that its service is ever used for any purpose other than to infringe" copyrights (emphasis added)); *see Matthew Bender & Co., Inc. v. West Pub. Co.*, 158 F. 3d 693, 706–707 (CA2 1998) (court did not require that noninfringing uses be "predominant," it merely found that they were predominant, and therefore provided no analysis of *Sony's* boundaries). Instead, the real question is whether we should modify the *Sony* standard, as MGM requests, or interpret *Sony* more strictly, as I believe Justice Ginsburg's approach would do in practice.

As I have said, *Sony* itself sought to "strike a balance between a copyright holder's legitimate demand for effective—not merely symbolic—protection of the statutory monopoly, and the rights of others freely to engage in substantially unrelated areas of commerce." Thus, to determine whether modification, or a strict interpretation, of *Sony* is needed, I would ask whether MGM has shown that *Sony* incorrectly balanced copyright and new-technology interests. In particular: (1) Has *Sony* (as I interpret it) worked to protect new technology? (2) If so, would modification or strict interpretation significantly weaken that protection? (3) If so, would new or necessary copyright-related benefits outweigh any such weakening?

A

The first question is the easiest to answer. *Sony's* rule, as I interpret it, has provided entrepreneurs with needed assurance that they will be shielded from copyright liability as they bring valuable new technologies to market. *Sony's rule is clear.* That clarity allows those who develop new products that are capable of substantial noninfringing uses to know, *ex ante*, that distribution of their product will not yield massive monetary liability. At the same time, it helps deter them from distributing products that have no other real function than—or that are specifically intended for—copyright infringement, deterrence that the Court's holding today reinforces (by adding a weapon to the copyright holder's legal arsenal).

*Sony's rule is strongly technology protecting.* The rule deliberately makes it difficult for courts to find secondary liability where new technology is at issue. It establishes that the law will not impose copyright liability upon the distributors of dual-use technologies (who do not themselves engage in unauthorized copying) unless the product in question will be used almost *exclusively* to infringe copyrights (or unless they actively induce infringements as we today describe). *Sony* thereby recognizes that the copyright laws are not intended to discourage or to control the emergence of new technologies, including (perhaps especially) those that help disseminate information and ideas more broadly or more efficiently. Thus *Sony's* rule shelters VCRs, typewriters, tape recorders, photocopiers, computers, cassette players, compact disc burners, digital video recorders, MP3 players, Internet search engines, and peer-to-peer software. But *Sony's* rule does not shelter descramblers, even if one could *theoretically* use a descrambler in a noninfringing way.

*Sony's rule is forward looking.* It does not confine its scope to a static snapshot of a product's current uses (thereby threatening technologies that have undeveloped future markets). Rather, as the VCR example makes clear, a product's market can evolve dramatically over time. And *Sony*—by referring to a *capacity* for substantial noninfringing uses—recognizes that fact.

*Sony's* word "capable" refers to a plausible, not simply a theoretical, likelihood that such uses will come to pass, and that fact anchors *Sony* in practical reality.

*Sony's rule is mindful of the limitations facing judges where matters of technology are concerned.* Judges have no specialized technical ability to answer questions about present or future technological feasibilility or commercial viability where technology professionals, engineers, and venture capitalists themselves may radically disagree and where answers may differ depending upon whether one focuses upon the time of product development or the time of distribution. Consider, for example, the question whether devices can be added to Grokster's software that will filter out infringing files. MGM tells us this is easy enough to do, as do several *amici* that produce and sell the filtering technology. Grokster says it is not at all easy to do, and not an efficient solution in any event, and several apparently disinterested computer science professors agree. Which account should a judge credit? *Sony* says that the judge will not necessarily have to decide.

Given the nature of the *Sony* rule, it is not surprising that in the last 20 years, there have been relatively few contributory infringement suits—based on a product distribution theory—brought against technology providers (a small handful of federal appellate court cases and perhaps fewer than two dozen District Court cases in the last 20 years). I have found nothing in the briefs or the record that shows that *Sony* has failed to achieve its innovation-protecting objective.

B

The second, more difficult, question is whether a modified *Sony* rule (or a strict interpretation) would significantly weaken the law's ability to protect new technology. Justice Ginsburg's approach would require defendants to produce considerably more concrete evidence—more than was presented here—to earn *Sony's* shelter. That heavier evidentiary demand, and especially the more dramatic (case-by-case balancing) modifications that MGM and the Government seek, would, I believe, undercut the protection that *Sony* now offers.

To require defendants to provide, for example, detailed evidence—say business plans, profitability estimates, projected technological modifications, and so forth—would doubtless make life easier for copyrightholder plaintiffs. But it would simultaneously increase the legal uncertainty that surrounds the creation or development of a new technology capable of being put to infringing uses. Inventors and entrepreneurs (in the garage, the dorm room, the corporate lab, or the boardroom) would have to fear (and in many cases endure) costly and extensive trials when they create, produce, or distribute the sort of information technology that can be used for copyright infringement. They would often be left guessing as to how a court, upon later review of the product and its uses, would decide when necessarily rough estimates amounted to sufficient evidence. They would have no way to predict how courts would weigh the respective values of infringing and noninfringing uses; determine the efficiency and advisability of technological changes; or assess a product's potential future markets. The price of a wrong guess—even if it involves a good-faith effort to assess technical and commercial viability—could be large statutory damages (not less than $750 and up to $30,000 *per infringed work*). 17 U.S.C. § 504(c)(1). The additional risk and uncertainty would mean a consequent additional chill of technological development.

C

The third question—whether a positive copyright impact would outweigh any technology-related loss—I find the most difficult of the three. I do not doubt that a more intrusive *Sony* test would generally provide greater revenue security for copyright holders. But it is harder to conclude that the gains on the copyright swings would exceed the losses on the technology roundabouts.

For one thing, the law disfavors equating the two different kinds of gain and loss; rather, it leans in favor of protecting technology. As *Sony* itself makes clear, the producer of a technology which *permits* unlawful copying does not himself *engage* in unlawful copying—a fact that makes the attachment of copyright liability to the creation, production, or distribution of the technology an exceptional thing. Moreover, *Sony* has been the law for some time. And that fact imposes a serious burden upon copyright holders like MGM to show a need for change in the current rules of the game, including a more strict interpretation of the test.

In any event, the evidence now available does not, in my view, make out a sufficiently strong case for change. To say this is not to doubt the basic need to protect copyrighted material from infringement. The Constitution itself stresses the vital role that copyright plays in advancing the "useful Arts." Art. I, § 8, cl. 8. No one disputes that "reward to the author or artist serves to induce release to the public of the products of his creative genius." *United States v. Paramount Pictures, Inc.*, 334 U.S. 131, 158 (1948). And deliberate unlawful copying is no less an unlawful taking of property than garden-variety theft. But these highly general principles cannot by themselves tell us how to balance the interests at issue in *Sony* or whether *Sony's* standard needs modification. And at certain key points, information is lacking.

Will an unmodified *Sony* lead to a significant diminution in the amount or quality of creative work produced? Since copyright's basic objective is creation and its revenue objectives but a means to that end, this is the underlying copyright question. *See Twentieth Century Music Corp. v. Aiken*, 422 U.S. 151, 156 (1975) ("Creative work is to be encouraged and rewarded, but private motivation must ultimately serve the cause of promoting broad public availability of literature, music, and the other arts"). And its answer is far from clear.

Unauthorized copying likely diminishes industry revenue, though it is not clear by how much. The extent to which related production has actually and resultingly declined remains uncertain, though there is good reason to believe that the decline, if any, is not substantial. *See*, Benkler, *Sharing Nicely: On Shareable Goods and the Emergence of Sharing as a Modality of Economic Production*, 114 Yale L. J. 273, 351–52 (2004) ("Much of the actual flow of revenue to artists—from performances and other sources—is stable even assuming a complete displacement of the CD market by peer-to-peer distribution. . . . [I]t would be silly to think that music, a cultural form without which no human society has existed, will cease to be in our world [because of illegal file swapping]"). More importantly, copyright holders at least potentially have other tools available to reduce piracy and to abate whatever threat it poses to creative production. As today's opinion makes clear, a copyright holder may proceed against a technology provider where a provable specific intent to infringe (of the kind the Court describes) is present. Services like Grokster may well be liable under an inducement theory.

In addition, a copyright holder has always had the legal authority to bring a traditional infringement suit against one who wrongfully copies. Indeed, since September 2003, the Recording Industry Association of America (RIAA) has filed "thousands of suits against people for sharing copyrighted material." These suits have provided copyright holders with damages; have served as a teaching tool, making clear that much file sharing, if done without permission, is unlawful; and apparently have had a real and significant deterrent effect. (number of people downloading files fell from a peak of roughly 35 million to roughly 23 million in the year following the first suits; 38% of current downloaders report downloading fewer files because of the suits); but *see* Evangelista, Downloading Music and Movie Files is as Popular as Ever, San Francisco Chronicle, Mar. 28, 2005, p. E1 (referring to the continuing "tide of rampant copyright infringement," while noting that the RIAA says it believes the "campaign of lawsuits and public education has at least contained the problem").

Further, copyright holders may develop new technological devices that will help curb unlawful infringement. Some new technology, called "digital 'watermarking'" and "digital fingerprint[ing]," can encode within the file information about the author and the copyright scope and date, which "fingerprints" can help to expose infringers. Other technology can, through encryption, potentially restrict users' ability to make a digital copy.

At the same time, advances in technology have discouraged unlawful copying by making *lawful* copying (*e.g.,* downloading music with the copyright holder's permission) cheaper and easier to achieve. Several services now sell music for less than $1 per song. (Walmart.com, for example, charges $0.88 each). Consequently, many consumers initially attracted to the convenience and flexibility of services like Grokster are now migrating to lawful paid services (services with copying permission) where they can enjoy at little cost even greater convenience and flexibility without engaging in unlawful swapping. *See* M. Madden & L. Rainie, March 2005 Data Memo, *supra,* at 6–7 (percentage of current downloaders who have used paid services rose from 24% to 43% in a year; number using free services fell from 58% to 41%).

Thus, lawful music downloading services—those that charge the customer for downloading music and pay royalties to the copyright holder—have continued to grow and to produce substantial revenue. *See* Bruno, Digital Entertainment: Piracy Fight Shows Encouraging Signs (Mar. 5, 2005), available at LEXIS, News Library, Billboard File (in 2004, consumers worldwide purchased more than 10 times the number of digital tracks purchased in 2003; global digital music market of $330 million in 2004 expected to double in 2005); Press Release, Informa Media Report, *supra* (global digital revenues will likely exceed $3 billion in 2010); Ashton, [International Federation of the Phonographic Industry] Predicts Downloads Will Hit the Mainstream, Music Week, Jan. 29, 2005, p. 6 (legal music sites and portable MP3 players "are helping transform the digital music market" into "an everyday consumer experience"). And more advanced types of *non*-music-oriented P2P networks have also started to develop, drawing in part on the lessons of Grokster.

Finally, as *Sony* recognized, the legislative option remains available. Courts are less well suited than Congress to the task of "accommodat[ing] fully the varied permutations of competing interests that are inevitably implicated by such new technology."

I do not know whether these developments and similar alternatives will prove sufficient, but I am reasonably certain that, given their existence, a strong demonstrated need for modifying *Sony* (or for interpreting *Sony's* standard more strictly) has not yet been shown. That fact, along with the added risks that modification (or strict interpretation) would impose upon technological innovation, leads me to the conclusion that we should maintain *Sony*, reading its standard as I have read it. As so read, it requires affirmance of the Ninth Circuit's determination of the relevant aspects of the *Sony* question.

* * *

For these reasons, I disagree with Justice Ginsburg, but I agree with the Court and join its opinion.

* * *

The entertainment industry battle was also going on in Congress. In 2005, President Bush signed into law a new bipartisan *Family Entertainment and Copyright Act*, also known as *Artists Rights and Theft Prevention Act*, making it a federal crime to use a video camera to copy a film on the screen in a movie theater, and also giving the theater staff the right to detain anyone reasonably suspected of doing so. But the industry's lack of confidence that *Grokster* solved its problems was shown by the filing of another 874 individual lawsuits, bringing the total to nearly 12,000.

This practice had begun in 2003 when the record labels had located online and filed lawsuits against four college students, asserting violation of their copyrights. Since the potential damage awards ranged from $750 to $150,000 for each copyrighted work made available online, these four defendants and their families were pleased to negotiate settlements requiring each to pay total damages ranging from $12,000 to $17,000 and a commitment never again to use computers to gain or provide free access to copyrighted material.

The viability of these lawsuits had just been dramatically expanded by a 2003 ruling which compelled Verizon Communications to hand over the names and addresses of any subscribers who had been sharing music on its Internet service. The court ruled that refusing to allow these subpoenas "would create a huge loophole in Congress's effort to prevent copyright infringement on the Internet." The industry then obtained more than 1000 subpoenas against Verizon, Comcast, and Time Warner Cable, as well as universities like Princeton, MIT, and Boston College. Supported by the ACLU and the Consumers Union, Verizon appealed, and the universities asserted a special defense based on students' privacy rights under the federal *Family Educational Rights and Privacy Act*. Verizon won its appeal in the D.C. Circuit, and the Supreme Court denied certiorari. Nevertheless, the major RIAA music industry members filed thousands of new lawsuits against individual file-sharers they had located.

In 2003, Apple Computer fashioned a new Internet service with licenses from the music labels, called the iTunes Music Store, inviting people to "Rip, Mix, and Burn" the licensed songs into a portable music player or onto a CD. Though they originally made this service available just to users of Apple's Macintosh computers, they sold over one million songs this way in their first week, and over 10 million within a few months. A key reason for iTunes' appeal was that not only did the consumers not have to go to a store, but they only had to pay 99 cents per song and $9.90 for a full album. The music labels and performers were still earning their own full financial return because nobody had to be paying for the manufacture and distribution of a physical album in a store, which typically accounts for around 40 percent of the list $18 price of a CD. Indeed, the major labels soon reduced the wholesale price of CDs to reflect the new market realities.

Despite the new digital medium, however, some of the same problems arose that were part and parcel of owning vinyl records—unwanted music. While in those days one could buy and sell used records from the local record store, it was not clear how one could do this with digital music. In October 2011, a company called ReDigi sought to capture this market, advertising itself as the virtual marketplace for "pre-owned" digital music. Soon after, Capitol Records filed a lawsuit, alleging copyright infringement.

## CAPITOL RECORDS, LLC V. REDIGI, INC.

United States District Court, Southern District of New York, 2013.
934 F. Supp.2d 640.

SULLIVAN, DISTRICT JUDGE.

Capitol Records, LLC ("Capitol"), the recording label for such classic vinyls as Frank Sinatra's "Come Fly With Me" and The Beatles' "Yellow Submarine," brings this action against ReDigi Inc. ("ReDigi"), a twenty-first century technology company that touts itself as a "virtual" marketplace for "pre-owned" digital music. What has ensued in a fundamental clash over culture, policy, and copyright law, with Capitol alleging that ReDigi's web-based service amounts to copyright infringement in violation of the Copyright Act of 1976 (the "Copyright Act"), 17 U.S.C. § 101 *et seq.* Now before the Court are Capitol's motion for partial summary judgment and ReDigi's motion for summary judgment, both filed pursuant to Federal Rule of Civil Procedure 56. Because this is a court of law and not a congressional subcommittee or technology blog, the issues are narrow, technical, and purely legal. Thus, for the reasons that follow, Capitol's motion is granted and ReDigi's motion is denied.

## I. BACKGROUND

### A. Facts

ReDigi markets itself as "the world's first and only online marketplace for digital used music." (Capitol 56.1 Stmt., Doc. No. 50 ("Cap. 56.1"), ¶ 6.) Launched on October 13, 2011, ReDigi's website invites users to "sell their legally acquired digital music files, and buy used digital music from others at a fraction of the price currently available on iTunes." (*Id.* ¶¶ 6, 9.) Thus, much like used record stores, ReDigi permits its users to recoup value on their unwanted music. Unlike used record stores, however, ReDigi's sales take place entirely in the digital domain. (*See* ReDigi Reply 56.1 Stmt., Doc. No. 83 ("RD Rep. 56.1"), 4 ¶ 16.)

To sell music on ReDigi's website, a user must first download ReDigi's "Media Manager" to his computer. (ReDigi 56.1 Stmt., Doc. No. 56 ("RD 56.1"), ¶ 8.) Once installed, Media Manager analyzes the user's computer to build a list of digital music files eligible for sale. (*Id.*) A file is eligible only if it was purchased on iTunes or from another ReDigi user; music downloaded from a CD or other file-sharing website is ineligible for sale. (*Id.*) After this validation process, Media Manager continually runs on the user's computer and attached devices to ensure that the user has not retained music that has been sold or uploaded for sale. (*Id.* ¶ 10.) However, Media Manager cannot detect copies stored in other locations. (Cap. 56.1 ¶¶ 59–61, 63; *see* Capitol Reply 56.1 Stmt., Doc. No. 78 ("Cap. Rep. 56.1"), ¶ 10.) If a copy is detected, Media Manager prompts the user to delete the file. (Cap. 56.1 ¶ 64.) The file is not deleted automatically or involuntarily, though ReDigi's policy is to suspend the accounts of users who refuse to comply. (*Id.*)

After the list is built, a user may upload any of his eligible files to ReDigi's "Cloud Locker," an ethereal moniker for what is, in fact, merely a remote server in Arizona. (RD 56.1 ¶¶ 9, 11; Cap. 56.1 ¶ 22.) ReDigi's upload process is a source of contention between the parties. (*See* RD 56.1 ¶¶ 14–23; Cap. Rep. 56.1 ¶¶ 14–23.) ReDigi asserts that the process involves "migrating" a user's file, packet by packet—"analogous to a train"—from the user's computer to the Cloud Locker so that data does not exist in two places at any one time. (RD 56.1 ¶¶ 14, 36.) Capitol asserts that, semantics aside, ReDigi's upload process "necessarily involves copying" a file from the user's computer to the Cloud Locker. (Cap. Rep. 56.1 ¶ 14.) Regardless, at the end of the process, the digital music file is located in the Cloud Locker and not on the user's computer. (RD 56.1 ¶ 21.) Moreover, Media Manager deletes any additional copies of the file on the user's computer and connected devices. (*Id.* ¶ 38.)

Once uploaded, a digital music file undergoes a second analysis to verify eligibility. (Cap. 56.1 ¶¶ 31–32.) If ReDigi determines that the file has not been tampered with or offered for sale by another user, the file is stored in the Cloud Locker, and the user is given the option of simply storing and streaming the file for personal use or offering it for sale in ReDigi's marketplace. (*Id.* ¶¶ 33–37.) If a user chooses to sell his digital music file, his access to the file is terminated and transferred to the new owner at the time of purchase. (*Id.* ¶ 49.) Thereafter, the new owner can store the file in the Cloud Locker, stream it, sell it, or download it to her computer and other devices. (*Id.* ¶ 50.) No money changes hands in these transactions. (RD Rep. 56.15 ¶ 18.) Instead, users buy music with credits they either purchased from ReDigi or acquired from other sales. (*Id.*) ReDigi credits, once acquired, cannot be exchanged for money. (*Id.*) Instead, they can only be used to purchase additional music. (*Id.*)

To encourage activity in its marketplace, ReDigi initially permitted users to preview thirty-second clips and view album cover art of songs posted for sale pursuant to a licensing agreement with a third party. (*See* RD 56.1 ¶¶ 73–78.) However, shortly after its launch, ReDigi lost the licenses. (*Id.*) Accordingly, ReDigi now sends users to either YouTube or iTunes to listen to and view this promotional material. (*Id.* ¶¶ 77, 79.) ReDigi also offers its users a number of incentives. (Cap. 56.1 ¶ 39.) For instance, ReDigi gives twenty-cent credits to users who post files for sale and enters active sellers into contests for prizes. (*Id.* ¶¶ 39, 42.) ReDigi also encourages sales by advising new users via email that they can "[c]ash in" their music on the website, tracking and posting the titles of sought after songs on its website and in its newsletter, notifying users when they are low on credits and advising them to either purchase more credits or sell songs, and connecting users who are seeking unavailable songs with potential sellers. (*Id.* ¶¶ 39–48.)

Finally, ReDigi earns a fee for every transaction. (*Id.* ¶ 54.) ReDigi's website prices digital music files at fifty-nine to seventy-nine cents each. (*Id.* ¶ 55.) When users purchase a file, with credits, 20% of the sale price is allocated to the seller, 20% goes to an "escrow" fund for the artist, and 60% is retained by ReDigi. (*Id.*)

* * *

## III. DISCUSSION

Section 106 of the Copyright Act grants "the owner of copyright under this title" certain "exclusive rights," including the right "to reproduce the copyrighted work in copies or phonorecords," "to distribute copies or phonorecords of the copyrighted work to the public by sale or other transfer of ownership," and to publicly perform and display certain copyrighted works. 17 U.S.C. §§ 106(1), (3)–(5). However, these exclusive rights are limited by several subsequent sections of the statute.

Pertinently, Section 109 sets forth the "first sale" doctrine, which provides that "the owner of a particular copy or phonorecord lawfully made under this title, or any person authorized by such owner, is entitled, without the authority of the copyright owner, to sell or otherwise dispose of the possession of that copy or phonorecord." *Id.* § 109(a). The novel question presented in this action is whether a digital music file, lawfully made and purchased, may be resold by its owner through ReDigi under the first sale doctrine. The Court determines that it cannot.

A. Infringement of Capitol's Copyrights

To state a claim for copyright infringement, a plaintiff must establish that it owns a valid copyright in the work at issue and that the defendant violated one of the exclusive rights the plaintiff holds in the work. *Twin Peaks Prods., Inc. v. Publ'ns Int'l, Ltd.,* 996 F.2d 1366, 1372 (2d Cir.1993) (citing *Feist Publ'ns, Inc. v. Rural Tel. Serv. Co.,* 499 U.S. 340, 361, 111 S.Ct. 1282, 113 L.Ed.2d 358 (1991)). It is undisputed that Capitol owns copyrights in a number of the recordings sold on ReDigi's website. (*See* Cap. 56.1 ¶¶ 68–73; RD Rep. 56.118–19, ¶¶ 68–73; Decl. of Richard S. Mandel, dated July 19, 2012, Doc. No. 52 ("Mandel Decl."), ¶ 16, Ex. M; Decl. of Alasdair J. McMullan, dated July 19, 2012, Doc. No. 51 ("McMullan Decl."), ¶¶ 3–5, Ex. 1.) It is also undisputed that Capitol did not approve the reproduction or distribution of its copyrighted recordings on ReDigi's website. Thus, if digital music files are "reproduce[d]" and "distribute[d]" on ReDigi's website within the meaning of the Copyright Act, Capitol's copyrights have been infringed.

1. Reproduction Rights

Courts have consistently held that the unauthorized duplication of digital music files over the Internet infringes a copyright owner's exclusive right to reproduce. *See, e.g., A & M Records, Inc. v. Napster, Inc.,* 239 F.3d 1004, 1014 (9th Cir.2001). However, courts have not previously addressed whether the unauthorized transfer of a digital music file over the Internet—where only one file exists before and after the transfer—constitutes reproduction within the meaning of the Copyright Act. The Court holds that it does.

The Copyright Act provides that a copyright owner has the exclusive right "to reproduce the copyrighted work *in . . . phonorecords*." 17 U.S.C. § 106(1) (emphasis added). Copyrighted works are defined to include, *inter alia,* "sound recordings," which are "works that result from the fixation of a series of musical, spoken, or other sounds." *Id.* § 101. Such works are distinguished from their material embodiments. These include phonorecords, which are the "*material objects* in which sounds . . . are fixed by any method now known or later developed, and from which the sounds can be perceived, reproduced, or otherwise communicated, either directly or with the aid of a machine or device." *Id.* § 101 (emphasis added). Thus, the plain text of the Copyright Act makes clear that reproduction occurs when a copyrighted work is fixed in a new *material object. See Matthew Bender & Co., Inc. v. W. Pub. Co.,* 158 F.3d 693, 703 (2d Cir.1998).

The legislative history of the Copyright Act bolsters this reading. The House Report on the Copyright Act distinguished between sound recordings and phonorecords, stating that "[t]he copyrightable work comprises the aggregation of sounds and not the tangible medium of fixation. Thus, 'sound recordings' as copyrightable subject matter are distinguished from 'phonorecords[,]' the latter being physical objects in which sounds are fixed." H.R.Rep. No. 94–1476, at 56 (1976), 1976 U.S.C.C.A.N. 5659, 5669. Similarly, the House and Senate Reports on the Act both explained:

Read together with the relevant definitions in [S]ection 101, the right "to reproduce the copyrighted work in copies or phonorecords" means the right to produce a material object in which the work is duplicated, transcribed, imitated, or simulated in a fixed form from which it can be "perceived, reproduced, or otherwise communicated, either directly or with the aid of a machine or device."

*Id.* at 61, 1976 U.S.C.C.A.N. at 5675; S.Rep. No. 94–473, at 58 (1975). Put differently, the reproduction right is the exclusive right to embody, and to prevent others from embodying, the copyrighted work (or sound recording) in a new material object (or phonorecord). *See* Nimmer on Copyright § 8.02 (stating that "in order to infringe the reproduction right, the defendant must embody the plaintiff's work in a 'material object' ").

Courts that have dealt with infringement on peer-to-peer ("P2P") file-sharing systems provide valuable guidance on the application of this right in the digital domain. For instance, in *London-Sire Records, Inc. v. John Doe 1,* the court addressed whether users of P2P software violated copyright owners' distribution rights. 542 F.Supp.2d 153, 166 & n. 16 (D.Mass.2008). Citing the "material object" requirement, the court expressly differentiated between the copyrighted work—or digital music file—and the phonorecord—or "appropriate segment of the hard disk" that the file would be embodied in following its transfer. *Id.* at 171. Specifically,

> [w]hen a user on a [P2P] network downloads a song from another user, he receives into his computer a digital sequence representing the sound recording. That sequence is magnetically encoded on a segment of his hard disk (or likewise written on other media). With the right hardware and software, the downloader can use the magnetic sequence to *reproduce* the sound recording. The electronic file (or, perhaps more accurately,

> the appropriate segment of the hard disk) is therefore a "phonorecord" within the meaning of the statute.

*Id.* (emphasis added). Accordingly, when a user downloads a digital music file or "digital sequence" to his "hard disk," the file is "reproduce[d]" on a new phonorecord within the meaning of the Copyright Act. *Id.*

This understanding is, of course, confirmed by the laws of physics. It is simply impossible that the same "material object" can be transferred over the Internet. Thus, logically, the court in *London-Sire* noted that the Internet transfer of a file results in a material object being "created elsewhere at its finish." *Id.* at 173. Because the reproduction right is necessarily implicated when a copyrighted work is embodied in a new material object, and because digital music files must be embodied in a new material object following their transfer over the Internet, the Court determines that the embodiment of a digital music file on a new hard disk is a reproduction within the meaning of the Copyright Act.

This finding holds regardless of whether one or multiple copies of the file exist. *London-Sire,* like all of the P2P cases, obviously concerned multiple copies of one digital music file. But that distinction is immaterial under the plain language of the Copyright Act. Simply put, it is the creation of a *new* material object and not an *additional* material object that defines the reproduction right. The dictionary defines "reproduction" to mean, *inter alia,* "to produce again" or "to cause to exist again *or* anew." *See Merriam-Webster Collegiate Edition* 994 (10th ed. 1998) (emphasis added). Significantly, it is not defined as "to produce again while the original exists." Thus, the right "to reproduce the copyrighted work in . . . phonorecords" is implicated whenever a sound recording is fixed in a new material object, regardless of whether the sound recording remains fixed in the original material object.

Given this finding, the Court concludes that ReDigi's service infringes Capitol's reproduction rights under any description of the technology. ReDigi stresses that it "migrates" a file from a user's computer to its Cloud Locker, so that the same file is transferred to the ReDigi server and no copying occurs. However, even if that were the case, the fact that a file has moved from one material object—the user's computer—to another—the ReDigi server—means that a reproduction has occurred. Similarly, when a ReDigi user downloads a new purchase from the ReDigi website to her computer, yet another reproduction is created. It is beside the point that the original phonorecord no longer exists. It matters only that a new phonorecord has been created.

* * *

Accordingly, the Court finds that, absent the existence of an affirmative defense, the sale of digital music files on ReDigi's website infringes Capitol's exclusive right of reproduction.

2. Distribution Rights

In addition to the reproduction right, a copyright owner also has the exclusive right "to distribute copies or phonorecords of the copyrighted work to the public by sale or other transfer of ownership." 17 U.S.C. § 106(3). Like the court in *London-Sire,* the Court agrees that "[a]n electronic file transfer is plainly within the sort of transaction that § 106(3) was intended to reach [and] . . . fit[s] within the definition of 'distribution' of a phonorecord." *London-Sire,* 542 F.Supp.2d at 173–74. For that reason, "courts have not hesitated to find copyright infringement by distribution in cases of file-sharing or electronic transmission of copyrighted works." *Arista Records LLC v. Greubel,* 453 F.Supp.2d 961, 968 (N.D.Tex.2006) (collecting cases); *see, e.g., Napster,* 239 F.3d at 1014. Indeed, in *New York Times Co., Inc. v. Tasini,* the Supreme Court stated it was "clear" that an online news database violated authors' distribution rights by selling electronic copies of their articles for download. 533 U.S. 483, 498, 121 S.Ct. 2381, 150 L.Ed.2d 500 (2001).

There is no dispute that sales occurred on ReDigi's website. Capitol has established that it was able to buy more than one-hundred of its own recordings on ReDigi's website, and ReDigi itself compiled a list of its completed sales of Capitol's recordings. (Cap. 56.1 ¶¶ 68–73; RD Rep. 56.1 ¶¶ 68–73.) ReDigi, in fact, does not contest that distribution occurs on its website—it only asserts that the distribution is protected by the fair use and first sale defenses. (*See, e.g.,* ReDigi Opp'n 15 (noting that "any distributions . . . which occur on the ReDigi marketplace are protected").)

Accordingly, the Court concludes that, absent the existence of an affirmative defense, the sale of digital music files on ReDigi's website infringes Capitol's exclusive right of distribution.

3. Performance and Display Rights

Finally, a copyright owner has the exclusive right, "in the case of . . . musical . . . works, to perform the copyrighted work publicly." 17 U.S.C. § 106(4). Public performance includes transmission to the public regardless of "whether the members of the public . . . receive it in the same place or in separate places and at the same time or at different times." *Id.* § 101. Accordingly, audio streams are performances because a "stream is an electronic transmission that renders the musical work audible as it is received by the client-computer's temporary memory. This transmission, like a television or radio broadcast, is a performance because there is a playing of the song that is perceived simultaneously with the transmission." *United States v. Am. Soc. Of Composers, Authors, & Publishers,* 627 F.3d 64, 74 (2d Cir.2010). To state a claim for infringement of the performance right, a plaintiff must establish that (1) the public performance or display of the copyrighted work was for profit, and (2) the defendant lacked authorization from the plaintiff or the plaintiff's representative. *See Broad. Music, Inc. v. 315 W. 44th St. Rest. Corp.*, No. 93 Civ. 8082(MBM), 1995 WL 408399, at *2 (S.D.N.Y. July 11, 1995).

The copyright owner also has the exclusive right, "in the case of . . . pictorial [and] graphic . . . works[,] . . . to display the copyrighted work publicly." 17 U.S.C. § 106(5). Public display includes "show[ing] a copy of [a work], either directly or by means of a film, slide, television image, or any other device or process." *Id.* § 101. The Ninth Circuit has held that the display of a photographic image on a computer may implicate the display right, though infringement hinges, in part, on where the image was hosted. *Perfect 10, Inc. v. Amazon.com, Inc.*, 508 F.3d 1146, 1160 (9th Cir.2007).

Capitol alleges that ReDigi infringed its copyrights by streaming thirty-second song clips and exhibiting album cover art to potential buyers. (Compl. ¶¶ 25–26.) ReDigi counters that it only posted such content pursuant to a licensing agreement and within the terms of that agreement. (ReDigi Mem. 24–25.) ReDigi also asserts that it promptly removed the content when its licenses were terminated, and instead sent users to YouTube or iTunes for previews. (*Id.*) Capitol, in response, claims that ReDigi's use violated the terms of those licenses and did not cease at the time the licenses were terminated. (*Compare* RD 56.1 ¶¶ 73–79, *with* Cap. Rep. 56.1 ¶¶ 73–79.) As such, there are material disputes as to the source of the content, whether ReDigi was authorized to transmit the content, when authorization was or was not revoked, and when ReDigi ceased providing the content. Because the Court cannot determine whether ReDigi infringed Capitol's display and performance rights on the present record, ReDigi's motion for summary judgment on its alleged infringement of these exclusive rights is denied.

### B. Affirmative Defenses

Having concluded that sales on ReDigi's website infringe Capitol's exclusive rights of reproduction and distribution, the Court turns to whether the fair use or first sale defenses excuse that infringement. For the reasons set forth below, the Court determines that they do not.

#### 1. Fair Use

"The ultimate test of fair use . . . is whether the copyright law's goal of 'promot[ing] the Progress of Science and useful Arts' would be better served by allowing the use than by preventing it." *Castle Rock Entm't, Inc. v. Carol Publ'g Grp., Inc.*, 150 F.3d 132, 141 (2d Cir.1998) (quoting U.S. Const., art. I, § 8, cl. 8). Accordingly, fair use permits reproduction of copyrighted work without the copyright owner's consent "for purposes such as criticism, comment, news reporting, teaching (including multiple copies for classroom use), scholarship, or research." 17 U.S.C. § 107. The list is not exhaustive but merely illustrates the types of copying typically embraced by fair use. *Castle Rock Entm't, Inc.,* 150 F.3d at 141. In addition, four statutory factors guide courts' application of the doctrine. Specifically, courts look to:

> (1) the purpose and character of the use, including whether such use is of a commercial nature or is for nonprofit educational purposes; (2) the nature of the copyrighted work; (3) the amount and substantiality of the portion used in relation to the copyrighted work as a whole; and (4) the effect of the use upon the potential market for or value of the copyrighted work.

17 U.S.C. § 107. Because fair use is an "equitable rule of reason," courts are "free to adapt the doctrine to particular situations on a case-by-case basis." *Sony Corp. of Am. v. Universal City Studios, Inc.,* 464 U.S. 417, 448 n. 31, 104 S.Ct. 774, 78 L.Ed.2d 574 (1984) (quoting H. Rep. No. 94–1476, at 65–66, 1976 U.S.C.C.A.N. at 5679–5680); *see Iowa State Univ. Research Found., Inc. v. Am. Broad. Cos.,* 621 F.2d 57, 60 (2d Cir.1980).

On the record before it, the Court has little difficulty concluding that ReDigi's reproduction and distribution of Capitol's copyrighted works falls well outside the fair use defense. ReDigi obliquely argues that uploading to and downloading from the Cloud Locker for storage and personal use are protected fair use. (*See* ReDigi Mem. 15.) Significantly, Capitol does not contest that claim. (*See* Tr. 12:8–23.) Instead, Capitol asserts only that uploading to and downloading from the Cloud Locker *incident to sale* fall outside the ambit of fair use. The Court agrees. *See Arista Records, LLC v. Doe 3,* 604 F.3d 110, 124 (2d Cir.2010) (rejecting application of fair use to user uploads and downloads on P2P file-sharing network).

Each of the statutory factors counsels against a finding of fair use. The first factor requires the Court to determine whether ReDigi's use "transforms" the copyrighted work and whether it is commercial. *Campbell v. Acuff-Rose Music, Inc.,* 510 U.S. 569, 578–79, 114 S.Ct. 1164, 127 L.Ed.2d 500 (1994). Both inquiries disfavor ReDigi's claim. Plainly, the upload, sale, and download of digital music files on ReDigi's website does nothing to "add [ ] something new, with a further purpose or different character" to the copyrighted works. *Id.; see, e.g., Napster,* 239 F.3d at 1015 (endorsing district court finding that "downloading MP3 files does not transform the copyrighted work"). ReDigi's use is also undoubtedly commercial. ReDigi and the uploading user directly profit from the sale of a digital music file, and the downloading user saves significantly on the price of the song in the primary market. *See Harper & Row Publishers, Inc. v. Nation Enters.,* 471 U.S. 539, 562, 105 S.Ct. 2218, 85 L.Ed.2d 588 (1985) ("The crux of the profit/nonprofit distinction is not whether the sole motive of the use is monetary gain but whether the user stands to profit from exploitation of the copyrighted material without paying the customary price."). ReDigi asserts that downloads for personal, and not public or commercial, use "must be characterized as . . . noncommercial, nonprofit activity." (ReDigi Mem. 16 (quoting *Sony,* 464 U.S. at 449, 104 S.Ct. 774).) However, ReDigi twists the law to fit its facts. When a user downloads purchased files from the Cloud Locker, the resultant reproduction is an essential component of ReDigi's commercial enterprise. Thus, ReDigi's argument is unavailing.

The second factor—the nature of the copyrighted work—also weighs against application of the fair use defense, as creative works like sound recordings are "close to the core of the intended copyright protection" and "far removed from the . . . factual or descriptive work more amenable to fair use." *UMG Recordings, Inc. v. MP3.Com, Inc.,* 92 F.Supp.2d 349, 351 (S.D.N.Y.2000) (alteration and internal quotation marks omitted) (citing *Campbell,* 510 U.S. at 586, 114 S.Ct. 1164). The third factor—the portion of the work copied—suggests a similar outcome because ReDigi transmits the works in their entirety, "negating any claim of fair use." *Id.* at 352, 114 S.Ct. 1164. Finally, ReDigi's sales are likely to undercut the "market for or value of the copyrighted work" and, accordingly, the fourth factor cuts against a finding of fair use. *Cf. Arista Records, LLC v. Doe 3,* 604 F.3d at 124 (rejecting application of fair use to P2P file sharing, in part, because "the likely detrimental effect of file-sharing on the value of copyrighted compositions is well documented." (citing *Metro-Goldwyn-Mayer Studios Inc. v. Grokster, Ltd.,* 545 U.S. 913, 923, 125 S.Ct. 2764, 162 L.Ed.2d 781 (2005))). The product sold in ReDigi's secondary market is indistinguishable from that sold in the legitimate primary market save for its lower price. The clear inference is that ReDigi will divert buyers away from that primary market. ReDigi incredibly argues that Capitol is preempted from making a market-based argument because Capitol itself condones downloading of its works on iTunes. (ReDigi Mem. 18.) Of course, Capitol, as copyright owner, does not forfeit its right to claim copyright infringement merely because it permits certain uses of its works. This argument, too, is therefore unavailing.

In sum, ReDigi facilitates and profits from the sale of copyrighted commercial recordings, transferred in their entirety, with a likely detrimental impact on the primary market for these goods. Accordingly, the Court concludes that the fair use defense does not permit ReDigi's users to upload and download files to and from the Cloud Locker incident to sale.

* * *

## IV. CONCLUSION

At base, ReDigi seeks judicial amendment of the Copyright Act to reach its desired policy outcome. However, "[s]ound policy, as well as history, supports [the Court's] consistent deference to Congress when major technological innovations alter the market for copyrighted materials. Congress has the constitutional authority and the institutional ability to accommodate fully the varied permutations of competing interests that are inevitably implicated by such new technology." *Sony,* 464 U.S. at 431, 104 S.Ct. 774. Such defence often counsels for a limited interpretation of copyright protection. However, here, the Court cannot of its own accord condone the wholesale application of the first sale defense to the digital sphere, particularly when Congress itself has declined to take that step. Accordingly, and for the reasons stated above, the Court GRANTS Capitol's motion for summary judgment on its claims for ReDigi's direct, contributory, and vicarious infringement of its distribution and reproduction rights. The Court also DENIES ReDigi's motion in its entirety.

Because issues remain with respect to Capitol's performance and display rights, and ReDigi's secondary infringement of Capitol's common law copyrights, as well as damages, injunctive relief, and attorney's fees, IT IS HEREBY ORDERED THAT the parties shall submit a joint letter to the Court no later than April 12, 2013 concerning the next contemplated steps in this case.

The Clerk of Court is respectfully directed to terminate the motions pending at Doc. Nos. 48 and 54.

SO ORDERED.

---

In reflecting on these legal battles, we should consider the debate about the actual economic consequences of free trading of music on the Internet. For example, the Justice Department has estimated that world-wide annual music sales have dropped by $19 billion since their peak in 1999, while the Business Software Alliance estimated that the retail value of pirated music was $29 billion. The reason for this disparity is that many Internet users would not have bought these songs if they had not been available free. Consider the relevance of a study by Entertainment Media Research (EMR), which found that many music pirates were also music lovers who paid for large amounts of music.

In the years after *Grokster*, music is even more widely available than ever before. Services like Spotify offer free music in exchange for listening to advertisements, or for a small fee, monthly access to their libraries. Bands now focus on live performances and merchandise as their primary revenue streams. The band U2 teamed with Apple to offer their most recent album, *Songs of Innocence*, to the public for free. Similarly, artists such as Taylor Swift seem to focus more on developing trademarks from within their work as a means to sell merchandise as opposed to focusing on album sales. As performances have become more lucrative than records, the next topic has taken on an enhanced importance.

## C. PERFORMANCE RIGHTS IN SONGS[b]

A century before videotaping and the Internet appeared, the world of entertainment welcomed phonographs and radio broadcasting. These new products posed a major challenge to the performance rights feature of copyright law, particularly in connection with music. In the late 19th century, the main economic value of music consisted of the sale of song sheets for play in the home or at school. Legal control over use of the music in live stage or club performances was simply an added bonus. With the emergence of recordings, speaker systems, and radio (then television) broadcasting, the economic environment changed dramatically. Radio stations and nightclubs could buy a single copy of a record and play it many times for the benefit of their listeners. These new technologies created both the opportunity and the need for enforcing the "public performance" feature of copyright law.

When people buy records (or videos or books), the purchasers have the right to play the work for their own (and their family's) private enjoyment. If they want to present the work to a broader public audience, they can do so only with the consent of the copyright owner. Unrestricted public performance would erode the market for the original work and thus lessen the investment in creative artistry. That is why copyright law tells radio and television stations, clubs, bars, and other public facilities that they can play songs only after securing (and paying for) a license from the songwriter.

No individual songwriter can afford to negotiate licenses, collect the fees, and enforce the prohibition on unauthorized performance in locations across the nation (indeed around the world). The institutional response was the creation of the American Society of Composers, Authors, and Publishers (ASCAP), and then its major competitor, Broadcast Music Incorporated (BMI), to perform that role on a collective basis for all their members. ASCAP, BMI, and smaller counterparts now have approximately 200,000 writers and 5 million songs in their repertoire. The price of a blanket license to play all of the works represented by ASCAP or BMI ranges from $50 a year for a small store to $20,000 for a large hotel-casino. Total revenues are around $1 billion a year, which, after deducting administrative costs, are distributed to writer-members in

b *See* Paul Warenski, *Copyrights & Background Music: Unplug the Radio Before I Infringe Again*, 15 Hast. Comm/Ent L.J. 523 (1992).

proportion to the extent their music is played. In addition to doing the music surveying needed to assess these music royalties, ASCAP and BMI regularly send out their staff members—"the music cops"—to drop in on locations that are not licensed and listen to whether one of their songs is being played. If such a song is heard, a demand for payment is made. If the demand is not met, a copyright suit is filed, with financial consequences we will see later in this chapter.

The organization of songwriters into collective licensing bodies poses intriguing questions of antitrust and labor law that we will encounter in Chapter 11. There would be no practical point, let alone any economic power, in such an organization if the writer-members did not have an enforceable right in the first place. One key legal issue in determining the scope of this right lies in defining precisely what constitutes a "public performance" of music (or other protected works).

The Supreme Court addressed this question in *Twentieth Century Music v. Aiken*, 422 U.S. 151 (1975), a case involving a small (600-square-foot) restaurant in which the owner played his radio, amplified by four speakers. The Court rejected a claim of copyright infringement on the ground that this was not really a *performance* of music, but rather just passive transmission of songs that the radio station had already been licensed to play. The Court relied on its prior decisions, *Fortnightly Corporation v. United Artists*, 392 U.S. 390 (1968), and *Teleprompter Corp. v. CBS*, 415 U.S. 394 (1974), to the effect that the newly-blossoming cable industry simply involved passive retransmission of over-the-air television signals via coaxial cable into the homes of cable subscribers. The *Aiken* Court (like the *Sony* Court a decade later) firmly believed that a contrary legal result would be both unenforceable and inequitable:

> The practical unenforceability of a ruling that all of those in Aiken's position are copyright infringers is self-evident. One has only to consider the countless business establishments in this country with radio or television sets on their premises—bars, beauty shops, cafeterias, car washes, dentists' offices, and drive-ins—to realize the total futility of any evenhanded effort on the part of copyright holders to license even a substantial percentage of them.
>
> And a ruling that a radio listener "performs" every broadcast that he receives would be highly inequitable for two distinct reasons. First, a person in Aiken's position would have no sure way of protecting himself from liability for copyright infringement except by keeping his radio set turned off. For even if he secured a license from ASCAP, he would have no way of either foreseeing or controlling the broadcast of compositions whose copyright was held by someone else. Secondly, to hold that

> all in Aiken's position "performed" these musical compositions would be to authorize the sale of an untold number of licenses for what is basically a single public rendition of a copyrighted work. The exaction of such multiple tribute would go far beyond what is required for the economic protection of copyright owners, and would be wholly at odds with the balanced congressional purpose behind 17 U.S.C. § 1(e):
>
> The main object to be desired in expanding copyright protection accorded to music has been to give to the composer an adequate return for the value of his composition, and it has been a serious and a difficult task to combine the protection of the composer with the protection of the public, and to so frame an act that it would accomplish the double purpose of securing to the composer an adequate return for all use made of his composition and at the same time prevent the formation of oppressive monopolies, which might be founded upon the very rights granted to the composer for the purpose of protecting his interests. H.R. Rep. No. 2222, 60th Cong., 2d Sess., 7 (1909).

422 U.S. at 163–64. *Aiken* came down just as Congress was doing its full-scale revision of federal copyright law. As part of that legislative project, the 1976 Copyright Act rejected the legal rationale for *Aiken* while essentially preserving its practical result.

Rejection of the rationale took the form of enactment of a new section 101 definition of "public performance," which included

> (1) [performance] at a place open to the public or at any place where a substantial number of persons outside of a normal circle of a family and its social acquaintances is gathered; or
>
> (2) [transmission of] . . . the work to a place specified by clause (1) or to the public, by means of any device or process . . .

The legal instrument for preserving the *Aiken* result in the face of this expansive definition of "public performance" was an exemption in section 110(5) for

> (5) communication of a transmission embodying a performance or display of a work by the public reception of the transmission on a single receiving apparatus of a kind commonly used in private homes, unless—
>
> (A) a direct charge is made to see or hear the transmission
>
> (B) the transmission thus received is further transmitted to the public.

The scope and limits of this "small business" exemption produced considerable litigation. One of the more prominent such rulings was

*Broadcast Music, Inc. v. Claire's Boutiques, Inc.*, 949 F.2d 1482 (7th Cir. 1991), which was presented in the first edition of *Entertainment*.

The practical issues, however, posed by that case were rendered largely moot by a bill unanimously passed by the 105th Congress just before it was to take up a somewhat more divisive impeachment issue in 1998. The *Digital Millennium Copyright Act* on the surface appeared to be generated by a 1996 agreement by the United States and other World Intellectual Property Organization (WIPO) members to a new *Copyright and Performance and Phonograph Treaties*. One part of the 61-page law did address changes mandated by those treaties, but it made other significant revisions in domestic copyright law.

For purposes of this copyright section, the significant change was contained in the *Fairness in Music Licensing Act*, which rendered largely moot many disputes regarding the scope of performance rights in the playing of music. Previously, copyright law had left stores, restaurants, and bars free to let their customers listen to music only through "a single receiving apparatus of a kind commonly used in private homes" (producing cases such as *Claire's Boutique)*. Otherwise, the business had to pay fees charged by the songwriter societies like ASCAP and BMI for the public performance of their works.

Responding to long-standing objections by the restaurant/bar industry, Congress created a new bright-line rule based on the size of the shop rather than the nature of the equipment. A store of less than 2000 square feet or a restaurant/bar less than 3750 square feet is free to play radio, television, or cable broadcasts for their customers, irrespective of the nature and size of the receiver/loudspeaker equipment used. Even larger stores, restaurants, and bars are exempted if they satisfy specific limits on the number and size of the sets and speakers. Performance rights and revenues from the use of music in public have thus significantly been cut back to large venues and to either live performances, or the use of records, tapes, or CD players, including by radio and television stations. At the same time Congress expanded the scope of performance rights to cover digital transmissions, and this was provided not just to the songwriters (represented by ASCAP), but also to the creators of the record (represented by RIAA and AFM).

---

A more fundamental question is raised by the performance of recorded music by radio broadcasters themselves. Under current law, radio stations are clearly required to pay for any such performance license, and this has become a major revenue source for ASCAP and BMI. A recurring argument by the National Association of Broadcasters (NAB) is that its members should not have to pay those licensing fees because their playing of a record constitutes free advertising for the record, something that helps spark sales of the record to the station's audience that enjoyed what it was hearing over the air.

Perhaps the question should be rephrased to focus on the other side of this equation: why do broadcasters provide such advertising for free? Everyone in the music industry realizes that stations that play Top 40 hits have a large share of the radio audience and are crucial to the ability of an album (especially by newer performers) to make the Billboard lists. In a host of entertainment contexts it is considered appropriate to require the producers of a consumer product to pay for such valuable exposure—whether it be the soft drink displayed in a movie or the shoes worn in a televised basketball game. Should not the free market have produced the answer to that NAB argument?

The explanation for why that has not occurred on radio is to be found in the broadcasting branch of entertainment law, the subject of Chapter 13. Songwriters, their publishers, and their performing rights societies have long sought to establish industry rules that would block payments being made to those who perform their music. In the 1950s, radio stations shifted from live broadcasts of the big band and pop ballad music of the Glenn Millers and Frank Sinatras to disc jockeys playing the rhythm and blues and rock and roll records of the Chuck Berrys and Elvis Presleys. The creators of these new genres regularly paid the disc jockeys to get their music on the air. A combination of a broadcast scandal involving Dick Clark and his ABC television show, pressure from music publishing bodies, and establishment distaste for these new kinds of music that teenagers enjoyed led Congress in 1960 to enact a new "payola" law.

Section 508 of the Communications Act declared it an offense for any employee of a radio or television station to accept money or other valuable consideration to broadcast material, unless the payments were disclosed to the station owner beforehand. This new provision was combined with the existing section 317 of the Act, which required stations to disclose any such payments to their audiences. Even more important, the FCC issued an opinion that stations had to disclose the fact and the source of any such payment just before or just after the song had been played—something stations would be loathe to do as it would disrupt the flow of their programs.

This law has produced numerous payola scandals in the music/broadcast worlds, involving undercover efforts made by "independent" promoters on behalf of record labels to get their new releases played, especially on the Top 40 stations in larger markets. The law has, however, generated little analysis of the fundamental issue of whether those restraints on the label/station market make sense as a matter of public policy.[c] Suppose record labels were as free to pay to get their music played on air as they still are to have it played in night clubs and elsewhere; who would be prepared to pay for which music, and why? Should the radio audience be entitled to have the fact and source of such payments disclosed immediately, rather than once a day or once a week? Who wins and who loses from the combination of copyright law that gives songwriters the right to insist on payment when their music is played and broadcast law that effectively denies labels and stations the freedom to insist on payments before music is played to their audiences?

---

The latter questions reflect a real political controversy stemming from the differential treatment under current copyright law of movie videos and sound recordings.[d] When movies are broadcast on network or on cable television, the broadcasters must secure a license from the film producers for a fee that is shared with the performers. However, when a radio station (or night club) plays a record, it does not need to obtain and pay for the consent of the record company and its musicians. While songwriters and song publishers (represented by ASCAP and BMI) enjoy and enforce public performance rights, musicians and record companies still do not have such a general property right.

An apt illustration is the song "(I Can't Get No) Satisfaction," written by Mick Jagger and Keith Richards and then played and recorded along with their Rolling Stones band mates. Every record that is sold generates royalties that are divided among the entire group. When radio stations or night clubs play the records, however, this generates performance royalties for the writers, Jagger and Richards, but none for other members of the Stones. It would be like paying only Margaret Mitchell, the author, when *Gone With The Wind* is shown on television, and not the film producer, MGM (and thence its stars, Clark Gable and Vivian Leigh).

The historical explanation for this differential treatment of sound recordings dates back to the Supreme Court's decision in *White-Smith Music Publishing Co. v. Apollo Co.*, 209 U.S. 1 (1908), and the following year's revised Copyright Act of 1909, which read federal copyright's coverage of "writings" to encompass only those works that could be seen rather than just heard. For the next seventy years, music records enjoyed

---

[c] *See* Ronald H. Coase, *Payola in Broadcasting*, 22 J. Law & Econ. 269 (1979); J. Gregory Sidak & David E. Kronemeyer, *The "New Payola" & the American Record Industry: Transaction Costs & Precautionary Ignorance in Contracts for Illicit Services*, 10 Harv. J. Law & Pub. Pol. 521 (1987). For a judicial illustration of this law in operation, see *United States v. Goodman*, 945 F.2d 125 (6th Cir. 1991). For a popular account of the payola scandal of the 1980s, see William Knoedelseder, *Stiffed: A True Story of MCA, the Music Business, & the Mafia* (Harper Collins, 1993).

[d] *See* William H. O'Dowd, *The Need for a Public Performance Right in Sound Recordings*, 31 Harv. J. Legis. 249 (1993).

only uneven state common law or statutory protection against piracy through copying and sale. Not until the 1971 Sound Recording Act was federal copyright protection extended to sound recordings (with its constitutional validity being sustained in *Shaab v. Kleindienst*, 345 F. Supp. 589 (D.D.C. 1972), and its preemptive effect on state regulation defined in *Goldstein v. California*, 412 U.S. 546 (1973)). But even with the passage of this special 1971 legislation and the 1976 rewriting of the Copyright Act (which now confers copyright on any "work fixed in a tangible medium of expression"), public performance rights were withheld by section 114(a) from sound recordings at the insistence of both the National Association of Broadcasters and the Songwriters Guild.[e]

While section 114(a) denied public performance rights in sound recordings, section 115 continued the compulsory licensing system that allows musicians to record songs authored by someone else. This special "mechanical" license applies to nondramatic musical works (thus excluding songs in musicals or arias in operas) that the composer has previously authorized for sound recording and distribution to the public. Once this has occurred, any other musical group can record the song as long as "the style or manner of interpretation of the performance involved" does not alter "the basic melody or fundamental character of the work." (Because section 115 refers to "phonorecords," this compulsory license does not encompass video recordings.) In return, the musician must simply pay the composer (or copyright owner of the song) a royalty which was set at two cents per copy in 1909, left unchanged until the 1976 Copyright Act, and is now periodically adjusted by the Copyright Royalty Tribunal for inflation. The current rate is 9.1 cents per record or 1.75 cents per minute of recorded song, whichever is greater. While this statutory royalty rate serves as the ceiling, in practice negotiations between composer/publisher and musician (or record company label) tend to set the actual licensing fee around 75 percent of the statutory rate (except for the most popular songs).

Returning now to the issue of public performance of recorded music, the debate on this score intensified in the early 1990s with the emergence of digital technology as an alternative to analog sound recordings. The first digital products to appear were prerecorded compact discs (CDs) and movie laser disks. Soon afterwards, digital audio recorders were developed that could replicate the digital "bits" of a song directly onto a blank tape without translating them into sounds. The value of such digital taping is that it can produce an unlimited number of precise copies of the original, unlike traditional records and tapes that gradually lose quality with each successive recording "generation" (like repeated copying

[e] Section 114(a) states that "the exclusive rights of the owner of copyright in a sound recording are limited to the rights specified by § 106(1), (2), and (3), and do not include any right of performance under § 106(4)."

of a photocopied page). It was precisely this capacity for digital replication that produced the 1992 Audio Home Recording Act (AHRA). As previously noted, the AHRA both required measures to block "serial copying" and imposed royalty charges on digital recorders and tapes, two-thirds to be distributed to musicians and record companies and one-third to songwriters and song publishers.

The music industry was concerned, though, that the AHRA was not responsive to the next major development, digital audio transmission. Such digital broadcasting is now available across the country through satellite transmission, creating a "celestial jukebox." It was precisely this prospect that made the recording industry and its supporters in Congress even more insistent on securing full-blown public performance rights under the Copyright Act. Finally, in 1995, Congress passed the *Digital Performance Right in Sound Recordings Act*, which amended Sections 106 and 114 of the Copyright Act to create a performance right for recordings. This new statutory right is limited to "digital audio transmission," and thus excludes AM and FM radio and other analog performances, as well as audiovisual works like movies. Even digital recordings are deemed public performances only when transmitted over the air or the Internet, not when performed in a public place on a digital player. In addition, digital transmission is covered only when it is an "interactive" or "subscription," rather than a standard broadcast service.[f] And in *Bonneville Int'l Corp. v. Peters*, 347 F.3d 485 (3d Cir. 2003), the court deferred to the judgment of the Copyright Office that the exemption for non-subscription broadcast transmissions from the DPRA performance right covers only over-the-air broadcast transmissions and not Internet streams.

### *QUESTIONS FOR DISCUSSION*

1. What policy rationale could have been offered for the historically different legal treatment of video and audio performances? Could one have distinguished between the potential impact on the movie industry of television stations showing movies and radio stations playing records? Does the digital audio format qualitatively change that situation? What justification can be offered for the severe constraints that Congress has placed on this new digital performance right?

2. The above legislation created a statutory license for digital *subscription* services to broadcast whatever recorded music the services wanted, at a royalty rate that ultimately would be determined by a Copyright Royalty Arbitration Panel (and distributed pursuant to the AHRA formula). Such a compulsory license was not extended to digital *interactive* services, which must secure such broadcasting licenses through voluntary contracts

---

[f] *See* Lionel S. Sobel, *A New Music Law for the Age of Digital Technology*, 17 Ent. L. Rep. 3 (Nov. 1995).

negotiated with the music owners at rates to be agreed upon. What might explain this difference in legal treatment?

3. How would you characterize the difference between the recording industry, with its AHRA, and the movie industry, with its combination of public performance and the *Sony* ruling? Is AHRA's distribution to the recording industry of royalty assessments on digital audio recorders and tapes an appropriately targeted response to the problem?

4. Does the music industry need and deserve an *additional* performance right in the sound recording as well as in the original song? Recall the Rolling Stones' "Satisfaction" example. Would (and should) such a legislative step increase rates of return and output in the music industry, or simply redistribute current revenues from the product? *See* Gary Myers & George Howard, *The Future of Music: Reconfiguring Public Performance Rights*, 17 J. Intell. Prop. L. 279 (2010).

5. Section 110(4) of the Copyright Act creates a different exception from the exclusive performance right of the owner. The exemption applies to performances that are done without any purpose of "commercial advantage" and without any "compensation for the performance to any of its performers, promoters, or organizers," as long as there is no "admission charge," or if there is a charge, the net proceeds "are used exclusively for educational, religious, or charitable purposes and not for private financial gain." In that latter circumstance, though, the copyright owner is afforded the right by prior notice to block the performance. What is the justification for the general exemption or for the qualification?

## D. DIGITAL SAMPLING AND IMAGING

Digital technology has important implications not just for the distribution and use of music, but also for its original creation. Digital samplers are combination musical instruments/computers that permit the recording of sounds in a host of aural formats. Sounds can be broken down and then manipulated in a vast array of pitches, echoes, and rhythmic combinations. A major beneficiary of this new technology was "rap" music. Rap originated in the Bronx in the late 1960s as a form of "audio collage" produced by performers and disc jockeys (DJ's) at live dance parties and clubs. Borrowing from the visual collage movement epitomized by Andy Warhol and Robert Rauschenberg, rappers would blend a variety of music forms and sounds that had been recorded on analog records and tapes. The first major rap recording, *Rapper's Delight,* by the Sugarhill Gang in the late 1970s, brought this brand of music onto the national scene. By the late 1980s, the popularity of the genre, combined with new digital technology, allowed new albums by MC Hammer (*Please Hammer Don't Hurt 'Em*) and Vanilla Ice (*To the Extreme*) to sell eight and five million copies respectively. Hammer's album featured recognizable sounds of the funk classic by Rick James,

"Super Freak," and Vanilla Ice's album had excerpts from the 1980s hit by Queen, in collaboration with David Bowie, "Under Pressure."

As often happens in the entertainment industry, innovation soon produces litigation. Should the producer of a later song have to secure and pay for using any sound from an instrument or voice in a prior recording? The first reported music sampling decision was *Grand Upright Music v. Warner Brothers Records*, 780 F. Supp. 182 (S.D.N.Y. 1991). In that case, the plaintiffs sought a preliminary injunction to prevent the defendants from selling Biz Markie's album *I Need a Haircut*, which contained a song entitled "Alone Again" that made unlicensed use of three words and part of the melody from Raymond "Gilbert" O'Sullivan's song, "Alone Again (Naturally)." Focusing on the ethical implications of the practice, Judge Duffy began his opinion with these words:

> "Thou shalt not steal" has been an admonition followed since the dawn of civilization. Unfortunately, in the modern world of business this admonition is not always followed. Indeed, the defendants in this action for copyright infringement would have this court believe that stealing is rampant in the music business and, for that reason, their conduct here should be excused. The conduct of the defendants herein, however, violates not only the Seventh Commandment, but also the copyright laws . . .

*Id.* at 183. The court first found that the plaintiff's copyrights were valid, noting that the defendants had sought to obtain a license to use the sample. The court reasoned that "One would not agree to pay to use the material of another unless there was a valid copyright! What more persuasive evidence can there be!" The judge concluded with these observations:

> From all of the evidence produced in the hearing, it is clear that the defendants knew that they were violating the plaintiff's rights as well as the rights of others. Their only aim was to sell thousands upon thousands of records. This callous disregard for the law and for the rights of others requires not only the preliminary injunction sought by the plaintiff but also sterner measures.

*Id.* at 185. Indeed, the judge felt strongly enough that he referred the case to the United States Attorney for the Southern District of New York for possible criminal prosecution of the defendants under 17 U.S.C. § 506(a) and 18 U.S.C. § 2319. Compare this ruling with the next decision.

## JARVIS V. A & M RECORDS

United States District Court, District of New Jersey, 1993.
827 F. Supp. 282.

ACKERMAN, DISTRICT JUDGE.

* * *

### I. Undisputed Factual Background

The facts of this case are undisputed and relatively simple. About a decade ago, Boyd Jarvis wrote a song entitled "The Music's Got Me." He recorded the song with his group, Visual, and copyrighted the composition together with the arrangement in November 1982. The song subsequently was released on Prelude Records, and the undisputed evidence shows that Prelude Records retains the copyright to the sound recording.

In 1989, defendant Robert Clivilles and David Cole wrote and recorded a song entitled "Get Dumb! (Free Your Body)" and the song was released in three formats on A & M Records and Vendetta Records, A & M's subsidiary label. The three relevant versions are: (1) "Get Dumb! Free Your Body" as it appears on the "b" side of a single record called "Heartbeat" by the defendant group Seduction; (2) a trio of versions of "Get Dumb! Free Your Body" that appear on another 12 single by Cole/Clivilles Music Enterprises, recorded by a group called The Crew (featuring Freedom Williams); (3) the cassette single of the song "Get Dumb!"

In all three of the releases of "Get Dumb!", defendants digitally sampled sections of Mr. Jarvis's "The Music's Got Me." Digital sampling has been described as:

> the conversion of analog sound waves into a digital code. The digital code that describes the sampled music . . . can then be reused, manipulated or combined with other digitalized or recorded sounds using a machine with digital data processing capabilities, such as a . . . computerized synthesizer.

Judith Greenberg Finell, *How a Musicologist Views Digital Sampling Issues*, N.Y.L.J. p.5 n. 3 (May 22, 1992). Thus, digital sampling is similar to taping the original composition and reusing it in another context. In this case, then, throughout the defendants' songs, one occasionally hears an actual piece of "The Music's Got Me."

In 1990, Mr. Jarvis sued the defendants for copyright infringement. Defendants now move for summary judgment, on a variety of grounds. . . .

* * *

This is a case of what Professor Nimmer has termed "fragmented literal similarity," *see Nimmer on Copyright*, § 13.03[A][2] at 13–46, that is, there is literal verbatim similarity between plaintiff's and defendants' works. In fact, the copied parts could not be more similar—they were digitally copied from plaintiff's recording. Two parts from plaintiff's song were copied: first, the bridge section, which contains the words "ooh . . . move . . . free your body," was taken. Second, a distinctive keyboard riff, which functions as both a rhythm and melody, included in the last several minutes of plaintiff's song, were also sampled and incorporated into defendants' work.

As courts and commentators have repeatedly noted, the test for substantial similarity is difficult to define and vague to apply. Nonetheless, it is repeatedly said that the test to determine substantial similarity is the response of the ordinary lay person.

Defendants build on the premise of the lay audience test by arguing that only if the two songs are similar in their entirety should the defendant's song be held to have infringed plaintiff's song. Indeed, defendants' cite apparent authority for this proposition. In a case decided a half-century ago, a court, in rejecting the plaintiff's argument of infringement, stated that "I have heard the compositions played, and to my ear there is a similarity, but not such a similarity as would impress one. In other words, I would not take the one for the other." *Allen v. Walt Disney Productions, Ltd.*, 41 F. Supp. 134, 140 (S.D.N.Y. 1941). Similarly, the district judge in *Arnstein v. BMI,* 46 F. Supp. 379 (S.D.N.Y. 1942), wrote that "infringement must be founded upon more than the adoption of a few measures here and there. The theme and general melody must be substantially lifted." Moreover, the defendants cite an influential article by Jeffrey Sherman:

> A defendant should not be held liable for infringement unless he copied a substantial portion of the complaining work and there exists the sort of aural similarity between the two works that a lay audience would detect. As to the first requirement, the portion copied may be either qualitatively or quantitatively substantial. As to the second, the two pieces must be similar enough to sound similar to a lay audience, since only then is it reasonable to suppose that the performance or publication of the accused work could in any way injure the rights of the plaintiff composer.

J. Sherman, *Musical Copyright Infringement: The Requirement of Substantial Similarity*, Common Law Symposium, No. 92, ASCAP, p. 145 (1977).

However, defendants misconstrue the scope of the examination, at least in the context of fragmented literal similarity, where there unquestionably is copying, albeit of only a portion of plaintiff's song. If it really were true that for infringement to follow a listener must have to confuse one work for the other, a work could be immune from infringement so long as the infringing work reaches a substantially different audience than the infringed work. In such a situation, a rap song, for instance, could never be held to have infringed an easy listening song or a pop song. *See, e.g., Grand Upright Music, Ltd. v. Warner Brothers Records, Inc.*, 780 F. Supp. 182 (S.D.N.Y. 1991) (finding that rap song infringed easy listening song).

Moreover, defendants' test, applied in cases of fragmented literal similarity, would eviscerate the qualitative/quantitative analysis, which revolves around the premise that a party may be held liable when he or she appropriates a large section or a qualitatively important section of plaintiff's work, *see Werlin v. Reader's Digest Association*, 528 F. Supp. 451, 463 (S.D.N.Y. 1981) (Ward, D.J.).

Finally, such a strict test would seem to go counter to another general principle—that the relevant question in copyright infringement cases is whether the segment in question constituted a substantial portion of the plaintiff's work, not whether it constituted a substantial portion of the defendant's work. . . .

Thus, infringement based on fragmented literal similarity depends on the truth of the principle that "the value of a work may be substantially diminished even when only a part of it is copied, if the part that is copied is of great qualitative importance to the work as a whole." *Werlin* at 463.

[The court then discussed *Grand Upright* and concluded that "[t]he proper question to ask is whether the defendant appropriated, either quantitatively or qualitatively, 'constituent elements of the work that are original', *see Feist Publications, Inc. v. Rural Telephone Service Co.*, 499 U.S. 340 (1991), such that the copying rises to the level of an unlawful appropriation."]

* * *

I now turn to the songs at issue in this case.

Plaintiff's song begins with a rhythm and melody utterly unlike defendants' songs. But halfway through the song, the tone changes as the verse-chorus repetition segues into a lengthy bridge. The bridge begins with a series of "oohs," sung over a distinctive rhythm, changes into a series of "moves" and then culminates with vocal repetitions of the phrase "free your body." A couple of minutes later in plaintiff's song, the tone again changes. This time, the song segues into a distinctive keyboard riff (musical phrase), that functions as both rhythm and melody, and for some time stays in the foreground of the song. It remains throughout the end of the song, as lyrics are sung over it.

Nonetheless, defendants argue that the vocal portions of plaintiff's song which defendants copied were non-copyrightable and therefore those portions must be factored out prior to performing the substantial similarity test.

Since it is not unlawful to copy non-copyrightable portions of a plaintiff's work, non-copyrightable elements must be factored out in an inquiry into infringement. *See Warner Brothers v. American Broadcasting Companies*, 720 F.2d 231, 240 (2d Cir. 1983). . . . The policy behind the rule is to prevent a deterring effect on the creation of new works because of authors' fears of copying innocuous segments.

There is no easily codified standard to govern whether the plaintiff's material is sufficiently original and/or novel to be copyrightable. "Cliched language, phrases and expressions conveying an idea that is typically expressed in a limited number of stereotypic fashions, are not subject to copyright protection." Easily arrived at phrases and chord progressions are usually non-copyrightable. Thus, in one case, a court held that defendant's appropriation of the phrase "night and noon," in a song entirely different from plaintiff's song, was not copyright infringement. *O'Brien v. Chappel & Co.*, 159 F. Supp. 58, 58 (S.D.N.Y. 1958)(Dawson, D.J.). In another case, a court held that when plaintiff's and defendant's mug coasters referenced ideas of enjoyment, a drinking mug, friendship, sunshine, and flowers, the plaintiff's ideas were unprotected.

However, if a piece is sufficiently distinctive, it is copyrightable.

This case bears no relationship to the cases cited above. It is unfair to characterize the "oohs," "moves" and "free your body" as cliched phrases typical in the field. To the contrary, they are used together in a particular arrangement and in the context of a particular melody. And the precise relationship of the phrases vis-á-vis each other was copied. There is no question that the combined phrase "ooh ooh ooh ooh . . . move free your body" is an expression of an idea that is copyrightable. Moreover, the keyboard line that was copied represents a distinctive melody/rhythm that sets it far apart from the ordinary cliched phrases held not copyrightable. It, too, is an expression of an idea, and is capable of being infringed. Again, the fact that defendants appropriated the exact arrangement of plaintiff's composition says more than what can be captured in abstract legal analysis.

It is certainly not clear as a matter of law that the portions copied from plaintiff's song were insignificant to plaintiff's song. To the contrary, the "oohs" and "move, free your body" occur in a bridge that attempts to be distinct and attention-grabbing. The keyboard riff begins the final portion of plaintiff's song, setting the rhythm as well as the melody.

Summary dismissal denied.

---

In 2005, the Sixth Circuit provided its judgment on this score, in *Bridgeport Music v. Dimension Films*, 410 F.3d 792 (6th Cir. 2005). The plaintiffs were suing the defendants for playing five times in their 1998 movie *I Got The Hook-Up*, a four-second line "Get off your Ass and Jam" from George Clinton, Jr. and the Funkedelics' rap song "100 Miles and Runnin." The trial judge summarily dismissed this suit on the grounds that no one would recognize the source. The Sixth Circuit reversed, saying first that one was free "to take three notes from a musical composition but not three notes by way of sampling from a bought recording," because the latter "is a physical taking rather than an intellectual one." They concluded by stating:

> Unfortunately, there is no Rosetta stone for the interpretation of the copyright statute. We have taken a "literal reading" approach . . . If this is not what Congress intended or is not what they would intend now, it is easy enough for the record industry, as they have done in the past, to go back to Congress for a clarification or change in the law. This is the best place for the change to be made rather than in the courts, because as this case demonstrates the court is never aware of much more than the tip of the iceberg.

*Id.* at 805.

## *QUESTIONS FOR DISCUSSION*

1. Recalling the key concepts of copyright law, how do they apply to digital sampling as exhibited in these cases? At what point does the original sound in music become protected expression? When does subsequent replication of that sound constitute copying? If 2 Live Crew were to sample James Brown's signature sound "Heeeeyyy," could they appeal to the "fair use" analysis used by the Court in the *Campbell* parody case? (By analogy, can a later movie use Tom Cruise's phrase from *Jerry Maguire*, "Show me the money," or Julie Andrew's word, "supercalifragilisticexpialidocious" from *Mary Poppins?*) Should the test in music recordings be whether there is substantial similarity in the two works taken as a whole? Should it depend on the ability of a listener to recognize the similarities in particular musical phrases (or riffs), or the ability of electronic fingerprinting to identify the sound on one record as having been lifted from another?

2. Does digital sampling present a distinctive opportunity as well as problem, such that it should receive tailored legislative treatment? One suggestion that has been made is the creation of a compulsory license for anyone who wants to digitally sample music sounds, with payment of fees that calculated according to a formula administered by the Copyright Royalty Tribunal. This proposal borrows from the treatment given early in this

century to songs that were copyrighted by their composers, but that a host of musicians now want to record.[g] As we saw earlier, section 115 of the Copyright Act allows a musician to produce a new "cover" of an old song as long as he pays the modest statutory royalty and does not alter the "basic melody or fundamental character" of the composition. By its terms, that provision cannot apply to the sampling case, because just a bit of the earlier recorded song is extracted and put in a brand-new setting. Proponents of this variation on section 115 contend, though, that it responds to analogous problems of transaction costs and licensing holdups that now often block use of the sampling technique, especially by new artists recording for small labels. Opponents attack the compulsory license idea as an unwarranted intrusion on the free market, one that cannot reflect the qualitative as well as quantitative significance of particular samples (e.g., the difference between a "hook" or "bridge" and mere background), and one that may force artists to hear their sounds on a product or genre they disapprove of. How would you assess these conflicting positions? What should judges do in the absence of Congressional action?

3. In *Jarvis*, the plaintiff also filed a claim of infringement of his rights of privacy and publicity under state law. What is your verdict in light of the materials in Chapters 2 and 3 above?

4. In the mid-1990s, the demand for digital sampling and the risks posed by copyright law generated another new technological device, the CD sampler. Such samplers gather on a single CD a host of music snippets with a variety of instruments and sound effects. Some of these sampler sound tracks focus on rap music, others on jazz, reggae, classical, and the like. While the price of a CD sampler ranges from $500 to $5,000, the technology allows artists who are adept at using electronic keyboards to create an intriguing product without employing costly musicians. The sampler producer, instead, will have recorded a variety of performances by musicians it has hired for this purpose. To what extent does the availability of these samplers (a $20 million niche in the industry) render the legal difficulties encountered in *Jarvis* a transitory problem? To what extent, though, may the use of a CD sampler to help create an unexpected hit record itself generate a legal problem?

---

Digital sampling of music already looks like a rather rudimentary feature of the computerized entertainment industry. Digital imaging of motion pictures is bringing us into an even braver new world. In the early 1990s, studios substituted digital editing of movies for the long-established Moviola technique of cutting and gluing together pieces of film. Film editors now create special effects scenes that were never filmed, simply by weaving together features of different takes on location.

[g] *See* Frederick F. Greenman, Jr. & Alvin D. Deutsch, *The Copyright Royalty Tribunal & the Statutory Mechanical Royalty: History & Prospect*, 1 Cardozo Arts & Ent. L. J. 1 (1982).

The public witnessed a more vivid display of the impact of this new technology in the 1994 hit, *Forrest Gump*. Tom Hanks, playing Forrest Gump, was shown conversing with John Kennedy in the Oval Office, getting a suggestion from Richard Nixon to use the Watergate Hotel, laughing with John Lennon, and gazing at George Wallace. Real images of Kennedy, Nixon, Lennon, Wallace, and other public figures from the last three decades appeared in the movie. This was made possible by technology that permits images as well as sounds to be superimposed into the movie. Thus, the deceased John Lennon and the living Tom Hanks can play parts in movies on whose location they never set foot.

Earlier "low-tech" versions of this art form have appeared, for example, in the movie *Dead Men Don't Wear Plaid* (with Steve Martin talking to Humphrey Bogart); the 1992 music video "Unforgettable" showed Natalie Cole singing along with her late father, Nat "King" Cole; and the 1993 movie, *In the Line of Fire*, digitally pasted Clint Eastwood's head onto one of the Secret Service agents appearing in historical footage of President Kennedy's assassination. These products involved stitching together old and new filmed material into a single product. New computerized digital animation, by contrast, allows for the creation of new actions and dialogue for the absent protagonists, based on raw material drawn from old pictures. That technology offers qualitatively different products to movie fans, as well as unique legal challenges.

The difficult copyright issues do not arise in movies like *Jurassic Park*, whose "digital cryogenics" were created from whole cloth by Industrial Light & Magic, the same firm that did this work for *Forrest Gump*. One is as legally free to create a prehistoric dinosaur as to create a new cartoon character. The situation is quite different, though, when the producer wants to use the film image of a real person whose face, voice, movements, and expressions are as familiar in people's minds as those of Kennedy and Bogart.

One set of legal problems relates to the rights of the individual persons themselves (or their estates). Those issues were addressed in the materials in Chapter 3 above, on Celebrity Publicity Rights, where we saw President Clinton worked into the movie *Contact* and Speaker Gingrich into *Men In Black* without their consent (in contrast to the treatment of Sylvester Stallone and Michael Jackson in the latter movie). The second issue relates to the rights of the copyright owners of the photographs and films from which come the old images.[h] Often the necessary material is not in the public domain, and certainly for dead characters and often for living ones, it is not possible to take new pictures with the needed physical and vocal features. Is it a violation of copyright

[h] *See* Joseph J. Beard, *Casting Call At Forest Lawn: The Digital Resurrection of Deceased Entertainers—A 21st Century Challenge for Intellectual Property Law*, 8 High Tech. L.J. 101 (1993).

law for one filmmaker to draw upon other people's movies and pictures for this purpose? How do the relevant copyright doctrines apply to this technological development?

## E. COPYRIGHT OWNERSHIP

Up to this point we have been focusing on the legal prerogatives that are associated with copyright. Equally important is determining which party will be able to exercise this control over a work, whether through the initial assignment of ownership or through licensing arrangements in an increasingly complex entertainment world.

The fundamental principle of copyright law is that ownership of a work is initially vested in its author. The romantic vision underlying this rule has always been of a writer or painter working alone to create a work of fiction or art. In the real world of entertainment, especially one that is using complex and expensive technology, bringing a creative work to fruition nowadays is often a collective venture. Not only are there often several members of the original creative group (e.g., The Beatles), but there also is a larger enterprise (e.g., a movie studio) whose financial and human resources are crucial to production and distribution of the finished product. In this more complex industrial setting, the questions are to whom does copyright law attribute initial authorship and how does it interpret agreements for assignment of ownership from author to financier. Two rules that serve as the backdrop to any such contracts are the copyright doctrines of "work for hire" and "joint authorship."

### 1. WORKS FOR HIRE

Under Section 201(1)(a) of the Copyright Act, initial ownership of a work rests in the work's "author." Under Section 201(1)(b), when works are "made for hire," the *hiring* party rather than the actual creator of the work is deemed to be the author. Section 101 defines a "work made for hire" as either a work "prepared by an employee within the scope of his or her employment," or a work that has been "specially ordered or commissioned for use" in several enumerated ways, most prominently, "as a part of a motion picture or other audiovisual work." In the latter non-employee case, the parties must "expressly agree in a written instrument signed by them that the work shall be considered a work made for hire."

As to the general employment category of works made for hire, the Supreme Court has addressed the questions of what should be the general legal approach to defining an "employee" as contrasted with an "independent contractor," and whether there should be a distinctive test for "work for hire."

## COMMUNITY FOR CREATIVE NON-VIOLENCE V. REID

Supreme Court of the United States, 1989.
490 U.S. 730, 109 S.Ct. 2166, 104 L.Ed.2d 811.

JUSTICE MARSHALL delivered the opinion of the Court.

In this case, an artist and the organization that hired him to produce a sculpture contest the ownership of the copyright in that work. To resolve this dispute, we must construe the "work made for hire" provisions of the Copyright Act of 1976, 17 U.S.C. §§ 101 and 201(b), and in particular, the provision in § 101, which defines as a "work made for hire" a "work prepared by an employee within the scope of his or her employment" (hereinafter § 101(1)).

I

[Petitioner is the Community for Creative Non-Violence (CCNV), a nonprofit association dedicated to eliminating homelessness in America. In the fall of 1985, CCNV decided to participate in the Christmastime Pageant of Peace in Washington, D.C., by sponsoring a display to dramatize the plight of the homeless.

CCNV members decided to commission a sculpture of a modern Nativity scene in which, instead of the traditional Holy Family, the two adult figures and the infant would appear as contemporary homeless people huddled on a street-side steam grate. The steam grate would be positioned atop a platform within which special-effects equipment would emit simulated "steam" through the grid. The title for the work was to be "Third World America," and a legend for the pedestal was to read: "and still there is no room at the inn."

CCNV was referred to respondent James Earl Reid, a Baltimore sculptor who agreed to complete the sculpture. The parties agreed that the sculpture would be made of "Design Cast 62," a synthetic substance that could meet CCNV's monetary and time constraints, could be tinted to resemble bronze, and could withstand the elements. The parties agreed that the project would cost no more than $15,000, not including Reid's services, which he donated. The parties did not sign a written agreement, and neither party mentioned copyright.

Reid made several sketches of figures in various poses. At CCNV's request, Reid sent CCNV a sketch of a proposed sculpture showing the family in a creche-like setting. CCNV also took Reid to see homeless people living on the streets and pointed out that they tended to recline on steam grates, rather than sit or stand. From that time on, Reid's sketches contained only reclining figures. Various CCNV member visited Reid to check on his. CCNV rejected Reid's proposal to use suitcases or shopping bags to hold the family's personal belongings, insisting instead on a shopping cart. After Reid finished the statue, it was taken to Washington,

D.C. and mounted on its base. After the pageant, the sculpture was returned to Reid for minor repairs. When CCNV asked for the return of the sculpture for a multi-city tour, Reid refused and filed a certificate of copyright registration for the work. CCNV then filed a competing copyright claim.]

* * *

II

A

The Copyright Act of 1976 provides that copyright ownership "vests initially in the author or authors of the work." As a general rule, the author is the party who actually creates the work, that is, the person who translates an idea into a fixed, tangible expression entitled to copyright protection. The Act carves out an important exception, however, for "works made for hire." If the work is for hire, "the employer or other person for whom the work was prepared is considered the author" and owns the copyright, unless there is a written agreement to the contrary. Classifying a work as "made for hire" determines not only the initial ownership of its copyright, but also the copyright's duration, and the owners' renewal rights, § 304(a), termination rights, and right to import certain goods bearing the copyright. The contours of the work for hire doctrine therefore carry profound significance for freelance creators—including artists, writers, photographers, designers, composers, and computer programmers—and for the publishing, advertising, music, and other industries which commission their works.

* * *

Petitioners do not claim that the statute satisfies the terms of § 101(2). Quite clearly, it does not. Sculpture does not fit within any of the nine categories of "specially ordered or commissioned" works enumerated in that subsection, and no written agreement between the parties establishes "Third World America" as a work for hire.

[The Court turned, then, from § 101(2)'s standards for "works made for hire" by independent contractors to the general § 101(1) standard for "employees," who presumptively make all their works for hire.] The starting point for our interpretation of a statute is always its language. The Act nowhere defines the terms "employee" or "scope of employment." It is, however, well established that "[w]here Congress uses terms that have accumulated settled meaning under . . . the common law, a court must infer, unless the statute otherwise dictates, that Congress means to incorporate the established meaning of these terms." In the past, when Congress has used the term "employee" without defining it, we have concluded that Congress intended to describe the conventional master-servant relationship as understood by common-law agency doctrine.

Nothing in the text of the work for hire provisions indicates that Congress used the words "employee" and "employment" to describe anything other than " 'the conventional relation of employer and employee.' " On the contrary, Congress' intent to incorporate the agency law definition is suggested by § 101(1)'s use of the term, "scope of employment," a widely used term of art in agency law.

* * *

[The Court then rejected CCNV's proposal alternatives, a "right to control the product" as "actual control" of the product, as incompatible with the specific additions to Section 101(1) that Congress had enacted in Section 101(2).] Section 101 clearly delineates between works prepared by an employee and commissioned works. Sound though other distinctions might be as a matter of copyright policy, there is no statutory support for an additional dichotomy between commissioned works that are actually controlled and supervised by the hiring party and those that are not.

We therefore conclude that the language and structure of § 101 of the Act do not support either the right to control the product or the actual control approaches. The structure of § 101 indicates that a work for hire can arise through one of two mutually exclusive means, one for employees and one for independent contractors, and ordinary canons of statutory interpretation indicate that the classification of a particular hired party should be made with reference to agency law.

* * *

Finally, petitioners' construction of the work for hire provisions would impede Congress' paramount goal in revising the 1976 Act of enhancing predictability and certainty of copyright ownership. In a "copyright marketplace," the parties negotiate with an expectation that one of them will own the copyright in the completed work. With that expectation, the parties at the outset can settle on relevant contractual terms, such as the price for the work and the ownership of reproduction rights.

To the extent that petitioners endorse an actual control test, CCNV's construction of the work for hire provisions prevents such planning. Because that test turns on whether the hiring party has closely monitored the production process, the parties would not know until late in the process, if not until the work is completed, whether a work will ultimately fall within § 101(1). Under petitioners' approach, therefore, parties would have to predict in advance whether the hiring party will sufficiently control a given work to make it the author. "If they guess incorrectly, their reliance on 'work for hire' or an assignment may give them a copyright interest that they did not bargain for." This understanding of the work for hire provisions clearly thwarts Congress' goal of ensuring predictability through advance planning. Moreover, petitioners' interpretation "leaves the door open for hiring parties, who have failed to get a full assignment of copyright rights from independent contractors falling outside the subdivision (2) guidelines, to unilaterally obtain work-made-for-hire rights years after the work has been completed as long as they directed or supervised the work, a standard that is hard not to meet when one is a hiring party." Hamilton, *Commissioned Works as Works Made for Hire Under the 1976 Copyright Act: Misinterpretation and Injustice*, 135 U. Pa. L. Rev. 1281, 1304 (1987).

In sum, we must reject petitioners' argument. Transforming a commissioned work into a work by an employee on the basis of the hiring party's right to control, or actual control of, the work is inconsistent with the language, structure, and legislative history of the work for hire provisions. To determine whether a work is for hire under the Act, a court first should ascertain, using principles of general common law of agency, whether the work was prepared by an employee or an independent contractor. After making this determination, the court can apply the appropriate subsection of § 101.

B

We turn, finally, to an application of § 101 to Reid's production of "Third World America." In determining whether a hired party is an employee under the general common law of agency, we consider the hiring party's right to control the manner and means by which the product is accomplished. Among the other factors relevant to this inquiry are the skill required; the source of the instrumentalities and tools; the location of the work; the duration of the relationship between the parties; whether the hiring party has the right to assign additional projects to the hired party; the extent of the hired party's discretion over when and how long to work; the method of payment; the hired party's role in hiring and paying assistants; whether the work is part of the regular business of the hiring party; whether the hiring party is in business; the provision of employee benefits; and the tax treatment of the hired party. *See* Restatement (Second) of Agency § 220(2) (1958) (setting forth a nonexhaustive list of factors relevant to determining whether a hired party is an employee). No one of these factors is determinative.

Examining the circumstances of this case in light of these factors, we agree with the Court of Appeals that Reid was not an employee of CCNV but an independent contractor. True, CCNV members directed enough of Reid's work to ensure that he produced a sculpture that met their specifications. But the extent of control the hiring party exercises over the details of the product is not dispositive. Indeed, all the other circumstances weigh heavily against finding an employment relationship. Reid is a sculptor, a skilled occupation. Reid supplied his own tools. He worked in his own studio in Baltimore, making daily supervision of his activities from Washington practicably impossible. Reid was retained for less than two months, a relatively short period of time. During and after this time, CCNV had no right to assign additional projects to Reid. Apart from the deadline for completing the sculpture, Reid had absolute freedom to decide when and how long to work. CCNV paid Reid $15,000, a sum dependent on "completion of a specific job, a method by which independent contractors are often compensated." Reid had total discretion in hiring and paying assistants. Indeed, CCNV is not a business at all. Finally, CCNV did not pay payroll or Social Security taxes, provide any employee benefits, or contribute to unemployment insurance or workers' compensation funds.

Affirmed.

## *QUESTIONS FOR DISCUSSION*

1. As an alternative to the general agency test for employees, CCNV proposed a test based on the right to control (or actual control) of the *product* being created. The principal reason why the Court rejected that position is that whatever its merits as a matter of policy, it would *de facto* eliminate the distinction between works of employees for hire (covered by § 101(1)) and works of contractors for hire (covered by § 101(2) only with respect to certain enumerated categories of work). Do you agree with that conclusion as a matter of statutory interpretation? Do you think that § 101(2) should be revised to allow any type of contracted-for artistic product to be deemed a work for hire? Is there a justifiable policy ground for treating a musical score commissioned for a movie, for example, differently from Reid's sculpture for purposes of copyright authorship?

2. What are the differences in the standards for assigning copyright in works authored by employees and works authored by contractors? Is there justification for the present dual standard? Should characterization of a worker as an "employee" for purposes of copyright law turn on whether the firm so treats the worker for purposes of fringe benefits (e.g., health coverage) and taxes (e.g., FICA)? *See Aymes v. Bonelli*, 980 F.2d 857 (2d Cir. 1992).

3. What difference would it make if the Copyright Act stated that for employee-created, as well as for specially-commissioned contract works, express written and signed agreements were required for a "a work made for hire?"

4. Riding on these characterizations of the relationship is not so much copyright *ownership* as *authorship*. It is always possible for firms or artists to agree among themselves that ownership will be transferred. Under the current Copyright Act, though, copyright ownership automatically (and non-waivably) reverts to the original author (or estate) 35 years after the work was transferred, often at a time when the work has displayed substantial and enduring economic value. As illustration (under the old copyright act's rules),

the Second Circuit has ruled that hundreds of thousands of dollars of post-1982 record royalties from the 1926 hit song "When the Red, Red Robin Comes Bob-Bob-Bobbin Along" belonged to the heirs of composer Harry Woods, rather than to the Bourne Company which had been assigned copyright when it first published the song in 1926. *See Woods v. Bourne Co.*, 60 F.3d 978 (2d Cir. 1995).

5. Does the written "contract for hire" have to be signed before the work is created in order to determine copyright authorship? Suppose, for example, that a composer is hired by a movie producer to write the theme music for a film, pursuant to a relationship which under the *Reid* test looks more like an *independent contractor* than an *employee* status. Reflecting the oral understanding of the parties, the studio sends the standard "work for hire" agreement to the composer to be signed when depositing the enclosed check for the music that has already been prepared and integrated into the film. Do these actions satisfy the requirements of Section 101(2) of the Copyright Act? *See generally Playboy Enterprises v. Dumas*, 53 F.3d 549 (2d Cir. 1995); *Schiller & Schmidt v. Nordisco Corp.*, 969 F.2d 410 (7th Cir. 1992).

6. Even if performers have no claim to copyright in particular entertainment products, they may have other rights. Suppose, for example, that a live play, opera, or concert has been videotaped for broadcast on television, without the explicit consent of the individual performers (or the union that represents them). Does this telecast potentially infringe the state law rights of publicity of the performers? If so, would that state law be preempted by federal copyright law's assignment of "authorship" to their employer? *See Baltimore Orioles v. Major League Baseball Players Ass'n*, 805 F.2d 663 (7th Cir. 1986).

7. A recent court decision in this area, *Twentieth Century Fox v. Dastar*, 429 F.3d 869 (9th Cir. 2005), involved a book written back in 1941 which we will see in Chapter 6 also producing a major trademark ruling by the Supreme Court. The author of *Crusade in Europe* just happened to be Dwight Eisenhower writing about his first professional career before embarking on his second one. The legal battle in this case was whether copyright of the book had expired because while Eisenhower had not renewed its original 28-year life, his publisher Doubleday had done so. Thus, the lawsuit against the Dastar movie copier depended on who actually owned the copyright, author or publisher, which itself turned on whether or not this was a "work for hire." The undisputed facts, whose legal implications divided both the parties and the judges in this case, was first, the original deal in December 30, 1947 was "a gentleman's agreement" by shaking hands in front of Eleanor, that Eisenhower then spent around 16 hours a day for three months writing the book based in part on his previous notes as well as memories of World War II. However, on the advice of his staff and to avoid paying the higher income as opposed to lower capital gains tax, no formal contract was signed until later that year just before the book was to be published. But while he was writing his *Memory*, Doubleday had provided

Eisenhower with three secretaries, a "fact checker" for the actual war facts, and regular meetings with its editors as the book was progressing. What is your view about both the likely and appropriate result in this "work for hire" case?

---

Ownership debates continue not just in the courts, but also in Congress. In 1999, the Recording Industry Association of America (RIAA) managed to persuade its congressional supporters to tuck into the Omnibus Budget Bill a provision which explicitly made records a form of potential "work made for hire" even by non-employees (as the 1976 Copyright Act had done with musical scores in movies). This law would effectively remove the contract termination rights of music composers after 35 years, though it would not be effective until 2013 because the 1976 Act did not begin operation until January 1, 1978.

When the composers and musicians learned about this bill and its implications, they formed a new Artists Coalition led by Sheryl Crowe and Don Henley to have it repealed. Their basic argument was that it was unfair to deprive them of their copyrights based on a contract signed when they had just come into this field without any bargaining leverage. Congress then passed a new Work for Hire and Copyright Corrections Act of 2000, which repealed this 1999 provision and returned the issue back to the wording of the 1976 Copyright Act. Utah Senator (and amateur musician) Orrin Hatch explained that there was a serious issue about whether the "recapture" rights of non-employee musicians should be preserved because "the initial assignment of copyright might not fully reward the unproven artist who is an unknown quantity in a risky business. Once the artist's commercial value is better proven, an opportunity is given the artist to reap the reward of his or her creations that has stood the test of time."

Even under the 1976 statutory wording, there will soon be litigation about the actual legal status of music created since 1978. One issue in litigation will be whether albums are a form of "compilation," which has always been one of the nine specifically-identified categories of work that can be "made for hire," even by non-employees. But the basic policy issue is the appropriate copyright treatment of the composer-record company relationship.

## 2. JOINT AUTHORSHIP

Even works created by people who are independent contractors often are the product of varying levels of collaboration with others. Members of a musical group may each take responsibility for writing a particular song that will be played and recorded by the group (like John Fogerty did for Creedence Clearwater Revival's song "Run Through the Jungle").

Typically, though, the lyrics, arrangement, specific sounds and other features of a song will benefit from suggestions from other group members as the work comes to fruition on a recorded album. The question, then, is who enjoys copyright in the song as contrasted with the record.

More specifically, the legal issue is whether the song (or other work) will be deemed to have joint authors, rather than a single author-owner.[i] Section 101 of the Copyright Act defines a "joint work" as

> a work prepared by two or more authors with the intention that their contributions be merged into inseparable or interdependent parts of a unitary whole.

If the "joint work" test is satisfied, then each contributor enjoys an individual legal interest in the entire work with all attendant rights (including the author's right of copyright renewal for pre-1978 works, and right of license termination for post-1978 works).

An important decision addressing the test for determining when a contribution reaches the level of joint authorship was *Childress v. Taylor*, 945 F.2d 500 (2d Cir. 1991). This case involved a legal battle between a playwright, Alice Childress (who had previously won an Obie award), and the actress Clarice Taylor. This suit was actually produced by their venture, *Moms: A Praise Play for A Black Commedienne*, about the legendary Jackie "Moms" Mobley. Taylor did extensive research about Mobley with a view to turning her life into a play. She then contracted with Childress to write the play (for an upfront $2,500 retainer), meeting with Childress to discuss key scenes and characters to be incorporated into the story. When Childress completed the script, Taylor produced the play, with herself in the title role.

Sometime later, Taylor hired another playwright to do a revised version of *Moms*. However, Childress then sued Taylor for violating her copyright. The issue presented by this case was whether Taylor was a joint author of the original work, and thus just as entitled to revise and reuse it.

The Second Circuit first addressed the fundamental issue of whether both authors had to contribute independently copyrightable material to their project, which it answered affirmatively.

> The insistence on copyrightable contributions by all putative joint authors might serve to prevent some spurious claims by those who might otherwise try to share the fruits of the efforts of a sole author of a copyrightable work, even though a claim of

---

[i] *See* Nancy Perkins Spyke, *The Joint Work Dilemma: The Separately Copyrightable Contribution Requirement & Co-Ownership Principles*, 11 U. Miami Ent. & Sports L. Rev. 31 (1993).

> having contributed copyrightable material could be asserted by those so inclined. More important, the prevailing view strikes an appropriate balance in the domains of both copyright and contract law. In the absence of contract, the copyright remains with the one or more persons who created copyrightable material. Contract law enables a person to hire another to create a copyrightable work, and the copyright law will recognize the employer as "author." Similarly, the person with non-copyrightable material who proposes to join forces with a skilled writer to produce a copyrightable work is free to make a contract to disclose his or her material in return for assignment of part ownership of the resulting copyright. And, as with all contract matters, the parties may minimize subsequent disputes by formalizing their agreement in a written contract. It seems more consistent with the spirit of copyright law to oblige all joint authors to make copyrightable contributions, leaving those with non-copyrightable contributions to protect their rights through contract.

*Id.* at 507. The Court then turned to the question of whether and to what extent there had to be a mutual intention to have joint authorship. After citing examples of research assistants for scholarly authors and editors of novels or scripts, the Court concluded that there must be a joint intent.

> Examination of whether the putative co-authors ever shared an intent to be co-authors serves the valuable purpose of appropriately confining the bounds of joint authorship arising by operation of copyright law, while leaving those not in a true joint authorship relationship with an author free to bargain for an arrangement that will be recognized as a matter of both copyright and contract law. Joint authorship entitles the co-authors to equal undivided interests in the work. That equal sharing of rights should be reserved for relationships in which all participants fully intend to be joint authors. The sharing of benefits in other relationships involving assistance in the creation of a copyrightable work can be more precisely calibrated by the participants in their contract negotiations regarding division of royalties or assignment of shares of ownership of the copyright.

*Id.* at 508–09. It found that Taylor's role in Childress' writing of the play had never "evolved into more than the helpful advice that might come from the cast, the directors, or the producers of any play. A playwright does not so easily acquire a co-author."

---

Two years later, in *Erickson v. Trinity Theatre*, 13 F.3d 1061 (7th Cir. 1994), the Seventh Circuit reached the same conclusion about the general test for joint authorship, again involving the contributions of several people to plays such as *Much Ado About Shakespeare*. But the biggest joint authorship case was produced by James Bond, the most valuable franchise in movie history. Since Bond's first appearance on the movie screen in *Dr. No* in 1962, there have been a total of 21 Bond movies, with well over two billion worldwide admissions. The value of Bond ticket prices are supplemented by its earnings from home video, television, merchandising, and the like. For example, *Tomorrow Never Dies*, the 1997 Bond release, had $350 million in box office receipts, but had generated over $100 million in product placement and advertising deals with companies like BMW before the movie even opened.

Ian Fleming, a former intelligence agent himself, began writing Bond books in the early 1950s. The 15 novels have also made Bond one of the best-selling characters in book publishing history. It was the combination of the Danjaq production company (created by Albert Broccoli and Harry Saltzmann) and MGM/UA, the financier-distributor studio, that turned Bond into a movie character in 1962, and they have made 19 of the 21 Bond films. With authorization from Fleming and his estate, Danjaq-MGM has recently been authoring new post-Cold War plots.

With the revival of the Bond franchise in 1995 with *Goldeneye*, starring Pierce Brosnan, MGM was auctioned off to Kirk Kerkorian and partners for $1.3 billion. The person who had headed the UA when it developed and released *Goldeneye* was John Calley. In 1996, Calley was hired by Sony Corp. to head its Entertainment wing, and a year later Calley announced that Sony was going to be making its own series of Bond movies. Needless to say, this immediately generated a lawsuit by Danjaq/MGM asserting that it had the exclusive rights to the James Bond movie franchise—in financial terms, the biggest intellectual property case ever to hit Hollywood.

Sony Entertainment's lawyers acknowledged that even with brand-new plots, there was an exclusive copyright in the Bond character and themes. If there has even been a movie character who really is "the story being told," rather than "a mere chessman in the game of telling a story," it is James Bond, as a district court had ruled in a lawsuit filed by MGM when Calley was still there. *MGM v. American Honda Motor Co.*, 900 F. Supp. 1287 (C.D. Cal. 1995). Much the same judgment would likely be made about Bond being the quintessential movie trademark recently provided protection by federal trademark law against "dilution," not just "confusion" (as we will see in Chapter 6).

Given this legal background, Calley's strategy was to have Sony pay $2 million to buy what it claimed was another special right to make Bond movies, held by Kevin McClory. McClory's involvement stemmed from an incident four decades earlier when Ian Fleming had himself made a major copyright mistake. That episode also provides an intriguing view of the challenge involved in transforming books into movies.

As noted above, Fleming had created Bond in the 1950s, beginning with *Casino Royale* in 1953 and then six more best-sellers in the next six years. He also gave a Russian actor, Gregory Ratoff, the option to turn *Casino Royale* into a movie, but Ratoff was not able to persuade any studio or production firm that James Bond stories could play on the screen, rather than in print. Nobody wanted to make a movie even about the best-selling book character of the 1950s.

In 1959, a producer-friend of Fleming, Ivan Bryce, sent Kevin McClory over to see Fleming, with a view to creating a new Bond story that was specifically tailored for motion pictures. McClory (who had previously assisted Mike Todd with the big hit of that decade, *Around the World in 80 Days*) brought with him a screenwriter, Jack Whittingham. Fleming accepted that proposal and drafted a 62-page film treatment called *Longitude 72 West*, which Whittingham then expanded into a screenplay in early 1960.

Unfortunately, neither Bryce nor other producers could still see the possibility of putting Bond onto the screens even with this specially-designed plot. Fleming decided to expand and turn the screenplay into a novel, now titled *Thunderball*, which became the eighth consecutive Bond best-seller. However, Fleming took that action without ever granting credit to, let alone securing consent from, McClory and Whittingham.

Thus, as soon as *Thunderball* hit the book stores, McClory filed a lawsuit in London, claiming a violation of his copyright in the "jointly-authored" work (with Whittingham having been McClory's employee). While that lawsuit was wending its way to trial, Fleming also received some good news. Albert Broccoli and Harry Saltzmann said they had figured out how to turn the Bond books into movies and that United Artists (now a branch of MGM) had agreed to finance and distribute them. The plan was not just to use a new screenwriter but a then-unknown actor whom they believed would make Bond come alive on the screen (Sean Connery). Fleming thus agreed to give Danjaq and UA the exclusive rights to all past and future Bond stories, with the exception of *Casino Royale* (already optioned) and *Thunderball* (now under litigation). *Dr. No* came out in 1962, followed by *From Russia With Love* in 1963, and *Goldfinger* in 1964. Illustrating the kind of box office appeal Bond had, President Kennedy said they were his "favorite-ever" movies.

While all of this was happening, not only was *Thunderball* going to trial in 1963, but Fleming had become fatally ill. Fleming and McClory settled their dispute. Fleming was acknowledged to be the "creator and proprietor" of James Bond, but McClory was recognized to be "joint author of the story comprising the film script" that had become the book *Thunderball*. In return for dropping his suit against the book, McClory was given the exclusive right to make *Thunderball* into a movie, to use Bond as the lead character in it, and also to use the Bond and 007 names for advertising and merchandising the movie.

Ironically, while Fleming was dying, McClory went to Danjaq/UA to get them to make the *Thunderball* movie with Connery, which in 1965 was the fourth big Bond hit. After a decade, though, the exclusive rights to *Thunderball* reverted back to McClory. In the early 1980s, McClory assigned to Warner Brothers the right to do a remake of *Thunderball* under the name *Never Say Never Again* (at a time when John Calley was head of film production at Warner). While *Never*, Connery's last Bond role, made $100 million in 1983, Danjaq/MGM's Bond release that same year, *Octopussy* starring Roger Moore, grossed $185 million.

With all of that as background, the issue posed in the battle between Danjaq/MGM and McClory/Sony was whether McClory had the joint right to make Bond movies: not just a third remake of *Thunderball*, but an ongoing franchise of new Bond plots. The premise to McClory's claim was that he was "joint author" with Fleming of the movie version of James Bond. However dubious that claim seemed given the actual sequence of events, even assuming it to be true the legal issue posed to the district court in *Danjaq v. Sony Corp.*, 49 U.S.P.Q.2d 1341, 1998 WL 957053 (C.D. Cal. 1998) was whether McClory would still retain any such movie rights to use Bond in movies (at least in the United States) in light of *Stewart v. Abend*, 495 U.S. 207 (1990), and its copyright reversion doctrine.

For that purpose, it is also important to know that all of Fleming's novels were copyrighted in the U.S. as well as the U.K. when they first appeared. After the 28-year initial copyright terms expired, the right of renewal of each was exercised by the Fleming Estate in the 1980s and 1990s. And in return for additional payments, the Estate assigned to Danjaq/MGM the *exclusive* right to make and release James Bond movies (whether based on novels or new stories). The Danjaq/MGM and Fleming Estate claim was that the *Stewart* ruling had reverted to the estate any derivative movie rights assigned by Fleming to McClory in the 1963 settlement. McClory and Sony asserted that their case was distinguishable from *Stewart* because McClory (through his employee Whittingham) was joint author with Fleming of the *Longitude 78 West* script that eventually became *Thunderball*. In *Stewart*, by contrast, the original author of the short story *It Had To Be Murder* had nothing to do with the movie *Rear Window* created by James Stewart and Alfred Hitchcock.

Just before this case was to go to trial, Sony decided to settle the matter by agreeing *not* to make any James Bond movies, and to reimburse Danjaq/MGM the $5 million in legal bills it had run up to establish that point. In return, Danjaq/MGM agreed to pay Sony $10 million to acquire the one Bond movie they did not now own, Columbia Pictures' 1967 *Casino Royale* spoof starring David Niven as Bond, as well as an undertaking by Sony not to release Bond movies anywhere outside the United States. This settlement eventually inspired Sony to acquire MGM itself in 2004, ensuring that it then owned the James Bond movie rights.

McClory refused to be part of any such settlement, but the Ninth Circuit in *Danjaq v. Sony*, 263 F.3d 942 (9th Cir. 2001), ruled that his lawsuit was barred by the doctrine of laches: "McClory waited too long to claim his piece of the pie—whatever that share might have been." Suppose, though, that he had filed a reasonably prompt lawsuit against Danjaq/MGM. Should McClory have been deemed to have a stronger (or weaker) claim to remake *Thunderball* or to make new Bond movies than James Stewart had to re-release his own *Rear Window*?

## F. COPYRIGHT LICENSING

The features of copyright law we have been exploring about James Bond, *Gone With The Wind, Shakespeare in Love,* and the like define the way in which the law assigns ownership in books, songs, and films. Intellectual property law, though, simply establishes the default rules for contractual transfers of either full ownership or specified rights to use the product for a host of purposes in our increasingly integrated entertainment industry. In *Effects Associates, Inc. v. Cohen,* 908 F.2d 555 (9th Cir. 1990), the Ninth Circuit grappled with the implications of the Copyright Act's explicit requirement (in section 204) that copyright owners can sell or license their property rights only by means of written documents.

Larry Cohen had written, directed, and produced *The Stuff*, a horror movie with a dash of social satire:

> Earth is invaded by an alien life form that looks (and tastes) like frozen yogurt but, alas, has some unfortunate side effects—it's addictive and takes over the mind of anyone who eats it. Marketed by an unscrupulous entrepreneur, the Stuff becomes a big hit. An industrial spy hired by ice cream manufacturers eventually uncovers the terrible truth; he alerts the American people and blows up the yogurt factory, making the world safe once again for lovers of frozen confections.

*Id.* at 555–56. He hired Effects Associates to do the footages for several special effects action sequences. Unhappy with the final "factory explosion" that Effects had created, he refused to pay them the last $8,000 of the $64,000 of their oral agreement. After Cohen put Effects' footage into the film, Effects filed a copyright suit, saying that Cohen had not gained the right to use their copyrighted work without paying "the full contract price."

Cohen sought to avoid Section 204's "writing requirement" by arguing, as the court put it with "tongue in cheek, . . . movie makers do lunch, not contracts." In other words, Section 204 should not be applied here because "it is customary in the motion picture industry . . . not to have written licenses." However, the court rejected that "plea to exempt movie makers from the normal operation of Section 204."

> Common sense tells us that agreements should routinely be put in writing. This simple practice prevents misunderstandings by spelling out the terms of a deal in black and white, forces parties to clarify their thinking and consider problems that could potentially arise, and encourages them to take their promises seriously because it's harder to backtrack on a written contract than on an oral one. Copyright law dovetails nicely with common sense by requiring that a transfer of copyright ownership be in writing. Section 204 ensures that the creator of a work will not give away his copyright inadvertently and forces a party who wants to use the copyrighted work to negotiate with the creator to determine precisely what rights are being transferred and at what price. Most importantly, section 204 enhances predictability and certainty of copyright ownership—"Congress' paramount goal" when it revised the Act in 1976. Rather than look to the courts every time they disagree as to whether a particular use of the work violates their mutual understanding, parties need only look to the writing that sets out their respective rights . . . As § 204 makes no special allowances for the movie industry, neither do we.

*Id.* at 557–58.

The court then granted Cohen his defense on another ground: though "copyright ownership" can only be transferred in writing, the combination of Sections 101 and 204 meant that a "nonexclusive license" to use copyrighted work could be "granted orally, or even implied from conduct." The fact that Effects had not only done the special effects work but then handed over the footage to Cohen, who paid $56,000 meant that Effects was "impliedly granting [Cohen] nonexclusive license . . . to incorporate the footage into *The Stuff*." This ruling left Effects with the right to sue Cohen for breach of their oral contract and to use the footage whose copyright they retained in other markets (though the court was skeptical there would be much market demand "for shots featuring great gobs of alien yoghurt oozing out of a defunct factory").

## *QUESTIONS FOR DISCUSSION*

1. In a later case, *Papa's-June Music, Inc. v. McLean*, 921 F. Supp. 1154 (S.D.N.Y. 1996), Harry Connick Jr. was unable to convince a federal judge that oral understandings are sufficient to transfer revenue shares among joint authors. Beginning in 1984, Ramsey McLean had submitted lyrics to Connick, which the latter used on his 1989 record album *We Are in Love* and his 1991 album *Blue Light, Red Light*. Pursuant to a written co-publishing agreement between the two, Connick received 70 percent of the songwriting royalties and McLean 30 percent. While Connick used yet another batch of McLean's songs for his 1994 album *She*, he did not have a signed songwriting contract for this album. When McLean started receiving 50 percent of *She's* royalties from Sony Music, the album's distributor, he refused to sign a post-release contract that Connick submitted to him. In the resulting litigation, the judge rejected Connick's argument that an oral understanding about a 70–30 percent share (based on prior dealings) was sufficient to avoid the statutory requirement of *written* transfers of copyright ownership, whether in whole or in part. Is this ruling consistent with *Effects Associates*?

2. In a successor to his *Effects Associates* opinion, *Konigsberg Int'l, Inc. v. Rice*, 16 F.3d 355 (9th Cir. 1994), Judge Kozinski began by stating:

> Inside many a practicing lawyer there's a novelist struggling to be born. The converse is also true: Novelists sometimes yearn to be lawyers. All things considered, it's best if all concerned stick with their own callings.

16 F.3d at 355. That comment was the product of a dispute that began with a meeting of film producers Frank Konigsberg and Larry Sonitsky with Anne Rice, author of the best-selling novel (and hit movie) *Interview With the Vampire*. Over lunch, the three developed the idea for "a romantic melodrama involving a love triangle between a resurrected mummy, an English Heiress, and Queen Cleopatra." It was agreed that Rice would write the "bible" that detailed the story for purposes of generating derivative works. Rice would then author the novel and Konigsberg and Sonitsky would try to develop a movie or television version of the story.

Without a written agreement being finalized and signed, Rice wrote and delivered the "bible" and was paid $50,000 by Konigsberg and Sonitsky. Rice then wrote her novel *The Mummy*, but the producers were unable to turn the story into a film project within the initial two-year period. A dispute then arose about whether Konigsberg and Sonitsky enjoyed, and had exercised, an option to extend their rights. Rice wrote an indignant letter to the Konigsberg and Sonitsky lawyers, stating that although the contracts were never signed, they "were honored to the letter" by Rice. The questions the Ninth Circuit was asked to resolve were whether the Copyright Act writing requirement applied to joint creative lunches such as occurred here, and even if it did, whether the later Rice letter satisfied that requirement. What would be your verdict? Should the standard be the same as the writing requirement for "works for hire?"

---

Even written licenses for exclusive use of an entertainment product can pose major issues of contract interpretation. This is because a product that turns out to be a hit can become a valuable asset for new uses made possible by technology or by new entertainment vehicles over the decades. Consider the fate of Scarlett O'Hara and Rhett Butler. As we saw in Chapter 4, in 1936 Margaret Mitchell, author of the novel *Gone With The Wind*, assigned to MGM the right to make the movie version. In 1939, the film appeared to the delight of the largest audience ever to watch a movie. From the outset, the studio pursued (and Mitchell resisted) the idea of making at least a movie sequel to see whether Scarlett and Rhett would ever reunite. Eventually, in the 1980s, the Eleventh Circuit ruled (in *Trust Company Bank v. MGM/UA Entertainment*, 772 F.2d 740 (11th Cir. 1985)), that Mitchell's estate had retained, not assigned, the right to determine whether there would be any kind of sequel and if so who would make it. The estate auctioned off the rights to Warner Brothers for $5 million. In turn, Warner Brothers commissioned Alexander Ripley to write the book sequel, *Scarlett*, which became the best-selling novel of 1991, and then sold the film rights to CBS for $8 million. *Scarlett* finally appeared as an eight-hour miniseries in 1994, giving CBS the victory in the "sweeps" ratings for that fall.

---

The long journey of Scarlett and Rhett to prime-time underscores the theme of this chapter—that a key feature of the entertainment world for the past century has been the regular emergence of new forms of communication technology. These developments have been a godsend for entertainment fans who now see their favorite works turned into movies, television shows, musical albums and videos, and merchandise. One recent example is computerized interactive multimedia, which stores in digital form text, graphics, sound, and film, and permits the user to decide what items to draw upon and how they should be manipulated. The most widely-used form of such technology is the video game, with annual sales of $9 billion (more than total movie admissions).

Exploitation of these entertainment opportunities poses a huge challenge to the industry: in particular, how best to integrate the talent, resources, and culture of major entertainment powers in Southern California with those of the smaller high-tech firms in Northern California. Entertainment lawyers play a key role. One part is devising contract language to define the rights of the various participants in a project comprised of brand-new material. Another is deciding how to apply old contract language to new technology when a project seeks to draw upon existing material.

It is a mistake to suppose, however, that either interactive multimedia or Internet entertainment poses novel legal issues just because it is based on new technology. Indeed, "multimedia" (though not "interactive") was just as apt a label for the technological breakthrough in the mid-1920s that permitted synchronization of film and sound in "talking" movies. At each stage in such advancing entertainment technology, similar legal questions are posed at the intersection of copyright and contract law. The following decision has a court wrestling with this issue in connection with the showing of movies on videocassette, the major addition to the world of entertainment in the 1980s.

## COHEN, D/B/A BIZARRE MUSIC V. PARAMOUNT PICTURES CORP.

United States Court of Appeals, Ninth Circuit, 1988.
845 F.2d 851.

HUG, CIRCUIT JUDGE.

[Herbert Cohen had created a musical composition entitled "Merry-Go-Round." In 1969, he signed a "synchronization" license which gave H & J Pictures the right to use his song in a film called *Medium Cool*, to be exhibited in theaters and on television. After having made the movie, H & J assigned the distribution and exhibition rights to Paramount Pictures which in the early 1980s had the film put on videocassettes. After *Medium Cool* had sold what was then a sizeable number of 2725 videocassettes (generating $69,000 in gross revenues), Cohen sued Paramount for violating his copyright in the song. Since Paramount could not claim that videocassettes were covered by § 8(4)(a) of the original contract which covered exhibition in movie theaters, the focus of the case was § 8(4)(b) which permitted exhibition "by means of television, including pay television, subscription television, and closed circuit into homes television."]

Paragraph 4(b) grants to Paramount the limited right to authorize broadcasters and cable television companies to broadcast the movie over the airwaves or to transmit it by cable, microwave, or some such means from a central location. The words of that paragraph must be tortured to expand the limited right granted by that section to an entirely different means of making that film available to the general public—the distribution of individual videocassettes to the general public for private "performances" in their homes. The general tenor of the section contemplates some sort of broadcasting or centralized distribution, not distribution by sale or rental of individual copies to the general public. Furthermore, the exhibition of the videocassette in the home is not "by means of television." Though videocassettes may be exhibited by using a television monitor, it does not follow that, for copyright purposes, playing videocassettes constitutes "exhibition by television." Exhibition of a film on television differs fundamentally from exhibition by means of a videocassette recorder ("VCR"). Television requires an intermediary network, station, or cable to send the television signals into consumers' homes. The menu of entertainment appearing on television is controlled entirely by the intermediary and, thus, the consumer's selection is limited to what is available on various channels. Moreover, equipped merely with a conventional television set, a consumer has no means of capturing any part of the television display; when the program is over it vanishes, and the consumer is powerless to replay it. Because they originate outside the home, television signals are ephemeral and beyond the viewer's grasp.

Videocassettes, of course, allow viewing of a markedly different nature. Videocassette entertainment is controlled within the home, at the viewer's complete discretion. A consumer may view exactly what he or she wants (assuming availability in the marketplace) at whatever time he or she chooses. The viewer may even "fast forward" the tape so as to quickly pass over parts of the program he or she does not wish to view. By their very essence, then, videocassettes liberate viewers from the constraints otherwise inherent in television, and eliminate the involvement of an intermediary, such as a network.

Television and videocassette display thus have very little in common besides the fact that a conventional monitor of a television set may be used both to receive television signals and to exhibit a videocassette. It is in light of this fact that Paramount argues that VCRs are equivalent to "exhibition by means of television." Yet, even that assertion is flawed. Playing a videocassette on a VCR does not require a standard television set capable of receiving television signals by cable or by broadcast; it is only necessary to have a monitor capable of displaying the material on the magnetized tape.

Perhaps the primary reason why the words "exhibition by means of television" in the license cannot be construed as including the distribution of videocassettes for home viewing is that VCRs for home use were not invented or known in 1969, when the license was executed. The parties both acknowledge this fact and it is noted in the order of the district judge. Thus, in 1969—long before the market for videocassettes burgeoned—Cohen could not have assumed that the public would have free and virtually unlimited access to the film in which the composition was played; instead, he must have assumed that viewer access to the film *Medium Cool* would be largely controlled by theatres and networks. By the same token, the original licensee could not have bargained for, or paid for, the rights associated with videocassette distribution. The holder of the license should not now "reap the entire windfall" associated with the new medium. As noted above, the license reserved to the grantor "all rights and uses in and to said musical composition, except those herein granted to the licensee . . ." This language operates to preclude uses not then known to, or contemplated by the parties. Thus, by its terms, the contract did not convey the right to reproduce and distribute videocassettes. That right, having not been granted to the licensee, was among those that were reserved.

Moreover, the license must be construed in accordance with the purpose underlying federal copyright law. Courts have repeatedly stated that the Copyright Act was "intended definitively to grant valuable, enforceable rights to authors, publishers, etc., . . . 'to afford greater encouragement to the production of literary works of lasting benefit to the world.' " *Washingtonian Publishing Co. v. Pearson*, 306 U.S. 30, 36 (1939). We would frustrate the purposes of the Act were we to construe this license—with its limiting language—as granting a right in a medium that had not been introduced to the domestic market at the time the parties entered into the agreement.

Paramount directs our attention to two district court cases, which, it contends, compel the opposite result. Both, however, involve licenses that contain language markedly different from the language in the license at hand.

*Platinum Record Company, Inc. v. Lucasfilm, Ltd.*, 566 F. Supp. 226 (D.N.J.1983), involved an agreement executed in 1973 in which plaintiff's predecessor in interest granted Lucasfilm, a film producer, the right to use four popular songs on the soundtrack of the motion picture, *American Graffiti*. The agreement expressly conferred the right to "exhibit, distribute, exploit, market and perform said motion picture, its air, screen and television trailers, perpetually throughout the world by any means or methods now or hereafter known." Lucasfilm produced *American Graffiti* under a contract with Universal. The film was shown in theatres and on cable, network, and local television. In 1980, a Universal affiliate released the film for sale and rental to the public on videocassettes. Plaintiffs brought suit against Universal and its affiliate, alleging that the agreement did not give them the right to distribute the film on videocassettes.

The district court granted summary judgment in favor of the defendants. It reasoned that the language in the agreement conferring the right to exhibit the film "by any means or methods now or hereafter known" was "extremely broad and completely unambiguous, and precludes any need in the Agreement for an exhaustive list of specific potential uses of the film . . . It is obvious that the contract in question may 'fairly be read' as including newly developed media, and the absence of any specific mention in the Agreement of videotapes and video cassettes is thus insignificant."

Similarly, the district court in *Rooney v. Columbia Pictures Industries, Inc.*, 538 F. Supp. 211 (S.D.N.Y. 1982), aff'd, 714 F.2d 117 (2d Cir. 1982), found that the contracts in question, which granted rights to exhibit certain films, also gave defendants the right to sell videocassettes of the films. Like the contract in *Platinum*, the contracts in *Rooney* contained sweeping language, granting, for example, the right to exhibit the films "by any present or future methods or means," and by "any other means now known or unknown." The court stated, "The contracts in question gave defendants extremely broad rights in the distribution and exhibition of [the films], plainly intending that such rights would be without limitation unless otherwise specified and further indicating that future technological advances in methods of reproduction, transmission, and exhibition would inure to the benefit of defendants."

In contrast to the contracts in *Platinum* and *Rooney*, the license in this case lacks such broad language. The contracts in those cases expressly conferred the right to exhibit the films by methods yet to be invented. Not only is this language missing in the license at hand, but the license also expressly reserves to the copyright holder all rights not expressly granted. We fail to find the Rooney and Platinum decisions persuasive.

Conclusion

We hold that the license did not give Paramount the right to use the composition in connection with videocassette production and distribution of the film *Medium Cool*. The district court's award of summary judgment in favor of Paramount is reversed.

Reversed and Remanded.

### *QUESTIONS FOR DISCUSSION*

What distinctions were there in the contract language employed in *Bizarre Music,* as compared to *Platinum Record* and *Rooney,* the district court decisions relied on by Paramount? Should those variations in wording matter? Other circuit court decisions on this issue are *Rey v. Lafferty*, 990 F.2d 1379 (1st Cir. 1993), which held that the license to produce films "for television viewing" of *Curious George* did not include home video rights; *Bloom v. Hearst Entertainment*, 33 F.3d 518 (5th Cir. 1994), which ruled that a grant of "exclusive worldwide motion picture and television rights" in a book, *Evidence of Love*, carried with it home video rights in the CBS made-for-television movie, *Killing In a Small Town* (the latter decision based on a consensus in the negotiation history that clarified the ambiguous contract language); and *Woods v. Bourne*, 60 F.3d 978 (2d Cir. 1995), which held that

Disney's 1930s agreement for use of Bourne's copyrighted music "in synchronism with . . . motion pictures" such as *Snow White and the Seven Dwarfs* and *Pinocchio* did not, as matter of law, exclude videocassettes from the scope of that license in the 1990s.

---

For much of this century, disputes about the scope of a copyright license have mirrored the changes taking place in communication technology and the entertainment industry. Following are some of the major cases and their interpretative problems. The first group involves disputes about presentation of the same derivative work through a new medium:

(a) In *Manners v. Morosco*, 252 U.S. 317 (1920), the author of the play *Peg O' My Heart* had granted the defendant the "sole and exclusive license and liberty to produce, perform and represent the said play," which the Supreme Court ruled did not entitle the defendant to turn the play into a (silent) motion picture.

(b) In *L.C. Page v. Fox Film Corp.*, 83 F.2d 196 (2d Cir. 1936), the author of the novel *Captain January* had agreed in 1914 (and then reiterated in 1923) to grant "exclusive moving picture rights." The Second Circuit concluded that this license would permit a talking motion picture to be made in the mid-1930s.

(c) In *Bartsch v. MGM, Inc.*, 391 F.2d 150 (2d Cir. 1968), a 1930 license given by the playwright-author of the musical comedy *Playtime* to MGM to produce and then to "copyright, vend, license and exhibit. . . . [a] motion picture photoplay" (which appeared in 1935), was interpreted as giving the studio the right to show the movie on network television in 1958.

(d) In *Subafilms v. MGM-Pathe Communications Co.*, 24 F.3d 1088 (9th Cir. 1994), the court ruled that video cassette transmission was not covered by a 1967 licensing agreement for the 1968 Beatles movie *Yellow Submarine,* which gave MGM the right to "rent, lease, license, exhibit, distribute, reissue and otherwise deal in and with respect to the Picture," and went on to state that such "theatrical rights in the Picture" include the right to "project, exhibit, reproduce, transmit, and perform the picture. . . . by television and by any other technological, mechanical or electronic means, method, or device now known or hereafter conceived or created."

(e) In *Philadelphia Orchestra Ass'n v. Walt Disney Co.*, 821 F. Supp. 341 (E.D. Pa. 1993), the court refused to grant summary judgment on whether home video sales in the 1990s were covered by an agreement negotiated in 1939 between Roy Disney (Walt's brother) and Leopold Stokowski, the conductor of the Philadelphia Symphony Orchestra, whereby Disney Studios paid the Orchestra to compose the music for the movie *Fantasia* and in return gave Disney the right to use the music for a "feature picture."

(f) In *Brown v. Twentieth Century Fox Film*, 799 F. Supp. 166 (D.D.C. 1992), the singer James Brown, in connection with his appearance on a 1965 television show, had assigned to the producers of the show (in return for $15,000) the right "to exhibit, transmit, reproduce, distribute, broadcast, and exploit, and license or permit others [to do the above]. . . . in connection with all or any portion of the Theatre film [the telecast]. . . . in and by all media means whatsoever." The court found that this language entitled the television producers to license Fox to use a 27-second clip of Brown's performance in its 1991 motion picture *The Commitments,* which was released in theaters, on television, and then on videocassette.

A second group of cases addressed whether an original license to create a movie or other derivative work conveys the right to do sequels or other variations on the original story and characters.

(a) In *Goodis v. United Artists Television*, 425 F.2d 397 (2d Cir. 1970), the author of the novel *Dark Passage* had sold to Warner Brothers in 1945 (for $25,000) the "exclusive, complete, and entire motion picture rights [in the book including the right] to broadcast and transmit any photoplay produced hereunder by the process of television." After Warner Brothers had produced a movie by that same name, which it also showed on television in the mid-1950s, the studio licensed United Artists to produce the hugely successful television series *The Fugitive* in the 1960s, which the court ruled was also covered by the author's assignment.

(b) In *Landon v. Twentieth Century-Fox Film Corp.*, 384 F. Supp. 450 (S.D.N.Y. 1974), the author of the book *Anne and the King of Siam* granted Fox in 1944 the "sole and exclusive motion picture rights," which were defined as "to make, produce, adapt . . . exhibit, perform, and generally deal in and with the copyright motion picture versions of said

> literary property. . . . and for such purposes to adapt one or more versions of said literary property. . . . and use all thereof in new versions, adaptations, and sequels . . . [and in addition] the sole and exclusive right to broadcast by means of . . . television, or any process analogous thereto, any of the motion picture versions of said literary property produced pursuant hereto." After the highly successful musical version, *The King and I*, Fox produced a 13-week television series called *Anna and the King*. Rejecting Fox's motion for summary dismissal, the court concluded that a fair reading of the original contract language might not encompass the later use.

The immediate question raised by these cases is what was the correct interpretation of the quoted contract licensing language for the planned new presentation or use of the original property. A common issue is whether the copyright licenses should be read narrowly or broadly with respect to uses that were not explicitly addressed in the contract language, in part because the new technology had not yet been developed or was not in serious use when the contract was drafted and signed. Consider, for example, video games and other interactive multimedia technology: should courts treat these as qualitatively similar to or different from such earlier advances as the move from live theater to motion pictures, silent to talking movies, movie exhibition to television, and television broadcasting to videocassette? What are the relevant interests of authors, producers, and consumers, and how are these interests best served in cases such as these?

Indeed, we now have a decision by the Supreme Court, *New York Times v. Tasini*, 533 U.S. 483 (2001), about the application of this part of copyright law to a useful Internet service, Lexis/Nexis. A group of newswriters led by Jonathan Tasini, President of the 7000-member National Writers Union, filed a lawsuit against the Times, Sports Illustrated (a branch of Time Warner), the Los Angeles Times, and other publications. The claim is that since they wrote their articles as independent contractors rather than "work for hire" employees, the licensing of their works on the Lexis/Nexis and other electronic databases violated the rights they now retained under the 1976 Copyright Act.

Under Section 201(c) in the Act, "copyright in each separate contribution to a collective work is distinct from the copyright in the collective work as a whole, and vests initially in the author." Unless the latter has made an explicit transfer of copyright in this work, the publisher acquires just the right to publish the article as part of that original "collective work" or "any revision" of it.

The majority opinion written by Justice Ginsburg concluded that the on-line material involved neither the original nor any revision of the overall New York Times issue by providing separate access to all articles. In response to the suggestion that there should be no legal problem about making these articles available "as a miniscule fraction of the ever-expanding Database," Justice Ginsburg remarked: "then a 400-page novel quoting a sonnet in passing would represent a 'revision' of the poem." *Id.* at 516. Nor was the Court worried "that a ruling for the authors will have 'devastating consequences' . . . [by] punching gaping holes in the electronic record of history." *Id.* at 519. Either the authors and publishers could negotiate agreements "allowing continued electronic reproduction of the authors' works," or if they could not, the courts or the Congress "may draw on numerous models for distributing copyrighted work and remunerating authors for their distribution." *Id.*

---

A crucial feature of copyright law that underlies many of the issues we have been addressing in this chapter is the length of the copyright term.[j] An intriguing case illustrating this point is *Stewart v. Abend*, 495 U.S. 207 (1990). The subject of the decision was the Alfred Hitchcock movie classic *Rear Window*, starring Jimmy Stewart. *Rear Window* was based on a 1942 short story by Cornell Woolrich, *It Had To Be Murder*, which had been published in a detective magazine. Woolrich granted Stewart and Hitchcock the right to turn his story into a movie, which was a hit when it appeared in 1954.

Unfortunately for the *Rear Window* movie producers, the 1909 Copyright Act not only gave authors an initial copyright for a 28-year period, but also the right to a 28-year renewal term. The historic purpose of this legislative arrangement was to give authors (or their heirs) the right to reassert control over works that had proven to be major but unexpected successes after their original appearance and assignment. Notwithstanding that policy, in *Fred Fisher Music v. M. Witmark & Sons*, 318 U.S. 643 (1943), a divided Supreme Court ruled that the author could, by contract, commit to renew the copyright for the benefit of the original assignee. In *Stewart*, though, the Court held that if the author died before expiration of the first copyright term, the heirs were not bound by any such author contract when they exercised their statutory

[j] *See* R. Anthony Reese, *Reflections on the Intellectual Commons: Two Perspectives on Copyright Duration & Reversion*, 47 Stan. L. Rev. 707 (1995); J.H. Reichman, *The Duration of Copyright & the Limits of Cultural Policy*, 14 Cardozo Arts & Ent. L.J. 625 (1996); Robert L. Bard & Lewis Kurlantzick, *Copyright Duration: Duration, Term Extension, the European Union & the Making of Copyright Policy* (Austin & Windfield 1999); Jon M. Garon, *Media & Monopoly in the Information Age: Slowing the Convergence at the Marketplace of Ideas*, 17 Cardozo Arts & Ent. L.J. 491 (1999); K.G. Greene, *Copyright, Culture & Black Music: A Legacy of Unequal Protection*, 21 Hast. Comm/EntL.J. 339 (1999); Michael H. Davis, *Extending Copyright & the Constitution: "Have I Stayed Too Long?"*, 52 Fla. L. Rev. 989 (2000).

renewal rights at the appointed time. That meant that in 1970, with Woolrich already dead, the new copyright was held by Woolrich's estate (actually, by its assignee Abend). Not until Paramount (and ABC) paid lucrative new fees for the privilege could the derivative work, *Rear Window*, be shown in theaters and on television screens without violating copyright in the original short story, *It Had To Be Murder*.

By the time the *Stewart* case was decided, its legal underpinnings had already been altered by Congress in the 1976 Copyright Act. With respect to works created after 1978, the new statute created a non-renewable copyright term for the author's life plus 50 years. Authors and their heirs were given a non-waivable and non-assignable right to terminate any assignments at a point between the 35th and 40th years from the transfer of the copyright (thus reversing *Fred Fisher*). One analysis of these complexities is *Woods v. Bourne Co.*, 60 F.3d 978 (2d Cir. 1995), in which the Second Circuit held that the music publisher to whom the composer of the 1926 hit "When the Red, Red Robin Comes Bob-Bob-Bobbin Along" had originally assigned copyright in the song was entitled to performance royalties earned after termination from movies and television programs that had been licensed to use the song before termination. The composer's estate was entitled to all other revenues from use of the song, including performance of musical recordings that had been made before termination of the copyright assignment. However, any such termination would not affect the validity of any derivative works that had already been licensed and produced (thus reversing *Stewart*).

The 1993 movie *Sleepless In Seattle* generated a lawsuit that illustrates the complexities in deciding what really is a licensed derivative work. *Sleepless In Seattle* included in its soundtrack parts of the 1969 recording of the song "Bye Bye Blackbird," by Joe Cocker for A & M Records. The movie producers had authorization for use of the song not just from Cocker and his record label, but also from Warner/Chappell Music, which had been assigned copyright in the song itself by its composer. Sometime between the Cocker recording and the movie production, the songwriter had exercised his right to terminate that copyright assignment to Warner/Chappell in favor of another publisher, Ahlert Music. Thus, Ahlert, which had not licensed use of the song in the movie, filed suit against Warner/Chappell, seeking the revenues received from the studio. There was no doubt that inclusion of Cocker's original version of "Bye Bye Blackbird" in a new album (e.g., his *Greatest Hits*) would be considered to be no more than the use of an existing derivative work (just like showing *Rear Window* on television, cable, or home video). The tougher question the parties had to address in settling this lawsuit was whether synchronization of parts of that recording in a movie such as *Sleepless In Seattle*, as well as its incorporation in the movie's soundtrack album, is the same kind of use of an existing work, or is the creation of a new (and now unauthorized) derivative version of the song.

This problem raises a host of important questions about copyright policy. One is the significance of authorship. As we saw earlier, if the creative artist is an employee, the firm is the author and enjoys these copyright prerogatives, in contrast to cases in which the artist is an independent contractor (using the *Reid* test). What are the reasons why an artist-contractor should enjoy a non-waivable right to terminate contract assignments after 35 years, and why do these reasons not also apply to the artist-employee?

The more fundamental issue is the appropriate life of copyright. The original Article I, Section 8 provision in the Constitution gave Congress the power to create intellectual property in order to "promote the progress of science and useful arts, by securing for *limited time* to authors and inventors the exclusive right to their respective writings and discoveries." Our first intellectual property statute, titled *An Act for the Encouragement of Learning*, set this initial term at 14 years for both copyrights and patents (with a copyright renewal of 14 years). Over the next two centuries, the copyright length steadily expanded until it recently reached a basic 95 years under the Sonny Bono Copyright Term Extension Act of 1998.

Sonny Bono had been the male partner in the entertaining duo, Sonny and Cher; he went on to Congress and later suffered a fatal skiing accident in 1997. In order to prevent the "untimely death" of copyright in creative works, Congress decided to extend copyright duration by another 20 years. In other words, where the copyright was owned by the initial author's personal estate, e.g. George Gershwin's "Rhapsody in Blue" or F. Scott Fitzgerald's *The Great Gatsby*, it now lives for another 70 rather than 50 years after the death of the author. At his 82nd birthday party in 2001, J.D. Salinger celebrated the 50th anniversary of his first hit novel, *Catcher in the Rye*, whose copyright will last for more than 120 years. When the work is created by a corporation or other organization, like Disney's Mickey Mouse and Donald Duck, or Time Warner's *The Jazz Singer*, which were due to expire in the early 2000s, the copyright lasts for 95 (rather than 75) years from publication (or 120 from creation, whichever is shorter).

The Sonny Bono Act was justified by similar extensions in Europe, which would not apply to American works unless similar action was taken in the United States. Congress did not consider the option, mentioned in the first edition of *Entertainment*, that American copyright protection might have been extended only to European works for that additional 20 years, in order to secure reciprocal protection for American-made work in those countries. Moreover, the Sonny Bono Act gave the 20-

year extension to "works for hire" owned by a studio (e.g., *The Jazz Singer)*, even though the European Union did not do that for its producers, (or for American studio works.)

In 2003, the Supreme Court rendered its decision about the constitutionality of this latest extension of copyright duration, *Eldred v. Ashcroft,* 537 U.S. 186 (2003). This challenge to the 1998 *Sony Bono Copyright Term Extension Act* targeted its 20-year expansion of the copyright for existing rather than future works.

The 7–2 majority opinion authored by Justice Ginsburg dismissed this constitutional claim, with dissents by Justices Stevens and Breyer (the latter had years earlier written a law review article criticizing the expansion of copyright law). This case was the first time the Court defined the scope of the "limited time" phrase in the Copyright Clause written into the Constitution by the Founding Fathers back in 1787. The *Eldred* majority was impressed by the fact that, beginning in 1831 and then continuing in 1909, 1976, and 1998, Congress has always given the benefit of each expanded duration to existing, not just future, copyrighted works. As Justice Ginsburg put it, "to comprehend the scope of Congress' power under the Copyright Clause, 'a page of history is worth a volume of logic.' History reveals an unbroken congressional practice of granting to authors of works with existing copyright the benefit of term extension so that all under copyright protection will be governed evenhandedly under the same regime." And as she later put it, "Congress' consistent historical practice of applying newly-enacted copyright terms to future and existing copyrights reflects a judgment stated concisely by Representative Huntington at the time of the 1837 Act: 'Justice, policy and equity alike forbid [that] an author who had sold his [work] a week ago be placed in a worse situation than the author who should sell his work the day after the passing of [the] act.' "

Justice Ginsburg found that this latest extension was justified first by the need to give American copyright holders the same duration as those given by the European Union so that American works would enjoy the latter's protection in European countries. Next, "in light of demographic, economic, and technological change," this would be encouraging "copyright holders to invest in the restoration and public distribution of their works." Having thus concluded that the Sonny Bono Act "is a rational enactment, we are not at liberty to second-guess congressional determinations and policy judgments of this order."

Finally, the Court rejected the claim that this continuing extension of copyright infringed the First Amendment. First, since the Copyright Clause and the First Amendment were adopted close in time, "[t]his proximity indicates that, in the Framers' view, copyright's limited monopolies are compatible with free speech principles." Referring to the

Court's precedents we have already seen in Chapter 4, like *Feist Publications v. Rural Telephone Service*, 499 U.S. 340 (1991), holding facts and ideas not to be copyrightable, and *Campbell v. Acuff-Rose Music*, 510 U.S. 569 (1994), on fair use, Justice Ginsburg wrote

> The First Amendment securely protects the freedom to make—or decline to make—one's own speech: it bears less heavily when speakers assert the right to make other people's speeches. To the extent such assertions voice First Amendment concerns, copyright's built-in free speech safeguards are generally adequate to address them.

*Id.* at 221.

Justice Stevens began his dissent by addressing Justice Ginsburg's claim that, as he put it, "historical practice effectively establishes the constitutionality of retroactive extension of unexpired copyrights." He cited *INS v. Chadha* for the principle that "the fact that Congress has repeatedly acted on a mistaken interpretation of the Constitution does not qualify our duty to invalidate an unconstitutional practice when it is finally challenged in an appropriate case." *See also Walz v. Tax Comm'n of City of New York*, 397 U.S. 664 (1970) ("it is obviously correct that no one acquires a vested or protected right in violation of the Constitution by long use, even when that span of time covers our entire national existence").

Justice Breyer's dissent noted that this "longest blanket extension since the nation's founding," which made copyright life "virtually perpetual required serious, not deferential, constitutional scrutiny." The reason, he claimed, is that "what may count as a rational where economic regulation is at issue it is not necessarily rational where we focus on expression—in a national constitution dedicated to the free dissemination of speech, information, learning, and culture."

---

Those now in charge of Time Warner were among the many applauding the *Eldred* ruling for preserving their copyright in such major revenue-generating works as *Gone With The Wind*, *The Wizard of Oz*, and *Casablanca*, as well as the still-copyrighted "Happy Birthday to You." So also were the leaders of all the movie, television, and music unions who issued a joint statement that "artists in the entertainment community have a clear stake in the protection of copyright. We believe that extension is good for artists and the industry." After the ruling, the policy issue that remains is what Congress should be doing regarding intellectual property in this new millennium.

Returning again to *Gone With The Wind*, if Margaret Mitchell had written that novel in the 1790s, just after America's first copyright law, she would have enjoyed exclusive rights in the story for 14 years, with a 14 year renewal term. When the book was actually written and published in the 1930s, copyright protection then lasted for 56 years (until 1992 for this work). When Houghton Mifflin was about to publish Alice Randall's *The Wind Done Gone,* the Mitchell Estate's constitutionally limited time for its copyright continued until 2032. Should we go even further, as the heirs of Jane Austen are now asking from the British Parliament after their ancestor's early 19th Century novels like *Sense and Sensibility, Emma,* and *Pride and Prejudice* were made into movies in the late 20th Century? Or should copyright be reduced close to the length of *patents* (now 20 years), or should an additional 20-year term be added in a few decades when lifespans might be longer? It should be noted that all of the Justices agreed that a perpetual copyright term would be unconstitutional, unlike the *publicity* rights of the Martin Luther King estate, which in states like Georgia apparently remain in existence forever.

From a broader public policy perspective, how long of a copyright term is needed to secure the goals of the system? Is the objective to reward authors for all of the value generated by their creative work? Or is it to establish sufficient incentives to ensure that such work will be done, while permitting consumers to benefit from free access to works that can then be placed in the public domain? Would it have added materially to the incentives of Jane Austen, or even of Margaret Mitchell, to know that their heirs would secure returns from their works 50, or 70, or 200 years after the authors died?

Consider also the interplay between the expanding *scope* and the expanding *duration* of copyright. When Jane Austen was writing *Sense & Sensibility,* there was no capacity to turn this book into a movie, but even if there had been, copyright law at that time did not extend to derivative uses (even translation of books into different languages, as happened to Harriet Beecher Stowe's *Uncle Tom's Cabin*). Could a case be made for accommodating the interests of authors and users by giving a relatively long term to exclusive rights over the original work, but a considerably shorter life for derivative versions of the work (e.g., Emma Thompson's Academy Award-winning screenplay for the movie *Sense and Sensibility*)?

These questions all echo the theme that has been running through this and the prior chapter: there are few easy answers about how to design a copyright system that best accommodates both author creativity and consumer welfare.

## G. ENFORCING COPYRIGHT

The tangible value of any intellectual property right turns as much on the effectiveness of its enforcement as on the scope of its doctrinal formulation. When copyright infringement suits are filed, what is actually at stake for both plaintiffs and defendants? What should be the measure of the plaintiff's harm in an infringement action: lost profits, damage to reputation, a reasonable royalty? Is the harm in a copyright infringement action essentially economic, or is it also personal? What difference might that policy judgment make in defining the scope of copyright relief, as contrasted with contract law?

## 1. DAMAGES

Under the Copyright Act, a successful plaintiff in an infringement action is entitled to wide-ranging legal and equitable relief. Section 502 of the Act authorizes courts to "grant temporary and final injunctions on such terms as [they] may deem reasonable to prevent or restrain infringement of a copyright." 17 U.S.C. § 502(a). The need for effective enforcement of intellectual property ownership generally overrides any First Amendment qualms about prior restraints on television broadcasts, *see In re Capital Cities/ABC, Inc.*, 918 F.2d 140 (11th Cir. 1990), or book publications, *see Salinger v. Random House*, 811 F.2d 90 (2d Cir. 1987). Indeed, courts may even order that all allegedly infringing copies be impounded while the infringement action is pending. 17 U.S.C. § 503(a). Then, if final judgment is entered against the infringer, the court may order the "destruction or other reasonable disposition" of all infringing copies. 17 U.S.C. § 503(b).

Section 504 of the Copyright Act, pertaining to damages, provides that "an infringer of copyright is liable for either—(1) the copyright owner's actual damages and any additional profits of the infringer . . .; or (2) statutory damages. . . ." 17 U.S.C. § 504(a). Actual damages reimburse the plaintiff for the "extent to which the market value of the copyrighted work at the time of the infringement has been injured or destroyed by the infringement." *See Fitzgerald Publishing Co., Inc. v. Baylor Publishing Co., Inc.*, 807 F.2d 1110, 1118 (2d Cir. 1986). This calculation may be based on the plaintiff's lost profits, the defendant's profits, or a combination of both, though double recovery is not permitted. When actual damages would be difficult or impossible to prove, a plaintiff can elect to recover statutory damages, which range from $700 to $30,000 *per work infringed.* 17 U.S.C. § 504(c)(1) (also providing for reduction to $200 for innocent infringement and increases to $150,000 for willful acts). The amount of statutory damages recovered depends on a variety of issues, including a rough approximation of the plaintiff's actual damages, the amount it would take to induce someone in the plaintiff's position to produce a similar work, or the necessity to deter future infringement. *See, e.g., Harris v. Emus Records Corp.*, 734 F.2d 1329, 1335 (9th Cir. 1984).

---

The following decision illustrates one assessment of copyright damages.

## GASTE V. MORRIS KAISERMAN A/K/A MORRIS ALBERT

United States Court of Appeals, Second Circuit, 1988.
863 F.2d 1061.

JON O. NEWMAN, CIRCUIT JUDGE.

[This case involved a copyright suit brought by Louis Gaste, French composer of the 1956 song "Pour Toi," against the Brazilian composer and singer Morris Kaiserman (known professionally as Morris Albert) as to his 1973 hit "Feelings." Though "Pour Toi" (which was part of the music score for the movie *Le Feu aux Poudres*) had earned only $15,000 in revenues over a quarter century, the circuit court upheld the jury's verdict that "Feelings" had copied the music, though not the lyrics, of "Pour Toi." A further issue was the appropriateness of a $268,000 damage award against Fermata International Melodies, the producer and publisher of "Feelings." (The jury had awarded another $233,000 against Kaiserman, which the trial judge reduced to $135,000 to exclude revenues attributable to foreign sources.) Fermata argued that its $268,000 award (which was based on U.S. revenues from "Feelings") should be reduced (a) to account for the contribution of the lyrics (not just the music) to "Feelings," and (b) to allow for the cost of producing and distributing the song.]

* * *

We note preliminarily that the jury apparently made some apportionment of profits to account for the contribution of the lyrics and for the expenses incurred by Fermata. The parties agreed that Fermata's gross revenues from "Feelings" for the relevant time period were, in round numbers, $337,000. Although the record is not entirely clear on Kaiserman's revenue, the relevant figure appears to be $265,000. The jury found damages in the amount of $268,000 against Fermata and $233,000 against Kaiserman. Thus, the jury awarded Gaste approximately 80 percent of Fermata's gross revenues from "Feelings," and 88 percent of Kaiserman's revenues.

The District Court instructed the jury that if it made an apportionment for the lyrics, that apportionment would apply equally to Fermata and to Kaiserman. The jury was also told that only Fermata was entitled to reductions to cover the costs it incurred. Therefore, although we cannot be certain of the jury's reasoning absent a special verdict, it seems likely that the jury made a 12 percent reduction for both defendants to account for the lyrics and then made a further reduction of 8 percent for Fermata to account for its costs. With that in mind, we take

Fermata's argument to be that the jury did not apportion enough and did not recognize enough of Fermata's costs.

A. *Lyrics.* A successful copyright plaintiff is entitled to recover only those profits that are "attributable to the infringement." 17 U.S.C. § 504(b) (1983). "In establishing the infringer's profits, the copyright owner is required to present proof only of the infringer's gross revenue, and the infringer is required to prove his or her deductible expenses and the elements of profit attributable to factors other than the copyrighted work." An infringing defendant is entitled to an apportionment of profits to account for his independent contributions only when "the evidence is sufficient to provide a fair basis of division so as to give the copyright proprietor all the profits that can be deemed to have resulted from the use of what belonged to him." Confronted with imprecision in the computation of expenses, a court should err on the side of guaranteeing the plaintiff a full recovery, but want of precision is not a ground for denying apportionment altogether.

There was no dispute at the trial that Kaiserman wrote the lyrics to "Feelings," and that those lyrics were non-infringing. Fermata and Kaiserman argued to the jury that as much as 80 percent of the income from the song should be attributed to the lyrics.

The evidence on the value of the lyrics was decidedly mixed. Kaiserman's expert, Lou Levy, a retired music publisher, testified that while there was no set rule, the normal practice in the record industry when the lyrics and music to a song are written by different artists is to split the royalties "50/50." He said a well-known lyricist or composer could draw a larger share and that a "bad" lyricist might get as little as 15 percent. Levy testified that he "loved" the song "Feelings" and that he believed the title and lyrics were "far better" than the music itself. Nonetheless, he was unable to recall the words to the song on the stand and yet was able to sing the opening tune. He also said that the music and the words were inseparable and refused to estimate any percentage division.

Defendants also argued at trial that the lyrics must have had some effect because "Pour Toi" had virtually no commercial success, while "Feelings" was a smash hit. On the other hand, there was also evidence that "Dis Lui," a French version of "Feelings" with completely different words, also had considerable success. This could indicate either that the French words were also popular or that it was the music that gave the song its appeal.

We note that in *ABKCO Music, Inc. v. Harrisongs Music, Ltd.*, 508 F. Supp. 798 (S.D.N.Y. 1981), modified, 722 F.2d 988 (2d Cir. 1983), the District Court determined that three-fourths of the income of the infringing song "My Sweet Lord" was due to the music plagiarized from an earlier hit song, "He's So Fine." The Court deducted 25 percent for the defendant's contribution of the lyrics to "My Sweet Lord" and for the marketability added to the song by the fact that the defendant was former Beatle George Harrison.

Judge Conner, contrasting this case to *ABKCO* and declining to alter the jury's damage award, noted that Kaiserman, a virtual unknown before "Feelings," did not independently add the selling power of a Harrison. On the other hand, Fermata points out that the music to "Pour Toi" did not have the independently confirmed selling power of the music to "He's So Fine," which had been a No. 1 song in its own right.

We find no grounds to reject the jury's decision to apportion no more than 12 percent for the lyrics. . . . The jury had an opportunity to judge for itself the independent appeal of the lyrics and the music. The evidence of the varied success of the three songs with the same music—"Feelings," "Pour Toi," and "Dis Lui"—could reasonably have been interpreted as favoring either side. . . .

B. *Fermata's Costs.* [T]he jury appears to have subtracted approximately 8 percent from Fermata's revenues to account for Fermata's costs related to "Feelings," in addition to the 12 percent deduction for the lyrics. Fermata argues that the jury's verdict was contrary to the evidence. . . .

Again, we decline to overturn the jury's verdict. . . . Fermata's evidence of its costs was sorely lacking in documentation. . . . The jury here did not act unreasonably in rejecting estimates of costs that were not fully documented.

We also reject Fermata's contention that nearly 90 percent of its costs must be attributed to "Feelings" because "Feelings" brought in nearly 90 percent of the company's revenues. In a very similar case, we held that " 'overhead' which does not assist in the production of the infringement should not be credited to the infringer; that which does, should be; it is a question of fact in all cases," *Wilkie v. Santly Bros.*, 139 F.2d 264, 265 (2d Cir. 1943). In *Wilkie*, a music publisher found liable for infringement also sought to attribute nearly all of his costs to the infringing song because it was by far his biggest seller. The Court found no reason not to allocate the costs equally across all 47 songs the publisher published, because it was shown that the better selling songs were not more responsible for the overhead costs than the others.

Here, Fermata published some 200 songs in addition to "Feelings." It was Fermata's burden to prove that its overhead was nonetheless attributable mainly to "Feelings." . . . In *Sygma Photo News v. High Society Magazine*, 778 F.2d 89, 95 (2d Cir. 1985), we held that even when defendants had not been able to establish their costs with precision, they should be able to deduct the minimum amount they in all likelihood spent. The jury's decision to allow Fermata only an 8 percent reduction for its costs is not inconsistent with that rule.

Affirmed.

### *QUESTIONS FOR DISCUSSION*

1. Having seen a copyright damage calculation, consider these questions about the roles such awards should play. Is the objective to compensate the copyright owner, to prevent unjust enrichment of the infringing party, or to deter future violations by other potential copiers? Which of these roles are well-suited to private suits for damages? How does a court calculate the plaintiff's actual losses: indeed, what kinds of losses deserve redress? How does one calculate the defendant's *net* profits from the particular feature of a song or movie that copied the plaintiff's original? When is the statutory damage award likely to be a better option for the plaintiff, and when should the latter have to make that election: before trial, before the jury verdict, or only before entry of final judgment (the latter being the rule)?

2. Music sampling cases, discussed earlier, present interesting problems in calculating damages. One complication is that it is not unusual for sales of the sampled (infringed) song to increase with the renewed recognition brought by the sampler. For example, sales of Queen's "Under Pressure" rose after Vanilla Ice sampled that tune in his hit "Ice, Ice Baby" and exposed a new generation to it.

In *Jarvis v. A & M Records*, 827 F. Supp. 282 (D.N.J. 1993), the plaintiff, whose song "The Music's Got Me" was sampled in Cole and Clivilles's dance song "Get Dumb (Free Your Body)," claimed that as damages he should receive:

> (1) the amount he would have made had he re-released his version of [the song]; (2) defendants' income derived from every performance of their infringing compositions, including a percentage of the defendants' advance; (3) a projected profit amount that defendants' copies would have earned had they remained on the market for a 3-year period, projected from the initial sales period; (4) punitive damages.

The court held that the plaintiff had not proved actual damages, noting that the plaintiff's deposition "convey[ed] an air of unfamiliarity and unconcern with any notion of actual, quantifiable damages." The plaintiff had testified that his damage was "not excessive. . . . It's just I have been damaged. What it's worth, that's up to the courts to decide, what it's worth or, you know." Jarvis was, however, entitled to the defendants' profits. The court did not deduct overhead from their revenues, because "there can be no more brazen stealing of music than digital sampling," and overhead may not be deducted by willful infringers. Defendants had also argued that because only 12% of their song contained Jarvis' material, 88% of their profits should be deducted. Should the judge have accepted this argument? (Recall the decision in *Harper*

*& Row*, which rejected the fair use argument by the *Nation* that it had used only 300 words from President Ford's memoirs.)

3. To provide some sense how jury awards have been soaring in intellectual property as well as personal injury suits, in 2001 a Detroit jury awarded $19 million in damages after finding that 20th Century Fox had used many key parts of an earlier script written by a local school teacher, Brian Webster, to make its 1996 movie *Jingle All the Way*, which generated $80 million in domestic box office (with Arnold Schwarzenegger and Sinbad as two dads competing to find and buy an action toy). The Sixth Circuit, however, reversed the jury verdict, finding that Fox was entitled to summary judgment on the issue of substantial similarity. Specifically, the Court found that the lack of similarity between the scripts was insufficient to establish a claim. *See Murray Hill Publications, Inc. v. Twentieth Century Fox Film Corp.*, 361 F.3d 312 (6th Cir. 2004). Do you agree with the appellate court's assessment?

The financial consequences of infringement in the aftermath of the *Bright Tunes* decision excerpted in Chapter 4, were that George Harrison paid $587,000 for subconsciously copying the Chiffon's song "He's So Fine" in his 1970s hit "My Sweet Lord." The spiraling cash value of successful claims was also displayed by the 1994 verdict against Michael Bolton. A Los Angeles jury found Bolton to have copied the Isley Brother's 1966 rhythm and blues song "Love Is A Wonderful Thing," in Bolton's own song of the same name, which was the hit on his 1991 album *Time, Love, & Tenderness*. Bolton's characteristically sweetened album sold 10 million copies. The jury awarded the Isley Brothers 66 percent of the profits from the song and 28 percent from the album. Ultimately, in *Three Boys Music v. Bolton*, 212 F.3d 477 (9th Cir. 2000), the circuit panel endorsed the $5.4 million total award.

## 2. ATTORNEY FEES[k]

Another crucial feature of copyright enforcement is that courts are empowered, though not required, to award attorney fees to prevailing parties. Indeed, in certain situations legal costs may well dwarf the parties' copyright infringement losses and profits. In 1994, the Supreme Court confronted the standards that courts were using in awarding attorney fees as a byproduct of the copyright dispute described in Chapter 4 involving John Fogerty. Fogerty was the lead singer and songwriter for Creedence Clearwater Revival, now installed in the Rock & Roll Hall of Fame in honor of the group's distinctive "swamp rock" style.

Fogerty had been sued by Fantasy Records, the original record label of the now-disbanded Creedence group. Fantasy claimed that a later song composed by Fogerty for Warner Records, "Old Man Down the Road," had copied elements of a song, "Run Through the Jungle," that Fogerty had

[k] *See* Peter Jaszi, *505 & All that—The Defendant's Dilemma*, 55 Law & Contemp. Probs. 107 (Spring 1992).

composed and sung with Creedence on an album whose copyright had been assigned to Fantasy. After the jury accepted Fogerty's defense that there had been no copying of "Jungle," the question remained whether Fogerty should be awarded "reasonable attorney's fees" under section 505 of the Copyright Act.

Relying on the Third Circuit decision in *Lieb v. Topstone Industries*, 788 F.2d 151 (3d Cir. 1986), Fogerty contended that this provision made defendant victors in copyright litigation just as entitled to their attorney fees as plaintiffs. But the Ninth Circuit rejected Fogerty's claim on the grounds that while prevailing plaintiffs should receive their attorney fees as a matter of course, prevailing defendants must show that the original suit was "frivolous or brought in bad faith" in order to recover fees. The Supreme Court agreed to resolve this circuit split about the "evenhanded" or "dual standard" approaches to attorney fees.

## FOGERTY V. FANTASY, INC.

Supreme Court of the United States, 1994.
510 U.S. 517, 114 S.Ct. 1023, 127 L.Ed.2d 455.

CHIEF JUSTICE REHNQUIST delivered the opinion of the Court.

* * *

Respondent advances three arguments in support of the dual standard followed by the Court of Appeals for the Ninth Circuit in this case. First, it contends that the language of § 505, when read in the light of our decisions construing similar fee-shifting language, supports the rule. Second, it asserts that treating prevailing plaintiffs and defendants differently comports with the "objectives" and "equitable considerations" underlying the Copyright Act as a whole. Finally, respondent contends that the legislative history of § 505 indicates that Congress ratified the dual standard which it claims was "uniformly" followed by the lower courts under identical language in the 1909 Copyright Act. We address each of these arguments in turn.

The statutory language—"the court may also award a reasonable attorney's fee to the prevailing party as part of the costs"—gives no hint that successful plaintiffs are to be treated differently than successful defendants. But respondent contends that our decision in *Christiansburg Garment Co. v. EEOC*, 434 U.S. 412 (1978), in which we construed virtually identical language, supports a differentiation in treatment between plaintiffs and defendants.

*Christiansburg* construed the language of Title VII of the Civil Rights Act of 1964, which in relevant part provided that the court "in its discretion, may allow the prevailing party . . . a reasonable attorney's fee as part of the costs. . . ." 42 U.S.C. § 2000e–5(k). We had earlier held, interpreting the cognate provision of Title II of that Act, that a prevailing plaintiff "should ordinarily recover an attorney's fee unless some special circumstances would render such an award unjust." *Newman v. Piggie Park Enterprises, Inc.*, 390 U.S. 400, 402 (1968). This decision was based on what we found to be the important policy objectives of the Civil Rights statutes, and the intent of Congress to achieve such objectives through the use of plaintiffs as " 'private attorneys general.' " In *Christiansburg*, supra, we determined that the same policy considerations were not at work in the case of a prevailing civil rights defendant. We noted that a Title VII plaintiff, like a Title II plaintiff in *Piggie Park*, is "the chosen instrument of Congress to vindicate 'a policy that Congress considered of the highest priority.' " We also relied on the admittedly sparse legislative history to indicate that different standards were to be applied to successful plaintiffs than to successful defendants.

Respondent points to our language in *Flight Attendants v. Zipes*, 491 U.S. 754, 758, n. 2 (1989), that "fee-shifting statutes' similar language is a 'strong indication' that they are to be interpreted alike." But here we think this normal indication is overborne by the factors relied upon in our *Christiansburg* opinion which are absent in the case of the Copyright Act. The legislative history of § 505 provides no support for treating prevailing plaintiffs and defendants differently with respect to the recovery of attorney's fees. The attorney's fees provision § 505 of the 1976 Act was carried forward verbatim from the 1909 Act with very little discussion. The relevant House Report provides simply:

> "Under section 505 the awarding of costs and attorney's fees are left to the court's discretion, and the section also makes clear that neither costs nor attorney's fees can be awarded to or against 'the United States or an officer thereof.' "

* * *

The goals and objectives of the two Acts are likewise not completely similar. Oftentimes, in the civil rights context, impecunious "private attorney general" plaintiffs can ill afford to litigate their claims against defendants with more resources. Congress sought to redress this balance in part, and to provide incentives for the bringing of meritorious lawsuits, by treating successful plaintiffs more favorably than successful defendants in terms of the award of attorney's fees. The primary objective of the Copyright Act is to encourage the production of original literary, artistic, and musical expression for the good of the public. In the copyright context, it has been noted that "entities which sue for copyright infringement as plaintiffs can run the gamut from corporate behemoths to starving artists; the same is true of prospective copyright infringement defendants."

We thus conclude that respondent's argument based on our fee-shifting decisions under the Civil Rights Act must fail.

Respondent next argues that the policies and objectives of § 505 and of the Copyright Act in general are best served by the "dual approach" to the award of attorney's fees.[13] The most common reason advanced in support of the dual approach is that, by awarding attorney's fees to prevailing plaintiffs as a matter of course, it encourages litigation of meritorious claims of copyright infringement . . . Indeed, respondent relies heavily on this argument. We think the argument is flawed because it expresses a one-sided view of the purposes of the Copyright Act. While it is true that one of the goals of the Copyright Act is to discourage infringement, it is by no means the only goal of that Act. In the first place, it is by no means always the case that the plaintiff in an infringement action is the only holder of a copyright; often times, defendants hold copyrights too, as exemplified in the case at hand.

More importantly, the policies served by the Copyright Act are more complex, more measured, than simply maximizing the number of meritorious suits for copyright infringement. The Constitution grants to Congress the power "To promote the Progress of Science and useful Arts, by securing for limited Times to Authors and Inventors the exclusive Right to their respective Writings and Discoveries." U.S. Const., Art. I, § 8, cl. 8. We have often recognized the monopoly privileges that Congress has authorized, while "intended to motivate the creative activity of authors and inventors by the provision of a special reward," are limited in nature and must ultimately serve the public good. *Sony Corp. of America v. Universal City Studios, Inc.*, 464 U.S. 417, 429 (1984).

* * *

Because copyright law ultimately serves the purpose of enriching the general public through access to creative works, it is peculiarly important that the boundaries of copyright law be demarcated as clearly as possible. To that end, defendants who seek to advance a variety of meritorious copyright defenses should be encouraged to litigate them to the same extent that plaintiffs are encouraged to litigate meritorious claims of infringement. In the case before us, the successful defense of "The Old Man Down the Road" increased public exposure to a musical work that could, as a result, lead to further creative pieces. Thus a successful defense of a copyright infringement action may further the policies of the Copyright Act every bit as much as a successful prosecution of an infringement claim by the holder of a copyright.

---

[13] Respondent points to four important interests allegedly advanced by the dual standard: (1) it promotes the vigorous enforcement of the Copyright Act; (2) it distinguishes between the wrongdoers and the blameless; (3) it enhances the predictability and certainty in copyrights by providing a relatively certain benchmark for the award of attorney's fees; and (4) it affords copyright defendants sufficient incentives to litigate their defenses.

* * *

[After analyzing and rejecting Fantasy's argument that the legislative history of § 505 supported the dual standard for awarding attorney fees, the Court turned to Fogerty's] argument that § 505 was intended to adopt the "British Rule." Petitioner argues that, consistent with the neutral language of § 505, both prevailing plaintiffs and defendants should be awarded attorney's fees as a matter of course, absent exceptional circumstances. For two reasons we reject this argument. . . .

First, just as the plain language of § 505 supports petitioner's claim for disapproving the dual standard, it cuts against him in arguing for the British Rule. The statute says that "the court may also award a reasonable attorney's fee to the prevailing party as part of the costs." The word "may" clearly connotes discretion. The automatic awarding of attorney's fees to the prevailing party would pretermit the exercise of that discretion.

Second, we are mindful that Congress legislates against the strong background of the American Rule. Unlike Britain where counsel fees are regularly awarded to the prevailing party, it is the general rule in this country that unless Congress provides otherwise, parties are to bear their own attorney's fees. . . .

Thus we reject both the "dual standard" adopted by several of the Courts of Appeals, and petitioner's claim that § 505 enacted the British Rule for automatic recovery of attorney's fees by the prevailing party. Prevailing plaintiffs and prevailing defendants are to be treated alike, but attorney's fees are to be awarded to prevailing parties only as a matter of the court's discretion. "There is no precise rule or formula for making these determinations," but instead equitable discretion should be exercised "in light of the considerations we have identified." *Hensley v. Eckerhart*, 461 U.S. 424, 436–437 (1983). Because the Court of Appeals erroneously held petitioner, the prevailing defendant, to a more stringent standard than that applicable to a prevailing plaintiff, its judgment is reversed and the case is remanded for further proceedings consistent with this opinion.

It is so ordered.

## *QUESTIONS FOR DISCUSSION*

1. How would you characterize the four alternative standards for attorney fee awards described in the opinion—the American Rule, the British Rule, the "dual standard," and the "even-handed" approach? What are the pros and cons of each, and how do these factors apply to copyright, as contrasted with commercial, personal injury, or civil rights litigation? (Consider that Justice Clarence Thomas concurred only in the Court's

judgment, because he believed that the Court had erred in *Christiansburg Garment v. EEOC*, 434 U.S. 412 (1978), in adopting the "dual standard" for Title VII of the Civil Rights Act).

2. Now that the Court has ruled, how should lower courts actually make the judgment about whether to award attorney fees? *See Fantasy v. Fogerty*, 94 F.3d 553 (9th Cir. 1996) (awarding $1.3 million in fees on remand). When the plaintiff wins a copyright suit, what are the affirmative reasons for awarding fees? How about when the defendant wins the suit?

3. In *Feltner v. Columbia Pictures Television*, 523 U.S. 340 (1998), the Court faced another copyright enforcement issue. The wording of the *Copyright Act* seems arguably to give the judge alone the power to assess the "statutory" (rather than "actual") damages appropriate for a copyright violation. Does the Seventh Amendment give either party a constitutional right to have a jury verdict on this issue?

# CHAPTER 6

# ALTERNATIVE SOURCES OF ENTERTAINMENT PROPERTY RIGHTS

■ ■ ■

The previous two chapters explored the key components of copyright law, the central core of protection for entertainment assets. As shown in Chapter 3, courts have also fashioned a right of publicity, which gives celebrities an increasingly valuable vehicle for controlling and marketing their personal identities. This chapter will explore additional modes of protection for the creative efforts, such as trademark and unfair competition law. For example, the actual creators of a work may seek such relief even when they were required by either their employment status or by contract to relinquish copyright to the firm that financed production and distribution of the work.

## A. ARTISTIC CREDIT

The previous chapter shows how far legal treatment of the entertainment industry has moved from the original image of creative artists enjoying exclusive property in their personal work. Writers, singers, and actors who want to get their work produced and paid for typically have to assign initial authorship of a work made for hire, or at least agree to the transfer of ownership prerogatives through contract. In the next part of the book, **Contractual Relations in the Entertainment Industry**, we will explore in detail the ramifications of these relationships.

Aside from determining how a work is to be distributed, an author may well have a claim to receive (or *not* receive) artistic credit for the work in question. In the entertainment industry—in particular, motion pictures—credits are of crucial importance. In movie negotiations, for example, stars jockey for "first position" or "second position" billing above the title. Thus, in an unpublished ruling, *Gold Leaf Group v. Stigwood Group*, (N.Y. Sup. Ct. 1987), a judge ordered the film company to live up to its agreement to give Peter Frampton top billing on the film *Sgt. Pepper's Lonely Hearts Club Band*. The court ordered the company to put Frampton's name *above*, not just to the left of, the Bee Gees, notwithstanding the latter's post-contractual surge in popularity after the movie *Saturday Night Fever*:

> In the film industry, a particular actor's performance, which may have received an award or other critical acclaim, may be the primary attraction for movie-goers. Some actors are said to have such drawing power at the box office that the appearance of their names on the theater marquee can almost guarantee financial success. Such big box office names are built, in part, through being prominently featured in popular films and by receiving appropriate recognition in film credits and advertising. Since actors' fees for pictures, and indeed, their ability to get any work at all, is often based on the drawing power their name may be expected to have at the box office, being accurately credited for films in which they have played would seem to be of critical importance in enabling actors to sell their "services," i.e., their performances.

*Smith v. Montoro*, 648 F.2d 602, 607 (9th Cir. 1981). Nearly fifty years earlier, a Ninth Circuit judge made essentially the same observation about the significance of screen credits to script writers:

> [Screen credit] is a method of advertising to the public the fact that the production they are about to witness is the result of the ingenuity, inventive genius, and literary skill of the person to whom screen credit is given. Thus it is believed other motion picture producers will seek to avail themselves of the services of the person given screen credit to produce other stories for such reproduction.

*Paramount Productions v. Smith*, 91 F.2d 863, 867 (9th Cir. 1937).

Artists are willing to risk a great deal to receive credits. For example, in *Smithers v. Metro-Goldwyn-Mayer Studios*, 139 Cal.App.3d 643, 189 Cal. Rptr. 20 (1983) (now decertified for publication), Smithers, a notable supporting actor, was discharged from the television series *Executive Suite* when he refused to accept reduced credit. Smithers had agreed that actors in three specified roles could be billed above his name, but ultimately ten or eleven actors were billed above him. Smithers received a jury award in the seven-figure range for tortious breach of the covenant of good faith and fair dealing. The jury found that the president of MGM had threatened to blacklist Smithers if he did not go along with the reduced credit. It also found that Smithers had detrimentally relied on the promised level of credit in entering into the contract at a reduced fee.

Artistic credits for writers do have intellectual property overtones. There are, however, several other legal sources that artists can draw upon for this purpose. These include individual performance contracts, collective bargaining agreements, and certain provisions of the federal Lanham Act relating to trademarks. *See* Robert Davenport, *Screen Credit in the Entertainment Industry*, 10 Loyola Enter. L. J. 129 (1990).

An important early precedent, *Paramount Productions v. Smith*, 91 F.2d 863 (9th Cir. 1937), illustrates the potential role of the performance contract. Smith had authored a story entitled "Cruise to Nowhere," which he sold to Paramount for $2,500 pursuant to a written contract. Under his contract, Smith granted Paramount

> all the motion picture rights throughout the world, in and to and in connection with the said story, together with the sole and exclusive rights to use, adapt, translate, subtract from, add to and change the said story and the title thereof in the making of motion picture photoplays and/or as a part of and/or in conjunction with any motion picture photoplay and/or to combine the said story with any other work, to use the said title and/or any similar title in conjunction with motion picture photoplays based upon the said story and/or other literary, dramatic and/or dramatico-musical works . . .

Paramount, in turn, agreed "to announce on the film of the motion picture photoplays that may be produced pursuant hereto that such motion picture photoplays are based upon or adapted from a story written by the Author. . . ."

In 1934, Paramount began exhibiting a movie entitled *We're Not Dressing*, which Smith alleged was based upon his story, "Cruise to Nowhere." The supporting evidence included a production sheet for the movie that noted that it was "From Story 'Cruise to Nowhere,' " and a publicity item stating that *We're Not Dressing* was "an original story by Walton Hall Smith." A jury found that the movie was "based upon or adapted from" Smith's story, and the Ninth Circuit upheld that finding.

Paramount contended that the damages awarded to Smith were unduly speculative, but the court disagreed:

> Appellee testified that he and another writer collaborated in writing a story and sold it without screen credit for $10,000, which the two writers divided. Appellee's story was sold for $2,500, but under a contract that required that he be given screen credit. From these figures, the jury might easily compute the advertising value of the screen credit. He also testified that he received screen credit for a play; that prior thereto his salary was $250 per week; and that afterward he received $350 per week at one time, and $500 per week for a period of two weeks, due to the screen credit he had received. That evidence is, if believed, likewise sufficient as a gauge for the measure of the damages.

*Id.* at 867.

Judge Wilbur, who dissented, thought that Smith had proved neither breach of contract nor resulting damages. With respect to the breach of contract issue, Judge Wilbur believed there was not sufficient evidence to show that the movie was "based upon" Smith's story to justify giving him screen credit:

> Beyond question, the defendant purchased the plaintiff's story for film reproduction and went to work to adapt it for screen reproduction. . . . But the evidence shows that it was later decided that plaintiff's story was not suitable for the type of production desired at that time, and that several screen writers were employed to write the scenario for reproduction. . . . That the story produced was vastly different from that purchased is clear from a comparison of the two stories. . . . I conclude, therefore, that the admissions of the defendant that the produced story . . . was based upon plaintiff's story . . . are without probative value in determining whether or not the plaintiff was entitled to screen credit.

*Id.* at 867. Judge Wilbur was also of the view that "in construing the terms of the contract for screen credit, some attention must be given to the question as to whether or not the giving of such credit to a play which has been substantially changed would, in effect, be a falsehood tending to deceive the public." He noted that the screenwriter had never seen Smith's story or been told of its substance, and that the similarities between the stories were in unoriginal aspects.

On the issue of damages, Judge Wilbur observed:

> The plaintiff's contention is that, if his reputation had been enhanced by the advertisement that he had produced the story . . . , it would have been an advantage to him in securing other contracts of a similar nature and upon that hypothesis introduced evidence as to a past contract in which he had sold a story for less with screen credit than he had received for another story without screen credit. . . . While it is manifest that favorable publicity of any kind in connection with the production of a screen play would be valuable to one seeking to sell a story or play, it is clear it would be impossible to measure the value of one story by the amount paid for an entirely different story even though the author is the same. . . . The same thing may be said concerning the evidence . . . concerning the salary received by the plaintiff before and after he had obtained screen credit. There is no evidence that the increase in salary was due to the fact that screen credit had been given on a previous play. I think this evidence was too remote and speculative and should not have been received. . . .

*Id.* at 870.

In the present-day movie industry, the principal bases for artistic credit are labor agreements that unions negotiate under the National Labor Relations Act. As we will see in Chapter 11, entertainment is one of the most unionized industries in this country. Two features of entertainment unionism are distinctive. The first is that union jurisdiction is broken down by artistic specialty. "Above-the-line" movie contributors are represented by the Screen Actors Guild, the Writers Guild of America, the Directors Guild, and the American Federation of Musicians. The other feature is that collective bargaining establishes only a compensation floor: above that scale individual performers (through their agents) negotiate compensation that varies dramatically from star to bit player.

With respect to certain recurring issues, the union negotiates with the industry the governing standards and procedures for resolving the problem. The Writers Guild and Directors Guild have long been preoccupied with artistic credit for their members, because such designation not only secures future reputational and employment benefits from credits, but also provides specified royalty shares in the downstream financial returns from the movie in question.

This practice brings to light another problem for both the entertainment industry and the law: one writer's credit is another writer's lack of credit. That conflict is accentuated in the movie world, where film scripts regularly go through countless versions from the time the producers are looking for initial financial backing to the director's final "take" on the set. To settle screenwriter disputes about who will get the billing, the Writers Guild has established an expedited arbitration procedure, which we will see in Chapter 11.

Along with or in place of individual or collective contracts, artists can also claim credit for their work under the federal Lanham Act. Section 43(a), 15 U.S.C. § 1125, provides, in relevant part:

> (1) Any person who, on or in connection with any goods or services . . . uses in commerce any word, term, name, symbol, or device . . . or any false designation of origin, false or misleading description of fact, or false or misleading representation of fact, which—
>
> (A) is likely to cause confusion, or to cause mistake, or to deceive as to the affiliation, connection, or association of such person with another person, or as to the origin, sponsorship or approval of his or her goods, services, or commercial activities by another person,

shall be liable in a civil action by any person who believes that he or she is or is likely to be damaged by such act.

As we shall explore in Section C (on **Trademark Instead of Copyright**), the principal role of the Lanham Act is to protect the right of companies like Coca-Cola and Apple to reserve their trademark names for use on their products, and thereby protect consumers from confusion about which soda or computer to order. More recently, studios like Disney (and sports leagues like the National Football League) have used this federal law to assert an exclusive right in the names and identifying features of characters like those in *The Lion King* (or teams like the Dallas Cowboys).

In *Smith v. Montoro*, 648 F.2d 602 (9th Cir. 1981), however, the Ninth Circuit held that actor Paul Smith had stated a valid claim under § 43(a) when his name was removed from a movie's screen credits and advertising material. Smith had contracted with an Italian film company for star billing, and the company had agreed to provide for this billing in contracts with distributors. When the company licensed Montoro and Film Venture International (FVI) to distribute the film in the United States, Montoro and FVI (with whom Smith did not have a contract) removed Smith's name and substituted the name "Bob Spencer." Smith claimed that this action harmed his reputation and cost him future movie employment opportunities.

The court agreed with Smith that Montoro had violated § 43(a) by falsely designating another name in place of Smith's. The court acknowledged that this was not a case of "palming off," in the sense of "the selling of a good or service of one's own creation under the name or mark of another." However, the court noted that a

> § 43(a) claim may be based on economic practices or conduct "economically equivalent" to palming off. Such practices would include "reverse passing off," which occurs when a person removes or obliterates the original trademark, without authorization, before reselling goods produced by someone else. . . . Reverse passing off is accomplished "expressly" when the wrongdoer removes the name or trademark on another party's product and sells that product under a name chosen by the wrongdoer. "Implied" reverse passing off occurs when the wrongdoer simply removes or otherwise obliterates the name of the manufacturer or source and sells the product in an unbranded state.

*Id.* at 605. The court held that removing Smith's name from the movie's credits and advertising and substituting another name for his constituted "reverse passing off." The court explained that

> as a matter of policy, such conduct, like traditional palming off, is wrongful because it involves an attempt to misappropriate or profit from another's talents and workmanship. Moreover, in reverse palming off cases, the originator of the misidentified product is involuntarily deprived of the advertising value of its name and of the goodwill that otherwise would stem from public knowledge of the true source of the satisfactory product. The ultimate purchaser (or viewer) is also deprived of knowing the true source of the product and may even be deceived into believing that it comes from a different source.

*Id.* at 607.

The next case illustrates the factors that are relevant to a § 43(a) action for artistic credit.

## LAMOTHE V. ATLANTIC RECORDING CORP.

United States Court of Appeals, Ninth Circuit, 1988.
847 F.2d 1403.

THOMPSON, CIRCUIT JUDGE.

* * *

### II

### Facts

Viewing the evidence in the light most favorable to Lamothe and Jones, the facts pertinent to this appeal [from summary dismissal] are that Lamothe, Jones and Crosby are co-authors of two songs entitled "Scene of the Crime," and "I'm Insane." These works were composed while Lamothe, Jones and Crosby were members of a band called Mac Meda. After Mac Meda disbanded, Crosby joined another musical group called RATT. While Crosby was a member of RATT, he and Juan Croucier licensed the songs at issue to Time Coast Music, which in turn sub-licensed the songs to other of the defendants in this case, including Atlantic Recording. In 1984, Atlantic released an album by the group RATT entitled "Out of the Cellar," which included the recordings of the songs "Scene of the Crime" and "I'm Insane." Because of the popularity of this album, the music and lyrics for all compositions on the album were released in sheet music form by the sub-licensee Chappell Music Co. In both versions . . . , authorship of the music and lyrics of "I'm Insane" was attributed solely to Robinson Crosby and the music and lyrics of "Scene of the Crime" were attributed to Robinson Crosby and Juan Croucier. Neither Robert Lamothe nor Ronald Jones received credit for their roles in the writing of these songs.

III

Analysis

The principal issue on appeal is whether Lamothe and Jones have stated a claim under section 43(a) of the Lanham Act. . . . [The Lanham Act] has been applied to motion picture representations, and the defendants cite no case holding that it does not similarly reach musical compositions. We also note that "[t]o recover for a violation of [section 43(a)] it is not necessary that a mark or trade-mark be registered. The dispositive question is whether the party has a reasonable interest to be protected against false advertising." Finally, we recently have made clear that in cases involving false designation, the actionable "conduct must not only be unfair but must in some discernible way be competitive." *Halicki v. United Artists Communications, Inc.*, 812 F.2d 1213, 1214 (9th Cir. 1987). In the present case, the plaintiffs clearly have a legitimate interest in protecting their work from being falsely designated as the creation of another. The defendants do not dispute that the plaintiffs and Crosby are competitors in the relevant market. Having determined that the plaintiffs have an interest protected by the Lanham Act, we turn our attention to whether the defendants' conduct in this case constitutes a violation of section 43(a).

*1. Prohibited Conduct Under Section 43(a)*

The Lanham Act applies to two different types of unfair competition in interstate commerce. The first is "palming off" or "passing off," which involves selling a good or service of one person's creation under the name or mark of another. *Smith v. Montoro*, 648 F.2d 602, 604 (9th Cir. 1981). Section 43(a) also reaches false advertising about the goods or services of the advertiser. *U-Haul Int'l, Inc. v. Jartran, Inc.*, 681 F.2d 1159, 1160 (9th Cir. 1982). Because we conclude that Lamothe and Jones . . . have produced evidence satisfying the elements of a "reverse passing off" claim, we need not decide whether the defendants' actions also constitute false advertising.

*2. Passing Off*

[The court summarized the facts and holding of *Smith v. Montoro*.]

* * *

In the present case, taking the allegations of the complaint as true, the defendants engaged in express reverse palming off, by which they deprived Lamothe and Jones of recognition and profits from the release of the two songs that were their due.

The defendants' argument on appeal . . . is that there can be no express reverse passing off when the designation of a product's source is partially correct. Defendants argue that the failure to attribute authorship to Lamothe and Jones is a "mere omission," which is not actionable under section 43(a). We disagree. We do not read the "falsity" requirement in origination cases so narrowly that a partially accurate designation of origin, which obscures the contribution of another to the final product, is a permissible form of competition.

* * *

In the present case, the defendants unilaterally decided to attribute authorship to less than all of the joint authors of the musical compositions. Had the defendants decided to attribute authorship to a fictitious person, to the group "RATT," or to some other person, this would be a false designation of origin. It seems to us no less "false" to attribute authorship to only one of several co-authors . . . The policies we identified in *Smith*, namely, ensuring that the producer of a good or service receives appropriate recognition and that the consuming public receives full information about the origin of the good, apply with equal force here. An incomplete designation of the source of the good or service is no less misleading because it is partially correct. Misbranding a product to only partially identify its source is the economic equivalent of passing off one person's product under the name or mark of another. And the *Smith* case makes clear that in assessing section 43(a) claims, courts are to consider whether the challenged "practices or conduct [are] 'economically equivalent' to palming off." *Smith*, 648 F.2d at 605.

### *3. Liability of Licensees*

Atlantic Recording and the other licensees or sublicensees of Crosby and Croucier argue that even if Lamothe and Jones have stated a section 43(a) claim, they cannot be held liable because they are licensees. We disagree. Some of the licensees may have been involved in affixing an incomplete designation of authorship. . . . The express language of section 43(a) also imposes liability upon those who "with knowledge of the falsity of such designation of origin . . . cause or procure the same to be transported or used in commerce.". . .

* * *

## IV

## Conclusion

Because we conclude that summary judgment was inappropriate, we reverse the decision of the district court and remand the case with instructions to reinstate Lamothe's and Jones's federal causes of action. . . .

Reversed and Remanded.

---

A later decision by the Ninth Circuit, *Cleary v. News Corp.*, 30 F.3d 1255 (9th Cir. 1994), illustrates the limits on the "reverse passing off" theory. News Corp. owns the book publishing companies Harper Collins and Scott Foresman, which publish and distribute *Robert's Rules of Order*. General Henry Martyn Robert first wrote this work in 1876, and his family has retained copyright and artistic control ever since. The Rules have regularly been revised in new editions, which have always listed as authors the General and other family members involved in the new versions.

In the 1960s, Dr. James Cleary was brought in to help the General's daughter-in-law, Sarah Corbin Robert, create the 1970 edition. Cleary, who did a large part of the work, was listed on the title page as having assisted the daughter-in-law, along with her son Henry Robert III and William J. Evans. Cleary received royalties in the amount of .75% of book sales. For the 1980 edition, Cleary was only peripherally involved but he received the same credit and payment. (Sarah Corbin Robert, who died in 1972, was still listed as author.) For the 1990 edition in which Cleary played no role, he was still paid royalties but his name was left off the title page and his contributions were simply acknowledged in an introduction.

When Cleary sued the publisher for having been denied credit for a work that still contained most of his major changes from the 1970 version, the Ninth Circuit stated that the relevant standard for "reverse passing off" claims under the Lanham Act was not whether the later work was "substantially similar" to the plaintiff's original work (as under the Copyright Act), but rather whether there had been "bodily appropriation" of the original. Since in this case there had been significant, not just slight, modifications of Cleary's work, leaving his name off the title page was not likely to cause the kind of consumer confusion that the Lanham Act is designed to prevent. The Act is not designed to protect authors from denial of credit to which they feel morally entitled. This decision is quite significant in limiting the potential scope of Lanham Act claims in the movie and music worlds, given the host of revisions that are made in development of both an original work and its derivatives.

---

In a variation on the artistic credit theme, the film production firm Virgin Vision won a $3.3 million damage award against the Samuel Goldwyn Company in a dispute about who should get production credits for the 1989 hit movie, Steven Soderbergh's *Sex, Lies, and Videotape*. Virgin Vision put up half the production costs in return for distribution rights in foreign countries (where the movie grossed $37 million, versus the $25 million in domestic distribution controlled by Miramax). Virgin had hired Goldwyn to act as its sales agent for this (and other) films;

following a dispute between the two, Goldwyn altered the opening credits to have them read "Samuel Goldwyn [rather than Virgin Vision] presents. . . ." The court found that this violation of both the Lanham Act and the contract had cost Virgin the cachet the company would have gained in foreign movie markets as the studio behind this artistic and financial success story.

Reinforcing the value afforded to artistic credit, a California court ruled in *Tamarind Lithography Workshop, Inc. v. Sanders*, 143 Cal.App.3d 571, 193 Cal. Rptr. 409 (1983), that over and above a jury award of $25,000 for denial of credit, the screenwriter was entitled to an affirmative order adding credit to him on the film, in order to avoid future irreparable harm from the continued omission of his name and role.

### *QUESTIONS FOR DISCUSSION*

1. *Dodd v. Fort Smith Special School District No. 100*, 666 F. Supp. 1278 (W.D. Ark. 1987), involved a Lanham Act claim brought by Trolene Dodd, a former journalism and speech teacher in Fort Smith, Arkansas. Dodd had presented to the school principal, Mulloy, her idea for a book about the younger life of William Orlando Darby, a historic figure from their town. Mulloy told Dodd that she could pursue the project, but she would have to find her own funding. Dodd and her class sold advertising space in the book and worked on the project outside of class. They gathered and compiled the background information, created and edited the manuscript, and titled it *Portrait of a Hero: William Orlando Darby*.

That summer, after Dodd had resigned from the school for personal reasons, the manuscript went to the printers. At that point, Mulloy, the principal, and Jackie Farrar, another teacher, asked to look at the forthcoming book. They "expressed dissatisfaction" with the placement of the advertisements in it and offered to solicit donations for a much larger publication run. Dodd agreed "on the condition that she be allowed a final proof reading prior to printing." Dodd was never again shown the book, which was published (with a number of substantive alterations) under the title *William Orlando Darby: A Man to Remember*, as "prepared and edited by Ms. Jackie Marie Farrar." Dodd was told that her original manuscript had been destroyed. The only mention of Dodd and her students appeared in the preface, which stated that they "began the project of compiling a booklet on Bill Darby."

Is this a violation of the Lanham Act? Should injunctive relief be granted, and if so, on what terms? Is it relevant that Dodd, Farrar, and Mulloy were all employees of the Fort Smith School District? Should the Copyright Act's "work for hire" doctrine govern under the Lanham Act as well?

2. The story behind *Follett v. Arbor House Publishing Co.*, 497 F. Supp. 304 (S.D.N.Y. 1980), began in 1976 with a notorious robbery in France,

involving a gang that tunneled under the streets of Nice into a bank vault, from which they took 60 million francs ($8 million). After the thieves had been caught and were being tried, their leader jumped out the courthouse window and escaped. Shortly afterwards, three French journalists collaborated on a book, *Cing Milliards au Bout de l'Egout*, published in 1977 under their joint pseudonym, Rene Louis Maurice. Fontana Paperbacks purchased the British rights to the book, and hired (for 850 pounds) a then little-known editor, Ken Follett, to work on a "refashioned typescript" for English-language readers.

For purposes of those revisions, Follett went to France to talk to the writers and to see the bank and court sites in Nice. He revised the story line to eliminate flashbacks and to leave a chronological account of what had happened, while adding a prologue, an epilogue, and further details gathered from his investigation. Follett also enhanced the quality of writing and character depiction throughout the book. Though he had been hired as an editor, Follett insisted on authorship credit. Ultimately, the book was published in Britain, under the title *The Heist of the Century,* "by Rene Louis Maurice with Ken Follett." At that time, no publisher was interested in bringing an edition to the American market.

After Follett's own books, *Eye of the Needle* and *Triple*, became best-setters, Arbor House secured the U.S. publication rights for *The Heist of the Century,* which it planned to publish that under the title *The Gentleman of 16 July*, with the following attribution on the book jacket:

THE GENTLEMAN OF 16 JULY

by the author of TRIPLE and EYE OF THE NEEDLE—KEN FOLLETT

with Rene Louis Maurice

In addition, only Follett's name appeared on the spine portion of the book jacket. Having learned of Arbor House's plans, Follett sued to block this authorship attribution.

Does Follett have any rights under the Lanham Act to avoid this brand of authorship credit for *The Gentleman of 16 July*, and if so, on what theory? Would Follett have been able to secure his original credit if he had been hired as editor by an American, not a British, publisher?

3. *King v. Innovation Books*, 976 F.2d 824 (2d Cir. 1992), involved an objection by novelist Stephen King to the naming and marketing of a movie as *Stephen King's The Lawnmower Man*. King had assigned the movie and television rights in his 1970 short story, *The Lawnmower Man*, to Great Fantastic Picture Corp., giving Great Fantastic the "exclusive right to deal with the [story] as [it] may think fit" in exchange for a share of the profits of any such film or television show "incorporating or based upon" his story. In 1990, Great Fantastic transferred its rights to Allied, which produced the movie at issue. The movie incorporated the bulk of King's short story but added a number of additional features to the considerably longer film storyline. When King found out about the movie project in 1991, he asked his

agent to tell the producer not to give any credit to King for the movie. When King screened the film and saw that he was given both "possessory" and "based upon" credit, King wrote to his agent:

> I think *The Lawnmower Man* is really an extraordinary piece of work, at least visually, and the core of my story, such as it is, is in the movie. I think it is going to be very successful and I want to get out of the way. I want you to make clear to [the] trolls at New Line Pictures that I am unhappy with them, but I am shelving (at least for the time being) any ideas of taking out ads in the trades or trying to obtain an injunction to stop New Line from advertising or exploiting the picture. I would like to talk to you late this week or early next about doing some brief interviews which will make my lack of involvement clear, but for the time being, I am just going to step back and shut up.

Shortly thereafter, though, King filed suit.

What is the appropriate result under the Lanham Act? What do you suppose is the industry's distinction between a "possessory" and a "based upon" credit, and should that make any difference in the outcome? Suppose that King (or Follett and Dodd in the preceding cases) had signed a contract that explicitly authorized what was done in these cases. Should such an agreement by the author alter the result under the Lanham Act?

4. An unusual variation on this artistic credit theme produced a suit in the Southern District of New York. In 1991, Natalie Cole released an album whose Grammy-award winning piece "Unforgettable" helped the album sell over five million copies. The song blended together lyrics by Natalie Cole and by her late father, Nat King Cole, who had first made this song a hit in the 1950s. The song itself had been composed by Irving Gordon, whose consent was secured and credits given. Though the band-leader, Nelson Riddle, had done the original arrangements for "Unforgettable," credit for the 1991 duet version was given solely to Johnny Mandel. Riddle's widow, Naomi, sued the Elektra Records division of Time Warner for violation of the credit rights of her deceased husband. The suit was settled with Elektra agreeing to give Riddle credit as "arranger," and Mandel just as "adaptor," of "Unforgettable" in all future products and promotions.

---

Ghostwriting is a common arrangement in the book publishing industry. In 1984, then-Chrysler head Lee Iaccoca received over $10 million in royalties for his autobiography, but the person who actually wrote the book, anonymously, was William Novak, for a one-time payment of $40,000. Novak was able to translate the huge success of *Iaccoca* into a series of autobiographies for which he received not only more money but also credit, e.g., for works involving Nancy Reagan, Oliver North, and O.J. Simpson. The current celebrity book market includes not just autobiographies, but also novels billed as authored by a celebrity, e.g., Ivana Trump's *For Love Alone*.

The whole point of this publishing exercise is to tap popular interest in the celebrity by securing publicity that ordinary authors do not receive. Indeed, ghostwriters often brief the celebrity before a book tour, including writing a synopsis of the book the person has supposedly authored. In return for these efforts, the ghostwriter may receive one of a variety of possible credits. Notable writers like Novak get billing as full co-author. Those with experience and a reputation but not that level of negotiating leverage usually have the book jacket put the celebrity name first, followed by *with* or *as told to* the actual author (whose name is in smaller print). Unknown writers, especially of celebrity novels, ordinarily get no more than "special thanks and acknowledgment" in the book's preface.

A more recent incident indicates that ghostwriting is not confined to books: it happens in the movie world as well. One of the most highly-regarded foreign language movies ever released in the United States was the Italian-made *Il Postino* (*The Postman*). *Il Postino* won 1995 Academy Award nominations for Best Picture, Best Actor, and Best Director. The director billing in American theaters was for Michael Radford, who also won the Oscar nomination in that category. However, listed as co-director with Radford on the original version released in Italy in 1994 was Massimo Troisi, who starred in *The Postman* and was the movie's Oscar nominee for best actor. As was later made public, Troisi played absolutely no role in direction of the film. Indeed, Troisi's serious heart condition put major constraints even on how much acting he could do and, tragically, killed him hours after filming was completed. The sole reason for listing Troisi as co-director was that he was a major figure in the Italian film world, thereby helping secure the necessary financing and distribution arrangements to get *Il Postino* made in the first place. Like Novak with his celebrity book, Radford explicitly agreed to have Troisi credited as director.

In the American film industry, there would now be some obstacle to such an arrangement because of the Directors Guild, whose agreement with the studios has a procedure for allocating credits if challenges are lodged. There is no such labor agreement in book publishing, where writers are independent contractors, not employees. If the wording of the book contract is ambiguous, the ghostwriter may seek at least partial credit. (This reportedly happened in the case of the 1988 novel *Mirror, Mirror*, published under the name Betsy Von Furstenberg, until the real author, Virginia Gardner, filed suit.) Once that has happened, though, the publisher's lawyers will revise the standard book contract to clarify its language, and unknown authors usually have no choice but to accept a contract which makes it crystal-clear that they are to get *no* authorship credit.

The as-yet unresolved question is whether such a ghostwriting clause is enforceable. Can the real author of a book, through private contract, waive the artistic credit right conferred on artists by statute? Is the purpose of the Lanham Act to protect the interests of book authors or book buyers? Even though the stated policy of trademark law is to avoid consumer confusion, courts have ruled that consumers themselves cannot file suit under the Lanham Act against misleading product labels. *See Serbin v. Ziebart Int'l Corp.*, 11 F.3d 1163 (3d Cir. 1993). The courts apparently believe that other possible plaintiffs, such as competitors, are sufficient for this purpose. So far, though, no suit has been filed by competing publishers against the widespread failure of books to credit ghostwriters. Why might that be so? Should courts strike down contract waivers as contrary to public policy, or should they enforce them against authors who helped mislead readers about who actually wrote the books?

## B. MORAL RIGHTS AND CREATOR CONTROL[a]

Authors naturally want the right to claim (or disclaim) credit for their efforts when the works appear before the public. Even more important to many entertainment artists is the right to determine the content of the work in question and to prevent any subsequent alterations that might materially affect its quality. This has now become a major issue not just in Hollywood, but also on Capitol Hill, where legislation on this topic has been hotly debated. One particular focus of debate had been colorization of black & white films, though other film alteration techniques have also figured in the controversy.

The more recent debates were preceded by a conflict in the 1950s about what would happen to theatrical films when they were shown on television. Television broadcasts require regular breaks for commercials; they often need shortening to fit the broadcast schedule, including the time allotted for advertising; they occasionally need to have scenes and language deleted to fit within network and FCC standards of decency. The sharp difference in "aspect ratio" (width to height) between the typical television and movie screen (1.33:1 on television versus the standard 1.85:1 in theaters, with 2.35:1 for widescreen panorama) has led to use of "panning and scanning" the original film for its telecast version.

---

[a] *Compare* Edward J. Damich, *The Right of Personality: A Common Law Basis for the Protection of the Moral Rights of Authors*, 23 Ga. L. Rev. 1 (1988); Rudolph Carmenaty, *Terry Gilliam's Brazil: A Film Director's Quest For Artistic Integrity in a Moral Rights Vacuum*, 14 Colum.-VLA J. Law & Arts 93 (1989); *with* Lawrence Adam Beyer, *Intentionalism, Art, & the Suppression of Innovation: Film Colorization & the Philosophy of Moral Rights*, 82 Nw. L. Rev. 1011 (1988); *see also* Neil Netanal, *Alienability Restrictions & the Enhancement of Author Autonomy in the United States & Continental Copyright Law*, 12 Cardozo Arts & Enter. L. Rev. 1 (1994); Thomas F. Cotter, *Pragmatism, Economics, & the* Droit Moral, 76 N.C. L. Rev. 1 (1997); Henry Hansmann & Marina Santilli, *Authors' & Artists' Moral Rights: A Comparative Legal & Economic Analysis*, 26 J. Legal Stud. 95 (1997); Amy M. Adler, *Against Moral Rights*, 97 Cal. L. Rev. 263 (2009).

The result for the Oscar-winning movie *Ben Hur* is that most of the contenders in its famous chariot race were not visible to television viewers. In order to fit a movie into the standard schedule of network television, an electronic process called "lexiconning" is sometimes used to increase the speed of a movie like *Avalon,* which director Barry Levinson initially envisaged and shot in a more languid style.

The most visible and controversial alteration technique was the process of film colorization. The principal exponent of this practice had been Ted Turner, whose Turner Entertainment Company (now part of Time Warner) owns a vast stock of old films (particularly from the MGM film library) that his Turner Broadcasting cable network regularly broadcast, including *Casablanca, Arsenic and Old Lace, The Philadelphia Story,* and *The Maltese Falcon.* As illustrated at Christmas every year, the 1947 classic *Miracle on 34th Street* received significantly higher Nielsen ratings and advertising grosses when it was colorized. This process involves editorial selection of a color scheme for every single frame of the movie and computerized overlay of this new palette onto a copy of the original black and white version. This technology has made colorization a technically and economically feasible procedure for any old film—indeed, even for newer films like *Schindler's List*—whose market potential seems to warrant it. Techniques of digital imaging make possible not simply deleting material from the original, but also adding new characters, scenes, dialogue, and music to enhance the film's market potential. It should also be noted that the Turner Classic Movies (TCM) cable channel played a vital role in preserving older movies that were beginning to disintegrate.

One film that Turner's enterprise colorized was *The Asphalt Jungle,* which director John Huston had made for MGM back in 1948. In protest of this action, Angelica Huston filed suit on behalf of her deceased father. The suit was filed not in the United States, but in France, where it secured a favorable ruling from France's highest civil court, the Cour de Cassation. The court concluded that film colorization violated the *droit moral* (moral right) of Huston, the creator of *The Asphalt Jungle.* The colorized version of the movie could not be shown in France without Huston's consent; since neither he nor his family had given their consent, the court ordered Turner to pay more than $100,000 in damages for a 1988 telecast in France.

As we have seen, the major thrust of U.S. intellectual property law is, in the words of the Constitution, to "promote the Progress of Science and the useful Arts, by securing for limited Times to Authors and Inventors the exclusive Right to their respective Writings and Discoveries." In France, and now in much of the industrialized world, over and above this economic function, the law also tries to protect what are judged to be the inalienable, natural rights of artists in works that are seen as expressions and extensions of their creative personalities. Indeed, the international *Berne Convention For the Protection of Literary and Artistic Works* provides:

> Independently of the author's economic rights, and even after the transfer of the said rights, the author shall have the right to claim authorship of the work and to object to any distortion, mutilation or other modification of, or other derogatory action in relation to, the said work, which would be prejudicial to his honor or reputation.

For decades, the United States resisted becoming a party to this treaty, partly because of its moral rights feature. Because of the value of the Berne Convention in helping fight piracy in an increasingly international entertainment industry, President Ronald Reagan signed the treaty in the late 1980s. At the insistence of the motion picture industry, though, the *Berne Convention Implementation Act of 1988* did not adopt as part of U.S. law the previously-quoted language. Instead, this Act asserted that the *droit moral* principle was already adequately protected by existing federal, state, or common law rights of the artist to claim authorship in, or to object to prejudicial alteration of, the work in question. As you read the cases in this section, consider whether this was a fair characterization of U.S. law.

Although Congress had asserted that the moral rights of American artists enjoyed sufficient protection, it soon recognized one exception to that general stance: the case of visual artists, such as painters and sculptors, for whom it passed the *Visual Artists Rights Act of 1990*. Later in this section, we shall analyze the contents of that legislation. In addition, we will examine the variety of bills that have been introduced (in one case, even briefly enacted) to deal specifically with motion pictures.

Before doing so, however, we shall begin with an historical overview of the treatment that alteration of artistic works has received under existing doctrine: contract, unfair competition, and trademark law. One of the early cases was *Vargas v. Esquire, Inc.*, 164 F.2d 522 (7th Cir. 1947), in which the court held that an artist who gave up rights in his art work by contract with the publisher of Esquire magazine could not enjoin the publisher's use of the pictures after the contract was terminated, even though the publisher did not credit the artist. The artist sought to establish an implied agreement to publish the pictures only under his name, but the court held that such a concept applied only when the artist reserved those rights. The artist also claimed a violation of his "moral rights," but the court concluded that this concept was not recognized in American law:

> Plaintiff advances another theory which needs little discussion. It is predicated upon the contention that there is a distinction between the economic rights of an author capable of assignment and what are called "moral rights" of the author, said to be those necessary for the protection of his honor and integrity. These so-called "moral rights," so we are informed, are recognized by the civil law of certain foreign countries. In support of this phase of his argument, plaintiff relies upon a work by Stephen P. Ladas entitled "The International Protection of Literary and Artistic Property" It appears, however, that the author's discussion relied upon by plaintiff relates to the law of foreign countries. . . .
>
> What plaintiff in reality seeks is a change in the law of this country to conform to that of certain other countries. We need not stop to inquire whether such a change, if desirable, is a matter for the legislative or judicial branch of the government; in any event, we are not disposed to make any new law in this respect.

*Id.* at 526. A similar verdict was rendered in *Shostakovich v. Twentieth Century-Fox Film Corp.*, 196 Misc. 67, 80 N.Y.S.2d 575 (1948), aff'd, 275 A.D. 692, 87 N.Y.S.2d 430 (1949), involving a suit by the Russian composer Dmitry Shostakovitch about an MGM movie, *The Iron Curtain*, which used and credited his uncopyrighted music as background to an anti-Soviet story in the early days of the Cold War. (The French courts did block exhibition of the movie in that country for violation of the composer's moral rights.)

The following case, especially the concurring opinion, offers several additional observations about the doctrinal viability of the moral rights concept.

## GRANZ V. HARRIS

United States Court of Appeals, Second Circuit, 1952.
198 F.2d 585.

SWAN, CHIEF JUDGE.

[Norman Granz was a well-known promoter and producer of jazz concerts under the designation "Jazz at the Philharmonic." He had one of his concerts recorded—in particular, two pieces titled "How High the Moon" and "Lady Be Good"—on twelve-inch masters that played at 78 revolutions per minute (RPM). Granz licensed Herbert Harris to manufacture and sell these recordings, with the credit line "Presented by Norman Granz." The defendant then produced ten-inch, 78 RPM records that omitted eight minutes of the original sound—not just audience reactions (e.g., whistles, cheers, and screams), but also some of the music, including saxophone, piano, and trumpet solos. Granz sued to block the release of these recordings.]

* * *

We are therefore faced with the question whether the manufacture and sale by the defendant of the abbreviated ten-inch records violated any right of the plaintiff. Disregarding for the moment the terms of the contract, we think that the purchaser of the master discs could lawfully use them to produce the abbreviated record and could lawfully sell the same provided he did not describe it as a recording of music presented by the plaintiff. If he did so describe it, he would commit the tort of unfair competition. But the contract required the defendant to use the legend "Presented by Norman Granz," that is, to attribute to him the musical content of the records offered for sale. This contractual duty carries by implication, without the necessity of an express prohibition, the duty not to sell records which make the required legend a false representation. In our opinion, therefore, sale of the ten-inch abbreviated records was a breach of the contract. . . . Hence we think the plaintiff was entitled to an injunction against having the abbreviated ten-inch records attributed to him unless he waived his right. . . . [for which determination the court found further proceedings were necessary].

FRANK, CIRCUIT JUDGE, (concurring).

1. I agree, of course, that, whether by way of contract or tort, plaintiff . . . is entitled to prevention of the publication, as his, of a garbled version of his uncopyrighted product. This is not novel doctrine: Byron obtained an injunction from an English court restraining the publication of a book purporting to contain his poems only, but which included some not of his authorship. American courts, too, have enforced such a right. Those courts have also enjoined the use by another of the characteristics of an author of repute in such manner as to deceive buyers into erroneously believing that they were buying a work of that author. Those courts, moreover, have granted injunctive relief in these circumstances: An artist sells one of his works to the defendant who substantially changes it and then represents the altered matter to the public as that artist's product. Whether the work is copyrighted or not, the established rule is that, even if the contract with the artist expressly authorizes reasonable modifications (e.g., where a novel or stage play is sold for adaptation as a movie), it is an actionable wrong to hold out the artist as author of a version which substantially departs from the original. Under the authorities, the defendant's conduct here, as my colleagues say, may also be considered a kind of "unfair competition" or "passing off." The irreparable harm, justifying an injunction, becomes apparent when one thinks what would be the result if the collected

speeches of Stalin were published under the name of Senator Robert Taft, or the poems of Ella Wheeler Wilcox as those of T. S. Eliot.

2. If, on the remand, the evidence should favor the plaintiff, I think we should grant him further relief, i.e., an injunction against publication by the defendant of any truncated version of his work, even if it does not bear plaintiff's name. I would rest the grant of that relief on an interpretation of the contract.

Plaintiff, in asking for such relief, relied in part not on the contract but on the doctrine of artists' "moral right," a compendious label of a "bundle of rights" enforced in many "civil law" countries.[7] Able legal thinkers, pointing out that American courts have already recognized a considerable number of the rights in that "bundle," have urged that our courts use the "moral right" symbol. Those thinkers note that the label "right of privacy" served to bring to the attention of our courts a common center of perspectives previously separated in the decisions, and that the use of that label induced further novel and valuable judicial perspectives.

To this suggestion there are these objections: (a) "Moral right" seems to indicate to some persons something not legal, something meta-legal. (b) The "moral right" doctrine, as applied in some countries, includes very extensive rights which courts in some American jurisdictions are not yet prepared to acknowledge; as a result, the phrase "moral right" seems to have frightened some of those courts to such an extent that they have unduly narrowed artists' rights. (c) Finally, it is not always an unmitigated boon to devise and employ such a common name. As we have said elsewhere: "A new name, a novel label expressive of a new generalization, can have immense consequences. Emerson said, 'Generalization is always a new influx of the divinity into the mind. Hence the thrill that attends it.' Confronted with disturbing variety, we often feel a tension from which a generalization, an abstraction, relieves us. It serves as a de-problemizer, aiding us to pass from an unstable, problematical, situation to a more stable one. It satisfies a craving, meets what Emerson called 'the insatiable demand of harmony in man,' a demand which translates itself into the so-called 'law' of 'the least effort.' But the solution of a problem through the invention of a new generalization is no final solution: The new generalization breeds new problems. Stressing a newly perceived likeness between many particular happenings which had theretofore seemed unlike, it may blind us to continuing unlikenesses. Hypnotized by a label which emphasizes identities, we may be led to ignore differences . . . For, with its stress on uniformity, an abstraction or generalization tends to become totalitarian in its attitude towards uniqueness."

---

[7] *See* Roeder, *Doctrine of Moral Right*, 53 Harv. L. Rev. 554, 565–72 (1940); Ladas, *International Protection of Literary & Artistic Property*, Vol. I, 575 *et seq.*; Katz, *Doctrine of Moral Right*, 24 So. Cal. L. Rev. 375 (1951).

Without rejecting the doctrine of "moral right," I think that, in the light of the foregoing, we should not rest decision on that doctrine where, as here, it is not necessary to do so.

---

In *Chesler v. Avon Book Division, Hearst Publications*, 76 Misc.2d 1048, 352 N.Y.S.2d 552 (N.Y.Sup.Ct. 1973), Phyllis Chesler, a feminist psychologist, author and lecturer, sued to enjoin Avon from publishing a paperback edition of her book *Women and Madness*, which was published in hard cover by Doubleday, Inc. in 1972. By contract, Doubleday had given Avon the right to publish a paperback edition of the book. Chesler also sought to enjoin the use of her name and likeness in connection with the paperback version. Chesler's claim was that "relevant portions of the text, as well as various illustrations and footnotes, are either omitted, altered or rearranged in the Avon publication" and that "these changes are so extensive as to amount to 'mutilation' of her work, making it so confusing and incomprehensible as to modify substantially and dilute seriously its meaning and intent." The publication of this version, Chesler claimed, would "subject her to negative criticism, damage her reputation and invalidate her book for use as an authoritative work by potential students and other serious readers."

The court agreed with Chesler in part, stating that, "[a]lthough the authorities are sparse, it is clear that even after a transfer or assignment of an author's work, the author has a property right that it shall not be used for a purpose not intended or in a manner which does not fairly represent the creation of the author." Thus, the court held,

> appropriate action must be taken by Avon in connection with the distribution of further paperbacks and advertising to indicate to the public and prospective purchasers of the paperback version that changes have been made involving chapter introductions, omission of illustrations and footnotes and column juxtaposition. To this extent, there has been a condensation or abridgement. Although the right to do so exists under the contracts, there is an obligation to make known to readers that the right has been exercised. This is simply telling the truth.

*Id.* at 557. The court refused, however, to issue an injunction against publication of the book, on contractual grounds. Chesler's agreement with Doubleday had not given her any rights as to reprints or condensed versions of her book. Instead, Doubleday was authorized to "publish the work . . . in the style and manner 'which Doubleday' shall deem best suited to its sale." Moreover, Chesler "granted Doubleday the right to sell to other publishers reprint rights 'in full length, condensed or abridged versions,' the right to sell her work or parts of it for publication in serial form or in excerpts in newspapers or periodicals, and the right to license an adaptation of all or part of the work or extracts for use in periodicals or books." Thus, the court found that Chesler had not reserved the right to object to changes in later editions. Chesler had also claimed a violation of her moral rights, but the court noted that it was not necessary to rest its decision on such a concept "which has not been afforded full recognition in this State."

---

As noted earlier, it was the showing of films on television, which became a major economic resource for studios in the 1950s, that made movie directors staunch advocates of moral rights in works they had originally created. *Preminger v. Columbia Pictures*, 49 Misc.2d 363, 267 N.Y.S.2d 594 (N.Y.Sup.Ct. 1966), convinced the Directors Guild that they needed specific federal legislation. Otto Preminger was one of the top film directors (and producers) of the 1950s, including *Anatomy of a Murder*, with Columbia Pictures as the distributor enjoying the "exclusive and irrevocable right" to show it on television. Preminger's contract with Columbia gave him "the right to make the final cutting and editing of the picture." However, unlike a couple of his earlier contracts with United Artists, this clause was not explicitly applied to any changes that "may be required for the distribution of the picture on television." Thus, the issue posed by this case was whether Preminger's standard "final cutting" right applied just to the original, or also to the commercial breaks in and deletions from the movie that were required to meet the distinctive time and content standards of television.

In *Preminger*, the court found that the relevant standard was "the common practice and custom at the time the parties herein signed their contract." For television purposes this was found to be reflected in Columbia's contract with the network, which permitted film breaks and cuts "to conform to time segment requirements/ or to orders of any duly authorized public censorship authority," but barred any changes that could "adversely affect the artistic or pictorial quality of the picture as materially interfere with its continuity." And if there was any viewer resentment about commercial breaks or edits in the film when shown on television, the court said these would be directed at the broadcaster, not at the film director or producer.

> The television industry serves a great public need and its services have ofttimes, and perhaps at some financial sacrifice, been offered in the public interest. Despite such apparent unselfish public service, it should not be overlooked that the industry, like every other business, has as its primary objective the accumulation of profits. Sponsorship of programs, by advertisers, provides a station with its only source of revenue and though it ofttimes interrupts its programs with what some

> viewers feel to be an inordinate amount of advertising, since its primary purpose is to advertise the products of its sponsors, such interruptions in the absence of governmental or industry regulation can only be controlled by contractual arrangement.
>
> It is of no import that some viewers may not approve of the advertising practices prevalent in the industry—that is, the number and types of commercials. However, the parties to this distribution agreement signed it knowing of the existence of such practices. The plaintiffs, as well as any independent producer or director, could have obviated this problem by specifically prohibiting such cuts or interruptions by contract. This, of course, might have had an adverse effect on the extent of television distribution—an eventuality which most producers would not welcome. Accordingly, in the absence of any contractual provision to the contrary, they must be deemed to have contemplated that what was permissible, under the existing practice, would continue in effect.

*Id.* at 602–03.

### *QUESTIONS FOR DISCUSSION*

1. George Stevens, a major film director of the 1940s and 1950s, made movies such as *Shane*, *Something To Live For*, and *A Place in the Sun*, for Liberty Films, which he co-owned with his fellow directors, Frank Capra and William Wyler. Eventually Stevens and his partners sold Liberty and its film library to Paramount Pictures, which in turn licensed NBC to broadcast many of its movies, including the ones just mentioned. The Paramount-NBC contract allowed the network to make deletions and interruptions in its film broadcasts to accommodate commercials and program time constraints. Stevens sued both Paramount and NBC, alleging that this action violated the terms of his employment contract with Liberty which gave him "sole control of the production and distribution of the photoplay [movie] consistent with the total budget . . . [including] the right to edit, cut and score said photoplay." Stevens had also agreed with Liberty that the movies he directed would "conform to the requirements and standards set by the terms of any contract for the distribution of such photoplay which [Liberty] may enter into. . . ." A California court decided that the appropriate way to accommodate these two clauses was to read Stevens' "sole control" over editing and cutting his films as relating just to their initial production; once the movie was completed, Stevens had given the studio the prerogative to make whatever post-production alterations were necessary to satisfy its distribution agreements (including on television). How would you compare the contract language and judicial reading here with those in *Preminger*? *See Stevens v. NBC*, 270 Cal. App.2d 886, 76 Cal. Rptr. 106 (1969).

2. What would have been your verdict as arbitrator of the following case? In 1985, a contract dispute arose between Warren Beatty and Paramount about the proposed broadcast of the movie *Reds*. Beatty had won the 1982 Academy Award for Best Director for the 195-minute long *Reds*, a project for which he was given the contractual "final cut." Paramount sold the television rights to ABC, which wanted to cut out six minutes of the film to accommodate commercials on what still would have been a very lengthy prime-time showing. Beatty refused to consent to any such cuts, blocked the ABC broadcast, and cost Paramount the sizable revenues from that broadcast license. Was this a breach of his implied covenant of "good faith and fair dealing" with Paramount?

3. At the end of the *Preminger* opinion, the court did say that if the 161-minute *Anatomy of a Murder* was cut to the standard 100 minutes of non-commercial time in a two-hour movie showing, it would be possible for Preminger to file a suit targeted specifically at what "could well be described as mutilation." What does the *Preminger* ruling tell us about the adequacy of the current legal regime in protecting the concerns of film creators, especially in light of the host of innovations that have taken place in the movie industry since then? What would be the legal basis upon which the court could grant any such relief?

4. Suppose that the owners of a film did not cut the film, but rather remade the work to make it more appealing to a contemporary audience (e.g., making use of *Forrest Gump's* digital imaging). For example, imagine that D.W. Griffith's *Birth of a Nation* was reshaped into a critique, rather than a defense, of the Jim Crow policies of the Reconstruction Era South. Could Griffith's heirs be able to block such "mutilation" of this notorious work that helped give birth to the American film industry?

---

Consider whether the next case, one that illustrates some of the differences between both the entertainment and the legal worlds in United States and Europe, offers any promise for such a mutilation claim.

## GILLIAM V. AMERICAN BROADCASTING COMPANIES, INC.

United States Court of Appeals, Second Circuit, 1976.
538 F.2d 14.

LUMBARD, CIRCUIT JUDGE.

[The Monty Python group of writers and performers became famous in their native Great Britain in the early 1970s through their comedy series *Monty Python's Flying Circus*, telecast on the British Broadcasting Corporation (BBC) network. The Python group wrote and supplied scripts to BBC pursuant to a contract that spelled out procedures for any alterations in the script as the 30-minute programs were being taped.

BBC had the right to license retransmission of the program in other countries.

In 1973, BBC granted such a license to Time-Life Films for broadcasts of *Flying Circus* in the United States, including the right to edit programs for purposes of commercial time, censorship, and time segment requirements (none of these factors being mentioned in the Monty Python-BBC script contract). Time-Life Films in turn sublicensed its *Flying Circus* rights to ABC, which proceeded to broadcast a 90-minute Monty Python special comprising three half-hour shows. This broadcast removed a total of 24 minutes from the original shows, principally for commercial time, but partly to delete material the network considered offensive. When Monty Python sued to block any further such broadcasts, the trial judge refused to grant an interim injunction. While Judge Lasker agreed with Python that the "integrity of their work" had been impaired, causing the programs "to lose their iconoclastic verve," he was unsure who owned copyright in the programs. On appeal, the Second Circuit agreed with the Python group that "even if BBC owned the copyright in the recorded program, its use of that work would be limited by the license granted to BBC by Monty Python for use of the underlying script."]

* * *

If the proprietor of the derivative work is licensed by the proprietor of the copyright in the underlying work to vend or distribute the derivative work to third parties, those parties will, of course, suffer no liability for their use of the underlying work consistent with the license to the proprietor of the derivative work. Obviously, it was just this type of arrangement that was contemplated in this instance. The scriptwriters' agreement between Monty Python and BBC specifically permitted the latter to license the transmission of the recordings made by BBC to distributors such as Time-Life for broadcast in overseas territories.

One who obtains permission to use a copyrighted script in the production of a derivative work, however, may not exceed the specific purpose for which permission was granted. Most of the decisions that have reached this conclusion have dealt with the improper extension of the underlying work into media or time, i.e., duration of the license, not covered by the grant of permission to the derivative work proprietor. *See Bartsch v. Metro-Goldwyn Mayer, Inc.*, 391 F.2d 150 (2d Cir. 1968); *G. Ricordi & Co. v. Paramount Pictures, Inc.*, 189 F.2d 469 (2d Cir. 1951). Appellants herein do not claim that the broadcast by ABC violated media or time restrictions contained in the license of the script to BBC. Rather, they claim that revisions in the script, and ultimately in the program, could be made only after consultation with Monty Python, and that ABC's broadcast of a program edited after recording and without consultation with Monty Python exceeded the scope of any license that BBC was entitled to grant.

The rationale for finding infringement when a licensee exceeds time or media restrictions on his license—the need to allow the proprietor of the underlying copyright to control the method in which his work is presented to the public—applies equally to the situation in which a licensee makes an unauthorized use of the underlying work by publishing it in a truncated version. Whether intended to allow greater economic exploitation of the work, as in the media and time cases, or to ensure that the copyright proprietor retains a veto power over revisions desired for the derivative work, the ability of the copyright holder to control his work remains paramount in our copyright law. We find, therefore, that unauthorized editing of the underlying work, if proven, would constitute an infringement of the copyright in that work similar to any other use of a work that exceeded the license granted by the proprietor of the copyright.

If the broadcast of an edited version of the Monty Python program infringed the group's copyright in the script, ABC may obtain no solace from the fact that editing was permitted in the agreements between BBC and Time-Life or Time-Life and ABC. BBC was not entitled to make unilateral changes in the script and was not specifically empowered to alter the recordings once made. . . . Since a grantor may not convey greater rights than it owns, BBC's permission to allow Time-Life, and hence ABC, to edit, appears to have been a nullity.

* * *

[In response,] ABC contends that appellants must have expected that deletions would be made in the recordings to conform them for use on commercial television in the United States. ABC argues that licensing in the United States implicitly grants a license to insert commercials in a program and to remove offensive or obscene material prior to broadcast. . . .

The proof adduced up to this point, however, provides no basis for finding any implied consent to edit. Prior to the ABC broadcasts, Monty Python programs had been broadcast on a regular basis by both commercial and public television stations in this country without interruption or deletion. . . . These facts, combined with the persistent requests for assurances by the group and its representatives that the programs would be shown intact, belie the argument that the group knew or should have known that deletions and commercial interruptions were inevitable.

Several of the deletions made for ABC, such as elimination of the words "hell" and "damn," seem inexplicable given today's standard television fare. If, however, ABC honestly determined that the programs were obscene in substantial part, it could have decided not to broadcast the specials at all, or it could have attempted to reconcile its differences with appellants. . . .

[T]he copyright law should be used to recognize the important role of the artist in our society and the need to encourage production and dissemination of artistic works by providing adequate legal protection for one who submits his work to the public. *See Mazer v. Stein*, 347 U.S. 201 (1954). We therefore conclude that there is a substantial likelihood that, after a full trial, appellants will succeed in proving infringement of their copyright by ABC's broadcast of edited versions of Monty Python programs. In reaching this conclusion, however, we need not accept appellants' assertion that any editing whatsoever would constitute infringement. Courts have recognized that licensees are entitled to some small degree of latitude in arranging the licensed work for presentation to the public in a manner consistent with the licensee's style or standards. *See Stratchborneo v. Arc Music Corp.*, 357 F. Supp. 1393, 1405 (S.D.N.Y. 1973); *Preminger v. Columbia Pictures Corp.*, 267 N.Y.S.2d 594 (Sup.Ct.), aff'd 219 N.E.2d 431 (N.Y. 1966). That privilege, however, does not extend to the degree of editing that occurred here especially in light of contractual provisions that limited the right to edit Monty Python material.

II

It also seems likely that appellants will succeed on the theory that, regardless of the right ABC had to broadcast an edited program, the cuts made constituted an actionable mutilation of Monty Python's work. This cause of action, which seeks redress for deformation of an artist's work, finds its roots in the continental concept of *droit moral*, or moral right, which may generally be summarized as including the right of the artist to have his work attributed to him in the form in which he created it.

American copyright law, as presently written, does not recognize moral rights or provide a cause of action for their violation, since the law seeks to vindicate the economic, rather than the personal, rights of authors. Nevertheless, the economic incentive for artistic and intellectual creation that serves as the foundation for American copyright law, cannot be reconciled with the inability of artists to obtain relief for mutilation or misrepresentation of their work to the public on which the artists are financially dependent. Thus courts have long granted relief for misrepresentation of an artist's work by relying on theories outside the statutory law of copyright, such as contract law, *Granz v. Harris*, 198 F.2d 585 (2d Cir. 1952) (substantial cutting of original work constitutes misrepresentation), or the tort of unfair competition, *Prouty v. National Broadcasting Co.*, 26 F. Supp. 265 (D.C.Mass.1939). *See* Strauss, "The Moral Right of the Author," 128–38, in *Studies on Copyright* (1963).

Although such decisions are clothed in terms of proprietary right in one's creation, they also properly vindicate the author's personal right to prevent the presentation of his work to the public in a distorted form. Roeder, *The Doctrine of Moral Right*, 53 Harv. L. Rev. 554, 568 (1940).

Here, the appellants claim that the editing done for ABC mutilated the original work and that consequently the broadcast of those programs as the creation of Monty Python violated the Lanham Act. This statute, the federal counterpart to state unfair competition laws, has been invoked to prevent misrepresentations that may injure plaintiff's business or personal reputation, even where no registered trademark is concerned. It is sufficient to violate the Act that a representation of a product, although technically true, creates a false impression of the product's origin. *See Rich v. RCA Corp.*, 390 F. Supp. 530 (S.D.N.Y. 1975) (recent picture of plaintiff on cover of album containing songs recorded in distant past held to be a false representation that the songs were new); *Geisel v. Poynter Products, Inc.*, 283 F. Supp. 261, 267 (S.D.N.Y. 1968).

These cases cannot be distinguished from the situation in which a television network broadcasts a program properly designated as having been written and performed by a group, but which has been edited, without the writer's consent, into a form that departs substantially from the original work. "To deform his work is to present him to the public as the creator of a work not his own, and thus makes him subject to criticism for work he has not done." Roeder, *supra*, at 569. In such a case, it is the writer or performer, rather than the network, who suffers the consequences of the mutilation, for the public will have only the final product by which to evaluate the work. Thus, an allegation that a defendant has presented to the public a "garbled," distorted version of plaintiff's work seeks to redress the very rights sought to be protected by the Lanham Act, and should be recognized as stating a cause of action under that statute. *See Autry v. Republic Productions, Inc.*, 213 F.2d 667 (9th Cir. 1954); *Jaeger v. American Int'l Pictures, Inc.*, 330 F. Supp. 274 (S.D.N.Y. 1971), which suggests the violation of such a right if mutilation could be proven.

During the hearing on the preliminary injunction, Judge Lasker viewed the edited version of the Monty Python program broadcast on December 26 and the original, unedited version. After hearing argument of this appeal, this panel also viewed and compared the two versions. We find that the truncated version at times omitted the climax of the skits to which appellants' rare brand of humor was leading and at other times deleted essential elements in the schematic development of a story line.[12]

[12] A single example will illustrate the extent of distortion engendered by the editing. In one skit, an upper class English family is engaged in a discussion of the tonal quality of certain words as "woody" or "tinny." The father soon begins to suggest certain words with sexual connotations as either "woody" or "tinny," whereupon the mother fetches a bucket of water and pours it over his head. The skit continues from this point. The ABC edit eliminates this middle

We therefore agree with Judge Lasker's conclusion that the edited version broadcast by ABC impaired the integrity of appellants' work and represented to the public as the product of appellants what was actually a mere caricature of their talents. We believe that a valid cause of action for such distortion exists and that therefore a preliminary injunction may issue to prevent repetition of the broadcast prior to final determination of the issues.[13]

* * *

Injunction directed.

GURFEIN, CIRCUIT JUDGE, concurring:

I concur in my brother Lumbard's scholarly opinion, but I wish to comment on the application of Section 43(a) of the Lanham Act.

I believe that this is the first case in which a federal appellate court has held that there may be a violation of Section 43(a) of the Lanham Act with respect to a common-law copyright. The Lanham Act is a trademark statute, not a copyright statute. Nevertheless, we must recognize that the language of Section 43(a) is broad. It speaks of the affixation or use of false designations of origin or false descriptions or representations, but proscribes such use "in connection with any goods or services." It is easy enough to incorporate trade names as well as trademarks into Section 43(a) and the statute specifically applies to common law trademarks, as well as registered trademarks.

In the present case, we are holding that the deletion of portions of the recorded tape constitutes a breach of contract, as well as an infringement of a common-law copyright of the original work. There is literally no need to discuss whether plaintiffs also have a claim for relief under the Lanham Act or for unfair competition under New York law. I agree with Judge Lumbard, however, that it may be an exercise of judicial economy to express our view on the Lanham Act claim, and I do not dissent therefrom. I simply wish to leave it open for the District Court to fashion the remedy.

---

sequence so that the father is comfortably dressed at one moment and, in the next moment, is shown in a soaked condition without any explanation for the change in his appearance.

[13] Judge Gurfein's concurring opinion suggests that since the gravamen of a complaint under the Lanham Act is that the original of goods had been falsely described, a legend disclaiming Monty Python's approval of the edited version would preclude violation of that Act. We are doubtful that a few words could erase the indelible impression that is made by a television broadcast, especially since the viewer has no means of comparing the truncated version with the complete work in order to determine for himself the talents of plaintiffs. Furthermore, a disclaimer such as the one originally suggested by Judge Lasker in the exigencies of an impending broadcast last December, would go unnoticed by viewers who tuned into the broadcast a few minutes after it began.

We therefore conclude that Judge Gurfein's proposal that the district court could find some form of disclaimer would be sufficient might not provide appropriate relief.

The Copyright Act provides no recognition of the so-called *droit moral*, or moral rights of authors. Nor are such rights recognized in the field of copyright law in the United States. *See* 1 *Nimmer on Copyright*, § 110.2 (1975 ed.). If a distortion or truncation in connection with a use constitutes an infringement of copyright, there is no need for an additional cause of action beyond copyright infringement. An obligation to mention the name of the author carries the implied duty, however, as a matter of contract, not to make such changes in the work as would render the credit line a false attribution of authorship, *Granz v. Harris*, 198 F.2d 585 (2d Cir. 1952).

So far as the Lanham Act is concerned, it is not a substitute for *droit moral* which authors in Europe enjoy. If the licensee may, by contract, distort the recorded work, the Lanham Act does not come into play. If the licensee has no such right by contract, there will be a violation in breach of contract. The Lanham Act can hardly apply literally when the credit line correctly states the work to be that of the plaintiffs which, indeed it is, so far as it goes. The vice complained of is that the truncated version is not what the plaintiffs wrote. But the Lanham Act does not deal with artistic integrity. It only goes to misdescription of origin and the like. *See Societe Comptoir De L'Industrie Cotonniere Etablissements Boussac v. Alexander's Dept. Stores, Inc.*, 299 F.2d 33, 36 (2d Cir. 1962).

The misdescription of origin can be dealt with, as Judge Lasker did below, by devising an appropriate legend to indicate that the plaintiffs had not approved the editing of the ABC version. With such a legend, there is no conceivable violation of the Lanham Act. If plaintiffs complain that their artistic integrity is still compromised by the distorted version, their claim does not lie under the Lanham Act, which does not protect the copyrighted work itself but protects only against the misdescription or mislabelling.

So long as it is made clear that the ABC version is not approved by the Monty Python group, there is no misdescription of origin. So far as the content of the broadcast itself is concerned, that is not within the proscription of the Lanham Act when there is no misdescription of the authorship.

I add this brief explanation because I do not believe that the Lanham Act claim necessarily requires the drastic remedy of permanent injunction. That form of ultimate relief must be found in some other fountainhead of equity jurisprudence.

## *QUESTIONS FOR DISCUSSION*

1. Having read the key rulings on the topic, you are now in a position to appraise the assertion by Congress in the *Berne Convention Implementation Act of 1988* that existing U.S. law is sufficient to protect the

moral rights of American creative artists. To what extent does moral rights protection in the United States rest on private agreements rather than public guarantees? Are contracts a sufficient instrument through which to secure moral rights?

2. A Canadian approach defines and establishes moral rights as a matter of public law, but then permits the author to waive the rights (in whole or in part) by express private agreement. Would you expect the Canadian model to generate significantly different outcomes than the American in the entertainment industry? Or does leaving any room for contract mean that the level of creative control turns on whether the author is a Margaret Mitchell or a film director like Steven Spielberg, rather than a relative unknown?

---

European countries have also faced some major controversies in this area. One was a case taken to the courts in Denmark, in connection with the movie *Three Days of the Condor*. This 1975 hit, starring Robert Redford and Faye Dunaway, was directed by Sidney Pollack. *Three Days* was filmed in the widescreen panavision format then common for movies shown in theaters. However, the producer used its contractual right to edit the Pollack work for "ancillary release" to license the state-owned Danish Broadcasting Corporation (DBC) to show the movie on television in that country in a heavily "panned and scanned" version that focused on what the key actors were doing in the center of the screen.

The Association of Danish Film Directors (ADFD) filed suit, claiming a violation of Pollack's moral rights. In its 1997 decision, the Danish high court agreed that a moral rights violation had occurred; many of *Three Days'* sequences were "mutilated, since the details of importance for the understanding of characters are left out, and discrepancies between dialogue and image have occurred . . . ," and this "vast pruning of the image was not technically necessary in order to make a showing on television possible" (although use of the original theater format would have left unoccupied the top and bottom portions of the home TV screens). However, the court found no violation of Pollack's rights, because his "work for hire" was being performed under a general standard contract provision that waived claims to preserve the original artistic integrity of his work. The outcome in Denmark, then, was essentially the same as that rendered in America regarding Otto Preminger's *Anatomy of a Murder,* rather than in France about the colorization of John Huston's 1948 "work for hire" for MGM, *The Asphalt Jungle.*

The French courts facing a much more fundamental challenge to moral rights in 2001 when the descendants of Victor Hugo sued to block publication of a new book, *Cosette, or Time of Illusion*, because of what it was doing to their ancestor's masterpiece, *Les Misérables.* One key feature of this *Cosette* sequel was that *Les Misérables'* villain, Javert, who had drowned himself at the end of the novel, was revived by French author Francois Cérésa as a religious hero. By contrast with the lawsuit being filed at the same time by the heirs of Margaret Mitchell, author of *Gone With The Wind*, copyright in *Les Misérables* had long expired, and it inspired a host of books, movies, and television series (most recently, Disney's *The Hunchback of Notre Dame*). The descendants sought to block this redoing of *Les Misérables* in what they considered a scandalous manner, but the French trial court dismissed their complaint. One key reason was what Hugo had written back in the 1870s, a decade before he played a major role in instigating the 1886 Berne Convention. Apparently he did not believe that "descendants by blood were also the heirs of the spirit" and thus because they "didn't write the book, they didn't have the author's rights." But in 2004 the Cour d'appel de Paris reversed that trial decision, ruling that the heirs did retain Hugo's moral rights, though it chose to impose a symbolic fine of *one* Euro for this violation of the *Les Miserables* intellectual property rights. With which legal view do you agree?

By contrast, in 1968, Twentieth Century Fox hired a new movie critic, Roger Ebert, to spend six weeks co-authoring his first screenplay along with director Russ Meyer. This was to be the sequel to a 1967 movie that Ebert had been very critical of, the *Valley of the Dolls*, and the title they gave to their 1970 movie was *Beyond the Valley of the Dolls*. When the author of the original *Valley* book, Jacqueline Susann, read what she considered to be a rather bizarre ending of this new story, she told the studio that in order to avoid a lawsuit it had to add this disclaimer right after the new movie's name.

> The film you are about to see is not a sequel to "Valley of the Dolls." It is wholly original and bears no relationship to real persons, living or dead. It does, like "Valley of the Dolls" deal with the oft-times nightmare world of show business, but in a different time and context.

---

Visual arts was the one setting in which Congress accepted that there was a need for new legislation, and thence it enacted the *Visual Artists Rights Act of 1990* (VARA).[b] This law, which applies to limited-edition paintings, sculptures, engravings, prints, artistic photographs, and the like, gives the artist guaranteed rights of *attribution* (to insist that his or her name be attached to the work) and of *integrity* (to prevent mutilation, distortion, or other modification of the work that would be

[b] *See* Amy L. Landers, *The Current State of Moral Rights Protection For Visual Artists in the United States*, 15 Hast. Comm/Ent L. J. 165 (1992).

prejudicial to the author's honor and reputation).[c] One incident specifically mentioned in the Congressional Report on this legislation was the case of two Australian entrepreneurs who bought a Picasso print, "Trois Femmes," cut it into hundreds of pieces, and sold the latter as original pieces of the Picasso. VARA would likely have blocked the 1980 destruction by the building owner of a 1600-pound metal sculpture, "Shinto," by Isamu Noguchi, that had hung in the lobby of the Bank of Tokyo Trust Company in New York's financial district. Under the current law, the building owner has to give the sculptor at least ninety days notice so the latter has an opportunity to remove the piece without it being destroyed.

Such notice is, of course, useless with respect to works such as giant murals, which may cover the inside or outside walls of a building. Absent written agreement with the artist, such works "of recognized stature" cannot be destroyed or mutilated at least until the artist has died. The first case to test the force and impact of VARA was *Carter v. Helmsley-Spear*, 71 F.3d 77 (2d Cir. 1995). *Carter* involved a massive sculpture that made up a large part of the lobby floor, walls, and ceiling in a former Macy's warehouse on Long Island that is now owned by Helmsley-Spear. Though the original commission contract had given the sculptors the copyright in their artistic creation, the Second Circuit said they had actually been working as employees rather than as independent contractors of the lessee (as illustrated by the way they were paid for the work assigned to them). As a legal "work for hire," the sculpture was not protected by VARA from being dismantled and removed from the warehouse by its new owner.

---

[c] One feature of European moral rights doctrine that was not included in VARA was the *droit de suite*. As evidenced by its name, this right originated in European law, was optional in the Berne Convention, and has now been adopted in more than 35 nations. The *droit de suite* gives visual artists a right to a resale royalty on their works—a continuing remunerative relationship between artists and their creative work. What that means is that even if a future Van Gogh or Cezanne sells an early painting for a "song," once the quality of his work and reputation rises, the painter will get some of the benefit of the soaring resale value of the work in the marketplace. The initial draft of VARA, as introduced by Senator Kennedy and Representative Markey, proposed a 7 percent royalty on the appreciated resale value of visual art, but that provision hit the congressional cutting room floor, pending further study. Unlike the rights discussed in the text, the *droit de suite* principally serves economic objectives, rather than moral values. The basic argument in its favor is that current copyright law generates little return to visual artists, especially in comparison to their creative peers who go into authoring books, music, or movies and enjoy the financial benefits of multiple copies, derivative works, and performance rights. The argument offered against *droit de suite* is that the prospect of such a mandatory royalty will reduce the prices initially paid for all young artists' work, while the benefits will be reaped only by the few older artists whose artistic reputation soars, along with the prices they get for their later works. What are your reactions to these competing arguments (and also to the possibility that the original purchasers of earlier works might themselves benefit from the *droit de suite* incentive for visual artists to enhance and preserve their reputation and thence the value of all their works)? For detailed appraisals, see Marilyn J. Kretsinger, Droit de Suite: *The Artist's Right to a Resale Royalty*, 15 Hast. Comm/Ent L.J. 967 (1993); Edward J. Damich, *Moral Rights Protection & Resale Royalties for Visual Art in the United States: Development & Current Status*, 12 Cardozo Arts & Ent. L.J. 387 (1994).

---

The original version of VARA included motion pictures in its conception of a visual art. To secure passage in the face of strong opposition from the film studios' Motion Pictures Association of America (MPAA), VARA was revised to exclude films from its scope. That has left the motion picture issues to be addressed on their own, with the original bone of contention being colorization.[d]

Movie directors (long represented by the Directors Guild) and screenwriters (represented by the Writers Guild), along with their supporters, have formed an Artistic Rights Foundation, whose charter members include Steven Spielberg, George Lucas, Angelica Huston, Harrison Ford, Sally Field, Kevin Costner, Michael Ovitz, and other powers-that-be in the film industry. These groups have had four different types of legislation introduced (indeed, one briefly enacted) in Congress:

(a) The *Film Integrity Act of 1987*, sponsored by Richard Gephardt, proposed to give the principal director and principal screenwriter the right to approve or block "material alteration" of the original work once it had been publicly released. This would have embodied essentially the same right of "integrity" as is now found in the *Visual Artists Rights Act* enacted in 1990.

(b) The *National Film Preservation Act of 1988*, enacted for a three-year trial period, established a National Film Registry and National Film Preservation Board under the auspices of the Library of Congress. The Board, whose members were drawn from the industry, would each year select 25 works (at least ten years old) that were judged "culturally, historically, and aesthetically significant" to the nation's heritage. (Among the works initially picked were *Citizen Kane*, *On the Waterfront*, *Gone With The Wind*, *The Maltese Falcon*, *Singing In the Rain*, *Star Wars*, *Snow White and the Seven Dwarfs*, and *The Birth of a Nation*.) Works that were so selected and registered could be shown even if materially altered, but only with a disclaimer that this had been done, and (if true) that it was done without participation and

---

[d] *See* Craig A. Wagner, *Motion Picture Colorization, Authenticity, & the Elusive Moral Right*, 64 N.Y.U. L. Rev. 628 (1989); David A Honicky, *Film Labelling as a Cure For Colorization (& Other Alterations): A Band-Aid For a Hatchet Job*, 12 Cardozo Arts & Ent. L. Rev. 409 (1994); Karen L. Gulick, *Creative Control, Attribution & the Need for Disclosure: A Study of Incentives in the Motion Picture Industry*, 27 Conn. L. Rev. 53 (1994); Matthew J. McDonough, *Moral Rights & the Movies: The Threat & Challenge of the Digital Domain,* 31 Suff. U.L. Rev. 455 (1997); Timothy E. Nielander, *Reflections on a Gossamer Thread in the World Wide Web: Claims for Protection of the "Droit Moral" Right of Integrity in Digitally Distributed Works of Authorship,* 20 Hast. Comm/Ent L.J. 59 (1997).

consent of the principal director, screenwriter, and other creators of the original.

(c) The *Film Disclosure Act of 1992* was introduced when the original three-year life and funding of the *National Film Preservation Act* ran out in 1991, and the latter program could only be re-enacted once this requirement of a "material alteration" disclaimer was removed. This new "film disclosure" proposal would amend section 43 of the Lanham Act and require labeling of any film that had been materially altered, and indicate whether the director, screenwriter, or cinematographer had consented to the changes. The prescribed wording would be along the following lines:

> This film is not the version originally released. It has been colorized by computer [or panned and scanned, lexiconned, and the like]. The director [or screenwriter or cinematographer] objects because this alteration removes visual information and/or changes the photographic image [or composition] of the actors and the film. Such labeling would be required on both the film package and at the outset of the film itself. Labeling would not however, be required for commercial breaks on television, editing to comply with FCC or other legal requirements, foreign distribution, and the like. While the film creators could grant and express their approval of any such changes, they could not be paid any money for that endorsement.

(d) The *Theatrical Motion Picture Authorship Act of 1995*, proposed by Congressman John Bryant as a variation on Gephardt's earlier *Film Integrity Act*, would add a new section 106B to the Copyright Act immediately after VARA. The economic rights of authorship in "theatrical motion pictures" would remain with the studios that commission these "works for hire." However, moral rights of *attribution* and *integrity* would be conferred on the principal director, screenwriter, and cinematographer who created the film. The integrity right would give the artistic author the right "to prevent any intentional distortion, mutilation, or other modification of a film which would be prejudicial to [the artist's] reputation." Transfer of these moral rights would be prohibited and waiver allowed only after the first performance of the film, and not in return for consideration. The moral rights of the artistic authors of a movie would, however, expire at the same time as would the copyright of the studio author, when the product was thus going into the public domain.

### *QUESTIONS FOR DISCUSSION*

1. Is there a significant motion picture problem that needs to be addressed from the point of view of producers or consumers? What gaps, if any, are there in the existing law?

2. As we have seen, VARA's protection currently extends only to creative works such as paintings and sculptures, not motion pictures. Clearly, film is just as "visual" an art as painting. What are the distinctive characteristics in the creation of these two kinds of works? Do the differences justify including painting and excluding film-making from VARA?

3. If you believe there is a significant legal problem, which approach do you favor among the ones embodied in the proposed Film Integrity Act, the National Film Preservation Act, the Film Disclosure Act, or the Theatrical Motion Picture Authorship Act?

4. What position do you think free speech advocates would take as to any of these legislative proposals?

5. In 1993, Jack Valenti announced that MPAA members had agreed to a voluntary industry labeling practice. In the case of colorization, the label would read, "This is a colorized version of the original black-and-white film." In the case of television broadcasts, the label would read: "This film has been modified from its original version. It has been formatted to fit your TV, and edited for content and to run in the time allotted." The label would run at the beginning of any showing and be attached to videocassettes. The reaction of Senator Orrin Hatch was that this initiative removed any need for federal legislation. Rep. Barney Frank, sponsor of a House bill, claimed that this step was entirely inadequate. Do you believe such labels are a sufficient response to the problem? Do you think there even is a problem?

---

In the new millennium, another moral rights issue involves "virtual advertising." By the 1990s, product placement had become a very common and profitable feature of the movie and television industries. Typically these products have been included in the original production, with the pioneering James Bond, for example, driving a BMW rather than a Mercedes after the one auto manufacturer had outbid the other for that advertising device. Digital technology now makes it feasible to alter the cars being driven, clothes being worn, or drinks being served, let alone adding a new label to such products.

Why would such action be taken after the director had completed the movie that has been released on the screen? One reason is that the occasional low-budget movie that did not get a product deal turns out to be a big hit, such as *The Full Monty* or *The Blair Witch Project*. Another reason is that there are some fundamental differences in the younger consumer audiences watching a movie in a theater and on home video (older on average), or on different continents. Thus, it may be economically rational to have different products and brand names on prints being sent to these various viewer settings. Any such studio action, though, is likely to raise the same kind of moral rights debates that we have been reading about. Is it the director-author or the producer-filmmaker of the work who should have the final judgment on this score (subject of course to individual contracts)? And does "virtual advertising" in a future James Bond movie have a greater or lesser impact on the author (and audience) than what John Huston's family felt about the colorization of *The Asphalt Jungle*?

Another moral rights issue was generated by the hit *Titanic*. When this 1997 film appeared on video, the Sunrise Family Video store in American Fork, Utah announced that (for $5) it would cut two "steamy" scenes from the home video requested by a customer. The scenes in questions were those in which Kate Winslet is posing nude for a sketch by Leonardo DiCaprio, and the other when the couple make love in the ship's cargo hold. Paramount's lawyers asked Sunrise not to do this "cutting and pasting," which directors like John Frankenheimer said was the equivalent of adding a bathing suit to a nude Picasso painting. Sunrise's response was that it was just satisfying the needs of its family customers (reportedly more than 1,000) to have a G-rated version of *Titanic* to watch and enjoy with their children.

When Paramount chose not to sue Sunrise, the latter expanded its service, and a market niche emerged. Following the lead of a prominent English physician, Dr. Thomas Bowdler, who had authored his own Family Shakespeare in 1818 so parents would feel more comfortable reading to their children such works as *Hamlet*, *Macbeth*, and *Romeo and Juliet*, the Pleasant Grove, Utah members of the Church of Jesus Christ of Latter-Day Saints formed their cooperative CleanFlicks arm. They not only edited out the nudity in Steven Spielberg's *Titanic*, but also the use of 28 "f" words in Steven Soderbergh's *Erin Brockovich*, and most of the opening four minutes of Spielberg's *Saving Private Ryan* with all the blood being shed at the beginning of that World War II Normandy battle. In just two years, CleanFlicks had expanded to 70 sites in 18 states, offering 450 edited films to its members. And these not only include deleting the beheading and similar battle scenes from Mel Gibson's performance in the R-rated *The Patriot*, but also taking some scenes out of the PG-13 hit, *Harry Potter and the Sorcerer's Stone* to earn it a G rating.

Similar services were developed by Trilogy Studios (MovieMask software to be downloaded into home computers), Family Shield (a set-top box), and ClearPlay (software embedded into DVD players). Each of these devices enables the purchaser or renter of the video to block out either the sound of offensive words or the images of unduly violent or sexual scenes that they consider offensive. The combination of these systems has now revealed there to be a sizeable market for more family-friendly versions of even such Oscar-winning hits as *Schindler's List* and *Million Dollar Baby*.

The basic rationale of these services is that they are doing no more for their customers than airlines had long done when they were showed a movie on a plane. However, unlike United or Delta Airlines, a CleanFlicks or a Trilogy never secured a contractual license from the studios, let alone the director, to do such editing. Among the many legal issues posed by CleanFlicks is whether these editorial deletions were just a fair use of the video owned by the consumer (as in *Bourne v. Walt Disney*, 68 F.3d 621 (2d Cir. 1995)), or the creation of a derivative work, which the court in *Mirage Editions v. Albuquerque A.R.T.*, 856 F.2d 1341 (9th Cir. 1988), made clear cannot be done.

The position of the MPAA has always been that film colorization and other movie changes should be addressed inside the industry, not in public legislation. One possible route is contractual negotiation between the studio and the individual director selected for a project; we saw earlier that Warren Beatty secured such a "final cut" for *Reds*, and James Cameron, after his successes with *Terminator* and *Alien*, got the same right for *True Lies*. Needless to say, Steven Spielberg, who has made many of the top-grossing movies in history, has long been able to negotiate whatever moral rights he wants in his films: *Schindler's List* will never be colorized without Spielberg's consent.

Another instrument that directors, writers, and cinematographers have long had available to them is collective bargaining with studios through their labor union, e.g., the Directors Guild of America (DGA). We shall take an in-depth look in Chapter 11 at labor law and collective bargaining in the entertainment industry. It is important to note here, though, that beginning in 1964 the Guild has secured some significant artistic rights for its members, whose role, as spelled out in the DGA-MPAA agreement, is to "contribute to all of the creative elements of a film and to participate in molding and integrating them into one cohesive dramatic and aesthetic whole." Article 7 of the agreement provides that "in no case will any creative decision be made regarding the preparation, production, and post-production of a motion picture without the consultation of the Director." To implement these principles, the director is given the exclusive right of "first cut" in a movie, with "no supervision or interference." While the producer retains the right of "final cut," the director is entitled to be present, to be consulted, to insist on a showing to the Directors Guild of the two versions, and to request the Guild to replace his name with a pseudonym on the producer's final version being released to the public if he is unhappy with the final cut.

The fact that the studios did not object to the new CleanFlicks process left the DGA and its 12,000 members feeling upset by what they saw happening to their movies without their participation or consent. Indeed, in 2002, the DGA released on its own website a memorandum about the concerns of Spielberg, Soderbergh, Martin Scorsese, Robert Altman, and other major members, and its likely upcoming lawsuit against CleanFlicks, Clear Play, and the others. Thus, in 2002, the CleanFlicks branch in Colorado City filed a suit there against Spielberg and the other directors mentioned in the DGA memorandum, seeking a declaratory judgment that they are not violating anybody's intellectual property rights with their edited videos (which were lawfully purchased). In response, the DGA filed its own suit in federal district court in Denver against CleanFlicks and other.

This technology and its inevitable lawsuits pose a host of complex legal policy questions. As a matter of copyright law, is this editing process the creation of a new derivative work that needs a license from its copyright owners, or just minor deletions that meet the "fair use" standards? One should note here that these groups have so far chosen not to edit such hits as *Austin Powers*, *The Blair Witch Project*, *Moulin Rouge*, and *Natural Born Killers* "because of the themes, overall message, and number of edits [needed] in the movie."

DGA asserted that this new process violated their members' publicity, trademark, and moral rights under the Berne Convention and the Visual Artists Rights Act (VARA). As DGA Executive Director Jay Roth put it, "this is very dangerous, what's happening here. This is not about an artist getting upset because someone dares to tamper with their masterpiece. This is fundamentally about artistic and creative rights and whether someone has the right to take an artists' work, change it, and then sell it." The response of CleanFlicks is that its efforts are not just legally but morally justifiable in providing parents paying the full consumer price for their videos to have it made safer for their children to be watching at home. How should courts have responded to the issues posed by this brand of entertaining technology?

In 2005 Congress enacted and President Bush signed a new *Family Movement Act* as part of a broader multi-part *Family Entertainment and Copyright Act*. This provides a degree of explicit legislative protection for the CleanFlicks process. In particular, players control its technology and its users are explicitly exempted from liability under either copyright or trademark law. However, Congress chose not to grant such a specific statutory exemption to the edited versions being provided and sold by digital technology businesses. Thus, these are being left up to the courts under general intellectual property law. Congress did add a provision that now makes it a federal crime, punishable by up to three years in prison for the first offense and up to six years for later ones, for using a camcorder or other video camera in the movie theater to record a film there.

## C. TRADEMARK INSTEAD OF COPYRIGHT

As we have seen in the previous sections, trademark law has offered performers some degree of protection for artistic credits and moral rights in the entertainment industry. Section 1127 of the Lanham Act defines trademark as "any word, name, symbol or device . . . used by a person . . . to identify and distinguish his or her goods . . . from those manufactured and sold by others and to indicate the source of the goods. . . ." Trademarks (and their equivalent, service marks) can be registered with the United States Patent & Trademark Office, in which case use by anyone else can be an infringement under section 32 of the Lanham Act. Even if the mark is not registered, an action can still be filed under section 43(a), which essentially codifies the common law doctrine against unfair competition.

From the point of view of entertainment firms as well as performers, trademark law can serve as a supplement to copyright in affording protection for features of a product (e.g., titles and character names) that cannot be copyrighted. One such lawsuit involved a notable entertainment figure, Harry Potter. In 1997, J.K. Rowling, a single mother living on welfare in Edinburgh, Scotland, published her first book, *Harry Potter and the Sorcerer's Stone*, which with its three successors had sold over 120 million copies five years later. In 2001, Time Warner released the first Harry Potter movie, which set box office records of $200 million in the first two weeks. In 1999, though, an author in Camp Hill, Pennsylvania, Susan Stouffer, had told Rowling and her publisher and movie studio that these works were infringing on the trademarks created by a rather different 25-page children's activity book she had published in 1984, *The Legend of Rah and the Muggles*. Stouffer had characters named Larry (rather than Harry) and Lilly (rather than Lily) Potter, and Rowling referred to ordinary humans as Muggles.

Rather than wait for Stouffer to sue after she had unsuccessfully sought compensation, Rowling's publisher and film producer filed suit in New York asking for a declaration that there had been no violation of any trademark or copyright. The court summarily dismissed this claim in *Scholastic v. Stouffer*, 221 F. Supp. 2d 425 (S.D.N.Y. 2002). The judge first synopsized the essence of the Harry Potter stories and then described the complex history of Stouffer's self-publishing her 25-page booklets with very few sales over the first 15 years. It was only in 2001 that an independent publisher, Thurman House, brought out updated versions of "The Legend of Rah and the Muggles" and "Larry Potter and His Best Friend Lilly," and Stouffer began to experience more substantial sales (though still less than 10,000 total) from the use of those trademarked names.

The court observed: "The similarities between Stouffer's books and the *Harry Potter* series are minimal and superficial, and when considered altogether they could not give rise to a likelihood of confusion." The following passage comparing Stouffer's Larry Potter and Rowling's Harry Potter graphically displays the reasons why.

> . . . Stouffer's "Larry Potter" appears in an 11-page booklet about a boy who is sad because he has to wear eyeglasses. "Larry" has brown or orange hair and glasses with non-circular lenses and speckled brown frames. In contrast, "Harry Potter" is a young orphan boy with dark brown or black hair, a scar in the shape of a lightning bolt on his forehead, and distinctive eyeglasses with black frames and circular lenses. After discovering that he has magical powers and enrolling at a school for young wizards, Harry has many adventures, which are described throughout the course of the four *Harry Potter* books, each of which is several hundred pages in length. Aside from the similar, though not identical, names of the main characters and the fact that both "Larry" and "Harry" are boys with glasses, Stouffer's booklet and plaintiffs' books, along with their accompanying illustrations, have almost nothing in common. Accordingly, no reasonable juror could find a likelihood of confusion between "Larry Potter" and "Harry Potter."

The judge found no fact issues that could justify a trial, let alone a verdict for Stouffer, and he awarded the defendants their attorney fees as well as a $50,000 monetary sanction against Stouffer for having "asserted claims and defenses without any reasonable basis in fact or law, and [having] attempted to support such claims and defenses with items and evidence that have been created or altered for purposes of this litigation." The Second Circuit affirmed, 81 Fed. App. 396 (2nd Cir. 2003).

Notwithstanding this decision, the major role played by trademark law in the entertainment world is as the legal underpinning for marketing features of such top-selling book and movie characters as Harry Potter and James Bond.[e] While Bond has long been a top-selling merchandising character (with BMW having to bid against Mercedes and other auto manufacturers to have Bond driving its car), Harry Potter secured a $150 million deal from Coca-Cola to place his name and image on its cans and bottles world-wide. These are dramatic illustrations of the

[e] *See* Janet Wasko, *Hollywood In the Information Age: Beyond the Silver Screen* (U. Texas Press 1995).

fact that, based on the popular appeal of movies like *Star Wars* and *The Lion King*, licensed merchandise generates around $20 billion a year in sales of products tied to fictional characters (and approximately the same for those tied to sports and its real athletes), with the licensing fees paid to the owners of the trademark name ranging from 8 to 10 percent of the retail price.

An additional Hollywood revenue stream comes from joint marketing campaigns. For example, in 1996, McDonald's secured a $2 billion, decade-long cross-promotional agreement with Disney, and Pepsi did the same thing with George Lucas and *Star Wars*. The principal economic benefit to movie studios from these tie-ins consists in the tens of millions of dollars spent by the fast food chains and other suppliers of goods and services to advertise and promote the films. It is understandable why the manufacturers of consumer products want to have that association with the characters, symbols, and themes with which their customers identify. However, the reason why the makers of such products agree to pay billions of dollars is that trademark law puts them at legal risk if they do not.

The essence of a trademark claim has long been very different from copyright's grant of an exclusive right in a work or publicity law's grant of an equivalent in an entertainer's personal identity. Walt Disney does not have a property right derived from trademark law that gives it the right to stop anyone from using the names and symbols of its characters. Disney can block that action only if the use is likely to cause confusion or deception of consumers in the sale of competing goods.

As explained in one of the leading scholarly treatments of this subject,[f] the basic aim of trademark law has been to protect consumers in their choice and use of goods. The technique for doing so is to encourage producers to develop brands and other identifiers for their products, such as Coca-Cola, that permit easy recognition of the product whose features consumers prefer. That kind of name recognition gives producers an incentive to preserve and enhance the attractive qualities of their products. It also gives imitators an incentive to use the name without necessarily matching the product quality. The role of trademark law is to bar any use of a name or symbol when the use may confuse consumers about the products they are seeking to purchase.

That distinctive objective serves not only to narrow but also to broaden the scope of protection of trademark relative to copyright. For example, in *Frederick Warne & Co. v. Book Sales, Inc.*, 481 F. Supp. 1191 (S.D.N.Y. 1979), the court concluded that even though the contents (the

---

[f] William M. Landes & Richard A. Posner, *Trademark Law: An Economic Perspective*, 30 J. Law & Econ. 265 (1987), and, by the same authors, *The Economics of Trademark Law*, 78 Trademark L. Rep. 267 (1988).

expression) of the century-old *Peter Rabbit* books had long since passed into the public domain, the cover illustrations might still be protected trademarks identified with the publisher and its goodwill and reputation.

> In the case of a copyright, an individual creates a unique design and, because the Constitutional fathers saw fit to encourage creativity, he can secure a copyright for his creation for a [limited period of time]. After the expiration of the copyright, his creation becomes part of the public domain. In the case of a trademark, however, the process is reversed. An individual selects a word or design that might otherwise be in the public domain to represent his business or product. If that word or design comes to symbolize his product or business in the public mind, the individual acquires a property right in the mark. The acquisition of such a right through use represents the passage of a word or design out of the public domain into the protective ambits of trademark law.

481 F. Supp. at 1196 (quoting *Boston Professional Hockey Association v. Dallas Cap & Emblem Manufacturing*, 510 F.2d 1004 (5th Cir. 1975)).

A circuit court decision, *The New Kids on the Block v. News America Publishing*, 971 F.2d 302 (9th Cir. 1992), explored whether trademark law might expand the scope of the celebrity publicity rights we encountered in Chapter 3. The New Kids on the Block, a hot music act of the late 1980s, had licensed their names for use on more than 500 products and services, including 900-numbers that fans could call to listen to the New Kids or to communicate with other fans. The Star Magazine and USA Today each decided independently to conduct their own polls about who was the most popular New Kid. Fans could call a 900 number, at 95 cents a minute, to cast their votes. The New Kids sued under trademark law to block that action, occasioning an analysis by Judge Kozinski of the rationale for federal trademark rights:

> Throughout the development of trademark law, the purpose of trademarks remained constant and limited: identification of the manufacturer or sponsor of a good or the provider of a service.[2] And the wrong protected against was traditionally equally limited: preventing producers from free-riding on their rivals' marks. Justice Story outlined the classic scenario a century and

---

[2] In economic terms, trademarks reduce consumer search costs by informing people that trademarked products come from the same source.

> The benefit of the brand name is analogous to that of designating individuals by last as well as first names, so that, instead of having to say "the Geoffrey who teaches constitutional law at the University of Chicago Law School—not the one who teaches corporations," you can say "Geoffrey Stone, not Geoffrey Miller."

Williams M. Landes & Richard A. Posner, *Trademark Law: An Economic Perspective*, 30 J.L & Econ. 265, 269 (1987).

a half ago when he described a case of "unmitigated and designed infringement of the rights of the plaintiffs, for the purpose of defrauding the public and taking from the plaintiffs the fair earnings of their skill, labor and enterprise." The core protection of the Lanham Act remains faithful to this conception. Indeed, this area of the law is generally referred to as "unfair competition"—unfair because, by using a rival's mark, the infringer capitalizes on the investment of time, money and resources of his competitor; unfair also because, by doing so, he obtains the consumer's hard-earned dollar through something akin to fraud.

A trademark is a limited property right in a particular word, phrase or symbol. And although English is a language rich in imagery, we need not belabor the point that some words, phrases or symbols better convey their intended meanings than others. Indeed, the primary cost of recognizing property rights in trademarks is the removal of words from (or perhaps non-entrance into) our language. Thus, the holder of a trademark will be denied protection if it is (or becomes) generic, i.e., if it does not relate exclusively to the trademark owner's product. This requirement allays fears that producers will deplete the stock of useful words by asserting exclusive rights in them. When a trademark comes to describe a class of goods rather than an individual product, the courts will hold as a matter of law that use of that mark does not imply sponsorship or endorsement of the product by the original holder.

A related problem arises when a trademark also describes a person, a place or an attribute of a product. If the trademark holder were allowed exclusive rights in such use, the language would be depleted in much the same way as if generic words were protectable. Thus trademark law recognizes a defense where the mark is used only "to describe the goods or services of [a] party, or their geographic origin. The 'fair-use' defense, in essence, forbids a trademark registrant to appropriate a descriptive term for his exclusive use and so prevent others from accurately describing a characteristic of their goods." . . .

With many well-known trademarks, such as Jell-O, Scotch tape and Kleenex, there are equally informative non-trademark words describing the products (gelatin, cellophane tape and facial tissue). But sometimes there is no descriptive substitute, and a problem closely related to genericity and descriptiveness is presented when many goods and services are effectively identifiable only by their trademarks. For example, one might refer to "the two-time world champions" or "the professional

> basketball team from Chicago," but it's far simpler (and more likely to be understood) to refer to the Chicago Bulls. In such cases, use of the trademark does not imply sponsorship or endorsement of the product because the mark is used only to describe the thing, rather than to identify its source.

*Id.* at 305–306.

The panel members then ruled on a fair use defense to federal trademark law:

* * *

> . . . [A] nominative use of a mark—where the only word reasonably available to describe a particular thing is pressed into service—lies outside the strictures of trademark law: because it does not implicate the source-identification function that is the purpose of trademark, it does not constitute unfair competition; such use is fair because it does not imply sponsorship or endorsement by the trademark holder.

* * *

> . . . [W]here the defendant uses a trademark to describe the plaintiff's product, rather than its own, we hold that a commercial user is entitled to a nominative fair use defense provided he meets the following three requirements: First, the product or service in question must be one not readily identifiable without use of the trademark; second, only so much of the mark or marks may be used as is reasonably necessary to identify the product or service; and third, the user must do nothing that would, in conjunction with the mark, suggest sponsorship or endorsement by the trademark holder.

*Id.* at 308. Applying that test, the court concluded that The New Kids' trademark rights had not been infringed, even though some fans would be spending their limited funds to call the defendants' 900 lines rather than The New Kids' own lines:

> While the New Kids have a limited property right in their name, that right does not entitle them to control their fans' use of their own money. Where, as here, the use does not imply sponsorship or endorsement, the fact that it is carried on for profit and in competition with the trademark holder's business is beside the point.

*Id.* at 309.

---

Whether asserted by celebrities or other owners of marketable names, trademark law can impose the same kinds of restraints on freedom of speech that we encountered earlier with both publicity and copyright law. A case that explicitly addressed this First Amendment question is *Rogers v. Grimaldi*, 875 F.2d 994 (2d Cir. 1989). Beginning in the 1930s, Ginger Rogers and Fred Astaire had become the most famous couple in show business history, "the paragons of style, elegance and grace." By the 1980s, Astaire was dead and Rogers no longer in Hollywood. Rogers had, however, licensed use of her name for various products, and was working on an autobiography she hoped might eventually be adapted for a movie.

In 1986, the Italian film-maker, Federico Fellini, created a movie entitled *Ginger and Fred*. This was a bittersweet story of two fictional Italian cabaret performers, Pippin and Amelia, who had been known as "Ginger and Fred" in their original career in the 1930s and 1940s, and were coming back for a television reunion in the 1970s. Rogers sued the distributor of *Ginger and Fred* for violation of her trademark rights by showing the movie in the United States under that title. To support the claim, Rogers offered a survey of approximately 200 likely moviegoers, of whom 30 said that upon being shown the title, they assumed that Ginger Rogers had been involved in the making of the film.

The court ruled that a balance had to be struck between the rights of trademark owners and the First Amendment rights of producers of films:

> Movies, plays, books, and songs are all indisputably works of artistic expression and deserve protection. Nonetheless, they are also sold in the commercial marketplace like other more utilitarian products, making the danger of consumer deception a legitimate concern that warrants some government regulation. *See Central Hudson Gas & Electric v. Public Service Commission*, 447 U.S. 557, 563 (1980) ("The government may ban forms of communication more likely to deceive the public than inform it . . ."). Poetic license is not without limits. The purchaser of a book, like the purchaser of a can of peas, has a right not to be misled as to the source of the product. Thus, it is well established that where the title of a movie or a book has acquired secondary meaning—that is, where the title is sufficiently well known that consumers associate it with a particular author's work—the holder of the rights to that title may prevent the use of the same or confusingly similar titles by other authors. Indeed, it would be ironic if, in the name of the First Amendment, courts did not recognize the right of authors to protect titles of their creative work against infringement by other authors.

> Though First Amendment concerns do not insulate titles of artistic works from all Lanham Act claims, such concerns must nonetheless inform our consideration of the scope of the Act as applied to claims involving such titles.[2] Titles, like the artistic works they identify, are of a hybrid nature, combining artistic expression and commercial promotion. The title of a movie may be both an integral element of the film-maker's expression as well as a significant means of marketing the film to the public. The artistic and commercial elements of titles are inextricably intertwined. Film-makers and authors frequently rely on word-play, ambiguity, irony, and allusion in titling their works. Furthermore, their interest in freedom of artistic expression is shared by their audience. The subtleties of a title can enrich a reader's or a viewer's understanding of a work. Consumers of artistic works thus have a dual interest: They have an interest in not being misled and they also have an interest in enjoying the results of the author's freedom of expression. For all these reasons, the expressive element of titles requires more protection than the labeling of ordinary commercial products.

*Id.* at 997–98. From that general premise, the test formulated by the court would make movie, book, or song titles a trademark violation only if they had no artistic relevance to the underlying work, or even when they had some relevance, if the titles were explicitly misleading as to the source or content of the work. (Illustrations offered of the latter included an exercise book that might be titled *Jane Fonda's Workout Book*, or a celebrity life story said to be "An Authorized Biography," when these assertions were untrue.) Here, though, Fellini had an artistic reason for use of the title *Ginger and Fred.* Fellini wanted to contrast the glamorous life on Hollywood screens in the 1930s and 1940s with the harsh life that many, including these cabaret performers, were experiencing in Italy at that time. In the eyes of the court, the fact that some consumers might be misled by the ambiguity in this title (or others by the movie title *Come Back to the Five and Dime, Jimmy Dean, Jimmy Dean*) could not justify restraining Fellini's artistic expression in the title, not just the content, of his work.

Our answers may well be shaped by learning about the most recent Supreme Court verdict in this area, *Dastar v. Twentieth Century Fox Film Corp.*, 539 U.S. 23 (2003). This decision was actually stimulated by something that a person had done back in 1948. Before embarking on his

---

[2] *See* Robert C. Denicola, *Trademarks as Speech: Constitutional Implications of the Emerging Rationales for the Protection of Trade Symbols*, 1982 Wis. L. Rev. 158 (1982); Harriette K. Dorsen, *Satiric Appropriation & the Law of Libel, Trademark, & Copyright: Remedies without Wrongs*, 65 B.U. L. Rev. 923, 949–52 (1985); Robert J. Shaughnessy, *Trademark Parody: A Fair Use & First Amendment Analysis*, 72 Va. L. Rev. 1079 (1986); Robert N. Kravitz, *Trademarks, Speech, & the Gay Olympics Case*, 69 B.U. L. Rev. 131 (1989).

new professional career, the greatest-ever American General, Dwight D. Eisenhower, at the beginning of 1948 spent about 16 hours a day for three months authoring his first memoir, *Crusade in Europe*, about his experience in beating Hitler in World War II. His contract with the publisher Doubleday gave the latter "all rights of every nature . . ." to the book that came out at the end of 1948. That same year Doubleday granted exclusive television rights to the book's story to Twentieth Century Fox which in 1949 brought out an extensive and popular television series of the same name.

However, while in 1975 Doubleday had exercised its copyright renewal rights, in 1977 Fox failed to do the same thing in what, as we have seen in Chapter 5, seems then to have been a relatively short basic copyright lifespan. That did not preclude Fox in 1988 securing from Doubleday the right to bring their *Crusade* series out on TV again, and then licensing the new home video rights to SFM Entertainment and New Line Home Video. However, a major lawsuit and this Supreme Court decision was produced by what began in 1995.

That was when Dastar, which until then had just been in the music disc field, decided to expand into what by then had become the very popular home video area. The product they chose as their first video, to celebrate the 50th anniversary of Eisenhower winning that war, they titled *Campaign in Europe*. But rather than creating a whole new product, instead they used around half of the Fox TV series, though with a new opening and closing, music, and chapter titles along with their own credits and no reference or credits at all to either the Fox TV series or the Doubleday book. And Dastar's home video price of $25 was far lower than what had been charged for the Fox *Crusade*.

So in 1998 Fox, SFM and New Line all sued Dastar under both copyright and trademark law. While the 9th Circuit in its ruling of 34 Fed. Appx. 312 (2002), said there was no longer a valid copyright claim, it found there to be one under Section 43(a) of the *Lanham Act* about trademark rights. This 9th Circuit panel said that "Dastar's bodily appropriation of Fox's original television series is sufficient to establish the reverse passing off" also prohibited by *Lanham*, and thus was warranting the trial judge's damage awards under Section 35 of *double* Dastar's profits in order to deter such trademark infringements as Dastar's "false designation of origin" through removing Fox's name from its home video and leaving just its own name on it.

However when this case reached the Supreme Court, a unanimous decision authored by Justice Scalia basically accepted the Dastar view that "bodily appropriation" without proof of "consumer confusion" was not sufficient to create trademark violation. Scalia said first . . .

> (t)hat claim would undoubtedly be sustained if Dastar had bought some of New Line's *Crusade* videotapes and merely repackaged them as its own. Dastar's alleged wrongdoing, however, is vastly different. It took a creative work in the public domain—the *Crusade* television series—copied it, made modifications (arguably minor), and produced its very own series of videotapes.

539 U.S. at 31. In the court's view "the problem with this argument according special treatment to communicative products is that it causes the *Lanham Act* to conflict with the law of copyright, which addresses that subject specifically." *Id.* at 33. In particular, even if it was true that Dastar was representing itself as the producer of this story, "allowing a cause of action under 43(a) for that representation would create a species of mutant copyright law that limits the public's federal right to copy and to use expired copyrights," *Id.* at 34.

After pointing out that Congress had itself adopted such an expansion of copyright law through its *Visual Artists Act* of 1990 which clearly was not applicable to this kind of TV series, Scalia then observed that none of these plaintiffs had . . .

> shot the film used in the Crusade television series. Rather that footage came from the United States Army, Navy, and Coast Guard, the British Ministry of Information and War Office, the National Film Board of Canada, and unidentified "Newsreel Pool Cameramen." If anyone has a claim to being the original creator of the material used in both the Crusade television series and the Campaigns videotapes, it would be those groups, rather than Fox. We do not think the Lanham Act requires this search for the source of the Nile and all its tributaries.

*Id.* at 35–36. So this court unanimously concluded that because trademark, unlike copyright (or patent), had a "perpetual" legal life span, reading the *Lanham Act* in that expansive way would generate a public policy conflict with the "limited time" constraint on intellectual property terms that we saw in Chapter 5 in *Eldred v. Ashcroft*, 537 U.S. 186 (2003).[g]

---

While the *New Kids on the Block* and *Ginger Rogers* decisions are intriguing illustrations of the underlying policy and proper scope of trademark law, they are of relatively little practical economic significance in the entertainment world. What is more important to a Universal Studios, for example, is to be able to block others from making and selling

[g] *See* Landau, *Copyrights, Moral Rights & the End of the Right of Attribution under US Trademark Law*, 19 Int. Rev. Law, Comp. & Tech. 37 (2005).

coffee mugs proclaiming "I Love E.T." *Universal City Studios, Inc. v. Kamar Industries, Inc.*, 217 U.S.P.Q. 1162 (S.D. Tex. 1982). Riding on such rulings are the billions of dollars in licensing fees and promotional expenditures by firms seeking to have their toys associated with the Ninja Turtles, or their burgers with Pocahontas.

Use of trademark law for that purpose poses a major analytical problem. Recall that the objective of trademark law is to encourage producers like Coca-Cola to develop distinctive names and symbols to identify their products by barring other producers from attaching similar marks and thereby misleading consumers seeking their favorite soft drink. Producers do not, however, receive a copyright-like monopoly in their name and symbol that blocks others from using it for non-confusing purposes. Pepsi, for example, can use the words "Coca-Cola" in an advertisement that seeks to draw an unfavorable comparison with its own product. *See Consumers Union of the United States, Inc. v. General Signal Corp.*, 724 F.2d 1044 (2d Cir. 1983).

In the case of entertainment merchandising, though, what is being sold are the character names and symbols themselves, thus allowing fans wearing a Batman t-shirt, eating Bubba Gump shrimp, and drinking coffee from an "I Love E.T." mug to identify with their favorite stories and personalities. If the t-shirt carried the name and likeness of Johnny Carson or Vanna White, the right of publicity gives them the exclusive authority to license or bar such uses for commercial purposes. Movie studios, on the other hand, are business organizations that cannot use this outgrowth of the right of personal privacy. Instead, they must rely on federal trademark law or on certain state law variations on this theme.[h] The following case illustrates how the Second Circuit applies trademark law to merchandising cases in a suit brought against, not by, a movie producer.

## HORMEL FOODS CORP. V. JIM HENSON PRODUCTIONS, INC.

United States Court of Appeals, Second Circuit, 1996.
73 F.3d 497.

VAN GRAAFEILAND, CIRCUIT JUDGE.

[A 1996 Muppet movie, *Muppet Treasure Island*, added a new character to those child treasures, Kermit the Frog, Miss Piggy, and Fozzie Bear. Spa'am is the high priest of a tribe of wild boars that worship Miss Piggy as Queen Sha Ka La Ka La, and he eventually helps the Muppets escape the film's villain, Long John Silver.

[h] *See* Robert C. Denicola, *Institutional Publicity Rights: An Analysis of the Merchandising of Famous Trade Symbols*, 62 N.C. L. Rev. 603 (1984); Peter A. Mims, *Promotional Goods & the Functionality Doctrine: An Economic Model of Trademarks*, 63 Tex. L. Rev. 639 (1984).

Whatever the reaction of Muppet fans, Hormel Foods was not amused by Spa'am. Hormel is the maker of the long-time luncheon meat SPAM, which was clearly intended to be parodied by Spa'am. Hormel found the Spa'am version to be unappetizing, one that it said might make its customers worry about the quality of its meat product, and certainly would cause confusion with merchandise issued under the name SPAM. While Hormel initially objected to the portrayal of Spa'am in the Muppet movie, this appeal focused only on use of the name for Muppet Treasure Island merchandise, such as like clothes and toys sold with the Spa'am name.]

* * *

Discussion

*A. Trademark Infringement*

A plaintiff's trademark is protected by federal law against infringement by use of colorable imitations of the mark which are "likely to cause confusion, or to cause mistake, or to deceive." 15 U.S.C. § 1114(1). The central inquiry is whether there is a "likelihood of confusion," a "likelihood that an appreciable number of ordinarily prudent purchasers are likely to be misled, or indeed simply confused, as to the source of the goods in question," *Mushroom Makers, Inc. v. R.G. Barry Corp.*, 580 F.2d 44, 47 (2d Cir. 1978), or that there may be confusion as to plaintiff's sponsorship or endorsement of the junior mark. *See Dallas Cowboys Cheerleaders, Inc. v. Pussycat Cinema, Ltd.*, 604 F.2d 200, 204–05 (2d Cir. 1979).

In this circuit, claims for infringement usually are analyzed under the eight-factor *Polaroid* test. *See Polaroid Corp. v. Polarad Electronics Corp.*, 287 F.2d 492, 495 (2d Cir. 1961) In the instant case, the district court found that each of the eight factors favored Henson as to both use of the Spa'am likeness alone and use of the Spa'am likeness in conjunction with the name "Spa'am" on its merchandise. Finding no other circumstances tending to create confusion, it concluded that there was no likelihood of confusion and rejected Hormel's claim . . . We now examine each of the *Polaroid* factors in turn.

*1. Strength of the Mark*

There is little doubt that SPAM is a distinctive, widely recognized trademark. Hormel has sold over five billion cans of its luncheon meat under the SPAM mark and invested millions of dollars in advertising. As a result, Hormel has a 75 percent share of the canned meat market and SPAM is eaten in 30 percent of all American homes. Thus, SPAM truly is a household name. In the usual trademark case, such an undeniably strong mark would be a factor favoring the trademark plaintiff. The more deeply a plaintiff's mark is embedded in the consumer's mind, the more likely it is that the defendant's mark will conjure up the image of the plaintiff's product instead of that of the junior user.

However, this does not always lead to confusion. As then District Judge Leval explained in *Yankee Publishing Inc. v. News America Publishing Inc.*, 809 F. Supp. 267, 273 (S.D.N.Y. 1992), "where the plaintiff's mark is being used as part of a jest or commentary . . . [and] both plaintiff['s] and defendant's marks are strong, well recognized, and clearly associated in the consumers' mind with a particular distinct ethic . . . confusion is avoided. . . ." Indeed, a parody depends on a lack of confusion to make its point. "A parody must convey two simultaneous—and contradictory—messages: that it is the original, but also that it is not the original and is instead a parody." *Cliffs Notes, Inc. v. Bantam Doubleday Dell Publishing Group, Inc.*, 886 F.2d 490, 494 (2d Cir. 1989).

Henson's use of the name "Spa'am" is simply another in a long line of Muppet lampoons. Moreover, this Muppet brand of humor is widely recognized and enjoyed. Thus, consumers of Henson's merchandise, all of which will display the words "Muppet Treasure Island," are likely to see the name "Spa'am" as the joke it was intended to be . . .

We find, therefore, that the clarity of Henson's parodic intent, the widespread familiarity with Henson's Muppet parodies, and the strength of Hormel's mark, all weigh strongly against the likelihood of confusion as to source or sponsorship between Hormel's mark and the name "Spa'am." Moreover, this reasoning applies to both use of the Spa'am character likeness alone and use of the likeness and name together on Henson's movie merchandise.

*2. Degree of Similarity Between the Marks*

Although Henson's wild boar puppet in no way resembles Hormel's luncheon meat or SPAM-man, Hormel contends that depiction of the puppet alone will conjure up the name "Spa'am," because consumers will associate the name that appears in the movie and media with the figure on Henson's merchandise. Thus, Hormel argues, use of the puppet likeness alone is in essence no different than its use in conjunction with its name. However, even combined use of the name and likeness does not present a strong case of similarity. Viewed alone, of course, the names "Spa'am" and "SPAM" bear more than a passing resemblance. Indeed, Henson's parody depends on the correspondence between the two. However, there are also some significant differences. "Spa'am" is divided in two by an apostrophe and it contains two a's instead of one. In addition, Spa'am is pronounced as two distinct syllables, SPAM only one.

Moreover, "an inquiry into the degree of similarity between two marks does not end with a comparison of the marks themselves. . . . 'the setting in which a designation is used affects its appearance and colors the impression conveyed by it.' " *Spring Mills, Inc. v. Ultracashmere*

*House, Ltd.*, 689 F.2d 1127, 1130 (2d Cir. 1982). . . . In this connection, placement of the marks next to other identifying but dissimilar symbols is clearly relevant. Here, Henson plans to always use the name "Spa'am" next to a likeness of the wild boar puppet. In addition, the words "Muppet Treasure Island" always will be prominently displayed wherever the name "Spa'am" appears. Thus, the two marks appear in strikingly different contexts and project wholly different visual displays. Moreover, the prominence of Henson's mark, widely recognized as a source of satire, will make it clear that the merchandise itself parodies Hormel's product, a message which depends for its success on distinguishing Spa'am from SPAM. Therefore, although the two marks are superficially similar, in all likelihood the parodic context in which the name "Spa'am" appears will distinguish the marks in the consumer's mind.

*3. Proximity of the Products*

Our finding that the marks are dissimilar in practice is buttressed by the fact that Henson and Hormel occupy distinct merchandising markets. The district court found that SPAM merchandise and Muppet merchandise featuring Spa'am "clearly . . . derive their associations from a primary product—luncheon meat, in the case of SPAM, and a Muppet motion picture, in the case of Spa'am." It noted that "purchasers of SPAM merchandise would generally be consumers of the luncheon meat," *id.*, and that "consumers of merchandise bearing the likeness and/or name of Spa'am will buy it because they like Spa'am, the Muppets, and/or Muppet Treasure Island." Thus, the separation between the markets for luncheon meat and puppet entertainment carries over into the secondary merchandising market.

This finding is not clearly erroneous. Our opinion in *Universal City Studios, Inc. v. Nintendo Co.*, 746 F.2d 112 (2d Cir. 1984) explains why. In that case, the competing marks "King Kong" and "Donkey Kong" appeared in different primary markets—motion pictures and video games respectively. As to secondary products featuring Donkey Kong, we noted that "since the videogame [Donkey Kong] is by far the dominant source of goodwill for these characters, consumer impressions of these other items are likely to be generated by the videogame, diminishing the possibility that the items will create more confusion among consumers than the videogame itself." Likewise, the character Spa'am, even as he appears on merchandise, will be defined almost entirely by his appearance in Muppet Treasure Island. This connection will be strengthened by the presence of the Muppet Treasure Island logo. Thus, it is unlikely that consumers will confuse merchandise featuring Spa'am with similar items displaying the SPAM trademark.

*4. Bridging the Gap*

Bridging the gap refers to the "senior user's interest in preserving avenues of expansion and entering into related fields." *C.L.A.S.S. Promotions, Inc. v. D.S. Magazines, Inc.*, 753 F.2d 14, 18 (2d Cir. 1985). Hormel has shown no intention of entering the field of puppet entertainment with its attendant merchandising, and there is no evidence that consumers would relate Hormel to such an enterprise. Because market proximity in the instant case depends on identification with the primary product, this factor too favors Henson.

*5. Actual Confusion*

Hormel points to the misspellings and mispronunciations of Spa'am as SPAM in the media as evidence of actual confusion. However, in none of the articles Hormel cites is the source or sponsorship of the two marks confused. Indeed, there is no evidence that consumers, members of the media, or anyone else has mistaken Spa'am as a promotional figure for SPAM, or as a character sponsored by Hormel. Accordingly, the district court found that there was no actual confusion. Although misspellings may demonstrate a possibility of confusion, the vastly different contexts in which the marks at issue herein will appear militate against any possible confusion as to source or sponsorship.

*6. Bad Faith*

As noted above, Henson's parody depends on consumer recognition that Spa'am is a Muppet lampoon and not simply a modified version of the SPAM-man. As the court noted in *Yankee Publishing*, supra, "[Henson] would have absolutely nothing to gain from creating a confusion among [merchandise consumers] causing them to believe there was a business association between [Henson] and [Hormel]." 809 F. Supp. at 275. Indeed, the lack of subtlety in Henson's parody is evidence in itself that Henson intended no deceit. There is nothing to indicate that Henson acted in bad faith.

*7. Quality of the Products*

The quality of a junior user's product can be relevant in two ways: (1) an inferior product may cause injury to the plaintiff trademark owner because people may think that the senior and junior products came from the same source; or (2) products of equal quality may tend to create confusion as to source because of this very similarity. Henson's Muppets, which now include Spa'am among their members, are high quality products, similar in this respect to Hormel's SPAM. However, similarity of quality as between SPAM and Spa'am is unlikely to cause confusion, because the products are not otherwise related as to makeup, usage, etc.

Yet, although Henson's Muppets present high quality entertainment, Hormel contends that Henson's Spa'am character will call into question the quality of its SPAM luncheon meat. However, Hormel overlooks the district court's findings that Spa'am is a positive character, that he is not unhygienic, and that a simple comic reference to the fact that SPAM is made from pork will not damage its image, especially in view of the lack of adverse effect from the numerous other humorous references to SPAM.

*8. Consumer Sophistication*

The district court found that a child or adult who would be likely to buy merchandise featuring Spa'am would do so "because he likes the Muppets, not because he mistakenly thinks that it is a SPAM [product]." Hormel complains that the district court focused on consumers who want to purchase Spa'am merchandise while overlooking possible confusion on the part of those who would like to buy SPAM products. However, although the district court did not discuss the latter consumers in its sophistication analysis, it found in its discussion of market proximity that consumers who want to purchase SPAM merchandise do so to affiliate themselves with Hormel's primary product and would not be confused by Henson's merchandise, all of which will prominently carry the Muppet Treasure Island mark. This finding is relevant in the sophistication analysis, especially because sophistication and market proximity are closely related concepts. Therefore, we find no error in the district court's reasoning.

*Likelihood of Confusion*

The elements of parody in Henson's Spa'am merchandise distinguish those products from ones manufactured by Hormel. The obvious, though inoffensive, nature of the parody and the prominence of the Muppet Treasure Island mark are strong evidence that consumers are not likely to be confused between merchandise carrying the SPAM logo and products featuring Spa'am. This is true both as to use of the Spa'am likeness and use of the Spa'am name in conjunction with that likeness, as portrayed in Henson's plans submitted to the district court. We therefore conclude that Hormel's infringement claim is without merit.

* * *

Affirmed.

---

Needless to say, the complaint lodged in *Hormel* is very much the exception rather than the rule. Indeed, product placement, as the strategy is called, has now become a key feature of the merchandising side of entertainment productions, as epitomized by the title of the 1985 movie hit, *The Coca-Cola Kid*. Movies and television shows portray dozens of products—beers or sodas being sipped, cars being driven, planes being flown. If those products are identifiable on the screen, this can provide an attractive advertising slot. There is no better illustration than the surge in sales of Reese's Pieces after their delightful role in *E.T.* Recognizing this marketing potential, entertainment producers often sell the right to have a product appear in their works. The amounts may exceed $100,000 for a single product placement (depending on its spot) and $5 million for all the film's products (depending on the anticipated size and makeup of the movie's audience). By 2010, the total amount spent on product placements in movies, television shows, video games, novels, and even Broadway musicals had topped $7.5 billion. Indeed, not only is James Bond a lucrative box office character, but his product placement appeal is also strong. For example, when *Tomorrow Never Dies* appeared in 1997, it had already secured $110 million in product placement, promotional and merchandising deals, roughly the same amount as the *domestic* box office take for *Tomorrow* (although it did earn $350 million in worldwide box office).

Producers do not have to rely on the law to sell such a placement. It simply tells the director whether Bond will be driving a BMW or a Mercedes, or whether Bruce Willis will be hoisting a can of Miller Lite or Bud Lite in his movies. The law comes into play only when the manufacturer of the product does not want it portrayed in a particular film, perhaps because of the unattractive setting or portrayal. For instance, the film *Jerry Maguire,* starring Tom Cruise as a beleaguered sports agent, opened in 1996 and quickly a box office success. Two weeks after *Maguire's* release, the studio (Sony's TriStar Pictures) faced a $10 million lawsuit by Reebok International, a footwear and apparel manufacturer. Reebok argued that it had agreed with TriStar that in an early scene in the movie, Cruise/Maguire's underachieving football player client, Rod Tidwell, would make disparaging remarks about Reebok for being unwilling to offer him an endorsement deal. Then, against a backdrop of the credits at the end of the movie, Tidwell (who by then had become a star) would appear in a humorous and positive Reebok commercial.

As part of the agreement, Reebok not only produced the commercial featuring Tidwell, but also supplied athletic equipment and a football coach for the production; it then heavily promoted the movie's Reebok connection. The film's producer, Gracie Films, decided to drop the Reebok commercial (though not the earlier Reebok slam) just before its release into theaters. Reebok's resulting lawsuit included claims of breach of contract, fraud, trademark infringement and disparagement, and unfair competition. TriStar's response to the suit was that it had never reached a binding agreement with Reebok to include the commercial, and that the actual references to Reebok in the film constituted free speech, not trademark violations. If this case had been litigated to a conclusion rather than settled, it would have offered a revealing look at the potential tension between commercial and artistic aims in the placing of products in present-day movies.

———

On the subject of disparaging remarks, disparaging trademarks also can be disallowed by the government under the Lanham Act. Recently, Simon Tam, lead singer of the Asian-American band "The Slants," attempted to register the band's name as a trademark. The Trademark Trial and Appeal Board denied his application. As explained by the Federal Circuit in Tam's case:

> Section 2(a) of the Lanham Act provides that the Patent and Trademark Office (PTO) may refuse to register a trademark that "[c]onsists of or comprises immoral, deceptive, or scandalous matter; or matter which may disparage or falsely suggest a connection with persons, living or dead, institutions, beliefs, or national symbols, or bring them into contempt, or disrepute." 15 U.S.C. § 1052(a). A disparaging mark " 'dishonors by comparison with what is inferior, slights, deprecates, degrades, or affects or injures by unjust comparison.' " *In re Geller,* 751 F.3d 1355, 1358 (Fed.Cir.2014) (quoting *Pro-Football, Inc. v. Harjo,* 284 F.Supp.2d 96, 124 (D.D.C.2003)) (alterations omitted). In *Geller,* we applied a two-part test to determine if a mark may be disparaging:
>
> (1) what is the likely meaning of the matter in question, taking into account not only dictionary definitions, but also the relationship of the matter to the other elements in the mark, the nature of the goods or services, and the manner in which the mark is used in the marketplace in connection with the goods or services; and
>
> (2) if that meaning is found to refer to identifiable persons, institutions, beliefs or national symbols, whether that meaning may be disparaging to a substantial composite of the referenced group. *Id.*

*In re Tam*, 785 F.3d 567 (Fed. Cir. 2015). The Federal Circuit upheld the denial of a trademark, but the court subsequently agreed to hear the case *en banc*. What is the correct outcome?

Another example of a trademark long considered offensive is the nickname of the Washington, D.C. NFL team, the Redskins. Is the offensive nature of this nickname grounds for revoking its federal trademarks?

## PRO-FOOTBALL, INC. V. BLACKHORSE

United States District Court, Eastern District, Virginia, 2015.
___ F. Supp. 3d ___, 2015 WL 4096277.

LEE, DISTRICT JUDGE.

THIS MATTER is before the Court on two sets of cross-motions for summary judgment. First, Plaintiff Pro-Football, Inc. ("PFI"), Defendants Amanda Blackhorse, Marcus Briggs-Cloud, Phillip Gover, Jillian Pappan, and Courtney Tsotigh ("Blackhorse Defendants"), and the United States of America filed cross-motions for summary judgment on PFI's claims challenging the constitutionality of Section 2(a) of the Lanham Act (Counts III–VI) (Docs. 54, 105, and 108). Second, Blackhorse Defendants and PFI filed cross-motions for summary judgment on PFI's claims contesting the Trademark Trial and Appeal Board's ("TTAB") Order cancelling the registrations of six of PFI's trademarks on the grounds that they consisted of matter that "may disparage" Native Americans and bring them into contempt or disrepute, and that the defense of laches does not bar the claims (Counts I, II, and VII) (Docs. 69 and 79). This case concerns Blackhorse Defendants' petition to cancel the registration of six trademarks owned by PFI on the grounds that the marks consisted of matter that "may disparage" a substantial composite of Native Americans and bring them into contempt or disrepute under Section 2(a) of the Lanham Act, 15 U.S.C. § 1052(a), at the time of their registrations (1967, 1974, 1978, and 1990).

* * *

### *BACKGROUND*

The "Washington Redskins" are a well-known professional football team. The "Redskins" mark was first used by the "Washington Redskins" National Football League ("NFL") franchise in 1933 when then-owner George Preston Marshall selected the name while the team was located in Boston, Massachusetts. "Redskins" was chosen to distinguish the football team from the Boston Braves professional baseball team. (Compl.¶ 35.) The team has used the name ever since. (*Id.* 34; Doc. 41 ¶ 34.) The United States Patent and Trademark Office ("PTO") approved and registered the mark in 1967. (Doc. 56 at 1.) Five additional variations of "Redskins" trademarks were approved and registered between 1974 and 1990 (collectively "Redskins Marks"). The registrations of the Redskins Marks have been renewed repeatedly since 1967, with the most recent renewal occurring in 2015. (Doc. 51 ¶ 8(a)-(f)). PFI owns, and has always owned, the Redskins Marks. (*Id.*)

* * *

The Redskins Marks have not evaded controversy. *See Walker v. Tex. Div., Sons of Confederate Veterans, Inc.*, ___ U.S. ___, ___, 135 S.Ct. 2239,

2262, 192 L.Ed.2d 274 (2015) (Alito, J., dissenting) (describing the "Washington Redskins" as a controversial team name). For example, in 1971 and 1972, there were a host of newspaper articles detailing opposition to the name "Redskins" by some Native Americans. (Docs. 73–12–73–14; 73–29–73–38.) Similarly, in 1972 Leon Cook, President of the National Congress of American Indians ("NCAI"), among others, met with Edward Bennett Williams, the president of PFI, to explain that the team name was a slur; Williams reported the meeting to the NFL Commissioner the following day. (Doc. 71–3 at 5–6; Doc. 73–24 at 12–14; Doc. 73–25.) Also, a 1972 official game program referenced the controversy surrounding the team's name. (Doc. 72–5 at 6.)

The registrability of the Redskins Marks has been litigated for over two decades. In 1992, Susan Harjo and six other Native Americans filed a petition to cancel the registrations of the Redskins Marks under Section 2(a) of the Lanham Act. Seven years later, the TTAB ruled that the Redskins Marks "may disparage" Native Americans when registered and ordered that the registrations of the marks be cancelled. *Harjo v. Pro-Football, Inc.,* 50 U.S.P.Q.2d 1705, 1999 WL 375907 (T.T.A.B.1999). On appeal, the United States District Court for the District of Columbia reversed the TTAB, holding that (1) the TTAB's finding of disparagement was unsubstantiated, and (2) the doctrine of laches precluded consideration of the case.

The case traversed back and forth between the district court and the D.C. Circuit, with the final outcome being that D.C. Circuit affirmed the district court's ruling that laches barred the claim. *Pro-Football, Inc. v. Harjo,* 565 F.3d 880 (D.C.Cir.2009). The D.C. Circuit never addressed the TTAB's finding of disparagement on the merits.

On August 11, 2006, while *Harjo* was pending, Amanda Blackhorse, Marcus BriggsCloud, Phillip Cover, Jillian Pappan, and Courtney Tsotigh ("Blackhorse Defendants") filed a petition to cancel the same six registrations of the Redskins Marks. The TTAB suspended action in the *Blackhorse* case until the *Harjo* litigation concluded in 2009. The parties here have agreed that the entire *Harjo* record could be entered into evidence in the case before the TTAB. The parties also waived all non-relevance evidentiary objections to that evidence.

On June 18, 2014, the TTAB scheduled the cancellation of the registrations of the Redskins Marks under Section 2(a) of the Lanham Act, 15 U.S.C. § 1052(a), finding that at the time of their registrations the marks consisted of matter that both "may disparage" a substantial composite of Native Americans and bring them into contempt or disrepute. *See Blackhorse v. Pro-Football, Inc.,* 111 U.S.P.Q.2d 1080, 2014 WL 2757516 (T.T.A.B.2014). This action seeks a *de novo* review, pursuant to 15 U.S.C. § 1071(b), of the TTAB's decision, based on the TTAB

*Blackhorse* record and the additional evidence the parties have submitted to this Court.

PFI asserts the following seven causes of action. In Count I, PFI seeks a declaration of non-disparagement. In Count II, PFI seeks a declaration of non-contempt or disrepute. Count III concerns PFI's claim that Section 2(a) of the Lanham Act, 15 U.S.C. § 1052(a), violates the First Amendment. Count IV is PFI's claim that Section 2(a) of the Lanham Act is void for vagueness. Count V is PFI's claim that the TTAB Order violates the Due Process Clause of the Fifth Amendment. In Count VI, PFI claims that the TTAB Order violates the Takings Clause of the Fifth Amendment. Lastly, Count VII is PFI's claim that Blackhorse's petition to cancel the registrations of the Redskins Marks was barred by the doctrine of laches.

PFI and Blackhorse Defendants filed cross-motions for summary judgment on PFI's constitutional claims (Counts III–VI) (Docs. 54 & 105). The United States of America intervened and filed a motion for summary judgment on PFI's constitutional claims (Doc. 108), defending the constitutionality of Section 2(a) of the Lanham Act. Additionally, PFI and Blackhorse Defendants filed cross-motions for summary judgment on PFI's Lanham Act and laches claims (Counts I, II, and VII) (Docs. 69 & 79). Each motion is now before the Court.

* * *

A. Trademark Registration vs. Trademarks Themselves

As a threshold matter, throughout the pleadings the parties conflated the legal principles surrounding trademarks with those surrounding trademark *registration*. Just as Allen Iverson once reminded the media that they were wasting time at the end of the Philadelphia 76ers' season "talking about *practice* " and not an actual professional basketball game, the Court is similarly compelled to highlight what is at issue in this case—trademark registration, not the trademarks themselves. It is the registrations of the Redskins Marks that were scheduled for cancellation by the TTAB's decision, not the trademarks. In fact, the TTAB itself pointed out that it is only empowered to cancel the statutory *registration* of the marks under Section 2(a); it cannot cancel the trademarks themselves. *See Blackhorse v. Pro-Football, Inc.*, 111 U.S.P.Q.2d 1080, 2014 WL 2757516, at *1 (T .T.A.B.2014) (citation omitted). Thus, regardless of this Court's ruling, PFI can still use the Redskins Marks in commerce.

It is also important to identify the effect of federal trademark registration. A trademark is "any word, name, symbol, or device or any combination thereof used by any person to identify and distinguish his or her goods, including a unique product, from those manufactured or sold by others and to indicate the source of the goods, even if that source is unknown." *Two Pesos, Inc. v. Taco Cabana, Inc.,* 505 U.S. 763, 768, 112 S.Ct. 2753, 120 L.Ed.2d 615 (1992). Federal law does not create trademarks. *See In re Trade-Mark Cases,* 100 U.S. 82, 92, 25 L.Ed. 550 (1879). Regardless of whether a mark is registered, the "right to a particular mark grows out of its use, not its mere adoption . . ." *United Drug Co. v. Theodore Rectanus Co.,* 248 U.S. 90, 97, 39 S.Ct. 48, 63 L.Ed. 141 (1918) (citation omitted); *see also Emergency One, Inc. v. Am. Fire Eagle Engine Co.,* 332 F.3d 264, 267 (4th Cir.2003) ("To acquire ownership of a trademark it is not enough to have invented the mark first *or even to have registered it first;* the party claiming ownership must have been the first to *actually use the mark* in the sale of goods or services." (emphasis added) (citation and internal quotation marks omitted)); 2 J. McCarthy, Trademarks And Unfair Competition § 16:1 (4th ed.2014) (same). Thus, use of a mark in commerce, by itself, creates a host of common law rights. *See Hanover Star Milling Co. v. Metcalf,* 240 U.S. 403, 36 S.Ct. 357, 60 L.Ed. 713 (1916) (explaining scope of common law trademark rights); *Harrods Ltd. v. Sixty Internet Domain Names,* 302 F.3d 214, 230 (4th Cir.2002) ("Generally speaking, trademark protection is a common law right that arises from the use of a mark to identify the source of certain goods or services." (citation omitted)); *see also Spartan Food Sys. v. HFS Corp.,* 813 F.2d 1279, 1282 (4th Cir.1987); *Armand's Subway, Inc. v. Doctor's Assocs.,* 604 F.2d 849, 849 (4th Cir.1979). The Lanham Act does, however, contain a cause of action for the enforcement of unregistered trademarks. *See* 15 U.S.C. § 1125(a).

The owner of a trademark can apply to register it with the PTO under the Lanham Act. *See* 15 U.S.C. § 1051. After reviewing an application, "[if] a trademark examiner believes that registration is warranted, the mark is published in the Official Gazette of the PTO" as well as the Principal Register. *B & B Hardware, Inc. v. Hargis Indus.,* ___ U.S. ___, ___, 135 S.Ct. 1293, 1300, 191 L.Ed.2d 222 (2015) (citing 15 U.S.C. § 1062); *see also* 15 U.S.C. § 1057. Registration confers several benefits upon the owner of a mark in addition to those available at common law:

> (1) constructive notice of the registrant's claim of ownership of the trademark; (2) *prima facie* evidence of the validity of the registration, of the registrant's ownership of the mark, and of his exclusive right to use the mark in commerce as specified in the certificate; (3) the possibility that, after five years, registration will become [incontestable] and constitute conclusive evidence of the registrant's right to use the mark; (4) the right to request customs officials to bar the importation of goods bearing infringing trademarks; (5) the right to institute trademark actions in federal courts without regard to diversity of

citizenship or the amount in controversy; and (6) treble damage actions against infringing trademarks and other remedies.

*Georator Corp. v. United States,* 485 F.2d 283, 285 (4th Cir.1973) (citing 15 U.S.C. § 1051 *et seq.*), *abrogated on other grounds by NCNB Corp. v. United States,* 684 F.2d 285 (4th Cir.1982). Incontestability and proof of ownership are among the most significant advantages of registration. *See Brittingham v. Jenkins,* 914 F.2d 447, 452 (4th Cir.1990); *see also B & B Hardware,* 135 S.Ct. at 1300 ("The Lanham Act confers important legal rights and benefits on trademark owners who register their marks." (citation and internal quotation marks omitted)).

What is at issue here is the registration of the Redskins Marks and the benefits associated with registration, not the use of the marks.

* * *

C. Lanham Act Challenges

* * *

Section 2(a) of the Lanham Act, 15 U.S.C. § 1052(a), provides that registration should be denied to any mark that "[c]onsists of or comprises immoral, deceptive, or scandalous matter; or matter which may disparage or falsely suggest a connection with persons, living or dead, institutions, beliefs, or national symbols, or bring them into contempt or disrepute . . ." *Id.* The TTAB has established a two-part test to determine whether a mark contains matter that "may disparage." The parties agree that the test in this case is as follows:

1. What is the meaning of the matter in question, as it appears in the marks and as those marks are used in connection with the goods and services identified in the registrations?
2. Is the meaning of the marks one that may disparage Native Americans?

*See Blackhorse v. Pro-Football, Inc.,* 111 U.S.P.Q.2d 1080, 2014 WL 2757516, at *4 (T.T.A.B.2014) (citations omitted); *see also In re Geller,* 751 F.3d 1355, 1358 (Fed.Cir.2014). This inquiry focuses on the registration dates of the marks at issue. *Blackhorse,* 2014 WL 2757516, at *4 (citations omitted). Here, the registration dates are 1967, 1974, 1978, and 1990.

When answering the second question, whether the term "redskins" "may disparage" Native Americans, courts should look to the views of Native Americans, not those of the general public. *Id.* Moreover, Blackhorse Defendants are only required to show that the marks "may disparage" a "substantial composite" of Native Americans. *See Geller,* 751 F.3d at 1358 (citations omitted). A substantial composite is not necessarily a majority. *See In re Boulevard Ent., Inc.,* 334 F.3d 1336, 1340 (Fed.Cir.2003) (citing *In re McGinley,* 660 F.2d 481, 485 (C.C.P.A.1981)); *In re Mavety Media Grp.,* 33 F.3d 1367, 1370 (Fed.Cir.1994) (citation omitted).

Courts consider dictionary evidence when determining whether a term "may disparage" a substantial composite of the referenced group. In *In re Boulevard,* the Federal Circuit held that when a mark has only "*one pertinent meaning[,] a standard dictionary definition and an accompanying editorial designation alone* sufficiently demonstrate[ ] that a substantial composite of the general public" considers a term scandalous. 334 F.3d 1336, 1340–41 (Fed.Cir.2003) (emphasis added) (citing 15 U.S.C. § 1052(a)) (finding that a mark had one "pertinent meaning" when all of the dictionaries consulted contained usage labels characterizing a term as "vulgar").

Courts can use usage labels to decide whether a term "may disparage" a specific referenced group, as opposed to the general public in Section 2(a) "scandalous" actions, because usage labels denote when words are disparaging or offensive to the group referenced in the underlying term. *See, e.g., Symbols and Labels Used in Oxford Learner's Dictionaries,* OXFORD LEARNER'S DICTIONARIES, http://www.oxfordlearnersdictionaries.com/us/about/labels (last visited July 6, 2015) ("offensive expressions are used by some people to address or refer to people in a way that is very insulting, especially in connection with their race, religion, sex or disabilities").

Thus, using a dictionary's usage labels to determine whether a term "may disparage" a substantial composite of Native Americans during the relevant time period is consistent with the Federal Circuit's holding in *Boulevard. See In re Fox,* 702 F.3d 633, 635 (Fed.Cir.2012) ("But where it is clear from dictionary evidence that the mark as used by the applicant in connection with the products described in the application invokes a vulgar meaning to a substantial composite of the general public, the mark is unregistrable." (citation and internal quotation marks omitted)); *In re Heeb Media, LLC,* 89 U.S.P.Q.2d 1071, 2008 WL 5065114, at *5 (T.T.A.B.2008) ("It has been held that, at least as to offensive matter, dictionary evidence alone can be sufficient to satisfy the USPTO's burden, where the mark has only one pertinent meaning." (citing *Boulevard,* 334 F.3d at 1340–41)).

However, when dictionaries are not unanimous in their characterization of a term, additional evidence must be adduced to satisfy the PTO's burden. Reversing the TTAB's finding that a mark was scandalous based *solely* on discordant dictionary characterizations, the Federal Circuit explained:

In view of the existence of such an alternate, *non-vulgar definition,* the Board, *without more,* erred in concluding that in the context of the adult entertainment magazine, the substantial composite of the general public would necessarily attach to the mark BLACK TAIL the vulgar meaning of "tail" as a female sexual partner, rather than the admittedly non-vulgar meaning of "tail" as rear end. *In the absence of evidence as to which of these definitions the substantial composite would choose,* the PTO failed to meet its burden of proving that Mavety's mark is within the scope of § 1052(a) prohibition.

*Mavety Media Grp.,* 33 F.3d at 1373–74 (emphasis added).

1. The Meaning of the Matter in Question is a Reference to Native Americans

The Court finds that the meaning of the matter in question in all six Redskins Marks-the term "redskins" and derivatives thereof—is a reference to Native Americans. PFI admits that "redskins" refers to Native Americans. The team has consistently associated itself with Native American imagery.

* * *

As stated by the TTAB in *Harjo* and confirmed by the D.C. District Court:

> This is not a case where, through usage, the word "redskin(s)" has lost its meaning, in the field of professional football, as a reference to Native Americans in favor of an entirely independent meaning as the name of a professional football team. Rather, when considered in relation to the other matter comprising at least two of the subject marks and as used in connection with respondent's services, "Redskins" clearly both refers to respondent's professional football team and carries the allusion to Native Americans inherent in the original definition of that word.

*Pro-Football, Inc. v. Harjo,* 284 F.Supp.2d 96, 127 (D.D.C.2003) (quoting *Harjo v. Pro-Football, Inc.,* 50 U.S.P.Q.2d 1705, 1999 WL 375907, at *41 (T.T.A.B.1999)). The Court agrees and finds that because PFI has made continuous efforts to associate its football team with Native Americans during the relevant time period, the meaning of the matter in question is a reference to Native Americans.

2. The Redskins Marks "May Disparage" a Substantial Composite of Native Americans During the Relevant Time Period

The Court finds that the meaning of the marks is one that "may disparage" a substantial composite of Native Americans in the context of the "Washington Redskins" football team. The relevant period for the disparagement inquiry is the time at which the marks were registered. *Blackhorse,* 2014 WL 2757516, at *4 (citations omitted). Here, the Court focuses on the time period between 1967 and 1990. When reviewing whether a mark "may disparage," the PTO does not, and practically cannot, conduct a poll to determine the views of the referenced group. *See In re Loew's Theatres, Inc.,* 769 F.2d 764, 768 (Fed.Cir.1985). Instead, three categories of evidence are weighed to determine whether a term "may disparage": (1) dictionary definitions and accompanying editorial designations; (2) scholarly, literary, and media references; and (3) statements of individuals or group leaders of the referenced group regarding the term. *See Am. Freedom Def. Initiative v. Mass. Bay Transp. Auth.,* 781 F.3d 571, 585 (1st Cir.2015) (dictionaries); *In re Geller,* 751 F.3d 1355, 1358 (Fed.Cir.2014) (dictionaries and news reports/articles); *In re Lebanese Arak Corp.,* 94 U.S.P.Q.2d 1215, 2010 WL 766488, at *5 (T.T.A.B.2010) (dictionary); *In re Heeb Media, LLC,* 89 U.S.P.Q.2d 1071, 2008 WL 5065114, at *5 (T.T.A .B.2008) (dictionaries and individual and group sentiment); *In re Squaw Valley Dev. Co.,* 80 U.S.P.Q.2d 1264, 2006 WL 1546500, at *10–*14 (T.T.A.B.2006) (dictionaries, literary and media references, and individual and group statements).

Furthermore, by using the term "may disparage," Section 2(a) does not require that the mark holder possess an intent to disparage in order to deny or cancel a registration. *See Harjo,* 284 F.Supp.2d at 125; *Blackhorse,* 2014 WL 2757516, at *9–*10 (citing *Heeb Media,* 2008 WL 5065114, at *8; *Squaw Valley,* 2006 WL 1546500)). Also, in order to be cancelled or denied registration, the marks must consist of matter that "may disparage" in the context of the goods and services provided. *See In re McGinley,* 660 F.2d 481, 485 (C.C.P.A.1981).

a. Dictionary Evidence

First, the record evidence contains dictionary definitions and accompanying designations of "redskins" that weigh in favor of finding that the Redskins Marks consisted of matter that "may disparage" a substantial composite of Native Americans when each of the six marks was registered. Dictionary evidence is commonly considered when deciding if a term is one that "may disparage." *See Am. Freedom Def. Initiative v. Mass. Bay Transp. Auth.,* 781 F.3d 571, 585 (1st Cir.2015); *In re Geller,* 751 F.3d 1355, 1358 (Fed.Cir.2014); *In re Lebanese Arak Corp.,* 94 U.S.P.Q.2d 1215, 2010 WL 766488, at *5 (T.T.A.B.2010); *In re Heeb Media, LLC,* 89 U.S.P.Q.2d 1071, 2008 WL 5065114, at *5 (T.T.A.B.2008); *In re Squaw Valley Dev. Co.,* 80 U.S.P.Q.2d 1264, 2006 WL 1546500, at *10–*14 (T.T.A.B.2006).

The record contains several dictionaries defining "redskins" as a term referring to North American Indians and characterizing "redskins" as offensive or contemptuous:

1. *Webster's Collegiate Dictionary* 682 (1898) ("often contemptuous");
2. *The Random House Dictionary of the English Language* 1204 (1966) ("Often Offensive");
3. *Random House Dictionary of the English Language* 1204 (1967) ("Often Offensive");
4. *Random House Dictionary of the English Language* 1204 (1973) ("Often Offensive");
5. *Thorndike-Barnhart Intermediate Dictionary* 702 (2d ed.1974) ("a term often considered offensive");
6. *Oxford American Dictionary* 564 (1980) ("contemptuous");
7. *The American Heritage Dictionary of the English Language: Second College Edition* 1037 (1982) ("Offensive Slang");
8. *Webster's Ninth New Collegiate Dictionary* 987 (1983) ("usu[ally] taken to be offensive");
9. *Merriam-Webster Collegiate Dictionary* (1983) ("usu[ally] taken to be offensive");
10. *Collier's Dictionary* (1986) ("considered offensive"); and
11. *Oxford English Dictionary* 429 (2d ed. 1989) ("Not the preferred term").

* * *

Furthermore, Dr. David Barnhart, one of PFI's linguistics experts, said that characterizing "redskins" as "disparaging" from 1967 to 1985 is too strong a term to apply. Criss Decl. Ex. 14 at 181:9–12. However, he did declare that in that same time period, the term "certainly might be offensive." *Id.* This weighs in favor of finding that "redskins" "may disparage" for two reasons. First, Dr. Barnhart stated that "disparage" required intent, Criss Decl. Ex. 14 at 181:13–182:3, and both parties agree that "may disparage," which is the standard posed by Section 2(a)—*not* does disparage—does not require intent. Second, as explained above, in Section 2(a) "may disparage" cases both the Federal Circuit and the TTAB use "disparage" and derivatives of "offend" interchangeably. Thus, the Court finds that Dr. Barnhart's declaration that "redskins" "certainly might be offensive" is highly probative and weighs in favor of finding that "redskins" "may disparage" a substantial composite of Native Americans during the relevant time period.

Finally, the expert linguists from both parties, Dr. Geoffrey Nunberg for Blackhorse Defendants and Ronald Butters for PFI, both agree that dictionaries tend to lag in updating usage labels for ethnic slurs. (Doc. 71 at 70.) This shows that *Webster's Collegiate Dictionary* (1898) ("often contemptuous"), *The Random House Dictionary of the English Language* (1966) ("Often Offensive"), and *The Random House Dictionary of the English Language* (1967) ("Often Offensive") were not inaccurate in recognizing that the term was "often contemptuous" or "often offensive." Instead, it suggests that the term "redskin" may have been viewed as offensive or contemptuous well in advance of the 1898 entry.

Because both Federal Circuit and TTAB precedent establish that usage labels are relevant, the Court rejects PFI's challenges and finds that the record evidence of eleven dictionary definitions and their usage labels describing "redskins" as "offensive" or "contemptuous," along with Dr. Barnhart's testimony that "redskins" "might be offensive," weigh towards finding that between 1967 and 1990, the Redskins Marks consisted of matter that "may disparage" a substantial composite of Native Americans.

b. Scholarly, Literary, and Media References

Second, the record evidence contains scholarly, literary, and media references that weigh in favor of finding that "redskins" "may disparage" a substantial composite of Native Americans when each of the six Redskins Marks was registered. Scholarly, literary, and media references evidence is often considered when evaluating whether a mark consists of or comprises matter that "may disparage." *See In re Geller,* 751 F.3d 1355, 1358 (Fed.Cir.2014) (citing articles from the Chicago Tribune and the Courier News to show that associating Islam with terrorism "may disparage" Muslims); *In re Heeb Media, LLC,* 89 U.S.P.Q.2d 1071, 2008 WL 5065114, at *5 (T.T.A.B.2008) (referencing an article in the New York Observer to demonstrate that "heeb" "may disparage" the Jewish community); *In re Squaw Valley Dev. Co.,* 80 U.S.P.Q.2d 1264, 2006 WL 1546500, at *10–*14 (T.T.A.B.2006) (holding that the record evidence, including articles from more than ten newspapers and periodicals, sufficiently demonstrated that "squaw" "may disparage" Native Americans).

[The court provides a long list of references, many of which are negative in connotation, both implicitly and explicitly]

* * *

Here, based on the evidence presented in *Geller, Heeb Media,* and *Squaw Valley,* the Court finds that the scholarly, literary, and media references evidence weighs in favor of finding that the Redskins Marks consisted of matter that "may disparage" a substantial composite of Native Americans between 1967 and 1990. For example, as early as 1911, sources such as Encyclopedia Britannica contemplated the poor standing of the term "redskins." The Court finds that Encyclopedia Britannica is a well-respected source. The Supreme Court has referenced Encyclopedia Britannica entries approximately 40 times since 1846, with over 25 of those references occurring before the first Redskins Mark was registered in 1967. *See, e.g., Kennedy v. Mendoza-Martinez,* 372 U.S. 144, 187, 83 S.Ct. 554, 9 L.Ed.2d 644 (1963) ("Magna Carta"); *Gaines v. Herman,* 65 U.S. 553, 581, 589, 24 How. 553, 16 L.Ed. 770 (1860) ("Inquisition"); *Moore v. Am. Transp. Co.,* 65 U.S. 1, 25, 24 How. 1, 16 L.Ed. 674 (1860) ("Navigation, Inland"). The Supreme Court has repeatedly relied on Encyclopedia Britannica as an authoritative source and this Court shall do the same.

Prior to the first mark's registration in 1967, there were two renowned journals and an Encyclopedia Britannica reference that illustrate the term's disfavor among Native Americans. Taken altogether, the Court finds that these three pieces of evidence establish that in 1967, the date of the first registration, evidence existed that showed that the Redskins Marks consisted of matter that "may disparage" a substantial composite of Native Americans during the relevant time period.

c. Statements of Individuals or Group Leaders

Third, the record evidence contains statements of Native American individuals or leaders of Native American groups that weigh in favor of finding that the Redskins Marks consisted of matter that "may disparage" a substantial composite of Native Americans during the relevant time period. The TTAB considers statements from individuals in the referenced group and leaders of organizations within that referenced group when it makes its "may disparage" finding. *See In re Heeb Media, LLC,* 89 U.S.P.Q.2d 1071, 2008 WL 5065114, at *5 (T.T.A.B.2008); *In re Squaw Valley Dev. Co.,* 80 U.S.P.Q.2d 1264, 2006 WL 1546500, at *10–*14 (T.T.A.B.2006).

Blackhorse Defendants reference a 1972 meeting between PFI's president and a few major Native American organizations about the "Washington Redskins" team name to show that it "may disparage." In March 1972, a delegation of Native American leaders met with the then President of PFI, Edward Bennett Williams, to demand that the team change its name. The group included: (1) Leon Cook, President of NCAI; (2) Dennis Banks, National Director of the American Indian Movement ("AIM"); (3) Ron Aguilar, District Representative of the National Indian Youth Council ("NIYC"); (4) LaDonna Harris, President of AIO; (5) Richard LaCourse, News Director in the Washington Bureau of the American Indian Press Association ("AIPA"); (6) Laura Wittstock, Editor of Legislative Review for ILIDS; (7) Hanay Geiogamah, Assistant to the Commissioner of Indian Affairs and the Youth Representative from the Bureau of Indian Affairs; and (8) Ron Petite, AIM. Criss Decl. Ex. 64 at 18:6–19:5; Ex. 66. Articles from the Washington Post and the Washington Daily News state that around the time of the meeting, NCAI's membership was approximately 300,000–350,000 members. *See Blackhorse,* 2014 WL 275716, at *19–*20.

The next day, Williams wrote to NFL Commissioner Pete Rozelle to inform him about the meeting, noting that the "delegation of American Indian leaders . . . vigorously object[ed] to the continued use of the name Redskins." Criss Decl. Ex. 3. Although Williams did not change the team name after the meeting, he did change the fight song and altered the cheerleaders' outfits so that they were less stereotypical. (Doc. 71 at 19.)

The Court finds this meeting probative on the issue of whether the mark consisted of matter that "may disparage" a substantial composite of Native Americans during the relevant time period. Representatives of several prominent Native American organizations protesting the "Redskins" name is strong evidence that the term "may disparage." Williams himself regarded the Native Americans he met with as "leaders," rather than a group of individuals representing their own interests. (*Id.*)

In support of their argument that prominent Native American organizations and leaders in the Native American community have long opposed the use of the term "redskins" as the name of an NFL football team name, Blackhorse Defendants have submitted several declarations. Below are quotes from the declarations of four prominent Native Americans: Raymond Apodaca (former Area Vice President of NCAI and Governor for the Yselta Del Sur Pueblo); Leon Cook (former NCAI President and former Council Member and Tribal Administrator for the Red Lake Nation); Kevin Gover (prominent attorney, former Assistant Secretary of the Interior for Indian Affairs, and current Director of the Smithsonian Institution's National Museum of the American Indian); and Suzanne Harjo (former Executive Director of the NCAI and 2014 recipient of the Presidential Medal of Freedom for her work on behalf of Native Americans). Each declaration affirms Blackhorse Defendants' argument that from 1967 to 1990, the Redskins Marks consisted of matter that "may disparage" a substantial composite of Native Americans.

Raymond Apodaca was born in 1946 and is a member of the Yselta Del Sur Pueblo. Apodaca Decl. ¶ 2. Apodaca is a former Executive Director of the Texas Indian Commission, serving in that capacity from 1982–1989. *Id.* ¶ 7. From 1991–1992, he was the Tribal Administrator for the Yselta Del Sur Pueblo. *Id.* ¶ 5. At the time, Tribal Administrator was the highest administrative role within the tribe. *Id.* He also served as Tribal Governor for the same pueblo from 1990–1992. *Id.* Apodaca has been an active member of the NCAI since 1973. *Id.* ¶ 6. Apodaca declared that "NCAI is the oldest and the preeminent Native American organization, representing the majority of Native Americans on a variety of political, cultural, and social policy issues." *Id.* ¶ 7.

He further stated that because NCAI represents the majority of Native Americans in federally recognized tribes, NCAI is the best organization to consult to discern an understanding of Native Americans' position on an issue. *Id.* ¶ 12. He held several leadership positions in NCAI, including Area Vice President. Apodaca has thought that "redskin," both the term and the professional football team name, was a racial slur against Native Americans since the 1960s. *Id.* ¶¶ 13–15.

Leon Cook was born in 1939 and is a member of the Red Lake Band of Chippewa Indians. Cook Decl. ¶ 2. Between 1970 and 1971, Cook worked for the Bureau of Indian Affairs. *Id.* ¶ 3. He has held various roles in the Red Lake Nation, including Tribal Council Representative, member of the tribal governing council, a Tribal Administrator, and Human Resources Director. *Id.* ¶ 4.

Cook has been an active member of NCAI since 1966 and was elected its president in 1971. *Id.* ¶¶ 5–6. While Cook was president of NCAI, 100–150 tribes were members. *Id.* ¶ 6. As president, Cook also served as the head of NCAI's Executive Council. *Id.* ¶ 8. Its role was to identify "issues of concern to the Native American membership and develops strategies to address those issues." *Id.* Cook invited representatives of AIM, NIYC, and AIO to a 1972 Executive Council meeting. At this meeting, the four groups concluded that they shared a common interest in opposing the "Washington Redskins" name as it was "bigoted, discriminatory, and offensive to Native Americans." *Id.* ¶ 10.

Cook further stated that in 1973, the NCAI General Assembly voted in favor of a resolution calling for the "Washington Redskins" to change the team name. *Id.* ¶ 14. According to Cook, NCAI has maintained its opposition to the name, formalizing the opposition with resolutions in the early 1990s. *Id.* ¶ 15. Finally, Cook declared, "Throughout my life, I have maintained my opposition to the Washington football team's name. I believe the use of the term 'redskin' in any context—professional athletics or otherwise—is derogatory, disparaging, and demeaning to Native Americans." *Id.* ¶ 16.

Kevin Gover was born in 1955 and is a citizen of the Pawnee Indian Nation. Gover Decl. ¶¶ 2–3. Gover grew up thinking that "redskin" was a racial slur. *Id.* ¶ 4. Gover was occasionally called a "redskin" during his upbringing. He stated:

> I vividly recall a time when I was in fourth grade when another child called me a "dirty redskin" on the playground. In addition, when I played for my junior high school football team, members of opposing teams sometimes would call me a "redskin" as a form of bullying or "trash talking" on the field.

*Id.* ¶ 5. Gover's parents moved to Washington, D.C. in 1971 so his father could work for the AIO. Gover claimed that he remembers his parents and other Native Americans in their social circle "expressing their dismay that the local NFL football team used an ethnic slur against Native Americans as its team name." *Id.* ¶ 6. This helped motivate Gover to write a letter to Edward Bennett Williams. In his letter, Gover noted that several hundred thousand Native Americans find the team name "Redskins" offensive and suggested that Williams change the team name to the "Washington Niggers" in order to stick with his "ethnic theme." Gover Decl. Ex. A.

Finally, Susan Harjo's declaration is also evidence of the disparaging nature of the "Washington Redskins" team name. Harjo was born in 1945 and is a citizen and enrolled member of the Cheyenne and Arapho Tribes of Oklahoma. Harjo Decl. ¶ 3. Harjo currently serves as the President and Executive Director of The Morning Star Institute, "a Native American cultural organization that is dedicated to Native Peoples' traditional and cultural rights, historical research and arts promotion." *Id.* ¶ 2. Growing up, Harjo and her family members often heard "redskin" being used as a slur. Harjo explained:

> In the 1950s, my brothers, cousins and Cheyenne friends were often called "redskins" by white children at school . . . and sometimes by their parents. On one especially upsetting and painful occasion, an elementary school teacher argued with me about our family history and the Battle of Little Big Horn, and he angrily called me names, including "redskin." He also slandered my great-great-grandfather, Chief Bull Bear, and called him a "redskin" and pushed me into a rosebush. I also remember shopkeepers calling me the epithet "redskin." Altogether, white people probably called me the slur "redskin," or called the group I was with "redskins," at least 100 times.

*Id.* ¶ 5.

In 1962, Harjo was selected by the Business Committee of the Cheyenne and Arapho Tribes of Oklahoma to be a part of a tribal delegation to federal meetings in Washington, D.C. *Id.* ¶ 10. She recalled members of the delegation complaining about the "Redskins" signage and promotion in Washington, with tribal leaders saying something to the effect of, "No wonder such bad Indian policy comes out of D.C.; look what bad things they call us." *Id.* Harjo also served as the Executive Director of the NCAI from 1984–1989. While in that role, Harjo "reflected and carried out the position of NCAI to oppose the name of the Washington NFL team and to call for its elimination." *Id.* ¶ 13. Lastly, Harjo noted that she has always regarded "redskin" as a racial slur and deems it "the most awful slur that can be used to refer to Native American nations, tribes, and persons." *Id.* ¶ 19.

The Court finds that the declarations from these prominent Native American individuals and leaders, replete with the actions of groups concerning the "Washington Redskins" football team and anecdotes of personal experiences with the term "redskin," show that the Redskins Marks consisted of matter that "may disparage" a substantial composite of Native Americans during the relevant time period.

Additional evidence that the marks consisted of matter that "may disparage" is found in the NCAI Resolution. In 1993, the Executive Council of the NCAI passed a resolution on the "Washington Redskins" team name. Founded in 1944, NCAI bills itself as "the oldest and largest intertribal organization nationwide representative of, and advocate for national, regional, and local tribal concerns." Criss Decl. Ex. 108. The resolution provided, in pertinent part, that, "[T]he term REDSKINS is not and has never been one of honor or respect, but instead *it has always been* and continues to be a pejorative, derogatory, denigrating, offensive, scandalous, contemptuous, disreputable, disparaging and racist designation for Native American[s]." Criss Decl. Ex. 108 (emphasis added). The Court finds that this resolution is probative of NCAI's constituent members' collective opinion of the term "redskin" and PFI's marks for many years, including when the last Redskins Mark was registered. *See In re Heeb Media LLC,* 89 U.S.P.Q.2d 1071, 2008 WL 5065114, at *1 (T.T.A.B.2008) (affirming denial of registration of a mark based in part on excerpts from "individuals representing Jewish groups or in their individual capacity," which provided that they "consider the term HEEB to be a disparaging").

* * *

The Court finds that Blackhorse Defendants have shown by a preponderance of the evidence that there is no genuine issue of material fact as to the "may disparage" claim: the record evidence shows that the term "redskin," in the context of Native Americans and during the relevant time period, was offensive and one that "may disparage" a substantial composite of Native Americans, "no matter what the goods or services with which the mark is used." *In re Squaw Valley Dev. Co.,* 80 U.S.P.Q.2d 1264, 2006 WL 1546500, at *16 (T.T.A.B.2006). "Redskin" certainly retains this meaning when used in connection with PFI's football team; a team that has *always* associated itself with Native American imagery, with nothing being more emblematic of this association than the use of a Native American profile on the helmets of each member of the football team.

Accordingly, the Court finds that the Redskins Marks consisted of matter that "may disparage" a substantial composite of Native Americans during the relevant time period, 1967–1990, and must be cancelled. Also, consistent with the parties' concession that Section 2(a)'s "may disparage" and "contempt or disrepute" provisions use the same legal analysis, the Court further finds that the Redskins Marks consisted of matter that bring Native Americans into "contempt or disrepute." Thus, Blackhorse Defendants are entitled to summary judgment on Count II.

* * *

---

As noted at the outset of this section, the most important use of merchandising rights based on trademark law involves not the portrayal of real life products in fictional scenes, but fictional scenes, characters, and themes in real life products. Suppose, then, that having lost its case in the Second Circuit, Hormel were to turn around and start selling a variety of food products it named Spa'am, or Miss Piggy. Each product was being marketed in a way which made it clear to customers that those foods were not being sponsored or authorized by the producers of Muppet movies (who are selling or licensing Muppet food). Would that action constitute trademark infringement? Can the consumer confusion theory in *Hormel* justify such a conclusion?

Nearly four decades ago, when entertainment and sports merchandising was beginning to take off, the Fifth Circuit faced precisely that issue. National Hockey League teams had begun to license use of their names and symbols on a host of clothes and sporting goods. A manufacturer, Dallas Cap & Emblem Mfg., having failed to secure such a license, decided to produce and sell the emblems to various sporting goods stores anyway. When the NHL licensing arm went to court, it was able to get a directive from the court that customers had to be told that the emblems were not officially authorized by the NHL. Dallas Cap was happy to do that, but the NHL wanted a total ban on the sale of its team names and symbols without the league's consent. That relief was granted by the court of appeals in *Boston Professional Hockey Association v. Dallas Cap & Emblem Mfg.*, 510 F.2d 1004 (5th Cir. 1975).

Quoted earlier in this section was a passage from the Fifth Circuit opinion acknowledging the fundamental differences between trademark and copyright law. The district judge had reasoned that to give the NHL more than the specific disclaimer to dispel consumer confusion would be tantamount to giving the NHL a monopoly in those symbols, something copyright did not do and trademark was not supposed to do. The appellate court, while acknowledging that "our decision here may slightly tilt the trademark laws from the purpose of protecting the public to the protection of the business interests of plaintiffs," decided that both sports fans and NHL teams would be better served by barring any unlicensed sales of team symbols:

> Underlying our decision are three persuasive points. First, the major commercial value of the emblems is derived from the efforts of plaintiffs. Second, defendant sought and ostensibly would have asserted, if obtained, an exclusive right to make and sell the emblems. Third, the sale of a reproduction of the trademark itself on an emblem is an accepted use of such team symbols in connection with the type of activity in which the business of professional sports is engaged. We need not deal here with the concept of whether every artistic reproduction of the symbol would infringe upon plaintiffs' rights. We restrict ourselves to the emblems sold principally through sporting goods stores for informal use by the public in connection with sports activities and to show public allegiance to or identification with the teams themselves.

*Id.* at 1011. With respect to the use of the disclaimers to dispel fan confusion about sponsorship, the court stated:

> . . . In this case, however, the district court overlooked the fact that the Act was amended to eliminate the source of origin as being the only focal point of confusion. The confusion question here is conceptually difficult. It can be said that the public buyer knew that the emblems portrayed the teams' symbols. Thus, it can be argued, the buyer is not confused or deceived. This argument misplaces the purpose of the confusion requirement. The confusion or deceit requirement is met by the fact that the defendant duplicated the protected trademarks and sold them to the public knowing that the public would identify them as being the teams' trademarks. The certain knowledge of the buyer that the source and origin of the trademark symbols were in plaintiffs satisfies the requirement of the Act. The argument that confusion must be as to the source of the manufacture of the emblem itself is unpersuasive, where the trademark, originated by the team, is the triggering mechanism for the sale of the emblem.

*Id.* at 1012.

* * *

---

Leagues must be careful when licensing their trademarks to third-party manufacturers to avoid antitrust issues. The National Football League faced exactly that difficulty after it chose to grant an exclusive ten-year license to Reebok. American Needle, a former manufacturer of officially licensed NFL hats, sued the NFL under the Sherman Act alleging antitrust violations.

The NFL adopted a "single entity" defense, arguing that it could not be subject to antitrust law in this context because it was a single entity—it was not colluding with any other licensor when it contracted with Reebok.

American Needle argued that the NFL was, in fact, 32 different entities—the teams—that were colluding to restrict open competition in the market for licensed products, including caps.

The United States Supreme Court agreed with American Needle, and found that the NFL, for antitrust purposes, consisted of 32 different entities, not one. *See American Needle v. NFL*, 560 U.S. 183 (2010).

---

*Boston Hockey* generated a major and still controversial expansion in the scope of trademark law, especially when contrasted with the decision in *Pagliero v. Wallace China*, 198 F.2d 339 (9th Cir. 1952), which had adopted an "aesthetic functionality" trademark defense for use of another product's colors and design. Indeed, in *International Order of Job's Daughters v. Lindeburg*, 633 F.2d 912 (9th Cir. 1980), the Ninth Circuit reiterated its *Pagliero* precedent in denying relief to an organization whose decorative insignia were being reproduced and sold on the defendant's jewelry.

More recent cases have tended to uphold the right of trademark plaintiffs to prevent use of distinctive insignia. For example, in *Warner Brothers, Inc. v. Gay Toys, Inc.*, 724 F.2d 327 (2d Cir. 1983), the court found that the defendant's "Dixie Racer" toy cars were likely to cause confusion (particularly among child purchasers) with Warner's "General Lee" from the Dukes of Hazzard television series.

Despite the *Boston Hockey* (Fifth Circuit) and *Warner Bros.* (Second Circuit) decisions, this branch of intellectual property law remains somewhat murky, as illustrated by a pair of encounters the First Circuit has had with the Boston Marathon, a century-old Patriots Day race from Hopkinton, Massachusetts, to Boston, managed by the non-profit Boston Athletic Association (BAA). After the BAA decided to enlarge its revenues by granting exclusive merchandising licenses, it sued to block a Hopkinton clothing distributor from continuing its practice of selling T-shirts depicting "Boston Marathon" with the year and the image of a runner. In *BAA v. Sullivan*, 867 F.2d 22 (1st Cir. 1989), a First Circuit panel, while acknowledging "that a trademark, unlike a copyright or patent, is not a 'right in gross' that enables a holder to enjoin all reproduction," asserted that "when a manufacturer intentionally uses another's mark as a means of establishing a link in consumers' minds with the other's enterprise, and directly profits from that link, there is an unmistakable aura of deception." In this case,

> [g]iven the undisputed facts that (1) defendants intentionally referred to the Boston Marathon on its shirts, and (2) purchasers were likely to buy the shirts precisely because of that reference, we think it fair to presume that purchasers are likely to be confused about the shirt's source or sponsorship. We presume that, at the least, a sufficient number of purchasers would be likely to assume—mistakenly—that defendant's shirts had some connection with the official sponsors of the Boston Marathon. In the absence of any evidence that effectively rebuts this presumption of a "likelihood of confusion," we hold that plaintiffs are entitled to enjoin the manufacture and sale of defendant's shirts.

*Id.* at 34.

Emboldened by this success, the BAA registered the words "Boston Marathon" in connection with the race and expanded its marketing efforts to generate more funds to enhance the quality of the event. One such agreement was an exclusive license given to WBZ-TV, a local station, to telecast the race. Nevertheless, WCVB-TV, Channel 5 in Boston, continued to televise the race using cameras in helicopters and along the marathon route, and regularly used the phrase Boston Marathon throughout its telecast. The BAA went back to court, this time in front of a different First Circuit panel headed by then-Chief Judge (now Justice) Breyer. *See WCVB-TV v. Boston Athletic Ass'n*, 926 F.2d 42 (1st Cir. 1991).

Judge Breyer first noted that this was not the garden variety brand of "confusion" seen in typical trademark cases, where one producer was using a similar name that had become associated with another producer. Channel 5 was not running its own Marathon to compete with the BAA's; the thrust of the BAA case, instead, was that Channel 5's use of the Boston Marathon trademark would somehow confuse viewers into believing the telecast had the BAA's "official 'O.K.' or imprimatur," something that had been held sufficient for a Lanham Act violation in *Sullivan*. Judge Breyer made it clear, though, that the allusions in *Sullivan* (and other cases relied on by the BAA) to "free riding" on the plaintiff's name and good will did not alter the trademark law focus on consumer confusion:

> As a general matter, the law *sometimes* protects investors from the "free riding" of others; and *sometimes* it does not. The law, for example, gives inventors a "property right" in certain inventions for a limited period of time; it provides copyright protection for authors; it offers certain protections to trade secrets. But, the man who clears a swamp, the developer of a neighborhood, the academic scientist, the school teacher, and

> millions of others, each day create "value" (over and above what they are paid) that the law permits others to receive without charge. Just how, when and where the law should protect investments in "intangible" benefits or goods is a matter that legislators typically debate, embodying the results in specific statutes, or that common law courts, carefully weighing relevant competing interests, gradually work out over time. The trademark statute does not give the appellants any "property right" in their mark except "the right to prevent confusion."

*Id.* at 45 (emphasis in original). Judge Breyer found that there was no reasonable likelihood that Channel 5 viewers would somehow believe this telecast had the official authorization or sponsorship of the BAA (especially since Channel 5 had offered to insert disclaimers during its program).

### *QUESTIONS FOR DISCUSSION*

1. Suppose that in *Warner Bros. v. Gay Toys* (or in *BAA v. Sullivan*) the manufacturer of the Dixie Racer toy car (or Boston Marathon T-shirt) had inserted on its package the notation "Not sponsored or authorized by Warner Bros. (or the BAA)." The Fifth Circuit in *Boston Professional Hockey* said that would be insufficient to justify intrusion on the plaintiff's trademark, although another panel in the Fifth Circuit expressed reservations about that apparent expansion of trademark law, in *Kentucky Fried Chicken v. Diversified Packaging Corp.*, 549 F.2d 368 (5th Cir. 1977). How would Judge Breyer have resolved such a case? What is the relevance of *Consumers Union of the United States v. General Signal Corp.*, 724 F.2d 1044 (2d Cir. 1983), in which the Second Circuit dismissed a trademark claim by the Consumers Union (CU) when a manufacturer quoted a favorable CU review of this product, naming the CU as the source, but disclaiming any relationship with or endorsement by the CU?

2. Whatever doctrinal differences remain across the circuits, there is a real question about whether it makes a significant practical difference in the level of protection enjoyed by entertainment firms. Even circuits that apply the *Job's Daughters* formulation requiring tangible proof of consumer confusion can be persuaded by survey evidence that this is the case. The reality is that because of the current blend of law and industry reaction, a large part of the consuming public probably does believe that the products they are buying with merchandising names and symbols carry the authorization of the parties that created those marks. On the other hand, had the law made it clear that any manufacturer could sell children's clothing with Kermit the Frog on it, or children's toys with General Lee, as long as they carried a specified disclaimer, customers might not assume that the product carried the *imprimatur* of the producers of the *Muppet* movies or the *Dukes of Hazzard*. The theoretical question is which way should the law have shaped consumer perceptions.

---

Vivid illustrations of the complexities of these legal policy issues can be found in two district court rulings in the late 1990s. One of them, *Mattel Inc. v. MCA Records*, 28 F. Supp. 2d 1120 (C.D. Cal. 1998), involved a hit song by the Danish music group Aqua for MCA Records, "Barbie Girl." This song displayed two characters, Barbie and Ken, singing to each other about their "life in plastic." Barbie, for example, sang:

I'm a Barbie girl, in a Barbie world
Life is plastic, it's fantastic
You can brush my hair, undress me anywhere
Imagination, life is your creation
I'm a blond bimbo girl,
in a fantasy world
Dress me up, make it light,
I'm your dolly . . .

She then went on to chant:

You can undress me everywhere . . .
You can touch, you can play
If you say, "I'm always yours"—
Make me talk, do whatever you please
I can act like a star I can beg on my knees.

Since Mattel's most famous product had long been the Barbie plastic doll, the company was concerned that these "adult-oriented lyrics" were incompatible with Barbie's wholesome image. They were also displeased that Ken, another of its dolls, was singing:

Kiss me here, touch me there Hanky Panky—
Come jump in, bimbo friend,
Let's do it again,
Hit the town, fool around,
Let's go party.

The court, however, rejected the trademark claim in *Mattel*. With respect to traditional "confusion" doctrine, the judge wrote that, even accepting that

> . . . some individuals inevitably will believe that titles and lyrics containing a celebrity or icon's name constitute an endorsement, [any such mark] is outweighed by the danger of restricting artistic expression. The First Amendment interests at stake outweigh the possibility that some people might not interpret the song's light-hearted lyrics as a comment or spoof of the popular

> Mattel product and might be confused as to whether Mattel put out or authorized the song Barbie Girl.

*Id.* at 1152. The reason is that "[f]rom the lyrics of the song and the various comments by the Aqua band members, it appears that song was intended to parody both the doll itself and the shallow, plastic values she has come to represent in some circles." *Id.* at 1139. As the judge put it:

> Even if Aqua knew that parodying a popular product would attract favorable attention, this knowledge alone cannot erase their First Amendment interests in commenting on Barbie; if it did, then no unknown group could criticize popular products because the accusation of trying to get attention would always exist. The First Amendment's protection must apply even to those whose parodies target the strong, popular, or well-established.

*Id.* at 1145.

Around that same time, another district court found a trademark violation in the title of a movie, in *Tri-Star Pictures v. Unger*, 14 F. Supp. 2d 339 (S.D.N.Y. 1998). In 1956, Sam Spiegel produced the Oscar-winning movie *Bridge on the River Kwai*, with a story about the fate of Allied prisoners of the Japanese near the end of World War II. In 1978, Joan and Clay Blair wrote and published a book *Return from the River Kwai*. This book had nothing to do with the fictional story in *Bridge*, but instead was a description of what happened to a real group of Allied prisoners who were forced to build a Japanese railway through the jungles of Burma and Thailand, and were then shipped to Japan to help fill a shortage of labor in its mines and weapons factories.

When Kurt Unger and his Leisure Time Productions learned that Spiegel was not interested in producing another movie based on this book, he secured the rights and made the movie. *Return* was shown at the 1988 Cannes Film Festival and in 50 countries around the world, and in Japan it was entitled *Bridge on the River Kwai II*. When Unger sought to release the movie in the United States, using the same title as the 1978 book, he was sued by Columbia, whose Tri-Star Pictures arm had distributed *Bridge* in this country.

In fact there is a River Kwai in Asia that had actually been crossed by these prisoners on the way to Japan, as was depicted in the *Return* movie. But the court concluded that "River Kwai" had acquired a secondary meaning in the movie world, and that there was no distinct historic or artistic reason for using that name in this movie's title. Given that the only apparent objective for doing so was to draw upon moviegoer identification with the historic *Bridge* movie, the court concluded that the resulting confusingly similar title violated Tri-Star's trademark rights. Not only did the judge enjoin release of the movie in this country, but he later awarded Columbia over $1 million in attorney fees. *See Tri-Star Pictures v. Unger*, 42 F. Supp.2d 296 (S.D.N.Y. 1999).

Are these two trademark rulings compatible in permitting a parody song titled "Barbie Girl", but barring a real-life movie titled *Return from the River Kwai*? Should the courts have blocked release of the 1978 book with the latter title, or the recent showing by Arts & Entertainment Network of a show titled *River Kwai: The True Story*? What are arguments for expanding or contracting the scope of this trademark (as opposed to copyright) protection?

## BROWNE V. MCCAIN

United States District Court, Central District, California, 2009.
612 F. Supp. 2d 1125.

KLAUSNER, DISTRICT JUDGE.

* * *

[In 2007, the Ohio Republican Party (ORP), acting on behalf of the Republican National Committee (RNC) and Senator John McCain, created a commercial criticizing Barack Obama. During the commercial, a sound recording of Jackson Browne's song "Running on Empty" played in the background. Browne, a long-time supporter of the Democratic Party, sued under copyright and trademark law. After denying the defendants' motion to dismiss the copyright claim, the court addressed the Lanham Act.]

* * *

RNC contends that the Court should dismiss Plaintiff's Lanham Act claim because (1) the Lanham Act applies only to commercial speech, (2) the First Amendment and artistic relevance test bar the claim, and (3) Plaintiff cannot, as a matter of law, establish likelihood of confusion. For the following reasons, the Court disagrees.

*1. Application of the Lanham Act to Political Speech*

RNC contends that Plaintiff cannot state a claim for false association or endorsement under 15 U.S.C. § 1125(a)(1)(A) of the Lanham Act ("Section 43(a)(1)(A)") because the Lanham Act applies only to commercial speech and does *not* apply to political speech. For the following reasons, the Court disagrees.

RNC appears to collapse several distinct arguments into one general contention that the Lanham Act does not apply to political speech. Each distinct argument is addressed separately below.

First, contrary to RNC's assertions, courts have recognized that the Lanham Act applies to noncommercial (i.e., political) *and* commercial speech. *See, e.g., United We Stand America, Inc. v. United We Stand, America New York, Inc.,* 128 F.3d 86, 92–3 (2d Cir. 1997); *MGM-Pathe Commns. Co. v. Pink Panther Patrol,* 774 F. Supp. 869, 876 (S.D.N.Y. 1991). Indeed, the Act's purpose of reducing consumer confusion supports application of the Act to political speech, where the consequences of widespread confusion as to the source of such speech could be dire. *See United We Stand America, Inc.,* 128 F.3d at 91–93. Thus, to the extent RNC's Motion is based on its theory that the Lanham Act applies only to commercial speech, that theory is rejected.

Second, to the extent that RNC argues that Plaintiff's Lanham Act claim must yield to important First Amendment concerns over protecting political speech, such concerns are addressed in the Court's discussion of the First Amendment and artistic relevance test.

Third, the mere fact that a defendant is engaged in political speech, alone, does not bar a plaintiff's Lanham Act claim. *See MGM-Pathe Commns. Co.,* 774 F. Supp. at 877. Thus, to the extent RNC's Motion is based on its theory that the mere fact that Browne's Lanham Act claim is based on political speech bars his claim as a matter of law, that theory is rejected.

Fourth, contrary to the implications of RNC's arguments, the Lanham Act's reference to use "in commerce" does not require a plaintiff who asserts a claim under Section 43(a)(1)(A) to show that the defendant actually used the mark in commerce. *United We Stand America, Inc.,* 128 F.3d at 92. Rather, the Act's reference to use "in commerce" actually "reflects Congress's intent to legislate to the limits of its authority under the Commerce Clause" to regulate interstate commerce. *Id.* The interstate commerce jurisdictional predicate for the Lanham Act merely requires a party to show that the defendant's conduct affects interstate commerce, such as through diminishing the plaintiff's ability to control use of the mark, thereby affecting the mark and its relationship to interstate commerce. *See Stauffer v. Exley,* 184 F.2d 962, 964–67 (9th Cir. 1950); *see, e.g., Maier Brewing Co. v. Fleischmann Distilling Corp.,* 390 F.2d 117, 120 (9th Cir. 1968); *F.E.L. Publications, Ltd. v. National Conference of Catholic Bishops,* 466 F. Supp. 1034, 1044 (D.C.Ill.1978). As such, the "scope of 'in commerce' as a jurisdictional predicate of the Lanham Act is broad and has a sweeping reach." *Planned Parenthood Federation of America, Inc. v. Bucci,* 1997 WL 133313 (S.D.N.Y.) (citing *Steele v. Bulova Watch Co.,* 344 U.S. 280, 73 S.Ct. 252, 97 L.Ed. 319 (1952)).

Thus, to the extent RNC's Motion is based on its theory that Browne cannot state a claim under the Lanham Act because he has not shown actual use in commerce, that theory is rejected. Moreover, since RNC has not actually argued that Plaintiff's claim fails to satisfy the interstate commerce requirement, the Court will not address that issue at this time.

*2. The First Amendment and Artistic Relevance Test*

RNC also contends that Plaintiff cannot state a claim under the Lanham Act because the Commercial is an expressive work and thus the claim is barred under the First Amendment and artistic relevance test. For the following reasons, the Court disagrees.

In the Ninth Circuit, a Lanham Act claim based on use of a mark in an artistic work is analyzed under the Second Circuit's *Rogers* artistic relevance test, which was developed to address the competing interests of the First Amendment's protection of artistic works and trademark protection. *See Mattel, Inc. v. MCA Records, Inc.*, 296 F.3d 894, 902 (9th Cir. 2002). Under this test, "[a]n artistic work's use of a trademark that otherwise would violate the Lanham Act is not actionable [1] 'unless the use of the mark has no artistic relevance to the underlying work whatsoever, or, [2] if it has some artistic relevance, unless it explicitly misleads as to the source or content of the work.'" *E.S.S. Entm't 2000, Inc. v. Rock Star Videos, Inc.*, 547 F.3d 1095, 1099 (9th Cir. 2008) (citing *MCA Records, Inc.*, 296 F.3d at 902).

Here, the Court finds that RNC has not established that the First Amendment and artistic relevance test bar Plaintiff's Lanham Act claim at this time. First, RNC has not established that the Commercial is an artistic work, requiring application of the artistic relevance test. Second, RNC has not shown that the First Amendment and artistic relevance test bar Browne's claim merely because the Commercial is noncommercial, political speech. In fact, courts that have applied the Lanham Act to noncommercial and political speech have implicitly rejected the theory that claims based on such speech are barred, as a matter of law, based on the First Amendment and artistic relevance test. *See, e.g., MGM-Pathe Commns. Co.*, 774 F. Supp. at 874–76; *see generally United We Stand America, Inc.*, 128 F.3d at 92. Finally, it appears that, in light of the Court's limited inquiry on a 12(b)(6) motion, the Court would have difficulty applying the artistic relevance test at this time.

Thus, the Court finds that RNC has not established that Plaintiff's Lanham Act claim is barred by the First Amendment and artistic relevance test at this time and rejects RNC's contention that the Court should dismiss this claim on that basis.

*3. Likelihood of Confusion*

RNC also contends that Plaintiff cannot state a claim under the Lanham Act because the Commercial clearly identifies its source as ORP, so there is no likelihood of confusion as to its origin. For the following reasons, the Court disagrees.

The Ninth Circuit considers the following factors, known as *Sleekcraft* factors, in determining whether likelihood of confusion exists

(1) strength of the mark, (2) proximity or relatedness of the goods, (3) similarity of the marks, (4) evidence of actual confusion, (5) marketing channels used, (6) degree of care customers are likely to exercise in purchasing the goods, (7) defendant's intent in selecting the mark, and (8) likelihood of expansion into other markets. *KP Permanent Make-Up, Inc. v. Lasting Impression I, Inc.,* 408 F.3d 596, 608 (9th Cir. 2005).

Here, the Court finds that RNC has not established, at this time, that Plaintiff cannot show likelihood of confusion. RNC's contention that the Commercial clearly identifies its source as ORP, alone, does not show that a consumer could not possibly be confused as to whether Browne endorsed Senator McCain, RNC, or ORP. Moreover, RNC has failed to address all of the *Sleekcraft* factors and whether they weigh against likelihood of confusion. Without the parties' arguments as to these factors, the Court is unable to thoroughly analyze likelihood of confusion at this time.

Thus, the Court finds that RNC has not established that Plaintiff cannot show likelihood of confusion at this time and rejects RNC's contention that the Court should dismiss this claim on that basis.

---

The Federal Trademark Dilution Act of 1995[i] amended section 43 of the Lanham Act to grant the "owner of a *famous work*" injunctive relief (and on occasion damages) if others used its mark in ways that "cause *dilution* of the distinctive quality of the mark." The factors listed by section 43(c) for determining whether a mark has become "famous" include the mark's degree of distinctiveness, the duration and extent of its use in connection with particular products, trade channels, and geographic areas, the mark's degree of recognition, and whether the mark had been registered. Dilution is defined as the "lessening of the capacity of a famous mark to identify and distinguish goods and services," regardless of any "likelihood of confusion, mistake, or deception."

The policy rationale for this expansion of federal trademark law is that this would be helpful in securing better enforcement of famous American marks (like Nike) in foreign countries, many of which have anti-dilution laws on their books and apparently object to the absence of such protection of their own marks under American law. Moreover, more than half the states have adopted different versions of the dilution law, though judges (especially in federal courts) have been reluctant to enforce those laws on any kind of national basis. One state with such a law is New York, and the Second Circuit's analysis of its scope and application

---

i *See* Kenneth L. Port, *The Congressional Expansion of American Trademark Law: A Civil Law System in the Making*, 35 Wake Forest L. Rev. 827 (2000).

in another part of a case we read earlier in this section provides a glimpse of how this law may affect the entertainment world.

## HORMEL FOODS CORP. V. JIM HENSON PRODUCTIONS, INC.

United States Court of Appeals, Second Circuit, 1996.
73 F.3d 497.

VAN GRAAFEILAND, CIRCUIT JUDGE.

[The dispute in this case was whether the character Spa'am in the movie *Muppet Treasure Island* had infringed upon Hormel Foods' trademark for SPAM luncheon meat. Here the court addressed the question of whether, even absent evidence of the consumer confusion then needed under federal law, the movie had diluted the distinctive quality of SPAM by either "blurring" or "tarnishing" this name under state law.]

B. Trademark Dilution

* * *

*Blurring*

Dilution by blurring occurs when "customers or prospective customers . . . see the plaintiff's mark used on a plethora of different goods and services." 3 McCarthy § 24.13[1][a][i] at 24–106. "Thus, dilution by 'blurring' may occur where the defendant uses or modifies the plaintiff's trademark to identify the defendant's goods and services, raising the possibility that the mark will lose its ability to serve as a unique identifier of the plaintiff's product." *Deere & Co. v. MTD Prods., Inc.*, 41 F.3d 39, 43 (2d Cir. 1994). This injury to the mark's selling power need not involve any confusion as to source or sponsorship. The unauthorized pullulation itself causes the harm. The legislative history of § 368–d underscores this understanding by giving examples of hypothetical violations: "DuPont shoes, Buick aspirin tablets, Schlitz varnish, Kodak pianos, Bulova gowns, and so forth." 1954 N.Y. Legis. Ann. 49–50.

There is very little likelihood that Henson's parody will weaken the association between the mark SPAM and Hormel's luncheon meat. Instead, like other spoofs, Henson's parody will " 'tend[ ] to increase public identification' " of Hormel's mark with Hormel. *See Jordache Enterprises, Inc. v. Hogg Wyld, Ltd.*, 828 F.2d 1482, 1490 (10th Cir. 1987). . . .

This conclusion is strengthened when we consider that Henson's parody undermines any superficial similarities the marks might share. As we noted above, the name "Spa'am" will always appear next to the character likeness and the words "Muppet Treasure Island." This dissimilarity alone could defeat Hormel's blurring claim, for in order to establish dilution by blurring, the two marks must not only be similar, they "must be 'very' or 'substantially' similar." *Mead Data Central, Inc. v. Toyota Motor Sales, U.S.A., Inc.*, 875 F.2d 1026, 1029 (2d Cir. 1989). Moreover, Henson is not using the name "Spa'am" as a product brand name. Rather, Spa'am is a character in products branded with Henson's own trademark "Muppet Treasure Island." This tends to dissipate the fear that SPAM will no longer be considered a unique product identifier. Viewed against the backdrop of Henson's transparent parodic intent and the contextual dissimilarity between the two marks, it is clear that use of the name "Spa'am" does not blur Hormel's mark.

*Tarnishment*

Dilution may also occur by tarnishment. A trademark may be tarnished when it is "linked to products of shoddy quality, or is portrayed in an unwholesome or unsavory context," with the result that "the public will associate the lack of quality or lack of prestige in the defendant's goods with the plaintiff's unrelated goods." *Deere & Co.*, supra, 41 F.3d at 43. The mark may also be tarnished if it loses its ability to serve as a "wholesome identifier" of plaintiff's product. *Id.*

Tarnishment can occur through a variety of uses. Some cases have found that a mark is tarnished when its likeness is placed in the context of sexual activity, obscenity, or illegal activity. Hormel argues that the image of Spa'am, as a "grotesque," "untidy" wild boar will "inspire negative and unsavory associations with SPAM luncheon meat." Both Hormel and Amicus Curiae rely heavily on our recent decision in *Deere*, supra, for the proposition that products that "poke fun at widely recognized marks of non-competing products, risk diluting the selling power of the mark that is made fun of." 41 F.3d at 44. Their reliance is misplaced.

In *Deere* we addressed the question "whether the use of an altered version of a distinctive trademark to identify a competitor's product and achieve a humorous effect can constitute trademark dilution." MTD produced a television commercial for its competing lawnmower tractor, altering the famous Deere trademark from a proud, majestic deer, to one that was cowardly and afraid. We found that there was no blurring because there was little risk of impairing the identification of Deere's mark with its products. Noting that tarnishment "is usually found where a distinctive mark is depicted in a context of sexual activity, obscenity, or illegal activity," we held that the "blurring/tarnishment dichotomy does not necessarily represent the full range of uses that can dilute a mark under New York law." We found a violation of the anti-dilution statute because "alterations of that sort, accomplished for the sole purpose of promoting a competing product . . . risk the possibility that consumers will come to attribute unfavorable characteristics to a mark and ultimately associate the mark with inferior goods and services." This holding mirrors the rationale of the tarnishment doctrine. Thus, although the court below understood *Deere* to create a new category of dilution, we find that our decision in *Deere* is better understood as a recognition of a broad view of tarnishment, where that doctrine had been sometimes narrowly confined.

The sine qua non of tarnishment is a finding that plaintiff's mark will suffer negative associations through defendant's use. Hormel claims that linking its luncheon meat with a wild boar will adversely color consumers' impressions of SPAM. However, the district court found that Spa'am, a likeable, positive character, will not generate any negative associations. Moreover, contrary to Hormel's contentions, the district court also found no evidence that Spa'am is unhygienic or that his character places Hormel's mark in an unsavory context. Indeed, many of Henson's own plans involve placing the Spa'am likeness on food products. In addition, the court also noted that a simple humorous reference to the fact that SPAM is made from pork is unlikely to tarnish Hormel's mark. Absent any showing that Henson's use will create negative associations with the SPAM mark, there was little likelihood of dilution.

Moreover, unlike *Deere*, Henson's merchandise will not be in direct competition with that of Hormel. This is an important, even if not determinative, factor. "Dilution of this sort is more likely to be found when the alterations are made by a competitor with both an incentive to diminish the favorable attributes of the mark and an ample opportunity to promote its products in ways that make no significant alteration." Here, Henson does not seek to ridicule SPAM in order to sell more of its competitive products; rather, the parody is part of the product itself. Without Spa'am, the joke is lost. Indeed, we were mindful of this problem in *Deere* when we noted that "the line-drawing in this area becomes especially difficult when a mark is parodied for the dual purposes of making a satiric comment and selling a somewhat competing product." *Id.* Thus, in *Deere* we did not proscribe any parody or humorous depiction of a mark. Overall, we took a cautious approach, stating that "we must be careful not to broaden section 368–d to prohibit all uses of a distinctive mark that the owner prefers not be made."

Therefore, in the instant case, where (1) there is no evidence that Henson's use will cause negative associations, (2) Henson is not a direct competitor, and (3) the parody inheres in the product, we find that there is no likelihood of dilution under a tarnishment theory.

Affirmed.

---

One group that did express concern to Congress about the 1995 dilution law was the media industry, which the new statute accommodated by making it clear that the following uses of even a "famous" mark could not be actionable under the section 43(c):

> A. Fair use of a famous mark by another person in comparative commercial advertising or promotion . . .
>
> B. Noncommercial use of a mark.
>
> C. All forms of news reporting and news commentary.

This provision also came into play in *Mattel Inc. v. MCA Records*, 28 F. Supp. 2d 1120 (C.D. Cal. 1998), the Barbie doll case. The judge ruled that, even accepting that Barbie was a *famous* mark, the song "Barbie girl" could not be said to have "diluted" or "tarnished" the doll's image. The song fell within the "noncommercial use exception" to this expansion of trademark protection. In placing these limits on both dilution and confusion standards, the judge relied on the following passage from *L.L. Bean Inc. v. Drake Publishers*, 811 F.2d 26 (1st Cir. 1987):

> The central role which trademarks occupy in public discourse (a role eagerly encouraged by trademark owners), makes them a natural target of parodists. Trademark parodies, even when offensive, do convey a message. The message may be simply that business and product images need not always be taken too seriously; a trademark parody reminds us that we are free to laugh at the image and associations linked with the mark . . . Denying parodists the opportunity to poke fun at symbols and names which have become woven into the fabric of our daily life, would constitute a serious curtailment of a protected form of expression.

*Id.* at 34.

### *QUESTIONS FOR DISCUSSION*

1. In appraising the desirability expanded dilution theories, consider first the general situation of movie studios and other entertainment firms. Should they be entitled to the same exclusive property rights in their names and symbols as are now given to entertainers by the law of publicity rights? Even if the user of the performer's name and likeness makes it clear that its product or advertisement does not carry the performer's endorsement, this caveat will not constitute a defense to a publicity rights suit. Are there distinctions between the interests of performers as persons and studios as business entities that warrant different treatment?

2. Consider now the interests of entertainment fans. Suppose that there are lots of consumers in the entertainment market who would like to wear a shirt or cap with their favorite show or character's logo on it, but do

not much care whether this is an "official" product, at least not enough to want to add the studio's five to fifteen percent licensing fee to the purchase price of the merchandise. Should the law deny fans this informed choice in a competitive marketplace, in order to assure that several billion dollars a year in licensing fees continue to be channeled to entertainment companies? What affirmative social values are served by such a legal regime?

---

A lawsuit filed in 1996 illustrates the fact that while trademark and copyright law differ, the two do share one critical problem: who owns the rights? Frank Capra's 1947 classic *It's A Wonderful Life* saw its copyright lapse in the 1970s when someone forgot to file for the 28-year renewal period that the Copyright Act then offered. With the movie apparently having fallen into the public domain, television stations around the country were delighted to be able to show it for free, especially at Christmas-time. Then, in the early 1990s, with their lawyers having read *Stewart v. Abend*, 495 U.S. 207 (1990), Spelling Entertainment, the current parent to Republic Pictures, asserted a right in the movie based on its ownership of the still copyrighted short story on which Capra had loosely based his film. That claim led television stations to shy away from televised replays. It also blocked a project planned by the actor Jimmy Hawkins, who in the movie had played Terry Bailey, the son of the Bailey parents, James Stewart and Donna Reed. Hawkins had developed a calendar for the 50th anniversary of *It's A Wonderful Life* that would feature trivia about the film, including the dates for events in the lives of its stars. Spelling warned Hawkins' producers and distributors away from doing anything with his calendar, saying that it violated the studio's trademark rights in the movie's names and images. Hawkins responded with a suit against Spelling for improperly inducing a breach of contract by his collaborators in this project. The claim was that even if Spelling and Republic might be able to assert copyright in the movie as a derivative product from the story they continue to own, this could not support trademark claims derived just from the well-known movie and its character portrayals. What do you believe was, and should have been, the results of this *Wonderful Life* lawsuit?

## D. CONTRACT RIGHTS IN STORY IDEAS[j]

A recurring problem in the entertainment industry is the "stolen" idea. Many disputes arise out of claims that a studio appropriated an idea and turned it into a successful movie or series. These cases are generally

[j] *See* Arthur Miller, *Common Law Protection For Products of the Mind*, 119 Harv. L. Rev. 703 (2006); Lionel S. Sobel, *The Law of Ideas, Revisited*, 1 UCLA Enter. L. Rev. 7 (1994); Melville B. Nimmer, *The Law of Ideas*, 27 So. Cal. L. Rev. 119 (1954); *see also* Margreth Barrett, *The "Law of Ideas" Reconsidered*, 71 J. Pat. & Tm. Off. Soc'y 691 (1989); Glen L Kulik, *Copyright Preemption: Is This the End of Desny v. Wilder?* 21 Loy. L.A. Ent. L. Rev. 1 (2000).

referred to as "idea-submission" claims. As we saw in Chapter 4, copyright law has never protected ideas as such. To state a tenable claim under copyright law, a plaintiff needs to show that the submission moved beyond the realm of "idea" and into the domain of "expression." Because of the way the entertainment industry operates, this is an insuperable hurdle for many plaintiffs.

In the motion picture and television industries, it is common for writers to submit ideas to producers in a condensed draft known as a "treatment." Often a treatment is not developed into a complete work until after a producer or studio formalizes its interest in the project. Because many of these treatments do not rise to the level of copyrightable expression, writers have had to seek protection for their ideas under other areas of the law. Although some early plaintiffs enjoyed success under property law or confidential relationship theories, it is now clear that contract doctrine provides writers with the broadest protection in idea-submission cases.

Historically, there was considerable doubt about the viability of contract law for protection of pure ideas. The uncertainty surrounding an idea-submission contract action was not erased until 1956, when the California Supreme Court issued its landmark ruling in *Desny v. Wilder*, 46 Cal.2d 715, 299 P.2d 257 (1956). That case involved a suit by writer Victor Desny against producer Billy Wilder and Paramount Pictures over their alleged use of one of Desny's story ideas for their movie, *Ace in the Hole*. The controversy began when Desny called Wilder's office in an attempt to set up an appointment to meet Wilder and to pitch his movie idea (which was then in the form of a 65-page script). Wilder's secretary advised him to prepare a synopsis of the story if he wanted Wilder to read it. Two days later, Desny's three-page synopsis was ready. At the secretary's request, he proceeded to dictate it to her over the phone. Desny told the secretary he expected compensation if the idea was used, and she assured him he would be paid if it was.

Based upon these factual assertions, the California Supreme Court reversed the trial court's grant of summary judgment against Desny and held that he was entitled to a trial on the implied contract claim. "[I]deas are as free as the air," the court ruled, but "there can be circumstances when neither air nor ideas may be acquired without cost."

In the course of determining whether the record contained any triable issue of material fact, California Supreme Court Justice Schauer engaged in a treatise-like portrayal of the law relating to idea-submission cases. "An idea is usually not regarded as property," he noted, "because all sentient beings may conceive and evolve ideas throughout the gamut of their powers of cerebration and because our concept of property implies something which may be owned and possessed to the exclusion of all other persons." The court noted, though, that ideas can be the subject of contract, because "disclosure may be of substantial benefit to the person to whom it is disclosed" (quoting Justice Traynor's dissent in *Stanley v. Columbia Broadcasting System, Inc.*, 35 Cal.2d 653, 674, 221 P.2d 73, 85 (1950)). Thus, Justice Schauer observed, "[t]he person who can and does convey a valuable idea to a producer who commercially solicits the service or who voluntarily accepts it knowing that it is tendered for a price should likewise be entitled to recover." The court went on to state:

> . . . conveyance of an idea can constitute valuable consideration and can be bargained for before it is disclosed to the proposed purchaser, but once it is conveyed, i.e., disclosed to him and he has grasped it, it is henceforth his own and he may work with it and use it as he sees fit. In the field of entertainment the producer may properly and validly agree that he will pay for the service of conveying to him ideas which are valuable and which he can put to profitable use. Furthermore, where an idea has been conveyed with the expectation by the purveyor that compensation will be paid if the idea is used, there is no reason why the producer who has been the beneficiary of the conveyance of such an idea, and who finds it valuable and is profiting by it, may not then for the first time, although he is not at that time under any legal obligation so to do, promise to pay a reasonable compensation for that idea—that is, for the past service of furnishing it to him—and thus create a valid obligation.

299 P.2d at 269. Under certain circumstances, the court explained, a contract might be implied even without an express promise to pay:

> [T]he idea purveyor cannot prevail in an action to recover compensation for an abstract idea unless (a) before or after disclosure he has obtained an express promise to pay, or (b) the circumstances preceding and attending disclosure, together with the conduct of the offeree acting with knowledge of the circumstances, show a promise of the type usually referred to as "implied" or "implied-in-fact."

*Id.* at 270. Aware of the difficulties faced by those who receive unsolicited ideas, the court cautioned that "[u]nless the offeree has opportunity to reject he cannot be said to accept. The idea man who blurts out his idea without having first made his bargain has no one but himself to blame for the loss of his bargaining power."

Justice Carter dissented from the majority's "lengthy discussion of numerous principles of law wholly inapplicable and unnecessary to a determination of this matter." He advocated that even broader protections be available to individuals who, with little bargaining power, seek to sell their story ideas to Hollywood insiders. In doing so, Justice

Carter offered these observations about the entertainment industry context in which these disputes arise:

> When we consider the difference in economic and social backgrounds of those offering such merchandise for sale and those purchasing the same, we are met with the inescapable conclusion that it is the seller who stands in the inferior bargaining position. It should be borne in mind that producers are not easy to contact; that those with authority to purchase for radio and television are surrounded by a coterie of secretaries and assistants; that magazine editors and publishers are not readily available to the average person. It should also be borne in mind that writers have no way of advertising their wares—that, as is most graphically illustrated by the present opinion, no producer, publisher, or purchaser for radio or television, is going to buy a pig in a poke. And, when the writer, in an earnest endeavor to sell what he has written, conveys his idea or his different interpretation of an old idea, to such prospective purchaser, he has lost the result of his labor, definitely and irrevocably. And, in addition, there is no way in which he can protect himself. If he says to whomever he is permitted to see, or, as in this case, talk with over the telephone, "I won't tell you what my idea is until you promise to pay me for it," it takes no Sherlock Holmes to figure out what the answer will be! This case is a beautiful example of the practical difficulties besetting a writer with something to sell—he is not permitted even to see the secretary in person—he must convey to her over the telephone the result of his efforts.
>
> * * *
>
> I disagree with the statement in the majority opinion that: "The idea man who blurts out his idea without having first made his bargain has no one but himself to blame for the loss of his bargaining power." It seems to me that in the ordinary situation, when the so-called "idea man" has an opportunity to see, or talk with, the prospective purchaser, or someone in his employ, it is at that time, without anything being said, known to both parties that the one is there to sell, and the other to buy. This is surely true of a department store when merchandise is displayed on the counter—it is understood by anyone entering the store that the merchandise so displayed is for sale—it is completely unnecessary for the storekeeper, or anyone in his employ, to state to anyone entering the store that all articles there are for sale. I am at a loss to see why any different rules should apply when it is ideas for sale rather than normal run of merchandise. It is quite true that one need not pay for ideas as such which are

> in the public domain but when those ideas have been so treated that they have worth or value to a prospective purchaser, it is difficult to understand why it is necessary that the seller should definitely state that he is selling his merchandise to a prospective buyer. . . .

*Id.* at 280–81.

### *QUESTIONS FOR DISCUSSION*

1. Whose position in *Desny* do you find more persuasive, Justice Schauer's or Justice Carter's? Should courts consider the relative bargaining power of the parties when establishing legal standards to govern their contract claims? In considering these questions, keep in mind that the protections offered by contract law have developed against a backdrop of copyright law whose features we have been exploring in the preceding chapters.

2. In *Desny v. Wilder*, the court also made the following observation:

> [W]e are not oblivious of the hazards with which producers of the class represented here by defendants and their related amici are confronted through the unsolicited submission of numerous scripts on public domain materials in which public materials the producers through their own initiative may well find nuclei for legitimately developing the "stupendous and colossal."

*Id.* at 267. When analyzing idea-submission claims, what consideration should courts give to the position of studios that are often inundated with story ideas sent by aspiring screenwriters? If you were counsel for a production company, what policy would you recommend toward unsolicited manuscripts?

---

The issues addressed in *Desny* have been revisited by courts numerous times in later decades. In fact, it has often been said that every major motion picture or television series spawns at least one idea-submission claim. The movie *Philadelphia*, a critically acclaimed 1994 film, provides a more contemporary illustration of how these claims can arise.

The movie starred Tom Hanks as a lawyer who brings suit against his former law firm when it fires him after discovering that he has AIDS. TriStar Pictures, a unit of Sony-Columbia Pictures, said that the idea for its film came from brainstorming sessions between director Jonathan Demme and screenwriter Ron Nyswaner that began in 1989 when they both learned that someone close to them was suffering from AIDS. According to the studio, Demme and Nyswaner spent the next two years trading articles and books about this subject, and consulting family and friends to develop a compelling human story.

The family of the late Geoffrey Bowers alleged otherwise in a $10 million contract claim filed against TriStar, Demme, Nyswaner, and individual producers (including Scott Rudin). The family claimed that *Philadelphia* was really based on Bowers's own AIDS discrimination lawsuit against his former employer, the Chicago-based law firm, Baker & McKenzie. Baker had fired Bowers in 1986 after learning he had AIDS, Bowers filed suit in 1987, Bowers died in 1988 shortly after testifying at trial, and several years later the Bowers estate won a $500,000 verdict against Baker. In 1988, Scott Rudin, the producer of movies such as *The Firm* and *Sister Act*, discussed with the Bowers family the idea of making a movie based on their son's struggle against the law firm. After meeting with Geoffrey Bowers's family, friends, and attorneys, Rudin allegedly reached an understanding with the family that he would make a movie about the saga. Rudin originally planned to make the movie for Orion Pictures, but after Orion went into bankruptcy in 1991, an Orion executive who moved to TriStar took the story idea with him. Rudin was paid $100,000 for his contribution and had no further involvement in *Philadelphia*; instead, he went off to make his 1996 hit *The First Wives Club*.

TriStar maintained that the movie was a composite of a number of different AIDS discrimination cases, and that almost all elements of the story were derived from court records and news articles that are part of the public domain. The family, however, alleged that *Philadelphia* mirrored the life of Geoffrey Bowers in ways that could only have been derived from personal interviews with his family and friends. Like Bowers, the movie character portrayed by Tom Hanks had a warm relationship with an understanding family, a Latino live-in lover, adored opera and wrote his own memorial service, and was fired by the law firm after developing visible lesions on his face. The key to both Bowers and the Hanks character winning their lawsuits was taking off their shirts to show body lesions while on the stand. And in the Bowers case, as in *Philadelphia*, the mother (played by Joanne Woodward) gave the go-ahead to the suit being filed and the story being publicly disclosed.

What would the Bowers family need to prove in order to win its suit? Would it be enough to establish the existence of an oral understanding between them and independent producer Rudin? In the alternative, would demonstrating that the movie contained unique facts about Bowers' life that went beyond the public record be necessary or sufficient to succeed on an implied-in-fact contract theory (in tandem with the rights of privacy and publicity)?

---

*Desny* established the principle that contract law is available to protect against misappropriation of a person's ideas. Following that landmark decision, courts were faced with the task of determining what actions are needed to constitute formation of a contract for the sale of an idea. In *Blaustein v. Burton,* 9 Cal.App.3d 161, 88 Cal. Rptr. 319 (1970), a California appellate court addressed whether, under New York law, an implied contract may be created from the fact of disclosure and discussion of a story idea.

In 1964, Producer Julian Blaustein conceived the idea of a movie production based on William Shakespeare's play *The Taming of the Shrew,* which would star Richard Burton and Elizabeth Taylor, to be directed by Franco Zeffirelli. The movie would eliminate Shakespeare's play-within-a-play device, would include two scenes that occur offstage in the play, and would be filmed in Italy in the actual settings described by Shakespeare. Blaustein presented his idea to Richard Burton's agent, Hugh French, in New York, and French responded enthusiastically. Blaustein also met with Zeffirelli, who said he would like to participate in the project. Blaustein then flew to New York to discuss the idea with Burton and Taylor. Burton expressed his support for the idea, said he would like to participate in such a project, and suggested that Blaustein speak with his general counsel to work out an appropriate arrangement.

Negotiations with Zeffirelli and the Burtons continued during the following months. Blaustein then learned that his position as producer of the movie was in jeopardy. In 1965, a lawyer for Burton and Taylor told Blaustein that even if another producer was used, he would be rewarded for his contributions.

Thereafter, Columbia Pictures produced a movie, *The Taming of the Shrew,* which it released in 1967. The film incorporated many of Blaustein's ideas, including the casting of the actors, the use of Zeffirelli as the director, the elimination of the play-within-a-play device found in the original work, and the enactment of two key scenes that occur offstage in the original. In addition, the film was shot in Italy, though not in the specific locations described by Shakespeare. Blaustein was given neither credit nor money for his efforts.

The defendants pointed out that Blaustein himself admitted that there was nothing novel in casting leading stars to adapt a Shakespearean play to the screen. In fact, a film version of *The Taming of the Shrew* had been made in the 1930s with two leading stars of the time, Douglas Fairbanks and Mary Pickford. That version also eliminated the play-within-a-play device and visually depicted the two scenes that are only described in the original.

After a trial judge summarily dismissed Blaustein's suit, the appeals court ruled that under New York law (which it found similar to California law, post-*Desny*) Blaustein did have a viable contract claim for disclosure of an idea that, while perhaps not "novel," was valuable:

* * *

> We are of the opinion that appellant's idea of the filming of Shakespeare's play "The Taming of the Shrew" is one which may be protected by contract.
>
> Express or implied contracts both are based upon the intention of the parties and are distinguishable only in the manifestation of assent. The making of an agreement may be inferred by proof of conduct as well as by proof of the use of words. Whether or not the appellant and respondents here, by their oral declarations and conduct, as shown by the depositions and affidavits, entered into a contract whereby respondents agreed to compensate appellant in the event respondents used appellant's idea, is a question of fact which may not be properly resolved in a summary judgment proceeding, but must be resolved upon a trial of the issue. . . .

*Id.* at 334–35.

Fifteen years after *Blaustein*, the Second Circuit in *Whitfield v. Lear*, 751 F.2d 90 (2d Cir. 1984), read California law as offering an even broader scope for contract creation from idea submission. The defendant, Norman Lear, and his television production team had been working on a proposed television comedy series, *The Righteous Apples*, about a multiracial junior high rock band. Independently, the plaintiff, Thurman Whitfield, had written the script for a dramatic series, *Boomerang*, about a multiracial crime-fighting rock band of recent high school graduates. In 1979, Whitfield sent his script to a number of producers, including Lear, who acknowledged receipt. A year later, *The Righteous Apples* appeared on television, allegedly having changed its orientation from comedy to drama, particularly through the band members' fighting of crime and corruption in their community. The Second Circuit ruled that while Whitfield's story was not copyrightable, he had stated a potentially valid claim for breach of contract for the use of his idea.

> There is no evidence of an express contract between Whitfield and any of the defendants. However, California law will imply a contract from the conduct of the parties in certain circumstances. Thus, if a producer accepts a submitted idea with full knowledge that the offeror expects payment in the event of use, California courts impose liability under a theory of implied-in-fact contract.

* * *

> Whitfield contends that the custom in the television industry is that a studio or producer not desiring any outside submissions states so explicitly and, when a studio or producer is not interested in reviewing a particular script, the script is returned unopened. If, however, a studio or producer is notified that a script is forthcoming and opens and reviews it when it arrives, that studio or producer has by custom implicitly promised to pay for the ideas if used.
>
> * * *
>
> We conclude that the communications in question and the allegation of custom in the industry are sufficient to withstand a motion for summary judgment on this point.

*Id.* at 92–93.

### *QUESTIONS FOR DISCUSSION*

1. Based upon the factual record described above, what should be the outcome of the *Blaustein* and *Whitfield* cases? Did Blaustein and Burton/Taylor actually reach an explicit agreement? If not, should Blaustein's story idea (or Whitfield's) receive protection under an implied contract theory?

2. One of Blaustein's claims was that the defendants breached a duty of confidence owed to him when they used his ideas without his consent. Blaustein claimed that based upon the parties' dealings, he placed his trust and confidence in the defendants and expected that his ideas would be kept in confidence. The court ruled that summary judgment was inappropriate on this claim. Do you think that the parties developed a confidential relationship? Did the defendants breach a confidence when they made the film without Blaustein's consent?

3. Consider a later California case, *Faris v. Enberg*, 97 Cal.App.3d 309, 158 Cal. Rptr. 704 (1979). Edgar Faris developed the idea for a television sports quiz show in 1964 and approached television sports announcer Dick Enberg in 1970 to see whether he would be interested in being the master of ceremonies. Faris gave Enberg a copy of his format for the show and told him he could participate as a producer and part owner of the program. Enberg said he "was going to talk the next week with some KTLA producers about a sports show" and asked Faris to leave him a copy of the show's format. Faris did so without asking Enberg not to discuss the show with anyone. Sometime later, there appeared on television a quiz show entitled "Sports Challenge," with Enberg as master of ceremonies and with other similarities to Faris' idea. How would you compare this case to *Blaustein*? Should the claim survive a motion to dismiss? Is Faris's prior background and accomplishments in the entertainment industry relevant? Should it make a

difference whether Faris had told Enberg he wanted the idea kept confidential? If so, on what theory?

4. One of the early implied contract cases involved a claim by writer Harry Yadkoe against actor W.C. Fields. Yadkoe had sent a letter to Fields enclosing comic material for him to use in his movie productions or radio broadcasts. Fields replied with a letter thanking Yadkoe for his submission and expressing his intention to use the material in one of his upcoming works. Fields ultimately used the routines without compensating Yadkoe for his contribution. Should a contract to pay for the use of Yadkoe's material be implied by the court? How would you respond to Fields' claim that he only used an insignificant amount of Yadkoe's work? Should a court evaluate this defense based on whether or not there is still value left in the work for Yadkoe to exploit after Fields use of the material? If you believe that Fields violated a contract that existed between the parties, how would you determine the appropriate damage award? *See Yadkoe v. Fields*, 66 Cal.App.2d 150, 151 P.2d 906 (1944).

5. Even when an express contract has been signed by the parties, courts may not enforce it if its terms are overly broad. In *Sellers v. American Broadcasting Co.*, 668 F.2d 1207 (11th Cir. 1982), plaintiff Sellers told investigative reporter Geraldo Rivera that he had an exclusive theory concerning Elvis Presley's death. In exchange for revealing his story to Rivera and ABC, Sellers insisted that Rivera sign an agreement that obligated Rivera and the network to credit Sellers with uncovering the true cause of Presley's death if they aired his story. According to Sellers, Presley's bodyguard and physician replaced a prescription of cortisone with placebos in order to kill Presley and prevent him from seeking repayment of a $1.3 million loan he made to them. Eleven months after signing the contract with Sellers, Rivera helped ABC air a feature story which claimed that Presley died of polypharmacy, the interaction of prescription drugs. The district court dismissed Sellers's breach of contract action on summary judgment after concluding that ABC and Rivera did not use Sellers's exclusive story in any of its broadcasts. On appeal, the Eleventh Circuit took a different approach to disposing of Sellers's claim. Without deciding whether ABC and Rivera used Sellers's theory, the court concluded that the parties' agreement was "so vague and uncertain as to be unenforceable as a matter of law." *Id.* at 1210. The court reasoned that the contract was too indefinite to create an enforceable duty. Do you agree?

---

The most widely publicized idea-submission case to date involved Eddie Murphy's hit movie *Coming to America*, which has attracted a host of lawsuits,[k] including one discussed in Chapter 4. A misappropriation claim was filed by Art Buchwald, who claimed that the idea for *Coming to*

[k] *See* Pierce O'Donnell (with Dennis McDougal), *Fatal Subtraction: The Inside Story of* Buchwald v. Paramount (Doubleday 1996).

*America* was his, not Murphy's (as the movie credits had stated). The case is different from *Desny* and *Blaustein*, because Buchwald's claim was premised on breach of an express contract, rather than on a contract implied from the parties' behavior. The focus of the case, then, was whether Paramount Pictures had violated the terms of its agreement with Buchwald, not whether such a contract actually existed.

## ART BUCHWALD V. PARAMOUNT PICTURES CORP.

California Superior Court, Appellate Department, 1990.
13 U.S.P.Q.2D 1497, 17 Media L. Rep. 1257, 1990 WL 357611.

SCHNEIDER, JUDGE.

[In 1982, Art Buchwald, a renowned writer and humorist, prepared an eight-page screen treatment entitled "It's a Crude, Crude World," whose principal character was inspired by Buchwald's observance of a state visit by the Shah of Iran. Buchwald sent the treatment to Alain Bernheim, a friend and co-plaintiff in this action, who registered it with the Writers Guild of America. Bernheim met with Jeffrey Katzenberg, then head of motion picture production at Paramount Pictures, for the purpose of "pitching" Buchwald's story to Paramount for development into a movie starring Eddie Murphy. Katzenberg described Buchwald's treatment as "a succinct, smart, straightforward idea with a lot of potential to it."

After changing the title to "King for a Day" and registering it with the MPAA, Paramount began searching for a writer for the movie. In 1983, Paramount reached an agreement with Buchwald that gave the studio the option to make a movie "based upon" the treatment, and an agreement with Bernheim that he would be producer for the film if it was made. In the meantime, Paramount continued to search for a writer and director for the movie. In addition, Katzenberg and others kept Eddie Murphy apprised of the studio's progress with the venture.

In the summer of 1983, Paramount chose a writer for the screenplay, and in a studio memorandum, "King for a Day" was described as the "Art Buchwald idea" that Paramount was "now developing for Murphy." In addition, John Landis was approached as a potential director for the film. In September 1983, the screen writer sent the first draft of the script for "King for a Day" to Paramount, but this draft was not well received. As a result, the studio paid $2,500 to Buchwald to extend its option on "King for a Day" and began searching for a new writer. The following month, negotiations with French writer and director Francis Veber led to a $300,000 contract, under which he was to write a new draft.

In early 1984, Paramount's financial agreement with Bernheim was amended. The studio also exercised its second option on Buchwald's story idea. When the script was still not ready by that summer, Katzenberg instructed a Paramount executive to obtain a one-year extension on its option from Buchwald "for cheap money." In August 1984, with release of the movie still scheduled for the summer of 1985, the Paramount-Buchwald agreement was amended to provide for a third option. That option was ultimately exercised in October 1984. By March 1985, however, Paramount announced that it had abandoned its plans for the "King for a Day" project.

Buchwald maintained an interest in the venture, and in 1986 he optioned his treatment of "King for a Day" to Warner Brothers. In the 1987, Paramount began the development process of a property called "The Quest," reportedly based upon a story by Eddie Murphy. The studio selected John Landis as director for this project, which was ultimately renamed *Coming to America*. In the meantime, Warner Brothers was still involved in developing the Buchwald treatment, and a revised script was ready in November 1987. That project, however, was cancelled when Warner Brothers learned that Paramount was shooting *Coming to America*, starring Eddie Murphy. *Coming to America* was finally released in the summer of 1988; the screenplay credit was given to David Sheffield and Barry Blaustein, and Eddie Murphy received the story credit.

Soon after the movie's release, Buchwald and Bernheim sued Paramount for breach of contract. Buchwald claimed that he was entitled to additional compensation under his option agreement with Paramount, since the studio produced a movie "based upon" his treatment of "King for a Day." Without questioning the validity of the contract, Paramount denied that it had breached its agreement with Buchwald. The studio claimed that *Coming to America* had not been "based upon" Buchwald's treatment, and therefore it owed him no additional compensation.]

* * *

Discussion

*Introduction*

At the outset the Court desires to indicate what this case is and is not about. It is not about whether Art Buchwald or Eddie Murphy is more creative. It is clear to the Court that each of these men is a creative genius in his own field and each is an uniquely American institution. This case is also not about whether Eddie Murphy made substantial contributions to the film *Coming to America*. The Court is convinced he did. Finally, this case is not about whether Eddie Murphy "stole" Art Buchwald's concept "King for a Day." Rather, this case is primarily a breach of contract case between Buchwald and Paramount (not Murphy) which must be decided by reference to the agreement between the parties and the rules of contract construction, as well as the principles of law enunciated in the applicable legal authorities.

* * *

*The Meaning of "Based Upon"*

Since the agreement provided Buchwald was entitled to payment only if Paramount produced "a feature length theatrical motion picture" "based upon Author's Work," the threshold inquiry in this case is what is meant by the term "based upon." Because the term is not defined in the contract, it was the Court's hope that the term had a specific meaning in the entertainment industry and that the experts who testified would so indicate. Unfortunately, there was as little agreement among the experts concerning the meaning of this term as there was between plaintiffs and Paramount concerning whether *Coming to America* is based upon Buchwald's treatment.

* * *

Since the Court found the testimony of the entertainment experts, both individually and collectively, to be of little value with respect to the "based upon" issue, the Court turned to the appellate decisions of this State for guidance. Fortunately, that guidance existed. Indeed . . . the Court believes these decisions provide a road map through the "based upon" mine field.

*Access and Similarity*

In cases involving infringement, which this case is not, it has been held that an inference of copying may arise where there is proof of access to the material with a showing of similarity. . . . These same rules have been applied in a case involving a cause of action alleging breach of an express contract. *Fink v. Goodson-Todman Enterprises, Ltd.*, 9 Cal. App. 3d 996, 1013 (1970).

*Access*

In the present case, there is no real issue concerning Eddie Murphy's access to Buchwald's concept. Indeed, the evidence is that Murphy knew about Buchwald's concept. . . .

* * *

*Similarity*

Since there is no real issue concerning access, the focus must then be on the question of similarity. . . .

The parties have directed a substantial amount of their attention to the issue of similarity. Paramount contends that there must be substantial similarity between Buchwald's treatment and *Coming to America* in order for Buchwald to succeed in this case.

* * *

Although the Court believes the cases relied upon by Paramount are inapplicable to the issue of the extent of similarity that is required in this case, the Court has concluded the two controlling cases with respect to this issue are *Fink* supra, and *Weitzenkorn v. Lesser*, 40 Cal.2d 778 (1953).

In *Fink*, as in the present case, the contract between the parties obligated the defendant to compensate the plaintiff if the defendant created a series "based on Plaintiff's Program or any material element contained in [it]." The Court stated that a " '[m]aterial element' could range from a mere basic theme up to an extensively elaborated idea, depending upon what might be proved as the concept of the parties." With respect to the contract cause of action, the Court framed the issue: "[W]hether . . . defendants have based their series on a material element of plaintiff's program." The Court noted that its "based on any material element" test was "quite close to the concept of 'inspiration for' which was the key to the upholding of an implied contract count in *Minniear v. Tors*, 266 Cal.App.2d 495, 505 [72 Cal. Rptr.287]."

Similarly, in *Weitzenkorn*, supra, the contract obligated the defendants to pay for plaintiffs' composition "if they used it or any portion of it, regardless of its originality."

Based on the decisions in *Fink* and *Weitzenkorn*, and the contract involved in this case, the Court concludes that Paramount's obligation to pay Buchwald arose if *Coming to America* is based upon a material element of or was inspired by Buchwald's treatment. As the Court in *Fink* noted, this determination is to be made by searching for "points of similarity" both quantitatively and qualitatively. . . .

*The Comparison of Buchwald's Treatment and "Coming to America"*

* * *

In Buchwald's treatment, a rich, educated, arrogant, extravagant, despotic African potentate comes to America for a state visit. After being taken on a grand tour of the United States, the potentate arrives at the White House. A gaffe in remarks made by the President infuriates the African leader. His sexual desires are rebuffed by a black woman State Department officer assigned to him. She is requested by the President to continue to serve as the potentate's United States escort. While in the United States, the potentate is deposed, deserted by his entourage and left destitute. He ends up in the Washington ghetto, is stripped of his clothes, and befriended by a black lady. The potentate experiences a number of incidents in the ghetto, and obtains employment as a waiter. In order to avoid extradition, he marries the black lady who befriended him, becomes the emperor of the ghetto and lives happily ever after.

In *Coming to America* the pampered prince of a mythical African kingdom (Zamunda) wakes up on his 21st birthday to find that the day for his prearranged marriage has arrived. Discovering his bride to be very subservient and being unhappy about that fact, he convinces his father to permit him to go to America for the ostensible purpose of sowing his "royal oats." In fact, the prince intends to go to America to find an independent woman to marry. The prince and his friend go to Queens, New York, where their property is stolen and they begin living in a slum area. The prince discovers his true love, Lisa, whose father—McDowell—operates a fast-food restaurant for whom the prince and his friend begin to work. The prince and Lisa fall in love, but when the King and Queen come to New York and it is disclosed who the prince is, Lisa rejects the prince's marriage invitation. The film ends with Lisa appearing in Zamunda, marrying the prince and apparently living happily ever after.

There are, to be sure, differences between Buchwald's "King for a Day" and *Coming to America.* However, as noted above, where, as here, the evidence of access is overwhelming, less similarity is required. Moreover, " '[e]ven if the similar material is quantitatively small, if it is qualitatively important . . . the trier of fact . . . may properly find substantial similarity' " (*Fink, supra,* at 1013).

In his opening statement, counsel for plaintiffs made the following comparison of "King for a Day" and *Coming to America*:

> "Both are modern day comedies. The protagonist is a young black member of royalty from a mythical African kingdom, pampered and extremely wealthy, well-educated. They both come to a large city on the American East Coast. And they arrive as a fish out of water from this foreign kingdom.
>
> Abruptly, finding themselves without royal trappings of money and power, they end up in the black, urban American ghetto, about as far culturally as they could ever hope to be from their pampered, royal status in their mythical kingdom. Each character abandons his regal attitudes. Both live in the ghetto as poor blacks experiencing the realities of ghetto life.
>
> Each takes a menial job as (sic) a series of harrowing and comedic adventures in the ghetto, is humanized and enriched by his experiences. Love always triumphing over all, each meets and falls in love with a beautiful young American woman whom he will marry and make his Queen and live happily ever after in his mythical African kingdom."

The Court agrees with this comparison. In fact, the Court believes that these similarities alone, given the language of the contract involved in this case and the law that liability in a contract case can arise even if a non-substantial element is copied, might well be sufficient to impose contract liability on Paramount. The fact is, however, that other compelling evidence of similarity exists.

In the original script . . . that was indisputably based upon Buchwald's treatment, the king ends up as an employee of a fast food restaurant where he ultimately foils a robbery attempt by use of a mop. In *Coming to America* the prince is also employed by a fast food restaurant and foils a robbery attempt by use of a mop. These similar "gimmicks" provide compelling evidence that the evolution of plaintiffs' idea provided an inspiration for *Coming to America*.

The Court has found an item of documentary evidence significant with respect to the similarity issue. In early September, 1984, a writer by the name of Jim Harrison sent a treatment to Robert Wachs, Murphy's manager, which he suggested was "closely aligned with Murphy's talents." This treatment envisioned Eddie Murphy playing an aide to a powerful Southern senator. The aide ultimately becomes the King of Somaili. In rejecting this idea, Wachs wrote Harrison in pertinent part as follows:

> "Unfortunately, there is a project under development at Paramount for Eddie entitled 'King for a Day', based on an unpublished Art Buchwald story, which is fairly close to your story line, hence I really can't give you a go-ahead on this one."

When asked what he meant by "fairly close," Wachs replied "that an ordinary person would find that any two items had more similarities than dissimilarities." If Murphy's manager thought that the Harrison treatment had more similarities than differences to Buchwald's treatment, it seems to the Court that a substantially stronger case can be made with respect to the similarities between Buchwald's treatment and *Coming to America*.

There are other factors that are present in this case that strongly support plaintiffs' position that Buchwald's original concept and its subsequent development at Paramount was the inspiration for *Coming to America*. For example, the evidence is overwhelming that for two years Paramount considered "King for a Day" to be a project that was being developed for Eddie Murphy. In fact, when *Coming to America* was made, its star was Eddie Murphy. Additionally, during the development of "King for a Day" it was contemplated Murphy would portray multiple characters. In *Coming to America* he did.

Moreover, when "King for a Day" was under development, Paramount sought to interest John Landis in directing the movie. . . . The fact that Landis was aware of Buchwald's concept for "King for a Day" is important. Since the evidence revealed that Landis had creative input into *Coming to America*, it is his access and knowledge, in addition to Eddie Murphy's, that it is relevant to the issue of similarity.

It is also important to observe that one of the promotional ideas utilized in connection with *Coming to America* was a "King for a Day" concept where a prize winner was afforded the opportunity to go on a shopping spree.

As indicated above, there are differences between Buchwald's treatment and *Coming to America*. One of the principal differences is that the king in Buchwald's original treatment was despotic, while the prince in *Coming to America* is kind and naive. The fact is, however, that early in the development process Paramount desired to make Buchwald's king more likable. . . .

The other significant difference between Buchwald's treatment and *Coming to America* is the motivation that brought the principal character to America. In Buchwald's treatment the motivation was to obtain military weapons from the United States. In *Coming to America* it was to find an independent wife. This dissimilarity does not, however, require a finding that *Coming to America* is not "based upon" Buchwald's work.

In many ways, the decision in *Weitzenkorn*, supra, is similar to the present case. *Weitzenkorn* was a breach of contract case in which the plaintiff sued to recover damages by reason of the defendant's use of her Tarzan/Fountain of Youth idea. Although both plaintiff's idea and the defendant's movie involved Tarzan, there were striking dissimilarities between the two. In plaintiff's story, Tarzan entered the area where the Fountain of Youth was located because he was captured by the evil persons who dwelled in the area. By contrast, in the defendant's version Tarzan voluntarily entered the area which was occupied by a king who was a friend of Tarzan. In plaintiff's version, Tarzan undertook his journey to rescue Boy. In defendant's version, Tarzan was on a mission of mercy to find a missing aviatrix. In plaintiff's version, the evil queen and her subjects disintegrated when Tarzan destroyed the Fountain of Youth. In defendant's version, the ending was totally different.

In *Weitzenkorn* the Court found no similarity as to form and manner of expression between plaintiff's composition and defendant's movie. Although both works included the same characters in Africa being involved with a mythical Fountain of Youth, the moral of each was entirely different. Specifically, the moral of plaintiff's work was that eternal youth was not a blessing. The moral of defendant's work was that eternal youth was a reward for good.

In spite of the significant differences between plaintiff's and defendant's work, the Court concluded that the trial court had erroneously sustained the demurrers of the defendants without leave to amend. Because the defendants had expressly agreed to compensate the plaintiff if they used plaintiff's composition, or any portion of it, the Court concluded that plaintiff's complaint stated a cause of action "no matter how slight or commonplace the portion which" the defendants used. [The court also found *Blaustein v. Burton*, 9 Cal. App. 3d 161 (1970) to be "instructive".]

Based upon the authorities discussed above and the provisions of the contract involved in this case, the court concludes that *Coming to America* is a movie that was "based upon" Buchwald's treatment "King for a Day". "Bearing in mind the unlimited access . . . [proved] in this case and the rule that the stronger the access the less striking and numerous the similarities need be, . . . [the Court concludes that Paramount has] appropriated and used a qualitatively important part of plaintiff's material in such a way that features discernible in . . . [Paramount's] work are substantially similar thereto." Finally, the Court wishes again to emphasize that its decision is in no way intended to disparage the creative talent of Eddie Murphy. It was Paramount and not Murphy who prepared the agreement in questions. It is Paramount and not Murphy that obligated itself to compensate Buchwald if any material element of Buchwald's treatment was utilized in or inspired a film produced by Paramount. *Coming to America* is no less the product of Eddie Murphy's creativity because of the Court's decision than it was before this decision was rendered.

*The Issue of the Originality of Buchwald's Treatment*

As indicated, in the agreement between Buchwald and Paramount, the former sold to Paramount his "original story and concept" and warranted that his work was original and not taken from or based upon any other material or motion picture. During the trial, Paramount was permitted to introduce into evidence a movie made in the 1950's by Charlie Chaplin entitled *A King in New York*. Although the Court understood it to be Paramounts's position during trial that Buchwald's treatment was not original in that it was based upon *A King in New York*, it appears that this position was abandoned by Paramount during oral argument. Paramount's present position, as the Court understands it, is that if the Court concludes *Coming to America* is based upon Buchwald's treatment, it must similarly conclude that Buchwald's treatment is based upon *A King in New York* since the same degree of similarity exists between Buchwald's treatment and each of the two movies. The Court does not agree.

It is true that Buchwald testified that he saw *A King in New York* in Paris in the 1950's and wrote a column concerning his review of the movie after seeing it. Besides these facts, there is not a scintilla of evidence that Buchwald's treatment was in any way based on *A King in New York* since the same degree of similarity exists between Buchwald's treatment and each of the two movies. The Court does not agree.

In sum, . . . the Court rejects the contention that Buchwald's treatment was not original and that it was in any way based upon *A King in New York*. Stated another way, while plaintiffs have proved by a preponderance [of the evidence] that *Coming to America* is "based upon" "King for a Day," plaintiffs have also proved by a preponderance of the evidence that "King for a Day" is not "based upon" *A King in New York*.

Contract claim upheld.

* * *

## *QUESTIONS FOR DISCUSSION*

1. In analyzing the degree of similarity between Buchwald's treatment and *Coming to America,* the court applies the "Inverse Ratio Rule" that was stated in *Fink*: "the stronger the access, the less striking and numerous the similarities need be." Do you agree that Paramount's unlimited access to the Buchwald treatment should entitle plaintiffs to make a lesser showing of similarity between the works? Do you think the application of the rule had an impact on the ultimate holding in this case?

2. How would you have decided Paramount's appeal? Would your view change if you were told that after *Coming to America*, seven different people filed lawsuits claiming to have been the actual creator of the story on which the movie was based?

3. An earlier case that explored the difference between the legal standards governing copyright claims and contract claims is *Chandler v. Roach,* 156 Cal.App.2d 435, 319 P.2d 776 (1957). Plaintiff Chandler, a professional writer, devised the idea for a dramatic series based on the activities of a public defender's office. After conducting research into the idea, Chandler hired an agent to help him pitch his concept to Hollywood insiders. The agent, and ultimately Chandler himself, met with defendant Roach, a television producer, who wished to produce a series based on Chandler's idea. The parties proceeded to negotiate the terms of an agreement, and they exchanged at least two drafts of a written contract. Roach asked Chandler to prepare a sample script, and he did so and then revised it pursuant to Roach's suggestions. About two years, communications between the parties broke down, but Roach began producing a television series about a public defender's office. He neither paid nor credited Chandler for any contribution to the program. After accepting the jury's conclusion that Roach had based his show on Chandler's idea, the court ruled that Roach had violated an implied contract to pay Chandler for the disclosure of his idea. The court held that a plaintiff in a breach of contract case need not prove that his idea was either novel or concrete:

> The producer and the writer should be free to make any contract they desire to make with reference to the buying of the ideas of the writer; the fact that the producer may later determine, with a little thinking, that he could have had the same ideas and could thereby

> have saved considerable money for himself, is no defense against the claim of the writer. This is so even though the material to be purchased is abstract and unprotected material.

*Id.* at 442. Do you agree with the court's conclusion that novelty and concreteness should not be required elements in an *implied,* as opposed to an *express*, contract claim (such as the one brought by *Buchwald*)?

4. A suit for copyright infringement and breach of contract was brought against Paramount Pictures following its release of the movie *Trading Places*, which starred Eddie Murphy and Dan Aykroyd. Marilyn Anderson, a professional writer, claimed that *Trading Places* was substantially similar to her screenplay entitled *High Stakes,* a romantic melodrama about a lonely female executive who bets her best friend that in six months, she can train an uneducated white man to appear sufficiently genuine as an entrepreneur to fool her company's board of directors. The subplot of the movie is the love that develops between these two characters. *Trading Places* is a comedy about a double bet between two wealthy brothers that a black derelict could become a successful executive, and that a successful white executive would become a criminal if they simply "traded places." The film's subplot involves the alliance that these two characters form in an effort to exact revenge on the wealthy brothers. Based on these facts and the materials from Chapter 4 above, do you think Anderson should succeed on her copyright infringement claim? In the alternative, if Anderson could satisfy the test for *creation* of an idea-submission contract with Paramount, do you think there is a sufficient resemblance between the story ideas to constitute a *violation* of such a contract? *See Anderson v. Paramount Pictures*, 617 F. Supp. 1 (C.D. Cal. 1985).

---

In the late 1980s, the Second Circuit found New York's legal treatment of idea-submission claims to be fundamentally different from California's. In *Murray v. NBC*, 844 F.2d 988 (2d Cir. 1988), the court concluded that New York law required that the idea must be truly "novel" to be valid consideration for such a contract claim. And this decision was generated by one of the most important programs in American television industry. In 1980, Hwesu Murray, a black employee of NBC (a financial analyst in its Sports division), wrote a brief two-page memo to entertainment division executives (led by Brandon Tartikoff), proposing a new situation comedy called *Father's Day*. This was to be "wholesome . . . entertainment which will focus upon the family life of a Black American family . . . The leading character will be the father, . . . a devoted family man and a compassionate, proud, authority figure . . . The program will show how a black father can respond with love . . ." This "closely-knit . . . middle class" black family would be living in a contemporary urban setting, with the wife and mother also working. And crucial to Murray's story idea was that the father would be played by Bill Cosby, who was already a television star, winning three Emmy awards. Murray told NBC executives that if they used this idea, he expected not only to be paid and credited, but to serve as the show's executive producer

NBC turned down the idea, saying "we are not interested in pursuing its development at this time." Four years later, though, NBC unveiled *The Cosby Show*, with Bill Cosby playing a doctor, his wife a lawyer, and their Huxtable family living in New York City. In its first season, The *Cosby Show* topped the Nielsen ratings, and over its lifetime had the largest average audience in television history. Murray was given no compensation, credit, or production role, and so he filed suit against what was now his former employer, claiming breach of an implied contract.

The Second Circuit summarily dismissed the claim as not displaying the kind of "genuine novelty and innovation" that is needed for rights in a story idea (by contrast with expression). It read New York law as affording "special protection . . . only to truly innovative ideas while allowing the free use of ideas that are 'merely clever or useful adaptations of existing knowledge'."

> We certainly do not dispute the fact that the portrayal of a nonstereotypical black family on television was indeed a breakthrough. Nevertheless, that breakthrough represents the achievement of what many black Americans, including Bill Cosby and plaintiff himself, have recognized for many years—namely, the need for more positive, fair and realistic portrayal of blacks on television. While NBC's decision to broadcast *The Cosby Show* unquestionably was innovative in the sense that an intact, nonstereotypical black family had never been portrayed on television before, the mere fact that such a decision had not been made before does not necessarily mean that the idea for the program is itself novel.
>
> Consequently, we do not agree with appellant's contention that the nonstereotypical portrayal of a black middle-class family in a situation comedy is novel because
>
> [t]o argue otherwise would be the equivalent of arguing that since there had always been baseball, and blacks in baseball, there was nothing new about Jackie Robinson playing in the major leagues—or that since there had always been schools in Little Rock, Arkansas, and blacks in schools, there was nothing new about integrating schools in Little Rock.
>
> As appellees persuasively point out in response to this analogy, Murray has "confused[d] the 'idea' with its execution. . . . Indeed, the idea of integration . . . had been discussed for decades prior to the actual events taking place." Similarly, we believe, as a matter of law, that plaintiff's idea embodied in his "Father's

Day" proposal was not novel because it merely represented an "adaptation of existing knowledge" and of "known ingredients" and therefore lacked "genuine novelty and invention."

We recognize of course that even novel and original ideas to a greater or lesser extent combine elements that are themselves not novel. Originality does not exist in a vacuum. Nevertheless, where, as here, an idea consists in essence of nothing more than a variation on a basic theme—in this case, the family situation comedy—novelty cannot be found to exist. The addition to this basic theme of the portrayal of blacks in nonstereotypical roles does not alter our conclusion, especially in view of the fact Bill Cosby previously had expressed a desire to do a situation comedy about a black family and that, as the district court found, Cosby's entire career has been a reflection of the positive portrayal of blacks and the black family on television.

Appellant would have us believe that . . . we are in effect condoning the theft of ideas. On the contrary, ideas that reflect "genuine novelty and intention" are fully protected against unauthorized use. But those ideas that are not novel "are in the public domain and may freely be used by anyone with impunity." Since such non-novel ideas are not protectible as property, they cannot be stolen.

*Id.* at 992–93.

A decade later, though, in *Nadel v. Play-By-Play Toys & Novelties*, 208 F.3d 368 (2d Cir. 2000), the Second Circuit in effect rejected that *Murray* reading of New York law. This case involved the idea for a new toy rather than a television program. The lower court cited *Murray* in dismissing the implied contract claim by Nadel in the "toy idea man," on the ground that the basic concept of a "spinning plush toy" was not that novel in the industry, but the Second Circuit panel reversed it. As then-Judge Sonia Sotomayor put it, by contrast with a claim of *misappropriation* of an idea, "for contract-based claims in submission-of-idea-cases, a showing of novelty to the buyer will supply sufficient consideration to support a contract." This standard of "novelty to the buyer" was felt to "comport with traditional principles of contract law. While an idea may be unoriginal or non-novel in a general sense, it may have substantial value to a particular buyer who is unaware of it and therefore willing to enter into a contract to acquire and exploit it." The reason is that "the buyer may reap benefits from such a contract in a number of ways—for instance, by not having to expend resources pursuing the idea through other channels or by having a profit-making idea implemented sooner rather than later." *Id.* at 377.

The year 2004 saw two conflicting court decisions involving contracts for story ideas. In *Grosso v. Miramax*, 383 F.3d 965 (9th Cir. 2004), the Ninth Circuit found that there was a viable claim against Miramax Films by author Jeff Grosso for its movie *Rounders* allegedly taking some ideas and themes from his screenplay *The Shell Game*. Grosso had sent an unsolicited copy of his script about Texas Hold-em Poker to Miramax. The court overturned the district court's summary dismissal of the idea contract claim:

> To establish a *Desny* claim for breach of implied-in-fact contract, the plaintiff must show that the plaintiff prepared the work, disclosed the work to the offeree for sale, and did so under circumstances from which it could be concluded that the offeree voluntarily accepted the disclosure knowing the conditions on which it was tendered and the reasonable value of the work.

*Id.* at 967. And an "express promise to pay" was not necessary.

That same year the Third Circuit reached the opposite result in its reading of New Jersey state law in the case of *Baer v. Chase*, 392 F.3d 609 (3d Cir. 2004). David Chase, who had gone from New Jersey to Los Angeles in 1971, eventually created the HBO television series *The Sopranos*. In doing so, he was certainly aided by a New Jersey lawyer, Robert Baer, who had just left a prosecutor's office there and was also aspiring to a career in Hollywood. Thus, he both gave a script to Chase and met with him where "he pitched the idea to shoot a film or television series about the New Jersey Mafia," and then arranged Chase's "research visit" to New Jersey, including meetings with detectives and visiting locations.

Accepting that this had played a role in the creation of *The Sopranos* and noting that Baer had also been sent and then given Chase comments on a *Sopranos* screenplay, the court said "Baer does not dispute that virtually all his ideas and locations that he too contributed to Chase existed in the public domain." In addition the court found crucial what Baer had alleged and Chase had accepted, that "I would perform the services while assuming the risk that if the show failed [Chase] would owe me nothing. If, however, the show succeeded he would remunerate me in a manner commensurate to the true value of my services." The court found that "an implied-in-fact contract in an idea submission case" had to "be definite as to price and duration." After reviewing the evidence, the court concluded

> New Jersey precedent does not support Baer's attempt to carve out an exception to traditional principles of contract law for submission-of-idea cases. The New Jersey courts have not provided even the slightest indication that they intend to depart from their well-established requirement that enforceability of a

> contract requires definiteness with respect to the essential terms of that contract. Accordingly, we will not relax the need for Baer to demonstrate definiteness as to price and duration with respect to the contract he entered into with Chase.

*Id.* at 620.

Thus, Baer's claim to any compensation for his help in creating *The Sopranos* was summarily dismissed.

It is important to remember that (unlike copyright law or the Lanham Act), contracts, express or implied, are recognized and enforced under state law. This means that different states acting through their legislatures as well as courts, are entitled to define their contractual standards in the manner they believe best serves their policy objectives. What are your views about the appropriate treatment of implied contract claims by those who have fashioned or supplied the idea, but not the detailed expression, for a new television show or a new toy?

---

As cases in this section have shown, a plaintiff can adduce evidence of access and similarity to support a claim that the defendant used plaintiff's idea in violation of an express or implied contract. The defendant, however, always has the opportunity to present evidence to rebut this inference of actual use. For example, even if a plaintiff demonstrates that there is similarity between two works, the defendant can show that it did not have access to plaintiff's idea or can introduce evidence of its independent creation of the allegedly misappropriated story idea. *Mann v. Columbia Pictures, Inc.*, 128 Cal.App.3d 628, 180 Cal. Rptr. 522 (1982), offers an interesting example of such a case.

In *Mann,* plaintiff argued that Columbia Pictures had misappropriated her idea in its development of the movie *Shampoo*. She demonstrated that she gave her treatment to a friend, who in turn gave it to her neighbor who was production manager for an independent filmmaker then based on Columbia's lot. Without reading the script, the production manager delivered it to a story editor for this independent production company, who agreed to evaluate plaintiff's movie idea.

The court held that there was insufficient evidence to infer that Columbia had access to plaintiff's work. While the court acknowledged that some Columbia staff may have had access to plaintiff's work, it also noted that the *Shampoo* screenwriters, Robert Towne and Warren Beatty, did not actually have access to plaintiff's script. Defendants presented uncontradicted evidence that neither Towne nor Beatty had any contact with the production manager or story editor who had possession of plaintiff's treatment. The mere possibility that one of the latter submitted the idea to Columbia's story department was insufficient to allow a jury to infer access by defendants to plaintiff's work.

In addition, the court held that Columbia rebutted plaintiff's inference of access with "clear positive and uncontradicted evidence" of independent creation. Defendants demonstrated that major elements of the screenplay for *Shampoo* pre-dated plaintiff's submission. This evidence of independent creation, coupled with the lack of access, led the court to uphold the trial judge's rejection of a $185,000 jury verdict for plaintiff.

Even if a defendant presents convincing evidence of independent creation, the plaintiff is not necessarily devoid of legal weapons. The plaintiff may attempt to show the two works are "strikingly similar" in order to overcome defendant's evidence of independent creation and thus permit an inference of actual use. Such an argument was put forth by William Kienzle in *Kienzle v. Capital Cities/ABC*, 774 F. Supp. 432 (E.D. Mich. 1991). Kienzle alleged that ABC and 20th Century Fox misappropriated his idea for a television series entitled *All Things,* about an inner-city Catholic rectory run by a group of priests. In response to Kienzles's suit, defendants presented evidence that *Have Faith*, a situation comedy Fox produced for ABC which aired briefly in 1989, was independently created by defendants. Although Kienzle was unable to rebut this affirmative defense of independent creation, he attempted to demonstrate that the works were so strikingly similar as to preclude the possibility of independent creation. In support of his contention, Kienzle focused on several undisputed facts:

> (1) the title "Have Faith" and the title of Kienzle's proposed series, "All Things," both contain two one-syllable words, (2) in promoting their series, both ABC and Kienzle referred to "Barney Miller," (3) both series have a character who is a Polish priest, (4) Kienzle's treatment and an ABC's advance press release describe a priest who is well built, (5) both series accentuate the "interaction of priests and people" rather than the "interplay between priest," (6) both series are situation comedies set in an inner-city rectory.

*Id.* at 437. The court, however, concluded that the similarities between the two ideas were not sufficiently striking to support the conclusion that the possibility of independent creation is precluded. The court noted that many television shows have titles containing only two one-syllable works, and several popular situation comedies feature regular interaction between key characters and the general public. Moreover, it was not surprising that in promoting the series, ABC compared *Have Faith* to *Barney Miller* because the writer and co-creator of the show wrote over 160 episodes of *Barney Miller*. Finally, the court reasoned that it was not an "unearthly" coincidence that two writers "intimately familiar with the priesthood independently thought of the same raw idea for a television series within a seven-year period." *Id.* at 438. Although the argument of striking similarity did not succeed in this case, it is still a tactic that plaintiffs can try to use to overcome a defendant's declaration of independent creation.

### *QUESTIONS FOR DISCUSSION*

Recall the lawsuit regarding the idea for the movie *Philadelphia*. Although the case was settled, what would be your appraisal of the likelihood of success if it had proceeded? Should the verdict turn on who initiated the conversations, the producer or the family? On whether or not there were conversations about payment to the family? On how much of the story idea was novel and how much was available through research in court documents? Which state's law should govern such a case?

---

To give some sense of the kinds of damages that can ride on such a case, in 1981, Sandy Veith, a contract screen writer for Universal Studios, wrote the script for a television plot, *Coletta*. The series was to be based on the story of a New York doctor who, in order to repay medical school bills, goes off to work in a southern town where he deals with a host of eccentric characters. Nothing was done with Veith's *Coletta*. However, a decade later two other Universal writers, Joshua Brand and John Falsey, wrote the script for CBS's 1990 Emmy Award-winning *Northern Exposure,* involving a New York doctor who, in much the same situation, went off to practice in an Alaskan town. The jury rejected the defendants' claim that their *Northern Exposure* story had been based on a friend's real-life experiences, and that any resemblances to *Coletta* were purely coincidental. The damages verdict was for $7.3 million.

To avoid the risk of such damage awards, many studios and networks now make it their corporate policy not to let their staff accept and read any unsolicited idea-submissions unless the writer signs a written waiver of any potential liability. How would you draft such a waiver for the firm? How would you treat it as a judge? Is such a policy good for authors as well as producers? *See Spinello v. Amblin Entertainment,* 29 Cal.App.4th 1390, 34 Cal. Rptr.2d 695 (1994) (upholding provision in idea-submission contract that required arbitration rather than litigation of any disputes about whether the producer used submitted idea in a film project).

---

The idea-submission material we have read in this section provides a valuable contract counterpoint to the laws of intellectual property that we have explored throughout this part. Several of these cases also foreshadow the problem with which the next part begins: what are the requirements for formation of any kind of entertainment contract, including those for personal services?

# PART 3

# CONTRACTUAL RELATIONS IN THE ENTERTAINMENT INDUSTRY

■ ■ ■

# CHAPTER 7

# CONTRACT FORMATION AND DURATION[a]

■ ■ ■

In the day-to-day life of the entertainment industry, the legal rules that govern transactions are principally those created by the parties and their lawyers in contract documents. Clearly the legislative and judge-made doctrines discussed throughout this book have an important influence on the private terms negotiated in the shadow of these laws. The parties do, however, have a large measure of flexibility in shaping their respective personal and property rights and obligations to their particular needs and interests.

In the previous Part, we caught a glimpse into how contracts shape the purchase and sale of story rights. There is, however, much effort that must still be undertaken to turn a story idea into a finished entertainment product that will prove attractive to the fans of movies, television shows, music albums, books, and plays. That creative venture draws upon the talent and effort of a consortium of performers, writers, editors, producers, and investors. The terms of such participation are embodied in personal service and other contracts developed by attorneys and other representatives of the key participants in the project. This part of the book discusses ways in which contract law has responded to the blend of cooperation and contention in the entertainment world.

Two distinctive features of the entertainment industry shape these contractual issues. The first is that any entertainment product is the sum of a host of creative efforts. The actors, writers, cinematographers, directors, and producers involved in a movie all have their own vision about how such a work (and their role in it) should be presented to the eventual audience. Contract negotiations about these roles can be a double-edged sword. Trying to work out all of the details in advance can lead to endless squabbling and delay in getting the project started; however, failing to address certain key issues can lead to disputes that interrupt a tight schedule once production is underway. A delicate balance must be struck between protecting individual creative integrity

[a] A vast amount has been written on both the day-to-day workings of the entertainment world and the fundamental principles of general contract law. On contracts, see E. Allan Farnsworth, *Contracts* (5th ed. 2005); Charles Fried, *Contract as Promise: A Theory of Contractual Obligation* (Harvard U. Press 1981). On the industries, see Jason Squire, ed., *The Movie Business Book* (Simon & Schuster, 3rd ed. 2004); Donald S. Passman, *All You Need to Know About the Music Business* (Simon & Schuster, 7th ed. 2009).

and establishing firm leadership of a project that can produce an appealing work on time and within budget. This clash between "art" and "commerce" is a regular theme in entertainment contract negotiation and litigation.

A second key feature of the entertainment industry is the unpredictability of success and ever-present risk of failure. If contracts strictly limited compensation to profitability, many entertainers would earn so little that the industry might shrink from attrition. A significant proportion of books, songs, plays, television series, and films end up earning less money than they cost to make and market. How much one must earn to reach the break-even point is illustrated by movies, for example, which have large production costs, even larger promotion costs, and generally must gross two and half times their production budget to break even. That means that the entertainment industry as a whole is financed by those products that are successful enough that their returns subsidize the majority, which do not break even.[b] Since neither side in negotiations can accurately predict the market's reaction to a particular product, the terms of their contracts typically reflect this uncertainty. This not only poses an obstacle to agreement before the fact, but also makes the parties to the occasional blockbuster prone to second-guess the terms of their deal after the fact.

Entertainment negotiations thus involve a personal creative process in which all participants find it hard to predict the market outcome of their projects. Ironically, these same features that complicate achievement of an entertainment agreement make the existence of a contract essential to both the artist and the firm, and render disputes about alleged contract breaches more heated and more intractable for judges. While this and the next two chapters focus on the separate legal domains of contract formation, obligation, and remedy, the cases all display the common theme of courts trying to tailor general contract doctrine to the distinctive features of the entertainment world.

## A. CONTRACT FORMALITY: THE MOVIE WORLD

The problems of creative vision and unpredictable outcome that are endemic to the entire field of entertainment law are further complicated by obstacles that are distinctive to each of the major entertainment industries. The motion picture industry, for example, no longer operates under the studio model of the 1930s and 1940s, when each major producer assembled talent under long-term employment agreements. Such relationships are still the norm in the music recording industry. Now, when a new story idea appears on the scene, the studios not only

---

[b] *See* David F. Prindle, *Risky Business: The Political Economy of Hollywood* (Westview Press 1993).

must secure exclusive rights to the story from its author, but also must sign up the key people who are needed to transform the idea into a film with box office appeal. In this world of movie deal-making, one that requires a host of commitments from performers, financiers, and distributors before production can get underway, the parties often have no opportunity to conduct extended negotiations regarding the details of their agreements. The time constraints on parties involved in a movie deal are further exacerbated by the large number of people who needed to complete a creative venture. The parties involved include producers, directors, screenwriters, actors, actresses, stunt persons, choreographers, composers, cinematographers, costume designers, editors, production managers, investors, distributors, and banking institutions. A producer is forced to sell his idea to these parties simultaneously because of the domino effect that is inherent in the process.

This process has been referred to as a "shell game": a key star will not participate until a particular director and co-star agree to do so, and the director will not commit until the stars do. Even more important, lining up major performers is crucial for securing financing for the project, for example through presale of distribution rights around the world. Since a commitment from one star must quickly be parlayed into agreements from others needed to make the whole deal materialize, there is little time for attorneys to negotiate and draft all the details of a long-form contract each time a party agrees to participate in a project. The common perception is that if parties stopped to haggle over the nuances of every agreement, moviemaking would grind to a halt and audiences would be left staring at blank movie screens. Consequently, movie deals are frequently constructed out of oral contracts signaled by handshakes.

Typically, agents put the initial pact together by negotiating the major deal points for each side. After an oral agreement is reached, participants then turn to their attorneys to finalize the agreement and draft a "deal memo," or letter of intent, documenting the material terms of the contract. These terms specify the salary, percentage of profit, tentative filming dates, and degree of credit the star will receive. Some deal memos also include arrangements for the level of creative control and personal perks that a party will enjoy. Often these deal memos are never signed by the parties. While contracting parties contemplate the completion of lengthy, signed agreements, in many cases pre-production work, even filming, commences before each side's attorneys are able to finish negotiating and drafting a final personal service contract.

The deal memo is Hollywood's technique for managing the tension between the need to have projects moving forward and the need to memorialize agreements to remedy any contract breaches. While the deal memo usually satisfies a studio's need for rapid agreement, it does a less satisfactory job of creating an enforceable legal instrument. Courts will only enforce a deal memo if it is executed and contains definite language explaining the material provisions that will govern each side's performance. In many cases, however, a deal memo is based on different people's recollections of verbal agreements and handshake modifications. When material terms are unclear, courts are unlikely to enforce the agreement, based on the contract doctrine that the courts cannot write a contract that the parties have not made. *See, e.g., Metro-Goldwyn-Mayer, Inc. v. Scheider*, 40 N.Y.2d 1069, 392 N.Y.S.2d 252, 360 N.E.2d 930 (1976).

Despite potential problems with enforceability, most parties continue to rely on deal memos when entering personal service contracts in the movie industry. If a dispute later arises, the parties often disagree about whether an enforceable contract exists, and if so, what terms govern its performance. Despite this propensity for disagreement, reputational pressures usually constrain parties from allowing their disputes to spill over into the courtroom. Six major studios dominate the motion picture industry, and a party who breaches a commitment with one of them faces the informal sanction of having his or her reputation impaired with all of them. Actors who breach their oral promises to a studio would have a difficult time securing work from this and other studios in the future. Conversely, a studio that mistreats its talent will gain a reputation for that pattern of behavior, thereby prompting actors to seek deals with "talent-friendly" studios. With so much riding on one's reputation in a comparatively compact industry, most disputes are settled informally before they ever reach the courthouse steps.[c]

Because litigation over personal service contracts is uncommon, the system's informal nature has rarely been tested by the law. An early 1990s dispute between Kim Basinger and Main Line Pictures over an oral personal service contract was litigated before a California jury. The startling verdict in this case may or may not have served as an impetus for Hollywood insiders to alter the way they do business.

## 1. *BASINGER* AND OTHER STAR LAWSUITS

The negotiations between Kim Basinger and Main Line Pictures with respect to Basinger's participation in the film *Boxing Helena* exemplify the way personal service contracts are formed in the motion picture industry. The initial contact between the parties took place in 1990 when Intertalent, Basinger's agency at the time, forwarded the script for *Boxing Helena* to her. Within a week, Carl Mazzocone, the founder and president of Main Line Pictures, wrote to Basinger's agent offering her the leading role in the film. Basinger would star alongside Ed Harris in the story of a woman who is hit by a car and then rescued by a surgeon.

[c] *See* David Charny, *Nonlegal Sanctions in Commercial Relationships*, 104 Harv. L. Rev. 375 (1990).

The surgeon then amputates her injured legs and unhurt arms and keeps her captive in a box, hoping she will fall in love with him. Intrigued by the role, Basinger decided to meet with Jennifer Lynch, the writer and would-be director of the movie. After their meeting, Basinger informed Lynch that she "loved" the script and was interested in participating in the project. At a second meeting at which issues of nudity were discussed (and, according to Lynch, resolved) Basinger said she would play the role of Helena.

Negotiations between the parties' agents escalated in intensity during the next several weeks. As progress toward a deal was made, the agents withdrew and the attorneys became the chief negotiators. Agreement on the main deal points was ultimately reached on February 28, 1991, and documented in a form entitled "Agreement/Deal Memo." The deal memo addressed everything from compensation and credit to the contents of the star-size dressing room that Basinger would occupy during the six weeks of filming. One feature of this deal (and industry practice generally) is that (for tax reasons) Basinger's services would be provided to Main Line by Basinger's own "loan out" corporation, Mighty Wind. Basinger, however, never actually signed the deal memo. Instead, attorneys spent the next several months negotiating and drafting the final long-form contract that would memorialize the fine points of the agreement. After six to eight versions of the long-form contract had been exchanged, Main Line's attorney sent an executory copy of the contract to Basinger's attorney. Basinger never signed or returned the contract. Instead, two weeks later, her attorney sent a letter to Main Line, informing them that Basinger was withdrawing from the project because certain issues had not been resolved to her satisfaction. By this time, Basinger had moved to a new talent agency, International Creative Management (ICM).

While this negotiation scenario, including the deal's last-minute collapse, was not atypical of Hollywood business transactions, the aftermath proved unconventional. Unlike the six major studios, with whom negotiated settlements follow most contract disputes, Main Line was in a precarious financial situation when the deal with Basinger was being made. Production of *Boxing Helena* had already been interrupted once before, when Madonna had reneged on her agreement to play Helena just before filming was to begin. Main Line needed to replace Madonna with a star big enough to attract financing commensurate with its prior budget. Everyone knew that as an independent filmmaker, Main Line was dependent upon outside sources to raise the money necessary to underwrite the costs of production. Consequently, Main Line sought to use Basinger's participation in the project to generate agreements with foreign distributors and domestic banks. Main Line's struggle to secure this financial backing coincided with its exchange of long-form agreements with Basinger's attorneys to secure her commitment to the film.

When the news broke that Basinger had withdrawn from the film, the banks and foreign distributors cancelled financial commitments made in reliance on Basinger's drawing power. Main Line had already spent much of the money on pre-production efforts or committed it in "play-or-pay" deals with other actors. Basinger's withdrawal also cost Main Line the services of Ed Harris, whose agreement was conditioned on Basinger's participation in *Boxing Helena.* Though Main Line was able to produce the film with the comparatively unknown performers Sherilyn Fenn and Julian Sands in the lead roles, the film was a box office bust when it was released in 1993. Main Line, meanwhile, sued for the damages caused by Basinger's change of heart.

Because Basinger had never signed the deal memo or the long form agreement, Main Line had to rely on an oral contract theory when the case went to trial. The company argued that a verbal agreement for Basinger to star in the movie had already been reached when the parties began negotiating the finer details that would comprise the long-form contract. It buttressed that contention by pointing out that Basinger had furnished Main Line with photographs to be used in promotional materials, had sought work for her costume designer, and had composed lyrics for a song that was to be used in the movie.

Basinger countered that those actions, even when fortified by deal memos and drafts of long-form agreements, did not create an enforceable personal service contract. She based her contention on the fact that neither of the written forms was executed and several material terms had yet to be agreed upon. Specifically, Basinger asserted that the amount of nudity that would be required was still unresolved when she withdrew from the deal. After Lynch had refused to alter the script to accommodate her wishes, Basinger said she realized the movie passed her personal nudity limit and she backed out of the deal. Basinger cited a Screen Actor's Guild (SAG) rule that a written contract must exist before a producer can require an actor to perform in the nude.

In court, however, Main Line was able to convince the jury that Basinger's nudity issue was simply an after-the-fact rationalization for her withdrawal. The California jury voted 9–3 to hold Basinger liable for bad faith breach of an oral contract to star in *Boxing Helena.* The jury awarded Main Line Pictures $8.9 million in damages. Some commentators say Basinger's prior willingness to pose nude in Playboy and star in the sultry *9½ Weeks* swayed the jury in Main Line's favor by undermining Basinger's claim that material terms relating to nudity were not settled. Others contend that Basinger's acknowledgement that she had not signed a written contract in seven of her last ten films made the difference.

After filing for personal bankruptcy because of the size of the judgment against her, Basinger appealed. Basinger's attorney, Howard Weitzman, had worked out a tentative bankruptcy settlement that effectively reduced Main Line's award to $3.8 million, but the appellate court reversed the trial judgment in 1994, thereby aborting the bankruptcy settlement. The court ruled that the trial judge gave "prejudicially ambiguous" instructions to the jury by not making it clear whether Basinger, or her "loan-out" company Mighty Wind, would be liable for the damages. Only if Mighty Wind was found to be just an alter ego for Basinger (an issue that was not put to the jury) would the actress be responsible for breaches of contracts entered into by her personal corporation. The court did not address the merits of the contract claim in making its ruling. In fact, there were some indications at oral argument that the appeals court believed enough evidence was present to support a finding that a contract between the parties existed. Main Line claimed the substance of the jury's finding was left intact and that it would not allow a reversal on a technicality to stop it from retrying the case. Settlement was finally reached in 1995, with Basinger paying Main Line the approximately $3.8 million recommended by the bankruptcy judge. Part of that money Main Line had to use to pay Ed Harris the $600,000 he was owed under the "play-or-pay" clause in his contract.

---

The *Basinger-Main Line* case was by no means the last act in Hollywood's oral contract drama, it was but one example of many such disputes. For instance, in 1996, John Travolta was in Paris rehearsing for a new film, *The Double*, co-starring Isabelle Adjani and John Goodman and directed by Roman Polanski. Travolta and his agent had agreed with the movie's production firm, Mandalay Entertainment, on a fee of $17 million plus a share in gross revenues. Though no written contract had been signed, Mandalay's owner Peter Guber had found Travolta's acceptance of the role extremely valuable in preselling distribution rights of *The Double* to finance its production. Unfortunately, during the rehearsals, Travolta and Polanski developed a rift about the story line and Travolta's role in it. One day Travolta simply walked off the set and flew home to Los Angeles, where he said he would not make the film unless Polanski was replaced as director. (Indeed, Travolta reportedly offered to pay off Polanski's $3 million fee to secure his removal.) Mandalay decided, instead, to sue Travolta for breach of contract.

In 1997, Sony Entertainment took over Mandalay Entertainment's rights to make *The Double* (with Steve Martin now playing the lead character) and also to sue Travolta. Travolta's lawyer Bert Fields was able to negotiate an apparently amicable settlement, with Travolta agreeing to take a somewhat discounted salary to star in Sony's planned film version of the Pulitzer Prize-winning novel *The Shipping News.* Two years later the parties had not been able to work out the specifics of this movie, and Sony relaunched its suit against Travolta. It was not until the eve of trial that the two sides reached another settlement, with Kevin Spacey replacing Travolta in *The Shipping News.*

Similarly, director Francis Ford Coppola became involved in a dispute involving the interplay of story-idea and performance contracts. In 1991, Coppola began work on a new project, *Pinocchio.* The 1940 animated version of this story had been one of Walt Disney's early hits. *Pinocchio* had originally been an Italian children's classic authored in 1883 by Carlo Collodi, meaning that the basic story line was now in the public domain. Coppola planned to combine live action with some computer-generated animation, with the actual setting having a band of children seeking to escape from the Nazis during World War II.

After discussions between Coppola and Warner Brothers executives, the studio agreed to support Coppola's development of this project. While Warner paid Coppola himself just $3,100 as an advance on his work, it spent nearly $400,000 on screen writers and others. Coppola signed a Certificate of Employment sent to him by Warner, which purported to make this a "work for hire." However, he never did sign a detailed contract, something Coppola apparently had also not done before when making two other movies for Warner Brothers. Besides a difference of opinion about the overall film budget, the two sides disagreed about whether, if Coppola performed as director (rather than just producer) of *Pinocchio,* he would get the same share of gross receipts he had secured from Columbia Pictures for *Dracula.*

In 1993, Coppola took this *Pinocchio* project over to Columbia Pictures. This studio was prepared to contribute $26 million to production costs (including Coppola's fee), in return for exclusive domestic distribution rights. That meant that Coppola would have to raise the additional money to make the movie from sale of its foreign distribution rights. While he was pursuing that option, Warner wrote the Columbia people, saying that it had bought and now owned the exclusive right to this Coppola *Pinocchio* project. Warner was prepared to release those rights for repayment of the $400,000, plus a right-of-first-refusal to the foreign distribution rights. That letter led Columbia and some foreign prospects to back off from this venture.

*Pinocchio* actually did return to the screen in 1996, with a live action version produced by New Line Cinema. While this film received decent reviews, it did not do that well at the box office. Coppola himself did better with his 1997 movie version of John Grisham's *The Rainmaker,* a film that ended with a huge jury verdict in favor of plaintiffs against a powerful business group.

Coppola was not just making *The Rainmaker*—he was actually trying to emulate it. Coppola sued Warner Brothers, saying that he had never entered into a contract with Warner, and that the studio's statements to the contrary to Columbia constituted a tortious infliction of harm on him. Warner's response was that it was quite common in Hollywood for studios to make informal but binding story-idea deals with producers and directors. Even if it now turned out there actually was no binding agreement with Coppola, Warner had acted in good faith in assuming there was one for a project on which it spent $400,000.

At trial, the judge found in favor of Coppola about the absence of any contract (including a legally-invalid Certificate of Employment), and the jury found Warner liable in tort for blocking the Columbia/Coppola making of *Pinocchio*. Not only did the jury award Coppola $20 million in compensatory damages, but also another $60 million in punitive damages. The judge then reversed the punitive damages award, but upheld the liability findings and the $20 million compensatory verdict. However, this ruling was reversed on appeal on the grounds that even if there was no binding contract, a party could not be made liable in tort if it "had probable cause" to believe there was one. In its unpublished opinion the court expressed its view that such probable cause was almost invariably going to exist in the movie industry.

> Motion picture development and production operates in a unique business universe. There was testimony defining the industry distinction between its "agreement" and a "deal." Film projects progress with substantial expenditures of money, talent, resources and time while formal contract negotiations are continuing. Multi-million dollar film projects are developed and completed (or cancelled) on the basis of loose, artistic understandings without written, signed contracts. The Coppola-Warner relationship in developing "Hoover" and "Secret Garden" is a case in point. There is a distinction between "creative executives" and "decision makers," the latter having authority to bind, the former having no such binding authority notwithstanding their testimony and opinions regarding the existence or nonexistence of contractual obligations. Black letter certainty doesn't seem to be a priority until a relationship disintegrates into court proceedings. Then, of course, the absence of a written, signed contract becomes paramount in the minds of at least one side to the dispute.

Meanwhile, in yet another such lawsuit, it was the performer who claimed that a binding contract had been reached by the parties, even though no such document was prepared and signed. Don Henley, drummer for The Eagles, had been approached by Paramount Pictures and asked to create a song for its forthcoming movie, *Double Jeopardy*. After extensive discussions between the two sides about both the nature of the song and the price to be paid for it, Henley made and delivered the master recording of a ballad "Taking You Home," which he assumed was to be played in the final scene and screen credits. However, when the movie was finished and given preliminary viewings, director Bruce Beresford decided that *Double Jeopardy* was now more an action adventure than a love story, and thus needed something other than a ballad in it.

While Beresford and Paramount people were quite pleased with the box office returns when *Double Jeopardy* appeared in 1999, Henley was not. Not only had "Taking You Home" not been used as he expected, but Paramount had declined to pay him the $1 million fee that they had discussed. The studio's position was that no final, legally-enforceable agreement had ever been reached by the two sides. With Henley immediately filing his suit claiming not just the fee but also broader damages for his song not being put in the movie, yet another jury was going to have to decide whether a binding performer contract has been reached in Hollywood. What should be the result in this unreported case?

---

Oral agreements, nonetheless, may still be enforceable in some cases, even though a written agreement is almost always preferable. Prior to the bursting of the housing bubble in 2008, Richard Davis developed the concept for a reality television show called "Flip This House," in which Davis or another real estate developer would buy a house, fix it up, and resell it for a higher price.

A&E Entertainment orally agreed with Davis to televise his show, with the unusual arrangement of splitting the profits 50–50. The show aired from 2005–06, and had a successful run until the relationship between the parties collapsed. Davis sued A&E for half of the show's profits, pursuant to their oral agreement.

In 2008, a jury awarded Davis $4 million—half of the first season's net revenues (while Davis appeared in almost all of the episodes of the first season, his role, on and off camera, diminished in the second and third seasons).

The United States Court of Appeals for the Fourth Circuit upheld the jury verdict in 2011, despite the absence of a written contract. Citing traditional contract law principles, the court explained:

> As Judge Learned Hand once explained: " 'A contract has, strictly speaking, nothing to do with the personal or individual

intent of the parties. A contract is an obligation attached by mere force of law to certain acts of the parties, usually words, which ordinarily accompany and represent a known intent.'" *S.S.I. Investors Ltd. v. Korea Tungsten Min. Co., Ltd.,* 80 A.D.2d 155, 438 N.Y.S.2d 96, 100 (N.Y.App.Div.1981) (quoting *Hotchkiss v. Nat'l City Bank,* 200 F. 287, 293 (S.D.N.Y.1911)), *aff'd* by 55 N.Y.2d 934, 449 N.Y.S.2d 173, 434 N.E.2d 242 (N.Y.1982). Therefore, ours is an objective inquiry. We do not care about the "parties' after-the fact professed subjective intent." *Cleveland Wrecking,* 23 F.Supp.2d at 292 (internal quotations omitted). Rather, in deciding whether parties have reached an agreement, we must look to the parties':

> [O]bjective intent as manifested by their expressed words and deeds at the time.... In determining whether the parties entered into a contractual agreement and what were its terms, "disproportionate emphasis is not to be put on any single act, phrase or other expression, but, instead, on the totality of all of these, given the attendant circumstances, the situation of the parties, and the objectives they were striving to attain. . . ."

*Id.* (quoting *Reprosystem, B.V. v. SCM Corp.,* 522 F.Supp. 1257, 1275 (S.D.N.Y.1981)). Therefore, "[w]hether an acceptance is ambiguous or equivocal ... depends not on the subjective, undisclosed intent of the offeree, but rather on the offeree's words and actions as viewed from the perspective of a reasonable person." *Johnson,* 629 F.Supp.2d at 330.

Particularly persuasive for the court was the uncontradicted testimony of Davis concerning what the parties had orally agreed to at their meeting. *See Trademark Properties, Inc. v. A&E Television Networks*, 422 Fed.Appx. 199 (4th Cir. 2011).

Two obvious lessons emerge from this case. It is always better to have a written contract so that the agreement is clear, but handshake deals can be enforceable—yet another reason to encapsulate the agreement in writing.

### *QUESTIONS FOR DISCUSSION*

1. All of these Hollywood lawsuits illustrate the complexities of both contract negotiation and litigation in this sphere. The informal quality of movie deal-making enables parties to move quickly to assemble the story ideas, talent, and financing to make a movie that can have worldwide appeal. At the same time, all sides are often left with a pervasive sense of uncertainty about the existence, let alone the precise terms, of their personal service contracts until after a film has actually appeared on screen and the

checks have cleared the banks. The reason is that even after the parties have reached an oral understanding about all the issues, the ensuing agreement will not constitute an enforceable contract if the parties did not intend their agreement to be binding until a written contract was signed. *See Scheck v. Francis*, 26 N.Y.2d 466, 311 N.Y.S.2d 841, 260 N.E.2d 493 (1970). Should all studios follow the policy adopted by Paramount and Disney that filming cannot begin until all the major participants have actually signed written contracts? Is such a policy sufficient to address film financing and script issues? Should courts be required to enforce informal handshake deals in the movie industry, thereby requiring judges and juries to reconstruct events from years earlier and decide at what point there was sufficient consensus or reliance to make an understanding legally binding?

2. As we shall see in Chapter 9, in suits for breach of contract, parties can seek damages, an injunction, or both. The speculative nature of success in the entertainment industry makes it difficult for courts to calculate damages. Similarly, courts rarely require personal service contracts to be specifically performed, partly because of judicial concern about "involuntary servitude," and partly because of the difficulty in monitoring and enforcing compliance on the job. To overcome these obstacles, should liquidated damage clauses be a required element of all personal service contracts in the entertainment industry? Would it be better for the parties to allocate the risks of breaching a contract *ex ante*, rather than having courts attempt to make uncertain damage calculations *ex post*? Remember that liquidated damage clauses are only enforceable if they represent a reasonable forecast of the damages that would result from a breach, and thereby providing compensation rather than a penalty against the breaching party.

3. The live theater industry has faced many of the same contracting problems experienced in Hollywood. In a case that represents a reversal of the *Basinger* scenario, Faye Dunaway filed suit in 1994 against Andrew Lloyd Webber for defamation, fraud, and breach of contract. Dunaway was scheduled to replace Glenn Close in the lead role of Norma Desmond in the Los Angeles production of *Sunset Boulevard*. Three days before her debut, Lloyd Webber announced that he was closing the production because of Dunaway's inability to meet the "musical demands" of the role.

The actress, who was to be paid $25,000 a week, plus a box office percentage of as much as $13,000 a week, alleged that the show was closed for purely economic reasons. She claimed that since the Los Angeles production was losing money, Lloyd Webber and his investors had decided to close it, sell the set to a Toronto group, and send the seasoned cast to Broadway to save money on their New York opening. Blaming the closing on Dunaway enabled the producer to deflect the attention of the New York critics from the show's mediocre success in Los Angeles.

The case posed a host of legal issues. Was there an enforceable contract in the first place? Even if there was a contract, would it be a breach for the producer to terminate it, allegedly at the instigation of the show's creative team in Los Angeles? What was the relevance of the fact that Lloyd Webber had been aware of Dunaway's limited singing experience and the fact that she was undertaking intensive voice training? Lloyd Webber and Dunaway settled their lawsuit out of court. If you had been a lawyer advising the parties, would you have assessed the case as warranting a generous or a modest settlement amount?

4. Oral contract disputes can also arise between an actor and their representatives. Sam Lutfi managed pop star Britney Spears. Now her ex-manager, Lutfi claims that he entered into an oral contract with Spears that entitled him to 15% of her $800,000 per month income.

In March, 2015, the California Court of Appeals reversed the trial court's grant of motion to dismiss, reinstating Lutfi's contract claim. The Court found that the evidence offered by Lutfi had not been completely rebutted by Spears, and chose to send the case to the jury. *See Lutfi v. Spears*, 2015 WL 1088127. How likely might the jury be to side with Lutfi? Clearly, not encapsulating the agreement in writing is an "oops" that Spears is not likely to "do again."

## 2. STATUTE OF FRAUDS

The Statute of Frauds presents another obstacle to legal enforcement of oral contracts. The Statute of Frauds requires that personal service contracts that are not performable within one year of the contract being made must be reduced to writing to be binding. It is common for parties defending against a breach of contract action to assert that the Statute of Frauds bars the enforcement of plaintiff's asserted claim.

Actor Roy Scheider asserted this defense in a 1970s case in New York, *Metro-Goldwyn-Mayer, Inc. v. Scheider*, 40 N.Y.2d 1069, 392 N.Y.S.2d 252, 360 N.E.2d 930 (1976). MGM sued Scheider for breach of contract when he refused to appear for the filming of a television series. The parties had agreed in 1971 on a contract with five one-year options for Scheider to star in a television series, *The Munich Project*, which MGM was to produce and ABC to broadcast. Scheider's contract with MGM, and the latter's with ABC, were stated to be for five years, but ABC's (and thence MGM's) commitments were based on the exercise of options to renew the series for each new television season. MGM sued to enjoin Scheider from working for others and for damages relating to his breach. Scheider's defense, which the trial court accepted, was that the contract was unenforceable since it did not satisfy the Statute of Frauds. The appeals court reversed, finding that performance of the contract could be complete less than a year from the initial agreement. Since the network, ABC, had an option to renew the series thereafter, the contract was deemed performable within one year and the Statute of Frauds could not serve to defeat MGM's claim. MGM was ultimately awarded $120,888 in damages, representing the difference between the amount the studio would have had to pay Scheider under their contract and the amount it paid to Robert Conrad to replace him.

The *Scheider* case is an illustration of a key question posed by the Statute of Frauds' requirement that contracts for one year or longer be reduced to writing. Suppose that at the outset it is uncertain whether an oral contract will endure for a year or more. Should the test for enforceability be whether the contract *must* last for a year, *might* last for a year, is *expected* to last for a year, or *has* lasted for a year? In analyzing this question, first consider why contracts of extended duration are singled out for a writing requirement (e.g., a multi-year Jimmy Fallon television deal, as contrasted to a single three-month film project, such as Kim Basinger in *Boxing Helena*). In light of the Statute of Frauds' broader policy objectives, do you agree with *Scheider's* selection of the "must last for a year" test for when a contract needs to be in writing? Does such a narrow construction reflect the (justifiable?) point of view that the Statute of Frauds is now an outmoded contract policy in the modern economy? Can emails satisfy the writing requirement? Finally, would your view of the legal issues in *Scheider* have been affected by this additional fact—after agreeing to perform in the television series, Scheider's stature rose dramatically with his role in the hit movie *The French Connection*, and he then became dissatisfied with the terms of the original contract?

---

Even plaintiffs who are unable to base a contract claim on an oral deal are not necessarily without legal recourse. In cases where they rely to their detriment on the assurances of another party, plaintiffs may pursue their claims under the theory of promissory estoppel. The Restatement Second of Contracts, section 90, states that "a promise which the promisor should reasonably expect to induce the promisee's action or forbearance and which does induce this action or forbearance is binding if injustice can only be avoided by the enforcement of the promised."[d] A party which knowingly allows another party to take action in reliance on their agreement may create a contract-like obligation. In cases where promissory estoppel is claimed, courts are frequently left to determine whether the plaintiff reasonably relied on the defendant's assurances, or whether the plaintiff jumped the gun and acted in the absence of an agreement.

[d] *See* Edward Yorio & Steve Thel, *The Promissory Basis of Section 90*, 101 Yale L.J. 111 (1991).

## ELVIN ASSOCIATES V. ARETHA FRANKLIN

United States District Court, Southern District of New York, 1990.
735 F. Supp. 1177.

KNAPP, DISTRICT JUDGE.

* * *

In early 1984 Ashton Springer, the principal of plaintiff Elvin Associates, began efforts to mount a Broadway musical production about the life and music of Mahalia Jackson, and wrote to defendant Aretha Franklin seeking her agreement to appear in the title role. Franklin called Springer and expressed her strong interest in the production, and told Springer to contact her agents at the William Morris Agency. Springer spoke with Phil Citron and Katy Rothacker of that agency and in several conversations with the latter discussed the basic financial terms of Franklin's engagement to appear. Several proposals and counter-proposals were exchanged, . . . [and] near the end of February 1984, Rothacker called Springer and informed him that his final proposal was acceptable.

In the interim, Springer had already set about making the necessary arrangements to get the production going. He was in frequent consultation with Franklin concerning artistic and production matters, although he negotiated the financial terms of the agreement strictly through her agents. During a conversation about rehearsal and performance dates, Franklin indicated to Springer that there were no other conflicting engagements on her schedule, stating: "This is what I am doing."

* * *

After returning to New York, Springer began negotiating limited partnership agreements with various investors to finance the *Mahalia* production. He also began calling promoters and theaters in various cities in an effort to reserve dates for performances. During discussions with several promoters he learned for the first time that Franklin had recently cancelled several performances, purportedly due to a newly acquired fear of flying. Springer spoke with Citron at William Morris regarding these incidents, and the latter stated that the cancellations resulted from commitments made by prior agents for Franklin without her approval, and reassured Springer that there was no such problem here. Springer also spoke with Franklin, who reassured him that she wanted to do the show and that she would fly as necessary. Springer offered to make alternative arrangements for transportation to the various performance sites, and to alter the performance schedule to accommodate slower forms of transportation. Franklin told Springer that she was uncomfortable traveling more than 200 miles per day by ground transportation, but strongly assured him that she would overcome her fear of flying.

Springer had also in the interim contacted Jay Kramer, his attorney, about the proposed production and the terms he had discussed with Franklin's representatives. Kramer set up a meeting for March 23, 1984 with Franklin's representatives for the purpose of finalizing the agreement. . . . [A]t the meeting, . . . [t]he basic financial terms that had been previously agreed upon in the Springer-Rothacker conversations were confirmed. . . . Springer and Kramer asked Franklin's representatives to call her and obtain her approval of these terms. The Franklin team left the meeting room, and shortly returned indicating that she had agreed to them.

After the March 23 meeting, Kramer drafted a contract in the form of a letter to defendant Crown Productions, Inc., the corporation through which Franklin's services were to be furnished. . . . [Like] every draft, [it] began with the sentence:

"This letter [addressed to Crown Productions, Inc.], when countersigned by you, shall constitute our understanding until a more formal agreement is prepared."

In the ensuing weeks a series of drafts circulated between the principals and their various agents. . . . Franklin reviewed at least some of these drafts, but could not identify any of them with certainty as having been reviewed by her.

Of the various changes made in the successive drafts, with or without intervening oral negotiation, all concerned relatively minor points. . . . [No] issue emerged as a potential "deal-breaker." A final draft of the contract was ready for signature as of June 7, the date that Franklin was scheduled to come to New York to begin rehearsals for the show.

Springer had in the intervening weeks made all of the arrangements necessary for rehearsals to begin. He had hired set, lighting and costume designers, stage and technical crew, and had reserved dance studios. Springer was in frequent communication with Franklin during this period, as were [director-choreographer George] Faison and other members of the production staff, concerning such varied matters as the compositions to be performed, the costumes she would wear, and the hiring of her own regular backup singers to be in the chorus. At one point, Franklin sang one of the production songs to Springer over the telephone. . . .

As planned, rehearsals actually began on June 4 without Franklin, and continued for several days. Franklin did not arrive in New York on June 7 and, indeed, never came to New York for the rehearsals. Kramer immediately sought an explanation from Franklin's representatives and was informed that she would not fly. Springer paid the cast through the end of that week, but then suspended the production. He attempted to secure some other well-known performer to fill the title role, but none of the performers whom he contacted would agree to step into the role at that juncture.

* * *

This lawsuit ensued, with Springer (suing in the name of Elvin Associates) alleging breach of the original agreement to appear in *Mahalia*. . . . In his pre-trial memorandum, Springer asserted an alternative right to recover on a theory of promissory estoppel.

Discussion

[Before reaching the promissory estoppel issue, the court determined that "[t]he cause of action for breach of contract must . . . be dismissed as against both defendants," because it found that the parties intended their contract not to be binding until the document was executed. The court stated that "[l]anguage inserted in a draft of the agreement referring to its validity upon execution has generally been found to be strong (though not conclusive) evidence of intent not to be bound prior to execution." Such language did exist here.]

* * *

That, however, does not end the case. As above noted, plaintiff has asserted, in the alternative, a right to recover on a theory of promissory estoppel. The elements of a claim for promissory estoppel are: "[A] clear and unambiguous promise; a reasonable and foreseeable reliance by the party to whom the promise is made; and an injury sustained by the party asserting the estoppel by reason of his reliance." *Reprosystem*, supra, at 264. The " 'circumstances [must be] such as to render it unconscionable to deny' the promise upon which plaintiff has relied." *Philo Smith & Co., Inc. v. USLIFE Corporation*, 554 F.2d 34, 36 (2d Cir. 1977).

It is difficult to imagine a more fitting case for applying the above-described doctrine. Although for her own business purposes Franklin insisted that the formal contract be with the corporate entity through which her services were to be "furnished," in the real world the agreement was with her, and we find that she had unequivocally and intentionally committed herself to appear in the production long before [the] day on which it was intended that the finalized agreement with her corporation would be signed.

First, it is clear from the testimony of all of the witnesses that Franklin was enthusiastic about appearing in the production and that at all times during the relevant period gave it the highest professional priority. She early on stated to Springer: "This is what I am doing."

Combined with her oral agreement, through her agents, to the basic financial terms of her engagement, her continued expression of this enthusiasm to Springer more than amply afforded Springer a reasonable basis for beginning to make the various arrangements and expenditures necessary to bring the production to fruition.

Second, Franklin could not possibly have assumed that Springer could have performed his obligations to her—which, among other things, included arranging a complicated schedule of performances to commence shortly after her arrival in New York—without committing himself to and actually spending considerable sums prior to her affixing her signature to the contract on the date of such arrival. Throughout the time that he was making those commitments and advancing the necessary sums, she accepted his performance without any disclaimer of her prior promises to him. Indeed, she actively participated in many aspects of the necessary arrangements.

Third, Franklin's expression to Springer of her fear of flying did not, as she has contended, make her promise conditional or coat it with a patina of ambiguity that should have alerted Springer to suspend his efforts to mount the production. Although Franklin rejected Springer's offer to make alternative ground transportation arrangements, her primary reason for doing so was that she was determined to overcome her fear of flying, and it was reasonable for Springer to rely on her reassurances that she would be able to fly. Moreover, it was also entirely reasonable for him to assume that if she could not overcome her fear she would travel to New York by other means, even if it meant spreading the trip over several days. In short, Franklin's fear of flying provides no basis whatsoever for avoiding liability for failing to fulfill her promise, reiterated on several occasions, to appear in "Mahalia." If she could not bring herself to fly, she should have traveled by way of ground transportation. It has not been established that she was otherwise unable to come to New York to meet her obligations.

We conclude that under the circumstances as we have outlined them it would be unconscionable not to compensate Springer for the losses he incurred through his entirely justified reliance on Franklin's oral promises. A determination of the exact amount to be awarded has been reserved for a later trial on damages.

---

The court awarded Elvin Associates $209,364.07 in damages against Franklin for the expenditures made and debts incurred by Elvin Associates in preparing for the production of *Mahalia*. The court also rejected Franklin's counterclaim brought for breach of contract relating to a later attempt to revive the *Mahalia* production. After the production was suspended, Springer had discussions with a Texas financier who expressed an interest in backing the show. Springer wrote to Franklin with a proposal to revive the production, with rehearsals and opening performances to take place in Detroit. The extra costs associated with this arrangement would be deducted from Franklin's share of the show's profits. Franklin agreed to sign a draft agreement, one that was expressly conditioned on Springer's finalization of a performance schedule. This final schedule was never arranged. Because of the collapse of the initial production, theater and concert halls were requiring substantial deposits to reserve dates for performances. Springer lacked the money to make these deposits, and his Texas financier abandoned his plan to back the project. Unable to obtain financing elsewhere, Springer abandoned his efforts to produce *Mahalia*.

The district court dismissed Franklin's breach of contract claim relating to the Detroit production of the show. Although Springer did not expressly condition his performance of the second agreement on his obtaining financial backing for the production, the court found that "the whole tenor of Springer's letter to Franklin . . . was one of contingency, based upon securing new and greater amounts from investors." The court held that Franklin had knowledge of Springer's dire financial situation and could not have reasonably believed that he was committing himself unconditionally to the obligations associated with the Detroit production. Finally, the court noted that the parties expressly conditioned the contract on Springer's arranging for a final performance schedule, which would not occur until the financing was in place.

### *QUESTIONS FOR DISCUSSION*

1. Consider first the use of promissory estoppel to resolve Springer's claim against Franklin for the aborted Broadway production. In operational terms, this doctrine means that a party who has made a promise that does not satisfy one or more conditions for enforcement as a contract can still be liable if the other party has reasonably relied on them. Does the promissory estoppel doctrine render illusory the basic features and safeguards of contract doctrine if a court happens to feel uncomfortable about their results? Are there differences in the tangible value of contract and estoppel claims that could justify the court's ruling that Franklin did make a "promise" for section 90 purposes, but yet had not entered into a binding agreement?

2. Do you agree with the court's implication of a condition in the contract for the Detroit production in order to insulate Springer from liability? Would it have been appropriate for the court to do so if Franklin had not been responsible for the collapse of the initial production?

---

When construing the meaning of a contract, courts seek to identify the intent of the parties and then issue rulings that reflect this original bargain. As we have previously seen, courts have an extremely difficult time deriving this intent when the agreement is not reduced to a signed writing. Problems of contract interpretation are also difficult to address when the parties have signed an initial document with express plans for a formal contract to follow. In these situations, courts must determine whether the parties agreed to an enforceable contract, or whether their negotiations simply resulted in a preliminary and unenforceable "agreement to agree." Restatement Second of Contracts, § 27.

The oral tradition in movie deals has been the source of numerous disputes over the definiteness of contracts. The competitive nature of the industry often compels parties to act quickly to secure the necessary rights to produce a film and the talent to participate in the project. Negotiations usually take place on an informal basis and without written documentation as the bargaining proceeds. When a deal is finally reached, it is consummated with a handshake and then turned over to the attorneys to draft a written contract. In the following case, the deal between the parties collapsed after they shook hands, but before they had executed a written agreement prepared by their attorneys. The court was left to determine if the terms of the oral agreement and the intent of the parties supported enforcement of a legal contract.

## GOLD SEAL PRODUCTIONS V. RKO RADIO PICTURES

District Court of Appeal of California, Second District, 1955.
134 Cal.App.2d 843, 286 P.2d 954.

WOOD, JUDGE.

[Plaintiff Jack Skirball was a movie producer and president of Gold Seal Productions. Skirball was engaged in production of the movie *Payment on Demand* for RKO Pictures, which was run by Howard Hughes. In March 1950, Skirball entered discussions with Sidney Rogell, an executive producer for RKO, regarding production of the movie *Appointment in Samarra.* Skirball owned the motion picture rights to *Appointment in Samarra*, which was a best-selling 1932 novel authored by John O'Hara. The parties bargained over the terms of a deal under which RKO would pay Skirball a sum of money and a percentage of profits to produce the movie on the RKO lot for distribution by the studio.

RKO was simultaneously negotiating with Vanguard films to lease the services of Gregory Peck to play the leading role, and with Skirball for the rights to the script and his production of the movie. On May 16, faced with a midnight deadline to complete a deal for Peck's services, RKO presented Skirball with a final offer for the film. That afternoon, the parties reached an oral understanding that would pay Skirball $125,000, plus 20% of the movie's profits, to produce the film. After Skirball confirmed that the other terms of the contract would be the same as those for *Payment on Demand*, (the "Gwenaud contract") and that the agreement was a deal "with or without Peck," Skirball and Rogell shook hands and each said, "We have a deal." After reaching an understanding about the budget for the movie and securing the rights to Peck's participation, RKO publicized the deal in various trade journals and news sources.

Gordon Youngman, the head of the legal department at RKO, then sent a memo outlining the agreement reached with Skirball to one of the studio's attorneys and instructed him to immediately reduce the deal to writing so it could be executed by the parties that week. A draft was then submitted to Skirball's attorney with a letter that stated that any enforceable agreement would be subject to the execution of a written contract. Some minor changes were made to the first draft, and on May 24 Skirball met with an RKO attorney and told him that the contract was satisfactory. Skirball reiterated his understanding that the parties had a deal with or without Peck.

The next day, RKO received a telegram from Peck expressing his reluctance to participate in the film. RKO then told Skirball that it would not sign a contract that obliged it to pay Skirball $125,000, without first approving a replacement for Peck. After some discussion about other leading actors, a change in management occurred at RKO. In February 1951, Skirball was informed that the deal for the movie was off. Skirball tried to sell the rights to the movie to other studios but was unable to secure any offers. He claimed that RKO's advertisement of their oral contract—and subsequent withdrawal from the deal—destroyed the value of the film rights because no other studios or directors would become associated with a questionable production.

Skirball then sued RKO for breach of their oral contract. The trial court entered a judgment for Skirball in the amount of $397,486, and RKO appealed.]

* * *

Appellant [RKO] contends . . . that the evidence was insufficient to support the finding that the parties entered into a contract. It concedes that the basic terms of such a contract, namely the story, leading actor and money consideration, were agreed upon. It argues, however, that the alleged agreement of May 16 left various terms of the final contract open for future agreement; and the parties did not intend to be bound until a written contract was signed. Some of the terms which, appellant asserts, were left open were: the starting date; budget; director and principal cast; minor revisions of the script; [and] assignment of television, radio, and stageplay rights to the novel. . . . With reference to those terms, which allegedly were left open, appellant refers to the Gwenaud contract (the pattern of which allegedly was to be followed herein) and states in effect that provisions therein, regarding terms allegedly left open herein, manifestly were not applicable to the present case by reason of different dates, names, amounts, etc., and therefore that the parties in the present case must have contemplated further agreement as to those matters.

With reference to the parties not intending to be bound until a contract was signed, appellant argues that the words "we have a deal" were ambiguous and did not import a present agreement; that the unexpressed subjective intent of the parties was immaterial; and that the surrounding circumstances showed that the parties did not intend to be bound immediately. As to the words "we have a deal," appellant asserts that they meant that the parties had agreed upon the basic points (story, star and money) and that the other points were details as to which, it was anticipated, the parties could agree without difficulty; but that a formal agreement would be prepared. It asserts further that the words were ambiguous in that it could not be determined therefrom whether the parties were not to be bound until the formal agreement was signed, or whether they were to be bound immediately and that the formal agreement to be prepared would be a memorial of their present agreement. As to the unexpressed subjective intent of the parties, appellant is referring to testimony of Skirball and Rogell to the effect that they "felt" or "understood" the parties were "bound" or "committed" when they said they had a deal and then shook hands; and appellant is also referring to the testimony of Rogell to the effect that the handshaking was "in a manner in which you shake hands when you have concluded a deal. . . ."

As above stated, the court found that on May 16 the parties entered into an oral contract, with the mutual intention that it should thereupon become binding, and at that time the parties contemplated that a memorial thereof would be prepared and executed; on May 24 a memorial, setting forth all the terms of the oral contract, was orally approved by the parties; the second draft of the agreement (May 24), incorporating changes in the first draft (May 20), was prepared in order to memorialize the oral contract entered into between the parties. The parties had entered into prior contracts, including the Gwenaud contract. Appellant concedes that on May 16 the parties agreed orally upon the basic points of the contract (story, star and money) and that the other points were details which the parties anticipated could be agreed upon without difficulty. The other points or "details" were to follow the pattern of the Gwenaud contract. (Youngman's letter to the resident attorney of RKO, directing him to draw the agreement herein, stated that "All of the other terms and provisions are the same as those in the last contract [Gwenaud contract].")

* * *

In *Mancuso v. Krackov*, 110 Cal. App. 2d 113, 115 [241 P.2d 1052], it was said: "[It] is not necessary that each term [of an oral contract] be spelled out in minute detail." In *Thompson v. Schurman*, 65 Cal. App. 2d 432 [150 P.2d 509], it was said:

> "The rule is well established and uniformly followed that when the respective parties orally agree upon all the terms and conditions of a contract with the mutual intention that it shall thereupon become binding, the mere fact that a formal written agreement to the same effect is to be thereafter prepared and signed does not alter the binding validity of the original contract. . . . The question as to whether an oral agreement, including all the essential terms and conditions thereof, which according to the mutual understanding of the parties is to be subsequently reduced to writing, shall take effect forthwith as a completed contract depends on the intention of the parties, to be determined by the surrounding facts and circumstances of a particular case."

65 Cal. App. 2d at 440. *Columbia Pictures Corp. v. DeToth*, 87 Cal. App. 2d 620 [197 P.2d 580], was an action for declaratory relief—the plaintiff Columbia contending that it and defendant DeToth had entered into an oral contract whereby DeToth agreed to render services as a director. Prior to making the contract there involved, the parties had entered into a written contract regarding another matter. Columbia had a standard form of contract which it used for directors, and at the time the parties were discussing the contract involved in that case DeToth understood that they were discussing the standard form of contract. After DeToth and a representative of Columbia had had some discussion regarding the new contract involved therein, wherein the essentials of a contract were stated, a representative of Columbia asked DeToth if he agreed, and he replied "Yes." Then said persons shook hands and one of them said "This is a deal." DeToth also said that he would sign a contract when he was "free of" another agent. The court said:

> "[When] the respective parties orally agree upon all of the terms and conditions of an agreement with the mutual intention that it shall thereupon become binding, the mere fact that a formal written agreement to the same effect is to be prepared and signed does not alter the binding validity of the oral agreement . . . Whether it was the mutual intention of the parties that the oral agreement should be binding is to be determined by the surrounding facts and circumstances of a particular case and is a question of fact for the trial court."

87 Cal.App.2d at 629. In the present case the findings with respect to the making of the oral contract are supported by the evidence.

[The Court then rejected appellant's contention that, since the alleged oral contract could not be performed within one year, Skirball's action was barred by the Statute of Frauds. The Court ruled that Youngman's May 16 memorandum, which outlined the basic terms of the oral contract and referred to the Gwenaud contract for all additional terms, was in practical effect a complete statement of their agreement that satisfied the requirements of California's Statute of Frauds.]

* * *

Affirmed and modified.

## *QUESTIONS FOR DISCUSSION*

1. Do you agree with the court's finding that there was sufficient certainty in the terms of the oral agreement for it to be enforced? Were all material terms of the contract agreed to?

2. The appellate court reduced the damage award from $375,000 to $275,000, plus interest. Do you think this award provided Skirball with the appropriate amount of compensation? Beyond the $125,000 that Skirball was guaranteed, how can a court fairly calculate the percentage of profits he would have received? Since it is almost impossible to predict how well a movie will do at the box office (and studios regularly claim that only one or two of ten movies make a net profit), should a court award damages for expected profits?

3. Gabriel Garcia Marquez, an internationally renowned novelist from Mexico City, won the 1982 Nobel Prize for Literature. After Marquez' novel *Love in the Time of Cholera* appeared in the mid-1980s, a Los Angeles-based producer, Richard Roth, sought to make a movie of it. Marquez' literary agent, Carmen Balcells, lived and worked in Barcelona. At an initial meeting between the three in Havana, Cuba, Marquez told Roth that he would be happy to authorize a movie version of *Cholera* if the movie was directed by a Latin American, if it was filmed in Columbia, and if he was paid $5 million. Over the next two years, there were a number of further meetings (mostly in Mexico, but a couple in California), telephone calls, and faxes, with the principal focus being money. In 1988, Roth made a formal offer of a $200,000 advance payment for a two-year option on the movie, another $1.05 million if the option was exercised, another $400,000 for video rights in the movie, $350,000 for television rights, and five percent of net profits in the overall project. Marquez and his literary agent, Balcells, were holding out for $400,000 for the option advance. Finally, Roth's representative faxed his acceptance of that figure to Balcells in Barcelona.

The relevant paragraph in the faxed contract stated: "the option shall commence upon signature by Marquez to the formal agreement . . . at which time the option payment shall be made to you as agent for Marquez." Accompanying that previously agreed-to contract language was a note saying that Roth was "very happy to confirm the final agreement" between himself and Marquez. Balcells faxed back that she also was "happy that this deal [was] finally concluded," and that she was "await[ing] the formal agreement at your earliest convenience." When the document was sent several weeks later, Balcells launched objections at several points, including the lack of mention of a Latin American director or film location. A formal agreement was never signed by Marquez, and Roth eventually sued him in California.

Had Marquez and Roth formed a binding contract, or was there no more than an agreement to agree? *See Roth v. Garcia Marquez*, 942 F.2d 617 (9th Cir. 1991). Compare the facts in *Roth* with those in *Gold Seal Productions* and *Basinger*. *See also Carter v. Milestone*, 170 Cal.App.2d 189, 338 P.2d 569 (1959). Does a California court have jurisdiction over a contract claim against Marquez, who lives and writes in Mexico?

4. In 1988, recording artist John Mellencamp brought suit against his music publishing company for, among other things, breach of an oral agreement for the sale of his copyrights and songwriting services. The court dismissed his oral claim, finding that the evidence suggested a mutual lack of intent to be bound absent an executed agreement. In reaching its conclusion, the court applied a four-factor test recently set forth by the Second Circuit. The factors include: 1) whether there has been an express reservation of the right not to be bound absent a writing; 2) whether there has been partial performance of the alleged contract; 3) whether all of the terms of the contract have been agreed upon; and 4) whether the contract concerns complex and substantial business matters that would not ordinarily be the subject of an oral agreement. *See Mellencamp v. Riva Music*, 698 F. Supp. 1154 (S.D.N.Y. 1988). Is this four-factor test an appropriate way to approach disputes over oral contract claims? Are there any other factors that courts should consider? How would such a test affect the outcome of *Basinger*, *Travolta*, *Franklin*, and *Roth*?

5. The record industry also has a history of loose and informal contract formation. When disputes arise and the parties end up in court, judges are often faced with the task of determining whether a contract was ever formed by the parties. In one such case, the plaintiff asked a musician to record music at his studio. When asked "What's in it for you?" plaintiff replied, "We'll worry about that down the line." Defendant then recorded twelve songs for plaintiff, who also paid for him to travel to New York to meet with representatives of a large record company. After defendant broke off relations with the plaintiff, the latter sued to recover his recording costs and the expenses associated with the trip to New York. How should a court rule on plaintiff's claim? Are the facts sufficient to establish the existence of an implied contract? Has plaintiff shown enough to prove the existence of an oral contract? *See Sound Doctor Recording Studio, Inc. v. Conn*, 391 So.2d 520 (La. App. 1980).

## B. DEFINITENESS

Even when the parties have an agreement reduced to writing, disputes often arise regarding the meaning of the written provisions. This is especially true in cases where only a deal memo, rather than a long-form contract, has been finalized. Since it is difficult to create a contract that anticipates the broad range of possible future events, parties often agree to incorporate general language in their original agreements. Years later, courts face the task of trying to interpret these ambiguous contract terms. Although traditional contract doctrine asserts that courts should not write a contract for the parties, judges today have considerable latitude in giving meaning to the terms of a contract.

In applying the principles of contract law, judges seek to protect a promisee's expectation interest. That is, courts attempt to put the promisee in the position it would have been in had the contract been properly performed. In order to achieve this result, a court must be able to determine the scope of the parties' bargain with some precision. As contract scholars point out, if recovery for breach of contract were limited to the promisee's restitution and reliance interests, the definiteness requirement would often be unnecessary.[e]

In the past, courts tended to require parties to create contracts with a high degree of specificity. The common law rules of definiteness were liberalized by the adoption of Article II of the Uniform Commercial Code and then the Restatement (Second) of Contracts. The Restatement Second states that the terms of a contract must "provide a basis for determining the existence of a breach and for giving an appropriate remedy" (§ 33(2)). Thus, as long as the contract is definite enough to allow a court to determine whether a party has breached it, it will not be voided for lack of definiteness. Instead, courts will use "interpretive aids" to resolve ambiguities: the express language of the contract as understood in a legal context; the extent to which the parties performed under the agreement and the understandings under which they performed, both stated and implied; the parties' dealings in past transactions; and custom and usage in the specific entertainment industry involved.

When a court is asked to intervene in a dispute over indefinite contract terms, a judge usually balances two competing considerations. On the one hand, judges are constrained by the traditional contract doctrine that courts must not *make* a contract for the parties. This concern was addressed in the previous discussion of the *Basinger* litigation. On the other hand, judges may be sympathetic to the difficulties of drafting specific contract terms when indefiniteness is

[e] *See* Ian Ayers & Robert Gertner, *Filling Gaps in Incomplete Contracts: An Economic Theory of Default Rules*, 99 Yale L. J. 87 (1989); Randy Barnett, *The Sound of Silence: Default Rules & Contractual Silence*, 78 Va. L. Rev. 821 (1992).

endemic in the industry. Typically, courts require parties to agree with substantial certainty to the material terms of a contract. Courts are, however, more willing to intervene to *save* the contract when non-material terms were omitted. Where parties have attempted to deal with a contract term but have failed to express their intent in a clear way, courts are less likely to intervene because of their concern about supplying a term that might conflict with the position of one or both of the parties.

Disputes over the definiteness of contracts frequently arise with regard to "best efforts" clauses. In the following two cases, courts were called upon to interpret these clauses intended to obligate the parties to negotiate with one another for renewal of their contractual relationship upon the expiration of the existing agreement.

## PINNACLE BOOKS, INC. V. HARLEQUIN ENTERPRISES LIMITED

United States District Court, Southern District of New York, 1981.
519 F. Supp. 118.

DUFFY, DISTRICT JUDGE.

[Plaintiff Pinnacle Books publishes paperback books. It sought an injunction and damages to remedy defendant Harlequin Enterprises' allegedly unlawful interference with the contractual relationship between Pinnacle and its most successful author, Don Pendleton. Since 1969, Pendleton had written and Pinnacle had published 38 different action/adventure books in *The Executioner* series. Pendleton was the copyright owner in the series, which had sold approximately 20 million copies.

In 1976, Pinnacle entered an agreement with Pendleton for the rights to publish books 29 through 38 in *The Executioner* series. The agreement provided that Pendleton would not offer rights in the series to any other publisher until, after extending their best efforts, the parties were unable to agree on terms for a new contract. If the parties were unable to agree after expending their best efforts, Pendleton could offer the series to new publishers, provided that no new books were published within three months following Pinnacle's first publication of book thirty-eight.

Initial negotiations for an extension of their 1976 agreement took place in 1978–79. When a dispute between the parties over foreign royalty rights was resolved, negotiations became more intense. According to Pinnacle, all conditions established by Pendleton were either satisfied in full or could have been met if the parties had continued to use their best efforts. But in January 1980, Harlequin, another paperback publisher, began meeting with Pendleton to discuss the possibility of obtaining the publishing rights to *The Executioner* series. By February,

Pendleton informed Pinnacle that he was halting their discussions on a renewal agreement while he entertained an offer from Harlequin. In May 1980, Pendleton signed an agreement with Harlequin as his new publisher.

Pinnacle alleged that Harlequin, although aware of Pendleton's obligation to negotiate with Pinnacle, induced him to terminate negotiations with Pinnacle just as a final agreement was near. In defending against Pinnacle's motion for summary judgment, Harlequin contended that the "best efforts" clause was unenforceable.]

* * *

Discussion

To succeed in an action for interference with contractual relations, the plaintiff must establish first and foremost the existence of a valid contract.

* * *

Harlequin's first contention that the "best efforts" clause is an unenforceable "agreement to agree" is inappropriate in this case. Clause VII of the 1976 Agreement does not require that any agreement actually be achieved but only that the parties work to reach an agreement actively and in good faith.

Harlequin is correct, however, in arguing that the "best efforts" clause is unenforceable because its terms are too vague. "Best efforts" or similar clauses, like any other contractual agreement, must set forth in definite and certain terms every material element of the contemplated bargain. It is hornbook law that courts cannot and will not supply the material terms of a contract.

Essential to the enforcement of a "best efforts" clause is a clear set of guidelines against which the parties' "best efforts" may be measured. The performance required of the parties by a "best efforts" clause may be expressly provided by the contract itself or implied from the circumstances of the case. *See Bloor v. Falstaff Brewing Corp.*, 454 F. Supp. 258 (S.D.N.Y. 1978), aff'd, 601 F.2d 609 (2d Cir. 1979) ("best efforts" under a distribution contract based on distributor's capabilities and prior merchandising of other similar products); *Perma Research & Development v. Singer Co.*, 402 F. Supp. 881 (S.D.N.Y. 1975), aff'd, 542 F.2d 111 (2d Cir. 1976), ("best efforts" under a patent assignment based on company's financial and other capabilities). In the case at bar, there simply are no objective criteria against which either Pinnacle or Pendleton's efforts can be measured.

Pinnacle's argument that the parties' obligations under the "best efforts" clause are clear from the circumstances of the case is without merit. While it is possible to infer from the circumstances the standard of performance required by a "best efforts" clause where the parties have agreed to work toward a specific goal, it is not so here where the parties have agreed only to negotiate. The performance required by a contract to negotiate with best efforts, unlike the performance required by a distribution contract or a patent assignment, simply cannot be ascertained from the circumstances. Unless the parties delineate in the contract objective standards by which their efforts are to be measured, the very nature of contract negotiations renders it impossible to determine whether the parties have used their "best" efforts to reach a new agreement. Certainly, no party to a negotiation, no matter what the circumstances, is required to make a particular offer nor to accept particular terms. What each party offers or demands in the course of any negotiation is a matter left strictly to the business judgment of that party. Thus, absent express standards, a court cannot decide that one party's offer does not constitute its best efforts; nor can it say that the other party's refusal to accept certain terms does not constitute its best efforts.

In the instant case, therefore, where the parties agreed only to negotiate and failed to state the standards by which their negotiation efforts were to be measured, it is impossible to determine whether Pinnacle or Pendleton used their "best efforts" to negotiate a new agreement. For instance, there simply is no objective standard by which the court can determine whether Pinnacle's offer constituted its best efforts; nor can it decide whether Pendleton's participation in negotiations with Pinnacle for over a year were his best efforts. In short, the option clause is unenforceable due to the indefiniteness of its terms. . . .

Summary judgment denied.

### *QUESTIONS FOR DISCUSSION*

1. This result reflects the reluctance of courts to become overly involved in disputes between private parties. Without objective standards against which to judge compliance with a "best efforts" clause, many courts refuse to make business judgments for the parties themselves. Do you agree with the position taken by the court in *Pinnacle*? Would it have been acceptable for the court to have interpreted the clause in a way that forced Pendleton to negotiate further with Pinnacle? Does the outcome depend on whether the best efforts clause was a material term in the contract?

2. Andrew Ettinger, the editorial director of Pinnacle, was responsible for negotiating with Pendleton in 1978–79. Ettinger then left Pinnacle and joined Harlequin, where he led its effort to become Pendleton's new publisher. Do these facts alter your view of the appropriate outcome of the case?

3. What could the parties do to ensure that a best efforts clause is enforceable? In a footnote, the court suggested that the parties could have

included a specific time period for exclusive negotiations before either side could deal with others. Pinnacle could also have contracted for the right to match any other offers received by Pendleton (a right of first refusal). If you were Pendleton, would you have any problems with these alternatives?

4. Courts have stated that "when called upon to construe a clause in a contract expressly providing that a party is to apply his best efforts, a clear set of guidelines against which to measure a party's best efforts is essential to the enforcement of such a clause." *Jillcy Film Enters. v. Home Box Office*, 593 F. Supp. 515 (S.D.N.Y. 1984) (citing *Mocca Lounge, Inc. v. Misak*, 94 A.D.2d 761, 462 N.Y.S.2d 704 (2d Dep't 1983)). Can the prior dealings of the parties provide a basis for interpreting a best efforts clause?

4. The cost of failing to provide definite terms in a contract can be significant in terms of time and energy. In 1982, Gary Schreiber purchased intellectual property rights to the recorded media of Robert "Evel" Knievel's daredevil and stunt performances, certain identified artworks, and his autobiography. The parties, however, subsequently disagreed upon what exactly was transferred in the "Bill of Sale" contract between Schreiber and Knievel. Sadly, the litigation, which lasted over 25 years, outlasted both men, who died prior to its resolution. In 2013, the District Court of Nevada finally resolved the matter, finding that the contract lacked the requisite definiteness with respect to the assignment of the film rights to be enforceable, allowing Knievel's estate to prevail. *See Raymond G. Schreiber Revocable Trust v. Estate of Robert Knievel*, 984 F.Supp.2d 1099 (D. Nevada 2013). Why do you think it took so long to resolve a contract claim? What does this show you about the value of resolving contract disputes rather than litigating them?

---

In *Academy Chicago Publishers v. Cheever*, 144 Ill.2d 24, 161 Ill.Dec. 335, 578 N.E.2d 981 (1991), the court was called upon to decide if Academy Chicago Publishers had entered into an enforceable contract with the widow of author John Cheever to publish a collection of her late husband's short stories. The agreement provided that Cheever would deliver to Academy, on a mutually acceptable date, a manuscript satisfactory to the publisher in form and content. Academy, in turn, agreed to publish the work within a reasonable time at its own expense, and in such a style, manner, and price as it deemed best. Several months later, Cheever informed Academy that she no longer wished to publish the book, and she attempted to return her advance.

The trial court found that an enforceable agreement had been executed by the parties. In an effort to give meaning to the open-ended nature of the agreement, the court determined that Cheever could fulfill her obligations by delivering a manuscript containing at least 10 to 15 stories, totaling at least 100 pages. The Illinois Supreme Court reversed, finding that although the parties intended to make a contract, the content of the agreement was so uncertain and indefinite that no contract was formed. The terms of the contract did not provide the court with a means of determining the intent of the parties, so the court was unwilling to enforce the agreement.

In particular, the court pointed to the significant number of material terms that were left unresolved by the parties. The parties failed to agree upon a minimum or maximum number of stories or pages, a specific date for delivery of the manuscript or for publication, criteria for determining if the manuscript submitted was satisfactory, the price of the book, or the length of time it would remain in publication. Although a contract may be enforced even if some of its terms have not been agreed upon, the missing terms in this agreement were so essential that the court found that the parties had illustrated no mutual assent. Do you agree with this conclusion? Will this hands-off approach compel parties to be more thorough when fashioning contracts in the future?

## C. CONSIDERATION AND MUTUALITY[f]

As a general principle, binding contracts must be supported by "consideration." Consideration means that in return for a promise, the other party has provided either a reciprocal promise or some expected performance. The purpose of this requirement is to distinguish between promises that are meant to be enforceable and promises that are not. In theory, the existence of consideration serves two principal functions. First, it provides a court with objective evidence of the parties' intent to enter into a binding agreement. This is referred to as the evidentiary function. Second, the parties themselves will act more carefully if they know that providing consideration will make their promises enforceable. This is the cautionary function of consideration.

A recurring issue in consideration cases is whether both sides must assume some legal detriment or mutual obligation in order for there to be an enforceable contract. *See* Restatement Second of Contracts § 79. One of the early mutuality cases in the music industry was *M. Witmark & Sons v. Peters*, 164 A.D. 366, 149 N.Y.S. 642 (1914), a contract dispute between Witmark, a music publisher, and Peters, a composer. The agreement called for Peters to provide Witmark with at least six compositions each year for a five-year period. Peters conveyed to Witmark all rights to his compositions during the term of the contract, and agreed not to permit anyone else to publish his work during this time. The contract obligated Witmark to publish at least three of the compositions that Peters provided each year. Plaintiff also agreed to pay Peters ¾ cent to 4 cents for each composition that was sold, plus half the royalties it collected.

---

[f] *See* Edwin W. Patterson, *An Apology For Consideration*, 58 Colum. L. Rev. 929 (1958).

After two years, Peters signed an agreement with a rival company that had known of his existing contract with Witmark. The trial court granted Witmark's request for specific performance by compelling Peters to assign his music to the company. The court also agreed to enforce the covenant in the contract that prevented Peters from composing for anyone other than Witmark. On appeal, the court held that the contract lacked mutuality, because it obligated Peters to convey rights in all of his music that he wrote during the term of the contract; Witmark, on the other hand, only had to publish three compositions that it selected each year, and was not bound to publish them in the year that they were submitted. In addition, the court noted that the agreement did not obligate plaintiff to publish or sell any minimum number of copies of the compositions. The court concluded that it was improper for a court of equity to enforce such an "inequitable and improvident" agreement. Plaintiff, therefore, was limited to any damages it could establish in an action at law.

Do you agree with the court's conclusion that the publishing contract lacked mutuality? Do you think a court today would be more likely to enforce the bargain without examining the degree of consideration provided by each side? Three years later, the New York Court of Appeals came to a different conclusion in the far better known case of *Wood v. Lucy, Lady Duff-Gordon*, 222 N.Y. 88, 118 N.E. 214 (1917). There, Lady Duff Gordon, a fashion designer, gave Wood the exclusive rights to market her designs. In return, the contract called for Wood to pay her half the profits he derived from selling the endorsed products. Lady Duff Gordon breached the agreement by endorsing the products of someone else. When Wood sued for breach of contract, Lady Duff Gordon argued that the contract failed for lack of consideration since Wood was not obligated to sell any of the endorsed products at all. Justice Cardozo rejected her argument and saved the contract by finding consideration through an implied promise—that Wood had implicitly undertaken to use "reasonable efforts" to market the designs. This undertaking by Wood offset her promise of exclusivity and enabled the contract to be enforced.

Should the court in *Peters* have reached the same conclusion? Would it have been better to save the contract by requiring Witmark to use reasonable efforts? Courts have supplied terms requiring best efforts by parties in various kinds of exclusive dealing agreements. Should it make a difference that Witmark was seeking equitable relief?

---

The following case provides an example of how a more contemporary court is likely to address a dispute over the mutuality of consideration in a recording contract.

## BONNER V. WESTBOUND RECORDS, INC.

Appellate Court of Illinois, First District, Third Division, 1979.
76 Ill.App.3d 736, 31 Ill.Dec. 926, 394 N.E.2d 1303.

SIMON, JUDGE.

[The Ohio Players, a previously unsuccessful music group, entered into a recording agreement with Westbound Records, Inc. and its music publishing affiliate, Bridgeport Music, Inc. The contract required The Ohio Players to make records only for Westbound for a five-year period. Bridgeport was the exclusive publisher of the group's work as long as the recording agreement remained in effect. The contract, signed in March 1972, was governed by Michigan law.

Within the first two years of the agreement, Westbound advanced $59,000 to cover the costs of recording sessions, artwork, the group's travel expenses, and recording session wages paid to members of the band. Westbound also advanced $22,000 to enable The Ohio Players to pay their income taxes and to settle litigation against them. Westbound had no obligation to make these payments, and could only recoup the advances out of royalties payable to The Ohio Players. The Ohio Players also received $4,000 from Westbound as an advance against royalties when they signed the recording agreement. During this two-year period, The Ohio Players recorded four singles and two albums that were released by Westbound. The releases were distributed nationally, and one album achieved gold status.

In January 1974, The Ohio Players signed a new deal to record exclusively for Phonogram, Inc., one of Westbound's competitors. Two months later, the group sought a declaratory judgment that its recording agreement with Westbound was invalid and unenforceable. The lower court entered summary judgment for The Ohio Players on the ground that the contract lacked mutuality, because even though The Ohio Players were obligated to make a minimum number of recordings, Westbound was not required to make even a single recording using The Ohio Players. Westbound appealed.]

* * *

Contrary to the conclusion reached by the circuit court judge, it is our view that consideration passed to The Ohio Players when they accepted $4,000 to enter into the agreements. The fact that this payment was made by Westbound and Bridgeport via a check containing the notation that it was "an advance against royalties" does not disqualify the payment from being regarded as consideration. If sufficient royalties were not earned to repay Westbound the $4,000, The Ohio Players would not have been obligated to return it. By making the $4,000 advance, Westbound suffered a legal detriment and The Ohio Players received a legal advantage. Therefore, under both Michigan and Illinois law, the $4,000 payment constituted valid consideration. It is not the function of either the circuit court or this court to review the amount of the consideration which passed to decide whether either party made a bad bargain unless the amount is so grossly inadequate as to shock the conscience of the court. The advance The Ohio Players received, taken together with their expectation of what Westbound would accomplish on their behalf, does not shock our conscience. On the contrary, to a performing group which had never been successful in making records, Westbound offered an attractive proposal. The adequacy of consideration must be determined as of the time a contract is agreed upon, not from the hindsight of how the parties fare under it.

Although the $4,000 payment to plaintiffs was not recited in either of the agreements, parol evidence was properly admitted to establish that the payment was made in consideration of the agreements. Where a contract is silent as to consideration, its existence may be established through parol evidence. The agreements are valid and enforceable even if they lack mutuality because they are supported by the executed consideration of $4,000 passing from the defendants to The Ohio Players.

Even had the defendants not made the $4,000 advance, the plaintiffs could not prevail. The circuit court judge erred in finding that "there was no obligation on the part of the defendants to do anything under their respective agreement" with The Ohio Players. During the first 21 months after the date of the recording agreement, Westbound expended in excess of $80,000 to promote The Ohio Players and to pay their taxes and compromise litigation against them, and during this period the performers recorded four single records and two albums. The consistent pattern of good faith best efforts exerted by the parties during the first third of the term of the agreements demonstrates that they intended to be bound and to bind each other. Even contracts which are defective due to a lack of mutuality at inception may be cured by performance in conformance therewith.

Disregarding the performance under the agreements, the conclusion that the parties intended to be and were mutually obligated is also compelled by the rule that the law implies mutual promises to use good faith in interpreting an agreement and good faith and fair dealing in carrying out its purposes; *Wood v. Lucy, Lady Duff-Gordon*, 222 N.Y. 88, 118 N.E. 214 (1917). [The court summarized the *Wood's* facts and then quoted the following passage from Justice Cardozo's opinion.] . . .

> "[The defendant insists] that the plaintiff does not bind himself to anything. It is true that he does not promise in so many words that he will use reasonable efforts to place the defendant's endorsements and market her designs. We think,

> however, that such a promise is fairly to be implied. The law has outgrown its primitive stage of formalism when the precise word was the sovereign talisman, and every slip was fatal. It takes a broader view today. A promise may be lacking, and yet the whole writing may be 'instinct with an obligation,' imperfectly expressed. If that is so, there is a contract."

*Id.* at 90–91.

Justice Cardozo relied upon features identical with those included in the recording agreement as a basis for implying that the manufacturer had a contractual obligation. Referring to the manufacturer's exclusive privilege to market the designer's creations, the court reasoned that absent the manufacturer's efforts, the designer would have had no right to market her own fashions. Justice Cardozo explained the significance of this factor:

"We are not to suppose that one party was to be placed at the mercy of the other."

The court noted that it was to be assumed that the plaintiff's business organization would be used for the purpose for which it was adapted, to manufacture and distribute the designer's creations. The court also regarded as relevant that the designer's compensation depended upon the manufacturer's efforts. The court next stressed the duty of the manufacturer to account for profits, commenting that this obligation supported the conclusion that the manufacturer had an obligation to use reasonable efforts to bring profits and revenues into existence.

* * *

The plaintiffs attempt to distinguish *Wood v. Lucy* in three ways. First, they contend that the agreements in this case resulted in the transfer of their total creative efforts, while the designer in *Wood v. Lucy* transferred only limited rights. The reverse is true. The designer transferred not only endorsement rights, but the exclusive right to sell her designs and to license others to sell them. In other words, she transferred the identity of her creative efforts and her major source of livelihood as a dress designer. In this case, The Ohio Players retained the right to perform in nightclubs and in concerts. This is significant, for at the time these agreements were signed, the major portion of The Ohio Players' income was from their live performances rather than their recording or song-writing efforts.

Next, the plaintiffs contend that the recording agreement is assignable and that an assignable contract is not subject to an implied promise of good faith. This distinction is not persuasive for the manufacturer in *Wood v. Lucy* had the exclusive right to sell or to license others to sell the designer's creations, which in effect meant that his contract rights were assignable.

Finally, plaintiffs, relying upon provisions of the recording agreement and the publishing agreement, argue that those agreements expressly negated any implied promise by defendants to perform in good faith, and *Wood v. Lucy* is, therefore, not applicable. The recording agreement provided:

> "Company is not obligated to make or sell records manufactured from the master recordings made hereunder or to license such master recordings or to have Artist record the minimum [number] of record sides referred to in Paragraph 2 (B)."

The publishing agreement provided:

> "The extent of exploitation of any Musical Composition, including the publication of sheet music or other printed editions, or the decision to refrain therefrom, shall be entirely within the discretion of Publisher."

Plaintiffs' argument is inconsistent with the meaning of the agreements, taken in their entirety, and also is at odds with the interpretation placed upon the agreements by the parties. Neither of the above-quoted provisions states that Westbound and Bridgeport may sit idly by for 5 years, and they did not. Neither agreement states that Westbound and Bridgeport may act in bad faith. Neither provision quoted above contradicts the implied promises of good faith which we attribute to the agreements.

As we interpret the provision of the recording agreement quoted above, it states only that Westbound is not obligated to record the full minimum number of records set forth in another provision of the contract which The Ohio Players were obligated to record, or after going to the expense of making master recordings, to license them or make or sell records from the master recordings in the event the master recordings proved not to be suitable for that purpose. It does not mean, as plaintiffs urge, that Westbound is not required to make even one recording with The Ohio Players. And, the Bridgeport provision merely left to the discretion of the publisher the amount of advertising and publicity that would be given to any musical composition written by The Ohio Players. These provisions reserve to Westbound and Bridgeport discretion to control the content of recordings and the timing and number of releases. Flexibility of this type was essential in order to achieve the greatest success for The Ohio Players as well as Westbound and Bridgeport. Nothing in either the recording agreement or the publishing agreement or in the conduct of the parties demonstrates that Westbound or Bridgeport could or did use this discretion arbitrarily or in bad faith.

This interpretation of the recording agreement finds support in a seemingly unrelated provision of that agreement. The agreement was to run for an initial term of 5 years, but Westbound had the option to extend it for 2 years. If, as the plaintiffs contend, Westbound had absolutely no obligations under the contract, that extension would be practically automatic, for Westbound would have nothing to lose by exercising its option, and perhaps something to gain. The agreement would be essentially for one 7-year term, and the "option" phrasing a meaningless complication. Under our interpretation of the contract, however, the option provision makes perfect sense: Westbound could extend its right to the plaintiffs' services, but only at the cost of renewing its own obligation to use reasonable efforts on their behalf. The law prefers an interpretation that makes sense of the entire contract to one that leaves a provision with no sense or reason for being a part of a contract.

* * *

The circuit court also erred in failing to give effect to the doctrine of promissory estoppel as a substitute for consideration. Decisions in Illinois as well as Michigan state that promissory estoppel may be relied upon to uphold a contract otherwise lacking in consideration or mutuality at the time of its execution, where injustice can be avoided only by enforcement of the promise.

Prior to their agreement with Westbound, The Ohio Players had made only a few recordings, none of which met with great success. Their performances were mainly in nightclubs and discotheques; they were virtually unknown in the recording field. Yet, Westbound, in reliance upon the execution of the recording agreement by The Ohio Players, undertook a substantial business risk, incurring more than $80,000 in expenses which it could recoup only if the recordings were successful. The recording agreement provided for royalty payments to The Ohio Players at percentage rates ordinarily found in the record industry in contracts providing for exclusive services of performers over a period of time. Assuming Westbound and Bridgeport were not obligated to do anything, the expenses and liabilities they incurred in reasonable reliance upon enjoying the exclusive services of The Ohio Players for a 5-year period obligated The Ohio Players to perform as they promised to do.

Plaintiffs assert that promissory estoppel is not an appropriate doctrine in this case because it applies only when there is unjust enrichment. No Michigan authority is cited. However, because the agreements are supported by consideration, the defendants need not rest on the doctrine of promissory estoppel as a substitute for consideration. Our purpose in considering the promissory estoppel issue is primarily to illuminate the fundamental unfairness of the plaintiffs' claim, and so we shall, for the sake of argument, accept the plaintiffs' legal doctrine that unjust enrichment is required.

The plaintiffs' theory is that there is no unjust enrichment once Westbound recoups its advances from the royalties The Ohio Players have earned, and thereby suffers no actual loss. This, however, is possible only because of the success The Ohio Players enjoyed in recording for Westbound. If we adopt the plaintiffs' view and refuse to enforce the agreement, the outlook at the time promissory estoppel arises, when Westbound, relying on plaintiffs' promises, works and advances money on their behalf, but before those efforts succeed or fail, is this: if the venture fails, Westbound's money will vanish, but if The Ohio Players become a hit, they will allow Westbound to break even. Conversely, The Ohio Players can do no worse than break even, having nothing invested, and they may perhaps enjoy a great profit, largely due to Westbound's work and backing. It is obvious that no one would ever voluntarily take Westbound's end of this deal. The Ohio Players should not be able to impose it on Westbound by backing out of their agreement. For The Ohio Players to obtain for themselves the possibility of a bonanza, while imposing the risk of loss on Westbound, by breaking their promises after Westbound's reliance on those promises for a period of almost 2 years, would unfairly enrich The Ohio Players at Westbound's expense.

The Ohio Players had nothing to offer Westbound but an interest in their future, the chance to make a great deal of money by making them famous. The Ohio Players had nothing to lose; Westbound was to take all the risks. Having induced Westbound to perform as fully and faithfully as anyone could desire by signing these agreements, The Ohio Players now seek to deny Westbound the sole reward of its success. Their aim is to keep for themselves the fame and money which, judging by their past experience, they could not have acquired without Westbound's aid, by asserting that Westbound did not originally promise to do what it has already actually done. This the plaintiffs are estopped to do; even if the agreements were not originally supported by consideration, they became enforceable when Westbound performed in reliance on the promises of The Ohio Players, and indeed advanced additional monies not called for by the contract, to protect its investment.

* * *

For the above reasons, we conclude that the recording agreement and the publishing agreement were supported by consideration consisting of the cash advances and the mutual promises of the parties, and that the agreements may also be upheld by the doctrine of promissory estoppel.

* * *

Reversed and remanded.

### *QUESTIONS FOR DISCUSSION*

1. The *Bonner* decision illustrates the influence that Justice Cardozo's *Wood v. Lucy* opinion has had in the field of contract law. Courts are more willing to look beyond the "four corners" of the contract to imply terms to make the agreement enforceable. In light of these changes in doctrine, do you think the *Peters* case would be decided differently today?

2. Consider the court's analysis of the nature and sufficiency of the payments made by the record company to establish consideration. Suppose the Ohio Players had demonstrated that Westbound had not used its best efforts to market and sell its recordings; would the court have reached the same result? Or might breach of the "best efforts" clause be deemed sufficiently material to the entire contract?

3. As a matter of contract theory, are *Peters*, *Wood*, and *Bonner* correct in their premise that a party (e.g., a producer) must make a tangible (albeit implied) undertaking to the performer in order to enforce the latter's explicit commitment? Is there anything wrong with a marketplace that allows performers to secure no more than the expectation that the producer will do what is necessary, though motivated not by contract but by pursuit of profits and preservation of the producer's business reputation?

4. As we saw earlier in *Franklin*, the *Bonner* court endorsed the alternative promissory estoppel route to reach what it considered the just result. Does the estoppel doctrine render superfluous the requirement of consideration and mutuality for the enforceability of promises? Would reliance on promissory estoppel alone have allowed Westbound to obtain the relief it was seeking? Would it also allow Westbound to pursue a separate lawsuit against Phonogram, which signed the new contract with the Ohio Players? *See Westbound Records, Inc. v. Phonogram, Inc.*, 76 Ill.App.3d 359, 31 Ill.Dec. 938, 394 N.E.2d 1315 (1979).

5. In the following passage, the court addressed another argument made by the Ohio Players:

> The plaintiffs refer us to two recent English decisions involving exclusive service contracts for an extended period of time between songwriters and music publishers. The cases are: *A. Schroeder Music Publishing Co. v. Macaulay*, 3 All E.R. 616 (H.L.[1974]); *Clifford Davis Management Ltd. v. WEA Records Ltd.*, 1 All E.R. 237 (C.A. [1975]). These decisions are distinguishable. They avoid contracts not for lack of consideration but as unconscionable restraints of trade. Both of these cases emphasize that the exclusive service agreements were oppressively one-sided, and that the songwriters in both cases were not represented by attorneys or advisers and lacked equality of bargaining power with the publishers. This is not the case here. The Ohio Players were represented by an attorney and advisers who conducted a portion of the negotiations with Westbound, and prior to signing their

> agreement with Westbound, The Ohio Players received competing offers from at least one other company engaged in the music recording business. Also, in contrast with the efforts expended and advances made by Westbound to promote and publicize The Ohio Players, there was no indication in either of the English decisions that there had been substantial activity by the music publisher which resulted in the distribution and sale of successful artistic creations produced by the songwriters.

31 Ill.Dec. at 935, 394 N.E.2d at 1312–13. Keep *Bonner* in mind as you read several later cases that challenge the fairness and enforceability of contracts in the music recording industry.

---

The problem of mutuality in contractual relationships has become exacerbated by the use of texting, email, and other less formal electronic forms of communication. Failure to use care in making such communications can give rise to contractual disputes. In the case below, the court must consider whether the phrase "Dope!" constitutes a valid acceptance demonstrating mutual agreement to contractual terms.

## BEASTIE BOYS V. MONSTER ENERGY

United States District Court, Southern District of New York, 2013.
983 F.Supp.2d 338.

ENGELMAYER, DISTRICT JUDGE.

This case involves claims by the Beastie Boys, the hip-hop group, against Monster Energy Company ("Monster"), the energy-drink company. Specifically, the Beastie Boys, along with affiliated plaintiffs, bring claims of copyright infringement and of violations of the Lanham Act, 15 U.S.C. § 1051 *et seq.,* and the New York Civil Rights Law (NYCRL) § 51, arising out of Monster's allegedly unauthorized publication of a promotional video that used as its soundtrack a remix including songs originally composed and recorded by the Beastie Boys.

At issue presently is a third-party Complaint which Monster, after it was sued by the Beastie Boys, brought against Zach Sciacca, a/k/a "Z-Trip," the disk jockey ("DJ") who, with the Beastie Boys' permission, originally made the remix. Z-Trip furnished the remix to Monster. Monster's Complaint alleges that Z-Trip authorized Monster to make unrestricted use of the remix, including the Beastie Boys' original compositions and recordings contained in it, in its promotional video. Monster sues Z-Trip for breach of contract and also for fraud, the latter based on the claim that Z-Trip falsely represented to a Monster employee that he had authority to permit Monster to use the remix for its own purposes.

Discovery is now complete. Z-Trip moves for summary judgment on Monster's claims against him. For the reasons that follow, the Court grants his motion for summary judgment, and dismisses Monster's third-party complaint.

## I. Background

### A. The Beastie Boys' Claims against Monster

The Beastie Boys are a famous hip-hop group "from the family tree of old school hip-hop." Beastie Boys, InterGalactic (Capitol Records 1998); *see also* Z-Trip Aff. ¶ 7; Levy Aff. Ex. J. Monster is the maker of the eponymous "Monster" energy drinks. Monster 56.1 ¶ 44; Philips Aff. ¶ 2.

The Beastie Boys' claims against Monster arise out of events in 2012. As part of its marketing efforts, Monster organizes and sponsors an annual snowboarding competition in Canada called "Ruckus in the Rockies." Phillips Aff. ¶¶ 3, 5. The competition "promote[s] the Monster lifestyle and brand." *Id.* ¶ 5. The 2012 event included an after-party, at which various DJs, including Z-Trip, performed. Z-Trip Aff. ¶ 15.

On May 9, 2012, Monster posted a promotional video (the "Video") recapping that year's Ruckus in the Rockies, featuring the competition and the after-party, on its YouTube channel. Phillips Aff. ¶ 20. The Video used as its soundtrack excerpts from a remix of Beastie Boys songs (the "Megamix") which had been created by Z-Trip. Z-Trip 56.1 ¶ 28; Monster 56.1 ¶ 28. Z-Trip had previously created the Megamix, and posted it on his (Z-Trip's) website, with the Beastie Boys' permission. The excerpt of the Megamix which Monster included in its Video included portions of four Beastie Boys songs: "So Watcha Want," "Sabotage," "Looking Down the Barrel of a Gun," and "Make Some Noise." Z-Trip 56.1 ¶ 28; Monster 56.1 ¶ 28. The credits on Monster's Video read, in pertinent part:

MUSICC

ALL-ACCESS BEASTIE BOYS MEGA MIX

COURTESY OF Z-TRIP

DOWNLOAD THE LINK FOR FREE AT

ZTRIP.BANDCAMP.COM

Video at 3:52. The next screen of the credits read, "RIP MCA." *Id.* at 3:54. MCA was the stage name of Beastie Boys member Adam Yauch, who died on May 4, 2012, after a three-year battle with cancer.

It is undisputed that Monster never contacted the Beastie Boys, their management, or any agent or representative to obtain permission to use the Beastie Boys' music compositions, sound recordings, or marks in the Video. Z-Trip 56.1 ¶ 40; Monster 56.1 ¶ 40; Phillips Dep. 185.

On June 13, 2012, Monster received a letter from counsel for the Beastie Boys, stating that Monster did not have permission to use Z-Trip's Megamix in the Video, presumably because Monster lacked permission to use the underlying Beastie Boys music. Monster Br. 5, Phillips Aff. ¶ 21. Monster thereupon removed the Video from its YouTube channel, and edited the Video, replacing the Megamix excerpts with music from the band Swollen Members. Phillips Aff. ¶¶ 22–23.

### B. Procedural Background

On August 8, 2012, the Beastie Boys sued Monster. Dkt. 1. The Complaint alleges that the Beastie Boys partnership co-owns the copyrights to the sound recordings of the four Beastie Boys songs used in the Video and that plaintiff Brooklyn Dust Music co-owns the copyrights to the musical compositions of those four songs; Compl. ¶¶ 12–19.; and that Brooklyn Dust Music and the Beastie Boys partnership co-own the copyrights to other Beastie Boys songs used in the Megamix. *Id.* ¶¶ 22–56.

The Complaint alleges that Monster, all without the Beastie Boys' consent, "synchronized and recorded" certain Beastie Boys songs and included them in the Video; that Monster thereby sought to and did associate its products with the Beastie Boys' original work; that the Video text for the same purpose referenced the names "Beastie Boys" and "Adam Yauch"; and that Monster posted links to the Megamix and the Video on various websites, so as to advertise and promote Monster's products, events, and corporate goodwill. *Id.* ¶¶ 58–68.

The Complaint asserts nine claims for copyright infringement, one claim for violation of the Lanham Act, and one claim for violation of New York Civil Rights Law § 51. The copyright claims consist of two for each of the four Beastie Boys songs used in the Video: one for infringement of the Beastie Boys partnership's sound recording copyright and one for infringement of Brooklyn Dust's musical work copyright. Compl. ¶¶ 70–100. Each of these eight claims alleges an "unauthorized reproduction, preparation of a derivative work . . . distribution to the public . . . and public performance" that was "intentional and willful." Compl. ¶¶ 70–100. The ninth copyright claim asserts multiple copyright infringements arising from Monster's posting of the Megamix on multiple websites. *Id.* ¶¶ 101–108. The Lanham Act claim alleges that Monster made unauthorized use of the mark "Beastie Boys" and "the marks comprised of the legal and professional names" of the individual Beastie Boys. *Id.* ¶¶ 109–117. The New York Civil Rights Law claim alleges that Monster made unauthorized use of the voices of Mike D. and Ad-Rock in connection with its advertising. *Id.* ¶¶ 118–122.

On October 4, 2012, Monster answered. Dkt. 5. Overwhelmingly, Monster's Answer denied the Complaint's factual allegations or denied knowledge sufficient to enable it to form a belief as to the truth of those allegations. Answer ¶¶ 1–122. Monster raised 12 affirmative defenses. Relevant here, several sought to deflect responsibility for any copyright infringement to Z-Trip, the disk jockey who had made the Megamix. In this vein, the Answer stated that any injury to the plaintiffs was due to Z-Trip's negligence, fraud or breach of contract; that Monster reasonably relied on Z-Trip's apparent authority as an agent for the Beastie Boys; and that Monster had received a license or permission, presumably from Z-Trip, to use the Beastie Boys' music. *Id.* at 13. Monster also raised the defense of a failure to join a necessary party, again presumably Z-Trip. *Id.* at 12.

On October 5, 2012, Monster brought a third-party Complaint against Z-Trip. It alleged that Z-Trip had caused any damage to plaintiffs for which Monster might be found liable, by contracting with Monster to allow it to make unrestricted use of the Megamix, and/or by fraudulently leading Monster to believe that he had authority to license Monster to use for its own purposes the Beastie Boys' recordings on the Megamix. Dkt. 9. Monster based these claims on a brief set of interactions, during Ruckus in the Rockies, between Nelson Phillips, a Monster employee, and Z-Trip. As relief, Monster sought, from Z-Trip, indemnification, compensatory and punitive damages, costs, and fees.

### C. Z-Trip's Motion for Summary Judgment

On August 1, 2013, following discovery, Z-Trip moved for summary judgment against Monster's Complaint. Dkt. 36–38. (Neither the Beastie Boys nor Monster moved for summary judgment on the Beastie Boys' claims against Monster; Monster did not move for summary judgment on its third-party claims against Z-Trip.)

In his motion, Z-Trip argues that, as a matter of law, he cannot have entered into a contract with Monster authorizing Monster to make the use it did of the Beastie Boys recordings on his Megamix, because (1) he lacked apparent authority to issue a license for the Beastie Boys' music and (2) his perfunctory exchanges with Phillips cannot be read to reflect agreement on material terms of such a license. As to Monster's fraud claim, Z-Trip argues that summary judgment must be granted in his favor, because, *inter alia,* a reasonable person could not have believed that he had the authority to license the Beastie Boys' music for use by Monster.

On August 1, 2013, the Beastie Boys filed a memorandum in support of Z-Trip's motion. Dkt. 39. On August 22, 2013, Monster filed its opposition, Dkt. 40–43, with an exhibit redacted pursuant to a confidentiality order. On August 27, 2013, after obtaining the Beastie Boys' consent, Dkt. 48, Monster filed unredacted opposition papers. Dkt. 43–47. On September 9, 2013, Z-Trip filed a reply. Dkt. 49–50.

## D. Facts Relevant to the Motion for Summary Judgment

The following facts relevant to Z-Trip's motion for summary judgment have been adduced in discovery.

Zach Sciacca, who performs under the name Z-Trip, is "well-known and one of the best remix DJs." Phillips Aff. ¶ 7. In 2009, the Beastie Boys asked Z-Trip to create a remix of Beastie Boys' songs that fans could download for free to promote the Beastie Boys' then-upcoming album, "Hot Sauce Committee Part II." Z-Trip 56.1 ¶ 9; Z-Trip Aff. ¶ 10; Beastie Br. 2. In April 2011, Z-Trip released the 23-minute long "Megamix" on his website. Z-Trip 56.1 ¶ 10; Z-Trip Aff. ¶ 11. The Megamix consists of more than a dozen Beastie Boys' songs. Monster Br. 4.

Nelson Phillips is director of marketing for Monster's Canadian business unit. Phillips Aff. ¶ 1. He is responsible for planning Ruckus in the Rockies. *Id.* ¶ 3. Phillips completed one semester of college and worked in the forestry and ski industries before joining Monster. Phillips Dep. 7–9.

In February 2012, Phillips decided to book Z-Trip for that year's after-party. Phillips Aff. ¶ 7. On February 28, 2012, Z-Trip contracted with Monster to DJ the after-party for $15,000 plus accommodations and transportation. Z-Trip 56.1 ¶ 15; Z-Trip Aff. ¶¶ 13–14; Agreement at 1.

On May 5, 2012, Ruckus in the Rockies was held. Phillips Aff. ¶ 9. Snowboarders competed. *Id.* Z-Trip and other DJs performed. Z-Trip Aff. ¶ 15. Monster videotaped the event, including Z-Trip's performance. Z-Trip 56.1 ¶ 17; Z-Trip Aff. ¶ 19.

That night, before Z-Trip's performance, Z-Trip and Phillips had a brief conversation in the green room of the Lake Louise Lodge. Z-Trip Aff. ¶ 18; Phillips Aff. ¶ 11. Phillips testified that the conversation lasted between four and five minutes, mostly devoted to the possibility of collaboration on future projects, but also with a 30-second segment related to the Megamix. Phillips Aff. ¶ 11. Phillips testified that he "asked Mr. Sciacca [Z-Trip] if he had any music that Monster could use for a web edit of the Ruckus in the Rockies event. Mr. Sciacca told me yes. He indicated that he had made a Megamix that was available on his website and it could be downloaded for free." *Id.; see also* Phillips Dep. 206 ("Q. How brief was the—how long is 'brief'? A. As simple as what I told you. I asked him if he had any music that we could use. He said there it is on my website, download it. Q. So we're talking about 30 seconds? A. Ish, yes.").

On either May 6 or May 7, 2012, Z-Trip and Phillips had breakfast together. Z-Trip Aff. ¶ 22; Phillips Aff. ¶ 12. They spent most of the time discussing future collaborations. Phillips Aff. ¶ 12; Z-Trip Aff. ¶ 23. They also briefly discussed the Video. Phillips testified that the conversation related to the Megamix: "I had a follow up conversation with Mr. Sciacca regarding the use of his Megamix for the Video. I told Mr. Sciacca that I would send him the Video after the first edit was complete. I also told him that we would not publish the Video until he was completely satisfied with it and approved it. Mr. Sciacca indicated his agreement." Phillips Aff. ¶ 12.

After the breakfast, Phillips went to Z-Trip's website and listened to the Megamix. Phillips Aff. ¶ 13. Phillips testified that, based on Z-Trip's having directed him to his website and Z-Trip's representation that the Megamix was available for free, Phillips "believed that Mr. Sciacca had given me permission to use his Megamix as part of the soundtrack for the Video." *Id.* ¶ 14. On that understanding, Phillips and the videographer then selected the portions of the Megamix to use in the video. *Id.* ¶ 15. Phillips testified that he did not believe he needed anyone else's approval to license the music on the Megamix for Monster's promotional Video, "[b]ecause Mr. Sciacca, who held himself out to be the creator of the Megamix, represented that it was permissible for me to use his Megamix." *Id.* ¶ 16. Indeed, Phillips testified, his view was that, because Z-Trip's remix was "available for free download on his website . . . it's there for use. For free." Phillips Dep. at 181, 183. *See also id.* at 183–184 ("Q. For any use. By anybody. A. Yes. Q. Whether it's your home video or a video promoting Monster products. A. Yes.").

On May 8, 2012, at 11:47 p.m., Phillips sent Z-Trip the following email:

> Hey Zach,
>
> Please have a look at the video from this past weekend and let me know if you approve. (I think we'll remove the logo[ ]s at the end since they're redundant and the rest will get cleaned up just a little bit more.)
>
> Thanks again for an amazing weekend!!
>
> Once you approve, we'll post on youtube and notify our 16M fans on fb [Facebook]. the password is: ruckus
>
> http://vimeo.com/41825355

Levy Aff. Ex. B. On May 9, 2012, at 3:50 a.m., Z-Trip replied:

> Dope!
>
> Maybe at the end when you put up the info about my Beasties mix, you could post below it "Download the mix for free at http://ztrip.bandcamp.com"
>
> That way people can pause it and go get it if they want . . . Also maybe a proper link on the description they can click thru once it's posted proper?

> Dope though . . . Love the can at the end.
>
> No 45 footage?
>
> And, btw [by the way] . . . Thanks again for everything . . . still high off the weekend! Z

*Id.* (ellipses in original).

Phillips and Z-Trip testified to different understandings of the meaning of Phillips's email and Z-Trip's response. Phillips testified that, "[b]ecause both [Z-Trip's] Megamix and his image were used in the Video, I believed that Monster needed [Z-Trip's] approval to use his Megamix in the Video in addition to using his image." Phillips Aff. ¶ 18. Therefore, Phillips testified, his purpose in sending the email was to get Z-Trip's "approval that [he] appeared in the way that [he is] comfortable with." Phillips Dep. at 128; *see also id.* at 129 ("Q. And is that the e-mail that you were just referring [to] where you wanted to get his approval as to his appearance in the video? A. Yup."). As to Z-Trip's response, Phillips testified, he understood the word "Dope" to "indicate[ ] [Z-Trip's] approval of the entire Video and all elements, including the use of his Megamix and his image." Phillips Aff. ¶ 19. Further, Phillips testified, he viewed Z-Trip's suggestion that the Video include a link to his website as being "in exchange for the use of his Megamix." *Id.*

Z-Trip, by contrast, testified that, upon receiving the Video, he "was surprised that excerpts of the Megamix were used as the soundtrack," both because the Megamix had not played at the Ruckus in the Rockies and because "no one from Monster Energy had ever asked whether portions of the Megamix could be downloaded for use in a video." Z-Trip Aff. ¶ 26. He testified that he assumed that Phillips' purpose in sending him the Video for review was merely "to rectify his error in not having obtained my approval to videotape my performance prior to my having begun my concert." *Id.* ¶ 28. As for his email response, Z-Trip testified, he used the word "Dope!" to "convey that I liked how I appeared in the Video." *Id.* ¶ 29.

On May 9, 2012, Phillips emailed Z-Trip to tell him that the Video had been posted on Monster's YouTube channel. Pohl Aff. Ex. B. Z-Trip again replied, "Dope!!!" *Id.*

On June 5, 2012, Z-Trip emailed his manager, Lorrie Boula:

> Lorrie,
>
> I feel really, really bad about this whole thing. I would never do anything intentionally to harm the Beasties, ever.
>
> The dude asked me when we were boarding and hanging. I thought a promo video about me was cool. I told him to reach out to you like always.

I don't know what went down on the Monster side, but I figured they'd also reach out to the Beasties to clear their tunes too . . . Didn't know they didn't.

I feel incredibly bad for having even the slightest bit of involvement in any of this. Please apologize to the Beasties entire camp for me, I feel like shit.

Sorry,

Zach

Pohl Aff. Ex. C. (ellipses in original).

**III. Discussion**

* * *

**A. Contract**

"To form a valid contract under New York law, there must be an offer, acceptance, consideration, mutual assent and intent to be bound." *Peterson v. Regina,* 935 F.Supp.2d 628 (S.D.N.Y.2013) (quoting *Register.com, Inc. v. Verio, Inc.,* 356 F.3d 393, 427 (2d Cir.2004)).

Monster argues that "the oral conversations and emails between Phillips and [Z-Trip] formed a contract." Monster Br. 8. The terms of the contract, according to Monster, were that "[i]n exchange for promotion on the Video and Monster's placement of a link, to his website containing the Megamix, on its website, [Z-Trip] provided that Monster could use his Megamix for free." *Id.* at 16. And, because Monster's use of the Megamix (containing as it did original recordings and songs of the Beastie Boys) implicated the copyright rights of the Beastie Boys, Monster argues that Z-Trip represented to Monster that he had the authority to license third parties such as Monster to themselves use the Beastie Boys' original recordings that were contained on the Megamix. Monster argues that Z-Trip breached this agreement because Z-Trip did not, in fact, convey to it a valid license.

In moving for summary judgment, Z-Trip argues that the admissible evidence would not permit a trier of fact to find a binding contract on these terms between him and Monster. The Court agrees with Z-Trip. The only relevant evidence is (1) the testimony by Phillips and Z-Trip about their fleeting oral communications during "Ruckus in the Rockies" and (2) their ensuing email exchange. Even viewing this evidence in the light most favorable to Monster, a reasonable juror could not find an offer, sufficiently clear acceptance, or consideration, *e.g.,* a legal duty which Monster incurred to Z-Trip, let alone all three. *See Restatement (Second) of Contracts* § 1 (1981) ("A contract is a promise or a set of promises for the breach of which the law gives a remedy, or the performance of which the law in some way recognizes as a duty.").

### 1. Offer

An offer is "[a] promise to do or refrain from doing some specified thing in the future, conditioned on an act, forbearance, or return promise being given in exchange for the promise or its performance; a display of willingness to enter into a contract on specified terms, made in a way that would lead a reasonable person to understand that an acceptance, having been sought, will result in a binding contract." Black's Law Dictionary (9th ed.2009).

There are four communications between Phillips and Z-Trip during which, conceivably, an offer could have been made: the green room conversation, the breakfast conversation, and the emails of May 8 and 9, 2012. Monster is, tellingly, noncommittal as to at which one of these the supposed offer was made. But the events at none could be plausibly read to involve an offer.

In the green room, Phillips testified, he "asked [Z-Trip] if he had any music that Monster could use for a web edit of the Ruckus in the Rockies event." Phillips Aff. ¶ 11. That, however, was a question; it was not an offer. In response, Phillips testified, "[Z-Trip] told me yes. He indicated that he had made a Megamix that was available on his website and it could be downloaded for free." *Id.* Z-Trip's response, at most, could be taken as a factual representation as to Monster's ability to download the Megamix. In no sense was it an offer to engage in a contract, let alone the one posited by Monster. It did not specify any legal duty that Monster took on in consideration for permitting the download. And, even if it had, the right ostensibly offered to Monster, to download the Megamix, is a far cry from the rights that Monster claimed it obtained from Z-Trip: to reproduce, for its own commercial purposes, including on various websites, the original recordings and songs of the Beastie Boys contained on the Megamix. Quite the contrary, the exchange in the green room is devoid of any discussion or acknowledgment of such rights.

At breakfast, Phillips testified, he "had a follow up conversation with [Z-Trip] regarding the use of his Megamix for the Video. I told [Z-Trip] that I would send him the Video after the first edit was complete. I also told him that we would not publish the Video until he was completely satisfied with it and approved it. [Z-Trip] indicated his agreement." *Id.* ¶ 12. This conversation, too, however, does not propose a bilateral exchange, let alone one in which Monster offered consideration in exchange for a license to use, in the manner it ultimately did, the Beastie Boys' recordings on the Megamix.

On May 8, 2012, Phillips emailed Z-Trip:

> Hey Zach,

> Please have a look at the video from this past weekend and let me know if you approve. (I think we'll remove the logo[ ]s at the end since they're redundant and the rest will get cleaned up just a little bit more.)
>
> Thanks again for an amazing weekend!!
>
> Once you approve, we'll post on youtube and notify our 16M fans on fb [Facebook]. the password is: ruckus
>
> http://vimeo.com/41825355

Levy Aff. Ex. B. This, too, was not an offer of contractual terms: It did not specify the legal duties that Monster was offering to undertake. Nor did it use language remotely sufficient to support a finding that Phillips was proposing to acquire, from Z-Trip, the right to use the underlying copyrighted material owned by the Beastie Boys. And, contrary to Monster's claim in opposition to summary judgment, no reasonable jury could find, in Phillips' statement that he would post the remix on YouTube, an offer of an exchange of promises. Read naturally, Phillips' email was instead merely describing his intended conduct.

Finally, there is Z-Trip's response to Phillips's email, sent on May 9, 2012, at 3:50 a.m.:

> Dope!
>
> Maybe at the end when you put up the info about my Beasties mix, you could post below it "Download the mix for free at http://ztrip.bandcamp.com"
>
> That way people can pause it and go get it if they want . . . Also maybe a proper link on the description they can click thru once it's posted proper?
>
> Dope though . . . Love the can at the end.
>
> No 45 footage?
>
> And, btw [by the way] . . . Thanks again for everything . . . still high off the weekend! Z

*Id.* (ellipses in original). But Z-Trip's email response did not constitute the offer that was a necessary predicate for contract formation. A reasonable jury could not read it to propose mutual promises in consideration for each other. Rather, Z-Trip's suggestion that Phillips include a link to his website—prefaced and qualified with the word "maybe"—cannot fairly be read as any more than that, a suggestion. The exchange of emails would not have imposed on Monster, in return for posting the video, a legal duty to Z-Trip to post a link to his website.

### 2. Acceptance

There is, in any event, no evidence on which a reasonable juror could find acceptance of contractual terms. Monster appears to argue that Z-Trip's use of the exclamation "Dope!" at the beginning of the May 9, 2012 email reflected his acceptance. Monster Br. 13. But that argument fails for at least two reasons. First, as noted, there was no clear and reasonably specific offer that preceded it. There was, therefore, nothing for Z-Trip to accept. Second, viewed in context, the word "Dope!" as used by Z-Trip was not " 'clear, unambiguous and unequivocal,' " as required under New York law. *Transition Investments, Inc. v. The Allen O. Dragge, Jr. Family Trust,* No. 11 Civ. 04775(AJN), 2012 WL 1848875, at *6 (S.D.N.Y. May 21, 2012) (quoting *Krumme v. WestPoint Stevens Inc.,* 143 F.3d 71, 83 (2d Cir.1998)). In proper context, the word "Dope!" could certainly be taken as an expression, albeit unorthodox, of approval and acceptance of another's antecedent offer. But here, Z-Trip's exclamation, "Dope!" was in response to Phillips's query, "Please have a look at the video from this past weekend and let me know if you approve." Levy Aff. Ex. B. Viewed in this context, Z-Trip's response of "Dope!" plainly communicated that, in some sense, he "approve[d]" of "the video." But such approval is quite distinct from conveying assent to a mutual exchange of promises or other consideration. And it certainly did not convey that Z-Trip had authority to approve, on behalf of the Beastie Boys, a free license to Monster to use the Beastie Boys' recordings and songs. There is no fair reading of the facts under which Z-Trip, by exclaiming "Dope!," accepted such a contractual offer. Z-Trip's locution, although memorable, was entirely too enigmatic and elliptical to constitute the "clear [and] unambiguous" acceptance necessary for contract formation.

### 3. Consideration

The supposed contract also fails for lack of consideration. Conceivably, as Monster argues, Z-Trip stood to benefit from Monster's linking its Video to his website. Monster Br. 13–14. But a fair reading of the email exchange between Phillips and Z-Trip is that any such benefit was incidental. The sparse communications between the two cannot be read to imply a binding promise by Monster in exchange for Z-Trip's approval of its proposed use of the Megamix. Had Monster decided not to post the Video, or to post it but not include a link to Z-Trip's website, Z-Trip would not have been able to claim a breach of an actionable agreement. Indeed, although Monster emphasizes that "consideration can consist of an exchange of promises," *id.* at 14, tellingly, it never argues that Monster made an actual promise to Z-Trip.

### 4. Terms

Finally, even if an offer and acceptance of an exchange of promises constituting consideration could be found in Phillips' sparse communications with Z-Trip, no reasonable person could understand Z-Trip to have granted Monster the rights necessary here-to wit, a license on behalf of the Beastie Boys to use the underlying copyrighted material owned by the Beastie Boys, or, as Monster alternatively appears to posit, indemnification against a future suit by the Beastie Boys for violating such copyrights. The two men's communications could not remotely support such a conclusion. It would take an heroic effort of explication to derive such a conclusion from their words and informal email exchanges. And to read Phillips's or Z-Trip's words to convey a contract to cede Monster such rights would flout common sense. Phillips, a former forestry and ski-industry worker with no evident legal expertise, never raised any such questions with Z-Trip, or reflected any awareness of the copyright interests that Monster would need to acquire or license to bring the promotional Video it contemplated into compliance with copyright law. It is implausible to imbue his statements with appreciation of the relevant copyright concepts and an intent to acquire, from the Beastie Boys, the necessary license.

Further, the Beastie Boys, as owners of the copyrights to the underlying songs, *see* Z-Trip 56.1 ¶ 3, Levy Aff. Ex. I (Silva Dep.) 34–56, held the exclusive right to authorize Monster to "reproduce," "prepare derivative works," "distribute," and publicly perform the music, 17 U.S.C. § 106, including by synchronizing it with an audiovisual work such as the Video. *ABKCO Music, Inc. v. Stellar Records, Inc.,* 96 F.3d 60, 62 n. 4 (2d Cir.1996). Z-Trip was never a member of the Beastie Boys, Z-Trip 56.1 ¶ 6, Z-Trip Aff. ¶ 9, Phillips Dep. 205, and did not hold any Beastie Boys copyrights, Z-Trip 56.1 ¶ 7, Z-Trip Aff. ¶ 9. And the summary judgment record does not supply any credible basis on which Phillips, even had he been savvy to his employer's necessary licensing needs, could reasonably conclude that Z-Trip had the right to license third parties such as Monster to use the underlying copyrighted material owned by the Beastie Boys.

The evidence thus, in multiple respects, precludes finding a contract between Monster and Z-Trip. On Monster's third-party claim of a breach of such a contract, summary judgment thus must be granted for Z-Trip.

* * *

## CONCLUSION

Third-party defendant Sciacca's motion for summary judgment is granted. The Clerk of Court is respectfully directed to dismiss him from this case and to terminate the motion pending at docket number 36.

## D. CONTRACT PARTIES: MINORS[g]

The biggest star in Hollywood in the 1930s and 1940s was Shirley Temple. Temple made more than fifty movies during that period, most for Twentieth Century Fox, and was credited with saving Fox from bankruptcy during the Depression. The vast majority of Temple's movies were made while she was a child, under contracts her father signed. The first contract, agreed upon when Temple was just four years old, would pay Temple $150 a week for seven years. After Temple's first big hit that same year, Fox made six Temple movies in 1934, and leased her services to other studios for $3500 a week, money kept by Fox. Temple's father and his lawyer renegotiated the contracts several times over the next decade. When Temple married shortly after World War II, she was stunned to discover that very little money was left from her time as Hollywood's box office superstar. The Temple case illustrates the distinctive legal challenges posed by contracts with minors.

Under the common law, a minor such as Temple could not bind herself to a contract. While minors did have to pay for "necessary" goods that had been received and used, they could not be constrained by contractual promises made for the future. Minors could perform work on a specific project (i.e., a movie) and be paid for it, but they could not legally commit themselves to do so for an extended period, such as Temple's seven years. Moreover, the child's parents were entitled to keep and spend the child's earnings, as a corollary to the parental obligation to support their children. The common law presumed that minors needed a legal prerogative to disaffirm their contract obligations (either before or soon after reaching the age of majority), because their youth and inexperience left them susceptible to ill-considered promises, or even deliberate exploitation. A party contracting with a child, then, bore the risk that the child (or the child's parents) could maintain and enforce contracts that were favorable, but reject those that turned out to be poor deals.

In the 1920s, the burgeoning movie industry developed a practice of seven-year contracts, as well as an appreciation of the appeal of child artists. The common law contract rule was seen as an obstacle to the development of mutually beneficial relationships with budding child performers. In 1927, California passed a law that allowed minors to enter into contracts for "artistic or creative services." Once the terms of that agreement had been reviewed and approved by a judge, they could not be disaffirmed by the child. This was the law under which Temple signed her judicially-approved 1933 contract with Fox.

---

[g] *See* Robert A. Martis, *Children in the Entertainment Industry: Are They Being Protected? An Analysis of the California & New York Approaches*, 8 Loy. Ent. L.J. 25 (1988).

Several years later, a scandal arose involving child actor Jackie Coogan, star of such hit movies as *The Kid* and *Oliver Twist* (later Uncle Fester in the Addams Family television series). Apparently Coogan's mother had dissipated her son's $4 million in earnings during that decade. California thus added a new feature to its statutes, one that authorized the court "to require the setting aside and preservation for the benefit of the minor of up to one half of the net earnings of the minor . . . ," with the court having "continuing jurisdiction over any [such] trust." Apparently Temple refused to sue her father for having ignored the judicial directive that he put in a trust fund half of Temple's earnings from her second seven-year contract with Fox.

California's law on minors' artistic contracts is now embodied in section 6750–53 of its Family Code. In *Warner Bros. Pictures v. Brodel*, 31 Cal. 2d 766, 192 P.2d 949 (1948), the Supreme Court of California held that the statute authorized judicial approval of studio options as well as contract commitments to use the services of child performers. In 1961, New York enacted similar legislation. In both states, the minority period lasts until the child reaches 18 years of age. State courts are empowered to approve contracts that protect the well-being of minors and that have the signed approval of a parent or guardian. Unlike California, New York places a three-year limit on the duration of any such agreement; thus, judicial approval must be sought again for renewal or revision of the original contract. Both states also seek to safeguard the financial interests of minors by requiring that a certain percentage of the child's net earnings be set aside in a trust that will be turned over to the child upon reaching the age of majority. Unlike New York, California limits the scope of any such judicial set-aside to no more than fifty percent of the child's net earnings.

The basic objective of these laws is to manage the tension between two competing goals. The law encourages entertainment firms to contract with minors by providing a legal guarantee against the threat of non-performance by child artists. At the same time, children are offered some protection against entering into unfavorable contracts. Since most minors, whatever their artistic talents, do not have financial experience and skills, they depend on their parents or representatives to safeguard their present and future well-being. By providing judicial scrutiny of the terms of contracts with minors, the legislature protects children from the mistakes or misdeeds of their parents, while precluding both child and parent from using the performer's youth as a sword to win a better deal if and when the child becomes a star.

---

Both parties have incentives, then, to secure prior judicial approval of a minor's contract, to reduce both the initial uncertainty and the eventual litigation costs. The two sides, however, have no obligation to do so. If they do not, the child performer retains the common law prerogative to disaffirm the contract. As the following case demonstrates, the power to disaffirm does not necessarily allow the minor to profit at the expense of the other party.

## SCOTT EDEN MANAGEMENT V. KAVOVIT

Supreme Court of New York, Westchester County, 1990.
149 Misc.2d 262, 563 N.Y.S.2d 1001.

COPPOLA, JUDGE.

[This case involved the effort by a child actor, Andrew Kavovit, to extricate himself from contract obligations to his personal manager, Scott Eden. Eden had begun to represent Kavovit in 1984, when the actor was 12 years old, and the extension of the management contract ran until February 1989. Eden was entitled to a 15 percent commission on Kavovit's gross compensation generated by any contracts negotiated during Eden's tenure. Kavovit also signed a contract with a talent agency selected by Eden, the Andreadis Agency, which entitled the agency to a further 10 percent commission on his earnings.

Kavovit was able to secure several performance contracts—most important, a role on the long-running television soap opera *As the World Turns*. Kavovit's initial role was to run from 1987 to 1990, with a strong likelihood of renewal. Eden received 15 percent of Kavovit's earnings until his management term expired in February 1989. At that point, Kavovit and his parents decided not to stay with Eden, and they terminated payments of any commission on future earnings from *As the World Turns*. Eden filed suit for breach of contract, and Kavovit responded with the defense that as a minor he was entitled to disaffirm the continuance of the management contract and its terms.]

* * *

In this case of first impression, an infant actor has disaffirmed a personal services contract. He thereby seeks to avoid responsibility to his manager for commissions due in the future on income from performance contracts already obtained for him by the manager.

[The judge then synopsized "the salient facts [that] are not in dispute," and quoted this key passage from the Andrew Kavovit-Scott-Eden contract.]

> "With respect to contracts entered into by [Andrew] . . . during the term of this agreement . . . [Scott Eden] shall be entitled to [its] commission from the residuals or royalties of such contracts, the full term of such contracts, including all extensions or

renewals thereof, notwithstanding the earlier termination of this agreement."

* * *

An infant's contract is voidable and the infant has an absolute right to disaffirm (General Obligations Law § 3–101; *Continental Natl. Bank v. Strauss*, 137 N.Y. 148; *Casey v. Kastel*, 237 N.Y. 305; *Joseph v. Schatzkin*, 259 N.Y. 241; and see, General Obligations Law § 3–107 [with regard to the absence of parental liability either as parties or guarantors]). This aspect of the law of contracts was well entrenched in the common law as early as the 15th century. In bringing this action, and defending the motion, plaintiffs fully recognize the principle of law involved here and in no way challenge the infant's right to disaffirm. Rather, plaintiffs rely upon a corollary to the main rule, which also evolved early in the common law "After disaffirmance, the infant is not entitled to be put in a position superior to such a one as he would have occupied if he had never entered into his voidable agreement. He is not entitled to retain an advantage from a transaction which he repudiates. 'The privilege of infancy is to be used as a shield and not as a sword.' "

* * *

The parties have not cited, nor has the court found, a case dealing with the exact issue at bar, i.e., whether disaffirmance may void the contractual obligation to pay agents' commissions without any concomitant exchange being made. However, an analogy may be drawn from the case of *Mutual Milk & Cream Co. v. Prigge*, (112 App.Div. 652). There, a minor had entered the employ of the plaintiff as a milk wagon driver and had signed a contract which included a restrictive covenant wherein the minor agreed not to solicit plaintiff's customers within three years after leaving plaintiff's employ. Several months after entering into the contract, the minor quit, pursuant to the terms of the contract, but then went to work for plaintiff's rival and solicited business from plaintiff's customers.

The Appellate Division affirmed the issuance of an injunction against the minor, who had pleaded infancy in avoidance of the contractual obligations. The court considered that the issue was not one of liability of an infant for a breach of his contract, but whether an infant should be allowed to repudiate his contract without restoring what he had received and, if restoration could not be made, without being enjoined from making use of the information he had gained from his employment by the plaintiff to the latter's damage. The court held that the infant should be enjoined "from making use of that information in violation of his agreement made at the time when he desired and obtained employment and upon the faith of which he obtained the information and acquaintance." The court further noted that "No man would engage the services of an infant if he could not impose the same condition for his own protection against the use of his formulas, trade secrets, and lists of customers that he could exact of an adult."

The rationale of the *Mutual Milk* case is applicable to this case. The work a personal manager does for and with his client is preparatory to the performance contract. Once a performance contract has been signed, the personal manager is entitled to his percentage fee, subject only to the condition subsequent that the client performs and earns his fee. This is clearly the understanding in the industry, unlike, for example, the standard in the insurance field where the initial commission is disproportionately high and the subsequent, smaller commissions are viewed as consideration for continued efforts in keeping the insurance contract current. When the client signs a performance contract, it is with the understanding that the gross amount to be paid is not solely for him. It is the expectation of all parties—the agent, the performer and, in this case, the soap opera production company, that 15% of that gross amount belongs to the personal manager. To the extent that the performer obtains that 15% for himself, he is unjustly enriched.

Here, the position adopted by defendants is no different than that advanced on behalf of the infant who had taken the airplane ride and wanted her money back or the truck driver who had milked his employer's efforts and tutelage and then refused to honor his reciprocal commitment. In each case, the infant consumed the fruits of the contract and refused to pay for that fruit, to the clear prejudice of the other party. In this case, the infant will continue to reap the benefits of his contract with plaintiff but is using his infancy as an excuse not to honor the promise made in return for that benefit.

If the argument asserted by defendants were adopted by the court, the infant would be put in a position superior to that which he would have occupied had he never entered into the contract with plaintiff. He would be retaining an advantage from the repudiated transaction, i.e., using the privilege of infancy as a sword rather than a shield. Not only is this manifestly unfair, but it would undermine the policy underlying the rule allowing disaffirmance. If the infant may rescind the contract with the manager immediately after a lucrative performance contract is signed, yet still retain the benefits of the performance contract, no reputable manager will expend any efforts on behalf of an infant.

In this case, adjustment of the equities so as to prevent unjust enrichment, leads to the conclusion that defendants must continue to pay to plaintiffs all commissions to which plaintiffs would be entitled under their contract, as they become due.

* * *

Summary dismissal denied.

### *QUESTIONS FOR DISCUSSION*

Do you agree the court's ruling against this child performer? (Chapter 10 will address the broader issues of agent and manager representation of entertainment talent, whether child or adult.) What policy considerations influenced the court's analysis? Does the outcome of this case make it more or less likely that parties will seek court approval of their contracts?

---

*Scott Eden Management* demonstrates that minors may not use their power to disaffirm a contract to gain a financial advantage over a party that has already performed its side of the bargain. In the case of *In re Prinze,* 38 N.Y.2d 570, 381 N.Y.S.2d 824, 345 N.E.2d 295 (1976), the New York Court of Appeals went a step further. There, the court was called upon to enforce an agreement (again between a minor and his personal manager) that did not satisfy the terms of the state's statute for minors and thus could not have been judicially approved *ex ante.* Despite the contract's statutory shortcomings, the court noted that it could still be enforced if the agreement was deemed to be "reasonable and provident" to the minor's interests. Thus, a minor may not always have the right to disaffirm a contract without incurring liability, simply because the agreement had not previously been approved by a court.

Despite the heightened certainty and other benefits that judicial approval offers parties who contract with minors in the entertainment industry, there is at least one obstacle that may limit the desirability of this mechanism. That obstacle is the public nature of our court system. As a general rule, parties who seek judicial approval of contracts with minors must disclose to the court (and therefore to the public) the terms of the contract and related financial information that the parties may wish to keep private. A 1993 case involving child actor Macaulay Culkin's contract with Twentieth Century Fox to perform in the movie *Home Alone II* illustrates the dilemma faced by the parties.

The first *Home Alone*, made in 1990, was a huge blockbuster, earning over $500 million at the worldwide box office. Culkin was a comparatively unknown child actor when he signed his contract with Fox to play the lead role in that movie for $100,000. Unlike Shirley Temple's 1933 contract with Fox, Culkin was the beneficiary of the new Hollywood practice of signing artists to perform in single movies rather than for extended periods. Thus Culkin's parents, who were his joint managers (in return for 15 percent of his earnings), were able to extract from Fox a contract for the *Home Alone* sequel that guaranteed their son $5 million, plus five percent of the film's gross revenues. To protect their respective interests in the enforceability of this contract, the parties sought court approval. In making its decision, the court examined the reasonableness of Culkin's performance and promotional obligations under the contract. In addition, the court had to study the Culkin family's financial status in order to determine the appropriate proportion of his earnings to be set aside in a trust. To protect their privacy interests in this information, both Fox and Culkin petitioned the court to seal many of the documents they were required to submit for the court's review.

A New York Surrogate Court denied that request, reasoning that the public interest in disclosure outweighed the parties' interest in confidentiality. The court made an exception for the film's screenplay, which it agreed to seal. Rather than disclose the information, the parties appealed the ruling on confidentiality. The appellate court reversed, finding that the parties had presented compelling arguments in support of protecting their privacy interests. *See Re Twentieth Century Fox Film Corp.*, 190 A.D.2d 483, 601 N.Y.S.2d 267 (1993). The court noted that disclosure of information relating to Fox's financial and business arrangements for the movie could jeopardize the studio's relations with other actors, as well as its competitiveness with other studios. The court also expressed its concern that disclosure of Culkin's earnings would subject him to undue pressure from investment advisers and others.

The court's decision was also driven by its desire to protect the force of New York's Arts and Cultural Affairs Law. It feared that requiring disclosure in this case would have a chilling effect on the willingness of parties to contract with minors, because going to court to protect their bargain would expose details of the transaction to public scrutiny. The court did, however, make it clear that future proceedings should not automatically be sealed. Instead, courts must make judgments on a case-by-case basis, balancing the parties' privacy interests against the public's interest in disclosure.

As it turned out, *Home Alone II* also did very well, grossing over $350 million, of which Culkin was entitled to five percent. While the child had one more movie hit, *Richie Rich* in 1994, by the time he had reached his teens, Culkin's box office appeal had dissipated. Happily, unlike Shirley Temple, Culkin had over $40 million set aside in a trust fund waiting for him to reach the age of majority. Unhappily, Culkin's parents ended their relationship and became embroiled in litigation over custody of their son and access to some of his assets to support family members in the style to which they had become accustomed.

---

The legal requirements for using minors in traditional scripted programs are well established. By contrast, an area that is relatively unexplored involves reality-based television programs. *See* Adam P. Greenberg, *Reality's Kids: Are Children Who Participate on Reality Television Shows Covered Under the Fair Labor Standards Act?*, 82 S. Cal. L. Rev. 595 (2009); Christopher C. Cianci, *Entertainment or Exploitation?: Reality Television & the Inadequate Protection of Child Participants Under the Law*, 18 S. Cal. Interdisc. L.J. 363 (2009).

## E. DURATION

A number of lawsuits have been brought by leading musical performers against their record companies: suits by Don Henley and Glen Frey of the Eagles, Luther Vandross, Metallica, Prince, George Michael (against Sony Music), and Courtney Love (against Vivendi's Universal Music Group). The focus of these suits has been a standard feature of musical recording agreements that is no longer found in movie performance agreements—multiyear duration.

As noted earlier, the production and distribution of recorded music requires collaboration by a variety of parties: songwriter, performer, producer, distributor, and retailer. The key document is the contract between the performing artist and the record company (or "label"). The artist receives compensation in the form of advances against royalties from the sale of the recording (now usually a compact disc or digital download). Royalties are based on an agreed upon percentage of the revenues generated by sale of the recording, less the costs of production and distribution. In return, the label receives the exclusive right to release and distribute the recording, and often secures copyright ownership as well.

The length of the contract commitment varies, depending on the side from which it is viewed. The label ordinarily commits itself just to an initial period, now usually defined in terms of albums rather than years. Within six months of delivery of the first album by the artist, the label has the option to renew the contract for another such period, and then for as many additional album options as the artist has given. The artist, by contrast, has unconditionally committed to record for as long as that specified option period, which in the case of new musicians is usually for eight, or perhaps even ten, albums. It now typically takes 18 to 20 months to produce an acceptable album, and the standard industry contract specifies that a second album cannot begin to be recorded until the prior one has been delivered. In sum, new musicians make a one-way commitment to record companies that may last as long as twenty years.

This contract is obviously attractive to the label. When the original contract is signed, the quality and appeal of a new artist's musical work is uncertain. The label must make a significant investment (perhaps one hundred thousand dollars) in producing and promoting the first album. If it turns out that the artist's work is not popular, the company does not want to have to invest in several more albums that likely will prove no more appealing. On the other hand, if the first album does sell, the company wants to have the prerogative to produce and profit from future works, thereby recouping its investment not only in artists who have succeeded but also those who failed.

From the perspective of successful performers, that is precisely the reason why this long-term, one-sided contract commitment is unattractive. At a time when these artists were among the thousands of unknown musicians competing for their first record deal, their negotiating leverage with respect to royalty rates, creative control, ownership of the master tapes, and other terms was at its lowest. If their musical performances failed, these artists reaped no long-term reward. If their work succeeded, they were locked into lengthy contracts that blocked competing bids from other labels for the right to produce what clearly promised to be lucrative recordings.

There is, of course, nothing in the law that requires artists to sign recording contracts with long durations. As we saw in *Bonner*, even new artists like the Ohio Players use the services of managers who are fully aware of these issues when negotiating deals for their clients with one of the major record companies or the small independent labels. It is the marketplace that generates this standard feature of record agreements. Nonetheless, artists have sought the help of the law to protect them from long-term commitments that are not now found in the movie, television, or theatrical industries.

One such lawsuit, filed in 1995 by the folk singer Michelle Shocked, actually appealed to the U.S. Constitution in her cause. Shocked signed a 1987 recording agreement with the Mercury label of Polygram Records. After several reasonably successful albums, Shocked claimed that Polygram refused to release the kind of albums that Shocked was then recording (e.g., one entitled *Prayers*). Polygram would also not let Shocked out of the long-term contract so she could find a label that might be interested in her current artistic style. Shocked claimed that Polygram's insistence on a contract constraint that she must continue to be "stylistically consistent" violated the Thirteenth Amendment, which bars "slavery and involuntary servitude" by private as well as state actors.

The more typical basis for such a lawsuit (including Shocked's) is either state common law or legislation. Most prominent is a provision in the California Labor Code, section 2855, which places a limit on the permissible duration of employment contracts. As originally enacted in 1872, such "personal service" commitments were limited to two years; the length was later increased to five years and then to seven years (in 1931), where it now remains.

The initial focus of that law in the entertainment world was the film industry. During the "Golden Age" of Hollywood from the 1920s to the late 1940s, movie studios sought to develop their stars by signing young performers to long-term contracts at specified annual salaries, and then embarking on publicity campaigns to make those performers "larger than life." Indeed, as we saw in the Shirley Temple case, once an actor became a star, a studio could loan (or "farm") her out to work at other studios at a rate greater than the performer's salary. The following case remains a major ruling on the meaning and scope of the California law.

## DE HAVILAND V. WARNER BROS. PICTURES

Court of Appeal of California, Second District, 1944.
67 Cal.App.2d 225, 153 P.2d 983.

SHINN, JUDGE.

[In 1936, the movie actress Olivia De Haviland signed a one-year contract with Warner Bros. Pictures that gave Warner the annual option to renew her contract for up to another six years (which Warner did). After *Gone With the Wind*, which made De Haviland a big star, Warner sought to assign her to more parts, but De Haviland became more willing to refuse roles she felt were not suited to her talents and future career. Warner then exercised its right to suspend De Haviland without pay during those missed production periods, as well as on one occasion when the actress was not able to perform because of illness. In 1945, De Haviland sued for a declaration that her contract was required to be terminated by reason of section 2855 of the Labor Code:

> A contract to render personal service, other than a contract of apprenticeship as provided in Chapter 4 of this division, may not be enforced against the employee beyond seven years from the commencement of service under it. Any contract, otherwise valid, to perform or render service of a special, unique, unusual, extraordinary, or intellectual character, which gives it peculiar value and the loss of which cannot be reasonably or adequately compensated in damages in an action at law, may nevertheless be enforced against the person contracting to render such service, for a term not to exceed seven years from the commencement of service under it. If the employee voluntarily continues his service under it beyond that time, the contract may be referred to as affording a presumptive measure of the compensation.

Warner's response was that it was entitled to add the 25 weeks of suspension periods to the seven calendar years specified in De Haviland's contract.]

* * *

It is the contention of defendant that under section 1980, as amended in 1931, a contract for "exceptional services" could be enforced against an employee for seven years of actual service, even though the employee would thereby be required to render services over a period of more than seven calendar years. Defendant's argument, in substance, is as follows: if it had not been the intention to take contracts for exceptional services out of the seven years' limitation, there would have been no occasion for the 1931 amendment, since employers holding contracts for the exclusive services of artists (a term we use to denote all of those who contract to render "exceptional services") could enjoin the rendering of the services of their employees to others during the term of the contract (*Lumley v. Gye*, 2 El. & Bl. 216, 118 Eng.Rep. 749; Civ. Code, § 3423); section 1980 of the Civil Code had always made an exception of contracts of apprenticeship; the 1931 amendment, in addition to changing the term of seven years, created another exception expressed in the first paragraph by the words "other than a contract entered into pursuant to the proviso hereinafter in this section contained." The effect of this language, it is claimed, was to take contracts for "exceptional services" out of the general limitation of seven years and to state a special rule for them as found in the proviso. Our attention is then directed to the wording of the proviso that contracts for exceptional services "may nevertheless be enforced against the person contracting to render such service for a term not beyond a period of seven years from the commencement of service under it." It is argued that the phrase "for a term not beyond a period of seven years" in the proviso, instead of the phrase "beyond the term of seven years" which was retained in the paragraph relating to contracts for services of a general nature, had a peculiar significance. . . .

If we are to accept defendant's construction of the section as amended, we must add words to the phrase used in the proviso so that it would read "for a term not beyond a period of seven years of actual service from the commencement of service under it." In fact, the words "of actual service" could have been used appropriately after the word "term" and also after the words "seven years" if it had been the intention to do away with the limitation of seven calendar years from the commencement of service. It is true that the exception in the first clause of contracts for exceptional services, to which the proviso relates, suggests a possible intention to take such contracts out of the general rule, but the proviso itself is the enacting clause and the controlling one. It is the clause which determines whether the general limitation was intended to be removed as to contracts for exceptional services. Defendant's contention is that there could have been only one purpose in amending the section, namely, to allow the enforcement against employees of contracts for personal services to the extent of seven years of actual service, regardless of the time over which such services might extend. With this we cannot agree. The difficulty with the argument, and which we think is insurmountable, is that the Legislature has not used the words "of service," and the failure to use those or equivalent words is far more significant as indicating the purpose of the enactment than the entire amendment as written. We cannot believe that the phrase "for a term not beyond a period of seven years" carries a hidden meaning. It cannot be questioned that the limitation of time to which section 1980 related from 1872 to 1931 was one to be measured in calendar years. It is conceded that contracts for general services are limited to seven calendar years. The substitution of years of service for calendar years would work a drastic change of state policy with relation to contracts for personal services. One would expect that such a revolutionary change, even as applied to a particular class of contracts, would be given expression in clear and unmistakable terms. It is difficult—in fact, too difficult—to believe that a purpose which could have been expressed so simply and clearly was intentionally buried under the camouflage of uncertainty and ambiguity.

* * *

What we have said does not fully answer the question why section 1980 was amended, if it was not to make a special rule for the enforcement of contracts of artists. Defendant's argument is that if it did not serve that purpose it served no purpose at all. The amendment would seem to have been unnecessary, for it worked no change in the substantive or procedural rights of either the employer or the employee. It is not questioned by either party that before the amendment was adopted, employers who had contracted for the exclusive services of artists could enforce their contracts for the term limited by section 1980 by means of injunction restraining the rendering of services of their employees to others. Both plaintiff and defendant cite *Lumley v. Gye*, supra, in support of this proposition. Prior to 1919, section 3423 of the Civil Code provided that an injunction may not be granted to prevent the breach of a contract which would not be subject to specific performance. In 1919 the section was amended so as to except contracts for exceptional services such as the one in issue, which provide a rate of compensation of not less than $6,000 per annum. But even though the amendment of section 1980 did not enlarge the rights of employers to enforce such contracts other than to extend the term to seven years, the amendment was nevertheless desirable because it constituted a statement of a well established rule of equity and there is a good purpose served by the codification of established rules of law or equity. . . .

We have not overlooked the earnest arguments of counsel as to whether a producer of motion pictures should or should not have the right to the exclusive services of an artist for a period of seven years of service. It is to be presumed that the Legislature considered such matters in legislating upon the subject, but the arguments do not aid us in determining what the code sections mean. While the purpose sought to be accomplished in the enactment of a statute may be considered as an aid to interpretation, the question whether the Legislature has acted at all in a given particular must find answer in the statute itself. We think the expressions of the various enactments cannot be bent to a shape that will fit defendant's argument, and that the several extensions of plaintiff's contract due to her suspensions were ineffective to bind her beyond May 5, 1943, seven years after her services commenced.

A second contention is that if defendant had not the right under the code to demand seven years of service, plaintiff has waived the right to question the validity of the extensions, which carried beyond the seven-year period. By her breaches of the contract, it is claimed, she brought into operation the provisions for extension and is now estopped to avoid them. Defendant relies upon section 3513 of the Civil Code, reading as follows: "Anyone may waive the advantage of a law intended solely for his benefit. But a law established for a public reason cannot be contravened by a private agreement." Defendant insists that the limitations of said sections 1980 and 2855 were enacted solely for the benefit of employees and not for a public reason, and may be waived.

* * *

The fact that a law may be enacted in order to confer benefits upon an employee group, far from shutting out the public interest, may be strong evidence of it. It is safe to say that the great majority of men and women who work are engaged in rendering personal services under employment contracts. Without their labors the activities of the entire country would stagnate. Their welfare is the direct concern of every community. Seven years of time is fixed as the maximum time for which they may contract for their services without the right to change employers or occupations. Thereafter they may make a change if they deem it necessary or advisable. There are innumerable reasons why a change of employment may be to their advantage. Considerations relating to age or health, to the rearing and schooling of children, new economic conditions and social surroundings may call for a change. As one grows more experienced and skillful there should be a reasonable opportunity to move upward and to employ his abilities to the best advantage and for the highest obtainable compensation. Legislation which is enacted with the object of promoting the welfare of large classes of workers whose personal services constitute their means of livelihood and which is calculated to confer direct or indirect benefits upon the people as a whole must be presumed to have been enacted for a public reason and as an expression of public policy in the field to which the legislation relates. It was said in *Re Miller* (1912), 162 Cal. 687, 695 [124 P. 427]: "The courts must always assume that the legislature, in enacting laws, intended to act within its lawful powers and not to violate the restrictions placed upon it by the constitution." The validity of legislation infringing upon the right of contract is to be judged from its tendency to promote the welfare of the general public rather than that of a small percentage of citizens.

The power to restrict the right of private contract is one which does not exist independently of the power to legislate for the purpose of preserving the public comfort, health, safety, morals and welfare. The power to provide for the comfort, health, safety and general welfare of any or all employees is granted to the Legislature by article XX, section 17½ of the state Constitution. Enactments exercising the power have been upheld in many instances. . . .

* * *

Finally, it may be pointed out that the construction of the code sections contended for by defendant would render the law unworkable and would lead to an absurd result. If an employee may waive the statutory right in question by his conduct, he may waive it by agreement, but if the power to waive it exists at all, the statute accomplishes nothing. An agreement to work for more than seven years would be an effective waiver of the right to quit at the end of seven. The right given by the statute can run in favor of those only who have contracted to work for more than seven years and as these would have waived the right by contracting it away, the statute could not operate at all. It could scarcely have been the intention of the Legislature to protect employees from the consequences of their improvident contracts and still leave them free to throw away the benefits conferred upon them. The limitation of the life of personal service contracts and the employee's rights thereunder could not be waived.

* * *

Affirmed.

---

As a result of this ruling, De Haviland's future contracts usually negotiated not just a generous salary, but a share of the gross revenues. For example, in her next role in *Lady in the Cage*, she was paid $25,000 up front and an additional $150,000 when the film turned out to be a box office hit.

Another case, *Autry v. Republic Productions*, 30 Cal. 2d 144, 180 P.2d 888 (1947), posed an interesting variation on *De Haviland*. Gene Autry, a star of cowboy movies, signed a five-year option deal with Republic Pictures in 1938. Autry promised to make ten movies each year, at $6,000 for each of the first two and $10,000 a film after that. Midway through the contract, in 1942, Autry was called to military duty. At the end of World War II, Autry sued for a declaration that his three years in the army were to be counted as part of the term of his seven-year contract. Autry won his case on grounds other than section 2855, including the economic conditions resulting from the war.

### *QUESTIONS FOR DISCUSSION*

1. The *De Haviland* facts posed a number of analytical questions. One was whether the seven-year time limit applied to contracts of movie stars. Second was whether an actor's failure to perform for a portion of the seven years—whether because of refusing particular movie roles, or illness, or military service—could extend the contract's duration to encompass actual service for a full seven years. Third was whether during the life of the contract, De Haviland could have explicitly agreed to extend the length of her service commitment (perhaps in the form of a new contract), perhaps to avoid suspension of her salary during her absences or even to secure a larger salary. What would be your reading of section 2855 be with respect to each of these questions?

2. In 1951, Hank Ketcham, the California creator of *Dennis the Menace*, entered into a contract with a New York firm, Hall Syndicate, whereby the latter would syndicate Ketcham's cartoon series across the country. The agreement was for an initial period of one year, with provision for automatic renewal after every year in which the plaintiff's share from the syndication proceeds met a stipulated minimum payment. In 1961, Ketcham sought to end the contract, even though his payments were more than five times the minimum amounts. Is this contract governed by California or New York law? Under California law, is this relationship the kind of personal service contract covered by the Labor Code's seven-year limit? Under New York law, what is the appropriate analysis under common law contract doctrine? *See Ketcham v. Hall Syndicate*, 37 Misc.2d 693, 236 N.Y.S.2d 206 (1962), *aff'd*, 19 A.D.2d 611, 242 N.Y.S.2d 182 (1963).

3. In 1973, Melissa Manchester signed a recording agreement with Arista Records under which Arista was entitled to exercise options for a period stated to be five years. The contract, however, also required Manchester to deliver two albums per year, and if she did not, Arista was allowed to extend each option period until the albums were received. It was not until 1980, then, that the contract had reached its fifth option year. In addition, Manchester had been sued by her record producer, who won a $145,000 judgment. Arista agreed to pay this sum in return for Manchester giving Arista yet another option year. When Arista exercised this option in 1980, extending the agreement through 1981, Manchester filed suit, seeking a ruling that this last contract extension was precluded by section 2855. Manchester's argument was that under *De Haviland*, no extension of existing contracts beyond seven years was valid. Arista Records argued that all such extensions were permissible. While ultimately resting its decision on a different ground, the court expressed the view that some, but not all, mid-contract extensions were legal under the Labor Code. Under this intermediate position, what factors would be relevant? *See Manchester v. Arista Records*, 3 Ent. L. Rep. 1 (November 1981).

4. The court did not have to render a decision in *Manchester* about section 2855 because it enforced another provision in the recording

agreement, under which the parties chose to have the contract governed by New York law and to have any disputes resolved in New York courts. Manchester had homes in both New York and Los Angeles, and while Arista did its recording in Los Angeles, its headquarters were in New York. Suppose, though, that the artist's principal residence and the label's principal office were in California, so that under usual choice-of-law and venue rules, California would have been selected. Should the artist be able to contract away the right to sue in a California court and assert the section 2855 provision under California law?

---

A George Michael suit illustrates the manner in which contract duration clauses may be challenged under the common law. Michael had begun his career as the lead singer for the British group WHAM!, which signed its first contract with Inner Vision Records, giving the label option rights for up to ten albums by the group. Inner Vision had a licensing agreement with the United Kingdom branch of CBS Music. In 1983, WHAM! released its first album, which was a success in Britain. The group then filed suit in England, asking the court to terminate its contract with Inner Vision as an undue restraint of trade. The case was settled before trial, with Inner Vision agreeing to let CBS Music sign WHAM! to a new contract with eight album options on better financial terms.

After two more popular WHAM! albums appeared in 1984 and 1986, Michael (as well as his colleague, Andrew Ridgeley) decided to leave the group and embark on solo careers. Under the WHAM! contract that Michael had signed, CBS had the prerogative to apply the 1984 contract to Michael and Ridgeley as individual artists. Happily for CBS, it did exercise that option, and in 1987, it released Michael's first solo album, *Faith*. *Faith*'s worldwide sales of 16 million records made it a best seller. Following that success, Michael and his agents renegotiated the terms of his WHAM! agreement. In return for higher royalty payments and $6 million in advance payments, Michael agreed to give CBS Music contract options it might extend for fifteen years (until 2003).

At that same time, Sony Corp. was negotiating to buy CBS Music for $2 billion, as the Japanese manufacturer's first major entertainment venture. With Michael considered one of its major artistic assets, the newly-titled Sony Music Entertainment accepted the terms of the 1988 agreement, and in 1990 it revised the contract to increase his royalty to the industry's superstar level. Michael's next album was released in 1990—*Listen Without Prejudice*. That album, whose musical style was similar to *Faith*, sold 8 million copies, less than half its predecessor. Sony believed that the reason for the drop in sales (which occurred mainly in the U.S. market) was that (by contrast with *Faith*) Michael had refused to put his image on the cover of *Listen Without Prejudice*, to do a music video version, or to perform at a series of concert appearances. Michael thought the problem stemmed from the label's deliberate failure to promote the album in the United States in retaliation for Michael's effort to downplay his image in pursuit of a longer-term career plan. Michael filed suit against Sony Music in London, alleging that the 15-year length of his record contract constituted an undue restraint of trade under British and European Union law.

Under American law, a contract is in restraint of trade "when its performance limit[s] competition in any business, or restrict[s] a promisor in the exercise of gainful employment." Restatement (Second) of Contracts § 186. A contract that restrains trade is void if the restriction is unreasonable. To determine reasonableness, "[t]he promise is viewed in terms of the effects that it could have had and not merely what actually happened. Account is taken of such factors as the protection that it affords for the promisee's legitimate interests, the hardship that it imposes on the promisor, and the likely injury to the public." *Id.*, Comment a.

The British music industry has produced several cases addressing the same contract principle under British law. *See Schroeder Music Pub. v. Macaulay*, 3 A11 E.R. 616 (H.L. 1974) ("everyone should be free so far as practicable to earn a livelihood and to give to the public the fruits of his particular abilities.") Michael's claim was that the contract was too one-sided and did not provide reciprocity: Sony could choose not to sign him to an extended contract term, but he had no comparable right to stop recording. Furthermore, Sony had the right to control the master recordings until termination of the contract, thereby granting Michael no access to his recordings and no freedom to supply them to third parties. Said Michael:

> Even though I both created and paid for my work, I will never own it or have any rights over it . . . Most importantly, I have no rights to resign. There is no such thing as a resignation for an artist in the music industry. You sign a piece of paper at the beginning of your career and you are expected to live with that decision for the rest of your life.

Others in the industry echoed this sentiment. Don Engel, attorney for singer Don Henley observed that "George Michael's complaints are typical of artists all over the world of these long-term contracts, because they are signed when the artists don't have clout or economic power. They become quite onerous to many artists." Even after the artist becomes a superstar they "are still, by and large, constrained by the first contract they sign, and therefore may never reach the market value they could receive if they were free to negotiate anew at the peak of their careers."

Michael also claimed that the contract was unreasonably restraining his creativity. In a statement released before trial, Michael explained that

> [m]usicians do not come in regimented shapes and sizes, but are individuals who change and evolve together with their audiences. Sony obviously views this as a great inconvenience. They have developed hard-sell, high-profile sales techniques, and their stance is that if George Michael, or any other artist for that matter, does not wish to conform to Sony's current ideas, there are plenty of hungry young acts who will.

Sony countered that when the parties were renegotiating in 1988 and 1990, both sides did so in good faith and without legal or economic pressure. The company contended that the renegotiation of the 1984 contract between WHAM! and CBS was also legally binding because the negotiation was done in good faith and Michael showed no prior signs of dissatisfaction. Michael, they claim, renegotiated for better payment terms: while even these new terms may not have been "as good as he had hoped for, or had been led to believe that he would get—they were genuinely negotiated."

In 1994, the British judge rendered a decision in favor of Sony, concluding that the negotiating process and the resulting terms of the 1988 agreement had been reasonable and fair, and that the potential contract duration did not constitute an unreasonable restraint of trade.

> It is to be borne in mind that the 1988 Agreement is a renegotiation of the 1984 Agreement; that by January 1988 George Michael was already an established artist who had just achieved commercial success as a solo artist with his album *Faith*; that his aim in the renegotiation was to achieve parity "with other superstars"; and that the essence of the renegotiations, as embodied in the 1988 Agreement, was a substantial improvement in George Michael's financial terms in exchange for additional product.

Michael filed an appeal, but the parties also began serious negotiations for release of Michael's recording rights. Finally, in 1995, the Michael-Sony saga ended when Sony fully released Michael from any obligations with its label. Michael signed a new record contract with DreamWorks in the U.S. and with Virgin Records for the rest of the world. DreamWorks planned to use Michael as their launching pad into the music industry. DreamWorks and Virgin paid Sony a release fee that reportedly was in the $30–40 million range, just to be able to sign Michael to a two-album contract (which paid him a $10 million advance against his 20 percent royalty rate). Michael's first album since 1990 finally appeared in 1996. While *Older* quickly reached Billboard's Top Ten list, its rather lackluster sales did not come close to *Listen Without Prejudice*, let alone *Faith*.

Another lawsuit involving stars seeking to free themselves from their lengthy contracts involved the heavy metal group Metallica's deal with Elektra. Metallica filed suit in California, seeking a declaration that its contract was invalid. Elektra argued that the choice-of-law provision invoking New York law precluded application of section 2855 of the California Labor Code. Metallica's response was that this clause was just as invalid as the overall contract, and the contract was also invalid under New York law, which precluded agreements that were either unconscionable or were unreasonable restraints of trade. The case was settled before trial, with Metallica securing ownership and control of its albums and more generous royalties. Metallica's 1996 album, *Load* (the group's first recording since its 1991 blockbuster, *Metallica*), went to the top of Billboard's sales charts in its first week of release.

Another major lawsuit against a music label was filed in 2001, by Courtney Love. In 1989, Love formed a partnership with Eric Erlandson in a rock duo called Hole. After a successful independent label release of their debut album, *Pretty on the Inside*, Hole created a corporation, Doll Head, to market its future services. After receiving a host of offers, Hole opted for the Geffen Records branch of what was then MCA Universal. The Hole partners felt especially attracted to David Geffen, who had founded this company to specialize in rock bands and was still leading it after the merger with Universal. The contract had the standard commitment by the Hole to deliver seven albums in seven years, while giving Geffen the option to terminate the contract at each album stage.

The first Hole album released by Geffen, *Live Through This*, came out in 1994, generating over two million record sales. Tragically, shortly afterwards, Love's husband Kurt Cobain committed suicide. This left Love with both their two year-old child and Cobain's large estate. Love worked on a second Hole album, *Celebrity Skin*, which generated strong sales and four Grammy nominations. During this time, though, Canadian liquor company Seagram acquired Universal; Geffen left the company shortly afterwards; the record company merged in 2000 with the France-based Vivendi Universal.

Universal assigned responsibility for its contracts to Interscope, which Hole felt was too oriented toward pop rather than rock music. Thus, in 1999, Doll Head delivered a notice of termination of their contract after the expiration of the seven-year period under the California Labor Code. Shortly afterwards, the record company filed suit, claiming breach of contract because Hole had delivered only two of the seven promised albums. Hole counterclaimed that Geffen had violated the terms of the contract by miscalculating the actual revenues and costs generated by the two Hole albums, defrauding them of the full royalty share they should have been paid. While these two albums generated over $50 million in sales, Hole had not received anything more than their original advance payments of $150,000 for the first and $225,000 for the second album. (This entertainment royalty issue is addressed in Chapter 8).

The record company's reliance on Section 2855(b)(3)'s record contract exemption to the seven-year limit was alleged to be invalid for several reasons. Hole argued that it was not practicable to do seven albums in seven years. It may be possible to compose and record one new album a year, but the Geffen contract also required Hole to do two videos for each such album, which takes several months. Even more important, it was in both sides' interest to have the group take a domestic and world tour for six to 12 months to enhance record sales, as well as performance earnings. Finally, even if Hole had decided to concentrate on recording a new album annually, the record company might reject them because they want a two-year gap between the releases to maximize sales.

Based on their assertion that the contract was, *de facto*, for at least 14 years, Hole claimed that it could not be supported even under the special music contract exception written into section 2855 in 1987. The first argument was that such a lengthy contract term is unconscionable under general contract law doctrine (the same argument made by Metallica under New York law). Second, it was said to be an invalid contract of adhesion and restraint of trade in the music industry, because all the top labels insist on the standard duration, leaving artists with no choice but to accept it if they want to enter this branch of the industry. Finally, enforcement of such a one-way, long-term commitment was claimed to be unconstitutional as a denial of a musician's equal protection rights and as "involuntary servitude" for a period that may cover a musician's entire recording career.

On the eve of trial, the parties reached a settlement whereby the label agreed to release Hole from the contract even though they had made only two of the agreed-on seven albums; Hole also received additional royalties, and Love agreed to release through Universal the last song composed for Nirvana by her deceased husband, Kurt Cobain, "You Know You're Right," as part of a retrospective album for Universal.

Don Henley, formerly of the Eagles, and his Recording Artists Coalition, sought legislative reform, but in 2002, the California State Senate withdrew from consideration a proposal to remove the special exemption for music contracts from the seven-year limit in section 2855. The Recording Industry Association of America (RIAA) successfully argued for continuing this exemption for contracts between musicians and record labels.

### *QUESTIONS FOR DISCUSSION*

1. Why have long-term contracts become the standard practice in the music industry, but nowhere else? Is such an arrangement necessary for the label and valuable to the artist by securing up-front investments in their recording projects? Why is the seven-album, 14-year commitment made only by the artist, with the record company retaining the option to choose whether to renew each year in light of the artist's market potential? Should such contracts be enforceable only if they bind both the artist and the label?

A point to consider in Chapter 12 is whether the music marketplace (with three major labels accounting for most music revenue from all sources) is sufficiently competitive to ensure reasonable and fair terms for both budding artists and established stars looking to renegotiate their contracts? Consider Mariah Carey's experience after she completed her successful 13-year contract with Sony Records, under which she sold 140 million albums. The resulting bidding war led to a five-album, $80 million contract from EMI's Virgin Records, with a $21 million up-front payment. After Carey's first Virgin album, *Glitter*, did poorly that fall, EMI was compelled by the terms of that contract to pay her another $28 million to secure its release from any further obligation.

2. In comparing the music and movie industries, consider the experience of actors John Travolta and Jim Carrey. In 1993, with Travolta considered a has-been actor, he received $150,000 for performing in *Pulp Fiction*; the relatively unknown Canadian, Jim Carrey, came to Hollywood to make *Ace Ventura* for $350,000. Just three years later, after these hit movies, Travolta and Carrey received approximately $20 million apiece for their respective new releases, *Broken Arrow* and *The Cable Guy*, and by 2000, Carrey had topped $25 million for *How The Grinch Stole Christmas*. Consider why the studios taking those initial chances with Travolta and Carrey did not insist on an option clause for future movies. These issues will arise again in Chapter 11 on *Performer Organizations*, which will consider the Screen Actors Guild's role.

3. The hit television show Modern Family also became the subject of litigation resulting from employment contracts longer than seven years. The show, which won Emmys and drew high ratings, was in some ways the victim of its own success. Five of the actors on the show, including stars Sofia Vegara and Julie Bowen, sued Twentieth Century Fox, arguing that their contracts were illegal under California Law because their duration exceeded the statutory limit of seven years. Small caps on the percentage raises the actors received under the contract certainly provided for some of the motivation of this lawsuit. Twentieth Century Fox quickly settled the suits by giving the actors significant raises and new contracts. Would the actors have had the same leverage if their original contracts had not violated state law? What does this tell you about the importance of careful contract drafting?

## F. BANKRUPTCY

The popular rhythm and blues group TLC filed for bankruptcy in 1996 with the aim of terminating its record contract with Pebbitone Inc. and LaFace Records. TLC was comprised of three young Atlanta women, Tionne "T-Boz" Watkins, Lisa "Left-Eye" Lopes, and Rozanda "Chilli" Thomas. TLC's first album, *Ooooooohhh . . . on the TLC Tip* (1992), sold four million copies worldwide, and its second, *Crazysexycool* (1995), sold ten million and won two Grammy awards. Under its contract, which required eight albums and thus likely would last for 16 years or so, the group was entitled to 7 percent of defined revenues for the first 500,000 in sales and 8 percent thereafter, far less than the 11–13 percent industry norm for newcomers, let alone the 20–25 percent secured by "superstars" like George Michael.

A complicating factor in this case is that TLC was originally discovered by Atlanta singer Perri Reid, who had performed under the name Pebbles, and had recently begun her own music-manager business through Pebbitone, Inc. In return for Reid agreeing to take TLC on as one of her clients, the group agreed to give Pebbitone the right to produce and sell their albums, with TLC to receive the 7–8 percent royalty rate. Pebbitone then assigned this record production right to LaFace, jointly owned by Reid's then-husband, Antonio "L.A." Reid, and Kenny "Babyface" Edmonds. LaFace, whose records were distributed by the Arista Records label of Bertelsmann A.G., agreed to pay Pebbitone 15 percent royalties on all TLC record sales, only half of which was paid over to the artists. As we shall see in Chapter 8, all production costs for each album must be covered by the performers' royalties. Consequently, the actual net earnings for a group are much lower than one might suppose even if an album reaches the top of the Billboard charts, regardless of the royalty percentage. Finally, the three artists who made up TLC had incurred major personal debts in the 1990s. (The largest of these debts was owed by Lopes to Lloyds of London, insurer of the $1.3 million home of Lopes' live-in boyfriend Andre Rison, a home that Lopes had accidentally burned down in a dispute with Rison.) Thus the group members sought to use the bankruptcy route to get a "fresh start."

The federal Bankruptcy Code establishes three alternative paths for pursuing these objectives. One is Chapter 7, which provides for liquidation of all the non-exempt assets of the debtor, division of the proceeds among the creditors, and then discharge of the debtor from any past obligations that cannot be satisfied from the liquidation fund. A second procedure is Chapter 11, which allows the "debtor-in-possession," or a court-appointed trustee, to continue a business venture that has more value as a going concern than it does in liquidated tangible assets, while developing a plan for court-approved reorganization that will pay creditors over a specified period. The third route, Chapter 13, allows individuals to work out a plan for paying off all their debts from future income, rather than forcing them to liquidate non-exempt assets to pay their creditors immediately.

A crucial feature of bankruptcy law is that it allows the debtor (or trustee) to reject "executory" contracts—contracts containing obligations for significant future performance. Under Chapter 7, rejection of executory contracts is automatic. Under Chapter 11, rejection is permitted with approval of the bankruptcy court, routinely given unless the damage to the contract beneficiary is substantially disproportionate to the benefits gained by the debtor and other creditors. Rejection of the contract means that neither party can be required to perform in the future. The rejecting party can, however, be the target of a claim for damages that then become part of the broader array of debts to be dealt with in the reorganization plan.

There has been little jurisprudence regarding the status of personal service contracts under bankruptcy law, even as to whether these are the types of executory contracts that can be rejected under the Code. The likely explanation is that for most workers, no future obligations are owed under the standard at-will employment relationship. The entertainment industry, as we have seen, is a distinct exception to that rule. That is why the use of bankruptcy procedures by musicians, as in the next case, provides a revealing glimpse into the policies involved in this "fresh start" feature of the law.[h]

## IN THE MATTER OF NOONAN P.K.A. WILLIE NILE

United States Bankruptcy Court, Southern District of New York, 1982.
17 B.R. 793, Bankr. L. Rep. (CCH) P 68,841, *aff'd*, 697 F.2d 287 (2d Cir. 1982).

BABITT, BANKRUPTCY JUDGE.

On its motion to convert the debtor's voluntary Chapter 7 case to an involuntary Chapter 11 case, the moving creditor invites this court to come up with a square holding in its favor on nice, round, undisputed facts. The court must decline the invitation and rule for the debtor as a round hole cannot accept the square peg which sets this case apart from others fitting more snugly into the statutory scheme. That uniqueness is based on who the debtor is, who the creditor is, what it wants from the debtor, and how it can go about getting it!

[Songwriter and musician Robert A. Noonan (professionally known as "Willie Nile") filed a voluntary petition for Chapter 11 bankruptcy in 1981. At the time of the filing, he was signed to an exclusive recording contract with Arista Records. This contract required Noonan to record at

[h] *See* Thomas H. Jackson, *The Fresh-Start Policy in Bankruptcy Law*, 98 Harv. L. Rev. 1393 (1985).

least two albums over 18 months, and granted Arista the right to renew the contract for three consecutive segments of 18 months each. Noonan recorded two albums and received an advance of $300,000. Arista could only recoup this and any future advances through royalties from the sale of Noonan's albums. Despite slower than expected album sales, Arista extended Noonan's contract for an additional 18 months, thereby requiring him to record another two albums with Arista. In order to recover the $300,000 and any future advances given to Noonan for the two new albums, Noonan's records would have had to sell more than one million copies.

In an effort to avoid his obligations under the extended contract, Noonan, as "debtor-in-possession," moved for and was granted an order declaring the extended contract to be executory. Facing opposition from Arista, Noonan then converted his Chapter 11 bankruptcy into a Chapter 7 proceeding, which granted him an automatic right to reject executory contracts. Arista moved to have Noonan put back into Chapter 11 bankruptcy and sought to file a reorganization plan that would give Noonan's creditors (including Arista) a more generous pay-off than they would receive under Chapter 7 via the liquidation of Noonan's estate. The court considered whether Arista should be allowed to submit its plan and force Noonan back into Chapter 11.]

* * *

Arista claims to find support for [its reorganization plan] in the authority in the 1978 Code for an involuntary Chapter 11 case, the impulse for which was Congress' feeling that a debtor's creditors should be able to realize on his assets through reorganization just as in a liquidation. In furtherance of this, Arista says that reconversion to Chapter 11, assumption of its contract with Noonan and confirmation of its plan will work and everyone will be happy.

Everyone except Noonan, that is. He says nothing can compel him to assume or reaffirm his contract with Arista and that this court, even if it could force him, should not as a matter of equity, for to do so would interfere with his fresh start and place him in involuntary servitude.

Therefore, Noonan argues that for the court to decree reconversion would be a futile act pre-ordained to result in his return to Chapter 7, as Arista's Chapter 11 dreams can never be realized. So, he says, Arista's motion should be denied, a view with which the court agrees.

The court has carefully considered these factors for all are clearly relevant, since the decision to convert under Section 706(b) is left to the sound discretion off the court, an exercise which should include consideration of the best interests of both the creditors and the debtor.

* * *

Arista says that in exercising its discretion the court should not consider the Noonan contract now. And so, the court now addresses what it considers relevant to Arista's contention.

The purpose of the usual Chapter 11 case is a business reorganization. It is premised upon the theory that the assets of a business in use are more valuable than those same assets sold in a liquidation sale for the benefit only of their purchaser. Efforts are made to preserve and conserve the value of assets. And by permitting involuntary reorganization, Congress reasoned that creditors should be able to realize on these assets through reorganization, as well as liquidation. But these typical factors are foreign to this case, as it simply refuses to be typical and application of customary Chapter 11 principles on the facts here cannot work. This debtor is an individual; an artist. He has no tangible assets available for distribution. He earns his living by his creativity, by his voice, and by the combination of the two. The Arista contract is merely the instrumentality for the exploitation of the debtor's talents.

The Arista contract is clearly an executory contract. 11 U.S.C. § 541 vests the debtor's estate with all the debtor's property as of the commencement of the case. A seeming exception to the sweep of this rule continues for executory contracts, for the Code continues prior law by postponing vesting of the debtor's rights and duties until assumption. . . . Where an executory contract between the debtor and another is of such a nature as to be based upon the debtor's personal skill, the trustee does not take title to the debtor's rights and cannot deal with the contract. The Arista contract is simply not the kind of an asset to which the creditors can look by insisting that the debtor assume it.

Since a personal service contract does not vest in the debtor's trustee, services performed under it would appear not to be "for the benefit of the estate, but rather for the personal benefit of the bankrupt. . . ." For policy, practical and constitutional reasons, these contracts are sui generis. Clearly, the answer to Arista is that its contract is not an asset that can be used for its benefit nor in the debtor's plan absent his consent. And, as it appears to be Noonan's only potential asset of value, the underpinning for Arista's conversion motion has been removed.

To be sure, Arista's frustration is understandable. However, it must have known it was dealing in an area which historically fashioned its own rules. It is a long-standing rule that courts of equity will not order specific performance of personal service contracts. Notwithstanding the lip service paid the old adage that "a bird that can sing and will not sing, must be made to sing", *De Rivafinoli v. Corsetti*, 4 Paige Ch. 264, 270 (N.Y.Ch.1833), "(W)e insist upon liberty even at the expense of broken promises." And, courts have always understood that an artist does not work well under compulsion.

And only the other day, the New York Court of Appeals reviewed the rules and the reasons for the rules that have developed in this area of personal service contracts and enforceability of such agreements. . . .

[The court then summarized *ABC v. Wolf*, 52 N.Y.2d 394, 438 N.Y.S.2d 482, 420 N.E.2d 363 (1981), where the plaintiff, a well-known New York City sportscaster, was sued by his former employer, ABC, for negotiating with and accepting a job with CBS in violation of the good faith negotiation clause of his contract. That clause required Wolf to negotiate with ABC for 90 days and granted ABC the first right of refusal on any other job offer. ABC sought specific performance and an injunction barring Wolf from working at CBS. The court refused to grant ABC this remedy, explaining that ordering specific performance would "violate the express command of the Thirteenth Amendment" barring involuntary servitude.]

* * *

These considerations are the indices of a mature, democratic society. And hand in hand with their reaffirmation is recognition that where problems have arisen in a contractual relationship calling for the performance of purely personal services, the termination of that relationship terminates the problems, to paraphrase Mr. Justice Frankfurter in *Perez v. Brownell*, 356 U.S. 44, 60 (1958). It follows from all these generalities not only that Noonan cannot be compelled to abide by his contract with Arista but that it must be rejected for it cannot be assumed unless Noonan wants it so. It therefore must also follow that Arista's attempt to restore Noonan to Chapter 11 status has to be denied for its rationale is rejected by Noonan on the facts and by this court on the law.

And that result is consistent with Congress' views found elsewhere. Congress was not unaware that the prohibition against involuntary servitude loomed large in bankruptcy, and Congress therefore magnified its concern on the area of involuntary Chapter 13 cases. Here Congress acted to dispel even the remotest possibility of involuntary servitude by prohibiting involuntary Chapter 13 cases.

Arista would have the court ignore this expression of a general Congressional mood by insisting that Congress' concerns in the Chapter 13 case are irrelevant to the motion to convert Noonan to a Chapter 11 debtor pursuant to 11 U.S.C. § 706(b), for Arista says that it is a party in interest and that Noonan, at least facially, is an eligible Chapter 11 debtor. So, Arista concludes, the statute is satisfied and it must prevail. But this syllogism ignores the reality. Courts are often faced with situations not envisioned by the most gifted legislative imagination.

The fact is that Congress perceived the usual Chapter 13 case as emanating from a non-business debtor and determined to make the relief of that chapter voluntary in order to avoid the spectre of involuntary peonage for a hapless debtor laboring for his creditors on their petition and their plan which would strip the debtor and his family of all that made their lives otherwise worth living.

It is also the fact that Congress perceived Chapter 11 of the 1978 Code . . . as a reorganization device, mainly for non-individually operated businesses, and occasionally for the small sole proprietor ineligible for Chapter 13 relief. . . . From that vantage point, it was Congress' view that the Chapter 11 petition could emanate from the debtor's creditors, thereby bringing the debtor involuntarily into the bankruptcy process.

* * *

The possibility, therefore, that the rare and unique kind of fact pattern present here in which there lurks the real possibility of the involuntary servitude with which Congress was concerned in Chapter 13, never occurred to it when it perceived Chapter 11.

But this is not to say that this court should ignore Congress' concerns on facts it did not foresee because comment was made about concerns on facts it did foresee. The policy against forcing an individual to work against his will is applicable, if the facts present themselves, in Chapter 11 as well as in Chapter 13. Congress' concerns are so strongly expressed in connection with Chapter 13 that this court would be remiss were it to apply them only there.

Congress voiced its concerns in these words:

> As under current law, Chapter 13 is completely voluntary. This Committee firmly rejected the idea of mandatory or involuntary Chapter 13 in the 90th Congress. The thirteenth amendment prohibits involuntary servitude. Though it has never been tested in the wage earner plan context, it has been suggested that a mandatory Chapter 13, by forcing an individual to work for creditors, would violate this prohibition. On policy grounds, it would be unwise to allow creditors to force a debtor into a repayment plan. An unwilling debtor is less likely to retain his job or to cooperate in the repayment plan; and more often than not, the plan would be preordained to fail.

It is thus clear from the strong policy considerations of Congress which, on the facts here, touch on constitutionally protected areas, that Arista's motion, addressed to this court's discretion, must fail. This is so because the relief it seeks, i.e., reinstatement of Noonan's Chapter 11 case, is itself destined to fail for the reasons already described.

Finally, it is clear that Arista's proposed plan would defeat a primary purpose of the Code "to allow the individual debtor to obtain a fresh start, free from creditor harassment and free from the worries and pressures of too much debt." If the debtor could be compelled to assume the Arista contract, he would leave this bankruptcy court subject to at least $300,000 of indebtedness, which Arista could recoup from his future earnings. Moreover, as Arista concedes, a confirmed plan reaffirming the contract would subject Noonan to the very real likelihood of protracted litigation. Clearly, the full potential reach of Arista's "scheme" would deprive Noonan of the full scope of his discharge.

As the full measure of a debtor's fresh start flowing from the bankruptcy process is vital to Congress' mission in enacting the Code, cf., *Powell v. U.S. Cartridge Co.*, 339 U.S. 497, 516 (1950), anything which would frustrate the mission must be scrutinized carefully. Arista's attempts to manipulate the bankruptcy process for its own ends is found seriously wanting.

Motion to convert denied.

### *QUESTIONS FOR DISCUSSION*

1. The court was not persuaded by Arista's argument that this was a test case for the record industry because an adverse decision could detract from a record company's ability to maintain contractual exclusivity with its artists. The judge responded that "this court is well aware that any business might be adversely affected by someone else's bankruptcy—the record industry is not unique to this plight." Do you agree with this view? Suppose a musician has run up large debts that become significantly larger than his or her total assets. Should that fact justify relief under bankruptcy law from the normal long-term recording contract? Should courts make exceptions for entertainment contracts, given the special characteristics of the industry? Should the courts permit labels to create an exception by fashioning a contract term that commits the artist not to seek bankruptcy relief against this type of executory contract?

2. A different view was expressed by the judge in *In re Carrere*, 64 B.R. 156 (Bankr. Cal. 1986). Tia Carrere had signed a contract in 1985, under which she agreed to play a minor role in ABC's daily soap opera *General Hospital*. The contract was to last for three years, pay Carrere up to $700 for each appearance, and guarantee her a minimum of three appearances every two weeks. Soon after having appeared on *General Hospital*, Carrere attracted the attention of the producers of the upcoming prime-time series *A-Team*, who offered Carrere a more prominent and more lucrative role if she freed herself of the ABC contract. Thus, in 1986, Carrere filed for bankruptcy under Chapter 11. While Carrere did establish that her debts ($77,000) far exceeded her total assets ($13,000), the bankruptcy judge was not prepared to allow the actress an escape from *General Hospital*. The judge asserted that a

personal service contract was not the kind of contract that either a bankruptcy trustee or the debtor-in-possession was entitled to terminate under section 365. More important, the judge was "concerned about the good faith issue of allowing a debtor to file for the primary purpose of rejecting a personal service contract. A personal service contract is unique and money damages will often not make the employer whole. . . . It would be inequitable to allow a greedy debtor to seek the equitable protection of this Court when her major motivation is to cut off the equitable remedies (e.g., negative injunction) of her employer."

3. The first appellate opinion on this topic, *In the Matter of Taylor*, 913 F.2d 102 (3d Cir. 1990), involved James (J.T.) Taylor who had been the lead singer and songwriter for the group Kool and the Gang. Under their 1985 contract with Polygram Records, the band was required to write and record up to eight albums at Polygram's option. In 1988, Taylor decided to leave the Gang, thereby triggering the "leaving member" contract clause that made him personally responsible for the eight albums. At that time Taylor, both a participant in and guarantor of the Gang's lavish life style, had accumulated over $4.5 million in debts and less than $750,000 in assets (principally his home). Thus, Taylor entered Chapter 11 bankruptcy, and as debtor-in-possession proceeded to reject his Polygram contract. In a brief opinion, the Third Circuit concluded, first, that personal service contracts could be rejected under Chapter 11 (as well as Chapter 7), and that the bankruptcy court's approval of that rejection was appropriate here, given Taylor's current debt-asset ratio and his future earnings prospects under a more attractive recording contract.

4. What is the tangible value of the record company's damage claim against recording artists for rejecting their contracts? Could the company file suit against any other firm that offered the artist a better deal, either before or after rejection? Given bankruptcy law's "fresh start" policy for personal (as opposed to corporate) debtors, should the financial value of the performer's estate include the expected returns from a more lucrative future record contract? What about the current value of future royalties from albums already produced, or of concert tours and merchandising deals that are anticipated from the artist's name recognition and popular appeal? In other words, suppose that Taylor's projected returns from future records, concerts, and endorsements exceed his current debts. Should this fact lead the bankruptcy judge to approve the rejection of the existing record contract under Chapter 11; could it entitle the judge to block rejection under Chapter 7? If the contract is terminated by the bankruptcy court, what effect does that have on the artist's entitlement to future royalties? *See Waldschmidt v. CBS*, 14 B.R. 309 (M.D. Tenn. 1981).

---

In 1996, the bankruptcy judge in the TLC case concluded that the three recording artists were genuinely indebted in significant amounts, and the bankruptcy petition had not been filed simply to avoid their contract obligations to Pebbitone and LaFace. However, the judge had reserved ruling on the question whether to permit the group to reject that contract for the future. Until such a final ruling was made, TLC remained bound by its current contract, and thus was not able to release new albums with any other label. To avoid losing TLC, the record label had offered the group a new contract, which would pay them an immediate $10 million as an advance against future royalties, and had also proposed a new 18 percent royalty rate if TLC agreed to add two more albums to the contract. TLC initially rejected that proposal, saying that since LaFace and Pebbitone had made a reported $50 million on TLC's first two albums, while the artists had received a total of $1.2 million, TLC should receive the same large retroactive bonus that other labels have recently given to male groups, such as Hootie & the Blowfish and Boys II Men. Complicating the situation was the presence of Pebbitone's Perri Reid, who not only had lost TLC as a management client, but had also lost LaFace's co-owner Antonio Reid as her husband. The parties finally settled, and TLC signed a new recording contract directly with LaFace, in return for an undisclosed cash advance and royalty rate, while Pebbitone was paid to leave the scene. Finally, in 1999, LaFace was able to release a popular new TLC album, *Fan Mail.*

LaFace Records faced a replay of the TLC legal saga, this time involving Toni Braxton. Braxton had also been a major music performer of the 1990s. Her two albums, *Toni Braxton* (1993) and *Secrets* (1996), had sold more than 17 million copies and won five Grammy Awards. While these albums may have generated over $170 million in worldwide sales, she earned $5 million. Braxton decided to follow the lead of TLC in the courts.

Braxton's original contract with LaFace included seven albums in return for a 12 percent royalty rate from LaFace (from which was to be deducted the percentage paid to the LaFace record producers). After the eponymous *Braxton* album appeared in 1993, with six million in sales, LaFace agreed to enlarge Braxton's royalty rate to 15 percent and also pay her a sizeable advance. Then, after the 1996 *Secrets* album had generated 11 million in worldwide sales, Braxton's managers and lawyers went back to LaFace looking for an even better deal. By 1997, they believed they had succeeded, with LaFace offering their client a 19 percent royalty rate and a $10 million signing advance.

Braxton, however, was not satisfied with the new contract her representatives had secured, and so she terminated them. Braxton's new manager went back to LaFace seeking a 22 percent royalty rate and $20 million, comparable to what Madonna, George Michael, and other stars had secured. LaFace believed that these artists had secured such superstar rates only after a longer track record of commercial success than Braxton's, and was prepared to make only modest improvements in its last offer to her. Braxton then filed suit in Los Angeles, claiming that the existing record contract had expired under the California Labor Code's seven-year limit on employment contracts. A month later, LaFace's lawyer filed suit against Braxton in New York, citing the forum-selection and choice-of-law clause in their contract. Braxton's then filed for bankruptcy in California.

One benefit for Braxton would be to use the Section 7 provision of the federal *Bankruptcy Code* to eliminate any future executory contract obligations to LaFace. Like anybody else filing for bankruptcy, she would also be able to avoid much of her existing debts, of which Braxton's total of more than $2 million included substantial unpaid fees to her prior managers and lawyer.

Throughout 1998, Braxton could not make any new recordings. Instead, she played Belle on Disney's Broadway hit *Beauty and the Beast*, where she sang a new song "A Change in Me," written especially for her. Meanwhile, Congress was focusing on the broader issues of bankruptcy law reform, and the parties eventually agreed on a new and lucrative record deal. *The Heat* sold two million copies in 2000, and won Braxton yet another Grammy award.

# CHAPTER 8

# ENTERTAINMENT CONTRACT OBLIGATIONS

■ ■ ■

Once an entertainment deal has been negotiated and the major players have signed their contracts, the creative process commences, with producers and performers seeking to develop and market their finished product. This creative process sometimes results in a clash between art and commerce. This clash is particularly apparent in disputes involving performer and producer obligations under personal service contracts. Performers are hired because of their unique talent, and because of the way they express themselves through their acting, singing, or writing. In hiring them, producers are hoping to create a viable and successful product. The creative and financial forces that drive an artistic work are often challenged by the unpredictable nature of the entertainment industry. As circumstances change, the parties must adjust their relationship, both artistically and financially, within the confines of a binding agreement. Here, the dispute is not over whether there *is* a contract, but over whether a party has *breached* the contract.

In 2002, a writer for the television show *L.A. Law*, Paul Haggis, in his spare time wrote a script for a movie he named *Crash,* but he was unable to persuade any studio to produce it. However, a former movie director and successful businessman, Bob Yari, liked the script and agreed to make that effort. He recruited Cathy Shulman to become his partner in Bull's Eye Entertainment to get *Crash* produced. Yari was the principal among six partners in charge of raising the $7.5 million needed to finance it, Shulman for getting it made, and Haggis directing it, at the same time he was writing the script for the 2004 Oscar-winning *Million Dollar Baby*. After *Crash* came out in 2005, earning $80 million in theatre revenues, two lawsuits were filed. One was by Shulman against Yari because Bull's Eye was still paying her and Haggis their very modest salaries, rather than a share of the movie profits; Yari was defending on the ground that the real profits had not yet started to come in. The other suit was brought by Yari against Shulman for having persuaded the Academy of Motion Picture Arts and Sciences, in applying its two producer Oscar ceiling (generated by five producers receiving the 1999 Oscar for *Shakespeare in Love)*, to name only her and Haggis rather than himself.

With respect to *Brokeback Mountain*, actor Randy Quaid, who played the disapproving manager of a sheep farm who had hired two cowboys in that movie, sued the artistic arm of Universal Pictures, Focus Features, for allegedly being underpaid for this 2005 hit. Quaid's claim was that while he normally was paid around $10 million for his role in major studio movies, the head of Focus, David Linde, told him that this movie was "a low-budget, art-house film with no prospect of making any money." Thus he took a very low salary and secured no share of the movie's profits. The Quaid contract/fraud lawsuit is based on the fact that while *Brokeback Mountain* cost slightly less than $15 million to make, by Oscar night it had already grossed more than $150 million just in theaters around the world, with more to be made through home video and on television.

In appraising the likely success of these *Crash* and *Brokeback Mountain* lawsuits, consider that the production of an entertainment work is a collaborative effort. Producers need writers and performers to make their entertainment work a reality, while entertainers need producers to fashion and market their works. This mutual need is often memorialized in two types of contracts—those securing the talent for a project, and those securing the rights necessary to produce a finished product. The latter involve contracts for the acquisition of intellectual property rights in story ideas. Contracts of the former type, which secure the talent for a project, are called personal service contracts.

Detailed personal service contracts are useful because the market is so unpredictable. It is hard to determine before release whether a film, program, book, or album will be a success. As a result, the contract should be designed to address each party's financial needs if the product succeeds or fails. Likewise, circumstances can change during the production phase; the lead actors may not have the chemistry needed to pull off a role, or a song may need altering to blend with a performer's voice. Drafting a personal service contract in the entertainment context is especially challenging because the contract must be both flexible enough to deal with the changes necessary to produce and market a quality product, yet precise enough to be an enforceable and effective instrument in resolving disputes if they should arise.

The outcomes of contract negotiations are heavily influenced by prior disputes that have generated litigation and court opinions. The cases and problems in this chapter regarding performer obligations involve creative input and control over projects, adherence to moral standards in one's personal behavior, and bars on moves to competing producers even for a period after a contract has expired. The corresponding producer obligations include judgments about whether a creative work is satisfactory for production, best promotional efforts for selling a work, and how to calculate the "net profits" or royalties due from sales. Each case forces the lawyers and judges to define the scope of the performer's or producer's obligations, and then to determine whether this obligation was violated, either through action or inaction.

## A. PERFORMER/AUTHOR OBLIGATIONS

As the cases in this section demonstrate, many clauses in performer contracts, particularly those involving creative control and moral behavior, are written in vague language. To help interpret obligations under any kind of contract, courts are supposed to put themselves in the shoes of the parties at the time that the contract was made. Restatement Second of Contracts § 202, Comment b. To assess these expectations and obligations, a court examines the course of performance, relations between the parties under the contract, and general trade usage. Using these factors, a court is able to consider not only how the parties dealt with each other but also how the entertainment industry as a whole views such situations.

In cases of ambiguous contract terms, courts lean towards the interpretation that does not favor the drafting party (even though the latter's views might seem to provide the best index of the contract's intended meaning). This is done for three reasons: (1) drafters are more likely to provide for careful protection of their interests when creating the document; (2) drafters are more likely to know of vague and uncertain terms; and (3) drafters may even have deliberately obscured certain terms with the intention of deciding later what meaning to attach to them. *Id.* § 206, Comment a. Interpreting terms against the drafting party is most frequently used when that party is in a stronger bargaining position than the other side. Inequality of bargaining positions in the entertainment industry is quite common. Many personal service contracts are negotiated when the performer is not yet a well-known and established talent. As a result, the performer is not in a position to demand changes in the producer's standard terms; to do so would block any deal at all.

### 1. CREATIVE CONTROL

Once a court determines a performer's contract obligations, it must decide whether the performer breached the contract by action or inaction. Contract disputes over performer obligations frequently involve the subjective creative process. A record company may not like a musician's song arrangements or a studio the script being authored for a movie project. Does the fact that a producer does not like the way an entertainment work is evolving mean that a performer can be fired for breaching the contract?

Making determinations about contract breaches is somewhat easier where the dispute does not involve questions of creative control. For example, in *CBS, Inc. v. Merrick*, 716 F.2d 1292 (9th Cir. 1983), David Merrick, a leading Broadway and film producer, contracted with CBS to produce a two-part mini-series based on the novel *Blood and Money*, whose rights were owned by Merrick. Under the contract, CBS paid for both the right to do the series and for Merrick's services. The contract was to terminate two years after its execution if the principal photography was not done by then. CBS would then pay Merrick in full and all rights in the work would revert to him. All contract modifications were to be in writing.

Merrick hired a director and screenwriter on CBS's behalf. When he hired them, Merrick knew that they could not meet the established deadlines because they were both working on another project. Merrick orally agreed to an extension of the two-year deadline, but never signed any of the modification documents CBS submitted to him. Five days before the deadline, CBS told Merrick that it would go on with the project, and Merrick had several planning meetings with CBS after the deadline had passed. The next month Merrick told CBS that because the deadline had passed, the project was off, and he wanted all his money. CBS sued and won both rescission and damages. The court based its determination on the fact that Merrick had waived the writing requirement and the two-year deadline by continuing to deal with CBS after the oral agreement. This finding of contract breach in *Merrick* rested, in part, on traditional notions of reliance and waiver, where one party takes action based on the other party's assurances.

*Merrick* was an easier case to decide than most because it did not involve creative or moral questions. Even when these questions arise, however, the court can still look to traditional contract doctrine. Hornbook contract law requires that a breach be material before the contract can be terminated. Among the relevant factors are: 1) the extent to which the non-breaching party is deprived of a benefit reasonably expected under the contract; 2) whether the non-breaching party will be adequately compensated for the loss through a damage award; 3) the degree to which the performer has partially performed obligations under the contract; 4) willfulness of the breach. Restatement Second of Contracts § 241. California law has altered the concept of material breach in the case of personal service contracts. Under California Labor Code § 2924, an employer can fire an employee at any time for willful breach or "in the case of his habitual neglect of his duty or continued incapacity to perform. . . ." Section 2925 allows the employee to terminate employment at any time when the employer breaches willfully or permanently.

The next two cases illustrate how courts determine contract breach. The *Goudal* case highlights the tug-of-war between director and actor for control over the production of a movie. The *Loew's* case involved a challenge by a screenwriter to the operation of a morals clause contained in his contract. While both cases are old, they remain apt illustrations of how courts try to resolve the creative aspects of personal service contract disputes.

## GOUDAL V. CECIL B. DEMILLE PICTURES CORP.

California Court of Appeals, Second District, 1931.
118 Cal.App. 407, 5 P.2d 432.

FRICKE, JUSTICE.

[Jetta Goudal, a movie star of the 1920s, entered into an employment contract with Cecil B. DeMille Pictures. After DeMille twice exercised its annual option to renew (at substantial increases in pay), the studio terminated the contract in 1927, midway through its third year. When Goudal won a trial verdict of slightly over $34,000 for wrongful dismissal, DeMille contended on appeal that Goudal had violated her obligations under the contract, thus justifying its termination.]

* * *

The claim that respondent failed or refused to perform her parts as requested is based upon many incidents set forth in detail in the record. They relate to occasions when the respondent, instead of unquestioningly performing as directed by the director in charge, called attention to inconsistencies, possible improvements, or lack of artistic quality in the performance called for as they appeared to her. In some instances this resulted in the suggested change being made by the director without argument; in other cases the change was made after some argument between them. In most instances where the director did not make the suggested change it appears that respondent took the question up with the president of the appellant corporation, and in a substantial number of instances he agreed with her and the changes were made. In other instances he did not agree. This presents the question—was respondent compelled by the contract to go through her scenes as a mere puppet responding to the director's pull of the strings, regardless of whether or not he pulled the right or the wrong string, or was she called upon by the language and spirit of the contract to give an artistic interpretation of the scenes, using her intelligence, experience, artistry, and personality to the ultimate end of securing a production of dramatic merit? We believe that the latter is the correct interpretation.

Suggestions and even objections as to the manner of enacting the various scenes, when made in good faith, were in the interest of the employer; in fact, it appears from the testimony that they were welcomed and encouraged in many instances, and, prior to commencing work, the president of appellant informed respondent that he did not want manikins to work for him, that he wanted thinking people, and that, if she would explain to him why she wanted to do a thing in a particular way, he would appreciate it. By the very wording of the contract "it is agreed that the services of the artist herein provided for are of a special, unique, unusual, extraordinary and intellectual character." . . . [T]he trial court was more than justified in finding that it was not true that respondent had refused or failed to perform her part of the contract.

* * *

The declarations of several of the directors as to their dissatisfaction with the work of respondent is rather inconsistent with the testimony elsewhere of one of them that the picture *White Gold*, in which respondent performed under his direction, was "the best picture I ever will make," and the testimony of the director of her last picture, that he considered it one of his best American pictures. When considering the testimony of the directors who expressed dissatisfaction with the performance of her parts by respondent, one may well wonder who was temperamental and out of step when we note in connection therewith that in the picture in which Cecil De Mille directed Miss Goudal there was no trouble whatever. There is, furthermore, a conflict in the evidence as to whether the performance given by respondent was to the best of her ability and or an artistic character. In this conflict the trial court was fully sustained in its findings against appellant.

The remaining ground urged as justifying her discharge is that respondent on certain occasions was late arriving on the sets at the time designated by her employer. The instances cited were explained by the testimony for respondent as being due, not to any neglect or intentional absence, but duties relating to costumes which had been voluntarily assumed by respondent with the approval of appellant, though not required by the contract. . . . There is in the case at bar no willful tardiness nor invalid excuse for absences, the instances of tardiness here being covered by the general description in that those delays were occasioned by the requirements of the scenes to be enacted on those particular days, delays while respondent was actually engaged in performing her employment business.

It may also be noted that the references to alleged breaches of the contract consist largely of incidents prior to May 1927, when appellant, for the second time, had exercised its option to continue and extend the contract for another year, and by which time respondent had completed seven of the eight pictures in which she performed for appellant. It is rather difficult to reconcile as sincere the appellant's criticism and faultfinding as to respondent's services in the pictures made during the two years prior to May 1927, with the fact that that month appellant voluntarily availed itself of its option to secure the talents and services of respondent for another year. Particularly is this significant when we consider that the salary under the latter option would amount to $39,000 more than respondent's salary for the preceding year. This circumstance alone would fully justify the trial court in considering as of little or no weight the testimony as to alleged breaches of contract prior to May 1927.

The exercise of the option not only evinced a desire on the part of appellant to retain respondent's services, but expressed an approval of the manner in which she had performed her services in the past, and was an indication that a continuation of the former services was desired. Having thus placed the stamp of approval upon respondent's conduct and services as rendered prior to May 1927, it is not reasonable that a continuance of such services and conduct was unsatisfactory, and, from appellant's viewpoint, constituted a breach of the contract warranting respondent's discharge. Furthermore, the exercise of the option may be considered as a declaration by act that the past conduct of the artist was not such conduct as was intended by the contracting parties as a justification for the termination of the contractual relations. This would be particularly true where, as here, the duties of the performing party are described in the contract by such general phraseology as that the artist shall render the services "conscientiously" and "artistically."

It might be said that an artist who performed her part as directed without remonstrance or suggestion, in spite of the fact that the action was inartistic, crude, and illogical, would not be rendering services either conscientious or artistic in character, while the artist who made an effort to secure a change in the action to produce an artistic result would be complying with the letter and spirit of the contract. These matters and the intent and good faith of the respondent were matters of fact to be passed upon by the trial court, and, since their decision adversely to appellant is sustained by the evidence, the findings of the trial court are not subject to review here.

To constitute a refusal or failure to perform the conditions of a contract of employment such as we have here, there must be, on the part of the actress, a willful act or willful misconduct . . . a condition which is absent when the actress uses her best efforts to give an artistic performance and to serve the interests of her employer. The trial court was fully warranted by the evidence in finding that respondent neither failed nor refused to perform the services required of her under the contract.

Even in the most menial forms of employment there will exist circumstances justifying the servant in questioning the order of the master. Would the discharge of a ditch digger be justified if, instead of immediately driving his pick into the ground at the point indicated, he in good faith suggested to the employer that the pipes they were to uncover lay on the other side of the highway? And when the employment is of the services of a "special, unique, unusual, extraordinary and intellectual character," . . . to be rendered "conscientiously, artistically and to the utmost of her ability," sincere efforts of the artist to secure an artistic interpretation of play, even though they may involve the suggestion of changes and the presentation of argument in favor of such changes, even though insistently presented, do not amount to willful disobedience or failure to perform services under the contract, but rather a compliance with the contract which basically calls for services in the best interests of the employer.

What may in the case of the extra girl be rank insubordination because of a refusal to do exactly what she is ordered to do by the director may even be praiseworthy co-operation in the interests of the employer when the refusal is that of an artist of the exceptional ability expressly stipulated in the contract here before us.

* * *

[The court rejected the argument that Goudal's recovery should be limited because she failed to mitigate damages by seeking other employment, and instead awarded Goudal damages equal to the contract price.]

Affirmed.

### *QUESTIONS FOR DISCUSSION*

1. The judge in *Goudal* noted that the contract did not require her to be a "puppet," but to lend her own creative interpretation to the film by "using her intelligence, experience, artistry and personality" in the film project. Do you agree with this interpretation, and if so what are its limits? When should the director/producer be entitled to demand certain behavior while remaining true to the language and spirit of the contract?

2. Goudal's appeal was also upheld, in part, because the producer exercised its option to renew her contract *after* the alleged activity occurred, suggesting acceptance of her previous behavior. The court considered the overall course of performance and dealing when making this decision. Is this a reliable source for determining breach? If you were counsel for a movie studio, how would you phrase the contract standard?

3. A more contemporary example involved a dispute between Raquel Welch and Metro-Goldwyn-Mayer. Raquel Welch was selected to co-star with Nick Nolte in a movie, *Cannery Row*, based on a novella by John Steinbeck. In charge of the film project were Michael Phillips (producer) and David Ward (director and screenwriter). While Phillips and Ward had previously collaborated on the movie *The Sting*, Ward had never before been director of a major film. This was also the first product that MGM undertook under its

new president, David Begelman, who had just moved to MGM from a troubled reign at Columbia Pictures.[a]

Unfortunately, the *Cannery Row* project quickly encountered problems: it was over budget, behind schedule, and its daily film cuts were poorly received at the studio. Three weeks into the shooting schedule, Begelman's team decided to replace Welch with Debra Winger. While MGM had the right under its "play or pay" contract clause to terminate Welch for any reason, as long as it paid her $250,000 salary, Begelman chose to fire Welch for allegedly taking three hours every day to be made up at home rather than on location. The resulting publicity was bad for both Welch (who did not get another movie deal for years) and for MGM (whose *Cannery Row* lost over $16 million). The studio's actions also produced a lawsuit by Welch claiming breach of contract, bad faith, and defamation. The court found that the director, Ward, had accepted Welch's makeup routine and that the studio had wrongfully dismissed her from the film. *See Welch v. Metro-Goldwyn-Mayer Film Co.*, 207 Cal.App.3d 164, 254 Cal. Rptr. 645 (1988), *cause transferred*, 264 Cal. Rptr. 353, 782 P.2d 594 (1989); *see also Mason v. Lyl Productions*, 69 Cal.2d 79, 69 Cal. Rptr. 769, 443 P.2d 193 (1968) (another wrongful dismissal claim).

4. Part of having creative control is also having the money to finance the director's vision of the production or film. The recent negotiations between David Lynch and Showtime over the third season of Twin Peaks provides a good example. Twin Peaks, which developed a cult following in its two year run on ABC, ceased production when Lynch quit after two seasons over a dispute with the network concerning the plotline of the show. The executives wanted Lynch's next season to resolve the question in the opening tagline—"Who killed Laura Palmer."

With Showtime, the dispute concerned the amount of money available to pay for the production costs of the show, given Lynch's creative control. In April 2015, Lynch quit the project. One month later, Showtime acceded to his demands and resumed production of the show, which is set to air in 2017.

5. Can an actor sue the film company if the film turns out poorly? Actor Wesley Snipes sued New Line Cinema and director / producer David Goyer after the release of Blade: Trinity, contending that decisions made by the producers resulted in the film bombing at the box office. The lawsuit settled, but what do you think about actors ex post lawsuits challenging creative decisions? With actors increasingly required by contract to promote their movies, what position does that put them in if they think that the movie is terrible?

---

[a] David Begelman was soon to achieve even greater notoriety as one of the main subjects of a best-selling book about his life at Columbia Pictures: David McClintick, *Indecent Exposure: A True Story of Hollywood & Wall Street* (Wm. Morrow 1982).

## 2. MORALS CLAUSES

The next decision was a byproduct of a notorious episode in American movie history, the blacklisting of the "Hollywood Ten."[b] A considerable number of actors and writers had joined the Communist Party or affiliated organizations in the 1930s and 1940s. By 1947, the U.S. House of Representatives' House Un-American Activities Committee (HUAC) was determined to stamp out the threat of Communist influences. One important figure in that real-life drama was a Warner Brothers movie actor and president of the Screen Actors Guild, Ronald Reagan.

A key event was a hearing that the HUAC held in Hollywood. The target was a group of eleven screenwriters—the most prominent being Dalton Trumbo and Ring Lardner Jr.—believed (likely accurately) to be or to have been Communists. The writers agreed amongst themselves not to answer directly the question, "Are you now or have you ever been a member of the Communist party?" After all had testified in that fashion, one (Bertolt Brecht) left to return to East Germany; the others were charged with contempt of Congress.

Before these hearings, the public posture of the studios was that they would not penalize performers for their political beliefs and affiliations as long as this did not affect the content and quality of their film products. Following the heavily-publicized HUAC hearings and under pressure from an American Legion-organized movie boycott, the studios reversed course. Under the auspices of their Association, the studios agreed on the "Waldorf-Astoria" Declaration:

> Members of the Association of Motion Picture Producers deplore the action of the ten Hollywood men who have been cited for contempt by the House of Representatives. We do not desire to prejudge their legal rights, but their actions have been a disservice to their employers and have impaired their usefulness to the industry.
>
> We will forthwith discharge or suspend without compensation those in our employ and we will not re-employ any of the Ten until such time as he is acquitted, or had himself purged of contempt and declares under oath that he is not a Communist.

---

[b] *See* Nancy Lynn Schwartz, *The Hollywood Writers' Wars* (Knopf 1982); Larry Ceplair & Steven Englund, *The Inquisition in Hollywood: Politics in the Film Community*, 1930–1960 (U. Cal. Press 1983); Stephen Vaughn, *Ronald Reagan in Hollywood: Movies & Politics* (Camb. Univ. Press 1994); Larry May, *The Big Tomorrow: Hollywood & the Politics of the American Way* (U. Chicago Press 2000); Harold W. Horowitz, *Legal Aspects of "Political Black Listing" in the Entertainment Industry*, 29 So. Cal. L. Rev. 263 (1956); Martin H. Redish & Christopher R. McFadden, *HUAC, the Hollywood Ten, & the First Amendment Right of Non-Association*, 85 Minn. L. Rev. 1669 (2001).

> On the broader issue of alleged subversive and disloyal elements in Hollywood, our members are likewise prepared to take positive action.
>
> We will not knowingly employ a Communist or a member of any party or group which advocates the overthrow of the government of the United States by force, or by any illegal or unconstitutional method.
>
> * * *
>
> The absence of a national policy, established by Congress, with respect to the employment of Communists in private industry makes our task difficult. Ours is a nation of laws. We request Congress to enact legislation to rid itself of subversive, disloyal elements.

That studio understanding led MGM to tell one of its writers, Lester Cole, that he had to return before the HUAC and testify under oath that he was not now a member of the Communist party. When Cole refused, MGM fired him under the standard "morals clause" in movie personal service contracts, which required the performer

> not to do or commit any act or thing that [would] tend to degrade him in society or bring him into public hatred, contempt, scorn or ridicule, or that [would] tend to shock, insult or offend the community or ridicule the public morals or decency, or prejudice the producer or the motion picture, theatrical or radio industry in general.

Cole filed suit in federal court for wrongful dismissal. The trial court found that Cole had acted within his rights and had not violated the morals clause, and that he had been led by MGM's behavior, both before and immediately after the HUAC hearings, to believe that his job would not be affected by his political associations. MGM appealed the $76,000 damage award in Cole's favor.

## LOEW'S, INC. V. COLE

United States Court of Appeals, Ninth Circuit, 1960.
185 F.2d 641.

POPE, CIRCUIT JUDGE.

* * *

It is argued that what Cole did at the hearing was not a violation of his contract. . . .

There is no room for doubt as to just what Cole did before the Committee. A transcript of his testimony is a part of the pre-trial order.

This discloses that the Committee sought to elicit from him answers to two questions: "Are you a member of the Screen Writers' Guild?", and "Are you now or have you ever been a member of the Communist Party?" All that need be said is that although Cole stated he would be very happy to answer these questions, the Committee did not succeed in getting an answer from him to either one.

* * *

We think that a jury might well find as fact that the natural result of Cole's refusal to say whether he was or had been a member of the Communist party was to give the Committee, and the public generally, the impression that he was a Communist, that his refusal was for the purpose of concealing his actual membership in the party. The event showed that this is exactly the interpretation which the public did place upon the conduct of Cole and of the other witnesses who took a like stand. The fact that his actions were in concert with the others, pursuant to the agreement hereafter mentioned, made this result doubly certain. And because, even in 1947, a large segment of the public did look upon Communism and Communists as things of evil, we think it cannot be said, as a matter of law, that in acting as he did Cole did not breach his agreement.

* * *

[In response, Cole contended that the statements by Loew's officials before and after the HUAC hearing meant that Loew's could not now claim that Cole had breached his contract. The court reviewed the evidence regarding Loew's attitude toward Communism and the investigation in general. Among the significant facts were the following. Loew's refused to agree to a proposition by the president of the Motion Picture Producer's Association that it not employ proven Communists in positions of influence and power. In an interview with Committee members, E. J. Mannix, the General Manager of Loew's, stated that he did not "give a damn whether [Cole and another employee, Dalton Trumbo, were] Communists or not." Louis B. Mayer, the head of the Loew's studio, also wrote in his report on the interview with the Committee members that he was "not going to fire men on the assumption that they are Communists, when they have done nothing Communistic that I can find and no one has proven they are Communists. . . ." Around this time, Loew's offered Cole an extension on his contract that increased his pay and the number of weeks of work guaranteed each year. Cole signed the amended contract with Loew's in September of 1947. Cole, along with other industry employees, published an advertisement in the *Hollywood Reporter* protesting the October 20th hearing, and charging the Committee with trying to control the film industry by intimidating its executive heads. Loew's knew of this article.

Leading figures in the industry were openly critical of the Committee's investigation and condemned it as attempting to control the industry and stop the free flow of creativity and ideas. Loew's never talked with Cole before he testified to determine how he intended to conduct himself and to advise him on the responses he should give to the Committee's inquiries.]

* * *

Upon the basis of the evidence which we have here related, it is argued that the conduct of the employer and its representatives prior to the time when Cole testified, was such as would reasonably cause him to believe that no exception would be taken to such conduct as that which he manifested on the witness stand.

We think that it cannot be said as a matter of law that these facts, uncontroverted as they are, establish either that there was a practical construction of the contract as having the meaning appellee says should be attached to it, or that there had been a waiver of performance in advance. Restatement of the Law of Contracts, § 297.

It is true that Mr. Johnston, Mr. McNutt and Mr. Mannix had all indicated that the employer did not intend to blacklist or discharge Communists. Mr. Johnston explained that he had been convinced of the correctness of this determination for "who was going to prove whether a man was a Communist or not?" While Mannix had said when Cole and Trumbo were mentioned to him with an inquiry as to whether he knew they were Communists: "No, and I don't give a damn whether they are Communists or not," it should be remembered that he made this statement to the investigators toward whose errands generally he was quite hostile. He did not make the statement to Cole, who had assured Mr. Mayer that he was not a Communist.

It also appears that the employers as well as the employees resented and disliked the whole investigation and Loew's indicated no objection to the proposal of Cole's attorneys to move to quash the subpoenas. While there was apparently no effort to advise or warn Cole as to how he should conduct himself, a fact to which the trial court seemed to attach must importance, we think that it cannot be said that the employer owed a duty to instruct Cole, for in the circumstances it might well have subjected itself to criticism by the Committee had it undertaken to do so. Had it been disclosed at the hearing that Cole had received instructions as to how to testify, Loew's might well expect to be charged with an improper effort to exert its power as an employer to induce the witness to slant his testimony.

We think all of this falls short of giving approval to conduct calculated to convict Cole of a contemptuous refusal to answer. Nor does it in our opinion compel the conclusion that the employer gave an advance approval to the conduct on the part of Cole which might generally be construed as a broadcasting of his membership in the Communist party.

The conduct of the employer during this period adds up to an attitude of definite hostility and unfriendliness to the Committee hearings, which the producers apparently feared was headed in the direction of censorship of the screen. Thus Cole may have felt that he was justified in carrying a torch for freedom of speech, and in protesting against the proceedings. But we cannot think that as a matter of law this gave him the implied consent of the employer to go so far as to subject himself to a misdemeanor charge. He was plainly ill advised to go to the extreme which he did. A more reasonable course of conduct would have enabled him to trumpet his protest without danger to himself. Thus Mr. Mayer, in his testimony as to his talk with Cole following the meeting, suggested what was patently the more reasonable alternative for Cole, when he asked him why he did not first protest and then answer.

The testimony of the employer's executives given before Cole testified, should have put him on notice that he was not expected to assume the sacrificial attitude which he took. Cole heard Mr. Johnston testify: "I have never objected to your investigating Hollywood. I told you we welcomed it, and we sincerely do," and say in reply to the statement of a Committee member that it was the job of Congress to be certain that agents of a foreign power are not circulating freely in this country, "I think you are right. We welcome that Mr. Congressman." Cole also heard both Johnston and Mayer testify that they would not employ proven Communists as writers.

Throughout the hearing the industry representatives had been undertaking to demonstrate to the Committee that their product contained no Communist propaganda. In the face of this obvious effort to play down the so-called Communist infiltration, Cole (evidently in concert with others), by his tactics of evasion, reasonably construed to be a refusal to answer, and calculated to carry the sting of contempt even more than a mere "I refuse to answer," chose in effect to broadcast to a listening world that it might place what construction it chose upon his refusal to answer whether he was or had been a Communist party member. We cannot say that as a matter of law such action was sanctioned by the prior conduct of his employer.

[The court then addressed the point that for several weeks after Cole's HUAC testimony, Loew's had "condoned his behavior by allowing him to continue to work on the screenplay *Zapata*, before finally suspending him."]

* * *

The theory upon which Cole's counsel tried this aspect of the case was that until after the Congressional hearing the employer was entirely satisfied if not actually pleased with what Cole had done, that he was put back to work and his services used without any idea of discharging him, and that only after a public uproar arose in consequence of the action of the writers who testified did the executives of the industry, in their surprise and chagrin, determine to try to save themselves by throwing these "unfriendly" witnesses to the wolves.

The verdict of the jury indicates that it may have adopted this view. Plainly this theory made much progress with the court, for a considerable portion of the court's opinion is devoted to an exposition of Cole's claim that Loew's agreed to a policy which involved suspending Cole, only after being persuaded, against its initial desires, to take such action in concert with similar action by other producers. We think that the manner in which appellant came to be persuaded to take the action which it obviously did is wholly without bearing on the case . . .

[The Court then turned to Cole's argument that it was impossible for him to comply with the conditions set by Loew's for his return to work]; that he had no control over procuring an acquittal and there were no means by which he could be purged of contempt. As for the required non-Communist oath, it is said that the employer was without power to demand it.

While the securing of an acquittal was, of course, not a matter within Cole's control, we think that Cole is in no position to assert that he was without power to purge himself of contempt. Had he sought from the Committee an opportunity to reappear before them with notification of his desire to purge himself of contempt, and had he them been refused that privilege, his argument of impossibility would have weight. It does not lie in his mouth to say that he could not have purged himself of contempt for he made no effort to do so.

We think that at the time notice of suspension was given him, the demand that he purge himself of contempt was not an unreasonable one. By that time the widespread and adverse reaction in the press and other organs of public opinion had become so violent that the executives of the industry had reason for genuine concern lest drastic action in the form of legislation or boycott might be taken. This had come about mainly because of the attitude of Cole and the other "unfriendly" witnesses at the hearing. We think it not unreasonable that the employer should attach the condition that Cole, to the extent possible, undo the harm he had succeeded in accomplishing. As for the non-Communist oath, if the employer was justified in believing Cole's own statement that he was not a Communist, the taking of the oath was likewise within Cole's power. . . .

It is our view that at the time the notice was given the employer would be fully within its rights in giving Cole just such a notice—that if he was a Communist his services were ended. For the situation had changed entirely from the time when Mannix, the manager, had said he did not care whether Cole was a Communist or not so long as he did good work. When Mannix made that statement there was no occasion to suspect that the public generally had reason to suppose that Cole was a Communist or that the industry was generally employing writers who were Communists. The conduct of Cole and the other witnesses completely changed the situation. A film company might well continue indefinitely the employment of an actor whose private personal immorality is known to his employer, and yet be fully justified in discharging him when he so conducts himself as to make the same misconduct notorious.

The net effect of the hearing was to make Cole a distinct liability to his employer. We think that the insertion of these conditions, which were calculated to furnish Cole with an opportunity to undo a portion of what he had succeeded in accomplishing, was not beyond the power of the employer.

* * *

.... We think these errors require us to reverse the judgment and to remand the cause for a new trial.

Reversed and remanded.

---

During the next two decades the Hollywood Ten wrote under pseudonyms, while in jail or exile (and at drastically reduced rates), the scripts for such Academy Award classics as *The Brave One*, *The Caine Mutiny*, *The Bridge Over the River Kwai*, and *Lawrence of Arabia*. Of course, working under a pseudonym, such as Trumbo's "Richie Rich" for *The Brave One*, was not a viable career option for *actors* on the blacklist. The studio boycott was lifted in 1960, when Otto Preminger hired Trumbo to write *Exodus* under his own name.

## *QUESTIONS FOR DISCUSSION*

1. Do you believe Cole violated the morals clause in his contract? Taking more contemporary examples, suppose he had been found guilty of possession of an illegal drug (like Robert Downey, Jr. from *Ally McBeal*)? Of driving while impaired? Of income tax evasion? Of spousal abuse? Of contributing to and speaking out on behalf of a radical left- or right-wing group? Does a studio, network, or record label have a valid claim that it is harmed by negative publicity associated with any such actions?

This question was anything but academic in 1995, when Walt Disney Studios released its new movie *Powder,* about an albino boy with telekinetic powers and the boy's relations with his teachers, played by Mary Steenburgen and Jeff Goldblum. Marring the movie's opening was the revelation that *Powder*'s writer-director, Victor Salva, had been convicted and jailed in 1987 for videotaping himself having oral sex with a 12-year-old boy who was in a movie that Salva was then directing. As it turned out, Disney had not known about the conviction until the now 20-year-old victim passed out leaflets condemning Salva at the Hollywood executives' previewing of *Powder*. The film's producer, Roger Birnbaum, who had learned of Salva's offense midway through the filming, said that his director had "paid for his crime, he paid his debt to society . . . what happened eight years ago has nothing to do with this movie." Disney's executives echoed that view. Suppose, though, that Disney had learned of Salva's past just before filming began, and thought the safest course was to substitute another director. Should the morals clause permit such dismissal? Does off-the-set behavior by directors or actors pose a threat to their movie's performance at the box office? Recall that audiences did not seem to react negatively to the arrest of Hugh Grant for engaging in paid sex with a prostitute, Divine Brown, in a car on Sunset Boulevard, just before the opening of Grant's new movie *Nine Months* in 1995.

2. A later example of political tensions in the entertainment world involved Vanessa Redgrave and the Boston Symphony Orchestra (BSO). For its 100th anniversary in 1982, the BSO planned a performance at Boston's Symphony Hall and New York's Carnegie Hall that would focus on the works of Igor Stravinsky, who had had a close relationship with the BSO. The centerpiece was to be Stravinsky's opera-oratorio *Oedipus Rex*, with music arranged by conductor Seiji Ozawa and theatrical features by director Peter Sellars. A significant rolc in the opera was that of the narrator, and the BSO felt that it had scored a real coup when it announced that actress Vanessa Redgrave had agreed to fill that role.

Shortly afterwards, though, the BSO began to hear rumblings of discontent from the Boston Jewish community, some of whom were important supporters of the Orchestra. The reason for their objection was Redgrave's public commitment to the Palestine Liberation Organization (PLO) in its long-time violent struggle against the state of Israel. When Redgrave won the 1978 Academy Award for her role in the movie *Julia* (in which she played a socialist member of the underground resistance to the Nazis), Redgrave was burned in effigy by the Jewish Defense League (JDL) outside the auditorium in Los Angeles. Faced with threats of similar demonstrations at *Oedipus Rex* (perhaps even inside Boston's Symphony Hall), as well as a vote of censure by the Anti-Defamation League, Ozawa and BSO General Manager (Thomas Moore) overrode Sellars' objections and cancelled *Oedipus Rex* "because of circumstances beyond the [Orchestra's] reasonable control" (the relevant contract language). Berlioz' *Requiem* was played in its place.

Although the BSO was prepared to pay her contract fee (about $30,000), Redgrave filed suit for breach of contract, seeking much larger consequential damages for damage to her reputation and career prospects. That issue will be addressed in the next chapter, ***Contract Damages***. Redgrave also filed a claim under the Massachusetts Civil Rights Act (MCRA), a state law that goes beyond the standard anti-discrimination legislation to ban interference with constitutional rights (including free speech) by private and public actors.

The following are among the legal policy issues posed by *Redgrave*. Should an orchestra (or studio or network) be permitted to terminate a performer's contract because of the latter's political views and affiliations (such as with the PLO or the Ku Klux Klan)? Should it matter that the reason for termination is not the producer's personal feelings on these issues, but its concerns about the reactions of subscribers, contributors, or protesters? Would a legal requirement that the BSO and Ozawa continue to use Redgrave in *Oedipus Rex* infringe on *their* freedom of speech under the Constitution? *See Redgrave v. Boston Symphony Orchestra*, 855 F.2d 888 (1st Cir. 1988) (en banc).

3. Even where an actor does not have a morals clause in his contract, immoral behavior can become a catalyst for termination. After allegedly showing up to work under the influence of drugs and alcohol, Charlie Sheen was fired from the popular television show "Two and a Half Men" by Warner Brothers and CBS. Sheen's struggles with substance abuse have been well-documented. Described by the *New York Times* as the "crack-smoking, prostitute-frequenting Mr Sheen," the actor apparently went on one too many binges for Warner Brothers and CBS, who replaced Sheen with Ashton Kutcher. Sheen subsequently sued Warner Brothers and CBS, and although terms were not disclosed, received a handsome settlement. According to multiple news reports, Sheen did not have a morals clause in his contract.

## 3. CIVIL RIGHTS IN ENTERTAINING ROLES

The ink was barely dry on the *Redgrave* decision when another controversy arose in the Broadway theater industry.[c] *Miss Saigon* had been a major theatrical hit in London in the late 1980s. In 1990, the producer, Cameron Mackintosh, announced that he would be bringing *Miss Saigon* to Broadway. By mid-summer, advance ticket sales (at a then-record price of $100) had reached $25 million. Suddenly, a debate over a key cast member endangered *Miss Saigon's* prospects. Mackintosh said that Jonathan Pryce would be brought to the United States to reprise his London role as the half Vietnamese-half French "Engineer," the owner of a Saigon bar and brothel who had reunited an American soldier with his Vietnamese girlfriend in Saigon during the last days of

[c] *See* Jennifer L. Sheppard, *Theatrical Casting: Discrimination or Artistic Freedom?*, 15 Colum.-VLA J. Law & Arts 267 (1991); Mabel Ng, *Miss Saigon: Casting for Equality on an Unequal Stage*, 14 Hast. Comm/Ent L.J. 451 (1992).

the Vietnam War. While Pryce had won the Olivier Award for his London performance, he was Welsh and Caucasian.

Responding to concerns expressed by author David Henry Hwong and actor B.D. Wong, who had won the Pulitzer Prize and Tony Award respectively for *M. Butterfly*, the Broadway performers' union Actors Equity said that it would not consent to certifying Pryce as a "star" for purposes of getting him an H–1 Visa from the Immigration and Naturalization Service (INS) to work as a nonresident alien. Actors Equity said that Mackintosh's refusal to consider any Asians for this part was "an affront to the Asian community" and violated principles of non-discrimination and multi-racial employment opportunities articulated in the collective agreement with the League of American Theaters and Producers (LATP). Mackintosh could have taken this decision to arbitration, where almost certainly he would have won because the union had already designated Pryce a star for another Broadway show a few years earlier. Instead, Mackintosh announced that he was going to cancel *Miss Saigon's* appearance on Broadway because the true issue here was "the artistic integrity of the authors and the creative team" and the undermining of "our right to cast whomever we consider to be the most suitable talent in any role, regardless of race or ethnic background."

Faced with loss of a major show, with its significant work opportunities for the union's members, and prodded by Mayor David Dinkins, Actors Equity relented and gave Pryce its star certificate. Mackintosh in turn agreed to seek Asian actors to serve as understudies for Pryce and to fill the role in future tours of *Miss Saigon*. The show opened on Broadway 1991 and became a major hit.

This dispute raised fundamental questions about the interplay of artistic freedom and equal opportunity. The practice of casting Caucasians as ethnic minorities was not new with Pryce in *Miss Saigon*. For example, Yul Brynner and Marlon Brando had played Asians in *The King and I* and *The Teahouse of the August Moon*, respectively. Since then, minority stars have performed in what traditionally were considered parts for white actors (e.g., Denzel Washington in *Richard III*, Morgan Freeman in *The Taming of the Shrew*, and Robert Guillaume in *Phantom of the Opera*).

The entertainment industry has also now produced civil rights lawsuits. One suit was brought by Hunter Tylo, an actress in her mid-30s who had appeared on CBS' *The Bold and the Beautiful*. In 1996, Tylo announced that she was leaving *Bold* to perform as a new character on Fox's prime time hit, *Melrose Place*. Spelling Entertainment, the producer of *Melrose*, had agreed to pay Tylo $13,500 for each of eight episodes during the 1996–97 season. Three weeks later, Tylo, who already had two young children, learned that she was pregnant again. When she told

Spelling, the producer dismissed Tylo on the grounds that her "material change in appearance" violated the terms of her performance contract; the *Melrose* character they had envisioned her playing is for "dramatic believability . . . by necessity not pregnant."

Spelling did offer Tylo a role for the next season, following the birth of her child. Tylo, however, filed a lawsuit, claiming a violation of the 1978 *Pregnancy Discrimination Act*'s expansion of Title VII of the *Civil Rights Act* (together with the equivalent California legislation).[d] While these statutes make discrimination on account of pregnancy the equivalent of discrimination on account of sex, the law also allows sex to be a "bona fide occupational qualification" where objectively necessary.

By 1998, Tylo had returned to *The Bold and the Beautiful*, and that November her daughter Izabella was born. Tylo's lawsuit went to trial a year later. The Spelling people testified that Tylo had been hired for her unique appearance as a "vamp and a vixen" who would be seducing the husband of *Melrose* star Heather Locklear; her pregnancy, however, had increased Tylo's weight by 46 pounds. Tylo said that this was yet another example of Hollywood treating actresses as "pieces of meat." Both sides pointed out that Locklear herself had continued to appear on the screen while pregnant and giving birth to her child a month before Tylo's. In addition, Tylo's replacement on *Melrose Place*, Lisa Rinna, had also become pregnant, giving birth to her child in 1999. The jury found in Tylo's favor, awarding $864,000 in economic damages and $4 million for emotional distress.

Spelling Entertainment appealed the liability and damages findings. With respect to liability, the question is whether an actress becoming pregnant violates her contract commitment, or instead, whether Spelling was guilty of discrimination against her on account of pregnancy? Can acting positions be judged "appearance-oriented," such that not being pregnant is a "bona fide occupational qualification" under the *Civil Rights Act*? Suppose Tylo had signed a contract that gave the studio the right to terminate the deal if her weight rose more than ten pounds: is it a violation of either "disparate treatment" or "disparate impact" civil rights doctrine to exercise that option when the weight gain is due to pregnancy? Were there production resources (whether filming strategy or technology) available to make a "reasonable accommodation" for Tylo's appearance during the time she was visibly pregnant? Assuming there is a basis for liability in the Tylo case, was the jury verdict an appropriate assessment of the level of damages inflicted on Tylo?

In 1994, Janet Peckinpaugh was a popular news anchor for a Hartford television station owned by Washington Post-Newsweek and

---

[d] *See* Diane Klein, *Pregnancy Discrimination in Show Business*, 4 UCLA Ent. L. Rev. 210 (1997).

affiliated with CBS. In her mid-40s, Peckinpaugh was the oldest of three anchorwomen when station executives decided to reduce the number of anchors. After appraising the relative performance of the three anchorwomen (but not the two males), the station terminated Peckinpaugh's contract; she thus lost her $250,000 annual salary, taking a $45,000-position at another Hartford station.

Peckinpaugh filed suit, claiming discrimination on account of both sex and age. The jury found in her favor on the former score. The jury awarded Peckinpaugh $4.3 million in compensatory damages and $4 million in punitives. While the trial judge reduced the total damages to $3.79 million, Post-Newsweek appealed, asserting that male-female anchor pairings are precisely what American viewers want. In 1999, the parties settled the case for an undisclosed amount that "thrilled" her, especially since she by then had an anchor job at another Hartford station, as well as a cameo role in a forthcoming movie.

The *Peckinpaugh* case poses some intriguing questions about the nature of television roles and the application of civil rights standards to them. For example, are female anchors, in contrast to their male counterparts, typically hired when they are young and attractive and then moved off the screen when they grow older? Is the news anchor role one of investigative journalism or entertaining performance, and what difference should that make?

Soon after the new millennium, Hollywood faced civil rights litigation alleging age discrimination against both men and women. The Writers Guild of America (WGA), the union that represents screenwriters, sought $200 million in damages for WGA members who found their incomes declining when they reached 40 or 50 years of age. This class action suit alleged that disparate access to script-writing assignments meant that WGA members in their thirties made three times as much as those in their fifties. While the median earnings of writers in their thirties rose by more than 200 percent in the 1980s and 1990s, the earnings of those in their fifties declined by 4 percent in the same period. Assuming that these allegations were true, one key issue is whether such a disparity in opportunities can be justified by "audience age demographics," the assumption that younger writers are more likely to have the same perspectives as the young audiences who are the main audience for films and television programs.

Ironically, not long after this class action suit was filed against the studios and networks, one major network was facing an apparently contrary suit. A claim was filed against CBS and its Survivors Entertainment Group (SEG), by a young woman, Stacey Stillman, who believed that the reason she lost the vote by her "tribe" colleagues in a *Survivor* episode was that the producers had sought to retain an elderly contestant, Rudy Boesch. This was allegedly done to attract older fans to see who was going to win the million-dollar prize. Stillman, who is also a lawyer, asserted that this preference for an "old-timer" violated her contract rights to a competitive rather than a rigged outcome (and that it violated Section 509 of the Federal Communications Act, which prohibits "any artifice or scheme for the purpose of predetermining . . . the outcome of a purportedly-*bona fide* contest"). When CBS was served with this suit for $75,000, they counterclaimed for $5 million in damages for what they alleged to be defamatory "extortion," and for breach of a contract term that required competitors to say nothing about the contest without the producer's consent. With respect to the FCC rule enacted in 1960 to deal with the "game-show rigging" scandal of the late 1950s, CBS' defense was that *Survivor* is actually a reality drama, not a "contest of intellectual skill."

Having read about these civil rights suits, should freedom of artistic expression preclude any scrutiny by government agencies of casting decisions? How would you compare the First Amendment concerns here with the academic freedom issues posed by university tenure decisions?

## 4. NON-COMPETITION CLAUSES

Another way that producers regulate performer conduct is through the use of non-competition clauses. Non-competition clauses are regularly found in contracts for employment in financial or product development positions in which the employer wants to protect its interests by preventing a former employee from luring away former customers, exposing trade secrets, or similar harmful conduct. Non-competition clauses in performer/writer contracts restrict their ability to produce similar types of works for a fixed time after termination of the contract.

These kinds of clauses are valid only if they are *ancillary* to an independent agreement (e.g., the sale of a business or employment in a position). Even then, the clause must be related to legitimate interests of the parties, and must not impose unduly broad and long restrictions on the party bound by the commitment. A judge determining whether to enforce a non-competition clause, and a performer who is deciding whether to take on a new project, must determine two things: 1) whether the new and old projects are too much alike, and 2) whether the projects would compete with each other for profits.

The court in *Harlequin Enterprises v. Warner Books*, 639 F. Supp. 1081 (S.D.N.Y. 1986), dealt with the alleged breach by an action-adventure book author of a non-competition clause in his contract with his former publisher. Don Pendleton had written a series of action stories called *The Executioner,* which depicted the elimination of the Mafia, and involved a main character named Mack Bolan. Pendleton signed a contract with Harlequin that gave the publisher the right to use Mack Bolan and Pendleton's other characters in a continuation of *The Executioner* series. Under the terms of the contract, Pendleton would submit story ideas and Harlequin would find the writers. Pendleton's contract also contained a clause precluding his creation of a series that would compete with *The Executioner*, though he was allowed to write non-competing works. Over time Harlequin decided to shift away from a Mafia vigilante theme to one dealing with terrorists. Harlequin's new *Gold Eagle* series still contained the Bolan character, but Pendleton's input significantly decreased. Pendleton became dissatisfied with this series and asked Harlequin not to use his name on the book cover, because it suggested that he wrote the books when he had not.

Several years later, Pendleton started writing for Warner Books. The new books involved a character named Ashton Ford, who was a detective with mystic powers. Warner was not told about the non-competition clause in Pendleton's Harlequin contract before it signed the contract with Pendleton. Pendleton's agent felt that the Ford character was so different from the Bolan character that Harlequin would not challenge the new series. Warner then began a publicity campaign to promote the new series and released materials proclaiming "Don Pendleton's Back—The Creator of *The Executioner*." The book covers for the new series created images and used language suggesting that Ford was an action/adventure character.

Harlequin notified Warner that it believed that the new Ford series conflicted with the Bolan series. Harlequin then sued Pendleton, charging violation of the non-competition clause. The court found for Pendleton and dismissed Harlequin's claim, conducting a two-part analysis under which it "examined whether the contents of the book appeal to similar readerships and whether the manner in which they are being promoted or marketed caused them to compete." The court relied on the testimony of publishing experts (editors, writers, professors, and publishers) to determine that the two series would not appeal to similar readerships. As to promotional efforts, the court concluded that the two series would not compete because the Ford series would appeal to supernatural, rather than to action/adventure, fans. The court deliberately adopted a narrow interpretation of competing works, because "prevent[ing] Pendleton from writing any new fiction, even of a different sort, simply because it could conceivably indirectly effect sales of 'The Executioner' series, is to carry the restrictions of the contract to excess."

Do non-competition clauses impose unreasonable restrictions on a performer's freedom to create? What advice would you give performers concerning non-competition clauses?

Interestingly, the Wall Street Journal reported in 2013 that the number of non-competition lawsuits had increased dramatically over the past decade. Increasingly, employees are reluctant to leave their positions in businesses with stringent non-compete agreements, even where such provisions might be unenforceable.

## B. STUDIO-PUBLISHER OBLIGATIONS

A year before the tragic 1994 suicide of Nirvana frontman Kurt Cobain, this top-selling group found itself in a conflict with its record label, David Geffen Company (DGC), about whether the latter had to accept as "satisfactory product" a new Nirvana album that was viewed by the company as "actively and stridently anticommercial." Much the same kind of conflict five years earlier between Geffen and veteran rocker Neil Young also produced a lawsuit alleging that Young was making "unrepresentative" and noncommercial albums that were generating lackluster sales. Both disputes were eventually settled, but the fundamental legal questions remain. Assuming that the master tapes submitted by musicians are satisfactory from a technical standpoint, can the label reject them if it feels they are not marketable to consumers? Does the artist's commitment to create representative works mean that George Michael or Michelle Shocked cannot change their artistic style without violating their record contracts? What is the appropriate role of the law in addressing these tensions between artistic creativity and commercial viability?

Satisfactory product concerns are not unique to music among the entertainment industries. Whether the product is satisfactory does tend to be a greater source of conflict in literary publishing and sound recording than in the film industry. One reason is that the book and music settings involve bilateral transactions with clearly definable entities on each side. In music, the artist has to answer to the label; in books, the author answers to the publishing house. In movies, however, while one side of the transaction has a clearly delineated entity (the studio), the other side includes a host of people working toward completing the movie. Should the studio hold the producer accountable for an unsatisfactory product? The director? The screenwriter? The actor? The gaffer? The legal and practical problems in singling out any one party as contractually responsible for a bad movie result are daunting and ultimately prohibitive.

Secondly, the dynamic among the players of the movie industry is quite different from that of books and music. Typically, there is a regular flow of dialogue between the studio and the producers and filmmakers to whom they are giving money. A studio will scrutinize and approve ("greenlight") a project's many steps to try to assure itself of the quality, or at least the commercial viability, of the product. By the end of the project, a studio may have only itself to blame for an expensive failure.[d] Music and books generally have no such system to aid in filtering out unsatisfactory works before they are submitted. Thirdly, even if a bona fide movie bomb works itself through the greenlighting process, the large sums that the studio invested to that point warrant a policy of never rejecting a film outright, but rather working with the filmmaking team to produce something releasable. Finally, while in books and music the return of advances may ride on whether the product is declared satisfactory, most of the major players in a movie are compensated by a flat fee and/or a percentage of either gross revenue or net profit.

---

The bulk of the judicial decisions in this area, including those reproduced here, come from the book publishing field. As a prelude, it is useful to describe the key elements of an author-publisher contract and the analytical issues posed by that framework. There is no better example than the lucrative book contract signed in 1995 by Speaker of the House, Newt Gingrich, with Harper Collins, a subsidiary of Rupert Murdoch's Fox. The original contract would have provided Gingrich with a $4.5 million payment for his book. That money would likely have been paid in three stages: one-third ($1.5 million) at signing, another third upon submission of a satisfactory manuscript (usually a year or so later), and a final third upon publication (probably six months after submission). Some book contracts break the payments down into four stages, with the last quarter paid after publication of the paperback edition.

These advance payments reflect the parties' estimate of the bulk of the royalties that the author can expect from sales on the book. The standard contract pays 10% of the retail sales price for the first 5,000 copies sold, 12.5% on the next 5,000, and 15% thereafter. Royalties on paperbacks run from 7.5% to 10% of the sales price. Assuming Gingrich would have received 15% of a $30 hardcover price and 10% of a $10 paperback price, his book would have had to be a huge best-seller for the publisher just to recoup the royalties: perhaps a half million in hardcover sales and two million in paperback.

Criticism of the Gingrich contract focused on a perceived conflict of interest from the Speaker dealing with Murdoch, whose company's purchase of television stations was then being contested by NBC before

[d] Two book-length treatments of such movie "bombs" offer revealing pictures of the way films get made. *See* Steven Bach, *Final Cut: Dreams & Disaster in the Making of "Heaven's Gate"* (William Morrow 1985); Julie Salamon, *The Devil's Candy: The "Bonfire of the Vanities" Goes to Hollywood* (Houghton Mifflin 1991). *See generally* Mark Litwak, *Reel Power: The Struggle for Influence & Success in the New Hollywood* (Silman-James Press 1986); Jason E. Squire, ed., *The Movie Business Book* (Simon & Schuster, 2d ed. 1992); John W. Cones, *The Feature Film Distribution Deal: A Critical Analysis of the Single Most Important Film Industry Agreement* (So. Ill. U. Press 1997).

the Federal Communications Commission (FCC) as a violation of the Communication Act's ban on foreign broadcast ownership (a rule addressed in Chapter 13). In response, the Gingrich contract was revised to eliminate any advance payment, perhaps in return for higher royalty percentages.

The broader issue is why there are such advance payments in the usual book (or music recording) contract. Why do the parties seek to agree on an estimate of the author's royalties before the manuscript has been completed and long before the book actually appears? Why are publishers prepared to commit themselves to what often are huge payments long before they know how the manuscript will read or what the market for it will be like?

One possible explanation is that the author needs the money to live on and to produce the work. In the music industry, for example, much of the advance goes to pay for recording costs. The reality, though, is that the lion's share of those payments go to the biggest names, to the Whitney Houstons or Stephen Kings who have the least need for such advances. Stephen King, for example, secured a $40 million contract commitment for four books about which the publisher knew nothing when it signed the deal (and in 2001 the Clinton family, just after leaving the White House, secured a total of $22 million in advances for Bill and Hilary's autobiographies). Are these huge advances a good business decision for publishers?

The explanation offered by Professors Hansmann and Kraakman[e] is that these contracts are designed to address a fundamental economic problem in publishing or recording contracts. At the outset, both sides agree that the project is worthwhile because the expected gains to be shared between them exceed their expected costs. Yet that the bulk of the costs expended by the author (or band) are incurred at the first stage, in authoring the manuscript (or record). The costs incurred by the publisher or record company come at the next stage, in producing and promoting the product. At that stage, if circumstances have changed (whether in the perceived quality of the work or the state of the market), the publisher knows it still has to make all of its investment but will recoup only a share of the (declining) proceeds. Absent an enforceable commitment, the publisher is naturally tempted to reduce its investment in the project accordingly. Appreciating that possibility, authors (and bands) will be disinclined to sink time and effort into their work. The solution to that entertainment industry version of the Prisoner's Dilemma, according to Hansmann-Kraakman, is for the parties to "tie the hands" of the publisher by making it commit in advance to pay the bulk of the royalties expected to be earned by the author.

[e] *See* Henry Hansmann & Reinier Kraakman, *Hands-Tying Contracts: Book Publishing, Venture Capital Financing, & Secured Debt*, 8 J. Law, Econ. & Org. 628 (1992).

Keep this economic theory in mind as you read the cases in the next two sections and assess the treatment of the key terms in publishing contracts: the author agreeing to create a "satisfactory product" in return for advances and royalties, and the publisher agreeing to furnish its "best efforts" in distributing and promoting the book.

## 1. SATISFACTORY PRODUCT[g]

### HARCOURT BRACE JOVANOVICH, INC. V. BARRY GOLDWATER

United States District Court, Southern District of New York, 1982.
532 F. Supp. 619.

GRIESA, DISTRICT JUDGE.

[This case involved a suit by the publisher, Harcourt Brace Jovanovich (HBJ), for return of an advance paid to the authors of a book whose manuscript HBJ had rejected as "unsatisfactory." In 1977, HBJ and the writing team of Barry Goldwater and Stephen Shadegg signed a contract, under which Shadegg was to be the writer and Goldwater was to supply information and commentary for the publication of Senator Goldwater's memoirs. The initial proposal for the book, submitted through literary agents Oscar and Lisa Collier, apparently had been greeted by HBJ with great enthusiasm for the subject, but with some reservation about Shadegg as the writer. However, the Colliers furnished HBJ editor Carol Hill and her editor-in-chief Daniel Okrent with four books previously written by Shadegg, and HBJ entered into the contract.

The pivotal contract clause in this dispute was found in paragraph two of the agreement, which stated:

> "The author will deliver to the publisher, on or before October 1, 1978, one copy of the manuscript of the work as finally revised by the author and satisfactory to the publisher in form and content."

The agreement provided for an advance of $200,000, a high amount for the time, broken down into $65,000 upon signing, $75,000 upon delivery of the manuscript, and $60,000 upon publication.

Hill and Goldwater exchanged letters, the former in effect offering to do a vigorous job of editing, and the latter emphasizing that while he might be a bit "bullheaded," he welcomed such assistance. Shadegg and Goldwater then set to work, using as the raw materials for the book a

[g] *See* Calvin R. House, *Good Faith Rejection & Specific Performance in Publishing Contracts: Safeguarding the Author's Reasonable Expectations*, 51 Brook. L. Rev. 95 (1984); Mark Fowler, *The "Satisfactory Manuscript" Clause in Book Publishing Contracts*, 10 Colum.-VLA J. Law & Arts 119 (1985); Melvin Simensky, *Redefining the Rights & Obligations of Publishers & Authors*, 5 Loy. Ent. L. J. 111 (1985).

collection of notes and memos Goldwater referred to as the Alpha File, which reflected many of his exchanges over the years with other political figures. Shadegg would write from these materials and from Goldwater's reminiscences, and then submit to Goldwater a rough draft for comments. In this fashion the duo completed a rough draft of seven chapters, approximately 30,000 words, and submitted it to Hill in 1977, with a letter that concluded as follows:

> "We would be most interested in having your comments and your suggestions. One of the problems we face now is how much to put in and how much to leave out. The available material is almost overwhelming. Your objective viewpoint will be extremely helpful."

Hill did not communicate with the authors regarding their submission and did not return Shadegg's phone call, instead conveying to Oscar Collier her unfavorable impression of the manuscript—criticizing the tone, the lack of drama, and "flat writing." She did not make specific comments as to what should be cut or added or as to which parts were unclear and in need of revision. Her only contact with the authors came in response their queries regarding an ad in the *Washington Post* which stated that Goldwater was looking for a ghost writer; she claimed that there was nothing to it, that she was enthusiastic about the book, and that she was confident it would be an important work.

Shadegg and Goldwater, with an October 1978 deadline, continued working on the manuscript, and in July 1978 submitted 24 chapters to Hill. Goldwater himself submitted the materials, along with a letter which read in part:

> "If you have any suggestions . . . we could arrange to meet in Arizona at your convenience, in Washington or even New York. Let me know your honest opinion of what has been done so far and let me have any suggestions as soon as possible that might be incorporated in further writing."

Hill did not respond to Goldwater's letter, but privately held strong misgivings about the work; she submitted it to two other editors at HBJ, who apparently also gave negative reviews. In her communication with agent Oscar Collier, she again conveyed her negative impression and explicitly suggested that another writer be brought in to take over the project. When Collier rejected this suggestion, Hill indicated that HBJ probably would reject the book as unsatisfactory, and that he should feel free to commence inquiries with other publishers. Meanwhile, Hill sent an in-house memo to the head of the firm, Mr. Jovanovich, explaining what had transpired and stating, in effect, that the publisher's original plan had been to have another author rewrite the manuscript upon submission, in lieu of substantial editorial work.

Shadegg and Goldwater, however, continued work on the manuscript pursuant to the existing contract and on September 29, 1978, submitted to HBJ their full manuscript, which contained revisions of materials previously submitted and some additional chapters. After further negative reviews from her HBJ colleagues, as well as from a free-lance manuscript reader, Hill sent the manuscript back to Oscar Collier, stating that it was unacceptable and demanding the return of the $65,000 advance.

Following HBJ's rejection, Collier shopped the work to several other publishers, eventually selling the book rights to William Morrow & Company (Morrow) for an advance of $80,000. Howard Cady, an experienced editor at Morrow, saw problems with the manuscript but found it generally fascinating. Cady and Shadegg exchanged correspondence in which the former made detailed comments, and the latter revised materials according to these editorial suggestions. Following a conference in Arizona, the final work was completed and ready for galley proofs in a relatively short time. Morrow published it in 1979, under the title *With No Apologies,* and it became a best-seller. Meanwhile, HBJ pursued a contract suit for return of the $65,000 advance.]

* * *

We come to the conclusions of law to be drawn. It is true that under the contract which was in force here between HBJ and the authors, the publisher has a very considerable discretion as to whether to refuse a manuscript on the ground that it is unsatisfactory to the publisher in form and content.

It cannot be, however, that the publisher has absolutely unfettered license to act or not to act in any way it wishes and to accept or reject a book for any reason whatever. If this were the case, the publisher could simply make a contract and arbitrarily change its mind and that would be an illusory contract. It is no small thing for an author to enter into a contract with a publisher and be locked in with that publisher and prevented from marketing the book elsewhere.

It is clear, both as a matter of law and from the testimony in this case, that there is an implied obligation in a contract of this kind for the publisher to engage in appropriate editorial work with the author of a book. Both plaintiff's and defendants' witnesses testified to this effect, based on the custom of the trade.

It is clear that an author who is commissioned to do a work under a contract such as this generally needs editing to produce a successful book. There has been testimony by Goldwater, as I have mentioned, to the effect that he feels the need of editing work and expected it here. The letters from both Shadegg and Goldwater to the publisher indicated their desire for editorial work on the part of the publisher.

In a general way, it is clear that the editorial work which is required must consist of some reasonable degree of communication with the authors, an interchange with the authors about the specifics of what the publisher desires; about what specific faults are found; what items should be omitted or eliminated; what items should be added; what organizational defects exist, and so forth. If faults are found in the writing style, it seems elementary that there should be discussion and illustrations of what those defects of style are. All of this is necessary in order to allow the author the reasonable opportunity to perform to the satisfaction of the publisher.

If this editorial work is not done by the publisher, the result is that the author is misled and, in fact, is virtually prevented from performing under the contract.

There is no occasion in this decision to determine the full extent or the full definition of the editorial work which is required of a publisher under the contract. Here there was no editorial work. I emphasize, no editorial work. There was nothing approaching any sensible editorial activity on the part of the publisher. There were no comments of a detailed nature designed to give the authors an opportunity to remedy defects, even though such comments were specifically invited and requested.

. . . As far as any qualms about having Shadegg as writer, it should be emphasized that the contract was with Shadegg as well as with Goldwater. The contract was not with Goldwater alone. And . . . the publisher entered into this contract with a full opportunity to determine the exact abilities and talents of Shadegg.

In a given situation it could be that after a contract is entered into of the kind we have here, and after draft material is submitted, the material is so hopeless that editorial work might be fruitless. It is difficult to imagine such a situation occurring but I suppose it is conceivable. But this was far from the case here.

. . . It is quite clear that the bulk of the manuscript which was submitted to HBJ must have contained valuable and interesting factual material. This is not the case of a manuscript of no merit which ended up unpublished or was published in a book of clearly low-grade quality.

A distinguished editor, Howard Cady, found the manuscript fascinating. He edited the manuscript in the normal way and produced a successful book.

Consequently, I conclude that HBJ breached its contract with Shadegg and Goldwater by wilfully failing to engage in any rudimentary editorial work or effort. Consequently, HBJ cannot rely on the concept that the manuscript was unsatisfactory in form and content and can be rejected. HBJ had no right under its contract to reject that manuscript.

I have examined the legal authorities cited by the parties. No case directly in point has been referred to. I would note particularly that the case most heavily relied upon by HBJ, *Random House, Inc. v. Gold*, 464 F. Supp. 1306 (S.D.N.Y.), aff'd mem., 607 F.2d 998 (2d Cir. 1979), holds that the type of contract involved in the present case requires the publisher to act in good faith, and notes the obvious point that, allowing unfettered license to publishers to reject a manuscript submitted under contract would permit "overreaching by publishers attempting to extricate themselves from bad deals." 464 F. Supp. at 1308 n.1. In the present case, for the reasons already stated, it must be concluded that HBJ did not act in good faith. . . .

Dismissed.

## *QUESTIONS FOR DISCUSSION*

1. The court in *Goldwater* emphasizes the fact that the manuscript, with nothing more than standard editorial assistance, went on to be a commercial success, indeed a bestseller. How important should this be to the outcome of the case? Would authors of a work that had later been published by Morrow to mediocre sales have still been entitled to prevail in a breach of contract suit with HBJ?

2. In *Dell Publishing Co. v. Whedon*, 577 F. Supp. 1459 (S.D.N.Y. 1984), the court reiterated its stance, and indeed set an even higher standard as to the degree of editorial assistance required before a manuscript could be rejected as unsatisfactory. Whereas in *Goldwater* the court emphasized the fact that despite the authors' persistent desire for editorial help, no substantive editorial work was done, in *Dell* there was no contact between the author and publisher beyond the initial submission of an outline of a novel for which a portion of an advance was given. Even though the author did not actively seek editorial help while writing the novel, the company could not reject the novel as unsatisfactory without giving the author a chance to remedy the defects. The court held that there was an implied duty for the publisher to offer good faith suggestions about revisions needed to generate a satisfactory product. Editorial assistance had to be offered, and a manuscript could not be rejected without this assistance. The publisher's failure to do so prevented it from recovering the advances.

---

The next case, involving a novel authored by a movie star rather than a memoir by a politician, produced a rather different legal as well as artistic result.

## DOUBLEDAY & COMPANY, INC. V. TONY CURTIS

United States Court of Appeals, Second Circuit, 1985.
763 F.2d 495.

IRVING R. KAUFMAN, CIRCUIT JUDGE.

[In the 1970s, long-time movie star Tony Curtis decided to expand and enrich his career by becoming a novelist. With the aid of notable literary agent Irving "Swifty" Lazar, Curtis was able to get Doubleday to accept his draft manuscript *Kid Cody* as the basis for a two-book contract signed in 1976. The standard publishing contract term, "satisfactory to Publisher in content and form," was readily met by *Kid Cody*, whose final version involved a major contribution by Doubleday editor Larry Jordan, which was facilitated by a series of meetings with Curtis.

Having seen *Kid Cody's* commercial success and having received an eight-page outline of Curtis's new novel *Starstruck*, Doubleday agreed in 1977 to renegotiate the original contract. Curtis was to receive a $100,000 advance against future royalties for *Starstruck*, half paid on signing of the contract, and half on publisher "acceptance of completed satisfactory manuscript" (which was due by October 1, 1978). Doubleday then took this deal to New American Library (NAL), which agreed to pay $200,000 for the paperback publishing rights if Doubleday published the book by December 1980. NAL did not reserve for itself the right to judge whether the Curtis manuscript was satisfactory.

Curtis took much longer to write this novel, and had sent only the first part to Doubleday by April 1980. Doubleday ignored its deadline, and NAL extended its own date to December 1981. This time Curtis's editor at Doubleday was Adrian Zackheim. After carefully reading the first half of *Starstruck*, Zackheim wrote Curtis with a number of suggested changes, but said he was "charmed with the wonderful possibilities" of the novel, and did not expect any substantial changes in its "basic outlines." From then on, there were only occasional conversations between Curtis and Zackheim, in marked contrast to Curtis' talks with Jordan.

Finally, in August 1981, Curtis delivered a manuscript to Doubleday. In internal memoranda, Zackheim and his superior, Elizabeth Drew, judged *Starstruck* to be unpublishable "junk, pure and simple," and not capable of being "edited into shape, even rewritten into shape." When Curtis's agent, Lazar, did not accept Zackheim's suggestion that *Starstruck* be turned over to a "novel doctor" for rewriting, Doubleday cancelled its deal with NAL, rejected the manuscript from Curtis, and demanded repayment of the $50,000 advance. When Curtis refused, Doubleday sued, and Curtis counterclaimed for his loss of anticipated earnings from *Starstruck*.]

* * *

Discussion

*A. The Publisher's Duty to Perform in Good Faith.*

We note at the outset that Curtis has never defended his August 1981 manuscript as a work of publishable quality. Rather, Curtis maintains that but for Doubleday's inability and unwillingness to provide adequate editorial assistance, Starstruck would have met the "satisfactory to publisher" condition. Curtis concedes that his proposed interpretation is not supported by a literal reading of the 1977 agreement. On its face, the document is completely silent regarding any obligation on Doubleday's part to ensure that Curtis's rough drafts are transformed, through the company's affirmative efforts, into a polished novel.

Our task, then, is to delineate the extent to which New York law requires us to infer such an obligation from the agreement. Because New York's appellate court have not yet addressed this question, we must attempt to divine the likely response of our state brethren.

The 1977 agreement expressly granted Doubleday the right to terminate the contract if it deemed Curtis's manuscript to be unsatisfactory. In similar circumstances—where the satisfactory performance of one party is to be judged by another party—New York courts have required the party terminating the contract to act in good faith. In *Baker v. Chock Full O'Nuts Corp.*, 292 N.Y.S.2d 58, 30 A.D.2d 329 (1st Dep't 1968), for example, where payment to an advertiser was contingent upon the client's "satisfaction" with the completed promotional campaign, the court implied a requirement that the client terminate its arrangement only if motivated by "an honest dissatisfaction with the performance."

This principle—that a contract containing a "satisfaction clause" may be terminated only as a result of honest dissatisfaction—would seem especially appropriate in construing publishing agreements. To shield from scrutiny the already chimerical process of evaluating literary value would render the "satisfaction" clause an illusory promise, and place authors at the unbridled mercy of their editors.

A corollary of this duty to appraise a writing honestly is an obligation on the part of the publisher not to mislead an author deliberately regarding the work required for a given project. A willful failure to respond to a request for editorial comments on a preliminary draft may, in many instances, work no less a hardship than would an unjustifiable rejection of a final manuscript. A publisher's duty to exercise good faith in its dealings toward an author exists at all stages of the creative process.

Although we hold that publishers must perform honestly, we decline to extend that requirement to include a duty to perform skillfully. The possibility that a publisher or an editor—either through inferior editing or inadvertence—may prejudice an author's efforts is a risk attendant to the selection of a publishing house by a writer, and is properly borne by that party. To imply a duty to perform adequate editorial services in the absence of express contractual language would, in our view, represent an unwarranted intrusion into the editorial process. Moreover, we are hesitant to require triers of fact to explore the manifold intricacies of an editorial relationship. Such inquiries are appropriate only where contracts specifically allocate certain responsibilities to the publisher.

Accordingly, we hold that a publisher may, in its discretion, terminate a standard publishing contract, provided that the termination is made in good faith, and that the failure of an author to submit a satisfactory manuscript was not caused by the publisher's bad faith.

### *B. Doubleday's Good Faith*

Evaluating the Doubleday-Curtis relationship in light of these principles, we are convinced that Starstruck's failure was [not] attributable to any dishonesty, willful neglect or any other manifestations of bad faith on the part of Doubleday. The factual landscape illustrates the complete frustration experienced by Doubleday's editors, who were forced to harmonize an inferior manuscript, a lucrative reprint agreement and a recalcitrant author. Zackheim sincerely endeavored to assist Curtis in the completion of his manuscript. Although Zackheim's suggested revisions may have been offered somewhat belatedly, the evidence indicates that he extended numerous offers to discuss the novel with Curtis, as well as to review portions of the second draft. Indeed, it was Curtis who refused these renderings of assistance. That Zackheim's editing was perhaps inadequate is beside the point, as is any comparison with Larry Jordan. Curtis neither alleged, nor does the record support a finding that Doubleday deliberately or even recklessly assigned Starstruck to an editor unfit or unsuited for the project.

Admittedly, the selection of an editor is a matter of paramount importance to a writer, but we note once again that the power to control this decision—like all aspects of the publication process—could have been reserved to Curtis in his contract.[5]

Turning our attention to the actual termination of the contract, we believe the district court's finding that Doubleday rejected Starstruck in good faith is amply supported by the record before us. Zackheim and Drew were in complete agreement that no amount of in-house editing could save the project. Moreover, the suggestion that Curtis consult a "novel doctor"—though perhaps somewhat humiliating—appears to have

---

[5] Indeed, Curtis's own expert witness at trial admitted that an author's desire to work with a particular editor is often achieved by making that preference an explicit condition of the publishing contract.

been made sincerely, rather than as a stratagem for avoiding the responsibilities attendant to a difficult editing job.[6]

Curtis argues with some force that Doubleday terminated his contract in November 1981 primarily because of the impending NAL deadline. Although we agree the two events were not unconnected, we choose to characterize the relationship between them quite differently. Were it not for the extremely lucrative arrangement with NAL, it is likely that Doubleday would have abandoned Starstruck without hesitation, and perhaps at a much earlier date. Only the prospect of a commercially profitable reprint deal prevented Zackheim from rejecting the August 1981 manuscript immediately. Doubleday's decision to sacrifice financial reward for "ethics," as Zackheim's superior Drew framed the choice, can hardly be said to constitute an act of bad faith.

[For the reasons stated, the court concluded that Doubleday had acted in good faith, and thus Curtis's counterclaim must be dismissed and Doubleday repaid its advance.]

* * *

Affirmed in part.

### *QUESTIONS FOR DISCUSSION*

1. Do you agree with the Second Circuit's view that a publishing house need provide only good faith, not skillful, editorial assistance? Does that square with the wording and rationale of book contracts?

2. In an agreement to publish a series of books with periodic advances dependent upon the delivery of satisfactory manuscripts, should a publisher be able to take account of its recoupment of advances for prior books in making a judgment about a new manuscript? In *Random House, Inc. v. Gold*, 464 F. Supp. 1306 (S.D.N.Y.), *aff'd mem.*, 607 F.2d 998 (2d Cir. 1979), the court rejected the proposition that ". . . a publisher's financial circumstances and the likelihood of a book's commercial success must be excluded from the range of factors that may be weighed in the decision to accept or reject a manuscript . . ." The court concluded that requiring that ". . . a manuscript be satisfactory to the publisher gives it the right to reject the work if it acts in good faith; the publisher is not bound to incur the significant costs of publication if it declines to accept the risk of financial loss." One way of construing the court's holding is that "unsatisfactory in form or content to the

---

[6] Curtis relies on two district court decisions that denied publishers recovery of their advances after rejecting manuscripts as "unsatisfactory." Dell Publishing Co. v. Whedon, 577 F. Supp. 1459 (S.D.N.Y. 1984); Harcourt Brace & Jovanovich v. Goldwater, 532 F. Supp. 619 (S.D.N.Y. 1982). Although both decisions appear to recognize a duty on the part of publishers to provide adequate editorial services, the results reached in those cases are consistent with the framework we have adopted. In marked contrast to the supervision Zackheim offered Curtis on Starstruck, the authors in *Whedon* and *Goldwater* received no response to their requests for guidance and assistance in the preparation and revision of their manuscripts.

publisher" turns not on the quality of the manuscript, but only on whether the publisher likes it and believes it will sell. How does that position square with the later observation by the *Doubleday* court that "to shield from scrutiny the already chimerical process of evaluating literary value would render the 'satisfaction' clause an illusory promise, and place authors at the unbridled mercy of their editors?"

3. One point the *Curtis* court treats as a foregone conclusion is that advances necessarily should have to be returned if the manuscript is deemed, in good faith, to be unsatisfactory. In *J.B. Lippincott Co. v. Lasher*, 430 F. Supp. 993 (S.D.N.Y. 1977), the author sought to challenge the fundamental notion that an advance should be returned even though he conceded that he had not delivered a manuscript at all; since the only explicit reference to return of advances was contingent upon the manuscript ultimately being sold to another publisher, the author contended that he should be able to keep his $18,000 advance. While the court termed this "an intriguing interpretation," it rejected this view, stating that fundamental principle is that advances must be returned if no satisfactory manuscript is delivered (and thus a breach of contract by the author has occurred).

The return of advances is the standard recovery for author breach, with other damage awards being rare. The court in *Lippincott* rejected the notion of damages for lost future profits by the publisher: "It is almost impossible to compute what profit would have been made by the publisher if the defendant had, in fact, completed the work and the publisher had properly promoted and published the book. This claim is far too speculative to be ruled upon, and it is entirely rejected." Do you agree? Recall the Kim Basinger case from Chapter 7; is there a reason for different treatment of authors than actors?

4. In a later case an author was forced to return an advance even though the publisher terminated the contract prior to the expiration of the author's submission deadline. In *Little, Brown and Co. v. Klein*, 22 Media L. Rep. 108 (N.Y.Sup.Ct. 1993), author Klein was to have written, with the cooperation of the President and Barbara Bush and the White House staff, a book entitled *A Day in the White House with George and Barbara Bush*. The anticipated publication date was fall 1992, coinciding with the presidential election. But White House aides later withdrew the promise of cooperation, indicating that no one would be able to participate until 1993, after the election. The author, who had been advanced $166,666 as a first installment, was to have submitted a satisfactory manuscript by January 1, 1992; because of the withdrawal of White House cooperation he would be unable to meet this deadline. Little, Brown terminated the contract, demanding return of the advance. The court sided with the publisher, stating that the Bushes' cooperation in meeting the deadline were "material and essential to the contract . . . [such that] Klein's failure to obtain said cooperation prior to the deadline constituted a material breach of the contract, giving Little, Brown the right to rescind the contract and recover the advance monies." Contract law principles would normally disallow termination by one party because of a minor breach by the other party, and would instead call for a chance for the

breaching party to remedy his default. However, since the court ruled the breach to be "material," the publisher had the "right, but not the obligation, to publish the book after 1992 if Klein failed to timely deliver the manuscript."

5. The tables were turned in a case involving Lech Walesa—*Fayard (Librairie Artheme) v. Henry Holt & Co.*, 726 F. Supp. 438 (S.D.N.Y. 1989). In 1984, Walesa was still the leader of the Solidarity union movement in Poland, and was on his way to the Nobel Peace Prize and eventually the presidency of his liberated homeland. That year he entered into a written agreement with Holt, an American publisher, to have his autobiography published if the book was finished by the end of 1985. While Walesa's associate, Marion Terlecki, who was writing the book, made a good start on it, the project was interrupted when Terlecki was imprisoned by the Communist government of Poland. Sometime after the Holt publishing deadline had passed, a French publisher, Fayard, approached Walesa, and he agreed to have his autobiography written by someone whom Fayard supplied for that purpose. While Holt secured from Fayard certain English language translation and distribution rights in *Un Chemin d'Espoir* (*A Way of Hope*), the dispute between the two publishers eventually led to litigation about Holt's failure to pay advances and royalties. Holt argued that where, as here, termination of its exclusive publication rights under its original contract was conditioned on publication of a manuscript, the failure of the author (Walesa) to write and deliver the manuscript meant that the author could not rely on that provision to sign a publishing contract with someone else. The court rejected that argument, saying that Holt was bound by the terms of the contract. Suppose, though, that the reason why an author did not deliver the book was that his agent had seen the market value rising in the subject matter of the book, and the author was simply waiting until he was free to get a better deal from another publisher. Should there be a binding condition of "good faith and fair dealing" that governs these termination provisions (and would this hypothetical example violate that condition)?

## 2. BEST PROMOTIONAL EFFORTS

It does not do a recording artist, songwriter, or book author much good to have a work placed on the market if the work is not promoted sufficiently to make the buying public aware of it. Because of the vagaries surrounding the commercial success of a product, publishers and labels typically want to limit their commitment to doing *some level* of promoting. Though this contract term would seem to leave publishers and the like free of any real obligation toward the artist, after *Wood v. Lucy, Lady Duff-Gordon*, 222 N.Y. 88, 118 N.E. 214 (1917), courts have typically read into such contracts an implied obligation of publishers/labels to act in good faith by expending "reasonable efforts" to promote. The following case, again from the book publishing world, explores the tension between the concept of best efforts and the business interests of the publisher.

## ZILG V. PRENTICE-HALL, INC.

United States Court of Appeals, Second Circuit, 1983.
717 F.2d 671.

WINTER, CIRCUIT JUDGE.

[The publisher, Prentice-Hall, Inc. (P-H), appealed the trial judgment that it had to pay damages of $24,250 to author Gerald Zilg for breach of contract. The lower court ruled that P-H had violated its good faith obligation to extend best efforts to promote the author's book when it reduced the number of copies in the first printing and lowered the advertising budget without valid cause.

In early 1972, Zilg's proposal for a book about the Dupont family had caught the interest of Bram Cavin, senior editor in P-H's Trade Book Division. The proposal, which described the work as a historical account of the Duponts' role in American social, political, and economic affairs, was ultimately approved by John Kirk, P-H's Editor-in-Chief at the time. The form contract signed by Zilg with P-H required him to deliver to P-H a manuscript "in final form and content acceptable to the publisher," which would then be published by P-H in the style "it deems best suited to the sale of the work" and with a price and method of advertising, publicizing and selling the work (including the number of copies to be published) that P-H determined.

By November of 1973, Zilg had submitted, and Cavin had accepted, the completed manuscript. In March of 1974, a P-H committee discussed sales estimates for the book, most of which ranged from 12 to 15 thousand in the first year and from 15 to 20 thousand over five years, at a proposed retail price. The committee decided on a first printing of 15,000 copies at $12.95 per copy and, at a later meeting, determined an advertising budget of $15,000.

The book was an extremely critical depiction of the Dupont family's role in various facets of American life, and tended to polarize its advance readership, which included wholesalers, reviewers, booksellers, and the directors of the Book of the Month Club (BOMC). For example, one judge at BOMC characterized it as "300,000 words of pure spite." Conversely, the book garnered good reviews in many newspapers, including the *New York Times Book Review*. The majority of this advance audience apparently reacted negatively to it, however, and even its selection into the Fortune Book Club (Fortune), a subsidiary of BOMC (which had not selected the book), was accompanied by the admonition from the Club's inside reader that it was "a bad book, politically crude and cheaply journalistic," and the recommendation that it "be fed back to the author page by page." The book's appeal in the American market was also somewhat limited by its Marxist slant, its size (586 pages of text, 2 inches thick, three and a half pounds in weight), complexity (close to 200 family members with the surname Dupont and history covering 170 years), and price ($12.95 in 1974 dollars).

Other difficulties with the manuscript from P-H's perspective soon surfaced, including P-H's belated discovery of mistakes of fact and possibly libelous mischaracterizations in the text, the reconsideration and withdrawal of Fortune's selection of the book for distribution, the subsequent "horrible two days" spent by P-H's new Editor-in-Chief actually reading the manuscript, and the looming presence of a brooding Dupont Company. By August of 1974, P-H was circulating a memo recommending that the adjective "polemical" henceforth be used in describing the book, since "the book is a polemical argument and no pretense is made that it is anything else." The first printing was cut from 15,000 to 10,000 copies, with P-H citing the 5,000 copies no longer needed for Fortune, and the advertising budget was reduced from $15,000 to $5,500.

The lower court's decision that P-H had breached its good faith obligation to extend best efforts to promote the book "fully and fairly" centered around Judge Brieant's finding that P-H had no "sound" or "valid" business reason to have slashed the first printing by 5,000 volumes and the advertising budget by $9,500 just as the book was gaining sales momentum. The judge noted that the reduced printing could not be explained by the fact that Fortune no longer needed copies (as the P-H memo had asserted), since BOMC and its subsidiaries printed up their own allotment of books for club selections. On the basis of industry expert testimony, the judge determined that the book had been "privished," a publishing term of art meaning the process by which publishers, upon concluding that a book is not up to qualitative or commercial snuff, mount a wholly inadequate merchandising effort and effectively allow the book to die on the vine. "Privishing" is intended to technically comply with the terms of the contract to publish and promote, but enables the publisher to cap its losses so as to avoid "throwing good money after bad."]

* * *

. . . Putting aside for the moment P-H's motive in slashing the first printing and advertising budget, we note that Zilg neither bargained for nor acquired an explicit "best efforts" or "promote fully" promise, much less an agreement to make certain specific promotional efforts. The contract here thus contrasts with that in issue in *Contemporary Mission, Inc. v. Famous Music Corp.*, 557 F.2d 918 (2d Cir. 1977), which contained specific promotional obligations with regard to a musical group. While P-H obligated itself to "publish" the book once it had accepted it, the contract expressly leaves to P-H's discretion printing and advertising decisions. Working as we must in the context of a surprising absence of case law on the meaning of this not uncommon agreement, we believe that the contract in question establishes a relationship between the publisher and author which implies an obligation upon the former to make certain efforts in publishing a book it has accepted notwithstanding the clause which leaves the number of volumes to be printed and the advertising budget to the publisher's discretion. This obligation is derived both from the common expectations of parties to such agreements and from the relationship of those parties as structured by the contract. *See generally* Goetz and Scott, *Principles of Relational Contracts*, 67 Va. L. Rev. 1089 (1981).

Zilg, like most authors, sought to take advantage of a division of labor in which firms specialize in publishing works written by authors who are not employees of the firm. Under contracts such as the one before us, publishing firms print, advertise and distribute books at their own expense. In return for performing these tasks and for bearing the risk of a book's failure to sell, the author gives a publisher exclusive rights to the book with certain reservations not important here. Such contracts provide for royalties on sales to the author, often on an escalating basis, i.e., higher royalties at higher levels of sales.

While publishers and authors have generally similar goals, differences in perspective and resulting perceptions are inevitable. An author usually has a bigger stake in the success or failure of a book than a publisher who may regard it as one among many publications, some of which may lose money. The author, whose eggs are in one basket, thus has a calculus of risk quite different from the publisher so far as costly promotional expenditures are concerned. The publisher, of course, views the author's willingness to take large risks as a function of the fact that it is the publisher's money at peril. Moreover, the publisher will inevitably regard his or her judgment as to marketing conditions as greatly superior to that of a particular author.

One means of reconciling these differing viewpoints is "up-front" money—$6,500 in Zilg's case—which provides a token of the publisher's seriousness about the book. Were such sums not bargained for, acquisition of publishing rights would be virtually costless and firms would acquire those rights without regard to whether or not they had truly decided to publish the work.

However, up-front money alone cannot fully reconcile the conflicting interests of the parties. Uncertainty surrounds the publication of most books and publishers must be cautious about the size of up-front payments since they increase the already considerable economic risks they take by printing and promoting books at their own expense. Negotiating such matters as the number of volumes to be printed and the level of advertising efforts might be possible but such bargaining in the case of each author and each book would be enormously costly. There is never a guarantee of ultimate agreement, and if a set of negotiations fails over these issues, the bargaining must begin again with another publisher. Moreover, publishers must also be wary of undertaking obligations to print a certain number of volumes or to spend fixed sums on promotion. They will strongly prefer to have flexibility in reacting to actual marketing conditions according to their own experience.

The contract between Zilg and P-H was a printed form with formal and negotiated matters—e.g., the parties' names and the amount of the advance to the author—typed in. Under the terms of the printed form, once P-H accepted the manuscript it was obliged to publish the book but had discretion to determine the number of volumes to be printed and the level of advertising expenditures. These clauses are, of course, interrelated and the extent to which the language regarding promotional efforts and the promise to publish modify each other is the central issue before us. In resolving it, we must attempt to preserve the major interests of both parties.

Once P-H had accepted the book, it obtained the exclusive right to publish it. Were the clause empowering the publisher to determine promotional expenses read literally, the contract would allow a publisher to refuse to print or distribute any copies of a book while having exclusive rights to it. In effect, authors would be guaranteed nothing but whatever up-front money had been negotiated, and the promise to publish would be meaningless. We think the promise to publish must be given some content and that it implies a good faith effort to promote the book including a first printing and advertising budget adequate to give the book a reasonable chance of achieving market success in light of the subject matter and likely audience. *See Contemporary Mission, Inc. v. Famous Music Corp.*; cf. *Van Valkenburgh Nooger & Neville, Inc. v. Hayden Publishing Co.*, 30 N.Y.2d 34, 281 N.E.2d 142, 330 N.Y.S.2d 329 (1972) (publication of competing works may be so foreseeably harmful to author's royalties as to breach the covenant to promote the book).

However, the clause empowering the publisher to decide in its discretion upon the number of volumes printed and the level of promotional expenditures must also be given some content. If a trier of fact is free to determine whether such decisions are sound or valid, the publisher's ability to rely upon its own experience and judgment in marketing books will be seriously hampered. We believe that once the obligation to undertake reasonable initial promotional activities has been fulfilled, the contractual language dictates that a business decision by the publisher to limit the size of a printing or advertising budget is not subject to second guessing by a trier of fact as to whether it is sound or valid.

The line we draw reconciles the legitimate conflicting interests of publisher and author as reflected in the contractual language, for it compels the publisher to make a good faith effort to promote the book initially whether or not it has had second thoughts, while relying upon the profit motive thereafter to create the incentive for more elaborate promotional efforts. Once the initial obligation is fulfilled, all that is required is a good faith business judgment. This is not an interpretation harmful to authors. Were courts to impose rigorous requirements as to promotional efforts, publishers would of necessity undertake to publish fewer books with unpredictable futures.

Given the line we draw, a breach of contract might be proven by Zilg in two ways. First, he might demonstrate that the initial printing and promotional efforts were so inadequate as not to give the book a reasonable chance to catch on with the reading public. Second, he might show that even greater printing and promotional efforts were not undertaken for reasons other than a good faith business judgment. Because he has shown neither, we reverse the judgment in his favor.

[The court then stated its reason for overturning the trial judge's conclusion that the publisher had undermined rather than promoted the Zilg book's sales potential.] Indeed, Judge Brieant's view of the book's potential is entirely inconsistent with [the industry's] definition of privishing—not throwing "good money after bad"—for he in essence found that P-H had managed to avoid a small bonanza by breaching its contract.

As explained above, we think the contract between P-H and Zilg left the decisions in question to the business judgment of the publisher, the author's protection being in the publisher's experience, judgment and quest for profits. P-H's promotional efforts were, in [the industry expert's] words, "adequate," notwithstanding the reduction of the first printing and the initial advertising budget. Indeed, those reductions, coming on the heels of BOMC's decision not to distribute the book, appear to be a rational reaction to that news. Decker himself testified that the Fortune Book Club selection was an important barometer of marketability since it was an independent judgment that the book had an audience. Zilg's contract with P-H did not compel the publisher to ignore the implications of BOMC's change of heart.

* * *

Reversed.

### *QUESTIONS FOR DISCUSSION*

1. What are the differences in the standards for best promotional efforts as articulated by the district court and the circuit court in *Zilg*? What

about the *Doubleday* standard for best editorial efforts? How would you appraise the impact that these standards have on the interests of authors and publishers? Does it have more impact on some kinds of authors than others, before and after book contracts are signed? From the point of view of broader contract doctrine, are rulings like *Doubleday* and *Zilg* compatible with the decisions in Chapter 7, e.g., *Pinnacle* and *Candid Production*, striking down best-effort or good-faith standards for negotiating contract renewals as too indefinite to be legally enforceable?

2. A decision involving the music industry, *Mellencamp v. Riva Music Ltd.*, 698 F. Supp. 1154 (S.D.N.Y. 1988), made it clear that even though the songwriter-performer John Cougar Mellencamp had conveyed copyright in his songs to Riva, a music publishing company, in return for a percentage of royalties earned from the songs, this did not warrant an independent fiduciary obligation analogous to the attorney-client relationship. The publisher's duties had to flow from a contractual relationship that either expressly or by implication (i.e., the covenant of good faith and fair dealing) generated a best efforts obligation that might be interpreted as fiduciary in quality.

3. A well-received book, *The Execution of Charles Horman*, produced a defamation suit by the American military representative in Chile who is allegedly misportrayed in the book. (*Cf. Davis v. Costa-Gavras*, 654 F. Supp. 653 (S.D.N.Y. 1987), reproduced in Chapter 2.) The publisher, faced with the suit, decided to stop promoting the book and to let it go out of print. Should the author be able to sue the publisher for violation of its best promotional efforts obligation? *See Hauser v. Harcourt Brace Jovanovich*, 140 Misc.2d 82, 530 N.Y.S.2d 431 (1988).

4. Although a publisher may produce works that compete with those of another of its authors without violating its good faith-best efforts obligation to the latter artist, the decision in *Van Valkenburgh, Nooger & Neville v. Hayden Publishing Co.*, 30 N.Y.2d 34, 330 N.Y.S.2d 329, 281 N.E.2d 142 (1972), explores the limits of this principle. In *Van Valkenburgh*, the court held that the publisher had breached both its implied obligation of good faith and an explicit contract provision to expend its best efforts to promote the author's work when it marketed another author's very similar series of books with better terms for the publisher than under the first author's agreement.

The *Van Valkenburg* court, similar to the stance taken in *Zilg*, was reluctant to intrude too far into business judgments, but provided a window by saying that although ". . . a publisher has a general right to act on its own interests in a way that may incidentally lessen an author's royalties, there may be a point where that activity is so manifestly harmful to the author . . . as to justify the court in saying there was a breach of the covenant to promote the author's work."

5. Compliance with *express* contract terms regarding promotion may not be enough to remove a party from judicial censure over whether the party has exerted best efforts. In *Contemporary Mission, Inc. v. Famous Music*

*Corp.*, 557 F.2d 918 (2d Cir. 1977), a record label had obligated itself to promote a record on a nationwide basis. Two specific provisions were in the contract: the label would assign at least one person to oversee a nationwide promotion and sales campaign and the company would spend at least $50,000 within the first year on such a campaign. Though these terms were adhered to by the label, the court still found it to be in breach of its implied contractual obligation to use good faith-best efforts to promote the record. That obligation, the court said, "could not be satisfied merely by technical compliance with the spending and appointment requirements . . . of the agreement."

6. The notion of what constitutes best efforts will not be an idealized one, but rather one that reflects common practices in the industry. Thus, one will not be held to anything more than what the "average, prudent comparable distributor" would have done. Does this undercut the position articulated by the court in *Zilg* that best efforts are something special to be bargained for? Even if they are bargained for, the court will hold the party only to a reasonableness standard. *See Arnold Productions, Inc. v. Favorite Films Corp.*, 176 F. Supp. 862 (S.D.N.Y. 1959).

7. For a different slant on the best efforts paradigm, see *Warner Bros. Pictures, Inc. v. Bumgarner*, 197 Cal.App.2d 331, 17 Cal. Rptr. 171 (1961). In *Bumgarner*, the actor James Garner (suing under his given name) had his pay suspended by Warner Bros., the studio that produced his popular television series *Maverick*, because Warner claimed that a writers' strike had triggered the *force majeure* clause in its contract with him, entitling the studio to suspend his pay. The court found that the strike, while potentially a legitimate impediment as contemplated by the *force majeure* clause, had not really been an impediment here and was in fact used by the studio as a pretext for what ultimately was bad faith dealing with Garner. The court ruled that such "catastrophe" clauses could not be used as smokescreens to obscure whether good faith-best efforts had actually been expended.

8. Most of the above cases involve disputes over the level of promotion of an already-accepted product. A case that explores the more speculative status of an agreement that (for $100,000) transferred the exclusive right to create a film from a literary work is *Reback (Taylor Caldwell) v. Story Productions, Inc.*, 15 Misc.2d 681, 181 N.Y.S.2d 980 (1958), *aff'd*, 9 A.D.2d 880, 193 N.Y.S.2d 520 (1959). When the defendant failed to produce and distribute a film based on the book, the author sued for breach of contract. In that situation, should the fact that a producer has the exclusive right (especially if "in perpetuity") to create a product mean that it also has (i) an obligation to do so; (ii) or at least to make all "reasonable" efforts; (iii) or just its own "best" efforts; (iv) or no obligation at all other than its initial payment?

9. Having now read about the major decisions, what are your views about the Hansmann-Kraakman "hands-tying" theory of book contracts?

## C. ROYALTIES AND PROFITS[f]

### 1. CALCULATING THE AMOUNT: FILM

The movie *Forrest Gump* earned $670 million in world-wide box office receipts in its first year, at the time one of the largest ever. Yet Forbes Magazine reported that as of the end of 1994, when *Gump* had grossed $350 million, its studio, Paramount, was facing huge losses from the film. Paramount itself received "only" $190 million of those admission prices (the theater exhibitors kept the other $160 million). *Gump's* production costs (about $50 million) were somewhat above the industry's $35 million average, it was a puzzle why Paramount's books indicated that at the end of 1994 *Gump* was more than $60 million in the red.

The source of these numbers is the concept of "net profits," as defined in the standard contracts signed by the book's author (Winston Groom), the screen writer (Eric Roth), and co-producers (Steve Tisch and Wendy Finerman). Groom, for example, had sold the book rights for $350,000, plus 3% of any profits the movie earned if it were ever made. By contrast, the movie's star Tom Hanks, and its director Robert Zemeckis, agreed to reduce their respective $7 million and $5 million fees in return for a share in the film's *gross* revenues, with Hanks' share eventually reaching $65 million. Because of the 1995 surge in *Gump's* earnings, propelled by its Oscar sweep and unexpected revenue from the sale of videos and merchandise, everyone anticipated that Groom and other "net profit" participants would eventually realize some money from the deal. When Groom consulted a lawyer, he found out why movies that generate a "mere" $350 million in revenues rarely show a profit. Even after a film has been made and its production costs are documented, studios have a "rolling break even point" that is constantly being pushed back as the studio deducts from incoming film revenues an elaborate set of distribution fees, promotional expenses, studio and advertising overhead, and interest charges.

The lawyer whom Groom consulted, Pierce O'Donnell, had also been counsel for Art Buchwald in the litigation over *Coming to America,* which (as seen in Chapter 6) was based on Buchwald's story idea, "King for a

---

[f] *See* Pierce O'Donnell & Dennis McDougal, *Fatal Subtraction: The Inside Story of* Buchwald v. Paramount (Doubleday 1996); Bill Daniels, David Leedy & Stephen D. Sills, *Movie Money: Understanding Hollywood's (Creative) Accounting Practices* (Silaman-James Press 1998); Harry G. Prince, *Unconscionability in California: A Need for Restraint & Consistency*, 46 Hast. L.J. 459 (1995). On broader issues of contract adhesion and unconscionability, see Robert L. Hale, *Bargaining, Duress & Economic Liberty*, 43 Colum. L. Rev. 603 (1943); Arthur A. Leff, *Unconscionabilty & the Code: The Emperor's New Clause,* 115 U. Penn. L. Rev. 485 (1967); Richard A. Epstein, *Unconscionability: A Critical Reappraisal,* 18 J. Law & Econ. 293 (1975); Melvin A. Eisenberg, *The Bargain Principle & its Limits,* 71 Harv. L. Rev. 741 (1982); Todd D. Rakoff, *Contracts of Adhesion: An Essay in Reconstruction,* 96 Harv. L. Rev. 1174 (1983); Jeffrey L. Harrison, *Class, Personality, Contract, & Unconscionability,* 35 Wm. & Mary L. Rev. 445 (1994).

Day." The phase of the case provides an instructive look at movie industry accounting and explores the question of whether the industry's current net profit formula is unconscionable.

## BUCHWALD V. PARAMOUNT PICTURES CORP.

Superior Court of the State of California, County of Los Angeles, 1990.
1990 WL 357611, Unpublished Decision.

SCHNEIDER, JUDGE.

[The initial stage of this case is found in Chapter 6. In the discovery period for the damages phase of the trial, Paramount claimed that the film had fallen $18 million short of attaining any net profits, as the term was defined in the industry's standard form contract. When it was revealed that the film had actually earned $350 million in box office receipts, the plaintiffs amended their complaint, seeking to have the "net profits" formula, a staple in the movie business for at least forty years, declared unconscionable.]

* * *

### III. Discussion

#### A. *Contract of Adhesion*

A "contract of adhesion" signifies a standardized contract, which, imposed and drafted by the party of superior bargaining strength, relegates to the subscribing party only the opportunity to adhere to the contract or reject it. *Graham v. Scissor-Tail Inc.*, 28 Cal. 3d 807, 817 (1981). As the Court in *Graham* stated:

> Such contracts are, of course, a familiar part of the modern legal landscape, in which the classical model of "free" contracting by parties of equal or near-equal bargaining strength is often found to be unresponsive to the realities brought about by increasing concentrations of economic and other power. They are also an inevitable fact of life for all citizens—businessman and consumer alike. While not lacking in social advantages, they bear within them the clear danger of oppression and overreaching. It is in the context of this tension—between social advantage in the light of modern conditions on the one hand, and the danger of oppression on the other—that courts and legislatures have sometimes acted to prevent perceived abuses.

28 Cal.3d at 817–18.

In the present case, the court finds that Bernheim's compensation package, as set forth in the Deal Memo, was negotiated by Bernheim's agent and Paramount's representative, as were other provisions of the

Deal Memo not relevant to this case. The court finds, however, that the "boilerplate" language of the Deal Memo was not negotiated.

The court further finds that the "turnaround" provision, the Additional Terms and Conditions, and the net profit participation agreement were not negotiated. With respect to the latter three parts of the Bernheim-Paramount contract, there is not the slightest doubt that they were presented to Bernheim on a "take it or leave it" basis. Indeed, the evidence reveals that Bernheim did not have the "clout" to make a better deal.

It is true Paramount has submitted evidence that it freely negotiates its net profit formula with the talent with which it deals. The court is not impressed with Paramount's evidence. To the contrary, the court concludes plaintiffs have proved by a preponderance of the evidence that Paramount negotiates its net profit formula with only a relatively small number of persons who possess the necessary "clout," and even these negotiations result in changes that are cosmetic, rather than substantive. Indeed, if, as Paramount contends, it freely negotiates with respect to its net profit formula, the court presumes it would have been inundated with examples of contracts where this was done. Succinctly stated, this has not occurred.

The evidence also discloses that the entire contract was drafted by Paramount and that the "turnaround" and net profit participation provisions were standard form provisions. Indeed, there is evidence in the record that Paramount's net profit formula is standard in the film industry. Further, there is evidence in the record to support the conclusion that essentially the same negotiations are conducted at all studios, and that when one studio revises a provision of its net profit formula, that revision is adopted by the other studios.

The above factors lead to the inescapable conclusion that the Bernheim-Paramount contract is a contract of adhesion. The fact that a portion of the contract was negotiated, i.e., Bernheim's compensation package in the Deal Memo, does not require a different conclusion. In *Graham, supra*, the Court held that the contract before it was a contract of adhesion, even though some of the terms were negotiated between the parties.

### *B. Unconscionability*

In *Graham*, supra, the Court stated:

> To describe a contract as adhesive in character is not to indicate its legal effect. It is, rather, "the beginning and not the end of the analysis in so far as enforceability of its terms is concerned." Thus, a contract of adhesion is fully enforceable according to its terms unless certain other factors are present

which, under established legal rules—legislative or judicial—operate to render it otherwise.

Generally speaking, there are two judicially imposed limitations on the enforcement of adhesion contracts or provisions thereof. The first is that such a contract or provision which does not fall within the reasonable expectations of the weaker or "adhering" party will not be enforced against him. The second—a principle of equity applicable to all contracts generally—is that a contract or provision, even if consistent with the reasonable expectation of the parties, will be denied enforcement if, considered in its context, it is unduly oppressive or "unconscionable."

28 Cal.3d at 819–20.

[The court opened its discussion of unconscionability by addressing two of Paramount's contentions. First, the court stated that while it agreed with the studio that unconscionability could not be claimed as an affirmative cause of action by the plaintiffs, a review of California case law made it clear that unconscionability could be invoked to counter Paramount's defense that the plaintiffs should be held to the agreement as written. Secondly, the court pointed out that although it recognized that prevention of surprise was one of the motivations behind unconscionability doctrine, the fact that the contract terms were not contrary to the reasonable expectations of these industry veteran plaintiffs did not necessarily remove them from the reach of unconscionability doctrine.]

* * *

*3. Unconscionability—Oppression*

The other principal target of the unconscionability doctrine is oppression. *A & M Produce Co. v. FMC Corporation*, 135 Cal. App. 3d 473, 486 (1982). " 'Oppression' arises from an inequality of bargaining power which results in no real negotiation and 'an absence of meaningful choice.' " *Id.* at 486. This has been referred to as the procedural aspect of unconscionability.

Unconscionability also has a substantive aspect. In *A & M Produce Co.*, the Court stated:

Commercial practicalities dictate that unbargained-for terms only be denied enforcement where they are also *substantively* unreasonable. No precise definition of substantive unconscionability can be proffered. Cases have talked in terms of "overly harsh" or "one-sided" results. One commentator has pointed out, however, that "unconscionability" turns not only on a "one-sided" result, but also on an absence of "justification" for

> it, which is only to say substantive unconscionability must be evaluated as of the time the contract was made. The most detailed and specific commentaries observed that a contract is largely an allocation of risks between the parties, and therefore that a contractual term is substantively suspect if it reallocates the risks of the bargain in an objectively unreasonable or unexpected manner. But not all unreasonable risk allocations are unconscionable; rather, enforceability of the clause is tied to the procedural aspects of unconscionability such that the greater the unfair surprise or inequality of bargaining power, the less unreasonable the risk allocation which will be tolerated.

*Burbank v. McIntyre*, 135 Cal.App. at 487.

*4. Unconscionability—All or Any Provision of the Contract*

There is no question that the law relating to the doctrine of unconscionability permits a court to strike down an entire contract or any provision thereof. Indeed, Civil Code section 1670.5 so provides. *See also Perdue v. Crocker National Bank*, 38 Cal. 3d 913, 925–26 (1985).

Paramount, while apparently recognizing the above quoted law, argues that it would be impermissible to apply the unconscionability doctrine to this case. As the court understands it, Paramount's argument has two prongs. First, Paramount argues that a court may strike an unconscionable clause of a contract only where that clause is "divisible." Paramount contends that in the present case, plaintiffs are impermissibly attacking "financially interrelated provisions" and demanding "an individual defense of each." Second, relying on a number of so-called "price" cases, Paramount argues that "profitability is not relevant to unconscionability."

Addressing the last argument first, it is apparent that the events that occurred at the November 8, 1990, hearing in this case have rendered Paramount's second argument moot. A little discussion of the history of this case is required in order to validate this conclusion.

In many documents filed with the court prior to November 8, 1990, Paramount argued that its net profit formula was justified, and indeed required, in order to permit it to remain in business. For example . . . in its 7/24/90 Memo Paramount stated:

> As forty years of studio-talent bargaining has established, a studio is entitled to a return commensurate with the risks of movie-making. Otherwise, it could not remain a viable business. There is nothing unfair or unreasonable about how the "Net Profits" formula strikes this balance. . . .
>
> The level of return allowed to Paramount under its "Net Profits" formula is more than offset by the risks that the studio

> alone takes. As plaintiffs' experts readily conceded, "Net Profits" participants bear no risk; if a film flops, participants have no obligation to take up the shortfall and their up-front fee is guaranteed.
>
> In contrast, the studio's risks are enormous. When it signed the Buchwald and Bernheim contracts, Paramount assumed the risk that, despite substantial script development costs (nearly $500,000), the picture might never be made and that, even if made, the picture would not make money. Paramount spent $40 million to produce *Coming to America* and committed another $35 million to an advertising and a promotional campaign with no assurance that a single theater admission would be sold.
>
> The risk of failure in the motion picture business is ever-present, immense, and unmitigable. . . .

The Court interpreted the above quoted statements of Paramount, and many others like them, to mean that Paramount was attempting to justify its net profit formula on the ground that this formula was necessary for Paramount's survival. Indeed, when Paramount's counsel stated, "[o]therwise it could not remain a viable business," the Court understood Paramount to mean what its counsel had stated.

It was because Paramount argued that its net profit definition was justified by the exigencies of the film industry that the court decided to appoint its own accounting expert, pursuant to Evidence Code section 730. Indeed, the November 8, 1990, hearing was scheduled for the specific purpose of defining the tasks to be performed by the court's expert. This would have included, of course, an examination of Paramount's books and records to determine the accuracy of Paramount's representation with respect to its profitability, the number of films that make and lose money, and whether it was necessary for successful films to subsidize unsuccessful films.[5] Remarkably, it was at this same hearing that counsel for Paramount abandoned the argument that Paramount's net profit formula was required by the nature of the motion picture business. Paramount's abandonment of its "justification" argument rendered inquiry into Paramount's profitability moot and the appointment of the court's expert unnecessary. This abandonment also renders inapplicable

[5] So long as Paramount maintained its net profit formula was justified by the nature of the motion picture industry, the court felt an inquiry into Paramount's profitability was necessary and proper. In effect, Paramount was arguing that the formula properly allocated the risks between Paramount and Bernheim, because it bore substantially all of the risk. The court reasoned that if Paramount's representations as to its profitability were untrue, i.e., if it really ran no meaningful risk because of its profit structure, then its argument would fall by its own force. The court concluded it was required to engage in this analysis because "[a] contract is largely an allocation of risks between parties, and therefore . . . a contractual term is substantially suspect if it reallocates the risks of the bargain in an objectively unreasonable or unexpected manner." 135 Cal. App.3d at 487.

the so-called "price" cases relied upon by Paramount. These "price" cases were submitted to the Court, according to Paramount, to establish the point that "profitability is not relevant to unconscionability." Since Paramount no longer seeks to defend its net profit formula on the ground it is justified by the nature of its business, it is clear Paramount's profitability is irrelevant to the determination of whether the contract involved in this case is unconscionable.

As indicated above, Paramount also argues that the court may not strike down all or any portion of the net profit definition because that definition is part of the entire compensation package between Paramount and Bernheim. Paramount further argues that it would not have paid Bernheim as much "up-front" money if it had known many of the components of the net profit formula would be invalidated, and that Bernheim will reap a windfall if the court finds unconscionable portions of the net profit formula.

Paramount's argument is based on the proposition that the dispute between the parties is one over price. The court is not convinced that this is the case. However, even if Paramount is correct, it is "clear that the price term, like any other term in a contract, may be unconscionable." *Perdue*, supra, at 926. In fact, in *Perdue* the Court stated:

> The courts look to the basis and justification for the price, including "the price actually being paid by . . . other similarly situated consumers in a similar transaction." The cases, however, do not support defendant's contention that a price equal to the market price cannot be held unconscionable. While it is unlikely that a court would find a price set by a freely competitive market to be unconscionable, the market price set by an oligopoly should not be immune from scrutiny. Thus courts consider not only the market price, but also the cost of the goods or services to the seller, the inconvenience imposed on the seller, and the true value of the product or service.

38 Cal.3d at 926–27.

In the present case, the court has already found the Bernheim-Paramount contract to be adhesive. Moreover, it is clear, as the court has already found, that contractual relations between certain talent and studios, at least talent such as Bernheim who lack the "clout" of major stars, do not take place in a freely competitive market. Rather, it is clear that if a talent such as Bernheim wishes to work in the film industry, he must do so on terms substantially dictated by the studio. This is particularly true with respect to the net profit formula contained in the contract involved in this case. As previously indicated, Paramount simply does not negotiate with respect to its net profit formula with talent such as Bernheim.

* * *

Moreover, Paramount's argument that net profits represented a relatively insignificant part of Bernheim's total compensation package flies in the face of other evidence in the record. For example, in his Supplemental Declaration, Carmen Desiderio, Paramount's Vice-President of Contract Accounting, testified that Paramount had paid more than $150 million in net profits over the past 15 years, using the net profit formula contained in Bernheim's contact, or one similar to it. Additionally, Paramount itself admitted that " 'Net Profits' are a valuable form of contingent compensation, not the 'cruel hoax' that plaintiffs insinuate." Indeed, Paramount's "turnaround" provision provides for Paramount to receive net profits in the event Bernheim was successful in convincing another studio to make a film based on Buchwald's treatment.

Further, the doctrine of unconscionability would be rendered nugatory if a contracting party could escape its application by negotiating some monetary provisions, while at the same time imposing unjustifiably onerous provisions with respect to other contract provisions.

[The judge concluded that the following provisions of the Paramount contract were unconscionable.]

* * *

1. Fifteen Percent Overhead on Eddie Murphy Productions Operational Allowance. The court finds this provision unconscionable because an additional 15 percent charge is made for overhead "on top of" this item. In effect, this results in charging overhead on overhead. The court is able to perceive no justification for this obviously one-sided double charge and Paramount has offered none.
2. Ten Percent Advertising Overhead Not in Proportion to Actual Costs. This flat overhead charge, which has no relation to actual costs, adds significantly to the amount that must be recouped by Paramount before the picture will realize net profits. Again, the court is able to discern no justification for this flat charge and Paramount has offered none.
3. Fifteen Percent Overhead Not in Proportion to Actual Costs. Paramount's charge of a flat 15 percent for overhead yields huge profits, even though the overhead charges do not even remotely correspond to the actual costs incurred by Paramount. In this connection it should be observed that although Paramount originally contended that this charge was justified because "winners must pay for losers" this

justification was abandoned by Paramount during the November 8, 1990 hearing held in this case.

4. Charging Interest on Negative Cost Balance Without Credit for Distribution Fees. Paramount accounts for income on a cash basis, while simultaneously accounting for cost on an accrual basis. This slows down the recoupment of negative costs and inflates the amount of interest charged. The court finds this practice to be "one-sided" in the absence of a justification for the practice.

5. Charging Interest on Overhead. Paramount receives revenues in the form of distribution fees and overhead charges, neither of which are taken into account in determining whether costs have been recouped. This results in "interest" becoming an additional source of unjustified profit. The court finds this practice to be "overly harsh" and "one sided," and thus unconscionable.

6. Charging Interest on Profit Participation Payments. Paramount charges the payments made to gross participants to negative costs. In fact, these payments are not paid until the film has derived receipts. Accordingly, Paramount has not in any real sense advanced this money. Nevertheless, Paramount charges interest on gross participation shares. This is unconscionable.

7. Charging an Interest Rate Not in Proportion to the Actual Cost of Funds. Paramount charges an interest rate which can be as much as 20 to 30 percent, even when no funds have been laid out by Paramount. This is a one-sided, and thus unconscionable, provision. In sum, the court concludes that the foregoing provisions of Paramount's net profit formula are unconscionable.

* * *

---

The court made affirmative findings about the unconscionability of only seven of the seventeen contract items that Buchwald challenged. Judge Schneider believed that once several significant features of the net profits formula had been struck down, he had discretion to fashion an equitable result for the plaintiffs' claim. The judge rejected the idea that plaintiffs should simply receive the same 19 percent share of net profits specified in the original contract, but now applied to an expanded profit base after the "unconscionable" deductions had been struck from the contract formula. This, the judge felt, would give plaintiffs a windfall profit far beyond what they contemplated when the contract was being negotiated. Thus, calculation of the actual damages due the plaintiffs was deferred to a third phase of the trial. The plaintiffs sought a total of $6.2 million, Paramount contended that the maximum recovery should be $430,000, and the final awards were $150,000 (Buchwald) and $750,000 (Bernheim), plus interest. Paramount appealed but then settled, paying Buchwald and Bernheim slightly over $1 million.

Another major suit involved *The Lord of the Rings*. By 2004, this trilogy grossed more than $13 billion worldwide from all sources; its first installment, *The Fellowship of the Ring's* $900 million in world theater revenues has made it the fifth-highest grossing film at the time. Director Peter Jackson's Wingnut Film company had entered into a deal with Time Warner's New Line Cinema to make movies out of author J.R.R. Tolkien's books. Jackson felt compelled to sue the studio because of its treatment of revenues and profits contractually shared with its director.

Movie studios use two different methods of accounting for their films' profits. The first is the standard Wall Street accounting required for shareholders; the second is the Hollywood-style accounting observed in *Buchwald* for calculating performer shares of profits. The starting point for both is the same: how much did the movie actually generate in revenues from consumers? Revenue sources include viewing in theaters, on video, cable, over-the-air television, the legal Internet, plus merchandising and other vehicles. Hollywood movies often earn more money from foreign rather than domestic viewing. Of course, the studio actually receives only a part of the gross revenues generated by a film. Slightly over half the total box office admissions and nearly two-thirds of video sales and rentals are retained by the movie theaters or video vendors to run their operations. Ninety percent or more of merchandise sales are retained by the manufacturers, wholesalers, and retailers of the goods.

To calculate the true profits from a film, one must then deduct the actual costs incurred. The largest such item is labeled the "negative cost"—what it takes to produce the first completed print of the movie. This now averages over $60 million per film, though that average disguises the huge range from the $210 million to make *Titanic* in 1997 to the $100,000 to make *The Blair Witch Project* in 1999. The next biggest item is distribution, averaging about $25 million and growing, given the need for major advertising campaigns for movies being released around the world. Besides these variable costs for each movie, the studios have fixed overhead costs that must be assigned (via some formula) across the various movies that studio personnel handle. Finally, the cost of money is an important item. The average movie requires an up-front investment of $85 million to get into theaters on its first weekend release, while the studio's receipts will be flowing in for years. So studio interest costs have to be factored into the calculation.

As we have seen, the judge's opinion focused on items like the studio's overhead and interest rates, but in estimating the variation between standard shareholder accounting and performer "net profits" accounting, these items are dwarfed by two other factors. One is that after its actual distribution *costs*, the studio also charged a 30-percent distribution *fee*—in effect, the studio's gross profit participation rate. The second is the fact that studios exclude from a movie's revenues 80 percent of the money the studio receives from video viewing (and the 20 percent counted as video royalties are themselves charged the studio's 30-percent distribution fee).

In standard accounting terms, the money excluded via these distribution and video revenue factors would certainly be included in the net earnings made by the studio from a particular movie. Of course, some movies will lose money even without these deductions. If in a given year a studio has more money-losers than winners, its overall books may show a net loss to shareholders. The standard rationale offered, then, for the net profits formula is that the large economic risks that studios shoulder in making a film requires that they be able to exclude much of the profit attributable to hits in order to be able to cover the losses from the busts. In perhaps the most crucial decision made in the *Buchwald* trial, counsel for Paramount dropped this line of argument, rather than allow the judge and opposing counsel to inspect the studio books on other films. Why do you think that was done? What are its implications for the broader fate of the net profits formula?

### *QUESTIONS FOR DISCUSSION*

1. The unconscionability doctrine is further addressed in Chapter 11, Section D. A seminal decision in this area is *Williams v. Walker-Thomas Furniture*, 350 F.2d 445 (D.C. Cir. 1965), whose standard for unconscionability is the "absence of *meaningful choice* on the part of one of the parties together with contract terms which are *inherently favorable* to the other party." When applying that doctrine in cases of consumers, courts will not permit automobile dealers (*Henningsen v. Bloomfield Motors*, 32 N.J. 358, 161 A.2d 69 (1960)), or medical centers (*Tunkl v. Regents of the Univ. of Cal.*, 60 Cal.2d 92, 32 Cal. Rptr. 33, 383 P.2d 441 (1963)), to extract liability waivers from even fully-informed customers or patients. An important question raised by *Buchwald* is whether movie producers or performers should enjoy that level of protection. Buchwald and Bernheim were both represented by top agencies, and those agents were able to negotiate a number of changes in the original contract drafted by Paramount, including addition of the net profit clause itself. While Paramount would not permit any alteration in its net profits formula, the contract did promise Buchwald and Bernheim more than a quarter of a million dollars if their story idea was made into a movie. What significance (if any) should we attach to these

negotiations in appraising the way the studio formula calculated the profits from *Coming to America*?

2. Net profit sharing has long been part of Hollywood contracts. Indeed, Al Jolson, the star of *The Jazz Singer*, the first-ever movie with sound, had negotiated for a share of the profits. In the early 1950s, when Hollywood was turning from long-term relationships to contracts for single film projects, Jimmy Stewart, through his MCA agent Lew Wasserman, negotiated such terms for several of his films. (Stewart's contract gave him a percentage of the movie's actual profits, but only after the studio had recovered *double* its production costs.) The practice had expanded by the 1970s, and the studios developed their current elaborate formula. *Buchwald* was not the first assault on Hollywood's formula (it was the first to produce a court opinion). In 1983, for example, James Garner sued Universal City Studios because he had not received a penny of the 37.5 percent of net profits he was supposed to get for starring in *The Rockford Files*, for which he had taken a reduced salary. *Rockford* was a top-rated NBC series, but even by 1988, when the show had earned a total of $120 million from network and syndication fees, Universal's books still had *Rockford* in the red. Not only were there $58 million in production costs and $15 million in syndication expenses (including studio overhead), but Universal also charged *Rockford* $33 million for its 40 percent syndication-distribution fee and another $16 million in accumulated interest on the 1970s production costs. The *Rockford* suit was settled in 1989 for a reported $10 million payment by Universal to Garner.

3. In 1994, a different California judge ruled that the net profits formula used by Warner Bros. was *not* unconscionable. The plaintiffs, two independent producers who had obtained options for the movie rights to the Batman comic book characters, were entitled under their contract to receive an upfront fee ($400,000) as well as 13 percent of the net profits of any Batman movies that were made. The judge noted that although the first Batman movie had generated over $1 billion in revenues, more than any other Warner Bros. movie, it had not generated any net profits as contemplated by the contract. Still, he found against the plaintiffs.

The following passage displays the judge's underlying philosophy about this type of claim:

> At the core of plaintiffs' case is their argument that the contract was not fair to them because Warner Bros. and others earned millions of dollars on *Batman* and plaintiffs did not. The answer to that argument is that ever since the King's Bench decided *Slade's Case* in 1602, right down to today, courts do not refuse to enforce contracts or remake contracts for the parties because the court or the jury thinks that the contract is not fair.
>
> That principle is not some medieval anachronism. This society, this country, this culture operates on the basis of billions of bargains struck willingly every day by people all across the country

> in all walks of life. And if any one of those people could have their bargain reexamined after the fact on the ground that it was not fair or on an assertion that it was not fair, we would have a far different type of society than we have now; we would have one that none of the parties to this case would like very much.
>
> When one talks about a motion picture and the claims of this type that are made, they all have one thing in common: the plaintiff comes in and says, "Without me, they would have had nothing, and look how they treated me." But the process of making a motion picture consists of the process of bargaining with many talented people on many different and inconsistent bases, and making bargains with them that cannot rationally be compared one to another. It would not be good for the motion picture business or for the parties to this case if any one of those people on any motion picture could come back and ask a court to remake the bargain that he made on the ground that he now asserts, after the fact and in light of the success of the picture, that he was not fairly treated in comparison with others.

*Batfilm Productions v. Warner Bros.,* Nos. BC 051653 & 051654, 16 Ent. Law Rep. 3 (L.A. County 1994). The judge conceded that contracts that went beyond unfairness to "shock the conscience" because they were "harsh, oppressive and unduly one-sided," would be unconscionable and thus unenforceable. For a number of reasons, though, he concluded that plaintiffs had not met that standard. One reason was their lack of surprise at the specific contract terms. One of the plaintiffs was former general counsel at MGM and thus "knew all the tricks of the trade," particularly that net profits might have no relation to real profits. Next, as to particular provisions to which the plaintiffs objected, the judge ruled that while he was entitled to strike only certain provisions of the contract if he found them unconscionable, he need not do so. He said it was unimportant that specific item charges by Warner Bros. had no real relationship to actual charges. The test must be "whether the production and advertising overheads charged by using the percentage allocations are, in total, unconscionably higher than Warner Bros.' actual production and advertising overhead costs on a motion picture." Finally, the judge offered that while there might indeed be a profit embedded within Warner's distribution fees, the plaintiffs had not proven the amount of it, nor that it prevented the movie from showing a net profit. The case was eventually settled during the appeal process, with Warner paying an undisclosed amount.

4. In appraising these conflicting rulings, consider why the standard net profits clause contains specific features that apparently are so egregious that neither Paramount nor Warner Bros. defended their accounting accuracy. Why have the major talent agencies like William Morris or Creative Artists Agency been unable to clean up these clauses in negotiations with studios?

Consider that a contract of adhesion involves not just a "take it or leave it" deal, but also an oligopolistic relevant market, offering few or no alternatives. Why is the presence of a half dozen majors competing in the movie market insufficient to assure that the return from performers' contracts will reflect fair market value for their services?

---

The answer to that last question might have been disclosed by a lawsuit, *Estate of Jim Garrison v. Warner Bros.*, filed on behalf of Jim Garrison, the late New Orleans district attorney who conducted an investigation to try to uncover a supposed conspiracy behind the assassination of President John F. Kennedy. Oliver Stone and Warner turned Garrison's book-length account of his crusade, *On the Trail of the Assassin*, into a 1991 hit movie hit, *JFK*. Besides getting to see himself portrayed by Kevin Costner, Garrison got a promise from Warner for a share of the net profits earned by *JFK*. Although *JFK* had grossed over $200 million at the box office, Garrison's estate saw no payouts from the net profits clause.

What was special about their lawsuit was that it involved not just Garrison, but all of the movie industry "talent" in a class action against all of the major studios and the MPAA, challenging "standard net profit contracts" signed since 1988. The claim was that the seven major studios, whose films account for 90 percent of box office revenues, conspired to develop and adhere to the formula. Thus, besides contract claims of unconscionability and lack of good faith and fair dealing, Garrison also charged the industry with price fixing and boycotts in violation of the federal Sherman Antitrust Act and California's Business and Professions Act (the Cartwright Act).

The *Garrison* case was settled in 1999, after the court denied class action certification. The judge was persuaded by the studios that "since upfront compensation, which varies in amount from class member to class member, is individually negotiated by all the class members in addition to the net profits clauses," class action treatment would be inappropriate. Assuming that there are significant market power problems in Hollywood, is the best course for artists to ask courts to alter contracts on an individual basis, to launch an antitrust attack, or to build labor organization to give performers countervailing power? The entertainment industry experiences with labor and antitrust law are the subjects of Chapters 11 and 12.

Needless to say, the terms of a contract secured by Jim Garrison do not resemble those negotiated by a writer like Michael Crichton, author whose derivative works include *Jurassic Park* and *ER*. Crichton's representative, Michael Ovitz, negotiated a precedent-setting deal with Paramount Pictures for the rights to Crichton's novel, *Timeline*. Together with another Ovitz client, director Richard Donner (*Lethal Weapon*), this team secured a package deal from Paramount that offers them an up-front payment of $1 million, and 15% of the "*first dollar gross*" from a *Timeline* movie. Do you think that Dan Brown should have followed that same path with his bestseller, *The Da Vinci Code*?

While there can be a major payoff from a "gross receipts" formula, there can be some risks, especially on the television side. Just as the bulk of movie earnings come from home video, in television most earnings come from syndication rights for replay on cable channels and local stations. But movie studios like Disney, 20th Century Fox, and Paramount are tied to the major networks of ABC, Fox, and CBS. Syndication deals made within these conglomerates have thus generated lawsuits by the creators of *Home Improvement* and *NYPD Blue* and the stars of *The X-Files* and *M*A*S*H*.

In 1997, Wind Dancer Production Group sued Disney/ABC regarding the television hit *Home Improvement*. In 1989, Wind Dancer reached an agreement with Disney Television to develop a new television series that Disney would finance and distribute. The Wind Dancer partners were to be paid up-front writer-producer fees and a share of the profits. Wind Dancer presented Disney with their plan for a *Home Improvement* comedy starring Tim Allen, and Disney accepted. *Home Improvement* became a long-running hit.

When negotiations for *Home Improvement*'s 1996–97 season were taking place, *Seinfeld* had secured a lucrative deal, and Wind Dancer wanted the same thing for their show. Disney/ABC negotiated a deal for *Home Improvement*'s seventh and eighth seasons at $3 million per episode. While this was a significant increase, it was substantially less than Wind Dancer believed it was actually worth. Indeed, the makers of *Frasier* had just secured a renewal of their contract at $3.25 million per episode, even though *Frasier*'s ratings were 30 percent lower than *Home Improvement*'s.

Wind Dancer pressed their counterparts at Disney Television to offer *Home Improvement* to other networks to seek the highest bidder. When Disney refused, Wind Dancer offered $4 million an episode for exclusive rights, which they could then offer to ABC's competitors (including UPN and WB, which had just come onto the television scene). When that offer was rejected, Wind Dancer filed suit, claiming breach of contract by Disney Television for failing to negotiate "in good faith and at arm's length with ABC," and tortious interference with that contract obligation by parent Walt Disney Company to secure a "sweetheart deal" for its struggling network. The case eventually was settled.

The underlying issue thus remained unresolved. The plaintiff's attorney, Stanton Stein, had filed a similar suit on behalf of Alan Alda,

Hawkeye on the 1970's hit, *M*A*S*H**, when the show's original producer, 20th Century Fox, sold syndication rights in the 1990's to Fox cable at allegedly below-market rates. While Alda's suit was also settled in 1999, the lawyer soon filed a third such suit on behalf of David Duchovny, the star of *The X-Files*.

In renewing his contract following the success of *X-Files*, Duchovny not only secured a guaranteed salary of $250,000 per episode, but also a share of gross receipts from future syndication deals. Duchovny believed that the prices secured by the Fox studio from its cable and local station siblings, as well for a book published by its affiliate Harper Collins and international networks such as Fox's Sky Network in the UK and Europe, were so low that they cost him around $25 million as his expected share of a franchise that Newsweek had estimated would be generating $1.5 billion in total revenue. This suit was settled in 2000, with Duchovny agreeing to perform in a small number of future *X-File* episodes, and Fox reportedly agreeing to pay him nearly $30 million for this and his past work. A similar suit was filed against on behalf of Stephen Bochco, producer of *NYPD Blue* for 20th Century Fox, claiming that he earned only $32 million, rather than his expected $48 million, from Fox's internal syndication arrangements.

Consider that Duchovny's agent had negotiated a clause that expressly permitted Fox to make such "end run" deals with its affiliates, but also obligated the studio to "establish fair, just and equitable market prices in such dealings, which shall be created on a reasonable and empirically-justified basis." There is always a significant factual question whether gross revenues secured by hit shows like *Home Improvement* and *NYPD Blue* in syndication deals were improperly discounted within conglomerates when compared to what a *Seinfeld or ER* has extracted from an outside bidder. Should the law consider such private contracts to be a social problem? If so, is the appropriate response an *ex post* jury verdict under contract doctrine or *ex ante* regulation by the FCC?

## 2. CALCULATING THE AMOUNT: MUSIC[g]

A unique feature of the music industry is that creative costs are recouped from the artists themselves. In movies the studio does not assert a right to recoup every cent of its investment before actors and directors get paid. The book publisher, while requiring that royalties cover the advances made to the author, does not require that sales royalties be used to cover the typesetting, galley proofing, manufacture, packaging, or

[g] *See* Donald S. Passman, *All You Need to Know about the Music Business* (Simon & Schuster, 8th ed. 2012); Marc Eliot, *Rockonomics: The Money Behind the Music* (Carol Pub. Group 1993); Jeffrey Brabec & Todd Brabec, *Music, Money, & Success: The Insider's Guide to the Music Industry* (Macmillan Pub., 7th ed. 2011); Lionel S. Sobel, *Recording Artist Royalty Calculations: Why Gold Records Don't Always Yield Fortunes*, 12 Ent. L. Rep. 3 (October 1990).

distribution costs of the book. These are seen as expenses properly borne by the publishing house. In music, however, written into every artist's standard contract are terms that either expressly or effectively result in the band financing the production of its own records. Thus, Hole received less than $400,000 in advance payments and no further royalties from the more than four million in sales of the two hit records they had made in the Nineties for Universal Music Group.

These terms are, of course, negotiable; how negotiable depends upon the comparative desires of the artist to sign with the label and the label to obtain the artist. Stars like Janet Jackson and R.E.M., who translated their market appeal into 1996 recording contracts valued at $70 million and $80 million respectively, can secure contract terms that ensure that they receive a significant share of album revenue. When groups like Metallica and TLC are just beginning their careers, however, they have little choice but to accept the contract terms offered to them by their labels (including the duration features noted in Chapter 7 and the royalty calculation discussed here).

Typically, the path to a major label contract for a new artist begins with a letter of intent, or "deal memo," which states in loose contractual language that the band will sign with the label once a contract has been agreed upon. Many new artists fail to understand the significance of deal memos, which can be legally-binding agreements. These memos obligate the artist to conclude a deal with the label, and prohibit deals with another label without the first label's consent. Consent is usually obtained for a fee; to release the artist, the new label must compensate the old label in cash or by a percentage of the royalties from the artist's subsequent records. Contract buyouts such as these are not uncommon; the enterprising label Sub Pop Records made several million dollars from its release of Nirvana to David Geffen's DGC label. Often, however, the second label will pass on encumbered deals such as this. The artist is left with the deal memo, no term of expiry in sight, and whatever contract terms the label offers.

As mentioned above, the music business has as its foundation the concept of recoupment. The label can be thought of as a bank that loans out money to performers to make records. When one reads about million dollar advances and large recording funds, these are sums that the record company doles out with the expectation that this money will be recouped by the label through the withholding of royalties earned by the artist. The artists do not receive additional money until the royalties have covered the advances. New artists typically are offered a royalty of 11% to 13% of the suggested retail list price (SRLP) of records sold. While a star's new contract might reflect marketplace clout by allowing for periodic escalations of the royalty rate as the albums reach various sales milestones, new artists are in no position to demand this. The initial royalty percentage hardly seems unfair: 13% of $15.98 is over $2.00 per record sold, resulting in well over $200,000 to the artist with sales of only 100,000 copies.

The problem is that significant deductions from the artist's "take" must still be accounted for. The following are fairly typical of standard contract terms.

(i) Actual production costs are recouped from the advance, not just for the master tape but also for the music video, which serves largely as album promotion.

(ii) The artist's royalty rate is what is known as an "all-in" rate, meaning that all those who will be getting royalties are considered "in," as part of the artist's royalty figure. Thus, the record producer, who typically expects a 3% royalty, accounts for part of the percentage, reducing the artist's take to 10% (13% minus 3%) of the SRLP.

(iii) Reasoning that the artists should only earn money on the part of the album to which they contribute, label executives concluded that artists should not garner royalties on the component of the SRLP due to "packaging" costs (including artwork on the album cover); for calculating royalties on the sales of compact discs, the SRLP is reduced by 25% to account for packaging.

(iv) Artists will also only earn royalties on 85% of all distributed records, since the company allows for the use of 15% of shipments as "free goods" for promotional and review purposes, and the artist should only get a royalty on records that are *sold*. These promotional uses range from submissions to music critics and radio stations to special wholesaler campaigns ("Get 3 free with every 20 you buy").

(v) To cover losses due to the breakage of records in shipment, early record labels paid royalties on only 90% of shipments; if the labels were not going to be paid by wholesalers and retailers for broken records, then artists should not be paid either. Even though relatively unbreakable CDs and digital downloads are the principal formats sold today, companies sometimes still pay royalties on only 90% of actual sales.

(vi) Reserves, typically around 35% of royalties due the artist, are also held by the label to cover the contingency of returns by retailers of a poorly selling album. These generally may be held by the label up to a year before they are remitted to the artist, with no interest payable.

(vii) While the artists will make a full 10% (13% minus the producer's 3%) royalty from cassette sales, they will only make "75% of the otherwise applicable rate" for sales of "new configurations," including compact discs, resulting in a compact disc royalty of 7.5% of the SRLP.

(viii) Finally, after all of these deductions by the label, the proportion actually going to the artists is reduced by another 15 to 25% as the commission received by their personal manager.

These factors help explain why TLC's manager, label, and distributor were able to realize an estimated $50 million in profit from the group's hits, "Oooooohhh . . ." and "Crazysexycool," while the artists themselves netted a only $1.2 million. They also shed light on why groups like Metallica joined the suits by the labels against Napster to head off any additional impact on their album sales and royalties.

---

A recurring problem that musicians face is actually documenting how many records are being sold to calculate the royalties owed pursuant to the above contract formula. In 1996, Meat Loaf sued Sony Music, the successor to CBS Records for whom Meat Loaf had recorded three albums, including *Bat Out of Hell.* Meat Loaf claimed that CBS/Sony deliberately under-reported sales, costing him over $14 million in unpaid royalties. Meat Loaf relied on evidence from Billboard's Sound Scan, which tracked record sales for purposes of its Top 40 lists. Meat Loaf also charged the company with undercalculation of royalties at the lower "black vinyl" rate, rather than the higher rates for audio cassette and compact disc rates on which most of his albums were sold. After a preliminary ruling in *Aday v. Sony Music Ent.*, 1997 WL 598410 (S.D.N.Y. 1997), the parties reached a confidential settlement. *See also Weatherly v. Universal Music Pub. Group*, 125 Cal.App.4th 913, 23 Cal. Rptr.3d 157 (2004) (songwriter Jim Weatherly's claim for underpayment of foreign royalties).

---

Record royalties are not the only source of income for musicians. Most musicians earn more from live performances than they do from record deals. With records made for major labels, the artist agrees in the contract to go on tour in support of the new release. The label gives the artist money to cover expenses for the tour, which (especially with sizeable bands) will often earn less revenue than total expenses. Thus, tour support costs, like record production advances, are recouped by contract from royalties for record sales. The same is true of music videos, a key but costly promotional device.

Another important asset for musicians who are also songwriters (presented in Part Two) are returns from the recording and the public performance of their musical compositions. Songwriters are entitled to royalties from anyone whose records include their music. Once the song has been recorded and publicly distributed, then other musicians have the right under the Copyright Act to record cover versions of that song on their own albums. If that compulsory license is used, the songwriter is entitled to a mechanical royalty specified in the statute—now 9.1 cents per song for a five-minute composition. If there is a licensing agreement between songwriter and musician, the rate will be negotiated. In practice, the statutory rate is a ceiling, and the typical fee is 75 percent (or even less) of the statutory rate. This discount helps get the song on another record and generates more mechanical royalties. When the artist making the record is also the songwriter, the recording agreement includes a licensing agreement between the writer-artist and the recording company. As the price of getting the record deal, the contract almost always discounts the rate that will be paid for such a "controlled composition" from the mechanical royalties.

(i) The contract rate is often as low as 50 percent of the statutory rate;

(ii) The denominator is the minimum statutory rate for five-minute songs, irrespective of the actual length of the composition, and the figure is not altered by later Copyright Tribunal adjustments for inflation;

(iii) The rate is paid only on records that are sold by the recording company, not on free goods distributed to radio stations, distributors, or record stores for advertising purposes.

(iv) The record contract sets a maximum price for all songs on the album (usually, ten times 75 percent of the minimum statutory rate). This means that if the album includes songs written by other composers who charge the full statutory rate, the additional amount is deducted from the royalties paid to the musicians for their own "controlled compositions," sometimes reducing these royalties to near zero.

Still, assuming that the record does become a hit, the songwriting artist will also receive substantial compensation for performances of the work on the radio airwaves and other public places. Institutional byproducts of this law are performance rights societies, ASCAP, BMI, and SESAC, which use their "music police" to enforce this right against violators, and grant blanket licenses to use their entire music catalogue to radio stations, clubs, and other venues that want to play music for their own commercial purposes. The net revenues collected by these agencies are disbursed to members based upon surveys of frequency of nationwide play. This money is paid directly to the songwriter even if he is also a recording artist, so the record company does not take contractual deductions from it.

### *QUESTIONS FOR DISCUSSION*

1. How might the reasoning in the *Buchwald* decision affect the music business? Are record royalty computations more or less defensible than net profit calculations by movie studios? How does the *Bonner* court's analysis (in Chapter 7) square with *Buchwald*?

2. How should royalties for satellite radio or webcasting be determined? *See SoundExchange, Inc. v. Librarian of Cong.*, 571 F.3d 1220 (D.C. Cir. 2009); *Intercollegiate Broad. Sys. v. Copyright Royalty Bd.*, 571 F.3d 69 (D.C. Cir. 2009); Andrew Stockment, *Internet Radio: The Case for a Technology Neutral Royalty Standard*, 95 Va. L. Rev. 2129 (2009).

## 3. ENTITLEMENTS TO PAYMENTS

The owner of copyright in a song, novel, photo, painting, or even a three-page treatment for a movie plot has significant rights under copyright law as seen earlier. An idea, once expressed in tangible form, has power. A copyright in something as short and simple as the familiar strains of the "Happy Birthday" song can have significant economic consequences. While sales of sheet music or recordings of that song surely do not amount to much these days, control of the right to perform the song publicly does have value. In fact, copyright in the song "Happy Birthday to You," by Mildred and Patty Smith, had long been owned by the Sengstack family, who earned $1 million a year from it for many years. In 1988, the family sold the copyright to Warner Communications for $28 million.

Royalty payments from copyrights can be complex, due to the multi-party nature of modern business deals. A Second Circuit ruling, *Septembertide Publishing, B.V. v. Stein & Day*, 884 F.2d 675 (2d Cir. 1989), illustrated some of the complications. Best-selling author Harry Patterson wrote books under the pseudonym Jack Higgins, and entered into contracts through his corporation, Septembertide. A contract was negotiated in 1984, for what was to become another success story, *Confessional*. Septembertide granted Stein and Day the publishing rights to *Confessional* in return for a promise of three installment payments of $125,000 each as advances against hardcover royalties. Stein and Day, in turn, granted the paperback rights to New American Library (NAL) in return for a $750,000 advance to be paid in five installments to them. One contract term (of which NAL was aware) provided that Stein and Day would pay Septembertide two-thirds of these NAL installment payments.

In 1985, though, Stein and Day encountered financial difficulties, which led it to borrow $1.2 million from Bookcrafter USA. As a guarantee for that loan, Bookcrafter took a security interest in Stein and Day's tangible and intangible property, including the publisher's contract with NAL for *Confessional.* In 1986, Stein and Day folded while still owing Septembertide one of the installments on its hardcover deal, and while NAL had not yet paid half the paperback installments.

The Second Circuit ruled, first, that Stein and Day's failure to make timely payment of all the money due for the hardcover rights was not sufficiently substantial or willful to justify Septembertide's rescission of the contract as a whole (which would have voided the assignment). The court rejected the analogy to *Frankel v. Stein & Day*, 470 F. Supp. 209 (S.D.N.Y. 1979), in which the same publisher was found to have willfully breached a contract by refusing to pay any royalties to an author who had submitted his book late and had been unruly with the editors. The court relied instead on *Nolan v. Williamson Music, Inc.*, 300 F. Supp. 1311 (S.D.N.Y. 1969), involving a failure to pay nearly three quarters of the royalties owed on Bob Nolan's song, "Tumblin Tumbleweed," in which "oversight, negligence, and less than meticulous bookkeeping" was found not to be willful misconduct justifying termination.

Even though the publishing contract remained in effect, the court held that the triangular relationship between author, hardcover publisher, and paperback publisher made Septembertide the intended third-party beneficiary of the NAL paperback contract. It was true that Septembertide had taken no security interest in the NAL contract for *Confessional* and the monies flowing from NAL were mingled with the other (rapidly declining) Stein and Day funds. However, the author's beneficial interest in those paperback installments limited the scope of the NAL contract rights that Stein and Day could assign to Bookcrafters as security for its loan. While Bookcrafter retained its general security interest vis-a-vis other Stein & Day creditors, its entitlement had to take second place to earnings due the author from his own creative work. As between author and trade creditor, it was up to the latter to "prudently ascertain the actual existence of its collateral before agreeing to take a security interest in it."

---

The *Noonan* decision in the previous chapter concerned a performer's attempt to use bankruptcy law to free himself from future obligations under an executory contract. The following case addresses royalty payments under a contract in which the performer has already done the creative work but the publisher goes bankrupt.

## IN RE WATERSON, BERLIN & SNYDER CO.

United States Court of Appeals, Second Circuit, 1931.
48 F.2d 704.

AUGUSTUS N. HAND, CIRCUIT JUDGE.

The bankrupt was a music publisher. Prior to bankruptcy it had purchased from the petitioner Fain, and others, musical compositions, including words and music, under agreements all of which were identical except as to royalty rates and advance royalties. There were agreements made with twenty-two such composers.

. . . On September 20, 1929, and after the adjudication in bankruptcy which occurred late in August or early in September, 1929, the Irving Trust Company, which had been appointed receiver of Waterson, Berlin & Snyder Company, sent a circular to various persons in the music trade inviting bids before October 1, 1929, for all of the right, title, and interest of the bankrupt estate in the copyrights for the songs free from royalty claims. The circular stated that on October 1, 1929, the receiver proposed to submit the bids for individual songs, including rights to mechanical royalties, to the court for acceptance.

Thereupon Fain and the other composers filed a petition in the District Court alleging that in entering into their contracts they had relied on the reputation and organization of Waterson, Berlin & Snyder Company as leading musical publishers to popularize their publications and to increase sales of the songs, that the bankruptcy of the publishers had disabled them from further performance of the contracts to publish, and that, if the receiver was permitted to sell the compositions and copyrights free from royalty claims, purchasers would publish them without obligation to pay further royalties to the composers, who would thus be deprived of all revenue from their productions. The petitioners prayed for an order directing the receiver or trustee in bankruptcy to reassign the copyrights to them, or, in the alternative, not to sell without provision for the payment of future royalties to the composers, and for other and further relief.

The District Judge, though finding that each agreement involves "a transfer, absolute on its face, in exchange for a covenant by the publisher for the payment of certain agreed royalties," held that the "royalty contracts . . . involve such personal elements of trust and confidence that they are not assignable without the consent of the parties," and that they may "be rescinded by the composers when the publisher, as here, is unable or definitely refuses to fulfill his obligations thereunder." He therefore granted the petition and ordered that the royalty contracts be rescinded and that the trustee in bankruptcy should reassign each copyright to the composer upon the return to the bankrupt estate of any unearned advance royalties paid thereon to such composer.

The trustee has taken this appeal, which raises the questions (1) whether the trustee has a right to sell the copyrights at all; (2) whether, if he has a right to sell them at all, he may sell them free and clear of royalties.

The questions involved are interesting, and few precedents can be found in the American courts that throw direct light on the problems involved. We find difficulty in taking the view adopted by the District Judge, in spite of his interesting and informing opinion, because it disregards the unqualified grant to the publisher, and because it appears to give no weight to the labor, skill, and capital which a publisher expends in putting a song on the market. The expense of maintaining an organization, of building up a business and making it available to the composers of songs, as well as the more direct cost of making plates, advertising, and distributing the songs so as to give them popularity, largely go for nought if a rescission of the contracts be ordered on the sole condition that the composers return unearned advance royalties. Such a disposition seems specially inequitable where in the case of some, if not many, of the songs there are no unearned advances whatever.

In attempting to allow the composers any relief, we are confronted by certain decisions holding that an agreement to pay royalties in exchange for a transfer of title is nothing but an executory contract to pay, enforceable only at law. Bigham, J., in *Re Grant Richards*, [1907] 2 Q.B. 33, held that the trustee in bankruptcy of a publisher, who had purchased the copyright of a book and agreed to pay royalties to the author upon sales, could sell the copyright and was not even liable for royalties upon sales of the publication made by him as trustee. In other words, the relation was held to be that of debtor and creditor and the author was allowed no more than the right to prove his claim against the bankrupt estate. The foregoing decision of Bigham, J., is referred to with approval by Scrutton, L.J., in the Court of Appeal in *Barker v. Stickney*, [1919] K.B. 121, where an author who had sold his copyright under an agreement with the purchaser to pay royalties was held to have no lien upon the copyright in the hands of a subvendee who took title with notice of the original agreement. It was said that "a person acquiring a chose in action is not bound by mere notice of a personal covenant by his predecessor in title."

The foregoing decisions would indicate that the assignor of a copyright has only the right to recover at law for the breach of an agreement to pay royalties, and would have no control over the use of the copyright by his vendee or a subvendee. This rigorous doctrine, attributed to the English courts, is certainly far less satisfactory than that adopted by the court below, for, in case of bankruptcy or insolvency of the purchaser of the copyright, it deprives the author of any substantial remedy, though the consideration he was to receive for parting with his compositions was to depend on royalties accruing from a business during a long period of years. Under such a doctrine rescission could not be had even in the event of a complete failure to publish the songs.

But *In re Grant Richards* and *Barker v. Stickney* do not represent the sole current of English authority regarding the rights of a person in the position of the trustee in the present case.

In *Werderman v. Society Generale d'Electricite*, 19 Ch.D. 246, a patentee had assigned letters patent to A and B, who covenanted with him that they and their assigns would use their best endeavors to introduce the invention by granting licenses or working the patent or by selling it, and that the patentee should be entitled to 5 per cent. of all net profits received by A and B, their executors or assigns, whether arising from royalties, sales, or otherwise . . . A and B had taken the assignment with a view to forming a company to work the patent. The company was formed and the patent made over to them. The patentee sued the company for an account of profits. The company demurred on the ground that there was no privity between it and the plaintiff and that the plaintiff's right, if any, was against A and B only. The Court of Appeal held that the plaintiff could sue the company for an account of profits because the stipulations of the assignment to A and B amounted to a covenant that the owners of the patent for the time being should account for and pay to the plaintiff a share of profits unless a sale within the meaning of the deed was effected, and that no person taking the patent with notice of this contract could refuse to give effect to it. The argument was made that the plaintiff had acquired nothing but the personal obligation of A and B, but Jessel, M.R., said:

> "It is a part of the bargain that the patent shall be worked in a particular way and the profits be disposed of in a particular way, and no one taking with notice of that bargain can avoid the liability."

Lindley, L.J., said that the assignment was "subject to the obligation to account to the plaintiff for his royalty." A difference between the agreement in that case and the contract in the case at bar is that royalties were here to be paid on sales of the songs at so many cents a copy, while in the English contract the royalties were to be based on 5 percent of the net profits. It may accordingly be argued that that decision turned on the covenant to pay a percentage of the net profits and that such a covenant gave the plaintiff an interest in the patent such as Justice Holmes recognized in *Pratt v. Tuttle*, 136 Mass. 233.

But most of the decisions do not regard an agreement to pay a royalty based upon a certain percentage of the profits as creating an equitable ownership in a patent or copyright. . . . The gist of the decision in the *Werderman* case . . . was that one who takes property with notice that it is to be used in a particular way receives it subject to something resembling an equitable servitude.

In the case at bar there was an agreement to pay "33⅓% . . . of all revenue received from Mechanical reproductions less any expenses incurred," as well as to pay one cent upon each copy of the songs sold. Such a provision involved an implied covenant to work the copyright so far as was reasonable under all the circumstances. Under the doctrine of the *Werderman* case any purchaser of the copyrights who took with notice of such a covenant would take them subject to it, and, we believe, also subject to payment of royalties, without which the obligation to work the copyright would be futile . . .

* * *

. . . To allow rescission, the default must be such that it "destroys the essential objects of the contract," *Rosenwasser v. Blyn Shoes, Inc.*, 246 N.Y. at page 346, 159 N.E. 84, 85, or it "must be so fundamental and pervasive as to result in substantial frustration." *Buffalo Builders' Supply Co. v. Reeb*, 247 N.Y. at page 175, 159 N.E. 899, 901.

In our opinion a rescission could only be decreed in the case at bar if there had been a gross failure to work the copyrights, which has nowhere been indicated.

. . . In the case at bar, within a month after August 1, 1929, which was the date when royalty payments became due under the contract, and only about three weeks after the adjudication, the receiver called for bids and attempted to sell the copyrights. Any default in working the copyrights had not been long enough in itself to justify a rescission and the proposed sale cannot be said to have been an act that would "result in substantial frustration" of the composer's rights upon the record before us . . .

It may be that the songs, or some of them, are worth much more than when they were copyrighted, and it is not unlikely that a large part of their value is due to the labor and expense laid out upon them by the bankrupt as entrepreneur. The trustee in bankruptcy ought to be able to retain for the creditors these contributions to the copyrighted songs, as well as any fortuitous increment, if the right of the composers to receive royalties from working the copyrights can be reasonably safeguarded.

Whether or not the copyrights may have become burdened with equities in favor of the composers, their title is in the bankrupt estate. The assignments were absolute, and Waterson, Berlin & Snyder Company would have had no right to take out the copyrights had it not been the "proprietor" within the meaning of the Copyright Act.

In our opinion there is a middle course between the extreme doctrine of *In re Grant Richards* and *Barker v. Stickney*, supra, and the cases which have allowed rescission for failure to work a patent, which we should take in the circumstances here. In view of the absolute terms of the transfer, the presence of the word "assigns" in the instrument of conveyance, and the statutory requirement that one who takes out a copyright must be the "proprietor," we see no reason to imply a covenant that Waterson, Berlin & Snyder Company must itself publish the songs. The composers cannot object if the trustee sells the copyrights.

But it is a different matter to say that the sale of the copyrights should be free from all equities on behalf of the composers. In ordinary circumstances, and between the original parties, it may be that the only remedy of the composers would be an action at law for breach of the promise to pay royalties. Even between the original parties, rescission would be granted at the suit of the composers, if the publisher failed to work the copyrights in good faith, so that they might so far as possible yield royalties and thus afford the measure of compensation agreed upon. But, even where the publisher failed to work the copyrights, it could not be said that there would be actually no remedy at law, for the courts allow actions at law because of failure to observe such implied covenants. The damages for the breach of such a covenant, however, would necessarily be determined by estimates that at best could be no more than speculative substitutes for the definite royalties prescribed by the contracts. Accordingly a court of equity would decree a rescission where the breach was so fundamental as to amount to frustration, because the remedy at law would be inadequate. A restrictive covenant affecting the use is imposed in such cases, and rescission is granted for failure to observe it.

It is true that the royalties on the songs are definitely provided to be paid only "in the event of the publication" by Waterson, Berlin & Snyder Company, but, where the words of assignment of the musical compositions are absolute, it is unreasonable to suppose that there may be no exploitation of the songs, except by Waterson, Berlin & Snyder Company. It seems to us equally unreasonable to suppose that the trustee may sell them free from all rights of the composers and thus deprive the latter of the only means of fixing the royalties which they have been promised. In our opinion, while the copyrights may be sold by the trustee, they should be sold subject to the right of the composers to have them worked in their behalf and to be paid royalties according to the terms of the contracts. . . .

---

In another bankruptcy case, the trustee for the bankrupt estate of country singer George Jones was involved in a dispute with CBS Records over Jones' royalties. CBS sought to recoup money it had advanced Jones from royalties on recordings made prior to the filing of Jones' bankruptcy petition; the trustee claimed that the royalties were property of the estate and that CBS was thus in the same position as any other creditor seeking a set-off of Jones' debt to it. The court agreed that the royalties (as long as confined to recordings made prior to filing) were indeed to be classified as property of the estate for general purposes, but that with regard to this particular case, in which Jones' account was significantly unrecouped as to the advances made him, this property was first subject to CBS's right of recoupment. Thus, if CBS had recouped all its advances from Jones' royalties, royalties from records made prior to filing the petition would go to the estate to help offset Jones' debts. *See Waldschmidt v. CBS, Inc.*, 14 B.R. 309 (M.D. Tenn. 1981).

# CHAPTER 9

# ENTERTAINMENT CONTRACT REMEDIES AND LIABILITIES

■ ■ ■

Because of the highly speculative nature of their business, entertainment firms invest heavily in developing and marketing the various products they create. Although revenues from successful products can be huge, these successes are often offset by expensive flops. In the record industry, for example, labels regularly use earnings from established talent to subsidize the development of new acts and to recoup losses from bands that have failed to generate sales.

Of course, when performers become superstars, they would rather increase their own profits than subsidize the development of successors. In the previous chapters, we encountered a variety of arguments through which parties have tried to secure revision of contract terms, or perhaps even avoid their agreements altogether. The issues are not, however, limited to whether a contract has actually been formed and how to interpret its terms. To determine the value of these rights, it is important to analyze the kinds of remedies that the law offers for contract breaches. As you read this chapter, ask yourself if the law of remedies strikes a sensible balance between the interests of corporations seeking to recoup their investments and performers seeking artistic autonomy and financial leverage.

## A. INJUNCTIVE ENFORCEMENT OF PERSONAL SERVICE CONTRACTS[a]

Entertainment corporations have consistently relied on equitable remedies to prevent artists from evading their contractual obligations. While monetary damages are effective in some situations, it is often difficult to measure the lost profits of a proposed, but unrealized, performance. In cases where monetary damages are considered an inadequate remedy, employers turn instead to "negative injunctions" to prevent their stars from walking.

[a] *See* David F. Partlett, *From Victorian Opera to Rock & Rap: Inducement to Breach of Contract in the Music Industry*, 66 Tul. L. Rev. 771 (1992); Christopher T. Wonnell, *The Contractual Disempowerment of Employees*, 46 Stan. L. Rev. 87 (1993); *see generally* Anthony T. Kronman, *Specific Performance*, 45 U. Chi. L. Rev. 351 (1978); Alan Schwartz, *The Case for Specific Performance*, 89 Yale L.J. 271 (1979).

## 1. GENERAL EQUITY DOCTRINE

It has long been a principle of equity that contracts to perform personal services are not to be specifically enforced. Courts will not compel unwilling employees to continue to provide services to employers. This refusal stems, first, from the inherent difficulty of monitoring and enforcing the compliance of an unwilling party, and, second, from public policy concerns reflected in the Thirteenth Amendment's ban on involuntary servitude. In *ABC, Inc. v. Wolf*, 52 N.Y.2d 394, 438 N.Y.S.2d 482, 420 N.E.2d 363 (1981), the Court quoted a passage from a century-old opinion to illustrate why this policy was necessary:

> The New York Court of Chancery in *De Rivafinoli v. Corsetti,* (4 Paige Ch. 264, 270) eloquently articulated the traditional rationale for refusing affirmative enforcement of personal service contracts: "I am not aware that any officer of this court has that perfect knowledge of the Italian language, or possesses that exquisite sensibility in the auricular nerve which is necessary to understand, and to enjoy with a proper zest, the peculiar beauties of the Italian opera, so fascinating to the fashionable world. There might be some difficulty, therefore, even if the defendant was compelled to sing under the direction and in the presence of a master in chancery, in ascertaining whether he performed his engagement according to its spirit and intent. It would also be very difficult for the master to determine what effect coercion might produce upon the defendant's singing, especially in the livelier airs; although the fear of imprisonment would unquestionably deepen his seriousness in the graver parts of the drama. But one thing at least is certain; his songs will be neither comic, or even semi-serious, while he remains confined in that dismal cage, the debtor's prison of New York."

438 N.Y.S.2d at 485 n. 4, 420 N.E.2d at 366 n. 4.

Nevertheless, beginning with the British case of *Lumley v. Wagner*, 42 Eng. Rep. 687 (1852), courts have been prepared to offer an alternative form of equitable relief. Johanna Wagner, niece of composer Richard Wagner, was Europe's leading opera singer in the mid-19th century. Wagner contracted to perform during the 1852 season at Lumley's Drury Lane opera house. Soon afterwards, Wagner was lured away to sing at Covent Garden in London, in violation of her commitment to Lumley not to perform anywhere else that season. While the court was not prepared to compel the singer to satisfy her promise to work for her employer, it was prepared to enjoin a breach of the negative promise not to work for another party. Indeed, to obtain this remedy, it is not even necessary to have a clause that commits the employee not to offer his services to other parties during an existing contract, so long as the contract or context makes it clear that the services were to be exclusive (i.e., the employee was not supposed to work elsewhere and that such services are not readily replaceable by the employer, even with the help of monetary damages for the contract breach).[b]

In cases where an employee refuses to perform, an employer will usually seek a preliminary injunction to prevent the performer from working for a competitor. To obtain a preliminary injunction, the moving party must demonstrate irreparable harm, as well as a likelihood of eventual success on the merits. As a practical matter, the hearing on the preliminary injunction is much like a mini-trial, with the outcome largely determinative of the ultimate result.

The following case, involving an effort by one Broadway theater to use the services of a star performer under contract to another producer, illustrates the kind of analysis that courts engage in to determine whether such an injunction is appropriate.

## HARRY ROGERS THEATRICAL ENTERPRISES V. COMSTOCK

Supreme Court of New York, Appellate Division, 1928.
225 App. Div. 34, 232 N.Y.S. 1.

FINCH, JUDGE.

* * *

[Harry Rogers], the plaintiff had a [long term] contract with the defendant [performer] Comstock, professionally known as "Billy House." . . . Defendant Shubert and defendant Shubert Theatrical Corporation wished to obtain the services of Comstock for a musical show which was in preparation. Defendant Shubert, together with one Lyons, the booking agent of Shubert, saw Rogers for the purpose of obtaining a release of Comstock or a transfer of Rogers' contract to Shubert. After various negotiations, the proposed deal fell through and then Shubert engaged Comstock. [Rogers sued for an injunction to block Comstock from performing for Shubert, and the latter two offered a number of legal defenses.]

* * *

The third ground of defense urged by the respondents is that there was nothing unique, special or extraordinary about the services of the defendant Comstock, but that said services were ordinary and could easily be replaced. Therefore, urge the respondents, these services fall within the principle that ordinary contracts for personal services are not enforceable in equity and that damages at law afford an adequate

b See generally Douglas Laycock, *The Death of the Irreparable Injury Rule*, 103 Harv. L. Rev. 688 (1990).

remedy. The record is replete with the usual conclusory opinion affidavits, pro and con, alleging and denying the uniqueness of the services. Facts when present, however, are always more persuasive than opinions. In the case at bar the contract whose existence is attacked admits the services of Comstock to be unique and extraordinary. While such recital is not controlling, it reflects upon the affidavit later made by Comstock, when his interest was to the contrary, swearing that his services were not unique. Next we have the uncontroverted fact that the ability of Comstock is regarded as unique upon the Albee—Keith circuit and that a substitute will not be accepted. Hence in this well-known vaudeville office Comstock cannot be replaced. Again, Comstock is now admittedly receiving a salary of $1,000 a week, which, in his work, is very large and compares most favorably with that received by the leaders in the scientific, artistic and political world. In *Winter Garden Co. v. Smith* (282 Fed. 166), where two defendants were to receive a joint salary of $1,100 a week, the Circuit Court of Appeals of the Second Circuit said:

> "When, therefore, actors such as these have been successful for many years because of individual characteristics, and command salaries of a size rarely known in the liberal arts and sciences, their peculiar ability in the field in which they perform is almost res ipsa loquitur."

It seems unnecessary to go further with a recital of facts when the defendant Shubert, who knew Comstock was under a contract with the plaintiff, was willing to risk a law suit and pay $1,000 a week to secure the services of Comstock. The conclusion is, therefore, sustained that defendant Comstock has that personality which denotes the unusual and unique artist and enables him to pick up the attention of an audience and hold it interested, amused or in pathos until released. Where, therefore, the services of the actor are shown to be unusual, unique or extraordinary and that the damage to the plaintiff will be irreparable and unascertainable, the latter may enjoin the performer from appearing elsewhere during the period of his contract and, even though a negative covenant not to appear elsewhere may be lacking, such will be implied and enforced not only against those who are parties to the contract, but also restraining third parties from doing those acts which induce and continue the breach. This has been the law since the well-known early case of *Lumley v. Wagner* (1 DeG., M. & G. 604) and has been repeatedly applied in this court and elsewhere. (*Shubert Theatrical Co. v. Rath*, 271 Fed. 827; *Shubert Theatrical Co. v. Gallagher*, 206 App. Div. 514; *Pom. Spec. Perf.* [3d ed.] § 24.)

It is obvious that a court of equity is governed by principles of law impartially applied to the facts in the particular case and that the facts, when accurately and truthfully ascertained, are alike masters of bench and bar. If the time shall ever come when a court of equity must stand helplessly by while unique and unusual theatrical performers may be induced to breach contracts with impunity, except for such damages as a jury may see fit to award at some distant date, theatrical corporations will find their business hampered by intolerable conditions. . . .

Reversed.

## *QUESTIONS FOR DISCUSSION*

1. The court assumed that damages were an inadequate remedy for Rogers because Comstock's services were unique and irreplaceable, since he was then being paid the *star* salary of $1,000 a week. Suppose, though, that it had become impossible for Comstock to perform: perhaps he had been struck by a drunk driver on Broadway. Could Comstock be replaced in his role? Might the theater be insured against (perhaps even sue the driver for) the loss of the services of its big-name star? Is injunctive relief against performers really is an indispensable remedy for their contract breaches?

2. Section 367(1) of the Restatement (Second) of Contracts states that "[a] promise to render personal services will not be specifically enforced," and § 367(2) says that negative injunctions are not to be issued against employees where the "probable result will be to compel a performance involving personal relations the enforced continuance of which is undesirable, or will be to leave the employee without other reasonable means of making a living." Comment a states that "[i]t is not the purpose in granting the injunction to enforce the [employee's] duty to render the service. . . ." Was that standard satisfied in *Rogers*? Should there be such a limitation upon injunctive relief against breach of employment contracts entered into by (often) high-salaried entertainers? What about Comment c's further qualification that "if the probable result of an injunction will be the employee's performance of the contract, it should appear that the employer is prepared to continue the employment in good faith so that performance will not involve personal relations the enforced continuance of which is undesirable"?

3. Recall material in Chapter 7 relating to the duration of entertainment contracts, particularly in the music industry. In that chapter, the issue was the validity of a contract provision that gave a label the right to have a musician produce recordings only for that company for periods of as much as fifteen to twenty years. Here, the question is whether, even assuming the underlying validity of that commitment (e.g., for purposes of awarding damages), how much relief should be afforded to enforce that contract clause. Apparently, the Thirteenth Amendment ban on "involuntary servitude" is one of the key reasons why courts will not specifically enforce personal service contracts. Should such a policy preclude injunctions to bar George Michael, for example, from recording for anyone other than Sony Music for fifteen years, given that American as well as British courts may be prepared to stop a Johanna Wagner from singing in another opera house just for a single season?

4. In *King Records, Inc. v. Brown*, 21 A.D.2d 593, 252 N.Y.S.2d 988 (1964), singer James Brown violated the exclusivity clause of his contract with King Records by agreeing to record for Fair Deal Records, a label created by Brown and his manager. King Records brought a suit to enjoin Brown from recording for Fair Deal. Brown responded by asking for a stay of court proceedings pending arbitration. Apparently, King Records was party to a collective bargaining agreement with the American Federation of Musicians, which required arbitration of any claim arising from an agreement relating to services of a musician member of the Federation. Citing the general rule that an individual member of a labor union has no right to compel arbitration under a collective labor agreement between a union and an employer, the court denied Brown's motion and granted an injunction restraining Brown from recording for another label. In his dissent, Justice Valente argued that "if an employee is precluded from suing an employer who has a collective agreement with a union, or may not compel the employer to arbitrate, then the employer should be equally barred, in contravention of the collective agreement, from asserting a claim against the employee in an action, where the employer has agreed to arbitrate such disputes with the union. . . . All the employee is asking here is that plaintiff's suit be stayed. He is not demanding that the employer arbitrate the dispute with him."

Whose judgment do you find more persuasive? Recently, courts are increasingly favoring arbitration and other alternative means of dispute resolution (ADR) to work out conflicts within the private sector, particularly where organized labor is involved. Do you think this case would be decided differently today? While labor unions play a major role in the film industry, union representation is much less significant in the record industry. What would the music industry look like if musicians wielded more collective bargaining power?

5. Warner Wolf, a television sportscaster, worked for ABC's New York outlet in the 1970s under a contract that was to expire in 1980. The agreement bound Wolf to negotiate in good faith with ABC about contract extension during the last 90 days of his existing contract—from December 6, 1979 to March 4, 1980. For the first 45 days of this period, the negotiations with ABC were to be exclusive. Following expiry in March 5, 1980 of both the 90-day negotiating period and the existing agreements, Wolf was bound not to accept a sportscasting job with another party without giving ABC a right to match the terms. That right of refusal period would expire on June 3, after which Wolf was free to take a job anywhere else.

Wolf and ABC began negotiating for renewal of their contract, but were some distance apart regarding an increase in Wolf's existing $250,000 salary. Meanwhile, Wolf met with CBS officials in early October, notwithstanding the above restrictions, and the two discussed employment possibilities. By January 1980, ABC executives had decided to agree to Wolf's earlier proposal, but Wolf said they were too late. On February 1, just after ABC's exclusivity period had expired, Wolf orally agreed to move to CBS's New York affiliate for more than $400,000 a year. He signed a production agreement with CBS for "sports specials," whereby he agreed, as of March 6, 1990, not to work for anyone else without CBS's consent, and CBS agreed to hold open for Wolf an offer of employment as a sportscaster until June 4, 1980 (when Wolf would be free of ABC's right of first refusal). Wolf wrote ABC a letter of resignation, effective March 5th.

Wolf did continue to talk with ABC officials about their offers, and the station kept him on the air until the end of May. However, once Wolf had moved to CBS in June and ABC learned of their prior dealings, ABC sued for specific enforcement of its right of first refusal and for an injunction to bar Wolf from working for CBS. Did Wolf violate his contract with ABC? Should ABC be entitled to injunctive relief, and if so, for how long? *See ABC, Inc. v. Wolf*, 52 N.Y.2d 394, 438 N.Y.S.2d 482, 420 N.E.2d 363 (1981).

6. The entertainment industry has long banked on its ability to prevent stars from walking. The courts, however, have been reluctant to issue negative injunctions that may be unduly harsh or burdensome. In weighing the equities, courts generally consider the following factors.

A. *Uniqueness*. To warrant an injunction, the services must be unique or extraordinary. How should courts make this determination? At some level, do not all paid entertainment performers have unique talents? Or, is anyone other than a "superstar" irreplaceable? Courts have held that a showing of some difficulty in finding a substitute performer of similar talents is sufficient. Does this imply that the uniqueness requirement is outdated?

B. *Irreparable Injury*. The reason for the emphasis on the uniqueness is that the producer's injury from loss of these services is not to be reparable by the standard remedy of monetary damages. Recall the question posed earlier about whether studios, networks, or Broadway producers can secure insurance for loss of their key performers. Should the availability of such financial redress influence the court's judgment about whether to grant injunctive relief against the performers? On the other hand, even if an award of damages can be secured from a jury for an entertainer's breach of contract (as happened to Kim Basinger in Chapter 7), are these damages always collectible? *See* Restatement (Second) of Contracts § 360 (c).

C. *Undue Restraint*. Here, the court looks to the length of time the injunction is to run, the type of work at issue, the geographic area in which the performer may not seek employment, and the likelihood that the injunction will achieve its intended purpose, rather than simply punish the employee. Courts generally do not allow an employer both to suspend a performer and to restrain the performer from working elsewhere. However, a distinctive feature of entertainment (as contrasted with executive) contracts is that the former involve artistic expression, which performers like Neil Young or Michelle Shocked claim is stifled more by corporate than government restraints. Should artists be permitted to escape such restraints if, but only if, they are prepared to pay their current employer all the financial benefits they expect to receive under a new contract?

D. *Investment in Talent.* A recurring theme in claims for injunctive relief is the investment made by the company in the development and promotion of a performer. For example, in *ABC v. Wolf*, ABC pointed out that it brought Warner Wolf to the New York City sportscasting market and sought to "enhance his popularity by featuring, advertising, and otherwise promoting him"; thus Wolf and CBS should not be permitted to realize the benefits from this investment. Is it a sufficient response to this line of argument that performers seeking to move might reimburse their former employer for the actual investments it made in their talent development?

E. *Competitive Impact.* Courts have occasionally ruled that injunctions should not be available unless the performer is moving to a competitor, and thus not only depriving the original employer of its return but also inflicting additional losses from more intense competition. *See J. Walter Thompson Co. v. Winchell*, 244 App. Div. 195, 278 N.Y.S. 781 (1935). In the *Wagner* case, for example, the court emphasized that the opera singer was going to perform at another opera house in London, rather than in Paris or New York. With the advent of the Internet, would such a doctrinal requirement place any significant restrictions on injunctive relief?

7. What remedies can be used against a company that induces the performer's breach? While there is a long-established tort action against outsiders who interfere with contracts, one decision, *Roulette Records v. Princess Production Corp.*, 15 A.D.2d 335, 224 N.Y.S.2d 204 (1962), *aff'd*, 12 N.Y.2d 815, 236 N.Y.S.2d 65, 187 N.E.2d 132 (1962), adopts a narrow interpretation of the circumstances that constitute actionable interference, requiring *actual knowledge* of the prior contract. After entering into an exclusive contract with Roulette, renowned jazz singer Sarah Vaughan recorded two songs for a movie soundtrack entitled *Murder Inc.*, produced by Princess Productions. In Roulette's suit against Princess, the trial judge awarded both damages and an injunction against the production and sale of *Murder Inc.* However, the appellate court reversed. Although Vaughan's signing to Roulette had been announced in trade publications, the court held that while proof of actual knowledge could be predicated on circumstantial evidence, "this record does not demonstrate it." In his dissent, Justice Steuer argued that the circumstances before the court were adequate to imply knowledge:

> There is quite a distinction between a negligent failure to know and a deliberate intent to stay in ignorance of what one

> suspects. . . . [I]t was proved that news of the contract was published in two trade papers, attesting to the general interest of such an occurrence in the milieu in which these people operated. It was also established through the testimony of defendant's own expert that the practice was to inquire of the performer, before using him to make a record, whether the performer had existing contractual commitments. . . . [I]t was certainly a reasonable conclusion for the trier of fact to draw that the failure of the defendants to inquire was due to a desire not to be told. If this is not the equivalent of knowledge, it would seem to be an extremely technical exception in the law, as well as one without any basis in policy.

*Id.* at 209. Which side do you find more persuasive? Would the case come out differently today?

---

Performers, of course, are not the only parties who can violate personal service contracts. Suppose a movie or theater producer replaces an actor in violation of the latter's contract rights. Should the actor be able to enjoin production of the film or play? That was an issue posed in a case from Broadway, *Gennaro v. Rosenfield*, 600 F. Supp. 485 (S.D.N.Y. 1984).

Maurice Rosenfeld, a theatrical producer, acquired the right to adapt for stage performance Gene Kelly's famous movie from the 1950s, *Singin' in the Rain*. Rosenfeld in turn licensed rights for a London production to Harold Fielding. To help create his theatrical version, Fielding wanted to use choreographer Peter Gennaro, whose prior work included such Broadway hits as *The Unsinkable Molly Brown* and *Annie*.

Gennaro was prepared to work on the London production, but only if he also choreographed the Broadway version. Fielding secured Rosenfeld's agreement to use Gennaro if the London production met certain "hit" standards, which it easily did. However, Rosenfeld changed his plans and hired someone else to do the Broadway choreography. Gennaro sued for breach of contract, seeking an injunction to block *Singin' in the Rain* from coming to Broadway without his creative efforts.

There were sufficient complications in the dealings between Rosenfeld, Fielding, and Gennaro (and their representatives) to create doubt in the judge's mind about whether a binding personal services contract had been entered into by Rosenfeld with Gennaro. Assume the facts were such as to give Gennaro as conclusive a case on the merits. Should a performer be able to block the producer using a replacement in his role, as the producer is able to enjoin the performer from playing in a replacement production? Are there significant factors that support different approaches to the injunction issue? What about the interests of other parties that might be affected by the decision to grant an injunction against the producer?

## 2. CALIFORNIA INJUNCTION LEGISLATION[c]

The *Rogers*, *Brown*, and *Wolf* cases evidence the remedial approach fashioned by courts for enforcement of personal service contracts. Early in this century, the California state legislature placed statutory constraints on injunctions against performers. Historically known as the "$6,000 per year statute," California Code of Civil Procedure § 526 and Civil Code § 3423 long provided that in order to sustain a claim for injunctive relief, a contract must: 1) be in writing; 2) encompass unique and extraordinary services; and 3) guarantee minimum compensation of at least $6,000 per year. As we will see, this legislation was significantly revised in the 1993–94 legislative term. Nevertheless, case law interpreting the statute remains fundamental to understanding the law of entertainment service contracts in California.

### MOTOWN RECORD CORP. V. TINA MARIE BROCKERT

Court of Appeal of California, Second Appellate District, 1984.
160 Cal.App.3d 123, 207 Cal. Rptr. 574.

JOHNSON, JUDGE.

[In 1976, Tina Marie Brockert, known professionally as "Teena Marie," entered into exclusive contracts as a recording artist and songwriter with Motown Records and its publishing arm Jobete. Motown was a tiny label founded in Detroit in 1959 by an autoworker, Berry Gordy. Gordy's label soared when he launched Diana Ross and the Supremes, the Jackson Five, and Stevie Wonder. Before Motown signed up Teena Marie, she had been unknown in the music business, having performed only with local bands at weddings, parties, and so on. Her contracts with Motown and Jobete were for a one-year period and granted each company six one-year renewal options. Under the contracts, the companies had the option to pay Brockert "compensation at the rate of not less than $6,000 per annum" for the remainder of the term.

Between 1979 and 1980, Teena Marie recorded four albums for Motown, including one that achieved gold record status. In 1982, Teena Marie informed Motown and Jobete that she would no longer perform under her contracts. The companies responded by suing for injunctive relief. They also exercised their option to pay Teena Marie the $6,000 per year minimum guarantee. The trial court enjoined Teena Marie from performing for other companies until the seventh year of her agreements had expired. Even though the case was settled and the seventh year had

[c] *See* Jonathan Blaufarb, *The Seven-Year Itch: California Labor Code Section 2855*, 6 Comm/Ent L.J. 653 (Spring 1984).

elapsed, the court nevertheless went on to examine the merits of the appeal.]

* * *

It has long been a principle of equity that a contract to perform personal services cannot be specifically enforced. In the mid-19th century an exception to this rule was born in England that where the employee both covenants to perform for the employer and not to perform elsewhere, equity will enjoin a breach of the negative covenant not to perform elsewhere although it cannot specifically enforce the affirmative covenant to perform for the employer. (*Lumley v. Wagner* (1852) 42 Eng. Rep. 687) The infant doctrine was not warmly embraced even in the country of its birth. (*Whitwood Chem. Co. v. Hardman* (1891) 2 Ch. 416; 5A *Corbin on Contracts* (1964) § 1208, p. 415). And, while it has gradually gained acceptance in the United States, it has been questioned by some eminent legal scholars. (*See, e.g.*, comments of Justice Holmes quoted in Note, *Lumley v. Wagner Denied* (1894) 8 Harv. L.Rev. 172 and 11 *Williston on Contracts* (3d ed. 1968) § 1447, pp. 1018–19.)

When the California Civil Code was adopted in 1872 it did not include a *Lumley* exception to the rule prohibiting specific performance of personal services contracts. Section 3423, as originally enacted, provided, "An injunction cannot be granted: . . . 5. To prevent the breach of a contract, the performance of which would not be specifically enforced." After discussing the *Lumley* line of cases and another line of cases holding to the contrary, the court in *Anderson v. Neal Institutes Co.* (1918) 37 Cal. App. 174, 178 [173 P. 779] observed:

> "Subdivision 5 of section 3423 is free from ambiguity or uncertainty. It clearly declares as the law in this state the rule laid down in one of two opposing lines of authority . . . that the court will not interfere by injunction to prevent the violation of an agreement of which, from the nature of the subject, there could be no decree of specific performance."

A year after *Anderson v. Neal Institutes Co.* was decided, the California Legislature amended section 3423 to allow a limited version of *Lumley*. (Stats. 1919, ch. 226, § 1, p. 328.) As originally introduced, the legislation would have prohibited an injunction "[to] prevent the breach of a contract, other than a contract in writing for the rendition or furnishing of personal services from one to another, the performance of which would not be specifically enforced." The original bill was amended to add the stipulation "where the minimum compensation for such service is at the rate of not less than six thousand dollars per annum." It was amended again to require that the promised service be of a unique character the loss of which cannot be adequately compensated in damages. (J. of the Sen., Forty-Third Sess. (1919) pp. 534, 1255, 1349.)

In the 65 years since the current version of section 3423, subdivision Fifth, was adopted, only two cases have interpreted the $6,000 minimum compensation requirement: *Foxx v. Williams* (1966) 244 Cal.App.2d 223 [52 Cal. Rptr. 896] and *MCA Records Inc. v. Newton-John* (1979) 90 Cal.App.3d 18 [153 Cal. Rptr. 153].

[In the] *Foxx* [case] the recording company which was distributing [comedian Redd Foxx's] albums, [sought] injunctive relief to prevent Foxx from breaching the exclusivity clause of his contract. The trial court granted the injunction restraining Foxx " 'from making sound recordings for any other person . . . so long as royalties earned by [Foxx] under the contract . . . equal or exceed the sum of $3000 [for each six-month royalty period].' " On appeal the appellate court found the royalty payments were entirely contingent upon sales of Foxx's albums and, therefore, did not guarantee Foxx would receive any money while the injunction was in effect. [Thus, the royalty contract did not meet the statutory requirement that a minimum of $6,000 per year be guaranteed to the performers], "even though it should ultimately appear that the royalties earned, over any given period, should exceed the rate of $6,000 per year."

Thirteen years later the minimum compensation requirement was again an issue in a suit for injunctive relief. (*MCA Records Inc. v. Newton-John*, supra, 90 Cal.App.3d 18.) Unlike Foxx, who at the time of his suit was a struggling nightclub comic, Olivia Newton-John was an international star when her case came before the court. The agreement at issue provided for her to record and deliver to MCA two albums a year for two years and, at MCA's option, additional albums in three periods of one year each. In return, MCA agreed to pay royalties and a nonreturnable advance of $250,000 for each album recorded in the initial two-year period and $100,000 for each album recorded in the option years. Newton-John was required to pay her recording costs out of her advances. In opposing injunctive relief to enforce the exclusivity clause of this contract, Newton-John argued [that] requiring her to bear the costs of production reduced the $100,000 payments in the option years below the $6,000 minimum required for an injunction. The appellate court interpreted section 3423, subdivision Fifth, as providing that "A party to a personal service contract may not be enjoined from rendering personal services to others unless, under the terms of the contract, she is guaranteed minimum annual compensation of $6,000." The court upheld the injunction on the basis of the trial court's finding of fact that after deducting recording costs Newton-John would still net at least $6,000 a year and she controlled whether that sum was received. All Newton-John had to do was make the promised record each year and keep her production costs below $94,000. The record company had to pay her the non-refundable $100,000 advance no matter whether the record succeeded in the marketplace. *Foxx* was distinguished on the ground the comedian's contract "did not guarantee him annual compensation of $6,000."

In response to *Foxx* and *MCA* many California record companies adopted the practice of including a clause in their contracts giving the company the right at any time during the contract to agree to pay the artist a minimum compensation of $6,000 a year. The clause in Teena Marie's contract is typical of such provisions. In this manner the company hedges its bets on the success of its artists. If the artist is not selling, the company does not exercise its option. If the artist catches on with the public and begins to make a substantial sum of money for the company, the company plays its "option" card to keep the artist from jumping to another label.

As the case at bar indicates, the company may wait until the last possible moment to exercise its option. Motown and Jobete filed suit against Teena Marie in August 1982 but waited until September 1982 to exercise the option clauses. The request for a preliminary injunction was filed two months later. Thus, the companies purchased an insurance policy worth a considerable sum[4] for a minimal premium just prior to the time they could be fairly certain a loss would occur. If the option clause meets the statutory requirement of minimum compensation, the company can buy its insurance policy on the courthouse steps on its way to seek an injunction. Indeed . . . the company may be able to buy its insurance policy after the "accident" has occurred; that is, after the artist has already signed and recorded with another company.

* * *

. . . The companies argue [that] by exercising their option to pay Teena Marie $6,000 a year a new contract came into existence which did guarantee her the statutory sum and it was this new contract guaranteeing $6,000 a year—not the old contract giving them an option to pay $6,000 a year—that they were seeking to enforce by injunction.[5] In support of this argument the companies cite cases describing an option contract as a kind of contract within a contract: the initial contract—an irrevocable and continuing offer to perform an act—and the final contract—the underlying promises to which the option relates. We reject this interpretation. . . .

The contracts between the companies and Teena Marie are not option contracts with respect to the exclusivity clause. In the contracts, Teena Marie does not give the companies the option to enjoy her services

4 Teena Marie's expert witness estimated Motown had earned a net profit of about $1.7 million on her last album.

5 We note this lawsuit was filed in August but the option clauses were not exercised until September. It is a novel litigation strategy to sue for injunctive relief to enforce a contract not yet in existence. At least the plaintiffs cannot be accused of laches.

exclusively on condition they pay her $6,000 a year. Rather, the promise to perform exclusively for the companies is one of the terms to which Teena Marie agrees from the outset of the contracts. . . .

Alternatively, the companies argue the letters they sent Teena Marie advising her they had elected to "revise" her contract and guarantee her no less than $6,000 per year constituted new contracts modifying the former ones. The California Supreme Court has interpreted the language of section 1698 literally, holding that an executory written modification must meet the requirements of a valid contract. Specifically, the court has held the modification must be supported by new consideration. (*Main St. etc. v. L. A. Trac. Co.* (1900) 129 Cal. 301, 305 [61 P. 937].). Accordingly, an executory agreement to pay more for the same performance is unenforceable. In this case, Teena Marie was required by the original contracts to perform exclusively for the companies. Consequently there was no consideration for the purported modification of the contracts. Were we to interpret defendants' letters as attempts to create new contracts, the new contracts would be unenforceable by Teena Marie and, thus, would not guarantee her compensation at the rate of $6,000 a year.

Even if exercising the option clauses created "new" contracts, we question whether the provisions of the contracts regarding compensation meet the requirement of section 3423. In order to obtain an injunction to prevent the breach of a personal services contract the compensation for services under that contract must be at the rate of not less than six thousand dollars. The fact the performer was being paid at least $6,000 under some other contract with the same employer would not satisfy the statute. For example, if the performer had two personal services contracts with the same employer, one to record songs and the other to write songs, the fact the performer was guaranteed $6,000 a year under the recording contract would not support injunctive relief to prevent breach of the songwriting contract. Nor would a $6,000 guarantee under the songwriting contract support injunctive relief to enforce the record making contract.

The contracts in the case at bench appear to attempt such a set off of compensation. The recording contract with Motown provides, "Any amounts paid under [the $6,000 compensation clause] may be credited against monies thereafter payable to you pursuant to this or any other agreement between [Motown] and you, or between [Motown's] associated, affiliated, or subsidiary corporations and you." The songwriting contract with Jobete contains virtually identical language. There is no dispute Motown and Jobete are associated or affiliated corporations. If Teena Marie received $6,000 in 1982 from Jobete for songwriting, she would be guaranteed nothing from Motown for recording. Moreover, there is evidence suggesting Teena Marie performed other services for Motown and possibly Jobete as a producer, technician and the like. Presumably she received compensation for these efforts unrelated to her singing, songwriting and recording work. If she was already receiving $6,000 a year as a sound technician, for example, then she would be guaranteed nothing under the contracts before us.

Accordingly, these cagily drafted option clauses might not guarantee a cent in additional compensation for Teena Marie's songwriting and recording services or, at best, she would be guaranteed a single $6,000 a year payment for her services under both contracts.

Still, because we hold a contract giving the employer the discretion to pay the performer $6,000 a year if and when it chooses does not meet the requirements of section 3423, we need not decide whether the provisions for setting off compensation in the contracts before us would, independently, require refusal of injunctive relief.

Thus, we turn to the question left unanswered by *Foxx* and *MCA*: does an *option* to guarantee $6,000 a year at some time in the future satisfy the statutory requirement of [a minimum compensation of 6,000 per annum].

One of Teena Marie's songs is entitled "Don't Turn Your Back On Me." Here, it could be said, we answer her plea.

[The court rejected Motown's reliance on the optional payment clause on three separate grounds. First, the court read the statutory language as intended to cover only contracts that guarantee the performer a minimum of $6,000 per year from the outset.] . . . In other words, agreeing to payment of the minimum compensation is not a condition precedent to the granting of injunctive relief; it is a threshold requirement for admission of the contract into the class of contracts subject to injunctive relief under the statute.[7]

This reading of the statute is implicit in the *Foxx* and *MCA* decisions. In *Foxx* the court found the contract did not meet the minimum compensation requirement of section 3423 even though the potential for earning $6,000 or more existed under the contract. Similarly, under the option clause, the artist has merely the potential of earning $6,000 a year; there is no guarantee this compensation will ever be paid. Distinguishing *Foxx*, the court in *MCA* observed, "Unlike [Olivia Newton-John], who is guaranteed minimum annual compensation of $200,000 in the form of nonreturnable advances in addition to any royalties she may receive, Foxx's sole compensation was in the form of royalties contingent upon prospective sales which could amount to nothing." We believe the option

[7] We do not mean to imply the statute is satisfied any time there is at least $6,000 at stake under the contract. Although the issue is not presented here, in order that this opinion not be misunderstood, we are of the view the minimum compensation requirement requires at least $6,000 per year be available to the artist after deduction of production costs.

clause is analogous to the contingent payment rejected in *Foxx*. It is nothing more than a new arrangement of an old song.

[Next, the court asserted that this] . . . option clause would defeat the legislative intent to limit injunctive relief to contracts where not only are the services special or unique, but the performer herself is a person of distinction in her field at the time of entering the contract. [In support of this position, the court pointed out that since *Lumley v. Wagner,* there had been a discernible trend toward enforcing negative covenants against the "prima donnas," but not the "spear carriers." The court believed that the California Legislature also sought to limit injunctive relief to performers of star quality, because ordering specific performance imposed on the courts a difficult task of having to pass judgment upon the quality of performance.]

As the court in *Lumley v. Wagner* candidly admitted, it had no power to compel Madame Wagner to sing at Lumley's theater but the injunction prohibiting her from performing elsewhere might well accomplish the same result. Thus there is a danger an artist prohibited from performing elsewhere may feel compelled to perform under the contract and, under the stress of the situation, turn in an unsatisfactory performance. This would lead to further litigation between the parties on the adequacy of the artist's performance; the very thing the courts traditionally sought to avoid. There is less likelihood of this conundrum arising if the performer is of great renown. Such a performer may well choose not to perform rather than risk her reputation by delivering a sub-par performance.

In 1919 the sum of $6,000 a year was more than five times the average national wage of $1,142. This is equivalent to setting the minimum compensation figure at $100,000 today (based on the 1982 median income level of $20,171). By selecting such a large sum, the Legislature indicated an intent that injunctive relief not be available against a performer, however capable, who had not yet achieved distinction . . .

Without doubt the passage of time has diluted the effect of this legislative intent but the option clauses before us would totally wash it away. It would allow a record company to bind the entire student body of "Rydell High" to personal services contracts (and pay them nothing) on the off-chance one of them turns out to be Olivia Newton-John.

It is no answer to say that by the time Motown and Jobete sought injunctive relief to enforce the exclusivity clauses Teena Marie had become a star. Motown and Jobete did not contract with a star. By their own admission they contracted with a "virtual unknown." Nothing in section 3423 prevents the companies from seeking damages from Teena Marie for breach of the exclusivity clause. That section merely says for reasons of public policy the exclusivity clause of a contract can only be enforced by injunction when the contract is with a performer of requisite distinction as measured by the compensation the employer is willing to pay.

[As a final basis for denying equitable relief, the court held that the option clause in Teena Marie's contract violated the concept of fundamental fairness embodied in Civil Code § 3423.]

* * *

We agree with the court in *Foxx* that the $6,000 minimum compensation requirement was intended to balance the equities between employer and performer. This is quite clear when section 3423 is read in connection with Civil Code section 3391, subdivision 2, which provides specific performance cannot be enforced against a party as to whom the contract is not "just and reasonable." Taken together those sections demand a minimum standard of fairness as a condition on equitable enforcement of an exclusivity clause in a personal services contract.

"[A]n injunction which forbids an artist to accept new employment is a harsh and powerful remedy. The monetary limitation in the status is intended to serve as a counterweight in balancing the equities. The Legislature has concluded that an artist who is not entitled to receive a minimum of $6,000 per year by performing his contract should not be subjected to this kind of economic coercion." (*Foxx*, supra, 244 Cal.App.2d at p. 236.)

If we were to hold the option clause satisfies section 3423, we would nullify the $6,000 compensation requirement as a counterweight on the employer. Whereas the $6,000 compensation requirement was intended to balance the equities, the $6,000 option clause is intended to allow record companies to avoid payment of minimum compensation while retaining the power of economic coercion over the artist. This is accomplished in two ways. First, the option clause gives the company the coercive power of a credible threat of injunctive relief without it having to guarantee or pay the artist anything. The threat of a prohibitory injunction may be just as effective as the injunction itself in discouraging the artist from seeking more lucrative employment. Second, in practice, the company will exercise its option to pay minimum compensation only when it is certain the artist intends to breach the exclusivity clause by performing for another and, even then, only when exercising the option is necessary to enable the company to assert in court the contract does indeed provide for the statutory minimum compensation. Of course, by then the company's agreement to pay the artist a minimum of $6,000 a year is meaningless. If the artist was not already earning far in excess of that amount from royalties, the artist's worth to the company would not justify the expense of litigating the case. The record company is in fact merely "electing" to pay that which it would have to pay anyway as a result of royalties from sales.

Reversed.

### *QUESTIONS FOR DISCUSSION*

1. Recall the standard terms and typical operation of recording contracts—in particular, how the money given to the musician as an advance against royalties is used up in production of the record itself. What are the implications of that story for the legal issues in *Motown Record*?

2. Record labels developed several techniques to dilute the effect of *Motown Record Corp. v. Brockert*. The first tactic was to guarantee the $6,000 minimum, but to require artists to notify their labels when royalties and advances fail to total $6,000 in a given year. The minimum was paid at the end of each year, and advanced against royalties that have accrued over the term. Another tactic was to guarantee the $6,000 only to key members of a group. This legally binds the group's core, while making it unlikely that secondary members will resort to the $6,000 rule. Finally, smaller labels have sought to avoid the statute by incorporating non-California choice of law and forum provisions. However, note that a contract with a California artist that is executed in California may be treated as subject to California law if a judge determines it to be, the locus of the contract, notwithstanding the choice of law and jurisdiction provisions.

3. Since label-jumping involves not only a defecting star but also a competing label, can one enjoin the rival company from inducing the breach rather than enjoining the performer? Apparently, no one thought of using this strategy to circumvent the California legislation until 1986, when Beverly Glen Music tried to enjoin Warner Communications from luring away Anita Baker with a more attractive contract. *See Beverly Glen Music v. Warner Communications*, 178 Cal.App.3d 1142, 224 Cal. Rptr. 260 (1986). Since Beverly Glen had failed to pay Baker the statutory minimum, it was unable to enjoin Baker directly. Thus, the issue was whether the plaintiff—although prohibited from enjoining Baker—could seek to bar all labels that might employ her, thus achieving the same result. The lower court denied Beverly Glen's attempt to enjoin Warner, on the theory that what one was forbidden by statute to do directly, one could not accomplish through the back door. In affirming this holding, the appellate court noted: "if Warner's behavior has actually been predatory, plaintiff has an adequate remedy by way of damages. An injunction adds nothing to plaintiff's recovery from Warner except to coerce Ms. Baker to honor her contract. Denying someone his livelihood is a harsh remedy."

Given the difficulties in accurately gauging Baker's future market performance as of the time of breach, how should a court calculate the damages proposed above? Note that simply granting Beverly Glen a sales royalty for the remainder of Baker's contract term may be an overly generous measure, since Warner has significantly greater promotional resources than

Beverly Glen, and is thus more likely to sell a large volume of records. But what if Warner, rather than vigorously promoting Baker, simply decided to shelve her next release or give it minimal promotion?

4. The court in *Motown Record* noted a trend toward enforcing negative covenants against the "prima donnas" but not against the "spear carriers." Is this a proper distinction for courts to make? That is, can "star quality" be adequately determined by using objective measures such as sales? Under the court's reasoning, can a performer who is on the verge of stardom be enjoined from label jumping—the point at which injunctive relief may count most? Consider also the case of an artist who achieves critical acclaim but has modest record sales. Although such an artist may provide prestige to the label and thus be a valuable asset in terms of attracting new artists, does the court's reasoning imply that the label would have no equitable recourse against the breaching performer regardless of whether it has paid the statutory minimum? On the other hand, even if the label should be able to pursue some form of injunctive relief, should the statutory minimum be adjusted to account for the success of the performer, the label's actual investment, or the duration of the contract?

---

When the California law was enacted in 1919, the sum of $6,000 a year was more than five times the average national wage. In the early 21st century, the statutory minimum seemed less than adequate consideration for injunctive relief at a time when average salaries are nearing $30,000. In 1993, the California legislature briefly raised the statutory minimum to $50,000 per year. The bill was signed into law without objection from the entertainment industry, whose lobbyists had apparently been caught "sleeping at the wheel." After realizing the impact of the new Act, lobbyists persuaded the legislature to repeal the original bill and to draft a substantially scaled-down version.[d]

The final version of the Act states that California companies may seek injunctive relief for breaches of contracts executed after January 1, 1994, only after conforming with a "$9,000 PLUS" provision, as codified in revised § 3423 of the California Civil Code and § 526 of the Code of Civil Procedure. This law did not undermine a company's right to sue for damages, even if it is prevented from seeking injunctive relief.

Under this law, a company must contractually guarantee a $9,000 minimum annual payment during the first contract year, increasing to $12,000 for the second year and $15,000 for years three through seven. The annual compensation must be guaranteed (i.e., in advance payments), not contingent (i.e., in royalties). Moreover, to retain its

---

[d] *See* William I. Hochberg, *Revising the "Jump Ship" Clause: How California Legislators & the Music Industry Raised the Ante For Record Companies Seeking Injunctions Against Defecting Artists*, 15 Ent. L. Rep. 3 (No. 8, Jan. 1994) and 15 Ent. L. Rep. 7 (Jan. 1994); Peter Paterno, *California's Artist Comp Law Not Without Flaws*, 1 Ent. Law & Fin. 3 (Dec. 1993).

injunctive option, the company must pay additional sums of $15,000 per year in years four and five, and additional sums of $30,000 per year in years six and seven. This compensation may include contingent royalties, so long as the minimum compensation has actually been paid. Guaranteed or contingent compensation that exceeds the statutory minimum for a given year may be carried forward to meet the required minimums for future years. In the first year of the contract, then, an artist must be paid a guaranteed $9,000, in the third year a guaranteed $15,000, in the fifth year a guaranteed $15,000 plus an additional $15,000, and in the seventh year a guaranteed $15,000 plus an additional $30,000, though some or all of the latter figure could be covered by any amounts that exceeded the $45,000 required for the sixth year.

The law also provides an alternative method for securing injunctive relief for companies that failed to pay the guaranteed minimum compensation to an artist who then became extremely successful in a subsequent year. Under the so-called "Superstar Insurance" provision, the company would have to make a single payment equal to ten times the aggregate minimum required to secure the right to injunctive relief in each of the years of the contract. For example, a label that did not pay the guaranteed minimums to an artist in years one through three (i.e., $9,000, $12,000, $15,000), but that released an extraordinarily successful album by the artist in year four, could qualify to seek an injunction by making a lump sum payment on the courthouse steps which, in this case, would total $510,000 (ten times the $15,000 required for year 4, plus $360,000 as ten times the total that was supposed to have been paid during the first three years of the contract). By year seven, this payment for an injunction would have to total $960,000 (less any amounts that had actually been paid in prior years).

Note that a struggling artist will probably not be able to profit from the "Superstar Insurance" provision because a record company will not risk a lawsuit to steal away an artist with a marginal track record. The prime beneficiary of the clause will be an artist on the brink of success who has received substantial promotional support from her label, but has yet to generate significant record sales. This represents a fairly small class of performers.

Many artists will not benefit from the new statutory minimums. Small labels often cannot afford them, and major labels will generally limit guaranteed minimums to "key" group members. In addition, because no injunction is available under California law to enforce a personal services contract for more than seven years, labels who have not paid the minimum will generally not waste their money to enjoin performers who only has a year or two left under their contracts. Instead, labels will only pursue injunctions in the early years, when the statutory minimums are low and the label will have time to recoup its investment.

One of the key concerns of legislators in revising the $6,000 provision was a practice called "shelving." When a record company has a hot talent on its hands, it will go out of its way to prevent that artist from having direct competition. This can mean signing possible competitors to long-term contracts simply to keep them off the market. By increasing the statutory minimum to $50,000 in the original bill, legislators hoped to curb this practice. One of the intentions of the law was to guarantee a living wage to shelved artists.

The shelving controversy has led some commentators to argue that if the failure to permit artists to record is the problem, then the legislature should simply require companies to record and release records by an artist in order to retain injunctive relief. (Indeed, under the standard for pursuing injunctions, can a label seeking such relief genuinely claim that it is suffering irreparable injury from the loss of unique services of a group whose records it has not been recording and selling?) Obviously, most artists are far more concerned about the commitment of the label to promoting their records and establishing their careers than they are about receiving the minimum compensation: $9,000 may buy some guitars and a decent amplifier, but it is a poverty level wage. Is there some way to improve the situation of "shelved" artists without skewing the labels' incentives by making them reluctant to sign bands that seem to be riskier investments? How do you think labels and artists would respond to a proposal that companies regularly had to release and promote records by their performers in order to be able to secure injunctive enforcement?

---

Consider the broader policy questions raised by injunctive relief for performer violations of personal service contracts. Litigation about entertainment contracts vividly displays the contest between two visions of contract and its enforcement. One view pictures contracts as personal promises that create moral obligations and entitlements that are worthy of as much legal teeth as the law can sensibly provide. From this perspective, judges should not hesitate to enjoin actors from performing for another firm even if the resulting financial pressures from compliance with the first contract. Even under this vision of contract, is such an enforcement strategy compatible with the countervailing principle of freedom of artistic expression?

An alternative conception of contract pictures this institution as an economic instrument for whose enforcement the law should be deployed only if intervention produces an efficient allocation of resources. Under this theory, a musician should be entitled to break his initial commitment with one record producer as long as he is willing to pay that producer for losses that are demonstrably suffered. The assumption is that such contract breaches will be committed only when it is efficient to do so-in other words, when another producer finds this musician's services worth enough extra money to leave the musician better off even after paying compensatory damages to the original firm. From this perspective, are there distinctive features of the music industry—i.e., the up-front investments and risks—that render that efficient breach thesis inappropriate in this context?

## B. DAMAGES FOR CONTRACT BREACH[e]

### 1. PERFORMERS VS. PRODUCERS

As was noted earlier, there is at least a theoretical possibility that a performer whose contract has been wrongfully terminated could secure negative injunctive relief against the producer. Understandably, though, judges are extremely reluctant to bar a producer from hiring a replacement, because that could bring the entire production to a grinding halt. Courts thus comfort themselves with the thought that monetary damages will give the performer the needed redress.

The validity of that judgment depends on the types and amounts of damages that can be awarded. Unlike most people employed at will in the American workplace, entertainers typically have explicit guarantees of employment from their producers. When those commitments are violated, the performer must rely on the remedies that are deemed appropriate in this distinctive branch of wrongful dismissal litigation. In particular, is the entertainer's award limited to the specific salary that had been guaranteed (e.g., under a "pay or play" clause), or may it also encompass other financial, reputational, and psychological benefits that a performer expected from this particular undertaking? The cases that follow illustrate different ways that courts have addressed this crucial issue.

#### QUINN V. STRAUS BROADCASTING GROUP, INC.

United States District Court, Southern District of New York, 1970.
309 F. Supp. 1208.

[WMCA, a New York radio station, hired Quinn to host a talk show. After Quinn had been on the air for four months, WMCA discharged him. Although WMCA had apparently offered Quinn the balance of the $50,000 provided in his contract, he chose instead to sue the station on

[e] *See* Melvin Simensky, *Determining Damages for Breach of Entertainment Agreements*, 8 Ent. & Sports Law. 1 (Spring 1990); Henry W. Lauterstein, *Pay or Play or Pay and Pay: Right of an Artist or Entertainer to Recover Consequential Damages in a Breach of Contract Action*, 8 Ent. & Sports Law. 1 (Winter 1990). *See generally* Lon L. Fuller & William R. Perdue, *The Reliance Interest in Contract Damages: Parts I & II*, 46 Yale L. J. 52: 373 (1936–37); Edward Yorio, *In Defense of Money Damages for Breach of Contract*, 82 Colum. L. Rev. 1365 (1982); Robert Cooter & Melvin Aron Eisenberg, *Damages for Breach of Contract*, 73 Cal. L. Rev. 1432 (1985).

three counts: 1) $500,000 in damages for wrongful discharge; 2) $500,000 for damage to his professional reputation from the cancellation due to "the unique nature of Quinn's services and his need to appear before the public to advance his professional reputation"; and 3) an additional $500,000 for subjecting Quinn to "public ridicule" and permanently impairing his reputation as a performer.

The contract provided that Quinn was employed as a "staff announcer" for one year at a salary of $50,000, with an option to renew for a second year at $57,500, and for a third year at $65,000.]

BONSAL, DISTRICT JUDGE.

* * *

. . . The New York rule is that damages for breach of an employment contract are limited to the unpaid salary to which the employee would be entitled under the contract less the amount by which he should have mitigated his damages. This rule was recently applied with respect to the conductor of the orchestra of the Metropolitan Opera in *Amaducci v. Metropolitan Opera Association*, 33 A.D. 2d 542, 304 N.Y.S. 2d 322 (1st Dept.1969), where plaintiff sought damages for mental anguish and defamation resulting from his discharge, the court stating:

> "It is well settled that the optimum measure of damages for wrongful discharge under a contract of employment is the salary fixed by the contract for the unexpired period of employment, and that damages to the good name, character and reputation of the plaintiff are not recoverable in an action for wrongful discharge."

304 N.Y.S.2d at 323.

While *Amaducci* does not directly answer plaintiff's contention that he is entitled to damages for the loss of opportunity to practice his profession before the public, there is no reason to believe that the State courts would adopt a different rule in this context. Moreover, it is clear that by signing a $30,000 contract with radio station WCAU in Philadelphia in September 1969, plaintiff has not lost his opportunity to practice his profession.

Plaintiff relies on a 1930 House of Lords case (*Clayton & Waller, Limited v. Oliver* [1930] AC 209) and a 1965 California Court of Appeals case (*Colvig v. RKO General, Inc.*, 232 Cal. App. 2d 56, 42 Cal. Rptr. 473 (Dist.Ct.App., 1st Dist. 1965)) for the proposition that the New York courts would make an exception to the New York rule in this case. *Colvig* is clearly distinguishable as it involved the enforcement of an arbitration award. *Clayton* was decided 40 years ago, and no New York cases have been cited to indicate that New York would follow *Clayton*. Taken together, these two cases cannot be said to be a precursor of an exception to the New York rule, and therefore this court is bound to follow the rule as stated in *Cornell* and *Amaducci.*

Since, under the New York rule, plaintiff's damages are limited to a maximum of $50,000, his ad damnum clause of $500,000 in the first cause of action is clearly excessive and will be stricken.

The second and third causes of action are not recognized in the New York rule as laid down in *Cornell* and *Amaducci*. The second alleges that plaintiff's services were unique and that by reason of the breach of contract plaintiff was deprived of an opportunity to perform before large audiences; and the third alleges that his reputation as a performer had been impaired. No authority has been suggested for the proposition that loss of opportunity to perform entitles the employee to a separate cause of action. *Amaducci* holds that no separate cause of action can be stated for loss of reputation. Divested of these allegations, the second and third causes of action merely repeat the first cause of action. Accordingly, they will be stricken.

Motions granted.

---

Two decades later the question of whether consequential damages could be awarded for breach of a performer's employment contract was presented again in the dispute between Vanessa Redgrave and the Boston Symphony Orchestra (BSO). As we saw in Chapter 8, the BSO cancelled Redgrave's *Oedipus Rex* performance because of protests about her support of the Palestine Liberation Organization (PLO) against the State of Israel. On the assumption that this BSO action violated Redgrave's contractual, if not her statutory rights, there remained an issue about the appropriate level of damages. The BSO offered Redgrave her full performance fee (approximately $30,000), but a Boston jury awarded another $100,000 for the harm done to Redgrave's future professional opportunities. After District Judge Robert Keeton reversed the jury verdict on the grounds that consequential damages infringed on the BSO's First Amendment rights, the case was appealed.

## VANESSA REDGRAVE V. BOSTON SYMPHONY ORCHESTRA, INC.

United States Court of Appeals, First Circuit, 1988.
855 F.2d 888.

COFFIN, CIRCUIT JUDGE.

* * *

### II. The Consequential Damages Claim

#### A. *Consequential Damages for Loss of Professional Opportunities*

In response to special interrogatories, the jury found that the BSO's cancellation of the *Oedipus Rex* concerts caused consequential harm to Redgrave's professional career and that this harm was a foreseeable consequence within the contemplation of the parties at the time they entered the contract. A threshold question is whether Massachusetts contract law allows the award of such consequential damages for harm to a claimant's professional career.

Redgrave's consequential damages claim is based on the proposition that a significant number of movie and theater offers that she would ordinarily have received in the years 1982 and following were in fact not offered to her as a result of the BSO's cancellation in April 1982. The BSO characterizes this claim as one for damage to Redgrave's reputation, and argues that the recent Massachusetts state court decisions in *McCone v. New England Telephone & Telegraph Co.*, 393 Mass. 231, 471 N.E.2d 47 (1984) and *Daley v. Town of West Brookfield*, 19 Mass. App. Ct. 1019, 476 N.E.2d 980 (1985), establish that Massachusetts law does not permit plaintiffs in breach of contract actions to recover consequential damages for harm to reputation.

* * *

The BSO notes that Massachusetts is in agreement with virtually all other jurisdictions in holding that damages for reputation are not available in contract actions. This impressive line of cases, however, becomes less impressive for our purposes when the reasoning in these cases is analyzed with reference to the particular claim put forth by Redgrave.

In cases that have analyzed the reasons for disallowing a contract claim for reputation damages, courts have identified two determinative factors. First, courts have observed that attempting to calculate damages for injury to reputation is "unduly speculative." In many cases, the courts have viewed the claims for damages to reputation as analogous to claims for physical or emotional distress and have noted the difficulty in ascertaining such damages for contract purposes.

The second factor that courts identify is that damages for injury to reputation "cannot reasonably be presumed to have been within the contemplation of the parties when they entered into the contract." These courts state that the basic rule of *Hadley v. Baxendale*, 9 Ex. 341, 156 Eng. Rep. 145 (1854), which requires that contract damages be of the kind that arise naturally from the breach of a contract or be of a kind that reasonably may have been in the contemplation of the parties when they entered the contract, cannot possibly be met in a claim for general damages to reputation occurring as the result of a breach of contract. The Massachusetts Supreme Judicial Court seems to have accepted this rationale as a legitimate one for disallowing claims for injury to reputation as a contract damage.

The claim advanced by Redgrave is significantly different, however, from a general claim of damage to reputation. Redgrave is not claiming that her general reputation as a professional actress has been tarnished by the BSO's cancellation. Rather, she claims that a number of specific movie and theater performances that would have been offered to her in the usual course of events were not offered to her as a result of the BSO's cancellation. This is the type of specific claim that, with appropriate evidence, can meet the *Hadley v. Baxendale* rule, as adopted by the Massachusetts Supreme Judicial Court in *John Hetherington & Sons, Ltd. v. William Firth Co.*, 210 Mass. 8, 21, 95 N.E. 961, 964 (1911) (in breach of contract action, injured party receives compensation for any loss that follows as a natural consequence from the breach, was within the contemplation of reasonable parties as a probable result of breach, and may be computed by "rational methods upon a firm basis of facts"). As the district court correctly noted in a preliminary memorandum:

> If plaintiffs proved other employers refused to hire Redgrave after termination of the BSO contract because of that termination (that loss of the other employment "followed as a natural consequence" from the termination of the contract), that this loss of other employment would reasonably have been foreseen by the parties at the time of contracting and at the time of termination, and that damages are rationally calculable, then plaintiffs may be entitled to damages that include monies for loss of the other employment. Although plaintiffs have a heavy burden to carry here, it cannot be said with certainty at this time that they will not be able to meet this burden.

*Redgrave v. BSO*, 557 F. Supp. 230, 234 (D.Mass.1983).

The jury was given appropriate instructions to help it determine whether Redgrave had suffered consequential damages through loss of future professional opportunities. They were told to find that the BSO's cancellation was a proximate cause of harm to Redgrave's professional career only if they determined that "harm would not have occurred but for the cancellation and that the harm was a natural and probable consequence of the cancellation." In addition, they were told that damages should be allowed for consequential harm "only if the harm was a foreseeable consequence within the contemplation of the parties to the contract when it was made." In response to special interrogatories, the jury found that the BSO's cancellation caused consequential harm to Redgrave's career and that the harm was a foreseeable consequence within the contemplation of the parties.

Although we find that Redgrave did not present sufficient evidence to establish that the BSO's cancellation caused consequential harm to her professional career in the amount of $100,000, we hold that, as a matter of Massachusetts contract law, a plaintiff may receive consequential damages if the plaintiff proves with sufficient evidence that a breach of contract proximately caused the loss of identifiable professional opportunities. This type of claim is sufficiently different from a nonspecific allegation of damage to reputation that it appropriately falls outside the general rule that reputation damages are not an acceptable form of contract damage.

* * *

### C. *Sufficiency of the Evidence*

The requirements for awarding consequential damages for breach of contract are designed to ensure that a breaching party pays only those damages that have resulted from its breach. Thus, to receive consequential damages, the plaintiff must establish a "basis for an inference of fact" that the plaintiff has actually been damaged, Williston, *Contracts*, § 1345 at 231, and the factfinder must be able to compute the compensation "by rational methods upon a firm basis of facts." *John Hetherington & Sons*, 210 Mass. at 21, 95 N.E. at 964.

* * *

In order for Redgrave to prove that the BSO's cancellation resulted in the loss of other professional opportunities, she must present sufficient facts for a jury reasonably to infer that Redgrave lost wages and professional opportunities subsequent to April 1982, that such losses were the result of the BSO's cancellation rather than the result of other, independent factors, and that damages for such losses are capable of being ascertained "by reference to some definite standard, either market value, established experience or direct inference from known circumstances." *John Hetherington & Sons*, 210 Mass. at 21, 95 N.E. at 964. During trial, evidence was presented regarding losses Redgrave allegedly suffered in film offers and American theater offers. Based on this testimony, the jury found that the BSO's cancellation of its contract with Redgrave caused Redgrave $100,000 in consequential damages. We find that the evidence presented by Redgrave was not sufficient to support a finding of damages greater than $12,000, less expenses.

Most of Redgrave's annual earnings prior to April 1982 were derived from appearances in films and the English theater.[6] Redgrave presented evidence at trial that she earned more than $200,000 on the average since her company's fiscal year 1976, and she testified that she had a constant stream of offers from which she could choose films that had secure financial backing. After the BSO's cancellation in April 1982, Redgrave contended, her career underwent a "startling turnabout." Redgrave testified that she did not work at all for the fourteen months following the cancellation and that the only offers she received during that time were for films with insufficient financial backing.

The evidence demonstrates that Redgrave accepted three firm film offers in the fourteen months following the BSO cancellation. If these three films had been produced, Redgrave would have earned $850,000 during that period. [In the summer of 1982, Redgrave had secured a role in a film, *Annie's Coming Out*, which was to earn her $250,000. With that contract having been signed, Redgrave turned down several other offers. However, in the late fall of 1982, the *Annie's Coming Out* project was cancelled because of inability to secure financing. The same thing happened to two other film projects—*No Alternatives* and *Track 39*—for which Redgrave secured contracts in the first half of 1983. While those commitments on her part precluded Redgrave from accepting other movie offers, in only one of those three contracts did Redgrave secure a forfeiture payment (and that was for $25,000). There was no suggestion that the reasons for the financing failures of those three movie projects was caused by the cancellation of Redgrave's BSO performance.]

* * *

Although there is no doubt that Redgrave did not have a successful financial year following the BSO cancellation, we cannot say that she presented sufficient evidence to prove that her financial difficulties were caused by the BSO cancellation. . . . Redgrave contends, however, that the film offers she received following the BSO cancellation lacked secure financial backing and were thus significantly different from offers she had received prior to the cancellation. . . . [S]he argues that the fact that she had to accept two films that ultimately were not produced was itself a result of the BSO cancellation.

---

6 Although Redgrave received a number of offers to appear in Broadway plays between 1975 and 1980, the only offer she accepted and received payment for was a 1976 play, *Lady From the Sea*, performed in off-Broadway's Circle in the Square theater, for which Redgrave received $9,000.

We have some doubt as to whether Redgrave presented sufficient evidence to prove that the type of film offers she received in the year following the BSO cancellation were radically different from the film offers received before the cancellation. On direct examination, Redgrave testified regarding her previous performances, starting from 1966. As to most of the years, Redgrave testified solely regarding the work she did, rather than the offers she received, noting that she could only "remember what [she] actually did at the moment" and not the offers she had received. Redgrave did testify that she received four film offers in 1980, none of which she accepted, and four film offers in 1981, two of which she accepted. No evidence was presented, however, regarding the financial backing of those films that were offered to Redgrave but which she did not accept. Thus, the evidence does not present an effective comparison between the type of film offers received before and after the BSO cancellation and we are left primarily with Redgrave's allegation that the film offers received in the two time periods were significantly different.

Even if we accept, however, that Redgrave proved she had experienced a drop in the quality of film offers following the BSO cancellation, Redgrave must also prove that the drop was proximately caused by the BSO cancellation and not by other, independent factors. Redgrave failed to carry her burden of presenting evidence sufficient to allow a jury reasonably to infer this causal connection.

The defense introduced evidence that Redgrave's political activities and statements had generated much media attention prior to the incident with the BSO. Redgrave conceded that her agents had informed her, prior to April 1982, that certain producers were hesitant to hire her because of the controversy she generated. And, in a newspaper interview in February 1982, Redgrave stated that she "had lost a lot of work because of her political beliefs" but that every time there had been a move to stop her working, "an equally terrific response [came] forward condemning any witch hunts."

To the extent that Redgrave may have experienced a decline in the quality of film offers received subsequent to April 1982, that decline could have been the result of Redgrave's political views and not the result of the BSO's cancellation. Even if the cancellation highlighted for producers the potential problems in hiring Redgrave, it was Redgrave's burden to establish that, in some way, the cancellation itself caused the difference in film offers rather than the problems as highlighted by the cancellation. Redgrave produced no direct evidence from film producers who were influenced by the cancellation. Thus, the jury's inference that the BSO cancellation had caused Redgrave consequential damages was one based more on "conjecture and speculation," than on a sufficient factual basis.

Redgrave also claims that the BSO's cancellation caused a drop in her offers to perform on Broadway. [In fact, Redgrave had received two to four American play offers in the years 1976 to 1980, and no offer to perform on Broadway in 1981, the year immediately preceding the BSO cancellation.] Redgrave accepted only one of the offers made during this time period, appearing in *Lady From the Sea* in off-Broadway's Circle in the Square in 1976.

Redgrave contends that, as a result of the BSO cancellation, she no longer received offers to appear on Broadway. She testified that in April 1983 she was appearing in a successful English theater production of *The Aspern Papers* and was led to believe by the producers that the show would move to New York. Although it was Redgrave's opinion that the reason the play did not move to Broadway was because of the "situation" caused by the BSO cancellation, there was no testimony from the producers or others as to why the production did not go to Broadway. Redgrave also testified that in August 1983 she was asked by the Jujamson producers to appear in *The Abdication*, but that the play was never produced. Again, there was no testimony from the producers or others as to why the production did not materialize. In addition, Redgrave testified that Lillian Hellman had wished Redgrave to portray Hellman in a theater production on Broadway, but that Hellman was concerned about the BSO incident. Finally, Redgrave testified that Theodore Mann had considered offering her a role in *Heartbreak House* at Circle in the Square, but decided not to extend the offer because of the ramifications of the BSO cancellation.

Theodore Mann was the one producer who testified regarding his decision not to employ Redgrave in a Broadway production. He explained that:

> the Boston Symphony Orchestra had canceled, terminated Ms. Redgrave's contract. This had a-this is the premier or one of the premier arts organizations in America who, like ourselves, seeks support from foundations, corporations, individuals; have subscribers; sell individual tickets. I was afraid . . . and those in my organization were afraid that this termination would have a negative effect on us if we hired her. And so we had conferences about this. We were also concerned about if there would be any physical disturbances to the performance. . . . And it was finally decided . . . that we would not hire [Redgrave] because of all the events that had happened, the cancellation by the Boston Symphony and the effects that we felt it would have on us by hiring her.

The evidence presented by Redgrave concerning her drop in Broadway offers after April 1982, apart from Mann's testimony, is not sufficient to support a finding of consequential damages. We do not, of course, question Redgrave's credibility in any way. Our concern is with the meager factual evidence. Redgrave had to introduce enough facts for a jury reasonably to infer that any drop in Broadway offers was proximately caused by the BSO cancellation and not by the fact that producers independently were concerned with the same factors that had motivated the BSO. Mann's testimony itself reflects the fact that many producers in New York may have been hesitant about hiring Redgrave because of a feared drop in subscription support or problems of physical disturbances. Apart from Mann's testimony, Redgrave presented nothing other than the fact that three expected offers or productions did not materialize. This type of circumstantial evidence is not sufficient to support a finding of consequential damages.

In addition, we note that it would be difficult for any assessment of damages resulting from the lack of Broadway theater offers to meet the standard that damages must be "capable of ascertainment by reference to some definite standard, either market value, established experience or direct inference from known circumstances." *John Hetherington & Sons*, 210 Mass. at 21, 95 N.E. at 964. The three specific performances to which Redgrave referred, other than Mann's, were never performed on Broadway and there is no indication of the compensation Redgrave would have received. In addition, Redgrave had accepted only one Broadway offer among the many she had received over the years because, according to Redgrave, the scripts were not good enough for her first Broadway appearance. There was no evidence that Redgrave would necessarily have accepted any Broadway offer made in 1982.

Mann's testimony regarding the production of *Heartbreak House* is the one piece of evidence from which reasonable fact-finders could draw conflicting inferences and upon which a reasonably ascertainable damage award could be granted. We therefore defer to the inferences drawn by the jury from that testimony and grant Redgrave damages on that basis.

Mann's testimony reveals that, in considering whether to hire Redgrave, he and his partners were concerned about losing support from foundations and subscribers, having difficulty selling tickets, and dealing with possible physical disruptions. These are factors that result from the community response to Redgrave's political views. They are the same factors that apparently motivated the BSO to cancel its contract with Redgrave and are not the result of that cancellation. Thus, one possibly could infer from Mann's testimony that the BSO cancellation was not a proximate cause of the damage suffered by Redgrave in being denied the part in *Heartbreak House*.

Mann also testified, however, that he and his partners were affected by the BSO cancellation because the BSO was a premier arts organization and was dependent on the same type of support as Circle in the Square. A jury reasonably could infer that the BSO's cancellation did more than just highlight for Mann the potential problems that hiring Redgrave would cause but was actually a cause of Mann's decision, perhaps because Mann's theater support was similar to that of the BSO or because Mann felt influenced to follow the example of a "premier arts organization." Because this is a possible inference that a jury could draw from Mann's testimony, we defer to that inference. We therefore find that Redgrave presented sufficient evidence to prove consequential damages of $12,000, the fee arrangement contemplated by Mann for Redgrave's appearance in Heartbreak House, minus expenses she personally would have incurred had she appeared in the play.

* * *

Affirmed in part.

### *QUESTIONS FOR DISCUSSION*

1. The major industry decision on this topic prior to *Redgrave* was *Amaducci v. Metropolitan Opera Assoc.*, 33 A.D.2d 542, 304 N.Y.S.2d 322 (1969), which held that consequential damages could not be recovered in a contract action for wrongful termination of a performer's services. Those who prefer *Amaducci* to *Redgrave* argue that awarding consequential damages for loss of future work opportunities contravenes the industry expectation that producers will simply "play or pay," and transforms a contract action into the functional equivalent of the tort of defamation. With which position do you agree?

2. Recall the *Basinger* decision in Chapter 7. The jury awarded a film producer over $8 million in damages for losses suffered when Basinger broke her alleged contractual commitment to star in the movie *Boxing Helena.* Should Basinger have been allowed to rely on the *Amaducci* precedent and confine her potential contract damages to the amount that the producer, Main Line, had committed itself to pay for her (or her substitute's) performance?[f]

---

There are many reasons why studios may change their minds about using particular actors in film projects. Following cancellation of its commitment, standard contract doctrine requires the performer seek to mitigate damages by finding work elsewhere. The next case (involving actress Shirley Parker, better known as Shirley MacLaine) addresses the

---

[f] *See generally* Charles Goetz & Robert Scott, *Liquidated Damages, Penalties, & the Just Compensation Principle: Some Notes on an Enforcement Model & a Theory of Efficient Breach*, 77 Colum. L. Rev. 554 (1977).

distinctive problems that the entertainment world poses for the mitigation principle.

### PARKER V. TWENTIETH CENTURY-FOX FILM CORP.

Supreme Court of California, 1970.
3 Cal.3d 176, 89 Cal. Rptr. 737, 474 P.2d 689.

BURKE, JUSTICE.

* * *

Plaintiff is well known as an actress . . . is sometimes referred to as the "Artist." Under the contract [between plaintiff and defendant], dated August 6, 1965, plaintiff was to play the female lead in defendant's contemplated production of a motion picture entitled *Bloomer Girl*. The contract provided that defendant would pay plaintiff a minimum "guaranteed compensation" of $53,571.42 per week for 14 weeks commencing May 23, 1966, for a total of $750,000. Prior to May 1966 defendant decided not to produce the picture and by a letter dated April 4, 1966, it notified plaintiff of that decision and that it would not "comply with our obligations to you under" the written contract.

By the same letter and with the professed purpose "to avoid any damage to you," defendant instead offered to employ plaintiff as the leading actress in another film tentatively entitled *Big Country, Big Man*. The compensation offered was identical, as were 31 of the 34 numbered provisions or articles of the original contract. Unlike *Bloomer Girl*, however, which was to have been a musical production, *Big Country* was a dramatic "western type" movie. *Bloomer Girl* was to have been filmed in California; *Big Country* was to be produced in Australia. Also, certain terms in the proffered contract varied from those of the original.[2] Plaintiff

---

[2] Article 29 of the original contract specified that plaintiff approved the director already chosen for *Bloomer Girl* and that in case he failed to act as director plaintiff was to have approval rights of any substitute director. Article 31 provided that plaintiff was to have the right of approval of the *Bloomer Girl* dance director, and Article 32 gave her the right of approval of the screenplay.

Defendant's letter of April 4 to plaintiff, which contained both defendant's notice of breach of the *Bloomer Girl* contract and offer of the lead in *Big Country*, eliminated or impaired each of those rights. It read in part as follows:

> "The terms and conditions of our offer of employment are identical to those set forth in the *Bloomer Girl* Agreement, Articles 1 through 34 and Exhibit A to the Agreement, except as follows:
>
> 1. Article 31 of said Agreement will not be included in any contract of employment regarding *Big Country, Big Man* as it is not a musical and it thus will not need a dance director.
>
> 2. In the *Bloomer Girl* agreement, in Articles 29 and 32, you were given certain director and screenplay approvals and you had preapproved certain matters. Since there simply is insufficient time to negotiate with you regarding your choice of director and regarding the screenplay and since you already expressed an interest in performing the role in *Big Country, Big Man*, we must exclude from our offer of employment in *Big Country, Big Man* any approval rights as are contained in said Articles 29 and 32;

was given one week within which to accept; she did not and the offer lapsed. Plaintiff then commenced this action seeking recovery of the agreed guaranteed compensation.

The complaint sets forth two causes of action. The first is for money due under the contract; the second, based upon the same allegations as the first, is for damages resulting from defendant's breach of contract. Defendant in its answer admits the existence and validity of the contract, that plaintiff complied with all the conditions, covenants and promises and stood ready to complete the performance, and that defendant breached and "anticipatorily repudiated" the contract. It denies, however, that any money is due to plaintiff either under the contract or as a result of its breach, and pleads as an affirmative defense to both causes of action plaintiff's allegedly deliberate failure to mitigate damages, asserting that she unreasonably refused to accept its offer of the leading role in *Big Country*.

. . . [S]ummary judgment for $750,000 plus interest was entered in plaintiff's favor. This appeal by defendant followed.

* * *

The general rule is that the measure of recovery by a wrongfully discharged employee is the amount of salary agreed upon for the period of service, less the amount which the employer affirmatively proves the employee has earned or with reasonable effort might have earned from other employment. *De La Falaise v. Gaumont-British Picture Corp.* 39 Cal.App.2d 461, 469 (1940) [103 P.2d 447], and cases cited. However, before projected earnings from other employment opportunities not sought or accepted by the discharged employee can be applied in mitigation, the employer must show that the other employment was comparable, or substantially similar, to that of which the employee has been deprived; the employee's rejection of or failure to seek other available employment of a different or inferior kind may not be resorted to in order to mitigate damages.

* * *

Applying the foregoing rules to the record in the present case, with all intendments in favor of the party opposing the summary judgment motion—here, defendant—it is clear that the trial court correctly ruled that plaintiff's failure to accept defendant's tendered substitute employment could not be applied in mitigation of damages because the offer of the *Big Country* lead was of employment both different and

however, we shall consult with you respecting the director to be selected to direct the photoplay and will further consult with you with respect to the screenplay and any revisions or changes therein, provided, however, that if we fail to agree . . . the decision of . . . [defendant] with respect to the selection of a director and to revisions and, changes in the said screenplay shall be binding upon the parties to said agreement."

inferior, and that no factual dispute was presented on that issue. The mere circumstance that *Bloomer Girl* was to be a musical review calling upon plaintiff's talents as a dancer as well as an actress, and was to be produced in the City of Los Angeles, whereas *Big Country* was a straight dramatic role in a "Western Type" story taking place in an opal mine in Australia, demonstrates the difference in kind between the two employments; the female lead as a dramatic actress in a western style motion picture can by no stretch of imagination be considered the equivalent of or substantially similar to the lead in a song-and-dance production.

Additionally, the substitute *Big Country* offer proposed to eliminate or impair the director and screenplay approvals accorded to plaintiff under the original *Bloomer Girl* contract, and thus constituted an offer of inferior employment. No expertise or judicial notice is required in order to hold that the deprivation or infringement of an employee's rights held under an original employment contract converts the available "other employment" relied upon by the employer to mitigate damages, into inferior employment which the employee need not seek or accept.

* * *

Affirmed.

SULLIVAN, ACTING CHIEF JUSTICE, dissenting.

The basic question in this case is whether or not plaintiff acted reasonably in rejecting defendant's offer of alternate employment. The answer depends upon whether that offer (starring in *Big Country, Big Man*) was an offer of work that was substantially similar to her former employment (starring in *Bloomer Girl*) or of work that was of a different or inferior kind. To my mind this is a factual issue which the trial court should not have determined on a motion for summary judgment. The majority have not only repeated this error but have compounded it by applying the rules governing mitigation of damages in the employer-employee context in a misleading fashion. Accordingly, I respectfully dissent.

* * *

Over the years the courts have employed various phrases to define the type of employment which the employee, upon his wrongful discharge, is under an obligation to accept. Thus in California alone it has been held that he must accept employment which is "substantially similar;" "comparable employment;" employment "in the same general line of the first employment;" "equivalent to his prior position;" "employment in a similar capacity;" employment which is "not . . . of a different or inferior kind. . . ."

For reasons which are unexplained, the majority . . . selects from among the various judicial formulations . . . one particular phrase, "Not of a different or inferior kind," with which to analyze this case. I have discovered no historical or theoretical reason to adopt this phrase, which is simply a negative restatement of the affirmative standards set out in the above cases, as the exclusive standard. Indeed, its emergence is an example of the dubious phenomenon of the law responding not to rational judicial choice or changing social conditions, but to unrecognized changes in the language of opinions or legal treatises. However, the phrase is a serviceable one and my concern is not with its use as the standard but rather with what I consider its distortion.

* * *

The relevant language excuses acceptance only of employment which is of a different kind. It has never been the law that the mere existence of differences between two jobs in the same field is sufficient, as a matter of law, to excuse an employee wrongfully discharged from one from accepting the other in order to mitigate damages. Such an approach would effectively eliminate any obligation of an employee to attempt to minimize damage arising from a wrongful discharge. The only alternative job offer an employee would be required to accept would be an offer of his former job by his former employer.

Although the majority appear to hold that there was a difference "in kind" between the employment offered plaintiff in *Bloomer Girl* and that offered in *Big Country*, an examination of the opinion makes crystal clear that the majority merely point out differences between the two films (an obvious circumstance) and then apodictically assert that these constitute a difference in the kind of employment. The entire rationale of the majority boils down to this: that the "mere circumstances" that *Bloomer Girl* was to be a musical review while *Big Country* was a straight drama "demonstrates the difference in kind" since a female lead in a western is not "the equivalent of or substantially similar to" a lead in a musical. This is merely attempting to prove the proposition by repeating it. It shows that the vehicles for the display of the star's talents are different but it does not prove that her employment as a star in such vehicles is of necessity different in kind and either inferior or superior.

I believe that the approach taken by the majority (a superficial listing of differences with no attempt to assess their significance) may subvert a valuable legal doctrine.[5] The inquiry in cases such as this

[5] The values of the doctrine of mitigation of damages in this context are that it minimizes the unnecessary personal and social (e.g., nonproductive use of labor, litigation) costs of contractual failure. If a wrongfully discharged employee can, through his own action and without suffering financial or psychological loss in the process, reduce the damages accruing from the breach of contract, the most sensible policy is to require him to do so. I fear the majority opinion will encourage precisely opposite conduct.

should not be whether differences between the two jobs exist (there will always be differences) but whether the differences which are present are substantial enough to constitute differences in the kind of employment or, alternatively, whether they render the substitute work employment of an inferior kind.

* * *

It is not intuitively obvious, to me at least, that the leading female role in a dramatic motion picture is a radically different endeavor from the leading female role in a musical comedy film. Nor is it plain to me that the rather qualified rights of director and screenplay approval contained in the first contract are highly significant matters either in the entertainment industry in general or to this plaintiff in particular. . . .

* * *

I cannot accept the proposition that an offer which eliminates any contract right, regardless of its significance, is, as a matter of law, an offer of employment of an inferior kind. Such an absolute rule seems no more sensible than the majority's earlier suggestion that the mere existence of differences between two jobs is sufficient to render them employment of different kinds. Application of such per se rules will severely undermine the principle of mitigation of damages in the employer-employee context.

I remain convinced that the relevant question in such cases is whether or not a particular contract provision is so significant that its omission creates employment of an inferior kind. This question is, of course, intimately bound up in what I consider the ultimate issue: whether or not the employee acted reasonably. This will generally involve a factual inquiry to ascertain the importance of the particular contract term and a process of weighing the absence of that term against the countervailing advantages of the alternate employment. In the typical case, this will mean that summary judgment must be withheld.

* * *

### *QUESTIONS FOR DISCUSSION*

1. In assessing whether the performer failed to make reasonable efforts to mitigate damages from the producer's breach—in particular, by refusing another engagement—should the test be whether the two engagements were substantially similar, or whether the substitute was substantially inferior to the one contracted for? (Under either standard, what is the significance of the fact that Parker would have a right of consultation, but not of final approval, of the second movie's director and screenplay?) Which mitigation rule best serves the fans as well as the participants in the entertainment industry?

2. In *De La Falaise v. Gaumont-British Picture Corp.*, 39 Cal.App.2d 461, 103 P.2d 447 (1940), income from Constance Bennett's employment was offset against her damage recovery for breach of contract for two films, *Everything is Thunder* and *The Hawk*. Though the first film was produced and released, *The Hawk* was never begun. During the period of the contract, Bennett received $4,000 for two radio engagements. In her suit for breach of contract for the producer's failure to make *The Hawk*, the court found that a discharged employee need not obtain employment of an inferior kind to mitigate damages, but that an offset of Bennett's radio earnings was proper because "while such work might be denominated different in character from that required of a moving picture actress, it cannot be said to be inferior thereto." *Id.* at 470. Suppose that Bennett had refused the radio assignments: would the foregone earnings be deductible from the damage award?

3. Relying on *Parker*, the court in *Boehm v. American Broadcasting Co.*, 929 F.2d 482 (9th Cir. 1991), found that ABC had failed to satisfy its burden of proving that the network had offered substantially equivalent employment to a terminated employee. Following his termination as Vice President of ABC Radio in charge of Los Angeles regional sales, Frank Boehm was offered a newly created position at ABC. The base salary of the new position was the same as Boehm's previous base salary. In dispute was the comparative responsibilities of the two positions and whether the total compensation, including commissions earned in Boehm's former position, was equivalent. In his new position, Boehm would have been required to report to his replacement in his former job. Noting the fact that the new position was never filled, Boehm stated at trial that he felt that it was "phony." The Ninth Circuit affirmed a jury award of $1.34 million in compensatory damages and $150,000 for negligent infliction of emotional distress. Regarding the alleged failure of Boehm to mitigate his damages, the court stated that under California law, an employee who has been wrongfully terminated has a duty to mitigate damages through reasonable efforts to find other employment, but the failure to accept an alternative job is significant only if the employer shows, quoting *Parker*, "that the other employment was comparable, or substantially similar, to that of which the employee has been deprived." *Id.* at 485.

4. In *Phillips v. Playboy Music*, 424 F. Supp. 1148 (N.D. Miss. 1976), the court found that Playboy had willfully and intentionally breached a contract with plaintiffs by refusing to continue advancing funds in accordance with a record producing contract. Under the contract, Phillips and his partner, who were well-known talent scouts, agreed to produce and deliver eight LPs a year for two years in exchange for a $40,000 advance on signing, as well as advances of $5,000 per month during the first year, $4,166.66 per month during the second year, and $5,000 each time an LP was delivered. In breaching the contract, Playboy refused to pay plaintiffs two monthly payments during the first year of the term, aggregating the sum of $10,000 and the $50,000 which was due in equal monthly installments for the second year of the term.

At trial, Playboy argued that plaintiffs could not recover in the action because they did not attempt to mitigate damages by seeking a substitute contract. The court stated that plaintiffs were only required to exercise reasonable diligence in mitigating damages and that the "nature, term, and other pertinent aspects of the contract must be considered in light of the circumstances surrounding the undertakings of the contracting parties." The court found that the agreement in question could not "be readily or easily negotiated in the average or usual marketplace." *Id.* at 1153. Evidence also showed that music industry contracts that provided non-returnable advances were difficult to obtain. In light of these circumstances, the court held that plaintiffs did not have a reasonable opportunity to seek a contract with another distributor in order to minimize their loss.

---

The previous chapter, discussed a lawsuit by Raquel Welch against MGM. The jury found and the appeals court agreed that MGM president David Begelman's removal of Welch from the film *Cannery Row* and replacement of Welch with Debra Winger violated both MGM's express contract and implied covenant of good faith and fair dealing with Welch. The jury awarded Welch $2 million in compensatory damages and over $8 million in punitive damages. This amount included $194,000 that was still owed under the *Cannery Row* contract, and the balance for additional claims of slander, conspiracy to induce breach of contract, and breach of the implied covenant of good faith and fair dealing. The parts of the opinion reproduced here deal with MGM's appeal of that damages award. The *Welch* case illustrates the value of framing her claim as something different from a standard breach of contract suit.

## RAQUEL WELCH V. METRO-GOLDWYN-MAYER FILM CO.

Court of Appeal of California, Second Appellate District, 1988.
254 Cal. Rptr. 645.

WOODS, JUDGE.

* * *

Negative reviews of the film which appeared in Variety and the New York Times in February 1982 stated that Welch should feel happy she had been fired from it. The film was a major failure at the box office, and MGM lost almost $16 million on it.

The evidence established that an accusation of breaking a contract would be very damaging to an actress's reputation, as people in the industry would assume she was undependable. Welch never made another movie because of her firing from *Cannery Row*. One deal fell through due to a lack of financing and the only other offers she received, to portray a Nazi and a vampire, were unacceptable. In contrast, she had made about six films between 1973 and 1980, with compensation [per film] ranging between $150,000 and $350,000. At the time of trial, in 1986, film actresses routinely received twice the 1980 level of compensation. Some stars were making from $2 million to $5 million per film.

Having no offers in Hollywood, Welch moved to New York City. For two weeks at the end of 1981 and six months in 1982, she had a very successful run in the Broadway musical *Woman of the Year*, for which she earned $25,000 per week. She later signed two $1 million contracts, one for food commercials and the other for a concert tour. She also made hundreds of thousands of dollars from a best-selling health and beauty book and accompanying videotape. These activities would not have prevented her from accepting a film role.

IX

* * *

Appellants maintain that there was insufficient evidence to support an award of $1 million for loss of professional income on the bad faith count, as Welch did not have a reasonably certain future career as a serious film actress. We disagree. The lost income award was supported by the amount of money Welch had made from previous film work, the absence of film offers subsequent to *Cannery Row*, the expert testimony that she would have obtained additional film roles but for the *Cannery Row* firing, and the amount of money film stars were making at the time of trial. The $1 million the jury awarded for lost income was considerably less than the $3,200,000 for which her counsel argued.

We similarly reject appellant's argument that there was insufficient evidence to support damages of $750,000 for loss of reputation on the bad faith count. Appellants ignore the difference between Welch's pre-*Cannery Row* reputation as a somewhat difficult but professional actress and her post-*Cannery Row* reputation as a contract breaker who had been fired for cause.

* * *

X

[The court then addressed defendants' claim that the jury's punitive damages awards (a total of $7.65 million against MGM and $500,500 against Phillips, producer of *Cannery Row*) were legally excessive.]

* * *

It was stipulated below that MGM had a net worth of $215 million and Phillips of $5 million. The punitive damages thus represented 3.6 percent of MGM's net worth and 10 percent of Phillips's net worth as an individual. As to MGM, the ratio of punitive damages to compensatory damages was 2.8:1. The same ratio as to Phillips was 2.1:1.

. . . [T]he size of the punitive damage awards here were not inconsistent with or disproportionate to awards which have been affirmed in the past. We realize that MGM lost money on the film, and Phillips's salary for producing it was $200,000. Still, given the net worths of the defendants, their complete disregard of the likelihood that the unjustified firing would ruin Welch's film career, and the relatively high actual damages, the jury could properly conclude that appellants' conduct justified the amount of punitive damages which was awarded.

* * *

Affirmed.

---

Less than a week after the *Welch* decision, the California Supreme Court issued its major wrongful dismissal ruling, *Foley v. Interactive Data Corp.*, 47 Cal.3d 654, 254 Cal. Rptr. 211, 765 P.2d 373 (1988), holding that an employee cannot secure redress in *tort* for breach of the implied covenant of good faith and fair dealing in an employment *contract*. *Foley* distinguished its earlier decision, *Seaman's Direct Buying Service v. Standard Oil*, 36 Cal.3d 752, 206 Cal. Rptr. 354, 686 P.2d 1158 (1984), which had established such a tort for bad faith violation of insurance contracts, on the grounds that employees, unlike insureds, had ample other opportunities in the marketplace, and that the interests of employees and employers were far more complementary than were the interests of insureds and insurers. *Newman v. Emerson Radio Corp.*, 48 Cal.3d 973, 258 Cal. Rptr. 592, 772 P.2d 1059 (1989), then applied *Foley* retroactively, consistent with the general practice in tort cases. Consequently, *Welch* was vacated and reconsidered in light of *Newman*: after deleting Welch's $8 million punitive damage award, the court entered judgment against MGM in the amount of $5.3 million. When one considers the legal costs that went into litigating the *Welch* case and the magnitude of the damages ultimately awarded, it would seem that MGM should have relied on the "pay or play" clause in the first instance, and paid the $194,000 Welch would be owed under her contract if she was simply replaced rather than fired.

## 2. AUTHORS VS. PUBLISHERS

The last section of this chapter considers damage claims filed by the authors of books or music against their publishers or record companies. Clearly the role of the author in writing a book or a musician recording an album is very different from the role of an actor in a movie or play. What difference, if any, should this make when a firm violated its obligation to publish and promote the work, or when the author or musician failed to mitigate damages?

## FREUND V. WASHINGTON SQUARE PRESS, INC.

Court of Appeals of New York, 1974.
34 N.Y.2d 379, 357 N.Y.S.2d 857, 314 N.E.2d 419.

RABIN, JUDGE.

In this action for breach of a publishing contract, we must decide what damages are recoverable for defendant's failure to publish plaintiff's manuscript. In 1965, plaintiff, an author and a college teacher, and defendant, Washington Square Press, Inc., entered into a written agreement which, in relevant part, provided as follows. Plaintiff ("author") granted defendant ("publisher") exclusive rights to publish and sell in book form plaintiff's work on modern drama. Upon plaintiff's delivery of the manuscript, defendant agreed to complete payment of a nonreturnable $2,000 "advance". Thereafter, if defendant deemed the manuscript not "suitable for publication", it had the right to terminate the agreement by written notice within 60 days of delivery. Unless so terminated, defendant agreed to publish the work in hardbound edition within 18 months and afterwards in paperbound edition. The contract further provided that defendant would pay royalties to plaintiff, based upon specified percentages of sales. (For example, plaintiff was to receive 10% of the retail price of the first 10,000 copies sold in the continental United States.) If defendant failed to publish within 18 months, the contract provided that "this agreement shall terminate and the rights herein granted to the Publisher shall revert to the Author. In such event all payments theretofore made to the Author shall belong to the Author without prejudice to any other remedies which the Author may have. . . ."

Plaintiff performed by delivering his manuscript to defendant and was paid his $2,000 advance. Defendant thereafter merged with another publisher and ceased publishing in hardbound. Although defendant did not exercise its 60-day right to terminate, it has refused to publish the manuscript in any form.

Plaintiff commenced the instant action . . . [and] initially sought specific performance of the contract. The Trial Term Justice denied specific performance but, finding a valid contract and a breach by defendant, set the matter down for trial on the issue of monetary damages, if any, sustained by the plaintiff. At trial, plaintiff sought to prove: (1) delay of his academic promotion; (2) loss of royalties which would have been earned; and (3) the cost of publication if plaintiff had made his own arrangements to publish. The trial court found that plaintiff had been promoted despite defendant's failure to publish, and that there was no evidence that the breach had caused any delay.

Recovery of lost royalties was denied without discussion. The court found, however, that the cost of hardcover publication to plaintiff was the natural and probable consequence of the breach and, based upon expert testimony, awarded $10,000 to cover this cost. It denied recovery of the expenses of paperbound publication on the ground that plaintiff's proof was conjectural.

The Appellate Division, (3 to 2) affirmed, finding that the cost of publication was the proper measure of damages. In support of its conclusion, the majority analogized to the construction contract situation where the cost of completion may be the proper measure of damages for a builder's failure to complete a house or for use of wrong materials. The dissent concluded that the cost of publication is not an appropriate measure of damages and consequently, that plaintiff may recover nominal damages only.* We agree with the dissent. In so concluding, we look to the basic purpose of damage recovery and the nature and effect of the parties' contract.

It is axiomatic that, except where punitive damages are allowable, the law awards damages for breach of contract to compensate for injury caused by the breach—injury which was foreseeable, i.e., reasonably within the contemplation of the parties, at the time the contract was entered into. Money damages are substitutional relief designed in theory "to put the injured party in as good a position as he would have been put by full performance of the contract, at the least cost to the defendant and without charging him with harms that he had no sufficient reason to foresee when he made the contract." (5 Corbin, *Contracts*, 1002, pp. 31–32; 11 Williston, *Contracts* [3d ed.], 1338, p. 198.) In other words, so far as possible, the law attempts to secure to the injured party the benefit of his bargain, subject to the limitations that the injury—whether it be losses suffered or gains prevented—was foreseeable, and that the amount of damages claimed be measurable with a reasonable degree of certainty and, of course, adequately proven . . . But it is equally fundamental that the injured party should not recover more from the breach than he would have gained had the contract been fully performed.

Measurement of damages in this case according to the cost of publication to the plaintiff would confer greater advantage than performance of the contract would have entailed to plaintiff and would place him in a far better position than he would have occupied had the defendant fully performed. Such measurement bears no relation to compensation for plaintiff's actual loss or anticipated profit. Far beyond compensating plaintiff for the interests he had in the defendant's performance of the contract—whether restitution, reliance or expectation (*see* Fuller & Perdue, *Reliance Interest in Contract Damages*, 46 Yale L.J.

* Plaintiff does not challenge the trial court's denial of damages for delay in promotion or for anticipated royalties.

52, 53–56)—an award of the cost of publication would enrich plaintiff at defendant's expense.

Pursuant to the contract, plaintiff delivered his manuscript to the defendant. In doing so, he conferred a value on the defendant which, upon defendant's breach, was required to be restored to him. Special Term, in addition to ordering a trial on the issue of damages, ordered defendant to return the manuscript to plaintiff and plaintiff's restitution interest in the contract was thereby protected.

At the trial on the issue of damages, plaintiff alleged no reliance losses suffered in performing the contract or in making necessary preparations to perform. Had such losses, if foreseeable and ascertainable, been incurred, plaintiff would have been entitled to compensation for them.

As for plaintiff's expectation interest in the contract, it was basically two-fold-the "advance" and the royalties. (To be sure, plaintiff may have expected to enjoy whatever notoriety, prestige or other benefits that might have attended publication, but even if these expectations were compensable, plaintiff did not attempt at trial to place a monetary value on them.) There is no dispute that plaintiff's expectancy in the "advance" was fulfilled—he has received his $2,000. His expectancy interest in the royalties—the profit he stood to gain from sale of the published book—while theoretically compensable, was speculative. Although this work is not plaintiff's first, at trial he provided no stable foundation for a reasonable estimate of royalties he would have earned had defendant not breached its promise to publish. In these circumstances, his claim for royalties falls for uncertainty.

Since the damages which would have compensated plaintiff for anticipated royalties were not proved with the required certainty, we agree with the dissent in the Appellate Division that nominal damages alone are recoverable. Though these are damages in name only and not at all compensatory, they are nevertheless awarded as a formal vindication of plaintiff's legal right to compensation which has not been given a sufficiently certain monetary valuation.

In our view, the analogy by the majority in the Appellate Division to the construction contract situation was inapposite. In the typical construction contract, the owner agrees to pay money or other consideration to a builder and expects, under the contract, to receive a completed building in return. The value of the promised performance to the owner is the properly constructed building. In this case, unlike the typical construction contract, the value to plaintiff of the promised performance (publication) was a percentage of sales of the books published and not the books themselves. Had the plaintiff contracted for the printing, binding and delivery of a number of hardbound copies of his manuscript, to be sold or disposed of as he wished, then perhaps the construction analogy, and measurement of damages by the cost of replacement or completion, would have some application.

Here, however, the specific value to plaintiff of the promised publication was the royalties he stood to receive from defendant's sales of the published book. Essentially, publication represented what it would have cost the defendant to confer that value upon the plaintiff, and, by its breach, defendant saved that cost. The error by the courts below was in measuring damages not by the value to plaintiff of the promised performance but by the cost of that performance to defendant. Damages are not measured, however, by what the defaulting party saved by the breach, but by the natural and probable consequences of the breach to the plaintiff. In this case, the consequence to plaintiff of defendant's failure to publish is that he is prevented from realizing the gains promised by the contract—the royalties. But, as we have stated, the amount of royalties plaintiff would have realized was not ascertained with adequate certainty and, as a consequence, plaintiff may recover nominal damages only.

* * *

Reversed in part.

---

Three years later a New York court ruled, in *Gilroy v. American Broadcasting Co.*, 58 A.D.2d 533, 395 N.Y.S.2d 658 (1977), that a $750,000 award against the network for misappropriating a writer's literary property failed the *Freund* "wholly speculative" test. The court was satisfied, though, that Gilroy had suffered some financial harm as a result of ABC's actions. Thus, it made a pragmatic judgment that "the interest of substantial justice will best be achieved" by fixing the recovery at $100,000. That same year, the Second Circuit addressed the same issue under New York law, in a case involving the music industry.

## CONTEMPORARY MISSION V. FAMOUS MUSIC CORP.

United States Court of Appeals, Second Circuit, 1977.
557 F.2d 918.

MESKILL, CIRCUIT JUDGE.

I. The Facts.

Contemporary is a nonprofit charitable corporation . . . composed of a small group of Roman Catholic priests who write, produce and publish musical compositions and recordings. In 1972 the group owned all of the rights to a rock opera entitled *Virgin*, which was composed by Father John T. O'Reilly, a vice-president and member of the group.

Contemporary first became involved with Famous in 1972 as a result of O'Reilly's efforts to market *Virgin*.

Famous . . . is a wholly-owned subsidiary of the Gulf + Western Corporation, and, until July 31, 1974, it was engaged in the business of producing musical recordings for distribution throughout the United States. Famous' president, Tony Martell, is generally regarded in the recording industry as the individual primarily responsible for the successful distribution of the well-known rock operas *Tommy* and *Jesus Christ Superstar*.

The relationship between Famous and Contemporary was considerably more harmonious in 1972 than it is today. At that time, Martell thought he had found, in *Virgin*, another *Tommy* or *Jesus Christ Superstar*, and he was anxious to acquire rights to it. O'Reilly, who was encouraged by Martell's expertise and enthusiasm, had high hopes for the success of his composition. On August 16, 1972, they executed the so-called "*Virgin* Recording Agreement" on behalf of their respective organizations.

The terms of the *Virgin* agreement were relatively simple. Famous agreed to pay a royalty to Contemporary in return for the master tape recording of *Virgin* and the exclusive right to manufacture and sell records made from the master. The agreement also created certain "Additional Obligations of Famous" which included, inter alia: the obligation to select and appoint, within the first year of the agreement, at least one person to personally oversee the nationwide promotion of the sale of records, to maintain contact with Contemporary and to submit weekly reports to Contemporary; the obligation to spend, within the first year of the agreement, no less than $50,000 on the promotion of records; and the obligation to release, within the first two years of the agreement, at least four separate single records from *Virgin*. The agreement also contained a non-assignability clause.

On May 8, 1973, the parties entered into a distribution contract which dealt with musical compositions other than *Virgin*. This, the so-called "Crunch agreement," granted to Famous the exclusive right to distribute Contemporary's records in the United States. Famous agreed to institute a new record label named "Crunch," and a number of records were to be released under it annually. Contemporary agreed to deliver ten long-playing records and fifteen single records during the first year of the contract. Famous undertook to use its "reasonable efforts" to promote and distribute the records . . . The contract prohibited assignment by Contemporary, but it contained no provision relating to Famous' right to assign.

Although neither *Virgin* nor its progeny was ever as successful as the parties had originally hoped, the business relationship continued on an amicable basis until July 31, 1974. On that date, Famous' record division was sold to ABC Records, Inc. (ABC). When O'Reilly complained to Martell that Famous was breaking its promises, he was told that he would have to look to ABC for performance. O'Reilly met with one of ABC's lawyers and was told that ABC was not going to have any relationship with Contemporary . . . This lawsuit followed.

* * *

II. The Jury Verdict.

[The jury awarded Contemporary nearly $200,000 in damages for Famous' breach of the *Virgin* agreement (for failing adequately to promote *Virgin*) and its obligations under the Crunch agreement (for ABC's failure to promote Contemporary's music after the assignment).]

III. Discussion.

On this appeal, Famous attacks the verdict on several grounds. Their first contention is that the evidence was insufficient to support the jury's response to [a number of liability questions] . . . [In addition, they contend] that Contemporary failed to comply with the notice provision of the Crunch agreement. Their final contention is that Contemporary is estopped from suing for a breach of the Crunch agreement. We find none of these arguments persuasive.

*A. The Virgin Agreement.*

. . . Famous vigorously contends . . . that the jury's conclusion, that it had failed to adequately promote *Virgin* prior to the sale to ABC, is at war with the undisputed facts and cannot be permitted to stand. In particular they argue that they spent the required $50,000 and appointed the required overseer for the project. The flaw in this argument is that its focus is too narrow. The obligations to which it refers are but two of many created by the *Virgin* agreement. Under the doctrine of *Wood v. Lucy, Lady Duff-Gordon*, 222 N.Y. 88, 118 N.E. 214 (1917), Famous had an obligation to use its reasonable efforts to promote *Virgin* on a nationwide basis. That obligation could not be satisfied merely by technical compliance with the spending and appointment requirements of paragraph 14 of the agreement. Even assuming that Famous complied fully with those requirements, there was evidence from which the jury could find that Famous failed to adequately promote *Virgin*. The question is a close one, particularly in light of Martell's obvious commitment to the success of *Virgin* and in light of the efforts that were in fact exerted and the lack of any serious dispute between the parties prior to the sale to ABC. However, there was evidence that Famous prematurely terminated the promotion of the first single record, "Got To Know," shortly after its release, and that Famous limited its promotion of the second record,

"Kyrie," to a single city, rather than promoting it nationwide.[10] Moreover, there was evidence that, prior to the sale to ABC, Famous underwent a budget reduction and cut back its promotional staff. From this, the jury could infer that the promotional effort was reduced to a level that was less than adequate. On the whole, therefore, we are not persuaded that the jury's verdict should be disturbed.

*B. The Crunch Agreement.*

[The court concluded that even after its assignment to ABC Records of all rights in the "Crunch agreement," Famous remained legally responsible for any failure by ABC to fulfill its contractual obligations to Contemporary.]

* * *

IV. The Cross-Appeal.

During the trial, Contemporary sought to introduce a statistical analysis, together with expert testimony, in order to prove how successful the most successful of its single recordings, "Fear No Evil," would have become if the *Virgin* agreement had not been breached as a result of the sale to ABC. Based upon its projection of the success of that recording, Contemporary hoped to prove what revenues that success would have produced. Judge Owen excluded this evidence on the ground that it was speculative. *Freund v. Washington Square Press, Inc.*, 34 N.Y.2d 379, 314 N.E.2d 419, 357 N.Y.S.2d 857 (1974).

There can be no dispute that Contemporary "is entitled to the reasonable damage flowing from the breach of" the *Virgin* agreement by Famous, and that "the measure of the damage is the amount necessary to put [Contemporary] in [the] exact position as [it] would have been if the contract had not been breached." *Perma Research & Dev. v. Singer Co.*, 542 F.2d 111, 116 (2d Cir.) Nor can there be any dispute as to the New York rules concerning the measure of proof required to prove the existence of damage and the measure of proof necessary to enable the jury to fix its amount. It is clear that the existence of damage must be certain-a requirement that operates with particular severity in cases involving artistic creations such as books, *Freund v. Washington Square Press*, Inc., supra, movies, *Broadway Photoplay Co. v. World Film Corp.*, 225 N.Y. 104, 121 N.E. 756 (1919), plays, *Bernstein v. Meech*, 130 N.Y. 354, 29 N.E. 255 (1891), and, by analogy, records. What all of these have in common is their dependence upon taste or fancy for success. When the existence of

[10] We recognize that the limited promotion of "Kyrie" was a result of "test marketing," i.e., the concentration of promotional efforts in one area before expanding the efforts to the rest of the country. However, because the promotion of "Kyrie" was thus limited, Famous only marketed three single records on a nationwide basis, and the contract required the nationwide promotion of four.

damage is uncertain or speculative, the plaintiff is limited to the recovery of nominal damages. On the other hand,

> if the plaintiff has given valuable consideration for the promise of performance which would have given him a chance to make a profit, the defendant should not be allowed to deprive him of that performance without compensation unless the difficulty of determining its value is extreme. Especially is this true where there is no chance of loss.

11 *Williston on Contracts* § 1346, at 242 (3d ed. 1968). Thus, under the long-standing New York rule, when the existence of damage is certain, and the only uncertainty is as to its amount, the plaintiff will not be denied a recovery of substantial damages. *See Lee v. Joseph E. Seagram & Sons, Inc.*, 552 F.2d 447, 456, slip op. 2319, 2334 (2d Cir. Mar. 15, 1977); *W. L. Hailey & Co. v. County of Niagara*, 388 F.2d 746, 753 (2d Cir. 1967) (collecting New York cases). Moreover, the burden of uncertainty as to the amount of damage is upon the wrongdoer, and the test for admissibility of evidence concerning prospective damages is whether the evidence has any tendency to show their probable amount. The plaintiff need only show a "stable foundation for a reasonable estimate of royalties he would have earned had defendant not breached." *Freund v. Washington Square Press, Inc.*, supra, 314 N.E.2d at 421. "Such an estimate necessarily requires some improvisation, and the party who has caused the loss may not insist on theoretical perfection." *Entis v. Atlantic Wire & Cable Corp.*, 335 F.2d 759, 763 (2d Cir. 1964). "[The] law will make the best appraisal that it can, summoning to its service whatever aids it can command." *Sinclair Rfg. Co. v. Jenkins Co.*, 289 U.S. 689, 697 (1933).

We are confident that under the principles enunciated above the exclusion of the evidence proffered by Contemporary was error. This is not a case in which the plaintiff sought to prove hypothetical profits from the sale of a hypothetical record at a hypothetical price in a hypothetical market. At the time of the sale to ABC, the record was real, the price was fixed, the market was buying and the record's success, while modest, was increasing. Even after the promotional efforts ended, and the record was withdrawn from the marketplace, it was carried, as a result of its own momentum, to an additional 10,000 sales and to a rise from approximately number 80 on the "Hot Soul's Singles" chart of Billboard magazine to number 61. It cannot be gainsaid that if someone had continued to promote it, and if it had not been withdrawn from the market, it would have sold more records than it actually did. Thus, it is certain that Contemporary suffered some damage in the form of lost royalties. The same is not true, however, of the existence of damage in the form of lost opportunities for concert tours, theatrical tours or similar benefits. While it is certain that some sales were lost as a result of the failure to promote, we cannot believe that under *Freund* the New York courts would accept what Famous' counsel aptly described at trial as Contemporary's "domino theory" of prospective damages. The theory is that if "Fear No Evil" had become a "hit," its success would have stimulated additional sales of the full two record *Virgin* album and would have generated sufficient popular acceptance to enable Contemporary to obtain bookings for a nationwide concert tour. We hold that these additional benefits are too dependent upon taste or fancy to be considered anything other than speculative and uncertain, and, therefore, proof of damage in the form of such lost benefits was properly excluded by Judge Owen.

We next turn to the question of whether the evidence as to the amount of lost royalties was relevant under the standards set out above. Because "Fear No Evil" ultimately reached number 61 on the record charts, Contemporary offered a statistical analysis of every song that had reached number 61 during 1974. This analysis showed that 76 percent of the 324 songs that had reached number 61 ultimately reached the top 40; 65 percent reached the top 30; 51 percent reached the top 20; 34 percent reached the top 10; 21 percent reached the top 5; and 10 percent reached number 1. If the trial judge had admitted this evidence, Contemporary was prepared to offer the testimony of an expert witness who could have converted these measures of success into projected sales figures. The sales figures could be converted into lost royalties in accordance with the terms of the *Virgin* agreement.

Famous vigorously maintains, and Judge Owen agreed, that the data was incomplete because it failed to account for such factors as the speed with which the various records rose upward (the most successful records generally rise quickly-passing number 61 in their third or fourth week-"Fear No Evil" had risen relatively slowly-number 61 in ten weeks); the reputations of the various artists performing the recordings (Contemporary had no prior hit records and was relatively unknown); and the size and ability of the company promoting the recordings. We agree that a more accurate prediction of the success of "Fear No Evil" would be likely to result if the statistical analysis accounted for these and other factors. The omission of these factors from Contemporary's study affects only the weight of the evidence, however, and not its admissibility. Evidence need not be conclusive in order to be relevant. Standing alone, the study tended to prove that it was more likely than not that "Fear No Evil" would be among the 51 percent of recordings that reached the top 20. If Famous wished to offer proof that would tend to cast doubt on the accuracy of that prediction, it would be free to do so. In this way, all of the evidence tending to show the probable amount of Contemporary's damages would be placed before the jury. While it is true that the jury would be required to speculate to some degree with respect to whether

"Fear No Evil" would be within any particular percentage, such is the nature of estimation. If the amount of damage were certain, no estimation would be required. But the uncertainty exists, and since it is a product of the defendant's wrongful conduct, he will not be heard to complain of the lack of precision.

Because *Freund* does not bar proof of lost royalties and because the proffered evidence was relevant on that issue, Judge Owen was required to admit it, unless he found that "its probative value was substantially outweighed by the danger of unfair prejudice, confusion of the issues, or misleading the jury." It may be, for example, that "[in] the frame within which [they were sought to be] used . . . the [statistics], though relevant, became an item of prejudicial overweight." Fed R. Evid. 403. Similarly, it may be that if Contemporary was unprepared to offer an analysis of factors other than the bare statistics, those statistics, standing alone, would be misleading and would therefore not provide a "stable foundation for a reasonable estimate of royalties" that would have been earned if Famous had not breached. *Freund v. Washington Square Press, Inc.*, supra, 34 N.Y.2d at 383, 314 N.E.2d at 421, 337 N.Y.S.2d at 861. Because Judge Owen did not reach these issues, and because we believe it would be inappropriate for this Court to engage in Rule 403 balancing in the first instance, the case must be remanded to the district court for the purpose of making a Rule 403 determination. The resolution of that issue will, in turn, determine whether Contemporary should be given the new trial on the issue of damages, which it seeks on its cross-appeal.

The judgment of the district court is affirmed in all respects except as to its ruling with regard to lost royalties, and the case is remanded to the district court for further proceedings in accordance with this opinion.

### *QUESTIONS FOR DISCUSSION*

1. Are *Freund* and *Contemporary Mission*, both decided under New York law, consistent with each other? The *Freund* court found that the plaintiff's expectancy interest in his royalties was too speculative to justify more than nominal damages because "he provided no stable foundation for a reasonable estimate of royalties he would have earned." The *Contemporary* court, in contrast, found that since the existence of some damages was certain, even though their amount was not, the jury could award the plaintiff a substantial monetary verdict. Do you agree with one or both of these appellate rulings?

2. Given the restrictions placed on consequential damages in cases like *Contemporary Mission* and *Redgrave*, if you had been the attorney for the producer Main Line, which sued Kim Basinger for walking out on *Boxing Helena*, how would you have documented the $8 million in damages you were seeking to recover for this contract breach?

3. With respect to the contract claim that Famous had not adequately promoted the sale of Contemporary's music, compare the legal standard and its application in this case with the approach in the *Zilg* decision in Chapter 8, dealing with a publisher's obligation to promote the books of its authors.

4. Given the practical problems encountered by the performers in *Freund*, *Contemporary Mission*, and *Redgrave* in documenting the actual harms inflicted on them by their producers' breach of contract, should this branch of contract law be rethought? Should courts provide performers the same broad array of damages available in a tort suit against a party that caused personal injury? Alternatively, should specific performance be made available? What impact might such a change have on negotiation of contract terms in the first place?

# CHAPTER 10

# ENTERTAINER REPRESENTATION AND REGULATION[a]

■ ■ ■

The preceding chapters illustrated the pivotal role that contract negotiation and administration play in the career and lives of entertainers. Contracts determine their level of compensation, their non-economic perquisites, their creative input and credit for projects, and their corresponding commitments and restrictions. The benefits of these contracts are realized not only in the immediate venture, but also in the artist's longer-term career.

An important feature of performer contracts is that most are short-term and project-related. The entertainment world provides a classic example of "contingent employment," in which people move from project to project and firm to firm, rather than establish enduring career relationships with regular employers. Clearly there are exceptions to that rule, such as multi-year and multi-album record contracts, and television performers' ongoing roles on network series or talk shows. Even television and music stars like Oprah Winfrey and Taylor Swift have a host of other film specials, live concerts and personal appearances, and merchandising ventures and commercial endorsements.

On almost all of these projects, the artist is dealing with a large organization: a film studio, book publisher, record company, or television broadcaster. Sometimes the artist faces a conglomerate that brings all of these entertainment branches under one multimedia umbrella. Major entertainment companies have a host of full-time professionals working to enhance their side of the contract relationship. That is precisely why performers need sophisticated representation of their interests in a setting in which millions of dollars, as well as their professional lives, may turn on whether the deals were properly designed.

---

[a] *See* Frank Rose, *The Agency: William Morris & the Hidden History of Show Business* (Harper Collins 1995); Frederic Dannen, *Hit Men* (Times Books 1990); Neville L. Johnson & Daniel W. Long, *The Personal Manager in the California Entertainment Industry*, 52 So. Cal. L. Rev. 375 (1979); James M. O'Brien III, *Regulation of Attorneys Under the California Talent Agencies Act: A Tautological Approach to Protecting Artists*, 80 Cal. L. Rev. 471 (1992); Gary E. Devlin, *The Talent Agencies Act: Reconciling the Controversies Surrounding Lawyers, Managers, & Agents Participating in California's Entertainment Industry*, 28 Pepp. L. Rev. 381 (2001); David B. Wilkins, *Who Should Regulate Lawyers?* 105 Harv. L. Rev. 799 (1992).

Entertainer representation has become a large and variegated profession. Not just the big stars but even the mid-level performers regularly draw upon a variety of forms of representation—talent agent, personal manager, business manager, and entertainment lawyer. Two or more of these roles may well be filled by the same individual or firm. As we shall see, though, it is important to distinguish among the several functions.

The role of the talent agent is to market the entertainer's services and procure employment offers and contracts. This agency work is the oldest form of entertainer representation. Big firms like William Morris Agency, International Creative Management (ICM), and Creative Artists Agency (CAA) have rosters of thousands of clients, each typically paying a commission of ten percent of gross earnings. Drawing upon that client base, the large agencies often function not just as individual client representatives, but as "deal packagers"—putting together teams of actors, writers, directors, and producers (together with a story idea), and selling the entire deal to a studio that will finance and develop a movie or television series.

Given the size of big-time talent agencies, the first representative used by a fledgling performer is often a personal manager. (Indeed, a CAA or an ICM will not take on performers until the latter have developed a sufficient track record and reputation.) The role of the personal manager is to help develop, guide, and enhance the career path of the entertainer. The tasks they perform range from advice about the kinds of training to get or projects to accept, to the logistics of travel and appearances (e.g., concert tours), to the handling of problems in the performer's personal life. Given what often is 24-hour-a-day attention to particular clients, the personal manager's roster is usually very small (perhaps five or six), and the share of proceeds correspondingly greater (usually 15 to 25 percent). In the music industry, in particular, the personal manager secures all of the performer's work and contracts except live personal appearances (e.g., concert tours), which are booked by music agents.

An important feature of an entertainer's need for representation is financial in character: collecting the artist's earnings, paying the bills (including taxes), investing the savings, and developing and administering a long-range financial program. At the early stage of a performer's career, the personal manager handles these tasks. If the career takes off, the entertainer has both a need and ability to pay for specialized financial advice. Business managers typically receive 5 percent of the artist's gross earnings.

With respect to all of these functions, a crucial factor is the law—whether it be the contract and intellectual property laws we have explored in this book, or the tax, family, corporate, real estate, and other doctrines that play a significant role in the lives of all well-to-do Americans. Lawyers play a major role in advising entertainers about drafting contracts, designing a retirement investment plan, and resolving disputes with producers. Entertainment lawyers typically are paid on the standard hourly fee basis, but a number of the top Los Angeles entertainment law firms charge their clients a percentage (usually 5 percent) commission on their gross earnings.

As noted earlier, while the *formal* titles and roles of talent representatives are distinct, the actual services they provide often overlap. For example, many leading agents and managers are lawyers who bring that expertise to their clients' representation. In addition, there must be a high level of cooperation and cohesion between the actions of the talent agent seeking work opportunities for the performer, the decisions of the manager about which offers to accept, and the judgment of the lawyer about which terms of a contract or project are most legally beneficial.

---

The oldest talent agency is the William Morris Agency, created in 1898 by William Morris. Working out of a small New York office, Morris represented stars like Will Rogers, Sophie Tucker, and Harry Lauder in what was then the largest component of entertainment, vaudeville. With the help of Morris' assistant and eventual successor, Abe Lastfogel, the William Morris Agency took its clients—by then including Al Jolson, Maurice Chevalier, and the Marx Brothers—into the worlds of movies and radio broadcasting that largely replaced vaudeville in the 1920s.

In that same decade, Jules Stein created the Music Corporation of America (MCA), a Chicago-based agency that specialized in booking orchestras in ballrooms. By the end of the 1930s, MCA dominated this field, with clients like Guy Lombardo, Tommy Dorsey, and Benny Goodman. Stein also found an assistant and eventual successor, Lew Wasserman, who opened a West Coast branch of MCA to work in the movie industry. One of Wasserman's first clients was Ronald Reagan, for whom he secured a million-dollar contract after Reagan's movie hit, *King's Row*. Within a decade, MCA was the leading agent in Hollywood, with a client roster that included Errol Flynn, Bette Davis, Gene Kelly, Greta Garbo, Jimmy Stewart, and Alfred Hitchcock.

The emergence of television in the late 1940s produced wrenching changes in the movie industry. One change was the switch from the lucrative long-term contracts that Wasserman had negotiated on behalf of the Ronald Reagans in the 1940s to the specific movie contracts he negotiated for the Jimmy Stewarts in the 1950s. The latter form of contract relationship enabled MCA (and William Morris) to put together package proposals that combined several agency clients looking for work as actor, director, or screenwriter. These packages were even more significant in the infant world of television, where a talent agency not only put together a story idea and a talent team, but also did the budgetary and market analysis. The agency would then take the entire project to an advertising firm to get the program financed by one of the latter's clients, and finally to the networks to see which one wanted to air the program. That is how William Morris developed the first hit television series, *Texaco Star Theater,* featuring Milton Berle, which appeared on NBC in 1948; the same path was followed in the development of *I Love Lucy*, *The Honeymooners*, and the like.

While agencies did more work on these projects, they also reaped large financial rewards: rather than 10 percent of their own clients' salaries, the agencies took ten percent of the program's entire budget. Indeed, MCA went the next step and retained ownership in its television programs. In a labor agreement negotiated in 1938 between the Screen Actors Guild (SAG) and the Hollywood agents (represented by Morris' Abe Lastfogel), the agents agreed that they would not function as both performer representatives and production employers. In 1952, SAG was planning to have the same principle applied to television, but Ronald Reagan, who was president of the union, agreed to give the production arm of his long-time agent, MCA, an exemption from that rule. By the end of the 1950s, MCA and William Morris had more than a dozen programs on prime-time, but MCA owned its shows, something that would prove very important for later syndication and other derivative rights.

A combination of developments brought this trend to a halt. One was the scandal generated in the late 1950s by MCA's hit quiz show *Twenty One,* with Charles Van Doren (eventually portrayed in the 1994 movie *Quiz Show*). Another was Lew Wasserman's plan for MCA to acquire Decca Records in 1962, which also owned an established studio, Universal Pictures. The third was a decision by Attorney General Robert F. Kennedy to institute an antitrust investigation of MCA that same year, as the firm was both producing movies and television shows and representing the performers who starred in them. Prodded by both the Justice Department and SAG, MCA decided to give up its agency work and confine MCA/Universal to production of movies, television programs, and records.

A group of MCA agents, led by Freddie Fields and David Begelman, set up a new agency, Creative Management Associates (CMA), whose initial roster included Paul Newman and Joanne Woodward. By the late 1970s, a variety of mergers turned CMA into an International Creative Management (ICM). Meanwhile, Michael Ovitz and Ron Meyer departed William Morris to set up the Creative Artists Agency (CAA), which became the most important agency in Hollywood, especially in putting together film packages (which, of course, it could not own). By the mid-1990s, another series of corporate changes in the entertainment world cost CAA both Ovitz and Meyer, who had left to become the number two executives respectively, in Walt Disney (who had merged with ABC) and MCA/Universal (bought by Seagram).

Ovitz's stay with Disney was quite short-lived. When he left the studio the next year, rather than return to CAA he decided to create a new arm, the Artists Management Group. The immediate reason for this new role was that in return for selling his shares of CAA for a very generous amount, he had agreed to a non-compete clause as an agent. Not only has AMG represented such major figures as Martin Scorsese and Tom Clancy (marketing his products to both book publishers and movie studios), but it has a deal with the French Canal Plus to produce its own films with Canal Plus' financial backing. Now that we are in a new millennium, we may be seeing other novel and controversial brands of entertainer representation.

While agents, managers and lawyers are supposed to be defending the interests of performers vis-a-vis producers, occasionally performers require some outside help to protect their interests vis-a-vis their representatives. Some of that help comes through general principles of contract, fiduciary, and professional responsibility law. In addition, the two main centers of the entertainment industry, New York and California, took statutory action early in the past century to establish a regulatory regime for agents. The legislatures were responding to problems experienced by performers in Broadway theaters and in the early motion picture industry. Parallel to those legislative actions were collective efforts undertaken by the performers themselves, through unions such as Actors Equity, SAG-AFTRA, and the American Federation of Musicians.

This chapter will first cover the New York and California talent agent regulations. Then we will consider cases involving conflict of interest and breach of fiduciary duty, whether by agents, managers, or attorneys. Finally, this chapter will cover the scope and limits of union authority over the performer-representative relationship, including regulating the role of an agent in producing a film in which one of his or her clients performs.

These issues were depicted on a 1998 Court TV special, *Pamela Anderson Lee on Trial*. The complexities of that case forced the parties and judges to address both contract law and the role of talent agents and managers in negotiating such contracts with film producers. The plaintiff in the suit was Private Movie Company, an independent film production firm that had made several low-budget but popular movies like Cheech

Marin's *Shrimp on the Barbie* and *Private Lessons II.* Michael Blaha, Anderson's lawyer in a lawsuit filed by her former agent for an asserted share of her *Baywatch* earnings, also represented Private Movie. Thus, when Blaha heard of a new Private Movie project, *Hello, She Lied,* he recommended to company president Ben Efraim that Anderson might take the role of a con artist named "Marsha."

In her contract negotiations, Anderson used both a talent agency and a personal manager. Her formal agent at United Talent Agency was Nick Stevens, but in practice the work was done by UTA staffer Brandt Joel. This was also true on the manager side, where Roy Manzella was her "signing manager," but his employee Denis Brody attended to the bulk of Anderson's needs.

In 1994, Private Movie sent the script for *Hello, She Lied* to Brody, offering Anderson $90,000 for the Marsha role. A "creative meeting" was held in Manzella's office, with Ephraim, his film director Lawrence Lanoff, and his casting director Sue Swan there for Private Movie, discussing the project with both Anderson and Brody (with Manzella actually on the phone on another matter). Though interested in the movie and her character, Anderson objected to what she considered gratuitous sex and excessive nudity depicted in the script of *Hello, She Lied.* Ephraim assured Anderson that the script would be rewritten to respond to her concerns, and she would be sent a copy to verify this fact.

Soon afterwards, a "business meeting" was held to finalize Anderson's contract. While Anderson knew this meeting was taking place, she was not present. Both manager Brody and agent Joel were there representing her in negotiations with Ephraim and his lawyer, Michael Blaha. (While Anderson already knew that Private Movie was a Blaha client, she did not learn of his role in that meeting until he mentioned it to her on November 21.) This November 18 "deal closing" meeting focused on the terms of employment for Anderson. The matters of production dates, expenses, benefits, and the like were all resolved. Regarding the movie's nudity and sex, Brody was to provide a list of Anderson's "do's and don't's" to Private Movie. After Ephraim placed a call to the film's investors, he agreed to meet Joel's demand of a $200,000 fee for his client. Everyone then assumed that a basic deal had been reached, as Brody and Joel told both their client and their respective employers. On December 6, Brody telephoned Blaha with Anderson's restrictions on nudity and sex in films, which Blaha entered in his laptop computer to send to the production team redoing the script.

Throughout December, several drafts of the long-form contract were exchanged between Blaha and Brody. The contract's nudity clause was worded as follows:

> 9. *NUDITY*. The parties hereto acknowledge that the Picture will include "nude or simulated sex scenes." Player has read the screenplay for the Picture prior to receipt of the Agreement and hereby consents to being photographed in such scenes, provided that such "nude and/or simulated sex scenes" will not be changed or photographed in a manner different from what has been agreed to unless mutually approved by Artists and producer . . .

As background, the following quote is from the *Nudity Rule* of the Screen Actor's Guild, of which Anderson is a member:

> SAG 41. NUDITY D: The appearance of a performer in a nude or sex scene or the doubling of a performer in such a scene shall be conditioned upon his or her prior written consent. Such consent may be obtained by letter or other writing prior to a commitment or written contract being made or executed. Such consent must include a general description as to the extent of the nudity and the type of physical contact required in the scene.

Along with the last contract draft of December 21st, Blaha wrote to Brody saying, "I am pleased we were able to reach an agreement on the main deal points."

A week later, Anderson was sent the revised script for *Hello, She Lied*, and a couple of weeks after that her people told Ephraim that Anderson would *not* be appearing in the movie because it still had too much "simulated sex." Apparently at that same time, Anderson was offered $500,000 to star in *Barb Wire*, a futuristic, post-feminist action film. There was no direct conflict in the production schedules of these two movies, and there was some nudity in *Barb Wire*. In addition, two months after rejecting *Hello, She Lied*, Anderson did make *Naked Souls*, which had some vivid and graphic sex scenes. Anderson said, though, that while the sex in *Naked Souls* was integral to its story, *Hello, She Lied*'s sex scenes were "gratuitous."

These statements were made in a lawsuit filed by Private Movie against Anderson. The firm's movie had been made under the name *Miami Hustle*, starring Sports Illustrated model Kathy Ireland. Production costs totaled $1.3 million, to which Showtime contributed $675,000 for domestic rights. However, replacing Anderson with Ireland not only did not generate much box office success for *Miami Hustle* (though *Barb Wire* also did rather poorly), but it made it impossible for Private Movie to secure the up-front foreign distribution agreement that it had expected for *Hello, She Lied* and four erotic successors. Thus, the damages claimed for Anderson's alleged breach of contract totaled nearly $5 million. Unfortunately for Private Movie and Ephraim, though, they were not able to persuade a California trial judge or appeals division that a binding contract had ever been reached on this movie scene.

There were two significant contract issues posed by the case. The first was whether there actually was a material disagreement between Anderson and Private Movie about sex scenes in the movie, especially since she was told she did not have to appear in any of them. The second was whether the absence of a signed long-form agreement precluded there being a binding contract to make the movie even if all the points had been settled.

For purposes of this chapter, the most important dispute was about the legal significance of the fact that Anderson had not been at the November 18 "business meeting" when, according to Private Movie, agreement had been reached on all the terms necessary (including nudity) to allow a binding contract to be formed. While both Brody and Joel admitted in their testimony that they felt that they had "closed the deal" there, what is the legal relevance of that fact? Should an understanding between a studio and a performer's representative be binding on the performer only if she personally ratified it? Or if the performer had told the studio that her representatives can reach a binding agreement on her behalf? Or if the performer created the ostensible authority of representatives to agree to the contract? Should it be enough that the industry assumes such apparent authority is operative in Hollywood unless the client lets the studio know to the contrary?

Finally, we should note the differences as well as the similarities in the roles of Joel and his employer United Talent Agency, and Brody and his talent manager Manzella. While Joel was at the November 18 meeting and played the key role in securing Anderson her $200,000 fee, Brody was the one who played the principal role before, at, and after that meeting (e.g., in conversations and draft exchanges with Blaha).

Is there anything distinctive about the role of the talent agent, as compared to the personal or business manager, that suggests a greater need for regulation of the former? What are the key problems in the relationship (e.g., competence, compensation, or conflicts of interests) that deserve the most attention, and what are the appropriate standards with respect to each?

## A. STATE REGULATION OF ENTERTAINER REPRESENTATIVES

### 1. NEW YORK'S EMPLOYMENT AGENT REGULATION

In 1909, New York enacted its employment agent statute, under which any person (including individuals, corporations, and societies) may serve as the agent for an individual or group, provided they have applied for and been granted a license to act as an agent. N.Y. Gen. Bus. Law §§ 170–190 (McKinney 1989). In defining the term "agent," the law included a separate definition for representation by a "theatrical employment agency":

> any person . . . who procures or attempts to procure employment or engagements for circus, vaudeville, the variety field, the legitimate theater, motion pictures, radio, television, phonograph recordings, transcriptions, opera, concert, ballet, modeling or other entertainments or exhibitions or performances, but such term does not include the business of managing such entertainments, exhibitions or performances, or the artists or attractions constituting the same, where such business only incidentally involves the seeking of employment therefor.

*Id.* § 171(8). The precise scope of "incidental" procurement of employment has been the subject of litigation in New York and will be explored further in this section. In addition to requiring licensing, the law sets limits on the fees an agency can charge for its services. An agent's fee for a single engagement cannot exceed ten percent of an artist's compensation for that event (§ 185(8)). If the agent is responsible for booking an orchestra, opera, or concert, the fee cannot exceed twenty percent (§ 185(8)).

Entertainment clients alleging violations of the Employment Agency Act must seek redress from the Commissioner of Labor (§ 189(1)). This structure requires a complainant to proceed through the relevant administrative agency prior to bringing a suit in a state court. After filing a complaint with the Commissioner, a hearing is conducted and further investigation occurs. If the Commissioner finds a violation and orders the suspension/revocation of a license, or levies a fine against the agent, the agent is allowed to seek judicial review of the Commissioner's ruling. A person who acts as an agent and fails to obtain a license, or who violates the fee limits, is guilty of a misdemeanor and can be subject to a fine of up to $1000 and imprisoned for up to one year (§ 190). The agent's license (if previously issued) may also be revoked or suspended upon a final determination of guilt.

Determining where the line falls between agents, managers, and lawyers is often difficult because of the interdependent nature of the industry. The following historic case examines what happens when an attorney acts as personal manager for an artist.

## MANDEL V. LIEBMAN

Court of Appeals of New York, 1951.
303 N.Y. 88, 100 N.E.2d 149.

CONWAY, JUDGE.

[The defendant Liebman was an author, writer and director who signed a contract with the plaintiff Mandel, an attorney who specialized in the personal management of entertainers. This contract, signed in 1946, stated that Liebman would employ Mandel "as his personal representative and manager" for five years. Mandel was to receive 10 percent of Liebman's gross earnings for engagements during the duration of the contract as well as 10 percent of all engagements commenced during the five years and continued, renewed, or resumed beyond the contract term.

Following several disagreements over business records, the parties entered into a written settlement on November 11, 1947, whereby Liebman recognized the validity of the 1946 contract and agreed to release Mandel from his obligation under the original contract. Mandel, in turn, agreed to waive the compensation scheme called for in the original contract in any year where Liebman earned less than $20,000 and to return all of Liebman's business records then in his possession.

Mandel later filed suit to recover compensation due him for the period from 1948 through 1949. The trial court dismissed Mandel's claims on the basis that the original contract was actually a legal retainer agreement between the two parties; as such, Liebman could discharge his attorney at any time and limit recovery to *quantum meruit* for those services delivered by the time of discharge. In affirming on other grounds, the appellate court reasoned that the original contract as modified by the 1947 agreement was "void, unconscionable and against public policy." Under the original contract, the court argued, "the plaintiff was not required to render any services to [the] defendant . . . and yet [the] defendant was required to pay to plaintiff 'what might be called a tribute in perpetuity.' " The plaintiff appealed to New York's highest court.]

* * *

It is apparent that the majority [in the intermediate appellate court], in holding the contracts to be "unconscionable," thought that the obligations assumed thereunder by the parties were so shockingly disproportionate that they could not be enforced. It is commonplace, of course, that adult persons, suffering from no disabilities, have complete freedom of contract and that the courts will not inquire into the adequacy of the consideration. . . .

Despite the general rule, courts sometimes look to the adequacy of the consideration in order to determine whether the bargain provided for is so grossly unreasonable or unconscionable in the light of the mores and business practices of the time and place as to be unenforceable according to its literal terms.

* * *

There might be some force to the claim of unconscionability in the case at bar if the contract could properly be construed as was done by the majority in the Appellate Division. That court held that under the express terms of the contract of May 8, 1946, plaintiff was not required to render any services to defendant. We do not think that that is a permissible construction under our decisions. *See Wood v. Lucy, Lady Duff-Gordon*, 118 N.E. 214, 215 (N.Y. 1917). . . . Here, the contract provides that it is "MUTUALLY AGREED BY THE PARTIES," among other things, that the defendant "hereby employs" the plaintiff "as his personal representative and manager to use his ability and experience as such manager and personal representative in the guidance and furtherance" of defendant's career and "to advise him in connection with all offers of employment and contracts for services, and conclude for him such contracts." Thus, there is a clear implication that plaintiff was required to do that for which he was employed. Even if the contract had merely provided that plaintiff was employed "as personal representative and manager," with no further description of his duties, that would have been sufficient, for it could be shown that to these parties, in a specialized field with its own peculiar customs and usages, that phrase was enough to measure the entire extent of plaintiff's required services.

The further provision in the contract—that plaintiff "shall only devote as much time and attention to the activities and affairs" of defendant "as the opinion and judgment" of plaintiff "deems necessary"—must be given a reasonable interpretation consonant with the purpose of the contract. It would be an unnatural and bizarre construction of the document to hold that that provision was intended to excuse plaintiff from any obligation to render service under the contract, while continuing to reap benefits thereunder. The provision seems merely to constitute an attempt on the part of plaintiff to protect himself from excessive and unreasonable demands upon his time. *See Meyers v. Nolan*, 18 Cal. App. 2d 319 where it was said:

> [t]he fact that the contract provided that the managers could devote as much time to defendant's affairs as they deemed necessary does not destroy its mutuality. The very nature of the business of the parties was such that representation of other actors was to be expected. The clause was evidently inserted to avoid misunderstanding on the subject and to more clearly define the rights and obligations of the managers.

18 Cal.App.2d at 323.

Of course, as defendant urges, it is theoretically possible that plaintiff, under this provision, could deem it necessary to devote no time to the activities and affairs of defendant, but in that event, it is clear that plaintiff would not be performing the contract but would be breaching it and foregoing his right to compensation.

Since plaintiff, as we hold, was required to render some service to defendant under the contract, it cannot be said that the contract was unconscionable. Defendant was the best judge of the necessity and worth of plaintiff's services, and of the price he wished to pay to obtain them. In return for plaintiff's contractual obligation to render such services, defendant agreed to pay as compensation an amount based upon a percentage of his earnings. It is not for the court to decide whether defendant made a good or bad bargain. We fail to see how the contract can be described as one " 'such as no man in his senses . . . would make' " and " 'no honest or fair man would accept' " or one which would "shock the conscience and confound the judgment of any man of common sense" or even one which is "so extreme as to appear unconscionable according to the mores and business practices of the time and place," particularly since, as we are told, without denial the contract of May 8, 1946, is similar in most respects to contracts in current and general use in the entertainment industry.

* * *

Finally, we do not think that the contract of May 8, 1946, at least upon its face, may be held to be a retainer agreement between attorney and client with respect to some matter in controversy under which the client may discharge the attorney at any time, with or without cause, and relegate the attorney to an action for his services to the time of discharge. Here, plaintiff was employed as defendant's personal representative and manager, a position which might well have been filled by a nonlawyer. As a lawyer, plaintiff might be called upon to use his legal training in handling defendant's affairs, but that is not sufficient, as a matter of law, to transform an otherwise binding contract of employment into a contract at will on the part of the employer. An attorney, like any other man, may enter into a contract of employment which can be enforced against the employer, and that is so even though the employment may envisage the exercise of his legal skills and ability. . . .

[The court also held that the contract was not invalid because Mandel lacked an agent's license. Mandel's activities as Liebman's "personal representative and manager," the court reasoned, fell under the personal manager exception to the "theatrical employment agency" definition. Additionally, the contract expressly provided that it "does not in any way contemplate that the second party [plaintiff] shall act as agent for the purpose of procuring further contracts or work" for defendant, the plaintiff was "not required in any way to procure" such contracts or work, and that in the event defendant "needs additional employment or work, then an agent shall be employed by the second party [plaintiff] to procure such employment, and the services of said agent shall be separately paid for" by defendant.]

Reversed.

### *QUESTIONS FOR DISCUSSION*

1. *Mandel* is another illustration of use of the notable precedent *Wood v. Lucy, Lady Duff-Gordon*, 222 N.Y. 88, 118 N.E. 214 (1917), to enforce a promise expressly made by one party by implying a reciprocal obligation on the other party to perform services as consideration for the promise. Among the entertainment cases we have already seen are *Bonner v. Westbound Records*, 76 Ill.App.3d 736, 31 Ill.Dec. 926, 394 N.E.2d 1303 (1979), and *Contemporary Mission v. Famous Music*, 557 F.2d 918 (2d Cir. 1977), both dealing with record producer obligations to undertake reasonable promotional efforts on behalf of artists under contract. Should that same principle be applied to save the agreement between an artist and a manager, especially when the manager (who is also a lawyer) drafted contract language of the type seen in *Mandel*?

2. The court was careful to note that Mandel's status as an attorney did not override his other duties as manager and representative. Such an observation is important in an industry in which many lawyers are employed as agents, managers, and executives to make non-legal decisions. As will be discussed in Section B, which deals with conflicts of interest, the multi-faceted nature of lawyers' work in the entertainment industry generates many questions concerning their ethical responsibilities.

3. The court in *Mandel* did not address the characterization of the contract's compensation scheme as "a tribute in perpetuity." While the court did not rule on this issue, it noted that "a question may be raised as to the validity or enforceability of one provision relating to compensation." Defendant had apparently agreed that his future earnings were "due to the opportunities now procured for him" by plaintiff. This provision seemed to create a conclusive presumption that any employment obtained by defendant during the term of the contract, and any renewal thereafter, were deemed to have been the result of the plaintiff's efforts, entitling the latter to the agreed percentage. Do you think that such a provision should be so interpreted and enforced?

---

Question 3 above highlights a problem often found in the compensation structures in agent contracts. The issue of the duration of the performer's obligation to pay an agent was addressed in the case of *Watts v. Columbia Artists Management*, 188 A.D.2d 799, 591 N.Y.S.2d

234 (1992). In 1983, Andre Watts, a concert pianist (through his "loan-out" corporation Andre Watts Performances, Inc.) entered into a contract with Columbia Artists Management. Under this contract Columbia was to act as Watts' exclusive agent and was to receive 15% of his earnings from U.S. concerts. Columbia was to receive no fee if Watts was not paid for his engagement. Watts' corporation dissolved in 1985 and the term of the contract was scheduled to end in 1986. Afterwards, Columbia continued to act as agent and Watts continued to compensate the agency in the manner required by the then-expired contract between them. In 1988, Watts notified Columbia that he wished to terminate their relationship.

As explained by the court, "[w]hen the parties' relationship was terminated, defendant had scheduled a total of 82 engagements for plaintiff for the next two concert seasons. Contracts had been executed as of Sept. 1, 1988, for 48 of the 82 scheduled engagements, and plaintiff performed and was paid for 46 of those 48 engagements. Of the remaining 34 scheduled engagements, for which no contract had been executed as of Sept. 1, 1988, plaintiff performed 33 of them and was paid for 32 of the performances." Thus Watts was eventually compensated for 78 of the 82 engagements Columbia had scheduled by September 1, 1988.

Columbia claimed that it was entitled to 15 percent of Watts' earnings from the 78 paid engagements. Watts, on the other hand, claimed that Columbia was entitled to no compensation for the 32 engagements for which contracts were not executed by September 1, 1988. Additionally, he claimed that Columbia was entitled to half of its 15 percent commission on the other engagements, "because additional managerial services, including travel arrangements, rehearsal schedules, piano delivery and tuning, receptions, master classes and other details, were required after Sept. 1, 1988. According to plaintiff, the additional services were performed by another manager retained by plaintiff after Sept. 1, 1988."

Watts sought declaratory relief to determine what his obligations were to Columbia. The court "found that a contract implied-in-fact existed between the parties with the same terms and conditions as the expired written contract between the Corporation and defendant, and that defendant was entitled to full commissions for all 78 engagements at issue." Watts appealed. In affirming this ruling, the appellate court stated that "an implied-in-fact contract rests upon the conduct of the parties and not their verbal or written words. Thus, the theories of express contract and of contract implied in fact are mutually exclusive." The court found an implied-in-fact contract between Watts and Columbia because of their dealings between the end of the contract term in 1986, and September 1, 1988, when Columbia continued to find employment for Watts, and Watts continued to pay it the 15 percent.

The court also determined that Columbia was entitled to $290,000, as its 15 percent commission for the 78 engagements. Columbia had argued that it fulfilled its duty as an agent when it "arranged the date, time and fee for a performance, informed plaintiff of the engagement and was informed by plaintiff that he accepted the engagement." The time, date and fee were the essential elements of the booking, and once finalized, the execution of a final contract "was largely a formality involving ministerial details." The court accepted this idea, noting that the fact that Watts "actually performed 33 of the 34 engagements booked by the defendant for which no contract was executed prior to September 1, 1988 tends to support defendant's view." In addition, the agreement did not make Columbia's commission dependent on execution of a formal contract: rather, the commission was to be based upon Columbia's scheduling of engagements for Watts and his payments from those engagements. The fact that Watts chose to have another manager perform Columbia's other duties did not affect Columbia's rights.

### *QUESTIONS FOR DISCUSSION*

1. Do you agree with the outcome in *Watts*? How might Watts have protected himself more effectively?

2. This case highlights the common industry practice of proceeding with performances and receiving payments without a signed contract. As shown in Chapter 7, the hurried and interdependent entertainment industry, might come to a halt if people waited to execute formal contracts. Does it concern you that the court was willing to overlook the contract formality argument?

## 2. CALIFORNIA TALENT AGENCIES ACT[b]

California also regulates talent agencies through its *Talent Agencies Act*. Cal. Labor Code §§ 1700–1700.47. This statute is similar to New York's, but it does not grant an exception to personal managers who undertake only *incidental* agent responsibilities. The Act defines a talent agency as

[b] *See* Adam Nimoy, *Personal Managers & the California Talent Agencies Act: For Whom the Bill Toils*, 2 Loyola Enter. L.J. 145 (1982); Richard L. Feller, *California's Revised Talent Agencies Act: Fine-Tuning the Regulation of Employment Procurement in the Entertainment Industry*, 5 Enter. & Sports Lawyer 3 (Fall 1986); Bruce C. Fishelman, *Agents & Managers: California's Split Personality*, 11 Loyola Ent. L.J. 401 (1991); Don Biederman, *Agent or Manager? There Is a Difference . . . Isn't There?* 15 Ent. L. Rep. 3 (Feb. 1994); Edwin F. McPherson, *The Talent Agencies Act: Time for Change*, 19 Hast. Comm/Ent L.J. 899 (1997); Chip Robertson, *Don't Bite the Hand that Feeds: A Call for a Return to an Equitable Talent Agencies Act Standard*, 20 Hast. Comm/Ent L.J. 223 (1997); Heath B. Zarin, *The California Controversy Over Procuring Employment: A Case for the Personal Managers Act*, 7 Ford. Int. Prop., Media & Ent. L.J. 927 (1997); Donald E. Biederman, *Agents v. Managers Revisited*, 1 Vand. J. Ent. L. & Prac. 5 (1999).

> a person or corporation who engages in the occupation of procuring, offering, promising, or attempting to procure employment or engagements for an artist or artists, except that the activities of procuring, offering, or promising to procure recording contracts for an artist or artists shall not of itself subject a person or corporation to regulation and licensing under this chapter. Talent agencies may, in addition, counsel or direct artists in the development of their professional careers.

Cal. Labor Code § 1700.4(a). In addition to the exemption for record contracts, the Act provides that an unlicensed agent (e.g., the performer's manager) may "act in conjunction with and at the request of a licensed talent agency in the negotiation of an employment contract." § 1700.44(d).

The Labor Commissioner is charged with enforcing the provisions of the Act. The talent agency must get pre-approval by the Commissioner of the terms of the standard contract the agency offers to all its clients, to ensure that these terms (including the fee) are not "unfair, unjust, and oppressive." While the Act does not set specific limits on the fees an agency can charge its clients, the Commissioner will not permit rates higher than 20–25 percent. Once a complainant has filed a case, a hearing is held and the Commissioner makes a ruling. The losing party can appeal the decision to the superior court. A violation of the Act is no longer a criminal offense, thereby limiting recovery to civil damages or injunctive relief. Provided the contract between an agency and the artist meets the requirements of the Act, a provision for arbitration of disputes is enforceable, and the arbitrator's decision can stand in place of a Labor Commissioner decision. An artist seeking to bring an action alleging that his personal manager acted as an unlicensed agent must do so within one year of the incident.

---

An early case dealing with personal managers is excerpted below. As you read the case, think about the implications for managers who get employment offers for their clients through personal connections or other business dealings. Should the manager who occasionally finds work for a client be subject to the Act?

## RADEN V. LAURIE

Court of Appeal of California, Second Appellate District, 1953.
120 Cal.App.2d 778, 262 P.2d 61.

SHINN, JUDGE.

[In 1948, the plaintiff, Ted Raden, entered into an agreement with Charlotte Jacobs and her daughter, Rosetta Jacobs (known professionally as Piper Laurie), to act as the manager for Laurie. Laurie was a minor at the time the agreement was signed. By its terms, Raden was to "secur[e] . . . engagements for [Laurie] in the motion picture, theatrical, radio, television and allied fields with and upon the consent of [Rosetta and her legal guardian]." Raden was to receive a 10 percent commission on the engagements he arranged. There were no durational limit on the first agreement.

Later that year, the parties entered into a second agreement wherein Raden agreed to continue acting as Laurie's "advisor and counsel and business counsel" (until her twenty-first birthday) with regard to "all business and financial matters . . . including but not limited to [Laurie's] dealings with [her] agent, representatives and employers." While Raden was neither required nor authorized to seek employment on Laurie's behalf, he was required to advise them as to the selection of an agent for Laurie. The commission structure remained the same under the second agreement.

The Jacobs terminated the relationship with Raden in 1949. Raden filed suit, claiming that Laurie had earned money through professional engagements and never paid him his commission of $3100. The Jacobs claimed that Raden promised to find employment for Laurie when he signed the original 1948 agreement. During 1948 and 1949, Raden took Laurie "several times to locations where entertainers might find employment," but was unsuccessful in procuring work for her.

Raden, who was not a licensed agent, stated that he had simply counseled and advised Laurie in order to develop her career. He asserted that when he took her to locations, his purpose was not to obtain employment for her, but to advance her "general development and education." Furthermore, Raden alleged that the second 1949 agreement superseded the previous agreement. Raden appealed from a summary judgment entered in favor of Laurie.]

* * *

Plaintiff was not licensed as an artists' manager, theatrical manager or employment agent. It is said by respondent that her motion was granted upon the ground that plaintiff was either an unlicensed artists' manager or employment agent. The definition of artists' manager is contained in § 1650 of the Labor Code. One is not an artists' manager unless he both advises, counsels and directs artists in the development or advancement of their professional careers, and also procures, offers, promises or attempts to procure employment or engagements for an artist "only in connection with and as a part of the duties and obligations of such person under a contract with such artist by which such person contracts to render services of the nature above mentioned to such artist." Such is the clear wording of the statute.

* * *

We have experienced some difficulty in understanding defendant's construction of the section. It appears to be contended that one who is employed to advise, counsel and direct an artist, thereby promises to procure or attempt to procure employment for his principal; therefore, despite the language of the agreement, plaintiff was bound to seek employment for Rosetta; his efforts to do so were a part of his duties of counseling and advising and he was therefore an artists' manager.

The July agreement is explicit and unambiguous. It specifically provides that plaintiff has no authority and no duty to seek or obtain employment for Rosetta Jacobs [Laurie]. He is required only to give counsel and advice and to assist generally in her training for a professional career and the selection and employment of agents. Although it was alleged in the affidavit of Charlotte that plaintiff endeavored, unsuccessfully, to obtain employment for Rosetta, there was no showing that he procured, offered, promised or attempted to procure employment or engagements for Rosetta "only in connection with and as a part of the duties and obligations of such person under a contract with such artist." It would seem clear that his duties were intentionally limited to the rendition of services which would not require his being licensed as an artists' manager.

Respondent says: "It is the act of seeking employment, not the contract provision, which brings the legislation into play." This might be true if the contract were a mere sham and pretext designed by plaintiff to misrepresent and conceal the true agreement of the parties and to evade the law. But there was no evidence which would have justified the court in reaching that conclusion. There was no evidence of misrepresentation, fraud or mistake as to the terms of the contract nor as to plaintiff's obligations thereunder, nor evidence that defendants did not understand and willingly accept the limitation of plaintiff's duties. The assertions in defendant's affidavit that in January, 1948, plaintiff represented that he could and would obtain employment for Rosetta, while immaterial, were denied in plaintiff's affidavit. By the former agreement plaintiff undertook to seek engagements for Rosetta and to act as her manager, but not so under the July agreement.

In the absence of any evidence that the July 30th agreement was a mere subterfuge or otherwise invalid the court was required to give effect to its clear and positive provisions. It was to be presumed that the parties acted in good faith. If there was a doubt whether the later agreement was entered into in good faith, as a substitute for the earlier one, and that it expressed the real intentions of the parties, it should have been resolved in favor of plaintiff. These were not questions to be decided on a motion for summary judgment.

* * *

Since [as far as the affidavits indicated] plaintiff was employed only to counsel and advise Rosetta and to act as her business manager in matters not related to obtaining engagements for her, he was not acting as a [talent agency] as defined by [the Act].

* * *

Reversed.

### *QUESTIONS FOR DISCUSSION*

1. Raden admitted that he had taken Laurie to locations where she might find employment in order to advance her career. Do you find this a plausible explanation? Should the act of taking an artist to such locations, for whatever reason, be used as evidence of a manager acting as an agent?

2. What exactly does it mean to "counsel and advise" an artist? If a manager is approached with an offer to employ an artist, should the offer be rejected because it does not fit the manager's job description? If the manager accepts the assignment for the client, should he or she be deemed an agent for regulatory purposes? *See Marathon Entertainment, Inc. v. Blasi*, 42 Cal.4th 974, 70 Cal. Rptr.3d 727, 174 P.3d 741 (2008) (holding that the Act applies to personal managers engaged in procurement of work for artists, even in a single instance).

---

Many provisions of the Act were addressed in *Buchwald v. Superior Court of San Francisco*, 254 Cal.App.2d 347, 62 Cal. Rptr. 364 (1967). The court clarified many of the terms defined in the Act and settled several procedural issues left unclear by the legislation. The members of the group Jefferson Airplane sued Matthew Katz, their "exclusive personal representative, advisor and manager." Each band member had signed a separate contract with Katz containing the following clause:

> It is clearly understood that you [Katz] are not an employment agent or theatrical agent, that you have not offered or attempted to promise to obtain employment or engagements for me, and you are not obliged, authorized or expected to do so.

In 1966, after a dispute between the band and Katz over the contract, Katz sought to compel arbitration. The band then filed a "Petition to Determine Controversy" with the Labor Commissioner. Jefferson Airplane alleged numerous infractions by Katz, including 1) that the latter had used "false and fraudulent statements" to induce the group to sign with him as its artist-manager, 2) that at the time of the contract Katz was not a licensed agent, 3) that Katz had promised and procured employment for the band, and 4) that Katz forbade the group from procuring its own employment. The group also argued that Katz failed to fulfill several requirements under the Act. Katz responded that he had never acted as an agent for the group, so the Act did not apply to him, and the Commissioner had no jurisdiction over the dispute.

From the outset, the court noted that the Act is a "remedial statute" whose "clear object . . . is to prevent improper persons from becoming artists' managers and to regulate such activity for the protection of the public." As such, "a contract between an unlicensed artists' manager and an artist is void." Following this determination, the court went on to address each of Katz' contentions and to establish guidelines for the applicability of the statute and the jurisdiction of the Labor Commission.

The court held that agents, whether licensed or not, are "bound and regulated" by the Act. Without such a ruling, the court reasoned, an agent, "by nonsubmission to the licensing provisions of the Act, [could] exclude himself from its restrictions and regulations enacted in the public interest." The court also rejected Katz' contention that because the written contract stated that he was not the agent for the band, as a matter of law he was not an agent, and therefore not subject to the Act. If agents could use the express language of their contracts to avoid regulation, "the form of the transaction, rather than its substance, would control." *Id.* at 355. Instead, the court ruled, if Katz acted as an agent, he could be regulated by the Act regardless of the contract terms.

As to jurisdiction, the court held that the doctrine of exhaustion of administrative remedies applied to disputes under the Act and that the Labor Commissioner "had original jurisdiction, to the exclusion of the superior court," over controversies arising under the Act. The court could hear the case on appeal from the Commission after a final administrative determination was rendered. The court also rejected Katz' contention that the dispute should go to arbitration as provided in the contract: "[i]f the agreement is void, no rights, including the claimed right to private arbitration, can be derived from it." *Id.* at 360.

Do you agree with the court's determination that the Act should apply to unlicensed as well as to licensed agents? With the court's willingness to go beyond contract terms to focus on the parties' conduct to determine responsibility? With the court's "protection of the public" rationale?

---

Noncompliance with agent licensing requirements continues to generate claims by performers who become dissatisfied with their representation. For example, in 1982, Richard Pryor won a $3 million award from the Labor Commissioner to recoup commissions (plus interest) that had been paid to Pryor's unlicensed agent. Is there any inequity in allowing a performer to use the licensing statute to recoup commissions for services rendered over many years?

In 1993, a major decision was rendered about the dividing line between agent and manager in a dispute involving talk-show host Arsenio Hall. In this case, Hall sued his former manager, X Management, alleging that it had acted as an unlicensed agent in violation of the Act. Following the Labor Commissioner's decision, X Management sued James Curry, the Acting Commissioner for California, challenging the constitutionality of the Act. In reading this material, compare the court's reasoning with that used in earlier decisions. Consider whether the Act is serving its purpose of protecting entertainers.

## WACHS V. CURRY

Court of Appeal of California, Second Appellate District, 1993.
13 Cal.App.4th 616, 16 Cal. Rptr.2d 496.

JOHNSON, ASSOCIATE JUSTICE.

[In 1987, Arsenio Hall entered into a Personal Management Agreement with X Management. The principals of X Management were Robert Wachs and Mark Lipsky, though for a period Eddie Murphy was also involved in the firm. The contract recited that Hall had not

> retained our personal management firm under this agreement as an employment agent or a talent agent. This firm has not offered or attempted or promised to obtain employment or engagements for you and this firm is not obligated, authorized or expected to do so.

Hall said that he had signed the standard form contract without reading this or other terms, and that he did not have a lawyer read it. Wachs, a lawyer, apparently told Hall that his commission rate would be 15 percent, and that Hall did not also need a talent agent at another 10 percent commission.

X Management secured an impressive number of contracts for Hall:

1. The contract with Paramount Pictures for Hall to act in Murphy's film, *Coming to America*;
2. The agreement with Fox Square Productions for Hall to serve as guest host on its nightly talk show;
3. The contract with Paramount Television for the syndicated *Arsenio Hall Show*;
4. A new movie contract with Paramount;
5. A $1.5 million endorsement and promotional deal for Hall with Coca-Cola;

6. An arrangement for Hall to serve as host for the 1990 MTV Video Music Awards.

From 1987 until 1990, X Management's 15 percent commission translated into $2.62 million in earnings for the firm.

The relationship broke down in 1990, when Hall discovered that Wachs and Lipsky were not only getting screen credit as Production Executives on *The Arsenio Hall Show*, but that they were being paid $5,000 a week for this role. (Apparently Eddie Murphy had dropped out of X Management in 1989.) In August 1990, Hall terminated the agreement and initiated a proceeding before the Labor Commissioner, claiming the agreement was void *ab initio* because X Management was not a licensed agent under the *Talent Agencies Act*.

The Labor Commissioner ruled that X Management—in particular, Wachs—had been involved in the occupation of "procuring employment" for Hall. While "negotiating and arranging for employment" might well be an integral part of the personal manager role, the legislature had not specifically exempted the latter for film performers, as it had for those who procured recording contracts. The Commissioner rejected defenses of waiver and estoppel based on Hall's awareness of and consent to Wachs' actions. The Commissioner also refused to hold that the statute was designed to protect only artists of limited means, rather than wealthy performers such as Hall.

The remedy the Commissioner awarded was not simply to terminate the contract for the future, but to direct that all fees earned under it during the (limitations period) year before proceedings had begun must be reimbursed. In Hall's case that meant that Wachs and Lipsky had to reimburse Hall for $2.12 million of the fees they had been paid.

After the Commissioner's decision, Wachs and X Management asked the court to rule that the statute was unconstitutional on two grounds: (1) there was no rational basis for exempting procurement only of recording contracts; and (2) one could not discern from the Act which activities triggered the licensing requirement as a talent agent.]

* * *

## III. A RATIONAL BASIS EXISTS FOR EXEMPTING THOSE WHO PROCURE RECORDING CONTRACTS FROM THE LICENSING REQUIREMENTS OF THE ACT.

* * *

Plaintiffs, who are not licensed talent agents, contend the licensing provisions of the Act are unconstitutional because there is no rational basis for exempting from the licensing requirement those who engage in procuring recording contracts but not other kinds of contracts.

The provision exempting the procurement of recording contracts was added to the Act in 1982 with a sunset provision of January 1, 1986. At the same time, the Legislature created the California Entertainment Commission to study and recommend revisions to the Act. The commission, after two years of study, submitted its recommendations to the Legislature which adopted them with minor language changes.

One of the issues the commission studied was whether any changes should be made to the provision exempting persons who procure recording contracts for an artist. The majority of the commission recommended this exemption should be retained in the Act. The commission gave the following reasons for its recommendation.

> A recording contract is an employment contract of a different nature from those in common usage in the industry involving personal services. The purpose of the contract is to produce a permanent and repayable showcase of the talents of the artist. In the recording industry, many successful artists retain personal managers to act as their intermediaries, and negotiations for a recording contract are commonly conducted by a personal manager, not a talent agent. Personal managers frequently contribute financial support for the living and business expenses of entertainers. They may act as a conduit between the artist and the recording company, offering suggestions about the use of the artist or the level of effort which the recording company is expending on behalf of the artist. . . . However, the problems of attempting to license or otherwise regulate this activity arise from the ambiguities, intangibles and imprecisions of the activity. The majority of the Commission concluded that the industry would be best served by resolving these ambiguities on the side of preserving the exemption of this activity from the requirements of licensure.

On the commission's recommendation, the exemption for those who procure recording contracts became permanent.

We believe the report from the Legislature's own commission of experts provides a sufficiently rational basis for the exemption from the licensing requirement. Numerous decisions support the proposition that persons in the same general type of business may be classified differently where their methods of operation are not identical.

## IV. THE LICENSING REQUIREMENTS OF THE ACT ARE NOT VOID FOR VAGUENESS.

Plaintiffs contend the term "occupation of procuring [employment]" as used in § 1700.4, subdivision (a), does not sufficiently define the conduct which requires a license. Thus, persons such as plaintiffs, who provide a variety of services to artists and entertainers, cannot determine in advance what conduct they may lawfully engage in without a license. As a result, plaintiffs operate at great financial risk because a subsequent finding by the labor commissioner they "procured" employment without a license may relieve the client of any obligation to repay funds advanced to promote the client's career and entitle the client to restitution of all fees paid the agent.

Although the Act contains no criminal penalty for the unlicensed procuring of employment, the financial penalties to which the unlicensed agent is exposed are clearly sufficient to raise due process concerns. "Statutes, regardless whether criminal or civil in nature, must be sufficiently clear as to provide adequate notice of the prohibited conduct as well as to establish a standard of conduct which can be uniformly interpreted by the judiciary and administrative agencies."

In *Hall v. Bureau of Employment Agencies*, 64 Cal.App.3d 482 (1976), the court summarized the test a statute must pass to satisfy due process:

> [I]f the words used may be made reasonably certain by reference to the common law, to the legislative history of the statute involved, or to the purpose of that statute, the legislation will be sustained . . .; and a standard fixed by language which is reasonably certain, judged by the foregoing rules, meets the test of due process notwithstanding an element of degree in the definition as to which estimates might differ. Further, even though all statutes regardless of nature must be sufficiently clear to provide fair notice of prohibited conduct . . . reasonable certainty is all that is required. A statute will not be held void for uncertainty if any reasonable and practical construction can be given its language. It will be upheld if its terms may be made reasonably certain by reference to other definable sources.

64 Cal.App.3d at 494.

Resort to the dictionary definitions of the words at issue and the legislative purpose and history of the Act convinces us the statute has an objective content from which ascertainable standards of conduct can be fashioned.

The relevant dictionary definition of "occupation" is "the principal business of one's life: a craft, trade, profession or other means of earning a living." (*Webster's New Internat. Dict.* (3d ed. 1981) p. 1560.)

The history of the Act further illuminates the legislative intent with respect to activities requiring a talent agent's license.

Regulation of what we now refer to as talent agencies originated with the Artists' Managers Act of 1943. The Artists' Managers Act defined an artist's manager as "a person, who engages in the occupation of advising, counseling, or directing artists in the development or advancement of their professional careers and who procures, offers, promises or attempts to procure employment or engagements for an artist only in connection with and as a part of the duties and obligations of such person under a contract with such artist by which such person contracts to render services of the nature above mentioned to such artist."

With the adoption of the [Talent Agencies] *Act*, the Legislature made a significant change in the definition of the covered activities. The Act provided,

> "A talent agency is hereby defined to be a person or corporation who engages in the occupation of procuring, offering, promising, or attempting to procure employment or engagements for an artist or artists. Talent agencies may, in addition, counsel or direct artists in the development of their professional careers."

Comparison of the activities regulated in the two acts shows a marked change of emphasis from the counseling function to the employment procurement function. Under the Artists' Managers Act the focus was on persons who engaged in the "the occupation of advising, counseling or directing artists" in the "development or advancement" of their careers and who engaged in procuring employment "only in connection with and as a part of" their duties as advisor and counselor. Under the Act, the focus is on persons engaged "in the occupation of procuring . . . employment or engagements for an artist. . . ." These persons "may, in addition, counsel or direct artists in the development of their professional careers."

We conclude from the Act's obvious purpose to protect artists seeking employment and from its legislative history, the "occupation" of procuring employment was intended to be determined according to a standard that measures the significance of the agent's employment procurement function compared to the agent's counseling function taken as a whole. If the agent's employment procurement function constitutes a significant part of the agent's business as a whole then he or she is subject to the licensing requirement of the Act even if, with respect to a particular client, procurement of employment was only an incidental part of the agent's overall duties. On the other hand, if counseling and directing the clients' careers constitutes the significant part of the agent's business then he or she is not subject to the licensing requirement of the Act, even if, with respect to a particular client, counseling and directing the client's career was only an incidental part of the agent's overall duties. What constitutes a "significant part" of the agent's business is an element of degree we need not decide in this case.

Plaintiffs' concentrate their attack on the alleged vagueness of the word "procure." They posit numerous examples of conduct which they claim have little if any relationship to the purpose of the Act but which the labor commissioner has held, or might hold, constitutes "procuring" employment. However, as we noted above, the only question before us is whether the word "procure" in the context of the Act is so lacking in objective content that it provides no standard at all by which to measure an agent's conduct.

To "procure" means "to get possession of: obtain, acquire, to cause to happen or be done; bring about." (*Webster's New Internat. Dict.*, supra, at p. 1809.)

The term "procure" in connection with employment is used in numerous California statutes. The fact none of these statutes has ever been challenged is some evidence the term is well understood.

We recognize the Legislature's failure to define the term "procure" for purposes of section 1700.4 has been criticized by several commentators. . . . None of these commentators have suggested, however, the term "procure" is so lacking in objective content as to render the Act facially unconstitutional.

We conclude the term "occupation of procuring [employment]" is not "so patently vague and so wholly devoid of objective meaning that it provides no standard at all." Whether the Act is unconstitutional as applied to plaintiffs is a question for another day.

Affirmed.

---

Although *Wachs* upheld the constitutionality of the Act, the court seemed to place a significant limit on the statute's scope by confining the licensing requirement to those for whom "the employment procurement function constitutes a significant part of the agent's business as a whole." Shortly after *Wachs*, the Labor Commissioner was presented with a case, *Church v. Brown* (1994), in which this question arose. Ross Brown had used his position as the casting director for a film *Stolen Moments* to get Thomas Church an audition and then a part in the movie. Afterwards, Church agreed to have Brown "counsel and advise him" (for 15 percent of his earnings), though not to serve as his talent agent. Then Church secured a role in the television series *Wings*, for which he paid Brown $68,000 over two years. When Church sought to have the management agreement nullified as a violation of the Act, the Commissioner found that notwithstanding the contract language, Brown had sometimes performed the agency functions. With respect to the *Wachs* formulation, the Commissioner stated:

> . . . procurement of employment constitutes a "significant" portion of the activities of an agent if the procurement is not due to inadvertence or mistake and the activities of procurement

> have some importance and are not simply a *de minimis* aspect of the overall relationship between the parties when compared with the agent's functions on behalf of the artist.

A year later, in *Waisbren v. Peppercorn Productions*, 41 Cal.App.4th 246, 48 Cal. Rptr.2d 437 (1995), another court explicitly disagreed with what was characterized as dicta in *Wachs*. This court ruled that personal managers must be licensed under the Act even if they devote a minimal or incidental proportion of their representation activities to procuring employment for their clients. While the Act requires such a license only for those engaged in the occupation of procuring employment, it is quite common for people to have more than one occupation. This panel believed that the legislative history, administrative interpretation, and basic purpose of the Act would be ignored by failing to subject the occasional, as well as the full-time, agent to regulatory control. Under the statute, an unlicensed manager could only "participate in negotiating an employment contract for an artist . . . 'in conjunction with, and at the request of, a licensed talent agency.' " *Id.* at 259, 48 Cal. Rptr.2d at 445.

The Labor Commissioner then went even further, in *Baker v. BNB Associates*, 18 *Ent. L. Rptr.* No. 9, at 18 (Feb. 1997). This case involved the relationship of singing star Anita Baker with Sherwin Bush, who did business as BNB Associates. In the 1980s and early 1990s, Baker had not been represented by a talent agency, and instead had relied on Bush as her manager, including for appearances on television networks or live concerts. In 1994, Baker sought to end their contract and relationship by petitioning the Commission to rule that Bush had been acting as an unlicensed agent.

Bush's clients had included other stars, such as Neil Diamond and Herb Alpert. Bush's response to Baker's claim was that while he had sometimes responded to these network or orchestra requests for his client's services by discussing and settling the payment and terms, he had "served solely as a 'conduit' for employment offers." The Commissioner found it implausible to "assume that a major musical artist went without any talent agent representation for a period of almost eleven years . . . during which time the artist received numerous major television and live concert engagements. Such a proposition not only defied logic, it flies in the face of common industry practice and experience." Even if Bush had not actively initiated the contracts and potential employment of Baker, the *Arsenio Hall* precedent meant that "negotiations that 'exploit' employment offers emanating from the outside constitute solicitation within the meaning of the Talent Agencies Act."

In a second such case, the court endorsed the Labor Commissioner's position on this issue, in *Park v. Deftones*, 71 Cal.App.4th 1465, 84 Cal. Rptr.2d 616 (2d Dist. 1999). Starting in 1992, David Park had represented a musical group called Deftones and secured for them a contract with Maverick Records. Deeming himself the group's "personal manager," Park had not secured a license from the Commissioner under the Act, which exempted record contracts from the type of work that required a license. After a dispute, Park sued for breach of contract.

The Deftones' defense was that the Commissioner had found Park to have been functioning as an unlicensed talent agent when he secured the group more than 80 live concert performances over three years. The court agreed that this made Park's entire contract with them "null, void, and unenforceable" for purposes of collecting the commission. Agreeing with its counterpart court in *Waisbren* that the Supreme Court's statement in *Wachs* was just "dictum," it found here that "even incidental procurement is regulated." *Id.* at 619. The *Deftones* court went one step further, ruling that even though Park was not paid by for securing concert (as opposed to record) deals, the Act's basic policies required an agent's license for that role.

> One may engage in an occupation which includes procuring engagements without receiving direct compensation for that activity. . . . The abuses at which these [licensing/regulating] requirements are aimed apply equally where the personal manager procures work for the artist without a commission, but rather for the deferred benefits from obtaining a recording contract.

*Id.* at 620.

Then, in *Yoo v. Robi*, 126 Cal.App.4th 1089, 24 Cal. Rptr.3d 740 (2nd Dist. 2005), the court took the next major step. This case involved a suit about whether Howard Wolf had lost his right to receive a commission from a 1986 record by Paul Robi and his Platters group. Even though, as we have seen, the Act did not require a license for marketing a client's album to a company like Tango Records, the unlicensed Wolf had violated that Act by securing for Robi several concerts at fairs like the ones at Santa Clara and Bristol, Connecticut: "the rationale for denying a personal manager recovery even for activities which were entirely legal is based on the public policy of the Act to deter personal managers from engaging in illegal activities," like obtaining for his client lucrative concerts without a license to undertake such an effort.

While these artists successfully used the Act to nullify the contracts with their managers, Wesley Snipes was not able to do so. The key difference in *Snipes v. Dolores Robinson Entertainment*, 20 *Ent. L. Rptr.* No. 1, 4 (June 1998), was that Snipes had always been represented by the Creative Artists Agency (CAA). After establishing his star status in the 1990s, Snipes hired personal manager Dolores Robinson, who had been recommended to him by CAA. Five years later, Snipes sought to remove

Robinson from that role by claiming that she was actually serving as his agent.

At the Commission hearing, there was a strong contradiction in the factual testimony of the two sides. Robinson claimed that she simply focused on matters like Snipes' personal chef, bodyguard, and trainer after CAA had settled the basic movie deal, while Snipes claimed that Robinson was actively involved in securing movie roles and improving his pay deals. The Commissioner did not have to render a decision on this score, because Robinson demonstrated that any such roles were performed by her "at the request of and in conjunction with" CAA; this action was exempted by § 1700.44(d) of the Labor Code from the licensed agent requirement. Not only had CAA originally proposed and continued to accept Robinson's role with Snipes, but CAA was "intimately involved in all of the negotiations and . . . Robinson was at all times working closely with them."

The basic message, then, is that if Snipes chooses to have both an agent and a manager who each collaborate in their client's representation, the performer can and will have to pay for both.

### *QUESTIONS FOR DISCUSSION*

1. Should Arsenio Hall have received an award of $2.1 million to return commissions already paid to X Management for lucrative assignments it had secured for Hall, given Hall's knowledge of the services performed for him?

2. Suppose Wachs had not actively sought out the projects being offered to Hall after *Coming to America*, but had negotiated the contracts with producers. Should the Act treat such negotiations as the *procuring* of employment or engagements?

3. Notwithstanding these cases, many movie stars are hiring managers and foregoing use of agents. A major reason is that personal managers have a small number of clients as compared to large talent agencies: the latter's client rosters allow them to broker package film deals but preclude paying a lot of attention to the idiosyncratic wishes of each client. Indeed, some stars (such as Sharon Stone) are now having their managers listed and paid by the studio as a producer of their films. As a practical matter, the fact that the studio paid a reported $750,000 to Stone's manager as part of the inducement for her to appear in *Diabolique* would likely reduce the amount it found financially sensible to pay directly to Stone for her acting services. From a legal point of view, though, the question is whether a talent manager who submits a movie proposal to a studio in his capacity as a "producer," but with his client included as the project's star attraction, can be said to be engaged in the "procuring of employment" for his client. Does it matter that the performer's attorney negotiates the terms of

the contract, albeit under the direction of the manager? (Stone returned to the talent agency roster in 1996.)

4. California's regulation of talent agents but not managers is not just an historical anomaly. As we saw in *Wachs*, the legislature preserved this differential treatment and refused to import New York's "incidental procuring of employment" standard into the permissible role of the manager. Has either state made the appropriate policy judgment? Are there real differences in the responsibilities of agents and managers that warrant such different treatment?

5. California excluded the representation of musicians for procurement of record contracts from the Act. New York, in contrast, makes no exception for record contracts unless securing such a deal happens to be "incidental" to the manager's broader functions. *Pine v. Laine*, 36 A.D.2d 924, 321 N.Y.S.2d 303 (1971). Even if that rationale might justify the minimal rational basis test for constitutionality of the Act, is it a sensible policy? Recall the music industry disputes we saw in prior chapters (involving George Michael, Olivia Newton John, TLC, Toni Braxton, and others). Does it make sense to say that Arsenio Hall needs a licensed agent to negotiate a movie contract for *Coming to America*, but Courtney Love does not need a licensed agent to negotiate a record deal with a label, a contract of much longer duration and greater compensation complexities? If California was going to exempt representation of musicians in securing record contracts, should it also have exempted the agents who procure club dates that often are the stepping stones to a record contract?

6. In 1996, Tennessee repealed its system of licensing and record-keeping that had previously been required for talent and employment agencies (though the statute had always excluded "musician booking agencies"). Is there any justification for California, New York, and other states maintaining their scrutiny of the qualifications, performance, and fees of talent agencies in the movie industry? Why is a competitive free market in agent services insufficient for this purpose? Why has this market not produced sharp differences in the standard 10 percent commission that agencies charge their clients (except for a small number of superstars)?

7. Why did Robert Wachs, a lawyer, simply obtain a talent agent license that would have entitled him to procure employment for Hall? Why might it be difficult to secure such a license?

## B. CONFLICT OF INTEREST IN ENTERTAINER REPRESENTATION[c]

Most of the major players in entertainer representation are lawyers. A major concern about the quality of representation involves conflicts of interest among the clients of the lawyer, agent, or manager. The combination of these two facts has been a recipe for litigation in the last two decades. For example, in the early 1990s, Billy Joel filed a $90 million lawsuit against Allen Grubman, one of the most powerful New York lawyers in the music world. Grubman's clients included Walter Yetnikoff, head of CBS Records, David Geffen, founder of Geffen Records, and Irving Azoff, head of MCA Records. It was Yetnikoff who steered to Grubman his first big performer client Billy Joel, and David Geffen his second, Bruce Springsteen. Besides doing legal work for CBS (later Sony) Records, which held Joel's recording rights, and Winterland, which held his merchandising rights, Grubman also represented Frank Weber, Joel's ex-manager and ex-brother-in-law, who had defrauded Joel of millions of dollars. Though Grubman and his firm denied any wrongdoing and responsibility for Joel's plight, they eventually settled the suit for a reported $3 million (apparently paid by Sony).

This blend of clients and ventures is even more striking in Hollywood. The most heavily-publicized example is Creative Artists Agency (CAA) and its original founding chair, Michael Ovitz. While CAA was representing such motion picture luminaries as Steven Spielberg, Tom Cruise, Barbra Streisand, Robin Williams, Robert Redford, and Sylvester Stallone, Ovitz was playing a major role in Sony's $3.4 billion purchase of Columbia Pictures in 1989, Matsushita's $6.8 billion purchase of MCA in 1991, and Credit Lyonnais' attempted rescue of MGM in 1993.

While CAA and Ovitz attracted comments and questions about representing both performers and studios, these allegedly conflicting roles did not attract any lawsuits. The same cannot be said of the powerful Ziffren law firm, which faced several conflict of interest suits in the 1990s. One, brought by Ziffren's former client Philip DeGuere, producer of the television series *Simon & Simon*, alleged that Ziffren orchestrated a deal between its other clients, CBS and Columbia Pictures, which cost DeGuere his new series *Triangle* that he had been making for Columbia to be shown on CBS. The suit was eventually settled, reportedly for more than a million dollars. Another suit was filed by Gregg Homer, a former

---

[c] *See* Donna G. Cole-Wallen, *Crossing the Line: Issues Facing Entertainment Attorneys Engaged in Related Secondary Occupations,* 8 Hast. Comm/Ent L.J. 481 (1986); Hal I. Gilenson, *Badlands: Artist-Personal Manager Conflicts of Interest in the Music Industry*, 9 Cardozo Arts & Ent. L.J. 501 (1991); Jonathan Kirsch, *Ethics in Entertainment Law,* 36 Los Ang. Law. 38 (April 1993); Corie Brown, *That's Entertainment*, 13 Cal. Law. 38 (June 1993); Owen J. Sloane, *What Price Glory?* 18 Los Ang. Law. 28 (April 1995).

Ziffren partner, who alleges that he was forced out of Ziffren in 1991, because he was insisting that the firm rigorously comply with professional standards about conflicts of interest. The parties worked out a reported seven-figure settlement of that dispute.

The flip side of the coin is that a major reason why many clients find the Ziffren and Grubman firms attractive in the first place is that their many clients and connections give them the inside track in securing attractive deals for their clients. For example, when *Cheers* was at the top of the television ratings, Ziffren represented Ted Danson and Woody Harrelson, as well as Brandon Tartikoff, chairman of Paramount, which produced the show, and Warren Littlefield, president of NBC, which was broadcasting the series. Typically, it is only after the fact and when the deal has gone wrong that the (by then) ex-client takes umbrage at the alleged conflict of interest.

What are the relevant legal standards? Traditionally, state regulation of talent agencies has not addressed this area of the law. Recently, though, California amended its *Talent Agencies Act* to bar agents from referring their artists to firms in which the agency has a financial interest (or from which the agent receives a referral fee) in return for other services to be rendered to the artists (such as making audition or demonstration materials). California law makes it clearly illegal, then, for agents covered by the statute to have conflicts between their own financial interests and those of their clients. In other states these particular conflicts may well constitute a violation of common law fiduciary duties in agent-principal relationships.

The tougher question is posed by cases where an agent (or manager or lawyer) has two clients who themselves have conflicting interests. Here the law basically controls only those representatives who are lawyers and thus governed by standards of *legal* ethics. State laws on this subject typically reflect the standards found in either the American Bar Association's Model Code of Professional Responsibility or the Model Rules of Professional Conduct. The basic principle is spelled out in the ABA's Model Rule 1.7.

Rule 1.7. Conflict of Interest: General Rule

(a) A lawyer shall not represent a client if the representation of that client will be directly adverse to another client, unless:

(1) the lawyer reasonably believes the representation will not adversely affect the relationship with the other client; and

(2) each client consents after consultation.

(b) A lawyer shall not represent a client if the representation of that client may be materially limited by the lawyer's responsibilities to another client or to a third person, or by the lawyer's own interests, unless:

> (1) the lawyer reasonably believes the representation will not be adversely affected; and
>
> (2) the client consents after consultation. When representation of multiple clients in a single matter is undertaken, the consultation shall include explanation of the implications of the common representation and the advantages and risks involved.

New York's Disciplinary Rules (those governing Alan Grubman and his firm) provide that:

> A lawyer shall decline proffered employment if the exercise of independent professional judgment in behalf of a client will be or is likely to be adversely affected by the acceptance of the proffered employment, or if it would be likely to involve the lawyer in representing differing interests, except . . . a lawyer may represent multiple clients if it is obvious that the lawyer can adequately represent the interests of each and if each consents to the representation after full disclosure of the possible effect of such representation on the exercise of the lawyer's independent professional judgment on behalf of each.

N.Y. DR 5–105(A). Essentially the same standard, and the requirement of at least oral disclosure and client consent, apply in cases where the lawyer has personal transactions with, or affecting the interests of, the client. DR 5–108 deals with the problem of conflicts in the representation of present adversaries to former clients.

California standards in this area have become even more specific. With respect to multiple representation, California Rule 3–310(C) states:

> A member shall not, without the informed written consent of each client:
>
> (1) Accept representation of more than one client in a matter in which the interests of the clients potentially conflict; or
>
> (2) Accept or continue representation of more than one client in a matter in which the interests of the clients actually conflict; or
>
> (3) Represent a client in a matter and at the same time in a separate matter accept as a client a person or entity whose interest in the first matter is adverse to the client in the first matter.

With respect to the attorney's business and personal, as well as professional, interests in the matter, Rule 3–310(B) provides that an attorney cannot agree to represent a client without written disclosure that the attorney:

(1) has a legal, business, financial, professional or personal relationship with a party or witness in the same matter;

(2) or the member knows or reasonably should know that:

(a) the member previously had a legal, business, financial, professional or personal relationship with a party or witness in the same matter; and

(b) the previous relationship would substantially affect the member's representation;

(3) the member has or had a legal, business, financial, professional or personal relationship with another person or entity the member knows or reasonably should know would be affected substantially by resolution of the matter; or

(4) the member has or had a legal, business, financial, professional or personal interest in the subject matter of the representation.

The conflict of interest standards in these and other states do allow lawyers to represent clients in the face of potential conflicts with the interests of either the attorney or other clients, provided the client has accepted this situation after full disclosure and consent (*written* consent, in California) of the relevant facts. However, such conflicting representation is not always permissible, even if there is consent; if representation of the new client would be "materially limited" by the lawyer's responsibility to a current client, or if representation of this client would be "directly adverse" to the interests of another client. Indeed, professional conduct rules might even prevent the necessary disclosure where to do so would violate the lawyer's duty to honor confidentiality of relations with the other client. Likewise, the standard requiring a lawyer to be able to act competently on behalf of a client may make waiver of the conflict rules insufficient where it is determined that the lawyer cannot provide objectively adequate representation to one or both clients because of the conflict. These limits on the use of disclosure and consent to avoid conflicts may force an attorney to make a judgment about whether a desirable client may be kept in the face of an apparent conflict.

---

The following case is one of the few reported decisions involving potential conflicts of interest among entertainment clients.[d]

## CROCE V. KURNIT

United States District Court, Southern District of New York, 1982.
565 F. Supp. 884.

SWEET, DISTRICT JUDGE.

This diversity action presented facts which evoked memories of "A Star Is Born," except that the star in this case, James Croce, died all too soon after his ascendancy.

* * *

[Jim Croce had gone to Villanova University in the 1960s, where he not only met his future wife, Ingrid, but also became a friend of Tommy West. During and after college, Croce began a career in music, while West got a job producing music at ABC and then CBS Records. In 1968, West created a new independent record company, CP & W with several partners, one of whom was lawyer Philip Kurnit, who was also at ABC and CBS Records.

In 1968, Croce and his wife came to New York, stayed with West, were introduced to Kurnit as "the lawyer," and discussed the possibility of CP & W producing Croce's first-ever album. Two months later, they had another meeting with Kurnit, who was still at CBS Records, though the Croces knew he was a partner in the CP & W. Kurnit spent two to three hours explaining the terms of the record contract, which the Croces signed and then Kurnit did so on behalf of CP & W. Kurnit was neither retained nor paid by the Croces as their lawyer, but he did not advise them to hire an independent counsel to review the terms of the agreement.]

* * *

The contracts that were executed on September 17, 1968 provided that Croce would perform and record exclusively for CP & W, as well as the terms under which all the Croce's songs would be published and managerial services would be provided for the Croces. The contracts placed no affirmative requirements on the defendants other than to pay each of the Croces approximately $600 a year and to make certain royalty

---

[d] Another notorious case, *Day v. Rosenthal*, 170 Cal. App. 3d 1125, 217 Cal. Rptr. 89 (1985), presents no significant legal issues, but does depict one of the most horrendous examples of breach of fiduciary duty by an entertainment lawyer. Doris Day eventually won a legal malpractice award of $26 million (upheld on appeal) against her long-time lawyer-manager for losses she suffered from his mismanagement of her earnings and assets, much of which ended up in the lawyer's own pockets. The law firm's malpractice insurer paid the award, except for the $1 million punitive damage component against the individual malefactor, Rosenthal.

payments in the event that music or records were sold. The duration of the contracts was seven years if options to extend were exercised by the defendants. All rights to the Croces' musical performances and writings were granted to the defendants. The management contract was assignable.

* * *

[In fact, Croce's recording contract was assigned to Cashwest, and his management contract to Showcase Management, both spin-offs of CP & W. Croce prepared a demonstration record with which the CP & W people were able to persuade Capital Records to produce a Croce album. Meanwhile, Kurnit was providing a number of legal services directly to the Croces. However, Croce's album for Capital Records was a failure, and Croce turned briefly to other pursuits.

In early 1970 the Croces consulted another lawyer, Rubert Cashman, about how they might get out of their current contracts, because they were unhappy about the management they had been receiving. While Cashman met with Kurnit to discuss cancellation or revision of the contracts, nothing materialized. By the end of 1970, Ingrid Croce had become pregnant, Jim had returned to music, and his relationship with the CP & W principals had been restored (though Croce's personal management contract had been assigned to an established agency, BNB Associates). With Kurnit's help, Croce was able to get ABC Records to produce a new album, which was a big hit in 1972. Croce's recording and performing career skyrocketed for a year until, while returning from a concert on September 20, 1973, his private plane crashed and Croce was killed.

Kurnit had continued to do legal work for the Croces, and he served as attorney for Jim Croce's estate in a number of matters, including a wrongful death action. By 1976, though, a number of issues had arisen between Ingrid Croce and her new husband and Kurnit and his colleagues. Ingrid Croce filed suit against Kurnit and the other CP & W principals and affiliated corporations, claiming both violations of the royalty terms of the Jim Croce contracts, and breach of fiduciary duty and unconscionability that warranted rescission of the contracts and delivery of rights in Croce's music back to her.]

* * *

During the period from 1968 to date the defendants received approximately $6.9 million as a consequence of the performance of the contracts. The recording and entertainment career of Croce is not atypical, representing as it does, initially a famine, and ultimately a feast. No expert who testified claimed the prescience to determine in advance what records the public will buy or in what amount. Though the returns on a successful record are unbelievably high, the risk of initial failure is also high. Judgment, taste, skill and luck far outweigh the time spent or the capital expended on any particular recording.

* * *

### *1. Representation by Kurnit*

The claims of breach of fiduciary duty and procedural unconscionability are based on the role and actions of Kurnit at the signing and during the performance of the contracts. Indeed, the nature of Kurnit's relationship with the Croces determines whether this action is barred by the statute of limitations. Therefore, this court will assess the September 17, 1968 transaction before proceeding to the merits of each claim.

Mrs. Croce asserts that after Kurnit had been introduced to the Croces on a prior occasion as "the lawyer," Kurnit acted as the Croces' attorney at the signing of the contracts or in such a manner as to lead the Croces to reasonably believe that they could rely on his advice. The Croces were aware of the fact that Kurnit was an officer, director and shareholder of Blendingwell and Cashwest on whose behalf Kurnit signed the contracts.

In light of the facts set forth above, Kurnit did not act as the Croces' attorney at the signing of the contracts. Even in the absence of an express attorney-client relationship, however, a lawyer may owe a fiduciary obligation to persons with whom he deals. In particular, a fiduciary duty arises when a lawyer deals with persons who, although not strictly his clients, he has or should have reason to believe rely on him. Kurnit's introduction as "the lawyer," his explanation to the Croces of the "legal ramifications" of the contracts which contained a number of legal terms and concepts, his interest as a principal in the transactions, his failure to advise the Croces to obtain outside counsel, and the Croces lack of independent representation taken together establish both a fiduciary duty on the part of Kurnit and a breach of that duty.[3]

* * *

Although I conclude that Kurnit did not act as counsel to the Croces before September, 1968, the events surrounding the execution of the contracts, in particular his failure to advise the Croces to obtain counsel, establish the applicability of [the standard in] *Howard v. Murray*, 372 N.E.2d 568 (N.Y. 1977), in determining the obligations of Kurnit.

---

[3] *See* Model Code Prof. Resp., DR 7–104(A)(2)(1979):

During the course of his representation of a client a lawyer shall not:

> . . . Give advice to a person who is not represented by a lawyer, other than the advice to secure counsel, if the interests of such person are or have a reasonable possibility of being in conflict with the interests of his client.

Moreover, the limits of the fiduciary relationship as defined in *Penato v. George*, 52 A.D. 2d 939, 383 N.Y.S.2d 900 (2d Dep't 1976) apply. The court there realized that the

> exact limits of such a relationship are impossible of statement. Broadly stated, a fiduciary relationship is one founded upon trust or confidence reposed by one person in the integrity and fidelity of another. It is said that the relationship exists in all cases in which influence has been acquired and abused, in which confidence has been reposed and betrayed. The rule embraces both technical fiduciary relations and those informal relations which exist whenever one man trusts in, and relies upon, another.

383 N.Y.S.2d at 904–95.

This definition of a fiduciary duty applies not only to Kurnit's relationship but also on the facts of this case to West and Cashman, in whom the Croces placed their trust. . . .

* * *

*3. Unconscionability and Breach of Fiduciary Duty*

Mrs. Croce contends that the contracts were unconscionable. An unconscionable contract "affronts the sense of decency," and usually involves gross one-sidedness, lack of meaningful choice and susceptible clientele. J. Calamari & J. Perillo, *Contracts* § 9–40 (2d ed. 1977). A claim of unconscionability "requires some showing of 'an absence of meaningful choice on the part of one of the parties together with contract terms which are unreasonably favorable to the other party.' "

Additionally, Mrs. Croce alleges that defendants breached their fiduciary duty to the Croces. A fiduciary relationship is bound by a standard of fairness, good faith and loyalty.

Substantial testimony was adduced on the subject of the inherent conflict presented by the control of the management contract by the publisher. The management contract, of course, served only the interest of the artist, although obviously the interest of the artist and his career were inextricably interwoven with the publication and promotion of his product. For example, BWB, when undertaking the assignment to manage Croce, immediately obtained a royalty rate increase, of course, thus affecting its own compensation.

The significance of management contracts depends on the needs of artists, some of whom are entirely capable of performing all the business and promotion duties while others seek to concentrate solely on their artistic efforts. As the relationship developed, Croce depended on his manager significantly, but the conflict between the artist and the producer does not so completely overbalance the mutuality of their interest as to make management and recording contracts held or controlled by the same interests, as occurred here, in and of itself, determinative of the issues of unfairness and unconscionability. Indeed, it was Kurnit who ultimately arranged for a separate management contract, albeit that the contract with BWB barred the manager from urging the artist to terminate the contracts.

As the facts stated above indicate, the contracts were hard bargains, signed by an artist without bargaining power, and favored the publishers, but as a matter of fact did not contain terms which shock the conscience or differed so grossly from industry norms as to be unconscionable by their terms. The contacts were free from fraud and although complex in nature, the provisions were not formulated so as to obfuscate or confuse the terms. Although Jim Croce might have thought that he retained the right to choose whether to exercise renewal options, this misconception does not establish that the contracts were unfair. Because of the uncertainty involved in the music business and the high risk of failure of new performers, the contracts, though favoring the defendants, were not unfair. Therefore, I conclude that the terms of the contracts were neither unconscionable nor unfair and that Cashman and West did not breach a fiduciary duty.

In considering procedural unconscionability this court notes that the instant situation lacks the elements of haste and high pressure tactics, and that the contracts did not provide for the sole benefit of the defendants. Indeed, they benefitted the Croces by millions of dollars. Thus Kurnit's actions do not rise to the level of procedural unconscionability. Kurnit, however, as a lawyer and principal, failed to advise the Croces to retain independent counsel and proceeded to give legal advice to the Croces in explaining the contracts to them. These actions, as discussed above, constitute a breach of the fiduciary duty Kurnit owed the Croces. *See Howard v. Murray*, 43 N.Y.2d 417, 372 N.E.2d 568, 401 N.Y.S.2d 781, 784 (1977).[7]

* * *

[The court then ruled that] the breach of fiduciary duty by Kurnit is not so fundamental as to defeat the intent or purpose of the contract [with CP & W]. Mrs. Croce, is, however, entitled to damages resulting from Kurnit's breach of fiduciary duty in failing to advise the Croces to seek

---

[7] Retention of independent counsel by the Croces, had they chosen to do so, might well have resulted in terms more advantageous to them. Although they were never pursued, the brief negotiations entered into by Cushman in 1970 on the Croces' behalf, seeking revisions and amendments to the contracts, evidence this fact. Kurnit's failure to advise the Croces of the advantage of independent representation, coupled with his introduction to them as "the lawyer," his explanation of contracts to them and his interests in the venture warrant a finding of breach of fiduciary duty.

independent counsel. Given the bifurcated nature of this lawsuit, and the fact that, but for Kurnit's breach, the second branch of Mrs. Croce's complaint, claiming fraud, unconscionability, and breach of fiduciary duty, would in all likelihood not have arisen, this court assesses Mrs. Croce's damages to be the costs and attorneys' fees expended in prosecuting those claims, and determines that Kurnit is liable for this amount.

* * *

[The court then awarded damages to Mrs. Croce against Kurnit in the amount of her costs and attorney's fees for pursuing the fraud, unconscionability, and fiduciary duty claims. While the court refused to rescind the songwriting and record agreements, it did uphold several of Mrs. Croce's contract claims regarding the royalties owed to the estate.]

So ordered.

### *QUESTIONS FOR DISCUSSION*

1. CP & W appealed this decision on the contract breach and set-off claims, and the lower court's ruling was affirmed by the Second Circuit in *Croce v. Kurnit*, 737 F.2d 229 (2d Cir. 1984).

2. The lower court dismissed Mrs. Croce's claim that if Kurnit had not violated his fiduciary duties, her late husband would have retained independent representation to negotiate the original contracts with CP & W, and that this action would likely have produced improvements in the contract terms drafted by Kurnit for the deal. Besides the parts of the opinion reproduced above, the judge said:

> [C]ertain of the provisions which were under attack were also contained in the forms published by various organizations involved in the entertainment industry, and there was no evidence presented in this action . . . which established that the terms of these contracts differed significantly from others prepared by Kurnit on behalf of the defendants. These contracts include many terms of art and are customarily the subject of hard bargaining in the event that the artist and the producer both have established economic power. Here, however, no significant changes were made in the contracts as initially proposed by Kurnit on behalf of the other defendants.

*Id.* at 888. Is that a sufficient response to the claim that an unfavorable contract was generated by a lawyer's conflict of interests?

3. Recall the Chapter 6 discussion of *Blaustein v. Burton*, 9 Cal.App.3d 161, 88 Cal. Rptr. 319 (1970). Blaustein's lawyer was Martin Gang, partner in a Los Angeles law firm, another of whose partners, Mickey Rudin, was the outside attorney for the Burtons. The Burtons also used a New York-based lawyer, Aaron French, as their day-to-day legal counsel, and French was the person most intimately involved in these negotiations. However, Blaustein

had asked Gang to speak to Rudin about the specifics of his personal contract and producer fees for this project. Later on, it was Rudin who told Blaustein that while the Burton group (in particular, French) had become reluctant to have him serve as producer, he would still be "rewarded for his contribution to the project." Still later, when Blaustein learned that the Burtons were negotiating with Columbia Pictures for financing and distributing the movie, Gang persuaded him not to write to Columbia, telling the latter of his claim, because the prospect of litigation might dampen Columbia's interest in the project. At or around that time, Rudin was leaving the law firm to work full-time with the Burtons on *The Taming of the Shrew* production. Did Rudin's various roles in this transaction create a conflict of interest?

---

The cases described so far have involved conflicts of interests raised by attorney representation of parties involved in the same transaction. An even stronger conflict arises when the entertainer's representative has a financial interest in the project in question. This brand of conflict arises more often in the case of managers, who may, for example, want a part of the venture in which they are representing their client (as we saw in the Arsenio Hall case earlier in this chapter and the TLC case at the end of Chapter 7). If the manager or agent is a lawyer (as was Hall's manager, Robert Wachs), he is bound by at least some of the standards of legal ethics, irrespective of whether he is technically affording legal representation to the client. Would Wachs be bound by the rules that limit attorney advertising and solicitation of business from new clients, or those that preserve confidentiality of communications with Hall and other existing clients, or just those that bar conflicts of interest and dishonesty? As to the latter, see *ABA Formal Opinion* 336 (June 3, 1974). If the manager/agent is not a lawyer, he or she will still be held to a judicially-fashioned standard of fiduciary responsibility.

The case that follows examines a conflict of interest between a manager and his client. The dispute was an offshoot of a 1971 copyright infringement suit excerpted in Chapter 4, a suit filed by Bright Tunes, copyright owner of the Ronald Mack song "He's So Fine," against former Beatles member George Harrison for the latter's composition, "My Sweet Lord."

## ABKCO MUSIC, INC. v. HARRISONGS MUSIC, LTD.

United States Court of Appeals, Second Circuit, 1983.
722 F.2d 988.

PIERCE, CIRCUIT JUDGE.

* * *

[When Bright Tunes commenced its copyright suit against Harrison in 1971, ABKCO Music and its President, Allen Klein, were the business managers of The Beatles. Indeed, the initial stages of the litigation were handled by ABKCO's general counsel. In 1973, though, a serious rift appeared in the Beatles-ABKCO relationship, ABKCO's management contract was not renewed; litigation ensued about their prior dealings. That dispute was settled in 1977, with a $4.2 million payment by The Beatles to ABKCO.

Meanwhile, the "My Sweet Lord" litigation was proceeding slowly, partly because the plaintiff firm was in receivership. While Klein had suggested to Bright Tunes as early as 1971 that one way to resolve the suit was for Harrison to purchase all the stock of the company, serious settlement negotiations did not get underway until 1975. At that time, the two sides were debating whether Bright Tunes should get 40 or 50 percent of the royalties from "My Sweet Lord." On the eve of trial in 1976, Harrison offered $148,000 to settle the U.S. suit, based on an estimated 40 percent of U.S. royalties.

By this time, though, Bright Tunes had drastically revised its position, now seeking 85 percent of royalties, plus future copyright in "My Sweet Lord." The reason was that ABKCO and Klein had appeared on the scene with an offer to buy Bright Tunes for payment of $100,000 up front and an additional $160,000 upon a finding of copyright infringement. As part of those negotiations, Klein had given Bright Tunes' President, Seymour Borach, ABKCO's records of the prior royalty income of "My Sweet Lord," plus his estimate of the song's future value. Borach thought that Klein's offer was just an opening bid and that the true value of his suit was double that amount.

In any event, trial proceeded without any agreement, and the judge's decision finding a copyright violation came down in August 1976, with hearings on damages yet to come. Meanwhile, ABKCO paid Bright Tunes $587,000 just for the copyright in "He's So Fine" and the infringement claim against Harrison. Harrison confessed to being "a bit amazed" to learn about this purchase when ABKCO offered to sell its rights to him for $700,000.

Harrison refused that offer, and the cased dragged on for another fifteen years, with ABKCO now the plaintiff. The judge's 1991 ruling assessed damages of just under $1.6 million. In response to a new counterclaim by Harrison, however, the judge concluded that the manner in which ABKCO had become the plaintiff meant that the latter's recovery must be sharply curtailed.]

* * *

Particularly "troublesome" to the [lower] court was "Klein's covert intrusion into the settlement negotiation picture in late 1975 and early 1976 immediately preceding the trial on the merits." He found, inter alia, that Klein's status as Harrison's former business manager gave special credence to ABKCO's offers to Bright Tunes and made Bright Tunes less willing to settle with Harrison Interests either before or after the liability trial. Moreover, the court found that in the course of negotiating with Bright Tunes in 1975–76, Klein "covertly furnished" Bright Tunes with certain financial information about MSL which he obtained while in Harrison's employ as business manager. The foregoing conduct, in the court's view, amounted to a breach of ABKCO's fiduciary duty to Harrison. The court held that although it was not clear that "but for" ABKCO's conduct Harrison Interests and Bright Tunes would have settled, he found that good faith negotiations had been in process between the parties and Klein's intrusion made their success less likely, since ABKCO's offer in January 1976 was viewed by Bright Tunes as an "insider's disclosure of the value of the case." Consequently, the district judge directed that ABKCO hold the "fruits of its acquisition" from Bright Tunes in trust for Harrison Interests, to be transferred to Harrison Interests by ABKCO upon payment by Harrison Interests of $587,000 plus interest from the date of acquisition.

## II. ABKCO's Arguments on Appeal

* * *

### *A. Breach of Fiduciary Duty*

There is no doubt that the relationship between Harrison and ABKCO prior to the termination of the management agreement in 1973 was that of principal and agent, and that the relationship was fiduciary in nature. The rule applicable to our present inquiry is that an agent has a duty "not to use confidential knowledge acquired in his employment in competition with his principal." *Byrne v. Barrett*, 268 N.Y. 199, 206, 197 N.E. 217, 218 (1935). This duty "exists as well after the employment is terminated as during its continuance." *Id.* On the other hand, use of information based on general business knowledge or gleaned from general business experience is not covered by the rule, and the former agent is permitted to compete with his former principal in reliance on such general publicly available information. The principal issue before us in the instant case, then, is whether the district court committed clear error in concluding that Klein (hence, ABKCO) improperly used confidential information, gained as Harrison's former agent, in negotiating for the purchase of Bright Tunes' stock (including HSF) in 1975–76.

One aspect of this inquiry concerns the nature of three documents—schedules of MSL earnings—which Klein furnished to Bright Tunes in connection with the 1975–76 negotiations. Although the district judge did not make a specific finding as to whether each of these schedules was confidential, he determined that Bright Tunes at that time was not entitled to the information. It appears that the first of the three schedules may have been previously turned over to Bright Tunes by Harrison. The two additional schedules which Klein gave to Bright Tunes (the detailed updating of royalty information and Klein's personal estimate of the value of MSL and future earnings) appear not to have been made available to Bright Tunes by Harrison. Moreover, it appears that at least some of the past royalty information was confidential. The evidence presented herein is not at all convincing that the information imparted to Bright Tunes by Klein was publicly available. . . .

Another aspect of the breach of duty issue concerns the timing and nature of Klein's entry into the negotiation picture and the manner in which he became a plaintiff in this action. In our view, the record supports the position that Bright Tunes very likely gave special credence to Klein's position as an offeror because of his status as Harrison's former business manager and prior coordinator of the defense of this lawsuit. *See e.g.*, letter from Barash to Sheldon, dated January 19, 1976 ("Since Mr. Klein is in a position to know the true earnings of My Sweet Lord, his offer should give all of us an indication of the true value of this copyright and litigation."). To a significant extent, that favorable bargaining position necessarily was achieved because Klein, as business manager, had intimate knowledge of the financial affairs of his client. Klein himself acknowledged at trial that his offers to Bright Tunes were based, at least in part, on knowledge he had acquired as Harrison's business manager.

Under the circumstances of this case, where there was sufficient evidence to support the district judge's finding that confidential information passed hands, or, at least was utilized in a manner inconsistent with the duty of a former fiduciary at a time when this litigation was still pending, we conclude that the district judge did not err in holding that ABKCO had breached its duty to Harrison.

We find this case analogous to those "where an employee, with the use of information acquired through his former employment relationship, completes, for his own benefit, a transaction originally undertaken on the former employer's behalf." *Group Association Plans, Inc. v. Colquhoun*, 466 F.2d 469, 474 (D.C.Cir. 1972). In this case, Klein had commenced a purchase transaction with Bright Tunes in 1971 on behalf of Harrison, which he pursued on his own account after the termination of his fiduciary relationship with Harrison. While the initial attempt to purchase Bright Tunes' catalogue was several years removed from the eventual purchase on ABKCO's own account, we are not of the view that such a fact rendered ABKCO unfettered in the later negotiations. Indeed, Klein pursued the later discussions armed with the intimate knowledge not only of Harrison's business affairs, but of the value of this lawsuit—and at a time when this action was still pending. Taking all of these circumstances together, we agree that appellant's conduct during the period 1975–78 did not meet the standard required of him as a former fiduciary.

In so concluding, we do not purport to establish a general "appearance of impropriety" rule with respect to artist/manager relationship. That strict standard—reserved principally for the legal profession—would probably not suit the realities of the business world. The facts of this case otherwise permit the conclusion reached herein. Indeed, as Judge Owen noted in his Memorandum and Order of May 7, 1979 (permitting Harrison Interests to assert counterclaims), "The fact situation presented is novel in the extreme. Restated in simplest form, it amounts to the purchase by a business manager of a known claim against his former client where, the right to the claim having been established, all that remains to be done is to assess the monetary award." We find these facts not only novel, but unique. Indeed, the purchase, which rendered Harrison and ABKCO adversaries, occurred in the context of a lawsuit in which ABKCO had been the prior protector of Harrison's interests. Thus, although not wholly analogous to the side-switching cases involving attorneys and their former clients, this fact situation creates clear questions of impropriety. On the unique facts presented herein, we certainly cannot say that Judge Owen's findings and conclusions were clearly erroneous or not in accord with applicable law.

Appellant ABKCO also contends that even if there was a breach of duty, such breach should not limit ABKCO's recovery for copyright infringement because ABKCO's conduct did not cause the Bright Tunes/Harrison settlement negotiations to fail. Appellant urges, in essence, that a finding of breach of fiduciary duty by an agent, to be actionable, must be found to have been the proximate cause of injury to the principal. We do not accept appellant's proffered causation standard. An action for breach of fiduciary duty is a prophylactic rule intended to remove all incentive to breach—not simply to compensate for damages in the event of a breach. . . . Having found that ABKCO's conduct constituted a breach of fiduciary duty, the district judge was not required to find a "but for" relationship between ABKCO's conduct and lack of success of Harrison Interests' settlement efforts.

ABKCO argues further that the offer to sell substantially what had been gained in the purchase from Bright Tunes to Harrison for $700,000, and Harrison's rejection of that offer, bars Harrison Interests from obtaining a constructive trust in this action. . . . [W]e find somewhat disingenuous ABKCO's claim that a $700,000 offer was a "price equivalent to his cost of acquisition," which had been $587,000. In any event, it is unclear whether that which ABKCO offered Harrison Interests was equivalent to that which ABKCO had brought from Bright Tunes.

Finally, on the facts herein, we agree that a constructive trust on the "fruits" of ABKCO's acquisition was a proper remedy. . . .

* * *

Affirmed as modified.

---

The Second Circuit rendered yet another decision on damages in *ABKCO Music v. Harrisongs Music*, 944 F.2d 971 (2d Cir. 1991), twenty years after the beginning of litigation that, in the words of the court, is "giving true meaning for those involved, to the title of the Beatles 'It's Been a Hard Day's Night.'" Even this ruling remanded several issues back to the district judge to recalculate the amounts payable by Harrison to Klein.

### *QUESTIONS FOR DISCUSSION*

1. Why do you think Klein felt it was proper to negotiate with Bright Tunes and use confidential information obtained while representing Harrison? Is it possible for a manager to behave as Klein did and still act in the best interests of the client? Should managers be subject to professional conduct rules similar to those imposed on lawyers? Does the current situation, which holds attorneys to higher standards, discourage lawyers from becoming managers? Does it encourage performers to hire lawyers as their managers, or perhaps have no effect at all on the market?

2. In *Gershunoff v. Panov*, 77 A.D.2d 511, 430 N.Y.S.2d 299 (1st Dept. 1980), The Panovs (husband and wife) were two well-known ballet dancers who emigrated from Russia to Israel in 1974. At that time they spoke only Russian. Gershunoff, an entertainment manager who spoke both Russian and English, convinced the dancers to sign a contract deeming him their exclusive "impresario manager" and granting him a 20% commission on the fees they received from engagements he procured. When the couple became more familiar with their industry situation, they became unhappy with Gershunoff and took steps to terminate their relationship. The manager sued the dancers for breach of contract and sought to enjoin them from accepting any engagements except those he had procured for them. The Panovs counterclaimed, charging Gershunoff with breach of his fiduciary obligations, both by taking payments for engagements he arranged for the Panovs and

not informing the artists of other engagements. An accounting was sought of Gershunoff's receipts from Panov performances. During the trial, it was revealed that, for example, Gershunoff had received a $25,000 fee as "promoter" from a theater in Philadelphia where the Panovs had agreed to perform for $10,000 for each performance. Gershunoff received a 20% commission from the Panovs for this engagement, and he never informed the Panovs of the theater's $25,000 payment to him. Gershunoff defended his actions on the ground that he was an "impresario manager," a non-traditional role that occupies a "status akin to a producer of events," whereby he "undertakes to pay the artist an agreed upon fee, produce the event at his risk, and retain as his compensation whatever profits are engendered." *Id.* at 301. Thus the $25,000 fee he had received was simply compensation for the risks he had undertaken in this role. The court disagreed, finding this a clear breach of Gershunoff's fiduciary duties to his clients, one that supported a $255,000 damage award.

3. Consider the fundamental ethical issue that is posed here.[e] Even with express written consent, the same law firm cannot represent opposing sides in *litigation* about a prior transaction. *Klemm v. Superior Court of Fresno County*, 75 Cal.App.3d 893, 142 Cal. Rptr. 509, 512 (1977). The most recent episode in the Kim Basinger saga may have tested the scope of this principle. In early 1996, after settling the dispute with Main Line Pictures (described in Chapter 7, Section A), Basinger's bankruptcy trustee filed a legal malpractice suit against Basinger's trial attorney, the Katten law firm. The basis for this complaint was an alleged conflict of interest stemming from Katten also representing Basinger's agency, International Creative Management, which had advised her not to appear in *Boxing Helena*. In fact, Katten had succeeded in having Main Line's suit against ICM for inducing Basinger's breach of contract dismissed before trial on grounds of the agent-client fiduciary relationship. Thus Basinger's trustee claimed that Katten should have added ICM as a third party, required to indemnify Basinger if her liability for breach of contract was established at trial. Should Katten have been responsible for any of this, assuming that Basinger knew of the firm's dual role?

4. Turn now from litigation to the original *negotiation* of the underlying transaction. Should the same party be able to represent both sides at that earlier stage? Suppose, for example, that Jim Croce had given written consent to Philip Kurnit to represent him in the negotiation of Croce's first music contract with CP & W, of which Kurnit was a part? What about negotiation of the breakup of a corporate venture that has gone wrong (i.e., an entertainment divorce)? Are there conflicts of interest in representation of various parties in situations such as the following:

---

[e] For a provocative exchange on this topic, see Edwin F. McPherson, *Conflicts in the Entertainment Industry? . . . Not!*, 10 Enter. & Sports Law. 5 (Winter 1993); Joseph B. Anderson & Darrell D. Miller, *Professional Responsibility 101: A Response to "Conflicts in the Entertainment Industry,"* 11 Enter. & Sports Law. 8 (Summer 1993); Richard E. Flamm & Joseph B. Anderson, *Conflict of Interest in Entertainment Law Practice, Revisited*, 14 Enter. & Sports Law. 3 (Spring 1996).

1. Representing a movie star like Julia Roberts in negotiating a film project with Disney Studios, whose studio head, Joe Roth, is also represented by that firm?
2. Representing a star with a share in the gross revenues (like Eddie Murphy in *Coming to America*), and a lesser performer (like Art Buchwald) with just net profit participation in that project?
3. Representing one member (say John Lennon) of a group (the Beatles), when Lennon is writing (and receiving copyright in) the songs the group as a whole is recording on its album?
4. An agency putting together a feature film proposal based on a script written by one of its screenwriter clients, and insisting that the script be rewritten in order to have an attractive part for one of its actors?

Are these cases simply illustrations of the rules of an entertainment game in which everyone involved is better off than they would otherwise be? (Some in Hollywood may feel that a representative with a potential *conflict* is at least someone with an actual *contact*). Should concerns about conflicts of interest involving agents and managers be confined to conflicting representative-client interests, and not to competing interests of two or more clients?

5. Consider now the Creative Artists Agency-Credit Lyonnais controversy mentioned at the start of this section. In 1992, Credit Lyonnais, a large state-owned French bank, took over Metro-Goldwyn-Mayer/United Artists (MGM/UA) and its affiliated producers when the studio filed for bankruptcy after having lost several billions of dollars that had been loaned by the bank. Credit Lyonnais hired Michael Ovitz, then head of CAA, to advise the bank on how to revive MGM/UA before it had to be sold in 1997 pursuant to the bankruptcy court's order. Many industry participants applauded this move, hoping it would increase the number of film projects and jobs. Under its new leadership MGM/UA was revived by 1996, after releasing such hits as *Get Shorty*, *GoldenEye*, *The Birdcage*, and *Leaving Las Vegas*, and the bank was able to sell the studio and recoup much of its losses.

Some concerns were raised about Ovitz' role in the revival of MGM/UA because of potential conflicts in having Ovitz advise the studio about projects at the same time that his agency representing actors, directors, and writers who might be involved in these ventures. Leading the criticism was Jeff Berg, head of ICM, one of CAA's two major agency rivals. Indeed, Berg and ICM filed a complaint with the Justice Department that the CAA-MGM relationship constituted a "combination in restraint of trade" in violation of antitrust laws. The precedent that Berg had in mind was the 1962 directive from the Kennedy's Justice Department requiring MCA, which Lew Wasserman had made into Hollywood's leading talent agency of the 1940s and then turned into a film producer in the 1950s, to divest itself of one side or the other of this business. As we saw earlier, MCA chose to concentrate on movie producing.

Berg was not really complaining that CAA was compromising the interests of its own clients, but rather those of ICM (and other agencies). The doctrines that allow performers to hold agents to loyal representation of *their* interests would not likely lead to suits by CAA clients against Ovitz having a major role advising the bank about possible deals with them. The question, then, is whether there should be an alternative legal regime (perhaps federal antitrust law or a state Talent Agencies Act) that preserves a level playing field for ICM and its clients in such a situation.

6. As was mentioned earlier, both Ovitz and his partner, Ron Meyer, left CAA in the midst of the 1995 merger storm to become executives at Disney/ABC and MCA/Universal Pictures, respectively. Prior to that, Ovitz owned 55 percent of the equity in CAA, Meyer 22.5 percent, and the third founding father, Bill Haber, the remaining 22.5 percent. The group taking over CAA agreed on a buyout package approaching $150 million, to be paid out over four years. The agreement specified that the payments came out of the ongoing proceeds from contract deals that had already been negotiated by CAA for its clients before Ovitz and Meyer left. The fact that Ovitz and Meyer were not to be paid by CAA in a lump sum, but instead over a period when they were officials at major studios, raised further questions about potential conflicts. (This was a short-lived problem as to Ovitz, who departed from Disney just a year later.) Would there be any problem with this arrangement? If there were a problem, would it likely be felt by CAA's clients, the clients of CAA's competitors, or the shareholders of Disney and MCA? In fact, the CAA-Ovitz-Meyer buyout was structured in a fashion that eliminated any such possible conflict. How could that be done?

---

Consider next the potential conflict of interest presented by Ovitz' new body, the Artists Management Group. As we have seen, AMG not only performs a host of functions on behalf of clients who work in movies and television, but is also now producing its own films. One key advantage to Ovitz from his functioning as a manager rather than as an agent is there is no limit (i.e., 10 percent) on the fees that are charged the AMG clients. Even more important, there is no ban on the manager producing the show on which its client is performing (with the manager being paid for both tasks). But talent managers are realizing from yet another major lawsuit that there may well be a fiduciary obligation owed to the client that makes certain features of this relationship a violation of the common law.[f]

---

[f] *See* M. William Krasilovsky & Robert S. Meloni, *Ethical Considerations for Music Industry Professionals,* 15 Colum.-VLA J. Law & Arts 335 (1991).

In the 1970s, Garry Shandling was a notable comic writer (e.g., on *Sanford and Son*), while Brad Grey had just begun as a personal manager. When Grey's one client introduced the two to each other in 1979, Shandling became Grey's second client, as he expanded his career to stand-up comic performances. In 1985, Grey teamed up with Bernie Brillstein, a more prominent manager as well as producer of television shows in which he retained the syndication rights. Shandling continued to be a client of Brillstein-Grey Enterprises (BG).

A year later, Shandling formed a partnership with another B-G branch, Brillstein-Grey Entertainment, to create and sell their new *It's Garry Shandling's Show* to Showtime. While Shandling was the star, writer, and co-producer of this show, Grey for the first time served (and was paid) as executive producer. In 1991, this group embarked on another joint venture to replace *It's Garry Shandling's Show* on Showtime with *The Larry Sanders Show* on HBO. Shandling provided the same services as before, through his personal corporation "How's My Hair." Besides the $500,000 he averaged for each of the 16 annual episodes of *Larry Sanders*, Shandling owned half of the future rights in this show. B-G Entertainment owned the other half, and Grey was paid approximately $50,000 per episode as executive producer. While B-G Enterprises charged a 15% commission for negotiating Shandling's compensation, they charged nothing for Grey's fees that he negotiated for himself.

By the early 1990s, B-G Enterprises had become a major management group in Hollywood, with over 100 clients. B-G Entertainment had had just two significant successes, both involving the Shandling shows. In 1991, though, it secured a deal with Columbia Pictures Television that gave B-G Enterprises tens of millions of dollars in up-front financing of new B-G Entertainment shows, in return for "first look" rights for syndication and other uses of the successful ones. Then, in 1994, the new entity B-G Communications was created, as a joint venture of the B-G and ABC/Capital Cities. In return for more than $100 million in investments, ABC had the "first look" rights at projects developed by the B-G people. In the next few years, B-G Communications created a number of well-regarded programs such as *NewsRadio*, *Just Shoot Me*, and *The Naked Truth*. In 1996, MCA/Universal Pictures paid $90 million to secure a 50 percent share of the B-G Entertainment arm and its rights in the Shandling and other shows.

During this time, there was still a friendly relationship between Shandling and Grey. *Larry Sanders* was a hit show on HBO, and Shandling was paid another $2 million by B-G Communications for his advice and contributions to new pilot scripts. Of course, B-G Enterprises took a management commission from those payments as well, and any new Shandling projects developed under that contract would be subject to the "first look" deal between B-G Communications and ABC. But not only were Shandling and Grey working and going to the Emmy Awards together, but they occasionally went on vacations together as well.

For reasons that are not clear, this relationship began to come apart in late 1996. During the shooting of the first "take" of the final episode of that season's *Larry Sanders Show*, Shandling became emotionally distraught, walked off the set, and flew to Hawaii and Fiji for three weeks of recovery. The final day of the shoot had to be done without its star, and the episode was edited somewhat around him. There had been some disaffection between Shandling and others involved in *Larry Sanders*, and a number of the latter ended up on other B-G Communications productions after quitting or being dismissed by Shandling. Most prominent of these was *Larry Sanders*' head writer Paul Simm who moved on to create *NewsRadio*.

In 1997, Shandling went to see a lawyer for the first time. While Grey offered to repay Shandling $1.2 million in management fees, and to pay him up to $20 million for future consultation and first-look rights, this was not enough. Grey terminated the manager-client relationship (which had never had a written agreement), and Shandling then filmed the last-ever episode of *Larry Sanders*. That episode, which HBO showed in 1998, had appearances by Warren Beatty, Jerry Seinfeld, Jim Carrey, Tim Allen, and Ellen DeGeneres.

Meanwhile, Shandling sued Grey and his firms (of which Grey was now sole owner) for $100 million in damages. The essence of the claim was that Grey as manager had violated his fiduciary obligations by using Shandling's personal talent, story ideas, and reputation as the major asset through which to secure partnerships with Columbia, ABC/Capital Cities, and MCA/Universal. Because Grey should have been concentrating on enhancing Shandling's return on those assets, Shandling believed he was now entitled to roughly half the proceeds.

Needless to say, this lawsuit generated intense interest and feelings among many managers and performers about the terms of their relationships. Illustrating this trend is the fact that the star of B-G Communications' *NewsRadio* was Phil Hartman, a client of B-G Enterprises, and the same was true of Adam Sandler, the star in B-G Entertainment's first movie hit *The Wedding Singer*. As with Shandling, Grey received the standard commission for these performers' earnings from contracts with his other entities. Of course, the nature of these relationships was well known to Shandling, Hartman, and Sandler. Thus, the basic issue is whether managers always owe a fiduciary duty to their clients to pursue just their interests in any such projects. Alternatively, if Grey (or Ovitz) wants to pursue his own interests in such a project, must he disavow any representation of the performer and have the latter to hire another manager to get the best deal possible for the client?

A top Hollywood litigator, Bert Fields, served as Grey's attorney in this case, and he filed a $10 million countersuit against Shandling for violating his contract obligation to preserve (rather than end with erratic behavior) *The Larry Sanders Show* while it still was an HBO hit. With the case scheduled to go to trial in 1999, Shandling had begun working on his first Hollywood film in some time, *What Planet Are You From?* Ironically, the executive producer of the film was Brad Grey. When Shandling's attorney David Boies took some time out of his ongoing antitrust suit against Microsoft, the lawyers were able to reach a settlement just before trial, saying that each had given the other "certain interests in various television programs," with Shandling reportedly getting the bulk of Grey's interest in *Larry Sanders* and *Shandling*, and giving up everything else (e.g., Grey's new HBO hit, *The Sopranos*). Since the terms of any settlement are shaped by the governing law, what share of *Larry Sanders* is Shandling likely to now own?

---

The presence of ulterior motives on the part of the agent can also lead to legal disputes. One example involved reality television producer Scott Einziger. Einziger, who produced the hit show *Big Brother*, sued his agent Michael Camacho and United Talent Agency for $10 million in 2011. Einzinger claimed that Camacho steered him from *Big Brother*, a hit show, to a risky job at RelativityReal, operated by Ellen Rakieten, who was in a serious romantic relationship with Camacho. Einzinger's time at RelativityReal was short-lived as a result of what he termed a "toxic" work environment.

Einzinger abruptly dropped the lawsuit on the eve of trial in September 2012. To what extent can claims such as his be successful? Is the romantic relationship enough of a conflict of interest to make Camacho liable?

---

Legal issues in representation of actors are not limited just to conflicts between actor and agent. Another recent conflict between leading talent agencies Creative Artists Agency (CAA) and United Talent Agency (UTA) is illustrative. In the spring of 2015, 10 agents left CAA to join UTA, including several agents still under contract with CAA. The exodus was particularly notable because the agents took a number of famous clients with them to CAA, including Will Ferrell, Chris Pratt, Zach Galifinakis, and Ed Helms.

CAA termed the exodus a "lawless midnight raid" and filed a lawsuit alleging, among other things, tortious interference with contracts, as well as breach of fiduciary duty and duty of loyalty against two of the defecting agencies. UTA's acquisition of the agents and their clients has certainly closed the gap between UTA and CAA, but it remains to be seen whether there will be any legal consequences to this exodus.

What facts would support a successful claim by CAA? What defenses might UTA and the agents have?

---

The conflict of interest questions we have just seen involved the movie industry. The world of music seems to consider this largely a non-issue.[g] Chapter 7 discussed bankruptcy litigation involving the group TLC, which was seeking to extricate itself from a long-term record contract that had bestowed huge profits on the group's label, but produced only modest returns to the three artists. A relevant fact for this chapter is that Perri Read, the person who discovered and managed TLC, had secured as part of her management contract with the group the right to produce their albums in return for a 7 percent royalty rate. Read resold those rights to her husband's LaFace Records, in return for *15 percent* royalty payments to Read's corporate arm, Pebbitone, Inc.

A more significant example involved Irving Azoff and his Front Line Management. In the late 1960s, Azoff was working for David Geffen, who was managing such music performers as Crosby, Stills, Nash, & Young, and Jackson Browne. When Geffen started a record label for his clients (to which he soon added newcomers like Linda Ronstadt, Joni Mitchell, and The Eagles), he left the managing business to Azoff, operating as Front Line Management and adding to its clientele Jimmy Buffett and Dan Fogelberg. In the early 1980s, Azoff was brought in by MCA/Universal to try to turn around its music division. (One thing Azoff would do in 1990 was have MCA acquire Geffen Records for $540 million, which in turn gave Geffen the financial base for co-founding the DreamWorks studio.) Even when he arrived as CEO of MCA Records, Azoff continued to own Front Line Management, eventually selling this asset to MCA itself (for $16 million). The result was that one arm of MCA was managing the affairs of Jimmy Buffett, for example, who had a record contracts with another arm of MCA. No one in the industry or in the Justice Department considered this to pose any conflict of interest. This is yet another illustration of the very different treatment of agency representation of movie performers and personal management of music performers. How, if at all, can such differences be explained and justified?

---

Talent representatives face another potential legal problem when they are allegedly too assiduous in promoting the interests of their

[g] *See* M. William Krasilovsky & Robert S. Meloni, *Ethical Considerations for Music Industry Professionals,* 15 Colum.-VLA J. Law & Arts 335 (1991).

clients, sometimes at the expense of the interests of third parties. In prior chapters we have encountered numerous examples of performers seeking to extricate themselves from long-term contracts. One such case provides an interesting lesson on the responsibility, if any, of the lawyer (or agent or manager) to third parties.

In the 1970s, Tim Scholz was an MIT engineering student who had gone on to work at Polaroid. In his spare time, Scholz experimented with a new style of rock and roll, performed with several friends under the name Boston. In 1976, Scholz secured a multi-album record deal from Epic Records, part of CBS Music group. Epic released the group's already-recorded first album, *Boston*, which stunned the music world by selling 8 million records, then the highest-ever for a debut album. It took the group two more years to produce its next album, *Don't Look Back*, which sold "only" 4 million copies. Scholz, a technical aficionado, believed that the problem was corporate pressure from Epic to release the album too early, before its sound had been perfected. The result was that the group's next album took far longer to complete. Eventually, in 1983, CBS Music decided to put pressure on Boston by cutting off payment of royalties owed on their earlier records (soon amounting to $3 million), and filing suit, seeking $20 million in damages for Boston's breach of its record contract.

Scholz and his colleagues hired Don Engel, a noted Los Angeles music attorney with a record of doing battle with the labels. (For example, Engel was the lawyer who freed TLC from its original record contract with Pebbitone and LaFace Records, and had earlier won Teena Marie's release from her Motown contract.) Besides defending (and counter-claiming) the CBS suit against his clients, Engel decided that CBS's refusal to pay past royalties owed to Boston allowed the group to rescind the contract, and in 1984 he negotiated a new deal with MCA Records for Boston's next album. CBS immediately sued MCA and Engel for allegedly inducing a breach of contract.

A New York judge quickly dismissed the claim against Engel, and the jury eventually rendered a $6.5 million award in favor of Boston. MCA's release of *The Third Stage* generated sales of 4 million copies. Engel in turn launched a malicious prosecution suit against CBS, which eventually produced a Ninth Circuit decision, *Engel v. CBS Inc.*, 981 F.2d 1076 (9th Cir. 1992). While Engel had filed his lawsuit in Los Angeles, the court said that New York law governed in this case. A key factor in a malicious prosecution claim is whether there was at least "probable cause" for the original suit. With respect to a suit against a client's lawyer, "under New York law an attorney generally cannot be held liable to a third party for purported injuries caused by services performed on behalf of a client, or advice offered to a client, absent a showing of fraud or collusion, or a malicious or tortious act." In this case, while CBS may well have had probable cause for its suit against MCA and Boston for possible breach of the latter's contract, it did not have a claim against Engel, who had just "openly shopped the market for a new record contract for his client." The Second Circuit dismissed the claim, because the CBS suit against the lawyer—though "reprehensible"—had not caused "the critical mass necessary to be cognizable as special injury" for purposes of a malicious prosecution claim, 182 F.3d 124 (2d Cir. 1999); *see* 93 N.Y.2d 195, 689 N.Y.S.2d 411, 711 N.E.2d 626, 632 (1999).

Clearly, then, an artist's attorney enjoys broad immunity from being sued by others for advice given or actions taken on behalf of the client. Should the same leeway be given to the artist's manager or agent if it is their advice that generates the breach of contract? Should lawyers be immune from suit by third parties if they know that their clients have no plausible grounds under their contract or the law, but they advise a refusal to perform because they are aware of production and market pressures that will force the other side to renegotiate on more generous terms?

## C. UNION REGULATION OF ENTERTAINER REPRESENTATION

The validity of the CAA-Ovitz-Meyer deal mentioned above was referred to the Hollywood unions—the Screen Actors Guild (SAG), Directors Guild (DG), and Writers Guild (WG)—that had earlier resolved the CAA-ICM dispute about Ovitz' work for Credit Lyonnais and MGM. These unions have rules that bar agents from receiving remuneration from producers of motion pictures, except in specifically defined circumstances, such as a fee for packaging a film project. (The virtue of these packaging fees from the point of view of agency clients and union members is that *they* do not have to pay a commission for the work the agency secured for them on such package deals.) The unions had Ovitz confine his advice to Credit Lyonnais to the general path that MGM/UA should be following, and not become involved in decisions about specific film projects and who would perform in them. Nor would he have access to confidential information about contracts between MGM and the clients of other agencies.

This shows that regulation of agent-manager qualifications, fees, and fiduciary responsibilities does not have to be left to courts or administrative agencies. These problems can be tackled by the entertainers themselves, through their trade unions. Indeed, as a debate went on in the 1990s in the California legislature about whether to amend the *Talent Agencies Act* to require agents to limit their fees to 10 percent, this was a non-issue among movie performers: their unions had already capped agent commissions at 10 percent of the performer's earnings. (The Association of Talent Agents' success in blocking that law did make a real difference to music performers, whose agents regularly charge 15 to 20 percent commissions for events they book, over and above the manager's share of musician earnings.)

The entertainment field is one of the most highly-unionized occupations in American industry. Live theater actors are in Actors Equity; movie actors, writers, and directors in the SAG, WG, and DG respectively; television and radio performers in the American Federation of Television and Radio Artists (AFTRA), now SAG-AFTRA; and musicians in the American Federation of Musicians (AFM). As we shall see in Chapter 11, the principal aim of the unions is to bargain collectively with studios, networks, Broadway producers and others to establish the basic conditions of employment above which individual performers may negotiate more favorable terms. Dating back to the 1920s, the unions have also sought to establish standards for the agents who represent performers in such individual negotiations.

The lever through which these unions have enforced such standards is a mutual undertaking by all union members not to use any agent who had not been certified (or "franchised") by the union, in return for the agent agreeing to certain terms, such as maximum fee percentages. On its face, such a performer agreement to boycott non-complying agents does seem to amount to "a combination . . . in restraint of trade," in violation of Section 1 of the Sherman Antitrust Act. The legal *imprimatur* for such union action would have to be the labor exemption from antitrust liability, an exemption originally developed by Congress and the courts to legalize collective worker actions vis-a-vis employers (and which we will see operating in that context in the following chapter). Not until the early 1980s did the Supreme Court face the question of whether entertainers enjoyed the same antitrust immunity as to their agents.

## H. A. ARTISTS & ASSOCS., INC. V. ACTORS' EQUITY ASS'N

Supreme Court of the United States, 1981.
451 U.S. 704, 101 S.Ct. 2102, 68 L.Ed.2d 558.

JUSTICE STEWART delivered the opinion of the Court.

I

A

Equity is a national union that has represented stage actors and actresses since early in this century. Currently representing approximately 23,000 actors and actresses, it has collective-bargaining agreements with virtually all major theatrical producers in New York City, on and off Broadway, and with most other theatrical producers throughout the United States. The terms negotiated with producers are the minimum conditions of employment (called "scale"); an actor or actress is free to negotiate wages or terms more favorable than the collectively bargained minima.

Theatrical agents are independent contractors who negotiate contracts and solicit employment for their clients. The agents do not participate in the negotiation of collective-bargaining agreements between Equity and the theatrical producers. If an agent succeeds in obtaining employment for a client, he receives a commission based on a percentage of the client's earnings. Agents who operate in New York City must be licensed as employment agencies and are regulated by the New York City Department of Consumer Affairs pursuant to New York law, which provides that the maximum commission a theatrical agent may charge his client is 10% of the client's compensation.

In 1928, concerned with the high unemployment rates in the legitimate theater and the vulnerability of actors and actresses to abuses by theatrical agents, including the extraction of high commissions that tended to undermine collectively bargained rates of compensation, Equity unilaterally established a licensing system for the regulation of agents. The regulations permitted Equity members to deal only with those agents who obtained Equity licenses and thereby agreed to meet the conditions of representation prescribed by Equity. Those members who dealt with nonlicensed agents were subject to union discipline.

The system established by the Equity regulations was immediately challenged. In *Edelstein v. Gillmore*, 35 F.2d 723 (2d Cir. 1929), the Court of Appeals for the Second Circuit concluded that the regulations were a lawful effort to improve the employment conditions of Equity members.

* * *

The essential elements of Equity's regulation of theatrical agents have remained unchanged since 1928. A member of Equity is prohibited, on pain of union discipline, from using an agent who has not, through the mechanism of obtaining an Equity license (called a "franchise"), agreed to comply with the regulations. The most important of the regulations requires that a licensed agent must renounce any right to take a commission on an employment contract under which an actor or actress receives scale wages.[8] To the extent a contract includes provisions under which an actor or actress will sometimes receive scale pay—for rehearsals

[8] The minimum, or "scale," wage varies. In August 1977, for example, the minimum weekly salary was $335 for Broadway performances, and $175 for performances off Broadway. Scale wages are set by a collective-bargaining agreement between Equity and the producers, to which the agents are not parties. When an agent represents an actor or actress whose professional reputation is not sufficient to demand a salary higher than scale, the agent hopes to develop a relationship that will become continually more remunerative as the performer's professional reputation grows, and with it the power to demand an ever higher salary. No agent is required to represent an actor or actress whom he does not wish to represent.

or "chorus" employment, for example—and sometimes more, the regulations deny the agent any commission on the scale portions of the contract. Licensed agents are also precluded from taking commissions on out-of-town expense money paid to their clients. Moreover, commissions are limited on wages within 10% of scale pay,[9] and an agent must allow his client to terminate a representation contract if the agent is not successful in procuring employment within a specified period. Finally, agents are required to pay franchise fees to Equity. The fee is $200 for the initial franchise, $60 a year thereafter for each agent, and $40 for any subagent working in the office of another. These fees are deposited by Equity in its general treasury and are not segregated from other union funds.

In 1977, after a dispute between Equity and Theatrical Artists Representatives Associates (TARA)—a trade association representing theatrical agents—a group of agents, including the petitioners, resigned from TARA because of TARA's decision to abide by Equity's regulations. These agents also informed Equity that they would not accept Equity's regulations, or apply for franchises. The petitioners instituted this lawsuit in May 1978, contending that Equity's regulations of theatrical agents violated §§ 1 and 2 of the Sherman Act, 26 Stat. 209, as amended, 15 U.S.C. §§ 1 and 2.

B

The District Court found [and the Second Circuit agreed] that Equity's creation and maintenance of the agency franchise system were fully protected by the statutory labor exemptions from the antitrust laws, and accordingly dismissed the petitioners' complaint. Among its factual conclusions, the trial court found that in the theatrical industry, agents play a critical role in securing employment for actors and actresses:

> As a matter of general industry practice, producers seek actors and actresses for their productions through agents. Testimony in this case convincingly established that an actor without an agent does not have the same access to producers or the same opportunity to be seriously considered for a part as does an actor who has an agent. Even principal interviews, in which producers are required to interview all actors who want to be considered for principal roles, do not eliminate the need for an agent, who may have a greater chance of gaining an audition for his client.

[9] It is Equity's view that commissions in the industry are not necessarily related to efforts by the agents, and that an agent often functions as little more than an "order taker," who is able to collect a percentage of a client's wages for the duration of a show for doing little more than answering a producer's telephone call. Indeed, an agent may collect a commission on the salary of an actor or actress he represents even if the client obtains the job without the agent.

* * *

> Testimony confirmed that agents play an integral role in the industry; without an agent, an actor would have significantly lesser chances of gaining employment.

The court also found "no evidence to suggest the existence of any conspiracy or illegal combination between Actors' Equity and TARA or between Actors' Equity and producers," and concluded that "[the] Actors Equity franchising system was employed by Actors' Equity for the purpose of protecting the wages and working conditions of its members."

* * *

II

A

Labor unions are lawful combinations that serve the collective interests of workers, but they also possess the power to control the character of competition in an industry. Accordingly, there is an inherent tension between national antitrust policy, which seeks to maximize competition, and national labor policy, which encourages cooperation among workers to improve the conditions of employment.[12] In the years immediately following passage of the Sherman Act, courts enjoined strikes as unlawful restraints of trade when a union's conduct or objectives were deemed "socially or economically harmful." *Duplex Printing Press Co. v. Deering*, 254 U.S. 443, 485 (Brandeis, J., dissenting). In response to these practices, Congress acted, first in the Clayton Act, 38 Stat. 731, and later in the Norris-LaGuardia Act, 47 Stat. 70, to immunize labor unions and labor disputes from challenge under the Sherman Act.

Section 6 of the Clayton Act, 15 U.S.C. § 17, declares that human labor "is not a commodity or article of commerce," and immunizes from antitrust liability labor organizations and their members "lawfully carrying out" their "legitimate [objectives]." Section 20 of the Act prohibits injunctions against specified employee activities, such as strikes and boycotts, that are undertaken in the employees' self-interest and that occur in the course of disputes "concerning terms or conditions of employment," and states that none of the specified acts can be "held to be [a] [violation] of any law of the United States." This protection is re-emphasized and expanded in the Norris-LaGuardia Act, which prohibits federal-court injunctions against single or organized employees engaged in enumerated activities, and specifically forbids such injunctions notwithstanding the claim of an unlawful combination or conspiracy.

[12] *See generally* Meltzer, *Labor Unions, Collective Bargaining, & the Antitrust Laws*, 32 U. Chi. L. Rev. 659 (1965); Winter, *Collective Bargaining & Competition: The Application of Antitrust Standards to Union Activities*, 73 Yale L. J. 14 (1963).

While the Norris-LaGuardia Act's bar of federal-court labor injunctions is not explicitly phrased as an exemption from the antitrust laws, it has been interpreted broadly as a statement of congressional policy that the courts must not use the antitrust laws as a vehicle to interfere in labor disputes.

In *United States v. Hutcheson*, 312 U.S. 219, the Court held that labor unions acting in their self-interest and not in combination with nonlabor groups enjoy a statutory exemption from Sherman Act liability. After describing the congressional responses to judicial interference in union activity, the Court declared that

> [so] long as a union acts in its self-interest and does not combine with non-labor groups, the licit and the illicit under § 20 [of the Clayton Act] are not to be distinguished by any judgment regarding the wisdom or unwisdom, the rightness or wrongness, the selfishness or unselfishness of the end of which the particular union activities are the means.

The Court explained that this exemption derives not only from the Clayton Act, but also from the Norris-LaGuardia Act, particularly its definition of a "labor dispute," in which Congress "reasserted the original purpose of the Clayton Act by infusing into it the immunized trade union activities as redefined by the later Act." Thus under *Hutcheson*, no federal injunction may issue over a "labor dispute," and "§ 20 [of the Clayton Act] removes all such allowable conduct from the taint of being a 'violation of any law of the United States,' including the Sherman [Act]." *Ibid.*

The statutory exemption does not apply when a union combines with a "non-labor group." *Hutcheson, supra,* at 232. Accordingly, antitrust immunity is forfeited when a union combines with one or more employers in an effort to restrain trade. In *Allen Bradley Co. v. Electrical Workers*, 325 U.S. 797, for example, the Court held that a union had violated the Sherman Act when it combined with manufacturers and contractors to erect a sheltered local business market in order "to bar all other business men from [the market], and to charge the public prices above a competitive level." The Court indicated that the union efforts would, standing alone, be exempt from antitrust liability, but because the union had not acted unilaterally, the exemption was denied. Congress "intended to outlaw business monopolies. A business monopoly is no less such because a union participates, and such participation is a violation of the Act."

The Court of Appeals properly recognized that the threshold issue was to determine whether or not Equity's franchising of agents involved any combination between Equity and any "non-labor groups," or persons who are not "parties to a labor dispute." And the court's conclusion that the trial court had not been clearly erroneous in its finding that there was no combination between Equity and the theatrical producers to create or maintain the franchise system is amply supported by the record.

The more difficult problem is whether the combination between Equity and the agents who agreed to become franchised was a combination with a "nonlabor group." The answer to this question is best understood in light of *Musicians v. Carroll*, 391 U.S. 99. There, four orchestra leaders, members of the American Federation of Musicians, brought an action based on the Sherman Act challenging the union's unilateral system of regulating "club dates," or one-time musical engagements. These regulations, inter alia, enforced a closed shop; required orchestra leaders to engage a minimum number of "sidemen," or instrumentalists; prescribed minimum prices for local engagements; prescribed higher minimum prices for traveling orchestras; and permitted leaders to deal only with booking agents licensed by the union.

Without disturbing the finding of the Court of Appeals that the orchestra leaders were employers and independent contractors, the Court concluded that they were nonetheless a "labor group" and parties to a "labor dispute" within the meaning of the Norris-LaGuardia Act, and thus that their involvement in the union regulatory scheme was not an unlawful combination between "labor" and "nonlabor" groups. The Court agreed with the trial court that the applicable test was whether there was "job or wage competition or some other economic interrelationship affecting legitimate union interests between the union members and the independent contractors."

The Court also upheld the restrictions on booking agents, who were not involved in job or wage competition with union members. Accordingly, these restrictions had to meet the "other economic interrelationship" branch of the disjunctive test quoted above. And the test was met because those restrictions were " 'at least as intimately bound up with the subject of wages' . . . as the price floors." *Id.* The Court noted that the booking agent restrictions had been adopted, in part, because agents had "charged exorbitant fees, and booked engagements for musicians at wages . . . below union scale."

## C

The restrictions challenged by the petitioners in this case are very similar to the agent restrictions upheld in the *Carroll* case. The essential features of the regulatory scheme are identical: members are permitted to deal only with agents who have agreed (1) to honor their fiduciary obligations by avoiding conflicts of interest, (2) not to charge excessive commissions, and (3) not to book members for jobs paying less than the union minimum.[25] And as in *Carroll*, Equity's regulation of agents

[25] The petitioners argue that theatrical agents are indistinguishable from "numerous [other] groups of persons who merely supply products and services to union members" such as

developed in response to abuses by employment agents who occupy a critical role in the relevant labor market. The agent stands directly between union members and jobs, and is in a powerful position to evade the union's negotiated wage structure.

The peculiar structure of the legitimate theater industry, where work is intermittent, where it is customary if not essential for union members to secure employment through agents, and where agents' fees are calculated as a percentage of a member's wage, makes it impossible for the union to defend even the integrity of the minimum wages it has negotiated without regulation of agency fees. The regulations are "brought within the labor exemption [because they are] necessary to assure that scale wages will be paid. . . ." *Carroll*, 391 U.S., at 112. They "embody . . . a direct frontal attack upon a problem thought to threaten the maintenance of the basic wage structure." *Teamsters v. Oliver*, 358 U.S. 283, 294. Agents must, therefore, be considered a "labor group," and their controversy with Equity is plainly a "labor dispute" as defined in the Norris-LaGuardia Act: "representation of persons in negotiating, fixing, maintaining, changing, or seeking to arrange terms or conditions of employment, regardless of whether or not the disputants stand in the proximate relation of employer and employee."

Agents perform a function—the representation of union members in the sale of their labor—that in most nonentertainment industries is performed exclusively by unions. In effect, Equity's franchise system operates as a substitute for maintaining a hiring hall as the representative of its members seeking employment.[28]

Finally, Equity's regulations are clearly designed to promote the union's legitimate self-interest. *Hutcheson*, 312 U.S., at 232. In a case such as this, where there is no direct wage or job competition between the union and the group it regulates, the *Carroll* formulation to determine the presence of a nonlabor group—whether there is " 'some . . . economic interrelationship affecting legitimate union interests . . . ,' " 391 U.S., at 106 (quoting District Court opinion)—necessarily resolves this issue.

---

landlords, grocers, accountants, and lawyers. But it is clear that agents differ from these groups in two critical respects: the agents control access to jobs and negotiation of the terms of employment. For the actor or actress, therefore, agent commissions are not merely a discretionary expenditure of disposable income, but a virtually inevitable concomitant of obtaining employment.

[28] In many industries, unions maintain hiring halls and other job referral systems, particularly where work is temporary and performed on separate project sites rather than fixed locations. By maintaining halls, unions attempt to eliminate abuses such as kickbacks, and to insure fairness and regularity in the system of access to employment. In a 1947 Senate Report, Senator Taft explained: "The employer should be able to make a contract with the union as an employment agency. The union frequently is the best employment agency. The employer should be able to give notice of vacancies, and in the normal course of events to accept men sent to him by the hiring hall." S. Rep. No. 1827, 81st Cong., 2d Sess., 13 (1947), *quoted in Teamsters v. NLRB*, 365 U.S. 667, 673–674.

* * *

Affirmed.

---

One immediate byproduct of the Court's ruling in *H.A. Artists* was adoption by sports unions (first in football, then in basketball and baseball, and most recently in hockey) of analogous regimes for agent regulation. There are, however, some interesting differences in both the content and the legal basis for sports agent regulation.[h]

As the basis for enforcing its agent regulations, the sports unions have utilized the exclusive bargaining authority rights they gain under the National Labor Relations Act (NLRA). When a union is designated by a majority of the employees as their collective bargaining representative, the employer cannot deal directly with the individual employees without the consent of the union. *J.I. Case v. NLRB*, 321 U.S. 332 (1944). Such consent is, of course, routine in the sports and entertainment industries, which collectively negotiate only the minimum terms of employment. The sports unions, though, permit the employer to deal only with those player agents who carry a certificate from the union.

In the 1990s, the legality of that restraint under antitrust law was challenged in *Collins v. National Basketball Players Ass'n & Grantham*, 976 F.2d 740 (10th Cir. 1992). Tom Collins had been an established agent whose clients included such NBA stars as Terry Cummings, Alex English, Ralph Sampson, and, most notably, Kareem Abdul-Jabbar. Unfortunately, Collins' management of Jabbar's money cost the latter much of his assets via unwise and allegedly unauthorized investments in risky California hotel developments. When Jabbar sued Collins, the latter voluntarily gave up his agency certification from the NBPA. When that suit was settled, Collins sought to return to agency work with some of his clients (such as Cummings) who wanted to use his services. After the NBPA refused to recertify Collins, Cummings's team, the San Antonio Spurs, could not negotiate with Collins. In Collins' antitrust suit, the Tenth Circuit held that the *H.A. Artists* rationale for the labor exemption applied equally to this sports union.

Building on that antitrust protection, sports unions have focused more closely on the conflict of interest rules than have their entertainment industry counterparts. Player agents, for example, cannot also represent teams or their executives and managers. In the mid-1990s, then Boston Red Sox player Jose Canseco announced that he was going into the representation business as a sideline: unlike Eddie Murphy in

---

[h] *See* Lionel S. Sobel, *The Regulation of Sports Agents: An Analytical Primer*, 39 Baylor L. Rev. 701 (1987); Paul C. Weiler & Gary R. Roberts, *Sports & the Law: Cases & Materials* (West Pub. 3rd ed. 2004).

the Arsenio Hall case, Canseco was going to employ a certified player agent in his firm. The Major League Baseball Players Association (MLBPA) quickly stated, though, that it would not allow active players to represent other players. Around the same time, the MLBPA stated that it would likely decertify an agent who continued to represent any player who chose to go back to work during the baseball strike.

Practically, most sports agents require athletes to waive conflict of interest claims. That way, agents can represent multiple athletes at the same position without giving rise to an impermissible conflict of interest. A good example was the free agent recruitment of Peyton Manning in the summer of 2012. Tom Condon, Manning's agent, also represented Alex Smith, the quarterback of the San Francisco 49ers who had just become a free agent like Manning.

An apparent conflict of interest arose with respect to Manning and Smith. Smith wanted to return to the 49ers, but their coach Jim Harbaugh held a secret tryout for Manning in North Carolina in an attempt to recruit him to become the 49ers quarterback. Without a waiver, Condon would have theoretically been unable to represent both Manning and Smith.

Manning ended up signing with the Broncos, and Smith with the 49ers. Smith ironically ended up as the quarterback of the Kansas City Chiefs the following year, an archrival of the Broncos.

### *QUESTIONS FOR DISCUSSION*

1. Should the labor exemption rationale in *H.A. Artists* protect a union-sponsored agent regulation program that relies on a bar to employer dealings (as in *Collins*), rather than simply on performer refusals to hire the agent? Given the growing reliance by movie stars on managers rather than agents, will the *H.A. Artists* rationale authorize SAG and other Hollywood unions to regulate the qualifications, services, and fees of their members' personal or business managers, rather than just the talent agents who are supposed to secure employment for performers? (Recall that in *Collins*, it was the agent's failings in managing money, not in negotiating contracts, that cost the agent his union certification.)

2. What are your views about the more intensive regulation of player agents regarding conflicts of interest or representation of replacements? Should these be emulated in the entertainment industry or dropped from the sports world? Do athletes need more or less protection from their agents than do entertainers? For example, should the players union be rethinking the Canseco rule after learning that rapper Eminem is represented by another rapper, Dr. Dre, and during this time their albums sold over seven million copies apiece?

3. Although the Court unanimously upheld the basic structure of Actors Equity regulation of theatrical agents, a majority of the Justices struck down the union rule that an agent who applies for an Actors' Equity "franchise" must pay a fee designed to cover the cost of administering the regulatory program (approximately $12,000 a year). The guild's objective of relieving its members from this added component to their duties was judged not to be a "legitimate interest" of the union for purposes of securing the labor exemption from antitrust. Is it consistent with the Court's rationale for upholding Actors Equity's overall regime, one that can deny some agents a franchise and that caps the fees charged by all agents, that this rationale will not also protect the union charging administrative fees to agents seeking certification? What relevance, if any, is there in the analogy offered by the dissent on this issue—that unions which operate "hiring halls" under their collective agreements (e.g., in construction) charge employers an administrative fee for referring employees to fill their work force needs?

4. What are the pros and cons of the regulation of agent (or manager) competence, compensation, and conflicts by unions, rather than by courts or administrative agencies?

---

The next chapter will cover the string of labor disputes in Hollywood in the new millennium. What few people were aware of, though, was the battle that took place between SAG and the Association of Talent Agents (ATA). Beginning in 1939 these two bodies had a regularly renegotiated "master franchise agreement," one of whose key terms precluded any talent agency also being the producer-owner of projects that SAG members and ATA clients might be performing on. Faced with competition from new management bodies like Ovitz' AMG and Grey's B-G Enterprises that were not governed by that SAG rule, when the 60-year-old SAG-ATA agreement was expiring at the end of 2000, ATA members wanted that restraint on their own market freedom finally removed.[i]

By 2002 the negotiators for these organizations reached a three-year settlement. In particular, this would allow independent production companies (rather than major studios like Disney or networks like ABC), as well as major advertisers like Coca-Cola, to own up to 20% of a licensed agency—and also vice versa. The hope was that this new standard would at least allow ATA members to attract new investors or make new investments elsewhere in their industry. In addition, agents would be permitted to earn a percentage of their clients' residual royalties from home video sales, as long as the performer was earning at least 10% more than the SAG minimum salary on that project.

---

[i] *See* Koh Siok Tian Wilson, *Talent Agents as Producers: A Historical Perspective of Screen Actors Guild Regulation & the Rising Conflict with Managers*, 21 Loyola L.A. Ent. L. Rev.

While this compromise was quickly approved by the ATA membership, it produced an intense battle within SAG. SAG President, Melissa Gilbert, who had negotiated that settlement, was endorsing it, along with members like Martin Sheen. Her main opponent in the contemporaneous SAG elections, Valerie Harper, supported by former SAG president Charlton Heston, strongly opposed it as making "our representatives also our employers." Even though Gilbert defeated Harper in the election, she lost the ratification referendum. Of the total of 98,000 SAG members, approximately 26,000 voted, with 14,000 (or 55%) voting no and slightly under 12,000 (or 45%) voting yes. This happened even though, at that same time, SAG's sister union, the American Federation of Television and Radio Artists (AFTRA), now SAG-AFTRA, was endorsing this new principle (doing so without a membership ratification vote).

This meant that, for the first time since the year that *Gone With the Wind* and *The Wizard of Oz* was appeared on the screen, talent agents as a group had not agreed to be licensed and governed by SAG-AFTRA. Gilbert and SAG told their union members that while they now do not have to hire only union "franchised agents" to represent their negotiating contracts with the studios, they can only use agencies who still comply with the SAG guidelines, including the 10 percent ceiling on commissions and the ban on apparent conflicts of interest from being both producer and agent on the same project.

Most ATA members continued to comply with "industry custom and practice" until a new SAG-ATA pact was worked out. Some did threaten to sue if SAG enforced a membership boycott against agents who deviated from the traditional rules. Should such a union action receive the same labor exemption from antitrust that was seen in *H.A. Artists*? Is there any need at all for such extrinsic regulation (whether private or public) of the agent-performer relationship? Why bar agents (though not yet managers) from producing movies, while allowing actor-SAG members to do so? Is there a free and competitive marketplace for agency services as compared to the marketplace for film studio, broadcast network, book publishing, or music recording opportunities?

# PART 4

# INDUSTRY ORGANIZATION, ECONOMIC POWER, AND LEGAL REGULATION IN THE ENTERTAINMENT WORLD

■ ■ ■

# CHAPTER 11

# PERFORMER ORGANIZATION

■ ■ ■

At the beginning of the 21st Century, the film industry risked joining the sports industry in having the most visible labor disputes in America. This confrontation between performer organizations and entertainment conglomerates was essentially about how to divide revenues from movies and television shows among the participants—ranging from actors and writers to investors, and from stars to bit players. We have already covered a variety of contractual relationships and disputes among performers and producers of entertainment works. Negotiation and implementation of these contracts take place within a broader industry environment that shapes the degree of market power enjoyed by the protagonists at the bargaining table, and thence the treatment that each side receives.

Hundreds of thousands of actors, musicians and writers make creative contributions to entertainment works. A large number of employees also work as skilled craftsmen doing the technical work of filming, recording, broadcasting, and publishing these artistic creations. On the other side of the employment relationship, there are four major television networks, three major record companies, six film studios, and five large book publishers. It is true that there are dozens of small independent firms engaged in producing movies, publishing books, recording albums, and distributing television programs. At the same time, the majors are being welded together into multimedia conglomerates—e.g., Time with Warner and Disney with ABC—each with the capacity to take an initial story idea and turn it into a book, then a movie, and then a television series (along with valuable soundtracks and merchandising).

One should not overestimate the market power of entertainment giants. After the successful Japanese firms, Sony and Matsushita, paid billions of dollars to take over Columbia Pictures and MCA respectively in the late 1980s, their entertainment arms consistently lost rather than made money for their high-technology parents. Despite these frequent corporate losses, even the most talented individual performers negotiate contracts (through their agents) with the various divisions of multi-billion dollar firms. This institutional environment leaves an imprint on the shape and content of these contracts. The background legal regimes—

labor, antitrust, and communication regulation—also influence the shape of the industry and the level of economic power that can be wielded within it. This is the subject of the final part of this book.

## A. THE ENTERTAINER LABOR MARKET[a]

This chapter will address a number of legal issues faced by performer organizations. In an era in which unionization of the American work force has been in steep decline, "above-the-line" entertainers constitute one of the most heavily unionized occupations in the private sector. Some of these bodies are traditional unions developed for purposes of bargaining collectively with their employers. Actors Equity (AE), dating back to 1913, has 49,000 members engaged in live theater; the Screen Actors Guild (SAG), formed in 1933, merged with the American Federation of Television and Radio Artists (AFTRA), formed in 1937, in 2012 and has 160,000 members; the Writers Guild of America (WGA), also born in the 1930s, but whose current incarnation of scriptwriters dates from 1954, now has 22,000 members; and the Directors Guild, with the same history, now has some 15,000 members directing movies and television. The American Guild of Musical Artists (AGMA) and the American Guild of Variety Artists (AGVA), both formed in 1936, now each have approximately 8,000 members in their respective spheres—the singers and dancers who perform in opera and dance companies or as solo artists, and performers in night clubs, circuses, and variety shows. The oldest and largest such body (dating back to 1896), the American Federation of Musicians, negotiates terms for work done by its 80,000 members in movies, broadcasts, and recording, as well as in symphony orchestras, nightclubs, and concerts. The Authors Guild (comprising 9,000 writers) and the Songwriters Guild (with more than 5,000 composers) seek to establish more favorable standard terms in the book and song-writer contracts. The American Society of Composers, Authors, and Publishers (ASCAP) was formed in 1914 for the specific purpose of negotiating and enforcing licensing arrangements for the performance rights in copyrighted songs covered in Chapter 5.

This great variety of performer organizations reflects a number of distinctive features of the industry and its working relationships. Indeed, there has actually been a major transformation in these relationships

---

[a] *See* Allan E. Koenig, ed., *Broadcasting and Bargaining: Labor Relations in Radio & Television* (Univ. Wis. Press 1970); Nancy Lynn Schwartz, *The Hollywood Writers' Wars* (Knopf 1982); David F. Prindle, *The Politics of Glamour: Ideology & Democracy in the Screen Actors Guild* (Univ. Wis. Press 1988); George Seltzer, *Music Matters: The Performer & the American Federation of Musicians* (Scarecrow Press 1989); Lois S. Gray & Ronald L. Seeber, eds., *Under the Stars: Essays on Labor Relations in Arts & Entertainment* (Cornell U. Press 1996). *See generally* Paul C. Weiler, *Governing the Workplace: The Future of Labor & Employment Law* (Harv. U. Press 1990).

inside the motion picture industry itself.[b] In the so-called Golden Age of Hollywood, from the 1920s to the early 1950s, movie-making was a form of mass production. Just as in the auto industry, a small number of studios made a large number of pictures every year—many reflecting the studio's standard movie formula. Studios were vertically integrated firms that controlled every phase of a film, from pre-production to production to distribution to exhibition in theaters (many of which the studios owned). To perform that work, the studios employed on a long-term basis (typically seven years) a large group of creative and technical workers who wrote the scripts, designed the sets, made up the actors, played the parts, shot and edited the film, and directed the overall work. These contractual relationships produced such film industry decisions as *Goudal*, *De Haviland*, and *Cole*, which we read in Part III.

These relationships also brought about unionization in Hollywood. Actors Equity organized Broadway performers and secured recognition from theatrical producers following a lengthy 1919 strike. Actors Equity then sought to organize the performers in Hollywood's fledgling movie industry. However, the newly-formed Motion Picture Producers Association (MPPA), under its first president, Will Hays, fended off that unionization effort by creating the Academy of Motion Picture Arts & Sciences, which signed agreements with the MPPA covering movie producers, directors, writers, and actors. The Academy was an especially vivid example of what business leaders in the 1920s dubbed the "American Way"—management formation of in-house organizations for workers, who thereby enjoyed a cooperative relationship with their employers.

The Depression of the 1930s and its legal byproduct, the National Labor Relations Act, put an end to what by then was believed to be an illusory brand of "company unionism." Hollywood provided a textbook illustration. Faced with severe financial pressures, the studios agreed amongst themselves and with the Academy to institute a temporary 50 percent cut in salary rates and then to establish a salary cap ($100,000 a year) on the amount that would be paid to any performer. The studios also gave themselves a "right of first refusal" on any offers made to their contract players once the seven-year term had expired, as well as the power to license the agents whom their performers might use to represent them in dealings with the studios.

The prospect of such radical changes in studio-performer relations (which were to be accomplished under President Franklin Roosevelt's

[b] *See* Michael Storper, *The Transition to Flexible Specialization in the US Film Industry: External Economies, the Division of Labor, & the Crossing of Industrial Divides*, 13 Camb. J. of Econ. 273 (1989); Asu Aksoy & Kevin Robins, *Hollywood for the 21st Century: Global Competition for Critical Mass in Image Markets*, 16 Camb. J. of Econ. 1 (1992); Murray Ross, *Stars & Strikes: Unionization of Hollywood* (Colum. U. Press 1941).

National Industrial Recovery Act (NIRA)) galvanized actors into organizing an independent union of their own, the SAG. (The Academy thenceforth focused on the annual Oscar awards.) The Guild was initially headed by the singer-comedian Eddie Cantor, with lead roles also played by James Cagney, Gary Cooper, Groucho Marx, and Robert Montgomery.

Cantor and his fellow Hollywood unionists (which also included a new Screen Writers Guild and Directors Guild triggered by the same studio actions) were able to persuade President Roosevelt not to give the NIRA seal of approval to the MPPA's plan to eliminate "destructive competition" in Hollywood through a salary cap. (The NIRA did, however, endorse industry restraints on film distribution deals between studios and theaters.) Two years later, the Supreme Court struck down the entire NIRA (in *A.L.A. Schechter Poultry Corp. v. United States*, 295 U.S. 495 (1935)) for overreaching the federal government's constitutional authority over interstate commerce.

None of these new unions were able, though, to persuade the studios to recognize and negotiate with them. Another key feature of the New Deal, the 1935 National Labor Relations Act, did promise all private sector employees the right to independent union representation if a majority wanted to bargain collectively. For two years the NLRA was largely a dead letter because of the shadow cast by Supreme Court constitutional jurisprudence. Finally, in 1937, faced with Roosevelt's notorious plan to expand the Court's membership to thirteen Justices, the Court made its startling "switch in time that saved nine," and upheld the constitutionality of federal labor law in *NLRB v. Jones & Laughlin Steel Corp.*, 301 U.S. 1 (1937). Shortly afterwards, the movie studios and the MPPA signed labor agreements with SAG and the Directors Guild establishing union shops, minimum wages, benefits, and working conditions for all unit members, together with an unrestricted right to negotiate individual contracts above that collectively-bargained scale.

The studios continued to resist dealing with the Screen Writers Guild, partly because of the perceived weakness of the Guild membership and partly because of the perceived radicalism (i.e., Communism) of its leadership. Thus, the SWG filed certification petitions with the NLRB. The Board analyzed the scope and structure of the film industry and ruled that Hollywood was part of interstate commerce and that even freelance writers were employees rather than independent contractors. *See Metro-Goldwyn-Mayer Studios*, 7 NLRB 662 (1938). The SWG won the Board-conducted certification election by a five-to-one margin. Even then it took three years and several unfair labor practice charges before the SWG and the MPPA signed their first contract in 1941. This labor agreement was in place in 1947 when the MPPA announced its blacklisting of the Hollywood Ten screenwriters, which included John Howard Lawson, the first SWG president, and Lester Cole, one of the

Guild's creators. That same year, Congress enacted the Taft-Hartley amendments to the NLRA, which placed restraints on union organizations and activities, including a ban on any Communists holding union offices.

As we saw in Chapter 8, these post-World War II traumas in Hollywood were the occasion for Ronald Reagan becoming a member of SAG's Executive Board and then its president, which served as the launching pad for his second career as a political leader. During Reagan's period of Guild leadership from the late 1940s to the early 1960s, movie production underwent a huge transformation, in response to the steep decline in movie-going and movie-making triggered by the appearance of television sets in homes. This new regime, labeled "flexible specialization," involves a host of different firms performing distinctive roles in the industry; the contributors come together on particular projects via *ad hoc* contracts, rather than as divisions of a single large enterprise.

The major studios still retain their gatekeeper role in the industry by providing the financial resources for particular film projects and then distributing the finished products. The actual creation of a film is carried out by an independent production firm, often incorporated just for this project. The producer assembles above-the-line talent in the form of actors, writers, and directors, and typically subcontracts out the technical side to firms that specialize in set construction, sound mixing and mastering, film processing, and the like. Once a particular project is finished, the entire team disbands, going off to work on other projects under different contracts. Contingent and episodic employment, rather than an enduring career with a single firm, is now the way of life in Hollywood movie-making.

Television production has tended in the same direction, especially for the numerous pilot shows for potential series. If a pilot gets awarded a time slot in a network's schedule, the project will continue for production of up to 22 episodes required for the season. Only a small number of new series are able to secure the audience ratings that are necessary to remain on the screen past that first year. Even then, series stars will be hired by other studios (initially during the summer off-season) to try to turn their name recognition and fan appeal into a successful movie (as happened with *Home Improvement's* Tim Allen's 1994 surprise hit *The Santa Clause*). There are exceptions to these short-term, contingent relationships; Johnny Carson, for example, spent thirty years on late-night television with NBC. These exceptions simply reinforce the general rule that the performers' principal career relationships are not with their employers, but with their agents and their unions.

As described above, the NLRA played a major role in establishing unionism in Hollywood. The premise of this federal legislation is that employees have a better chance of securing a fair deal from their employers if they bargain collectively rather than individually. Many employment issues (e.g., pension or health plans) cannot realistically be the subject of individually-tailored negotiations. Even with respect to the division of the economic pie between the firm and its work force, employees have greater leverage if they refuse as a group to work on the employer's terms. Thus, if the majority of employees in an *appropriate* workplace unit (as defined by the NLRB) decide that they want to bargain collectively, the union they select becomes the *exclusive* bargaining agent for all employees in that unit. The contract the union negotiates with the employer governs the terms and conditions of all the employees in the unit, whether or not every employee chooses to be part of the union itself.

There are, however, special features of the performer-producer relationship that give a distinctive flavor to entertainment industry labor relations. One such feature is the huge difference in the market value of superstars (like Tom Hanks and Julia Roberts) and the bit players in movies. In the late 1980s Bruce Willis astonished Hollywood by securing a $5 million contract to make the first *Die Hard,* and by 2000 Mel Gibson made $25 million from *The Patriot*. In 2015, A-listers such as Leonardo DiCaprio and Liam Neeson receive in the range of $20–25 million per picture. Others like Robert Downey, Jr. (*Ironman*) and Sandra Bullock (*Gravity*) have received even larger paydays by negotiating for a share of the gate receipts for the movie.

Illustrative of how fast one can move up the ladder, Jim Carrey was paid $350,000 in 1994 as the lead in *Ace Ventura: Pet Detective*. After that unexpected hit was followed by even bigger Carrey successes in *The Mask*, *Dumb and Dumber*, and *Batman Forever*, in 1995 Columbia Pictures signed Carrey to star as *The Cable Guy* for $20 million. Entertainment industry unions have succeeded in blocking any of the sports world's salary caps or luxury taxes that would hinder individual performers from realizing the full economic returns on their talents and appeal (which means that a single performer is occasionally paid more than the total remaining labor and other costs of making the movie).

A similar salary spiral has taken place in the television industry. In the 1996–97 season, both Jerry Seinfeld and Bill Cosby were guaranteed $1 million for each of the 22 episodes in their respective series that year, plus a percentage of future syndication earnings. Casts of shows such as *The Big Bang Theory* and *Modern Family* have maximized their per show salaries by banding together and demanding large pay increases after the initial success of their shows.

Indeed, it is not just the star actors (or directors or writers) who are receiving such huge returns. Even the invisible but highly talented animators who create the cartoons for money-making films like *Aladdin* and *The Lion King* are now attracting salary offers of several hundred thousand dollars (and a share of gross profits) from studios seeking to break into this lucrative movie niche that has long been the preserve of Disney. Voice talent has even been receiving a greater share of the profits, causing those undercompensated to demand more. In the spring of 2015, Harry Shearer (the voice of Montgomery Burns, among others) threatened to leave *The Simpsons*, the longest running television show, because he was not being paid market value.

Of course, the top studio executives also do very well: for example, Michael Eisner, who came to Disney in 1984, earned a reported billion dollars in salary and stock options over the next 15 years as he built Disney into an entertainment giant. The flip side of that coin is that "below the line" employees responsible for the technical support side of movie or television production have faced a difficult time preserving the real value of their collectively-negotiated salary scale and benefits as studios focus their cost containment efforts on the workers with less bargaining leverage.

Within the "above-the-line" performer bargaining unit, the traditional union-negotiated salary schedule, even one with considerable dispersion in its scale, simply will not fit with this industry. (In the early 2000s, around 20 of the SAG-AFTRA's 135,000 total members earned more than $5 million annually; 2,700 earned more than $100,000; 8,000 earned between $30,000 and $70,000, and 96,000 earned less than $7,500 or nothing at all.) Instead, SAG, the Directors Guild, and other unions negotiate a modest floor of salaries and benefits that must be paid to anyone on the set, and leave it to the Tom Cruises and Steven Soderberghs (through their agents) to extract the huge premiums that producers are willing to pay for their services. In a decision interpreting the NLRA, *J.I Case v. NLRB*, 321 U.S. 332 (1944), the Supreme Court held that such individual negotiations were compatible with the union's exclusive bargaining authority, but only if the union's agreement explicitly permitted such individual improvements on the minimum scale. This entertainment industry model found its way into the sports world in the late 1960s, where player unions encountered essentially the same differences between superstars and ordinary players.

The resulting disparities in earnings between a few entertainment or sports celebrities and the vast bulk of their fellow team members epitomize what has been happening in the broader "winner-takes-the-lion's-share" labor market for the last two decades. A tiny number of superstars have secured large increases in salaries, fees, stock options, and profit shares, while the real earnings of average workers have been steadily declining. In sports, players unions focus their attention on issues such as free agency and salary caps that affect the interests of the entire membership. In entertainment, the labor unions focus on general problems like residual rights, the quality of life on location, and the terms of agent representation. Entertainment has another distinctive feature that is not shared with sports: its talent often moves back and forth between working on projects and running them. The assumption of the NLRA is that there is a clear line between those who manage or supervise an operation and those who actually perform it. The policy of the NLRA is that managers/supervisors are not entitled to unionize because the firm needs their undivided loyalty in running the business. As illustrated by some Court decisions (e.g., *NLRB v. Health Care & Retirement Corp. of America*, 511 U.S. 571 (1994) (which found "charge nurses" in nursing homes to be excluded supervisors)), that rigid demarcation line fits quite uncomfortably with the changing structure of the contemporary workplace. Nowhere is that displayed more graphically than in entertainment, where stars like Clint Eastwood or Bill Cosby not only put together their own productions, but may well direct the movies or television series in which they are performing.

A final feature of entertainment work is that many performers are not employees at all, but rather independent contractors. The latter category is epitomized by the book author who contracts for delivery of a specified manuscript but controls the manner of producing it. The same holds true for the band that stages its own concert at a club or stadium. Deciding on exactly which side of the line falls the songwriter, the playwright, even the screenwriter, can well be a significant legal contest. One consequence of such a ruling we saw in Part II: is the product a "work for hire" for purposes of copyright law? Another even more important consequence is whether this entertainer group has the right under labor law to engage in collective bargaining about the compensation that will be paid for its work, or instead is subject to the obligation, under antitrust law, not to collude on the terms of trade for their personal services.

## B. LABOR LAW IN THE ENTERTAINMENT WORLD[c]

Unlike contract or intellectual property law, the entertainment world offers a rather small and skewed sample of labor and antitrust law in operation. In the rest of this chapter, we shall encounter selected cases that illustrate key legal features of the marketplace, as well as the problems encountered by performers who want to organize so as to improve their economic lot.

---

[c] *See* Jan Wilson, *Special Effects of Unions in Hollywood*, 12 Loyola Los Ang. L. Rev. 403 (1992).

From the 1950s to the early 21st Century, the major labor relations issue in the motion picture industry has always been *residuals*—compensation for reuse of a film in a variety of settings other than the one for which it was originally produced.[d] From the point of view of owners of the film, the virtue of such derivative uses of their intellectual property is that almost all of this additional revenue is pure profit after the original sunk costs have been recouped. From the point of view of creative talent, though, the ability of the producer to satisfy new markets without needing more work presents them with a problem rather than a profit. The solution sought by performer unions has been to channel some of the additional revenue from such new uses to the people who created the work, perhaps years earlier.

Negotiations on this issue between unions and the Alliance of Motion Picture and Television Producers (AMPTP) have been anything but easy. Of 22 strikes in the film industry from the early 1950s to the early 2000s, 19 turned, at least in significant part, on the residuals issue. One such strike in 1960, the first-ever by SAG (led by Ronald Reagan), secured residuals for the showing of movies on television. After a series of additional work stoppages by different unions about residuals on cable and video, the Writers Guild in 1988 shut the film industry down for five months to establish the principle that residuals would be paid for distribution of movies in foreign markets. In 2000, a branch of SAG broke that work stoppage record by going on strike for six months about residuals for television and cable commercials (and expansion of the collective agreement to cover Internet ads). And in 2001, the performers and producers were working hard to get their films completed before the expected summer strike by SAG and WGA members looking for a much more substantial share of the revenues generated by movies and programs on television and cable in both domestic and foreign markets. Fortunately, just before the work stoppages were about to begin, the parties reached a compromise.

Residuals are a crucial feature of what is now a three-tier compensation system in entertainment. The first tier is the collectively-bargained minimum salary rate, expressed either in time performed (under the SAG contract), or in the piece of work produced (under the WGA or the DGA contracts). The second tier is individually-negotiated compensation, which may consist not only of salary but also a share of gross revenues or net profits (as seen in Chapter 8). The third tier is the union-negotiated right to a percentage of revenues from residual uses of the film, which in 2000 were generating over a billion dollars a year.

[d] *See* Alan Paul & Archie Kleingartner, *Flexible Production & the Transformation of Industrial Relations in the Motion Picture & Television Industry*, 47 Ind. & Lab. Rel. Rev. 663 (1994); Karen L. Gulick, *Creative Control, Attribution, & the Need for Disclosure: A Study of Incentives in the Motion Picture Industry*, 27 Conn. L. Rev. 53 (1994).

Those sums play a vital role in the lives of entertainers, because the checks keep flowing even when no work is available on new projects.

Recent news stories highlight the continuing value of residuals for movies like *The Shawshank Redemption* and television series such as *Friends*.

In return for agreeing to increase their minimum salaries just 3 percent a year from 2001 to 2004 (which will make the latter floor $677 a day), substantial increases were secured in various residuals (including finally treating Fox as a major television network). These various changes were estimated to be expanding the residual sum by around $65 million a year for the members of these two unions (with the Directors Guild getting essentially the same terms in December 2001, six months before their collective agreement was even due to expire).

In 2007, major labor battles took place in the entertainment industry, shutting down not only the making of movies and television episodes, but also the staging of plays on Broadway. Broadway had the shortest work stoppage, ending after 19 days, by the stagehands in Local One of the International Alliance of Theatrical Stage Employees. Meanwhile, the Hollywood writers' strike lasted much longer, although its impact on movie and television fans was not as immediate, because most up-coming movies already had finished scripts.

The Guild was seeking a major expansion of their residual share of films and programs resold on DVDs (whose discounted rate negotiated in 1985 was giving them only around 4 cents per disc) and on new outlets like the Internet. However, the Alliance of Motion Picture and Television Producers (AMPTP) initially rejected that position, considering these outlets basically "promotional." Happily, a settlement was reached in 2008 ending this 100-day strike. The new three-year collective agreement gave writers a fixed Internet residual for the first two years, but then, contrary to the previous Directors Guild of America settlement and in tandem with the Writers Guild's major goal, a 2 percent share for screenwriters of the total revenues from streaming of their entertainment products on the Internet. Thus, 92.5 percent of the 3,775 writers who cast ballots voted to end the strike. Later agreements were reached between producers and the two actors unions, SAG and the American Federation of Television and Radio Artists (AFTRA), which merged in 2012.

Entertainment unions played a critical role in the development of this contractual alternative (for works made for hire) to the copyright authors' claim to all derivative uses of their creative works. The unions play an equally vital role in distribution of the revenues flowing in from producers. Indeed, the SAG-AFTRA collective agreements have the funds paid directly to the union, which then divides up the money according to a contractual formula that awards points per time on a project, not with reference to who happens to have the starring roles. (Individuals can, of course, use their star power to negotiate additional residual shares on their own, but this comes out of the film producer's pockets, not the pockets of their fellow SAG members.) The Writers Guild and Directors Guild contracts require the producer to make payments directly to those members who are receiving artistic credit for the project. But judgments about who is to get which of the limited number of credits are made by committees inside the respective unions.

Artistic credits, then, affect not only the personal feelings and employment prospects of screenwriters and movie directors, but also the actual financial returns from their immediate projects. The problem is that one person's credit is another's lack of credit. That tension is accentuated in film screenwriting, where scripts regularly go through numerous versions from the time the producers are looking for initial financial backing to the time the director is shooting the final "take" on the set. To settle disputes about who will get artistic billing, and to do so in time to get credits on the film before it hits the movie screen, the Writers Guild established an expedited arbitration procedure, as shown in the following case.

## MARINO V. WRITERS GUILD OF AMERICA, EAST, INC.

United States Court of Appeals, Ninth Circuit, 1993.
992 F.2d 1480.

FERNANDEZ, CIRCUIT JUDGE.

[Arbitration by the Writers Guild of America (WGA) had awarded screenwriting credit for *Godfather III* to director Francis Ford Coppola and author Mario Puzo, rather than to writers Nick Marino and Thomas Wright. Marino, a WGA member since 1985, then sued his union. He sought to discover the identities of the arbitrators, and to challenge the fairness of the arbitration procedure and of the representation afforded him by the WGA. After summary judgment was granted to defendants, Marino appealed.]

### Background

* * *

A portion of the WGA collective bargaining agreement titled "Theatrical Schedule A, Theatrical Credits," sets forth the general rules of credit determination. The procedures for arbitration of credit disputes are set out in WGA's "Credits Manual." They are not part of the collective bargaining agreement, but are approved by WGA's board of directors and by vote of its membership. According to the Credits Manual, the arbitration has three phases.

What we will call the first phase is a procedure through which common factual disputes can be resolved. If there are disputes as to "authenticity, identification, sequence, authorship or completeness of any literary material to be considered," a special committee conducts "a hearing at which all participating writers may present testimony and documentary evidence." That committee's factual determination is binding and forms a part of the basis of the material that goes to those who conduct the second phase of the process.

The second phase of the process is conducted by the use of three individuals, called arbiters. Unlike the decision makers in the first phase, the arbiters do not hear oral testimony or argument. They read and cogitate. Their task is to decide who should get screen credit for the screenplay. Their names are kept confidential from the public, the participating writers, and even from one another. Each arbiter makes this difficult decision on creativity in isolation and based upon written materials. Those are materials submitted by the film company and they include "all material written by participants as well as . . . source material." The participating writers are encouraged to review that material and may ask that appropriate materials be added. A participating writer may also submit a position statement for the purpose of helping the arbiters in their consideration of the written materials. Writers are encouraged to do so. Each arbiter then makes a decision and notifies the Credit Arbitration Secretary. A majority decides the question. After the arbiters have made their decision, the participating writers are informed and the third phase becomes available.

The third phase is a review procedure. Within twenty-four hours of notification of the credit determination, any of the writers involved may request a review by a Policy Review Board ("PRB"). The PRB's scope of review is limited to determining whether there has been "any serious deviation from the policy of the Guild or the procedure as set forth in this Manual." More specifically, the PRB may consider questions involving dereliction of duty on the part of the arbiters, or any of them, any use of undue influence upon the arbiters, any misinterpretation, misapplication, or violation of WGA policies, and any "important new written material" which was, for valid reasons, not previously available. The PRB has the authority to direct the original three arbiters to reconsider the case or to order a new proceeding. The entire arbitration process must occur within 21 business days. If it does not, the producer's own selection may become final.

In 1985, Marino and Wright wrote an adaptation of literary material, referred to as a treatment, for *Godfather III*, which Paramount Pictures Corporation ("Paramount") purchased.

Paramount hired Marino to write a motion picture script, or screenplay, based on the treatment. Marino completed the screenplay in 1985, but Paramount chose not to produce it at that time.

In 1987, Marino wrote a second treatment and sent it to executives at a production studio owned by Coppola and related to the prior *Godfather* pictures. The production studio neither solicited nor purchased Marino's 1987 treatment. In 1989 and 1990, Coppola and Puzo co-wrote a screenplay for *Godfather III*. The movie was produced and completed in 1990.

Before the movie was distributed, Marino was notified that WGA would be conducting an arbitration to determine the writing credits for *Godfather III*, pursuant to the collective bargaining agreement. Accordingly, Marino, Coppola and Puzo submitted written materials and statements for the arbiters' review. On November 5, 1990, the Arbitration Secretary informed Marino that Coppola and Puzo would receive sole writing credit. Marino requested a hearing before the PRB where he objected to the arbitration procedure. . . . The PRB discovered that one arbiter had not read Marino's 1985 treatment. That arbiter was sent the 1985 treatment for review, and the arbiter then reaffirmed the prior conclusion.

* * *

Discussion

Marino makes a number of attacks upon the arbitration procedures in general and upon their particular application to this case. A number of those revolve around his claim that it is fundamentally unfair to keep the identities of the arbiters confidential. That has the potential, he says, for concealing bias. Moreover, the result is that he cannot appear before them or cross-examine witnesses before them. . . .

A. *Waiver; the Anonymity Claims.*

Arbitration is a favored method for the resolution of disputes, particularly in the labor area. It is undoubtedly true that all notions of procedural fairness cannot be jettisoned simply because the parties have agreed to arbitrate. However, because arbitration is contractual, rather than imposed by law, what we have come to see as the hallmarks of judicial justice are not necessarily required in arbitral justice. One reason is that arbitration can take account of unique problems. Arbitration can supply high-powered expertise to a particular and narrow area—such as deciding who should get credit for creating an imaginative work. At the same time, it can supply unique ways for avoiding the kinds of biases and pressures that judges are all too aware of. Lifetime appointments help insulate federal judges from those vices; arbitration procedures may offer other ways.

If arbitration is to work, it must not be subjected to undue judicial interference. Moreover, parties must be encouraged, nay required, to raise their complaints about the arbitration during the arbitration process itself, when that is possible.

Thus, . . . a party may not sit idle through an arbitration procedure and then collaterally attack that procedure on grounds not raised before the arbitrators when the result turns out to be adverse. This rule even extends to questions, such as arbitrator bias, that go to the very heart of arbitral fairness.

* * *

Here, the major thrust of Marino's objection is his assertion that WGA precluded him from ascertaining the qualifications or partiality of the arbiters. The WGA's refusal to disclose the arbiters' identity was pursuant to the procedures which we have outlined. Under the procedures, "as has always been [WGA] practice, the names of the arbiters selected remain confidential." WGA's confidentiality policy is "supported by important and legitimate considerations, including the necessity that arbitrators be entirely freed from both real and perceived dangers of pressure, retaliation, and litigation."

The procedures allow the participating writers to strike a reasonable number of names from the list of arbiters. The list is long, and if one did not have substantial familiarity with the writing community, it may be well nigh impossible to ferret out possible bias in all of the persons on it. Still, Marino, without objection, took advantage of that opportunity. Between him and Wright, 85 names were stricken. From the remaining names on the list, three arbiters were chosen. Each potential arbiter was screened for potential bias by an arbitration coordinator.

While the notion of an anonymous judge may jar those who are used to judicial proceedings, no doubt WGA and its members understand the practical difficulties involved in having the arbiters' names disclosed. Very important people may be unhappy with a decision and may be in a good position to pressure or take revenge against the arbiters. Moreover, the WGA and its members have decided that the best arbiters will be experienced working members of the screenwriters community. The heavy responsibility of the arbiter's mantle might well be declined by hard-working writers if they knew that they could be hauled through recriminatory judicial proceedings, accused of bias, and the like. The procedures that reflected and dealt with these concerns had existed for decades. They were grounded on the collective bargaining agreement and were designed to implement its terms. Presumably they were fair.

In the face of this, Marino made no objection until the arbiters had found against him. Presumably the procedure was satisfactory to him, just as it was to the other members of the WGA. That is, it was satisfactory to him until the arbiters' decision went against him.

It is important to notice that Marino's attack on the anonymity of the arbiters, and the other concomitants of that anonymity, is very much like a claim of arbitrator bias. In fact, its central proposition is that the arbiters might be biased against him but he cannot tell for sure because he does not know whom they are. Of course, he cannot know for sure whether they are biased or not because he has not had an opportunity to investigate or grill them on that issue. . . . We hold that this claim, like that of actual bias, was waived when Marino failed to protest the procedure before the arbiters were selected and performed their task. A claim of true bias can be considered and dealt with before individuals have invested their time and decided the case. So too could this claim have been taken account of. Here the individuals who were being asked to decide a knotty screen credit question with celerity and certainty could have been informed that their impartiality and qualifications were being challenged. The WGA could have taken steps to ameliorate those claims. Just as importantly, the prospective arbiters, once being made aware of the claims, could have decided that they did not wish to become a part of a process which is, as the Manual says, "arduous and unpleasant." Perhaps individuals who had no objection to disclosure of their names could be found. We do not know. What we do know is that this bias issue, like others, should have been raised before the arbiters acted, not after. We understand Marino's focus on what he perceives as an issue of fairness to himself. We, however, must focus on fairness to all involved, including the arbiters and all of the other union members and officers who have relied on the arbitration process for so long.

As we see it, Marino's complaint of his inability to have a face-to-face hearing before the arbiters, complete with cross-examination—issues also not raised before his loss—must fall with the anonymity claim. They are its accompaniments.

We hasten to add two additional thoughts. We recognize that it would be possible to create a procedure so palpably unfair on its face that no prior objection should be expected or required. An anonymous coin toss might be an example of that. [T]hat is not the procedure we are dealing with. While Marino focuses on the arbiters' phase of the process, he loses sight of the overall arbitration process itself. He ignores the phase one evidentiary hearing process and likewise ignores the phase three procedural review process. The former, of course, provides for all of the usual confrontation and evidentiary rights. The latter provides some assurance of procedural fairness. Marino's claim that he is not in a position to assert procedural problems because he did not appear before the arbiters is not persuasive. He did assert problems. . . . Also, while it is true that the arbiters could have failed to consider materials or proceeded to commit other wrongs in a hidden way, that could occur despite hearings and despite knowledge of the arbiters' identities. In effect, Marino's claims in this regard do, once again, come back to the single issue of arbiter anonymity.

* * *

Conclusion

Movies are expensive creative works. Once they are ready for release their owners wish to move quickly. When the WGA wrested the unilateral power to decide screen credits from the producers, it did so at the price of an agreement that WGA itself would move quickly. The need for speed is part of the right it negotiated for on behalf of its members. That need drives the whole process; in the absence of quick determinations, it is likely that the right itself would wither away.

The procedures adopted by WGA were designed to make the difficult screen credit decision in a speedy and fair fashion. Although the three-phase arbitration procedure is not the same as the more deliberate judicial procedures that we are accustomed to, this case helps show why it cannot be. *Godfather III* was released over three years ago, and only now is the second phase of federal judicial procedures moving toward completion. That is not the fault of the parties or of the judicial system. Our procedures require time; other needs demand other procedures.

On this record, and based upon the issues properly before us for decision, we cannot say that the procedures designed for speed overwhelmed the ideal of justice.

Affirmed.

---

The same judicial deference to the WGA artistic credit system was exhibited by the California state courts in *Ferguson v. Writers Guild of America, West, Inc.*, 226 Cal.App.3d 1382, 277 Cal. Rptr. 450 (1991). There, Larry Ferguson, who had received joint screenplay credit for *Beverly Hills Cop II*, sought sole credit for both the screenplay and story. The WGA, however, awarded story credit to *Beverly Hills Cop*'s star, Eddie Murphy, and his manager, Robert Wachs. Wachs, recall, was the person whom Murphy introduced to his *Coming to America* sidekick, Arsenio Hall, discussed in Chapter 10.

Then, in *Wellman v. Writers Guild of America, West*, 146 F.3d 666 (9th Cir. 1998), the Ninth Circuit reaffirmed and even expanded *Marino*'s deferential approach to the WGA's award of screenwriter credits. Wendell Wellman was one of a number of writers contributing to the script for the Warner Brothers' movie *Fair Game*, which was adapted from a novel by the same name. However, Warner decided that Charlie Fletcher was entitled to sole screenwriter credit for the movie, a decision endorsed by the WGA process, and then subjected to very limited scrutiny in the courts.

The court did recognize that, "in Hollywood, a screenwriter's name is his most coveted asset," and that putting that name in a film's credits "does not merely satisfy a writer's longing to see his name in lights; it can propel him to other work—perhaps to the next blockbuster." *Id.* at 668. However, the Court saw the role of the WGA, as the writers' own union representative, as preventing studios "from using their superior bargaining power to assign credit arbitrarily." Given that relationship, there should be very modest judicial scrutiny to see whether there had been unfair representation of the members.

In fact, with respect to the (still anonymous) arbitration panel, there was to be no judicial review at all, with this role performed by the WGA's Policy Review Board. As regards the latter body, the court would review the record only to see whether there had been a "discriminatory or bad faith" judgment of who was entitled to credits, and, in addition, any "arbitrary" behavior of the Board in its "procedural and ministerial conduct" of the process. Applying those standards here, even to a Board that had taken just two hours to sustain the arbitration panel's verdict, the Ninth Circuit found that there had been no unfair union representation of Wellman in *Fair Game*.

### *QUESTIONS FOR DISCUSSION*

1. Suppose Marino had made an up-front objection to the writer credits for *Godfather III.* How should the court treat his legal claim then? How should the WGA members judge the pros and cons of this unique process of arbitrator anonymity? Does anonymity enhance or detract from the process for deciding who is to get artistic credit and residual financial rights in the screenplay? Should the arbitrators also be unaware of the names and identities of the writer-contenders for such credits? Is the latter brand of anonymity feasible in such decision-making? What ethical rules should apply to arbitrators and how might they be enforced?

2. Are there any labor law grounds upon which an employee like Marino can challenge decisions made by a private body such as the Writers Guild, pursuant to an agreement the union has negotiated with Marino's employers? What if Marino, while considered a part of the writers bargaining *unit*, had chosen not to join and participate in the writers *union*? What about intellectual property grounds? Should an arbitration award of screen credits be a sufficient defense to a Lanham Act claim (recall Chapter 6)?

---

Another major issue in WGA-AMPTP labor negotiations involved the status of overall credits for the making of movies. In 1995, the Writers

Guild won priority over producers in credits for a film—something the Directors Guild had secured through collective bargaining three decades earlier. The screenwriters who secure designation from the WGA now have second-to-last billing on all movies, with the non-union producers moved one more position back before them. The producers' effort to use an antitrust suit to overturn this term of a labor agreement was unsuccessful (because of the labor exemption).

What the parties agreed to postpone and study in their 1995 settlement was the issue of "possessory credits." WGA members do accept that the DGA director-members have a legitimate right to the final artistic credit for a film. However, they strongly object to what has now become a commonplace statement at the start of movies—saying this is "A film by. . ." whichever director (or sometimes producer) was individually able to negotiate that credit. While they agreed to postpone this issue in 2001 and concentrate on residuals, the WGA is pursuing an eventual agreement among affected parties that possessory credit should only be available to those who have established their status as an Oscar or box office leader (i.e., a Steven Spielberg or Steven Soderbergh).

What is the appropriate role of collective bargaining and labor law in determining who should get the artistic or possessory credits? What is the significance of the fact that the WGA and DGA bargain in different years? When you have watched a movie, who do you think it was "by"—the director, the writer, or the producer? Which of these should the Academy designate as the appropriate person to accept the Oscar for the Best Picture?

---

Residuals are simply one of the dozens of issues that now fill the many hundreds of pages in the SAG-AFTRA agreements. Consider the problems encountered in Part III in contract cases involving performers: the morals clause and Lester Cole; free speech and Vanessa Redgrave or *Miss Saigon*; net profits and Art Buchwald; perpetually renewable options and Dennis the Menace (and George Michael); film colorization and Steven Spielberg. Should courts and legislatures leave these issues up to the performer unions to resolve? What are the comparative virtues of private collective bargaining and public law-making? Why was the Writers Guild able in its 1981 negotiations to eliminate the "morals" clause from screenwriter contracts, but not SAG? How much significance should be attached to the fact that employer decisions about the *content* rather than the *effects* of its product are deemed permissive rather than mandatory subjects of bargaining with the union? *See Kiro, Inc. & AFTRA, Seattle Local*, 317 NLRB 1325 (1995); *Retlaw Broadcasting v. NLRB*, 172 F.3d 660 (9th Cir. 1999).

## C. LABOR SOLIDARITY AND ENTERTAINMENT HYPHENATES

To a considerable extent, the answer to the last question turns on the degree of bargaining leverage wielded by a union. Residuals are a valuable asset to film performers and a costly item for film producers. Rather than being handed over on a legislative platter (e.g., via copyright law), residuals have been secured through decades of labor struggles by film industry unions. Once a union's presence is established, both sides are subject to a duty to bargain collectively in good faith. This duty does not carry with it an obligation to make any particular concessions at the negotiating table. The statutory policy of *free* collective bargaining assumes that the way to break bargaining deadlocks is through the economic pressure of a strike or lockout. During a work stoppage, both sides may experience sufficient pain—in lost revenues and lost pay—from their disagreement that it soon seems less painful to make compromises to reach agreement. As the Supreme Court put it in *NLRB v. Insurance Agents' Int'l Union*, 361 U.S. 477 (1960):

> It must be realized that collective bargaining under a system where the Government does not attempt to control the results of negotiations, cannot be equated with an academic collective search for truth—or even with what might be thought to be the ideal of one. The parties . . . still proceed from contrary and to an extent antagonistic viewpoints and concepts of self interest. The system has not reached the ideal of the philosophic notion that perfect understanding among people would lead to perfect agreement among them on values. The presence of economic weapons in reserve, and their actual exercise on occasion by the parties, is part and parcel of the system that the Wagner and Taft-Hartley Acts have recognized.

*Id.* at 488–89.

Crucial to the success of a union strike is solidarity among the members. If enough performers cross a union's picket lines to keep film projects going, for example, this step alleviates the economic pressures on the producers, and accentuates those felt by the performers. The latter see their colleagues getting the immediate benefit of work, credits, and pay during the strike, and know they will also get the benefit of whatever contract breakthroughs the union is seeking in negotiations. This happened in the 1987 NFL strike, later depicted in the 2000 movie, *The Replacements*. While John Elway and Dan Marino remained committed to their union's effort to secure free agency for their successors, Joe Montana and Tony Dorsett crossed over the line and began to play, which led NFLPA leader Gene Upshaw to give up striking and resort instead to litigating.

In other industries, where there is no likely prospect for a successful suit about a collectively-negotiated issue, in order to deter a break in the bargaining unit's ranks, all unions (including entertainer unions) have rules that make it an offense to cross the line during a legal strike. Disciplinary measures include suspension from the union and fines in amounts that typically reflect the sums earned by working during the strike.

The competing incentives felt by performers differ in several ways from other workplaces. Because entertainers are paid more when they do work, they lose more when they go on strike, though they may also have more resources with which to absorb short-term losses. On the other hand, because there is little "permanent" work in entertainment anyway, performers feel little concern about being permanently replaced for having exercised their right to strike.

A distinctive feature of the entertainment world is the ambiguous status of performers, particularly writers and directors. On one project, a person may be a scriptwriter, on the next, a story editor, on a third, a producer; thence the label, "hyphenate," for writer-directors and writer-producers, as well as director-producers. The legal significance of that label stems from the fact that producers and directors supervise other employees and manage key features of the project on behalf of the production company. Under the NLRA, supervisors and managers are excluded from the scope of its statutory protections. The assumption of federal labor law is that employers need and should have the undivided loyalty of their representatives. This does not mean that the latter are prohibited from forming a union and going on strike: otherwise there would not be a Directors Guild. It does mean that there is no affirmative right to undertake such collective action, free of employer retaliation and punishment (as there is for ordinary workers). The question, though, is whether unions are barred from enforcing their rules to prevent their hyphenate-members from working during a strike.

This issue generated an important decision by the Court, *American Broadcasting Co. v. Writers Guild of America, West, Inc.*, 437 U.S. 411 (1978). This case was the byproduct of a three-month strike by the Guild against the motion picture and television industry. A number of hyphenates had gone to work on ongoing film projects and faced union discipline and fines thereafter. As background, four years earlier a closely-divided Court had ruled, in *Florida Power & Light Co. v. International Brotherhood of Electrical Workers*, 417 U.S. 790 (1974), that the union could legally discipline its supervisor-members who crossed the picket line to do the strikers' work. In *American Broadcasting*, by contrast, the hyphenate writers had gone to work just to perform their duties as story editors, film directors, and executive producers, overseeing production of television shows and motion pictures for which scripts had already been written.

In *American Broadcasting*, the Supreme Court found (by a 5–4 margin) that Writers Guild discipline of hyphenates violated the NLRA. Section 8(b)(1)B of the Act bars unions from restraining employers in selection of their "representatives for purposes of collective bargaining or the adjustment of grievances." The legislative concern underlying this section was ensuring that groups of employers like film producers were free to negotiate through bodies like the Alliance of Motion Picture and Television Producers (AMPTP). However, the provision had been interpreted as protecting the individual employer's prerogative to select its own personnel to negotiate or handle grievances. In the movie world, one of the occasional functions of hyphenates was to handle employee grievances at the initial level, and, in the case of the executive producer, to deal with the union about contract issues that might arise on the set. The majority stated:

> Respondent objects that this construction of the Act impermissibly intrudes on the union's right to resort to economic sanctions during a strike. However, an employer also has economic rights during a strike, and the statute declares that, in the unrestrained freedom to select a grievance-adjustment and collective-bargaining representative, the employer's rights dominate. Ample leeway is already accorded to a union in permitting it to discipline any member, even a supervisor, for performing struck work—to carry that power over to the case of purely supervisory work is an inappropriate extension and interference with the employer's prerogative.

437 U.S. at 430–31.

The dissent objected that the majority eroded the "union's ability to maintain a unified front in its confrontation with management and to impose disciplinary sanctions on those 'who adhere to the enemy in time of struggle.' " There was, however, an ambiguity in the Court's decision, and a potential answer to the union's concerns. Suppose that for the future the Guild permitted its hyphenate-members to cross the line and adjust grievances, but barred them from managing production of the struck film project. In *NLRB v. IBEW (Royal Electric)*, 481 U.S. 573 (1987), the Court ruled that such union action would fall on the *Florida Power & Light* rather than the *American Broadcasting* side of the line regarding union obstruction of employer prerogatives.

Why do these issues about union discipline turn on the *employer's* rights under the NLRA. What about the *supervisor's* or *manager's* rights? Indeed, the NLRA not only gives workers a protected right to form unions, to bargain collectively, and to strike or picket in disputes with their employer; it gives workers the equal right to *refrain* from any such activities. Where, then, does the union get its prerogative to discipline employees (supervisors or not) for working during a strike, whatever the apparent threat to worker solidarity?

The tenuous answer comes from a complex body of Court decisions that seem to be more creative judicial *writing*, rather than the literal *reading*, of the NLRA. First, union disciplinary authority derives from the members' contractual commitment to honor the terms of the union constitution. *See NLRB v. Allis-Chalmers*, 388 U.S. 175 (1967). Next, the union may not negotiate a union shop clause that makes it a condition of employment that the employee join and remain in the union. *See NLRB v. General Motors*, 373 U.S. 734 (1963). (In states without "right-to-work" laws, unions can negotiate agency shop clauses that require payment of that share of the union dues devoted to collective bargaining. *See Communications Workers of America v. Beck*, 487 U.S. 735 (1988).) This means that if employees decline to join the union, or even resign from the union during a strike, the union cannot discipline them for violating its rules. *See NLRB v. Textile Workers*, 409 U.S. 213 (1972). Finally, while unions can operate "hiring halls," which serve as the exclusive source of workers for the employer, they cannot discriminate in their referrals against non-members. *See Local 357, Int'l Brotherhood of Teamsters v. NLRB*, 365 U.S. 667 (1961).[e]

The next case in which the Court revisited this issue came from the entertainment world—*Marquez v. Screen Actors Guild*, 525 U.S. 33 (1998). Lakeside Production had hired Naomi Marquez for a one-line role in a single 1994 episode of its television series, *Medicine Ball*. Under Lakeside's standard labor agreement, each performer was supposed to become a "member in good standing" of SAG "30 days after his employment," which here was defined as "employment as a performer in a motion picture industry." While Marquez was very much a part-time actress, back in 1989 she had worked for more than 30 days on a movie.

In practice, SAG and the film producers interpreted and applied this union "membership" condition as requiring only payment of the appropriately-adjusted union dues. When Marquez asked what these dues were, she was told the amount to join the union was around $500 in her case. Since Marquez was making just $550 from her *Medicine Ball* part, she objected to that SAG condition. After Lakeside hired someone else to utter that one line on *Medicine Ball*, Marquez sued SAG for

---

[e] *See* Mark Meredith, *From Dancing Halls to Hiring Halls: Actors Equity & the Closed Shop Dilemma*, 96 Colum. L. Rev. 178 (1996); Emily C. Chi, *Star Quality & Job Security: The Role of the Performers' Unions in Controlling Access to the Acting Profession*, 18 Cardozo Arts & Ent. L.J. 1 (2000). *See also NLRB v. Actors' Equity Ass'n*, 644 F.2d 939 (2d Cir. 1981) (Actors Equity's dues assessment on Yul Brynner, a European resident and non-AE member, from his earnings on the Broadway revival of *The King and I* found illegal under the NLRA).

violating its labor law duty of "fair representation" in its union security clause.

With respect to this clause, the Court ruled that it was not illegal for a union to negotiate a contract that used the Congress' own wording in the NLRA, as long as employees like Marquez were told that, in practice, "membership" meant what the Court had said in *General Motors, Beck*, and other precedents noted above. With respect to the application of the 30-day employment condition—whether it includes employment in the industry or just by the immediate firm—the Court found this had to be addressed first by the NLRB, rather than the courts. How should this crucial issue in the entertainment world (where so much employment is now "contingent" on particular projects and firms) be resolved? What does this dispute suggest about the *costs* of unions, particularly for low-paid entertainers?

While unions cannot force employees to join, if they are working regularly in this industry, they have considerable incentive to do so, if only to have a voice in and vote about their representative's bargaining stance. Knowing that fact, most unions, like the Writers Guild, have drafted membership rules to make it clear that resignation will be effective only if it takes place before bargaining has reached the strike stage. The union wants its members to know how firm a commitment all of them are making to the group's bargaining position. In the 1980s, though, the Court upheld a decision by the NLRB that any such restriction on union resignation was a violation of employees' statutory rights. *See Pattern Makers' League v. NLRB*, 473 U.S. 95 (1985). With that endorsement, the Board struck down the Writers Guild limits on resignation during the 1988 strike against the film industry, thus precluding union discipline of any cross-overs, whether supervisor-hyphenates or not. *See Writers Guild of America, West, Inc.*, 297 NLRB 92, 1989 WL 224417 (1989).

The reason for the foregoing synopsis of labor law is that the Court in *Pattern Makers'* made it clear that it was upholding the Board position only on the grounds that it was a *rational* interpretation of the NLRA—not that it was the only *right* one on this score. Suppose this issue arose again, perhaps in the context of another entertainment industry work stoppage. What do you think is the appropriate policy judgment with respect to regular writers and actors? With respect to hyphenates? Does protecting the rights of entertainers *vis-á-vis* their unions enhance or detract from their rights vis-á-vis their studio or network employers?

## D. JUDICIAL CONTROL OF ENTERTAINMENT LABOR POWER

From the point of view of their members, labor unions have generally proven a helpful instrument for enhancing negotiating leverage and thence improving their earnings and treatment on the job. From the point of view of the parties purchasing the services of union members, the prospect is less pleasing. Sometimes the union may present them with a take-it-or-leave-it proposal, both sides of which seem highly unattractive. Such a result is not particularly likely in the film industry, where studios and television networks have formed an alliance, the AMPTP, that defends the needs of its members (which include many independent producers) in bargaining with movie unions. The music industry and the American Federation of Musicians (AFM) pose somewhat different problems—again, not as far as major record labels are concerned, but arguably with respect to AFM-established rules of the game for concert tours, for example, or private "club dates" for social events such as weddings.

The policy question is whether parties that are purchasing performer services should enjoy any protection against the union's market power. The principal avenue for this purpose is federal antitrust law, which will be introduced shortly. First, though, is a case involving state contract law that offers a reprise of some of the doctrinal issues examined in Part III.

### GRAHAM V. SCISSOR-TAIL, INC.

Supreme Court of California, 1981.
28 Cal.3d 807, 171 Cal. Rptr. 604, 623 P.2d 165.

[The plaintiff, Bill Graham, was one of California's leading producers and promoters of music concerts. The band (and AFM member) Scissor-Tail hired Graham to provide his services on two of the dates on their 1973 tour—one in Oakland, the other in Ontario. The contract was pursuant to the AFM Form B, which left blank the "wages agreed to." Graham agreed to pay Scissor-Tail the greater of the applicable AFM scale or 85 percent of "gross receipts less bona fide receipted expenses and taxes." The contract also specified that any disputes under it were to be resolved by the International Executive Board (IEB) of the AFM.

Unfortunately, while the Oakland concert netted $98,000, the Ontario concert lost $63,000. The contract had not specified what was to happen when one event suffered a loss while the other made a gain. Graham, taking the view that an offset was appropriate, went to court seeking a ruling to that effect. The court sent the case to the AFM for arbitration. Although Scissor-Tail asked the IEB for hearing dates, the IEB instead awarded the group the full amount of its $53,000 claim (constituting 85 percent of Oakland profits, less an advance). After

Graham protested and Scissor-Tail had raised its claim to $73,000 (saying that some of the claimed expenses were invalid), plus interest and attorney fees, the IEB sent the matter to its "referee," a former AFM official who regularly heard such matters. After a hearing, the referee recommended that the IEB maintain its $53,000 judgment, which the IEB did. Graham then went back to court.]

* * *

II

We first turn our attention to the validity of the order compelling arbitration. Plaintiff, as we have indicated, is entitled to challenge this order on the instant appeal.

Plaintiff's basic contention in this respect is that the order compelling arbitration was in error because the underlying agreement, at least insofar as it required arbitration of disputes before the A.F. of M., was an unenforceable contract of adhesion. Two separate questions are thus presented, each of which requires separate consideration: (1) is this a contract of adhesion? (2) if so, is it unenforceable?

A.

The term "contract of adhesion," now long a part of our legal vocabulary,[10] has been variously defined in the cases and other legal literature. The serviceable general definition first suggested by Justice Tobriner in 1961, however, has well stood the test of time and will bear little improvement: "The term signifies a standardized contract, which, imposed and drafted by the party of superior bargaining strength, relegates to the subscribing party only the opportunity to adhere to the contract or reject it." (*Neal v. State Farm Ins. Cos.*, 188 Cal. App. 2d 690, 694, 10 Cal. Rptr. 781 (1961).)

Such contracts are, of course, a familiar part of the modern legal landscape, in which the classical model of "free" contracting by parties of equal or near-equal bargaining strength is often found to be unresponsive to the realities brought about by increasing concentrations of economic and other power. They are an inevitable fact of life for all citizens, businessman and consumer alike. While not lacking in social advantages,[15] they bear within them the clear danger of oppression and

[10] The term, apparently resting upon concepts in French civil law, was first introduced into the common law vocabulary by Professor Patterson over 90 years ago: "Life-insurance contracts are contracts of 'adhesion.' The contract is drawn up by the insurer and the insured, who merely 'adheres' to it, has little choice as to its terms." Patterson, *The Delivery of a Life-Insurance Policy*, 33 Harv. L. Rev. 198, 222 (1919).

[15] "Through advance knowledge on the part of the enterprise offering the contract that its relationship with each individual consumer or offeree will be uniform, standard and fixed, the device of form contracts introduces a degree of efficiency, simplicity, and stability. When such contracts are used widely, the savings in cost and energy can be substantial. An additional benefit is that the goods and services which are covered by these contracts are put within the

overreaching. It is in the context of this tension between social advantage in the light of modern conditions on the one hand, and the danger of oppression on the other that courts and legislatures have sometimes acted to prevent perceived abuses.

We believe that the contract here in question, in light of all of the circumstances presented, may be fairly described as adhesive. Although defendant and its supporting amicus curiae are strenuous in their insistence that Graham's prominence and success in the promotion of popular music concerts afforded him considerable bargaining strength in the subject negotiations, the record before us fairly establishes that he, for all his asserted stature in the industry, was here reduced to the humble role of "adherent." It appears that all concert artists and groups of any significance or prominence are members of the A.F. of M.; that pursuant to express provision of the A.F. of M.'s constitution and bylaws members are not permitted to sign any form of contract other than that issued by the union; that the A.F. of M. Form B Contract in use at the time here relevant included the arbitration provisions here in question; and that Scissor-Tail insisted upon the use of 8 5/15 and 9 0/10 contractual arrangements. In these circumstances it must be concluded that Graham, whatever his asserted prominence in the industry, was required by the realities of his business as a concert promoter to sign A.F. of M. form contracts with any concert artist with whom he wished to do business and that in the case before us he, wishing to promote the Russell concerts, was presented with the nonnegotiable option of accepting such contracts on an 8 5/15 or 9 0/10 basis or not at all.

It is argued, however, that other provisions of the contract, e.g., those relating to the length, time, and date of the concert and the selection of a special guest artist to appear on the program preceding the Russell group were subject to negotiation and that this consideration operated to mitigate or remove all adhesive characteristics from the contract. We do not agree. Although there may be circumstances in which the parties to a contract, negotiating in the context of certain "nonnegotiable" provisions insisted upon by one of them, may yet achieve an agreement of nonadhesive character through accommodation and bargaining with respect to other significant terms, we do not believe that the instant case involves such a situation. The terms here asserted to be subject to negotiation, assuming that they were in fact so, were of relatively minor significance in comparison to those imposed by Scissor-Tail, which included not only the provision concerning the manner and rate of

---

reach of the general public, whose sheer size might prohibit widespread distribution if the necessary contractual relationships had to be individualized. Transactional costs, and therefore the possible prices of these goods and services, are reduced. In short, form contracts appear to be a necessary concomitant of a sophisticated, mass-consumption economy. They have social and economic utility." Sybert, *Adhesion Theory in California: A Suggested Redefinition & its Application to Banking*, 11 Loyola L.A. L. Rev. 297, 297–298 (1978).

compensation but that dictating a union forum for the resolution of any disputes. In these circumstances we cannot conclude that the presence of other assertedly negotiable terms acted to remove the taint of adhesion.

B.

To describe a contract as adhesive in character is not to indicate its legal effect. It is, rather, "the beginning and not the end of the analysis insofar as enforceability of its terms is concerned." (*Wheeler v. St. Joseph Hospital*, 63 Cal.App.3d 345, 357 (1976).) Thus, a contract of adhesion is fully enforceable according to its terms unless certain other factors are present which, under established legal rules, legislative or judicial, operate to render it otherwise.

Generally speaking, there are two judicially imposed limitations on the enforcement of adhesion contracts or provisions thereof. The first is that such a contract or provision which does not fall within the reasonable expectations of the weaker or "adhering" party will not be enforced against him. The second, a principle of equity applicable to all contracts generally, is that a contract or provision, even if consistent with the reasonable expectations of the parties, will be denied enforcement if, considered in its context, it is unduly oppressive or "unconscionable." We proceed to examine whether the instant contract, and especially that provision thereof requiring the arbitration of disputes before the A.F. of M., should have been denied enforcement under either of these two principles.

We cannot conclude on the record before us that the contractual provision requiring arbitration of disputes before the A.F. of M. was in any way contrary to the reasonable expectations of plaintiff Graham. By his own declarations and testimony, he had been a party to literally thousands of A.F. of M. contracts containing a similar provision; indeed it appears that during the 3 years preceding the instant contracts he had promoted 15 or more concerts with Scissor-Tail, on each occasion signing a contract containing arbitration provisions similar to those here in question. It also appears that he had been involved in prior proceedings before the A.F. of M. regarding disputes with other musical groups arising under prior contracts. Finally, the discussions taking place following the Oakland concert, together with his telegram indicating that he himself would file charges with the A.F. of M. if the matter were not settled to his satisfaction, all strongly suggest an abiding awareness on his part that all disputes arising under the contracts were to be resolved by arbitration before the A.F. of M. For all of these reasons it must be concluded that the provisions requiring such arbitration were wholly consistent with Graham's reasonable expectations upon entering into the contract.

We are thus brought to the question whether the contract provision requiring the arbitration of disputes before the A.F. of M., because it designates an arbitrator who, by reason of its status and identity, is presumptively biased in favor of one party, is for that reason to be deemed unconscionable and unenforceable. Graham, although couching his arguments in other terminology, essentially maintains that it is, the thrust of his position being that to allow the A.F. of M. to sit in judgment of a dispute arising between one of its members and a contracting nonmember is so inimical to fundamental notions of fairness as to require nonenforcement. We proceed to a consideration of this contention.

* * *

[T]he parties shall have considerable leeway in structuring the dispute settlement arrangements by which they are bound; while recognizing that the leeway may permit the establishment of arrangements which vary to some extent from the dead-center of "neutrality," we at the same time must insist, and most especially in circumstances smacking of adhesion, that certain "minimum levels of integrity" be achieved if the arrangement in question is to pass judicial muster.

* * *

We thus return to the narrow question here before us: Is the contract we here consider, insofar as it requires the arbitration of all disputes arising thereunder before the A.F. of M., to be deemed unconscionable and unenforceable?

The answer to this question, we have concluded, must clearly be yes. Although our review of the record has disclosed nothing which would indicate that A.F. of M. procedures operate to deny any party a fair opportunity to present his position prior to decision, we are of the view that the "minimum levels of integrity" which are requisite to a contractual arrangement for the nonjudicial resolution of disputes are not achieved by an arrangement which designates the union of one of the parties as the arbitrator of disputes arising out of employment, especially when, as here, the arrangement is the product of circumstances indicative of adhesion.

As we have indicated above . . . a contract which purports to designate one of the parties as the arbitrator of all disputes arising thereunder is to this extent illusory, the reason being that the party so designated will have an interest in the outcome which, in the view of the law, will render fair and reasoned decision, based on the evidence presented, a virtual impossibility. Because, as we have explained, arbitration (as a contractually structured substitute for formal judicial proceedings) contemplates just such a decision, a contractual party may not act in the capacity of arbitrator and a contractual provision which designates him to serve in that capacity is to be denied enforcement on grounds of unconscionability. We have also indicated that the same result would follow, and for the same reasons, when the designated arbitrator is not the party himself but one whose interests are so allied with those of the party that, for all practical purposes, he is subject to the same disabilities which prevent the party himself from serving. Again, a contractual provision designating such an entity as arbitrator must be denied enforcement on the ground that it would be unconscionable to permit that entity to so serve.

A labor union is an association or combination of workers organized for the purpose of securing through united action the most favorable conditions as regards wages or rates of pay, hours, and conditions of employment for its members; the primary function of such an organization is that of bargaining with employers on behalf of its membership in order to achieve these objectives. By its very nature, therefore, a labor union addresses disputes concerning compensation arrangements between its members and third parties with interests identical to those of the affected members; to suppose that it would do otherwise is to suppose that it would act in a manner inconsistent with its reason for being.

In the view of these considerations we think it must be concluded that a contractual provision designating the union of one of the parties to the contract as the arbitrator of all disputes arising thereunder, including those concerning the compensation due under the contract, does not achieve the "minimum levels of integrity" which we must demand of a contractually structured substitute for judicial proceedings. Such a provision, being inimical to the concept of arbitration as we understand it, would be denied enforcement in any circumstances; clearly it cannot stand in a case which, like that before us, requires the careful and searching scrutiny appropriate to a contract with manifestly adhesive characteristics. The trial court's order compelling arbitration in the instant case was therefore in error and must be reversed.

* * *

Reversed and remanded.

### *QUESTIONS FOR DISCUSSION*

1. What precisely was the basis for the court's decision? How would you advise the AFM (or other unions) to revise their procedures to pass judicial muster? Is there a preemption issue here, and if so, how should it be resolved?

2. In the course of its opinion, the *Graham* court referred to a New York decision, *Cross & Brown Company v. Nelson*, 4 A.D.2d 501, 167 N.Y.S.2d 573 (1957), which struck down a provision in an employment contract that made the employer the final arbiter. (The contract was for employment in a real estate brokerage firm, and the issues to be resolved related to the size and distribution of commissions earned on real estate transactions.) Suppose, though, that in the standard non-union environment of employment at will (in which employees can be fired for *good* reasons or for *no* reasons, though no longer for *bad* reasons that are in violation of public policy), an employer has established an internal peer review procedure for review of the fairness of managerial discipline or dismissal. In its statement of this policy to its work force, the employer makes it clear that its executives retain the final authority about whether to reverse or uphold the managerial decisions. Could a fired employee go to court to get this employer prerogative struck down as unconscionable? *See Circuit City Stores v. Adams*, 532 U.S. 105 (2001). Are there fundamental differences, though, between the relationship of the employer to its workforce and the relationship of musicians and other workers (through their union) to concert promoters (like Graham)? *See Jerry Kravat Ent. Services v. Cobbs*, 118 Misc. 2d 23, 459 N.Y.S.2d 993 (1983) (*Cross* held distinguishable in declining to invalidate clause in concert promoter-music performer contract that made AFM the arbitrator of disputes between parties).

3. Does *Graham* affect your views about *Buchwald* (which, recall, relied heavily on the *Graham* decision)? Does the fact that musicians and other entertainers have unions mean that they should not be entitled to complain of unconscionability in the terms of their individually-negotiated contracts? Could Graham and his fellow concert promoters have organized themselves into an association in order to negotiate a more acceptable contract with AFM?

4. Suppose that in the earlier *Marino* case, the plaintiff had filed suit in California state court, relying on *Graham* to strike down as an unconscionable contract of adhesion the provision that authorized the Writers Guild to arbitrate disputes about screenplay credits. What are the relevant similarities and differences in the *Marino* and *Graham* situations? Should Marino have won if he had followed this state law route?

---

*Graham* has given us a glimpse of the operation of the American Federation of Musicians, the oldest, largest, and most complex labor organization in the entertainment industry. While all performers will occasionally agree to short-term engagements, such as Scissor Tail's two concert dates with Bill Graham, that kind of freelance contract is the standard operating procedure for most musicians.

Indeed, when unionism first put down roots among musicians in the first half of the 19th century, musicians performed all of their work as independent contractors. There were no symphony orchestras, recording studios, broadcast networks, and other organizations that now employ musicians on a reasonably steady basis. The original union-like bodies really served as mutual aid societies that offered training to beginners in the craft, loans to those getting established, help to members who became ill, and death benefits to families. Another illustration of such a cooperative venture was the creation by musicians of the New York Philharmonic, the country's first symphony orchestra, in 1842.

The pioneering musicians' *labor* union—in the sense of a body that sought to improve the conditions under which musicians performed their *work*—was the Aschenbroedel Club of New York, created in 1860. The (originally just German-speaking) members of this Club soon saw the value of agreeing among themselves not to accept engagements on anything but the minimum standards they had set for their services. In 1896, the burgeoning number of local musician organizations formed themselves into a national AFM that was affiliated with the American Federation of Labor; at the turn of the century, the AFM had over 45,000 members. By the late 1930s, the AFM expanded its jurisdiction to encompass orchestra conductors, instrumental soloists, and accompanists who previously had been part of another AFL affiliate, the American Guild of Musical Artists (AGMA), along with singers, dancers, and choreographers.

The AFM has included conductors like Leonard Bernstein and Louis Armstrong, classical soloists like Vladimir Horowitz and Isaac Stern, popular artists like Bruce Springsteen and Willie Nelson, and almost all of their superstar counterparts. Crucial to attracting and maintaining such membership is securing agreement from the purchasers of musicians' services that they will meet the standards of pay and working conditions that the union members would like to enjoy. On occasion that requires union use of the economic power it derives from its membership's commitment to their cause.

A notable historical example was the lengthy struggle by the AFM to win recognition from the Boston Symphony Orchestra (BSO). The BSO, formed in 1881, was the country's second symphony, but following the Boston Pops spin-off five years later, the first to offer steady paid employment to its musicians. Unlike its counterparts in the other large cities, the BSO leadership long resisted the idea of unionization among its musicians. In the early 1920s, the BSO successfully fended off a union recognition effort by dismissing and replacing all of its musicians who went on strike to try to win a labor agreement. In the late 1930s, though, the AFM, under its new President James Petrillo, returned to the fray, this time with considerably more leverage. All AFM members had agreed that they would not do guest appearances with the BSO and would not play in their own orchestra if it invited the BSO conductor (Serge

Koussevitsky) or its star performers to appear with them; the AFM also told the radio networks and record studios that they would not get any work from AFM members if the BSO were to play on one of the company's broadcasts or recordings. Faced with those pressures, the BSO leadership finally signed a collective agreement with the AFM.

In labor relations parlance, the tactic used by the AFM was a "boycott" of the BSO—a collective refusal by the AFM membership to work for a nonunion employer or for any other employer doing business with it. Under the original version of the 1935 NLRA, there were no labor law bars to such union tactics. However, the well-established Sherman Antitrust Act of 1890 had regularly been used to prohibit secondary boycotts and other union restraints in the labor and product markets. *See Duplex Printing Press Co. v. Deering*, 254 U.S. 443 (1921). Enactment in the 1930s of both the NLRA and the 1932 Norris-LaGuardia Act sharply altered that antitrust environment. Because Congress had placed its legislative imprimatur on collective employee self-help to enhance worker bargaining power and improve working conditions, the Supreme Court concluded that such actions must be immunized from attack under an antitrust law designed to block combinations in restraint of trade. In *United States v. Hutcheson*, 312 U.S. 219, 232 (1941), the Court held that the labor exemption from antitrust law insulated any self-interested union action, irrespective of a court's "judgment regarding the wisdom or unwisdom, the rightness or wrongness, the selfishness or unselfishness of the end of which the particular union activities are the means." And in *Local Union No. 189, Amalgamated Meat Cutters v. Jewel Tea Co.*, 381 U.S. 676 (1965), the Court made it clear that the eventual product of such union pressure, a collective agreement with the employer governing wages and working conditions, was equally protected by the labor exemption.

Not only did the BSO have no viable legal route through which to withstand the AFM's pressures for recognition, but the AFM itself was able to utilize *Hutcheson* to win a major victory against the Justice Department. *See United States v. American Federation of Musicians*, 318 U.S. 741 (1943). The Court has, however, always made it clear that the labor exemption is available only for collective employee action directed at the *labor* market, not combinations between labor and non-labor groups whose principal focus is the *product* market. *See Allen Bradley v. Local Union No. 3*, 325 U.S. 797 (1945); *United Mine Workers of America v. Pennington*, 381 U.S. 657 (1965). There remains, though, the peculiar feature of the music industry, in which most musicians are selling their services as freelance contractors performing single engagements rather than as employees of a body such as the BSO. This feature brought the AFM back to the Court for the following illustration of the difficulties in drawing a sensible line between labor and product markets.

## AMERICAN FEDERATION OF MUSICIANS V. CARROLL

Supreme Court of United States, 1968.
391 U.S. 99, 88 S.Ct. 1562, 20 L.Ed.2d 460.

JUSTICE BRENNAN delivered the opinion of the Court.

[This case tested the legality under antitrust law of AFM rules regarding "club date" engagements. Club dates are one-time performances of music at social events like weddings, fashion shows and school graduations. The purchaser of the music (e.g., the parents of the bride) contracts with the band leader to provide the music. The "leader," in turn, hires the "sidemen" who fill out the band. In addition to doing this administrative work (sometimes through a booking agent), the leader usually conducts the band and sometimes plays an instrument. If the leader is not present, he designates a "subleader" for this group.

The AFM has long negotiated collective agreements with symphonies, record companies, film studios, resort hotels, and other organizations that regularly employ its members. Because such collective bargaining is not feasible with short-term, one-time, club dates, the union unilaterally promulgated and enforced the work standards that must be met on those engagements. A Price List Booklet specifies the minimum number of sidemen that have to be used and the minimum rates that have to be charged by the band leader—the latter comprising the wage scale for each sideman, a leader's fee at double the sideman rate, and an additional percentage amount to cover insurance and benefits for the musicians. If a sub-leader is being used, he must be paid one and a half times the base rate out of the leader's fee. Finally, the leader must use booking agents who are licensed by the union and governed by the commission limits.

Implementation of these union standards requires band leaders to adhere to them in their contracts with club date purchasers. The vast majority of such leaders have been members of the AFM from the time they had begun to work as sidemen (which many continue to do on engagements for which they are not serving as leader). Maintaining membership in good standing in the AFM by complying with its rules is also essential for leaders who want to secure the services of AFM—members to play in their bands and on their club dates. Carroll and his fellow plaintiffs, members of an AFM Local, maintained offices to secure their engagements and sidemen, and also worked as conductors or players in their bands. Unhappy with a number of features of the AFM club date rules with which they felt compelled to comply, they sued AFM under antitrust law.

In connection with the AFM's labor exemption defense, the lower courts found that in their capacity as leaders, the plaintiffs were independent contractors with their music purchasers and employers of their sidemen. The question was whether this status meant that the leaders were a nonlabor rather than a labor group for purposes of the antitrust exemption.]

* * *

The criterion applied by the District Court in determining that the orchestra leaders were a 'labor' group and parties to a 'labor dispute' was the "presence of a job or wage competition or some other economic inter-relationship affecting legitimate union interests between the union members and the independent contractors. If such a relationship existed the independent contractors were a 'labor group' and party to a labor dispute under the Norris-LaGuardia Act." The Court of Appeals held, and we agree, that this is a correct statement of the applicable principles. The Norris-LaGuardia Act took all 'labor disputes' as therein defined outside the reach of the Sherman Act and established that the allowable area of union activity was not to be restricted to an immediate employer-employee relation. *United States v. Hutcheson*, 312 U.S. 219, 229–236. *Allen Bradley Co. v. Local Union No. 3*, 325 U.S. 797 at 805–806; *Los Angeles Meat & Provision Drivers Union v. United States*, 371 U.S. 94, at 103; *Milk Wagon Drivers' Union etc. v. Lake Valley Farm Prods.*, 311 U.S. 91. "This Court has recognized that a legitimate aim of any national labor organization is to obtain uniformity of labor standards and that a consequence of such union activity may be to eliminate competition based on differences in such standards." *United Mine Workers of America v. Pennington*, 381 U.S. 657, 666.

The District Court found that the orchestra leaders performed work and functions which actually or potentially affected the hours, wages, job security, and working conditions of petitioners' members. These findings have substantial support in the evidence and in the light of the job and wage competition thus established, both courts correctly held that it was lawful for petitioners to pressure the orchestra leaders to become union members, *Los Angeles Meat Drivers*, supra, and *Milk Wagon Drivers'*, supra, to insist upon a closed shop, *United States v. American Federation of Musicians*, 318 U.S. 741, to refuse to bargain collectively with the leaders, *see Hunt v. Crumboch*, 325 U.S. 821, to impose the minimum employment quotas complained of, *United States v. American Federation of Musicians*, supra, to require the orchestra leaders to use the Form B contract, *see Local 24, International Brotherhood of Teamsters etc. v. Oliver*, 362 U.S. 605 (*Oliver II*), and to favor local musicians by requiring that higher wages be paid to musicians from outside a local's jurisdiction, *Rambusch Decorating Co. v. Brotherhood of Painters*, 2 Cir., 105 F.2d 134.

The District Court also sustained the legality of the 'Price List' stating,

> In view of the competition between leaders and sidemen and subleaders which underlies the finding that the leaders are a labor group, the union has a legitimate interest in fixing minimum fees for a participating leader and minimum engagement prices equal to the total minimum wages of the sidemen and the participating leader.

241 F. Supp. at 890.

The Court of Appeals, one judge dissenting, disagreed that the 'Price List' was within the labor exemption, stating that " 'the unions' establishment of price floors on orchestral engagements constitutes a per se violation of the Sherman Act." The premise of the majority's conclusion was that the 'Price List' was disqualified for the exemption because its concern is 'prices' and not 'wages.' But this overlooks the necessity of inquiry beyond the form. Mr. Justice White's opinion in *Local Union No. 189, Amalgamated Meat Cutters v. Jewel Tea Co.*, 381 U.S. 676, 690, n. 5, emphasized that "(t)he crucial determinant is not the form of the agreement-e.g., prices or wages-but its relative impact on the product market and the interests of union members." It is therefore not dispositive of the question that petitioners' regulation in form establishes price floors. The critical inquiry is whether the price floors in actuality operate to protect the wages of the subleader and sidemen. The District Court found that the price floors were expressly designed to and did function as a protection of sidemen's and subleaders' wage scales against the job and wage competition of the leaders. The Court said:

> As a consequence of this relationship, the practices of (orchestra leaders) when they lead and play must have a vital effect on the working conditions of the non-leader members of the union. If they undercut the union wage scale or do not adhere to union regulations regarding hours or other working conditions when they perform they will undermine these union standards. They would put pressure on the union members they compete with to correspondingly lower their own demands.

241 F. Supp., at 888. The Court of Appeals itself expressed a similar view in saying:

> even those orchestra leaders who, as employers in club dates, lead but never perform as players, are proper subjects for membership because they are in job competition with union subleaders; each time a non-union orchestra leader performs, he displaces a 'union job' with a 'non-union job.'

372 F.2d, at 168. And of particular significance, the Court of Appeals noted that where the leader performs, "the services of a sub-leader would not be required and the leader may in this way save the wages he would otherwise have to pay. Consequently, he could make the services of his

orchestra available at a lower price than could a non-performing leader." 372 F.2d, at 166.

[The Court believed that this situation was analogous to *Local 24 of International Brotherhood of Teamsters v. Oliver*, 358 U.S. 283 (*Oliver I*), where the Court upheld a labor agreement in the trucking industry that established a minimum truck rental price as well as a minimum wage in cases where both services were being provided by the owner-operator of a truck. The Court noted that in *Oliver* and *Carroll*, the minimum charge for truck rental and leadman services respectively reflected fair market value for those non-labor items, and had not been set artificially high.]

* * *

The reasons which entitle the Price List to the exemption embrace the provision fixing the minimum price for a club-date engagement when the orchestra leader does not perform, and does not displace an employee-musician. That regulation is also justified as a means of preserving the scale of the sidemen and subleaders. There was evidence that when the leader does not collect from the purchaser of the music an amount sufficient to make up the total of his out-of-pocket expenses, including the sum of his wage-scale wages and the scale wages of the sidemen,[12] he will, in fact, not pay the sidemen the prescribed scale. The District Court found:

> It is unquestionably true that skimping on the part of the person who sets up the engagement (the leader) so that his costs are not covered is likely to have an adverse effect on the fees paid to the participating musicians. By fixing a reasonable amount over the sum of the minimum wages of the musicians participating in an engagement to cover these expenses, the union insures that 'no part of the labor costs paid to a (leader) would be diverted by him for overhead or other non-labor costs.

241 F. Supp., at 891. In other words, the price of the product—here the price for an orchestra for a club-date—represents almost entirely the scale wages of the sidemen and the leader. Unlike most industries, except for the 8% charge, there are no other costs contributing to the price. Therefore, if leaders cut prices, inevitably wages must be cut.

The analyses of Mr. Justice White and Mr. Justice Goldberg in *Jewel Tea* support our conclusion. *Jewel Tea* did not hold that an agreement respecting marketing hours would always come within the labor exemption. Rather, that case held that such an agreement was lawful because it was found that the marketing-hours restriction had a

---

[12] Only two things can happen when the leader does not charge the specified minimum—either he works below union scale or the musicians he employs work below union scale. In either event the result is price competition through differences of standards in the labor market.

substantial effect on hours worked by the union members. Similarly, the price-list requirement is brought within the labor exemption under the finding that the requirement is necessary to assure that scale wages will be paid to the sidemen and the leader. If the union may not require that the full-time leader charge the purchaser of the music an amount sufficient to compensate him for the time he spends selecting musicians and performing the other musical functions involved in leading, the full-time leader may compete with other union members who seek the same jobs through price differentiation in the product market based on differences in a labor standard. His situation is identical to that of a truck owner in *Oliver I* who does not charge an amount sufficient to compensate him for the value of his labor services in driving the truck, and is a situation which the union can prevent consistent with its antitrust exemption. There can be no differentiation between the leader who appears with his orchestra and the one who on occasion hires a subleader. In either case part of the union-prescribed 'leader's fee' is attributable to service rendered in either conducting or playing and part to the service rendered in selecting musicians, bookkeeping, etc. The only difference is that in the former situation the leader keeps the entire fee while in the latter he is required to pay that part of it attributable to playing or conducting to the subleader. In this respect we agree with the view espoused by Judge Friendly in his separate opinion.

* * *

Reversed.

### *QUESTIONS FOR DISCUSSION*

1. Recall that the majority in *Carroll* was heavily relied upon by the Court in *H.A. Artists & Assoc., Inc. v. Actors' Equity Ass'n*, 451 U.S. 704 (1981), which we read in Chapter 10 as another example of the use of the labor exemption. The dissent in *Carroll* was prepared to apply labor immunity from antitrust to the AFM's requirement of minimum club date charges for bandleaders when they actually do lead their group in an engagement for which they have contracted. Even with respect to the engagements at which a leader did not appear, the dissent said the union was fully entitled to impose its minimum scale for work performed by the sidemen and subleaders. However, the dissent believed the labor exemption could not cover the additional component built into the minimum price for the leader's role with respect to club dates in which he was not performing, but was simply being compensated for administrative work. With whose judgments do you agree about the broad principles governing the line between labor and antitrust law?

2. Suppose SAG-AFTRA (hereinafter) has proposed and the Alliance of Motion Picture and Television Producers (AMPTP) has agreed to a formula that establishes the minimum rates that must be charged for replay of a

movie on cable and then on free television. SAG's objective is to ensure the appropriate revenue base for purposes of calculation of its members' residual financial rights in these replays of their creative works (especially given the integration of movie studios and television and cable outlets under the same corporate umbrella). Would that clause in the SAG-Alliance agreement pass muster under the labor exemption?

3. Recall the *H.A. Artists* case from the last chapter, involving a challenge by talent agents to regulation by Actors Equity. Having seen more of labor unions in operation, do you think that Actors Equity merited the same exemption afforded to the AFM in *Carroll*? Or the exemption that would certainly have been afforded to the Writers Guild in *Marino*? Are there relevant distinctions between what agents and producers do?

4. Whatever the merits of the *Carroll* ruling about the demarcation line between labor and antitrust law, the more fundamental question is whether the underlying legal principle is still good social policy. Should federal law continue to protect and facilitate concerted activity by musicians (and other entertainers) that precludes economic competition among themselves for available jobs, thereby enhancing not only the compensation they earn but also the prices that must be paid for their services—whether the purchaser be the parents of the bride or a film studio producing a movie?

---

Producers have long been organized into associations (like the AMPTP) for a variety of purposes, including collective bargaining with their employees' unions. While under the National Labor Relations Act employers are entitled to engage in multi-employer collective bargaining, including locking out and replacing their employees in negotiating disputes, a key question is whether under antitrust law the employers are entitled to agree among themselves on a contract they will impose on the unionized employees in their industry. Illustrating the fact that this is not an entirely academic question is the salary cap that the movie studios sought to establish in 1933, with hoped-for antitrust immunity via endorsement from the NRA. As we saw earlier, that studio effort actually *produced* unionization in Hollywood, with labor agreements that were firmly in place by World War II. In 1947, the MPPA issued its Waldorf Declaration—that all member studios had agreed to discharge the Hollywood Ten until each "declares under oath that he is not a Communist" and for the future not to "knowingly employ a Communist or a member of any party or group which advocates the overthrow of the government of the United States by force, or by any illegal or unconstitutional method."

The key to any such blacklist was the fact that all the studios had agreed not to use the services of these stars. (Indeed, the writers, though not the actors, were later hired under pseudonyms to write a number of

Academy Award-winning movie scripts.) At the time, the application of either antitrust law or a labor exemption was in a very underdeveloped state. By the mid-1990s, there was a much more sophisticated appreciation of and debate about the issues, largely generated in another branch of the entertainment world—*sports*. Faced with league-wide rookie drafts, restrictions on free agency, and salary caps, the courts developed two alternative theories of the scope of the labor exemption for such collective employer practices. The first point of view, formulated in the 1970s, was that employer restraints were protected only if they enjoyed the consent of the employees union. *See Mackey v. National Football League*, 543 F.2d 606 (8th Cir. 1976); *McCourt v. California Sports*, 600 F.2d 1193 (6th Cir. 1979). The assumption was that if the employees have agreed to a restraint on their market through their own independent union engaged in arm's length bargaining, this likely is a better index than is a jury verdict about the reasonableness of such an employer restraint. In the mid-1990s, an alternative view was announced—that the mere *presence* of an employee union insulated employers from antitrust scrutiny of restraints they collectively instituted. *See National Basketball Ass'n v. Williams*, 45 F.3d 684 (2d Cir. 1995); *Brown v. Pro Football, Inc.*, 50 F.3d 1041 (D.C. Cir. 1995). The assumption of the latter position was that employees can enjoy their right to union representation under labor law only if they give up their right to a competitive employer market under antitrust law.

The Court eventually adopted the union presence theory, in *Brown v. Pro Football*, 518 U.S. 231 (1996). The Court's opinion did not mention the concerns expressed in the amicus brief from the entertainment unions about the reasons why some backdrop antitrust protection was necessary for their members. The Court's doctrinal formulation (that multiemployer bargaining associations are entitled to impose their plan to restrict competition for employees in their industry) is just as applicable to the entertainment as to the sports world. Having witnessed the evolution of the labor markets in the movie, broadcasting, and music industries, does this accommodation of federal labor and antitrust policy strike you as sensible? Suppose the movie studios, for example, seek to reduce the spiraling costs of movie production by having the AMPTP ask SAG to agree to a salary cap for each performer and film. Assuming SAG rejects that idea, may the studios adopt and enforce that restraint in individual salary negotiations?

---

Returning to the role of the AFM in the music industry, musicians want increased compensation and also greater demand for their performances. More than in any other part of the entertainment world, musicians' work has faced a constant threat from technological change.

For over a century, new "music machines" have regularly reduced the need for live music performances: the player pianos and juke boxes of the 1890s; the audiovisual equipment that made sound movies possible in the late 1920s; the records and disc jockeys that in the 1930s began to replace musicians and bands on radio broadcasts; the digital synthesizers that in the late 1980s started to reduce the need for live background music in making records; and now the Internet, downloads, and streaming services offering ready access to songs for fans around the world.

The earlier chapter on intellectual property law discussed some of the economic and legal implications of technology in expanding the scope and value of entertainment products. From the point of view of musicians, though, these innovations regularly reduce the demand for their services at the same time as the population of trained musicians expands. What is especially ironic about these developments is that (unlike automation in a factory), musicians themselves create the records and other products that tend to make their own talents superfluous.

This issue was especially pronounced in the late 1930s and early 1940s, when the AFM was making itself into a dominant force in the music world.[f] As noted earlier, with the appearance of Al Jolson's *The Jazz Singer* in 1927, the ability to combine sound with film in the movie studio quickly eliminated the need for over 20,000 jobs in movie theaters for musicians who had been playing live music to accompany silent films. Much of that economic pain was alleviated, though, by the coincidental appearance of radio broadcasting, which made extensive use of live music played over the air. But the emergence of the record industry in the 1930s made it feasible for radio stations to play a few popular records repeatedly, rather than employ musicians to perform the songs.

The AFM first tried to solve this problem through collective bargaining. In particular, the union inserted in its agreement with record companies a provision that required every record to have an attached label that it was being sold for "home use only," and was "not licensed for radio broadcast." While the AFM membership won an initial ruling in a state court enforcing this restraint, *Waring v. WDAS Broadcasting Station*, 327 Pa. 433, 194 A. 631 (1937), shortly thereafter Judge Learned Hand found any such use of state contract or unfair competition law to be preempted by federal copyright law with its "first sale" doctrine and the absence of a public performance right for recorded music. *See RCA Manufacturing Co. v. Paul Whiteman*, 114 F.2d 86 (2d Cir. 1940).

Having lost in court, the AFM stunned the nation when it announced in 1942 that its members would no longer be making records until something was done to alleviate these economic consequences. The

[f] *See* Robert A. Gorman, *The Recording Musician & Union Power: A Case Study of the American Federation of Musicians*, 37 S.W. L.J. 697 (1983).

Justice Department went to court on behalf of record companies to force AFM to end that boycott of recording work. However, under the much more favorable legal environment of an NLRA and an expansive labor exemption from antitrust, the government's request for an injunction was denied. *United States v. American Federation of Musicians*, 47 F. Supp. 304 (1942), *aff'd* 318 U.S. 741 (1943). After months of negotiations, the record companies finally agreed to pay a fixed amount for each record into an AFM-created Recording and Transcription Fund. This Fund was used to hire unemployed musicians at the union pay scale to offer live concerts at public sites such as parks, schools, and homes for the aged. Over the next decade, the Fund supported thousands of free music performances around the country.

The new Republican Congress elected after the end of World War II was not, however, pleased with the tactics the AFM had used. In 1946, a Lea Act amendment was made to the Communications Act of 1934, which barred any use of economic pressure by employees to secure payment from radio stations playing the music they had recorded. The Supreme Court upheld the constitutionality of this provision and its applicability to the AFM in *United States v. Petrillo*, 332 U.S. 1 (1947). Responding to the broader phenomenon of trade union action, Congress enacted the 1947 Taft-Hartley amendments to the NLRA, which imposed restraints on union secondary boycotts, "featherbedding" obstacles to new technology and work procedures, and other tactics.

While the combination of the Lea and Taft-Hartley Acts forced the AFM to restructure its program into an independent Music Performance Trust Fund, it did not block the AFM from securing essentially the same financial arrangements in early 1950s negotiations with movie studios and television networks. The more difficult obstacle soon facing the union was the tension within its own membership about this tactic. Actual creation of the music for a record, movie or television commercial was done by a small number of musicians working in Los Angeles, New York, Nashville, and other music production centers. It soon became clear that the additional costs borne by producers to subsidize live performances by the large number of mostly part-time musicians (and AFM members) around the country was thereby reducing the amount of money available to pay additional compensation to the employees actually doing the recording work.

In the late 1950s, this internal union dissension produced both unfair representation suits against the AFM (*see Atkinson v. Superior Court*, 49 Cal.2d 338, 316 P.2d 960 (1957)), and a brief breakaway from the union—in the form of a newly-created Musicians Guild of America that won an NLRB election to represent the musician employees at record and film studios in Los Angeles. To win this key membership group back (which it did in 1960), the AFM had to make substantial changes in its bargaining priorities. The amounts flowing into the Music Performance Trust Fund were essentially cut in half, at the same time that new Special Payment Funds were being created specifically for those working on records and motion pictures. These funds emulated the residual rights model that was being established at that time for actors, writers, and directors in the movie business. An interesting variation on that theme, though, was embodied in the Phonograph Records Fund: the distribution was based on the overall amount of work done by musicians on all the records produced and sales generated for signatory record companies, not on the fortuity of doing the background music on an album that happened to become a best-selling hit. The Music Performance Trust Fund continues to operate, and has financed well over a million public concerts since its inception.

---

A challenge to another AFM policy illustrates both the scope and the limits of labor regulation of union actions in the entertainment market. In 1988, the musicians making up the Seattle Symphony Orchestra broke away from the AFM and formed their own union, the Seattle Symphony and Opera Players Organization, which negotiated collective agreements with symphony management. That agreement established somewhat lower wages and benefits than those negotiated by the AFM for every other major symphony orchestra in the country. For more than 50 years, the AFM had also fashioned a Phonograph Record Labor Agreement (PRLA) which governed recordings not just of classical, but also of jazz, rock, country and western, and every other music genre. These agreements are negotiated every three years by the AFM with an association of the major record companies, and then accepted on a "me too" basis by the 1600 or so minor record labels. Paragraph 17 of the PRLA obligates all signatory record companies to produce and distribute only those domestic records that used musicians who are paid at or above the AFM scale.

The consequence of Paragraph 17 was that even though the Seattle Symphony musicians were not represented by the AFM, they had to receive the somewhat higher AFM wages and benefits when they were making records, though not when they were performing at live concerts. The orchestra discovered, though, that no label was prepared to pay such a price for Seattle Symphony classical recordings. Rather than absorb that cost differential itself to try to secure this broader audience exposure for its orchestra, the Seattle Symphony management decided to file an unfair labor practice claim with the NLRB.

The basis of the charge was section 8(e) of the NLRA, which prohibits unions and employers from "enter[ing] into any agreements, express or implied, to cease doing business with any other person." Read literally, Paragraph 17 of the PRLA might seem to constitute such a bar to the

Seattle Symphony doing business with any recording company in the United States. However, the NLRB and the Supreme Court have interpreted this provision as intended to prohibit just "secondary" rather than "primary" boycotts; i.e., union-employer agreements targeted at third parties who will not recognize and contract with the union, rather than agreements designed simply to protect and preserve the work and employment standards of the union's own members. *See National Woodwork Manufacturers Ass'n v. NLRB*, 386 U.S. 612 (1967); *NLRB v. International Longshoremen's Ass'n*, 447 U.S. 490 (1980), and 473 U.S. 61 (1985). In more contemporary terms, unions are permitted to secure agreements that restrict outsourcing of work to cheaper labor, in order to protect their own members from such corporate downsizing.

In analyzing the Seattle Symphony charge, the NLRB first concluded that the record companies would in fact be "joint employers" of the orchestra members when the latter were making records, rather than playing at concerts. In addition, the scope and intent of Paragraph 17 was simply to ensure that all records made or distributed by PRLA signatories met the AFM's *employment* rather than its membership standards. Since this was not the kind of secondary boycott agreement encompassed by § 8(e), the NLRB refused to issue a formal complaint on the Seattle Symphony charges. *See American Federation of Musicians (Seattle Symphony Orchestra)*, Opinion of NLRB office of General Counsel, 1996 WL 323650 (NLRB 1996).

Of course, the fact that Seattle Orchestra members must be paid the higher AFM rates when making a record does not guarantee that they will get a record contract in the first place. Indeed, classical music dropped from 7 percent of the overall record market in the 1980s to under 3 percent in the late 1990s. The likely explanation for the surge in sales in the 1980s was the development of compact disc technology that induced classical music fans to restock their libraries with digital sound. The availability of CDs made by such top-flight orchestras as the New York Philharmonic and Berlin Philharmonic playing the works of Beethoven, Mozart, Schubert and other composers cost other major orchestras such as the Boston and Philadelphia symphonies their record contracts.

Indeed, the Philadelphia orchestra went on a lengthy strike in 1996 when their employer insisted on eliminating the record stipend from the contract. Eventually that impasse was settled, with the performers agreeing to give up a contractual guarantee in return for gaining the primary role in securing such contracts and a higher share of any proceeds that might be generated. The significance of the AFM-RIAA agreement, and its status under labor and antitrust law, is that when the Philadelphia Orchestra members are competing for record contracts with their counterparts on the Boston, Seattle, or other Symphonies, the competition must be based on a more attractive style and quality of music, not lower costs.

---

The foregoing conveys a sense of the role played by labor organizations in the careers of performers, both the unions' accomplishments for their members generally and the tensions felt by specific categories of performers, as well as by the purchasers and consumers of their artistic products. Like other unions, AFM membership has been dropping steadily from its mid-1970's peak of 360,000 to its current level of around 80,000. That phenomenon is not true of the regularly-employed and higher-paid musicians (no more than of their counterparts in movies and television). The members of a major symphony orchestra have a union-negotiated pay scale that is now around $100,000 (up from $4,000 in the early 1960s), with a substantial number of members negotiating individual salaries well above that floor. However, the level of union membership among musicians performing in club dates is down sharply from the era that gave rise to the *Carroll* case, as are the relative earnings of those who play at those freelance engagements. The extent to which the current state of labor law does (or should) make a difference in the free market for performer services is a hotly-contested issue in both the scholarly and political arenas.

## E. CONTINGENT WORKERS: EMPLOYEES OR CONTRACTORS

We turn now to a status question that plays a crucial role in determining whether entertainers will enjoy an affirmative right under federal labor law to act collectively to enhance the returns on their labor, or will instead be subject to antitrust controls on combinations in restraint of trade. In their relations with producers, are performers to be considered employees or independent contractors?

This is a critical question under many other bodies of law. One example in Chapter 5 dealt with the "work for hire" standard for allocating copyright authorship as between creative artists and the firms that pay for their services. The Supreme Court decision in *Community For Creative Non-Violence v. Reid*, 490 U.S. 730 (1989), specifying the standard under the Copyright Act, was then expanded in *Nationwide Mutual Insurance Company v. Darden*, 503 U.S. 318 (1992), dealing with the Employment Retirement Income Security Act (ERISA). Decades earlicr the Court had expressed the view that the modern test for whether someone was an employee or an independent contractor should rest on the "economic realities" of the relationship, in particular whether or not the worker was in a position of "dependence" on the firm. In *Reid*, and even more in *Darden*, the Court has made it clear that (absent explicit statutory language to the contrary) the "employment" test is the one used under common law:

> The hiring party's right to control the manner and means by which the product is accomplished . . . [as well as] the skill required; the source of the instrumentalities and tools; the location of the work; the duration of the relationship between the parties; whether the hiring party has the right to assign additional projects to the hired party; the extent of the hired party's discretion over when and how long to work; the method of payment; the hired party's role in hiring and paying assistants; whether the work is part of the regular business of the hiring party; whether the hiring party is in business; the provision of employee benefits; and the tax treatment of the hired party.

*Id.* at 323–24. Essentially the same approach applies with respect to claims lodged under antidiscrimination legislation (both the Civil Rights Act and Age Discrimination in Employment Act) and state workers compensation legislation (which, as illustrated by the death of actor Vic Morrow during the making of *Twilight Zone*, can come into play in the filming of movies, especially those with dangerous stunt scenes).

The contingent features of entertainment work make the *Darden* standard (which the Court acknowledged was "no short-hand formula or magic phrase") especially problematic. Performers move from project to project and firm to firm several times during any year. While on a project, they exercise a good deal of creative autonomy—especially as directors, writers, and composers, but even as actors. Star performers are regularly assigned to a project by their own personal (or loan out) corporation, which allows them a variety of tax breaks (e.g., the right to deduct as business expenses all their agent/manager costs, not just those that exceed 2 percent of their employment income). If the relationship is characterized as non-employment, both performer and producer get the benefit of not having to pay Social Security and Medicare contributions (under the Federal Insurance Contribution Act) or unemployment taxes (under the Federal Unemployment Tax Act).

Producers would get the benefit of an independent contractor classification that will subject collective performer actions to the governance of antitrust rather than labor law. The following case was a byproduct of a major entrant into the entertainment world in the 1970s—cable television programming, particularly its pioneering Home Box Office (HBO).

The immediate source of the litigation was an effort by the Directors Guild of America (DGA) to secure a collective agreement with HBO. Unlike the major networks, HBO had few full-time directors working on regular HBO series. Instead, the made-for-television movies that HBO itself produced and financed used freelance directors, often provided by the directors' own loan-out companies. The Guild had initially permitted its members to work on such HBO (or Showtime) programming without a collective agreement in order to allow these new entertainment vehicles the leeway to get themselves established. By the late 1970s, the Guild had decided that it was time to have the cable programmers governed by a labor agreement as had long been true of the networks.

In 1977, HBO signed an agreement with the American Federation of Television and Radio Actors (AFTRA) that provided for payment of 80 percent of broadcast network rates. HBO then sought the same favorable treatment from the Directors Guild. The Guild, however, after initially insisting on the standard network terms, changed its position to ask for the higher of the network rates or 4% of the gross revenues earned by HBO from a program worked on by a Guild director. While the Guild (and other entertainer unions) had previously secured for its membership defined percentages of revenues from *supplemental* uses of filmed works, this was the first-ever proposal for payment of a percentage of revenues from its intended *primary* use. The reason for this position was that its economic analysis indicated that pay television was going to be more, not less, profitable than regular television.

When HBO refused to meet, let alone exceed, the network rates for director services, the Guild rescinded its earlier permission to its members to work for HBO as a non-union company. A few directors who did work on HBO projects received disciplinary charges and fines from the Guild. When HBO sought to bring in directors from other countries, the Guild lodged complaints with the Immigration and Naturalization Service (INS). Those Guild actions produced an antitrust suit by HBO against the Guild. The Guild asserted that its actions and contracts were immune from antitrust scrutiny. The district judge's review of the law made it clear that the key to the labor exemption was whether directors on film projects (including "loan-outs") were employees or contractors.

## HOME BOX OFFICE, INC. v. DIRECTORS GUILD OF AMERICA, INC.

United States District Court, Southern District of New York, 1982.
531 F. Supp. 578.

SOFAER, DISTRICT JUDGE.

* * *

III. Application of Labor-Antitrust Law to Guild Activities

* * *

*1. Freelance Directors*

[As in the movie world, most television directors are freelance rather than full-time employees. As such, they contract to work on an individual program rather than for a fixed period, and theoretically have the right to direct different programs for different networks at the same time. Unlike composers who were found independent contractors in *Bernstein v. Universal Pictures*, 517 F.2d 976 (2d Cir. 1975), who are paid for their songs when they are completed and accepted, freelance directors are paid flat fees for the days they work as well as certain fringe benefits. In addition, network producers decide when and where they must work and when the show must be completed; thus, as a practical matter, rendering work for different networks at the same time impossible. And while some directors do have substantial creative control over their programs, the Guild agreement with the networks reserves to the latter the power to decide the budget, the participants, and the final edited content of the show.]

[Thus,] most characteristics of the work performed by freelance directors support the conclusion that they are employees of the production companies for which they work. Freelance directors risk no monetary capital in shows and do not share in any profits, although if the Guild is successful in its aims, directors would receive a percentage of the gross license fee for shows produced for pay television. Although they receive additional compensation in the event of a rerun or other supplemental use of a program on which they work, that arrangement is similar to those of others in the entertainment industry who unquestionably are employees.

* * *

[The court went on to explain that while television studios and networks had production and financial reasons for shifting directors on television series and movies to freelance status, and for reserving staff positions to those who direct news shows, soap operas, and sports programs, the actual functions, compensation, and control over these two director categories were quite similar.]

* * *

For all of the foregoing reasons, freelance directors are employees, not independent contractors or entrepreneurs. Yet even without regard to that conclusion, the similarity of functions and overlap of capacities among staff and freelance directors creates a mutuality of interest that readily justifies their bargaining collectively. If minimum wages or other conditions of employment differed materially for these two groups, the terms of employment enjoyed by the more advantaged group could well be affected by the availability of directorial services in the other group at lower prices. Staff and freelance directors are to a considerable extent interchangeable; indeed, employer decisions more than anything else determine throughout the industry whether a set of directors is staff or freelance. Thus, staff and freelance directors are in much stronger job competition than were the musicians and bandleaders in *American Federation of Musicians v. Carroll*, 391 U.S. 99 (1968), which permitted a bargaining combination of the two groups.

### 2. *Loan-Out Companies*

[The court then discussed 400 directors who had established personal service corporations to sell their services. These "loan-out" companies had no assets other than the talents of the director-owner whose services were being rented to a user such as HBO. The role of the loan-out device was to filter the director's compensation for tax reasons. The Directors Guild required the loan-out companies themselves to sign the collective agreement in order to preclude these directors from evading their commitment to fellow union members. However, the court found that the labor exemption would also permit the Guild to force HBO to sign a collective agreement governing the terms of HBO's contracts with loan-outs. As a practical matter, the loan-out company was functionally identical to its director-owner, and HBO could be required to pay the company the same levels of pay and benefits as it paid to individuals.]

* * *

### 3. *Producer-Directors*

[The Court then turned to the category of producer-director. Sometimes, the title of producer (or executive or associate producer) was just a figurehead label. In these situations, the above conclusions would not be affected by HBO giving someone the title of producer-director. The situation was different, though, if the producer-director, while operating within broad budgetary and artistic parameters established by HBO, had "actual control over the allocation of the budget, all hiring, work schedules, filming, editing, and other elements of the production." The markedly greater degree of control wielded by the director-producer over these features of program production would render the latter an "independent contractor under common law standards," even if he were "paid by time and not by output."]

* * *

Despite the independent-contractor status of such producer-directors, however, they may properly be the subject of the Guild's collective organizing efforts. Even the narrow class of producer-directors HBO defines—and, a fortiori, less independent producer-directors—are in job or wage competition or some other economic interrelationship affecting legitimate union interests with the union members. All producer-directors, by definition, perform all the functions generally performed by directors, particularly freelance directors. They are therefore in direct competition with other Guild members for Guild-category jobs. Any directing job performed by a producer-director is one that a Guild director who is not also a producer might otherwise perform. The Guild has a legitimate interest in seeking to preserve the directorial parts of the producer-director's job for its members working under Guild-established terms and conditions. It has a legitimate interest as well in preventing the erosion of standards threatened by the existence of productions on which directors work under substandard conditions. Like the bandleaders in *American Federation of Musicians v. Carroll*, supra, producer-directors have a dual function, one of which puts them in job competition with union members who perform only that function and who seek to maintain the wages and working conditions they have collectively established. Moreover, unlike the owner-drivers or bandleaders, producer-directors are not employers; they assume none of the entrepreneurial risks associated with ownership, and although they may possess considerable budgetary authority, they do not ultimately control the budget or pay the price for budgetary deficits.

[The Court noted that the Guild had disclaimed any effort to control whether its own members served as producers, even for a non-union company like HBO, as long as the members were not also acting as directors. On that assumption, the court held that the Guild was entitled to control the compensation for and functions of *director*-producers in order to protect its members' standards for the former type of work.]

* * *

### 4. *Director-Packagers*

[Last, the court turned to the category of "director-packager." These were directors who put together and marketed a finished program to a nonunion broadcaster like HBO or a union broadcaster like CBS. Such packagers occasionally operated on an individual basis, but more often through a partnership or corporation.]

* * *

A television packager is an employer and a businessman. Unlike a loan-out company, which contracts only for the service of its director-owner, a production company is a multi-faceted operation engaged in making television films for sale in the market. A production company generally has several full-time and many freelance employees, and leases or owns offices and production facilities as well as office and production equipment normally associated with a business. Frequently, the packager conceives of a program and then attempts to sell it; at other times, customers for television films approach the packager with ideas for programs, which the packager may agree to make. Once an idea is accepted, the packager and his customer normally agree on a price, which includes the estimated cost of the production and the packager's profit. The packager then generally arranges for a script, selects a production group, produces the program, and sometimes helps to advertise and sell it. Purchasers of shows generally retain some form of approval to ensure that they obtain approximately what they agreed to buy. But their approvals do not materially interfere with the packager's business and creative control; they merely require the packager to stay within the parameters of the pre-production agreement.

Packagers are often entrepreneurs. They earn no salary, but profit or lose on the programs they make depending on their success in producing acceptable programs for less than the agreed fee. A flat fee is usually established for a program before production begins. If the show is produced for less than the fee, the packager retains the difference; if not, the packager loses the difference. The packager does not merely make up or keep within a production budget, as some producers are called upon to do. Packagers are often ultimately responsible for the budget, reaping the benefits of successful management and bearing the burden of failure. They negotiate with employees, unions, suppliers, and purchasers. Martin Pasetta explained that, as a director-packager, he was "responsible for legal contracts with everyone, including talent unions." He does the payroll and insurance and bears the usual corporate liabilities: "I have the responsibility of delivering a package either in a profit or loss situation, and I either make a profit or I have to eat it, as they say."

When a director member of the Guild works as a director-packager, he is nonetheless a packager. As such, the director-packager is an entrepreneur and cannot claim [the *United States v. Hutcheson* (312 U.S. 219)] protection as an employee who may combine with other employees or with labor organizations. The Guild contends, however, that its combination with director-packagers in collective bargaining activities is lawful under the principles articulated in *Carroll*, even if director-packagers are entrepreneurs.

The Guild disclaims any intention to prevent director members, through its membership rules, from "working in a non-Guild capacity for a non-signatory employer, including HBO, or . . . (to prevent) a Guild member from being a principal of a non-signatory company." Nothing in the record casts doubt on this disclaimer. The Guild seeks protection under *Carroll* only for its efforts to prevent any of its members, including director-packagers, from working in a "Guild covered capacity" for any nonsignatory employer, including HBO. For the limited purpose of Guild representation of director-packagers "with respect to their activities as directors," the Guild argues, director-packagers are a labor group within the meaning of *Carroll*, and hence within the *Hutcheson* standard.

[Relying on the Supreme Court's *Carroll* and *H.A. Artists* decisions, the court endorsed the Guild's legitimate objective of protecting its work standards by restricting the terms upon which its members could serve as directors, even when part of a package deal they were putting together for a nonunion television purchaser.]

* * *

Director-packagers who are Guild members constitute a labor group for purposes of the Guild's representation of them in their directorial capacity because "when working as directors, they compete with other members of the Guild for job opportunities and wages and necessarily perform 'duties and functions' which actually or potentially (affect) the hours, wages, job security and working conditions of other members of the Guild." This is apparent in particular from the fact that director-packagers sometimes work as directors for production companies other than their own. When they do so, they are legitimately members of the Guild, and the Guild may lawfully insist, through enforcement of its constitution and by-laws, on their working only for signatories. The Guild has a legitimate interest in preventing them from performing Guild-category work for any employer not signatory to a collective bargaining agreement; all unions have such power over their members. *See Scofield v. NLRB*, 394 U.S. 423 (1969); *NLRB v. Allis-Chalmers Mfg. Co.*, 388 U.S. 175 (1967). This case, therefore, does not involve a situation in which the regulated entrepreneurs are not union members or in which they may not legitimately be union members because there is no competition or any other economic interrelationship with other union members.

Relatively few director-packagers exist. But that does not alter the conclusion that they stand in a *Carroll* relation to Guild members. A union has power to prohibit even a single one of its members from working in a union capacity for a nonsignatory. Nothing in the Supreme

Court's analysis in *H. A. Artists* and *Carroll* suggests that a union must wait to regulate the terms of employment of those in job and wage competition with union members until the subjects of the regulation have already made substantial inroads. All that is necessary is that there be evidence that there is actual or potential job or wage competition, that the union's objective be to protect its legitimate interests, and that the regulations be an attack on "a problem thought to threaten" the union's established standards. To hold otherwise would be to prevent the union from attacking at its inception "competition through differences of standards in the labor market." In any event, even a few directors free to work without Guild constraints could, in this area of commerce, substantially affect the interests of other Guild members, and the number of director-packagers might well increase if the Guild's combination with them were found unlawful. HBO's definition of "director-packager" would enable HBO, for example, to provide directors with the financing to become director-packagers. Indeed, HBO has provided the necessary financial backing to at least two of the mere handful of current director-packagers, and HBO could easily provide them with talent, script, and other components of a production. The director-packager position might thereby become a tool for evading Guild standards.

For the foregoing reasons, director-packager Guild members are a "labor group" insofar as they work as directors. The Guild may therefore forbid them to work as directors for nonsignatories and require them to comply, to the extent they work as directors on their own productions, with all lawful terms of the Guild's agreements.

Suit dismissed.

---

The court's dismissal of HBO's claim was upheld by the Second Circuit without opinion (*see* 708 F.2d 95 (2d Cir. 1983)), not only with respect to the "statutory exemption" (based on *Hutcheson* and *H.A. Artists*) for unilateral union actions, but also with respect to the "nonstatutory exemption" that applies to union-employer contracts covering an industry sector. As we saw in *Carroll*, the latter branch of the labor exemption allows unions to press for and secure contract terms designed to insulate the *labor* market from competitive pressures that serve to reduce wages and worsen working conditions. Unions may not, however, agree with companies on contract terms that are designed to protect the latter from competitive pressures in the *product* market.

HBO had also attacked the Guild's efforts on that latter ground, claiming that the Guild proposals were designed to place pay cable television at a competitive disadvantage with over-the-air television. HBO did not suggest any collusion between the Guild and the networks, and the bulk of the Guild's contract proposal related specifically to work for HBO. There were, however, several items there that evoked detailed analysis by Judge Sofaer.

The first was the Guild's insistence that directors be paid 4 percent of HBO's revenues from the primary use of its programs, something that the Guild had not asked of the networks:

> The possibility that HBO and other pay-television companies might be placed at a disadvantage relative to free television poses a potential violation of the antitrust laws. Had the Guild conspired with film producers or the networks to devise this price discrimination, the Guild's conduct would fall outside both the statutory and the nonstatutory exemptions. *See Allen Bradley Co. v. Local Union No. 3, Electrical Workers*, 325 U.S. 797 (1945). But HBO has expressly disclaimed any conspiracy by the networks to obtain an advantage in their competition with pay television. Furthermore, although HBO alleges a combination between the Guild and television-program packagers, it does not claim, and has introduced no evidence to prove, that the percentage-of-gross provision has been or will be arrived at through complicity rather than through arm's-length bargaining. The Guild's motivation in seeking a percentage of gross for its director members has been solely to exploit what the Guild perceives as pay television's higher profit margins relative to free television. The Guild's rationale is overtly discriminatory, but it is based on the unrebutted claim that HBO makes more money than free television on the programs that Guild members direct; those programs therefore are proper objects for collective action aimed at extracting more money for the services of those members.
>
> The Guild has informed the Court, moreover, that it has succeeded in obtaining a percentage-of-gross payment for its director members' work for pay-television programs in a series of new agreements with "all major companies in the television industry." This action makes clear that the Guild's motivation has been to advance the interests of its members, not to ally with any set of employers against pay television. It also appears to put to rest the notion that the Guild's policy has been to discriminate against HBO in particular or against pay television in general. Nevertheless, even assuming a different compensation demand for HBO and pay television, such a union demand is lawful and protected, if asserted for the union's benefit, and not at the behest of an employer seeking to destroy pay television.

> The payment of a percentage-of-gross license fees is a form of compensation. A union may lawfully seek higher compensation from employers it believes to be more able to pay, *see Cutler v. NLRB*, 395 F.2d 287, 290 (2d Cir. 1968), and may lawfully seek different wages for work performed in different fields. In addition, "(profit) sharing, it is well established, is a form of employee compensation and, as such, is a mandatory subject of bargaining." *Impressions, Inc. v. Twin Cities Printing Trades Union, Local No. 29,* 221 N.L.R.B. 389, 407 (1975). If profit sharing, which gives employees a portion of net receipts, is a form of compensation, so too is a percentage-of-gross-receipts arrangement, which cuts less directly into entrepreneurial rewards. The Guild percentage-of-gross provision, moreover, is no different in kind from other percentage-of-gross arrangements in the entertainment industry going back to the earliest days of television. The challenged provision is thus an accepted form of compensation in this distinctive industry, a mandatory subject of bargaining sanctioned by labor law, and therefore within the nonstatutory labor-antitrust exemption.

531 F. Supp. at 606–07.

The second issue was the proposed restraint on the length of the license that the director would grant to HBO to show the work, no more than fifteen days in any six-month period, and for no longer than twelve months overall. The Guild's rationale for placing this restriction only on pay, not free, television was that the former had far more frequent reruns of its programs, thus reducing its need for more productions. In practice, the Guild had been prepared to be flexible about this item in negotiating agreements with pay television channels, rather than insist upon it as "a term in a labor treaty, subscribed to by all employers in an industry-wide bargaining unit." But even if the Guild were to alter that posture, the court endorsed the legality of this objective, based on testimony

> . . . that the provision has both the purpose and the effect of preserving work for Guild directors. "(Temporal) limitations on reruns contribute to maintaining the demand for new programs and thereby preserve, indeed increase, work opportunities for Guild members." Like residual payments for supplemental market exhibition, those limitations reflect the Guild's deep concern with the "technological unemployment" made possible by taping and rebroadcast. Work preservation is a legitimate union objective. Whether or not the particular provision in the Guild agreements would be a mandatory subject of bargaining, provisions with just such a purpose and effect were found within the nonstatutory exemption in Jewel Tea, supra, and Berman, supra. The exhibition-restriction provisions are likewise

> "intimately related to wages, hours, and working conditions," *Local 189, Amalgamated Meat Cutters and Butcher Workmen v. Jewel Tea Co.*, 381 U.S. 676, 684 (1965).

*Id.* at 608–09.

The third question related to the Guild's requirement that a signatory must secure from any third party to whom it was going to license work made by Guild members an agreement that the licensee would assume the signatory's obligations to the Guild, particularly payment of a percentage of gross revenues and abiding by the time limits on showing the program. The language and history of this clause satisfied the court that its sole objective was to guarantee Guild director-members the contract terms they had secured from direct signatories to the Guild agreement. Given the distinctive features of the entertainment industry, the judge was satisfied that the Guild's "Assumption Agreement" served "legitimate union objectives" and thus came within the umbrella of the nonstatutory labor exemption from antitrust: "A different conclusion might be warranted if HBO had demonstrated a significant impact on the product market-by showing, for example, that the Guild was using the Assumption Agreement for organizational purposes among purchasers' employees and was thereby restraining the product market." *Id.* at 611.

* * *

The court did say that any effort by the Guild to use this Assumption Agreement with its signatories to force nonunion program purchasers (like HBO) to subscribe to the entire collective agreement and thus become fully unionized might well be a violation of both § 8(e) of the NLRA (the bar against secondary "hot cargo" clauses) and § 1 of the Sherman Act.

> Nevertheless, the Assumption Agreement does not in fact force a purchaser such as HBO into a collective bargaining relationship with the Guild and has not in fact been used for that purpose. It merely imposes on parties purchasing pay-television rights on programs directed by Guild members the obligations to pay the director's compensation and to comply with the exhibition restrictions, both of which depend on the exercise of those television rights. It imposes none of the special duties to which employers in a collective bargaining relationship are subject. The Guild is not seeking to promote its organizational interests outside the unit; neither is it motivated by a rivalry with a competing union. The evidence shows that the Guild has done nothing other than seek to protect or advance the wage and job interests of director employees of signatories.

*Id.* at 612.

### *QUESTIONS FOR DISCUSSION*

1. The Dramatists Guild of the Authors League of America (under its then-President, Richard Rodgers, the partner of Oscar Hammerstein), established rules whereby its members agree not to offer their plays or musicals to producers unless the latter sign the Basic Agreement with the Guild. That Agreement spells out minimum advance payments and royalties, precludes sale of movie or broadcast rights until after a play's first stage presentation, and addresses other recurring issues in playwright-producer contracts (including arbitration). Can the Basic Agreement be challenged under antitrust law by a producer who signed it in order to get rights to a play? Are playwrights (like the musicians in *Carroll*) employees protected by labor law, or (like the doctors in *American Medical Ass'n v. United States*, 317 U.S. 519 (1943)) contractors governed by antitrust? Should it make a difference that the Guild's current Approved Production Contract (as it is now called), provides that the playwright gets copyright in the work, including control over derivative uses? *See Ring v. Spina*, 148 F.2d 647 (2d Cir. 1945), with its eventual denouement at 186 F.2d 637 (2d Cir. 1951), and then its sequel in *Barr v. Dramatists Guild, Inc.*, 573 F. Supp. 555 (S.D.N.Y. 1983).

2. In 1984, the Society of Composers and Lyricists filed with the NLRB an unsuccessful application for certification as the collective bargaining agent of its members working for film studios in writing the music for movies and television shows. The Regional Director for the Board made the initial (and unappealed) decision dismissing the application because these film composers were independent contractors, not employees under the NLRA.

The facts relevant to the traditional common law test of employment status were that composers were hired for specific film projects, they did the bulk of their composing at home on their own pianos, and they might even be working on music for different films (and studios) during the same period. The composers were required to attend regular meetings at the studio or on location to discuss with producers and directors the kind of music wanted and the revisions to be made, to instruct performers about exactly how certain pieces should be sung or played, to monitor the recording of the sound track, and so on. The studio had the right to determine the "final shape" of the music and to require necessary revisions.

The Regional Director emphasized additional factors that made composers independent contractors. Composers had agents and managers; their contracts provided for a flat fee that did not vary with the time taken and had to be paid irrespective of whether the music was used in the final version; and, most important, they were "highly skilled artistic individuals who receive no training whatsoever from the studios and whose talents and experience play an important role in their initial selection for work."

If this case were to arise again, how should it be resolved? Does a composer have a different legal status than the screenwriter? The director? The actors? Should denial of status as an employee covered labor law mean that the organization is subject to the restraints of antitrust law? *See Aaron Spelling Productions & Society of Composers & Lyricists* (NLRB 1984), synopsized in 6 Enter. L. Rep. 7 (March, 1985); *Dic Animation City v. Animation Writers of America*, 295 NLRB 989 (1989) (dealing with a similar dispute involving writers on animated television and motion picture productions). And it may be worth noting that in a related industry, Microsoft agreed in 2001 to pay $97 million to settle a suit seeking statutory benefits that had not been paid to thousands of workers whom the company had deemed independent contractors rather than employees, a classification found inappropriate by a federal district judge.

3. The Federacion de Musicos launched a labor organization effort among musicians who work in large tourist hotels in Puerto Rico. The musicians are part of orchestras that are hired for engagements that last from one week to a year or more. The hotel determines where they will perform, during what hours, and what types of music they will play. The hotel pays each musician individually and withholds taxes from their pay. However, the band leaders not only direct individual members in their rehearsals and performances, but also decide which musicians will become and remain members of the group. The hotel's decision is whether to hire or terminate the orchestra as a whole. Group members provide their own musical instruments and they may also work on other engagements that do not conflict with their duties in the hotel. Given these fairly standard features of musical engagements, would you characterize orchestra members as employees of the hotel for either labor or antitrust law purposes? *See Hilton International Co. v. NLRB*, 690 F.2d 318 (2d Cir. 1982).

4. In recent years the influx of money into intercollegiate athletics has raised questions concerning whether student-athletes should receive remuneration (outside of room, board, and scholarship) to play sports, particularly football and basketball, which generate large amounts of money.

As with the preceding cases, the question centers on whether student-athletes are employees. In 2014, a group of Northwestern University football players petitioned the NLRB to allow them to form a union. The Regional Director held that for purposes of the NLRA, the athletes were employees of the university and had the right to organize. *See* Northwestern University and CAPA, case 13-RC-121359 (2014). On appeal, the five-member board of the NLRB vacated the decision of the Regional Director, but declined to exercise jurisdiction on the merits, while reserving the ability to consider the issue in the future. In particular, the NLRB cited the few number of private institutions with the current ability to unionize as a basis for deferring a decision on the merits.

Are college athletes employees? What are the legal consequences of categorizing them in this way? How do the consequences compare to the case above?

## F. PERFORMING RIGHTS SOCIETIES[g]

There are, of course, situations in which there is no doubt that performers are acting as contractors rather than as employees, and thus may be subject to antitrust scrutiny. Indeed, performers who serve as employees in one capacity may be contractors in another e.g., those who market their rights of publicity for commercial use. Thus, if entertainers were to come together as a group (as athletes have) for such licensing purposes, they may well face an antitrust challenge. *See Topps Chewing Gum v. Major League Baseball Players Ass'n*, 641 F. Supp. 1179 (S.D.N.Y. 1986). The most prominent illustration in the entertainment world, and an important contributor to antitrust doctrine, are the songwriter groups that collectively license broadcast stations and other businesses to publicly perform copyrighted works.

Performance rights in music first became part of copyright law in 1897. The development of phonographs and then of radio transmission soon made performance royalties the primary source of composer revenues, rather than the sales of sheet music that had predominated in the 19th century. Chapter 5 focused on two policy issues in this area. One was the scope of public performance: i.e., did it encompass playing music from the radio in retail stores? The other was whether musicians as well as composers should enjoy performance rights when their recordings are played, especially in this era of digital sound. Here, we address the major challenge to implementation of the performance right that Congress had promised to composers and lyricists. As Justice White put it in the key Supreme Court ruling in this area, *Broadcast Music, Inc. v. Columbia Broadcasting System*, 441 U.S. 1, 4 (1979):

> Since 1897, the copyright laws have vested in the owner of a copyrighted musical composition the exclusive right to perform the work publicly for profit, but the legal right is not self-enforcing. . . . [T]hose who performed copyrighted music for profit were so numerous and widespread, and most performances so fleeting, that as a practical matter it was impossible for many individual copyright owners to negotiate with and license the users and to detect unauthorized uses.

These difficulties in licensing authorized performances of music and in detecting unauthorized performances led composers to join together in collective licensing organizations. The first such society had been formed in France in 1851 and the model soon spread to the rest of Europe. No such body was needed in the United States until music performance

---

[g] *See generally* Bernard Korman & I. Fred Koenigsberg, *Performing Rights in Music & Performing Rights Societies*, 33 J. Copyright Soc'y 332 (1986); Stanley M. Besen, Sheila N. Kirby, & Steven C. Salop, *An Economic Analysis of Copyright Collectives*, 78 Va. L. Rev. 383 (1992); Robert P. Merges, *Contracting into Liability Rules: Intellectual Property Rights & Collective Rights Organizations*, 84 Cal. L. Rev. 1293 (1996).

rights were first granted in federal copyright law. In 1914, reacting to the suggestion of Italian opera composer Puccini, one of Broadway's leading composers, Victor Herbert, persuaded his colleagues (such as Irving Berlin and John Philip Sousa) to form the American Society of Composers, Authors and Publishers. ASCAP is a body composed of and run by its members, the composers and publishers who own the performance rights in the music industry. ASCAP also represents affiliated foreign societies for enforcement of their rights in the United States in return for reciprocal efforts by those societies in their home countries.

Just three years after its founding, ASCAP won a big lawsuit on behalf of its founder, *Herbert v. Shanley Co.*, 242 U.S. 591 (1917), in which the Supreme Court held that Herbert's performance rights in his musical *Sweethearts* had been violated by the defendant restaurant when it played music for its customers. Soon afterwards, ASCAP expanded its role from enforcing performance rights to licensing them on a collective basis, thus serving as the vehicle through which restaurants, radio stations, and anyone else wanting to perform music could secure the right to do so. Initially, radio stations around the country bargained with ASCAP about the terms of such licenses through their own arm, the All-Industry Radio Music Licensing Committee. By the late 1930s, unhappy with ASCAP's negotiating demands, the broadcasters created their own collective licensing arm, Broadcast Music Inc. (BMI), as a rival body to represent music composers and publishers for this licensing purpose. BMI, whose membership started to surge in the 1960s, is still owned and controlled by the broadcast industry, with its composers being affiliates, not members. By serving as clearinghouses for the licensing and enforcement of the public performance of music, ASCAP and BMI enabled copyright owners to reap the benefits of their statutorily guaranteed performance rights.

As the use of copyrighted music has grown, the role played by ASCAP and BMI has become increasingly important. (Another privately-owned body, the Society of European Stage Authors and Composers (SESAC), represents a small but growing proportion of composers and music.) With millions of performances of copyrighted music occurring each day, it would be a practical impossibility for individual copyright holders to determine which of those performances involved their music, and then to take the steps necessary to protect their rights through issuance of licenses or initiation of copyright suits. Likewise, users of copyrighted music who wish to comply with copyright law would find it futile to try to negotiate individual licenses with the thousands of copyright owners whose music they wanted to play.

Significant efficiencies result from the collective administration of these rights. Performing rights societies help copyright holders earn money for their creative efforts, enable users to contract for the legal use of a wide repertoire of music, and serve the public interest by encouraging the creation of music and making it widely available. ASCAP and BMI, which evolved to serve the needs of copyright owners in this regard, together account for 95% of the United States market for performing rights. Before describing how these performing rights societies operate, it is important to note how copyright law influences the ownership of the rights at issue.

Copyright vests initially in the composers and lyricists (collectively called "writers") who create the musical work. These parties usually lack the time and expertise to exploit their works in the marketplace. As a result, they rely on music publishers to tend to these business affairs. In addition to publishing the original sheet music, a music publisher licenses the mechanical,[h] synchronization[i] and dramatic[j] rights to a composition. Copyright law allows the creator of a work to assign copyright to a third party. Thus, in exchange for an immediate advance as well as specified royalties in the future, composers and lyricists will often assign their copyright to a music publisher, who will then market the work worldwide. This arrangement has been characterized as a joint venture whereby one party creates the music and the other administers the rights for their mutual benefit.

Composers, lyricists and publishers become members of ASCAP or BMI by assigning to the organization the right to license the nondramatic public performance of their works. For many artists, royalties from this public performance right provide the greatest financial return on their creative efforts. As we saw in Chapter 5, the 1976 Copyright Act offers a broad definition of public performance that covers many forms of public presentation of a copyrighted song. Indeed, in its committee reports, Congress explicitly noted that performances at "semi-private" locations

[h] Mechanical licenses, which we encountered in Chapters 5 and 8, are the consents given by composer or publisher-owners of a song to a musician or record company to produce recorded versions of the song. While a voluntary license and negotiated fee are required for the initial recording of a song, once that first record has been made and distributed, any other musician has the right to make a cover version upon payment of the statutory fee set by a Copyright Arbitration Royalty Panel. In practice, the actual fee is usually negotiated at something lower than the statutory fee. The Harry Fox Agency serves as the representative for some 3500 music publishing houses (including all the majors) for issuing and negotiating recording licenses for songs, and auditing, collecting, and distributing the royalties for the songs' use.

[i] The synchronization (or "synch") right is the right to reproduce the musical composition on the soundtrack of a film or video in synchronization with the action being depicted. Unlike sound recordings, there is no *statutory* synchronization license and prescribed royalty rate (even for music videos). Until the last decade, the Harry Fox Agency offered synchronization licenses, which must now be negotiated directly with copyright owners.

[j] Performance of music for dramatic purposes occurs when the music is an integral part of the story in a particular production, such as an opera or musical theater. Because dramatic performances are limited and publicized, it has always been feasible for the music copyright owners to grant performance rights on an individualized basis, just as is true of a non-musical drama.

like schools, country clubs, and factories are included. Only a few classes of public performances are exempted by the federal statute. These include performances that are part of face-to-face and some online teaching activities at a non-profit educational institution (e.g., in an entertainment law course), and performances in the course of religious services.

After its members have assigned performance rights in their songs to ASCAP or BMI, the societies then grant licenses to any user who wishes to publicly play music that is part of their repertoire. Music users include television networks, local television and cable broadcasters, radio stations, restaurants, hotels, theaters, and bars. The primary license agreement between ASCAP or BMI and these users is the blanket license, which for a set fee allows the licensee unlimited access to any song in the performing rights society's repertoire. The fee for a blanket license is either a flat rate or is based on a percentage of the licensee's gross revenue or size; it is not affected by the number or popularity of the songs that are actually used. For example, the fee for a restaurant or nightclub is generally based on objective criteria such as seating capacity, the number of nights a week that music is used, whether admission is charged, and whether there is dancing. Radio and television broadcasters, by contrast, typically pay fees based upon a percentage of their net revenues. Fees for a blanket license can range from a few hundred dollars per year for a small store, to $5,000 for a concert hall that charges admission, to many millions per year for a television network.

A per-program license, a modified version of the blanket license, is also made available to certain users. The per-program license grants a licensee the right to utilize any music in the society's repertoire for use in the particular program for which the license was issued. While the per-program fee is a higher percentage of a user's revenues, it is limited to revenues derived from the specific licensed programs. Typically both blanket and per-program licenses are issued on a yearly basis.

After deducting operating expenses (less than20 percent of revenue), ASCAP and BMI distribute the remaining fees to their members. In light of the number of members in each organization and the multitude of songs in their repertoires, the task of distributing royalties is an extremely complicated one. ASCAP represents over 540,000 writers and publishers, and has a repertoire of more than 8 million songs. It collects about $1 billion annually in fees. BMI represents over 700,000 writers and publishers, and has a repertoire of over 10.5 million songs. Its revenues also total about $1 billion annually. Each society uses a slightly different procedure to identify the songs being performed by licensees, and then to determine the share of income each of its members should receive.

The key element in the distribution process for both ASCAP and BMI is their surveys of performances on network and local television stations, streaming services, cable television, radio stations, concert halls, nightclubs, and even of background music services like Muzak. Estimates of total performances are derived from these surveys. After this information is compiled, the results are weighted based on the value of each performance. The value is influenced by the market size and stature of the performance. Ultimately, writers and publishers receive royalty payments from ASCAP or BMI based on the outcome of these formulas. Court-supervised mechanisms for challenging royalty payments are available to dissatisfied members.

In addition to licensing music users and distributing royalties, ASCAP and BMI play an important role in the enforcement of their members' copyrights. Through random audits and surveys, the societies' "music police" identify establishments that are making unauthorized uses of music in their repertoires. Unlicensed users are subject to lawsuits for copyright infringement; typically an injunction, statutory damages, and attorneys' fees are sought. The vast majority of claims are settled with payment for past violations as well as a licensing agreement for the future. Of those lawsuits that go to trial, ASCAP and BMI are successful in nearly all of their cases. By policing copyright infringement on a broad scale, these organizations eliminate the inefficiencies that would result from duplicative enforcement efforts by thousands of individual copyright owners. Ultimately, the costs of licensing authorized users and policing unauthorized ones are spread over this large group of writers and publishers.

## G. ANTITRUST CHALLENGES TO PERFORMING RIGHTS SOCIETIES[k]

While performing rights societies have a strong position under federal copyright law, they have faced a long series of challenges under federal antitrust law. Almost all of these antitrust challenges have centered on the *blanket* licensing of performing rights. The benefits of using a blanket license to reduce transaction costs have already been noted. However, because the blanket license produces a pooling of copyrights by members that also improves their bargaining leverage *vis-a-vis* licensees, the Department of Justice scrutinized ASCAP and BMI to evaluate their compliance with antitrust law. The government ultimately filed suit against ASCAP and BMI in 1941, alleging that their members had conspired to restrain trade in violation of the Sherman Act. The principal focus of the case was the fact that ASCAP and BMI had secured

[k] *See* Lionel S. Sobel, *The Music Business & the Sherman Act: An Analysis of the "Economic Realities" of Blanket Licensing*, 3 Loyola Ent. J. 1 (1983); Simon H. Rifkind, *Music Copyrights & Antitrust: A Turbulent Courtship*, 4 Cardozo Arts & Ent. L.J. 1 (1985).

from their members the right to be the exclusive licensor of public performance of their members' songs. Before analyzing the outcome of the government's challenge, it is important to understand how antitrust law is structured.

American antitrust law has its roots in Congress' passage of the Sherman Act in 1890. The objective of the Sherman Act is to limit private economic power in order to protect competition. Market competition benefits consumers by lowering prices, increasing the supply of goods and services, and encouraging innovation. The Sherman Act has two major provisions designed to remove constraints on the marketplace. Section 1 makes unlawful "every contract, combination . . . or conspiracy in restraint of trade or commerce among the several states, or with foreign nations." Section 2 prohibits monopolizing, attempting to monopolize, or conspiring to monopolize any part of interstate or foreign commerce. The Sherman Act is enforced by the Justice Department's Antitrust Division and the Federal Trade Commission, and through actions by private parties. Remedies include criminal penalties, equitable relief, monetary damages (which are trebled), and the plaintiff's costs.

Most antitrust challenges brought against ASCAP and BMI have been pursued under § 1 of the Sherman Act, which prohibits competitors from conspiring to restrain trade. Courts have developed two major lines of antitrust analysis under § 1—the *per se* rule and the "rule of reason." Rather than conducting a lengthy inquiry into activities that are plainly anti-competitive, courts will characterize such agreements among competitors as *per se* illegal. Examples of restraints of trade that can be deemed *per se* violations include horizontal price fixing, group boycotts, and territorial market divisions among competitors.

Under the "rule of reason" test, a court will evaluate the impact a business practice has on competition to determine if the activity *unreasonably* restrains trade. First, a court will determine whether the challenged conduct involves a substantial restraint of trade. If it does, the court will then ascertain whether less restrictive alternatives are available that would achieve the same results for the defendant. If alternatives are available, the challenged practice will be considered a violation of federal antitrust laws. If such alternatives are not available, the court will then balance the anticompetitive effects of the activity against its procompetitive effects to determine whether an antitrust violation exists.

## 1. JUSTICE DEPARTMENT CHALLENGE

The Justice Department's 1941 antitrust challenges to ASCAP and BMI alleged that their practice of issuing blanket licenses illegally restrained trade because the pooling of copyrights under an exclusive licensing system permitted the organizations to charge excessive prices. Any radio station that needed to play music had no other viable alternatives. The government sought to do away with the exclusive license and to force the societies to offer alternatives. Both ASCAP and BMI quickly settled the suits against them by entering into separate but similar consent decrees with the government.

In exchange for certain limits on their licensing rights, ASCAP and BMI were permitted to continue offering blanket licenses. Because once such a body reached a readily marketable size its founding members had an incentive to limit admission of newcomers except at lower rates of return for their music, ASCAP and BMI were required to open their membership to any songwriters with published songs and to distribute the blanket licensing revenues on a non-discriminatory basis. Next, the decrees required that ASCAP and BMI members assign their society only the non-exclusive right to issue performance licenses. As a result, since 1941 members have retained the right to negotiate directly with potential users about the terms under which the users could publicly perform the copyright holder's work. This process is referred to as "direct licensing." The decrees also prohibit the societies from discriminating "in price or terms" between similarly situated licensees. In addition, the decrees required ASCAP and BMI to offer per-program licenses to broadcasters, and per-program and per-composition licenses to non-broadcasters. These licenses must be offered at a reasonable rate in order to ensure that users have a real alternative in choosing a license.

Major changes in the industry and in technology over the last seven decades have regularly produced reexaminations and amendments to the consent decrees. The first one took place in 1950[1] after television had come onto the scene, with ASCAP's radio licensing rights and regulations expanded accordingly. ASCAP was, however, prohibited from selling blanket licenses to movie theaters rather than just individual licenses to the movie producers (among other reasons, because of a major change that antitrust law was fashioning in the motion picture industry covered in Chapter 12). Another fundamental change was the establishment of a judicial mechanism to fix the blanket fees if ASCAP and a prospective licensee could not agree. A New York district court has served as the "rate court" responsible for arbitrating ASCAP fees, with the user entitled to use ASCAP's copyrighted music while this process was going on.

Because ASCAP remained the dominant performance rights power in the 1950s, another major change in the decree was made in 1960 to deal with its relationship with its members. Procedures were established

---

[1] *See* Sigmund Timberg, *The Antitrust Aspects of Merchandising Modern Music: The ASCAP Consent Judgment of 1950*, 19 Law & Cont. Prob. 294 (1954); Herman Finklestein, *The Composer & the Public Interest-Regulation of Performing Rights Societies*, 19 Law & Cont. Prob. 275 (1954).

governing the way ASCAP officials would survey the actual performance of songs, how the revenues would be distributed, an internal procedure for resolving disputes, and even determining the voting rights of members in the governance of the organization. This is a weighted voting system, based on the relative size of performance credits, thus giving far more control of ASCAP to those members who have composed major hits.

In the 1990s, the Justice Department and ASCAP negotiated yet another Amended Consent Decree to address ongoing changes in both the technology and the industry. For example, "on-line music users and transmitters" are entitled to the same blanket "Through-to-the-Audience License" as radio, television, and cable operators had already secured. What had become a rather time-consuming as well as expensive "rate court" procedure was streamlined in a variety of ways. Because BMI became an almost equal competitor to ASCAP, the Justice Department agreed with ASCAP that the ability of members to terminate their relationship at the end of each calendar year with full back revenues and move over to one of these competitors made judicial supervision of the terms of their relationship no longer necessary.

## 2. TELEVISION NETWORKS CHALLENGE

The Justice Department's consent decree with ASCAP and BMI does not immunize them from private antitrust challenges. Several groups of licensees have regularly been dissatisfied with the blanket license, which charged users the same fee regardless of the number of songs in the repertoire they used. As a result, the groups have brought antitrust actions against ASCAP and BMI, alleging that the blanket license was an anticompetitive device that violated § 1 of the Sherman Act.

The courts had little difficulty dismissing such claims filed by radio stations (*see K-91 v. Gershwin Publishing*, 372 F.2d 1 (9th Cir. 1967)) or nightclubs and bars (*see Broadcast Music, Inc. v. Moor-Law, Inc.*, 527 F. Supp. 758 (D. Del. 1981), aff'd, 691 F.2d 490 (3d Cir. 1982)). Given the vast array of music performed by stations and clubs, courts concluded that the blanket license was the only viable option for this market. Courts have been unwilling to accept the plaintiff's invitation to direct ASCAP and BMI to develop specialty licenses for jazz, country music, or other genres in which particular stations or clubs may specialize.

The movie theaters' antitrust suit evoked quite a different response. Initially, movie theaters needed performing rights licenses for the same reasons as did night clubs. Until the late 1920s, the silent movies being shown on the screen were accompanied by live music being played in the theater by a pianist or orchestra hired by the theater owner. When "talkies" emerged in the late 1920s, though, movie theaters objected to having to purchase performance rights for the music that was now on the film's sound track. The reason such performance rights were required had to do with the division of intellectual property rights in Hollywood. Sometimes the feature music (and almost always the theme and background music), is specially commissioned for the movie: thus the producer owns copyright in this "work for hire." The invariable practice, though, was for the producers to retain just the synchronization rights in the music that allowed them to put the music on the film's sound track, and to give back (or leave with) the composer the performance rights in this music when the film played in a theater. The result was that the producer could pay the composer a smaller up-front fee for the music, and the composer could hope to earn larger returns if the movie became a hit and the music had to be performed often. The composer would then have ASCAP or BMI serve as the licensing agency to secure those returns from the movie theaters under its blanket license.

In *Alden-Rochelle, Inc. v. ASCAP*, 80 F. Supp. 888 (S.D.N.Y. 1948), a judge found this practice to be a violation of antitrust law. Not only did the judge bar ASCAP (and by implication, BMI) from selling blanket licenses to theaters, but he also ordered producers to keep or secure from ASCAP's members the performance rights for the film's music, as they were already doing with the synchronization rights. One reason why the judge concluded that ASCAP's non-exclusive blanket license was an unreasonable restraint of trade was that while its composer-members could grant a direct individual license to the theater, they had no incentive to do so: ASCAP's rules still required all licensing revenues, individual or collective, to be distributed through its fund.

That latter gap in the 1941 consent decree was quickly closed in 1950, when the Justice Department required ASCAP to allow individual members to retain their own financial returns on direct licenses. This was the legal setting in which the performance rights issue would be played out on television. The *Alden-Rochelle* decree neither mentioned nor affected performance rights with respect to movies that would eventually be shown on television, which was still in its infancy in 1948. And as television moved more of its shows from live broadcasts from the networks' New York studios to filmed series and features produced in Hollywood, the film industry division of synchronization and performance rights between producers and composers meant that both television networks and local stations faced exactly the same performance rights licensing issue as had radio stations and movie theaters.

CBS led the charge on behalf of the networks. During its first two decades in existence, CBS television operated without incident under a blanket licensing system. In fact, in 1969, CBS and ASCAP agreed on terms for a new blanket license for the network. This new agreement, however, indirectly triggered CBS's antitrust challenge to blanket licensing that would last eleven years and include an eight-week trial, an appeal to the Second Circuit, a major antitrust decision by the Supreme Court, and another decision on remand to the Second Circuit.

The 1969 agreement between CBS and ASCAP created a disparity between the fees collected from CBS by ASCAP and BMI. Historically, BMI had sought to maintain parity with its more established counterpart. When BMI attempted to increase the amount it charged CBS for its blanket license, CBS resisted. On December 31, 1969, the day its licenses with BMI and ASCAP expired, CBS filed an antitrust action against both organizations. The network sought to enjoin the practice of blanket licensing, which it claimed was an unreasonable restraint of trade. CBS alleged that by pooling their compositions and avoiding price competition among themselves, ASCAP's members enabled the organization to fix at excessive levels the price it charged users to obtain performance rights. In addition, the network asserted that the blanket license constituted an unlawful tying arrangement, because ASCAP used its market leverage to require music users to pay fees for music they did not want to license in order to be able to play the compositions they wished to use.

The relief CBS sought from the court was to require the performing rights societies to offer "per-use" licenses as an alternative to the traditional blanket license. This arrangement would allow the networks to use any composition they wanted from the ASCAP or BMI repertoire, but be charged only for the songs they actually performed. The court never assessed the viability of this per-use proposal because it ruled that blanket licensing was not a restraint of trade because CBS had an alternative to purchasing a blanket license: it could obtain performance licenses for the music it wished to use directly from composers and publishers. According to the court, CBS failed to substantiate its contention that direct licensing was not a feasible alternative for a network television station that performed thousands of different compositions each year.

CBS won round two of the litigation when it convinced the Second Circuit to reverse the district court's holding on the issue of price fixing. *See CBS, Inc. v. ASCAP*, 562 F.2d 130 (2d Cir. 1977). The court ruled that the blanket license issued to television networks constituted price fixing, which was a *per se* violation of the Sherman Act. According to a majority of the court, blanket licensing results in "at least the threshold elimination of price competition" for public performance licenses, and its existence "dulls the incentive" of composers and publishers to compete with one another through direct licensing. Quoting from the Supreme Court's decision in *United States v. Socony-Vacuum Oil*, 310 U.S. 150, 221 (1940), Judge Gurfein added:

> The charge that there is a restraint of trade by price-fixing is founded upon the conception that when any group of sellers or

> licensors continues to sell their products through a single agency with a single price, competition on price by the individual sellers has been restrained.... [E]ven if the members of the combination are willing not only to join in the blanket license, but also to sell their individual performing rights separately, the combination is nevertheless a "combination which tampers with price structures [and therefore] engages[s] in an unlawful activity."

562 F.2d at 135–36.

The Second Circuit qualified its holding that the blanket license was a *per se* violation of the Sherman Act by noting that it would not be illegal when the use of a blanket license is "absolutely necessary for the market to function at all." While this market necessity exception might well apply to radio broadcasters, for example, such was not the case for television networks because the availability of direct licensing meant that blanket licensing was not a necessity. Instead of enjoining the use of blanket licensing, the Second Circuit remanded the case to the district court for it to fashion an appropriate remedy, indicating that if ASCAP and BMI were required to provide some form of per-use licensing that ensured competition among its individual members, blanket licensing might still be made available to users who preferred that form of licensing.

The case never made it back to the district court, however, because the Supreme Court reversed and held that the blanket licenses issued to the television networks were not *per se* violations of the Sherman Act. *See Broadcast Music v. Columbia Broadcasting System*, 441 U.S. 1 (1979). The Court rejected the Second Circuit's "literal approach" to price fixing, which it called "overly simplistic" and overbroad. In an important decision in the evolution of antitrust law generally, the Court ruled that simply because a business practice could literally be labelled price-fixing did not automatically render it illegal. Instead, one had to examine the market role that the practice in question played to see whether it was obviously anticompetitive. If so, it was *per se* illegal. If not, the practice had to be evaluated under the "rule of reason" analysis, which considered both the history of the industry and the economic realities that gave rise to the restraint.

Writing for an 8–1 majority, Justice White stated:

> [T]he line of commerce allegedly being restrained, the performance rights to copyrighted music, exists at all only because of the copyright laws.... Although the copyright law confers no rights on copyright owners to fix prices among themselves or otherwise violate the antitrust laws, we would not expect that any market arrangements reasonably necessary to effectuate the rights that are granted would be deemed a per se

> violation of the Sherman Act. Otherwise, the commerce anticipated by the Copyright Act and protected against restraint by the Sherman Act would not exist at all or would exist only as a pale reminder of what Congress envisioned.

*Id.* at 18–19. The Court then assessed the roles played by ASCAP and BMI in protecting the statutory rights of copyright holders. After noting the organizations' importance in both integrating sales to authorized users and enforcing the law against unauthorized users, the Court concluded that blanket licensing was not a "naked restraint of trade with no purpose except the stifling of competition." *Id.* at 20.

Most important, the Supreme Court found that the blanket license was a different product from the individual compositions that copyright holders could offer through direct licensing. Justice White noted:

> The blanket license is composed of the individual compositions plus the aggregating service. Here, the whole is truly greater than the sum of its parts; it is, to some extent, a different product. The blanket license has certain unique characteristics: It allows the licensee immediate use of covered compositions, without the delay of prior individual negotiations, and great flexibility in the choice of musical material. Many consumers clearly prefer the characteristics and cost advantages of this marketable package. . . . Thus, to the extent the blanket license is a different product, ASCAP is not really a joint sales agency offering the individual goods of many sellers, but is a separate seller offering its blanket license, of which the individual compositions are raw material.

*Id.* at 21–22. All that the Court ruled, though, was that blanket licensing to the television networks was not *automatically* illegal under federal antitrust laws. That left it to the Second Circuit, on remand, to evaluate blanket licensing under the "rule of reason."

## COLUMBIA BROADCASTING SYSTEM, INC. V. ASCAP

United States Court of Appeals, Second Circuit, 1980.
620 F.2d 930.

NEWMAN, CIRCUIT JUDGE.

* * *

Some understanding is required of the facts concerning CBS's use of music. Two types of classification are involved: one concerns the function of the music, and the second concerns the circumstances under which the selection of music is made. CBS, like all broadcasters, uses music as theme, background, or feature. Theme music is played at the start or conclusion of a program and serves to enhance the identification of the program. Background music accompanies some of the action on the screen. Feature music is a principal focus of audience attention, such as a popular song sung on a variety show.

Music on network television is selected in one of three ways. Most of it, as much as 90%, is selected by production companies, or "packagers," which produce television programs and sell them to the networks. The music on these programs is almost always theme and background music, much of it composed specially for the production company. Typically the company employs a composer to write theme and background music, acquires the copyright from him, and assigns it to its own music publishing subsidiary. Such music is called "inside" music. In some instances the packager decides to use music that has already been composed, so-called "outside" music. In these instances the packager must acquire from the copyright owner the right to record the music on the soundtrack of the program's film or tape. This right is known as a "synch" right, the music often being carefully fitted to synchronize with the action on the screen. Acquisition of the synch right, however, does not carry with it the separate right to perform the music on the air. That performing right could be acquired by the packager when he acquires the synch right, and reassigned to the network; however, the industry practice has been that the network automatically acquires the performing right for all music used on packaged programs under the network's blanket license for the performing rights to all ASCAP music, and the packager therefore has no need to acquire a performing right for reassignment to the network.

A small portion of network music is selected by the network itself, in those few instances when the network is producing its own programs. A still smaller portion is selected by the person or group performing the music, in those very few instances where music is spontaneously used. Examples are a football half-time show or a late night talk show on which a guest sings an unscheduled song.

DISCUSSION

Our starting point for determining whether the blanket license violates § 1 is the decision of the Supreme Court remanding the case to us. That decision obliges us to make "an assessment under the rule of reason of the blanket license as employed in the television industry." Since the parties are agreed that the relevant market is the licensing of performing rights to the television networks, we assume our consideration should be similarly confined to the blanket license as employed by the television networks.[6] A rule of reason analysis requires a determination of whether an agreement is on balance an unreasonable

[6] The distinction may have significance, since the lawfulness of the blanket license has also been challenged by non-network broadcasters.

restraint of trade, that is, whether its anti-competitive effects outweigh its pro-competitive effects. *National Society of Professional Engineers v. United States*, 435 U.S. 679 (1978); *Continental T.V., Inc. v. GTE Sylvania, Inc.*, 433 U.S. 36 (1977); *Chicago Board of Trade v. United States*, 246 U.S. 231 (1918).

* * *

There can be no dispute with the observation of Justice Stevens, in his dissenting opinion, that "there is no price competition between separate musical compositions." 441 U.S. at 32. The blanket license is the only device by which performing rights are licensed to the networks, and, under a blanket license, no selector of music to be performed on a network considers what the price of using one song would be compared to the price of using any other song. No price considerations affect the choice among songs because the network holds a blanket license to perform all songs.

The absence of price competition among songs, however, does not mean that the blanket license is a restraint upon any potential competition. For price competition to exist there must be at least one buyer interested in purchasing a product from two or more sellers. In this case, there is no evidence that CBS has ever attempted to purchase performing rights to any song from the copyright owners, either the composers or the music publishing companies to which they may have assigned their copyrights. If the opportunity to purchase performing rights to individual songs is fully available, then it is customer preference for the blanket license, and not the license itself, that causes the lack of price competition among songs. Of course, even customer preference cannot save some practices from illegality under the antitrust law. If competing sellers fix the prices of their products, they violate § 1 no matter how much a buyer may prefer accepting their fixed price to negotiating with each for a lower price. But a practice that is not a *per se* violation, and this blanket license has authoritatively been found not to be such, does not restrain trade when the complaining customer elects to use it in preference to realistically available marketing alternatives.

Trade is restrained, frequently in an unreasonable manner, when rights to use individual copyrights or patents may be obtained only by payment for a pool of such rights, *United States v. Paramount Pictures, Inc.*, 334 U.S. 131 (1948) (copyrighted motion pictures); *Alden-Rochelle, Inc. v. ASCAP*, 80 F. Supp. 888 (S.D.N.Y. 1948) (copyrighted music); *Zenith Radio Corp. v. Hazeltine Research, Inc.*, 395 U.S. 100 (1969) (patents), but the opportunity to acquire a pool of rights does not restrain trade if an alternative opportunity to acquire individual rights is fully available. *Automatic Radio Manufacturing Co. v. Hazeltine Research, Inc.*, 339 U.S. 827 (1950) (patents); *Standard Oil Co. v. United States*, 283 U.S. 235 (1931) (same).

CBS challenges this approach on the ground that some alternatives can always be imagined that would satisfy the market needs of an antitrust plaintiff. As CBS argues, the blanket license cannot possibly be saved from illegality under § 1 simply because CBS has the alternative of hiring composers to fill its needs for music. CBS is right. An antitrust plaintiff is not obliged to pursue any imaginable alternative, regardless of cost or efficiency, before it can complain that a practice has restrained competition. But in this case the defendants do not suggest that CBS should do anything more extraordinary than offer to buy from competing sellers. We agree with the defendants that if that opportunity is fully available, and if copyright owners retain unimpaired independence to set competitive prices for individual licenses to a licensee willing to deal with them, the blanket license is not a restraint of trade.

In fact, if there is a realistic opportunity to obtain performance rights from individual copyright holders, then the remedy CBS seeks in this case, modification of the blanket license into an option to use all songs plus a charge for each use of any one song, would be a clear instance of unjustified price-fixing in violation of § 1. If ASCAP were to make a per use charge for each song,[7] it would have to determine a price to be charged. Whether or not that price varied for each song, the determination of any price for use of a song by a membership organization of competing songwriters would be classic price-fixing. If licensing directly from individual copyright owners were not feasible, then it would be arguable that per use pricing by ASCAP might be that rare instance when price-fixing does not necessarily violate § 1. But CBS's proposed remedy cannot possibly avoid the strictures of § 1 if direct licensing is feasible. We therefore turn to an examination of the feasibility of direct licensing.

It could be argued that the best evidence against the feasibility of direct licensing is the fact that CBS has brought this lawsuit at great expense to avoid taking the blanket license. That surely suggests that the blanket license is not something for which CBS has a preference. But that argument ignores the principle that "the purpose of the Sherman Act is to protect competition, not competitors." *Checker Motors Corp. v. Chrysler Corp.*, 283 F. Supp. 876, 885 (S.D.N.Y. 1968) (Mansfield, J.), aff'd, 405 F.2d 319 (2d Cir. 1969). If the market for selling performing rights to the television networks would be competitive among copyright owners whenever any network chose to deal with them, the antitrust laws are satisfied even though one network has reasons of its own for forgoing that

[7] Not the least of the ironies of the CBS claim is that the per use charge it finds acceptable is simply the formula now used by ASCAP to distribute royalties among its members. That formula, based on type of music and frequency of use, does not value any song differently than any other. Thus, if ASCAP were to base charges to CBS on the ASCAP royalty formula, CBS would obtain no price competition whatsoever. Neither CBS nor the packagers would be able to shop competitively for cheaper songs when selecting music.

competitive market in preference to the blanket license. The defendants suggest that CBS's preference for the blanket license derives from its unwillingness to seek competitive prices from individual copyright owners while its network competitors enjoy the advantages of obtaining their performing rights under their blanket licenses. In defendants' view, CBS is bringing this lawsuit, not because competition among songwriters has been restrained, but because CBS wants protection from the prospect of its competitors' continuing with blanket licenses. We need not determine whether defendants' speculation is correct, but we agree that the issue is whether competition among copyright owners is realistically feasible, regardless of whether CBS may have some business reason of its own for preferring not to enter an available competitive market.

The entire trial in the District Court concerned primarily the issue of whether direct licensing was feasible. Judge Lasker placed the burden of proof upon CBS, as the plaintiff, to prove that it was not, for he concluded that there was no restraint of trade if direct licensing was feasible. After carefully analyzing the evidence CBS offered, Judge Lasker concluded that "CBS has failed to prove the factual predicate of its claims the non-availability of alternatives to the blanket license. . . ." 400 F. Supp. at 780–81. That ultimate finding is abundantly supported by subsidiary findings and by the record, which completely refute all of CBS's allegations of barriers to direct licensing.

CBS maintained that the existing market structure created by the blanket license effectively prevented it from seeking direct licensing because any money spent to acquire performance rights from individual copyright owners would be wasted once CBS had already paid ASCAP and BMI for performance rights to all music. However, nothing prevented CBS from attempting to obtain from the copyright owners performance rights for some interval following expiration of the term of the blanket license.

CBS also contended that there existed no machinery to handle the numerous transactions that would be required to obtain performance rights directly. The record establishes that such machinery is entirely feasible; indeed a single agency now serves as the broker for the thousands of transactions in which copyright owners sell television synch rights and motion picture performance rights. Nevertheless, the claim is pressed that it would take some amount of time and money to establish a similar mechanism for the individual brokering of network television performance rights. We note that Justice Stevens relied on this circumstance to conclude that "real and significant," albeit not "insurmountable" barriers to direct licensing existed. 441 U.S. at 35. With deference, we conclude that the evidence and Judge Lasker's analysis of it demonstrate that neither the time nor the expense of creating machinery for direct licensing establishes a barrier of which CBS can complain. It must be recalled that CBS has obtained its performance rights by blanket licenses ever since the late 1940's. Having transacted business in that fashion for that length of time, CBS cannot expect the antitrust laws to assure it that a changeover to direct licensing can be accomplished instantly or at no expense. Moreover, Judge Lasker found that the changeover could be begun very rapidly with CBS meeting its music needs as the machinery for direct licensing was put into place. When Justice Stevens refers to the machinery being created within a year, 441 U.S. at 35, he is citing the outer limit testified to by a CBS witness, whereas Judge Lasker found that "the relatively modest machinery required could be developed during a reasonable planning period." And when Justice Stevens refers to an expenditure of millions of dollars by CBS, he does not mean the cost of creating direct licensing machinery, but only the payment CBS will make during the final term of its blanket license. But that is an expense for which it bargained and for which it has received considerable value.

Next, CBS argued that individual copyright owners would be reluctant to deal directly with CBS in the licensing of performance rights. At trial this was the so-called "disinclination" issue. Wholly apart from the record, we have some difficulty even contemplating the feared situation of individual songwriters displaying reluctance to arrange to have their songs performed on a national television network, especially one owned by "the giant of the world in the use of music rights." But we need not rely on an intuitive rejection of this CBS claim. Judge Lasker found, after hearing substantial evidence from composers and music publishers, that if CBS were to seek direct licensing, "copyright proprietors would wait at CBS' door."

Finally, CBS alleged a barrier to direct licensing based upon what was called the music-in-the-can problem. CBS apprehended that, without a blanket license, it would be subject to demands for unconscionably high fees from the owners of copyrighted music already recorded on the soundtracks of taped programs and feature films in CBS's inventory. Judge Lasker properly rejected this claim both on the facts and the law. As a matter of fact, he found, based on the testimony, that "hold-ups" were not realistically to be feared, that synch rights were regularly obtained at fair prices after the recording had been accomplished, that copyright proprietors would not wish to incur CBS's disfavor by attempting a "holdup," and that the whole claim was undercut by the turnover in the CBS inventory. Apart from the lack of factual support for the argument, Judge Lasker also correctly rejected it on the ground that it is not a consequence of the blanket license. If CBS would be vulnerable to a "hold-up" when it tries to acquire performance rights for music on a feature film it wishes to rerun, that is a consequence of CBS's failure to acquire rerun performance rights at the time it acquired the film. At that time CBS accepted the risk that it would one day have to purchase performance rights for reruns, either as part of the purchase price for a blanket license or at a separate price for a license obtained directly from the copyright owner.

Pervading these assessments of each of the CBS contentions of alleged barriers to direct licensing is one indisputable fact that perhaps overshadows all others. If CBS were to forgo the blanket license, seek direct licenses, and then discover, contrary to the facts found by Judge Lasker, that a competitive market among copyright owners was not a feasible alternative to the blanket license, it would be entitled, under the consent decree, to assure itself of continued performing rights by immediately obtaining a renewed blanket license. Indeed, Paragraph IX of the ASCAP decree permits CBS to use any music covered by a license application, without payment of fee, subject to whatever fees are subsequently negotiated or determined to be reasonable by the court if negotiations fail. In short, the District Court has found that CBS can feasibly obtain individual licenses from competing copyright owners and that it incurs no risk in endeavoring to do so. There is no basis in the record for concluding that these findings by the District Court are clearly erroneous.

Of course, the fact that CBS has failed to prove that the blanket license restrains competition among copyright owners does not guarantee that such competition will occur if CBS or the other networks elect to forgo their blanket licenses in the future. Uncertainty is created not only by the normal risks of predicting the future but also by the special circumstances currently governing the selection of music for network television programs. As previously mentioned, approximately 90% of this music is selected by the program packagers. If CBS forgoes its blanket license, we cannot predict—indeed, the record gives us no adequate basis for making a prediction—as to how performance rights for this 90% will be purchased. Perhaps CBS will inform the packagers that it will buy programs only when performance rights have been acquired by the production company. That would create an incentive for the packagers to consider price of performance rights for individual songs in selecting music, especially outside theme or feature music. But the packagers might decline to buy performance rights, preferring to sell their programs to other networks that continue to hold blanket licenses. To the extent that happened, CBS, if it wanted a program for which performance rights had not been purchased, would have to purchase the rights for music already selected and recorded, in which event no meaningful price competition among copyright owners would occur. Or it may happen that packagers will be so anxious to sell their programs to CBS that they will acquire performance rights, even though that might not be their initial preference.

Another situation for which prediction is hazardous concerns the CBS-produced programs that use music spontaneously selected by the performers. The blanket license, among its other virtues, assures CBS of the right to air such programs, regardless of what music the performers elect to play. Without a blanket license, CBS would have to purchase performance rights after the program was aired, or negotiate with ASCAP for some modified form of program license to secure the right to perform any music in the ASCAP repertory only on designated programs where music is spontaneously selected, or forgo the telecasting of such programs.

We mention these alternatives (and there are surely others) not to express any judgment upon them, but simply to point out the difficulty of determining what the market for performance rights will look like if CBS elects to forgo the blanket license. Neither the District Court nor we can predict that perfect competition will ensue. But what the District Court has found, and what we affirm, is that CBS has failed to prove that the existence of the blanket license has restrained competition. Since the blanket license is not a per se unlawful arrangement, its restraining effect must be proved before § 1 liability can be found. When, after a full trial, such proof is lacking, the challenge to the blanket license is properly dismissed.

Affirmed.

### *QUESTIONS FOR DISCUSSION*

1. How do you account for the change in outcome the second time the court reviewed the claim against ASCAP? Is the explanation simply the change from the *per se* doctrine to a rule of reason analysis? Or might the sudden deaths of Judge Gurfein and Judge Anderson, who wrote the majority opinion in the first case, and their replacement by Judges Newman and Lumbard, have had a significant impact on the Second Circuit's shift in result?

2. In his dissent, Justice Stevens accepted the basic premise that songwriters and publishers did not violate the Sherman Act simply because they had agreed to sell a collective license to CBS at a single blanket price. However, he believed that ASCAP's (and BMI's) refusal to give CBS the option of purchasing a license to use the music of selected songwriters violated the rule of reason. According to Stevens, the result of ASCAP's decision to put CBS (and individual television stations) to that "all-or-nothing" choice, and to base the price on a percentage of CBS' overall revenues, was that the market could not focus on differences in production costs, quantity, and quality of the music that was actually played over the air. Stevens believed that the best way to secure a competitive music market while retaining the administrative advantages of a performing rights society was to require ASCAP to have each of its members list a price at which they

were willing to license their music. Besides adding an administrative charge to these list prices, ASCAP would still be able to offer the blanket license as an alternative.

The Supreme Court refused to require ASCAP or BMI to make such an offer to CBS because the societies' non-exclusivity provision allowed CBS to obtain these rights directly from the songwriters. However, both before and after these antitrust rulings, the marketplace has simply not developed individual licensing as a viable option for television programming (in contrast to movie production and exhibition). Does that market phenomenon indicate that the blanket license is actually the optimal regime for both sides? Or does it suggest that there would be unduly high transaction costs in an effort by an individual network to move from blanket to individualized music licensing? From the point of view of songwriters, who gets the benefits from the current system that collects a blanket fee from all music users, and distributes the revenues to authors based on how often their music is actually used?

## 3. LOCAL TELEVISION STATIONS CHALLENGE

The Second Circuit made it clear that its decision in *CBS v. ASCAP* was limited to an antitrust analysis of the blanket license used by networks. This limitation opened the door to further antitrust challenges to blanket licensing by local television broadcasters. In fact, the seminal case in this context, *Buffalo Broadcasting Co. v. ASCAP*, 546 F. Supp. 274 (S.D.N.Y. 1982), *aff'd*, 744 F.2d 917 (2d Cir. 1984), was already underway when the Second Circuit issued its second decision in *CBS*. At the time the case was brought, there were approximately 750 television stations in the United States. While 600 of these stations were network affiliates, the vast majority even of these stations were independently owned local television stations for purposes of the *Buffalo Broadcasting* litigation. The blanket licenses issued by ASCAP and BMI applied to the entire programming day of the 150 independent stations, and to the approximately six and one-half hours of each programming day of the 600 network affiliates during which the networks did not supply programming. Television stations had followed the lead of their radio brethren and erected in 1949 an All-Industry Television Stations' Music Licensing Committee to conduct the periodic negotiations with ASCAP and BMI.

There are three different types of programming broadcast by local television stations: network programming supplied by networks to their affiliates; syndicated programming that is not produced by the local stations; and local programming that is produced independently by the stations themselves. While the *CBS* case disposed of the issue of network programming, *Buffalo Broadcasting* addressed the legality of blanket licensing for syndicated and local programming.

*Buffalo Broadcasting* was a class action suit brought against ASCAP and BMI by a group of local television stations. Because the Supreme Court's *CBS* decision had precluded their claim of *per se* price fixing, the plaintiffs challenged the blanket licensing scheme under the rule of reason approach. They argued that for ASCAP and BMI to permit only blanket licensing of local television stations was an unreasonable restraint of trade. The local stations sought to distinguish their case from *CBS* by asserting that unlike the networks, they did not possess the resources and market power to make direct licensing a feasible alternative to blanket licensing.

Following a lengthy trial, the court surprised many observers by holding that blanket licenses to local television stations constituted an unreasonable restraint of trade in violation of § 1 of the Sherman Act. *See Buffalo Broadcasting Co. v. ASCAP*, 546 F. Supp. 274 (S.D.N.Y. 1982). The court examined three alternatives to blanket licensing that were theoretically available to the local stations. The first, per-program licensing, was judged not to be feasible because of its transaction costs. Direct licensing, the second alternative, was rejected because "it would be unreasonably impractical and expensive for local stations to search for and obtain licenses from thousands of composers and publishers." *Id.* at 290. The court accepted the plaintiffs' argument that they did not possess sufficient market power to compel copyright holders to issue direct licenses for performance rights. Source licensing, the final alternative, would require *producers* of programs to obtain performance licenses for the music in their programs prior to transferring those programs to the local television stations. The court found that source licensing was not a feasible alternative because local television stations did not have the economic power to persuade producers to adopt this approach. The court concluded its rule of reason analysis by balancing the anticompetitive effects of blanket licensing against its procompetitive effects. The court ruled that the anticompetitive effect of not having price competition among individual copyright holders outweighed the procompetitive benefits of reducing transaction and monitoring costs. ASCAP and BMI were enjoined from issuing blanket licenses to local television stations. The district court's decision, which jeopardized $80 million in local television performing rights revenues annually—or 25 percent of ASCAP and BMI's total revenues—was immediately appealed.

The Second Circuit reversed, holding that blanket licensing for local television stations did not constitute an unreasonable restraint on the market for performing rights. *See Buffalo Broadcasting Co. v. ASCAP*, 744 F.2d 917 (2d Cir. 1984). Although the court followed the same approach as the district court in carrying out its rule of reason analysis, it arrived at different conclusions about the availability of alternatives to blanket licensing. First, the court rejected the claim that per-program licenses were not feasible because they were too costly in relation to blanket licenses. The district court's comparison of a nine percent rate for per-program licenses and a one to two percent rate for blanket licenses was faulty, the Second Circuit reasoned, because the per-program fee was a percentage of revenue from a particular program, while the blanket fee was a percentage of a station's total revenue. In addition, the court noted that under the terms of the consent decree, plaintiffs were entitled to initiate proceedings before the rate court if they believed ASCAP's per-program fee was unreasonably high. Next, the court rejected the finding that direct licensing was not a realistic alternative for local television stations. The court termed inadequate plaintiff's evidence that a brokering mechanism would not develop for copyright owners to deal directly with music users if the television stations offered to license performance rights directly. The Second Circuit was struck by the revelation that plaintiffs had never once attempted to license the performance rights to a song directly from the composer or publisher. Finally, the court overturned the finding that source licensing was not a realistically available alternative to blanket licensing. The court concluded that the failure of local stations to obtain from producers the performance rights in a program at the same time they acquired all other rights was actually due to their failure to press for such an arrangement.

Given what it believed were realistic alternatives to blanket licensing, the court concluded that ASCAP's and BMI's insistence on blanket licenses for local television stations was not a restraint of trade. Under the rule of reason, this finding made it unnecessary for the court to balance the anticompetitive effects of the conduct against its procompetitive benefits.

### *QUESTIONS FOR DISCUSSION*

1. Do you agree with the court's holding that ASCAP and BMI did not violate the Sherman Act because feasible alternatives to the blanket license are available to local television broadcasters? Was it reasonable for the court to expect plaintiffs to pursue these other forms of licensing prior to filing suit? If direct and source licensing alternatives do not materialize, will courts fault individual copyright owners for refusing to agree to such a deal, or are they more likely to blame local broadcasters for not making a strong enough effort to secure it?

2. In *BMI v. CBS*, the Supreme Court stated, "The necessity for and advantages of a blanket license for [television and radio networks] may be far less obvious than is the case when the potential users are individual television or radio stations." 441 U.S. 1, 21 (1979). In light of this comment, should *Buffalo Broadcasting* have been an easy case for a lower court to decide? What reasons do you think the Second Circuit gave for taking a fresh approach in *Buffalo Broadcasting*?

3. How much bargaining leverage do television stations enjoy on this issue, whether negotiating with ASCAP and BMI about the terms of a blanket performance license or with film producers about whether syndicated shows will already carry a performance license with them? Do local television stations have more or less bargaining power than television networks? Radio stations? Movie theaters? What significance should be given to the fact that all television stations are represented by an All-Industry Music Licensing Committee?

4. One consequence of the *CBS* and *Buffalo Broadcasting* rulings was the decision by NBC to require all advertising agencies that it deals with to secure performance rights for copyrighted music used in commercials to be broadcast by the network. This move meant that an NBC station would not have to possess a performance license from ASCAP or BMI to broadcast a commercial which used music from their repertoires. Is this sudden change in four decades of industry practice a sound one? What are the implications of this shift to source licensing for NBC, for advertising agencies, and for copyright owners?

---

The local television stations did not end their campaign against blanket licensing with *Buffalo Broadcasting*. After the Supreme Court denied their petition for review, broadcasters sought a legislative solution to their grievance. In 1986, they persuaded Congressmen Frederick Boucher and Henry Hyde and Senator Strom Thurmond to introduce bills that would have mandated source licensing for syndicated programs being shown on local television stations. Although the legislation, known as the Boucher bill, generated over one hundred co-sponsors in the House; it was never passed by either branch of Congress. The intent of the legislation was to require copyright owners to directly license performance rights to program producers at the same time synchronization rights were being licensed. In effect, television stations would receive the same result that movie theaters received from the court in *Alden-Rochelle*. The bill would have banned the use of both direct licensing to local television broadcasters and blanket licensing by ASCAP or BMI.

While television stations have continued to press for source licensing legislation, they have been unable to secure passage of any bills to date. Proponents contend that blanket licensing results in copyrighted music being priced at a value disproportionate to its contribution to the total work. Source licensing, the argument goes, is preferable in the context of syndicated programming because these shows contain a small number of compositions that are readily identifiable in advance. Opponents assert that broadcasters are simply trying to achieve through legislation what they were unable to secure through litigation or negotiation. Mandating source licensing is unnecessary because broadcasters can secure this alternative through agreements with producers and copyright holders. Such special interest legislation, they argue, would reduce the income earned by musicians, thereby reducing the incentive to develop new music.

Should Congress intervene in this dispute between copyright owners and music users, or should it defer to the outcome of the *Buffalo Broadcasting* litigation? If Congress were to step in, what type of legislation should it enact? Is a proposal like the Boucher bill likely to promote competition among songwriters and give more musicians an opportunity to participate in the market for syndicated music, as its sponsors contend?

## 4. CABLE COMPANIES CHALLENGE[m]

Another challenge to blanket licensing was mounted by the cable television industry in the 1990s. In two separate cases, cable companies attacked the legality of blanket licensing under Section 1 of the Sherman Act. While representatives of the cable industry, like their network and local television counterparts, were unsuccessful in overturning the legality of the blanket license, they have demonstrated that ASCAP's and BMI's licensing practices remain open to antitrust challenge at any time.

The first cable television case was brought as a counterclaim by Lifetime Television against BMI in a lawsuit charging Lifetime with copyright infringement. *See BMI v. Hearst/ABC Viacom Ent. Services (Lifetime Television)*, 746 F. Supp. 320 (S.D.N.Y. 1990). Lifetime argued that BMI's blanket license represented a concerted effort by BMI and its members to increase the prices of performance rights, and to restrict the market choices available to cable programmers. In response, BMI filed a motion to dismiss the counterclaim, asserting that the court's decision in *Buffalo Broadcasting* foreclosed challenges to the blanket license as an unreasonable restraint of trade.

The court rejected the motion, reminding BMI that even though the cable companies closely resemble television networks and local stations, they could still attempt to prove that blanket licensing restrains competition when applied to them:

> Here, an array of factual issues await the crystallizing effect of discovery, including the history of music licensing to cable program services, BMI's reasons for insisting upon the blanket license for cable program services, the presence of disincentives to individual copyright proprietors to market their compositions separately, the concomitant absence of alternatives available to cable program services and the effect of the blanket license on

---

[m] *See generally*, Janet L. Avery, *The Struggle Over Performing Rights to Music: BMI & ASCAP vs. Cable Television*, 14 Hast. Comm/Ent L.J. 47 (1991).

> the availability and prices of music performing rights for cable program services.

*Id.* at 326. The court never had the opportunity to examine the merits of Lifetime's antitrust claim because the parties settled the case.

The second cable television case was brought by a group of cable programmers and cable operators against BMI in the District of Columbia. *See National Cable Television Assoc., Inc. v. BMI*, 772 F. Supp. 614 (D.D.C. 1991). In a decision that closely paralleled *Buffalo Broadcasting*, the court held that blanket licensing for cable companies did not violate antitrust law because of the availability of realistic alternative forms of licensing.

A different licensing controversy arose between cable companies and performing rights societies, centering on the issue of "through to the viewer" licensing of performance rights. In order to understand this dispute, some background about the structure of the cable industry is necessary. The cable industry has a two-tiered structure composed of cable programming services and cable system operators. Cable programmers assemble a package of programming that they supply to cable operators via satellite. Cable operators, who are licensed to operate in specific geographic areas, then retransmit this programming over cable lines to subscribers.

Almost every kind of cable program uses up to three types of music: theme music, which introduces or closes a program; background music, which accompanies a program's visual action; and feature music, which is the principal focus of a program. When a producer wishes to use a composer's music in its program, the producer negotiates with the composer or his agent to obtain a license for the necessary rights. Typically, the parties negotiate for synchronization rights, dramatic performance rights, and mechanical rights. However, as we saw earlier, non-dramatic performance rights must be obtained separately from the composers, typically via ASCAP or BMI.

According to the provisions of their consent decrees, ASCAP and BMI are required to offer traditional "over the air" radio and television networks a single performance license that authorizes the transmission of its programming "through to the viewer." These provisions prohibit ASCAP and BMI from requiring separate licenses from the networks and their individual affiliates who simultaneously broadcast programming. Historically, this same source licensing arrangement was extended to members of the cable industry. Performing rights societies offered cable programmers a single license that covered both the satellite transmission of their programs to system operators, and the subsequent retransmission of those programs by cable operators to their subscribers.

The catalyst of this dispute was ASCAP's 1988 announcement that it would no longer issue "through-to-the-viewer" licenses to cable programmers. ASCAP believed that it was entitled to issue separate licenses to each tier of the cable industry. Ted Turner and his WTBS superstation responded by seeking a ruling that ASCAP had to continue issuing through-to-the-viewer licenses. *See United States v. ASCAP (In re Turner)*, 782 F. Supp. 778 (S.D.N.Y. 1991), *aff'd*, 956 F.2d 21 (2d Cir. 1992). Turner's application was joined by sixteen other cable programmers, including HBO, Showtime, MTV, and Disney. Because cable television had not existed at the time the consent decrees were adopted, it was an open question whether the decrees' prohibition on split licensing should be interpreted to apply to cable companies.

The cable programmers asserted that they were the functional equivalent of the networks, and that cable system operators were the equivalent of local television affiliates. As a result, the programmers asserted that they were entitled to the same protection against split licensing as television and radio networks had received under the consent decree. ASCAP responded by contending that television and cable are two extremely different media. Finding none of these differences dispositive, the court turned to the underlying purpose of the disputed provision of the consent decree and concluded:

> [T]he term "telecasting network" is to be read in its functional sense, that is, to cover the supplying of programming by a packager to another entity for transmission under the packager's name, to household televisions, and should not be limited based on either the particular terminology used to transmit the programs into the homes of the ultimate audience or the particular financial arrangement existing between the packager and the local transmitter of programs.

*Id.* at 795. Thus, because the goal of the consent decree was not dependent on the financial or technical structure of the broadcast medium, the court read the prohibition against split licensing broadly, to include the cable industry as well as "over the air" broadcasters. The Second Circuit affirmed.

The lawfulness of split licensing was addressed in *National Cable Television Assoc., Inc. v. BMI*, 772 F. Supp. 614 (D.D.C. 1991). In addition to their antitrust challenge to BMI's blanket licensing scheme, this group of cable programmers and operators sought relief from BMI's proposed shift to split licensing. The court ruled that split licensing survived scrutiny under a rule of reason analysis, and therefore did not violate federal antitrust law. Although barely mentioned at trial, the court proceeded to examine whether split licensing was lawful under BMI's consent decree. Endorsing the New York district court's treatment of the issue in its *Turner* decision, the court also ruled that BMI was required by the terms of its consent decree to offer through-to-the-viewer licenses to cable programmers.

### *QUESTIONS FOR DISCUSSION*

1. Do you agree with the way the courts have interpreted the consent decrees to prohibit dual licensing of cable programmers and cable operators? What impact did these decisions have on fee negotiations between the cable industry and the performing rights societies? Can ASCAP and BMI increase their revenues by simply raising the amount they charge for performing rights licenses? Did BMI have greater latitude to do so because it was not subject to the jurisdiction of a rate court?

2. A related aspect of the *Turner* case involved the cable programmers' request that the court instruct ASCAP to make a per-program license available to them, in addition to the blanket license. As noted earlier in this chapter, ASCAP's consent decree requires it to "issue to any unlicensed radio or television broadcaster, upon written request, per program licenses." Paralleling its analysis of the split licensing provision, the court issued a judgment requiring ASCAP to offer per program licensing to cable networks.

3. Recent trends have indicated that more media broadcasters have begun using per-program licensing to replace blanket licensing. Part of this trend may be attributable to the formation of organizations like Clearing House Ltd., which have created comprehensive databases to track the performance of copyrighted music by television broadcasters. As it becomes less costly to account for a station's use of copyrighted music, per-program licenses will become more attractive to broadcasters. If you were counsel for a television station, what factors would you consider in choosing between a blanket license and a per-program license? Would your views change if you represented a cable programmer instead?

## 5. JUDICIAL ARBITRATION OF PERFORMANCE RIGHTS FEES

ASCAP's 1950 amended consent decree requires it to set "reasonable" fees for the licensing of compositions in its repertoire. If after sixty days a music user has been unable to reach a negotiated agreement with ASCAP on a license fee, the prospective licensee may apply to the Southern District of New York (the "rate court") for determination of a reasonable fee. During the first 38 years of the amended consent decree, not a single case was tried before the rate court. Over forty rate proceedings were filed during that time, but all were settled prior to trial. The court was required to exercise its rate-setting power for the first time in 1989, when Showtime/The Movie Channel (SMC) challenged the reasonableness of ASCAP's proposed blanket license fee for performance of music in motion pictures appearing on SMC's programming. According to the terms of its consent decree, ASCAP has the burden of proving the reasonableness of its proposed fee. ASCAP attempted to justify its request for a fee of 25 cents per SMC subscriber, which HBO had agreed to pay. SMC, on the other hand, sought a fee of just 8 cents per subscriber.

In setting an appropriate fee, the rate court consciously sought to account for the "significant degree of bargaining leverage" that ASCAP possessed. The court tried to:

> arrive at a rate that would not reward ASCAP for the exercise of any leverage that may be inconsistent with generally accepted antitrust principles, while still providing its members with a return for their labors that is generally commensurate with the value that a competitive market would place on both the musical fruits of those efforts and the benefits offered by the blanket license.

912 F.2d at 583 (quoting magistrate's opinion). For this reason, the court rejected ASCAP's argument that the fee it had negotiated with HBO should serve as the relevant benchmark for this case. Instead, the court ruled that the appropriate benchmark was the fee BMI had negotiated with SMC. The court then adjusted the BMI fee upward to account for ASCAP's slightly larger repertoire. The Second Circuit affirmed the rate court's holding, which resulted in a licensing fee of 15 cents per SMC subscriber. *ASCAP v. Showtime/The Movie Channel*, 912 F.2d 563 (2d Cir. 1990).

Another decision, *United States v. ASCAP*, 831 F. Supp. 137 (S.D.N.Y. 1993), offers a detailed picture of the challenge faced by a rate court which has to set the price to be charged for a service. Not only are there no specific criteria in the ASCAP consent decree about the formula for a reasonable royalty, but there is no external market base for assessing individual prices for a form of intellectual property that is sold on an aggregate basis for the efficiency reasons described above.

ASCAP had not been able to reach an agreement with CBS and ABC since 1985 about the appropriate price of blanket licenses for use of ASCAP members' music on network television programming. During the interim the networks paid a tentative rate of $9.8 million a year for this "open" period, and the parties had finally come to the rate court to fix the final price. One key ruling the court made was to reject ASCAP's position that the rate should be a specific percentage of the network's overall revenues. That formula had long been the practice for radio licenses and had recently been accepted by NBC for its television programming (the rate being 0.44%). However, the court concluded that there was no strong connection between a network's television revenues and the value of the music it used in its programming.

The court, instead, used as its starting point the actual licensing fees generated by the 1985 agreements between the parties. These fees were then adjusted by the percentage changes in the networks' gross revenues since that time. The total amounts that advertisers were paying networks to reach their audience were judged to be more relevant than trends in either the consumer prices or gross domestic product or the networks' Nielsen ratings (which had been falling steadily with the emergence of cable channels). The court smoothed out the network revenue trends over five-year periods to alleviate the yearly fluctuations from events like the Super Bowl or the Olympic Games. Using that mode of analysis, the rates finally arrived at were $9.7 million for CBS and $10.3 million for ABC for these "open years." As a share of their respective revenues, this was close to what NBC was paying via its percentage formula.

### *QUESTIONS FOR DISCUSSION*

1. One of the major reasons that ASCAP offered for the percentage of revenue formula was that this had earlier been voluntarily agreed to by CBS and ABC (as well as NBC). The networks' response was that their earlier fee arrangements with ASCAP had been artificially inflated as the byproduct of the marketing leverage that the blanket license afforded ASCAP. How viable are these claims in light of the Second Circuit's decision in *CBS* and *Buffalo Broadcasting*? Should those cases prevent ABC and CBS from advancing this market power position in a rate court proceeding?

2. In response to the court's effort to adjust the networks' 1985 licensing fees to account for changed circumstances, ABC and CBS sought to persuade Judge Conner to focus on the networks' profitability rather than on their gross revenues. The judge declined to do so because of his belief that profitability is difficult to measure and susceptible to manipulation. What are the advantages of basing fee calculations on profitability rather than on gross revenues? Do you think the court's concerns about measuring profitability are warranted? Would gauging profitability require the court to conduct an audit of the networks' financial statements? Do your recollections of the *Buchwald v. Paramount* case from Chapter 8 affect your views about this issue?

3. The *Buffalo Broadcasting* litigation culminated in a similar rate court proceeding brought by local television stations. Following the Second Circuit's 1984 antitrust decision in favor of ASCAP, local television broadcasters petitioned the rate court to set fees for the blanket and per program licenses issued to them by ASCAP. After a 22-day trial, Judge Michael Dollinger issued an opinion in 1993 making these fee determinations for the parties. Judge Dollinger agreed with the local stations that they should pay a flat fee, rather than one based on a percentage of revenues, because station revenues are not directly influenced by the amount of ASCAP music they play. However, he agreed with ASCAP that the parties' 1969 agreement, rather than the networks' more recent agreement, should serve as the benchmark for the court's fee determination. While the court set a fee

for the local television stations, it offered no guidance on how that fee should be divided among these 1,000 commercial, non-cable broadcasters. How should the licensing fees be divided?

4. In 1994, BMI had its antitrust consent decree modified to provide for a rate court similar to ASCAP's, substituting direct judicial review of proposed rate changes to the expense, delay, and uncertainty of new antitrust litigation launched every time such changes had to be made. Illustrating how long these processes can take is a ruling in *United States v. Broadcast Music, Inc.*, 2001 WL 829874 (S.D.N.Y. 2001), involving a rate dispute with Music Choice, which provides 55 commercial-free music channels on basic cable (to 6 million subscribers), satellite (9 million), and Internet (1500), with the latter paying a direct fee to Music Choice. While Music Choice had agreed in 1990 (before there was a rate court) to pay BMI 4 percent of gross cable revenues, by 1997 when its music channels were moving from premium to basic cable-satellite service, it sought the same 1.75 percent rate that BMI accepted for what was then a new "Backstage Pass" Internet service. BMI responded that there was a fundamental difference between cable-satellite operations and Internet sites and that the benchmark should be the 4 percent rate that Music Choice's major competitor, Digital Music Express (DMI), had negotiated in 1985. Judge Stanton concluded that the BMI-DMI figure "should not be regarded as reflecting normal competitive market terms." Instead, he ruled that the appropriate rate was the same 1.75 percent that BMI had accepted for Music Service's Internet service. Needless to say, BMI appealed to the Second Circuit, saying there is a fundamental difference between basic cable-satellite service bringing rock, pop, country and western, classical, and other music genres into the television set, and Internet web sites bringing them into the computer. The opinion was vacated on appeal, remanded, and vacated again. *See United States v. Broadcast Music, Inc.*, 426 F.3d 91 (2d Cir. 2005). What are your views about who should be winning this dispute about the appropriate fees being paid by Music Choice to BMI from 1994 through 2004?

5. The performing rights rate court resolves not only fee disputes between ASCAP and users of music, but also disputes about the distribution of blanket licensing revenues among individual members. The ASCAP antitrust decree requires that such distribution be done through a fair and nondiscriminatory formula whose operation is based on regular surveys of the amount and value of music being used in the marketplace. For an illustration of such judicial scrutiny, see *United States v. ASCAP*, 156 F.R.D. 64 (S.D.N.Y. 1994), in which the court was largely deferential to ASCAP's changes in its weighting formula (based on a detailed analysis done by ASCAP's management consultants, Booz-Allen), but resisted any alterations that might reduce future judicial assessments. *See also United States v. ASCAP*, 32 F.3d 727 (2d Cir. 1994), involving a struggle about the appropriate weight for commercial music jingles in the overall distribution formula (this being the special cause of Steve Karmen, the author of "I Love

New York," "Nationwide Is On Your Side," and scores of equally notable jingles).

---

With the rise of digital music outlets has come a changing of the landscape with respect to delivery and sale of music. One area that publishers and artists believe has been particularly harmful is streaming of music with unfairly low licensing rates. In a recent lawsuit involving Pandora, at the time the most popular Internet radio service with over 250 million users (79 million are active listeners), ASCAP challenged these rates.

## PANDORA MEDIA, INC. V. ASCAP

United States Court of Appeals, Second Circuit, 2015.
785 F.3d 73.

PER CURIAM.

These appeals are taken from an opinion and order of the United States District Court for the Southern District of New York (Cote, *J.*), dated March 14, 2014, filed under seal and entered March 14, 2014, and filed publicly March 18, 2014 and entered March 19, 2014, along with all preliminary findings, rulings, and orders subsumed therein, including an opinion and order dated and entered September 17, 2013.

At issue are two separate decisions of the district court. The first granted summary judgment to Petitioner-Appellee Pandora Media, Inc. ("Pandora") on the issue of whether the consent decree governing the licensing activities of Respondent-Appellant American Society of Composers, Authors and Publishers ("ASCAP") unambiguously precludes partial withdrawals of public performance licensing rights. *See In re Pandora Media, Inc.*, No. 12 CIV. 8035(DLC), 2013 WL 5211927 (S.D.N.Y. Sept. 17, 2013). The second decision, issued after a bench trial, set the rate for the Pandora-ASCAP license for the period of January 1, 2011 through December 31, 2015 at 1.85% of revenue. *See In re Pandora Media, Inc.*, 6 F.Supp.3d 317 (S.D.N.Y.2014).

ASCAP and Intervenors-Appellants Universal Music Publishing, Inc. ("Universal"), Sony/ATV Music Publishing LLC ("Sony"), and EMI Music Publishing ("EMI") (collectively with ASCAP, "Appellants") challenge the summary judgment order, and ASCAP challenges the rate-setting order with respect to the years 2013–2015.

For the reasons set forth below, we AFFIRM the orders of the district court.

## BACKGROUND

Though we assume the parties' familiarity with the underlying facts, the procedural history of the case, and the issues on appeal, we offer a brief overview to serve as context for the discussion that follows.

### I. The ASCAP Consent Decree

ASCAP is a performing rights organization that represents almost half of all composers and music publishers in the United States. *See ASCAP v. MobiTV, Incorporation,* 681 F.3d 76, 78 (2d Cir.2012). "These composers grant to ASCAP the non-exclusive right to license public performances of their music." *Id.* "Because of concerns that ASCAP's size grants it monopoly power in the performance-rights market, it is subject to a judicially-administered consent decree, the most recent version of which was entered into on June 11, 2001." *Id.* at 79; *see United States v. ASCAP,* No. 41–1395(WCC), 2001 WL 1589999 (S.D.N.Y. June 11, 2001) ("AFJ2").

The core operative provision of AFJ2 provides, in pertinent part, that ASCAP must "grant to any music user making a written request therefor a non-exclusive license to perform all of the works in the ASCAP repertory." AFJ2 § VI. The decree defines "ASCAP repertory" as "those works the right of public performance of which ASCAP has or hereafter shall have the right to license at the relevant point in time." *Id.* § II(C). "Right of public performance" is defined, in pertinent part, as "the right to perform a work publicly in a nondramatic manner." *Id.* § II(Q).

When a music user requests "a license for the right of public performance of any, some or all of the works in the ASCAP repertory," ASCAP is required to notify the user of what it deems to be a reasonable fee for the license requested. *Id.* § IX(A). If certain prescribed periods of time elapse without the parties reaching an agreement, each party is granted the right to petition the United States District Court for the Southern District of New York, which retained jurisdiction, to set a reasonable fee. *Id.* §§ IX(A), XIV. While the rate determination is pending, the license applicant "shall have the right to perform any, some or all of the works in the ASCAP repertory to which its application pertains." *Id.* § IX(E).

ASCAP is permitted, "when so directed by the member in interest in respect of a work, [to restrict] performances of a work in order reasonably to protect the work against indiscriminate performances, or the value of the public performance rights therein, or the dramatic or 'grand' performing rights therein." *Id.* § IV(F).

### II. The Partial Withdrawals and Direct Licenses

Beginning around 2010, certain ASCAP members grew concerned that ASCAP was receiving below-market rates for public performance licenses to new media companies such as Pandora. These members sought to withdraw from ASCAP the right to license their works to new media music users, preferring to negotiate with new media music users outside the ASCAP framework. EMI, in particular, threatened to withdraw from ASCAP completely if ASCAP did not change its practices, so as to allow publishers to withdraw from ASCAP the right to license new media music users while continuing to license ASCAP to license other media. In response, ASCAP modified its internal compendium of rules to permit this practice. EMI withdrew its new media licensing rights shortly thereafter, effective May 1, 2011. Sony withdrew its new media licensing rights effective January 1, 2013, and Universal withdrew its new media licensing rights effective July 1, 2013.

Also in 2010, Pandora terminated its existing ASCAP license and requested a new license for the period running from January 1, 2011 to December 31, 2015. Each of EMI, Sony, and Universal ultimately entered into a direct license with Pandora.

### III. The District Court Proceedings

Pandora filed its rate court petition in the United States District Court for the Southern District of New York in November 2012, prior to the execution of its direct licenses with Sony and Universal. In June 2013, Pandora moved for summary judgment on the issue of the partial withdrawals. The district court granted Pandora's motion. *In re Pandora Media, Inc.,* No. 12 CIV. 8035(DLC), 2013 WL 5211927 (S.D.N.Y. Sept. 17, 2013). Sony, EMI, and Universal were subsequently granted leave to intervene in the district court *nunc pro tunc* to September 13, 2013.

The district court conducted a bench trial on the rate issue beginning January 21, 2014 and ending February 10, 2014. On March 14, 2014, the court issued a sealed opinion and order setting the licensing rate. A public version of that decision was filed on March 18, 2014 and was entered the following day. *See In re Pandora Media, Inc.,* 6 F.Supp.3d 317 (S.D.N.Y.2014). Pandora had sought a 1.70% rate for all five years of the license, while ASCAP proposed an escalating rate: 1.85% for 2011–2012, 2.50% for 2013, and 3.00% for 2014–2015. *See id.* at 320. The district court set the rate for all five years at 1.85%. *See id.*

ASCAP, Sony/EMI,1 and Universal each filed a notice of appeal on April 14, 2014. ASCAP's appeal of the rate determination pertains solely to the years 2013–2015.

## DISCUSSION

### I. Summary Judgment on Partial Withdrawals

We review *de novo* a district court's grant of summary judgment. *See Aulicino v. N.Y.C. Dep't of Homeless Servs.,* 580 F.3d 73, 79 (2d Cir.2009). Summary judgment should be granted "if the movant shows that there is no genuine dispute as to any material fact and the movant is entitled to judgment as a matter of law." Fed.R.Civ.P. 56(a). The Court must "construe the facts in the light most favorable to the non-moving party and must resolve all ambiguities and draw all reasonable inferences against the movant." *Beyer v. Cnty. of Nassau,* 524 F.3d 160, 163 (2d Cir.2008) (citation and internal quotation marks omitted). A district court's interpretation of a consent decree is also subject to *de novo* review. *See E.E.O.C. v. Local 40, Int'l Ass'n of Bridge, Structural & Ornamental Iron Workers,* 76 F.3d 76, 80 (2d Cir.1996).

Appellants contend that publishers may withdraw from ASCAP its right to license their works to certain new media music users (including Pandora) while continuing to license the same works to ASCAP for licensing to other users. We agree with the district court's determination that the plain language of the consent decree unambiguously precludes ASCAP from accepting such partial withdrawals. The decree's definition of "ASCAP repertory" and other provisions of the decree establish that ASCAP has essentially equivalent rights across *all* of the works licensed to it. The licensing of works through ASCAP is offered to publishers on a take-it-or-leave-it basis. As ASCAP is required to license its entire repertory to all eligible users, publishers may not license works to ASCAP for licensing to some eligible users but not others.

Appellants would have us rewrite the decree so that it speaks in terms of the right to license the particular subset of public performance rights being sought by a specific music user. This reading is foreclosed by the plain language of the decree, rendering Appellants' interpretation unreasonable as a matter of law. *Cf. Perez v. Danbury Hosp.,* 347 F.3d 419, 424 (2d Cir.2003) ("A court may not replace the terms of a consent decree with its own. . . ." (citation and internal quotation marks omitted)).

This outcome does not conflict with publishers' exclusive rights under the Copyright Act. Individual copyright holders remain free to choose whether to license their works through ASCAP. They thus remain free to license—or to refuse to license—public performance rights to whomever they choose. Regardless of whether publishers choose to utilize ASCAP's services, however, ASCAP is still required to operate within the confines of the consent decree.

The partially withdrawn works at issue remain in the ASCAP repertory pursuant to the plain language of the consent decree. Since section VI of the decree provides for blanket licenses covering *all* works contained in the ASCAP repertory, it necessarily follows that the partial withdrawals do not affect the scope of Pandora's license.

## II. Rate-Setting

We review the district court's rate determination for reasonableness. *See Broad. Music, Inc. v. DMX Inc.,* 683 F.3d 32, 45 (2d Cir.2012). This review involves two components: "we must find both that the rate is substantively reasonable (that it is not based on any clearly erroneous findings of fact) and that it is procedurally reasonable (that the setting of the rate, including the choice and adjustment of a benchmark, is not based on legal errors)." *United States v. Broad. Music, Inc.,* 426 F.3d 91, 96 (2d Cir.2005). The district court's factual findings are reviewed for clear error, and conclusions of law are reviewed *de novo. See ASCAP v. MobiTV, Incorporation,* 681 F.3d 76, 82 (2d Cir.2012).

Having reviewed the record and the district court's detailed examination thereof, we conclude that the district court did not commit clear error in its evaluation of the evidence or in its ultimate determination that a 1.85% rate was reasonable for the duration of the Pandora-ASCAP license. We likewise conclude that the district court's legal determinations underlying that ultimate conclusion—including its rejection of various alternative benchmarks proffered by ASCAP—were sound. *Cf. ASCAP v. Showtime/The Movie Channel, Inc.,* 912 F.2d 563, 571 (2d Cir.1990) ("Ultimately, the Magistrate weighed all of the evidence and found, as a matter of fact, that ASCAP had not sustained its burden of proving that its price . . . was reasonable. No legal error contributed to that finding, and the finding itself, adequately supported by the record, is not clearly erroneous.").

Although ASCAP challenges the district court's presumption that a rate found to be reasonable for part of a license term remains reasonable for the duration thereof, the district court expressly observed that its holding did not depend on the existence of such a presumption. ASCAP failed to carry its burden of proving that its proposed rate was reasonable. Under these circumstances, it was not clearly erroneous for the district court to conclude, given the evidence before it, that a rate of 1.85% was reasonable for the years in question.

Nor was it an abuse of discretion for the district court to refuse ASCAP's request for additional discovery regarding recent Pandora licenses. *See generally Goetz v. Crosson,* 41 F.3d 800, 805 (2d Cir.1994) ("Discovery rulings are reviewed for abuse of discretion."). As the district court correctly observed, contextual evidence would have been necessary in order to determine whether those licenses could serve as reliable benchmarks. The district court acted well within its discretion in declining to delay trial to accommodate this discovery, and it therefore follows *a fortiori* that the court did not commit legal error in failing to consider these potential benchmarks when setting the Pandora-ASCAP licensing rate.

## CONCLUSION

We have considered Appellants' remaining arguments and find them to be without merit. For the foregoing reasons, we AFFIRM the orders of the district court.

---

Consider the broader policy questions raised by these branches of entertainment law. First, as a matter of economic analysis, how much difference do variations in the legal background make in actual financial outcomes? Recall the divergence in treatment of music rights on films being shown in theaters and films being shown on television. Ever since *Alden-Rochelle*, theater owners can require that film producers get and keep the performance rights from composers and convey to the theater the right to play the music on the sound system at the same time as it is playing the film on the screen. By contrast, before and after the Supreme Court's verdict in *CBS*, for films that are shown on television (including those that were first exhibited in a theater) the composers get and keep the performance rights in their music on the soundtrack, and with the help of ASCAP and BMI are paid a fee whenever the film is shown on network, cable, or local television. How do these different practices affect the comparative amounts paid for soundtrack performance by theater owners and television owners as a whole? The amounts paid to composers for having written the music on the soundtracks? The amounts earned by famous composers (e.g. John Williams) as compared to unknown ones?

Consider the even starker differences in the legal situation of performer unions under labor law. ASCAP can negotiate on behalf of its songwriter members for the sale of performance rights in music to CBS and Paramount. However, these collective licensing agreements must leave CBS and Paramount the option of direct negotiations with individual composers at rates that may be more favorable to the firms than are the group rates. If the collective negotiations with ASCAP do not produce an attractive enough offer, CBS and Paramount have the option of going to the rate court to arbitrate the new rate.

Suppose that CBS and Paramount had sought the same arrangement from their performer unions, such as SAG (whose members include Julia Roberts and Tom Hanks as well as the bit players), the Directors Guild (with Steven Spielberg and Steven Soderbergh), and the Writers Guild (with Joe Eszterhas and Cameron Crowe). What do you think would be the unions' reaction? Should labor law be amended to give employers the same rights as the purchasers of music performance rights? Or antitrust law to give music writers the same rights as movie performers? Are there real differences between the situations of performers selling their services and songwriters selling their music that justify their different treatment under federal law?

# CHAPTER 12

# ENTERTAINMENT CONGLOMERATES UNDER CORPORATE AND ANTITRUST LAW[a]

■ ■ ■

The previous chapter examined the organization of talent in the entertainment industry, and the treatment that performer unions receive under labor and antitrust law. In this and the following chapter, we shall study the organization of the firms that produce, distribute, and exhibit creative works. This chapter will focus on the movie industry and its treatment under antitrust law. The next chapter will focus on the broadcast and cable industry and its regulation under federal communications law.

The entertainment industry is at a crossroads in this new millennium. Home computer and Internet services are now not only major instruments for work, but also for entertainment. There are now a host of new methods to enjoy entertainment products, ranging from books to movies, television shows, music and videos, and interactive media. This "information superhighway," combining rapidly developed new technologies, and consumers' increasing demand for these products, has forced firms to make major investment decisions to keep up in their industry. The favored course taken by most firms in this environment has been integration along both vertical and horizontal lines. "Horizontal" integration involves expansion across the same product setting in which the firm now operates, and "vertical" integration either goes backward to incorporate suppliers or forward to the firm's product users. Both these key moves have now been made in this industry, which is dominated by a small number of huge entertainment conglomerates.

In the mid-1980s, Rupert Murdoch's Australian-based News Corporation acquired the Twentieth Century Fox movie studio, created the Fox Television network, and combined these with a worldwide collection of broadcasters, publishers, and magazines. Shortly thereafter,

---

[a] *See* Harold L. Vogel, *Entertainment Industry Economics: A Guide for Financial Analysis* (Camb. U. Press, 8th ed. 2010); Dan Steinbock, *Triumph & Erosion of the American Media & Entertainment Industries* (Quorum Books 1995); Janet Wasko, *Hollywood in the Information Age* (U. Tex. Press 1995); Jason E. Squire, ed., *The Movie Business Book* (Simon & Schuster, 3d ed. 2004); Richard C. Caves, *Creative Industries: Contracts Between Art & Commerce* (Harv. Univ. Press 2000).

Japan's Sony Corporation bought CBS' record labels (for $2 billion) and Coca-Cola's Columbia Pictures studio (for $3.4 billion).[b] In 1989, the largest entertainment company in the world was created when Time, Inc. and Warner Communications completed a $14 billion merger following a protracted battle with Paramount for corporate control. Time Warner's holdings included a film studio, record label, cable television system, a variety of book publishers and magazines, and eventually a new Warner network on which to distribute its television programming. Five years later, Sumner Redstone's Viacom spent $10 billion to take over Paramount Communications and the retail home video giant, Blockbuster.

By 1995, these earlier mergers seemed merely a dress rehearsal for the explosion in entertainment conglomerates then taking place. First came the $5.7 billion purchase by Seagram, a Canadian liquor manufacturer, of 80 percent ownership of Universal-MCA, a movie and music producer whose performance had disappointed its prior owner, Matsushita Electric Industrial. Then, in a single week in August, two of the four major networks changed hands. CBS was purchased by Westinghouse for $5.4 billion and ABC-Capital Cities bought by Walt Disney Company for $19 billion. The latter deal married one of the largest and most successful movie studios (and theme park operators) with what was then the highest-rated broadcast network, the top sports cable channel (ESPN), and a variety of other cable channels and publishing arms. Just one month later, Time Warner sought to regain its title as the largest entertainment conglomerate in the world when (for $7.5 billion) it agreed to buy the Turner Broadcasting System (TBS), with its roster of cable channels (WTBS, CNN, and TNT) and film production arms (New Line Cinema and Castle Rock).

The end of the 1990s witnessed another series of entertainment purchases and mergers. Seagram acquired Polygram for $10.5 billion, with this combination of two of the top six record companies making it the largest music power. Seagram then merged with the French corporate giant Vivendi SA, which had begun as a water utility system, but by then owned Europe's largest pay-television channel, a portion of its largest satellite arm BSkyB, and a major Internet service. In 2001, Vivendi Universal spent $370 million to acquire MP3.com which it had sued the year before for facilitating consumer access to albums on the Internet, and $2.2 billion for Houghton Mifflin, the last major independent publisher. This Boston-based firm had begun in 1832 with authors like Emerson, Hawthorne, Longfellow, Thoreau and the Alcotts, and just before this Vivendi deal had published *The Wind Done Gone*. Vivendi spent $11.7 billion to acquire the cable television units of USA Networks

---

[b] *See* Nancy Griffin & Kim Masters, *Hit & Run: How Jon Peters & Peter Guber Took Sony For a Ride in Hollywood* (Simon & Schuster 1996).

and $1.5 billion for a 10 percent share in EchoStar's satellite operation (which was then seeking to merge with DirecTV). Meanwhile, in 1999, Redstone and his Viacom team paid a record-setting $40 billion to acquire CBS. That record was quickly topped by the unprecedented merger of Time Warner and America Online (AOL), the Internet service, at a $165 billion value. That last pioneering marriage of entertainment content and Internet access was then caught up in a year-long struggle not only as to stock pricing, but also with the Federal Trade Commission (FTC) administering antitrust law.

More recently, mergers have continued, with some of the above-named entities being sold. In 2015, for example, Verizon purchased AOL for $4 billion. Regulators allowed AT&T to acquire DirecTV for $49 billion, also in 2015, which enabled AT&T to diversify the markets in which it participates. On the other hand, in 2014, Comcast announced a deal to merge with Time Warner; regulators quashed this transaction because of concerns regarding competition. As this book goes to press, Charter Communications is seeking to acquire Time Warner Cable for $78.7 billion. Only time will tell how many of these combinations will last longer than the original AOL-Time Warner deal.

The trend toward integration of entertainment entities may reflect the desire of industry leaders not just to coordinate but also to control both the creation of entertainment products and their dissemination to consumers. It is precisely that concentration of market power that antitrust law had been designed to combat. From the 1940s through the 1970s, the federal government intervened in a variety of ways to block integration. More recent administrations have taken a more laissez-faire approach in the 1980s to the present day. Scaling back the reach of government regulation, the Justice Department has placed greater confidence in a self-regulating marketplace. This hands-off approach proved conducive to the consolidation of disparate entertainment holdings in that period. However, especially with what was then a strongly-debated Time Warner-AOL merger, the Justice Department wrestled with whether antitrust law (or telecommunications law, which we will study in the next chapter) should be used to contain such corporate expansions.

The desirability of this trend is also a hotly-debated issue within the entertainment world. Some scholars see the emergence of large multimedia conglomerates as a step toward greater efficiency in the industry. They contend that the diversity of entertainment products and modes of distribution ensures that strong competition will always be present in the industry. Unlike the 1940s and 1950s, when a few film studios were dominant, there is little need today to worry about the anticompetitive implications of corporate integration. Other analysts place less confidence in market self-regulation and believe that government intervention is important to protect the public from conglomerates with economic power within the industry. This is the fundamental policy debate to keep in mind as you read the next two chapters.

## A. PARAMOUNT AND CORPORATE TAKEOVER LAW

As noted above, Redstone made Paramount one of the key steps in his creation of an entertainment conglomerate that started with his family's National Amusement movie theaters and has now brought in CBS. On the way, though, Paramount played a major role in shaping the entertainment world. One major focus of this chapter will be Paramount's antitrust litigation and its consequences. As a prelude, though, we will briefly examine the way that corporate law facilitates purchases or mergers of existing media firms and secures for shareholders the best price for their capital. Paramount has figured in two of the major decisions in this area by the Supreme Court of Delaware, the legal home of most major corporations and thus a principal source of U.S. corporate law.[c]

In 1989, the boards of Warner Communications and Time, Inc. declared their intention to merge the two companies. The principal architect of this deal, Steve Ross, considered his new acquisition's principal value to lie in Warner Music, which was then emerging as a significant label in the burgeoning record industry. Ross also had Warner stake out an important role in the new field of cable delivery systems. While each of these industries had its ups and downs over the next two decades, by the end of the 1980s Warner was a major player in the entertainment world.

So also was Time, Inc. In the popular mind, Time was identified with its publication side (its namesake magazine), as well as Life, People, Sports Illustrated, and Entertainment Weekly. By the 1980s, though, Time's major revenue source lay in the distribution of audiovisual products. Not only did Time have the third largest collection of cable systems around the country (Warner was number six), but it also had created the pioneering arm in cable programming, Home Box Office. Rather than simply use cable to transmit broadcast programming, Time assigned several of its young employees (including Gerald Levin and

---

[c] For popular accounts of the two Paramount takeover battles, see Connie Bruck, *Master of the Game: Steve Ross & the Creation of Time Warner* (Simon & Schuster 1994); Connie Bruck, *Jerry's Deal*, The New Yorker 54 (2/19/1996); Ken Auletta, *Redstone's Secret Weapon*, The New Yorker 46 (1/26/1995). On the legal issues, see Paul L. Regan, *The Unimportance of Being Earnest:* Paramount *Rewrites the Rules For Enhanced Scrutiny In Corporate Takeovers*, 46 Hast. L.J. 125 (1994); Steven J. Fink, *The Rebirth of the Tender Offer?* Paramount Communications Inc. v. QVC Network, Inc., 20 Del. J. Corp. L. 133 (1995).

Michael Fuchs) to develop HBO's new pay cable programming service, consisting principally of recent Hollywood movies, special sporting events such as boxing matches, and eventually a number of programs made specifically for cable. Levin made the key move in 1975 when he paid to have HBO signals sent to satellite systems for instantaneous transmission to every cable system around the country. Not only did HBO become the major cash flow source for Time, Inc., but also the driving force for cable systems themselves. While most people in metropolitan areas could readily pick up television channels with no more than an antenna, the only way they could watch HBO and its successors was by signing up for cable.

Ross initiated merger negotiations between Warner and Time based on his perception of the value of distribution channels to the creators of entertainment products. Warner Bros. Pictures could enjoy preferred access to HBO, through which it could reach this crucial audience for films (including those made just for cable), and HBO would have the leverage of its parent's huge collection of local cable systems (second only to John Malone's TeleCommunications, Inc. (TCI)) to secure favorable terms for such access.

The heads of the two companies quickly negotiated a merger deal whereby the shareholders of each company would exchange their stock for a specified percentage of the shares in the new Time Warner. Time shareholders would own 38 percent of the new entity and Warner shareholders 62 percent, and each company would appoint 12 members to Time Warner's board of directors. Ross would be the company's initial head, but his designated successor was Nick Nicholas, then the heir-apparent at Time. Several "poison pill" features were added to Time's corporate bylaws to deter any outside bidders from seeking to supplant Warner in this merger. A key benefit to this mode of creating a $15 billion entertainment conglomerate (one that would supplant the German corporation, Bertelsmann A.G., as then the largest in the industry) is that it would have only $2.5 billion in debt.

As it turned out, Time's combination of cable programming and cable delivery was attractive not just to Warner, but also to Paramount. Twenty years earlier, Paramount Pictures had been just one subsidiary of a wide-ranging conglomerate, Gulf & Western. After Martin Davis took over Gulf & Western in 1984, he soon pared down the company to its entertainment industry core: the Paramount movie studio, a major book publisher (Simon & Schuster), and a sports arm (Madison Square Garden with its New York Knicks and Rangers). By the end of the 1980s, the now renamed Paramount Communications was considering how to enlarge and diversify its strategic position. When Davis heard of Time's proposed "friendly" merger with Warner, he decided to try to acquire Time's assets for his own company. Thus, just two weeks before the Time and Warner shareholders were to cast their votes on the proposed merger, Paramount made a surprise "hostile" bid of $175 per share in cash for all outstanding Time stock, which was then trading at $125. The only condition on this offer was that the Time board had to remove the poison pill provisions that would render the company's acquisition financially unattractive to Paramount.

Time's executives and board members did not like the Paramount proposal, but they realized that Time shareholders were not likely to cast their votes in favor of a speculative Time Warner merger and against this immediate financial windfall. Thus, Time and Warner recast their corporate venture into a $14 billion cash acquisition of Warner by Time. Unlike a merger, Time shareholders had no right under the company's bylaws to vote on such a business acquisition. While Davis boosted Paramount's offer for Time to $200 per share, the board members remained firmly against it. The rationale they offered was that, unlike the terms of the agreement with Warner, submerging Time into Paramount would endanger the culture of "journalistic integrity" at Time, one that had always sought to separate editorial independence (the "church") from the business side (the "state").

Paramount (joined by a number of aggrieved Time shareholders) sued Time to force its board to conduct an open auction for its shares, rather than go through with the acquisition by Warner. Paramount's claim rested on a recent Supreme Court of Delaware decision, *Revlon v. MacAndrews & Forbes Holdings, Inc.*, 506 A.2d 173, 184 (Del. 1986), which held that in the circumstances of that case, "the directors' role changed from defenders of the corporate bastion to auctioneers charged with getting the best price for the stockholders at a sale of the company." However, in *Paramount Communications v. Time, Inc.*, 571 A.2d 1140 (Del. 1989), the court read its earlier *Revlon* decision as addressing two situations; first, "when a corporation initiates an active bidding process seeking to sell itself," and second, "where in response to a bidder's offer a target . . . seeks an alternative transaction involving the breakup of the company." *Id.* at 1150. Here the court concluded that the Time-Warner merger constituted a long range strategic plan about the best way to enhance the value of the two companies' assets, and shareholders would retain essentially the same ownership and control in the new entity as in the prior one. In these circumstances, the Delaware courts would not require directors to conduct a takeover auction. The Time-Warner merger went through and the largest-ever entertainment conglomerate was born-though now it was saddled with a $15 billion debt service for having paid a premium to acquire Warner's stock.

After losing the battle for Time, Paramount continued its search for an acquisition partner. One of the companies it focused on was Viacom, controlled by Sumner Redstone. Redstone built his family-owned theaters into the largest privately held chain in the country. In 1987, Redstone made his first major foray into entertainment takeovers when he acquired Viacom, best known for channels like Showtime and MTV. The company had been formed in 1971 when the government forced CBS to divest its syndicated program holdings because of the FCC's new Financial Interest and Syndication rules (examined in Chapter 13). After an investment group led by inside management proposed to take Viacom private by buying out the existing shareholders for $2.7 billion, Redstone initiated a bidding war that eventually won him the company for $3.4 billion, as it turned out, a very profitable investment.

Paramount's Martin Davis found the prospect of a corporate marriage with Viacom and Redstone an alluring one. In 1993, after several years of sporadic discussions, Paramount and Viacom announced their plans for blending the two entertainment giants, with Redstone as Chairman and Davis as President. Paramount shareholders would receive a combination of cash and (largely non-voting) Viacom stock, whose market value was roughly $69 per share and slightly under $8 billion for the entire company. "Lock up" terms were included in the merger agreement, designed to give Viacom an edge if any outside bidders appeared on the scene. These terms included both a $100 million fee for Viacom if its agreement was terminated, plus an option to buy 20 percent of Paramount's stock at $69/share—even better, the right to require Paramount to buy out that stock option by paying Viacom in cash for any increase in its stock price above $69, something that would be inevitable in a takeover battle.

Before long Paramount found itself on the other side of the corporate law issues that it had faced in its battle for Time. QVC, the home shopping network, made its own bid for control of Paramount at approximately $80 a share (or about $8.5 billion). Interestingly, QVC was led by its Chairman, Barry Diller, who had previously worked with Martin Davis at Paramount. In the mid-1970s, Diller (and his protege, Michael Eisner) moved over to Paramount where Diller ran Paramount Pictures for a decade before a falling out with Davis about their respective roles in the firm. In 1984, Diller joined Twentieth Century Fox (and Eisner went to Walt Disney), where Diller helped launch Rupert Murdoch's Fox Television Network. Diller left Fox in 1992, when Murdoch also refused to grant him a more prominent role in the company. Longing to be his own boss, Diller bought a large stake in QVC in 1993, and began seeking opportunities to re-enter the entertainment industry at the top. In that plan, Diller was backed by John Malone, whose TCI was the largest cable distributor in the country and whose Liberty Media Corp. was the largest shareholder in QVC.

When Paramount failed to respond to QVC's merger bid in 1993, QVC filed suit against Paramount in an effort to enjoin its use of lockup obstacles to bidders against Viacom, and thus permit QVC to participate in an auction for Paramount on equal footing. At the same time, Diller made a hostile tender offer for Paramount at $80 per share for 51 percent of the stock. Redstone and Paramount then revised Viacom's friendly tender offer to $85 per share for 51 percent of the Paramount stock, prompting Diller to raise QVC's bid to $90 per share. Believing they were in the same legal position as Time had been four years earlier, Davis and the Paramount directors recommended that Redstone's lower offer be accepted because they concluded that Viacom provided a better strategic alliance.

When the Delaware Supreme Court heard this case, though, it sided with QVC and held that the Paramount board had not fulfilled its legal obligation to its shareholders to conduct an open and fair bidding war for the company. *See Paramount Communications v. QVC Network*, 637 A.2d 34 (Del. 1994). The court was critical of the defensive measures that the Paramount board had adopted in an effort to favor Viacom's bid. The court distinguished *Time-Warner* by holding that the proposed Viacom-Paramount merger was actually a sale, because the transaction would deliver a controlling interest in Paramount to Viacom, rather than to the "fluid aggregation of unaffiliated stockholders" in *Time-Warner*. Since the company was deemed "in play," Paramount directors had a duty to conduct an auction on a level playing field to maximize shareholder gains:

> [W]hen a corporation undertakes a transaction which will cause: (a) a change in corporate control; *or* (b) a breakup of the corporate entity, the directors' obligation is to seek the best value reasonably available to stock-holders. This obligation arises because the effect of the Viacom-Paramount transaction, if consummated, is to shift control of Paramount from the public stockholders to a controlling stockholder, Viacom.

*Id.* at 48. Unlike Time, then, control over Paramount would go to the highest bidder.

What do *Time-Warner* and *Paramount* mean for future takeover efforts in the entertainment industry? Directors are still permitted to reject hostile bidders, based on a business judgment that the shareholders will eventually realize more value if the company stays on its current course. Management's pursuit of a merger, however, can trigger the duty to conduct a fair and open bidding war if control of the new company will pass to a dominant shareholder, as was contemplated between Paramount and Viacom. At that point the remaining shareholders are considered to have lost the additional value that comes from their ability to influence majority votes about the firm's business strategy, and thus are deemed entitled to competitive bidding to set a market value for that feature of their holdings. In effect, corporate boards cannot "Just Say Yes" to one apparently friendly bidder.

These legal standards can have a substantial impact on the decisions of entertainment companies in planning for the future. Corporate law scholars have criticized the current state of the law on contrasting grounds. On the one hand, the law seems to allow top management to protect its own position through poison pills (whose rationale is to protect shareholders from two-tier takeover bids that offer a premium just to the first 51 percent of shares that are tendered to the bidder). On the other hand, the law makes directors less willing and able to secure friendly mergers that might provide shareholders with substantial premiums, because of their concern that a court will intervene and force them to subject the company to a potential takeover from a hostile bidder. Do you agree with these criticisms? Should shareholders be entitled to have a vote on any tender offer for a majority (or all) of their shares? Or should directors have more flexibility in choosing whether to accept or reject takeover bids? How can the board's obligation to maximize shareholder premiums be balanced with its desire to pursue long-term plans believed to be in the best interests of the company?[d]

---

The Delaware Supreme Court's decision in *QVC* only intensified the battle for control of Paramount. In preparation for a bidding war, both Viacom and QVC secured capital infusions from third parties who recognized Paramount's value. After QVC made what appeared to be the winning bid in 1994, Viacom countered with a $107 per share offer that enabled Redstone to best Diller for the Paramount prize. Viacom's final winning bid amounted to a total price of approximately $10 billion. Paramount had just been bought by the man whose career took off when he purchased many of the movie theaters that Paramount had been forced to divest itself of by an antitrust decision more than 40 years earlier (a decision we will read shortly). Both Paramount and Redstone had come full circle (but ironically, Martin Davis was now out of the picture).

---

[d] *See* Ralph Cassady Jr., *Impact of the* Paramount *Decision on Motion Picture Distribution & Price Making*, 31 So. Cal. L. Rev. 150 (1958); Michael Conant, *The* Paramount *Decrees Reconsidered*, 44 Law & Contemp. Probs. 79 (1981); Arthur De Vany & Ross D. Eckert, *Motion Picture Antitrust: The* Paramount *Cases Revisited*, 14 Res. Law & Econ. 51 (1991); Patricia M. Cox, *What Goes Up Must Come Down: Grounding the Dizzying Height of Vertical Mergers in the Entertainment Industry*, 25 Hofstra L. Rev. 261 (1996); Thomas A. Piraino, Jr. *A Proposed Antitrust Analysis of Telecommunications Joint Ventures*, 1997 Wis. L. Rev. 639; Jon M. Garon, *Media & Monopoly in the Information Age: Slowing the Convergence of the Marketplace of Ideas*, 17 Cardozo Arts & Ent. L.J. 491 (1999); Douglas L. Rogers, *Give the Smaller Players a Chance: Shaping the Digital Economy Through Antitrust & Copyright Law*, 5 Marq. Int. Prop. L. Rev. 13 (2001); Barak Y. Orbach, *Antitrust & Pricing in the Motion Picture Industry*, 21 Yale J. Reg. 317 (2004).

In order to best QVC and its allies, Redstone also had to seek additional financial support. His key ally, one that he eventually absorbed into Viacom, was then one of the entertainment industry's biggest "cash cows"—the Blockbuster Entertainment Group. The world's largest video retailer had been a 19 outlet video chain with $7 million in annual revenue when its Chairman, Wayne Huizenga, bought a 35% stake in 1987. Within six years, he had turned Blockbuster into an industry giant. At the time of its acquisition by Viacom, Blockbuster had 3600 video stores, 500 music stores, over $2 billion in annual sales, and $230 million in 1993 profits. Blockbuster was attractive to Redstone because it would help Viacom pay off its debt from the Paramount acquisition. The home video market, which produces half of all movie studio revenue, also offered a key route for Viacom to distribute its Paramount products to consumers.

The addition of Paramount and Blockbuster enlarged Redstone-Viacom from 5,000 to 75,000 employees, and its overall revenues reached the number two position in the entertainment world. Three years later Redstone acquired CBS for $45 billion, without any financial bidding or corporate law challenges.

---

Shortly after the Time-Warner merger, Steve Ross was diagnosed with what proved to be fatal cancer. Gerald Levin was able to outmaneuver Ross' designated successor, Nick Nicholas, and to assume leadership of Time-Warner when Ross died. In that role, though, Levin was to find that a company carrying over $15 billion in debt did not fare well in the financial markets. By 1995, Time Warner's stock was still 20 percent below the $200/share level that had been offered by Paramount in 1989, although the Dow Jones index had more than doubled in that period. The solution that Levin fashioned was yet further expansion of Time Warner, through acquisition of Ted Turner's TBS in exchange for $7.5 billion of new Time Warner stock.

In the 1970s, TBS was a small independent television station in Atlanta. Turner capitalized on the new technological capacity for satellite distribution of programming to cable systems across the country to make his WTBS the country's first "superstation," showing old movies and live sporting events (i.e., Turner's baseball Braves and basketball Hawks). With that lucrative cash base, Turner expanded into new cable channels, such as CNN, TNT, and the Cartoon Network, and into moviemaking through his New Line Cinema and Castle Rock Entertainment, which produced films for both his cable channels and theaters. Turner also bought a huge stockpile of classic movies from MGM/UA, some of which he proceeded to show in new "colorized" versions on Turner Movie Classics (TMC).

To finance this $7.5 billion entertainment vehicle from a small Atlanta base, Turner had to secure significant investment from outside sources. One such source was Time Warner, which in return received 18 percent of TBS shares. Another key investor was John Malone's TCI, with smaller contributions from Comcast and Continental Cablevision. Malone's cable systems posed a problem, because by 1995 TCI was covering 25 percent of the nation's homes. Time Warner was the nation's second largest cable system operator, covering roughly 15 percent of homes. The combination of the two would far exceed the 30 percent cable coverage limit then imposed by the FCC. Because the Time Warner/TBS merger was an exchange of stock, TCI's existing stake in TBS would give it 8 percent of Time Warner (behind only Turner at 10 percent and Seagram's at 9 percent). That level of minority ownership in Time Warner made it likely that federal authorities would reject the Time Warner/TBS merger.

The solution devised by the corporate lawyers was to make TCI a purely passive investor in Time Warner by having its stock put in a trust, with Levin having authority to exercise the voting rights in Time Warner decisions (about cable or other matters). To secure Malone's consent, Levin and Turner had to agree to give TCI a twenty-year distribution contract at a 15 percent discount for TBS cable channels such as TNT and CNN. TCI's cable system rivals, Comcast and Continental, who both were to own much less than 5 percent of Time Warner's stock, were upset because they did not get the same deal from TBS. The FTC investigated this Time Warner/TCI voting arrangement, but eventually granted antitrust approval to the merger in return for a number of concessions extracted from Time Warner. TCI's cable discount deal was to be revoked; TCI's stock in Time Warner would be made non-voting; Time Warner would not bundle its cable channels but instead would offer each on an *a la carte* basis to other cable systems; and it would provide room on its own cable network for another news channel to compete with Turner's CNN.

---

The assumption behind mergers of different entertainment arms—from publishing, to filmmaking or music recording, to radio, television, and cable, and now the Internet—is that these various components possess qualities that, when utilized together, can generate a whole that is greater than the sum of its parts. As Disney CEO Michael Eisner put it when asked why he was putting up $19 billion to acquire ABC, he was totally optimistic that one plus one will add up to four, because the two bodies will find "synergies under every rock" in their relationship. These entertainment mergers display two fundamental issues: whether pursuing such expansion makes sense as a matter of business strategy, and whether facilitating the expansion makes sense as a matter of legal policy.

With respect to business strategy, a decade prior to Viacom an intriguing counter-example had already emerged in a related telecommunications industry. Recall that in 1995, Time Warner agreed to pay a significant premium to acquire TBS and again make it the world's largest entertainment company. That very same week, AT&T announced that it was going to break up into three fully independent entities. One firm would focus on telecommunication services, a second on telecommunication equipment, and a third on computers. Management of these three new firms could continue the existing production and distribution relationships among these current divisions of AT&T. They would be equally free, though, to buy or sell their products and services from and develop new joint ventures with other participants in the marketplace. By 2001, AT&T had decided to dispose of its cable operations to Comcast, though it still had a minority share of the new AT&T Comcast. The latter had outbid AOL Time Warner to make itself the dominant power in this industry.

*AT&T* and *Viacom* pose the critical business question of whether (and when) there really is more economic value in single corporate ownership and control than in contractual relationships negotiated in a competitive market. How would you assess the relevant variables in such an analysis? Does common ownership create more opportunities for collaboration, better guarantees of product distribution, greater diversification across product markets, or simple economies of scale? Are there distinctive features of the entertainment world that suggest that a bigger and more diversified, or a smaller and more focused, organization is best suited for its unpredictable creative process?

Of course, one vehicle through which individual firms can justify paying a premium for expansion is by reducing the market options left open to other firms and their consumers. In the entertainment world this may involve control over the outlets available to producers (e.g., films needing to be shown in theaters, on television, or via video rental), or control of cable programming available to cable services. This is the point where the law comes in, with two different branches addressing such corporate power in the marketplace. The branch that is the focus of this chapter is antitrust law, which historically has been especially relevant to the movie industry. The other branch, FCC regulation of the broadcasting and cable industry, is the subject of the next chapter.

---

Before looking at antitrust law in the next section, it is helpful to learn something about a radically new corporate offering that has appeared in the entertainment industry. In 1997, rock star David Bowie turned his record (and copyright) portfolio into a major business asset through a device called "securitization." Securitization had initially been created in the 1970's as a technique for pooling home mortgages to make this resource more available to ordinary Americans at somewhat lower prices. In the 1980s, corporate securitization was expanded to include automobile loans, small business loans, credit card receivables, and the like. By the late 1990s, this financial instrument was annually generating several hundred billion dollars in financial investments, topping, for example, corporate bonds. By 2010, securitization received negative publicity because of its role in the financial crisis, but it remains important in financial markets.

The nature of securitization can be understood through the David Bowie example. Bowie retained copyright in several hundred of his songs that had been released by EMI Music. This meant that every year Bowie received royalties from reproduction and sale of the records, performance rights when the songs were played on radio stations, and even for printed versions of the song. A financial expert, David Pullman, created a Special Purpose Vehicle (SPV) to which his client, Bowie, as Originator (i.e., owner) transferred these individual "receivable" assets. The SPV then issued a bond whose value was given a financial rating by Moody Investor Services. Pleased by Moody's AAA rating, Prudential Insurance then paid $55 million in cash to Bowie to purchase this SPV bond, whose interest and repayment would be satisfied by the revenue streams generated by his music.

The following are among the key features of securitization. First, all assets are pooled to reduce the risks from any one song and to enhance the financial value of the whole. Second, these assets are isolated from any others owned by the artist, leaving the latter available for use by Bowie. Third, because ownership of the asset is transferred to the SPV, it is insulated from any bankruptcy or other debt proceedings that the artist's other activities may generate. This combination of pooling and insulation of the copyright assets makes them a diversified, safe, and attractive investment by Prudential, thus raising its price.

Rather than have to wait for the potential flow of music revenues over future decades (with two more added by the 1998 *Sonny Bono Act* covered in Chapter 5), an artist like Bowie can use this asset to raise all the immediate capital he needs for current professional, financial, or personal ventures. Because this is an SPV *bond* being purchased by the outside investor as a loan rather than a sale, there are no capital gains taxes on the transaction. After Bowie (and Pullman) displayed the value of this new financial asset, its use soon expanded. Not only did Pullman create a new Pullman Structured Asset Sales Group (PSASG) designed to sell "celebrity bonds," e.g., for three Motown songwriters who raised $30 million from the sale of 300 of their songs. Prudential's Entertainment

Finance International (EFI) raised $10 million for Dusty Springfield from the "loan" of her songs.

It should be noted that in the case of Bowie, one key reason for his SPV's AAA rating was that Bowie's long-time record company EMI had provided a backstop guarantee of the bulk of the record bond. By 1999, though, truly independent SPV's had been fashioned for both the Motown songwriters and the group Iron Maiden. While the latter's bond attracted just a BBB rating from Standard & Poor's, it still did quite well in the financial market.

Of course, it is one thing to use corporate, securities, and tax law to pool the value of a large roster of intellectual property rights owned by long-time stars like Bowie and Springfield. The bigger challenge is whether this device can be made available to newer artists, not just for making records, but for producing, distributing, and promoting far more expensive movies. Soon after the new DreamWorks studio had been created by Steven Spielberg, Jeff Katzenberg, and David Geffen, it used a (guaranteed) variation of securitization (a Dreamworks Film Trust) to raise $325 million for a total of 18 films (including *Amistad* produced before the bond was issued and *Saving Private Ryan* afterwards). But when a new and unknown TLC or Toni Braxton first appears on the music scene, or their counterparts in the movie world, there seems to be no possibility that an individual and non-guaranteed SPV created just for their forthcoming songs or films would have any significant value in the financial world. Thus, we will next consider whether a large group of such artists, each with one or two albums recorded or film scripts written, can effectively combine these works into a single portfolio, so as to be able to gain access to the capital markets in a manner analogous to Americans taking out home mortgages since the 1970s. In the meantime, newcomer artists will have to deal individually with the entertainment conglomerates to have their works produced.

## B. ANTITRUST LAW RESHAPES THE MOVIE BUSINESS

The role of corporate law is to facilitate the accumulation of capital in business enterprises and to safeguard the rights of shareholders in decisions made by *their* representatives—directors and managers. The role of antitrust law is to safeguard the rights of consumers and others who deal with these enterprises from the exercise of excessive market power derived from the organization of capital and the elimination of competition. Perhaps no other industry has been as subject to close antitrust scrutiny and restrictions as entertainment, particularly the movie world.

Before scrutinizing this more current use of antitrust law, we should look back to the early use of antitrust law in the movie industry. Indeed, the emergence of the movie industry in the early 1920s had been made possible by antitrust litigation against the Motion Picture Patent Trust created in New Jersey by Thomas Edison and his fellow inventors of movie technology. Two decades later, the way in which the five major Hollywood studios (Paramount, MGM, RKO, Warner, and Fox) had organized the production, distribution, and exhibition of their films attracted a series of antitrust complaints in 1938.

After ten years of discovery and litigation, the studios chose to avoid the potentially devastating outcome of a trial and instead opted to enter into consent decrees with the government. However, these were not consent decrees in the traditional sense. They were largely dictated by the courts after a series of findings had been made and remedies suggested: the Justice Department was given only limited leeway in negotiating the specifics of the final settlements.

Sixty years later, the consent decrees still operate as a limit on movie industry practices. Their immediate effect was the divestiture of film production and distribution from theater exhibition, and to prohibit studio practices such as block-booking, excessive clearance times, and the fixing of minimum admission prices. To adapt to future situations, the decrees empowered the courts to play a continuing supervisory role. For example, with respect to vertical integration, each consent judgment prohibited the defendant from acquiring a beneficial interest in a theater "unless [the defendant] shall show to the satisfaction of the Court, and the Court shall first find, that the acquisition will not unduly restrain competition."

The world has changed dramatically since these decrees were entered more than a half century ago. Judges and scholars have substantially altered their underlying conception of the role of antitrust law and the specifics of many antitrust doctrines. These changes will become evident from the courts' treatment of particular movie industry practices in this chapter. In the entertainment world, the film industry's dominant role was successfully challenged by television, which was just emerging when the decrees were signed in the late 1940s. With the passage of time, the defendants have sought to win exceptions to the prohibition against vertical integration in the film industry. With an approving nod from the Justice Department, movie companies are once again acquiring the exhibition companies they were forced to divest (as well as movie exhibitors like Sumner Redstone buying major studios like Paramount). However, the federal court overseeing the decrees has resisted undermining their force altogether. At their core, the consent decrees remain a contract by the movie companies with the government not to do those things that the parties had agreed at the time were violations of a Sherman Act whose judicial flavor seems quite different now.

---

As we saw in Chapter 11, the core provisions of antitrust law are contained in the Sherman Antitrust Act of 1890.[e] Section 1 makes illegal any "contract, combination, or conspiracy in restraint of trade," and Section 2 prohibits the effort by any person to "monopolize or attempt or conspire to monopolize trade." The premise of those crucial provisions (as well as of the Clayton Antitrust Act of 1914, which bars mergers whose effect "may be substantially to lessen competition or to tend to create a monopoly") is that a competitive marketplace is the ideal organization of our economic system.

In a world of perfect (or at least extensive) competition, the firms offering goods and services must struggle against other producers for the hearts and wallets of consumers. These competitive pressures force producers to enhance the quality of their products (both the film and the popcorn) and to reduce prices to a level just sufficient to pay for the costs of production, including the necessary return on capital investments. The source of these market pressures is the fact that if consumers do not like the price or quality of goods offered by one firm, they can take their patronage to another firm offering a better options.

The threat to a competitive marketplace stems from excessive power in the hands of a single entity or a group of producers who have entered into an agreement about how they will perform in that market. "Monopoly" is not the same as sheer size: companies as large as General Motors, IBM, and Sony have learned to their chagrin how little protection size provides against the forces of competition. Firms have a measure of monopoly power only if they have the ability to raise their prices above production costs without experiencing a decrease in profits, if not sales. The absence of competitive alternatives for the goods and services means that consumers will have to pay a higher price for the same product or buy lower quality products for the prices they can afford; this generates a transfer of wealth from customers to monopolist producers. Further, the amount of the good or service produced for and used by consumers will also drop. This "deadweight loss" for the economy as a whole is due to the fact that some factors of production (e.g., labor, equipment, and capital) that would have been most efficient at making the monopolist's products are diverted into producing less expensive goods for which they are not as well-suited.

---

[e] The major scholarly work on this subject is the multi-volume treatise by Phillip Areeda & Herbert Hovenkamp, *Antitrust Law* (2nd ed. 2003).

There is little disagreement about these immediate factual consequences of excessive market power. There is, however, an ongoing policy debate about whether and why legal intervention via antitrust litigation will actually leave the marketplace better or worse off.[f] One "populist" school contends that beyond harms done to allocative efficiency by monopoly power, antitrust law is also supposed to promote distributional equity-not just in economic terms but also in the dispersion of power in a democracy in which the entertainment media play a major role. Indeed, in a still controversial Supreme Court ruling about the Clayton Act, *Brown Shoe v. United States*, 370 U.S. 294, 344 (1962), Chief Justice Warren endorsed that position:

> [W]e cannot fail to recognize Congress' desire to promote competition through the protection of viable, small, locally owned businesses. Congress appreciated that occasional higher costs and prices might result from the maintenance of fragmented industries and markets. It resolved these competing considerations in favor of decentralization. We must give effect to that decision.

Beginning in the 1970s, though, there emerged a "Chicago School" of antitrust law and economics, which rejected the claim that distribution of either financial returns or cultural influence was a legitimate objective of antitrust policy. The only role of this branch of the law was to allow the market to maximize the total value of economic output, not to influence who would enjoy its fruits. Even with respect to the admitted deadweight economic losses from monopoly power, the Chicago School was skeptical of the view that legal intervention would always do more good than harm. In both their scholarship and their judicial opinions, such notable antitrust figures as Richard Posner, Frank Easterbrook, and Robert Bork have contended that many seemingly restrictive practices actually have pro-competitive values that legal barriers will deny to consumers, while even those restraints that on balance are anticompetitive will often dissipate if the market is left to itself.

This view of antitrust has influenced every administration since Ronald Reagan, though there remains a sharp debate among scholars, judges, and antitrust enforcers about whether self-correcting market forces or careful antitrust scrutiny are necessary to give American consumers and workers the protections they need in dealing with conglomerates.

---

[f] *See* Richard Posner, *The Chicago School of Antitrust Analysis*, 127 U. Penn. L. Rev. 925 (1979); Louis Kaplow, *Antitrust, Law & Economics, & the Courts*, 50 Law & Contemp. Probs. 181 (1987); Michael S. Jacobs, *An Essay on the Normative Foundations of Antitrust Economics*, 74 N.C. L. Rev. 219 (1995).

One of the most contentious issues is whether vertical integration poses a significant antitrust problem.[g] Chicago-school antitrust scholars and administrations tend to agree that a horizontal merger of two large movie studios or record labels may generate higher prices for movies or records. By contrast, when a movie studio or record company acquires a television network or Internet service to facilitate distribution of its product, this does not pose the obvious kinds of market risk that antitrust law is designed to address. Consumers still have the same number of studios and networks competing for their movie and television viewing or music listening.

It is possible, though, that the advantage secured by integrated firms will permit preferential (or exclusionary) practices that endanger the long-term viability of competitors. This potential damage to a competitive marketplace is, however, sufficiently speculative that it leaves a difficult question of whether courts should intervene to block the potentially "synergistic" collaboration of those who specialize in the production or distribution of entertainment works.

Even with respect to horizontal mergers, another crucial question is whether the firm thereby acquires market power that enables it to raise prices above cost. From an economic perspective, the immediate source of such power is "inelasticity of demand": consumers are not able to reduce their purchases even when a firm with market power raises its prices or lowers its product quality. The long-run source is "inelasticity of supply": despite the immediate presence of monopoly profits, barriers to entry obstruct the emergence of new competitors to give consumers an alternative source for their favored product.

In practice, it is extremely difficult in a courtroom to detect and measure monopoly power in the precise economic sense of the term. That is why the courts have adopted a surrogate doctrinal test: does the firm have a large share of the market, and are there entry barriers? That poses another difficult question, market definition. In our context, for example, is the relevant market just the making of movies to be shown in theaters, or film production for television, cable, home video, and the Internet, as well as theaters? Indeed, does the market encompass all forms of creative entertainment *works* (e.g., music and books as well as movies), or even all entertainment *activities* (such as theme parks, sports events, and gambling casinos)? What is the true scope of market competition faced in an entertainment industry in which both creative expression and technology are continually changing?

---

[g] *See* Michael H. Riordan & Stephen C. Salop, *Evaluating Vertical Mergers: A Post-Chicago Approach*, 63 Ant. L.J. 513 (1995); David Reiffen & Michael Vita, *Comment: Is There New Thinking on Vertical Mergers?* 63 Ant. L.J. 917 (1995); Michael H. Riordan & Stephen C. Salop, *Evaluating Vertical Mergers: Reply to Reiffen & Vita Comment*, 63 Ant. L.J. 943 (1995).

A major ruling on this topic is *United States v. E.I. du Pont de Nemours & Co.*, 351 U.S. 377 (1956). This case involved an antitrust complaint against du Pont, which at the time produced 75 percent of the nation's cellophane; however, cellophane constituted just 20 percent of all "flexible packaging materials." The following passages from the Court's opinion indicate how the scope of the market is to be defined:

> Market delimitation is necessary under du Pont's theory to determine whether an alleged monopolist violates § 2. The ultimate consideration in such a determination is whether the defendants control the price and competition in the market for such part of trade or commerce as they are charged with monopolizing. Every manufacturer is the sole producer of the particular commodity it makes, but its control in the above sense of the relevant market depends upon the availability of alternative commodities for buyers: i.e., whether there is a cross-elasticity of demand between cellophane and the other wrappings. This interchangeablity is largely gauged by the purchase of competing products for similar uses, considering the price, characteristics and adaptability of the competing commodities.
>
> * * *
>
> If a large number of buyers and sellers deal freely in a standardized product, such as salt or wheat, we have complete or pure competition. Patents, on the other hand, furnish the most familiar type of classic monopoly. As the producers of a standardized product bring about significant differentiations of quality, design, or packaging in the product that permit differences of use, competition becomes to a greater or less degree incomplete and the producer's power over price and competition greater over his article and its use, according to the differentiation he is able to create and maintain. A retail seller may have in one sense a monopoly on certain trade because of location, as an isolated country store or filling station, or because no one else makes a product of just the quality or attractiveness of his product, as for example in cigarettes. Thus one can theorize that we have monopolistic competition in every nonstandardized commodity with each manufacturer having power over the price and production of his own product. However, this power that, let us say, automobile or soft-drink manufacturers have over their trademarked products is not the power that makes an illegal monopoly. Illegal power must be appraised in terms of the competitive market for the product.

> Determination of the competitive market for commodities depends on how different from one another are the offered commodities in character or use, how far buyers will go to substitute one commodity for another. For example, one can think of building materials as in commodity competition, but one could hardly say that brick competed with steel or wood or cement or stone in the meaning of the Sherman Act litigation; the products are too different. This is the interindustry competition emphasized by some economists. On the other hand, there are certain differences in the formulae for soft drinks, but one can hardly say that each one is an illegal monopoly.

*Id.* at 380–81, 392–93.

Once the relevant market has been defined and the court has determined that a degree of monopoly power or restraint of trade exists in that market, a key question that remains is whether the firm's (or group's) practices constitute an "unreasonable" barrier to other firms entering the market and thence eliminating any short-term monopoly profits. This "rule of reason" inquiry often involves examination of the pro-competitive and anti-competitive impact of the business practice in question. We shall now look at how antitrust law has viewed the organization of the movie industry, particularly in its "Golden Age" in the 1930s and 1940s.

---

The organizational structure of the movie industry exists today much as it did in the early twentieth century. There are three basic tiers in the industry: production, distribution, and exhibition. The production arm generates ideas for motion pictures and turns them into the final product, making use of writers, producers, directors, cinematographers, and actors. The distribution arm finances and promotes the films and licenses them for exhibition around the world. Finally, exhibitors purchase the rights to show a film at particular theaters and times. It is the interplay among these groups, as well as their relationship to consumers, that has been an antitrust focus.

The first "combination . . . in restraint of trade" in the movie industry took place shortly after its inception.[h] In 1908, Thomas Edison and his fellow inventors of motion picture technology created a Motion Picture Patents Company, through which they collectively licensed use of their patents. On its face the trust was dedicated to enhancing both the technological and moral standards of an industry that then consisted of one or two-reel films being shown in "nickelodeons." In practice, the

[h] *See* Robert Sklar, *Movie-Made America: A Cultural History of American Movies* (Random House, Rev. ed. 1994).

partners had all agreed to license use of their cameras and projectors only to producers and exhibitors who paid the trust a weekly fee for that privilege, and who themselves agreed not to deal with any producer or exhibitor that had not made the same commitment to the trust. Edison reportedly earned $1 million a year from his share of the trust proceeds.

These constraints on an increasingly popular mode of entertainment made the trust an issue in the 1912 presidential election, which was won by Woodrow Wilson with the help of a platform that called for a stronger antitrust law to deal with the corporate "robber barons." Besides passage of the 1914 Clayton Act through Congress, the Wilson administration secured a judicial break-up of Edison's trust in *United States v. Motion Picture Patents Co.*, 225 Fed. 800 (E.D. Pa. 1920), as well as a Supreme Court ruling that prohibited patent-holders from using their legal monopoly to secure "tie-in" restraints on what users did with that licensed product. *See Motion Picture Patents Co. v. Universal Film Mfg.*, 243 U.S. 502 (1917). This dramatic change in the industry environment took place while film-makers were beginning to create full-length movies, such as D.W. Griffith's path-breaking *Birth of a Nation*.

Freed from the constraints imposed by those who controlled motion picture technology, the nation's prominent theater owners created their own organization, the First National Exhibition Circuit. Again, the stated role of First National was to facilitate the distribution and showing of movies, as well as to aid in the creation of even more movies. The organization was soon using its collective power to refuse to exhibit any films that were made by a new producer, Paramount Pictures, because the licensing terms that Paramount was seeking were not to the theater group's liking. Instead, First National chose to exhibit only its own films. To counteract this use of downstream market power, Paramount began to acquire its own exhibition houses. This practice was emulated several years later by William Fox, RKO, and Warner Brothers, which ultimately acquired First National. In 1920, the last studio "major" was created, when Loew's, a large exhibition company, purchased what became Metro-Goldwyn-Mayer to serve as its production-distribution arm. In the next two decades, these majors helped transform the movie industry from an obscure institution into the dominant force in American culture.

In the mid-1940s, movie-going played a far more important role in American lives than it does today. In 1946, the average American saw 30 of the 500 films released that year; the total of 4.5 billion admissions, at about 35 cents a ticket, generated $1.7 billion in box office revenues. In 2000, domestic box office receipts had reached $7.5 billion (nearly tripling the $2.7 billion in 1980). However, not only was that $7.5 billion figure worth not much more than $1 billion in 1946 dollars, but it was the product of 1.4 billion admissions (at an average $5.40 a ticket). In 2014, the top 701 movies generated approximately $10.4 billion, which is equivalent to $1.1 billion in 1946 dollars. So despite a larger number of movie releases in 2014, real dollar revenues are still lower than in 1946. The average ticket price in 2014 was $8.17.

During the Golden Age of Hollywood in the 1940s, the majors were dominant. Of the 18,000 theaters across the country, they owned just one-sixth (slightly more than 3,000). The majors' theaters, though, were the large, first-run, downtown facilities in the cities: over 70 percent of the theaters in the 100 largest cities. The majors each concentrated their theaters in different regions of the country and agreed with each other to have their movies shown first in their respective circuits (as did the minors like Columbia and Universal that produced and distributed, but did not themselves exhibit, movies). This is a classic example of market allocation.

An extensive set of rules governed the distribution of films for exhibition in theaters. Rather than a single film, a package (of ten to twenty) films was usually licensed together-*block booking*. This package was offered early in the season, when exhibitors could rarely see the finished products they were agreeing to show-*blind booking*. Theater circuits (both those owned by the majors and others) were regularly given the exclusive license to show the package in their theaters in the region-*franchise booking*. A complex *clearance system* ensured that the movies would have a first run in the large downtown theaters for a defined period, then a certain amount of time would have to go by (e.g., 28 days) before the second run would begin in the suburbs, and then more time (e.g., 14 days) before the third run began. Finally, the licensing agreements usually required a *minimum admission price* as part of a distribution fee system that often, though not always, gave the studio a percentage of box office revenues. This elaborate structure of the distributor-exhibitor relationship, one that was embodied in countless licensing agreements, produced a major event in antitrust law and then a transformation of the movie world (price fixing).

---

The next crucial antitrust challenge to the movie industry was initiated by the Justice Department in 1938, charging the "major" and "minor" movie studios with violations of both §§ 1 and 2 of the Sherman Act-combining and conspiring to restrain and monopolize trade and commerce in the production, distribution and exhibition of motion pictures. In 1940, before the commencement of the trial, the majors entered into a consent decree that lasted for three years. The minors did not consent to this decree. The decree enjoined the consenting defendants from having distributors of motion pictures license for exhibition a package of more than five movies ("block-booking"), and having distributors condition the licensing of movies to exhibitors on their promise to show the movie for a specified duration (a "run"). In addition, the decree required the defendants to subject the reasonableness of clearances to arbitration upon complaint by an exhibitor, and to notify the Justice Department of any acquisition of theaters.

Dissatisfied with what was happening in the industry following this decree, the Justice Department sought further relief under a provision in the decree. A three-judge panel held that the majors and minors had committed "various infractions of the Sherman Act" and modified the consent decrees to enjoin certain trade practices and establish a mandatory system of competitive bidding for movies. *See* 66 F. Supp. 323 (S.D.N.Y. 1946). This decision was appealed to the Supreme Court, which issued an historic ruling for both antitrust law and the movie industry.

## UNITED STATES V. PARAMOUNT PICTURES, INC.

Supreme Court of the United States, 1948.
334 U.S. 131, 68 S.Ct. 915, 92 L.Ed. 1260.

MR. JUSTICE DOUGLAS delivered the opinion of the Court.

* * *

The suit was instituted by the United States under § 4 of the Sherman Act to prevent and restrain violations of it. The defendants fall into three groups: (1) Paramount Pictures, MGM Loew's; Radio-Keith-Orpheum [RKO], Warner-Bros. Pictures, Twentieth Century-Fox Film, which produce motion pictures, and their respective subsidiaries or affiliates which distribute and exhibit films. These are known as the five major defendants or exhibitor-defendants. (2) Columbia Pictures and Universal, which produce motion pictures, and their subsidiaries which distribute films. (3) United Artists, which is engaged only in the distribution of motion pictures. The five majors, through their subsidiaries or affiliates, own or control theaters; the other defendants do not.

* * *

### I

*Restraint of Trade—(1) Price Fixing.*

No film is sold to an exhibitor in the distribution of motion pictures. The right to exhibit under copyright is licensed. The District Court found that the defendants in the licenses they issued fixed minimum admission prices, which the exhibitors agreed to charge, whether the rental of the film was a flat amount or a percentage of the receipts. . . .

The District Court found that two price-fixing conspiracies existed—a horizontal one between all the defendants; a vertical one between each distributor-defendant and its licensees. The latter was based on express agreements and was plainly established. The former was inferred from the pattern of price-fixing disclosed in the record. We think there was adequate foundation for it too. It is not necessary to find an express agreement in order to find a conspiracy. It is enough that a concert of action is contemplated and that the defendants conformed to the arrangement. *Interstate Circuit v. United States*, 306 U.S. 208, 226–227; *United States v. Masonite Corp.*, 316 U.S. 265, 275. That was shown here. [The basis for that district court finding of horizontal price-fixing was threefold: first, that the minimum admission charges contained in licenses granted by different distributors for the same type of theater were "in substantial conformity"; second, that when one distributor-exhibitor, e.g., RKO, licensed its film to be shown in a local theater owned by another distributor-exhibitor, e.g., Paramount, that same minimum pricing pattern was found in these agreements; and, finally, the total effect of this host of separate licensing contracts was to create a visible minimum pricing structure that effectively regulated any local competition in admission prices by separately-owned theaters.]

On this phase of the case the main attack is on the decree which enjoins the defendants and their affiliates from granting any license, except to their own theaters, in which minimum prices for admission to a theater are fixed in any manner or by any means. The argument runs as follows: *United States v. General Electric Co.*, 272 U.S. 476, held that an owner of a patent could, without violating the Sherman Act, grant a license to manufacture and vend, and could fix the price at which the licensee could sell the patented article. It is pointed out that defendants do not sell the films to exhibitors, but only license them and that the Copyright Act (35 Stat. 1075, 1088, 17 U.S.C. § 1), like the patent statutes, grants the owner exclusive rights. And it is argued that if the patentee can fix the price at which his licensee may sell the patented article, the owner of the copyright should be allowed the same privilege. It is maintained that such a privilege is essential to protect the value of the copyrighted films.

We start, of course, from the premise that so far as the Sherman Act is concerned, a price-fixing combination is illegal per se. *United States v. Socony-Vacuum Oil Co.*, 310 U.S. 150; *United States v. Masonite Corporation*, supra. We recently held in *United States v. Gypsum Co.*, 333 U.S. 364, 400, that even patentees could not regiment an entire industry by licenses containing price-fixing agreements. What was said there is adequate to bar defendants, through their horizontal conspiracy, from fixing prices for the exhibition of films in the movie industry. Certainly the rights of the copyright owner are no greater than those of the patentee.

Nor can the result be different when we come to the vertical conspiracy between each distributor-defendant and his licensees. The District Court stated in its findings:

> "In agreeing to maintain a stipulated minimum admission price, each exhibitor thereby consents to the minimum price level at which it will compete against other licensees of the same distributor whether they exhibit on the same run or not. The total effect is that through the separate contracts between the distributor and its licensees a price structure is erected which regulates the licensees' ability to compete against one another in admission prices."

That consequence seems to us to be incontestable. We stated in *United States v. Gypsum Co.*, supra, p. 401, that "The rewards which flow to the patentee and his licensees from the suppression of competition through the regulation of an industry are not reasonably and normally adapted to secure pecuniary reward for the patentee's monopoly." The same is true of the rewards of the copyright owners and their licensees in the present case. For here too the licenses are but a part of the general plan to suppress competition. The case where a distributor fixes admission prices to be charged by a single independent exhibitor, no other licensees or exhibitors being in contemplation, seems to be wholly academic, as the District Court pointed out. It is, therefore, plain that *United States v. General Electric Co.*, supra, as applied in the patent cases, affords no haven to the defendants in this case. For a copyright may no more be used than a patent to deter competition between rivals in the exploitation of their licenses.

*(2) Clearances and Runs.*

* * *

[The court then turned to the presence in the standard contract between studios and theater exhibitors of terms that specified when and where there would be the first run of a movie in a given area, and also set up clearances between different runs.] The clearances which were in vogue had, indeed, acquired a fixed and uniform character and were made applicable to situations without regard to the special circumstances which are necessary to sustain them as reasonable restraints of trade. The evidence is ample to support the finding of the District Court that the defendants either participated in evolving this uniform system of clearances or acquiesced in it and so furthered its existence. That evidence, like the evidence on the price-fixing phase of the case, is therefore adequate to support the finding of a conspiracy to restrain trade by imposing unreasonable clearances.

The District Court enjoined defendants and their affiliates from agreeing with each other or with any exhibitors or distributors to maintain a system of clearances, or from granting any clearance between theaters not in substantial competition, or from granting or enforcing any clearance against theaters in substantial competition with the theater receiving the license for exhibition in excess of what is reasonably necessary to protect the licensee in the run granted. In view of the findings this relief was plainly warranted.

Some of the defendants ask that this provision be construed (or, if necessary, modified) to allow licensors in granting clearances to take into consideration what is reasonably necessary for a fair return to the licensor. We reject that suggestion. If that were allowed, then the exhibitor-defendants would have an easy method of keeping alive at least some of the consequences of the effective conspiracy which they launched. For they could then justify clearances granted by other distributors in favor of their theaters in terms of the competitive requirements of those theaters, and at the same time justify the restrictions they impose upon independents in terms of the necessity of protecting their film rental as licensor. That is too potent a weapon to leave in the hands of those whose proclivity to unlawful conduct has been so marked. It plainly should not be allowed so long as the exhibitor-defendants own theaters. For in its baldest terms it is in the hands of the defendants no less than a power to restrict the competition of others in the way deemed most desirable by them. . . .

* * *

*(4) Formula Deals, Master Agreements, and Franchises.*

[The studios and theaters had contracts under which the circuit gave the studio a "formula deal" percentage of the firm's national gross. In return the studio gave the circuit a "master agreement" which gave it the power to allocate playing time and film rental among all theaters in their area, a "franchise right" which could extend for years. While holding that franchise terms were not automatically an antitrust violation, the Court reached the opposite conclusion about these other two contract elements.]

The formula deals and master agreements are unlawful restraints of trade in two respects. In the first place, they eliminate the possibility of bidding for films theater by theater. In that way they eliminate the opportunity for the small competitor to obtain the choice first runs, and put a premium on the size of the circuit. They are, therefore, devices for stifling competition and diverting the cream of the business to the large operators. In the second place, the pooling of the purchasing power of an entire circuit in bidding for films is a misuse of monopoly power insofar as it combines the theaters in closed towns with competitive situations. . . . It is hardly necessary to add that distributors who join in such arrangements by exhibitors are active participants in effectuating a restraint of trade and a monopolistic practice.

* * *

*(5) Block-Booking.*

Block-booking is the practice of licensing, or offering for license, one feature or group of features on condition that the exhibitor will also license another feature or group of features released by the distributors during a given period. The films are licensed in blocks before they are actually produced. All the defendants, except United Artists, have engaged in the practice. Block-booking prevents competitors from bidding for single features on their individual merits. The District Court held it illegal for that reason and for the reason that it "adds to the monopoly of a single copyrighted picture that of another copyrighted picture which must be taken and exhibited in order to secure the first." . . . The court enjoined defendants from performing or entering into any license in which the right to exhibit one feature is conditioned upon the licensee's taking one or more other features.[11]

We approve that restriction. The copyright law, like the patent statutes, makes reward to the owner a secondary consideration. . . . It is said that reward to the author or artist serves to induce release to the public of the products of his creative genius. But the reward does not serve its public purpose if it is not related to the quality of the copyright. Where a high quality film greatly desired is licensed only if an inferior one is taken, the latter borrows quality from the former and strengthens its monopoly by drawing on the other. The practice tends to equalize rather than differentiate the reward for the individual copyrights. Even where all the films included in the package are of equal quality, the

---

[11] Blind-selling is a practice whereby a distributor licenses a feature before the exhibitor is afforded an opportunity to view it. To remedy the problems created by that practice the District Court included the following provision in its decree:

> "To the extent that any of the features have not been trade shown prior to the granting of the license for more than a single feature, the licensee shall be given by the licensor the right to reject twenty per cent of such features not trade shown prior to the granting of the license, such right of rejection to be exercised in the order of release within ten days after there has been an opportunity afforded to the licensee to inspect the feature."

The court advanced the following as its reason for inclusion of this provision:

> "Blind-selling does not appear to be as inherently restrictive of competition as block-booking, although it is capable of some abuse. By this practice a distributor could promise a picture of good quality or of a certain type which when produced might prove to be of poor quality or of another type—a competing distributor meanwhile being unable to market its product and in the end losing its outlets for future pictures. The evidence indicates that trade-shows, which are designed to prevent such blind-selling, are poorly attended by exhibitors. Accordingly, exhibitors who choose to obtain their films for exhibition in quantities, need to be protected against burdensome agreements by being given an option to reject a certain percentage of their blind-licensed pictures within a reasonable time after they shall have become available for inspection."

We approve this provision of the decree.

requirement that all be taken if one is desired increases the market for some. Each stands not on its own footing but in whole or in part on the appeal which another film may have. As the District Court said, the result is to add to the monopoly of the copyright in violation of the principle of the patent cases involving tying clauses.

* * *

We do not suggest that films may not be sold in blocks or groups, when there is no requirement, express or implied, for the purchase of more than one film. All we hold to be illegal is a refusal to license one or more copyrights unless another copyright is accepted.

*(6) Discrimination.*

[The Court upheld the finding of antitrust violations from the fact that the studio contracts with large theater circuits (unaffiliated as well as affiliated) had a number of beneficial features not found in exhibition contracts with smaller independent theaters: e.g., occasional pre-general release showing of potential hits at higher admission prices, deductions from standard rentals for double bills, and use of excess film rental at one circuit theater to offset rental deficits at another.]

* * *

II

*Competitive Bidding.*

The District Court concluded that the only way competition could be introduced into the existing system of fixed prices, clearances and runs was to require that films be licensed on a competitive bidding basis. Films are to be offered to all exhibitors in each competitive area. The license for the desired run is to be granted to the highest responsible bidder, unless the distributor rejects all offers. The licenses are to be offered and taken theater by theater and picture by picture. Licenses to show films in theaters in which the licensor owns directly or indirectly an interest of ninety-five percent or more are excluded from the requirement for competitive bidding.

* * *

At first blush there is much to commend the system of competitive bidding. The trade victims of this conspiracy have in large measure been the small independent operators. They are the ones that have felt most keenly the discriminatory practices and predatory activities in which defendants have freely indulged. They have been the victims of the massed purchasing power of the larger units in the industry. It is largely out of the ruins of the small operators that the large empires of exhibitors have been built. Thus it would appear to be a great boon to them to substitute open bidding for the private deals and favors on which the large operators have thrived. But after reflection we have concluded that competitive bidding involves the judiciary so deeply in the daily operation of this nation-wide business and promises such dubious benefits that it should not be undertaken.

Each film is to be licensed on a particular run to "the highest responsible bidder, having a theater of a size, location and equipment adequate to yield a reasonable return to the licensor." The bid "shall state what run such exhibitor desires and what he is willing to pay for such feature, which statement may specify a flat rental, or a percentage of gross receipts, or both, or any other form of rental, and shall also specify what clearance such exhibitor is willing to accept, the time and days when such exhibitor desires to exhibit it, and any other offers which such exhibitor may care to make." We do not doubt that if a competitive bidding system is adopted all these provisions are necessary. For the licensing of films at auction is quite obviously a more complicated matter than the like sales for cash of tobacco, wheat, or other produce. Columbia puts these pertinent queries: "No two exhibitors are likely to make the same bid as to dates, clearance, method of fixing rental, etc. May bids containing such diverse factors be readily compared? May a flat rental bid be compared with a percentage bid? May the value of any percentage bid be determined unless the admission price is fixed by the license?"

The question as to who is the highest bidder involves the use of standards incapable of precise definition because the bids being compared contain different ingredients. Determining who is the most responsible bidder likewise cannot be reduced to a formula. The distributor's judgment of the character and integrity of a particular exhibitor might result in acceptance of a lower bid than others offered. Yet to prove that favoritism was shown would be well-nigh impossible, unless perhaps all the exhibitors in the country were given classifications of responsibility. If, indeed, the choice between bidders is not to be entrusted to the uncontrolled discretion of the distributors, some effort to standardize the factors involved in determining "a reasonable return to the licensor" would seem necessary.

We mention these matters merely to indicate the character of the job of supervising such a competitive bidding system. It would involve the judiciary in the administration of intricate and detailed rules governing priority, period of clearance, length of run, competitive areas, reasonable return, and the like.

The system would be apt to require as close a supervision as a continuous receivership, unless the defendants were to be entrusted with vast discretion. The judiciary is unsuited to affairs of business management; and control through the power of contempt is crude and clumsy and lacking in the flexibility necessary to make continuous and detailed supervision effective. Yet delegation of the management of the system to the discretion of those who had the genius to conceive the present conspiracy and to execute it with the subtlety which this record reveals, could be done only with the greatest reluctance. At least such choices should not be faced unless the need for the system is great and its benefits plain.

The system uproots business arrangements and established relationships with no apparent overall benefit to the small independent exhibitor. If each feature must go to the highest responsible bidder, those with the greatest purchasing power would seem to be in a favored position. Those with the longest purse-the exhibitor-defendants and the large circuits-would seem to stand in a preferred position. If in fact they were enabled through the competitive bidding system to take the cream of the business, eliminate the smaller independents, and thus increase their own strategic hold on the industry, they would have the cloak of the court's decree around them for protection. Hence the natural advantage which the larger and financially stronger exhibitors would seem to have in the bidding gives us pause. If a premium is placed on purchasing power, the court-created system may be a powerful factor towards increasing the concentration of economic power in the industry, rather than cleansing the competitive system of unwholesome practices. For where the system in operation promises the advantage to the exhibitor who is in the strongest financial position, the injunction against discrimination is apt to hold an empty promise. In this connection it should be noted that, even though the independents in a given competitive area do not want competitive bidding, the exhibitor-defendants can invoke the system.

* * *

In light of these considerations we conclude that the competitive bidding provisions of the decree should be eliminated so that a more effective decree may be fashioned.

* * *

III

*Monopoly, Expansion of Theater Holdings, Divestiture.*

There is a suggestion that the hold the defendants have on the industry is so great that a problem under the First Amendment is raised. Cf. *Associated Press v. United States*, 326 U.S. 1. We have no doubt that moving pictures, like newspapers and radio, are included in the press whose freedom is guaranteed by the First Amendment. That issue would be focused here if we had any question concerning monopoly in the production of moving pictures. But monopoly in production was eliminated as an issue in these cases, as we have noted. The chief argument at the bar is phrased in terms of monopoly of exhibition, restraints on exhibition, and the like. Actually, the issue is even narrower than that. The main contest is over the cream of the exhibition business—that of the first-run theaters. By defining the issue so narrowly we do not intend to belittle its importance. It shows, however, that the question here is not what the public will see or if the public will be permitted to see certain features. It is clear that under the existing system the public will be denied access to none. If the public cannot see the features on the first-run, it may do so on the second, third, fourth, or later run. The central problem presented by these cases is which exhibitors get the highly profitable first-run business. That problem has important aspects under the Sherman Act. But it bears only remotely, if at all, on any question of freedom of the press, save only as timeliness of release may be a factor of importance in specific situations.

The controversy over monopoly relates to monopoly in exhibition and more particularly monopoly in the first-run phase of the exhibition business.

[The Court here summarized the record, which disclosed that the five majors owned 3,137 (or 17 percent) of the nation's 18,076 theaters, but that these theaters accounted for 45 percent of domestic box office receipts. The reason was that in the 92 cities with a population of 100,000 or more, 70 percent of first run theaters were affiliated with the majors.]

* * *

The District Court held that the five majors could not be treated collectively so as to establish claims of general monopolization in exhibition. It found that none of them was organized or had been maintained "for the purpose of achieving a national monopoly" in exhibition. It found that the five majors by their present theater holdings "alone" (which aggregate a little more than one-sixth of all the theaters in the United States), "do not and cannot collectively or individually, have a monopoly of exhibition." The District Court also found that where a single defendant owns all of the first-run theaters in a town, there is no sufficient proof that the acquisition was for the purpose of creating a monopoly. It found rather that such consequence resulted from the inertness of competitors, their lack of financial ability to build theaters comparable to those of the five majors, or the preference of the public for the best-equipped theaters. And the percentage of features on the market which any of the five majors could play in its own theaters was found to be relatively small and in nowise to approximate a monopoly of film exhibition.

* * *

It is clear, so far as the five majors are concerned, that the aim of the conspiracy was exclusionary, i.e. it was designed to strengthen their hold on the exhibition field. In other words, the conspiracy had monopoly in exhibition for one of its goals, as the District Court held. Price, clearance, and run are interdependent. The clearance and run provisions of the licenses fixed the relative playing positions of all theaters in a certain area; the minimum price provisions were based on playing position-the first-run theaters being required to charge the highest prices, the second-run theaters the next highest, and so on. As the District Court found, "In effect, the distributor, by the fixing of minimum admission prices, attempts to give the prior-run exhibitors as near a monopoly of the patronage as possible."

It is, therefore, not enough in determining the need for divestiture to conclude with the District Court that none of the defendants was organized or has been maintained for the purpose of achieving a "national monopoly," nor that the five majors through their present theater holdings "alone" do not and cannot collectively or individually have a monopoly of exhibition. For when the starting point is a conspiracy to effect a monopoly through restraints of trade, it is relevant to determine what the results of the conspiracy were even if they fell short of monopoly.

An example will illustrate the problem. In the popular sense there is a monopoly if one person owns the only theater in town. That usually does not, however, constitute a violation of the Sherman Act. But . . . even such an ownership is vulnerable in a suit by the United States under the Sherman Act if the property was acquired, or its strategic position maintained, as a result of practices which constitute unreasonable restraints of trade. Otherwise, there would be reward from the conspiracy through retention of its fruits. Hence the problem of the District Court does not end with enjoining continuance of the unlawful restraints nor with dissolving the combination which launched the conspiracy. Its function includes undoing what the conspiracy achieved. The requirement that the defendants restore what they unlawfully obtained is no more punishment than the familiar remedy of restitution. What findings would be warranted after such an inquiry in the present cases, we do not know. For the findings of the District Court do not cover this point beyond stating that monopoly was an objective of the several restraints of trade that stand condemned.

Moreover, the problem under the Sherman Act is not solved merely by measuring monopoly in terms of size or extent of holdings or by concluding that single ownerships were not obtained "for the purpose of achieving a national monopoly." It is the relationship of the unreasonable restraints of trade to the position of the defendants in the exhibition field (and more particularly in the first-run phase of that business) that is of first importance on the divestiture phase of these cases . . . In this connection there is a suggestion that one result of the conspiracy was a geographical division of territory among the five majors. We mention it not to intimate that it is true but only to indicate the appropriate extent of the inquiry concerning the effect of the conspiracy in theater ownership by the five majors.

* * *

Exploration of these phases of the cases would not be necessary if, as the Department of Justice argues, vertical integration of producing, distributing and exhibiting motion pictures is illegal per se. But the majority of the Court does not take that view. In the opinion of the majority the legality of vertical integration under the Sherman Act turns on (1) the purpose or intent with which it was conceived, or (2) the power it creates and the attendant purpose or intent. First, it runs afoul of the Sherman Act if it was a calculated scheme to gain control over an appreciable segment of the market and to restrain or suppress competition, rather than an expansion to meet legitimate business needs. *United States v. Reading Co.*, 253 U.S. 26, 57; *United States v. Lehigh Valley R. Co.*, 254 U.S. 255, 269–270. Second, a vertically integrated enterprise, like other aggregations of business units (*United States v. Aluminum Co. of America*, 148 F.2d 416), will constitute monopoly which, though unexercised, violates the Sherman Act provided a power to exclude competition is coupled with a purpose or intent to do so. [S]ize is itself an earmark of monopoly power. For size carries with it an opportunity for abuse. And the fact that the power created by size was utilized in the past to crush or prevent competition is potent evidence that the requisite purpose or intent attends the presence of monopoly power. Likewise bearing on the question whether monopoly power is created by the vertical integration, is the nature of the market to be served and the leverage on the market which the particular vertical integration creates or makes possible.

These matters were not considered by the District Court. For that reason, as well as the others we have mentioned, the findings on monopoly and divestiture which we have discussed in this part of the opinion will be set aside. There is an independent reason for doing that. As we have seen, the District Court considered competitive bidding as an alternative to divestiture in the sense that it concluded that further consideration of divestiture should not be had until competitive bidding had been tried and found wanting. Since we eliminate from the decree the provisions for competitive bidding, it is necessary to set aside the findings on divestiture so that a new start on this phase of the cases may be made on their remand.

* * *

Affirmed in part, reversed in part, and remanded.

---

The Court rendered two related decisions on the same day as the *Paramount Pictures* opinion, *United States v. Griffith*, 334 U.S. 100 (1948), and *Schine Chain Theatres v. United States*, 334 U.S. 110 (1948). These involved companion suits filed by the Justice Department against exhibitors whom the Court agreed had wielded monopoly power in their one-theater towns to secure master agreements from the major studios. These agreements gave the exhibitors exclusive first runs for their preferred films across their entire circuits, thus putting independent exhibitors at an unfair disadvantage. The Court reached the same result in *Schine*, involving a single large chain in six northeast states, as it did in *Griffith*, involving a group of small exhibitors in three southwest states who had pooled their negotiating efforts with distributors. In these cases, as in *Paramount*, the underlying premise seemed to be that a fair and competitive market for movie exhibition required individualized agreements for each film and each theater, rather than broad-based, long-term relationships between the major studios and larger theater chains.

Left unsettled by *Paramount* was whether it was necessary to separate the business of movie production and distribution from theater exhibition. The district court had been denied the option of judicially-supervised competitive bidding for films. On remand, the panel concluded, in *United States v. Paramount Pictures*, 85 F. Supp. 881 (S.D.N.Y. 1949), *aff'd*, 339 U.S. 974 (1950), that vertical integration had been a key to the antitrust conspiracies in the movie world, and had to be dissolved.

The ultimate outcome of the *Paramount* cases was that motion picture practices and structures that had survived for decades were held to be anti-competitive and banned for the future. The district court carefully phrased its opinion not to condemn vertical integration as directly violative of the Sherman Act. Instead, the court found that in the absence of a competitive bidding system, vertical integration of film distribution and exhibition would continue to facilitate various forms of anti-competitive behavior.

After ten years of litigation, the courts had set the stage for a complete overhaul of the motion picture industry. Findings of both unreasonable restraints of trade and monopolistic behavior led the courts to impose drastic measures to open up the market to competition. Ultimately, the major movie studios and exhibitors entered into a series of antitrust consent decrees with the Justice Department providing as follows:

1. proscription of the practice of licensing feature films on condition that the exhibitor accept one or more other pictures offered by the studio (i.e. block-booking);

2. allowing exhibitors to set their own admission prices, free from contractually-mandated minimum prices;

3. an end to cooperative theater management and pooling agreements with other circuits or independents;

4. elimination of runs and clearances not justified by pro-competitive reasons;

5. a requirement that all defendants begin licensing motion pictures on a picture-by-picture basis, solely upon the merits of the bid, and without discrimination in favor of affiliated theaters or circuit theaters;

6. and the complete divestiture of motion picture exhibition from production and distribution, including bars on franchise agreements as well as corporate integration between distributors and exhibitors.

The decrees affected all the parties named in the complaints, majors and minors; however, it said nothing about future entrants into this field. With respect to vertical integration, the parties who had entered into late settlements with the government—Warner, Fox, and Loew's—were treated more severely by the courts, which prohibited them from purchasing any exhibition houses in the future without prior court approval. Paramount and RKO, which settled early by agreeing to divest their existing theater holdings, were not subject to these future pre-clearance restrictions. The minors—Columbia, Universal, and United Artists—which were not then in the exhibition business were not prohibited from future vertical integration.

The immediate result of the decrees was revolutionary. The organizational structure that had been in place for decades was eliminated. In its place, a system was established which required movies to be licensed film-by-film: thus separate agreements governed each movie. The system also required negotiation between licensor (buyer) and licensee (seller) to set the price (and other components of the exhibitor contract) at whatever level the market would bear. The expectation was that this more fluid mechanism for allocating movies to theaters would enhance the bargaining leverage of smaller independent exhibitors, and in the longer run improve both the quality of films and the theater settings in which fans could enjoy this brand of entertainment (perhaps even at a lower price).

We have already seen one major change in the movie industry that occurred shortly after *Paramount*. The studio's practice of employing (and paying) a large team of actors, directors, writers, and technicians was quickly dismantled. In its place was the more "flexible" mode of production projects, often packaged together by large Hollywood talent agencies, and financed and distributed by Paramount and its counterparts. The number of movies distributed each year by the majors dropped from 300 or so in the 1940s to around 100 in the 1980s, before rising again to 200 at the end of the 1990s. The cost of making movies (though perhaps not the quality) is dramatically higher. In 2005, average expenditures on a film distributed by an MPAA-member totaled $59 million just for making the movie, and high-budget movies regularly exceed $100 million. Another $27 million is spent on advertising and other distribution costs. One beneficiary of this regime has been the star performers, who now make $20 million or more for a single film as a result of the financial value of their international appeal and the negotiating leverage of contingent employment relationships.

These soaring film-making costs have accentuated two features of the movie industry that its protagonists have been wrestling with since the end of World War I. First, the vast bulk of those $77 million in production and distribution costs are expended (i.e., "sunk") before the producer, let alone the theater owner and audience, has seen the finished product. Second, even after the producer, distributor, and exhibitor (and also the reviewers) have viewed the movie, they have very little idea of whether it will be among the minority of movies that makes money, even after taking in receipts from domestic and foreign box office admissions, video sales and rentals, cable and over-the-air television, and merchandising. By contrast a Coca-Cola or a McDonald's, for example, entertainment fans do not have any significant consumer identification with a movie studio, e.g., Paramount rather than Warner. The decision about which movie to see depends entirely on its (largely unpredictable) quality and appeal. Keep in mind these features of the movie industry—particularly, the huge cost and uncertain market value of its product. In such an industry, what is the appropriate legal treatment of its organizational relationships, both vertically within the same product line and across different markets (e.g., combining movies, music, books, live theater, and broadcasting)?

## C. POST-*PARAMOUNT* MOTION PICTURE PRACTICES

Market forces often have greater practical significance than legal rules. The antitrust restructuring of the motion picture industry coincided with the sudden appearance in tens of millions of American homes of a far stronger competitive force—television. In 1948, less than 200,000 homes had television sets; by 1956, nearly 40 million homes had them (and in 2005, over 100 million). Throughout the 1950s, movie attendance dropped steadily, as families chose to stay in the comfort of their living rooms and watch Ed Sullivan, Milton Berle, Lucille Ball, Sid Caesar, and others perform for free. This decline in demand for seats in theaters (from more than 4 billion in the late 1940s to less than 1 billion in the early 1960s) in turn produced a drop in exhibitor demand for movies. Since that dismal decade for the industry, film producers have found that television can be a major source of work and revenue. From 1980 to 2005, for example, the number of homes with VCRs soared from 2 million to 85 million, and the number with cable movie channels from 9 to 67 million; total studio earnings from home viewing now far exceeds earnings from theaters.

There has, however, been a transformation in the overall structure of the movie industry. One of the majors from the 1940s, RKO, is out of movie-making, while one of the bit players of that era, Disney, is now a top firm (including its affiliate, Miramax). Steven Spielberg's Dreamworks is now a major player. The big studios still generate the lion's share (approximately 90 percent) of movie revenues. As seen in Chapter 11, the vast majority of movies are made by independent producers, while the majors finance and distribute the product. While the number of theaters is down sharply, the number of screens (most in multiplexes) has nearly tripled over the last three decades (from 14,000 in 1970 to over 39,000 in 2013).

Movies are no longer released for a first run in downtown theaters, then a second run in suburbs, and then to other theaters of descending size and appeal. Instead, films are shown on the same release day on one to four thousand screens across the country, with national advertising campaigns based on early media reviews. Film distributors now negotiate licensing deals with large chains. The transformation of the role of film-making in the broader entertainment world has led industry participants, judges, and scholars to question whether practices that were anticompetitive in the 1940s remain so today. Should antitrust decrees be replaced with the more flexible "rule of reason" analysis in light of modern trends?

The Supreme Court has taken a more flexible and functional approach to antitrust regulation. *Broadcast Music, Inc. v. CBS, Inc.*, 441 U.S. 1 (1979), emphasized the market efficiencies of the blanket performance license issued by composers as an alternative to individual licenses. A second decision was *Continental T.V. v. GTE Sylvania*, 433 U.S. 36 (1977), which permitted a manufacturer to place restrictions on the territory in which its distributors could market its product. While such a restraint might limit intrabrand competition among the sellers of that one manufacturer's brand, it could be justified if the restriction was part of an overall marketing strategy that made this manufacturer more competitive *vis-á-vis* its rivals. This is because such interbrand competition among producers would ultimately generate lower prices and better quality for consumers. An entertainment industry example of this newer approach is *Orson, Inc. v. Miramax Film Corp.,* 79 F.3d 1358 (3d

Cir. 1996), in which the court found no antitrust violation in the movie producer granting exclusive first-release exhibition rights in almost all its films to a particular theater in downtown Philadelphia.

At the same time, the Court made it clear in *National Society of Professional Engineers v. United States*, 435 U.S. 679 (1978), that it is only pro-competitive benefits that can justify restrictive trade practices. Thus, the Society of Professional Engineers could not defend its ban on engineers bidding for work by offering lower prices, on the ground that the engineers might cut corners to meet the unduly low price they had bid to win the contract. The Court stated:

> The assumption that competition is the best method of allocating resources in a free market recognizes that all elements of a bargain-quality, service, safety and durability-and not just the immediate cost, are favorably affected by the free opportunity to select among alternative offers. In our complex economy the number of items that may cause serious harm is almost endless-automobiles, drugs, aircraft components, heavy equipment, and countless others cause serious harm to individuals or to the public at large if defectively made. The judiciary cannot indirectly protect the public against this harm by conferring monopoly privileges on the manufacturers.

*Id.* at 695–96. Does this mean that motion picture studios or television networks cannot (absent statutory exemption) agree among themselves to reduce the level of violence in programming?

Illustrating the way that contemporary entertainment law can shape the nature of the entertainment industry is what finally happened with Time Warner and AOL. This new venture was required by the FTC to provide open access to each of its cable systems to at least three competing Internet access providers (beginning with Earthlink), at reasonable fees and other contract terms. AOL Time Warner was also told to provide similar open access on its cable systems to other forms of new "interactive television" (something that Disney, in particular, sought). Ironically, shortly after AOL and Time Warner executives accepted the terms of the deal negotiated by their lawyers with the FTC, both companies' stock market prices dropped sharply, and as we saw earlier, they never fully recovered. Whether antitrust law has operated to the benefit of entertainment fans (rather than shareholders) is up in the air. The next few pages describe how antitrust operates even when there are no major mergers involved.

## 1. PRICE-FIXING

Perhaps the most obvious form of restraint of trade deemed to be *per se* illegal under the Sherman Act is "horizontal" price-fixing among competitors. In *United States v. Trenton Potteries Co.*, 273 U.S. 392, 397 (1927), the Supreme Court stated:

> The aim and result of every price-fixing agreement, if effective, is the elimination of one form of competition. The power to fix prices, whether reasonably exercised or not, involves power to control the market and to fix arbitrary and unreasonable prices. The reasonable price fixed today may through economic and business changes become the unreasonable price of tomorrow.

Both the market and the legal landscape change when prices are fixed by non-competitors, e.g., by the supplier and buyer in a "vertical" chain of production. The broader question posed by *Paramount's* decision to ban any film licensing agreements from specifying minimum admission prices is whether the Court judged these agreements to be anti-competitive without any redeeming virtues, and if so, whether the Court was right in that judgment.

There are pro-competitive values that may be served by allowing producers to fix (not just to suggest) the minimum prices that distributors must charge for their goods. One argument is that price-fixing is essential to prevent forms of "free-riding" that ultimately are harmful to consumers. Suppose, for example, that there are certain services, like offering demonstrations and detailed explanations of video equipment, that retailers cannot charge for separately, but that provide significant benefits to consumers. Retailers may want to offer these services, but will be forced to charge a higher price to pay for them. Other retailers, including those on the Internet, that choose not to offer these services are then able to charge a lower price for the product. The problem is that a customer can take advantage of the services of the first retailer and the lower prices of the second retailer, who is "free riding" on the services of the first. These services, no matter how useful to consumers, are likely to be short-lived in such a competitive environment.

Despite differences in the role played by vertical, rather than horizontal, pricing agreements, such "resale price maintenance" arrangements between producers and retailers were *per se* antitrust violations under *Dr. Miles Medical v. John D. Park & Sons*, 220 U.S. 373 (1911). As we saw earlier, though, the Supreme Court has been prepared to accept exclusive territorial dealerships that serve many of the same functions as direct price controls. *See Continental T.V. v. GTE Sylvania*, 433 U.S. 36 (1977); *Business Electronics Corp. v. Sharp Electronics Corp.*, 485 U.S. 717 (1988). Finally, in *Leegin Creative Leather Products, Inc. v. PSKS, Inc.*, 551 U.S. 877, 885–87 (2007), the Court adopted the rule of reason for minimum resale price agreements.

### *QUESTIONS FOR DISCUSSION*

1. As rational economic actors, film distributors and exhibitors seek to generate the highest revenues and profits (not necessarily attendance) at their movies. There is, however, a potential divergence of interest that influences their preferred pricing policies. When a movie is released, the studio has already incurred the sunk costs of production and delivery, while the theater owner is about to incur the costs of opening its facility and serving its customers. The studio will be receiving a percentage of box office admissions; the percentage figure is highest in the first week and typically drops thereafter. Each theater owner gets the remaining percentage and all profits from concession sales (and from lead-in advertising on-screen). What are the complementary and conflicting interests of distributors and exhibitors in setting the price for admission to the theater? Are there reasons why film distributors may want to regulate price levels—minimum or maximum—in their licensing contracts with exhibitors? Should these reasons provide an antitrust justification for restrictions on the use of free passes or discount tickets for certain movies or in certain weeks?

2. Home sales and rentals of movies on DVD/Blu-ray have become an enormous segment of film industry earnings. Movie producers look to retail sales and rentals of videos for about half of their movie revenue. To promote a particular video sale, movie distributors such as Buena Vista (which distributes for Disney) have arrangements with retailers called "minimum advertised pricing," or MAP. MAP goes one step beyond "suggested retail pricing" by telling retailers not to sell below the nationally advertised minimum price, a policy the distributor can enforce by refusing to deal with price-cutting retailers. *See United States v. Colgate*, 250 U.S. 300 (1919); *Monsanto Co. v. Spray-Rite Service Corp.*, 465 U.S. 752 (1984) (requiring an agreement before a "restraint of trade" can be judged illegal under § 1 of the Sherman Act). To enhance the effectiveness of MAP, distributors have begun to tie cooperative advertising dollars to a retailer's acceptance of MAP. In other words, if a retailer wishes to partake of a distributor's advertising fund for a particular movie, it would have to agree to sell the video at no lower than MAP. What are the competitive advantages of cooperative advertising programs? Who benefits most from setting minimum prices—the distributor or the retailer? Should tying co-op dollars to MAP be unlawful?

3. Refreshment sales have always been a significant component of an exhibitor's revenues—15 to 20 percent. Recently, particularly in urban areas, megaplex theaters have been offering additional luxuries and restaurant-quality foods. Does any of this point toward another reason why distributors might be interested in forcing minimum prices on exhibitors? Should antitrust law be concerned with such developments?

---

Another relevant entertainment antitrust suit involved book publishing. Ironically, this suit was filed around the same time that a movie vividly displayed what was happening in the book-selling market. The *Sleepless in Seattle* team of director-writer Nora Ephron and stars Tom Hanks and Meg Ryan made *You've Got Mail*, a hit 1998 movie. This story took place in Manhattan, with Hanks opening up a large bookstore that put Ryan's neighborhood store out of business. The same thing happened in the real bookstore business. In the 1990s, the number of independent stores dropped from 5,500 to 3,200, and their share of book sales dropped from 33 percent to just 15 percent. The key source of the decline was the surge in bookstore chains, led by Barnes & Noble and Borders. Today, technology such as ebooks and Internet sites such as Amazon threaten all types of book stores.

There is nothing illegal about a large bookstore whose consumer appeal puts its competitors out of business (like Hanks' store did to Ryan's in *You've Got Mail*). However, the American Booksellers Association claimed that antitrust law can be violated if a bookstore chain uses its size and market leverage to extract and pass on to its consumers discounts and other preferences secured from publishers (even giants like Bertelsmann-Random House). The thrust of this suit was that Barnes & Noble and Borders were getting market advantages that are not available (at least proportionately) to the smaller neighborhood stores. The two sides eventually settled this case in 2001, with the two lead chains paying the ABA members a total of $4.7 million, less than their prior legal expenses in the proceedings. The postscript to this story is the decline of the brick and mortar retailers that now face massive Internet competition, albeit without accompanying cafes.

---

Another interesting antitrust question concerns the degree to which sports leagues can limit the televising of their games. Both professional hockey and professional baseball have strictly regulated the televising of their games, which has given rise to questions concerning the relationship between television audiences and the game. In both sports, for instance, a television blackout of a local game will occur when the sales for the event are under a certain level.

In 2009, the National Football League (NFL) attempted to insulate itself from liability by using a "single entity" defense. The argument went that if all of the teams are part of one league—the same entity—that an antitrust claim would be impossible, because one cannot collude with oneself.

The United States Supreme Court, however, thought otherwise. After closely examining the NFL franchises and their relationship to the NFL, the Court concluded that the league was not a single entity, but a group comprised of many individual franchises. *See American Needle v. NFL*, 560 U.S. 183 (2010).

Given the possibility of attacking collusion among teams and the desire to watch the preferred game irrespective of ticket sales, audience members who subscribed to live broadcasts over the radio, television, or Internet sued the leagues and the programming distributors in a complaint that focused on antitrust claims. The next case explores some of these ideas.

## LAUMANN V. NATIONAL HOCKEY LEAGUE

District Court for the Southern District of New York, 2012.
907 F.Supp.2d 465.

JUDGE SCHEINDLIN.

### I. INTRODUCTION

Plaintiffs bring this consolidated putative class action against the National Hockey League ("NHL") and Major League Baseball ("MLB"), various clubs within the Leagues, regional sports networks ("RSNs") that televise the games, and Comcast and DirecTV, multichannel video programming distributors ("MVPDs"). Plaintiffs challenge "defendants' . . . agreements to eliminate competition in the distribution of [baseball and hockey] games over the Internet and television [by] divid[ing] the live-game video presentation market into exclusive territories, which are protected by anticompetitive blackouts" and by "collud[ing] to sell the 'out-of-market' packages only through the League [which] exploit[s] [its] illegal monopoly by charging supra-competitive prices." Plaintiffs claim that these agreements "result in reduced output, diminished product quality, diminished choice and suppressed price competition" in violation of the Sherman Antitrust Act, and request statutory damages and injunctive relief on behalf of themselves and the class. Defendants jointly move to dismiss all claims pursuant to Federal Rule of Civil Procedure 12(b)(6).

### II. BACKGROUND

#### A. The Agreements to Telecast Baseball and Hockey

Plaintiffs are subscribers to television and/or Internet services that include live hockey and baseball telecasts. Defendant National Hockey League is an unincorporated association of thirty major league professional ice hockey clubs, nine of which are named as defendants in *Laumann* Defendant Office of the Commissioner of Baseball, doing business as Major League Baseball, is an unincorporated association of thirty professional baseball clubs, nine of which are named as defendants in *Garber*. The Complaints also name subsidiaries of the Leagues that pursue their commercial opportunities, including Internet operations (together with the NHL, MLB and the named individual clubs, the "League defendants"). Plaintiffs allege that "[p]ursuant to a series of agreements between and among Defendants, the League[s] ha[ve] obtained centralized control over distribution of live video programming of [hockey and baseball] games" and "the clubs have agreed not to compete in business matters related to the video presentation of live major-league men's professional [hockey and baseball] games."

Both the NHL and MLB are "ultimately controlled by, and operate for the benefit of the clubs." "Though necessarily cooperating to produce inter-club games, each club operates as an independently owned and managed business, competing against each other in various markets." In both the NHL and MLB, each team owns the initial right to control telecasts of its home games, and keeps the revenues it generates from the sale of these rights. The teams in each League have mutually agreed to permit the visiting team to produce a separate telecast of the games.

1. "In-Market" Agreements

The vast majority of telecasts are produced by arrangement between individual teams and RSNs, a number of which are named as defendants. RSNs are local television networks that negotiate contracts with individual NHL or MLB clubs to broadcast the majority of the local club's games within that club's telecast territory. Several defendant RSNs are owned and controlled by defendant Comcast, several are owned and controlled by defendant DirecTV, and two are independent of the MVPDs, but share ownership with an individual club.

RSNs produce the games and sell their programming to MVPDs including Comcast, a cable distributor, and DirecTV, a satellite distributor (the upstream market). MVPDs, in turn, sell programming to consumers (the downstream market). Pursuant to agreements with the RSNs, MPVDs make RSN programming available as part of standard packages sold to consumers within the RSN's designated territory, and black out games in unauthorized territories, in accordance with the agreements between the RSNs and the Leagues. The Complaints allege that the "regional blackout agreements," made "for the purpose of protecting the local television telecasters," are "[a]t the core of Defendants' restraint of competition." "But for these agreements," plaintiffs allege, "MVPDs would facilitate 'foreign' RSN entry and other forms of competition." Plaintiffs argue that the "MVPDs also directly benefit from the blackout of Internet streams of local games, which requires that fans obtain this programming exclusively from the MVPDs."

A small percentage of games are produced under national contracts between the Leagues (pursuant to rights granted by the individual teams) and national networks. These limited nationally televised games provide the only opportunity for fans to watch a game not involving a local team without purchasing an out-of-market package.

2. "Out-of-Market" Agreements

With the limited exception of nationally televised games, standard MVPD packages only televise "in-market" games (i.e., games played by the team in whose designated home territory the subscriber resides). For a consumer to obtain out-of-market games, there are only two options—television packages and Internet packages—both of which are controlled by the Leagues. Television packages—NHL Center Ice and MLB Extra Innings—are available for purchase from MVPDs, in accordance with agreements between the MVPDs and the Leagues. These packages require the purchase of all out-of-market games even if a consumer is only interested in viewing a particular game or games of one particular non-local team. They also require a subscription to the standard digital television package. Internet packages—NHL Gamecenter Live and MLB.tv—are available directly through the Leagues and also require the purchase of all out-of-market games. Neither local games nor nationally televised games are available through these packages. Thus, "there is *no* authorized method for viewing [local] games on the Internet." For example, an NHL Gamecenter Live subscriber in New York cannot watch New York Rangers games through any Internet source, but instead must subscribe to MSG through an MVPD. The alleged purpose of the limitation on Internet programming is to protect the RSNs' regional monopolies and insulate MVPDs that carry them from Internet competition.

Plaintiffs allege that the market divisions and centralization of rights to distribute out-of-market games in the Leagues have "adversely affected and substantially lessened competition in the relevant markets" by reducing output of live MLB and NHL game presentations, raising prices, and rendering output "unresponsive to consumer preference to view live [MLB and NHL] games, including local games, through both Internet and television media."

B. The Alleged Markets and Products

The Complaints allege relevant product/service markets for "the provision of major league professional ice hockey [and baseball] contests in North America." In addition, and "[m]ost importantly for this action, there is a relevant market for live video presentations of [professional baseball and hockey] games over media such as cable and satellite television and the Internet." These markets are "characterized by high barriers to entry" in which the NHL and MLB, as the only providers of these games, acting through and with the independent clubs that own and control the Leagues, have market power. The NHL's and MLB's dominance in the production of professional hockey and baseball games respectively "give [them] the ability, together with [their] television partners, to exercise market power in the market for live video presentations of [professional baseball and hockey] games."

C. The Claims

Based on the foregoing facts, plaintiffs allege four antitrust violations: (1) for Television plaintiffs, violation of Section 1 of the Sherman Antitrust Act based on agreements to "forbid[ ] the carrying or online streaming of any [NHL/MLB] game in any geographic market except those licensed by the [NHL/MLB] team in that geographic market" (Claim I);39 (2) for Television plaintiffs, violation of Section 1 based on agreements "that [NHL/MLB] will be the exclusive provider of live 'out-of-market' games distributed through television providers" (Claim II); (3) for Internet plaintiffs, violation of Section 1 based on agreements "that [NHL/MLB] will be the exclusive provider of live 'out-of-market' games over the Internet" (Claim III); and (4) for all plaintiffs, violation of Section 2 for conspiracy to monopolize the "market for video presentations of major league [hockey/baseball] games and Internet streaming of the same" (Claim IV).

Defendants make six arguments why plaintiffs' claims must be dismissed. *First,* plaintiffs have not alleged harm to competition. *Second,* [plaintiffs lack standing].

* * *

*Third,* plaintiffs allege "no cognizable conduct by Comcast, DirecTV or any of the RSN Defendants" because "[t]he only plausible allegations as to these Defendants relate to their *vertical* distribution, which is presumptively legal." *Fourth,* the alleged horizontal activities of the NHL and MLB defendants are "lawful on their face" as the "very core of what professional sports league ventures do—sell their jointly created product." *Fifth,* plaintiffs' "proposed relevant market is insufficient as a matter of law" because plaintiffs fail to "allege facts regarding reasonable interchangeability or cross-elasticity of demand." *Sixth,* plaintiffs' Section 2 claims must be dismissed for: (1) failure to allege any anticompetitive effect; (2) failure to allege any plausible "conspiracy" among the Leagues, the clubs and the RSNs and distributors; and (3) failure to allege any of the necessary elements of a monopolization claim.

* * *

## IV. APPLICABLE LAW

* * *

### B. Sherman Act Section 1

Section 1 of the Sherman Act prohibits "[e]very contract, combination in the form of trust or otherwise, or conspiracy, in restraint of trade or commerce among the several States." The Supreme Court has clarified that Section 1 "outlaw[s] only *unreasonable* restraints." To establish a Section 1 violation, a plaintiff must allege: "(1) concerted action between at least two legally distinct economic entities; (2) that constitute[ ] an unreasonable restraint of trade either per se or under the rule of reason."

Certain agreements which courts, after "considerable experience with the type of restraint at issue," determine to have "manifestly anti-competitive effects and lack any redeeming virtue," are deemed *per se* violations of the Sherman Act. Outside this category of "necessarily illegal" restraints, "[t]he rule of reason is the accepted standard for testing whether a practice restrains trade in violation of § 1." "The rule [of reason] distinguishes between restraints with anticompetitive effect that are harmful to the consumer and restraints stimulating competition that are in the consumer's best interest." A court must "determine whether the [ ] restriction is a naked restraint on trade, and thus invalid, or one that is ancillary to the legitimate and competitive purposes of the business association and thus valid."

Under the rule of reason plaintiffs bear an initial burden to demonstrate the defendants' challenged behavior had an *actual* adverse effect on competition as a whole in the relevant market . . . evidence that plaintiffs have been harmed as individual competitors will not suffice. . . . If the plaintiffs satisfy their initial burden, the burden shifts to the defendants to offer evidence of the pro-competitive effects of their agreement. . . . Assuming defendants can provide such proof, the burden shifts back to the plaintiffs to prove that any legitimate competitive benefits offered by defendants could have been achieved through less restrictive means. . .

Finally, certain challenged practices warrant an "abbreviated or quick-look rule of reason analysis" either "because the great likelihood of anticompetitive effects can be easily ascertained" *or,* on the flip side, where "restraints on competition are essential if the product is to be available at all [such that] the agreement is likely to survive the Rule of Reason."

### C. Sherman Act Section 2

Section 2 of the Sherman Act states that "[e]very person who shall monopolize, or attempt to monopolize, or combine or conspire with any other person or persons, to monopolize any part of the trade or commerce among the several States, or with foreign nations, shall be deemed guilty of a felony. . . ." In order to state a claim for monopolization under Section 2, plaintiffs must establish " '(1) the possession of monopoly power in the relevant market and (2) the willful acquisition or maintenance of that power as distinguished from growth or development as a consequence of a superior product, business acumen, or historic accident.' " Specifically, "a plaintiff must establish '(1) that the defendant has engaged in predatory or anticompetitive conduct with (2) a specific intent to monopolize and (3) a dangerous probability of achieving monopoly power.'

## V. DISCUSSION

* * *

### B. Section One Claims Regarding "In-Market" and "Out-of-Market" Agreements

1. Agreements Among Defendants

As discussed briefly in the context of standing, plaintiffs allege a multi-level conspiracy consisting of horizontal and vertical agreements implicating the League defendants, the RSNs and the MVPDs. "The question whether an arrangement is a contract, combination, or conspiracy is different from and antecedent to the question whether it unreasonably restrains trade."

a. League Defendants

Plaintiffs' allegations arise initially out of agreements by the individual clubs, as a league, to establish exclusive local telecast territories for each club and to grant the Leagues the exclusive rights to market those games outside the local territories. In *American Needle, Inc. v. National Football League* the Supreme Court held that when it comes to "marketing property owned by the separate teams," individual sports teams that together comprise a league "do not possess either the unitary decisionmaking quality or the single aggregation of economic power" of a single entity and "their objectives are not common." Where teams compete against each other in the relevant market, their concerted action may "deprive the marketplace of independent centers of decisionmaking and therefore of actual or potential competition." Like the intellectual property at issue in *American Needle,* the rights at issue here belong initially to the individual clubs. Plaintiffs have alleged that absent these agreements the clubs would compete against each other in the markets for hockey and baseball programming.

The fact that the NHL and MLB are lawful joint ventures does not preclude plaintiffs from challenging the Leagues' particular policies under the rule of reason. Defendants' argument that the teams cannot unlawfully conspire with respect to out-of-market games because only the Leagues can own those games assumes the legality of the very agreements challenged here. There is no distinction between in-market and out-of-market games other than that the clubs have agreed to cede to the Leagues the right to market the games, to which they have initial rights, outside their local territories. *American Needle* conclusively established that these kinds of arrangements are subject to Section 1 scrutiny.

b. Role of RSNs

Plaintiffs argue that the RSNs have participated in a conspiracy to divide the market for professional baseball and hockey programming. They assert that RSNs do not merely "pass through" the relevant product unchanged from the Leagues to the consumers: rather, RSNs purchase *rights* from the clubs, and produce video presentations of the games—the product in question—subject to anticompetitive agreements not to sell programming for a given hockey or baseball club outside the defined territory surrounding that club. Plaintiffs argue that "[t]he fact that the clubs have a central role in orchestrating this horizontal agreement" does not negate the horizontal character of the alleged agreements by the RSNs, because "each RSN plainly understood that it was getting a regional monopoly in exchange for an agreement to respect other RSN's regional monopolies." Thus, "[e]ven when the focus is on the horizontal agreement at the club level, the RSNs are still liable, as their role in carrying out the clubs' division of the market is not innocent."

Plaintiffs do not plausibly allege that the RSNs entered into actual agreements with one another to enforce the territorial market divisions established by the League defendants, but it is not necessary that they do so in order to implicate the RSNs in the conspiracy to divide the market. First of all, courts have recognized that "vertical agreements can [ ] injure competition by facilitating horizontal collusion." It is well established, for example, that a distributor's coordination of horizontal agreements in restraint of trade at the next distribution level by entering into a series of identical vertical agreements with multiple parties may subject all participants to antitrust liability. Moreover, where parties to vertical agreements have knowledge that other market participants are bound by identical agreements, and their participation is contingent upon that knowledge, they may be considered participants in a horizontal agreement in restraint of trade. It defies reason to suggest that the RSNs lack knowledge that all other RSNs have analogous agreements with the respective individual clubs, and it is at least plausible that the terms of the agreement between the clubs and the RSNs are contingent upon that knowledge. Plaintiffs have therefore adequately alleged participation on the part of the RSNs in the conspiracy to geographically divide the market for professional hockey and baseball games.

c. Role of MVPDs

Plaintiffs claim that Comcast and DirecTV are active participants in the challenged schemes in two ways. "*First,* they actively control their subsidiary RSN's in the very matters that are the subject of this lawsuit . . . [and] *second,* the MVPDs are the only parties that can actively implement the geographical divisions for television programming . . . [and] have agreed to do just that." In addition, plaintiffs claim that

"MVPDs are the direct beneficiaries of restrictions that prevent Internet streaming of local games."

Plaintiffs do not allege that the MVPDs have agreed amongst themselves in any way, and in fact, it is clear that MVPDS compete with each other to sell packages containing hockey and baseball programming. However, plaintiffs allege that Comcast and DirecTV own and control a number of RSNs, and that the League restrictions on Internet dissemination of hockey and baseball games benefit both the RSNs and the MVPDs. These allegations indicate that the MVPD defendants are doing more than passively implementing the agreements among the Leagues and the RSNs. They suggest "a unity of purpose or a common design and understanding, or a meeting of minds in an unlawful arrangement" sufficient to allege an agreement between the MVPDs and the RSNs and League Defendants to restrain trade. Thus, while plaintiffs have not alleged horizontal agreements among the MVPDs, they have plausibly alleged vertical agreements that not only facilitate, but are essential to the horizontal market divisions.

2. Harm to Competition

Plaintiffs do not argue that the agreements to divide the geographic market and cede control over out-of-market games to the Leagues constitute *per se* antitrust violations. The question is whether these agreements have "anticompetitive effect that are harmful to the consumer" or whether they "stimulat[e] competition . . . in the consumer's best interest"—in other words, whether they survive the rule of reason.130 In order to overcome defendants' motion to dismiss, plaintiffs' "allegations must 'raise a reasonable expectation that discovery will reveal evidence of an injury to competition.' "

Defendants argue that because the NHL and MLB are legitimate joint ventures, and some cooperation with respect to the production of games is necessary, that the conduct here—the production and distribution of live telecasts of games—is "core activity" immune from antitrust scrutiny. However, the notion that "the *exhibition* of [ ] league games on television and the Internet" is clearly a "league issue" is contrary to longstanding precedent that agreements limiting the telecasting of professional sports games are subject to antitrust scrutiny, and analyzed under the rule of reason. Even *if certain* agreements by sports leagues with respect to telecasting games may be "essential if the product is to be available at all" this does not give league agreements regarding television rights blanket immunity from antitrust scrutiny. To the contrary, the Supreme Court has held that an agreement that "define[s] the number of games that may be televised, establish[es] the price for each exposure, and . . . the basic terms of each contract between the network and a home team" with the result that "[m]any games for which there is a large viewer demand are kept from the viewers, and many games for which there is little if any demand are nonetheless televised" may constitute an antitrust violation.

a. "In-Market" Agreements

Plaintiffs allege that the Leagues' arrangements define the territory in which each individual team may televise its games, meaning that individual clubs are prohibited from telecasting their baseball and hockey games outside the designated home territory, irrespective of consumer demand for those games. Plaintiffs echo defendants MSG and the New York Rangers' argument, as plaintiffs in a different case, that " '[i]n a fully competitive marketplace, the [individual clubs] could and would . . . increas[e] the opportunity to view [their] games throughout the country, whether through cable, satellite or on the Internet.' " In other words, the agreements result in an arrangement by which the clubs have authority over the output of their own games in their home territory, but must "forego their own output" outside their home territory and cede to the Leagues' authority over out-of-market games. As numerous courts have recognized, "a horizontal agreement that allocates a market between competitors and restricts each company's ability to compete for the other's business may injure competition."

b. "Out-of-Market" Agreements

Defendants argue that the fact that the market division is part of a larger joint-selling arrangement, which makes all games available to the vast majority of viewers as "all-or-nothing" out-of-market packages, eliminates any harm to competition. In contrast, plaintiffs allege that the agreements to centralize control of all baseball and hockey out-of-market programming in the Leagues, as exclusive distributors, are themselves unreasonable restraints of trade. While Congress has exempted these types of joint agreements from antitrust scrutiny in *sponsored telecasting,* that exemption is inapplicable to the telecasts of the hockey and baseball games at issue here.

Contrary to defendants' argument, *Brantley v. NBC Universal, Inc.* does not sanction the alleged out-of-market "all or nothing" packages as a replacement for individual competition among the clubs. In *Brantley,* the court rejected allegations of unlawful tying where the tied television programs were owned in the first instance by the programmers who chose to market the programs as a package. The court analogized to the professional sports context noting that there is no question that individual teams may package desirable and undesirable game tickets as part of a season package. However, the arrangement here is more akin to the League commandeering the individual clubs' rights to sell tickets to sports fans outside their home territory, and, as a replacement, conditioning the purchase of a popular team's tickets on the purchase of other teams' tickets.

The Second Circuit established in *Major League Baseball Properties, Inc. v. Salvino,* that agreements by individual clubs to grant the League the exclusive right to license use of certain rights originally held by the individual clubs are analyzed under the rule of reason. At issue in *Salvino* was an agreement by MLB clubs to grant the League "the exclusive right—subject to limited exceptions—to license Club names and logos for use on retail products for national and international (*i.e.* not merely local) distribution . . . and to be sold at retail within the Clubs' respective local markets." The court concluded that the agreement was lawful, but only after careful consideration of the district court's factual conclusions concerning the impact of the licensing agreement on output, and the viability of MLB's justifications for its decision to consolidate licensing rights in the League. *Salvino* suggests that granting the Leagues exclusive rights to distribute out-of-market programming, and the Leagues' decision to do so largely in the form of blanket licensing, may very well be reasonable and in compliance with antitrust law. However, plaintiffs have alleged the anticompetitive effect of "forc[ing] . . . consumers to forego the purchase of [these games] from other distributors [the individual clubs]" resulting in decreased consumer choice and increased price—an allegation that states an injury to competition. Defendants have not even alleged that these restraints on trade are justified, for example, by arguing that " 'individual [teams] are inherently unable to compete fully effectively' " or that the agreements are "necessary to maintain a competitive balance."

Plaintiffs have adequately alleged harm to competition with respect to the horizontal agreements among individual hockey and baseball clubs, as part of the NHL and MLB, to divide the television market. Making all games available as part of a package, while it may increase output overall, does not, as a matter of law, eliminate the harm to competition wrought by preventing the individual teams from competing to sell their games outside their home territories in the first place. And plaintiffs in this case—the consumers—have plausibly alleged that they are the direct victims of this harm to competition.

### C. Section 2 Claim for Conspiracy to Monopolize the Market for Video Presentation and Internet Streaming of Games

The final claim, brought on behalf of all plaintiffs, is a Section 2 claim for conspiracy to monopolize the "market for video presentations of major league [hockey/baseball] games and Internet streaming of the same" and "use of that power for the purposes of unreasonably excluding and/or limiting competition." Defendants argue that the Section 2 claims must be dismissed for failure to allege any of the necessary elements of a monopolization claim.

It is well established that "[t]here are peculiar and unique characteristics that set major league men's ice hockey [and baseball] apart from other sports or leisure activities, . . . that [c]lose substitutes do not exist" and that the Leagues possess monopolies of their respective sports. It is also established that "[a] monopolist may not . . . use its market power, whether obtained lawfully or not, to prevent or impede competition in the relevant market." Having defined the relevant market as the market for television broadcasting of professional hockey and baseball games, plaintiffs have adequately alleged that NHL and MLB exercise monopoly power defined as " '[w]hen a product is controlled by one interest, without substitutes available.' " Finally, as already discussed, plaintiffs have plausibly alleged that the NHL and MLB have used their monopoly power to restrict the broadcast of television programming in a manner that harms competition. However, plaintiffs have not alleged any monopoly power on the part of RSNs or MVPDs in the market for production of baseball and hockey games, nor have they alleged facts in support of a conspiracy to monopolize the market. Claim Four is therefore dismissed against the RSNs and MVPDs.

VI. CONCLUSION

For the foregoing reasons, . . . The Section Two claim (Claim Four) is dismissed against the RSN and MVPD defendants, but may proceed against the League defendants. The Section One claims may proceed against all defendants.

SO ORDERED.

## 2. CONSCIOUSLY PARALLEL BEHAVIOR

Section 1 of the Sherman Act does not prohibit individual behavior. Rather, it requires a "contract, combination, . . . or conspiracy," i.e., an agreement of some kind between two or more separate entities, before it renders illegal a restraint of trade. When a plaintiff lacks evidence of an express agreement, courts sometimes look to circumstantial evidence to prove a conspiracy. Firms may be behaving in "consciously parallel" ways in setting their prices at higher than competitive levels. "Interdependent" action is crucial to the success of such joint practices because the system will fall apart if one firm breaks ranks and lowers its prices. Consumers will flock to the lower-priced firm and its competitors will have to match that price with a decrease of their own. Courts are often asked to infer an agreement from evidence that firms have been consciously behaving in a parallel, interdependent, and noncompetitive manner. Courts examine other factors when deciding whether to infer an agreement in restraint of trade. For example, if there are special channels for communication in the industry (such as a trade association), there is a greater likelihood that courts will find an agreement. In addition, products that are standardized in quality and have comparatively simple and inexpensive ingredients are easier to coordinate.

The leading case on "conscious parallelism" is *Interstate Circuit, Inc. v. United States*, 306 U.S. 208 (1939). In that case, the Supreme Court addressed the above questions in the context of the movie exhibition business. Interstate Circuit owned all first-run, and many second-run, movie theaters in several large Texas cities. Its standard admission price was 40 cents for the first run and 25 cents for the second. Interstate Circuit simultaneously announced to the eight large film distributors that it would no longer deal with any distributor that licensed films to its competitors in the second-run theater market without meeting certain conditions. In particular, Interstate Circuit demanded that the distributors require second-run theaters to charge a higher admission price (25 cents rather than their normal 15 cents), and not exhibit in double bills those films that were previously first-run movies. Each distributor, knowing that these terms were also being imposed on its competitors, responded to Interstate's demands in the same parallel fashion: accepting them in some towns (the same ones), but not others.

The Court held that an unlawful agreement among the distributors could be inferred from the facts of the case. While there was no direct evidence of a conspiracy, the Court emphasized the distributors' knowledge of, and motive for, concerted adherence to Interstate's higher price program. It also pointed out that the distributors reached almost identical arrangements with third party exhibitors after Interstate made its proposal; these represented a departure from past methods of doing business. In a key passage of its decision, the Court set forth what has become known as the "*Interstate* formula":

> It was enough that, knowing that concerted action was contemplated and invited [by Interstate], the distributors gave their adherence to the scheme and participated in it. Each distributor was advised that the others were asked to participate; each knew that cooperation was essential to successful operation of the plan. They knew that the plan, if carried out, would result in a restraint of commerce . . . and knowing it, all participated in the plan.

*Id.* at 226–27. Thus, the jury properly inferred a § 1 agreement from the consciously parallel and interdependent behavior of the eight distributors. The Court could be fairly certain of the conspiracy because it would not be in the interest of any one firm to adhere to Interstate's contract demands by itself.

In a later decision addressing similar issues, the Court made it clear that conscious parallelism alone will not establish an agreement in violation of the Sherman Act. In that case, *Theatre Enterprises, Inc. v. Paramount Film Distributing Corp.*, 346 U.S. 537 (1954), the plaintiff was a motion picture exhibitor who claimed that movie producers and distributors had conspired to restrict first-run pictures to downtown Baltimore theaters, leaving later runs for the suburbs. Prior to the suit, the plaintiff had sought to obtain from each distributor the right to show first-run films in its theaters outside Baltimore. Each distributor rejected Theater Enterprises' offer, "adher[ing] to an established policy of restricting first-runs in Baltimore to the eight downtown theaters." Paramount and the other defendants offered a number of economic reasons for their decisions: basically, that exhibitors in any metropolitan area would insist on an exclusive first run, and that (in 1949) returns from those runs in a large downtown theater would be much larger than those from a smaller suburban theater not served by public transportation. The Court reasoned:

> The crucial question is whether respondents' conduct toward petitioner stemmed from independent decision or from an agreement, tacit or express. To be sure, business behavior is admissible circumstantial evidence from which the fact finder may infer agreement. *Interstate Circuit, Inc. v. United States*, 1939, 306 U.S. 208; *United States v. Paramount Pictures, Inc.*, 1948, 334 U.S. 131. But this Court has never held that proof of parallel business behavior conclusively establishes agreement or, phrased differently, that such behavior itself constitutes a Sherman Act offense. Circumstantial evidence of consciously parallel behavior may have made heavy inroads into the traditional judicial attitude toward conspiracy; but 'conscious parallelism' has not yet read conspiracy out of the Sherman Act entirely. Realizing this, petitioner attempts to bolster its argument for a directed verdict by urging that the conscious unanimity of action by respondents should be 'measured against the background and findings in the *Paramount* case.' In other words, since the same respondents had conspired in the *Paramount* case to impose a uniform system of runs and clearances without adequate explanation to sustain them as reasonable restraints of trade, use of the same device in the present case should be legally equated to conspiracy. But the *Paramount* decrees, even if admissible, were only prima facie evidence of a conspiracy covering the area and existing during the period there involved. Alone or in conjunction with the other proof of the petitioner, they would form no basis for a directed verdict. Here each of the respondents had denied the existence of any collaboration and in addition had introduced evidence of the

> local conditions surrounding the Crest operation which, they contended, precluded it from being a successful first-run house. They also attacked the good faith of the guaranteed offers of the petitioner for first-run pictures and attributed uniform action to individual business judgment motivated by the desire for maximum revenue. This evidence, together with other testimony of an explanatory nature, raised fact issues requiring the trial judge to submit the issue of conspiracy to the jury . . .

*Id.* at 540–42. Other evidence besides parallel behavior must be produced, then, before a court will find a § 1 violation. In *Theater Enterprises*, each of the defendants offered independently justifiable business explanation for their conduct. Consequently, their actions, unlike those in *Interstate Circuit*, did not support a finding of an agreement based simply on consciously parallel and interdependent behavior.

A recent example of antitrust conspiracy involves Apple's entry into the ebook market. The following case, decided by the Second Circuit, demonstrates the harm caused by unlawfully co-ordinated behavior in the market.

## UNITED STATES V. APPLE, INC.

United States Court of Appeals for the Second Circuit, 2015.
791 F.3d 290.

LIVINGSTON, CIRCUIT JUDGE.

Since the invention of the printing press, the distribution of books has involved a fundamentally consistent process: compose a manuscript, print and bind it into physical volumes, and then ship and sell the volumes to the public. In late 2007, Amazon.com, Inc. ("Amazon") introduced the Kindle, a portable device that carries digital copies of books, known as "ebooks." This innovation had the potential to change the centuries-old process for producing books by eliminating the need to print, bind, ship, and store them. Amazon began to popularize the new way to read, and encouraged consumers to buy the Kindle by offering desirable books—new releases and *New York Times* bestsellers—for $9.99. Publishing companies, which have traditionally stood at the center of the multi-billion dollar book-producing industry, saw Amazon's ebooks, and particularly its $9.99 pricing, as a threat to their way of doing business.

By November 2009, Apple, Inc. ("Apple") had plans to release a new tablet computer, the iPad. Executives at the company saw an opportunity to sell ebooks on the iPad by creating a virtual marketplace on the device, which came to be known as the "iBookstore." Working within a tight timeframe, Apple went directly into negotiations with six of the major publishing companies in the United States. In two months, it announced that five of those companies—Hachette, Harpercollins, Macmillan, Penguin, and Simon & Schuster (collectively, the "Publisher Defendants")—had agreed to sell ebooks on the iPad under arrangements whereby the publishers had the authority to set prices, and could set the prices of new releases and *New York Times* bestsellers as high as $19.99 and $14.99, respectively. Each of these agreements, by virtue of its terms, resulted in each Publisher Defendant receiving *less* per ebook sold via Apple as opposed to Amazon, even given the higher consumer prices. Just a few months after the iBookstore opened, however, every one of the Publisher Defendants had taken control over pricing from Amazon and had raised the prices on many of their ebooks, most notably new releases and bestsellers.

The United States Department of Justice ("DOJ" or "Justice Department") and 33 states and territories (collectively, "Plaintiffs") filed suit in the United States District Court for the Southern District of New York, alleging that Apple, in launching the iBookstore, had conspired with the Publisher Defendants to raise prices across the nascent ebook market. This agreement, they argued, violated § 1 of the Sherman Antitrust Act, 15 U.S.C. § 1 *et seq.* ("Sherman Act"), and state antitrust laws. All five Publisher Defendants settled and signed consent decrees, which prohibited them, for a period, from restricting ebook retailers' ability to set prices. Then, after a three-week bench trial, the district court (Cote, *J.*) concluded that, in order to induce the Publisher Defendants to participate in the iBookstore and to avoid the necessity of itself competing with Amazon over the retail price of ebooks, Apple orchestrated a conspiracy among the Publisher Defendants to raise the price of ebooks—particularly new releases and *New York Times* bestsellers. *United States v. Apple Inc.,* 952 F.Supp.2d 638, 647 (S.D.N.Y.2013). The district court found that the agreement constituted a *per se* violation of the Sherman Act and, in the alternative, unreasonably restrained trade under the rule of reason. *See id.* at 694. On September 5, 2013, the district court entered final judgment on the liability finding and issued an injunctive order that, *inter alia,* prevents Apple from entering into agreements with the Publisher Defendants that restrict its ability to set, alter, or reduce the price of ebooks, and requires Apple to apply the same terms and conditions to ebook applications sold on its devices as it does to other applications.

On appeal, Apple contends that the district court's liability finding was erroneous and that the provisions of the injunction related to its pricing authority and ebook applications are not necessary to protect the public. Two of the Publisher Defendants—Macmillan and Simon & Schuster—join the appeal, arguing that the portion of the injunction related to Apple's pricing authority either unlawfully modifies their consent decrees or should be judicially estopped. We conclude that the district court's decision that Apple orchestrated a horizontal conspiracy among the Publisher Defendants to raise ebook prices is amply supported and well-reasoned, and that the agreement unreasonably restrained trade in violation of § 1 of the Sherman Act. We also conclude that the district court's injunction is lawful and consistent with preventing future anticompetitive harms.

* * *

Because we conclude that the district court did not err in deciding that Apple violated § 1 of the Sherman Act, and because we also conclude that the district court's injunction was lawful and consistent with preventing future anticompetitive harms, we affirm.

## BACKGROUND

### I. Factual Background

We begin not with Kindles and iPads, but with printed "trade books," which are "general interest fiction and non-fiction" books intended for a broad readership. *Apple,* 952 F.Supp.2d at 648 n. 4. In the United States, the six largest publishers of trade books, known in the publishing world as the "Big Six," are Hachette, HarperCollins, Macmillan, Penguin, Random House, and Simon & Schuster. Together, the Big Six publish many of the biggest names in fiction and non-fiction; during 2010, their titles accounted for over 90% of the *New York Times* bestsellers in the United States. *Id.* at 648 n. 5.

For decades, trade book publishers operated under a fairly consistent business model. When a new book was ready for release to the public, the publisher would sell hardcover copies to retailers at a "wholesale" price and recommend resale to consumers at a markup, known as the "list" price. After the hardcover spent enough time on the shelves—often a year—publishers would release a paperback copy at lower "list" and "wholesale" prices. In theory, devoted readers would pay the higher hardcover price to read the book when it first came out, while more casual fans would wait for the paperback.

* * *

### D. Apple's Negotiations with the Publishers

#### 1. Initial Meetings

Apple held its first meetings with each of the Big Six between December 15 and 16. The meetings quickly confirmed Cue's suspicions about the industry. As he wrote to Jobs after speaking with three of the publishers, "[c]learly, the biggest issue is new release pricing" and "Amazon is definitely not liked much because of selling below cost for NYT Best Sellers." J.A. 326–27. Many publishers also emphasized that they were searching for a strategy to regain control over pricing. Apple informed each of the Big Six that it was negotiating with the other major publishers, that it hoped to begin selling ebooks within the next 90 days, and that it was seeking a critical mass of participants in the iBookstore and would launch only if successful in reaching this goal. Apple informed the publishers that it did not believe the iBookstore would succeed unless publishers agreed both not to window books and to sell ebooks at a discount relative to their physical counterparts. Apple noted that ebook prices in the iBookstore needed to be comparable to those on the Kindle, expressing the view, as Reidy recorded, that it could not "tolerate a market where the product is sold significantly more cheaply elsewhere." *Apple,* 952 F.Supp.2d at 657 (internal quotation marks omitted). Most importantly for the publishers, however, Cue's team also expressed Apple's belief that Amazon's $9.99 price point was not ingrained in consumers' minds, and that Apple could sell new releases and *New York Times* bestsellers for somewhere between $12.99 and $14.99. In return, Apple requested that the publishers decrease their wholesale prices so that the company could make a small profit on each sale.

These meetings spurred a flurry of communications reporting on the "[t]errific news[,]" as Reidy put it in an email to Leslie Moonves, her superior at parent company CBS Corporation ("CBS"), that Apple "was not interested in a low price point for digital books" and didn't want "Amazon's $9.95 [sic] to continue." *Apple,* 952 F.Supp.2d at 658 (first alteration in original) (internal quotation marks omitted). Significantly, these communications included numerous exchanges *between* executives at different Big Six publishers who, the district court found, "hashed over their meetings with Apple with one another." *Id.* The district court found that the frequent telephone calls among the Publisher Defendants during the period of their negotiations with Apple "represented a departure from the ordinary pattern of calls among them." *Id.* at 655 n. 14.

### 2. The Agency Model

Meanwhile, Cue, Moerer, and Saul returned to Apple's headquarters to develop a business model for the iBookstore. Although the team was optimistic about the initial meetings, they remained concerned about whether the publishers would reduce wholesale prices on new releases and bestsellers by a large enough margin to allow Apple to offer competitive prices and still make a profit. One strategy that the team considered was to ask publishers for a 25% wholesale discount on all of these titles, so if a physical book sold at $12 wholesale (the going rate for the majority of *New York Times* bestsellers) Apple could purchase the ebook version for $9 and offer it on the iBookstore at a small markup. But Cue was aware that some publishers had increased Amazon's digital wholesale prices in 2009 in an unsuccessful effort to convince Amazon to change its pricing. *Id.* at 650; J.A. 1771. Cue felt it would be difficult to negotiate wholesale prices down far enough "for [Apple] to generally compete profitably with Amazon's below-cost pricing on the most popular e-books." J.A. 1772. As Cue saw it, Apple's most valuable bargaining chip came from the fact that the publishers were desperate "for an alternative to Amazon's pricing policies and excited about . . . the prospect that [Apple's] entry [into the ebook market] would give them leverage in their negotiations with Amazon." *Apple,* 952 F.Supp.2d at 659.

It was at this point that Cue's team, recognizing its opportunity, abandoned the wholesale business model for a new, agency model. Unlike a wholesale model, in an agency relationship the *publisher* sets the price that consumers will pay for each ebook. Then, rather than the retailer paying the publisher for each ebook that it sells, the publisher pays the retailer a fixed percentage of each sale. In essence, the retailer receives a commission for distributing the publisher's ebooks. Under the system Apple devised, publishers would have the freedom to set ebook prices in the iBookstore, and would keep 70% of each sale. The remaining 30% would go to Apple as a commission.

This switch to an agency model obviated Apple's concerns about negotiating wholesale prices with the Big Six while ensuring that Apple profited on every sale. It did not, however, solve all of the company's problems. Because the agency model handed the publishers control over pricing, it created the risk that the Big Six would sell ebooks in the iBookstore at far higher prices than Kindle's $9.99 offering. If the prices were too high, Apple could be left with a brand new marketplace brimming with titles, but devoid of customers.

To solve this pricing problem, Cue's team initially devised two strategies. First, they realized that they could maintain "realistic prices" by establishing price caps for different types of books. J.A. 359. Of course, these caps would need to be *higher* than Amazon's $9.99 price point, or Apple would face the same difficult price negotiations that it sought to avoid by switching away from the wholesale model. But at this point Apple was not content to open its iBookstore offering prices higher than the competition. For as the district court found, if the Publisher Defendants "wanted to end Amazon's $9.99 pricing," Apple similarly desired "that there be no price competition at the retail level." *Apple,* 952 F.Supp.2d at 647.

Apple next concluded, then, as the district court found, that "[t]o ensure that the iBookstore would be competitive at higher prices, Apple . . . needed to eliminate all retail price competition." *Id.* at 659. Thus, rather than simply agreeing to price caps above Amazon's $9.99 price point, Apple created a second requirement: publishers must switch all of their other ebook retailers—including Amazon—to an agency pricing model. The result would be that Apple would not need to compete with Amazon on price, and publishers would be able to eliminate Amazon's

$9.99 pricing. Or, as Cue would later describe the plan to executives at Simon & Schuster, Macmillan, and Random House, the plan "solve[d][the] Amazon issue" by allowing the publishers to wrest control over pricing from Amazon. *Id.* at 661 (internal quotation marks omitted).

On January 4 and 5, Apple sent essentially identical emails to each member of the Big Six to explain its agency model proposal. Each email described the commission split between Apple and the publishers and recommended three price caps: $14.99 for hardcover books with list prices above $35; $12.99 for hardcover books with list prices below $35; and $9.99 for all other trade books. The emails also explained that, "to sell ebooks at realistic prices . . . all [other] resellers of new titles need to be in [the] agency model" as well. J.A. 360. Or, as Cue told Reidy, "all publishers" would need to move "all retailers" to an agency model. J.A.2060.

3. The "Most-Favored-Nation" Clause

Cue's thoughts on the agency model continued to evolve after the emails on January 4 and 5. Most significantly, Saul—Cue's in-house counsel—devised an alternative to explicitly requiring publishers to switch other retailers to agency. This alternative involved the use of a "most-favored nation" clause ("MFN Clause" or "MFN"). In general, an MFN Clause is a contractual provision that requires one party to give the other the best terms that it makes available to any competitor. In the context of Apple's negotiations, the MFN Clause mandated that, "[i]f, for any particular New Release in hardcover format, the . . . Customer Price [in the iBookstore] at any time is or becomes higher than a customer price offered by any other reseller . . . , then [the] Publisher shall designate a new, lower Customer Price [in the iBookstore] to meet such lower [customer price]." J.A. 559. Put differently, the MFN would require the publisher to offer any ebook in Apple's iBookstore for no more than what the same ebook was offered elsewhere, such as from Amazon.

On January 11, Apple sent each of the Big Six a proposed eBook Agency Distribution Agreement (the "Contracts"). As described in the January 4 and 5 emails, these Contracts would split the proceeds from each ebook sale between the publisher and Apple, with the publisher receiving 70%, and would set price caps on ebooks at $14.99, $12.99, and $9.99 depending on the book's hardcover price. But unlike the initial emails, the Contracts contained MFN Clauses in place of the requirement that publishers move all other retailers to an agency model. Apple then assured each member of the Big Six that it was being offered the same terms as the others.

The Big Six understood the economic incentives that the MFN Clause created. Suppose a new hardcover release sells at a list price of $25, and a wholesale price of $12.50. With Amazon, the publishers had been receiving the wholesale price (or a slightly lower digital wholesale price) for every ebook copy of the volume sold on Kindle, even if Amazon ultimately sold the ebook for less than that wholesale price. Under Apple's initial agency model—with price caps but no MFN Clause—the publishers already stood to make *less* money per ebook with Apple. Because Apple capped the ebook price of a $25 hardcover at $12.99 and took 30% of that price, publishers could only expect to make $8.75 per sale. But what the publishers sacrificed in short-term revenue, they hoped to gain in long-term stability by acquiring more control over pricing and, accordingly, the ability to protect their hardcover sales.

The MFN Clause changed the situation by making it imperative, not merely desirable, that the publishers wrest control over pricing from ebook retailers generally. Under the MFN, if Amazon stayed at a wholesale model and continued to sell ebooks at $9.99, the publishers would be forced to sell in the iBookstore, too, at that same $9.99 price point. The result would be the worst of both worlds: *lower* short-term revenue and *no* control over pricing. The publishers recognized that, as a practical matter, this meant that the MFN Clause would force them to move Amazon to an agency relationship. As Reidy put it, her company would need to move all its other ebook retailers to agency "unless we wanted to make even less money" in this growing market. *Apple,* 952 F.Supp.2d at 666 (internal quotation marks omitted). This situation also gave each of the publishers a stake in Apple's quest to have a critical mass of publishers join the iBookstore because, "[w]hile no one Publisher could effect an industry-wide shift in prices or change the public's perception of a book's value, if they moved together they could." *Id.* at 665; *see also* J.A.1981.

Apple understood this dynamic as well. As the district court found, "Apple did not change its thinking" when it replaced the explicit requirement that the publishers move other retailers to an agency model with the MFN. Indeed, in the following weeks, Apple assiduously worked to make sure that the shift to agency occurred. *Apple,* 952 F.Supp.2d at 663. But Apple also understood that, as Cue bluntly put it, "any decent MFN forces the model" away from wholesale and to agency. *Id.* (internal quotation marks omitted). Or as the district court found, "the MFN protected Apple from retail price competition as it punished a Publisher if it failed to impose agency terms on other e-tailers." *Id.* at 665.

Thus, the terms of the negotiation between Apple and the publishers became clear: Apple wanted quick and successful entry into the ebook market and to eliminate retail price competition with Amazon. In exchange, it offered the publishers an opportunity "to confront Amazon as one of an organized group . . . united in an effort to eradicate the $9.99 price point." *Id.* at 664. Both sides needed a critical mass of publishers to achieve their goals. The MFN played a pivotal role in this *quid pro quo* by "stiffen[ing] the spines of the [publishers] to ensure that they would demand new terms from Amazon," and protecting Apple from retail price competition. *Id.* at 665.

#### 4. Final Negotiations

The proposed Contracts sparked intense negotiations as Cue's team raced to assemble enough publishers to announce the iBookstore by January 27. The publishers' first volley was to push back on Apple's price caps, which they recognized would become the "standard across the industry" for pricing. J.A. 571. In a set of meetings between January 13 and 14, the majority of the Big Six expressed a general willingness to adopt an agency model, but refused to do so with the price limits Apple demanded. Cue responded by asking Jobs for permission to create a more lenient price cap system. Under this new regime, *New York Times* bestsellers could sell for $14.99 if the hardcover was listed above $30, and for $12.99 if listed below that price. As for new releases, a $12.99 cap would apply to hardcovers priced between $25 and $27.50; a $14.99 cap would apply to hardcovers selling for up to $30; and, if the hardcover sold for over $30, publishers could sell the ebook for between $16.99 and $19.99. Jobs responded that he could "live with" the pricing "as long as [the publishers] move Amazon to the agen[cy] model too." J.A. 499.

Cue proposed this new pricing regime to the Big Six on January 16 and, with only 11 days remaining before the iPad launch, turned up the pressure. In each email conveying the new prices, Cue reminded the publishers that, if they did not agree to the iBookstore by the 27th, other companies, including Amazon and Barnes & Noble, would certainly build their own book store apps for the iPad. Correspondence from within the publishing companies also shows that Cue promoted the proposal as the "best chance for publishers to challenge the 9.99 price point," and emphasized that Apple would "not move forward with the store [unless] 5 of the 6 [major publishers] signed the agreement." J.A. 522–23. As Cue said at trial, he attempted to "assure [the publishers] that they weren't going to be alone, so that [he] would take the fear awa[y] of the Amazon retribution that they were all afraid of." J.A.2068 (internal quotation marks omitted). "The Apple team reminded the Publishers," as the district court found, "that this was a rare opportunity for them to achieve control over pricing." *Apple,* 952 F.Supp.2d at 664.

By January 22, two publishers—Simon & Schuster and Hachette—had verbally committed to join the iBookstore, while a third, Penguin, had agreed to Apple's terms in principle. As for the others, Cue was frustrated that they kept "chickening out" because of the "dramatic business change" that Apple was proposing. J.A. 547. To make matters worse, "[p]ress reports on January 18 and 19 alerted the publishing world and Amazon to the Publishers' negotiations with Apple," *Apple,* 952

F.Supp.2d at 670–71, and Amazon learned from Random House that it was facing "pressure from other publishers . . . to move to [the] agency model because Apple had made it clear that unless all of the Big Six participated, they wouldn't bother with building a bookstore," J.A. 1520. Representatives from Amazon descended on New York for a set of long-scheduled meetings with the publishers. As the district court found, "[i]n separate conversations on January 20 and over the next few days, the Publisher Defendants all told Amazon that they wanted to change to an agency distribution model with Amazon." *Apple,* 952 F.Supp.2d at 672.

Macmillan, however, presented an issue for Apple. The district court found that at a January 20 lunch between John Sargent and Amazon, Sargent "announced that Macmillan was planning to offer Amazon the option to choose either an agency [or wholesale] model." *Id.* But at dinner with Cue that night, according to the district court, Cue made sure that Sargent understood the consequences of the MFN, explaining "that Macmillan had no choice but to move Amazon to an agency model if it wanted to sign an agency agreement with Apple." *Id.* The next day, Sargent emailed Cue to express his continued reservations about switching Macmillan's other retailers to an agency relationship.

With the iPad launch fast approaching, Cue enlisted the help of others. Cue had received an email from Simon & Schuster's Carolyn Reidy, who had already verbally committed to Apple's terms and whom Cue would later call the "real leader of the book industry," moments after hearing from Sargent. J.A. 621. Cue then spoke with Reidy for twenty minutes before reaching out to Brian Murray, who, as the district court found, "was fully supportive of the requirement that all e-tailers be moved to an agency model." *Apple,* 952 F.Supp.2d at 673 n. 39. After the discussions, Cue asked Sargent to speak with both Reidy and Murray. Sargent complied, and "spoke to both Murray and Reidy by telephone for eight and fifteen minutes, respectively." *Id.* at 673. Minutes later, Sargent called the Amazon representative to inform him that Macmillan planned to sign an agreement that "required" the company to conduct business with Amazon through an agency model. *Id.* By January 23, Macmillan had verbally agreed to join the iBookstore.

Cue followed a similar strategy with Penguin. While Penguin's CEO David Shanks agreed to Apple's terms on January 22, he informed Cue that he would join the iBookstore only if four other publishers agreed to participate. By January 25, Apple had signatures from three publishers but Penguin was still noncommittal. Cue called Shanks, and the two spoke for twenty minutes. "Less than an hour [later], Shanks called Reidy to discuss Penguin's status in its negotiations with Apple." *Id.* at 675. Penguin signed the Contract that afternoon.

HarperCollins was the fifth, and final, publisher to agree in principle to Apple's proposal. Murray, its CEO, "remained unhappy over the size of Apple's commission and the existence of price caps." *Id.* at 673 n. 39. Unable to negotiate successfully with Murray, Cue asked Jobs to contact James Murdoch, the CEO of the publisher's parent company, and "tell him we have 3 signed so there is no leap of faith here." *Id.* at 675 (internal quotation marks omitted). After a series of emails, Jobs summarized Apple's position to Murdoch:

[W]e simply don't think the ebook market can be successful with pricing higher than $12.99 or $14.99. Heck, Amazon is selling these books at $9.99, and who knows, maybe they are right and we will fail even at $12.99. But we're willing to try at the prices we've proposed. . . . As I see it, [HarperCollins] has the following choices: (1) Throw in with [A]pple and see if we can all make a go of this to create a real mainstream ebooks market at $12.99 and $14.99. (2) Keep going with Amazon at $9.99. You will make a bit more money in the short term, but in the medium term Amazon will tell you they will be paying you 70% of $9.99. They have shareholders too. (3) Hold back your books from Amazon. Without a way for customers to buy your ebooks, they will steal them.

*Id.* at 677. Cue also emailed Murray to inform him that four other publishers had signed their agreements. Murray then called executives at both Hachette and Macmillan before agreeing to Apple's terms.

As the district court found, during the period in January during which Apple concluded its agreements with the Publisher Defendants, "Apple kept the Publisher Defendants apprised about who was in and how many were on board." *Id.* at 673. The Publisher Defendants also kept in close communication. As the district court noted, "[i]n the critical negotiation period, over the three days between January 19 and 21, Murray, Reidy, Shanks, Young, and Sargeant called one another 34 times, with 27 calls exchanged on January 21 alone." *Id.* at 674.

By the January 27 iPad launch, five of the Big Six—Hachette, HarperCollins, Macmillan, Penguin, and Simon & Schuster—had agreed to participate in the iBookstore. The lone holdout, Random House, did not join because its executives believed it would fare better under a wholesale pricing model and were unwilling to make a complete switch to agency pricing. Steve Jobs announced the iBookstore as part of his presentation introducing the iPad. When asked after the presentation why someone should purchase an ebook from Apple for $14.99 as opposed to $9.99 with Amazon or Barnes & Noble, Jobs confidently replied, "[t]hat won't be the case . . . the price will be the same. . . . [P]ublishers will actually withhold their [e]books from Amazon . . . because they are not happy with the price." A day later, Jobs told his biographer the publishers' position with

Amazon: "[y]ou're going to sign an agency contract or we're not going to give you the books." J.A. 891 (internal quotation marks omitted).

E. Negotiations with Amazon

Jobs's boast proved to be prophetic. While the Publisher Defendants were signing Apple's Contracts, they were also informing Amazon that they planned on changing the terms of their agreements with it to an agency model. However, their move against Amazon began in earnest on January 28, the day after the iPad launch. That afternoon, John Sargent flew to Seattle to deliver an ultimatum on behalf of Macmillan: that Amazon would switch its ebook sales agreement with Macmillan to an agency model or suffer a seven-month delay in its receipt of Macmillan's new releases. Amazon responded by removing the option to purchase Macmillan's print and ebook titles from its website.

Sargent, as the district court found, had informed Cue of his intention to confront Amazon before ever leaving for Seattle. *Apple,* 952 F.Supp.2d at 678. On his return, he emailed Cue to inform him about Amazon's decision to remove Macmillan ebooks from Kindle, adding a note to say that he wanted to "make sure you are in the loop." J.A. 640. Sargent also wrote a public letter to Macmillan's authors and agents, describing the Amazon negotiations. Hachette's Arnaud Nourry emailed the CEO of Macmillan's parent company to express his "personal support" for Macmillan's actions and to "ensure [him] that [he was] not going to find [his] company alone in the battle." J.A. 643. A Penguin executive wrote to express similar support for Macmillan's position.

The district court found that while Amazon was "opposed to adoption of the agency model and did not want to cede pricing authority to the Publishers," it knew that it could not prevail in this position against five of the Big Six. *Apple,* 952 F.Supp.2d at 671, 680. When Amazon told Macmillan that it would be willing to negotiate agency terms, Sargent sent Cue an email titled "URGENT!!" that read: "Hi Eddy, I am gonna need to figure out our final agency terms of sale tonight. Can you call me please?" J.A. 642. Cue and Sargent spoke that night and, while Cue denied at trial that the conversation concerned Macmillan's negotiations with Amazon, the district court found that "his denial was not credible." *Apple,* 952 F.Supp.2d at 681 n. 52. By February 5, Amazon had agreed to agency terms with Macmillan.

The other publishers who had joined the iBookstore quickly followed Macmillan's lead. On February 11, Reidy wrote to the head of CBS that Simon & Schuster was beginning agency negotiations with Amazon. She informed him that she was trying to "delay" negotiations because it was "imperative . . . that the other publishers with whom Apple has announced deals push for resolution on their term changes" at the same time, "thus not leaving us out there alone." J.A. 701. Each of the

Publisher Defendants then informed Amazon that they were under tight deadlines to negotiate new agency agreements, and kept one another informed about the details of their negotiations. As David Naggar, one of Amazon's negotiators, testified, whenever Amazon "would make a concession on an important deal point," it would "come back to us from another publisher asking for the same thing or proposing similar language." J.A. 1491.

Once again, Apple closely monitored the negotiations with Amazon. The Publisher Defendants would inform Cue when they had completed agency agreements, and his team monitored price changes on the Kindle. When Penguin languished behind the others, Cue informed Jobs that Apple was "changing a bunch of Penguin titles to 9.99" in the iBookstore "because they didn't get their Amazon deal done." *Apple,* 952 F.Supp.2d at 682 (internal quotation marks omitted). By March 2010, Macmillan, HarperCollins, Hachette, and Simon & Schuster had completed agency agreements with Amazon. When Penguin completed its deal in June, the company's executive proudly announced to Cue that "[t]he playing field is now level." *Id.* (internal quotation marks omitted).

F. Effect on Ebook Prices

As Apple and the Publisher Defendants expected, the iBookstore price caps quickly became the benchmark for ebook versions of new releases and *New York Times* bestsellers. In the five months following the launch of the iBookstore, the publishers who joined the marketplace and switched Amazon to an agency model priced 85.7% of new releases on Kindle and 92.1% of new releases on the iBookstore at, or just below, the price caps. *Apple,* 952 F.Supp.2d at 682. Prices for *New York Times* bestsellers took a similar leap as publishers began to sell 96.8% of their bestsellers on Kindle and 99.4% of their bestsellers on the iBookstore at, or just below, the Apple price caps. *Id.* During that same time period, Random House, which had not switched to an agency model, saw virtually no change in the prices for its new releases or *New York Times* bestsellers.

The Apple price caps also had a ripple effect on the rest of the Publisher Defendants' catalogues. Recognizing that Apple's price caps were tied to the price of hardcover books, many of these publishers increased the prices of their newly released *hardcover* books to shift the ebook version into a higher price category. *Id.* at 683. Furthermore, because the Publisher Defendants who switched to the agency model expected to make less money per sale than under the wholesale model, they also increased the prices on their ebooks that were *not* new releases or bestsellers to make up for the expected loss of revenue. Based on data from February 2010—just before the Publisher Defendants switched Amazon to agency pricing—to February 2011, an expert retained by the

Justice Department observed that the weighted average price of the Publisher Defendants' new releases increased by 24.2%, while bestsellers increased by 40.4%, and other ebooks increased by 27.5%, for a total weighted average ebook price increase of 23.9%. Indeed, even Apple's expert agreed, noting that, over a two-year period, the Publisher Defendants increased their average prices for hardcovers, new releases, and other ebooks.

Increasing prices reduced demand for the Publisher Defendants' ebooks. According to one of Plaintiffs' experts, the publishers who switched to agency sold 77,307 fewer ebooks over a two-week period after the switch to agency than in a comparable two-week period before the switch, which amounted to selling 12.9% fewer units. *Id.* at 684. Another expert relied on data from Random House to estimate how many ebooks the Publisher Defendants who switched Amazon to agency would have sold had they stayed with the wholesale model, and concluded that the agency switch and price increases led to 14.5% fewer sales. *Id.*

Significantly, these changes took place against the backdrop of a rapidly changing ebook market. Amazon introduced the Kindle in November 2007, just over two years before Apple launched the iPad in January 2010. During that short period, Apple estimated that the market grew from $70 million in ebook sales in 2007 to $280 million in 2009, and the company projected those figures to grow significantly in following years. Apple's expert witnesses argued that overall ebook sales continued to grow in the two years after the creation of the iBookstore and that the average ebook price fell during those years. But as Plaintiffs' experts pointed out, the ebook market had been expanding rapidly even before Apple's entry and average prices had been falling as lower-end publishers entered the market and larger numbers of old books became available in digital form. "Apple's experts did not present any analysis that attempted to control for the many changes that the e-book market was experiencing during these early years of its growth," *Apple,* 952 F.Supp.2d at 685, nor did they estimate how the market would have grown *but for* Apple's agreement with the Publisher Defendants to switch to an agency model and raise prices. To the contrary, the undisputed fact that the Publisher Defendants raised prices on their ebooks, which accounted for roughly 50% of the trade ebook market in the first quarter of 2010, necessitated "a finding that the actions taken by Apple and the Publisher Defendants led to an increase in the price of e-books." *Id.*

* * *

DISCUSSION

* * *

II. Apple's Liability Under § 1

This appeal requires us to address the important distinction between "horizontal" agreements to set prices, which involve coordination "between competitors at the same level of [a] market structure," and "vertical" agreements on pricing, which are created between parties "at different levels of [a] market structure." *Anderson News, L.L.C. v. Am. Media, Inc.,* 680 F.3d 162, 182 (2d Cir.2012) (internal quotation marks omitted). Under § 1 of the Sherman Act, the former are, with limited exceptions, *per se* unlawful, while the latter are unlawful only if an assessment of market effects, known as a rule-of-reason analysis, reveals that they unreasonably restrain trade. *See Leegin Creative Leather Prods., Inc. v. PSKS, Inc.,* 551 U.S. 877, 893, 127 S.Ct. 2705, 168 L.Ed.2d 623 (2007).

Although this distinction is sharp in theory, determining the orientation of an agreement can be difficult as a matter of fact and turns on more than simply identifying whether the participants are at the same level of the market structure. For instance, courts have long recognized the existence of "hub-and-spoke" conspiracies in which an entity at one level of the market structure, the "hub," coordinates an agreement among competitors at a different level, the "spokes." *Howard Hess Dental Labs. Inc. v. Dentsply Int'l, Inc.,* 602 F.3d 237, 255 (3d Cir.2010); *see also Toys "R" Us, Inc. v. FTC,* 221 F.3d 928, 932–34 (7th Cir.2000). These arrangements consist of *both* vertical agreements between the hub and each spoke and a horizontal agreement among the spokes "to adhere to the [hub's] terms," often because the spokes "would not have gone along with [the vertical agreements] except on the understanding that the other [spokes] were agreeing to the same thing." VI Phillip E. Areeda & Herbert Hovenkamp, *Antitrust Law* ¶ 1402c (3d ed.2010) (citing *PepsiCo, Inc. v. Coca-Cola Co.,* 315 F.3d 101 (2d Cir.2002)); *see also* Am. Bar Ass'n, *Antitrust Law Developments* 24–26 (6th ed.2007); XII Areeda & Hovenkamp, *supra,* ¶ 2004c.

Apple characterizes its Contracts with the Publisher Defendants as a series of parallel but independent vertical agreements, a characterization that forms the basis for its two primary arguments against the district court's decision. First, Apple argues that the district court impermissibly inferred its involvement in a horizontal price-fixing conspiracy from the Contracts themselves. Because (in Apple's view) the Contracts were vertical, lawful, and in Apple's independent economic interest, the mere fact that Apple agreed to the same terms with multiple publishers cannot establish that Apple consciously organized a conspiracy among the Publisher Defendants to raise consumer-facing ebook prices—even if the *effect* of its Contracts was to raise those prices. Second, Apple argues that, even if it did orchestrate a horizontal price-fixing conspiracy, its conduct should not be subject to *per se* condemnation. According to Apple, proper application of the rule of reason reveals that its conduct was not unlawful.

For the reasons set forth below, we reject these arguments. On this record, the district court did not err in determining that Apple orchestrated an agreement with and among the Publisher Defendants, in characterizing this agreement as a horizontal price fixing-conspiracy, or in holding that the conspiracy unreasonably restrained trade in violation of § 1 of the Sherman Act.

A. The Conspiracy with the Publisher Defendants

Section 1 of the Sherman Act bans restraints on trade "effected by a contract, combination, or conspiracy." *Bell Atl. Corp. v. Twombly,* 550 U.S. 544, 553, 127 S.Ct. 1955, 167 L.Ed.2d 929 (2007) (internal quotation marks omitted). The first "crucial question in a Section 1 case is therefore whether the challenged conduct 'stem[s] from independent decision or from an agreement, tacit or express.' " *Starr v. Sony BMG Music Entm't,* 592 F.3d 314, 321 (2d Cir.2010) (alteration in original) (quoting *Theatre Enters., Inc. v. Paramount Film Distrib. Corp.,* 346 U.S. 537, 540, 74 S.Ct. 257, 98 L.Ed. 273 (1954)).

Identifying the existence and nature of a conspiracy requires determining whether the evidence "reasonably tends to prove that the [defendant] and others had a conscious commitment to a common scheme designed to achieve an unlawful objective." *Monsanto Co. v. Spray-Rite Serv. Corp.,* 465 U.S. 752, 764, 104 S.Ct. 1464, 79 L.Ed.2d 775 (1984) (internal quotation marks omitted). Parallel action is not, by itself, sufficient to prove the existence of a conspiracy; such behavior could be the result of "coincidence, independent responses to common stimuli, or mere interdependence unaided by an advance understanding among the parties." *Twombly,* 550 U.S. at 556 n. 4 (internal quotation marks omitted). Indeed, parallel behavior that does not result from an agreement is not unlawful even if it is anticompetitive. *See In re Text Messaging Antitrust Litig.,* 782 F.3d 867, 873–79 (7th Cir.2015); *In re Flat Glass Antitrust Litig.,* 385 F.3d 350, 360–61 (3d Cir.2004). Accordingly, to prove an antitrust conspiracy, "a plaintiff must show the existence of additional circumstances, often referred to as 'plus' factors, which, when viewed in conjunction with the parallel acts, can serve to allow a fact-finder to infer a conspiracy." *Apex Oil Co. v. DiMauro,* 822 F.2d 246, 253 (2d Cir.1987).

These additional circumstances can, of course, consist of "direct evidence that the defendants entered into an agreement" like "a recorded phone call in which two competitors agreed to fix prices." *Mayor & City*

*Council of Baltimore, Md. v. Citigroup, Inc.* ., 709 F.3d 129, 136 (2d Cir.2013). But plaintiffs may also "present circumstantial facts supporting the *inference* that a conspiracy existed." *Id.* Circumstances that may raise an inference of conspiracy include "a common motive to conspire, evidence that shows that the parallel acts were against the apparent individual economic self-interest of the alleged conspirators, and evidence of a high level of interfirm communications." *Id.* (internal quotation marks omitted). Parallel conduct alone may support an inference of conspiracy, moreover, if it consists of "complex and historically unprecedented changes in pricing structure made at the very same time by multiple competitors, and made for no other discernible reason." *Id.* at 137 (internal quotation marks omitted).

Because of the risk of condemning parallel conduct that results from independent action and not from an actual unlawful agreement, the Supreme Court has cautioned against drawing an inference of conspiracy from evidence that is equally consistent with independent conduct as with illegal conspiracy—or, as the Court has called it, "ambiguous" evidence. *Matsushita Elec. Indus. Co. v. Zenith Radio Corp.,* 475 U.S. 574, 597 n. 21, 106 S.Ct. 1348, 89 L.Ed.2d 538 (1986). Thus, a finding of conspiracy requires "evidence that tends to exclude the possibility" that the defendant was "acting independently." *Monsanto,* 465 U.S. at 764. This requirement, however, "[does] not mean that the plaintiff must disprove all nonconspiratorial explanations for the defendants' conduct"; rather, the evidence need only be sufficient "to allow a reasonable fact finder to infer that the conspiratorial explanation is more likely than not." *In re Publ'n Paper Antitrust Litig.,* 690 F.3d 51, 63 (2d Cir.2012) (quoting Phillip E. Areeda & Herbert Hovenkamp, *Fundamentals of Antitrust Law* § 14.03(b), at 14–25 (4th ed.2011)); *accord Matsushita,* 475 U.S. at 588 (requiring that "the inference of conspiracy is reasonable in light of the competing inferences of independent action"); *In re High Fructose Corn Syrup Antitrust Litig.,* 295 F.3d 651, 655–56 (7th Cir.2002).

Apple portrays its Contracts with the Publisher Defendants as, at worst, "unwittingly facilitat[ing]" their joint conduct. Apple Br. at 23. All Apple did, it claims, was attempt to enter the market on profitable terms by offering contractual provisions—an agency model, the MFN Clause, and tiered price caps—which ensured the company a small profit on each ebook sale and insulated it from retail price competition. This had the *effect* of raising prices because it created an incentive for the Publisher Defendants to demand that Amazon adopt an agency model and to seize control over consumer-facing ebook prices industry-wide. But although Apple knew that its contractual terms would entice the Publisher Defendants (who wanted to do away with Amazon's $9.99 pricing) to seek control over prices from Amazon and other ebook retailers, Apple's success in capitalizing on the Publisher Defendants' preexisting incentives, it contends, does not suggest that it joined a *conspiracy* among the Publisher Defendants to raise prices. In sum, Apple's basic argument is that because its Contracts with the Publisher Defendants were fully consistent with its independent business interests, those agreements provide only "ambiguous" evidence of a § 1 conspiracy, and the district court therefore erred under *Matsushita* and *Monsanto* in inferring such a conspiracy.

We disagree. At the start, Apple's benign portrayal of its Contracts with the Publisher Defendants is not persuasive—not because those Contracts themselves were independently unlawful, but because, in context, they provide strong evidence that Apple consciously orchestrated a conspiracy among the Publisher Defendants. As explained below, and as the district court concluded, Apple understood that its proposed Contracts were attractive to the Publisher Defendants *only* if they collectively shifted their relationships with Amazon to an agency model—which Apple knew would result in higher consumer-facing ebook prices. In addition to these Contracts, moreover, ample additional evidence identified by the district court established both that the Publisher Defendants' shifting to an agency model with Amazon was the result of express collusion among them and that Apple consciously played a key role in organizing that collusion. The district court did not err in concluding that Apple was more than an innocent bystander.

Apple offered each Big Six publisher a proposed Contract that would be attractive only if the publishers acted collectively. Under Apple's proposed agency model, the publishers stood to make *less* money per sale than under their wholesale agreements with Amazon, but the Publisher Defendants were willing to stomach this loss because the model allowed them to sell new releases and bestsellers for more than $9.99. Because of the MFN Clause, however, each new release and bestseller sold in the iBookstore would cost only $9.99 as long as Amazon continued to sell ebooks at that price. So in order to receive the perceived benefit of Apple's proposed Contracts, the Publisher Defendants had to switch *Amazon* to an agency model as well—something no individual publisher had sufficient leverage to do on its own. Thus, each Publisher Defendant would be able to accomplish the shift to agency—and therefore have an incentive to sign Apple's proposed Contracts—*only* if it acted in tandem with its competitors. *See Starr,* 592 F.3d at 324; *Flat Glass,* 385 F.3d at 360–61; *see also* J.A.1974 (noting that the agreements would "not fix the publishers' problems" if they could not move Amazon to an agency model). By the very act of signing a Contract with Apple containing an MFN Clause, then, each of the Publisher Defendants signaled a clear commitment to move against Amazon, thereby facilitating their collective action. As the district court explained, the MFNs "stiffened the spines" of the Publisher Defendants. *Apple,* 952 F.Supp.2d at 665.

As a sophisticated negotiator, Apple was fully aware that its proposed Contracts would entice a critical mass of publishers only if these publishers perceived an opportunity collectively to shift Amazon to agency. In fact, this was the very purpose of the MFN, which Apple's Saul devised as an elegant alternative to a provision that would have explicitly *required* the publishers to adopt an agency model with other retailers. As Cue put it, the MFN "force[d] the model" from wholesale to agency. J.A. 865. Indeed, the MFN's capacity for forcing collective action by the publishers was precisely what enabled Jobs to predict with confidence that "the price will be the same" on the iBookstore and the Kindle when he announced the launch of the iPad—the same, Jobs said, because the publishers would make Amazon "sign ... agency contract[s]" by threatening to withhold their ebooks. J.A. 891. Apple was also fully aware that once the Publisher Defendants seized control over consumer-facing ebook prices, those prices would rise. It knew from the outset that the publishers hated Amazon's $9.99 price point, and it put price caps in its agreements because it specifically anticipated that once the publishers gained control over prices, they would push them higher than $9.99, higher than Apple itself deemed "realistic." *Apple,* 952 F.Supp.2d at 692 (internal quotation marks omitted).

* * *

[The court completes its antitrust analysis explaining why the *per se* rule applies (it is horizontal price fixing) and why Apple's conduct is illegal].

* * *

## CONCLUSION

We have considered the appellants' remaining arguments and find them to be without merit. Because we conclude that Apple violated § 1 of the Sherman Act by orchestrating a horizontal conspiracy among the Publisher Defendants to raise ebook prices, and that the injunctive relief ordered by the district court is appropriately designed to guard against future anticompetitive conduct, the judgment of the district court is AFFIRMED.

### *QUESTIONS FOR DISCUSSION*

1. What does the Court require to prove a conspiracy? Can the conduct seen in these cases be explained *without* inferring a conspiracy? What would stop a firm from acting on its own in the hopes that others follow? Would the standards set forth in *Interstate Circuit* and *Theater Enterprises* guard against such behavior? Should pure parallel behavior (e.g., oligopolistic pricing) without any agreement be prohibited?

2. On what evidence did the Supreme Court find there to be an agreement among the distributors in *Interstate Circuit*? Did the Court hold that there was an express agreement or merely interdependent behavior? Is the Court saying that tacit, parallel behavior is enough to establish an agreement?

3. In 1986, the Supreme Court heard another oligopoly case where proof of an agreement was at issue. *Matsushita Electric Industrial Co. v. Zenith Radio Corp.*, 475 U.S. 574 (1986). There, a U.S. corporation alleged that Japanese companies had conspired to charge *low* prices in the United States. The Court stated that "conduct that is as consistent with permissible competition as with illegal conspiracy does not, without more, support even an inference of conspiracy." The Court went on to say that the plaintiff "must present evidence 'that tends to exclude the possibility' that the alleged conspirators acted independently. . . ." Is this a step in the right direction for the interpretation of the Sherman Act? More recently, in *Bell Atlantic Corp. v. Twombly,* 550 U.S. 544, 561–63 (2007), the Court required evidence of conspiracy to be pled specifically (and not simply in a conclusory allegation in the complaint).

4. For a lower court case that found a conspiracy between movie distributors regarding licensing to exhibitors, see *Basle Theatres, Inc. v. Warner Bros. Pictures Distributing Corp.*, 168 F. Supp. 553 (W.D. Pa. 1958). In that case, the distributors' apparent agreement included a uniform timing schedule for releasing first-run movies in downtown Pittsburgh, and releasing them to the surrounding suburbs only weeks later.

5. In the *Apple* case, the dissent did not find that the behavior of Apple was anti-competitive. Do you agree? Why or why not?

## 3. BLOCK BOOKING AND BLIND BIDDING

One of the industry practices identified in the *Paramount* decision as anticompetitive was "block booking." Exhibitors, particularly the larger chains, agreed beforehand to take much if not all of a studio's film production that season. This was usually based on a written synopsis of what a movie was about and who its featured performers were. These contracts meant that the producer-distributor's license for a potential hit movie with a popular star was conditioned on the exhibitor agreeing to take other less appealing features in the film package.

The legality of this practice, known as a "tying arrangement,"[i] produced another major antitrust ruling from the Supreme Court. A tying arrangement is "an agreement by a party to sell one product, but only on the condition that the buyer also purchases a different (or tied) product,

[i] *See* Vol. 10 Philip Areeda, *Antitrust Law* (1996); George J. Stigler, United States v. Loew's, Inc.: *A Note on Block Booking*, 1963 S. Ct. Rev. 152; Roy W. Kenney & Benjamin Klein, *The Economics of Block Booking*, 26 J. Law & Econ. 497 (1983); F. Andres Hanssen, *The Block Booking of Films Reexamined*, 43 J. Law & Econ. 395 (2000); Roy W. Kenney & Benjamin Klein, *How Block Booking Facilitated Self-Enforcing Film Contracts*, 43 J. Law & Econ. 427 (2000).

or at least agrees that he will not purchase that product from any other supplier." *Northern Pacific Railway Co. v. United States*, 356 U.S. 1, 5–6 (1958). In order to get the more desirable good, the buyer must also purchase a less desired second one. The desired good is called the "tying" product and the undesired good is called the "tied" product.

A "tie" only has economic significance if it compels the buyer to acquiesce in the seller's wishes. The seller of the tying product must have the market power to force the buyer to purchase the tied product. A mere statement from the seller that the latter purchase is required is not enough from either an economic or an antitrust point of view. As Justice Black stated in *Northern Pacific*, "[i]f one of a dozen food stores in a community were to refuse to sell flour unless the buyer also took sugar, it would hardly tend to restrain competition in sugar if its competitors were ready and able to sell flour by itself." *Id.* at 7.

The law on tying arrangements is concerned with the effects that a tie has on the market for the tied product. Tie-ins can block other sellers of the tied product from having the chance to compete for customers on the merits of the tied product standing alone. Tie-ins affect current competitors and can create barriers to entry because potential competitors will shy away if they think that they must enter both markets. A further concern about tying is its effect on innovation in the tied market due to artificial control over sales and the lack of competition on the merits. Consumers may be harmed because they are unable to obtain the best bargain in the tied product market, and there is no longer competition on the merits in the tied product. At the same time, there may well be pro-competitive reasons for allowing a tie. For example, selling two products as a package may result in a cost savings, from marketing or production efficiencies. Notwithstanding these benefits, the Court traditionally judged tie-ins to be *per se* illegal, most prominently in another decision about block booking in the motion picture industry.

As noted earlier, the courts had struck down an especially egregious form of tie-in fashioned by Thomas Edison's Motion Picture Patents Trust. In the early 1930s, the FTC investigated the practice of block booking by Paramount Pictures, as a condition to exhibition of pictures in which this single studio held copyright. When the case reached the Second Circuit, the court ruled that block booking in those circumstances was not the kind of anticompetitive restraint that violated antitrust law. *See FTC v. Paramount Famous-Lasky Corp.*, 57 F.2d 152 (2d Cir. 1932). The court implicitly held that Paramount's copyright monopoly in its films was insufficient to confer market power on the studio, because the "tying" pictures were not attractive enough to induce acceptance of the tied films.

Thirty years later, the Court addressed a variation on block booking of movies. Here, Loew's packaged old films together for sale to television stations. The stations were required to purchase several films they did not want in order to obtain the more desirable ones. As one example, in order to get a package that included *Casablanca* and the *Treasure of Sierra Madre*, the station had to accept another package that included *Tugboat Annie Sails Again* and *Tear Gas Squad*. The United States sued under § 1 of the Sherman Act, producing the following decision.

## UNITED STATES V. LOEW'S, INC.

Supreme Court of the United States, 1962.
371 U.S. 38, 83 S.Ct. 97, 9 L.Ed.2d 11.

MR. JUSTICE GOLDBERG delivered the opinion of the Court.

* * *

This case raises the recurring question of whether specific tying arrangements violate § 1 of the Sherman Act. This Court has recognized that "tying agreements serve hardly any purpose beyond the suppression of competition," *Standard Oil Co. of California v. United States*, 337 U.S. 293, 305–306. They are an object of antitrust concern for two reasons-they may force buyers into giving up the purchase of substitutes for the tied product . . . and they may destroy the free access of competing suppliers of the tied product to the consuming market. . . . A tie-in contract may have one or both of these undesirable effects when the seller, by virtue of his position in the market for the tying product, has economic leverage sufficient to induce his customers to take the tied product along with the tying item. The standard of illegality is that the seller must have "sufficient economic power with respect to the tying product to appreciably restrain free competition in the market for the tied product. . . ." *Northern Pacific R. Co. v. United States*, 356 U.S. 1, 6. Market dominance-some power to control price and to exclude competition-is by no means the only test of whether the seller has the requisite economic power. Even absent a showing of market dominance, the crucial economic power may be inferred from the tying product's desirability to consumers or from uniqueness in its attributes.[4]

The requisite economic power is presumed when the tying product is patented or copyrighted. . . . This principle grew out of a long line of

[4] Since the requisite economic power may be found on the basis of either uniqueness or consumer appeal, and since market dominance in the present context does not necessitate a demonstration of market power in the sense of § 2 of the Sherman Act, it should seldom be necessary in a tie-in sale case to embark upon a full-scale factual inquiry into the scope of the relevant market for the tying product and into the corollary problem of the seller's percentage share in that market. This is even more obviously true when the tying product is patented or copyrighted, in which case, as appears in greater detail below, sufficiency of economic power is presumed. . . .

patent cases which had eventuated in the doctrine that a patentee who utilized tying arrangements would be denied all relief against infringements of his patent, *Motion Picture Patents Co. v. Universal Film Mfg. Co.*, 243 U.S. 502 (1917), . . . . These cases reflect a hostility to use of the statutorily granted patent monopoly to extend the patentee's economic control to unpatented products. The patentee is protected as to his invention, but may not use his patent rights to exact tribute for other articles.

Since one of the objectives of the patent laws is to reward uniqueness, the principle of these cases was carried over into antitrust law on the theory that the existence of a valid patent on the tying product, without more, establishes a distinctiveness sufficient to conclude that any tying arrangement involving the patented product would have anti-competitive consequences. . . . In *United States v. Paramount Pictures, Inc.*, 334 U.S. 131, 156–59, the principle of the patent cases was applied to copyrighted feature films which had been block booked into movie theaters. . . .

Appellants attempt to distinguish the *Paramount* decision in its relation to the present facts: the block booked sale of copyrighted feature films to exhibitors in a new medium-television. Not challenging the District Court's finding that they did engage in block booking, they contend that the uniqueness attributable to a copyrighted feature film, though relevant in the movie-theater context, is lost when the film is being sold for television use. Feature films, they point out, constitute less than 8% of television programming, and they assert that films are "reasonably interchangeable" with other types of programming material and with other feature films as well. Thus they argue that their behavior is not to be judged by the principle of the patent cases, as applied to copyrighted materials in *Paramount Pictures*, but by the general principles which govern the validity of tying arrangements of nonpatented products. . . . They say that the Government's proof did not establish their "sufficient economic power" in the sense contemplated for nonpatented products.

Appellants cannot escape the applicability of *Paramount Pictures*. A copyrighted feature film does not lose its legal or economic uniqueness because it is shown on a television rather than a movie screen.

The district judge found that each copyrighted film block booked by appellants for television use "was in itself a unique product"; that feature films "varied in theme, in artistic performance, in stars, in audience appeal, etc.," and were not fungible; and that since each defendant by reason of its copyright had a "monopolistic" position as to each tying product, "sufficient economic power" to impose an appreciable restraint on free competition in the tied product was present, as demanded by the

*Northern Pacific* decision.[6] We agree. These findings of the district judge, supported by the record, confirm the presumption of uniqueness resulting from the existence of the copyright itself.

Moreover, there can be no question in this case of the adverse effects on free competition resulting from appellants' illegal block booking contracts. Television stations forced by appellants to take unwanted films were denied access to films marketed by other distributors who, in turn, were foreclosed from selling to the stations. Nor can there be any question as to the substantiality of the commerce involved. The 25 contracts found to have been illegally block booked involved payments to appellants ranging from $60,800 in the case of Screen Gems to over $2,500,000 in the case of Associated Artists. A substantial portion of the licensing fees represented the cost of the inferior films which the stations were required to accept. These anti-competitive consequences are an apt illustration of the reasons underlying our recognition that the mere presence of competing substitutes for the tying product, here taking the form of other programming material as well as other feature films, is insufficient to destroy the legal, and indeed the economic, distinctiveness of the copyrighted product. . . . By the same token, the distinctiveness of the copyrighted tied product is not inconsistent with the fact of competition, in the form of other programming material and other films, which is suppressed by the tying arrangements.

It is therefore clear that the tying arrangements here both by their "inherent nature" and by their "effect" injuriously restrained trade. . . . Accommodation between the statutorily dispensed monopoly in the combination of contents in the patented or copyrighted product and the statutory principles of free competition demands that extension of the patent or copyright monopoly by the use of tying agreements be strictly confined. There may be rare circumstances in which the doctrine we have enunciated under § 1 of the Sherman Act prohibiting tying arrangements involving patented or copyrighted tying products is inapplicable. However, we find it difficult to conceive of such a case, and the present case is clearly not one.

The principles underlying our *Paramount Pictures* decision have general application to tying arrangements involving copyrighted products, and govern here. Applicability of *Paramount Pictures* brings with it a meeting of the test of *Northern Pacific*, since *Paramount Pictures* is but a particularized application of the general doctrine as reaffirmed in *Northern Pacific*. Enforced block booking of films is a vice in both the motion picture and television industries, and that the sin is more serious (in dollar amount) in one than the other does not expiate the guilt for

---

6 To use the trial court's apt example, forcing a television station which wants *Gone With The Wind* to take *Getting Gertie's Garter* as well is taking undue advantage of the fact that to television as well as motion picture viewers there is but one *Gone With The Wind*.

either. Appellants' block booked contracts are covered by the flat holding in *Paramount Pictures*, 334 U.S., at 159, that "a refusal to license one or more copyrights unless another copyright is accepted" is "illegal."

Vacated and remanded.

---

As part of the broader recasting of antitrust doctrine in the 1970s and 1980s, the Court took a more nuanced approach to tying arrangements. In *Jefferson Parish Hospital District No. 2 v. Hyde*, 466 U.S. 2 (1984), a narrow majority of the Court enunciated what looks to be only nominal *per se* liability for these arrangements. A tie-in is *per se* illegal, said the Court, only if (1) the tying seller has sufficient economic power in the tying product to be able to force buyers to take the tied product; and (2) the tying arrangement affects a " 'not insubstantial' amount of interstate commerce." *Id.* at 16. Under this partial *per se* test, the courts perform what resembles a rule of reason analysis, considering both market power and possible business justifications. (One important difference that remains is that tie-in plaintiffs need not show an actual anticompetitive effect in the tied market.) Justice O'Connor, in a concurrence joined by Chief Justice Burger and Justices Powell and Rehnquist, stated that "[t]he time has . . . come to abandon the *per se* label" for tying arrangements. *Id.* at 35. According to Justice O'Connor, the use of the *per se* rule in tying cases "incurs the costs of a rule-of-reason approach without achieving its benefits." *Id.* at 34.

In practice, courts are now analyzing tying arrangements on more of a case-by-case basis. A threshold issue in analyzing tying arrangements is whether there actually are two separate products being sold. In cases where consumers want and expect the two products (the alleged tying and tied product) to be sold together, they may be deemed a single product. For example, while the body of the car and its tires are literally separate goods, they are not considered two products in the mind of a consumer looking to buy a car. Even if the threshold requirement of distinct products is met, a further judgment must be made about whether the seller has sufficient economic power to force purchase of both of them. There may well be readily-available alternative sources of supply that consumers can turn to without having to buy the second, tied-in product. For the movie industry, in particular, a crucial but controversial[j] assumption was that a copyrighted (or patented) work carries with it substantial economic leverage because under intellectual property law, a company cannot get the same film from any source other than its owner.

---

[j] *See* J. Dianne Brinson, *Proof of Economic Power in a Sherman Act Tying Arrangement Case: Should Economic Power Be Presumed When the Tying Product Is Patented or Copyrighted?* 48 La. L. Rev. 29 (1982).

The Court finally rejected this presumption in *Illinois Tool Works Inc. v. Independent Ink, Inc.*, 547 U.S. 28, 42–43 (2006).

### *QUESTIONS FOR DISCUSSION*

1. Why might a motion-picture studio want to offer only package film deals to theaters and television stations? Is it really trying to exploit its "monopoly" in the popular films to extract excessive prices for its less attractive products? Or to exclude from the marketplace the films of those producers that do not have big hits to which to tie their packages? Note that the Court in *Loew's* held that the fact that a studio enjoyed copyright in its films satisfied the key "market power" factor in the Court's appraisal of the studio's "block-booking" practice. Is such an antitrust ruling compatible with the goals of intellectual property law? Is the Court's approach in *Illinois Tool Works v. Independent Ink* more reflective of market realities?

2. Economists have suggested that the real purpose of tie-ins is to engage in price discrimination, either by charging buyers in different markets according to their demand or metering overall demand. Tie-in deals can also be a pro-competitive device for reducing search costs on the part of both vendor and purchaser in trying to determine the right price for each individual item. (Grocery stores sell potatoes by the bag, at a single price, for example.) What are the relevant characteristics of the film distribution market for purposes of this analysis? Should there be different treatment of the block-booking described in *Paramount*—in which theaters agreed to take a studio season package of as yet unmade movies and to pay the studio a share (roughly half) of box office revenues—than of the *Loew's* example of licensing for television viewing of a package of already-made movies for a fixed overall price?

3. Recall the earlier discussion of performing rights to music in Chapter 11. Are ASCAP and BMI engaged in unlawful tying when they require users to purchase blanket licenses? Should that case turn on the reasonableness of the price charged for the blanket license? Is it relevant that it is often costly and unfeasible for users to obtain direct licenses from copyright holders? Recall that in *BMI*, the Court stated, "the whole is truly greater than the sum of its parts; it is, to some extent a different product." Do the same rationales apply to block booking?

4. In *Loew's*, the court allowed cost justifications for discounts associated with the purchase of packages of movies. Does this provision undermine the court's decree? What are examples of legitimate cost justifications that parties might advance for block booking?

5. Consider the following case under the "tying" rubric. A television network enters into negotiations with a producer of a drama show based on the popular movie *Fame*. The producer wants to condition the licensing of "first run" episodes of the show on the network's agreement to accept "syndicated" versions of previously-aired shows. The subject matter of the first-run and syndicated episodes involves the same general theme, but the

syndicated shows usually are run at a different time, attracting a different audience and advertisers. Is this a tie-in of separate products? Should the antitrust outcome rest on copyright or consumer market tests of substantial similarity? *See Metromedia Broadcasting Corp. v. MGM/UA Entertainment Co.*, 611 F. Supp. 415 (C.D. Cal. 1985).

---

Another allegedly restrictive practices in the film industry is "blind bidding."[k] Under this practice, studios put their films up for bidding (individually or in a block) without exhibitors having a chance to see the film, often because it is not even finished before the contracts are signed. This practice was briefly discussed in *Paramount* but was not explicitly barred by the decree. Beginning in the 1970s, though, 25 states have enacted legislation barring blind bidding and requiring a trade screening within the state before binding agreements can be reached for exhibition. A number of those statutes also ban advances or guarantees by exhibitors. Distributors have attacked the constitutionality of this legislation in Ohio (*see Allied Artists Picture Corp. v. Rhodes*, 679 F.2d 656 (6th Cir. 1982)), Utah (*see Warner Bros., Inc. v. Wilkinson*, 782 F.2d 136 (10th Cir. 1985)), and Pennsylvania (*see Associated Film Distribution Corp. v. Thornburgh* 800 F.2d 369 (3d Cir. 1986)). The challenges were based on the distributor's rights under the First Amendment and the Copyright Act, and on Congress's legislative authority over interstate commerce. What are your views about the validity of such state legislation? On the policy merits of state or federal regulation of the distribution market? What exactly is unfair about an exhibition contract (including dates and specified revenue shares) that is entered into before the movie is even made? Is that any different from a publishing contract in which advances are paid by the publisher based on the author's book proposal?

One ruling struck down an even more extreme feature of Pennsylvania's regulation of theater deals. Miramax Film had been sued by Orson, owner and operator of a second-run art theater in Philadelphia, for violating a provision in the state's *Feature Motion Picture Fair Business Practices Act*. In particular, Miramax had regularly given a first-run art theater in the city the exclusive right to show its films for longer periods than the 42-day ceiling imposed by § 203.7 of the Act. In *Orson v. Miramax Film*, 189 F.3d 377 (3d Cir. 1999), the Third Circuit found this provision to be preempted by § 106(4) of the Copyright Act, which gives copyright owners exclusive control over distribution of their works.

---

[k] *See* Note, *Blind Bidding & the Motion Picture Industry*, 92 Harv. L. Rev. 1129 (1979); Suzanne I. Schiller, *The Relationship Between Motion Picture Distribution & Exhibition: An Analysis of the Effects of Anti-Blind Bidding Legislation*, 9 Hast. Comm/Ent L.J. 131 (1986); Charles H. Grant, *Anti-Competitive Practices in the Motion Picture Industry & Judicial Support of Anti-Blind Bidding Statutes*, 13 Colum.-VLA J.L. & the Arts 349 (1989).

The court made it clear that the state's ban on blind bidding and block booking was not preempted by the Copyright Act: a law that "seeks to remedy problems caused by the economic disparity that impedes fairness in bargaining and honesty in business dealings is not impermissible merely because it has an economic effect on those regulated." *Id.* at 384–385. As a practical matter, is there a qualitative difference between these two branches of state law restraints on movie exhibition deals? As a matter of constitutional principle, is there a reason why a state cannot regulate the licensing of intellectual property, when it clearly may do so with physical property (including rental of the theater itself)? At the same time, is there a real need for these restrictions on negotiations between producers like Miramax and exhibitors like Orson?

## D. MOVIE INDUSTRY INTEGRATION REVISITED[1]

Returning to the broader question of how the movie industry can be organized, there are two different kinds of corporate expansion and integration that take place in this and other industries, horizontal and vertical. Vertical integration occurs when a firm working at one stage in the production and distribution process expands either backward or forward to do the work performed by its suppliers or customers. That was the issue in *Paramount Pictures,* where studios engaged in movie production and distribution had developed franchise relationships with or ownership of the theaters. Horizontal integration, by contrast, occurs when the firm expands laterally by acquiring or merging with a competing firm, e.g., two movie producers. This kind of corporate expansion is the more traditional focus of both economic analysis and antitrust protection of competitive markets. The following case illustrates the law and economics of this issue, again in the context of movie exhibition.

### UNITED STATES V. SYUFY ENTERPRISES

United States Court of Appeals, Ninth Circuit, 1990.
903 F.2d 659.

KOZINSKI, CIRCUIT JUDGE.

[Raymond Syufy opened a luxury six-screen theater in Las Vegas in 1981. This set off a bidding war for film exhibition in that area which eventually drove his competitors from the market. Three years later, Syufy had bought the theaters of his competitors, leaving him, briefly at

[1] *See* Gerald E. Phillips, *The Recent Acquisition of Theater Circuits by Major Distributors*, 5 Enter. & Sports Law. 1 (Winter 1987); Barry J. Brett & Michael D. Friedman, *A Fresh Look at the* Paramount *Decrees*, 9 Enter. & Sports Law. 1 (Fall 1991); Kraig G. Fox, Paramount *Revisited: The Resurgence of Vertical Integration in the Motion Picture Industry*, 21 Hofstra L. Rev. 505 (1992); Brian J. Wolf, *The Prohibition Against Studio Ownership of Theaters: Are They An Anachronism*, 13 Loy. L.A. Ent. L.J. 413 (1993).

least, as the sole first-run movie exhibitor in Las Vegas. The Justice Department filed suit, alleging that these acquisitions made Syufy a monopolist in violation of § 2 of the Sherman Act. The Ninth Circuit dismissed that claim, partly because there was no evidence of excessive increases in Syufy's prices or decreases in his licensing fees, and partly because, following the Justice Department action, another exhibitor had actually appeared in the market. The following passages from the court's ruling convey some of the flavor of a more skeptical present-day view of antitrust intervention, especially when used as here to "rescue this platoon of [studio] Goliaths from a single [exhibitor] David."]

* * *

Competition is the driving force behind our free enterprise system. Unlike centrally planned economies, where decisions about production and allocation are made by government bureaucrats who ostensibly see the big picture and know how to do the right thing, capitalism relies on decentralized planning-millions of producers and consumers making hundreds of millions of individual decisions each year-to determine what and how much will be produced. Competition plays the key role in this process: It imposes an essential discipline on producers and sellers of goods to provide the consumer with a better product at a lower cost; it drives out inefficient and marginal producers, releasing resources to higher-valued uses; it promotes diversity, giving consumers choices to fit a wide array of personal preferences; it avoids permanent concentrations of economic power, as even the largest firm can lose market share to a feistier and hungrier rival. If, as the metaphor goes, a market economy is governed by an invisible hand, competition is surely the brass knuckles by which it enforces its decisions.

When competition is impaired, producers may be able to reap monopoly profits, denying consumers many of the benefits of a free market. It is a simple but important truth, therefore, that our antitrust laws are designed to protect the integrity of the market system by assuring that competition reigns freely. While much has been said and written about the antitrust laws during the last century of their existence, ultimately the court must resolve a practical question in every monopolization case: Is this the type of situation where market forces are likely to cure the perceived problem within a reasonable period of time? Or, have barriers been erected to constrain the normal operation of the market, so that the problem is not likely to be self-correcting? In the latter situation, it might well be necessary for a court to correct the market imbalance; in the former, a court ought to exercise extreme caution because judicial intervention in a competitive situation can itself upset the balance of market forces, bringing about the very ills the antitrust laws were meant to prevent. *See* R. Coase, *The Firm, The*

*Market, and the Law* 117–19 (1988); R. Posner, *Economic Analysis of Law* 324–25, 338–39 (3d ed. 1986).

It is with these observations in mind that we turn to the case before us. Perhaps the most remarkable aspect of this case is that the accused monopolist is a relatively tiny regional entrepreneur while the alleged victims are humongous national corporations with considerable market power of their own. While this is not dispositive-it is conceivable that a little big man may be able to exercise monopoly power locally against large national entities-chances are it is not without significance. Common sense suggests, and experience teaches, that monopoly power is far more easily exercised by larger, economically more powerful entities against smaller, economically punier ones, than vice versa.

* * *

1. Power to Exclude Competition

It is true, of course, that when Syufy acquired Mann's, Plitt's and Cragin's theatres he temporarily diminished the number of competitors in the Las Vegas first-run film market. But this does not necessarily indicate foul play; many legitimate market arrangements diminish the number of competitors. It would be odd if they did not, as the nature of competition is to make winners and losers. If there are no significant barriers to entry, however, eliminating competitors will not enable the survivors to reap a monopoly profit; any attempt to raise prices above the competitive level will lure into the market new competitors able and willing to offer their commercial goods or personal services for less.

* * *

The government concedes that there are no structural barriers to entry into the market: Syufy does not operate a bank or similar enterprise where entry is limited by government regulation or licensing requirements. Nor is this the type of industry, like heavy manufacturing or mining, which requires onerous front-end investments that might deter competition from all but the hardiest and most financially secure investors. Nor do we have here a business dependent on a scarce commodity, control over which might give the incumbent a substantial structural advantage. Nor is there a network of exclusive contracts or distribution arrangements designed to lock out potential competitors. To the contrary, the record discloses a rough-and-tumble industry, marked by easy market access, fluid relationships with distributors, an ample and continuous supply of product, and a healthy and growing demand. It would be difficult to design a market less susceptible to monopolization.

Confronted with this record and the district court's clear findings, the government trots out a shopworn argument we had thought long abandoned: that efficient, aggressive competition is itself a structural barrier to entry. According to the government, competitors will be deterred from entering the market because they could not hope to turn a profit competing against Syufy. In the words of government counsel:

> There is no legal barrier. There is no law that says you can't come into this market, it's not that kind of barrier. . . . But, the fact of mere possibility in the literal sense, is not the appropriate test. Entry, after all, must, to be effective to dissipate the monopoly power that Syufy has, entry must hold some reasonable prospect of profitability for the entrant, or else the entrant will say, as Mann Theatres said . . . this is not an attractive market to enter. There will be shelter. And the reason is very clear. You have to compete effectively in this market. And witness after witness testified you would need to build anywhere from 12 to 24 theatres, which is a very expensive and time consuming proposition. And, you would then find yourself in a bidding war against Syufy.

The notion that the supplier of a good or service can monopolize the market simply by being efficient reached high tide in the law 44 years ago in Judge Learned Hand's opinion in *United States v. Aluminum Co. of Am.*, 148 F.2d 416 (2d Cir. 1945).[14] In the intervening decades the wisdom of this notion has been questioned by just about everyone who has taken a close look at it. *See*, 3 P. Areeda & D. Turner, *Antitrust Law* Para. 608e, at 22 (1978) ("It is absurd to classify such behavior as unlawfully 'exclusionary.' "); L. Sullivan, supra n. 5, at 103 ("The Hand formulation . . . fails to clearly identify the differences between guilty and innocent conduct."). It has been soundly repudiated by the Second Circuit. *See Berkey Photo, Inc. v. Eastman Kodak Co.*, 603 F.2d 263, 273–74 (2d Cir. 1979).

The argument government counsel presses here is a close variant of *Alcoa*: the government is not claiming that Syufy monopolized the market by being too efficient, but that Syufy's effectiveness as a competitor creates a structural barrier to entry, rendering illicit Syufy's acquisition of its competitors' screens. We hasten to sever this new branch that the government has caused to sprout from the moribund *Alcoa* trunk.

It can't be said often enough that the antitrust laws protect competition, not competitors. As we noted earlier, competition is essential to the effective operation of the free market because it encourages efficiency, promotes consumer satisfaction and prevents the accumulation of monopoly profits. When a producer is shielded from competition, he is likely to provide lesser service at a higher price; the victim is the consumer who gets a raw deal. This is the evil the antitrust laws are

---

[14] *See* Stanley Ornstein, *Motion Picture Distribution, Film Splitting, & Antitrust Policy*, 17 Hast. Comm/Ent L.J. 415 (1995).

meant to avert. But when a producer deters competitors by supplying a better product at a lower price, when he eschews monopoly profits, when he operates his business so as to meet consumer demand and increase consumer satisfaction, the goals of competition are served, even if no actual competitors see fit to enter the market at a particular time. While the successful competitor should not be raised above the law, neither should he be held down by law.

The Supreme Court has accordingly distanced itself from the *Alcoa* legacy, taking care to distinguish unlawful monopoly power from "growth or development as a consequence of a superior product, business acumen, or historic accident," *United States v. Grinnell Corp.*, 384 U.S. 563, 571 (1966), which are off limits to the enforcer of our antitrust laws. If a dominant supplier acts consistent with a competitive market-out of fear perhaps that potential competitors are ready and able to step in-the purpose of the antitrust laws is amply served. We make it clear today, if it was not before, that an efficient, vigorous, aggressive competitor is not the villain antitrust laws are aimed at eliminating. Fostering an environment where businesses fight it out using the weapon of efficiency and consumer goodwill is what the antitrust laws are meant to champion.

* * *

More fundamentally, in a free economy the market itself imposes a tough enough discipline on all market actors, large and small. Every supplier of goods and services is integrated into an endless chain of supply and demand relationships, making it dependent on the efficiency and goodwill of upstream suppliers, as well as the patronage of customers. Absent structural constraints that keep competition from performing its levelling function, few businesses can dictate terms to customers or suppliers with impunity. It's risky business even to try. As Syufy learned in dealing with Orion and his other suppliers, a larger company often is more vulnerable to a squeeze play than a smaller one. It is for that reason that neither size nor market share alone suffice to establish a monopoly. Without the power to exclude competition, large companies that try to throw their weight around may find themselves sitting ducks for leaner, hungrier competitors. Or, as Syufy saw, the tactic may boomerang, causing big trouble with suppliers.

* * *

The record here demonstrates in graphic detail that Syufy's entry into the Las Vegas first-run movie market resulted in a vast improvement for movie distributors and consumers alike. By all accounts, Raymond Syufy's theatres are among the finest built and best run in the nation, making him somewhat of a local hero. At the same time, movie distributors have nothing but praise for Syufy, as his being there has invigorated theatre attendance in Las Vegas, substantially driving up their revenues. As is often the case when a vigorous competitor enters the market, more complacent theatre operators were eliminated, but there was no credible evidence that Syufy did anything improper to drive them out. Indeed, by buying them out, Syufy may well have helped cushion the losses they would have suffered had they been required to sell the theatres at fire sale prices or leave them abandoned.

What then was the problem the government sought to solve by bringing this lawsuit? At oral argument, the lawyer for the government explained it thus:

> Basically if you drive down by anti-competitive conduct the price at which theatre owners buy film licenses, then there will be less film[s] ultimately produced, because there will be a distortion in the natural market in the competitive forces, and people who go to movies like you and me would ultimately have less choice.

It is, we suppose, not out of the question that what Raymond Syufy and other local theatre operators do in their respective markets could stem the avalanche of movies that comes to us out of Hollywood every year. Yet movie distributors are not exactly a powerless lot, likely to surrender the first time they are presented with hard choices by a theatre operator; nor are they reluctant to precipitate a showdown when they believe their rights are being infringed. And, as we have seen, the market has its own fail-safe mechanisms. Where the government inserts an antitrust enforcement action into this type of situation, there is a real danger of stifling competition and creativity in the marketplace.

It is well known that some of the most insuperable barriers in the great race of competition are the result of government regulation. Regulation often helps entrench existing businesses by placing new entrants at a competitive disadvantage. It is perhaps less well appreciated that litigation itself can be a form of regulation; lawsuits brought by the government impose significant costs on enterprises that are sued, and create significant disincentives for those that are not.

In this case, the government was suspicious because Syufy bought out the movie theatres of his retreating competitors. But, in a competitive market, buying out competitors is not merely permissible, it contributes to market stability and promotes the efficient allocation of resources. The fact is, a relentless, growing competitor is frequently the most logical buyer of a business that is declining. For competitors in a free market to fear buying each other out lest they be hit with the expense and misery of an antitrust enforcement action amounts to a burden only slightly less palpable than a direct governmental prohibition against such a purchase. In a free enterprise system decisions such as these should be made by market actors responding to market forces, not by government bureaucrats pursuing their notions of how the market should operate. Personal initiative, not government control, is the fountainhead of progress in a capitalist economy.

Affirmed.

### *QUESTIONS FOR DISCUSSION*

In footnote 9 of its opinion, the Ninth Circuit expressed the following judgment about the district court's definition of the relevant market:

> The court defined the market broadly to include not only first-run theatrical exhibition, but also "exhibition on home video, cable television, and pay-per-view television." We agree with the government that this is not the proper market definition in examining Syufy's power over film distributors. While moviegoers may well view these alternative methods of film exhibition as readily substitutable, film distributors do not. Distributors use first-run theatrical exhibition to make sure that audiences are exposed to a film so that, even if it gets bad reviews and fails to turn a profit in theatres, people switching channels or checking out videos will recognize the title and be induced by its fame to watch it. That first-run theatrical exhibition enhances a film's performance in auxiliary markets does not mean that auxiliary markets can substitute for theatrical release. The district court was therefore mistaken in relying on testimony that "of the 578 films produced in 1987, 214 were released on home video and not in the theatres," as there was no suggestion that any of these 214 films were suitable for theatrical release, or that any film has ever been released first on home video and then later played in first-run theaters. Jane Fonda's *Low Impact Aerobic Workout* may be a best-selling videocassette, but it is unlikely to be the hit at a local movie theatre.

*Id.* at 665–66.

While *Syufy* provides a valuable insight into the antitrust policies that govern the entertainment industry, its relevance to the movie theater segment is now dwarfed by that of bankruptcy law.

Given the choice, especially in metropolitan areas, fans were far more likely to watch a movie at a luxurious new theater with stadium-raised seating, even at somewhat higher prices (especially for food and beverages). Thus, by 2001 the second largest exhibitor, Loew's Cineplex, and six other major theater chains (with nearly 10,000 total screens) had petitioned for bankruptcy release from long-term leases for their older theater space in shopping malls and elsewhere. Should the theaters enjoy the same success with that legal instrument that such music stars as TLC and Toni Braxton secured in the 1990s?

---

Suppose that Syufy sustained its position as owner of all the large movie theatres in Las Vegas, and that the studios felt that the terms of their contracts were less favorable than those in more competitive markets. Besides trying to win an antitrust suit, another possibility would be for the studios to create a joint distribution arm for release of movies in that city, thereby eliminating competition among themselves. The legality of this action would be assessed not under § 2 of the Sherman Act, but under the more expansive § 1, which bars "any combination in [unreasonable] restraint of trade."

This is not an academic question given the movie studios' reaction to what they perceived as near-monopoly control of pay cable television. Home Box Office, created by Time, Inc., pioneered the development of specialized cable *programming* (by contrast with cable systems simply transmitting broadcast signals). Indeed, as we shall see in the next chapter, HBO won a crucial ruling, *HBO v. FCC*, 567 F.2d 9 (D.C. Cir. 1977), which struck down an administrative regulation designed to prevent "siphoning" by cable channels of programming that might otherwise be shown on "free" over-the-air stations. HBO was soon joined by a host of cable programmers like ESPN, Lifetime, and CNN, but rather than simply rely on payments from the local cable systems, HBO has always been financed by monthly subscriber fees.

The viability of that market niche depended on HBO showing new movies within a year or so of their release in theaters. Unlike the video tape recorder, which was making its appearance at roughly the same time, the studios applauded the emergence of pay cable because it provided a new vehicle for reaching a broader movie audience. Indeed, pay cable was a better vehicle than broadcast television for targeting the audience for such movies, because viewers paid the fees, rather than advertisers simply trying to reach their favored audience.

Subscribers to HBO soared from 25,000 in 1975 to 6 million in 1980. Another pay channel, Showtime, was created in 1978, as a joint venture of Viacom and Westinghouse Broadcasting, but it had only one quarter of the subscriber audience of HBO. Thus, unlike network television, pay cable had a single dominant force. As a result, four of the major studios—Paramount, Columbia, Universal, and Twentieth Century Fox—collaborated to create a new pay cable channel called Premiere. These studios agreed to give Premiere the exclusive right to play their films for the first nine months on cable, with subscriber revenues to be divided in proportion to the movies' box office receipts. Just before Premiere was scheduled to begin operations, a federal judge granted an injunction against this joint venture, which was found to be a blatant violation of the Sherman Act. *See United States v. Columbia Pictures*, 507 F. Supp. 412 (S.D.N.Y. 1980). The judge characterized the payment formula as "price fixing" and the nine-month exclusive window for Premiere as a "group boycott" by the studios of HBO and Showtime. The judge rejected the studios' principal defense, which was that these provisions were necessary to establish Premiere in the pay cable market and thus reduce the power being exercised by HBO:

> The argument the defendants return to repeatedly is that the network program service market is dominated by a single company, HBO, which has both monopsony power and monopoly power. Undoubtedly, as indicated above, HBO, by its pioneering efforts, has achieved a very substantial portion of the existing market. It has already obtained a substantial profit margin and a high return on investment, which it probably will be able to continue for some years to come. Its use of volume discounts has assisted it in obtaining affiliations with large cable systems. Certain of its practices, such as the obtaining of exclusive licenses, which it refuses to share with other networks, and its selective tactics in purchasing from motion picture producers, do suggest the exercise of monopoly or monopsony power. However, it is to be expected that the first entrant in the industry would have a substantial head start and that new entrants would have some catching up to do. Nevertheless, there appears to be no shortage of companies willing to undertake this task. Some may make a successful entry and, undoubtedly, others will fail, but neither the history nor the present condition of the market justifies the belief that HBO can successfully bar all new entrants.

*Id.* at 425.

The judge's principal concern was that Premier's exclusivity feature would lock up well over half the new movies being released by the Hollywood majors, and would then risk substituting Premiere for HBO as the dominant force in pay cable. Such exclusivity arrangements were legal for a new cable channel created by a single studio—e.g., The Movie Channel (TMC) created by Warner in 1980, and The Disney Channel created by Walt Disney in 1983—but not one created by a *combination* of studios. The harder legal question was whether an agreement by the four studios to create Premiere without any exclusivity rights would have been acceptable under § 1 of the Sherman Act.

The Justice Department gave its answer to that question when, in 1983, it blocked an agreement for common ownership of Warner's TMC and Showtime (now owned just by Viacom) along with Paramount and Universal. The merger of Showtime and TMC was permitted under the ownership of a single studio (Warner) and a cable programmer (Viacom), but not with the addition of two major studios. And as further evidence of the much more favorable treatment given to vertical rather than horizontal integration, in that same year the Justice Department approved another joint venture of a new studio called Tri-Star, jointly owned by producer Columbia Pictures, cable programmer HBO, and CBS, the television network.

Antitrust law does consider productive joint ventures among competitors to be more legitimate—e.g., a partnership among two studios to finance and distribute a movie. Indeed, with the soaring production costs of action movies with big name stars or special effects, such collaboration is becoming essential to finance expensive movies with uncertain box office appeal. One of the pioneering joint ventures was the 1995 Academy Award-winning *Braveheart*, involving Paramount and Twentieth Century Fox. A year later, Fox executives went back to Paramount for joint financing and distribution of an expensive and somewhat risky project, *Titanic*. Paramount put up $65 million to cover half the anticipated production costs in return for all revenues from Canada and the United States. Fox, which was in charge of production, would pay the balance of costs and receive all international market revenues. By the time *Titanic* appeared on the screens, total costs had soared to $210 million (and thus Fox's share to $145 million). However, both studios ended up with huge profits, with more than $600 million in domestic and one billion in foreign box office receipts. Should ongoing collaboration between major studios raise antitrust concerns?

---

Until the advent of file sharing, the world of music had experienced explosive growth while movie-viewing in theatres had been dropping sharply. In 1955, record sales in the United States amounted to less than $300 million for classical, country, and pop stars like Frank Sinatra and Perry Como. Then came the combination of rock and roll and audiocassettes, with a host of variations since. In 2005, U.S. compact disc and tape sales totaled more than $12 billion, and nearly $33 billion worldwide.

That same time frame witnessed major changes in the corporate structure of the music industry. In the 1950s there were a host of record labels, the largest being RCA Victor, Capital Records, and Columbia Records. Columbia Records was founded by Alexander Graham Bell in the late 19th century, taken over by the Columbia Broadcasting System in 1938, and together with a sister label, Epic Records, put under the umbrella of CBS Records. By the end of the 1960s, CBS Records was the dominant force in the music industry because it had been the first to make a full-blown commitment to rock and roll. Meanwhile, Warner Music and its sister label, Atlantic Records, had been losing money until they began to sign up groups such as The Grateful Dead, Crosby, Stills,

Nash, and Young, and Led Zeppelin. By the end of the 1960s, Warner Music was seen as an even more valuable asset than Warner Pictures.

Another important new player in the industry was Polygram. This joint venture of two European firms, Phillips N.V. and Siemens AG, originally focused on classical music. After buying MGM Records and entering the American market in the mid-1970s, Polygram struck gold with two huge-selling albums, the soundtracks to *Saturday Night Fever* and *Grease*. By 1979, when gross record sales reached $4 billion, Polygram had overtaken CBS Records at the top of the list.

For a variety of market reasons, the next several years experienced a roughly 20 percent drop in record sales. This was felt most severely by Polygram, which had built a costly distribution network but found that its mainstay, disco music, had fallen out of favor. Phillips bore the brunt of the losses (because recorded music was seen as a useful complement to Philips' development of the compact disc). By 1984, with Polygram having fallen to 7 percent of total sales and number six among the major labels, there was a real prospect that Philips would exit the market. Then another possibility arose—a merger of Polygram with Warner Music, blending Polygram's classical collection and European distribution capacity with Warner's strong position in both popular music and the U.S. market. CBS Records filed an FTC complaint that this merger would violate Section 7 of the Clayton Act as "substantially lessening competition" by increasing the top four music companies' share of the U.S. market from 68 to 75 percent. Warner/Polygram enlisted an all-star witness lineup to explain the procompetitive benefits of their proposed merger: the Nobel Prize-winning economists Kenneth Arrow and George Stigler, antitrust specialists like William Baxter, who had just returned to Stanford Law School from being the head of the antitrust division and William Landes, Richard Posner's long-time scholarly partner at Chicago, as well as a future Chair of the Federal Reserve Board, Alan Greenspan. That group convinced the head of the FTC's Economic Bureau, Wendy Gramm (wife of Texas Senator Phil Gramm) and the FTC Chairman, James Miller, that the merger should be permitted.

The other four members of the FTC were not persuaded, though, and they filed a Section 7 charge and secured a preliminary injunction from the Ninth Circuit. *See FTC v. Warner Communications, Inc.*, 742 F.2d 1156 (9th Cir. 1984). The Court found the Section 7 claim to be legally plausible, and ruled that it was important to hold off the merger before it happened, rather than try to unravel it after a trial. Strikingly, the Court rejected Polygram's argument that saving its presence in the industry via a merger was more important than letting the label die without Warner's organizational support.

Faced with the prospect of years of antitrust litigation, Warner and Polygram dissolved their merger deal. Warner soon displaced CBS Records as the number one selling label, at around the same time as Sony was buying the latter. (One reason for this purchase and the new name, Sony Music, was to guarantee that at least some recorded music would have a compatible format with Sony's new digital audio tape system.) Philips did not, however, carry forward on its threat to shut down Polygram. Instead, buoyed by its signing of Bon Jovi with his 1986 *Slippery When Wet*, Polygram turned its music business around so that by 1995 it was back on top, just ahead of Warner Music and Sony Music.

Four years later, Seagram bought Polygram for $10.5 billion, combining it with Universal and MCA to form Universal Music Group, the clear leader in overall sales. Illustrating how dramatically antitrust policy had changed, no antitrust challenge was filed against this merger. However, a different fate awaited another proposed music takeover. At the same time as it was working out its merger deal with America Online, Time Warner was trying to buy the British music leader, EMI Group PLS. This combination of EMI and Warner Music sales would place it slightly ahead of the Universal Music Group. However, authorities in Britain used their version of antitrust law to block that takeover. This means that after three decades of conglomerate purchases of independent music labels, we are left with three majors who control the bulk of the music market.

———

In 1994, the Justice Department received an antitrust complaint from another part of the music industry. This dispute pitted rock band Pearl Jam, against Ticketmaster, the dominant off-site seller of tickets to music concerts. The case was precipitated by Pearl Jam's efforts to stage a 1994 concert tour at low prices for its "grunge rock" fans. In a summer in which Eagles' concert tickets were topping $100 a seat and Barbara Streisand's reached $350, Pearl Jam wanted to keep its prices under $20. The group sought to accomplish this by setting the tickets' face value at $18 and Ticketmaster's service fee at $1.80 (10 percent of the base price). Ticketmaster refused to agree to any fee less than $2.50 plus its handling charges. Because Ticketmaster had exclusive contracts with almost all the facilities where Pearl Jam was planning to play, that summer's tour had to be cancelled. Pearl Jam filed an antitrust complaint with the Justice Department, and publicity about the dispute sparked hearings in Congress.

As background, off-site ticket selling was started in the 1960s by Ticketron, which focused initially on Broadway shows, sporting events, and concerts. Ticketron's business expanded to over $100 million in ticket sales by 1980, with the company's service charge set at one dollar or less.

Customers liked the convenience of buying tickets off-site, rather than at the facility's box office. The one significant problem was that people could buy only those tickets available at that particular site, with the best seats usually remaining at the box office.

In the late 1970s, two Arizona State computer science students developed a software program that allowed sellers at any location to find and sell any seat that was still available for the event. The students started Ticketmaster, which by 1981 was selling $1 million in tickets a year (or one percent of Ticketron's). A Chicago billionaire, Jay Pritzker, bought the founders out for $4 million, and installed a corporate lawyer, Fred Rosen, at the helm. Rosen combined Ticketmaster's computer technology with a new marketing strategy that within one decade made his company the dominant force in the industry.

The strategy was to focus on concert ticket sales. Unlike sports, where the good seats are reserved for season-ticket holders, or Broadway shows, which can go on for years to permit fans to have the dates and seats they want, concerts are usually one-time events in any city and season, making it crucial for fans to get their tickets quickly. Ticketmaster saw the possibility for raising its service charges sharply for these concerts, just as Michael Jackson, Bruce Springsteen, and U-2 were doing with basic ticket prices. Ticketmaster was prepared to pay a share of its service charges to the facilities to induce their owners to sign three to five year contracts that gave Ticketmaster exclusive rights to sell tickets off-site.

By the early 1990s, Ticketmaster had exclusive contracts with two-thirds of the concert facilities around the country. Ticketmaster was selling $1.5 billion worth of tickets each year (some of which were for facilities where it did not have exclusive rights). The average service charge was over $5.00, with a range from $2.00 to $20.00 (for Streisand), depending on the attraction of the facility and the event. In 1991, Ticketron went into bankruptcy and out of business, with its assets acquired by Ticketmaster. In 1993, Pritzker sold Ticketmaster for $325 million to Paul Allen, co-founder of Microsoft.

Thus, Pearl Jam complained that it had been excluded from the concert market in 1994 because of Ticketmaster's exclusive contracts with prime facilities in larger cities. After releasing a new best-selling album, *Vitalogy,* Pearl Jam scheduled a 1995 concert tour. This time it used a new Entertainment Ticket Network phone system for sales (with a $2.00 service charge). This new system was effective in selling out concerts within fifteen to thirty minutes. However, rather than concerts being staged in New York and Los Angeles, Pearl Jam found facilities that satisfied its safety and sound standards largely in places like Casper, Wyoming and Boise, Idaho. Even then, logistical difficulties forced the tour to be cancelled shortly after it began. However, just a couple of weeks later, the Justice Department announced that it was "closing its antitrust investigation into [Ticketmaster's] contracting practices" though the Department was going "to monitor competitive developments in the ticket industry."

### *QUESTIONS FOR DISCUSSION*

1. Does Ticketmaster have monopoly power in a relevant market? Ticketmaster asserts that it sells only about 2 percent of the 1.5 billion tickets purchased for events each year. The denominator for that figure, though, includes not just tickets for concerts, theater, and sports, but also for museums, state fairs, and amusement parks. Pearl Jam claimed the relevant market was rock concert tickets in large metropolitan areas, in which Ticketmaster sold the lion's share. Do you agree? But even so, was the right to buy a ticket at the box office rather than through Ticketmaster a viable option for Pearl Jam fans?

2. Even if Ticketmaster has monopoly power in a narrower market, was that power improperly secured, or was it simply the byproduct of the company's success in satisfying consumer demand? Recall the standard from *United States v. Grinnell Corp.*, 384 U.S. 563, 570–71 (1966) (cited in *Syufy*), that *illegal* monopoly power requires "the willful acquisition or maintenance of that power as distinguished from growth or development as a consequence of a superior product, business acumen, or historic accident." Is Ticketmaster's current market dominance a transient phenomenon, one that could readily be displaced as has happened to Blockbuster, if Ticketmaster does not continue to satisfy its customers? Are there obstacles to new entrants that were not present in *Syufy*?

3. A different problem is posed by "scalping," purchasing a ticket and then reselling it at a higher price. Many states and cities have made it illegal to resell such tickets above face value. Although constitutional, *see People v. Concert Connection, Ltd.*, 211 A.D.2d 310, 629 N.Y.S.2d 254 (1995), are such laws desirable as a matter of public policy (e.g., as applied to E-bay)? Whose interests are advanced by such regulation, producers or consumers of entertainment events? Is there a case for regulating the resale price of a concert ticket while not regulating the original price set by the promoter and Ticketmaster?

4. *Slattery v. Apple Computer*, 2005 WL 2204981 (N.D. Cal.), involved an antitrust class action against the online music leader Apple. The latter had designed its iPod digital music players to play songs purchased from its iTunes store, not those bought from online rivals like Real Network, whose price was less than half that of iTunes 99 cents. What result?

---

Returning to the movie industry, a curious byproduct of *Paramount Pictures* was an industry practice called "splitting," which in turn led to another antitrust complaint, this time by the studios against the theaters. The assumption in *Paramount Pictures* was that dissolution of relationships between studios and theaters, and the substitution of individualized negotiation of exhibition licenses, would constrain the economic power of studios and theater chains and generate a rational allocation of films. As it turned out, the transaction costs required to negotiate licenses for hundreds of films to be shown in thousands of theaters were high. Moreover, the competitive bidding model inevitably required *ex ante* guarantees by exhibitors that could not feasibly be adjusted *ex post* if the film was a failure.

In the 1950s, exhibitors developed an informal "splitting" arrangement among themselves. Forthcoming films were initially allocated to theaters, which would then negotiate with the distributor on license terms. Only if acceptable terms could not be reached with the first theater would the distributor go on to negotiate with a second member of the group. In another arrangement called "tracking," studios developed an informal relationship with individual theaters (or chains) for the regular showing of their movies. Under either splitting or tracking, the regular practice of the parties was to relieve the theater of the initial contract commitments for movies that turned out to be failures.

On its face, splitting seemed an obvious violation of Section 1 of the Sherman Act, but the Justice Department and the studios accepted this system for the next quarter century, so long as every exhibitor had the right to participate in the group and enjoyed ready access to new films. In the late 1970s, though, the Justice Department reversed course and initiated an action against a distributor group in Milwaukee. *United States v. Capitol Service, Inc.*, 568 F. Supp. 134 (E.D. Wis. 1983), *aff'd*, 756 F.2d 502 (7th Cir. 1985). A similar suit was filed by Walt Disney's distribution arm as a counter to a contract suit lodged by an exhibitor in *General Cinema v. Buena Vista Distribution Co.*, 532 F. Supp. 1244 (C.D. Cal. 1982). In both cases, the evidence showed that splitting generated almost no competitive bidding, few payment guarantees or advances by exhibitors to distributors, shorter average playing times for individual movies, but roughly the same admission prices for viewers and division of box office revenues between distributors and exhibitors (comparing, for example, Milwaukee with splitting and Minneapolis without it). In both cases, the courts held that splitting was a *per se* violation of § 1 and should be banned nationwide.

Although it was an obvious antitrust violation, the distinctive features of the movie market have raised questions about whether a competitive bidding system which produces guarantees that movies be shown and studios be paid irrespective of audience reaction really is the best way to enhance consumer welfare. In an earlier decision, *Greenbrier Cinemas, Inc. v. Attorney General*, 511 F. Supp. 1046 (W.D. Va. 1981), the judge concluded that splitting should not be deemed automatically illegal, and instead required an in-depth "rule of reason" analysis.

Splitting, of course, is not the only technique through which to address the challenge of encouraging the production of high quality films and theaters. One possibility is a vertical relationship between distributor and exhibitor involving informal tracking, formal franchising, or full-blown corporate ownership. The last path seemed to have been limited by the *Paramount Pictures* decision and its aftermath.

However, as the supply of films began to dwindle in the 1950s, the divorce of exhibition from production-distribution began to erode. In 1963, National General Corporation, a small exhibitor enjoined from engaging in production and distribution, sought leave of court under the decree to produce and distribute motion pictures on a limited scale. The order was granted on condition that National General compete for its own pictures "theater by theater, solely upon the merits and without discrimination in favor of affiliated theaters, including theaters operated by National, circuit theaters or others." In 1969, National General wanted further expansion of its leeway for vertical integration. Judge Palmieri, who was assigned to oversee the consent decrees, approved the request. He noted that the 1963 grant "rested largely on the premise that film product had been increasingly in short supply and that in consequence there had been developed a growing need by exhibitors for new and marketable film product." *See 1969 Trade Cas.* (CCH) ¶ 72,767.

After 1969, there were even more changes in the industry. Judge Palmieri summed up these developments in one of his opinions:

> Since the original *Paramount* decrees, the motion picture industry has changed considerably. Not only have important technical advances been made in the field of color, sound projection, and image projection, but it is anticipated that feature motion pictures may soon become a household commodity through cable television and the use of cassette or comparable equipment. Additionally, new national circuits, unaffected by the decrees, have become important factors in the industry and the drive-in theaters, relatively unknown in the early days of the decree, have become very numerous. The multiscreen theater-two to as many as eight screens under one roof-as well as the ethnic and sex oriented theaters, have all had their impact and have underscored the fact that the movie-going public is no longer an aggregate of families in search of entertainment suitable to a wide age spectrum of viewers, but a

> younger and highly sophisticated group of viewers representing an aggregate of disparate consumers.

*United States v. Paramount Pictures*, 1980–2 Trade Cases ¶ 63553, 1980 WL 1899, *4 (S.D.N.Y. 1980).

---

Indeed, American screens have grown sharply in number, from 14,000 in 1970, to over 39,000 in 2014. Most of these screens were owned by chains like United Artists Theater Circuit, Loew's Cineplex, General Cinema, and American MultiCinema. In 1994, the top ten theater chains owned 49 percent of the nation's movie screens (up from 30 percent in 1985), though the largest, United Artists, still had just 9 percent (up from 5 percent). And the movie distribution system has changed dramatically from the 1940s: most movies are now released at the same time across the country, often shown on more than 3,000 screens on a Friday before a summer or holiday weekend. In the 2000s, the problem is not whether independently-owned theaters can get pictures to exhibit, but rather how independent filmmakers can get screens to show their work.

Partly because of these trends, the Justice Department took the position that *Paramount* had outlived its usefulness, especially in its restraints on distributor acquisition of theaters. Some of the studios—Columbia, Universal, Disney, even Paramount—were not formally required to seek judicial approval before buying theaters, and in the mid-1980s their corporate owners began to accumulate them again. (Universal's media parent, MCA, is half owner of Cineplex Odeon.) By the early 1990s, it was estimated that 5,000 of 26,000 movie screens were owned by distributors, as high a percentage as in the 1940s. However, other studios, like Warner Brothers, were bound by this feature of the *Paramount* decree and had to seek approval for entrance into the exhibition market. Judge Palmieri was prepared to grant such permission, but only on condition that there was insulation of the distribution and exhibition sides of the enterprise. In the following case, backed by the Justice Department, Warner Brothers appealed such an order. The studio sought unrestricted half ownership (in partnership with Paramount) of Cinamerica Theaters, which owned 119 theaters (with 469 screens) in 43 cities and towns.

## UNITED STATES V. LOEW'S, INC., ET AL.

United States Court of Appeals, Second Circuit, 1989.
882 F.2d 29.

LUMBARD, CIRCUIT JUDGE:

* * *

. . . The gist of [Warner's evidence] is that the market has changed in the forty years since Paramount Pictures so that the antitrust concerns then present do not exist today. Specifically, Warner's affiants argued that the industry has changed, largely due to the influence of the so-called "aftermarkets" of television and videocassettes, so that there is much less market concentration and many fewer barriers to entry. Warner argued that Cinamerica wields too little market power to enable Warner, should its motion be granted, to be able to restrain competition and drive out competitors. Warner also stressed that many independent distributors and exhibitors, including large independent national and regional exhibition circuits, have sprung up and flourished since the entry of the consent judgments and that these businesses are not in need of the court's protection. . . . [A] Warner executive, asserted that "Warner wishes to be able to compete on an equal footing with its principal rivals," who are not subject to the decretal restrictions on vertical integration.

Landes, the economist retained by Warner, stated in his affidavit that the Herfindahl-Hirschman Index (HHI), a measure of market concentration adopted by the Antitrust Division in the 1984 Merger Guidelines, is now about 1100 in the movie distribution market, which indicates a "relatively unconcentrated market"; the district court relied upon a finding that the HHI in the exhibition market is under 200, indicating low market concentration.[2]

. . . The Antitrust Division of the Department of Justice stated that the government, after having made "a complete competitive analysis of the acquisition," did not oppose the motion. Counsel argued in part that the existence of the aftermarkets has shifted much of the potential revenues from motion picture distribution away from theaters, making foreclosure of certain exhibition markets, which could hinder a distributor's access to the aftermarkets, undesirable and counterproductive.

---

[2] Under the HHI, which is calculated by adding the squares of the individual market shares of all the firms in an industry, values of 1000 and 1800 are considered by the Justice Department to reflect moderate and high concentration, respectively. These numbers roughly correspond to the fifty percent and seventy percent concentration level benchmarks in the traditional "four-firm concentration" test, in which the shares of the four largest firms are simply added, the seventy percent mark indicating that the four largest firms in the relevant market control seventy percent of that market.

[District Judge Palmieri, while prepared to accept Warner's acquisition of a half interest in Cinamerica, did so only on condition that Warner maintain an entirely arm's length relationship with Cinamerica, exercising no control over the latter's exhibition assets or management, and leaving it an entirely independent board of directors. Warner appealed those conditions.]

* * *

II

The sole issue is whether Warner's acquisition of a fifty percent interest in Cinamerica is likely unreasonably to restrain competition in either the motion picture distribution or exhibition industries. This is the standard set forth in Part VI(B) of the consent decree and in Section 7 of the Clayton Act, 15 U.S.C. § 18.

In order to protect the public interest the district court properly examined Warner's motion with great care, especially in light of the practices in the production, distribution and exhibition of motion pictures disclosed in the extensive litigation leading up to the 1948 Supreme Court decision in *United States v. Paramount Pictures, Inc.*, 334 U.S. 131 (1948), and the consent decrees which followed. Judge Palmieri cited *United States v. American Cyanamid Co.*, 719 F.2d 558, 563–65 (2d Cir. 1983), a consent decree entered before trial, in support of his view that his inquiry regarding Warner's motion should be more vigorous because Warner and its co-defendants had entered into the consent decree after a trial which resulted in finding them guilty of antitrust violations. We believe that in view of the court's power to relax the provisions of its decrees in light of changing circumstances, we see no reason to make a distinction between consent decrees entered into before trial and consent decrees entered into after trial.

We conclude that Warner's one-half ownership interest in Cinamerica is not offensive under Part VI(B) of the consent judgment. The merger is unlikely to increase barriers to entry into the exhibition business or reduce competition by (1) foreclosing competing exhibitors from access to features; (2) foreclosing Warner's competitors from access to theaters; or (3) limiting entry and presence in the distribution and exhibition markets to integrated concerns.

There can be no question that Cinamerica, even with Warner behind it, will not be able to restrain competition among its competitors in the exhibition business. Cinamerica owns only two percent of the nation's screens, by any measure a low degree of concentration. In light of the continuing prohibition against licensing features to exhibitors on any basis other than theater-by-theater, we believe that Warner's stake, through Cinamerica, in motion picture exhibition is highly unlikely to result in foreclosure of the exhibition market.

The continuing injunction to license features theater-by-theater also makes it unlikely that Warner's interest in Cinamerica will result in foreclosure of distributors' access to exhibitors. Moreover, the changed nature of the motion picture exhibition industry has made such foreclosure highly improbable. The growth of the motion picture aftermarkets of videocassettes, network, syndicated and cable television, and the development of national television advertising, have changed the business realities of the industry so that movie producers and distributors have every incentive to disseminate their products as quickly, and as widely, as possible. Many more exhibitors exhibit on many more screens than was the case when the consent judgments were entered into. There is now at least one screen in most homes in the United States, many millions in addition to the 22,000 screens owned by motion picture exhibitors.

If the industry begins to show any signs of returning to the sort of licensing arrangements that were addressed and prohibited by the consent judgments, the Attorney General would be remiss if he did not seek to invoke the consent judgments to thwart such anti-competitive activities. Moreover, Warner's competitors remain free to seek redress under the antitrust laws if Warner begins to engage in anti-competitive activities. Consequently, the remote possibility that the anti-competitive practices eliminated by the consent judgment could be resumed is insufficient to compel the denial of Warner's motion.

The uncontroverted evidence presented to the district court is that Warner's motive for purchasing a stake in Cinamerica is to enable it to compete with distributors not subject to the decretal restrictions, a legitimate business purpose that offends neither the Warner Consent Judgment nor Section 7. The government agrees that Warner is highly unlikely to attempt any anti-competitive activity and argues that Warner's stated motive for the acquisition—improved ability to compete with distributors not subject to the decretal restrictions—is likely to be pro-competitive rather than anti-competitive. As the district court noted, "with Warner and Paramount still dependent on their relationships with . . . circuits [not owned by distributors], there is a convincing argument that it is not in Warner's interest to attempt foreclosure today."

Although Warner will be free, through its interest in Cinamerica, to add to its exhibition holdings in the future, the consent judgment is not affected in any other respect, and the injunction against licensing features to exhibitors in any manner other than on the merits, theater-by-theater, continues in full force and effect. Moreover, any further integration Warner may embark upon in the future will of course be governed by Section 7 and the full panoply of restrictions and regulations. . . .

Remanded, with directions to modify the order of the district court by eliminating any restrictions upon Warner's ownership and operation of its one-half interest in Cinamerica.

### *QUESTIONS FOR DISCUSSION*

1. Should Warner have been permitted to purchase a stake in an exhibitor chain? If so, should its integration of production, distribution, and exhibition be subject to judicial limits? By the way, what exactly is the HHI measure of market concentration (referred to in the *Loew's* opinion), and how did the distribution and exhibition sides of the industry score on this index? The HHI guidelines discussed in footnote 2 of the court's opinion were slightly revised in 2010.

2. Why are studios interested in owning theaters? What are the pro-competitive reasons for such a merger? What are the anti-competitive worries? Are consumers helped or hurt by renewed vertical acquisitions? What would the market look like if every major studio again owned a national theater chain?

3. One of the main issues in *Loew's* centered on Warner's potential possession of market power. What is the relevant market—all entertainment, including Broadway shows? Should movie exhibition be considered a national, regional, or local market? Should the court have focused on the fact that Cinamerica had 9 of the 17 screens in Westwood, California, which (along with the Upper East Side of Manhattan) has the country's largest concentration of movie personalities and critics?

4. In the past, a major concern about the movie studio power was that it was translated into studio determination of the content of movies. In the new world of movie-making, is this still a problem?

---

In 2002 the FCC issued conflicting decisions on two major conglomerate deals in the broadcast industry. The first involved the biggest-ever merger in cable history, between AT&T, which led the nation with nearly 14 million subscribers, and Comcast, whose 8 million was the third largest. Comcast offered $47 billion in stock and took on $25 billion in AT&T debt to assume control over this new partnership serving nearly one third of American homes with cable systems, and the only one with subscribers in metropolitan areas around the country.

A year later, the value of this deal had sunk from $47 billion to $30 billion because of the stock market decline of these companies (though that decline was dwarfed by what happened to AOL Time Warner). Some consumer groups continued to challenge this proposed merger as violating the public interest in competition. The FCC, however, ruled that there was no serious competitive risk to local cable subscribers because AT&T and Comcast had not been competing in the same regions. There might be some risk with respect to the availability of Internet service providers, but the FCC would deal with that later.[m]

More importantly, the FCC was persuaded that this merger would serve consumer interests by accentuating the improvement of cable services, especially among AT&T's subscribers. While 97 percent of Comcast's customers already had fiber-optic connections which gave them access to high-speed Internet and digital television, only 67 percent of AT&T customers had this. Indeed, that was the main reason AT&T had lost a half million customers to satellite since the merger deal had been reached a year earlier. Thus, Comcast President Brian Roberts, who was in charge of this new cable giant (named Comcast allegedly to avoid confusion with AT&T), committed to spending $2 billion over the next two years on fiber-optic technology.

In that same month of November 2002, the FCC unanimously rejected the proposed acquisition of the number-one satellite network, DirecTV, by number-two EchoStar. The basic reason was that this combination would have control of 16.7 million of the 17.4 million (or 96 percent) satellite subscribers, and thus would be exercising de facto monopoly power in this setting. The FCC rejected EchoStar's argument that it faced substantial competition from cable across the country. The one exception existed in a few isolated rural areas, where DirecTV agreed to be governed by the same fee and channel standards that were found in the metropolitan areas where cable competition clearly existed.

Consider the competitive implications and the broader policy questions raised in this chapter. Was the 1948 *Paramount Picture* decision a wise form of intervention in the affairs of the motion picture industry at that time? How much impact did this antitrust decree have on the subsequent evolution of the entertainment world? Is the more recent hands-off approach towards entertainment mergers the right policy stance for the new millennium? The major mergers of the last twenty years have produced entertainment conglomerates whose level of vertical integration dwarfs what the Supreme Court struck down in *Paramount Pictures*. The same company can publish a novel, turn it into a movie, show the movie through its theaters, videos, cable or television channels, and now Internet services, create an album and video out of the movie's music score, and a video game out of its story characters; indeed, if the movie is a big enough popular success, like *Star Trek*, the company (Paramount) can even generate a television series that eventually forms

[m] The only immediate condition imposed was that AT&T had to put into an immediate trust fund its 21 percent share of the stock of Time Warner's cable division (the second largest system with nearly 11 million subscribers) and sell these shares within the next five years.

the base for a new network. Have these conglomerates actually produced the sorts of problems theoretically raised by critics? What about newspapers, which are actually more concentrated that the electronic media? *See* Richard Brand, *All The News That's Fit To Split: Newspaper Mergers, Antitrust Laws And The First Amendment*, 26 Cardozo Arts & Ent. L.J. 1 (2008). On the subject of media ownership generally, see Adam Candeub, *Media Ownership Regulation, the First Amendment, & Democracy's Future*, 41 U.C. Davis L. Rev. 1547 (2008); David Pritchard, Christopher Terry & Paul R. Brewer, *One Owner, One Voice? Testing a Central Premise of Newspaper-Broadcast Cross-Ownership Policy*, 13 Comm. L. & Pol'y 1 (2008). In the next chapter we will continue the story and policy analysis by adding another crucial feature—telecommunications law.

# CHAPTER 13

# ENTERTAINMENT IN A NEW TELECOMMUNICATIONS WORLD[a]

■ ■ ■

The mid-1990s witnessed a major political battle involving the Telecommunications Reform Act of 1996. Chapter 1 addressed the Act's ban on indecent material on the Internet and the requirement that violence in television programs be rated for possible V-Chip screening. The major aim of this statutory reform, though, was relaxing rather than tightening government control of the communications universe. The specific path chosen was removal of many of the barriers among television, cable, and telephone companies. The expectation was that market competition in a broader media world will better serve the interests of consumers than will administrative regulation. As Reed Hundt, Chair of the Federal Communications Commission (FCC), remarked when President Clinton signed this bill into law, it felt like "the Berlin Wall of telecommunications was finally coming down."

After the passage of that Act, the production of television grew rapidly, with a proliferation of channels and offerings. The growth of the Internet has added to the explosion of television, creating ubiquitous entertainment and giving rise to a new telecommunications battleground: net neutrality.

This combination of innovation and deregulation has been the driving force behind the rise in entertainment conglomerates discussed in Chapter 12. In particular, it was the desire to integrate the production and distribution of audiovisual products that led Rupert Murdoch to create the Fox Network after acquiring 20th Century Fox, Disney to merge with ABC, Warner Brothers to do the same with Time (with its HBO and cable delivery systems), and Viacom to acquire Paramount, and then CBS for what was then a record-setting $40 billion. Certainly, the

---

[a] *See* Stuart Brotman, *Communications Law & Practice* (Law Jour. Press 2005); Ithiel de Sola Pool, *Technologies of Freedom* (Harv. Univ. Press 1983); Howard J. Blumenthal & Oliver R. Goodenough, *This Business of Television* (Billboard Books 1991); Thomas G. Krattenmaker & Lucas A. Powe, Jr., *Regulating Broadcast Programming* (MIT Press 1994); Bruce M. Owen & Steven S. Wildman, *Video Economics* (Harv. Univ. Press 1992); Ken Auletta, *Three Blind Mice: How the TV Networks Lost Their Way* (Random House 1991); Tino Balio, ed., *Hollywood in the Age of Television* (Unwin Hyman 1990); Peter Huber, *Law & Disorder in Cyberspace: Abolish the FCC & Let Common Law Rule the Telecoms* (Oxford Univ. Press 1997); Kerry Segrave, *Movies at Home: How Hollywood Came to Television* (McFarland 1999).

world of telecommunication has changed dramatically from its beginnings a century ago.

The first broadcast medium was radio, whose technology was devised by Guglielmo Marconi. Intriguingly, the first American broadcast legislation, the Radio Act of 1912, was precipitated by the tragedy of the Titanic. The government's concern was to prevent interference by the variety of radio signals being transmitted on a common electromagnetic spectrum. At the end of World War I, it was expected that the production, sale, and use of radios would soar. In 1919, the U.S. government forced the sale of the manufacturing operations of the American Marconi division to a newly-formed Radio Corporation of America (RCA), jointly-owned by General Electric, Westinghouse and AT&T. In 1920, Westinghouse created the first commercial radio station, KDKA in Pittsburgh, to facilitate the use and sale of radios, and GE and AT&T quickly followed suit. In just a few years, radio broadcasting had spread across the country.

The late 1920s saw the development of both the industry and a regulatory structure for broadcasting. A key feature was enactment in 1927 of a revised Radio Act, which created a Federal Radio Commission (FRC) to allocate and license radio frequencies to stations operating in the same location. The year before, RCA had spun off a subsidiary, the National Broadcasting Corporation (NBC), to operate two networks (Blue and Red), which coordinated and distributed broadcast programming to affiliated stations throughout the country. The next year saw the creation of a network rival, the Columbia Broadcasting System (CBS). Then the government forced AT&T, GE, and Westinghouse to divest themselves of ownership of RCA and NBC because of the competitive threat posed by common control of both broadcasting and the manufacture of radio equipment (as well as a potentially conflicting role as common carrier of telephone communications). Finally, in 1934 Congress enacted a comprehensive Communications Act, which gave the renamed Federal Communications Commission (FCC) responsibility for both telephone and radio regulation.

The FCC's authority was not limited to deciding *who* was entitled to broadcast radio signals *where*. It had a broader responsibility to influence *what* was being broadcast, in order to serve the "public interest, convenience, and necessity." As the Commission put it in an early decision:

> Broadcasting stations are licensed to serve the public and not for the purpose of furthering the private or selfish interests of individuals. . . . [A] broadcasting station may be regarded as a sort of mouthpiece on the air for the community it serves, over which its public events of general interest, its political

> campaigns, its election results, its athletic contests, its orchestras and artists, and discussion of its public issues may be broadcast.

*Great Lakes Broadcasting Co.*, 3 F.R.C. Annual Report 32 (1929), *modified on other grounds*, *Great Lakes Broadcasting Co. v. Federal Radio Commission*, 37 F.2d 993 (D.C. Cir. 1930). Given the interventionist New Deal attitude towards business regulation, President Roosevelt's Commission felt quite comfortable in spelling out the rules that would define broadcast industry ventures and relationships.

An important early example was FCC regulation of the permissible terms of the network-affiliate relationship. The original role contemplated for the agency was allocation of the use of the radio spectrum in local communities. However, just as is true of television now, in the early days of radio, national networks were crucial for creation of the kind and quality of programs that listeners wanted to hear. In return for permitting stations to broadcast its programs, the network insisted not only on a financial fee, but also on conditions that tied the stations to the network. In response, the FCC proclaimed a set of "chain broadcasting" rules designed to preserve local station autonomy to decide which network programs it would broadcast in its community. In *NBC v. United States*, 319 U.S. 190, 226 (1943), the Supreme Court held that these FCC conditions on the license to use the radio medium was not abridgment of the freedom of speech of broadcasters.

> Unlike other modes of expression, radio inherently is not available to all. That is its unique characteristic, and that is why . . . it is subject to regulation. Because it cannot be used by all, some who wish to use it may be denied.

Unlike a newspaper, the government had to license those who would have the exclusive right to speak on public airwaves. Having won a license in preference to other applicants, the licensee could not assert that its constitutional freedoms were being infringed by having to abide by the terms of that license.

Even after the crucial decisions of the 1950s and the 1960s, which expanded the scope of free speech protections, the Court stuck to this conception of broadcasting under the First Amendment. Perhaps the starkest illustration is the combination of *Red Lion Broadcasting v. FCC*, 395 U.S. 367 (1969) (which upheld the FCC's "fairness" doctrine requiring stations that took a position on one side of a public controversy to give the other side an opportunity to state its views on air), and *Miami Herald Pub. Co. v. Tornillo*, 418 U.S. 241 (1974) (which struck down an analogous state law applied to newspapers). The theme that runs through these opinions is that broadcasting requires special legal treatment.[b] In contrast to the movie industry, for example, telecasters have been entrusted with the exclusive right to use arguably scarce spectrum to beam their programs directly into 100 million homes. In return, broadcasters freedom is subject, at least to some extent, to public concerns about the quality and diversity of their programming. Chapter 1 covered the constitutional treatment of the original ban on indecent programming in *FCC v. Pacifica Foundation,* 438 U.S. 726 (1978), not long after the Court had found it to be a violation of the First Amendment to bar use of the same words on a jacket worn in a courtroom in *Cohen v. California*, 403 U.S. 15 (1971).

This decades-long debate about the legal status of broadcasting has been accompanied by fundamental transformations in the nature of the broadcast media themselves. Television became technologically feasible in the 1930s, and just like radio after World War I, commercial television took off after World War II. The dominant networks were NBC and CBS, both expanding from their radio bases. A third was DuMont, though this network expired in the mid-1950s and sold its stations to John Kluge (who named his group Metromedia). A fourth network was the American Broadcasting Corporation (ABC), which was the byproduct of a Justice Department antitrust directive forcing NBC to sell off one of its networks. Ironically, ABC was purchased by United Paramount Theaters, the new chain that the Department had required Paramount Pictures to unload in order to comply with the antitrust decree splitting the production and exhibition facets of the movie industry. UPT was headed by Leonard Goldenson, who had his struggling ABC branch establish the first television network-movie studio relationships: contracts with Disney to produce Saturday morning's *Disneyland*, and with Warner Brothers to produce prime-time series like *77 Sunset Strip* and *Maverick*.[c]

Television viewership soared throughout the 1950s and 1960s, while movie attendance sharply declined. During the baby boomer era, American families apparently preferred to watch films on television rather than go out to a theater. By the early 1970s, ABC's Barry Diller and Michael Eisner developed the concept of Hollywood-made Movies of the Week, which helped ABC finally rise to the top of national television ratings at a time when the overall network share of prime-time viewing was over 90 percent.

This was precisely the point at which another development was about to transform the television world—cable programming. Cable systems had originally appeared in the 1950s as a vehicle for bringing clearer

[b] *See* Jonathan Weinberg, *Broadcasting & Speech*, 81 Cal. L. Rev. 1103 (1993); Jim Chen, *The Last Picture Show (On the Twilight of Federal Mass Communications Regulation)*, 80 Minn. L. Rev. 1415 (1996); Cass Sunstein, *Television & the Public Interest*, 88 Cal. L. Rev. 499 (2000).

[c] *See* Leonard H. Goldenson with Marvin J. Wolf, *Beating the Odds* (MacMillan 1991).

signals for over-the-air shows into remote areas. In the 1960s the FCC imposed stringent restrictions on cable importation of distant television signals into urban markets (rules that were upheld in *United States v. Southwestern Cable Co.,* 392 U.S. 157 (1968)). The pioneer in the transformation of cable into a vehicle for new television programming was Home Box Office (HBO), which showed movies that had just left the theaters and produced new programs different from the standard fare on the networks.[d] HBO was quickly followed by Ted Turner's WTBS, CNN, and TNT cable channels, Viacom's Showtime and Nickelodeon, the USA Network, and ESPN. The eventual result of this greater range of television offerings was that by the end of the 1990s the network share of the prime-time audience had dropped under 60 percent.

This smaller share also had to be divided up among a larger number of networks. When Barry Diller moved from Paramount to Twentieth Century Fox in the 1980s, he developed a new Fox Broadcasting network for Rupert Murdoch that combined the studio's film production capacities with the Metromedia television station group. Around the same time, Capital Cities acquired ABC (which by then owned ESPN) for $3.5 billion. Meanwhile, Michael Eisner moved from Paramount to Disney, which was then somewhat in the doldrums. In the next decade, Eisner and his Disney team developed animated blockbusters such as *Beauty & the Beast* and *The Lion King,* giving Disney the leverage to acquire ABC-Capital Cities (for $19 billion). To show how far back the clock could turn in the broadcast world, the mid-1990s also saw Westinghouse acquiring CBS and the Infinity radio network, thus rejoining its long-ago partner, General Electric (which had bought RCA-NBC in 1986), as owners of broadcast networks the government had forced them to divest seven decades earlier.

In the 21st Century, radio and television are radically different from what they were in their respective infancies in the 1920s and 1940s. The corporate result has been an integration of broadcasters with other branches of the entertainment world. From the consumer perspective, there has been a radical expansion in the number of broadcast, cable, Internet, and satellite offerings, providing numerous program options for the typical American home. Even more important, perhaps, is the prospect of having several suppliers providing the same services via telephone, broadcast, cable, Internet, and satellite.

It was precisely these developments that sparked the debate in Washington during the mid-1990s about how to reshape the legal framework for this new telecommunications world. One view was that the most sensible step would simply be to repeal the Communications Act and eliminate the FCC, just as had been done with airline regulation in the

---

[d] *See* George Mair, Inside HBO: The Billion Dollar War Between HBO, Hollywood, & the Home Video Revolution (Dodd, Mead 1988).

late-1970s. An oft-cited comment of President Reagan's FCC Chair expressed a radically different perspective than what we saw earlier from President Hoover's Commission.

> It is time to move away from thinking about broadcasters as trustees. It is time to treat them the way almost everyone else in society does—that is, as businesses. Television is just another appliance. It's a toaster with pictures.

The Internet has further transformed television, moving it from an appointment-based model to an on-demand model (recall NBC promos from the 1990s of "must-see" Thursday night television with Friends, Seinfeld, and ER). Beginning with the development of DVRs and expanding through the growth of outlets like Netflix and Hulu, television typically is watched whenever the consumer wants. This has also led to the binge-watching phenomenon of choosing a new television show and watching multiple episodes in a row (and perhaps even a weekend marathon).

The one exception, of course, is live sporting events. Consequently, these remain among the most-watched television shows and garner the most advertising revenue.

Given that the Internet is now the home to all things entertainment, the telecommunications battle has migrated from regulation of content to availability of content, in the form of net neutrality debates.

## A. FINANCIAL INTEREST AND SYNDICATION RULES[e]

A major issue historical issue related to FCC rules about the "financial interest and syndication" (Fin/Syn) rights of television networks in the programming they broadcast. To understand the Fin/Syn rules, one must first know something about the television network relationship with affiliated stations. The networks each own a small number of stations in large markets. They also have affiliation agreements with some 200 independently-owned stations, which enable the networks to have nationwide simultaneous transmission of programming. When the local stations are showing network programs, the networks receive the bulk of the advertising dollars from national commercials (though some time is reserved for local commercials). When the local station is broadcasting its own shows, whether produced (e.g., local news and sports) or purchased from an independent producer, the local stations keep all of the advertising revenue.

---

[e] *See* David F. Prindle, *Risky Business: The Political Economy of Hollywood* (Westview Press 1993).

In the late 1960s, there were three major networks, NBC, CBS, and ABC, and their programming was watched by 90 percent of those viewing television in prime time. In 1970, after a decade of investigation, the FCC issued regulations that required two changes in the industry. *Network Television Broadcasting*, 23 F.C.C.2d 382 (1970). The first change was that on stations in the 50 largest markets, network programming could be shown for no more than three of the four prime-time hours (7 p.m. to 11 p.m.) The objective was to open up this crucial prime-time audience to a larger and more diverse range of programming and producers than those ordained by the three networks. Exceptions were made for special events like political conventions or sporting events.

The second change was a ban on the networks securing financial and syndication rights in the programming they broadcast. A considerable amount of programming (news and sports) is broadcast and watched live, with only limited audience interest in a replay during the next season. By contrast, television series and movies are regularly shown not only in a first run, but repeated for audiences that may have missed them or that want to see them again. Some replays take place on network prime-time to fill vacancies left in the year-long season, but most take place on local stations (affiliated or independent) outside of prime-time. The owner of a program puts together an *ad hoc* syndication network across the country for rebroadcast of a popular show years in the future. The syndicator charges the local station a licensing fee that depends on the size of its audience and the demand for the show, and the station recoups this investment through advertising. Cable channels like USA Network and Lifetime have become an alternative outlet for syndicated programs.

In practice, television series and films are made by the same creative talent—actors, directors, writers, composers—that are assembled for the production of movies for exhibition in theaters. Syndication revenues (now more than $8 billion a year) have become a crucial feature in the financing of television series and other features. The reason is that once a program is made and paid for, all of that additional revenue is pure profit. And these revenues can be huge—e.g., totaling over $3 billion for *Seinfeld* since that program went into syndication.

Indeed, syndication has now become a factor that kills as well as creates highly-rated series like *MASH*, *Miami Vice*, *Cheers* and *Friends*. After their stars (like Alan Alda, Don Johnson, Ted Danson and all six "Friends") become extremely popular, their compensation soars far more than do the networks' advertising revenues and the producers' licensing fees. Once the owner of a series has enough years—normally five or six—of shows on film to make the series an enduring replay, it can shut down the much more expensive production of new shows on network prime-time that actually function as competitors against syndicated viewing of the old shows.

A crucial question, then, is who actually owns these syndication and financial rights—the networks based in New York or the film production companies in Los Angeles? This issue would normally be settled by contract negotiations between the network and producers at the time a series is first appearing. As syndicated replays were becoming more popular and valuable in the 1960s, networks were beginning to insist on a share of those rights as the price of access to its prime-time schedule. Thus, for essentially the same reasons that underlay its three-hour limit on prime-time network programming, the FCC established a ban on network Fin/Syn rights in the programs it broadcast. Both sets of rules were upheld against constitutional and administrative challenges in *Mt. Mansfield Television, Inc. v. FCC*, 442 F.2d 470 (2d Cir. 1971).

By the early 1980s, both the broadcast industry and the politics of regulation had been transformed. The force of the *Paramount* antitrust decrees was greatly diluted. Civil Aeronautics Board regulation of air traffic routes and fares was totally eliminated. Thus, in 1983, the FCC issued for notice and comment a tentative ruling that would repeal the Fin/Syn, though not the prime-time access, rule. That administrative action set off a fierce political struggle between California's film industry and New York's broadcast industry. President Reagan's Administration eventually acquiesced to the urging of his former Hollywood colleagues.

The matter returned to the agenda of the first Bush Administration, this time precipitated by Fox, which now included an incipient television network as well as a motion picture studio. Fox Broadcasting could remain exempt from the Fin/Syn rules only as long as it had less than fifteen hours of weekly prime-time programming, a limit it eventually needed to exceed in order to attract affiliated stations across the country. (The significance of this issue for Fox was that its production arm had produced and was syndicating series like *The Simpsons* for the Fox network, *L.A. Law* for NBC, *Picket Fences* for CBS, and *NYPD Blue* for ABC.) By a narrow 3–2 margin, the FCC voted to retain the Fin/Syn concept, but in a somewhat reduced fashion.

1. There would be no such restraints on non-entertainment (e.g., news and sports) programs.
2. There would be only limited restraints on foreign syndication of all programs or domestic syndication of non-prime-time programs.
3. The network could contract with its producer for a financial interest in domestic syndication of prime-time programs, but only if such rights were negotiated at least thirty days *after* the network-producer contract had been finalized for the initial prime-time broadcasts.

4. Even in the latter case, the network could not secure the syndication rights for itself, but instead had to leave that function—i.e. selecting and negotiating the terms with local stations—to an independent body.

5. Replacing a recently terminated antitrust decree that barred all direct prime-time film production by the networks, *see United States v. National Broadcasting Co.*, 449 F. Supp. 1127 (C.D. Cal. 1978), the FCC would permit the networks to do up to 40 percent of their own prime-time film production.

Buoyed by a dissent from the FCC Chairman, who called for total repeal of the rules, the broadcast industry filed suit.

## SCHURZ COMMUNICATIONS, INC. V. FEDERAL COMMUNICATIONS COMMISSION

United States Court of Appeals, Seventh Circuit, 1992.
982 F.2d 1043.

POSNER, CIRCUIT JUDGE.

* * *

Many syndicated programs are reruns, broadcast by independent stations, of successful comedy or dramatic series first shown on network television. Very few series are sufficiently successful in their initial run to be candidates for syndication. Independent stations like to air five episodes each week of a rerun series that originally had aired only once a week or less, so unless a series has a first run of several years—which few series do—it will not generate enough episodes to sustain a rerun of reasonable length. The financial interest and syndication rules thus severely limited the networks' involvement in supplying television programs other than for their own or their affiliated stations.

The concern behind the [financial-syndication] rules was that the networks, controlling as they did through their owned and operated stations and their affiliates a large part of the system for distributing television programs to American households, would unless restrained use this control to seize a dominating position in the production of television programs. That is, they would lever their distribution "monopoly" into a production "monopoly." They would, for example, refuse to buy programs for network distribution unless the producers agreed to surrender their syndication rights to the network. For once the networks controlled those rights, the access of independent television stations, that is, stations not owned by or affiliated with one of the networks, to reruns would be at the sufferance of the networks, owners of a competing system of distribution. Market power in buying has the same misallocative effects as the more common market power in selling. The relation is especially close in this case because the networks can just as well be viewed as sellers of a distribution service as they can be as buyers of programs—the less they pay for programs, the more in effect they charge for distributing them.

The Commission hoped the rules would strengthen an alternative source of supply (to the networks) for independent stations—the alternative consisting of television producers not owned by networks. The rules would do this by curtailing the ability of the networks to supply the program market represented by the independent stations, and by protecting the producers for that market against being pressured into giving up potentially valuable syndication rights. And the rules would strengthen the independent stations (and so derivatively the outside producers, for whom the independent stations were an important market along with the networks themselves) by securing them against having to purchase reruns from their competitors, the networks.

The basis for this concern that the networks, octopus-like, would use their position in distribution to take over programming, and would use the resulting control of programming to eliminate their remaining competition in distribution, was never very clear. If the networks insisted on buying syndication rights along with the right to exhibit a program on the network itself, they would be paying more for their programming. (So one is not surprised that in the decade before the rules were adopted, the networks had acquired syndication rights to no more than 35 percent of their prime-time series, although they had acquired a stake in the syndicator's profits in a considerably higher percentage of cases.) If the networks then turned around and refused to syndicate independent stations, they would be getting nothing in return for the money they had laid out for syndication rights except a long-shot chance—incidentally, illegal under the antitrust laws—to weaken the already weak competitors of network stations. Nor was it clear just how the financial interest and syndication rules would scotch the networks' nefarious schemes. If forbidden to buy syndication rights, networks would pay less for programs, so the outside producers would not come out clear winners—indeed many would be losers. Production for television is a highly risky undertaking, like wildcat drilling for gas and oil. Most television entertainment programs are money losers. The losses are offset by the occasional hit that makes it into syndication after completing a long first run. The sale of syndication rights to a network would enable a producer to shift risk to a larger, more diversified entity presumptively better able to bear it. The resulting reduction in the risks of production would encourage new entry into production and thus give the independent stations a more competitive supply of programs. Evidence introduced in this proceeding showed that, consistent with this speculation, networks in the pre-1970 era were more likely to purchase syndication rights from small producers than from large ones.

Whatever the pros and cons of the original financial interest and syndication rules, in the years since they were promulgated the structure of the television industry has changed profoundly. The three networks have lost ground, primarily as a result of the expansion of cable television, which now reaches 60 percent of American homes, and videocassette recorders, now found in 70 percent of American homes. Today each of the three networks buys only 7 percent of the total video and film programming sold each year, which is roughly a third of the percentage in 1970. (The inclusion of films in the relevant market is appropriate because videocassettes enable home viewers to substitute a film for a television program.) And each commands only about 12 percent of total television advertising revenues. Where in 1970 the networks had 90 percent of the prime-time audience, today they have 62 percent, and competition among as well as with the three networks is fierce. They are, moreover, challenged today by a fourth network, the Fox Broadcasting Corporation, which emerged in the late 1980s.

Notwithstanding the fourth network, which might have been expected to reduce the number of independent stations by converting many of them to network—Fox network—stations, the number of independent stations has increased five-fold since 1970. At the same time, contrary to the intention behind the rules, yet an expectable result of them because they made television production a riskier business, the production of prime-time programming has become more concentrated. There are 40 percent fewer producers of prime-time programming today than there were two decades ago. And the share of that programming accounted for directly or indirectly by the eight largest producers, primarily Hollywood studios—companies large enough to bear the increased risk resulting from the Commission's prohibition against the sale of syndication rights to networks—has risen from 50 percent to 70 percent.

The original rules had been supported by the Antitrust Division of the Department of Justice. But as the years passed, antitrust thinking changed. The "leverage" theory, which taught that a firm having economic power in one market would use it to acquire a monopoly of another market, was widely discredited. The evolution of the television industry, sketched above, suggested that the rules, if they were having any effect at all, were working perversely from a competitive standpoint.

* * *

The Commission's majority opinion describes them as "deregulatory," arguing that they expand the networks' opportunities to participate in the program market and promising to reexamine them in four years to see whether a further relaxation of restrictions might then be justifiable. Although the Commission conceded that the networks may already have lost so much of their market power as no longer to pose a threat to competition as it is understood in antitrust law, it concluded that some restrictions remain necessary to assure adequate diversity of television programming. The Commission's chairman, understandably irate because the majority had ignored most of the points in his long and detailed dissent, predicted that the majority's decision would "produce a milestone case on what constitutes arbitrary and capricious decisionmaking."

[Having spelled out the standard for judicial review of administrative action—that not only the agency's rule but its stated explanation must be rational—Judge Posner essentially endorsed that dissenting view.]

* * *

Stripped of verbiage, the [FCC] opinion, like a Persian cat with its fur shaved, is alarmingly pale and thin. It can be paraphrased as follows. The television industry has changed since 1970. There is more competition—cable television, the new network, etc. No longer is it clear that the networks have market power in an antitrust sense, which they could use to whipsaw the independent producers and strangle the independent stations. So there should be some "deregulation" of programming—some movement away from the 1970 rules. But not too much, because even in their decline the networks may retain some power to extort programs or program rights from producers. The networks offer advertisers access to 98 percent of American households; no competing system for the distribution of television programming can offer as much. Anyway the Commission's concern, acknowledged to be legitimate, is not just with market power in an antitrust sense but with diversity, and diversity is promoted by measures to assure a critical mass of outside producers and independent stations. So the networks must continue to be restricted—but less so than by the 1970 rules. The new rules will give the networks a greater opportunity to participate in programming than the old ones did, while protecting outside producers and independent stations from too much network competition.

All this is, on its face, plausible enough, but it is plausible only because the Commission, ostrich fashion, did not discuss the most substantial objections to its approach, though the objections were argued vigorously to it, by its own chairman among others. To begin with, the networks object that the new rules do not in fact increase their access to the programming market and may decrease it, in the face of the Commission's stated objective. The 40 percent limitation on the amount of prime-time entertainment that a network can supply from its in-house production is a new restriction on the networks, having no counterpart in the original rules. It does have a counterpart in consent decrees that the networks entered into some years ago, e.g., *United States v. National Broadcasting Co.*, 449 F. Supp. 1127 (C.D.Cal.1978), when the Justice Department was still enamored of the leverage theory, but those decrees expired two years ago. The carving out of nonentertainment programming from the restrictions imposed by the new rules is a throwaway, because there is no syndication market for news and sports programs. Also illusory, the networks argue, is the newly granted right to acquire syndication rights from outside producers, given the restrictions with which the new right is hedged about. A producer cannot wait until 30 days after negotiating the network license fee to sell off syndication rights, because the sale of those rights, the networks contend, is critical to obtaining the financing necessary to produce the program in the first place. These arguments may be right or wrong; our point is only that the Commission did not mention them. We are left in the dark about the grounds for its belief that the new rules will give the networks real, not imaginary, new opportunities in programming.

The new rules, like their predecessors, appear to harm rather than to help outside producers as a whole (a vital qualification) by reducing their bargaining options. It is difficult to see how taking away a part of a seller's market could help the seller. One of the rights in the bundle of rights that constitutes the ownership of a television program is the right to syndicate the program to nonnetwork stations. The new rules restrict—perhaps, as a practical matter, prevent—the sale of that right to networks. How could it help a producer to be forbidden to sell his wares to a class of buyers that may be the high bidders for them? It is not as if anyone supposed that syndication rights, like babies or human freedom or the vital organs of a living person, should not be salable at all. They are freely salable—except to networks. Since syndication is the riskiest component of a producer's property right—for its value depends on the distinctly low-probability event that the program will be a smash hit on network television—restricting its sale bears most heavily on the smallest, the weakest, the newest, the most experimental producers, for they are likely to be the ones least able to bear risk. It becomes understandable why the existing producers support the financial interest and syndication rules: the rules protect these producers against new competition both from the networks (because of the 40 percent cap) and from new producers. The ranks of the outside producers of prime-time programming have been thinned under the regime of financial interest and syndication rules. The survivors are the beneficiaries of the thinning. They do not want the forest restored to its pristine density. They consent to have their own right to sell syndication rights curtailed as the price of a like restriction on their potential competitors, on whom it is likely to bear more heavily.

This analysis of risk and its bearing on competition in the program industry is speculative, theoretical, and may for all we know be all wet—though it is corroborated by the increasing concentration of the production industry since the rules restricting the sale of syndication rights were first imposed in 1970. The Commission was not required to buy the analysis. But as the analysis was more than plausible and had been pressed upon it by a number of participants in the rulemaking proceeding—including a putatively disinterested Justice Department that in the past had frequently seen the bogeyman of monopoly lurking everywhere, as well as the Commission's own chairman—the Commission majority was not entitled to ignore it. Not even to consider the possibility that the unrestricted sale of syndication rights to networks would strengthen the production industry (the industry—not necessarily its present occupants) and thereby increase programming diversity by enabling a sharing between fledgling producers and the networks of the risks of new production was irresponsible. For if the argument about risk sharing is correct, the rules are perverse; by discouraging the entry of new producers into the high-risk prime-time entertainment market, they are likely to reduce the supply of programs to the independent stations and so reduce diversity both of program sources and of program outlets. The Commission's stated desiderata are competition and diversity. The rules adopted by the Commission in order to achieve these desiderata have the remarkable property—if the risk-sharing argument that the Commission did not deign to address is correct—of disserving them both.

Central to the Commission's decision to continue restricting the networks' participation in programming is its belief that whether or not they have market power in some antitrust sense they have the power to force producers to sell them programs for less than the programs would be worth in a fully competitive market. The networks call this a contradiction: either they have market power, or they don't; there is no middle ground. A rational commission could disagree. Market power is a matter of degree. Some firms have a lot of it, some a little, some none. It is plausible that each network, even when not colluding with the others (there is no evidence that they are colluding), has some market power and thus can drive a harder bargain with producers than it could do if it had none. Even though each of the three major networks has only about 20 percent of the prime-time audience and a producer who does not sell his program to a network can still hope to distribute it to the public via independent stations and cable networks, or for that matter movie theaters and videocassette dealers, network distribution offers advertisers unique simultaneous access to a large fraction of American households and increases the prospects for successful syndication, which apparently is where the real money in the creation of television entertainment is to be made.

The difficulty is that if the networks do have market power, the new rules (in this respect like the old) do not seem rationally designed to prevent its exercise. A rule telling a person he may not do business with some firm believed to have market power is unlikely to make the person better off. Suppose that in a competitive market a network would pay $2 million for first-run rights to some program and $1 million for syndication rights, for a total of $3 million, but that because of the lack of perfect substitutes for using this network to distribute his program the producer is willing to sell each of these rights to the network for half their competitive-market value (i.e., for $1 million and $500,000 respectively). The producer is made no better off by being forbidden to sell the syndication rights to the network. He gets the same meager first-run license fee ($1 million) and now must cast about for another buyer for the syndication rights. That other buyer is unlikely to pay more than the network would ($500,000); otherwise the producer would have sold the syndication rights to him in the first place. It is no answer that the network would not have given the producer the option of selling it only first-run rights, that it would have insisted on the whole package so that it could control the program supply of the independent stations, which are heavily dependent on reruns and hence on syndication. The producer might indeed be desperate for network distribution, but that desperation would be reflected in the low price at which he was willing to sell the network whatever rights the network wanted. He cannot do better by being forbidden to make such a deal. If he could do better by selling syndication rights to someone else he would not accede to such unfavorable terms as the network offered.

If this is right, the new rules, at least insofar as they restrict network syndication, cannot increase the prices that producers receive. All they can do is increase the costs of production by denying producers the right to share risks with networks.

* * *

Everything that we have said about the effect of forbidding producers to sell syndication rights to networks may be wrong. That we freely grant. But the argument we have sketched—an argument vigorously pressed upon the Commission by the networks—is sufficiently persuasive to have placed a burden of explanation on the Commission. It did not carry the burden. It did not mention the objection.

And we have said nothing as yet of the treatment of the Fox network. That network is built around the production capability and film library of Twentieth Century Fox. At present the network supplies only 12 to 14 hours a week of prime-time programming to its owned and affiliated stations and is therefore exempt from the new rules. Should it reach 15 hours, however, it would be subject to them. Fox argues that, given the importance of program production in its overall corporate activity, the effect of the rules is to limit it to supplying fewer than 15 hours of prime-time programming and therefore to limit its growth as a network. Corroboration of this argument is found in the fact that the Fox network hit 15 hours a week shortly before the rules went into effect, then cut back to the present 12 to 14 hours. By limiting Fox in this way the new financial interest and syndication rules limit competition with the major networks and thus entrench the market power that is the rules' principal rationale. Or so Fox argues; it may be bluffing; maybe the effect of the rules will be to induce Fox to divest its production or network arms, so that the network can grow without constraining Fox's production activities. But once again the Commission failed even to mention the argument that its rules perversely limit competition with the established networks.

More than competition in the economic sense is at stake. Fox's affiliates are for the most part the traditionally weak UHF stations. They do not consider themselves "network" stations in the same sense that a CBS or NBC or ABC affiliate does. Many of them are members of the trade association of independent television stations. Anything that weakens Fox's incentives to furnish prime-time programming weakens them, contrary to the Commission's desire, protectionist though it may be, to strengthen independent stations. This perverse consequence of the rules also went unmentioned.

* * *

We remarked earlier that even if the networks had zero market power, the Commission might in the discharge of its undefined, uncanalized responsibility to promote the public interest restrict the networks' programming activities in order to create a more diverse programming fare.... [W]hile the word diversity appears with incantatory frequency in the Commission's opinion, it is never defined. At argument one of the counsel helpfully distinguished between source diversity and outlet diversity. The former refers to programming sources, that is, producers, and the latter to distribution outlets, that is, television stations. The two forms of diversity are related because the station decides what programs to air and therefore affects producers' decisions about what to produce. A third and one might suppose the critical form of diversity is diversity in the programming itself; here "diversity" refers to the variety or heterogeneity of programs. The Commission neither distinguished among the types of diversity nor explained the interrelation among them. As it is very difficult to see how sheer number of producers or outlets could be thought a good thing—and anyway the rules seem calculated, however unwittingly, to decrease, or at least to freeze, but certainly not to increase, the number of producers—we assume that the

Commission thinks of source diversity and outlet diversity as means to the end of programming diversity.

Are they? It has long been understood that monopoly in broadcasting could actually promote rather than retard programming diversity. If all the television channels in a particular market were owned by a single firm, its optimal programming strategy would be to put on a sufficiently varied menu of programs in each time slot to appeal to every substantial group of potential television viewers in the market, not just the largest group. For that would be the strategy that maximized the size of the station's audience. Suppose, as a simple example, that there were only two television broadcast frequencies (and no cable television), and that 90 percent of the viewers in the market wanted to watch comedy from 7 to 8 p.m. and 10 percent wanted to watch ballet. The monopolist would broadcast comedy over one frequency and ballet over the other, and thus gain 100 percent of the potential audience. If the frequencies were licensed to two competing firms, each firm would broadcast comedy in the 7 to 8 p.m. time slot, because its expected audience share would be 45 percent (one half of 90 percent), which is greater than 10 percent. Each prime-time slot would be filled with "popular" programming targeted on the median viewer, and minority tastes would go unserved. Some critics of television believe that this is a fair description of prime-time network television. Each network vies to put on the most popular programs and as a result minority tastes are ill served.

Well, so what? Almost everyone in this country either now has or soon will have cable television with 50 or 100 or even 200 different channels to choose among. With that many channels, programming for small audiences with specialized tastes becomes entirely feasible. It would not have been surprising, therefore, if the Commission had taken the position that diversity in prime-time television programming, or indeed in over-the-air broadcasting generally, was no longer a value worth promoting. It did not take that position. Instead it defended its restrictions on network participation in programming on the ground that they promote diversity. But it made no attempt to explain how they do this. It could have said, but did not, that independent television stations depend on reruns, which they would prefer to get from sources other than the networks with which they compete, and—since reruns are the antithesis of diversity—they use their revenue from reruns to support programming that enhances programming diversity. It could have said that programs produced by networks' in-house facilities are somehow more uniform than programs produced by Hollywood studios. It didn't say that either. It never drew the link between the rules, which on their face impede the production of television programs—not only by constraining negotiations between networks and outside producers but also by reducing the networks' incentive to produce by limiting the extent to which a network can exhibit its own programs in prime time—and the interest in diverse programming. The Commission may have thought the link obvious, but it is not. The rules appear to handicap the networks and by handicapping them to retard new entry into production; how all this promotes programming diversity is mysterious, and was left unexplained in the Commission's opinion.

That opinion, despite its length, is unreasoned and unreasonable, and therefore, in the jargon of judicial review of administrative action, arbitrary and capricious. The Commission's order is therefore vacated and the matter is returned to the Commission for further proceedings. The Commission may of course reopen the record of the rulemaking proceeding to receive additional comments if that will help it reach an articulate reasoned decision.

* * *

Vacated and remanded.

---

This ruling precipitated a major change in administrative policy. When the case went back to the FCC in 1993, it declared an eventual end to the Fin/Syn regulations. (This ruling, including certain interim restraints on the three established networks, was upheld by the Seventh Circuit in *Capital Cities/ABC v. FCC*, 29 F.3d 309 (7th Cir. 1994).) All networks were immediately allowed to secure passive financial interests in syndication, to do as much in-house production as they wanted, and to secure active syndication rights in any shows by the end of 1995. New networks like Fox (and then United Paramount and Warner) were immediately freed even of the latter restraint in order to remove any disincentive to their emergence as major players in prime-time television. By the early 2000s, Fox Broadcasting was a member of what now are four major networks.

## QUESTIONS FOR DISCUSSION

1. In reflecting on the Fin/Syn issues, it is important to distinguish two different eras: 1970, when the regulations were first instituted, and 1995, when they were dismantled. With respect to the first time frame, the *Schurz* opinion summarized the factors that persuaded the FCC to adopt the Fin/Syn rules. The objective of communications policy is to promote program diversity; the necessary means include source diversity and outlet diversity; network leverage from control of the nation's prime-time audience threatened both the policy means and objectives; and the response was a combination of restraints on network prime-time access and the Fin/Syn rule. Judge Posner's opinion indicates his skepticism about that thesis from the outset. With the benefit of hindsight, if you had been a member of President Nixon's FCC in

1970, would you have adopted the policy? Did it contribute to a subsequent expansion or reduction in program, source, and outlet diversity?

2. In the FCC hearings after *Schurz*, the principal argument that film producers put forward for retaining some Fin/Syn restrictions was that the networks still had market power derived from their access to the prime-time audience. The latter is crucial to the success of a new series, which is a prerequisite for making the series an attractive candidate for syndication. If free to do so, the networks will use their leverage to force producers who need a contract for their initial appearance on prime-time to sign away back-end Fin/Syn rights for minimal additional returns. And because there are so few networks being pursued by so many producers with new shows, the networks will be able to engage in interdependent and consciously parallel behavior about the terms of such back-end deals. As evidence of this, the film producers pointed to the nearly identical terms in current network licensing contracts for such issues as fee schedules, option terms, rerun reimbursements, spin-off protections, and exclusivity rights, all of which were non-negotiable as far as the networks were concerned. According to this argument, the crucial technique for containing network power would be to establish a minimum thirty-day period between the time that a producer-network contract is signed for a new series on prime-time, and the time that another contract can be signed between the parties regarding back-end Fin/Syn rights in the show should it become a hit.

In its 1993 decision, the FCC majority echoed and elaborated on *Schurz*' rejection of that argument. The Commission's position found that there is as much, if not more, competition on the network-purchaser side as on the producer-supplier side of the market for new series, and that Fin/Syn regulation had actually exacerbated rather than ameliorated the problems faced by producers. Nonetheless, how often do the production arms of Disney, 20th Century Fox, or Paramount license their new television series to any major network besides their respective affiliates, ABC, Fox, and CBS?

Without any prodding from the courts, in 1995, the FCC took the final step in repealing these 1970 regulations. Networks are no longer barred by the "prime-time access rule" from showing their programs during the fourth hour (7 p.m. to 8 p.m.), nor from syndicating network hits. Whatever the original objective of that rule, its practical effect had been to cause that hour in the nation's television viewing to be dominated by a handful of producers and their shows: King World Production's *Wheel of Fortune*, *Jeopardy*, and *Inside Edition*; Paramount's *Entertainment Tonight* and *Hard Copy*; and Fox's *A Current Affair*. Was the prime-time access rule ever justified? What kind of programming changes have occurred since then?

3. Recall that back in the early days of radio networks (and before there were any television broadcasts), the FCC adopted a number of rules that defined the terms of network-affiliate relationships (rules that the Supreme Court upheld in *NBC v. United States*, 319 U.S. 190 (1943)). The object of these regulations was to ensure that local stations retained their

autonomy to serve the "public interest, convenience, and necessity" in their programming decisions. The following are the key rules the FCC has put on its agenda for "notice and comment."

(i) "Right to reject": the local affiliate has the right to refuse to broadcast any program it does not want;

(ii) "Exclusive affiliation": an affiliate cannot be forbidden by its network from broadcasting programs made available by another network;

(iii) "Territorial exclusivity": the network cannot be precluded from offering programs rejected by its affiliate to another station in the same community or region;

(iv) "Time option": a network cannot secure an option to use a specified time period in its affiliate's schedule without also making a commitment to the affiliate to use that time.

What is your view of these FCC limits on network affiliate contracting?

---

The Fin/Syn and Prime-Time Access broadcast rules were soon followed by a more visible "family viewing hour," agreed to by the broadcasters, rather than imposed by the FCC.[f] In the 1950s and 1960s, most American families watched television together. Before 9:00 p.m., the home's only set was tuned into shows like *The Brady Bunch* and *Bewitched.* In the early 1970s, programming before that hour changed dramatically, with the popularity of *All in the Family* and its themes of racism and sexism, *Maude's* emphasis on abortion and alcoholism, and *M.A.S.H.* on the comic horrors of war. Popular concern about the showing of such situation comedies at this hour led FCC Chairman Richard Wiley to meet regularly with the networks and the National Association of Broadcasters (NAB). In 1975, the NAB announced a new "family viewing" policy to which all of its members would adhere—the networks between 8:00 and 9:00 p.m. and local stations between 7:00 and 8:00 p.m. under the "prime-time access" rule. Programming appropriate for viewing by a family audience would be broadcast during the first hour of network programming in prime time and in the immediate preceding hour. If a program is deemed to be inappropriate for such an audience, advisories should be used to alert viewers.

*All in the Family* and *Maude* experienced the immediate impact of this policy, when they were replaced in their 8:00 p.m. slots by series like *Little House on the Prairie* and *Good Times.* The move to later hours hurt

---

[f] *See* Newton N. Minow & Craig L. LaMay, *Abandoned in the Wasteland: Children, Television & the First Amendment* (Hill & Wang 1995); Ronald J. Krotoszynski, Jr., *Into the Woods: Broadcasters, Bureaucrats & Children's Television Programming*, 45 Duke L.J. 1193 (1996).

the shows' network ratings and endangered their syndication value on local stations (before 8:00 p.m.). Norman Lear, the producer of *Family* and *Maude*, persuaded the performer unions to file suit against the FCC as well as the NAB and the networks. *See Writers Guild of America v. FCC*, 423 F. Supp. 1064 (C.D. Cal. 1976). Relying on the Supreme Court ruling in *Adickes v. S.H. Kress & Co.*, 398 U.S. 144 (1970), the court first determined that the family viewing policy was *state*, not *private* action—not just because of Wiley's personal involvement in the NAB meetings, but because stations likely agreed to this constraint for fear of license renewal problems with the FCC if they chose to show *All in the Family* before 9:00 p.m. The judge then found that the policy infringed Lear's First Amendment rights, because the decision to move his show was not made by CBS as an individual network, but rather as part of an industry-wide policy.

Rather than appeal this debatable decision, the NAB decided to revoke its policy. As it turned out, though, for the next decade the networks tended to reserve their 8:00–9:00 p.m. time slot for more "family friendly" programs, such as *Family Ties*, *Happy Days*, and *The Cosby Show*. What changed the situation in the late 1980s was the appearance of the new Fox Network, which sought to carve out a niche for itself in that hour with shows like *Married . . . With Children*, *Melrose Place*, and *Beverly Hills 90210*. The popularity of such sexual content led the other networks (including the new Paramount and Warner contenders) to follow the same path in an effort to revive their ratings. Despite calls for Congress to direct the FCC to revisit the family viewing hour issue, no further action has taken place. A number of practical and constitutional questions are raised by this suggestion, especially given the dramatic increase in the number of television channels available to the typical American home. Does a ratings system for parents armed with the V-chip solve the problem?

---

Programs directly aimed at children have become a lucrative feature of the television world; advertisers spend approximately $700 million each year on over-the-air or cable shows aimed specifically at children. As commercial interest in the children's television market has risen, many parents have felt that the value of the programming has declined. Thus, in 1990, Congress passed the Children's Television Act, designed to secure more "educational and informational programming that serves the special needs of children."

Initially, the FCC did not adopt regulations to enforce that legislative policy. A 1995 Center for Media Education poll indicated that 82 percent of Americans felt that we needed more educational programming for children on commercial television, and 60 percent supported a requirement of a minimum of one hour a day as a condition of a station license. The NAB claimed that its survey of television stations indicated that children's educational programming had risen from an average of two to four hours a week since 1990. However, commentators cast serious doubts on those numbers, as some of the asserted educational programs were *Mighty Morphin Power Rangers*, *Doogie Howser, M.D.*, and *Yogi Bear*, and others appeared at times when most children were asleep.

The FCC finally acted in 1995, proposing that each station must have a minimum of three hours a week of regularly-scheduled educational programming, targeted at children 16 and younger, as a condition for retaining its broadcast license. Despite serious First Amendment problems with requiring stations to broadcast specific types of programs, this rule was put into place. To meet this requirement, the programming must "further the educational and informational needs of children 16 years of age and under, in any respect, including the child's educational/cognitive or social/emotional needs." The FCC made it clear that it was looking for programs like CBS's *Bill Nye, The Science Guy* and NBC's *Saved By the Bell*, not *Mighty Morphin Power Rangers.* In fact, *Mighty Morphin's* producer, Saban Entertainment, used the new FCC rule as the occasion to launch a new children's educational program, *The Why Why Family.* The FCC did allow stations a modest shortfall in the amount programming that meets this educational standard, if they offered other public service specials, paid for educational programming on other channels, or sponsored other public service events.

Do you agree with FCC Chairman Hundt's observation that "market values are not the same as family values, and [the FCC] concern ought to be with both. . . . The scarce airwaves are owned by the public, and as trustees of those airwaves, broadcasters can be required to provide public interest programming"? Is there a shortage of educational offerings on television? Should this be the target of governmental regulation or should it be left to the media marketplace? Is the preferred technique for teaching children via television to offer them programs that are explicitly educational in character, or to rely on shows that are principally entertaining, but have the occasional educational lessons worked into their story line? Suppose that a station is found not to have met the FCC standard; is a direct government requirement that a certain proportion of programming be devoted to educating children more or less defensible under the First Amendment than the earlier agreement on a "family viewing hour?" Might it make more sense as a matter of policy if the FCC simply charged stations a fee for use of the electromagnetic spectrum, and used this to provide funding for educational or artistic programming, such as *Sesame Street*?

## B. BROADCAST SPEECH, CABLE DISTRIBUTION, AND "MUST CARRY"[g]

One of the intriguing features of the *Schurz* litigation is that the networks did not challenge the Fin/Syn rules as an abridgement of their constitutional freedom to speak through their own television programs, rather than just through those owned by a Hollywood studio. The likely reason for taking that legal tack was the longstanding view that for First Amendment purposes broadcasting is qualitatively different from other media of expression. As mentioned previously, a vivid illustration of that difference is the Court's treatment of the FCC's fairness doctrine, which required licensed stations to offer a "balanced presentation of opposing viewpoints" about "controversial issues of public importance," and also to give a right of reply to any individual whose "honesty, character, integrity, or like personal qualities" had been attacked on that station. In 1964, the Court had rendered its momentous ruling in *New York Times v. Sullivan*, 376 U.S. 254 (1964), which held that because it was crucial to democratic self-governance that people be able to say what they wanted on issues of public controversy, there must be First Amendment constraints on state defamation actions launched by people whose reputations were harmed by such speech. During the presidential campaign that same year, Fred Cook, the author of a book critical of the Republican candidate, Barry Goldwater, was attacked on a conservative radio program as someone who worked for "a Communist-affiliated publication" (*The Nation*). Five years later, in *Red Lion Broadcasting v. FCC*, 395 U.S. 367, 389 (1969), the Court upheld the constitutionality of an FCC directive to the station that it had to give Cook the right to reply.

> There is nothing in the First Amendment which prevents the Government from requiring a licensee to share his frequency with others and to conduct himself as a proxy or fiduciary with obligations to present those views and voices which are representative of his community, and which would otherwise, by necessity, be barred from the airwaves.

The distinctive constitutional status of broadcasting was highlighted in another ruling handed down the same year as *Red Lion*. The FCC had revoked the license of a Jackson, Mississippi, television station, WLBT,

---

[g] *See* Thomas G. Krattenmaker & L.A. Powe, Jr., *Converging First Amendment Principles for Converging Communications Media*, 104 Yale L.J. 1719 (1995); Cass R. Sunstein, *The First Amendment in Cyberspace*, 104 Yale L.J. 1757 (1995); Symposium, *The 1992 Cable Act: Freedom of Expression Issues*, 17 Hast. Comm/Ent L.J. 1 (1994); *see also* C. Edwin Baker, Turner Broadcasting: *Content-Based Regulation of Persons & Presses*, 1994 S. Ct. Rev. 57; Ashutosh Bhagwat, *Of Markets & Media: The First Amendment, the New Mass Media & the Political Components of Culture*, 74 N.C. L. Rev. 141 (1995); Daniel L. Brenner, *Ownership & Content Regulation in Merging & Emerging Media*, 45 DePaul L. Rev. 1009 (1996); Charles W. Logan, Jr., *Getting Beyond Scarcity: A New Paradigm for Assessing the Constitutionality of Broadcast Regulation*, 85 Cal. L. Rev. 1687 (1997); Lawrence Lessig, *The Future of Ideas: The Fate of the Commons in a Connected World* (Random House 2001).

because the consistent theme of the station's programming was segregationist. Indeed, on one occasion WLBT cut off a network show because Thurgood Marshall was about to go on the air favoring racial integration. In *Office of Communication of United Church of Christ v. FCC*, 425 F.2d 543 (D.C. Cir. 1969), then-Judge Warren Burger upheld the constitutionality of removal of the station's license.

> A broadcaster seeks and is granted the free and exclusive use of a limited part of the public domain; when he accepts that franchise it is burdened by enforceable obligations. A newspaper can be operated at the whim or caprice of its owners; a broadcast station cannot. After nearly five decades of operation, the broadcast industry does not seem to have grasped the simple fact that a broadcast license is a public trust subject to termination for breach of duty.

Illustrating the stark constitutional dividing line between broadcasting and newspapers, just five years later Chief Justice Burger wrote a unanimous decision of the Supreme Court, *Miami Herald Publishing Co. v. Tornillo*, 418 U.S. 241 (1974), which struck down as a violation of the First Amendment a Florida law that gave a right of reply to political candidates being attacked in newspapers. *Tornillo* did not even mention *Red Lion.*

Ironically, at about the same time that *Tornillo* was being decided, the broadcast world was being radically altered in a fashion that would eventually persuade President Reagan's FCC to repeal the fairness doctrine as no longer a necessary feature of broadcast policy. *See In re Complaint of Syracuse Peace Council*, 2 F.C.C.R. 5043 (1987), *aff'd*, *Syracuse Peace Council v. FCC*, 867 F.2d 654 (D.C. Cir. 1989). The new industry element was cable, which itself was destined to produce a major First Amendment debate about "must carry." Cable television began in the late 1950s (under the label community antenna television, or CATV) as a vehicle for transmitting into rural homes the signals from distant stations. The FCC first adopted a "must carry" rule in 1962, making it a condition of granting a license to a rural cable system that the system must carry any local broadcast signals. As cable television expanded from rural to urban areas (particularly to improve reception of signals being deflected by large buildings), this administrative must-carry regulation remained in place.

The focal point of the original debates about cable focused on copyright law. When a cable system carried an over-the-air telecast for transmission into the homes of cable subscribers, it was uncertain whether this step constituted either copying or a public performance of the television station's copyrighted show. In two major decisions, *Fortnightly Corp. v. United Artists Television*, 392 U.S. 390 (1968), and

*Teleprompter Corp. v. Columbia Broadcasting System*, 415 U.S. 394 (1974), the Court held that it was neither. In its 1976 revision of the Copyright Act, Congress modified that judgment. Cable systems were given a compulsory license to retransmit over-the-air broadcasts, but with respect to distant non-network stations (including the emerging superstations such as WTBS and WGN), cable had to pay a fee that the Copyright Royalty Tribunal would distribute to copyright owners.

A second issue involved broadcast policy itself. In the early 1970s, only a small percentage of homes had cable, and they paid significant monthly charges. The FCC was not particularly concerned about cable systems transmitting network shows that were already on the air. The concern was about cable "siphoning" some programs away from free television to be shown exclusively to cable subscribers, and thus no longer available to those families that were unable or unwilling to pay for the new cable service.

FCC regulatory action had to find its statutory base in the Communications Act of 1934, which had not been revised specifically to encompass cable. However, in *United States v. Southwestern Cable*, 392 U.S. 157 (1968), the Court held that the FCC did have authority to regulate cable to the extent that such action would serve the Commission's responsibility for enhancing broadcast television. In *Southwestern Cable,* the Court upheld an FCC rule that barred a cable system in San Diego from bringing in a Los Angeles station that was believed to threaten the viability of fledgling UHF and public stations in San Diego. The Court found that this rule was "reasonably ancillary to the Commission's various responsibilities for the regulation of television broadcasting." *Id.* at 178. Then, in *United States v. Midwest Video Corp.*, 406 U.S. 649, 667–69 (1972), the Court upheld more elaborate FCC rules that required cable system operators to originate some programming of their own on available channels, on the theory that this would "further the achievement of long-established regulatory goals in the field of television broadcasting."

Much more controversial was the FCC's next set of rules, originally developed with reference to subscription television services that were being experimented with during the 1960s. The rules, however, found their principal target, Home Box Office. In 1975, with just 25,000 subscribers, the venture was poised to take off with the use of new satellite technology that permitted instantaneous transmission of programming to cable systems around the country. Such an upsurge, though, was hamstrung by FCC rules which barred live broadcasts on cable of sporting events that had been telecast over the air during the past five years, and also precluded the cable showing of movies less than three years and more than ten years after their theatrical release (these being the periods when television networks were most likely to show either recent movies or those that had become classics).

On this occasion, the FCC did not fare so well in court. *Home Box Office v. FCC*, 567 F.2d 9 (D.C. Cir. 1977), struck down this application of the anti-siphoning rules, principally as unwarranted action by an administrative agency, but to some extent also on freedom of speech grounds. The administrative law problem was that the FCC had simply applied to this new pay cable technology a set of rules that had been devised for quite a different subscription service, without having undertaken a full-scale review of whether this transplant was warranted. The court's analysis of the issues persuaded it that there was no plausible ground upon which the imposition of these constraints on HBO could be justified. In *Southwest*, for example, without having paid anything for the privilege, the cable system had brought into its local area many of the same programs for which the local stations thought they had secured the exclusive local rights. By contrast, not only did HBO have to pay for the right to broadcast either a movie or a sporting event, but it had to outbid the three networks to win these rights from the producers. Indeed, one major change HBO made in the industry was to reduce the oligopoly position of the networks vis-a-vis the program suppliers who wanted access to the networks' national audience (a problem the FCC itself had recognized and sought to deal with via its Fin/Syn regulations).

The court went on to say that *Red Lion's* very relaxed First Amendment standard for evaluating government restraints on broadcast speech should not be applied to cable. Unlike television stations, which sent their signals over the publicly-owned electromagnetic spectrum, cable programming was transmitted over an enclosed physical medium—a cable—that was connected up to subscribers' homes. The court believed that these anti-siphoning rules were aimed at the collateral economic consequences, not at the internal content, of HBO's speech. However, the FCC had not met the First Amendment standard laid down in *United States v. O'Brien*, 391 U.S. 367 (1968), that such collateral restraints on speech must "further an important and substantial governmental interest" without any more restrictive impact "than is essential to the furtherance of that interest."

After remand, the FCC decided to eliminate rather than to refashion its anti-siphoning policy to satisfy these judicial standards. Over-the-air television was no longer to be protected from the competitive challenge of cable. HBO was quickly joined by a number of new pay (e.g. Showtime and The Movie Channel) and non-pay (e.g., USA Network and ESPN) cable programmers. This expansion in the number of cable channels attracted huge numbers of new cable subscribers, especially in cities where viewers had not felt the need to enhance reception the network stations. That expanding audience in turn generated expanded cable offerings, with over 100 available to different systems across the country. By the end of the century, over 65 million homes were connected to cable and over 95 percent of homes could have cable if they wanted to pay for it. Nearly four decades after winning this ruling, HBO has over 133 million subscribers worldwide.

The stunning increase in cable availability and viewing has had a major impact on both the television industry and its legal environment. Within the industry, the key difference is that viewers are paying for channels, rather than having programmers paid by advertisers. For several decades, network prime-time programming was largely oriented to middle-class women between the ages of 25 and 45, because this was the most attractive audience for advertisers. When cable expanded the number of channels and allowed viewers to register their interest in particular types of programming, this created the market opening for channels targeted at different market niches, such as news (FOX and CNN), music (MTV), sports (ESPN), education (The Learning Channel), law (Court TV), and home shopping (QVC).

The expansion in the number and diversity of television channels had legal consequences as well. It was a key factor in persuading the FCC, in *In re Complaint of Syracuse Peace Council*, 2 F.C.C.R. 5043 (1987), that whatever may have been the Supreme Court's assumption in *Red Lion* in the late 1960s, the country no longer needed "fairness" regulation to ensure that a wide range of viewpoints were expressed over the air on issues of public concern, including the point of view of someone who was personally attacked on a particular show. At the same time, the more than 150 cable programmers seeking space on cable systems whose average size was still around 35 channels, gave far more economic and political significance to the FCC's "must carry" rules. The cable systems owned by John Malone's TeleCommunications Inc. (TCI) or Time Warner's cable arm now felt they could earn considerably more money by selling access to their scarce channels to a specialty programmer (e.g., a golf channel) than by giving away the channel to a local independent station that did not have a particularly large audience.

This economic tension from "must carry" set off a legal conflict that lasted for nearly two decades, with an interplay among Congress, the FCC, and the courts that is eerily reminiscent of what happening to "indecency" rules (in Chapter 1). Though the D.C. Circuit had upheld the original must-carry requirements against an early challenge, *Carter Mountain Transmission v. FCC*, 321 F.2d 359 (D.C. Cir. 1963), two decades later, in *Quincy Cable TV v. FCC*, 768 F.2d 1434 (D.C. Cir. 1985), a panel of the same circuit struck down this rule on the grounds that it did not now have a sound enough base to justify its encroachment on First Amendment freedom of speech. When the FCC revised the rules, a similar result was reached regarding the new version in *Century*

*Communications Corp. v. FCC*, 835 F.2d 292 (D.C. Cir. 1987), *order clarified*, 837 F.2d 517 (D.C. Cir. 1988).

In 1992, Congress enacted the Cable Television Consumer Protection & Competition Act. This legislation was a reaction to earlier federal deregulation of cable, through the Cable Communication Policy Act of 1984. Prior to that time, localities typically granted one cable company the exclusive right to place cable wires and connections on streets and buildings, and in return had restrained the rates that subscribers could be charged. The 1984 federal statute precluded both exclusive local licenses and local rate-setting. The consequence, however, was that almost no communities gained additional competing cable services, while rates escalated significantly.

Congress reversed course in 1992, instituting comprehensive federal regulation of a cable industry that by then reached nearly 60 million homes and collected $30 billion in subscriber and advertising revenues. The law mandated that the FCC should reduce rates for basic cable services. Another part required cable systems to secure (and if necessary, pay for) consent from the stations (particularly network affiliates) whose signals they wanted to transmit into the homes of subscribers. A third feature required cable program suppliers (like John Malone's Liberty Media) that were affiliated with cable operating systems (like TCI) to offer their programming at comparable rates to cable systems affiliated with rival producers (such as those of Time-Warner and Viacom-Paramount). Finally, the law enshrined a must-carry requirement for local independent and noncommercial stations.

Immediately after enactment, several constitutional attacks were launched as to its various provisions. The lead plaintiff in the suit against must-carry was Turner Broadcasting, but a divided panel of the D.C. Circuit found must-carry to be constitutional. *See Turner Broadcasting System v. FCC*, 819 F. Supp. 32 (D.D.C. 1993). That set the stage for a major ruling by the Supreme Court on the constitutional standards for regulation in this crucial branch of the entertainment industry.

## TURNER BROADCASTING SYSTEM, INC. V. FEDERAL COMMUNICATIONS COMMISSION

Supreme Court of the United States, 1994.
512 U.S. 622, 114 S.Ct. 2445, 129 L.Ed.2d 497.

JUSTICE KENNEDY announced the judgment of the Court and delivered the opinion of the Court, except as to Part III–B.

I

* * *

C

Congress enacted the 1992 Cable Act after conducting three years of hearings on the structure and operation of the cable television industry. The conclusions Congress drew from its fact finding process are recited in the text of the Act itself. In brief, Congress found that the physical characteristics of cable transmission, compounded by the increasing concentration of economic power in the cable industry, are endangering the ability of over-the-air broadcast television stations to compete for a viewing audience and thus for necessary operating revenues. Congress determined that regulation of the market for video programming was necessary to correct this competitive imbalance.

In particular, Congress found that over 60 percent of the households with television sets subscribe to cable, and for these households cable has replaced over-the-air broadcast television as the primary provider of video programming. This is so, Congress found, because "most subscribers to cable television systems do not or cannot maintain antennas to receive broadcast television services, do not have input selector switches to convert from a cable to antenna reception system, or cannot otherwise receive broadcast television services." In addition, Congress concluded that due to "local franchising requirements and the extraordinary expense of constructing more than one cable television system to serve a particular geographic area," the overwhelming majority of cable operators exercise a monopoly over cable service. "The result," Congress determined, "is undue market power for the cable operator as compared to that of consumers and video programmers."

According to Congress, this market position gives cable operators the power and the incentive to harm broadcast competitors. The power derives from the cable operator's ability, as owner of the transmission facility, to "terminate the retransmission of the broadcast signal, refuse to carry new signals, or reposition a broadcast signal to a disadvantageous channel position." The incentive derives from the economic reality that "cable television systems and broadcast television stations increasingly compete for television advertising revenues." By refusing carriage of broadcasters' signals, cable operators, as a practical matter, can reduce the number of households that have access to the broadcasters' programming, and thereby capture advertising dollars that would otherwise go to broadcast stations.

Congress found, in addition, that increased vertical integration in the cable industry is making it even harder for broadcasters to secure carriage on cable systems, because cable operators have a financial incentive to favor their affiliated programmers. Congress also determined that the cable industry is characterized by horizontal concentration, with many cable operators sharing common ownership. This has resulted in greater "barriers to entry for new programmers and a reduction in the number of media voices available to consumers."

In light of these technological and economic conditions, Congress concluded that unless cable operators are required to carry local broadcast stations, "there is a substantial likelihood that . . . additional local broadcast signals will be deleted, repositioned, or not carried," the "marked shift in market share" from broadcast to cable will continue to erode the advertising revenue base which sustains free local broadcast television, and that, as a consequence, "the economic viability of free local broadcast television and its ability to originate quality local programming will be seriously jeopardized."

* * *

II

There can be no disagreement on an initial premise: Cable programmers and cable operators engage in and transmit speech, and they are entitled to the protection of the speech and press provisions of the First Amendment. *Leathers v. Medlock*, 499 U.S. 439, 444 (1991). Through "original programming or by exercising editorial discretion over which stations or programs to include in its repertoire," cable programmers and operators "seek to communicate messages on a wide variety of topics and in a wide variety of formats." *Los Angeles v. Preferred Communications, Inc.*, 476 U.S. 488, 494 (1986). By requiring cable systems to set aside a portion of their channels for local broadcasters, the must-carry rules regulate cable speech in two respects: the rules reduce the number of channels over which cable operators exercise unfettered control, and they render it more difficult for cable programmers to compete for carriage on the limited channels remaining. Nevertheless, because not every interference with speech triggers the same degree of scrutiny under the First Amendment, we must decide at the outset the level of scrutiny applicable to the must-carry provisions.

A

We address first the Government's contention that regulation of cable television should be analyzed under the same First Amendment standard that applies to regulation of broadcast television. It is true that our cases have permitted more intrusive regulation of broadcast speakers than of speakers in other media. Compare *Red Lion Broadcasting Co. v. FCC*, 395 U.S. 367 (1969) (television), and *National Broadcasting Co. v. United States*, 319 U.S. 190 (1943) (radio), with *Miami Herald Publishing Co. v. Tornillo*, 418 U.S. 241 (1974) (print), and *Riley v. National Federation of Blind of N.C.*, Inc., 487 U.S. 781 (1988)(personal solicitation). But the rationale for applying a less rigorous standard of First Amendment scrutiny to broadcast regulation, whatever its validity in the cases elaborating it, does not apply in the context of cable regulation.

The justification for our distinct approach to broadcast regulation rests upon the unique physical limitations of the broadcast medium. *See FCC v. League of Women Voters of Cal.*, 468 U.S. 364, 377 (1984); *Red Lion*, supra, at 388–389, 396–399; *National Broadcasting Co.*, 319 U.S., at 226. As a general matter, there are more would-be broadcasters than frequencies available in the electromagnetic spectrum. And if two broadcasters were to attempt to transmit over the same frequency in the same locale, they would interfere with one another's signals, so that neither could be heard at all. The scarcity of broadcast frequencies thus required the establishment of some regulatory mechanism to divide the electromagnetic spectrum and assign specific frequencies to particular broadcasters In addition, the inherent physical limitation on the number of speakers who may use the broadcast medium has been thought to require some adjustment in traditional First Amendment analysis to permit the Government to place limited content restraints, and impose certain affirmative obligations, on broadcast licensees. As we said in *Red Lion*, "where there are substantially more individuals who want to broadcast than there are frequencies to allocate, it is idle to posit an unabridgeable First Amendment right to broadcast comparable to the right of every individual to speak, write, or publish."

Although courts and commentators have criticized the scarcity rationale since its inception,[5] we have declined to question its continuing validity as support for our broadcast jurisprudence, and see no reason to do so here. The broadcast cases are inapposite in the present context because cable television does not suffer from the inherent limitations that characterize the broadcast medium. Indeed, given the rapid advances in fiber optics and digital compression technology, soon there may be no practical limitation on the number of speakers who may use the cable

[5] *See Telecommunications Research & Action Center v. FCC*, 801 F.2d 501, 508–09 (D.C. Cir. 1986); L. Bollinger, Images of a Free Press 87–90 (1991); L. Powe, American Broadcasting & the First Amendment 197–209 (1987); M. Spitzer, Seven Dirty Words & Six Other Stories 7–18 (1986); Note, *The Message in the Medium: The First Amendment on the Information Superhighway*, 107 Harv. L. Rev. 1062, 1072–74 (1994); Winer, *The Signal Cable Sends—Part I: Why Can't Cable Be More Like Broadcasting?*, 46 Md. L. Rev. 212, 218–40 (1987); Ronald Coase, *The Federal Communications Commission*, 2 J. Law & Econ. 1, 12–27 (1959).

medium. Nor is there any danger of physical interference between two cable speakers attempting to share the same channel. In light of these fundamental technological differences between broadcast and cable transmission, application of the more relaxed standard of scrutiny adopted in *Red Lion* and the other broadcast cases are inapt when determining the First Amendment validity of cable regulation.

This is not to say that the unique physical characteristics of cable transmission should be ignored when determining the constitutionality of regulations affecting cable speech. They should not. But whatever relevance these physical characteristics may have in the evaluation of particular cable regulations, they do not require the alteration of settled principles of our First Amendment jurisprudence.

Although the Government acknowledges the substantial technological differences between broadcast and cable, it advances a second argument for application of the *Red Lion* framework to cable regulation. It asserts that the foundation of our broadcast jurisprudence is not the physical limitations of the electromagnetic spectrum, but rather the "market dysfunction" that characterizes the broadcast market. Because the cable market is beset by a similar dysfunction, the Government maintains, the *Red Lion* standard of review should also apply to cable. While we agree that the cable market suffers certain structural impediments, the Government's argument is flawed in two respects. First, as discussed above, the special physical characteristics of broadcast transmission, not the economic characteristics of the broadcast market, are what underlies our broadcast jurisprudence. Second, the mere assertion of dysfunction or failure in a speech market, without more, is not sufficient to shield a speech regulation from the First Amendment standards applicable to nonbroadcast media.

By a related course of reasoning, the Government and some appellees maintain that the must-carry provisions are nothing more than industry-specific antitrust legislation, and thus warrant rational basis scrutiny under this Court's "precedents governing legislative efforts to correct market failure in a market whose commodity is speech," such as *Associated Press v. United States*, 326 U.S. 1 (1945), and *Lorain Journal Co. v. United States*, 342 U.S. 143 (1951). This contention is unavailing. *Associated Press* and *Lorain Journal* both involved actions against members of the press brought under the Sherman Antitrust Act, a law of general application. But while the enforcement of a generally applicable law may or may not be subject to heightened scrutiny under the First Amendment, compare *Cohen v. Cowles Media Co.*, 501 U.S. 663, 670 (1991), with *Barnes v. Glen Theatre, Inc.*, 501 U.S. 560 (1991), laws that single out the press, or certain elements thereof, for special treatment "pose a particular danger of abuse by the State," *Arkansas Writers' Project, Inc. v. Ragland*, 481 U.S. 221, 228 (1987), and so are always subject to at least some degree of heightened First Amendment scrutiny. Because the must-carry provisions impose special obligations upon cable operators and special burdens upon cable programmers, some measure of heightened First Amendment scrutiny is demanded.

B

At the heart of the First Amendment lies the principle that each person should decide for him or herself the ideas and beliefs deserving of expression, consideration, and adherence. Our political system and cultural life rest upon this ideal. Government action that stifles speech on account of its message, or that requires the utterance of a particular message favored by the Government, contravenes this essential right. Laws of this sort pose the inherent risk that the Government seeks not to advance a legitimate regulatory goal, but to suppress unpopular ideas or information or manipulate the public debate through coercion rather than persuasion. These restrictions "raise the specter that the Government may effectively drive certain ideas or viewpoints from the marketplace." *Simon & Schuster, Inc. v. Members of the New York State Crime Victims Bd.*, 502 U.S. 105, 116 (1991).

For these reasons, the First Amendment, subject only to narrow and well-understood exceptions, does not countenance governmental control over the content of messages expressed by private individuals. *R.A.V. v. St. Paul*, 505 U.S. 377 (1992); *Texas v. Johnson*, 491 U.S. 397 (1989). Our precedents thus apply the most exacting scrutiny to regulations that suppress, disadvantage, or impose differential burdens upon speech because of its content. Laws that compel speakers to utter or distribute speech bearing a particular message are subject to the same rigorous scrutiny. In contrast, regulations that are unrelated to the content of speech are subject to an intermediate level of scrutiny, because in most cases they pose a less substantial risk of excising certain ideas or viewpoints from the public dialogue.

Deciding whether a particular regulation is content-based or content-neutral is not always a simple task. We have said that the "principal inquiry in determining content-neutrality . . . is whether the government has adopted a regulation of speech because of [agreement or] disagreement with the message it conveys." *Ward v. Rock Against Racism*, 491 U.S. 781, 791 (1989). The purpose, or justification, of a regulation will often be evident on its face. But while a content-based purpose may be sufficient in certain circumstances to show that a regulation is content-based, it is not necessary to such a showing in all cases. Nor will the mere assertion of a content-neutral purpose be enough to save a law which, on its face, discriminates based on content.

As a general rule, laws that by their terms distinguish favored speech from disfavored speech on the basis of the ideas or views expressed are content-based. . . . By contrast, laws that confer benefits or impose burdens on speech without reference to the ideas or views expressed are in most instances content-neutral.

C

Insofar as they pertain to the carriage of full power broadcasters, the must-carry rules, on their face, impose burdens and confer benefits without reference to the content of speech Although the provisions interfere with cable operators' editorial discretion by compelling them to offer carriage to a certain minimum number of broadcast stations, the extent of the interference does not depend upon the content of the cable operators' programming. The rules impose obligations upon all operators, save those with fewer than 300 subscribers, regardless of the programs or stations they now offer or have offered in the past. Nothing in the Act imposes a restriction, penalty, or burden by reason of the views, programs, or stations the cable operator has selected or will select. The number of channels a cable operator must set aside depends only on the operator's channel capacity; hence, an operator cannot avoid or mitigate its obligations under the Act by altering the programming it offers to subscribers.

The must-carry provisions also burden cable programmers by reducing the number of channels for which they can compete. But, again, this burden is unrelated to content, for it extends to all cable programmers irrespective of the programming they choose to offer viewers. And finally, the privileges conferred by the must-carry provisions are also unrelated to content. The rules benefit all full power broadcasters who request carriage—be they commercial or noncommercial, independent or network-affiliated, English or Spanish language, religious or secular. The aggregate effect of the rules is thus to make every full power commercial and noncommercial broadcaster eligible for must-carry, provided only that the broadcaster operates within the same television market as a cable system.

It is true that the must-carry provisions distinguish between speakers in the television programming market. But they do so based only upon the manner in which speakers transmit their messages to viewers, and not upon the messages they carry: broadcasters, which transmit over the airwaves, are favored, while cable programmers, which do not, are disfavored. Cable operators, too, are burdened by the carriage obligations, but only because they control access to the cable conduit. So long as they are not a subtle means of exercising a content preference, speaker distinctions of this nature are not presumed invalid under the First Amendment.

That the must-carry provisions, on their face, do not burden or benefit speech of a particular content does not end the inquiry. Our cases have recognized that even a regulation neutral on its face may be content-based if its manifest purpose is to regulate speech because of the message it conveys. . . .

Appellants contend, in this regard, that the must-carry regulations are content-based because Congress's purpose in enacting them was to promote speech of a favored content. We do not agree. Our review of the Act and its various findings persuades us that Congress's overriding objective in enacting must-carry was not to favor programming of a particular subject matter, viewpoint, or format, but rather to preserve access to free television programming for the 40 percent of Americans without cable.

In unusually detailed statutory findings, Congress explained that because cable systems and broadcast stations compete for local advertising revenue and because cable operators have a vested financial interest in favoring their affiliated programmers over broadcast stations, cable operators have a built-in "economic incentive . . . to delete, reposition, or not carry local broadcast signals." Congress concluded that absent a requirement that cable systems carry the signals of local broadcast stations, the continued availability of free local broadcast television would be threatened. Congress sought to avoid the elimination of broadcast television because, in its words, "such programming is . . . free to those who own television sets and do not require cable transmission to receive broadcast television signals," and because "there is a substantial governmental interest in promoting the continued availability of such free television programming, especially for viewers who are unable to afford other means of receiving programming."

By preventing cable operators from refusing carriage to broadcast television stations, the must-carry rules ensure that broadcast television stations will retain a large enough potential audience to earn necessary advertising revenue—or, in the case of noncommercial broadcasters, sufficient viewer contributions—to maintain their continued operation. In so doing, the provisions are designed to guarantee the survival of a medium that has become a vital part of the Nation's communication system, and to ensure that every individual with a television set can obtain access to free television programming.

This overriding congressional purpose is unrelated to the content of expression disseminated by cable and broadcast speakers. Indeed, our precedents have held that "protecting noncable households from loss of regular television broadcasting service due to competition from cable systems," is not only a permissible governmental justification, but an "important and substantial federal interest." *Capital Cities Cable, Inc. v. Crisp*, 467 U.S. 691, 714 (1984).

The design and operation of the challenged provisions confirm that the purposes underlying the enactment of the must-carry scheme are unrelated to the content of speech. The rules, as mentioned, confer must-carry rights on all full power broadcasters, irrespective of the content of their programming. They do not require or prohibit the carriage of particular ideas or points of view. They do not penalize cable operators or programmers because of the content of their programming. They do not compel cable operators to affirm points of view with which they disagree. They do not produce any net decrease in the amount of available speech. And they leave cable operators free to carry whatever programming they wish on all channels not subject to must-carry requirements.

Appellants and the dissent make much of the fact that, in the course of describing the purposes behind the Act, Congress referred to the value of broadcast programming. In particular, Congress noted that broadcast television is "an important source of local news[,] public affairs programming and other local broadcast services critical to an informed electorate," and that noncommercial television "provides educational and informational programming to the Nation's citizens." We do not think, however, that such references cast any material doubt on the content-neutral character of must-carry. That Congress acknowledged the local orientation of broadcast programming and the role that noncommercial stations have played in educating the public does not indicate that Congress regarded broadcast programming as more valuable than cable programming. Rather, it reflects nothing more than the recognition that the services provided by broadcast television have some intrinsic value and, thus, are worth preserving against the threats posed by cable.

The operation of the Act further undermines the suggestion that Congress's purpose in enacting must-carry was to force programming of a "local" or "educational" content on cable subscribers. The provisions, as we have stated, benefit all full power broadcasters irrespective of the nature of their programming. In fact, if a cable system were required to bump a cable programmer to make room for a broadcast station, nothing would stop a cable operator from displacing a cable station that provides local or education-oriented programming with a broadcaster that provides very little. Appellants do not even contend, moreover, that broadcast programming is any more "local" or "educational" than cable programming.

In short, Congress's acknowledgment that broadcast television stations make a valuable contribution to the Nation's communications system does not render the must-carry scheme content-based The scope and operation of the challenged provisions make clear, in our view, that Congress designed the must-carry provisions not to promote speech of a particular content, but to prevent cable operators from exploiting their economic power to the detriment of broadcasters, and thereby to ensure that all Americans, especially those unable to subscribe to cable, have access to free television programming—whatever its content.

[The Court added that, because the FCC did not have the authority to require broadcast stations (even "noncommercial educational" stations) to carry particular types of programs, a statutory requirement that cable carry these broadcast stations was not designed as "content control" over cable viewing. Congress' objective, instead was to protect broadcast television from "unfair competition" from the rapidly expanding cable television. Having concluded that must-carry was not content-based regulation, the relevant First Amendment standard was intermediate scrutiny under *United States v. O'Brien*, 391 U.S. 367, 377 (1968), under which regulation will be sustained if:

> it furthers an important or substantial governmental interest; if the governmental interest is unrelated to the suppression of free expression; and if the incidental restriction on alleged First Amendment freedoms is no greater than is essential to the furtherance of that interest.

The Court agreed that, in the abstract at least, must-carry was designed to serve three "important governmental interests": (i) preserving free over-the-air television; (ii) promoting a multiplicity of information sources; and (iii) promoting fair competition in the television market.

The Court was not, however, prepared simply to accept Congress' declaration that absent must-carry, local broadcasting would be "seriously jeopardized." The Court thus remanded the case for evidence as to whether cable operators would choose to deny carriage to significant numbers of local stations, and that stations denied such carriage would deteriorate economically and perhaps even fail. The Court also asked the three-member panel to consider whether under must-carry there might be greater suppression of cable programming speech than preservation of local broadcast speech.]

* * *

Vacated and remanded.

---

Justice O'Connor authored a dissent, joined by Justices Scalia, Ginsburg, and Thomas. Recognizing that cable operators originate little of the programming on their systems, they still were speakers for First Amendment purposes: "Selecting which speech to retransmit is, as we know from the example of publishing houses, movie theaters, bookstores, and Reader's Digest, no less communication than is creating the speech in the first place." 512 U.S. at 675. Even worse was the impact on cable programmers who were denied equal access to one-third of the space on cable systems:

> It is as if the government ordered all movie theaters to reserve at least one-third of their screening for films made by American production companies, or required all bookstores to devote one-third of their shelf space to nonprofit publishers.

*Id.* Moreover, the dissent believed that Congress' reasons for that broadcasting preference were content-based:

> Preferences for diversity of viewpoints, for localism, for educational programming, and for news and public affairs all make reference to content. They may not reflect hostility to particular points of view, or a desire to suppress certain subjects because they are controversial or offensive. They may be quite benignly motivated. But benign motivation, we have consistently held, is not enough to avoid the need for strict scrutiny of content-based justifications. The First Amendment does more than just bar government from intentionally suppressing speech of which it disapproves. It also generally prohibits the government from excepting certain kinds of speech from regulation because it thinks the speech is especially valuable.

I*d.* at 677. The dissent was quite sure that must-carry could not pass the "exacting test" of being narrowly tailored to a compelling state interest. While "localism" and "diversity" are legitimate, they are not compelling governmental objectives. And even if one assumed, arguendo, that preservation of space for educational or news programming was compelling, the Cable Act was not narrowly tailored because it imposed the same burden on CNN, C-SPAN, and the Discovery Channel as it did on cable entertainment programmers.

Justice O'Connor's concluding passage stated emphatic terms her views about the demands of the First Amendment in the new media world:

> The question is not whether there will be control over who gets to speak over cable—the question is who will have this control. Under the FCC's view, the answer is Congress, acting within relatively broad limits. Under my view, the answer is the cable operator. Most of the time, the cable operator's decision will be largely dictated by the preferences of the viewers; but because many cable operators are indeed monopolists, the viewers' preferences will not always prevail. Our recognition that cable operators are speakers is bottomed in large part on the very fact that the cable operator has editorial discretion.

> I have no doubt that there is danger in having a single cable operator decide what millions of subscribers can or cannot watch. And I have no doubt that Congress can act to relieve this danger. In other provisions of the Act, Congress has already taken steps to foster competition among cable systems. Congress can encourage the creation of new media, such as inexpensive satellite broadcasting, or fiber-optic networks with virtually unlimited channels, or even simple devices that would let people easily switch from cable to over-the-air broadcasting. And of course Congress can subsidize broadcasters that it thinks provide especially valuable programming.
>
> Congress may also be able to act in more mandatory ways. If Congress finds that cable operators are leaving some channels empty—perhaps for ease of future expansion—it can compel the operators to make the free channels available to programmers who otherwise would not get carriage. Congress might also conceivably obligate cable operators to act as common carriers for some of their channels, with those channels being open to all through some sort of lottery system or timesharing arrangement. Setting aside any possible Takings Clause issues, it stands to reason that if Congress may demand that telephone companies operate as common carriers, it can ask the same of cable companies; such an approach would not suffer from the defect of preferring one speaker to another.
>
> But the First Amendment as we understand it today rests on the premise that it is government power, rather than private power, that is the main threat to free expression; and as a consequence, the Amendment imposes substantial limitations on the Government even when it is trying to serve concededly praiseworthy goals. . . .

*Id.* at 684.

---

When the case was remanded for an in-depth examination of the justifications for the must-carry rule, the panel majority concluded that the government had satisfied the *O'Brien* standard, and the Supreme Court agreed, in *Turner Broadcasting System v. FCC*, 520 U.S. 180 (1997). By this time, one member of the original majority, Justice Blackmun, had retired and been replaced by Justice Breyer, who agreed with what was still a narrow five-member majority verdict. Justice Breyer did so not in order to promote competition in the face of a "significant market defect," but rather because he accepted the legitimacy of "the basic noneconomic purpose," which was "to prevent too precipitous a decline in the quality and quantity of programming choice for an ever shrinking non-cable subscribing segment of the public." His rationale was that it "has long been a basic tenet of national communication policy . . . [that] the widest possible dissemination of information from diverse and antagonistic sources is essential to the welfare of the public." *Id.* at 227–28.

These complex questions of constitutional principle and telecommunications policy still remain with us. From a constitutional perspective, it is important to compare the *Turner* case with some of the First Amendment rulings we looked at in Part One, such as *Joseph Burstyn, Inc. v. Wilson*, 343 U.S. 495 (1952), where the state of New York had banned the movie *The Miracle* as sacrilegious, and *Time, Inc. v. Hill*, 385 U.S. 374 (1967), where Richard Nixon's client had won a damage award for a docudrama intrusion on the privacy of a hostage family. By contrast, in *Turner*, as in much of the other First Amendment litigation of the 1990s, the government action in question had sought to alter the balance of economic power within which private decisions are made about what programs will appear on television screens. A key issue of constitutional policy is whether this brand of media regulation should be left to the political process, or should be subjected to closer First Amendment scrutiny because the business in question is "speech for fun and profit."

The other side of the coin is whether, even if constitutional, a policy like must-carry is sensible. How does the economic power of cable systems in this new century compare with that of television in the late 1960s (when the FCC's Fin/Syn rules were being developed), or the movie studios in the late 1940s (the time of the *Paramount* litigation)? Though Congress spent three years debating a host of broadcast issues, the Telecommunications Act of 1996 did not revisit the must-carry question.

### *QUESTIONS FOR DISCUSSION*

1. The following questions address the appropriate "free speech" status of must-carry.

(a) Is there a stronger justification, as a matter of constitutional principle or of broadcasting policy, for giving must-carry rights to noncommercial public or educational stations than to local non-network stations? *See Chicago Cable Communications v. Chicago Cable Commission*, 879 F.2d 1540 (7th Cir. 1989).

(b) How does the cable situation compare with the following freedom of speech precedents? In *Wooley v. Maynard*, 430 U.S. 705 (1977), the Court struck down a New Hampshire motor vehicle law that placed on all license plates the state's motto "Live Free or Die." In *PruneYard Shopping Center v. Robins*, 447 U.S. 74 (1980), the Court upheld a California law that required shopping centers to allow groups (there, high school students) to use its public space for passing out leaflets and securing petition signatures. Which analogy is closer to the judgment about whether cable operators are wielding property rights or "speaking" when deciding which broadcast services will fill their scarce channel space?

(c) Recall the FCC rule requiring television stations to offer at least three hours of educational programming each week. This regulation will presumably be defended from constitutional attack on the same scarcity rationale that the Court used to justify the FCC's "fairness" and "indecency" rules in *Red Lion* and *Pacifica*. Is this programming obligation of broadcasters more or less an invasion of either free speech principles or consumer market incentives than the channel obligation imposed on cable system operators? Does scarcity even exist any longer?

Perhaps a more fundamental question is whether either of these situations involve core speech for which the First Amendment was designed.[h] Alternatively, is each more like commercial speech—designed to sell a product rather than the speech itself—which enjoys more limited constitutional protection? *See Central Hudson Gas & Elec. Corp. v. Public Service Comm'n*, 447 U.S. 557 (1980); *Rubin v. Coors Brewing Co.*, 514 U.S. 476 (1995). In other words, when a television station chooses to carry *Mighty Morphin Power Rangers* rather than *Bill Nye, The Science Guy*, is it making a judgment based on the content of the program or on the commercial value that the program offers to its advertisers? In the case of cable, is the decision to carry Turner Classic Movies instead of a local television station based on programming or on the number of cable subscribers the two are likely to deliver? Are either of those judgments distinguishable for First Amendment purposes from CBS' decisions about what issues *60 Minutes* will address on its next show?

(d) What is the significance of the fact that must-carry was a specific requirement enacted by Congress and administered by the FCC, whereas the antitrust law used in *Paramount* and other cases in Chapter 12 rests on a broad mandate given by the Sherman Act to the courts? For example, in *Associated Press v. United States*, 326 U.S. 1 (1945), the Court held that the 1200 newspapers who had created the Associated Press newsgathering cooperative violated the Sherman Act by agreeing to limit admission to A.P. membership for newspaper-competitors of existing members and to refrain from selling

[h] *See* Ronald J. Krotoszynski, Jr., *Into the Woods: Broadcasters, Bureaucrats, & Children's Television Programming*, 45 Duke L.J. 1193 (1996).

news stories to non-members. In response to a First Amendment challenge to a decree that required the newspapers to make A.P. membership and its news product more freely available, the Court stated:

> Surely a [First Amendment] command that the government itself shall not impede the free flow of ideas does not afford non-governmental combinations a refuge if they impose restraints upon that constitutionally guaranteed freedom. . . . Freedom of the press from governmental interference under the First Amendment does not sanction repression of that freedom by private interest.

*Id.* at 20. Is this antitrust analogy similar to the must-carry requirements imposed on cable systems? Should the fact that speech is the product being sold by a business render the latter more or less subject to regulation of its market power?

2. Even if must-carry passes constitutional muster, it still may not be the appropriate policy for our fast-changing broadcast world.[i] Consider these issues:

(a) Should the decision about whether a local station or a national cable channel is to be carried on a local cable service be left to competitive bidding? Are cable subscribers better off if they lose cable programming like C-SPAN, Court-TV, and Ted Turner's classic movie channel because scarce cable channels must be devoted to independent local stations?

(b) Was it fair under the 1992 Act to require cable systems to secure (and pay for) the consent of stations that they wanted to carry, and yet to require carriage of those stations they did not want (perhaps because the stations had little audience appeal)?

(c) What significance should be given to the fact that although around 67 percent of television homes now have cable, this service is now physically accessible to nearly all homes? What about the existence of satellite television as a competitor? And Internet television?

---

The complexities of the cable world were explored again in *Denver Area Educational Telecommunications Consortium v. FCC*, 518 U.S. 727 (1996), a constitutional challenge to yet another provision in the 1992 Cable Act. The dispute concerned requirements dating back to the origins of cable, when localities made it a condition of granting a franchise that

---

[i] *See* Robert W. Crandall & Harold Furchtgott-Roth, *CABLE TV: Regulation or Competition* (Brookings Inst. Press 1996).

several channels be reserved for public use. In the late 1960s, the FCC announced rules that required a percentage of cable channels in the top 100 markets to be reserved by the franchising authority for "public, educational, and governmental" (PEG) programming. These and other cable regulations were eventually struck down in *FCC v. Midwest Video Corp.*, 440 U.S. 689 (1979), as going beyond the FCC's authority over broadcasting.

However, § 531 of the 1984 Cable Act explicitly authorized cities to reserve PEG channels in their cable franchises, and § 532 *required* that the franchise reserve a certain percentage of the channels (on systems with at least 36 channels) for leasing to programmers who did not want 24-hours access to a channel. The 1992 Cable Act authorized the FCC to regulate the prices and terms set by cable systems for access to leased channels. Under both local laws and the 1984 statute, the cable systems were precluded from imposing editorial constraints on either the "public access" or "leased access" channels. The Helms Amendment to the 1992 Cable Act conferred express authority on cable operators to exclude sexually indecent programs from those channels, thus leading to the *Denver* case and a deeply-divided Supreme Court.

Justice Thomas, writing for Chief Justice Rehnquist and Justice Scalia, voted to uphold both provisions. (Justice O'Connor concurred, with a brief separate opinion). These Justices concluded that what was really at stake was the freedom of cable *operators* to speak over their own private systems. For reasons expressed in *Turner*, all were dubious about the validity of either the local or federal requirement that cable systems reserve several of their channels for either PEG or leased programming. However, once those requirements were in place, all that the Helms Amendment did was restore to the operator the freedom to decide whether or not *its* system would "speak" indecently—something they had always been entitled to do in deciding whether to carry a pay channel.

Justice Kennedy, writing for Justice Ginsburg, wanted to find both provisions unconstitutional. His starting point was starkly different from that of Justice Thomas. By virtue first of local laws and then of the 1984 federal law, certain parts of each community's cable system had been designated as a public forum for private speech, with the cable system serving as a "common carrier" of the programming without regard to its content. Now Congress had singled out sexually explicit speech for editorial control by the cable operator. Applying strict scrutiny, these two Justices found no sufficient justification for authorizing those constraints on either PEG or leased channels.

Justice Breyer, joined by Justices Stevens and Souter, voted to uphold the editorial control conferred on cable operators over the leased channels, but to strike down that effort with respect to the PEG channels;

these swing votes determined the Court's result. In the rapidly-changing technological and regulatory world of telecommunications, Justice Breyer thought it was premature for the Court to commit itself to a single conception of cable operators as either common carriers or program speakers. Using a contextual approach, Justice Breyer concluded that there were constitutionally significant differences in the situation of these two channel categories. While operator control over leased access channels had first been taken away by the 1984 law and was now being restored in part by the 1992 law, control of the PEG channels had always been withheld from the cable systems as the *quid pro quo* for conferring the cable franchise. And while leased access channels had been made answerable to no one under the 1984 law, thus warranting some scrutiny of the indecent quality of their programming, the PEG channels had always been overseen by local bodies, thus rendering the additional operator control more harmful than helpful. Finally, indecent programming was almost unheard of on PEG channels but had become a significant and controversial feature of leased programming (e.g., in Manhattan). Justice Breyer agreed with Justice Kennedy that these laws involved state action, and he agreed with Justice Thomas that a law that invites editorial discretion from a private operator (like Time Warner) is preferable to one that produces regulation by the FCC. On balance, Justice Breyer upheld cable control over leased channels, but not PEG channels.

The Helms Amendment contained another feature, which required the operators to scramble indecent programming on their leased (though not their PEG) channels unless subscribers had made written requests to receive those channels. Justice Breyer viewed this precursor to the V-chip component in the later legislation as an excessive constraint on the speech of cable operators as well as programmers (and on the freedom of those customers who wanted the "indecent" channel but did not want to say so in writing). On this issue Justice O'Connor parted ranks with Justice Thomas and voted with the majority. However, the fundamental question that *Denver* poses is who exactly the speaker is in the complex world of cable, and whether the Court's decisions are consistent the values embedded in the First Amendment.

By 1999, several other major changes took place in the cable world. One was the product of the 1996 Telecommunications Act, which relieved cable systems from federal and state restraints on rates charged to subscribers. This step was taken because Washington believed that local telephone companies would provide effective competition, an expectation that was not realized. Average cable rates went up a total of 38 percent from 1997 through 2001, despite low inflation during that time.

However, a new competitor to cable had appeared in the early 1990s—satellite dish systems. Just as had been true of cable in the 1950s, satellite dishes were originally designed to provide service to people living in rural areas who were outside the range of cable (or broadcast). But by the end of 2005, there were over 25 million American homes using satellite dishes, about a third of them in urban areas. Strikingly, the original FCC reaction to this new technology was to ban them showing over-the-air television stations. This meant that for the vast majority of families, cable was the most viable option, because this was the only way they could watch their local news, weather, and sports. Well-to-do urban dwellers who had cable were happy to spend another $100 each month for a satellite system that brought numerous additional channels. The 1999 Satellite Television Home Viewer Act removed the ban on satellite dishes carrying local stations, and extended to satellite providers a variation of the must-carry obligation of cable systems. In contrast to cable's blanket "must carry" rule, satellite providers were given a choice: if they wanted to carry one station in a city like New York or Los Angeles, then they had to carry all of its twenty or so channels, rather than just "cherry pick" the four or five popular stations there. With the larger number of channels available on satellite than on cable at the time, it was expected that this rule would enhance the variety, quality, and price of programming in this new millennium of telecommunications. Just before this new satellite obligation was to take effect, the Fourth Circuit in *Satellite Broadcasting & Communications Assoc. v. FCC*, 275 F.3d 337 (4th Cir. 2001), found this to be a constitutionally legitimate restraint on satellite free speech under *Turner Broadcasting*.

In 2000, Time Warner (owner of Turner Broadcasting) had taken an action that drew attention to the clash between cable systems and networks. In May, the beginning of the Nielsen "sweeps" ratings, Time Warner removed the ABC network from all its cable systems. The immediate reason was an impasse between the two sides negotiating the new term of their "retransmission consent agreement." Disney wanted significantly higher fees for its existing channels (especially ABC), sought to move its Disney Channel to basic cable, and wanted to add a new soap opera channel, Soap Net. Time Warner resisted these requests around the same time as the pending Time Warner-AOL merger was being debated, with Disney being one of the major opponents.

Time Warner's action generated a viewer outcry across the country, especially in metropolitan New York which was basically limited to this cable system. Time Warner claimed that it deserved the same access for its Warner Brothers television shows to Disney's ABC network as the latter wanted to Time Warner's cable system. The FCC responded with a ruling that the cutoff of television shows during the sweeps month was illegal. Soon afterwards, the parties signed a new six-year agreement that gave Disney essentially what it had sought. Since their main objective was to get FCC (and FTC) approval of their record-setting merger with

AOL, Time Warner executives vowed that they would never again "lockout" a network from their cable systems; instead, the network would have to "strike"—i.e., pull their channels off—to secure better terms in future cable negotiations. Time Warner eventually secured approval of its merger, with the FTC (rather than the FCC) imposing as a key condition that the Time Warner cable system had to provide access to AOL's Internet competitors such as EarthLink.

In 2001 Time Warner won a major ruling striking down a regulation that the FCC had created under the Cable Television Consumer Protection & Competition Act of 1992. *Time Warner Entertainment v. FCC*, 240 F.3d 1126 (D.C. Cir. 2001). This FCC rule placed two kinds of limits on the size and operation of cable systems, one horizontal and the other vertical. The horizontal rule imposed a 30 percent limit on the number of cable subscribers across the country who could be served by a "multiple cable system operator." Since the denominator now also included 13 million subscribers to the new satellite systems, this meant that Time Warner could have its cable system cover 37 percent of the 67 million cable subscribers. The vertical rule limited to 40 percent the amount of cable channels that Time Warner could allocate to its own programming affiliates (a limit that applied only to the first 75 channels). The rest of these channels had to be offered to producers like Disney. The court started with the premise that the horizontal and vertical limits interfered with Time Warner's freedom of speech. Applying the *O'Brien* and *Turner Broadcasting* standard of intermediate scrutiny, the panel was not persuaded that these limits were necessary to foster either "the promotion of diversity in ideas and speech" or "the preservation of competition." The court thus sent the issues back to the FCC to rethink and redesign these rules—e.g., adopting "a 60% limit [that] might be appropriate as necessary to ensure that programmers had an adequate 'open field' even in the face of rejection by the largest company. . . ." *Id.* at 1137.

Coincidental with the litigation about must-carry and other cable regulation was a debate being conducted in both the courts and the Congress, this one finding the cable companies on the opposite side. In the 1960s, the FCC adopted a policy that precluded local telephone companies from offering television to their subscribers. The objective of this cross-ownership ban was to protect the incipient cable industry from what was perceived to be unfair competition from telephone companies who could subsidize this new venture with their governmentally provided monopoly telephone rates. *See General Telephone Co. v. United States*, 449 F.2d 846 (5th Cir. 1971) (upholding these FCC rules). The 1984 Cable Act embodied this rule in statutory form, though the legislation made it clear that the new "Baby Bells" could own cable systems in other regions of the country (as several eventually did). In the early 1990s, the Bush

Administration's FCC recommended to Congress that the ban be removed to enhance competition for the supply of cable services, *In re Telephone Company-Cable Television Cross-Ownership Rules*, 7 F.C.C.R. 5781 (1992). Unfortunately, the Cable Act of 1992 did not take that step, opting instead for FCC regulation of the rates that cable systems could charge their subscribers.

As a result, several of the Baby Bells went to court, contending that a law which barred them from cable delivery abridged that their freedom of speech. One of their First Amendment victories, *Chesapeake & Potomac Telephone Co. v. United States*, 42 F.3d 181 (4th Cir. 1994), was taken for review by the Supreme Court in the 1995 Term. Midway through that Term, though, Congress enacted the Telecommunications Act of 1996, which not only cleared the way for telephone companies to offer cable services, but also for cable companies to offer telephone services. This step was considered crucial to eliminating the need for rate regulation in both telecommunication spheres. The Court found that the *Chesapeake* dispute was moot. Whether this blend of new technology and market competition will eliminate the need for must-carry as well as cable rate regulation is something we can now assess.

The prior bar to telephone-cable cross-ownership was one of many constraints imposed pursuant to the Communications Act of 1934. As noted at the outset of this chapter, the premise of broadcast policy was that spectrum scarcity means that licenses should be given only to those judged most likely to serve the community's interests. A key feature of this public interest has been diversity in the communications being offered to the public. That is why, for example, the FCC has long forbidden a company from owning both a television station and a newspaper in the same market. Thus, when News Corp. purchased the Boston Herald in the 1980s, it had to sell its Boston Channel 25 television station; when it later developed the Fox Broadcasting Network, it had to sell the Herald in order to reacquire Channel 25 as the network's local affiliate.

In *FCC v. National Citizens Committee for Broadcasting*, 436 U.S. 775, 802 (1978), the Court rejected the claim that this FCC policy infringed on the freedom of speech of media entities:

> In making [its] licensing decision between competing applicants, the Commission has long given "primary significance" to "diversification of control of the media of mass communications." [The FCC's policy is consistent] with the statutory scheme [and with] the First Amendment goal of achieving "the widest possible dissemination of information from diverse and antagonistic sources." [Petitioners argue that the FCC's regulation of ownership seriously limits the opportunities for expression of

> both broadcasters and newspapers. But as] we stated in *Red Lion*, "to deny a station a license because 'the public interest' requires it 'is not a denial of free speech.'" . . . [The] regulations are a reasonable means of promoting the public interest in diversified mass communications; thus they do not violate the First Amendment rights of those who will be denied broadcast licenses pursuant to them.

The policy favoring diversification of media ownership also precludes common ownership of more than one television station in the same community. Hence, as a prelude to FCC approval of the Disney/ABC and Westinghouse/CBS mergers, the new entities had to divest one of the two television stations that each pair previously had owned in cities like Los Angeles.

The FCC has also placed a limit on the total number of stations that can be owned within the national market. In 1953, it set the limit at seven television, AM radio, and FM radio stations. The Court upheld that policy in *United States v. Storer Broadcasting*, 351 U.S. 192 (1956), finding it to be a legitimate attempt to limit concentration in the broadcast industry, making it easier for more groups to voice their views over the air. In 1984, the FCC decided to expand the ownership limits to 12 stations in each category, but to "sunset" the entire rule in 1990. Faced with the threat of Congressional reversal, the FCC altered its policy by eliminating the sunset clause and adding to the 12-station limits a further cap of 25 percent of the national audience. At the time, Metromedia had the highest share, with 24 percent.

Again in the early 1990s, many suggested that the ownership caps be removed entirely, with any concerns about economic concentration left to the antitrust enforcers. By analogy, there were no limits on how many cities could be served by chains of newspapers, theaters, or video rental stores. Among those who advocated that position was Vice-Chair of President Clinton's FCC, Michael Powell. When President Bush made Powell his FCC Chair (shortly after making Michael's father, Colin, Secretary of State), he reiterated his advocacy of removing any kind of ceiling (Congress itself had raised to 35 percent). Rather than wait for the FCC to rethink these regulations, the television networks prevailed in *Fox Television v. FCC*, 280 F.3d 1027 (D.C. Cir. 2002), which found no rational basis for even the 35 percent figure and sent the matter back to the FCC to decide whether any ownership cap at all was needed in this new millennium.

In 2003, after an extensive review process with more than 520,000 public comments, the FCC issued a lengthy Rulemaking Order that relaxed the media concentration rules, but still preserved the basic principle. It maintained its ban on mergers among the top four national broadcast networks. In local markets with five or more TV stations, one company can own two of them (and if 18 or more stations, three), but in neither case own two of the top four in ratings. For the national market, the ceiling on the number of households that a single company owning television stations can reach was raised from 35 to 45 percent. What are your views about the value and the long-term prospects of these rules?

## C. PURSUING DIVERSITY IN THE BROADCAST INDUSTRY

Yet another wrinkle in the broadcast ownership area stems from a provision in the 1934 law that bans foreign ownership of U.S. broadcast stations. (That rule has not been made applicable to cable systems.) As a practical matter, this rule also precludes significant foreign ownership of a broadcast network because the stations owned and operated by the network in major markets are the financial lifeblood of a network's overall operations. This provision sparked a controversy about whether Rupert Murdoch and Fox Broadcasting had complied with the letter of the rule, and if they had not, whether enforcement of the rule made sense as a matter of broadcast policy.

In the 1980s, Murdoch, a native Australian who was just then becoming a U.S. citizen, purchased several stations that would be the base for his new Fox network. The necessary capital was supplied by an equity stake held by Murdoch's Australian-based News Corp. In the 1990s, the NAACP filed a complaint about Fox's station ownership with the FCC (seeking to promote more ownership opportunities for minorities in large markets); NBC joined the complaint, because it was unhappy about Fox's use of its new National Football League television contract to woo away several of NBC's key local affiliates. In 1995, the FCC found that Murdoch's corporate structure was in violation of the anti-foreign ownership rule. Rather than force News Corp. to divest itself of at least 75 percent of its station ownership (which would have generated hundreds of millions of dollars in capital gains taxes), the FCC granted a waiver from the rule on the grounds that the creation of the new Fox network had enhanced broadcast competition and improved the diversity and quality of programming in the United States.

Meanwhile, Congress was proposing to relax the foreign ownership rule as an unwarranted government intrusion in the broadcast marketplace. The specific change that was enacted allowed ownership of American broadcast stations by the citizens of countries that allow their stations to be owned by U.S. citizens. Given the broadcast policy in other countries (most still adhering to the same philosophy that the United States adopted in 1934), this particular feature will have little practical effect. From the point of view of the broader and increasingly integrated entertainment industry, these foreign ownership policies seem rather anomalous. In the movie industry, for example, besides Twentieth Century Fox which is owned by News Corp. (Australian), Columbia Pictures is owned by Sony (Japanese), and MCA-Universal Pictures by Vivendi (French), and until recently, MGM/UA by Credit Lyonnais (French). All of these studios produce programs and movies broadcast on television. However, absent a waiver such as the one given the Fox network, other foreign-owned studios will not be able to follow the lead of Disney and acquire or create a television network based on their owned-and-operated stations in the major markets. The uneasy case for such a domestic constraint on foreign broadcasting will be addressed in the **Epilogue**.

---

Another long-standing feature of broadcast ownership policy is the FCC's comparative licensing evaluation, which gives weight to ownership by local individuals, especially those who are going to be personally involved in station management. The FCC saw this factor as a valuable instrument for ensuring that local issues and perspectives would be reflected in station programming. By the late 1960s, though, the Commission had become concerned about the fact that African-Americans and other minorities owned not a single one of the country's 750 television stations (and just ten of 7,000 radio stations). No one at the Commission believed that the FCC had itself discriminated against minorities in its award of television or radio licenses. It was obvious, though, that minorities faced major barriers in resources, connections, and experience, which made it difficult for them to win the comparative licensing contests held by the FCC for each station. Thus, in 1972, the FCC adopted a policy of treating minority status as a positive advantage in the licensing competition, but only if it were shown that this characteristic would actually influence the station's programming. That latter qualification by the FCC was struck down in *TV 9, Inc. v. FCC*, 495 F.2d 929 (D.C. Cir. 1973); the court held that if the FCC already *presumed* that other preferential factors (such as local ownership) positively influenced programming, it could not discriminate against the minority preference by requiring actual proof of this connection on a case-by-case basis.

That set the stage for a full-scale review of the issue in 1978, by which time minority broadcast ownership had risen modestly, to 40 of the 8500 stations (or 0.5 percent). The new FCC policy had three crucial components:

1. In licensing decisions, a comparative advantage would be given to an applicant that had minority ownership or management with "an important voice in the station's affairs."

2. In cases where an existing license was in danger of being taken away by the FCC because of the current ownership's poor performance, a hearing and possible revocation decision could be avoided through a "distress sale" of the station to a minority-controlled purchaser for no more than 75 percent of the station's fair market value.

3. The final component was a tax certificate awarded by the FCC for the sale of any station to a minority-controlled purchaser. While there was no requirement of a reduction in sale price, as a practical matter the expected value of the tax break would be split between the two sides to the transaction.

The FCC's rationale for this policy was that "adequate representation of minority viewpoints in programming serves not only the needs and interests of the minority, but also enriches and educates the non-minority audience."

In 1984, the FCC granted an additional licensing advantage to minorities. As described above, the Reagan Commission was trying to eliminate the limits on multi-station ownership. Eventually, the Commission was forced by Congress to confine its revisions of that policy to expanding station numbers from 7 to 12 and to adding a cap of 25 percent of the national audience. However, the FCC voted to allow firms to extend their ownership to 14 stations covering 30 percent of the national audience if the additional stations were at least half owned by minorities.

These affirmative-action policies were successful in securing their objectives. Between 1978 and 1994, approximately 300 tax certificates, 40 distress sales, and 115 comparative-advantage hearings gave minority-controlled firms either existing or new broadcast licenses. About half the minorities involved were African-American, one third Hispanic-American, 10 percent Asian-American, and 5 percent Native American. By 1994, 323 of the 11,128 broadcast stations (approximately 3 percent) were minority-controlled. Within that aggregate broadcast total, 31 of 1,155 (2.7 percent) television stations were minority-owned, up from *zero* a quarter of a century earlier.

The FCC adopted these policies to increase minority control of broadcast stations at the very time that the constitutional status of government-sponsored affirmative action reached the Supreme Court. A closely-divided Court struck down a set-aside for minorities of a number of admission spots in a state medical school in *Regents of the Univ. of California v. Bakke*, 438 U.S. 265 (1978). Just two years later, an equally-fragmented Court upheld a federal government policy that set aside for "minority business enterprises" ten percent of federal funds granted for local public works in *Fullilove v. Klutznick*, 448 U.S. 448 (1980). Just like the country as a whole, the Justices had sharply divergent views about the legitimacy of race-conscious policies, the objectives these policies were supposed to serve, and the constitutional standard they had to meet to be upheld.

The next debate was on extension of the policy to include women. In 1979, the FCC decided to grant women-controlled entities a comparative advantage in license hearings for new stations, but not in the tax certificate, distress sale, or expanded multi-ownership policies for minorities. After a successful equal protection challenge launched by a male-owned firm that lost a license contest, *Steele v. FCC*, 770 F.2d 1192 (D.C. Cir. 1985), the FCC asked to have the matter remitted to the Commission for full-scale review of its affirmative action policy for both women and minorities. *Steele v. FCC*, 806 F.2d 1126 (D.C. Cir. 1986). Because the FCC's brief made it clear that it was skeptical about the entire policy, Congress intervened, inserting in the 1987 Omnibus Budget Reconciliation Act a provision precluding FCC repeal or relaxation of any of the existing preferences.

That left the struggle to be waged on the judicial rather than the administrative front. While the Court struck down the city of Richmond's 30 percent minority set-aside for construction subcontracts, *City of Richmond v. J.A. Croson Co.*, 488 U.S. 469 (1989), two different panels in the D.C. Circuit were confronting challenges to the FCC's affirmative action program for minorities. One panel upheld the constitutionality of the program, *Winter Park Communications, Inc. v. FCC*, 873 F.2d 347 (D.C. Cir. 1989), while another panel struck it down, *Shurberg Broadcasting of Hartford v. FCC*, 876 F.2d 902 (D.C. Cir. 1989). The cases were consolidated for the Court's first-ever review of affirmative action in this distinctive setting.[j]

## METRO BROADCASTING, INC. V. FCC

Supreme Court of the United States, 1990.
497 U.S. 547, 110 S.Ct. 2997, 111 L.Ed.2d 445.

JUSTICE BRENNAN delivered the opinion of the Court.

The issue in these cases, consolidated for decision today, is whether certain minority preference policies of the Federal Communications Commission violate the equal protection component of the Fifth Amendment. The policies in question are (1) a program awarding an

[j] *See* Charles Fried, Metro Broadcasting, Inc. v. FCC: *Two Concepts of Equality*, 104 Harv. L. Rev. 107 (1990); Michael Rosenfeld, Metro Broadcasting, Inc. v. FCC: *Affirmative Action at the Crossroads of Constitutional Liberty & Equality*, 38 UCLA L. Rev. 583 (1991); Matthew L. Spitzer, *Justifying Minority Preferences in Broadcasting*, 64 So. Cal. L. Rev. 293 (1991); Patricia M. Worthy, *Diversity & Minority Stereotyping in the Television Media: The Unsettled First Amendment Issue*, 18 Hast. Comm/Ent L.J. 509 (1996).

enhancement for minority ownership in comparative proceedings for new licenses, and (2) the minority "distress sale" program, which permits a limited category of existing radio and television broadcast stations to be transferred only to minority-controlled firms. We hold that these policies do not violate equal protection principles.

* * *

II

[The majority began by stating that after *Fullilove v. Klutznick*, 448 U.S. 448 (1980), the test for] benign race conscious measures mandated by Congress—even if those measures are not "remedial" in the sense of being designed to compensate victims of past governmental or societal discrimination—are constitutionally permissible to the extent that they serve important governmental objectives within the power of Congress and are substantially related to achievement of those objectives. [The strict scrutiny test established in the] last Term in *Richmond v. J. A. Croson Co.*, 488 U.S. 469 (1989), concerning a minority set-aside program adopted by a municipality, does not prescribe the level of scrutiny to be applied to a benign racial classification employed by Congress.

* * *

We hold that the FCC minority ownership policies pass muster under the test we announce today. First, we find that they serve the important governmental objective of broadcast diversity. Second, we conclude that they are substantially related to the achievement of that objective.

A

Congress found that "the effects of past inequities stemming from racial and ethnic discrimination have resulted in a severe underrepresentation of minorities in the media of mass communications." Congress and the Commission do not justify the minority ownership policies strictly as remedies for victims of this discrimination, however. Rather, Congress and the FCC have selected the minority ownership policies primarily to promote programming diversity, and they urge that such diversity is an important governmental objective that can serve as a constitutional basis for the preference policies. We agree.

[The opinion then capsulized the decisions described earlier in this chapter which have] recognized that "[b]ecause of the scarcity of [electromagnetic] frequencies" . . . safeguarding the public's right to receive a diversity of views and information over the airwaves is therefore an integral component of the FCC's mission. . . .

* * *

Against this background, we conclude that the interest in enhancing broadcast diversity is, at the very least, an important governmental objective and is therefore a sufficient basis for the Commission's minority ownership policies. Just as a "diverse student body" contributing to a " 'robust exchange of ideas' " is a "constitutionally permissible goal" on which a race-conscious university admissions program may be predicated, *Regents of University of California v. Bakke*, 438 U.S. 265, 311–313 (1978) (opinion of Powell, J.), the diversity of views and information on the airwaves serves important First Amendment values. The benefits of such diversity are not limited to the members of minority groups who gain access to the broadcasting industry by virtue of the ownership policies; rather, the benefits redound to all members of the viewing and listening audience. As Congress found, "the American public will benefit by having access to a wider diversity of information sources."

B

[The Court then went on to "find that the minority ownership policies are substantially related to the achievement of the Government's interest."]

* * *

1

The FCC has determined that increased minority participation in broadcasting promotes programming diversity. As the Commission observed in its 1978 Statement of Policy on Minority Ownership of Broadcasting Facilities, "ownership of broadcast facilities by minorities is [a] significant way of fostering the inclusion of minority views in the area of programming," and "[f]ull minority participation in the ownership and management of broadcast facilities results in a more diverse selection of programming." Four years later, the FCC explained that it had taken "steps to enhance the ownership and participation of minorities in the media" in order to "increas[e] the diversity in the control of the media and thus diversity in the selection of available programming, benefiting the public and serving the principle of the First Amendment." The FCC's conclusion that there is an empirical nexus between minority ownership and broadcasting diversity is a product of its expertise, and we accord its judgment deference.

Furthermore, the FCC's reasoning with respect to the minority ownership policies is consistent with longstanding practice under the Communications Act. From its inception, public regulation of broadcasting has been premised on the assumption that diversification of ownership will broaden the range of programming available to the broadcast audience. Thus, "it is upon ownership that public policy places primary reliance with respect to diversification of content, and that historically has proved to be significantly influential with respect to editorial comment and the presentation of news." The Commission has never relied on the market alone to ensure that the needs of the audience are met. Indeed, one of the FCC's elementary regulatory assumptions is that broadcast content is not purely market driven; if it were, there would be little need for consideration in licensing decisions of such factors as integration of ownership and management, local residence, and civic participation. In this vein, the FCC has compared minority preferences to local residence and other integration credits:

> "[B]oth local residence and minority ownership are fundamental considerations in our licensing scheme. Both policies complement our concern with diversification of control of broadcast ownership. Moreover, similar assumptions underlie both policies. We award enhancement credit for local residence because . . . [i]t is expected that [an] increased knowledge of the community of license will be reflected in a station's programming. Likewise, credit for minority ownership and participation is awarded in a comparative proceeding [because] 'minority ownership is likely to increase diversity of content, especially of opinion and viewpoint.' "

2

* * *

[The court then reviewed the history of Congressional appraisal and endorsement of these minority licensing policies, and found that because] both Congress and the Commission have concluded that the minority ownership programs are critical means of promoting broadcast diversity, [w]e must give great weight to their joint determination.

C

The judgment that there is a link between expanded minority ownership and broadcast diversity does not rest on impermissible stereotyping. Congressional policy does not assume that in every case minority ownership and management will lead to more minority-oriented programming or to the expression of a discrete "minority viewpoint" on the airwaves. Neither does it pretend that all programming that appeals to minority audiences can be labeled "minority programming" or that programming that might be described as "minority" does not appeal to nonminorities. Rather, both Congress and the FCC maintain simply that expanded minority ownership of broadcast outlets will, in the aggregate, result in greater broadcast diversity. A broadcasting industry with representative minority participation will produce more variation and diversity than will one whose ownership is drawn from a single racially and ethnically homogeneous group. The predictive judgment about the overall result of minority entry into broadcasting is not a rigid assumption about how minority owners will behave in every case but rather is akin to Justice Powell's conclusion in *Bakke* that greater admission of minorities would contribute, on average, "to the 'robust exchange of ideas.'" 438 U.S., at 313. To be sure, there is no ironclad guarantee that each minority owner will contribute to diversity. But neither was there an assurance in *Bakke* that minority students would interact with nonminority students or that the particular minority students admitted would have typical or distinct "minority" viewpoints.

Although all station owners are guided to some extent by market demand in their programming decisions, Congress and the Commission have determined that there may be important differences between the broadcasting practices of minority owners and those of their nonminority counterparts. This judgment—and the conclusion that there is a nexus between minority ownership and broadcasting diversity—is corroborated by a host of empirical evidence. Evidence suggests that an owner's minority status influences the selection of topics for news coverage and the presentation of editorial viewpoint, especially on matters of particular concern to minorities. . . . While we are under no illusion that members of a particular minority group share some cohesive, collective viewpoint, we believe it a legitimate inference for Congress and the Commission to draw that as more minorities gain ownership and policymaking roles in the media, varying perspectives will be more fairly represented on the airwaves. . . .

* * *

D

We find that the minority ownership policies are in other relevant respects substantially related to the goal of promoting broadcast diversity. First, the Commission adopted and Congress endorsed minority ownership preferences only after long study and painstaking consideration of all available alternatives.

* * *

In short, the Commission established minority ownership preferences only after long experience demonstrated that race-neutral means could not produce adequate broadcasting diversity. The FCC did not act precipitately in devising the programs we uphold today; to the contrary, the Commission undertook thorough evaluations of its policies three times—in 1960, 1971, and 1978—before adopting the minority ownership programs. In endorsing the minority ownership preferences, Congress agreed with the Commission's assessment that race-neutral alternatives had failed to achieve the necessary programming diversity.

* * *

The minority ownership policies, furthermore, are aimed directly at the barriers that minorities face in entering the broadcasting industry. The Commission's task force identified as key factors hampering the growth of minority ownership a lack of adequate financing, paucity of information regarding license availability, and broadcast inexperience. The Commission assigned a preference to minority status in the comparative licensing proceeding, reasoning that such an enhancement might help to compensate for a dearth of broadcasting experience. Most license acquisitions, however, are by necessity purchases of existing stations, because only a limited number of new stations are available, and those are often in less desirable markets or on less profitable portions of spectrum, such as the UHF band. Congress and the FCC therefore found a need for the minority distress sale policy, which helps to overcome the problem of inadequate access to capital by lowering the sale price and the problem of lack of information by providing existing licensees with an incentive to seek out minority buyers. The Commission's choice of minority ownership policies thus addressed the very factors it had isolated as being responsible for minority underrepresentation in the broadcast industry.

The minority ownership policies are "appropriately limited in extent and duration, and subject to reassessment and reevaluation by the Congress prior to any extension or reenactment." *Fullilove*, 448 U.S., at 489 (opinion of Burger, C. J.). Although it has underscored emphatically its support for the minority ownership policies, Congress has manifested that support through a series of appropriations Acts of finite duration, thereby ensuring future reevaluations of the need for the minority ownership program as the number of minority broadcasters increases . . . [and thus] opportunities to revisit the merits of those policies. Congress and the Commission have adopted a policy of minority ownership not as an end in itself, but rather as a means of achieving greater programming diversity. Such a goal carries its own natural limit, for there will be no need for further minority preferences once sufficient diversity has been achieved. The FCC's plan, like the Harvard admissions program discussed in *Bakke*, contains the seed of its own termination.

Finally, we do not believe that the minority ownership policies at issue impose impermissible burdens on nonminorities. Although the nonminority challengers in these cases concede that they have not suffered the loss of an already-awarded broadcast license, they claim that they have been handicapped in their ability to obtain one in the first instance. But just as we have determined that "[a]s part of this Nation's dedication to eradicating racial discrimination, innocent persons may be called upon to bear some of the burden of the remedy," we similarly find that a congressionally mandated, benign, race-conscious program that is substantially related to the achievement of an important governmental interest is consistent with equal protection principles so long as it does not impose undue burdens on nonminorities.

In the context of broadcasting licenses, the burden on nonminorities is slight. The FCC's responsibility is to grant licenses in the "public interest, convenience, or necessity," and the limited number of frequencies on the electromagnetic spectrum means that "[n]o one has a First Amendment right to a license." *Red Lion Broadcasting Co. v. FCC*, 395 U.S. 367, 389 (1969). Applicants have no settled expectation that their applications will be granted without consideration of public interest factors such as minority ownership. Award of a preference in a comparative hearing or transfer of a station in a distress sale thus contravenes "no legitimate firmly rooted expectation[s]" of competing applicants.

* * *

III

The Commission's minority ownership policies bear the imprimatur of longstanding congressional support and direction and are substantially related to the achievement of the important governmental objective of broadcast diversity. The judgment in *Metro Broadcasting* is affirmed, the judgment in *Shurburg* is reversed, and the cases are remanded for proceedings consistent with this opinion.

It is so ordered.

JUSTICE O'CONNOR, with whom THE CHIEF JUSTICE, JUSTICE SCALIA, and JUSTICE KENNEDY join, dissenting.

[The dissent began by stating that the *Richmond* strict scrutiny standard must apply to any governmental racial classification, whether or not it is characterized as "benign."] . . . To the person denied an opportunity or right based on race, the classification is hardly benign. . . . We are a Nation not of black and white alone, but one teeming with divergent communities knitted together by various traditions and carried forth, above all, by individuals. Upon that basis, we are governed by one Constitution, providing a single guarantee of equal protection, one that extends equally to all citizens.

* * *

[The dissent acknowledged] that . . . it is undisputed that minority participation in the broadcasting industry falls markedly below the demographic representation of those groups, and this shortfall may be traced in part to the discrimination and the patterns of exclusion that have widely affected our society. . . . [While the government does possess "a compelling interest in remedying the effects of identified race discrimination," such that "narrowly tailored race-conscious measures" might pass strict scrutiny to remedy identifiable discrimination "in the allocation of broadcasting licenses," that argument was not available here. The FCC had "disclaimed the possibility that discrimination infected the allocation of licenses" and this policy had been developed simply to "achiev[e] diverse programming." This interest the dissent was not prepared to find sufficiently compelling to justify a racial preference in broadcast licensing.]

* * *

The interest is certainly amorphous: the FCC and the majority of this Court understandably do not suggest how one would define or measure a particular viewpoint that might be associated with race, or even how one would assess the diversity of broadcast viewpoints. Like the vague assertion of societal discrimination, a claim of insufficiently diverse broadcasting viewpoints might be used to justify equally unconstrained racial preferences, linked to nothing other than proportional representation of various races. And the interest would support indefinite use of racial classifications, employed first to obtain the appropriate mixture of racial views and then to ensure that the broadcasting spectrum continues to reflect that mixture. We cannot deem to be constitutionally adequate an interest that would support measures that amount to the core constitutional violation of "outright racial balancing."

The asserted interest would justify discrimination against members of any group found to contribute to an insufficiently diverse broadcasting spectrum, including those groups currently favored. In *Wygant v. Jackson Bd. of Education*, 476 U.S. 267 (1986), we rejected as insufficiently weighty the interest in achieving role models in public schools, in part because that rationale could as readily be used to limit the hiring of teachers who belonged to particular minority groups. The FCC's claimed interest could similarly justify limitations on minority members' participation in broadcasting. It would be unwise to depend upon the Court's restriction of its holding to "benign" measures to forestall this result. Divorced from any remedial purpose and otherwise undefined, "benign" means only what shifting fashions and changing politics deem acceptable. Members of any racial or ethnic group, whether now preferred under the FCC's policies or not, may find themselves politically out of fashion and subject to disadvantageous but "benign" discrimination.

Under the majority's holding, the FCC may also advance its asserted interest in viewpoint diversity by identifying what constitutes a "black viewpoint," an "Asian viewpoint," an "Arab viewpoint," and so on; determining which viewpoints are underrepresented; and then using that determination to mandate particular programming or to deny licenses to those deemed by virtue of their race or ethnicity less likely to present the favored views. Indeed, the FCC has, if taken at its word, essentially pursued this course, albeit without making express its reasons for choosing to favor particular groups or for concluding that the broadcasting spectrum is insufficiently diverse.

We should not accept as adequate for equal protection purposes an interest unrelated to race, yet capable of supporting measures so difficult to distinguish from proscribed discrimination. The remedial interest may support race classifications because that interest is necessarily related to past racial discrimination; yet the interest in diversity of viewpoints provides no legitimate, much less important, reason to employ race classifications apart from generalizations impermissibly equating race with thoughts and behavior. And it will prove impossible to distinguish naked preferences for members of particular races from preferences for members of particular races because they possess certain valued views: no matter what its purpose, the Government will be able to claim that it has favored certain persons for their ability, stemming from race, to contribute distinctive views or perspectives.

Even considered as other than a justification for using race classifications, the asserted interest in viewpoint diversity falls short of being weighty enough. The Court has recognized an interest in obtaining diverse broadcasting viewpoints as a legitimate basis for the FCC, acting pursuant to its "public interest" statutory mandate, to adopt limited measures to increase the number of competing licensees and to encourage licensees to present varied views on issues of public concern. *See, e.g., FCC v. National Citizens Committee for Broadcasting*, 436 U.S. 775 (1978); *Red Lion Broadcasting Co. v. FCC*, 395 U.S. 367 (1969); *United States v. Storer Broadcasting Co.*, 351 U.S. 192 (1956); *Associated Press v. United States*, 326 U.S. 1 (1945); *National Broadcasting Co. v. United States*, 319 U.S. 190 (1943). We have also concluded that these measures do not run afoul of the First Amendment's usual prohibition of Government regulation of the marketplace of ideas, in part because First Amendment concerns support limited but inevitable Government regulation of the peculiarly constrained broadcasting spectrum. But the conclusion that measures adopted to further the interest in diversity of broadcasting viewpoints are neither beyond the FCC's statutory authority nor contrary to the First Amendment hardly establishes the interest as important for equal protection purposes.

IV

[Not only was the FCC's interest in diversity of viewpoint not compelling, but its racial classifications were not narrowly tailored to this objective.]

* * *

A

The FCC claims to advance its asserted interest in diverse viewpoints by singling out race and ethnicity as peculiarly linked to distinct views that require enhancement. The FCC's choice to employ a racial criterion embodies the related notions that a particular and distinct viewpoint inheres in certain racial groups, and that a particular applicant, by virtue of race or ethnicity alone, is more valued than other applicants because "likely to provide [that] distinct perspective." The policies directly equate race with belief and behavior, for they establish race as a necessary and sufficient condition of securing the preference. The FCC's chosen means rest on the "premise that differences in race, or in the color of a person's skin, reflect real differences that are relevant to a person's right to share in the blessings of a free society. [T]hat premise is utterly irrational and repugnant to the principles of a free and democratic society." The policies impermissibly value individuals because they presume that persons think in a manner associated with their race.

The FCC assumes a particularly strong correlation of race and behavior The FCC justifies its conclusion that insufficiently diverse viewpoints are broadcast by reference to the percentage of minority-owned stations. This assumption is correct only to the extent that minority-owned stations provide the desired additional views, and that stations owned by individuals not favored by the preferences cannot, or at least do not, broadcast underrepresented programming. Additionally, the FCC's focus on ownership to improve programming assumes that preferences linked to race are so strong that they will dictate the owner's behavior in operating the station, overcoming the owner's personal inclinations and regard for the market. This strong link between race and behavior, especially when mediated by market forces, is the assumption that Justice Powell rejected in his discussion of health care service in *Bakke* In that case, the state medical school argued that it could prefer members of minority groups because they were more likely to serve communities particularly needing medical care. Justice Powell rejected this rationale, concluding that the assumption was unsupported and that such individual choices could not be presumed from ethnicity or race.

The majority addresses this point by arguing that the equation of race with distinct views and behavior is not "impermissible" in these particular cases. Apart from placing undue faith in the Government and courts' ability to distinguish "good" from "bad" stereotypes, this reasoning repudiates essential equal protection principles that prohibit racial generalizations. The Court embraces the FCC's reasoning that an applicant's race will likely indicate that the applicant possesses a distinct perspective, but notes that the correlation of race to behavior is "not a rigid assumption about how minority owners will behave in every case." The corollary to this notion is plain: individuals of unfavored racial and ethnic backgrounds are unlikely to possess the unique experiences and background that contribute to viewpoint diversity. Both the reasoning and its corollary reveal but disregard what is objectionable about a stereotype: the racial generalization inevitably does not apply to certain individuals, and those persons may legitimately claim that they have been judged according to their race rather than upon a relevant criterion. Similarly disturbing is the majority's reasoning that different treatment on the basis of race is permissible because efficacious "in the aggregate." In *Weinberger v. Wiesenfeld*, 420 U.S. 636 (1975), we rejected similar reasoning: "Obviously, the notion that men are more likely than women to be the primary supporters of their spouses and children is not entirely without empirical support. But such a gender-based generalization cannot suffice to justify the denigration of the efforts of women who do work and whose earnings contribute significantly to their families' support." 420 U.S., at 645. Similarly in these cases, even if the Court's equation of race and programming viewpoint has some empirical basis, equal protection principles prohibit the Government from relying upon that basis to employ racial classifications. This reliance on the "aggregate" and on probabilities confirms that the Court has abandoned heightened scrutiny, which requires a direct rather than approximate fit of means to ends. We would not tolerate the Government's claim that hiring persons of a particular race leads to better service "in the aggregate," and we should not accept as legitimate the FCC's claim in these cases that members of certain races will provide superior programming, even if "in the aggregate." The Constitution's text, our cases, and our Nation's history foreclose such premises.

B

Moreover, the FCC's selective focus on viewpoints associated with race illustrates a particular tailoring difficulty. The asserted interest is in advancing the Nation's different "social, political, aesthetic, moral, and other ideas and experiences," *Red Lion*, 395 U.S., at 390, yet of all the varied traditions and ideas shared among our citizens, the FCC has sought to amplify only those particular views it identifies through the classifications most suspect under equal protection doctrine. Even if distinct views could be associated with particular ethnic and racial groups, focusing on this particular aspect of the Nation's views calls into question the Government's genuine commitment to its asserted interest.

Our equal protection doctrine governing intermediate review indicates that the Government may not use race and ethnicity as "a 'proxy for other, more germane bases of classification.'" *Mississippi University For Women v. Hogan*, 458 U.S. 718, 726 (1982), quoting *Craig v. Boren*, 429 U.S. 190, 198 (1976). The FCC has used race as a proxy for whatever views it believes to be underrepresented in the broadcasting spectrum. This reflexive or unthinking use of a suspect classification is the hallmark of an unconstitutional policy. The ill fit of means to ends is manifest. The policy is overinclusive: many members of a particular racial or ethnic group will have no interest in advancing the views the FCC believes to be underrepresented, or will find them utterly foreign. The policy is underinclusive: it awards no preference to disfavored individuals who may be particularly well versed in and committed to presenting those views. The FCC has failed to implement a case-by-case determination, and that failure is particularly unjustified when individualized hearings already occur, as in the comparative licensing process . . .

Moreover, the FCC's programs cannot survive even intermediate scrutiny because race-neutral and untried means of directly accomplishing the governmental interest are readily available. The FCC could directly advance its interest by requiring licensees to provide programming that the FCC believes would add to diversity. The interest the FCC asserts is in programming diversity, yet in adopting the challenged policies, the FCC expressly disclaimed having attempted any direct efforts to achieve its asserted goal. The Court suggests that administrative convenience excuses this failure, yet intermediate scrutiny bars the Government from relying upon that excuse to avoid measures that directly further the asserted interest. The FCC and the Court suggest that First Amendment interests in some manner should exempt the FCC from employing this direct, race-neutral means to achieve its asserted interest. They essentially argue that we may bend our equal protection principles to avoid more readily apparent harm to our First Amendment values. But the FCC cannot have it both ways: either the First Amendment bars the FCC from seeking to accomplish indirectly what it may not accomplish directly; or the FCC may pursue the goal, but must do so in a manner that comports with equal protection principles. And if the FCC can direct programming in any fashion, it must employ that direct means before resorting to indirect race-conscious means.

Other race-neutral means also exist, and all are at least as direct as the FCC's racial classifications. The FCC could evaluate applicants upon their ability to provide, and commitment to offer, whatever programming the FCC believes would reflect underrepresented viewpoints. If the FCC truly seeks diverse programming rather than allocation of goods to persons of particular racial backgrounds, it has little excuse to look to racial background rather than programming to further the programming interest. Additionally, if the FCC believes that certain persons by virtue of their unique experiences will contribute as owners to more diverse broadcasting, the FCC could simply favor applicants whose particular background indicates that they will add to the diversity of programming, rather than rely solely upon suspect classifications. Also, race-neutral means exist to allow access to the broadcasting industry for those persons excluded for financial and related reasons. The Court reasons that various minority preferences, including those reflected in the distress sale, overcome barriers of information, experience, and financing that inhibit minority ownership. Race-neutral financial and informational measures most directly reduce financial and informational barriers.

* * *

The FCC has posited a relative absence of "minority viewpoints," yet it has never suggested what those views might be or what other viewpoints might be absent from the broadcasting spectrum. It has never identified any particular deficiency in programming diversity that should be the subject of greater programming or that necessitates racial classifications.

[The dissent concluded its analysis by noting two other troubling features of the FCC's racial and ethnic licensing criteria. One was "that the nexus between owners' race and programming is considerably less than substantial. . . . [T]he market shapes programming to a tremendous extent. Members of minority groups who own licenses might be thought, like other owners, to seek to broadcast programs that will attract and retain audiences, rather than programs that reflect the owners' tastes and preferences." Second, the result of the FCC policy was to "provide the eventual licensee with an exceptionally valuable property," and thereby "unduly burdens individuals who are not members of the favored racial and ethnic groups," and thence did not enjoy equal access to the licenses being distributed under this program. For these and the reasons reproduced above, the dissent found that the FCC policies violated the "equal protection" requirements of the Constitution.]

---

*Metro Broadcasting* itself had dealt only with the minority side of the FCC's licensing preferences. Two years later, a white male who lost a contest for a Maryland radio station license to a white woman challenged the FCC's gender credit policy. In *Lamprecht v. FCC*, 958 F.2d 382 (D.C. Cir. 1992), the majority decision, authored by then-Judge Clarence Thomas, struck down the gender preference on the ground that *Metro Broadcasting* did not govern this issue. The court focused on the data assembled in a 1988 Congressional Report, *Minority Broadcast Station Ownership and Broadcast Programming: Is There a Nexus?*

1. Of stations owned primarily by women, 35 percent broadcast "women's" programs, as compared to 28 percent of stations owned by men;
2. Of stations owned by Blacks, 79 percent broadcast Black-oriented programs, as compared to 20 percent by stations owned by non-Blacks;

3. In the case of Hispanic-owned stations, the programming gap was 74 to 10 percent, for Asian-owned stations, 25 to 3 percent, and Native-American-owned stations, 46 to 4 percent.
4. While one-third of women-owned stations broadcast "women's" programming, the percentage of minority-owned stations showing women's programming ranged from 40 to 60 percent, depending on the minority group.

Based on these statistical comparisons, Judge Thomas concluded that there was no "statistically meaningful link" between female ownership and programming content that could support the licensing preference that the Supreme Court upheld for minorities. Chief Judge Mikva, dissenting in *Lamprecht*, argued that women-owned stations were 20 percent more likely than male-owned stations (35 percent versus 28 percent) to broadcast women's programming. He also noted that, unlike the FCC licensing preference, the CRS data had not singled out stations that are both owned and *managed* by women (or minorities).

---

Then, in 1995, the Supreme Court overturned the doctrinal premise of its 1990 *Metro Broadcasting* verdict. In *Adarand Constructors, Inc. v. Pena*, 515 U.S. 200 (1995), the Court revisited the affirmative action controversy in connection with a challenge to a federal highway law. Adarand Construction had lost the subcontract to build guardrails on a highway in Colorado, even though its bid was $1700 lower than its Hispanic-owned competitors; the latter's bid carried with it a $10,000 governmental bonus for the general contractor who awarded a subcontract to "socially and economically disadvantaged individuals," which, under the statute, all minorities and women were presumed to be.

In *Adarand*, Justice O'Connor reiterated her *Metro Broadcasting* position that strict scrutiny must apply to any racial classification by the government, whether federal or state, and even if the classification was intended to be "benign." *Strict* rather than *intermediate* scrutiny requires that the law be "narrowly tailored to serve a compelling governmental interest." Justice Thomas (and Justice Scalia) wrote a concurring opinion to the effect that affirmative racial (or gender) preferences were flatly unconstitutional. Justice O'Connor (joined by Chief Justice Rehnquist and Justice Kennedy), on the other hand, expressly stated that she wanted to "dispel the notion that strict scrutiny [of affirmative action] is 'strict in theory but fatal in fact' ":

> The unhappy persistence of both the practice and the lingering effects of racial discrimination against minority groups in this country is an unfortunate reality, and government is not

> disqualified from acting in response to it. . . . When race-based action is necessary to further a compelling interest, such action is within constitutional constraints if it satisfies the "narrow tailoring" test this Court has set out in previous cases.

*Id.* at 237. The Court remanded the case for a strict scrutiny determination.

*Adarand* led the D.C. Circuit to render two rulings on the constitutionality of efforts to promote diversity in broadcasting—though these times focusing on the labor market. In the first case, *Lutheran Church-Missouri Synod v. FCC*, 141 F.3d 344 (D.C. Cir. 1998), the panel decision authored by Judge Silberman struck down the FCC's long-time Equal Employment Opportunity (EEO) program for women and minorities seeking positions with radio and television stations. Later that year, the full Circuit rejected (by a 6–4 margin) a petition for *en banc* review, with dissents written by Judges Edwards and Tatel claiming that the FCC guidelines did not amount to race or gender-conscious preferences, and thus could not be found to be unconstitutional.

The Lutheran Church owned two radio stations in the St. Louis metropolitan area. One was a religious and non-commercial station, the other a commercial station that played classical music, often with a religious format. In 1989, the Church filed the standard petition with the FCC for renewal of the two station licenses. This time, though, the NAACP intervened to claim that the stations had not been hiring enough blacks. While the FCC renewed the station licenses, it did so only with the condition that the Church begin to comply with the EEO guidelines. One guideline required each station to "compare the composition of the relevant labor area with the composition of the station's work force," and if "there is under-representation of either minorities and/or women, examine the company's personnel policies and practices to assure that they do not inadvertently screen out any group, and take appropriate action where necessary." The FCC had itself stated that "our broadcast EEO rules require that broadcast licensees . . . establish and maintain an affirmative action program for qualified minorities and women."

As it turned out, 16 percent of the St. Louis area population was minority, with 14 percent black. Over the prior three years, 9 percent of the hirings by the Lutheran Church stations had been minorities, but without any systematic attention to the FCC's EEO guidelines. One response of the Church to the NAACP's argument before the FCC was that its "hiring criteria of 'knowledge of Lutheran doctrine' and 'classical music training' narrowed the local pool of available minorities" for its positions. The Commission's response was that while preferences for Lutheran training and knowledge would be justifiable "when hiring employees who are reasonably connected to the espousal of religious philosophy over the air," this rationale did *not* apply to the hiring of "receptionists, secretaries, engineers, and business managers."

The court first ruled that *Adarand* had effectively overturned the principle formulated by the majority in *Metro Broadcasting*. Even *federal* affirmative action programs designed to provide "benign" preferences for minorities must pass a "strict scrutiny" test. The *Lutheran Church* panel concluded that even accepting the FCC's argument that its guidelines did not "require hiring in accordance with fixed quotas," they did "oblige stations to grant some degree of preference to minorities in hiring."

> A station would be flatly imprudent to ignore any one of the factors it knows may trigger intense review—especially if that factor, like racial breakdown, is particularly influential. As a matter of common sense, a station can assume that a hard-edged factor like statistics is bound to be one of the more noticed screening criteria.

*Id.* at 353. As a result, whether a "government hiring program imposes hard quotas, soft quotas, or goals . . . [a]ny one of these techniques induces an employer to hire with an eye toward meeting the numerical target." *Id.* at 354.

Nor was the court persuaded that the FCC's stated "desire to foster 'diverse' programming content" satisfied *Adarand*'s "compelling" (or even *Metro Broadcasting*'s "important") public policy interest. The court reminded the FCC of the reason why the latter had rejected the *Lutheran Church*'s preference for religion in hiring: such a policy could not apply to the hiring of "receptionists, secretaries, engineers, or business managers," because these employees were not reasonably "connected to the espousal of religious philosophy over the air." *Id.* at 356.

Rather than appeal to the Supreme Court, FCC members debated whether and how to refashion its policy, eventually adopting a new Equal Employment Opportunity rule to promote programming diversity. The objective was to replace the typical word-of-mouth station recruiting system with one of two options, to secure "broad outreach." Under Option A, the station had to use at least four of 12 initiatives specified by the FCC (such as job fairs, job banks on the Internet, internships, or scholarships). Under option B, the station would design its own "outreach program," but then would have to report to the FCC the source, race, and gender of job applicants for potential appraisal of its effectiveness. In addition, the FCC restored its requirement of an Annual Employment Report by all stations, including identification of the gender and race of all employees. The FCC indicated that this information would be used to study overall industry trends, not to appraise individual licensees.

However, the broadcasters immediately challenged the constitutionality of this new rule, and a year later, in *MD/DC/DE*

*Broadcasters Association v. FCC*, 236 F.3d 13, 19–20 (D.C. Cir. 2001), the court struck it down:

> Measuring output to determine whether readily measurable inputs were used is more than self-evidently illogical; it is evidence that the agency with life and death power over the licensee is interested in results, not process, and is determined to get them. As a consequence the threat of being investigated creates an even more powerful incentive for licensees to focus their recruiting efforts upon women and minorities, at least until these groups generate a safe proportion of the licensee's job applications.

The court found that Option B, in particular, was "compelling broadcasters to redirect their necessarily finite recruiting resources so as to generate a larger percentage of applications from minority candidates." That meant that "prospective non-minority candidates who would have learned of job opportunities but for the Commission's directive now will be deprived of an opportunity to compete simply because of their race." *Id.* at 21.

The strict scrutiny test had not been satisfied because this rule was not "narrowly tailored to prevent racial or gender discrimination" by a "particular broadcaster [who had] discriminated in the past or reasonably could be expected to do so in the future." *Id.* at 23. Having ruled that Option B was unconstitutional, the Court deemed Option A non-severable, and thus it had to be struck down as well. This decision was not appealed, and no new FCC effort has been undertaken.

The broadcast industry was, however, facing a private effort on that score. In 1999, the NAACP announced that it was challenging the four major networks for under representation of on-screen minority characters. Apparently only two of the top ten prime-time shows in the 1998–99 season had even a single African-American lead character—*ER* and *Touched by an Angel*—and not a single such character was on any of the 26 new shows scheduled for the fall of 1999. The NAACP said it would ask its 500,000 members and their families and friends to boycott these networks and their sponsors, unless the networks began to enhance the diversity of their programs. As NAACP member (and Harvard Medical School professor) Dr. Alvin F. Poussaint put it, "why should we give you our money if you don't reflect our lives?" Faced with this private effort, the networks agreed to institute an explicit affirmative hiring program.

## *QUESTIONS FOR DISCUSSION*

1. These policies and rulings raise fundamental questions in the debate about affirmative action generally, as well as in the entertainment world. Are preferences justifiable in an industry where there has long been

under-representation of minorities and women, but in which there was no government discrimination in the granting of licenses? Should the FCC be able to grant advantages to current members of groups that have historically faced obstacles in becoming part of the business ventures that won the lion's share of broadcast licenses?

2. The FCC's official policy justification was not that it was designed to compensate for past discrimination, but that it would enhance diversity in broadcasting in the future. Should one presume that minority personnel or ownership of a station will significantly influence program content?

3. Should one distinguish for purposes of this diversity objective between minority and female ownership? From your own viewing of television shows, are minority characters well represented? Are the elderly, disabled, poor, and rural characters well represented? Whatever one's diagnosis of diversity on television, is minority *ownership* or minority *employment* by the stations and networks more significant to decisions about content? Should priority be given to minority *writers* or *actors*? How has the explosion of entertainment options in the Internet age affected the analysis?

4. Recall Justice O'Connor suggestion that the preferable avenue for securing diversity in broadcast programming was directly requiring licensees to provide underrepresented types of programming, rather than seeking this result indirectly through racial preferences in granting station licenses. Is that content-based regulatory alternative compatible with Justice O'Connor's own free speech analysis of the must-carry policy in *Turner Broadcasting*?

## D. A NEW SPECTRUM FOR THIS NEW MILLENNIUM

When the first edition of this text was being completed in 1996, Washington was debating the new digital spectrum for television. The original objective of this change was to create high definition television (HDTV), but the switch from analog to digital would also multiply five-fold the number of available channels, and spectrum space could be free up for high speed data services and wireless links to the Internet.

The immediate question, though, was how to allocate this new digital spectrum. Intriguingly, this was a question that had been addressed in the early 1960s by the Nobel Prize-winning founder of Law and Economics—Ronald Coase.[k] He had questioned why television stations had received valuable analog space for free. Coase explained why the standard theory, that the electromagnetic spectrum was "scarce," was largely a myth, and that FCC efforts to deal with the situation by

[k] *See* Ronald H. Coase, *The Federal Communications Commission*, 2 J. Law & Econ. 1 (1959); Ronald H. Coase, *Evaluation of Public Policy Relating to Radio & Television Broadcasting: Social & Economic Issues*, 41 Land & Pub. Util. Econ. 161 (1965); Mark S. Fowler & Daniel L. Brenner, *A Marketplace Approach to Broadcast Regulation*, 60 Tex. L. Rev. 207 (1982).

granting licenses subject to a host of regulatory conditions aggravated the problem. While it is true that there is a limited amount of spectrum space upon which to send television signals, there is also a limited amount of land on which to build the television station (or a newspaper plant or theater). The standard solution to the problem of scarce land is for the law to define property rights that can be sold to the firms willing to pay the highest amounts because they believe they can generate the greatest return from that resource. As Coase pointed out, a benefit of the market approach is that it generates a more economical use of existing physical resources, as well as investment in the methods that will eventually increase the supply. Indeed, it is often pointed out that the number of newspapers in any city is far smaller than the number of television (let alone radio) stations. Coase's argument was that this fact should shape not only the First Amendment rights of broadcasters, but also Congress' judgment about whether and how much the broadcasters should have to pay for that right.

However, in the 1990s, the National Association of Broadcasters (NAB), sought to have the new digital channels given to current licensees for what they estimated would be a fifteen- to twenty-year transition to the new medium (the stations had to install new digital transmission technology, and homeowners had to replace their television or install digital converter boxes). At the end of that period, the stations would return their analog channels to the government. Republican Senate Majority Leader Robert Dole adopted Professor Coase's concept that digital space should not be given for free to current analog broadcast licensees; instead, this new part of the electromagnetic spectrum should be auctioned to the highest bidders. If current broadcasters wanted to use this new technology, they should have to pay a significant part of the $70 billion that the Senator estimated would be generated by an auction. To ensure that financial returns were that high, the law should remove the host of restrictions imposed on who can own a broadcast license.

After Dole had left the Senate for an unsuccessful campaign against President Clinton, Clinton reached an agreement with Dole's Senate successor Trent Lott and House Speaker Newt Gingrich to give the digital channels to current analog licensees for free, though on condition that the analog space be returned for an auction after the transition. As we have seen in this chapter, the stations and networks have been able to use the First Amendment to free them from many of the FCC regulations on channels they have received for free.

In 2001, the FCC rejected an NAB request to interpret the "must carry" standard as requiring cable systems to transmit the digital as well as the analog signals from local stations. The Commission found such a "dual carriage" rule did not serve the interests of viewers, because it would require sacrificing a number of specialty cable channels. The stations were given the option of choosing whether to use their must-carry rights for their traditional analog or new digital systems. The full transition to digital finally took place in the late 2000s.

By 2011, the Internet has become a major source of entertainment content delivery. Should the FCC regulate the Internet? What are the dangers of such regulation? *See* Peter Hettich, *YOUTUBE To Be Regulated? The FCC Sits Tight, While European Broadcast Regulators Make the Grab for the Internet*, 82 St. John's L. Rev. 1447 (2008). Does the FCC presently have the power to regulate the Internet? Consider the FCC's recently announced plan to regulate "network neutrality." *See* Gary S. Becker, *Net Neutrality And Consumer Welfare*, 6 J. Compet. L. & Econ. 497 (2010); Christopher S. Yoo, *Free Speech & the Myth of the Internet as an Unintermediated Experience*, 78 Geo. Wash. L. Rev. 697 (2010). The next section considers these issues.

---

The use of the Internet has become central to the lives of a large majority of Americans. The question remains, though, as to who controls the Internet. Specifically, there is a threat to "net neutrality"—the idea that all have equal access to the Internet. Specific Internet service providers (ISPs), such as Verizon and Comcast, have been accused of slowing the speed by which others' services cross their systems. The worry is that ultimately, such providers will have a two-tiered system by which to access content—with the paying entities being able to transmit content at significantly higher speeds that non-paying entities. This is particularly important with content providers like Netflix that require significant bandwidth to stream movies on the Internet.

At the center of the fight to maintain net neutrality is the Federal Communications Commission, which promulgates the rules that ISPs, among others, must follow, pursuant to its authority under the Telecommunications Act. This next subsection explores the regulatory challenges inherent in regulating the Internet.

---

In the 1960s and 1970s, the FCC made inquiries into how computers might change its regulatory role. On the heels of these discussions, the FCC decided in 1976 to split communication into two categories: basic services and enhanced services. Basic services, such as the telephone, merely carried the information, while enhanced services included computation on top of the carrying. If one sent information through wires, and then a computer changed that information in some way, then one was using an enhanced service. Voice mail is an example of an enhanced service.

In the Telecommunications Act of 1996, the FCC maintained this dichotomy, but changed the monikers. Basic services became telecommunication services, and enhanced services became information services.

The confusion begins when one attempts to categorize the Internet. Initially, the FCC categorized the World Wide Web as information services, and the dial-up modem (which used phone lines) as telecommunications service. This changed, however, when the FCC started categorizing broadband web access. In 2002, the FCC decided that broadband access was an information service, not a telecommunications service. Brand X, a broadband provider, challenged this decision.

## NATIONAL CABLE & TELECOMMUNICATIONS ASS'N V. BRAND X INTERNET SERVICES

Supreme Court of the United States, 2002.
545 U.S. 967.

JUSTICE THOMAS delivered the opinion of the Court.

Title II of the Communications Act of 1934, 48 Stat. 1064, as amended, 47 U.S.C. § 151 *et seq.*, subjects all providers of "telecommunications servic[e]" to mandatory common-carrier regulation, § 153(44). In the order under review, the Federal Communications Commission concluded that cable companies that sell broadband Internet service do not provide "telecommunications servic[e]" as the Communications Act defines that term, and hence are exempt from mandatory common-carrier regulation under Title II. We must decide whether that conclusion is a lawful construction of the Communications Act under *Chevron U.S.A. Inc. v. Natural Resources Defense Council, Inc.*, 467 U.S. 837 (1984), and the Administrative Procedure Act, 5 U.S.C. § 555 *et seq.* We hold that it is.

### I

The traditional means by which consumers in the United States access the network of interconnected computers that make up the Internet is through "dial-up" connections provided over local telephone facilities. *See* 345 F.3d 1120, 1123–1124 (CA9 2003) (cases below); *In re Inquiry Concerning High-Speed Access to the Internet Over Cable and Other Facilities*, 17 FCC Rcd. 4798, 4802–4803, ¶ 9 (2002) (hereinafter *Declaratory Ruling*). Using these connections, consumers access the Internet by making calls with computer modems through the telephone wires owned by local phone companies. *See Verizon Communications Inc. v. FCC,* 535 U.S. 467, 489–490 (2002) (describing the physical structure of a local telephone exchange). Internet service providers (ISPs), in turn, link those calls to the Internet network, not only by providing a physical connection, but also by offering consumers the ability to translate raw

Internet data into information they may both view on their personal computers and transmit to other computers connected to the Internet. *See In re Federal-State Joint Board on Universal Service*, 13 FCC Rcd. 11501, 11531, ¶ 63 (1998) (hereinafter *Universal Service Report*); P. Huber, M. Kellogg, & J. Thorne, Federal Telecommunications Law 988 (2d ed. 1999) (hereinafter Huber); 345 F.3d, at 1123–1124. Technological limitations of local telephone wires, however, retard the speed at which data from the Internet may be transmitted through end users' dial-up connections. Dial-up connections are therefore known as "narrowband," or slower speed, connections.

"Broadband" Internet service, by contrast, transmits data at much higher speeds. There are two principal kinds of broadband Internet service: cable modem service and Digital Subscriber Line (DSL) service. Cable modem service transmits data between the Internet and users' computers via the network of television cable lines owned by cable companies. *See id.*, at 1124. DSL service provides high-speed access using the local telephone wires owned by local telephone companies. *See WorldCom, Inc. v. FCC*, 246 F.3d 690, 692 (CADC 2001) (describing DSL technology). Cable companies and telephone companies can either provide Internet access directly to consumers, thus acting as ISPs themselves, or can lease their transmission facilities to independent ISPs that then use the facilities to provide consumers with Internet access. Other ways of transmitting high-speed Internet data into homes, including terrestrial- and satellite-based wireless networks, are also emerging. *Declaratory Ruling* 4802, ¶ 6.

II

At issue in these cases is the proper regulatory classification under the Communications Act of broadband cable Internet service. The Act, as amended by the Telecommunications Act of 1996, 110 Stat. 56, defines two categories of regulated entities relevant to these cases: telecommunications carriers and information-service providers. The Act regulates telecommunications carriers, but not information-service providers, as common carriers. Telecommunications carriers, for example, must charge just and reasonable, nondiscriminatory rates to their customers, 47 U.S.C. § 201–209, design their systems so that other carriers can interconnect with their communications networks, § 251(a)(1), and contribute to the federal "universal service" fund, § 254(d). These provisions are mandatory, but the Commission must forbear from applying them if it determines that the public interest requires it. §§ 160(a), (b). Information-service providers, by contrast, are not subject to mandatory common-carrier regulation under Title II, though the Commission has jurisdiction to impose additional regulatory obligations under its Title I ancillary jurisdiction to regulate interstate and foreign communications, *see* §§ 151–161.

These two statutory classifications originated in the late 1970's, as the Commission developed rules to regulate data-processing services offered over telephone wires. That regime, the "*Computer II*" rules, distinguished between "basic" service (like telephone service) and "enhanced" service (computer-processing service offered over telephone lines). *In re Amendment of Section 64.702 of the Commission's Rules and Regulations (Second Computer Inquiry)*, 77 F.C.C. 2d 384, 417–423, ¶¶ 86–101 (1980) (hereinafter *Computer II Order*). The *Computer II* rules defined both basic and enhanced services by reference to how the consumer perceives the service being offered.

In particular, the Commission defined "basic service" as "a pure transmission capability over a communications path that is virtually transparent in terms of its interaction with customer supplied information." *Id.*, at 420, ¶ 96. By "pure" or "transparent" transmission, the Commission meant a communications path that enabled the consumer to transmit an ordinary-language message to another point, with no computer processing or storage of the information, other than the processing or storage needed to convert the message into electronic form and then back into ordinary language for purposes of transmitting it over the network—such as via a telephone or a facsimile. *Id.*, at 419–420, ¶¶ 94–95. Basic service was subject to common-carrier regulation. *Id.*, at 428, ¶ 114.

"[E]nhanced service," however, was service in which "computer processing applications [were] used to act on the content, code, protocol, and other aspects of the subscriber's information," such as voice and data storage services, *id.*, at 420–421, ¶ 97, as well as "protocol conversion" (*i.e.*, ability to communicate between networks that employ different data-transmission formats), *id.*, at 421–422, ¶ 99. By contrast to basic service, the Commission decided not to subject providers of enhanced service, even enhanced service offered via transmission wires, to Title II common-carrier regulation. *Id.*, at 428–432, ¶¶ 115–123. The Commission explained that it was unwise to subject enhanced service to common-carrier regulation given the "fast-moving, competitive market" in which they were offered. *Id.*, at 434, ¶ 129.

The definitions of the terms "telecommunications service" and "information service" established by the 1996 Act are similar to the *Computer II* basic- and enhanced-service classifications. "Telecommunications service"—the analog to basic service—is "the offering of telecommunications for a fee directly to the public . . . regardless of the facilities used." 47 U.S.C. § 153(46). "Telecommunications" is "the transmission, between or among points specified by the user, of information of the user's choosing, without change in the form or content of the information as sent and received." § 153(43). "Telecommunications carrier[s]"—those subjected to mandatory

Title II common-carrier regulation—are defined as "provider[s] of telecommunications services." § 153(44). And "information service"—the analog to enhanced service—is "the offering of a capability for generating, acquiring, storing, transforming, processing, retrieving, utilizing, or making available information via telecommunications. . . ." § 153(20).

In September 2000, the Commission initiated a rulemaking proceeding to, among other things, apply these classifications to cable companies that offer broadband Internet service directly to consumers. In March 2002, that rulemaking culminated in the *Declaratory Ruling* under review in these cases. In the *Declaratory Ruling*, the Commission concluded that broadband Internet service provided by cable companies is an "information service" but not a "telecommunications service" under the Act, and therefore not subject to mandatory Title II common-carrier regulation. In support of this conclusion, the Commission relied heavily on its *Universal Service Report*. *See Declaratory Ruling* 4821–4822, ¶¶ 36–37 (citing *Universal Service Report* or *Report*). The *Universal Service Report* classified "non-facilities-based" ISPs—those that do not own the transmission facilities they use to connect the end user to the Internet—solely as information-service providers. *See Universal Service Report* 11533, ¶ 67. Unlike those ISPs, cable companies own the cable lines they use to provide Internet access. Nevertheless, in the *Declaratory Ruling*, the Commission found no basis in the statutory definitions for treating cable companies differently from non-facilities-based ISPs: Both offer "a single, integrated service that enables the subscriber to utilize Internet access service . . . and to realize the benefits of a comprehensive service offering." *Declaratory Ruling* 4823, ¶ 38. Because Internet access provides a capability for manipulating and storing information, the Commission concluded that it was an information service. *Ibid.*

The integrated nature of Internet access and the high-speed wire used to provide Internet access led the Commission to conclude that cable companies providing Internet access are not telecommunications providers. This conclusion, the Commission reasoned, followed from the logic of the *Universal Service Report*. The *Report* had concluded that, though Internet service "involves data transport elements" because "an Internet access provider must enable the movement of information between customers' own computers and distant computers with which those customers seek to interact," it also "offers end users information-service capabilities inextricably intertwined with data transport." *Universal Service Report* 11539–11540, ¶ 80. ISPs, therefore, were not "offering . . . telecommunications . . . directly to the public," § 153(46), and so were not properly classified as telecommunications carriers, *see id.*, at 11540, ¶ 81. In other words, the Commission reasoned that consumers use their cable modems not to transmit information "transparently," such as by using a telephone, but instead to obtain Internet access.

The Commission applied this same reasoning to cable companies offering broadband Internet access. Its logic was that, like non-facilities-based ISPs, cable companies do not "offe[r] telecommunications service to the end user, but rather . . . merely us[e] telecommunications to provide end users with cable modem service." *Declaratory Ruling* 4824, ¶ 41. Though the Commission declined to apply mandatory Title II common-carrier regulation to cable companies, it invited comment on whether under its Title I jurisdiction it should require cable companies to offer other ISPs access to their facilities on common-carrier terms. *Id.*, at 4839, ¶ 72. Numerous parties petitioned for judicial review, challenging the Commission's conclusion that cable modem service was not telecommunications service. By judicial lottery, the Court of Appeals for the Ninth Circuit was selected as the venue for the challenge.

* * *

IV

We next address whether the Commission's construction of the definition of "telecommunications service," 47 U.S.C. § 153(46), is a permissible reading of the Communications Act under the *Chevron* framework. *Chevron* established a familiar two-step procedure for evaluating whether an agency's interpretation of a statute is lawful. At the first step, we ask whether the statute's plain terms "directly addres[s] the precise question at issue." 467 U.S., at 843. If the statute is ambiguous on the point, we defer at step two to the agency's interpretation so long as the construction is "a reasonable policy choice for the agency to make." *Id.*, at 845. The Commission's interpretation is permissible at both steps.

A

We first set forth our understanding of the interpretation of the Communications Act that the Commission embraced. The issue before the Commission was whether cable companies providing cable modem service are providing a "telecommunications service" in addition to an "information service."

The Commission first concluded that cable modem service is an "information service," a conclusion unchallenged here. The Act defines "information service" as "the offering of a capability for generating, acquiring, storing, transforming, processing, retrieving, utilizing, or making available information via telecommunications. . . ." § 153(20). Cable modem service is an information service, the Commission reasoned, because it provides consumers with a comprehensive capability for manipulating information using the Internet via high-speed telecommunications. That service enables users, for example, to browse the World Wide Web, to transfer files from file archives available on the

Internet via the "File Transfer Protocol," and to access e-mail and Usenet newsgroups. *Declaratory Ruling* 4821, ¶ 37; *Universal Service Report* 11537, ¶ 76. Like other forms of Internet service, cable modem service also gives users access to the Domain Name System (DNS). DNS, among other things, matches the Web page addresses that end users type into their browsers (or "click" on) with the Internet Protocol (IP) addresses[1] of the servers containing the Web pages the users wish to access. *Declaratory Ruling* 4821–4822, ¶ 37. All of these features, the Commission concluded, were part of the information service that cable companies provide consumers. *Id.*, at 4821–4823, ¶¶ 36–38; *see also Universal Service Report* 11536–11539, ¶¶ 75–79.

At the same time, the Commission concluded that cable modem service was not "telecommunications service." "Telecommunications service" is "the offering of telecommunications for a fee directly to the public." 47 U.S.C. § 153(46). "Telecommunications," in turn, is defined as "the transmission, between or among points specified by the user, of information of the user's choosing, without change in the form or content of the information as sent and received." § 153(43). The Commission conceded that, like all information-service providers, cable companies use "telecommunications" to provide consumers with Internet service; cable companies provide such service via the high-speed wire that transmits signals to and from an end user's computer. *Declaratory Ruling* 4823, ¶ 40. For the Commission, however, the question whether cable broadband Internet providers "offer" telecommunications involved more than whether telecommunications was one necessary component of cable modem service. Instead, whether that service also includes a telecommunications "offering" "tur[ned] on the nature of the functions the *end user* is offered," *id.*, at 4822, ¶ 38 (emphasis added), for the statutory definition of "telecommunications service" does not "res[t] on the particular types of facilities used," *id.*, at 4821, ¶ 35; *see* § 153(46) (definition of "telecommunications service" applies "regardless of the facilities used").

Seen from the consumer's point of view, the Commission concluded, cable modem service is not a telecommunications offering because the consumer uses the high-speed wire always in connection with the information-processing capabilities provided by Internet access, and because the transmission is a necessary component of Internet access: "As provided to the end user the telecommunications is part and parcel of cable modem service and is integral to its other capabilities." *Declaratory Ruling* 4823, ¶ 39. The wire is used, in other words, to access the World Wide Web, newsgroups, and so forth, rather than "transparently" to transmit and receive ordinary-language messages without computer processing or storage of the message. *See supra*, at 4 (noting the *Computer II* notion of "transparent" transmission). The integrated character of this offering led the Commission to conclude that cable modem service is not a "stand-alone," transparent offering of telecommunications. *Declaratory Ruling* 4823–4825, ¶¶ 41–43.

B

This construction passes *Chevron*'s first step. Respondents argue that it does not, on the ground that cable companies providing Internet service necessarily "offe[r]" the underlying telecommunications used to transmit that service. The word "offering" as used in § 153(46), however, does not unambiguously require that result. Instead, "offering" can reasonably be read to mean a "stand-alone" offering of telecommunications, *i.e.*, an offered service that, from the user's perspective, transmits messages unadulterated by computer processing. That conclusion follows not only from the ordinary meaning of the word "offering," but also from the regulatory history of the Communications Act.

1

Cable companies in the broadband Internet service business "offe[r]" consumers an information service in the form of Internet access and they do so "via telecommunications," § 153(20), but it does not inexorably follow as a matter of ordinary language that they also "offe[r]" consumers the high-speed data transmission (telecommunications) that is an input used to provide this service, § 153(46). We have held that where a statute's plain terms admit of two or more reasonable ordinary usages, the Commission's choice of one of them is entitled to deference. *See Verizon,* 535 U.S., at 498 (deferring to the Commission's interpretation of the term "cost" by reference to an alternative linguistic usage defined by what "[a] merchant who is asked about 'the cost of providing the goods'" might "reasonably" say); *National Railroad Passenger Corporation v. Boston & Maine Corp.,* 503 U.S. 407, 418 (1992) (agency construction entitled to deference where there were "alternative dictionary definitions of the word" at issue). The term "offe[r]" as used in the definition of telecommunications service, 47 U.S.C. § 153(46), is ambiguous in this way.

It is common usage to describe what a company "offers" to a consumer as what the consumer perceives to be the integrated finished product, even to the exclusion of discrete components that compose the product, as the dissent concedes. *See post*, at 3 (opinion of Scalia, J.). One might well say that a car dealership "offers" cars, but does not "offer" the integrated major inputs that make purchasing the car valuable, such as the engine or the chassis. It would, in fact, be odd to describe a car dealership as "offering" consumers the car's components in addition to the car itself. Even if it is linguistically permissible to say that the car dealership "offers" engines when it offers cars, that shows, at most, that the term "offer," when applied to a commercial transaction, is ambiguous about whether it describes only the offered finished product, or the product's discrete components as well. It does not show that no other usage is permitted.

The question, then, is whether the transmission component of cable modem service is sufficiently integrated with the finished service to make it reasonable to describe the two as a single, integrated offering. *See ibid.* We think that they are sufficiently integrated, because "[a] consumer uses the high-speed wire always in connection with the information-processing capabilities provided by Internet access, and because the transmission is a necessary component of Internet access." *Supra*, at 16. In the telecommunications context, it is at least reasonable to describe companies as not "offering" to consumers each discrete input that is necessary to providing, and is always used in connection with, a finished service. We think it no misuse of language, for example, to say that cable companies providing Internet service do not "offer" consumers DNS, even though DNS is essential to providing Internet access. *Declaratory Ruling* 4810, n. 74, 4822–4823, ¶ 38. Likewise, a telephone company "offers" consumers a transparent transmission path that conveys an ordinary-language message, not necessarily the data transmission facilities that also "transmi[t] . . . information of the user's choosing," § 153(43), or other physical elements of the facilities used to provide telephone service, like the trunks and switches, or the copper in the wires. What cable companies providing cable modem service and telephone companies providing telephone service "offer" is Internet service and telephone service respectively—the finished services, though they do so using (or "via") the discrete components composing the end product, including data transmission. Such functionally integrated components need not be described as distinct "offerings."

In response, the dissent argues that the high-speed transmission component necessary to providing cable modem service is necessarily "offered" with Internet service because cable modem service is like the offering of pizza delivery service together with pizza, and the offering of puppies together with dog leashes. *Post*, at 3–4 (opinion of Scalia, J.). The dissent's appeal to these analogies only underscores that the term "offer" is ambiguous in the way that we have described. The entire question is whether the products here are functionally integrated (like the components of a car) or functionally separate (like pets and leashes). That question turns not on the language of the Act, but on the factual particulars of how Internet technology works and how it is provided, questions *Chevron* leaves to the Commission to resolve in the first instance. As the Commission has candidly recognized, "the question may not always be straightforward whether, on the one hand, an entity is providing a single information service with communications and computing components, or, on the other hand, is providing two distinct services, one of which is a telecommunications service." *Universal Service Report* 11530, ¶ 60. Because the term "offer" can sometimes refer to a single, finished product and sometimes to the "individual components in a package being offered" (depending on whether the components "still possess sufficient identity to be described as separate objects," *post*, at 3), the statute fails unambiguously to classify the telecommunications component of cable modem service as a distinct offering. This leaves federal telecommunications policy in this technical and complex area to be set by the Commission, not by warring analogies.

We also do not share the dissent's certainty that cable modem service is so obviously like pizza delivery service and the combination of dog leashes and dogs that the Commission could not reasonably have thought otherwise. *Post,* at 3–4. For example, unlike the transmission component of Internet service, delivery service and dog leashes are not integral components of the finished products (pizzas and pet dogs). One can pick up a pizza rather than having it delivered, and one can own a dog without buying a leash. By contrast, the Commission reasonably concluded, a consumer cannot purchase Internet service without also purchasing a connection to the Internet and the transmission always occurs in connection with information processing. In any event, we doubt that a statute that, for example, subjected offerors of "delivery" service (such as Federal Express and United Parcel Service) to common-carrier regulation would unambiguously require pizza-delivery companies to offer their delivery services on a common carrier basis.

2

The Commission's traditional distinction between basic and enhanced service, *see supra*, at 4–5, also supports the conclusion that the Communications Act is ambiguous about whether cable companies "offer" telecommunications with cable modem service. Congress passed the definitions in the Communications Act against the background of this regulatory history, and we may assume that the parallel terms "telecommunications service" and "information service" substantially incorporated their meaning, as the Commission has held. *See, e.g., In re Federal-State Joint Board on Universal Service*, 12 FCC Rcd. 8776, 9179–9180, ¶ 788 (1997) (noting that the "definition of enhanced services is substantially similar to the definition of information services" and that "all services previously considered 'enhanced services' are 'information services' "); *Commissioner v. Keystone Consol. Industries, Inc.,* 508 U.S. 152, 159 (1993) (noting presumption that Congress is aware of "settled judicial and administrative interpretation[s]" of terms when it enacts a statute). The regulatory history in at least two respects confirms that the term "telecommunications service" is ambiguous.

First, in the *Computer II Order* that established the terms "basic" and "enhanced" services, the Commission defined those terms functionally, based on how the consumer interacts with the provided information, just as the Commission did in the order below. *See supra*, at 4–5. As we have explained, Internet service is not " 'transparent in terms of its interaction with customer-supplied information,' " *Computer II Order* 420, ¶ 96; the transmission occurs in connection with information processing. It was therefore consistent with the statute's terms for the Commission to assume that the parallel term "telecommunications service" in 47 U.S.C. § 153(46) likewise describes a "pure" or "transparent" communications path not necessarily separately present, from the end user's perspective, in an integrated information-service offering.

The Commission's application of the basic/enhanced service distinction to non-facilities-based ISPs also supports this conclusion. The Commission has long held that "all those who provide some form of transmission services are not necessarily common carriers." *Computer II Order* 431, ¶ 122; *see also id.*, at 435, ¶ 132 ("acknowledg[ing] the existence of a communications component" in enhanced-service offerings). For example, the Commission did not subject to common-carrier regulation those service providers that offered enhanced services over telecommunications facilities, but that did not themselves own the underlying facilities—so-called "non-facilities-based" providers. *See Universal Service Report* 11530, ¶ 60. Examples of these services included database services in which a customer used telecommunications to access information, such as Dow Jones News and Lexis, as well as "value added networks," which lease wires from common carriers and provide transmission as well as protocol-processing service over those wires. *See In re Amendment to Sections 64.702 of the Commission's Rules and Regulations (Third Computer Inquiry)*, 3 FCC Rcd. 1150, 1153, n. 23 (1988); *supra*, at 4 (explaining protocol conversion). These services "combin[ed] communications and computing components," yet the Commission held that they should "always be deemed enhanced" and therefore not subject to common-carrier regulation. *Universal Service Report* 11530, ¶ 60. Following this traditional distinction, the Commission in the *Universal Service Report* classified ISPs that leased rather than owned their transmission facilities as pure information-service providers. *Id.*, at 11540, ¶ 81.

Respondents' statutory arguments conflict with this regulatory history. They claim that the Communications Act unambiguously classifies as telecommunications carriers all entities that use telecommunications inputs to provide information service. As respondent MCI concedes, this argument would subject to mandatory common-carrier regulation all information-service providers that use telecommunications as an input to provide information service to the public. Brief for Respondent MCI, Inc. 30. For example, it would subject to common-carrier regulation non-facilities-based ISPs that own no transmission facilities. *See Universal Service Report* 11532–11533, ¶ 66. Those ISPs provide consumers with transmission facilities used to connect to the Internet, *see supra*, at 2, and so, under respondents' argument, necessarily "offer" telecommunications to consumers. Respondents' position that all such entities are necessarily "offering telecommunications" therefore entails mandatory common-carrier regulation of entities that the Commission never classified as "offerors" of basic transmission service, and therefore common carriers, under the *Computer II* regime. *See Universal Service Report* 11540, ¶ 81 (noting past Commission policy); *Computer and Communications Industry Assn. v. FCC*, 693 F.2d 198, 209 (CADC 1982) (noting and upholding Commission's *Computer II* "finding that enhanced services . . . are not common carrier services within the scope of Title II"). We doubt that the parallel term "telecommunications service" unambiguously worked this abrupt shift in Commission policy.

Respondents' analogy between cable companies that provide cable modem service and facilities-based enhanced-service providers—that is, enhanced-service providers who own the transmission facilities used to provide those services—fares no better. Respondents stress that under the *Computer II* rules the Commission regulated such providers more heavily than non-facilities-based providers. The Commission required, for example, local telephone companies that provided enhanced services to offer their wires on a common-carrier basis to competing enhanced-service providers. *See, e.g., In re Amendment of Sections 64.702 of the Commission's Rules and Regulations (Third Computer Inquiry)*, 104 F. C. C. 2d 958, 964, ¶ 4 (1986) (hereinafter *Computer III Order*). Respondents argue that the Communications Act unambiguously requires the same treatment for cable companies because cable companies also own the facilities they use to provide cable modem service (and therefore information service).

We disagree. We think it improbable that the Communications Act unambiguously freezes in time the *Computer II* treatment of facilities-based information-service providers. The Act's definition of "telecommunications service" says nothing about imposing more stringent regulatory duties on facilities-based information-service providers. The definition hinges solely on whether the entity "offer[s] telecommunications for a fee directly to the public,"

47 U.S.C. § 153(46), though the Act elsewhere subjects facilities-based carriers to stricter regulation, *see* § 251(c) (imposing various duties on facilities-based local telephone companies). In the *Computer II* rules, the Commission subjected facilities-based providers to common-carrier duties

not because of the nature of the "offering" made by those carriers, but rather because of the concern that local telephone companies would abuse the monopoly power they possessed by virtue of the "bottleneck" local telephone facilities they owned. *See Computer II Order* 474–475, ¶¶ 229, 231; *Computer III Order* 968–969, ¶ 12; *Verizon*, 535 U.S., at 489–490 (describing the naturally monopolistic physical structure of a local telephone exchange). The differential treatment of facilities-based carriers was therefore a function not of the definitions of "enhanced-service" and "basic service," but instead of a choice by the Commission to regulate more stringently, in its discretion, certain entities that provided enhanced service. The Act's definitions, however, parallel the definitions of enhanced and basic service, not the facilities-based grounds on which that policy choice was based, and the Commission remains free to impose special regulatory duties on facilities-based ISPs under its Title I ancillary jurisdiction. In fact, it has invited comment on whether it can and should do so. *See supra*, at 7.

In sum, if the Act fails unambiguously to classify non-facilities-based information-service providers that use telecommunications inputs to provide an information service as "offer[ors]" of "telecommunications," then it also fails unambiguously to classify facilities-based information-service providers as telecommunications-service offerors; the relevant definitions do not distinguish facilities-based and non-facilities-based carriers. That silence suggests, instead, that the Commission has the discretion to fill the consequent statutory gap.

* * *

The questions the Commission resolved in the order under review involve a "subject matter [that] is technical, complex, and dynamic." *Gulf Power*, 534 U.S., at 339. The Commission is in a far better position to address these questions than we are. Nothing in the Communications Act or the Administrative Procedure Act makes unlawful the Commission's use of its expert policy judgment to resolve these difficult questions. The judgment of the Court of Appeals is reversed, and the cases are remanded for further proceedings consistent with this opinion.

It is so ordered.

JUSTICE SCALIA, with whom JUSTICE SOUTER and JUSTICE GINSBURG join as to Part I, dissenting.

The Federal Communications Commission (FCC or Commission) has once again attempted to concoct "a whole new regime of regulation (or of free-market competition)" under the guise of statutory construction. *MCI Telecommunications Corp. v. American Telephone & Telegraph Co.*, 512 U.S. 218, 234 (1994). Actually, in these cases, it might be more accurate to say the Commission has attempted to establish a whole new regime of *non*-regulation, which will make for more or less free-market competition, depending upon whose experts are believed. The important fact, however, is that the Commission has chosen to achieve this through an implausible reading of the statute, and has thus exceeded the authority given it by Congress.

I

The first sentence of the FCC ruling under review reads as follows: "Cable modem service provides high-speed access to the Internet, *as well as* many applications or functions that can be used with that access, over cable system facilities." *In re Inquiry Concerning High-Speed Access to the Internet Over Cable and Other Facilities,* 17 FCC Rcd. 4798, 4799, ¶ 1 (2002) (hereinafter *Declaratory Ruling*) (emphasis added, footnote omitted). Does this mean that cable companies "offer" high-speed access to the Internet? Surprisingly not, if the Commission and the Court are to be believed.

It happens that cable-modem service is popular precisely because of the high-speed access it provides, and that, once connected with the Internet, cable-modem subscribers often use Internet applications and functions from providers other than the cable company. Nevertheless, for purposes of classifying what the cable company does, the Commission (with the Court's approval) puts all the emphasis on the rest of the package (the additional "applications or functions"). It does so by claiming that the cable company does not "offe[r]" its customers high-speed Internet access because it offers that access only in conjunction with particular applications and functions, rather than "separate[ly]," as a "stand-alone offering." *Id.,* at 4802, ¶ 7, 4823, ¶ 40.

The focus on the term "offer" appropriately derives from the statutory definitions at issue in these cases. Under the Telecommunications Act of 1996, 110 Stat. 56, " 'information service' " involves the capacity to generate, store, interact with, or otherwise manipulate "information via telecommunications." 47 U.S.C. § 153(20). In turn, " 'telecommunications' " is defined as "the transmission, between or among points specified by the user, of information of the user's choosing, without change in the form or content of the information as sent and received." § 153(43). Finally, " 'telecommunications service' " is defined as "the offering of telecommunications for a fee directly to the public ... regardless of the facilities used." § 153(46). The question here is whether cable-modem-service providers "offe[r] ... telecommunications for a fee directly to the public." If so, they are subject to Title II regulation as common carriers, like their chief competitors who provide Internet access through other technologies.

The Court concludes that the word "offer" is ambiguous in the sense that it has " 'alternative dictionary definitions' " that might be relevant. *Ante,* at 18 (quoting *National Railroad Passenger Corporation v. Boston &*

*Maine Corp.,* 503 U.S. 407, 418 (1992)). It seems to me, however, that the analytic problem pertains not really to the meaning of "offer," but to the identity of what is offered. The relevant question is whether the individual components in a package being offered still possess sufficient identity to be described as separate objects of the offer, or whether they have been so changed by their combination with the other components that it is no longer reasonable to describe them in that way.

Thus, I agree (to adapt the Court's example, *ante,* at 18) that it would be odd to say that a car dealer is in the business of selling steel or carpets because the cars he sells include both steel frames and carpeting. Nor does the water company sell hydrogen, nor the pet store water (though dogs and cats are largely water at the molecular level). But what is sometimes true is not, as the Court seems to assume, *always* true. There are instances in which it is ridiculous to deny that one part of a joint offering is being offered merely because it is not offered on a " 'stand-alone' " basis, *ante,* at 17.

If, for example, I call up a pizzeria and ask whether they offer delivery, both common sense and common "usage," *ante,* at 18, would prevent them from answering: "No, we do not offer delivery—but if you order a pizza from us, we'll bake it for you and then bring it to your house." The logical response to this would be something on the order of, "so, you *do* offer delivery." But our pizza-man may continue to deny the obvious and explain, paraphrasing the FCC and the Court: "No, even though we bring the pizza to your house, we are not actually 'offering' you delivery, because the delivery that we provide to our end users is 'part and parcel' of our pizzeria-pizza-at-home service and is 'integral to its other capabilities.' " Cf. *Declaratory Ruling* 4823, ¶ 39; *ante,* at 16, 26. Any reasonable customer would conclude at that point that his interlocutor was either crazy or following some too-clever-by-half legal advice.

In short, for the inputs of a finished service to qualify as the objects of an "offer" (as that term is reasonably understood), it is perhaps a sufficient, *but surely not a necessary,* condition that the seller offer separately "each discrete input that is necessary to providing . . . a finished service," *ante,* at 19. The pet store may have a policy of selling puppies only with leashes, but any customer will say that it *does* offer puppies—because a leashed puppy is still a puppy, even though it is not offered on a "stand-alone" basis.

Despite the Court's mighty labors to prove otherwise, *ante,* at 17–29, the telecommunications component of cable-modem service retains such ample independent identity that it must be regarded as being on offer—especially when seen from the perspective of the consumer or the end user, which the Court purports to find determinative, *ante,* at 18, 22, 27,

28. The Commission's ruling began by noting that cable-modem service provides *both* "high-speed access to the Internet" *and* other "applications and functions," *Declaratory Ruling* 4799, ¶ 1, because that is exactly how any reasonable consumer would perceive it: as consisting of two separate things.

The consumer's view of the matter is best assessed by asking what other products cable-modem service substitutes for in the marketplace. Broadband Internet service provided by cable companies is one of the three most common forms of Internet service, the other two being dial-up access and broadband Digital Subscriber Line (DSL) service. *Ante,* at 2–3. In each of the other two, the physical transmission pathway to the Internet is sold—indeed, *is legally required* to be sold—separately from the Internet functionality. With dial-up access, the physical pathway comes from the telephone company and the Internet service provider (ISP) provides the functionality.

"In the case of Internet access, the end user utilizes two different and distinct services. One is the transmission pathway, a telecommunications service that the end user purchases from the telephone company. The second is the Internet access service, which is an enhanced service provided by an ISP. . . . Th[e] functions [provided by the ISP] are separate from the transmission pathway over which that data travels. The pathway is a regulated telecommunications service; the enhanced service offered over it is not." Oxman, The FCC and the Unregulation of the Internet, p. 13 (FCC, Office of Plans and Policy, Working Paper No. 31, July 1999), available at http://www.fcc.gov/Bureaus/OPP/working_papers/oppwp31.pdf (as visited June 24, 2005, and available in the Clerk of Court's case file).

As the Court acknowledges, *ante,* at 29, DSL service has been similar to dial-up service in the respect that the physical connection to the Internet must be offered separately from Internet functionality. Thus, customers shopping for dial-up or DSL service will not be able to use the Internet unless they get both someone to provide them with a physical connection and someone to provide them with applications and functions such as e-mail and Web access. It is therefore inevitable that customers will regard the competing cable-modem service as giving them *both* computing functionality *and* the physical pipe by which that functionality comes to their computer—both the pizza and the delivery service that nondelivery pizzerias require to be purchased from the cab company.

Since the delivery service provided by cable (the broad-band connection between the customer's computer and the cable company's computer-processing facilities) is downstream from the computer-processing facilities, there is no question that it merely serves as a conduit for the information services that have already been "assembled" by the cable company in its capacity as ISP. This is relevant because of the statutory distinction between an "information service" and "telecommunications." The former involves the capability of getting, processing, and manipulating information. § 153(20). The latter, by contrast, involves no "change in the form or content of the information as sent and received." § 153(43). When cable-company-assembled information enters the cable for delivery to the subscriber, the information service is already complete. The information has been (as the statute requires) generated, acquired, stored, transformed, processed, retrieved, utilized, or made available. All that remains is for the information in its final, unaltered form, to be delivered (via telecommunications) to the subscriber.

This reveals the insubstantiality of the fear invoked by both the Commission and the Court: the fear of what will happen to ISPs that do not provide the physical pathway to Internet access, yet still use telecommunications to acquire the pieces necessary to assemble the information that they pass back to their customers. According to this *reductio, ante,* at 22–24, if cable-modem-service providers are deemed to provide "telecommunications service," then so must *all* ISPs because they all "use" telecommunications in providing Internet functionality (by connecting to other parts of the Internet, including Internet backbone providers, for example). In terms of the pizzeria analogy, this is equivalent to saying that, if the pizzeria "offers" delivery, *all* restaurants "offer" delivery, because the ingredients of the food they serve their customers have come from other places; no matter how their customers get the food (whether by eating it at the restaurant, or by coming to pick it up themselves), they still consume a product for which delivery was a necessary "input." This is nonsense. Concluding that delivery of the finished pizza constitutes an "offer" of delivery does not require the conclusion that the serving of prepared food includes an "offer" of delivery. And that analogy does not even do the point justice, since " 'telecommunications service' " is defined as "the offering of telecommunications for a fee *directly to the public.*" 47 U.S.C. § 153(46) (emphasis added). The ISPs' use of telecommunications in their processing of information is not offered directly to the public.

The "regulatory history" on which the Court depends so much, *ante,* at 21–25, provides another reason why common-carrier regulation of all ISPs is not a worry. Under its *Computer Inquiry* rules, which foreshadowed the definitions of "information" and "telecommunications" services, *ante,* at 4–5, the Commission forbore from regulating as common carriers "value-added networks"—non-facilities-based providers who leased basic services from common carriers and bundled them with enhanced services; it said that they, unlike facilities-based providers, would be deemed to provide only enhanced services, *ante,* at 22. That same result can be achieved today under the Commission's statutory authority to forbear from imposing most Title II regulations. 47 U.S.C. § 160. In fact, the statutory criteria for forbearance—which include what is "just and reasonable," "necessary for the protection of consumers," and "consistent with the public interest," §§ 160(a)(1), (2), (3)—correspond well with the kinds of policy reasons the Commission has invoked to justify its peculiar construction of "telecommunications service" to exclude cable-modem service.

The Court also puts great stock in its conclusion that cable-modem subscribers cannot avoid using information services provided by the cable company in its ISP capacity, even when they only click-through to other ISPs. *Ante,* at 27–29. For, even if a cable-modem subscriber uses e-mail from another ISP, designates some page not provided by the cable company as his home page, and takes advantage of none of the other standard applications and functions provided by the cable company, he will still be using the cable company's Domain Name System (DNS) server and, when he goes to popular Web pages, perhaps versions of them that are stored in the cable company's cache. This argument suffers from at least two problems. First, in the context of telephone services, the Court recognizes a *de minimis* exception to contamination of a telecommunications service by an information service. *Ante,* at 26–27. A similar exception would seem to apply to the functions in question here. DNS, in particular, is scarcely more than routing information, which is expressly excluded from the definition of "information service." 47 U.S.C. § 153(20). Second, it is apparently possible to sell a telecommunications service separately from, although in conjunction with, ISP-like services; that is precisely what happens in the DSL context, and the Commission does not contest that it *could* be done in the context of cable. The only impediment appears to be the Commission's failure to require from cable companies the unbundling that it required of facilities-based providers under its *Computer Inquiry*.

Finally, I must note that, notwithstanding the Commission's self-congratulatory paean to its deregulatory largesse, *e.g.,* Brief for Federal Petitioners 29–32, it concluded the *Declaratory Ruling* by asking, as the Court paraphrases, "whether under its Title I jurisdiction [the Commission] should require cable companies to offer other ISPs access to their facilities on common-carrier terms." *Ante,* at 7; *see also* Reply Brief for Federal Petitioners 9; Tr. of Oral Arg. 17. In other words, what the Commission hath given, the Commission may well take away—unless it doesn't. This is a wonderful illustration of how an experienced agency can (with some assistance from credulous courts) turn statutory constraints into bureaucratic discretions. The main source of the Commission's regulatory authority over common carriers is Title II, but the Commission has rendered that inapplicable in this instance by concluding that the definition of "telecommunications service" is ambiguous and does not (in its current view) apply to cable-modem service. It contemplates, however, altering that (unnecessary) outcome, not by changing the law (*i.e.,* its construction of the Title II definitions), but by reserving the right to change the facts. Under its undefined and sparingly used "ancillary" powers, the Commission might conclude that it can order cable companies to "unbundle" the telecommunications component of cable-modem service. And presto, Title II will then apply to them, because they will finally be "offering" telecommunications service! Of course, the Commission will still have the statutory power to forbear from regulating them under § 160 (which it has already tentatively concluded it would do, *Declaratory Ruling* 4847–4848, ¶¶ 94–95). Such Möbius-strip reasoning mocks the principle that the statute constrains the agency in any meaningful way.

After all is said and done, after all the regulatory cant has been translated, and the smoke of agency expertise blown away, it remains perfectly clear that someone who sells cable-modem service is "offering" telecommunications. For that simple reason set forth in the statute, I would affirm the Court of Appeals.

* * *

It is a sadness that the Court should go so far out of its way to make bad law.

I respectfully dissent.

---

Which opinion do you find more persuasive? Is the question such a complicated one that complete deference to the FCC is warranted? Or is Scalia correct in attacking the question and in finding that the FCC's interpretation is incorrect? Do you agree with his pizzeria analogy?

The consequences for the FCC of choosing the regulatory path it did continue to haunt it. The most recent example is the next case.

## VERIZON V. FEDERAL COMMUNICATIONS COMMISSION

U.S. Court of Appeals, D.C. Circuit, 2014.
740 F.3d 623.

TATEL, CIRCUIT JUDGE.

For the second time in four years, we are confronted with a Federal Communications Commission effort to compel broadband providers to treat all Internet traffic the same regardless of source—or to require, as it is popularly known, "net neutrality." In *Comcast Corp. v. FCC,* 600 F.3d 642 (D.C.Cir.2010), we held that the Commission had failed to cite any statutory authority that would justify its order compelling a broadband provider to adhere to open network management practices. After *Comcast,* the Commission issued the order challenged here—*In re Preserving the Open Internet,* 25 F.C.C.R. 17905 (2010) ("the *Open Internet Order*")—which imposes disclosure, anti-blocking, and anti-discrimination requirements on broadband providers. As we explain in this opinion, the Commission has established that section 706 of the Telecommunications Act of 1996 vests it with affirmative authority to enact measures encouraging the deployment of broadband infrastructure. The Commission, we further hold, has reasonably interpreted section 706 to empower it to promulgate rules governing broadband providers' treatment of Internet traffic, and its justification for the specific rules at issue here—that they will preserve and facilitate the "virtuous circle" of innovation that has driven the explosive growth of the Internet—is reasonable and supported by substantial evidence. That said, even though the Commission has general authority to regulate in this arena, it may not impose requirements that contravene express statutory mandates. Given that the Commission has chosen to classify broadband providers in a manner that exempts them from treatment as common carriers, the Communications Act expressly prohibits the Commission from nonetheless regulating them as such. Because the Commission has failed to establish that the anti-discrimination and anti-blocking rules do not impose *per se* common carrier obligations, we vacate those portions of the *Open Internet Order*.

## I.

Understanding this case requires an understanding of the Internet, the Internet marketplace, and the history of the Commission's regulation of that marketplace.

Four major participants in the Internet marketplace are relevant to the issues before us: backbone networks, broadband providers, edge providers, and end users. Backbone networks are interconnected, long-haul fiber-optic links and high-speed routers capable of transmitting vast amounts of data. *See In re Verizon Communications Inc. and MCI, Inc. Applications for Approval of Transfer of Control,* 20 F.C.C.R. 18433, 18493 ¶ 110 (2005). Internet users generally connect to these networks—and, ultimately, to one another—through local access providers like petitioner Verizon, who operate the "last-mile" transmission lines. *See Open Internet Order,* 25 F.C.C.R. at 17908, 17915 ¶¶ 7, 20. In the Internet's early days, most users connected to the Internet through dial-up connections over local telephone lines. *See In re Inquiry Concerning High-speed Access to the Internet over Cable and Other Facilities,* 17 F.C.C.R. 4798, 4802–03 ¶ 9 (2002) ("*Cable Broadband Order*"). Today, access is generally furnished through "broadband," i.e., high-speed communications technologies, such as cable modem service. *See In re Inquiry Concerning the Deployment of Advanced Telecommunications*

*Capability to All Americans in a Reasonable and Timely Fashion,* 25 F.C.C.R. 9556, 9557, 9558–59 ¶¶ 1, 4 (2010) ("*Sixth Broadband Deployment Report*"); 47 U.S.C. § 1302(d)(1). Edge providers are those who, like Amazon or Google, provide content, services, and applications over the Internet, while end users are those who consume edge providers' content, services, and applications. *See Open Internet Order,* 25 F.C.C.R. at 17910 ¶ 13. To pull the whole picture together with a slightly oversimplified example: when an edge provider such as YouTube transmits some sort of content—say, a video of a cat—to an end user, that content is broken down into packets of information, which are carried by the edge provider's local access provider to the backbone network, which transmits these packets to the end user's local access provider, which, in turn, transmits the information to the end user, who then views and hopefully enjoys the cat.

These categories of entities are not necessarily mutually exclusive. For example, end users may often act as edge providers by creating and sharing content that is consumed by other end users, for instance by posting photos on Facebook. Similarly, broadband providers may offer content, applications, and services that compete with those furnished by edge providers. *See Open Internet Order,* 25 F.C.C.R. at 17915 ¶ 20.

Proponents of net neutrality—or, to use the Commission's preferred term, "Internet openness"—worry about the relationship between broadband providers and edge providers. They fear that broadband providers might prevent their end-user subscribers from accessing certain edge providers altogether, or might degrade the quality of their end-user subscribers' access to certain edge providers, either as a means of favoring their own competing content or services or to enable them to collect fees from certain edge providers. Thus, for example, a broadband provider like Comcast might limit its end-user subscribers' ability to access the *New York Times* website if it wanted to spike traffic to its own news website, or it might degrade the quality of the connection to a search website like Bing if a competitor like Google paid for prioritized access.

Since the advent of the Internet, the Commission has confronted the questions of whether and how it should regulate this communications network, which, generally speaking, falls comfortably within the Commission's jurisdiction over "all interstate and foreign communications by wire or radio." 47 U.S.C. § 152(a). One of the Commission's early efforts occurred in 1980, when it adopted what is known as the *Computer II* regime. The *Computer II* rules drew a line between "basic" services, which were subject to regulation under Title II of the Communications Act of 1934 as common carrier services, *see* 47 U.S.C. §§ 201 et seq., and "enhanced" services, which were not. *See In re Amendment of Section 64.702 of the Commission's Rules and Regulations,* 77 F.C.C.2d 384, 387

¶¶ 5–7 (1980) ("*Second Computer Inquiry*"). What distinguished "enhanced" services from "basic" services was the extent to which they involved the processing of information rather than simply its transmission. *Id.* at 420–21 ¶¶ 96–97. For example, the Commission characterized telephone service as a "basic" service, *see id.* at 419 ¶ 94, because it involved a "pure" transmission that was "virtually transparent in terms of its interaction with customer supplied information," *id.* at 420 ¶ 96. Services that involved "computer processing applications . . . used to act on the content, code, protocol, and other aspects of the subscriber's information"—a definition that encompassed the services needed to connect an end user to the Internet—constituted enhanced services. *Id.* at 420 ¶ 97.

By virtue of their designation as common carriers, providers of basic services were subject to the duties that apply to such entities, including that they "furnish . . . communication service upon reasonable request," 47 U.S.C. § 201(a), engage in no "unjust or unreasonable discrimination in charges, practices, classifications, regulations, facilities, or services," *id.* § 202(a), and charge "just and reasonable" rates, *id.* § 201(b). Although the Commission applied no such restrictions to purveyors of enhanced services, it imposed limitations on certain entities, like AT&T, which owned the transmission facilities over which enhanced services would be provided. *Second Computer Inquiry,* 77 F.C.C.2d at 473–74 ¶¶ 228–29. These restrictions included, most significantly, requirements that such entities offer enhanced services only through a completely separate corporate entity and that they offer their transmissions facilities to other enhanced service providers on a common carrier basis. *Id.*

For more than twenty years, the Commission applied some form of the *Computer II* regime to Internet services offered over telephone lines, then the predominant way in which most end users connected to the Internet. *See, e.g., In re Appropriate Framework for Broadband Access to the Internet Over Wireline Facilities,* 17 F.C.C.R. 3019, 3037–40 ¶¶ 36–42 (2002). Telephone companies that provided the actual wireline facilities over which information was transmitted were limited in the manner in which they could provide the enhanced services necessary to permit end users to access the Internet. *Id.* at 3040 ¶ 42. They were also required to permit third-party Internet Service Providers (ISPs), such as America Online, to access their wireline transmission facilities on a common carrier basis. *Id.*

It was against this background that Congress passed the Telecommunications Act of 1996, Pub.L. No. 104–104, 110 Stat. 56. Tracking the *Computer II* distinction between basic and enhanced services, the Act defines two categories of entities: telecommunications carriers, which provide the equivalent of basic services, and information-service providers, which provide the equivalent of enhanced services. 47

U.S.C. § 153(24), (50), (51), (53); *see National Cable & Telecommunications Ass'n v. Brand X Internet Services,* 545 U.S. 967, 976–77, 125 S.Ct. 2688, 162 L.Ed.2d 820 (2005). The Act subjects telecommunications carriers, but not information-service providers, to Title II common carrier regulation. 47 U.S.C. § 153(53); *Brand X,* 545 U.S. at 975–76, 125 S.Ct. 2688.

Pursuant to the Act, and paralleling its prior practice under the *Computer II* regime, the Commission then classified Digital Subscriber Line (DSL) services—broadband Internet service furnished over telephone lines—as "telecommunications services." *See In re Deployment of Wireline Services Offering Advanced Telecommunications Capability,* 13 F.C.C.R. 24012, 24014, 24029–30 ¶¶ 3, 35–36 (1998) ("*Advanced Services Order*"). DSL services, the Commission concluded, involved pure transmission technologies, and so were subject to Title II regulation. *Id.* at 24030–31 ¶ 35. A DSL provider could exempt its Internet access services, but not its transmission facilities themselves, from Title II common carrier restrictions only by operating them through a separate affiliate (i.e., a quasi-independent ISP). *Id.* at 24018 ¶ 13.

Four years later, however, the Commission took a different approach when determining how to regulate broadband service provided by cable companies. Instead of viewing cable broadband providers' transmission and processing of information as distinct services, the Commission determined that cable broadband providers—even those that own and operate the underlying last-mile transmission facilities—provide a "single, integrated information service." *Cable Broadband Order,* 17 F.C.C.R. at 4824 ¶ 41. Because cable broadband providers were thus not telecommunications carriers at all, they were entirely exempt from Title II regulation. *Id.* at 4802 ¶ 7.

In *National Cable & Telecommunications Ass'n v. Brand X Internet Services,* 545 U.S. 967, 125 S.Ct. 2688, 162 L.Ed.2d 820 (2005), the Supreme Court upheld the Commission's classification of cable broadband providers. The Court concluded that the Commission's ruling represented a reasonable interpretation of the 1996 Telecommunications Act's ambiguous provision defining telecommunications service, *see id.* at 991–92, 125 S.Ct. 2688, and that the Commission's determination was entitled to deference notwithstanding its apparent inconsistency with the agency's prior interpretation of that statute, *see id.* at 981, 1000–01, 125 S.Ct. 2688.

Following *Brand X,* the Commission classified other types of broadband providers, such as DSL and wireless, which includes those offering broadband Internet service for cellular telephones, as information service providers exempt from Title II's common carrier requirements. *See In re Appropriate Framework for Broadband Access to the Internet*

*Over Wireline Facilities,* 20 F.C.C.R. 14853, 14862 ¶ 12 (2005) ("*2005 Wireline Broadband Order*"); *In re Appropriate Regulatory Treatment for Broadband Access to the Internet Over Wireless Networks,* 22 F.C.C.R. 5901, 5901–02 ¶ 1 (2007) ("*Wireless Broadband Order*"); *In re United Power Line Council's Petition for Declaratory Ruling Regarding the Classification of Broadband over Power Line Internet Access Service as an Information Service,* 21 F.C.C.R. 13281, 13281 ¶ 1 (2006). Despite calls to revisit these classification orders, *see, e.g., Open Internet Order,* 25 F.C.C.R. at 18046 (concurring statement of Commissioner Copps), the Commission has yet to overrule them.

But even as the Commission exempted broadband providers from Title II common carrier obligations, it left open the possibility that it would nonetheless regulate these entities. In the *Cable Broadband Order*, for example, the Commission sought comment on whether and to what extent it should utilize the powers granted it under Title I of the Communications Act to impose restrictions on cable broadband providers. *Cable Broadband Order,* 17 F.C.C.R. at 4842 ¶ 77. Subsequently, in conjunction with the *2005 Wireline Broadband Order*, the Commission issued a Policy Statement in which it signaled its intention to "preserve and promote the open and interconnected nature of the public Internet." *In re Appropriate Framework for Broadband Access to the Internet Over Wireline Facilities,* 20 F.C.C.R. 14986, 14988 ¶ 4 (2005). The Commission announced that should it "see evidence that providers of telecommunications for Internet access or IP-enabled services are violating these principles," it would "not hesitate to take action to address that conduct." *2005 Wireline Broadband Order,* 20 F.C.C.R. at 14904 ¶ 96.

The Commission did just that when, two years later, several subscribers to Comcast's cable broadband service complained that the company had interfered with their use of certain peer-to-peer networking applications. *See In re Formal Complaint of Free Press and Public Knowledge Against Comcast Corp. for Secretly Degrading Peer-to-Peer Applications,* 23 F.C.C.R. 13028 (2008) ("*Comcast Order*"). Finding that Comcast's impairment of these applications had "contravene[d] . . . federal policy," *id.* at 13052 ¶ 43, the Commission ordered the company to adhere to a new approach for managing bandwidth demand and to disclose the details of that approach, *id.* at 13059–60 ¶ 54. The Commission justified its order as an exercise of what courts term its "ancillary jurisdiction," *see id.* at 13034–41 ¶¶ 14–22, a power that flows from the broad language of Communications Act section 4(i). *See* 47 U.S.C. § 154(i) ("The Commission may perform any and all acts, make such rules and regulations, and issue such orders, not inconsistent with this chapter, as may be necessary in the execution of its functions."); *see generally American Library Ass'n v. FCC,* 406 F.3d 689, 700–03

(D.C.Cir.2005). We have held that the Commission may exercise such ancillary jurisdiction where two conditions are met: "(1) the Commission's general jurisdictional grant under Title I covers the regulated subject and (2) the regulations are reasonably ancillary to the Commission's effective performance of its statutorily mandated responsibilities." *American Library Ass'n,* 406 F.3d at 691–92.

In *Comcast,* we vacated the Commission's order, holding that the agency failed to demonstrate that it possessed authority to regulate broadband providers' network management practices. 600 F.3d at 644. Specifically, we held that the Commission had identified no grant of statutory authority to which the *Comcast Order* was reasonably ancillary. *Id.* at 661. The Commission had principally invoked statutory provisions that, though setting forth congressional policy, delegated no actual regulatory authority. *Id.* at 651–58. These provisions, we concluded, were insufficient because permitting the agency to ground its exercise of ancillary jurisdiction in policy statements alone would contravene the " 'axiomatic' principle that 'administrative agencies may [act] only pursuant to authority delegated to them by Congress.' " *Id.* at 654 (alteration in original) (quoting *American Library Ass'n,* 406 F.3d at 691). We went on to reject the Commission's invocation of a handful of other statutory provisions that, although they could "arguably be read to delegate regulatory authority," *id.* at 658, provided no support for the precise order at issue, *id.* at 658–61.

While the *Comcast* matter was pending, the Commission sought comment on a set of proposed rules that, with some modifications, eventually became the rules at issue here. *See In re Preserving the Open Internet,* 24 F.C.C.R. 13064 (2009). In support, it relied on the same theory of ancillary jurisdiction it had asserted in the *Comcast Order. See id.* at 13099 ¶¶ 83–85. But after our decision in *Comcast* undermined that theory, the Commission sought comment on whether and to what extent it should reclassify broadband Internet services as telecommunications services. *See In re Framework for Broadband Internet Service,* 25 F.C.C.R. 7866, 7867 ¶ 2 (2010). Ultimately, however, rather than reclassifying broadband, the Commission adopted the *Open Internet Order* that Verizon challenges here. *See* 25 F.C.C.R. 17905.

The *Open Internet Order* establishes two sets of "prophylactic rules" designed to "incorporate longstanding openness principles that are generally in line with current practices." 25 F.C.C.R. at 17907 ¶ 4. One set of rules applies to "fixed" broadband providers—i.e., those furnishing residential broadband service and, more generally, Internet access to end users "primarily at fixed end points using stationary equipment." *Id.* at 17934 ¶ 49. The other set of requirements applies to "mobile" broadband providers—i.e., those "serv[ing] end users primarily using mobile stations," such as smart phones. *Id.*

The *Order* first imposes a transparency requirement on both fixed and mobile broadband providers. *Id.* at 17938 ¶ 56. They must "publicly disclose accurate information regarding the network management practices, performance, and commercial terms of [their] broadband Internet access services." *Id.* at 17937 ¶ 54 (fixed providers); *see also id.* at 17959 ¶ 98 (mobile providers).

Second, the *Order* imposes anti-blocking requirements on both types of broadband providers. It prohibits fixed broadband providers from "block[ing] lawful content, applications, services, or non-harmful devices, subject to reasonable network management." *Id.* at 17942 ¶ 63. Similarly, the *Order* forbids mobile providers from "block[ing] consumers from accessing lawful websites" and from "block[ing] applications that compete with the provider's voice or video telephony services, subject to reasonable network management." *Id.* at 17959 ¶ 99. The *Order* defines "reasonable network management" as practices designed to "ensur[e] network security and integrity," "address [ ] traffic that is unwanted by end users," "and reduc[e] or mitigat[e] the effects of congestion on the network." *Id.* at 17952 ¶ 82. The anti-blocking rules, the *Order* explains, not only prohibit broadband providers from preventing their end-user subscribers from accessing a particular edge provider altogether, but also prohibit them "from impairing or degrading particular content, applications, services, or non-harmful devices so as to render them effectively unusable." *Id.* at 17943 ¶ 66.

Third, the *Order* imposes an anti-discrimination requirement on fixed broadband providers only. Under this rule, such providers "shall not unreasonably discriminate in transmitting lawful network traffic over a consumer's broadband Internet access service. Reasonable network management shall not constitute unreasonable discrimination." *Id.* at 17944 ¶ 68. The Commission explained that "[u]se-agnostic discrimination"—that is, discrimination based not on the nature of the particular traffic involved, but rather, for example, on network management needs during periods of congestion—would generally comport with this requirement. *Id.* at 17945–46 ¶ 73. Although the Commission never expressly said that the rule forbids broadband providers from granting preferred status or services to edge providers who pay for such benefits, it warned that "as a general matter, it is unlikely that pay for priority would satisfy the 'no unreasonable discrimination' standard." *Id.* at 17947 ¶ 76. Declining to impose the same anti-discrimination requirement on mobile providers, the Commission explained that differential treatment of such providers was warranted because the mobile broadband market was more competitive and more rapidly evolving than the fixed broadband market, network speeds and penetration were lower, and operational constraints were higher. *See id.* at 17956–57 ¶¶ 94–95.

As authority for the adoption of these rules, the Commission invoked a plethora of statutory provisions. *See id.* at 17966–81 ¶¶ 115–37. In particular, the Commission relied on section 706 of the 1996 Telecommunications Act, which directs it to encourage the deployment of broadband telecommunications capability. *See* 47 U.S.C. § 1302(a), (b). According to the Commission, the rules furthered this statutory mandate by preserving unhindered the "virtuous circle of innovation" that had long driven the growth of the Internet. *Open Internet Order,* 25 F.C.C.R. at 17910–11 ¶ 14; *see id.* at 17968, 17972 ¶¶ 117, 123. Internet openness, it reasoned, spurs investment and development by edge providers, which leads to increased end-user demand for broadband access, which leads to increased investment in broadband network infrastructure and technologies, which in turn leads to further innovation and development by edge providers. *Id.* at 17910–11 ¶ 14. If, the Commission continued, broadband providers were to disrupt this "virtuous circle" by "[r]estricting edge providers' ability to reach end users, and limiting end users' ability to choose which edge providers to patronize," they would "reduce the rate of innovation at the edge and, in turn, the likely rate of improvements to network infrastructure." *Id.* at 17911 ¶ 14.

Two members of the Commission dissented. As they saw it, the *Open Internet Order* rules not only exceeded the Commission's lawful authority, but would also stifle rather than encourage innovation. *See Open Internet Order,* 25 F.C.C.R. at 18049–81 (Dissenting Statement of Commissioner McDowell); *id.* at 18084–98 (Dissenting Statement of Commissioner Baker).

Verizon filed a petition for review of the *Open Internet Order* pursuant to 47 U.S.C. § 402(a) as well as a notice of appeal pursuant to 47 U.S.C. § 402(b). Because "we plainly have jurisdiction by the one procedural route or the other," "we need not decide which is the more appropriate vehicle for our review." *Cellco Partnership v. FCC,* 700 F.3d 534, 541 (D.C.Cir.2012) (internal quotation marks omitted).

Verizon challenges the *Open Internet Order* on several grounds, including that the Commission lacked affirmative statutory authority to promulgate the rules, that its decision to impose the rules was arbitrary and capricious, and that the rules contravene statutory provisions prohibiting the Commission from treating broadband providers as common carriers. In Part II, we consider Verizon's attacks on the Commission's affirmative statutory authority and its justification for imposing these rules. We consider the common carrier issue in Part III. Given our disposition of the latter issue, we have no need to address Verizon's additional contentions that the *Order* violates the First Amendment and constitutes an uncompensated taking.

Before beginning our analysis, we think it important to emphasize that although the question of net neutrality implicates serious policy questions, which have engaged lawmakers, regulators, businesses, and other members of the public for years, our inquiry here is relatively limited. "Regardless of how serious the problem an administrative agency seeks to address, . . . it may not exercise its authority in a manner that is inconsistent with the administrative structure that Congress enacted into law." *Ragsdale v. Wolverine World Wide, Inc.*, 535 U.S. 81, 91, 122 S.Ct. 1155, 152 L.Ed.2d 167 (2002) (internal quotation marks omitted). Accordingly, our task as a reviewing court is not to assess the wisdom of the *Open Internet Order* regulations, but rather to determine whether the Commission has demonstrated that the regulations fall within the scope of its statutory grant of authority.

## II.

The Commission cites numerous statutory provisions it claims grant it the power to promulgate the *Open Internet Order* rules. But we start and end our analysis with section 706 of the 1996 Telecommunications Act, which, as we shall explain, furnishes the Commission with the requisite affirmative authority to adopt the regulations.

Section 706(a) provides:

> The Commission and each State commission with regulatory jurisdiction over telecommunications services shall encourage the deployment on a reasonable and timely basis of advanced telecommunications capability to all Americans (including, in particular, elementary and secondary schools and classrooms) by utilizing, in a manner consistent with the public interest, convenience, and necessity, price cap regulation, regulatory forbearance, measures that promote competition in the local telecommunications market, or other regulating methods that remove barriers to infrastructure investment.

47 U.S.C. § 1302(a). Section 706(b), in turn, requires the Commission to conduct a regular inquiry "concerning the availability of advanced telecommunications capability." *Id.* § 1302(b). It further provides that should the Commission find that "advanced telecommunications capability is [not] being deployed to all Americans in a reasonable and timely fashion," it "shall take immediate action to accelerate deployment of such capability by removing barriers to infrastructure investment and by promoting competition in the telecommunications market." *Id.* The statute defines "advanced telecommunications capability" to include "broadband telecommunications capability." *Id.* § 1302(d)(1).

Verizon contends that neither subsection (a) nor (b) of section 706 confers any regulatory authority on the Commission. As Verizon sees it, the two subsections amount to nothing more than congressional statements of policy. Verizon further contends that even if either provision grants the Commission substantive authority, the scope of that grant is not so expansive as to permit the Commission to regulate broadband providers in the manner that the *Open Internet Order* rules do. In addressing these questions, we apply the familiar two-step analysis of *Chevron, U.S.A., Inc. v. Natural Resources Defense Council, Inc.,* 467 U.S. 837, 104 S.Ct. 2778, 81 L.Ed.2d 694 (1984). As the Supreme Court has recently made clear, *Chevron* deference is warranted even if the Commission has interpreted a statutory provision that could be said to delineate the scope of the agency's jurisdiction. *See City of Arlington v. FCC,* ___ U.S. ___, 133 S.Ct. 1863, 1874, ___ L.Ed.2d ___ (2013). Thus, if we determine that the Commission's interpretation of section 706 represents a reasonable resolution of a statutory ambiguity, we must defer to that interpretation. *See Chevron,* 467 U.S. at 842–43, 104 S.Ct. 2778. The *Chevron* inquiry overlaps substantially with that required by the Administrative Procedure Act (APA), pursuant to which we must also determine whether the Commission's actions were "arbitrary, capricious, an abuse of discretion, or otherwise not in accordance with law." 5 U.S.C. § 706(2)(A); *see National Ass'n of Regulatory Utility Commissioners v. Interstate Commerce Commission,* 41 F.3d 721, 726–27 (D.C.Cir.1994).

### A.

This is not the first time the Commission has asserted that section 706(a) grants it authority to regulate broadband providers. Advancing a similar argument in *Comcast,* the Commission contended that section 706(a) provided a statutory hook for its exercise of ancillary jurisdiction. Although we thought that section 706(a) might "arguably be read to delegate regulatory authority to the Commission," we concluded that the Commission could not rely on this provision to justify the *Comcast Order* because it had previously determined, in the still-binding *Advanced Services Order*, that the provision " 'does not constitute an independent grant of authority.' " *Comcast,* 600 F.3d at 658 (quoting *Advanced Services Order,* 13 F.C.C.R. at 24047 ¶ 77). We rejected the Commission's claim that the *Advanced Services Order* concluded only that section 706(a) granted it no forbearance authority—authority to relieve regulated entities of statutory obligations to which they would otherwise be subject, *see* 47 U.S.C. § 160—over and above that given it elsewhere in the Communications Act. *Comcast,* 600 F.3d at 658. Indeed, the *Advanced Services Order* was clearly far broader, explicitly declaring: "section 706(a) does not constitute an independent grant of forbearance authority *or of authority to employ other regulating methods.*" *Advanced Services Order,* 13 F.C.C.R. at 24044 ¶ 69 (emphasis added). Because the Commission had "never questioned, let alone overruled, that understanding of section 706," we held that it "remain[ed] bound" by its prior interpretation. *Comcast,* 600 F.3d at 659.

But the Commission need not remain *forever* bound by the *Advanced Services Order*'s restrictive reading of section 706(a). "An initial agency interpretation is not instantly carved in stone." *Chevron,* 467 U.S. at 863, 104 S.Ct. 2778. The APA's requirement of reasoned decision-making ordinarily demands that an agency acknowledge and explain the reasons for a changed interpretation. *See FCC v. Fox Television Stations, Inc.,* 556 U.S. 502, 515, 129 S.Ct. 1800, 173 L.Ed.2d 738 (2009) ("An agency may not . . . depart from a prior policy *sub silentio* or simply disregard rules that are still on the books."); *Brand X,* 545 U.S. at 981, 125 S.Ct. 2688 ("Unexplained inconsistency is, at most, a reason for holding an interpretation to be an arbitrary and capricious change from agency practice under the Administrative Procedure Act."). But so long as an agency "adequately explains the reasons for a reversal of policy," its new interpretation of a statute cannot be rejected simply because it is new. *Brand X,* 545 U.S. at 981, 125 S.Ct. 2688. At the time we issued our *Comcast* opinion, the Commission failed to satisfy this requirement, as its assertion that section 706(a) gave it regulatory authority represented, at that point, an attempt to " 'depart from a prior policy *sub silentio.*' " *Comcast,* 600 F.3d at 659 (quoting *Fox,* 556 U.S. at 515, 129 S.Ct. 1800).

In the *Open Internet Order*, however, the Commission has offered a reasoned explanation for its changed understanding of section 706(a). To be sure, the *Open Internet Order* evinces a palpable reluctance to accept this court's interpretation of the *Advanced Services Order*, as the Commission again attempts to reconcile its current understanding of section 706(a) with its prior interpretation. *See Open Internet Order,* 25 F.C.C.R. at 17969 ¶ 119 (characterizing the *Advanced Services Order* as being "consistent with [the Commission's] present understanding"). Of course, such reluctance hardly makes the Commission's decision unreasonable, as it is free to express its disagreement with this court's holdings. After all, even a federal agency is entitled to a little pride. Moreover, although the *Open Internet Order* inaccurately describes the *Advanced Services Order*'s actual conclusion, it does describe what the *Order* likely *should* have concluded. Specifically, the *Advanced Services Order* 's rejection of section 706(a) as a source of substantive authority rested almost entirely on the notion that a contrary interpretation would somehow permit the Commission to evade express statutory commands forbidding it from using its forbearance authority in certain circumstances. *See Advanced Services Order,* 13 F.C.C.R. at 24045–46 ¶¶ 72–73. This makes little sense. By the same reasoning, one might say that Article I of the Constitution gives Congress no substantive authority because Congress might otherwise be able to use that authority in a way that violates the Ex Post Facto Clause. The *Open Internet Order* characterizes the *Advanced Services Order* as simply "disavowing a reading of Section 706(a) that would allow the agency to trump specific mandates of the Communications Act," thus honoring "the interpretive canon that '[a] specific provision . . . controls one[ ] of more general application.'" *Open Internet Order,* 25 F.C.C.R. at 17969 ¶¶ 118–119 (quoting *Bloate v. United States,* 559 U.S. 196, 207, 130 S.Ct. 1345, 176 L.Ed.2d 54 (2010)). Perhaps the Commission should have more openly acknowledged that it was not actually describing the *Advanced Services Order*, but instead rewriting it in a more logical manner. In this latter task, however, the Commission succeeded: its reinterpretation of the *Advanced Services Order* was more reasonable than the *Advanced Services Order* itself.

In any event—and more important for our purposes—the Commission expressly declared: "To the extent that the *Advanced Services Order* can be construed as having read Section 706(a) differently, we reject that reading of the statute for the reasons discussed in the text." *Open Internet Order,* 25 F.C.C.R. at 17969 ¶ 119 n. 370. Setting forth those "reasons" at some length, the Commission analyzed the statute's text, its legislative history, and the resultant scope of the Commission's authority, concluding that each of these considerations supports the view that section 706(a) constitutes an affirmative grant of regulatory authority. *Id.* at 17969–70 ¶¶ 119–121. In these circumstances, and contrary to Verizon's contentions, we have no basis for saying that the Commission "casually ignored prior policies and interpretations or otherwise failed to provide a reasoned explanation" for its changed interpretation. *Cablevision Systems Corp. v. FCC,* 649 F.3d 695, 710 (D.C.Cir.2011) (internal quotation marks omitted).

The question, then, is this: Does the Commission's current understanding of section 706(a) as a grant of regulatory authority represent a reasonable interpretation of an ambiguous statute? We believe it does.

Recall that the provision directs the Commission to "encourage the deployment . . . of advanced telecommunications capability . . . by utilizing . . . price cap regulation, regulatory forbearance, measures that promote competition in the local telecommunications market, or other regulating methods that remove barriers to infrastructure investment." 47 U.S.C. § 1302(a). As Verizon argues, this language could certainly be read as simply setting forth a statement of congressional policy, directing the Commission to employ "regulating methods" already at the Commission's disposal in order to achieve the stated goal of promoting "advanced telecommunications" technology. But the language can just as easily be read to vest the Commission with actual authority to utilize such "regulating methods" to meet this stated goal. As the Commission put it in the *Open Internet Order*, one might reasonably think that Congress, in directing the Commission to undertake certain acts, "necessarily invested the Commission with the statutory authority to carry out those acts." *Open Internet Order,* 25 F.C.C.R. at 17969 ¶ 120.

Section 706(a)'s reference to state commissions does not foreclose such a reading. Observing that the statute applies to both "[t]he Commission *and* each State commission with regulatory jurisdiction over telecommunications services," 47 U.S.C. § 1302(a) (emphasis added), Verizon contends that Congress would not be expected to grant both the FCC and state commissions the regulatory authority to encourage the deployment of advanced telecommunications capabilities. But Congress has granted regulatory authority to state telecommunications commissions on other occasions, and we see no reason to think that it could not have done the same here. *See, e.g., id.* § 251(f) (granting state commissions the authority to exempt rural local exchange carriers from certain obligations imposed on other incumbents); *id.* § 252(e) (requiring all interconnection agreements between incumbent local exchange carriers and entrant carriers to be approved by a state commission); *see also AT&T Corp. v. Iowa Utilities Board,* 525 U.S. 366, 385–86, 119 S.Ct. 721, 142 L.Ed.2d 835 (1999) (describing the Commission's power and responsibility to dictate the manner in which state commissions exercise such authority). Thus, Congress has not "directly spoken" to the question of whether section 706(a) is a grant of regulatory authority simply by mentioning state commissions in that grant. *Chevron,* 467 U.S. at 842, 104 S.Ct. 2778.

This case, moreover, is a far cry from *FDA v. Brown & Williamson Tobacco Corp.,* 529 U.S. 120, 120 S.Ct. 1291, 146 L.Ed.2d 121 (2000), on which Verizon principally relies. There, the Supreme Court held that "Congress ha[d] clearly precluded the [Food and Drug Administration] from asserting jurisdiction to regulate tobacco products." *Id.* at 126, 120 S.Ct. 1291. The Court emphasized that the FDA had not only completely disclaimed any authority to regulate tobacco products, but had done so for more than eighty years, and that Congress had repeatedly legislated against this background. *See id.* at 143–59, 120 S.Ct. 1291. The Court also observed that the FDA's newly adopted conclusion that it did in fact have authority to regulate this industry would, given its findings regarding the effects of tobacco products and its authorizing statute, logically require the agency to ban such products altogether, a result clearly contrary to congressional policy. *See id.* at 135–43, 120 S.Ct. 1291. Furthermore, the Court reasoned, if Congress had intended to "delegate a decision of such economic and political significance" to the agency, it would have done so far more clearly. *Id.* at 160, 120 S.Ct. 1291.

The circumstances here are entirely different. Although the Commission once disclaimed authority to regulate under section 706(a), it never disclaimed authority to regulate the Internet or Internet providers altogether, nor is there any similar history of congressional reliance on such a disclaimer. To the contrary, as recounted above, *see supra* at 629–31, when Congress passed section 706(a) in 1996, it did so against the backdrop of the Commission's long history of subjecting to common carrier regulation the entities that controlled the last-mile facilities over which end users accessed the Internet. *See, e.g., Second Computer Inquiry,* 77 F.C.C.2d at 473–74 ¶¶ 228–29. Indeed, one might have thought, as the Commission originally concluded, *see Advanced Services Order,* 13 F.C.C.R. at 24029–30 ¶ 35, that Congress clearly contemplated that the Commission would continue regulating Internet providers in the manner it had previously. *Cf. Brand X,* 545 U.S. at 1003, 125 S.Ct. 2688 (Breyer, J., concurring) (concluding that the Commission's decision to exempt cable broadband providers from Title II regulation was "perhaps just barely" within the scope of the agency's "statutorily delegated authority"); *id.* at 1005, 125 S.Ct. 2688 (Scalia, J., dissenting) (arguing that Commission's decision "exceeded the authority given it by Congress"). In fact, section 706(a)'s legislative history suggests that Congress may have, somewhat presciently, viewed that provision as an affirmative grant of authority to the Commission whose existence would become necessary if other contemplated grants of statutory authority were for some reason unavailable. The Senate Report describes section 706 as a "necessary fail-safe" "intended to ensure that one of the primary objectives of the [Act]—to accelerate deployment of advanced telecommunications capability—is achieved." S.Rep. No. 104–23 at 50–51. As the Commission observed in the *Open Internet Order,* it would be "odd . . . to characterize Section 706(a) as a 'fail-safe' that 'ensures' the Commission's ability to promote advanced services if it conferred no actual authority." 25 F.C.C.R. at 17970 ¶ 120.

Verizon directs our attention to a number of bills introduced in Congress subsequent to the passage of the 1996 Act that, if enacted, would have imposed requirements on broadband providers similar to those embodied in the Commission's *Open Internet Order. See, e.g.,* Internet Non-Discrimination Act of 2006, S. 2360, 109th Cong. (2006). Such subsequent legislative history, however, provides " 'an unreliable guide to legislative intent.' " *North Broward Hospital District v. Shalala,* 172 F.3d 90, 98 (D.C.Cir.1999) (quoting *Chapman v. United States,* 500 U.S. 453, 464 n. 4, 111 S.Ct. 1919, 114 L.Ed.2d 524 (1991)). Moreover, even assuming that Congress's failure to impose such restrictions would itself cast light on Congress's understanding of the Commission's power to do so, any such inferences would be largely countered by Congress's similar failure to adopt a proposed resolution that would have specifically disapproved of the Commission's promulgation of the *Open Internet Order. See* H.J. Res. 37, 112th Cong. (2011). These conflicting pieces of subsequent failed legislation tell us little if anything about the original meaning of the Telecommunications Act of 1996.

Thus, although regulation of broadband Internet providers certainly involves decisions of great "economic and political significance," *Brown &*

*Williamson,* 529 U.S. at 160, 120 S.Ct. 1291, we have little reason given this history to think that Congress could not have delegated some of these decisions to the Commission. To be sure, Congress does not, as Verizon reminds us, "hide elephants in mouseholes." *Whitman v. American Trucking Ass'ns, Inc.,* 531 U.S. 457, 468, 121 S.Ct. 903, 149 L.Ed.2d 1 (2001). But FCC regulation of broadband providers is no elephant, and section 706(a) is no mousehole.

Of course, we might well hesitate to conclude that Congress intended to grant the Commission substantive authority in section 706(a) if that authority would have no limiting principle. *See Comcast,* 600 F.3d at 655 (rejecting Commission's understanding of its authority that "if accepted . . . would virtually free the Commission from its congressional tether"); *cf. Whitman,* 531 U.S. at 472–73, 121 S.Ct. 903 (discussing the nondelegation doctrine). But we are satisfied that the scope of authority granted to the Commission by section 706(a) is not so boundless as to compel the conclusion that Congress could never have intended the provision to set forth anything other than a general statement of policy. The Commission has identified at least two limiting principles inherent in section 706(a). *See Open Internet Order,* 25 F.C.C.R. at 17970 ¶ 121. First, the section must be read in conjunction with other provisions of the Communications Act, including, most importantly, those limiting the Commission's subject matter jurisdiction to "interstate and foreign communication by wire and radio." 47 U.S.C. § 152(a). Any regulatory action authorized by section 706(a) would thus have to fall within the Commission's subject matter jurisdiction over such communications—a limitation whose importance this court has recognized in delineating the reach of the Commission's ancillary jurisdiction. *See American Library Ass'n,* 406 F.3d at 703–04. Second, any regulations must be designed to achieve a particular purpose: to "encourage the deployment on a reasonable and timely basis of advanced telecommunications capability to all Americans." 47 U.S.C. § 1302(a). Section 706(a) thus gives the Commission authority to promulgate only those regulations that it establishes will fulfill this specific statutory goal—a burden that, as we trust our searching analysis below will demonstrate, is far from "meaningless." Dissenting Op. at 662.

## B.

Section 706(b) has a less tortured history. Until shortly before the Commission issued the *Open Internet Order*, it had never considered whether the provision vested it with any regulatory authority. The Commission had no need to do so because prior to that time it had made no determination that advanced telecommunications technologies, including broadband Internet access, were not "being deployed to all Americans in a reasonable and timely fashion," the prerequisite for any purported invocation of authority to "take immediate action to accelerate deployment of such capability" under section 706(b). 47 U.S.C. § 1302(b).

In July 2010, however, the Commission concluded that "broadband deployment to *all* Americans is not reasonable and timely." *Sixth Broadband Deployment Report,* 25 F.C.C.R. at 9558 ¶ 2. This conclusion, the Commission recognized, represented a deviation from its five prior assessments. *Id.* at 9558 ¶ 2 & n. 8. According to the Commission, the change was driven by its decision to raise the minimum speed threshold qualifying as broadband. *Id.* at 9558 ¶ 4. "Broadband," as defined in the 1996 Telecommunications Act, is Internet service furnished at speeds that "enable[ ] users to originate and receive high-quality voice, data, graphics, and video telecommunications using any technology." 47 U.S.C. § 1302(d)(1). In 1999, the Commission found this requirement satisfied by services "having the capability of supporting . . . a speed . . . in excess of 200 kilobits per second (kbps) in the last mile." *In re Inquiry Concerning the Deployment of Advanced Telecommunications Capability to All Americans in a Reasonable and Timely Fashion,* 14 F.C.C.R. 2398, 2406 ¶ 20 (1999). The Commission chose this threshold because it was "enough to provide the most popular forms of broadband—to change web pages as fast as one can flip through the pages of a book and to transmit full-motion video." *Id.* That said, the Commission recognized that technological developments might someday require it to reassess the 200 kbps threshold. *Id.* at 2407–08 ¶ 25.

In the *Sixth Broadband Deployment Report*, the Commission decided that day had finally arrived. The Commission explained that consumers now regularly use their Internet connections to access high-quality video and expect to be able at the same time to check their email and browse the web. *Sixth Broadband Deployment Report,* 25 F.C.C.R. at 9562–64 ¶¶ 10–11. Two hundred kbps, the Commission determined, "simply is not enough bandwidth" to permit such uses. *Id.* at 9562 ¶ 10. The Commission thus adopted a new threshold more appropriate to current consumer behavior and expectations: four megabytes per second (mbps) for end users to download content from the Internet—twenty times as fast as the prior threshold—and one mbps for end users to upload content. *Id.* at 9563 ¶ 11.

Applying this new benchmark, the Commission found that "roughly 80 million American adults do not subscribe to broadband at home, and approximately 14 to 24 million Americans do not have access to broadband today." *Sixth Broadband Deployment Report,* 25 F.C.C.R. at 9574 ¶ 28. Given these figures and the "ever-growing importance of broadband to our society," the Commission was unable to find "that broadband is being reasonably and timely deployed" within the meaning of section 706(b). *Id.* This conclusion, it explained, triggered section 706(b)'s mandate that the Commission "take immediate action to accelerate deployment." *Id.* at 9558 ¶ 3 (quoting 47 U.S.C. § 1302(b)) (internal quotation marks omitted).

Subsequently, in the *Open Internet Order* the Commission made clear that this statutory provision does not limit the Commission to using other regulatory authority already at its disposal, but instead grants it the power necessary to fulfill the statute's mandate. *See Open Internet Order,* 25 F.C.C.R. at 17972 ¶ 123. Emphasizing the provision's "shall take immediate action" directive, the Commission concluded that section 706(b) "provides express authority" for the rules it adopted. *Id.*

Contrary to Verizon's arguments, we believe the Commission has reasonably interpreted section 706(b) to empower it to take steps to accelerate broadband deployment if and when it determines that such deployment is not "reasonable and timely." To be sure, as with section 706(a), it is unclear whether section 706(b), in providing that the Commission "shall take immediate action to accelerate deployment of such capability by removing barriers to infrastructure investment and by promoting competition in the telecommunications market," vested the Commission with authority to remove such barriers to infrastructure investment and promote competition. 47 U.S.C. § 1302(b). But the provision may certainly be read to accomplish as much, and given such ambiguity we have no basis for rejecting the Commission's determination that it should be so understood. *See Chevron,* 467 U.S. at 842–43, 104 S.Ct. 2778. Moreover, as discussed above with respect to section 706(a), *see supra* at 638–40, nothing in the regulatory background or the legislative history either before or after passage of the 1996 Telecommunications Act forecloses such an understanding. We think it quite reasonable to believe that Congress contemplated that the Commission would regulate this industry, as the agency had in the past, and the scope of any authority granted to it by section 706(b)—limited, as it is, both by the boundaries of the Commission's subject matter jurisdiction and the requirement that any regulation be tailored to the specific statutory goal of accelerating broadband deployment—is not so broad that we might hesitate to think that Congress could have intended such a delegation.

Verizon makes two additional arguments regarding the Commission's interpretation of section 706(b), both of which we can dispose of in relatively short order.

First, Verizon contends that if section 706(b) gives the Commission any regulatory authority, that authority must be understood in conjunction with section 706(c), which directs the Commission to "compile a list of geographical areas that are not served by any provider of advanced telecommunications capability." 47 U.S.C. § 1302(c). Thus, Verizon claims, any regulations that the Commission might adopt pursuant to section 706(b) may not "reach beyond any particular 'geographical areas that are not served' by any broadband provider and apply throughout the country." Verizon's Br. 33 (emphasis omitted). By its own terms, however, section 706(c) describes simply "*part* of the inquiry" that section 706(b) requires the Commission to conduct concerning broadband deployment. 47 U.S.C. § 1302(c) (emphasis added). It nowhere purports to delineate all aspects of that inquiry. Nor does it limit the actions that the Commission may take if, in the course of that inquiry, it determines that broadband deployment has not been "reasonable and timely."

Second, Verizon asserts that the *Sixth Broadband Deployment Report*'s finding that triggered section 706(b)'s grant of regulatory authority "arbitrarily contravened five prior agency determinations of reasonable and timely deployment." Verizon's Br. 33. The timing of the Commission's determination is certainly suspicious, coming as it did closely on the heels of our rejection in *Comcast* of the legal theory on which the Commission had until then relied to establish its authority over broadband providers. But questionable timing, by itself, gives us no basis to reject an otherwise reasonable finding. Beyond its general assertion that the Commission's finding was "arbitrar[y]," Verizon offers no specific reason for thinking that the Commission's logical and carefully reasoned determination was illegitimate. We can see none.

C.

This brings us, then, to Verizon's alternative argument that even if, as we have held, sections 706(a) and 706(b) grant the Commission affirmative authority to promulgate rules governing broadband providers, the specific rules imposed by the *Open Internet Order* fall outside the scope of that authority. The Commission's theory, to reiterate, is that its regulations protect and promote edge-provider investment and development, which in turn drives end-user demand for more and better broadband technologies, which in turn stimulates competition among broadband providers to further invest in broadband. *See Open Internet Order,* 25 F.C.C.R. at 17910–11, 17970 ¶¶ 14, 120. Thus, the Commission claims, by preventing broadband providers from blocking or discriminating against edge providers, the rules "encourage the deployment on a reasonable and timely basis of advanced telecommunications capability to all Americans," 47 U.S.C. § 1302(a), and "accelerate deployment of such capability," *id.* § 1302(b), by removing "barriers to infrastructure investment" and promoting "competition," *id.* § 1302(a), (b). *See Open Internet Order,* 25 F.C.C.R. at 17968, 17972 ¶¶ 117, 123. That is, contrary to the dissent, *see* Dissenting Op. at 660–62, the Commission made clear—and Verizon appears to recognize—that the Commission found broadband providers' potential disruption of edge-provider traffic to be itself the sort of "barrier" that has "the potential to stifle overall investment in Internet infrastructure," and could "limit competition in telecommunications markets." *Open Internet Order,* 25 F.C.C.R. at 17970 ¶ 120.

Verizon mounts a twofold challenge to this rationale. It argues that the *Open Internet Order* regulations will not, as the Commission claims, meaningfully promote broadband deployment, and that even if they do advance this goal, the manner in which they do so is too attenuated from this statutory purpose to fall within the scope of authority granted by either statutory provision.

We begin with the second, more strictly legal, question of whether, assuming the Commission has accurately predicted the effect of these regulations, it may utilize the authority granted to it in sections 706(a) and 706(b) to impose regulations of this sort on broadband providers. As we have previously acknowledged, "in proscribing . . . practices with the statutorily identified effect, an agency might stray so far from the paradigm case as to render its interpretation unreasonable, arbitrary, or capricious." *National Cable & Telecommunications Ass'n v. FCC,* 567 F.3d 659, 665 (D.C.Cir.2009). Here, Verizon has given us no reason to conclude that the *Open Internet Order* 's requirements "stray" so far beyond the "paradigm case" that Congress likely contemplated as to render the Commission's understanding of its authority unreasonable. The rules not only apply directly to broadband providers, the precise entities to which section 706 authority to encourage broadband deployment presumably extends, but also seek to promote the very goal that Congress explicitly sought to promote. Because the rules advance this statutory goal of broadband deployment by first promoting edge-provider innovations and end-user demand, Verizon derides the Commission's justification as a "triple-cushion shot." Verizon's Br. 28. In billiards, however, a triple-cushion shot, although perhaps more difficult to complete, counts the same as any other shot. The Commission could reasonably have thought that its authority to promulgate regulations that promote broadband deployment encompasses the power to regulate broadband providers' economic relationships with edge providers if, in fact, the nature of those relationships influences the rate and extent to which broadband providers develop and expand their services for end users. *See Cablevision,* 649 F.3d at 709 (holding that Commission had not impermissibly "reached beyond the paradigm case" in "interpreting a statute focused on the provision of satellite programming to authorize terrestrial withholding regulations," because cable companies' ability to withhold terrestrial programming would, in turn, discourage potential competitors from entering the market to provide satellite programming) (internal quotation marks omitted).

Whether the Commission's assessment of the likely effects of the *Open Internet Order* deserves credence presents a slightly more complex question. Verizon attacks the reasoning and factual support underlying the Commission's "triple-cushion shot" theory, advancing these arguments both as an attack on the Commission's statutory interpretation and as an APA arbitrary and capricious challenge. Given that these two arguments involve similar considerations, we address them together. In so doing, "we must uphold the Commission's factual determinations if on the record as a whole, there is such relevant evidence as a reasonable mind might accept as adequate to support [the] conclusion." *Secretary of Labor, MSHA v. Federal Mine Safety & Health Review Comm'n,* 111 F.3d 913, 918 (D.C.Cir.1997) (internal quotation marks omitted); *see* 5 U.S.C. § 706(2)(E). We evaluate the Commission's reasoning to ensure that it has "examine[d] the relevant data and articulate[d] a satisfactory explanation for its action including a rational connection between the facts found and the choice made." *National Fuel Gas Supply Corp. v. FERC,* 468 F.3d 831, 839 (D.C.Cir.2006) (quoting *Motor Vehicle Manufacturers Ass'n of U.S. v. State Farm Mutual Auto. Insurance Co.,* 463 U.S. 29, 43, 103 S.Ct. 2856, 77 L.Ed.2d 443 (1983)) (internal quotation marks omitted). When assessing the reasonableness of the Commission's conclusions, we must be careful not to simply " 'substitute [our] judgment for that of the agency,' " especially when the "agency's predictive judgments about the likely economic effects of a rule" are at issue. *National Telephone Cooperative Ass'n v. FCC,* 563 F.3d 536, 541 (D.C.Cir.2009) (quoting *State Farm,* 463 U.S. at 43, 103 S.Ct. 2856). Under these standards, the Commission's prediction that the *Open Internet Order* regulations will encourage broadband deployment is, in our view, both rational and supported by substantial evidence.

To begin with, the Commission has more than adequately supported and explained its conclusion that edge-provider innovation leads to the expansion and improvement of broadband infrastructure. The Internet, the Commission observed in the *Open Internet Order*, is, "[l]ike electricity and the computer," a " 'general purpose technology' that enables new methods of production that have a major impact on the entire economy." *Open Internet Order,* 25 F.C.C.R. at 17909 ¶ 13. Certain innovations—the lightbulb, for example—create a need for infrastructure investment, such as in power generation facilities and distribution lines, that complement and further drive the development of the initial innovation and ultimately the growth of the economy as a whole. *See* Timothy F. Bresnahan & M. Trajtenberg, *General purpose technologies: 'Engines of Growth'?* 65 J. ECONOMETRICS 83, 84 (1995), *cited in Open Internet Order,* 25 F.C.C.R. at 17909 ¶ 13 n. 12; *see also* Amicus Br. of Internet Engineers and Technologists 17 (citing *Hearing on Internet Security Before the H. Comm. on Science, Space, and Technology,* 103d Cong. (Mar. 22, 1994) (written testimony of Dr. Vinton G. Cerf)). The rise of streaming online video is perhaps the best and clearest example the Commission used to illustrate that the Internet constitutes one such technology: higher-speed residential Internet connections in the late 1990s "stimulated" the development of streaming video, a service that requires particularly high bandwidth, "which in turn encouraged broadband providers to increase network speeds." *Open Internet Order,* 25 F.C.C.R. at 17911 ¶ 14 n. 23. The Commission's emphasis on this connection between edge-provider innovation and infrastructure development is uncontroversial. Indeed, in its comments to the Commission, Verizon, executing a triple-cushion shot of its own, acknowledged:

> [T]he social and economic fruits of the Internet economy are the result of a virtuous cycle of innovation and growth between that ecosystem and the underlying infrastructure—the infrastructure enabling the development and dissemination of Internet-based services and applications, with the demand and use of those services . . . driving improvements in the infrastructure which, in turn, support further innovations in services and applications.

Verizon Comments at 42, Docket No. 09–191 (Jan. 14, 2010) (internal quotation marks omitted).

The Commission's finding that Internet openness fosters the edge-provider innovation that drives this "virtuous cycle" was likewise reasonable and grounded in substantial evidence. Continued innovation at the edge, the Commission explained, "depends upon low barriers to innovation and entry by edge providers," and thus restrictions on edge providers' "ability to reach end users . . . reduce the rate of innovation." *Open Internet Order,* 25 F.C.C.R. at 17911 ¶ 14. This conclusion finds ample support in the economic literature on which the Commission relied, *see, e.g.,* Joseph Farrell & Philip J. Weiser, *Modularity, Vertical Integration, and Open Access Policies: Towards a Convergence of Antitrust and Regulation in the Internet Age,* 17 HARV. J.L. & TECH. 85, 95 (2003), *cited in Open Internet Order,* 25 F.C.C.R. at 17911 ¶ 14 n. 25, as well as in history and the comments of several edge providers. For one prominent illustration of the relationship between openness and innovation, the Commission cited the invention of the World Wide Web itself by Sir Tim Berners-Lee, who, although not working for an entity that operated the underlying network, was able to create and disseminate this enormously successful innovation without needing to make any changes to previously developed Internet protocols or securing "any approval from network operators." *Open Internet Order,* 25 F.C.C.R. at 17910 ¶ 13 (citing, *inter alia,* TIM BERNERS-LEE, WEAVING THE WEB 16 (2000)). It also highlighted the comments of Google and Vonage—both innovative edge providers—who emphasized the importance of the Internet's open design to permitting new content and services to develop at the edge. *Id.* at 17911 ¶ 14 n. 24 & n. 25. The record amassed by the Commission contains many similar examples, and Verizon has given us no basis for questioning the Commission's determination that the preservation of Internet openness is integral to achieving the statutory objectives set forth in Section 706. *See id.* at 17910–11, 17968, 17972 ¶¶ 14, 117, 123.

Equally important, the Commission has adequately supported and explained its conclusion that, absent rules such as those set forth in the *Open Internet Order*, broadband providers represent a threat to Internet openness and could act in ways that would ultimately inhibit the speed and extent of future broadband deployment. First, nothing in the record gives us any reason to doubt the Commission's determination that broadband providers may be motivated to discriminate against and among edge providers. The Commission observed that broadband providers—often the same entities that furnish end users with telephone and television services—"have incentives to interfere with the operation of third-party Internet-based services that compete with the providers' revenue-generating telephone and/or pay-television services." *Open Internet Order,* 25 F.C.C.R. at 17916 ¶ 22. As the Commission noted, Voice-over-Internet-Protocol (VoIP) services such as Vonage increasingly serve as substitutes for traditional telephone services, *id.,* and broadband providers like AT&T and Time Warner have acknowledged that online video aggregators such as Netflix and Hulu compete directly with their own "core video subscription service," *id.* at 17917 ¶ 22 & n. 54; *see also id.* at 17918 ¶ 23 n. 60 (finding that a study concluding that cable companies had sought to exclude networks that competed with the companies' own affiliated channels, *see* Austan Goolsbee, *Vertical Integration and the Market for Broadcast and Cable Television Programming,* Paper for the Federal Communications Commission 31–32 (Sept. 5, 2007), "provides empirical evidence that cable providers have acted in the past on anticompetitive incentives to foreclose rivals"). Broadband providers also have powerful incentives to accept fees from edge providers, either in return for excluding their competitors or for granting them prioritized access to end users. *See id.* at 17918–19 ¶¶ 23–24. Indeed, at oral argument Verizon's counsel announced that "but for [the *Open Internet Order*] rules we would be exploring those commercial arrangements." Oral Arg. Tr. 31. And although broadband providers might not adopt pay-for-priority agreements or other similar arrangements if, according to the Commission's analysis, such agreements would ultimately lead to a decrease in end-user demand for broadband, the Commission explained that the resultant harms to innovation and demand will largely constitute "negative externalities": any given broadband provider will "receive the benefits of . . . fees but [is] unlikely to fully account for the detrimental impact on edge providers' ability and incentive to innovate and invest." *Open Internet Order,* 25 F.C.C.R. at 17919–20 ¶ 25 & n. 68. Although Verizon dismisses the Commission's assertions regarding broadband providers' incentives as "pure speculation," Verizon's Br. 52, *see also* Dissenting Op. at 666–67, those assertions are, at the very least, speculation based firmly in common sense and economic reality.

Moreover, as the Commission found, broadband providers have the technical and economic ability to impose such restrictions. Verizon does not seriously contend otherwise. In fact, there appears little dispute that broadband providers have the technological ability to distinguish between and discriminate against certain types of Internet traffic. *See Open Internet Order,* 25 F.C.C.R. at 17923 ¶ 31 (broadband providers possess "increasingly sophisticated network management tools" that enable them to "make fine-grained distinction in their handling of network traffic"). The Commission also convincingly detailed how broadband providers' position in the market gives them the economic power to restrict edge-provider traffic and charge for the services they furnish edge providers. Because all end users generally access the Internet through a single broadband provider, that provider functions as a " 'terminating monopolist,' " *id.* at 17919 ¶ 24 n. 66, with power to act as a "gatekeeper" with respect to edge providers that might seek to reach its end-user subscribers, *id.* at 17919 ¶ 24. As the Commission reasonably explained, this ability to act as a "gatekeeper" distinguishes broadband providers from other participants in the Internet marketplace—including prominent and potentially powerful edge providers such as Google and Apple—who have no similar "control [over] access to the Internet for their subscribers and for anyone wishing to reach those subscribers." *Id.* at 17935 ¶ 50.

To be sure, if end users could immediately respond to any given broadband provider's attempt to impose restrictions on edge providers by switching broadband providers, this gatekeeper power might well disappear. *Cf. Open Internet Order,* 25 F.C.C.R. at 17935 ¶ 51 (declining to impose similar rules on "dial-up Internet access service because telephone service has historically provided the easy ability to switch among competing dial-up Internet access services"). For example, a broadband provider like Comcast would be unable to threaten Netflix that it would slow Netflix traffic if all Comcast subscribers would then immediately switch to a competing broadband provider. But we see no basis for questioning the Commission's conclusion that end users are unlikely to react in this fashion. According to the Commission, "end users may not know whether charges or service levels their broadband provider is imposing on edge providers vary from those of alternative broadband providers, and even if they do have this information may find it costly to switch." *Id.* at 17921 ¶ 27. As described by numerous commenters, and detailed more thoroughly in a Commission report compiling the results of an extensive consumer survey, the costs of switching include: "early termination fees; the inconvenience of ordering, installation, and set-up, and associated deposits or fees; possible difficulty returning the earlier broadband provider's equipment and the cost of replacing incompatible customer-owned equipment; the risk of temporarily losing service; the risk of problems learning how to use the new service; and the possible loss of a provider-specific email address or website." *Open Internet Order,* 25 F.C.C.R. at 17924–25 ¶ 34 (footnotes omitted) (citing, *inter alia,* Federal Communications Commission, *Broadband Decisions: What Drives Consumers to Switch—Or Stick With—Their Broadband Internet Provider* (FCC Working Paper, Dec. 2010), *available at* hraunfoss.fcc.gov/edocs—public/attachmatch/DOC–303264A1.pdf). Moreover, the Commission emphasized, many end users may have no option to switch, or at least face very limited options: "[a]s of December 2009, nearly 70 percent of households lived in census tracts where only one or two wireline or fixed wireless firms provided" broadband service. *Id.* at 17923 ¶ 32. As the Commission concluded, any market power that such broadband providers might have with respect to end users would only increase their power with respect to edge providers. *Id.*

The dissent focuses on this latter aspect of the Commission's reasoning, arguing at some length that the Commission's failure to expressly find that broadband providers have market power with respect to end users is "fatal to its attempt to regulate." Dissenting Op. at 665. But Verizon has never argued that the Commission's failure to make a market power finding somehow rendered its understanding of its statutory authority unreasonable or its decision arbitrary and capricious. Verizon does fleetingly mention the market power issue once in its opening brief, asserting as part of its First Amendment claim that *Turner Broadcasting System, Inc. v. FCC,* 520 U.S. 180, 117 S.Ct. 1174, 137 L.Ed.2d 369 (1997)—in which the Supreme Court, applying intermediate scrutiny, upheld a congressional statute compelling cable companies to carry local broadcast television stations, *id.* at 185, 117 S.Ct. 1174—is distinguishable in part because, unlike the Commission here, Congress had found "evidence of 'considerable and growing market power.'" Verizon Br. 46 (quoting *Turner,* 520 U.S. at 197, 117 S.Ct. 1174). But to say, as Verizon does, that an allegedly speech-infringing regulation violates the First Amendment because of the absence of a market condition that would increase the need for that regulation is hardly to say that the absence of this market condition renders the regulation wholly irrational. Verizon's bare citation to a Justice Department submission—relied upon by the dissent, *see* Dissenting Op. at 664, 666–67—is even less on point, as that submission simply advised the Commission to take care to avoid stifling incentives for broadband investment; it never asserted, as the dissent does, that such market power is required for broadband providers to have the economic clout to restrict edge-provider traffic in the first place. *See* Department of Justice Comments at 28, Docket No. 09–51 (Jan. 14, 2010). Indeed, when pressed at oral argument to embrace our dissenting colleague's position, Verizon's counsel failed to do so, stating only that it was "possible" that if the Commission had made a market power finding, the *Order* could be justified. Oral Arg. Tr. 10. As we "do not sit as [a] self-directed board[ ] of legal inquiry and research," and Verizon "has made no attempt to address the issue," the argument is clearly forfeited. *Carducci v. Regan,* 714 F.2d 171, 177 (D.C.Cir.1983).

In any event, it seems likely that the reason Verizon never advanced this argument is that the Commission's failure to find market power is not "fatal" to its theory. Broadband providers' ability to impose restrictions on edge providers does not depend on their benefiting from the sort of market concentration that would enable them to impose substantial price increases on end users—which is all the Commission said in declining to make a market power finding. *See Open Internet Order,* 25 F.C.C.R. at 17923 ¶ 32 & n. 87; *see also* Department of Justice & Federal Trade Commission, Horizontal Merger Guidelines § 4.1 (2010) (defining product markets and market power in terms of a firm's ability to raise prices for consumers). Rather, broadband providers' ability to impose restrictions on edge providers simply depends on end users not being fully responsive to the imposition of such restrictions. *See supra* at 646. If the dissent believes that broadband providers' ability to restrict edge-provider traffic without having their end users react would itself represent an exercise of market power, then the dissent's dispute with the Commission's reasoning appears to be largely semantic: the Commission expressly found that end users are not responsive in this fashion even if it never used the term "market power" in doing so. *See Open Internet Order,* 25 F.C.C.R. at 17924–25 ¶ 34.

Furthermore, the Commission established that the threat that broadband providers would utilize their gatekeeper ability to restrict edge-provider traffic is not, as the Commission put it, "merely theoretical." *Open Internet Order,* 25 F.C.C.R. at 17925 ¶ 35. In support of its conclusion that broadband providers could and would act to limit Internet openness, the Commission pointed to four prior instances in which they had done just that. These involved a mobile broadband provider blocking online payment services after entering into a contract with a competing service; a mobile broadband provider restricting the availability of competing VoIP and streaming video services; a fixed broadband provider blocking VoIP applications; and, of course, Comcast's impairment of peer-to-peer file sharing that was the subject of the *Comcast Order. See id.* Although some of these incidents may not have involved "adjudicated findings of misconduct," as Verizon asserts, Verizon's Br. 50, that hardly means that no record evidence supports the Commission's conclusion that the incidents had in fact occurred. Likewise, the fact that we vacated the *Comcast Order*—rendering it, according to Verizon, a "legal nullity," Verizon's Br. 51—did not require the Commission to entirely disregard the underlying conduct that produced that order. In *Comcast,* we held that the Commission had failed to cite any statutory authority that justified its order, not that Comcast had never impaired Internet traffic. *See Comcast,* 600 F.3d at 644. Nor, finally, did the Commission's invocation of these examples demonstrate that it was attempting to "impose an 'industry-wide solution for a problem that exists only in isolated pockets.'" Verizon's Br. 51 (quoting *Associated Gas Distributors v. FERC,* 824 F.2d 981, 1019 (D.C.Cir.1987)). Rather, as the Commission explained, these incidents—which occurred "notwithstanding the Commission's adoption of open Internet principles," Commission enforcement proceedings against those who violated those principles, and specific Commission orders "requir[ing] certain broadband providers to adhere to open Internet obligations," *Open Internet Order,* 25 F.C.C.R. at 17926–27 ¶ 37—buttressed the agency's conclusion that broadband providers' incentives and ability to restrict Internet traffic could produce "[w]idespread interference with the Internet's openness" in the absence of Commission action, *id.* at 17927 ¶ 38. Such a "problem" is doubtless "industry-wide." *Associated Gas Distributors,* 824 F.2d at 1019.

Finally, Verizon argues that the *Open Internet Order* rules will necessarily have the opposite of their intended effect because they will "harm innovation and deter investment by increasing costs, foreclosing potential revenue streams, and restricting providers' ability to meet consumers' evolving needs." Verizon's Br. 52; *see also* Dissenting Op. at 666–67. In essence, Verizon believes that any stimulus to edge-provider innovation, as well as any consequent demand for broadband infrastructure, produced by the *Open Internet Order* will be outweighed by the diminished incentives for broadband infrastructure investment caused by the new limitations on business models broadband providers may employ to reap a return on their investment. As Verizon points out, two members of the Commission agreed that the rules would be counterproductive, and several commenters contended that certain regulations of broadband providers would run the risk of stifling infrastructure investment. *See Open Internet Order,* 25 F.C.C.R. at 18054–56 (Dissenting Statement of Commissioner McDowell); *id.* at 18088–91 (Dissenting Statement of Commissioner Baker); Verizon Comments at 40–86, Docket No. 09–191 (Jan. 14, 2010); MetroPCS Comments at 24–35, Docket No. 09–191 (Jan 14, 2010); *see also Open Internet Order,* 25 F.C.C.R. at 17931 ¶ 42 n. 143 (discussing the comments of the Department of Justice and Federal Trade Commission).

The record, however, also contains much evidence supporting the Commission's conclusion that, "[b]y comparison to the benefits of [its] prophylactic measures, the costs associated with the open Internet rules . . . are likely small." *Open Internet Order,* 25 F.C.C.R. at 17928 ¶ 39. This is, in other words, one of those cases—quite frequent in this circuit—where "the available data do[ ] not settle a regulatory issue and the agency must then exercise its judgment in moving from the facts and probabilities on the record to a policy conclusion." *State Farm,* 463 U.S. at 52, 103 S.Ct. 2856. Here the Commission reached its "policy conclusion" by emphasizing, among other things, (1) the absence of evidence that similar restrictions of broadband providers had discouraged infrastructure investment, and (2) the strength of the effect on broadband investment that it anticipated from edge-provider innovation, which would benefit both from the preservation of the "virtuous circle of innovation" created by the Internet's openness and the increased certainty in that openness engendered by the Commission's rules. *Open Internet Order,* at 17928–31 ¶¶ 40–42. In so doing, the Commission has offered "a rational connection between the facts found and the choice made," *State Farm,* 463 U.S. at 52, 103 S.Ct. 2856 (internal quotation marks omitted), and Verizon has given us no persuasive reason to question that judgment.

## III.

Even though section 706 grants the Commission authority to promote broadband deployment by regulating how broadband providers treat edge providers, the Commission may not, as it recognizes, utilize that power in a manner that contravenes any specific prohibition contained in the Communications Act. *See Open Internet Order,* 25 F.C.C.R. at 17969 ¶ 119 (reiterating the Commission's disavowal of "a reading of Section 706(a) that would allow the agency to trump specific mandates of the Communications Act"); *see also D. Ginsberg & Sons, Inc. v. Popkin,* 285 U.S. 204, 208, 52 S.Ct. 322, 76 L.Ed. 704 (1932) ("General language of a statutory provision, although broad enough to include it, will not be held to apply to a matter specifically dealt with in another part of the same enactment."). According to Verizon, the Commission has done just that because the anti-discrimination and anti-blocking rules "subject[ ] broadband Internet access service . . . to common carriage regulation, a result expressly prohibited by the Act." Verizon's Br. 14.

We think it obvious that the Commission would violate the Communications Act were it to regulate broadband providers as common carriers. Given the Commission's still-binding decision to classify broadband providers not as providers of "telecommunications services" but instead as providers of "information services," *see supra* at 630–31, such treatment would run afoul of section 153(51): "A telecommunications carrier shall be treated as a common carrier under this [Act] only to the extent that it is engaged in providing telecommunications services." 47 U.S.C. § 153(51); *see also Wireless Broadband Order,* 22 F.C.C.R. at 5919 ¶ 50 (concluding that a "service provider is to be treated as a common carrier for the telecommunications services it provides, but it cannot be treated as a common carrier with respect to other, non-telecommunications services it may offer, including information services"). Likewise, because the Commission has classified mobile broadband service as a "private" mobile service, and not a "commercial" mobile service, *see Wireless Broadband Order,* 22 F.C.C.R. at 5921 ¶ 56, treatment of mobile broadband providers as common carriers would violate section 332: "A person engaged in the provision of a service that is a private mobile service shall not, insofar as such person is so engaged, be treated as a common carrier for any purpose under this [Act]." 47 U.S.C. § 332(c)(2); *see Cellco,* 700 F.3d at 538 ("[M]obile-data providers are statutorily immune, perhaps twice over, from treatment as common carriers.").

Insisting it has transgressed neither of these prohibitions, the Commission begins with the rather half-hearted argument that the Act referred to in sections 153(51) and 332 is the Communications Act of 1934, and that when the Commission utilizes the authority granted to it in section 706—enacted as part of the 1996 Telecommunications Act—it is not acting "under" the 1934 Act, and thus is "not subject to the statutory limitations on common-carrier treatment." Commission's Br. 68. But section 153(51) was also part of the 1996 Telecommunications Act. And regardless, "Congress expressly directed that the 1996 Act . . . be inserted into the Communications Act of 1934." *AT&T Corp.,* 525 U.S. at 377, 119 S.Ct. 721 (citing Telecommunications Act of 1996 § 1(b)). The Commission cannot now so easily escape the statutory prohibitions on common carrier treatment.

Thus, we must determine whether the requirements imposed by the *Open Internet Order* subject broadband providers to common carrier treatment. If they do, then given the manner in which the Commission has chosen to classify broadband providers, the regulations cannot stand. We apply *Chevron*'s deferential standard of review to the interpretation and application of the statutory term "common carrier." *See Cellco,* 700 F.3d at 544. After first discussing the history and use of that term, we turn to the issue of whether the Commission's interpretation of "common carrier"—and its conclusion that the *Open Internet Order*'s rules do not constitute common carrier obligations—was reasonable.

### A.

Offering little guidance as to the meaning of the term "common carrier," the Communications Act defines that phrase, somewhat circularly, as "any person engaged as a common carrier for hire." 47 U.S.C. § 153(11). Courts and the Commission have therefore resorted to the common law to come up with a satisfactory definition. *See FCC v. Midwest Video Corp.,* 440 U.S. 689, 701 n. 10, 99 S.Ct. 1435, 59 L.Ed.2d 692 (1979) ("*Midwest Video II*").

In the Nineteenth Century, American courts began imposing certain obligations—conceptually derived from the traditional legal duties of innkeepers, ferrymen, and others who served the public—on companies in the transportation and communications industries. *See Cellco,* 700 F.3d at 545. As the Supreme Court explained in *Interstate Commerce Commission v. Baltimore & Ohio Railroad Co.,* 145 U.S. 263, 275, 12 S.Ct. 844, 36 L.Ed. 699 (1892), "the principles of the common law applicable to common carriers . . . demanded little more than that they should carry for all persons who applied, in the order in which the goods were delivered at the particular station, and that their charges for transportation should be reasonable." Congress subsequently codified these duties, first in the 1887 Interstate Commerce Act, ch. 104, 24 Stat. 379, then the Manns-Elkins Act of 1910, ch. 309, 36 Stat. 539, and, most relevant here, the Communications Act of 1934, ch. 652, 48 Stat. 1064. *See Cellco,* 700 F.3d at 545–46.

Although the nature and scope of the duties imposed on common carriers have evolved over the last century, *see, e.g., Orloff v. FCC,* 352 F.3d 415, 418–21 (D.C.Cir.2003) (discussing the implications of the relaxation of the tariff-filing requirement), the core of the common law concept of common carriage has remained intact. In *National Association of Regulatory Utility Commissioners v. FCC,* 525 F.2d 630, 642 (D.C.Cir.1976) ("*NARUC I*"), we identified the basic characteristic that distinguishes common carriers from "private" carriers—i.e., entities that are not common carriers—as "[t]he common law requirement of holding oneself out to serve the public indiscriminately." "[A] carrier will not be a common carrier," we further explained, "where its practice is to make individualized decisions, in particular cases, whether and on what terms to deal." *Id.* at 641. Similarly, in *National Association of Regulatory Utility Commissioners v. FCC,* 533 F.2d 601, 608 (1976) ("*NARUC II*"), we concluded that "the primary *sine qua non* of common carrier status is a quasi-public character, which arises out of the undertaking to carry for all people indifferently." (Internal quotation marks omitted).

For our purposes, perhaps the seminal case applying this notion of common carriage is *Midwest Video II.* At issue in *Midwest Video II* was a set of regulations compelling cable television systems to operate a minimum number of channels and to hold certain channels open for specific users. 440 U.S. at 692–93, 99 S.Ct. 1435. Cable operators were barred from exercising any discretion over who could use those latter channels and what those users could transmit. They were also forbidden from charging users any fee for some of the channels and limited to charging an "appropriate" fee for the remaining channels. *Id.* at 693–94, 99 S.Ct. 1435. Because at that time the Commission had no express statutory authority over cable systems, it sought to justify these rules as ancillary to its authority to regulate broadcasting. *Id.* at 696–99, 99 S.Ct. 1435.

Rejecting this argument, the Supreme Court held that the Commission had no power to regulate cable operators in this fashion. The Court reasoned that if the Commission sought to exercise such ancillary jurisdiction over cable operators on the basis of its authority over broadcasters, it must also respect the specific statutory limits of that authority, as "without reference to the provisions of the Act directly governing broadcasting, the Commission's jurisdiction . . . would be unbounded." *Midwest Video II,* 440 U.S. at 706, 99 S.Ct. 1435. Congress had expressly prohibited the Commission from regulating broadcasters as common carriers, a limitation that must then, according to the Court, also extend to cable operators. *Id.* at 707, 99 S.Ct. 1435. And the challenged regulations, the Court held, "plainly impose common-carrier obligations on cable operators." *Id.* at 701, 99 S.Ct. 1435. In explaining this conclusion, the Court largely reiterated the nature of the obligations themselves: "Under the rules, cable systems are required to hold out dedicated channels on a first-come, nondiscriminatory basis. Operators are prohibited from determining or influencing the content of access programming. And the rules delimit what operators may charge for access and use of equipment." *Id.* at 701–02, 99 S.Ct. 1435 (internal citations omitted).

In *Cellco,* we recently confronted the similar question of whether a Commission regulation compelling mobile telephone companies to offer data roaming agreements to one another on "commercially reasonable" terms impermissibly regulated these providers as common carriers. 700 F.3d at 537. From the history and decisions surveyed above, we distilled "several basic principles" that guide our analysis here. *Id.* at 547. First, "[i]f a carrier is forced to offer service indiscriminately and on general terms, then that carrier is being relegated to common carrier status." *Id.* We also clarified, however, that "there is an important distinction between the question whether a given regulatory regime is *consistent* with common carrier or private carrier status, and the *Midwest Video II* question whether that regime *necessarily confers* common carrier status." *Id.* (internal citations omitted). Thus, "common carriage is not all or nothing—there is a gray area in which although a given regulation might be applied to common carriers, the obligations imposed are not common carriage *per se.*" *Id.* In this "space between *per se* common carriage and *per se* private carriage," we continued, "the Commission's determination that a regulation does or does not confer common carrier status warrants deference." *Id.*

Given these principles, we concluded that the data roaming rule imposed no *per se* common carriage requirements because it left "substantial room for individualized bargaining and discrimination in terms." *Cellco,* 700 F.3d at 548. The rule "expressly permit[ted] providers to adapt roaming agreements to 'individualized circumstances without having to hold themselves out to serve all comers indiscriminately on the same or standardized terms.' " *Id.* That said, we cautioned that were the Commission to apply the "commercially reasonable" standard in a restrictive manner, essentially elevating it to the traditional common carrier "just and reasonable" standard, *see* 47 U.S.C. § 201(b), the rule might impose obligations that amounted to common carriage *per se,* a claim that could be brought in an "as applied" challenge. *Cellco,* 700 F.3d at 548–49.

**B.**

The Commission's explanation in the *Open Internet Order* for why the regulations do not constitute common carrier obligations and its defense of those regulations here largely rest on its belief that, with respect to edge providers, broadband providers are not "carriers" at all. Stating that an entity is not a common carrier if it may decide on an individualized basis " 'whether and on what terms to deal' with potential *customers,*" the Commission asserted in the *Order* that "[t]he customers at issue here are the end users who subscribe to broadband Internet access services." *Open Internet Order,* 25 F.C.C.R. at 17950–51 ¶ 79 (quoting *NARUC I,* 525 F.2d at 641) (emphasis added). It explained that because broadband providers would remain able to make "individualized decisions" in determining on what terms to deal with end users, the *Order* permitted the providers the "flexibility to customize service arrangements for a particular customer [that] is the hallmark of private carriage." *Id.* at 17951 ¶ 79. Here, the Commission reiterates that "as long as [a broadband provider] is not required to serve end users indiscriminately, rules regarding blocking or charging edge providers do not create common carriage." Commission's Br. 61. We disagree.

It is true, generally speaking, that the "customers" of broadband providers are end users. But that hardly means that broadband providers could not also be carriers with respect to edge providers. "Since it is clearly possible for a given entity to carry on many types of activities, it is at least logical to conclude that one may be a common carrier with regard to some activities but not others." *NARUC II,* 533 F.2d at 608. Because broadband providers furnish a service to edge providers, thus undoubtedly functioning as edge providers' "carriers," the obligations that the Commission imposes on broadband providers may well constitute common carriage *per se* regardless of whether edge providers are broadband providers' principal customers. This is true whatever the nature of the preexisting commercial relationship between broadband providers and edge providers. In contending otherwise, the Commission appears to misunderstand the nature of the inquiry in which we must engage. The question is not whether, absent the *Open Internet Order*, broadband providers would or did act as common carriers with respect to edge providers; rather, the question is whether, given the rules imposed by the *Open Internet Order*, broadband providers are *now* obligated to act as common carriers. *See Midwest Video II,* 440 U.S. at 701–02, 99 S.Ct. 1435.

In support of its understanding of common carriage, the Commission first invokes section 201(a), which provides that it is the "duty of every common carrier . . . to furnish . . . communication service upon reasonable request therefor." 47 U.S.C. § 201(a). No one disputes that a broadband provider's transmission of edge-provider traffic to its end-user subscribers represents a valuable service: an edge provider like Amazon wants and needs a broadband provider like Comcast to permit its subscribers to use Amazon.com. According to the Commission, however, because edge providers generally do not "request" service from broadband providers, and may have no direct relationship with end users' local access providers, broadband providers cannot be common carriers with respect to such edge providers. But section 201(a) describes a "duty" of a common carrier, not a prerequisite for qualifying as a common carrier in the first place. More important, the *Open Internet Order* imposes this very duty on broadband providers: given the *Open Internet Order*'s anti-blocking and anti-discrimination requirements, *if* Amazon were now to make a request for service, Comcast *must* comply. That is, Comcast must now "furnish . . . communication service upon reasonable request therefor." 47 U.S.C. § 201(a).

Similarly flawed is the Commission's argument that because the Communications Act defines a "common carrier" as a "common carrier *for hire*," 47 U.S.C. § 153(11) (emphasis added), a common carrier relationship may exist only with respect to those customers who purchase service from the carrier. As Verizon aptly puts it in response, the fact that "broadband providers . . . generally have not charged edge providers for access or offered them differentiated services . . . has no legal significance because the avowed purpose of the rules is to deny providers the discretion to do so now and in the future." Verizon's Reply Br. 5 n. 3. In other words, but for the *Open Internet Order*, broadband providers could freely impose conditions on the nature and quality of the service they furnish edge providers, potentially turning certain edge providers—currently able to "hire" their service for free—into paying customers. The Commission may not claim that the *Open Internet Order* imposes no common carrier obligations simply because it compels an entity to continue furnishing service at no cost.

Likewise, the Commission misses the point when it contends that because the Communications Act "imposes non-discrimination requirements on many entities that are not common carriers," the *Order's* requirements cannot "transform[ ] providers into common carriers." Commission's Br. 66–67. In support, the Commission cites 47 U.S.C. § 315(b), which requires that broadcasters charge political candidates nondiscriminatory rates if broadcasters permit them to use their stations, as well as 47 U.S.C. § 548(c)(2)(B), which prohibits satellite programming vendors owned in part or in whole by a cable operator from discriminating against other cable operators in the delivery of programming. Commission's Br. 66–67. But Congress has no statutory obligation to avoid imposing common carrier obligations on those who might not otherwise operate as common carriers, and thus the extent to which the cited provisions might regulate those entities as such is irrelevant. The Commission, on the other hand, has such an obligation with respect to entities it has classified as statutorily exempt from common carrier treatment, and the issue here is whether it has nonetheless "relegated [those entities], *pro tanto,* to common-carrier status." *Midwest Video II,* 440 U.S. at 700–01, 99 S.Ct. 1435.

In these respects, *Midwest Video II* is indistinguishable. The *Midwest Video II* cable operators' primary "customers" were their subscribers, who paid to have programming delivered to them in their homes. There, as here, the Commission's regulations required the regulated entities to carry the content of third parties to these customers—content the entities otherwise could have blocked at their discretion. Moreover, much like the rules at issue here, the *Midwest Video II* regulations compelled the operators to hold open certain channels for use at no cost—thus permitting specified programmers to "hire" the cable operators' services for free. Given that the cable operators in *Midwest Video II* were carriers with respect to these third-party programmers, we see no basis for concluding that broadband providers are not similarly carriers with respect to third-party edge providers.

The Commission advances several grounds for distinguishing *Midwest Video II.* None is convincing.

The Commission asserts that, unlike in *Midwest Video II,* here the content is delivered to end users only when an end user requests it—i.e., by clicking on a link to an edge provider's website. But the same was essentially true in *Midwest Video II:* cable companies' customers would not actually receive the content on the dedicated public access channels unless they chose to watch those channels. The access requested by the programmers in *Midwest Video II,* like the access requested by edge providers here, is the ability to have their communications transmitted to end-user subscribers if those subscribers so desire.

Nor, contrary to the Commission's contention, is it at all relevant that in *Midwest Video II* only a limited number of cable channels were available, while in this case the number of edge providers a broadband provider could serve is unlimited. Whether an entity qualifies as a carrier does not turn on how much content it is able to carry or the extent to which other content might be crowded out. A short train is no more a carrier than a long train, or even a train long enough to serve every possible customer.

Finally, *Midwest Video II* cannot be distinguished on the basis that the Court there emphasized the degree to which the Commission's rules impinged on cable operators' "editorial discretion," and "transferred control" over the content transmitted. Commission's Br. 65. The Court made two related points regarding editorial discretion, neither of which helps the Commission. First, it observed that the need to protect editorial discretion was one reason Congress forbade common carrier treatment of broadcasters in the first place, a rationale that also applied to cable operators, thus confirming the Court's decision to extend that statutory prohibition to the Commission's attempt to exercise its ancillary jurisdiction over such entities. *Midwest Video II,* 440 U.S. at 700, 706–08, 99 S.Ct. 1435. Here, whatever might be the *justifications* for prohibiting common carrier treatment of "information service" providers and "commercial" mobile service providers, such treatment is undoubtedly prohibited. *See* 47 U.S.C. §§ 153(51), 332(c)(2). Second, the Court emphasized that, unlike the regulations approved in *United States v. Midwest Video Corp.,* 406 U.S. 649, 92 S.Ct. 1860, 32 L.Ed.2d 390 (1972) ("*Midwest Video I*")—which required certain cable companies to create their own programming and maintain facilities for local production, *id.* at 653–55, 92 S.Ct. 1860—the regulations in *Midwest Video II* "transferred control of the content of access cable channels from cable operators to members of the public." *Midwest Video II,* 440 U.S. at 700, 99 S.Ct. 1435. The Court's point was simply that the *Midwest Video I* regulations had created no common carrier obligations because they had imposed no obligation on cable operators to provide carriage to any third party. By giving third parties "control" over the transmissions that cable operators carried, however, the *Midwest Video II* regulations did. The regulations here accomplish the very same sort of transfer of control: whereas previously broadband providers could have blocked or discriminated against the content of certain edge providers, they must now carry the content those edge providers desire to transmit. The only remaining question, then, is whether the *Open Internet Order* 's rules have so limited broadband providers' control over edge providers' transmissions that the regulations constitute common carriage *per se.* It is to that question that we now turn.

## C.

We have little hesitation in concluding that the anti-discrimination obligation imposed on fixed broadband providers has "relegated [those providers], *pro tanto,* to common carrier status." *Midwest Video II,* 440 U.S. at 700–01, 99 S.Ct. 1435. In requiring broadband providers to serve all edge providers without "unreasonable discrimination," this rule by its very terms compels those providers to hold themselves out "to serve the public indiscriminately." *NARUC I,* 525 F.2d at 642.

Having relied almost entirely on the flawed argument that broadband providers are not carriers with respect to edge providers, the Commission offers little response on this point. In its briefs, the Commission contends only that if the *Open Internet Order* imposes common carriage requirements, so too would the regulations at issue in *United States v. Southwestern Cable Co.,* 392 U.S. 157, 88 S.Ct. 1994, 20 L.Ed.2d 1001 (1968), which the Supreme Court declined to strike down. *Southwestern Cable* involved a Commission rule that, among other things, compelled cable operators to transmit the signals of local broadcasters when cable operators imported the competing signals of other broadcasters into the local service area. *Id.* at 161, 88 S.Ct. 1994. Such a rule is plainly distinguishable from the *Open Internet Order* 's anti-discrimination rule because the *Southwestern Cable* regulation imposed no obligation on cable operators to hold their facilities open to the public generally, but only to certain specific broadcasters if and when the cable operators acted in ways that might harm those broadcasters. As the Court later explained in *Midwest Video II,* the *Southwestern Cable* rule "was limited to remedying a specific perceived evil," and "did not amount to a duty to hold out facilities indifferently for public use." 440 U.S. at 706 n. 16, 99 S.Ct. 1435. The *Open Internet Order*'s anti-discrimination provision is not so limited, as the compelled carriage obligation applies in all circumstances and with respect to all edge providers.

Significantly for our purposes, the Commission never argues that the *Open Internet Order*'s "no unreasonable discrimination" standard somehow differs from the nondiscrimination standard applied to common carriers generally—the argument that salvaged the data roaming requirements in *Cellco.* In a footnote in the *Order* itself, the Commission suggested that it viewed the rule's allowance for "reasonable network management" as establishing treatment that was somehow inconsistent with *per se* common carriage. *See Open Internet Order,* 25 F.C.C.R. at 17951 ¶ 79 n. 251. But the Commission has forfeited this argument by failing to raise it in its briefs here. *See Comcast,* 600 F.3d at 660; *Roth v. U.S. DOJ,* 642 F.3d 1161, 1181 (D.C.Cir.2011).

In any event, the argument is without merit. The *Order* defines the "reasonable network management" concept as follows: "A network management practice is reasonable if it is appropriate and tailored to achieving a legitimate network management purpose, taking into account the particular network architecture and technology of the broadband Internet access service." *Open Internet Order,* 25 F.C.C.R. at 17952 ¶ 82. This provision, the Commission explained, would permit broadband providers to do two things, neither of which conflict with *per se* common carriage. First, "the reasonable network management" exception would permit broadband providers to "address [ ] traffic that is unwanted by end users . . . such as by providing services or capabilities consistent with an end user's choices regarding parental controls or security capabilities." *Id.* Because the relevant service broadband providers furnish to edge providers is the ability to access end users if those end users so desire, a limited exception permitting *end users* to direct broadband providers to block certain traffic by no means detracts from the common carrier nature of the obligations imposed on broadband providers. Second, the *Order* defines "reasonable network management" to include practices designed to protect the network itself by "addressing traffic that is harmful to the network" and "reducing or mitigating the effects of congestion." *Id.* at 17952 ¶ 82. As Verizon correctly points out, however, this allowance "merely preserves a common carrier's traditional right to 'turn [ ] away [business] either because it is not of the type normally accepted or because the carrier's capacity has been exhausted.'" Verizon's Br. 20 (quoting *NARUC I,* 525 F.2d at 641). Railroads have no obligation to allow passengers to carry bombs on board, nor need they permit passengers to stand in the aisles if all seats are taken. It is for this reason that the Communications Act bars common carriers from engaging in "*unjust or unreasonable* discrimination," not *all* discrimination. 47 U.S.C. § 202 (emphasis added).

The Commission has provided no basis for concluding that in permitting "reasonable" network management, and in prohibiting merely "unreasonable" discrimination, the *Order's* standard of "reasonableness" might be more permissive than the quintessential common carrier standard. *See Cellco,* 700 F.3d at 548 (characterizing the "just and reasonable" standard as being that "applicable to common carriers"). To the extent any ambiguity exists regarding how the Commission will apply these rules in practice, we think it is best characterized as ambiguity as to *how* the common carrier reasonableness standard applies in this context, not *whether* the standard applied is actually the same as the common carrier standard. Unlike the data roaming requirement at issue in *Cellco,* which set forth a "commercially reasonable" standard, *see id.* at 537, the language of the *Open Internet Order* 's anti-discrimination rule mirrors, almost precisely, section 202's language establishing the basic common carrier obligation not to "make any unjust or unreasonable discrimination." 47 U.S.C. § 202. Indeed, confirming that the two standards are equivalent, the Commission responded to commenters who argued that the "no unreasonable discrimination" requirement was too vague by quoting another commenter who observed that "[s]eventy-five years of experience have shown [the 'unreasonable' qualifier in Section 202] to be both administrable and indispensable to the sound administration of the nation's telecommunications laws." *Open Internet Order,* 25 F.C.C.R. at 17949 ¶ 77 n. 240. Moreover, unlike the data roaming rule in *Cellco*—which spelled out "sixteen different factors plus a catchall . . . that the Commission must take into account in evaluating whether a proffered roaming agreement is commercially reasonable," thus building into the standard "considerable flexibility," *Cellco,* 700 F.3d at 548—the *Open Internet Order* makes no attempt to ensure that its reasonableness standard remains flexible. Instead, with respect to broadband providers' potential negotiations with edge providers, the *Order* ominously declares: "it is unlikely that pay for priority would satisfy the 'no unreasonable discrimination' standard." *Open Internet Order,* 25 F.C.C.R. at 17947 ¶ 76. If the Commission will likely bar broadband providers from charging edge providers for using their service, thus forcing them to sell this service to all who ask at a price of $0, we see no room at all for "individualized bargaining." *Cellco,* 700 F.3d at 548.

Whether the *Open Internet Order* 's anti-blocking rules, applicable to both fixed and mobile broadband providers, likewise establish *per se* common carrier obligations is somewhat less clear. According to Verizon, they do because they deny "broadband providers discretion in deciding which traffic from . . . edge providers to carry," and deny them "discretion over carriage terms by setting a uniform price of zero." Verizon's Br. 16–17. This argument has some appeal. The anti-blocking rules establish a minimum level of service that broadband providers must furnish to all edge providers: edge providers' "content, applications [and] services" must be "effectively [ ]usable." *Open Internet Order,* 25 F.C.C.R. at 17943 ¶ 66. The *Order* also expressly prohibits broadband providers from charging edge providers any fees for this minimum level of service. *Id.* at 17943–44 ¶ 67. In requiring that all edge providers receive this minimum level of access for free, these rules would appear on their face to impose *per se* common carrier obligations with respect to that minimum level of service. *See Midwest Video II,* 440 U.S. at 701 n. 9, 99 S.Ct. 1435 (a carrier may "operate as a common carrier with respect to a portion of its service only").

At oral argument, however, Commission counsel asserted that "[i]t's not common carriage to simply have a basic level of required service if you can negotiate different levels with different people." Oral Arg. Tr. 86. This contention rests on the fact that under the anti-blocking rules broadband providers have no obligation to actually provide any edge provider with the minimum service necessary to satisfy the rules. If, for example, all edge providers' "content, applications [and] services" are "effectively usable," *Open Internet Order,* 25 F.C.C.R. at 17943 ¶ 66, at download speeds of, say, three mbps, a broadband provider like Verizon could deliver all edge providers' traffic at speeds of at least four mbps. Viewed this way, the relevant "carriage" broadband providers furnish might be access to end users more generally, not the minimum required service. In delivering this service, so defined, the anti-blocking rules would permit broadband providers to distinguish somewhat among edge providers, just as Commission counsel contended at oral argument. For example, Verizon might, consistent with the anti-blocking rule—and again, absent the anti-discrimination rule—charge an edge provider like Netflix for high-speed, priority access while limiting all other edge providers to a more standard service. In theory, moreover, not only could Verizon negotiate separate agreements with each individual edge provider regarding the level of service provided, but it could also charge similarly-situated edge providers completely different prices for the same service. Thus, if the relevant service that broadband providers furnish is access to their subscribers generally, as opposed to access to their subscribers at the specific minimum speed necessary to satisfy the anti-blocking rules, then these rules, while perhaps establishing a lower limit on the forms that broadband providers' arrangements with edge providers could take, might nonetheless leave sufficient "room for individualized bargaining and discrimination in terms" so as not to run afoul of the statutory prohibitions on common carrier treatment. *Cellco,* 700 F.3d at 548.

Whatever the merits of this view, the Commission advanced nothing like it either in the underlying *Order* or in its briefs before this court. Instead, it makes no distinction at all between the anti-discrimination and anti-blocking rules, seeking to justify both types of rules with explanations that, as we have explained, are patently insufficient. We are unable to sustain the Commission's action on a ground upon which the agency itself never relied. *Lacson v. Department of Homeland Security,* 726 F.3d 170, 177 (D.C.Cir.2013); *see also United States v. Southerland,* 486 F.3d 1355, 1360 (D.C.Cir.2007) ("argument[s] . . . raised for the first time at oral argument [are] forfeited"). Nor may we defer to a reading of a statutory term that the Commission never offered. *Shieldalloy Metallurgical Corp. v. Nuclear Regulatory Comm'n,* 624 F.3d 489, 495 (D.C.Cir.2010).

The disclosure rules are another matter. Verizon does not contend that these rules, on their own, constitute *per se* common carrier obligations, nor do we see any way in which they would. Also, because Verizon does not direct its First Amendment or Takings Clause claims against the disclosure obligations, we have no need to address those contentions here.

Verizon does argue that the disclosure rules are not severable, insisting that if the anti-discrimination and anti-blocking rules fall so too must the disclosure requirements. We disagree. "Whether the offending portion of a regulation is severable depends upon the intent of the agency and upon whether the remainder of the regulation could function sensibly without the stricken provision." *MD/DC/DE Broadcasters Ass'n v. FCC,* 236 F.3d 13, 22 (D.C.Cir.2001) (emphasis omitted). At oral argument, Commission counsel explained that the rules function separately, Oral

Arg. Tr. 81–82, and we are satisfied that the Commission would have adopted the disclosure rules absent the rules we now vacate, which, we agree, operate independently. *See Davis County Solid Waste Management v. EPA,* 108 F.3d 1454, 1457–59 (D.C.Cir.1997) (finding promulgated standard to be severable where EPA asserted in rehearing petition that, contrary to its position at oral argument, the standards could stand alone).

### IV.

For the forgoing reasons, although we reject Verizon's challenge to the *Open Internet Order*'s disclosure rules, we vacate both the anti-discrimination and the anti-blocking rules. *See Northern Air Cargo v. U.S. Postal Service,* 674 F.3d 852, 860–61 (D.C.Cir.2012) (appropriateness of vacatur dependent on whether "(1) the agency's decision is so deficient as to raise serious doubts whether the agency can adequately justify its decision at all; and (2) vacatur would be seriously disruptive or costly"); *Comcast,* 600 F.3d at 661 (vacating the *Comcast Order*). We remand the case to the Commission for further proceedings consistent with this opinion.

*So ordered.*

---

Clearly, the battle for net neutrality, and the FCC's attempts to regulate the Internet are only just beginning. Is the dream of net neutrality sustainable over the long-term? Should corporate interests be able to dictate (and charge for) using higher speed service? To what extent will the future debate mirror elements of the regulation of other forums, including broadcast television explored in this chapter?

# EPILOGUE

# ENTERTAINMENT IN INTERNATIONAL TRADE[a]

■ ■ ■

A recurring theme in this book involves the increasingly international scope of the entertainment industry. When someone makes a movie, a recording, or even a television series, the key to its economic—if not its artistic—success is whether the work can gain a worldwide audience. That is why Congress considers it important to establish intellectual property standards that are reasonably uniform with those of other countries, so that American artists and firms can obtain the full financial returns from the international popularity of their creations. Moreover, the ability of firms to distribute and sell entertainment products globally has been one of the driving forces behind corporate expansion and integration in this industry.

While a large share of the major movie and music studios are now owned by foreign corporations like Sony and News Corp., the lion's share of entertainment works are made by American performers guided by American management. This gives the United States one of its highest comparative advantages, in both creative and executive talent, in the world economy. To reap the financial gains from that talent advantage requires a body of international trade law whose playing field ensures that the appeal of the entertainment product, not the country of its origin, will be the governing factor in its success. But securing such a trade standard in this new century is the kind of complex challenge that helped generate the Seattle demonstrations at the end of the last one.

The United States produces the vast majority of popular, money-making films: of the top 100 world-grossing films each year, more than 90 are made and/or distributed by American studios. From a trade perspective, even more important is the fact that more than half the audience (in theaters and on video) for American movies is in other countries, whereas only a tiny part of the U.S market is devoted to foreign films. For example, while U.S. movies now generate around three

[a] *See* Steven S. Wildman & Stephen E. Siwek, *International Trade in Films & Television Programs* (Ballinger 1988); Kerry Segrave, *American Films Abroad: Hollywood's Domination of the World's Movie Screens from the 1890's to the Present* (McFarland 1997); Kerry Segrave, *American Television Abroad: Hollywood's Attempt to Dominate World Television* (McFarland 1998); J. Gregory Sidak, *Foreign Investment in American Telecommunications* (U. Chi. Press 1997); Keith Acheson & Christopher Moule, *Much Ado About Culture: North American Trade Disputes* (U. Mich. Press 1999).

quarters of European box office revenues, European-made movies were watched by only five percent of the American audience, down substantially from the 1970s.

Much the same is true of television. In Europe, U.S. programs are recycled (and dubbed) for an annual return of about $4 billion to American studios, while European programs earn only $300 million from the American television market based on most recent available data. In the music and book market, as well, there are many billions of dollars in international trade, with American products having a significant edge in earnings from foreign markets (though not as stark as in the movie and television markets). Thus, the entertainment industry is an important feature of the U.S. Gross National Product ($504 billion, based on a 2013 study of 2011 GDP), and it makes a major contribution (over $14 billion, based on a 2013 study of 2011 data) towards containing the country's trade imbalance.

While this trend is attractive to American producers, it is correspondingly unattractive to foreign film producers and to the governments who have been prepared to intervene on their behalf, even at the expense of foreign consumers who prefer the American product.

*China Video/Music Trade Dispute*

The issue in U.S.-China relations in the 1990s that produced continual negotiations, impasses, and threatened sanctions was not human rights or foreign policy, but rather entertainment piracy. A group of thirty or so factories located near military compounds in the Guangdong Province in southern China have specialized in manufacturing video and audio tapes and disks. Several hundred million such tapes and disks have been sold every year, not just in China but in other Asian countries. This manufacturing has taken place without licenses from the owners of the intellectual content contained on the tapes and disks. The Motion Picture Association of America (MPAA) and the Recording Industry Association of America (RIAA) estimated that such entertainment "bootlegging" by Chinese factories was costing their members up to $2 billion in annual sales in the burgeoning Asian market.

For reasons elaborated in Part Two, content is qualitatively more prone to this kind of operation than is entertainment hardware (e.g., manufacturing the video or audio players themselves). The primary cost of production of a movie or musical work is the creation of the original work. Though costs are falling, some major albums have cost six and even seven figures to produce; average movie production and marketing costs can exceed $100 million. The average disk or tape costs very little to produce. Once the original artistic efforts and financial investment have borne fruit in a popular entertainment product, it is easy and cheap to reproduce the content in a new video or disk that the "pirates" can sell without having to pay the licensing fee that covers a proportionate cost of the original creative endeavor (including the risk that the latter might fail).

That is precisely why every industrialized nation has established a system of intellectual property law to ensure that the revenues from commercial exploitation of entertainment works will be channelled to the original author rather than to the later copier. This legislative action is considered crucial for consumers as well as producers, because it preserves the incentives for future creative efforts by authors (including the movie studios that pay directors, writers, and performers to make "works for hire").

When the customers are in one country and the creators in another, however, the political incentives are different. Domestic consumers have to pay a higher price so that the financial rewards can go to foreign producers. This division was not something first discovered by the Chinese Communist government.[b] An oft-forgotten fact about U.S. intellectual property law is that for the first 100 years of the Copyright Act, protection was not given to works by foreign authors. It was perfectly legal for most of the 19th century for American printers to reproduce and sell books by such rather notable European authors as Dickens, Balzac, and Dostoevsky without securing and paying for that right. Charles Dickens traveled to Washington in the 1840s to try to secure revisions in American law that would prohibit piracy of such works as *A Tale of Two Cities* and *Bleak House*. Dickens and his allies did not succeed in persuading a Congress which recognized that European authors were selling a large number of books in the United States, but American authors very few in Europe. In 1886, Victor Hugo and other leading artists persuaded European (and several other) governments to adopt the *Berne Convention for the Protection of Literary and Artistic Works,* which established minimum standards and reciprocal enforcement of intellectual property rights across their respective borders. The United States, while present at Berne, initially refused to sign the new Convention. Not until the end of the 19th century did America finally extend a modicum of copyright protection to foreign works, and not until 1989 did this country finally accept *Berne*.

An international convention such as *Berne* (or the more modest *Universal Copyright Convention* that the United States developed after World War II) sets standards for intellectual property law, but does not itself have binding instruments for enforcing these standards against individual violators in other countries. (For example, a European movie director could not sue in the United States under *Berne*, charging a

---

[b] *See* William P. Alford, *To Steal a Book Is An Elegant Offence: Intellectual Property Law in Chinese Civilization* (Stan. U. Press 1995) (noting influence of China's Confucian heritage, as well as communism, in leading to piracy).

violation of his moral rights if his original black and white film was colorized for screening on television by Ted Turner, who happened now to own the work.) Instead, foreign governments must be pressed to take appropriate action against pirates within their borders. The preferred American weapon for this purpose are measures deployed under its own trade law.

There are three major instruments in trade law—unfair trade practice sanctions and anti-dumping or countervailing duties.[c] The one deployed against China was Section 301 of the 1974 Trade Act, which authorizes the President to impose duties or other trade barriers against products being exported into the United States market from another country whose practices are deemed unjustifiable, unreasonable, discriminatory, or burdensome for U.S. exports to that country. The impetus for enacting this provision was a "Chicken War" in the late 1960s between U.S. and European poultry producers. By the early 1990s, China had developed a huge trade surplus with America, second only to Japan's. Whatever its impact on the overall U.S. trade deficit, this gave the U.S. significant leverage vis-à-vis the Chinese authorities because of its prerogative to cut off Chinese producers' access to the American market by imposing large taxes on their imports into this country.

The first President Bush used this trade law lever to pressure China to sign on to the *Berne Convention* in 1992. When the MPAA and RIAA demonstrated to the Commerce Department that the Chinese signatures to *Berne* had not precluded the emergence of this video and music bootlegging operation, President Clinton used the same Section 301 threat to secure agreements from the Chinese government in 1995 and 1996 to take a host of measures to block the manufacture and sale of pirated American music and films. In 1999, the U.S. reached a broad trade agreement with China, which by then wanted to be fully admitted to the WTO.

Technology has made it difficult to enforce these rules not just in China, but in the United States as well. Ironically, China was admitted to the WTO the same week in 2001 when *Harry Potter & the Sorcerer's Stone* was breaking the all-time box office record for the first weekend of release in the United States. A week later, *Harry Potter* videos were being sold on the streets of Beijing. Someone used a video camera to tape the movie in an American theater, the disc is shipped to China, subtitles (or even voiceovers) are worked in, and the quite high quality DVDs are offered for sale (for less than one U.S. dollar each) Apparently, there were over 20 million sales of illegal copies of *Titanic,* which was 40 times the number of legal DVDs offered for sale in China nine months after its

---

[c] *See* Alan O. Sykes, *Constructive Unilateral Threats in International Commercial Relations: The Limited Case for Section 301,* 23 L. & Pol. in Int'l Bus. 263 (1992); Alan O. Sykes, *Countervailing Duty Law: An Economic Perspective,* 89 Colum. L. Rev. 199 (1989).

release in its theaters (which did get the highest box office receipts in China, just as in the United States).

*Canada/Sports Illustrated Trade Dispute*

Another trade law governs the situation where producers in other countries sell their own goods to *American* consumers "too cheaply." Section 701 of the Tariff Act authorizes the government to impose countervailing duties on imported goods to offset subsidies given to producers by their home government or when the firms themselves are judged to be "dumping" the goods in the American market at significantly lower prices than those charged in their domestic markets. The initial effect of the duty (like § 301 trade sanctions) is to raise prices for American consumers, but the long-term policy objective is to secure a level playing field between American and foreign producers in the market. Though countervailing duties have not yet been required for the American entertainment industry, an example of the use of this law was the decade-long dispute about allegedly below-market prices of Canadian softwood lumber products exported into the United States (not just to build homes, but also to print newspapers, magazines and books).

A U.S.-Canada dispute that was on-going at the time the first edition of *Entertainment* was being published illustrates the operation of both antidumping and unfair trade practice law in a setting closer to the entertainment world. In 1995, the United States threatened to impose § 301 sanctions because the Canadian government had adopted a countervailing measure against the alleged dumping by Time Warner into the Canadian market of below-cost editions of its magazine, Sports Illustrated. This was because Sports Illustrated, long one of the top-selling magazines in Canada, had begun to publish a "Canadian" edition, with essentially the same sports content as the American version but with Canadian-only advertising at far lower prices than those charged in the American edition for its larger market. Canadian magazines complained to their government about potential "unfair" competition because their advertising (and subscription) prices have to cover the cost of producing their entire editorial content as well as other production expenditures. Agreeing with that view, the Canadian government imposed an 80-percent excise tax on advertising revenues for special Canadian editions of magazines whose editorial content is more than 20 percent foreign-produced.

The Sports Illustrated case was actually a replay of a similar dispute in the 1960s involving the broadcasting industry. Three network television stations were established in such small border cities as Burlington, Vermont, and Bellingham, Washington, which along with those in Buffalo, New York, found by far their largest audience in their Canadian neighbors, Montreal, Vancouver, and Toronto respectively.

(Because nearly 90 percent of Canadians live within 75 miles of the American border, they were within range of northern U.S. television stations long before the age of cable, let alone satellite, broadcasting.) In the 1970s, these stations began to sell much of their local advertising to businesses in the Canadian cities at significantly lower prices than those charged by the producers of shows on the affiliates of the CBC and CTV networks in Canada. The precedent for the 1995 Canadian action against Sports Illustrated was a 1976 Canadian law that eliminated any tax deduction for advertisements placed on U.S. television stations by Canadian companies aimed at Canadian audiences (as opposed to Canadian corporate commercials aimed at American audiences via the U.S. networks, for example).

Rather than the ineffective "measured response" taken by President Carter to that 1970s Canadian action, President Clinton filed a 1996 complaint against Canada with the World Trade Organization (WTO) under the General Agreement on Tariffs and Trade (GATT). In 1998, Canada received the decision of WTO's Appellate Body that an excise tax imposed only on these foreign magazines violated the free trade principles of GATT, which require equal treatment (including taxation) of foreign and domestic products in the same market. The Canadian Parliament responded to this ruling by repealing this restraint on magazines, but it also passed a new *Foreign Publishers Advertising Services Act*, which made it an offense for any Canadian firm to purchase advertising in a foreign magazine where the advertising was aimed at the Canadian, rather than a broader international, market. Apparently, the U.S. trade lawyers concluded that this new Canadian bill did not likely violate GATT because it was restricting just the advertising *service* rather than the magazine *good*. American magazines like Sports Illustrated would continue to have around 50% of total magazine sales in Canada, and over 80% of these products that were sold in newsstands. However, the Clinton Administration sought to remove this restraint on advertising sales in Canada by imposing § 301 sanctions on a number of Canadian products coming into the U.S. (e.g., lumber, steel, and textiles).

This threatened trade war triggered intense negotiations between these two countries, which have the largest level of trade of any two nations in the world. Finally, in 1999, negotiators achieved a settlement whereby Canada was permitted to bar anything more than 18% of advertising by Canadian companies in a magazine with less than 50% of Canadian content, when the advertising was aimed at the Canadian market. Among the policy questions posed by this settlement is whether Canadian magazines still do face a major challenge from American publishers like Sports Illustrated deciding that there still is a financial payoff from a split-run magazine limited to 18% of advertising just for this Canadian audience, and whether the MPAA is rightly worried that this North American "cultural" trade agreement will serve as a precedent, for example, for Europe's or Asia's dealings with the American film industry.

*Canadian Movie-Making Subsidies*[d]

Another trade issue concerned "runaway productions," film productions moving to Canada, especially just north of Seattle in Vancouver, causing concerns for U.S. movie unions. Around the time the above magazine trade settlement was being reached, SAG and DG released a joint report, U.S. Runaway Film and Television Production,[e] which disclosed that Vancouver had become the third biggest location for American studio movies ($700 million worth of production there in 1999), with Toronto and Montreal not far behind at numbers four and five. Consider why the Oscar-winning movies like *Good Will Hunting*, the story about life at Harvard and MIT in the Boston area, or Tom Hanks' *My Big Fat Greek Wedding*, a fictional story about life in Chicago, came to be filmed in Toronto. They were lured there by the pioneering 1992 Canadian film-making subsidy system. Thus, Vancouver and Toronto trail only Los Angeles and New York as major studio filming sites, and Canada as a whole accounts for three quarters of those movies being filmed outside the United States.

Apparently there is a substantial body of movie talent in Canada for positions both above and below the production line, and of course, a close resemblance in the look and feel of urban and rural locations. Canada's key comparative advantage is production cost. One source was the substantial drop in the 1990s of the value of the Canadian dollar. Second, the Canadian Artists Alliance of Cinema, Television and Radio (ACTRA) labor agreements allow more flexible terms for film production (especially for shooting schedules). The most important factor, however, was the creation in the 1990s of both federal and provincial Production Service Tax Credits (PSTC), each originally amounting to 11% of salaries paid by foreign film producers to Canadian residents for services performed within Canada, which have now gone up to over 30 percent.

When these credits are added to the currency and labor contract features, it is about 25 percent less expensive to film a movie in Toronto rather than in Boston, or in Vancouver rather than in Seattle. Digital technology now makes it easy to substitute U.S. names and symbols on signs, billboards, car licenses, as well as the appearance of major buildings and other structures. The 2001 movie *The Score*, which was originally set in San Francisco but was lured to Montreal by subsidies,

[d] Oliver R. Goodenough, *Defending the Imaginary to the Death? Free Trade, National Identity & Canada's Cultural Preoccupation*, 15 Ariz. J. Int'l Comp. L. 203 (1998).

[e] *See* U.S. Commerce Dept., *The Migration of U.S. Film & Television Production* (2001); Pamela Conley Ulich & Lance Simmens, *Motion Picture Production: To Run or Stay Made in the U.S.A.*, 21 Loyola L.A. Ent. L. Rev. 357 (2001).

depicted Robert De Niro and Marlon Brando planning the theft of jewels from the Canadian Custom House.

Of course, these numbers reflect the typical cost of film production that can be saved in Canada, and would be a far smaller percentage for a *Good Will Hunting* or *The Truman Show* where the bulk of the costs are those paid in American dollars to stars (and SAG members) like Robin Williams or Jim Carrey. So less than 20 percent of Hollywood theater movies are made in Canada, but half of the studios' made-for-television movies are shot north of the border, because these films rarely use high-priced actors. Thus, the financial benefits of having most of the supporting actors and all of the production personnel being paid in Canadian dollars (that are then subsidized) generates significantly more than a 30 percent savings in production costs.

Other countries are following Canada's lead, beginning with Australia, which put up $12 million of the $62 million spent to produce the 1999 hit *The Matrix* and then did much the same thing with the *Star Wars* trilogy. The Czech Republic has also lured film-making there, such as Matt Damon's *The Bourne Identity* and *The Brothers Grimm*. *Slumdog Millionaire* attracted some Indian government subsidies and was made for the equivalent of $14 million. Time Warner and Fox battled against each other, eventually acquiring shared distribution rights for this hit Oscar winner.

Numerous American states have now adopted the film subsidy strategy. In 2002, Louisiana passed legislation giving studios up to 15 percent of total investments there and 20 percent of the wages paid to Louisiana residents working on the filming. That quickly induced the studio planning a story about singer Ray Charles to move the making of *Ray* from Georgia (where he was born and raised) to Louisiana. In aggregate, while approximately $12 million was spent on making movies in Louisiana in 2002, by 2005 that number had surged to a $425 million, with the state taxpayers spending well over $100 million as subsidies in that period.

As a result of these interstate and international efforts, the number of feature-film, on-location production days in Los Angeles fell by 37 percent from 1996 through 2004, leading California to consider its own tax credits. Moreover, in 2004 Congress passed Section 181 of the *Jobs Creation Act*, which provides a federal tax break to films where at least 75 percent of the production costs were incurred in the United States. However, this new law is limited to film with budgets under $15 million, or $20 million if made in an economically depressed area.

The Hollywood unions (through their Film & Television Action Committee) have also petitioned the Federal Trade Commission to impose countervailing duties under the Tariff Act that matched subsidies being given the studios by the Canadian government. Not only then Canadian Prime Minister Jean Chretien, but also then MPAA leader Jack Valenti strongly opposed this action as likely to generate a trade war between the two countries. As has generally been true for the American labor movement, the Hollywood unions have had no domestic success in their effort to protect their jobs from foreign competition.

In appraising the legal and policy merits of this issue in the entertainment field, consider the analogy to the sports field, where Tennessee taxpayers lured the Vancouver Grizzlies to Memphis by promising to build a new $300 million arena for them, or Washington spending at least $350 million in public funds to build a new stadium to attract the Montreal Expos baseball team to Washington (as the Nationals). Should taxpayers have to support these sports or entertainment enterprises and stars?[f] Who reaps the benefits and who bears the burdens?

*European Television and the Cultural Exception*[g]

The complexities of free trade in "cultural" works was shown back in the 1980s, when Canada and the U.S. negotiated a Free Trade Agreement (FTA) designed to remove trade barriers to the movement of goods and services across their borders; Canada insisted and President Reagan agreed that a "cultural exception" would be incorporated into the FTA, excluding books, magazines, and periodicals, movies and home video, published songs and recordings, and television, radio, cable, and satellite transmission. The FTA, then, would not bar such Canadian policies as the special broadcast advertising taxes, nor did it remove the U.S. prerogative to respond with its own trade sanctions of "equivalent commercial effect" if and when such cultural barriers were adopted. While the cultural exception was maintained when the FTA was expanded into a NAFTA that included Mexico, it has attained far more significance in trade relations with Europe.

American entertainment products now dominate the Canadian audience, with 90 percent of movie admissions from American-made or distributed films. In terms of revenue, though, this is dwarfed by the 75 percent share that American studios now enjoy of the 350-million person European market. Thus, American television producers sell European stations approximately $4 billion in programming, while Europeans receive only $300 million from the American market (almost all for British-made shows).

---

[f] *See* Paul Weiler, *Leveling the Playing Field: How the Law Can Make Sports Better for Fans* (Harv. Univ. Press 2000).

[g] Shalin Venturelli, *Liberalizing the European Media: Politics, Regulating, & the Public Sphere* (Clarendon Press 1998); Thomas C. Fischer, *The United States, the European Union, & the "Globalization" of World Trade: Allies or Adversaries?* (Quorum Books 2000).

Understandably, then, in the 1990s Uruguay Round of GATT negotiations, there was a deep trade conflict between the United States, which wanted to enhance its producers' access to the huge European entertainment market, and the EU, which wanted to retain its authority to protect domestic entertainment production. What all sides had agreed upon by 1993 were major reductions in prevailing tariff rates on goods, the extension of GATT principles to a wide range of services, a new Trade-Related Aspects of Intellectual Property Rights (TRIPS) accord, and the creation of the WTO. European governments (particularly France) insisted on including in GATT a version of the "cultural" exemption that had been secured by Canada in NAFTA.

The original 1947 GATT had created a special exemption for governmental limitation of "exhibition of [foreign] cinematograph films" to a specified percentage of total screen time in theaters. The lead proponent of this feature was Great Britain, which was seeking to revive its movie industry after World War II. The principal European objective in the Uruguay Round four decades later was to expand the exemption to provide the necessary leeway for a 1989 EU Directive, Television Without Frontiers.[h] The broader aim of this EU Directive was to facilitate the emergence of a single European market in the television industry. Among other things, the Directive coordinated EU-member laws regarding the level of television advertising, the moral suitability of children's programming, and the right of reply for persons whose reputations had been harmed by inaccurate stories. A key feature of the Directive was Article 4(C):

> Member states shall ensure, where practicable and by appropriate means, that broadcasters reserve for European works, within the meaning of Article 6, a majority proportion of their transmission time, excluding the time appointed to news, sports events, games, advertising, and teletext services.

Though American programs constituted nearly three quarters of European television time, the objective was to secure at least half time for European audiovisual works.

The strongest proponent of this policy is France, which had established a 60 percent floor for European-made television programming shown in that country, as well as taxes on movie admissions, television

---

[h] *See* Richard Collins, *The Screening of Jacques Tati: Broadcasting & Cultural Identity In the European Community*, 11 Cardozo Arts & Ent. L.J. 361 (1993); "Jonas M. Grant, *Jurassic" Trade Dispute: The Exclusion of the Audiovisual Sector From the GATT*, 70 Ind. L.J. 1333 (1995); W. Ming Shao, *Is There No Business Like Show Business? Free Trade & Cultural Protectionism*, 20 Yale J. Inter. L. 105 (1995); John David Donaldson *"Television Without Frontiers": The Continuing Tension Between Liberal Free Trade & European Cultural Integrity*, 20 Fordham Int. L.J. 90 (1996); Sandrine Cahn & Daniel Schimmel, *The Cultural Exception: Does it Exist in the GATT & GATS Framework? How Does it Affect or is it Affected by the Agreement on TRIPS?* 15 Cardozo Arts & Ent. L.J. 281 (1997).

shows, and blank tape/disk sales, to fund support for domestic film production. American studios strongly objected to the box office tax because with a 60 percent share of movie admissions in France, the studios felt they were paying for the bulk of a subsidy being provided to French film-makers. However, in 1993, in order to secure other trade gains in the Uruguay Round, the U.S. conceded the point about the "cultural" exemption, while reserving for itself the right to use § 301 trade sanctions for excessive burdens placed on American movie and television production.

In the 1990s France expanded its entertainment regulation by requiring that at least 40 percent of songs played on the radio be from French artists. Spain went a step further, requiring its movie theaters to exhibit European films on one day for every two days given to U.S. films. Distributors wanting to dub American films into Spanish must also generate a certain level of distributional revenues for European movies. However, Germany moved away from the ironically named Television Without Frontiers Directive, after its Constitutional Court ruled that only its state governments, not Bonn, can regulate television in that country (and most of the states, led by Bavaria, are opposed to the Directive).

---

The foregoing provides a sense of the economic significance and political controversy surrounding trade in entertainment products. We conclude with a synopsis of the arguments made and questions raised by the opposing sides at the negotiating table.

The free trade argument in entertainment services is the same as is made for all the other goods and services for which GATT has steadily been reducing trade barriers for the last half-century. Free trade serves all sides in an increasingly integrated world economy by inducing people in different nations to concentrate on those areas where they have a comparative advantage. In entertainment, authors work at those tasks where they are, relatively speaking, the most skilled, and the organizations in which they work gain the economies of scale from producing and distributing their works to a much larger international market. The consumers get the benefit of a wider range of entertainment choices and of competitive pressures on producers to make higher quality products at lower prices. Viewers in the U.S. have experienced the way in which the emergence of Fox, HBO, TNT, and other television options have increased the variety and quality of programming in this country. Would not the availability of those American-made programs for fans in Canada, Europe, Japan, and elsewhere in the world equally enhance entertainment consumer satisfaction, even when they are watching their home channels that must operate in a more competitive environment?

The argument in favor of government intervention to protect its own entertainment industry rests on a combination of strategic trade theory and cultural integrity. It is asserted, first, that the U.S. audiovisual industry has a huge strategic advantage. To some extent this is due to historical accident dating back to the birth of the Hollywood film studios in the early 1920s. To a greater extent it is because American producers have a large (and somewhat insular) home audience, which facilitates production of expensive and appealing films that have long dominated the English-speaking market around the world. With that financial base, Hollywood is easily able to attract top-flight foreign actors as soon as they become stars in their home countries: e.g., Mel Gibson and Russell Crowe from Australia, Antonio Banderas from Spain, Hugh Grant from England, and Jim Carrey from Canada. Given that pool of artistic talent (which also includes leading foreign directors, writers, cinematographers, and the like) and a ready capacity to dub works into other languages, it is easy to understand why many movie fans in France prefer to watch a film produced in Los Angeles rather than one made in Paris.

Adding to that enduring strategic advantage is the fact that *content* is the key attraction and the major cost item in a movie or television program. As noted above, once the creative work has been done on a film (for Hollywood-made movies now averaging over $100 million in production and marketing costs), the additional expense for dubbing into another language is modest (about $100,000), and for each additional theater print it is insignificant (about $1,000, and even less for a new digital copy). This means that if a film can pay for itself in its home market (especially one as large as the U.S.), the additional revenue from foreign markets is pure profit. American producers can thus offer their audiovisual product at however low a price is necessary to outsell the domestic producers. (Variety reported that in the 1980s, the price charged by Hollywood studios for showing of their movies on foreign television ranged from $100 in Bermuda to $40,000 in France.) If a Japanese manufacturer of computers or other consumer hardware were following that variable pricing practice to undercut domestic producers in the American market, it would be subject to sanctions for "dumping" their surplus output. However, given the distinctive "intellectual" feature of films, can one make the economic claim that producers really are underpricing their goods relative to true marginal costs of production and distribution in foreign markets?

Whatever the explanation, foreign film producers do seem to face major obstacles to becoming competitive with American producers. (Another intriguing question is why this comparative disadvantage seems confined to audiovisual works, not records or books.) Why should consumers find anything objectionable about an international market in which they can choose to watch better programs at lower prices than those made in their home country? French moviegoers, for example, seem to be expressing their views: from 1985 to 2000, the domestic share of annual admissions in France dropped from 60 percent to 30 percent while American movies were rising proportionately (though the French share has risen slightly since then).

The rationale for government intervention on behalf of domestic entertainment producers is that there is a unique feature to a movie or television program that one does not find in the television set or other consumer hardware. Even when created to entertain rather than enlighten, a film draws upon the experiences of the author, his family, friends, and neighbors. Preservation and enhancement of a nation's artistic creativity and cultural integrity is a value distinct from the country's GNP. The question, though, is whether the cultural environment has the qualities of a public good that are not sufficiently served by individual choices in the consumer market, such that there is a need for government action.

There are also complications in labeling particular entertainment products domestic or foreign. Recall that Hollywood majors as Twentieth Century Fox (now part of News Corp.), Columbia Pictures (Sony), and Universal (Vivendi), are subsidiaries of foreign-based corporations. The European Directive test is whether a film is made mainly by people "residing" in an EU state, and "supervised and actually controlled" by "producer(s) established" in an EU state. The Vivendi Universal executives are asking the EU to remove the limit on how much time its Canal-Plus pay television service may use to show its own programs. And as stated earlier, many performers, directors, and writers working on "American" movies are from a host of other countries, and many movies are now filmed outside the United States. Since stars like Mel Gibson and Jim Carrey, as well as Julia Roberts and Tom Hanks, realize that their movies are going to be shown around the world, this means that their market price ($20 million or more a film) has driven up the cost of Hollywood-produced movies and thereby removed much of the latter's strategic cost advantage mentioned earlier.

Executives in Los Angeles still make the key decisions about what movie projects will go forward, even if many of the creative artists come from other countries. However, the target audiences whose tastes influence those financial decisions are now found as much in foreign countries as in the U.S. That fact is having an increasing powerful impact on the role that movies play in the American cultural identity. It is much easier to secure a studio investment in an action movie like *Die Hard*, a special effects movie like *The Matrix*, or an animation movie like *The Lion King,* than in a thoughtful story like *Driving Miss Daisy*. While *Daisy* won the Academy Award for Best Picture, it did poorly at the box office in other countries whose audiences were not able to empathize with a story about race relations in the American South. On the other hand, a later Academy Award winner, *Schindler's List*, was able to do much better in Europe than it did even in the U.S.

In closing, it is useful to contrast two disparate claims about whether there should be special treatment of entertainment products to preserve cultural identities. Jacques Delors, then-President of the European Commission, said that "culture is not a piece of merchandise like any other and must not be treated as such." Jack Valenti, former President of the MPAA, argued that trade in entertainment "has nothing to do with culture unless French soap operas and game shows are the equivalent of Moliere. This is all about the hard business of money." Jack Lang, France's Minister of Culture, replied: "The soul of France cannot be sold for a few pieces of silver." Recall the materials and issues we have been tracing from Chapter 1 onward, about the legal treatment of the entertainment industry under the First Amendment, intellectual property, private contract, and public regulation. Ironically, it was an Italian movie, *The Miracle*, that first brought free speech rights to the American entertainment industry, in *Joseph Burstyn v. Wilson*, 343 U.S. 495 (1952). Is there something special about *speech* for fun and profit? And even if so, does that mean the *trade* must be as free as the speech itself?

# SUBJECT MATTER INDEX

**The inclusion of names of individuals, organizations, parties and topics in this index is by no means exhaustive. Index listings include those individuals, organizations, parties and topics which form a part of a detailed textual discussion, and may exclude those which are mentioned in passing or as case support. Named parties to a case may be found in the Table of Cases, although they may also be included here if discussed elsewhere in the text.**